THE OXFORD HANDBOOK OF

POLITICAL NETWORKS

THE OXFORD HANDBOOK OF

POLITICAL

NETWORKS

Edited by

JENNIFER NICOLL VICTOR,
ALEXANDER H. MONTGOMERY,

and

MARK LUBELL

OXFORD
UNIVERSITY PRESS

Oxford University Press is a department of the University of Oxford.
It furthers the University's objective of excellence in research, scholarship,
and education by publishing worldwide. Oxford is a registered trade mark of
Oxford University Press in the UK and in certain other countries.

Published in the United States of America by Oxford University Press
198 Madison Avenue, New York, NY 10016, United States of America.

Library of Congress Cataloging-in-Publication Data
Names: Victor, Jennifer Nicoll, editor. | Montgomery, Alexander H., editor. |
Lubell, Mark, editor.
Title: The Oxford handbook of political networks /
edited by Jennifer Nicoll Victor, Alexander H. Montgomery, and Mark Lubell.
Description: Oxford ; New York : Oxford University Press, 2018. |
Includes bibliographical references.
Identifiers: LCCN 2017007626 | ISBN 9780190228217 (hardcover)
Subjects: LCSH: Policy networks. | Policy sciences.
Classification: LCC H97.7 .O84 2017 | DDC 320.6—dc23
LC record available at https://lccn.loc.gov/2017007626

1 3 5 7 9 8 6 4 2
Printed by Sheridan Books, Inc., United States of America

Contents

PART I NETWORK THEORY AND THE STUDY OF POLITICS

PART II POLITICAL NETWORK METHODOLOGIES

PART III NETWORKS AND AMERICAN POLITICS

PART IV NETWORKS IN PUBLIC POLICY AND PUBLIC ADMINISTRATION

PART V NETWORKS IN INTERNATIONAL RELATIONS

PART VI NETWORKS IN COMPARATIVE POLITICS

PART VII WHAT CAN POLITICAL SCIENCE LEARN FROM OTHER DISCIPLINES?

About the Editors

Jennifer Nicoll Victor holds a Ph.D. in political science from Washington University in St. Louis (2003) and is Associate Professor of Political Science at the George Mason University Schar School of Policy and Government. She is the coauthor of *Bridging the Information Gap: Legislative Member Organizations as Social Networks in the United States and the European Union* with Nils Ringe (University of Michigan Press 2013) and her research on legislative politics, political parties, organized interests, and campaign finance has been published in the *American Journal of Political Science, American Politics Research, Party Politics, PS: Political Science & Politics, British Journal of Political Science*, and elsewhere.

Alexander H. Montgomery holds a Ph.D. in political science from Stanford University (2006) and is Department Chair and Associate Professor of Political Science at Reed College. His research on international relat ions, network analysis, and nuclear proliferation has been published in *International Organization, Journal of Conflict Resolution, International Security, Intelligence and National Security*, and elsewhere.

Mark Lubell holds a Ph.D. in political science from the State University of New York at Stony Brook (1999) and is Professor at the University of California, Davis, Department of Environmental Science and Policy as well as Director of the UC Davis Center for Environmental Policy and Behavior. He is the coauthor of *Swimming Upstream: Collaborative Approaches to Watershed Management* with Paul Sabatier, Will Focht, Zev Trachtenberg, Arnold Vedlitz, and Marty Matlock (MIT Press 2005) and his research on environmental policy, collective action, and social networks has been published in the *American Journal of Political Science, Public Administration Review, Ecology and Society, Policy Studies Journal*, and elsewhere.

CONTRIBUTORS

Isabella Alcañiz holds a Ph.D. in Political Science from Northwestern University (2004) and is Assistant Professor in the Department of Government and Politics at the University of Maryland. She has a forthcoming book with Cambridge University Press, *Environmental and Nuclear Networks in the Global South: How Skills Shape International Cooperation*. Her research on environmental politics, states in the global south, social network analysis, political economy of skills, and Latin American politics has been published in the *British Journal of Political Science, Latin American Perspective, Latin American Research Review*, and elsewhere.

Barry Ames holds a Ph.D. in Political Science from Stanford University (1972) and is Professor of Comparative Politics at the University of Pittsburgh. He is author of *The Deadlock of Democracy in Brazil* (University of Michigan Press 2001) and his research on Latin American politics has been published in the *American Journal of Political Science, American Political Science Review, Legislative Politics in Latin America*, and elsewhere.

Andy Baker holds a Ph.D. in Political Science from the University of Wisconsin, Madison (2001) and is Associate Professor in the Department of Political Science at the University of Colorado at Boulder. He is author of *Shaping the Developing World: The South, the West, and the Natural World* (Congressional Quarterly Press 2014) and his research on Latin American politics, political economy, political behavior, international political economy, and Brazil has been published in the *American Journal of Political Science, World Politics, Electoral Studies*, and elsewhere.

Paul A. Beck holds a Ph.D. in Political Science from the University of Michigan (1971) and is Professor Emeritus at the Ohio State University. He is coauthor of *Party Politics in America* with Marjorie Randon Hershey (Longman 2003) and his research on political parties, voting behavior, and public opinion has been published in the *American Journal of Political Science, International Journal of Public Opinion Research, Party Politics, American Political Science Review*, and elsewhere.

Ramiro Berardo holds a Ph.D. in Political Science from Florida State University (2006) and is Assistant Professor in the School of Environment and Natural Resources at the Ohio State University. His research on policy networks, collaborative governance, public policy, and collective action dilemmas has been published in the *American Journal of Political Science, The Journal of Politics, Policy Studies Journal, Political Research Quarterly*, and elsewhere.

Steven P. Borgatti holds a Ph.D. in Mathematical Social Science from the University of California, Irvine (1989) and is Professor and Paul Chellgren Endowed Chair at the University of Kentucky in the Management Department of the Gatton College of Business and Economics. He is coauthor of *Analyzing Social Networks* with Martin Everett and Jeff Johnson (Sage Publications 2013) and his research on social networks, knowledge management, and computational models has been published in *Science, Social Networks, Organization Science, Academy of Management Review*, and elsewhere.

Janet M. Box-Steffensmeier holds a Ph.D. in Government from the University of Texas (1993) and is Vernal Riffe Professor of Political Science at the Ohio State University. She is coauthor of *Event History Modeling: A Guide for Social Scientists* with Bradford S. Jones (Cambridge University Press 2004) and her research on American politics, public opinion, elections, and time series methodology has been published in the *American Journal of Political Science, American Political Science Review, Journal of Politics*, and elsewhere.

Jeffrey Broadbent holds a Ph.D. in Sociology from Harvard University (1982) and is Professor of Sociology at the University of Minnesota. He is author of *Environmental Politics in Japan: Networks of Power and Protest* (Cambridge University Press 1997), which won two academic awards, and is coauthor of *Comparing Policy Networks: Labor Politics in the U.S., Germany, and Japan* with David Knoke, Franz Pappi, and Yutaka Tsujinaka (Cambridge University Press 1996). His research on political networks, climate change, comparative sociology, Japan, and social movements has been published in the *Journal of Japanese Studies, Policy Sciences, Journal of Civil Society, American Sociological Review*, and elsewhere.

Stephanie Chan is a candidate for a Bachelor of Arts degree at the University of Massachusetts, Amherst (2017) and will begin Princeton University's Politics doctoral program in Fall 2017.

Wendy K. Tam Cho holds a Ph.D. in Political Science from the University of California, Berkley (1997) and is Professor in the Departments of Political Science and Statistics at the University of Illinois at Urbana-Champaign. Her research on statistical and computational models for social science has been published in the *American Journal of Political Science, The American Statistician, Journal of Politics, Political Analysis*, and elsewhere.

Dino P. Christenson holds a Ph.D. in Political Science from the Ohio State University (2010) and is Associate Professor of Political Science at Boston University. He is coauthor of *Applied Social Science Methodology: An Introductory Guide* with John Gerring (Cambridge University Press 2017) and his research on American political behavior and quantitative methods has been published in *American Political Science Review, American Journal of Political Science, Political Behavior, Social Networks*, and elsewhere.

Skyler J. Cranmer holds a Ph.D. in Political Science from the University of California, Davis (2007) and is Carter Phillips and Sue Henry Associate Professor in the Department of Political Science at the Ohio State University. His research on network analysis, political networks, political methodology, international relations, and conflict processes has been published in *Political Analysis, Conflict Management and Peace Science, Policy Studies Journal*, and elsewhere.

Bruce A. Desmarais holds a Ph.D. in Political Science from the University of North Carolina at Chapel Hill (2010) and is Associate Professor of Political Science at Pennsylvania State University. His research on political institutions, political methodology, computational social science, network analysis, and machine learning has been published in *Political Analysis, American Political Science Review, American Journal of Political Science, Social Networks*, and elsewhere.

Cassy Dorff holds a Ph.D. in Political Science from Duke University (2015) and is Assistant Professor of Political Science at the University of New Mexico. Her research on conflict studies, international relations, social movements, network analysis, and forecasting has been published in the *American Journal of Political Science, International Studies Review, Political Science Research and Methods, International Interactions*, and elsewhere.

Mette Eilstrup-Sangiovanni holds a Ph.D. in Political Science from the European University Institute (2001) and is Lecturer in International Studies in the Department of Politics and International Studies at the University of Cambridge. Her research on international organization, international relations theory, international security, and institutional design has been published in *International Studies Quarterly, International Spectator, International Security, European Journal of International Relations*, and elsewhere.

Giorgio Fagiolo holds a Ph.D. in Economics from the European University Institute (2001) and is Professor of Economics at the Laboratory of Economics and Management at the Sant'Anna School of Advanced Studies. His research on agent-based computational economics and economic networks has been published in *Science, Journal of Artificial Societies and Social Simulation, Journal of Economic Dynamics and Control, Physical Review*, and elsewhere.

Richard C. Feiock holds a Ph.D. in Political Science from the University of Kansas (1986) and is the Augustus B. Turnbull Professor of Public Administration and Policy and Director of the Sustainable Energy and Governance Program in the Askew School of Public Administration and Policy at Florida State University. He is coauthor of *Institutional Constraints and Local Policy Choices: An Exploration of Local Governance* with James Clingermayer (State University of New York Press 2001) and his research on governance, local government, and institutions has been published in the *Journal of Urban Affairs, Urban Affairs Review, Public Administration Review, American Journal of Political Science*, and elsewhere.

Manuel Fischer holds a Ph.D. in Political Science from the University of Geneva (2011) and is Lecturer in the Institute of Political Science at the University of Berne and Tenure Track Researcher at the Swiss Federal Institute of Aquatic Science and Technology. He is coauthor of *Political Decision-Making in Switzerland* with Pascal Sciarini and Denise Traber (Springer 2015) and his research on governance arrangements, decision-making processes, and political networks has been published in the *Journal of Public Policy, Water Science and Technology, Journal of Politics, Social Networks*, and elsewhere.

Sandra González-Bailón holds a D.Phil. in Sociology from the University of Oxford (2007) and is Assistant Professor in the Annenberg School for Communication at the University of Pennsylvania. Her research on network science, data mining, computational tools, and political communication has been published in *American Behavioral Scientist, Journal of Information Technology, Journal of Complex Networks, Social Networks,* and elsewhere.

Justin H. Gross holds a Ph.D. in Statistics and Public Policy from Carnegie Mellon University (2010) and is Assistant Professor of Political Science at the University of Massachusetts, Amherst. His research on mass media and political communication, public opinion, and public policy has been published in the *American Journal of Political Science, Social Networks, British Journal of Political Science,* and elsewhere.

Jennifer Hadden holds a Ph.D. from Cornell University's Department of Government (2011) and is Assistant Professor in the University of Maryland's Department of Government and Politics. She is the author of *Networks in Contention: The Divisive Politics of Climate Change* (Cambridge University Press 2015) and her research on international relations, environmental politics, and non-state actors has been published in *Global Environmental Politics, Journal of Politics, Mobilization,* and elsewhere.

Michael T. Heaney holds a Ph.D. in Political Science and Public Policy from the University of Chicago (2004) and is Assistant Professor of Organizational Studies at the University of Michigan. He is coauthor of *Party in the Street: The Antiwar Movement and the Democratic Party after 9/11* with Fabio Rojas (Cambridge University Press 2015) and his research on social networks, interest groups, social movements, and political parties has been published in the *American Political Science Review, American Journal of Sociology, Social Networks,* and elsewhere.

Adam Douglas Henry holds a Ph.D. in Transportation Technology and Policy from the University of California, Davis (2009) and is Associate Professor in the School of Government and Public Policy at the University of Arizona. His research on sustainability science, network analysis, public policy, and social learning has been published in the *American Journal of Political Science, Policy Studies Journal, Journal of Public Administration Research and Theory,* and elsewhere.

Paul S. Herrnson holds a Ph.D. in Political Science from the University of Wisconsin, Madison (1986) and is Professor in the Department of Political Science at the University of Connecticut. He is the author of *Congressional Elections: Campaigning at Home and in Washington* (CQ Press, 2016 7th edition) and his research on political parties and elections, money and politics, public opinion, and voting technology and ballot design has appeared in the *American Journal of Political Science, Journal of Politics, Electoral Studies, Election Law Journal,* and elsewhere.

Matthew Jackson holds a Ph.D. in Economics from Stanford University (1988) where he also serves as William D. Eberle Professor of Economics. He is also an external faculty member at the Santa Fe Institute and a Senior Fellow of CIFAR. He is author of *Social* *and Economic Networks* (Princeton University Press 2008) and his research on game theory, microeconomic theory, and social and economic networks has been published in Science, PNAS, Social Networks, *Journal of Economic Theory, American Economic Review,* and elsewhere.

Joshua M. Jansa holds a Ph.D. in Political Science from the University of North Carolina at Chapel Hill (2016) and is Assistant Professor of Political Science at Oklahoma State University. His research on interest groups and lobbying, state politics and policymaking, class politics and income inequality, and economic development has been published in *Economic Development Quarterly* and *State Politics and Policy Quarterly.*

Lorien Jasny holds a Ph.D. in Sociology from the University of California, Irvine (2012) and is Lecturer at the University of Exeter in Political and Environmental Network Analysis. Her research on social networks, political sociology, and environmental sociology has been published in *Policy Studies Journal, Society and Natural Resources,* and *Social Movement Studies: Journal of Social, Cultural and Political Protest.*

Alexandra P. Joosse holds a Ph.D. in Public Policy Analysis from the University of Arizona (2015). Her research on collaborative networks between government, non-profit, and for profit organizations has been published in *Conflict Resolution Quarterly,* and *Studies in Conflict and Terrorism.*

David Kinsella holds a Ph.D. in Political Science from Yale University (1993) and is Professor of Political Science and International Studies and Chair of the Division of Political Science at Portland State University. He is coauthor of *World Politics: The Menu for Choice* with Bruce Russett and Harvey Starr (Wadsworth 2013, 10th edition) and his research on arms trade, international conflict, international law, and democratic peace has been published in the *American Journal of Political Science, Journal of Politics, American Political Science Review,* and elsewhere.

Justin H. Kirkland holds a Ph.D. in Political Science from the University of North Carolina at Chapel Hill (2012) and is Assistant Professor of Political Science at the University of Houston. His research on legislative politics, state politics, social network analysis, and statistical methods has been published in the *Journal of Politics, International Interactions, Social Networks,* and elsewhere.

Casey A. Klofstad holds a Ph.D. in Political Science from Harvard University (2005) and is Associate Professor in the Department of Political Science at the University of Miami. He is author of *Civic Talk: Peers, Politics, and the Future of Democracy* (Temple University Press 2011) and his research on social networks and political behavior has been published in the *American Journal of Political Science, Political Research Quarterly, Public Opinion Quarterly,* and elsewhere.

David Knoke holds a Ph.D. in Sociology and Social Work from the University of Michigan (1972) and is Professor at the University of Minnesota Department of

Sociology. He is the coauthor of *Network Analysis* with James H. Kuklinski (Sage Publications 1982) and author of *Political Networks: The Structural Perspective* (Cambridge University Press 1990). His research on social networks, organizations, political sociology, and economic sociology has been published in *Management Decision, Applied Network Analysis, American Behavioral Scientist, American Sociological Review*, and elsewhere.

Gregory Koger holds a Ph.D. in Political Science from the University of California, Los Angeles (2002) and is Associate Professor of Political Science at the University of Miami. He is the author of *Filibustering: A Political History of Obstruction in the House and Senate* (University of Chicago Press 2010) and his research on legislative politics, political institutions, political parties, interest groups, and elections has been published in the *American Journal of Political Science, Legislative Studies Quarterly, British Journal of Political Science*, and elsewhere.

Tetiana Kostiuchenko is a doctoral candidate in Sociology at National University of Kyiv-Mohyla Academy in Kyiv, Ukraine, where she is also a senior lecturer in the Department of Sociology. She was a Carnegie Visiting Fellow at the University of Minnesota in 2014. Her research on political elites and power networks in Ukraine and Georgia has been published in *Polish Sociological Review, Europe-Asia Studies, Journal of Contemporary Central and Eastern Europe,* and elsewhere.

David Lazer holds a Ph.D. in Political Science from the University of Michigan (1996) and is Distinguished Professor in the Department of Political Science and College of Computer and Information Science at Northeastern University. His research on network science, computational social science, political science, and organizational behavior has been published in *Science, Law and Society Review, Administrative Science Quarterly*, and elsewhere.

Claire Leavitt holds an M.A. in Political Science from Boston University (2015) and is currently a Ph.D. candidate in the Department of Government at Cornell University.

Philip Leifeld holds a Ph.D. in Politics and Public Administration from the University of Konstanz (2011) and is Senior Lecturer in the School of Social and Political Sciences at the University of Glasgow. He is author of *Policy Debates as Dynamic Networks: German Pension Politics and Privatization Discourse* (University of Chicago Press 2016) and his research on methodology, political networks, public policy, and polarization has been published in the *American Journal of Political Science, European Journal of Political Research, American Behavioral Scientist*, and elsewhere.

Zeev Maoz holds a Ph.D. in Political Science from the University of Michigan (1981) and is Distinguished Professor of Political Science at the University of California, Davis. He is author of *Defending the Holy Land: A Critical Analysis of Israel's National Security and Foreign Policy* (University of Michigan Press 2006) and his research on network analysis, international politics, Israeli national security and foreign policy, and international relations in the Middle East has been published in *American*

Political Science Review, Journal of Conflict Resolution, International Interactions, and elsewhere.

Seth Masket holds a Ph.D. in Political Science from the University of California, Los Angeles (2004) and is Professor and Chair of the Department of Political Science at the University of Denver. He is author of *The Inevitable Party: Why Attempts to Kill Political Parties Fail and How They Weaken Democracy* (Oxford University Press 2016) and his research on American politics, party organizations, state legislatures, campaigns and elections, and social networks has been published in the *American Journal of Political Science, British Journal of Political Science, Perspectives on Politics*, and elsewhere.

Scott D. McClurg holds a Ph.D. in Political Science from Washington University in St. Louis (2000) and is Professor of Political Science at Southern Illinois University. His research on political behavior, elections, social networks, and political geography has been published in the *American Journal of Political Science, Political Research Quarterly, Political Behavior*, and elsewhere.

H. Brinton Milward holds a Ph.D. in Public Administration from the Ohio State University (1978) and is Director of the School of Government and Public Policy at the University of Arizona. His research on interorganizational networks, public management, collaboration, and terrorist networks has been published in *Administrative Science Quarterly, Public Administration Review, Journal of Public Administration Research and Theory*, and elsewhere.

Shahryar Minhas holds a Ph.D. in Political Science from Duke University and will be an Assistant Professor in the Department of Political Science and Social Science Data Analytics Program at Michigan State University in 2017. His research on quantitative methods, political economy, and international relations has been published in *International Interactions, Journal of Conflict Resolution, Journal of Peace Research*, and *Research and Politics*.

James Moody holds a Ph.D. in Sociology from the University of North Carolina at Chapel Hill and is Robert O. Keohane Professor of Sociology at Duke University and Distinguished Adjunct Professor at King Abdulaziz University. His research on sociology, social networks, and quantitative methods has been published in *American Sociological Review, American Journal of Sociology, American Behavioral Scientist*, and elsewhere.

Peter Mucha holds a Ph.D. in Applied and Computational Mathematics from Princeton University (1998) and is Bowman and Gordon Gray Distinguished Term Professor of Mathematics at the University of North Carolina at Chapel Hill. His research on applied and computational mathematics, networks, and complex systems has been published in *Physical Review, Journal of Applied Mathematics, Network Science*, and elsewhere.

Amanda Murdie holds a Ph.D. in Political Science from Emory University (2009) and is Professor of International Affairs at the University of Georgia. She is author of *Help* *or Harm: The Human Security Effects of International NGOs* (Stanford University Press 2014) and her research on international relations, INGOs, human rights, and human security has been published in *International Studies Quarterly, Journal of Conflict Resolution, Human Rights Quarterly*, and elsewhere.

Hans Noel holds a Ph.D. in Political Science from the University of California, Los Angeles (2006) and is Associate Professor of Government at Georgetown University. He is author of *Political Ideologies and Political Parties in America* (Cambridge University Press 2013) and his research on political parties, ideology, methodology, presidential nominations, and political networks has been published in the *British Journal of Political Science, Perspectives on Politics, Social Networks*, and elsewhere.

John F. Padgett holds a Ph.D. in Sociology and Public Policy from the University of Michigan (1978) and is Professor of Political Science at the University of Chicago. He is the coauthor of *The Emergence of Organizations and Markets* with Walter Powell (Princeton University Press 2012) and coauthor of the article "Robust Action and the Rise of the Medici, 1400–1434" with Christopher Ansell, published in *American Journal of Sociology* (University of Chicago Press 1993). His research on networks, organizations, complexity, and history has been published in *Administrative Science Quarterly, American Political Science Review, American Politics Research*, and elsewhere.

John W. Patty holds a Ph.D. in Economics and Political Science from the California Institute of Technology (2001) and is Professor of Political Science at the University of Chicago. He is coauthor of *Learning While Governing: Information, Accountability, and Executive Branch Institutions* with Sean Gailmard (University of Chicago Press 2012) and his research on formal political theory, Congress, bureaucracy, political institutions, and American politics has been published in the *American Journal of Political Science, Games and Economic Behavior, Public Choice*, and elsewhere.

Elizabeth Maggie Penn holds a Ph.D. in Social Science from the California Institute of Technology (2003) and is Professor of Political Science at the University of Chicago. She is coauthor of *Social Choice and Legitimacy: The Possibilities of Impossibility* with John Patty (Cambridge University Press 2014) and her research on formal political theory has been published in the *American Journal of Political Science*, the *Journal of Politics, Public Choice*, and elsewhere.

Arie Perliger holds a Ph.D. in Political Science from the University of Haifa (2007) and is Associate Professor in the Department of Social Sciences at the U.S. Military Academy at West Point. He is coauthor of *Jewish Terrorism in Israel* with Ami Pedahzur (Colulmbia University Press 2009) and his research on terrorism, political violence, and Israeli politics has been published in *Political Studies, Security Studies, Israel Affairs*, and elsewhere.

Jürgen Pfeffer has a Ph.D. in Business Informatics from Vienn a University of Technology. In 2012 he became Assistant Research Professor for Societal Computing at the School of Computer Science at Carnegie Mellon University in Pittsburgh. Since March 2016 Pfeffer serves as Professor for Computational Social Science and Big Data at the Bavarian School of Public Policy at the Technical University of Munich. Pfeffer's research on the intersection of social science and computer science has been published in *Science, Journal of Marketing Communications, Digital Journalism,* and elsewhere.

Mark Pickup holds a Ph.D. in Political Science from the University of British Columbia (2005) and is Associate Professor in the Department of Political Science at Simon Fraser University. He is author of *Introduction to Time Series: Quantitative Applications in the Social Sciences* (Sage Publications 2014) and his research on the economy and democratic accountability, polls and electoral outcomes, and conditions of democratic responsiveness has been published in the *Journal of Politics, Electoral Studies, Journal of Conflict Resolution,* and elsewhere.

Marc Polizzi holds a Ph.D. in Political Science from the University of Missouri and is Assistant Professor in the Department of Political Science and Sociology at Murray State University.

Armando Razo holds a Ph.D. in Political Science from Stanford University (2003) and is Associate Professor in the Department of Political Science at Indiana University. He is author of *Social Foundations of Limited Dictatorship* (Stanford University Press 2008) and his research on political economy of development, informal institutions, social network analysis, and Latin American politics has been published in the *Journal of Theoretical Politics, Journal of Latin American Studies, World Politics,* and elsewhere.

Nils Ringe holds a Ph.D. in Political Science from the University of Pittsburgh (2006) and is Associate Professor at the University of Wisconsin, Madison. He is coauthor of *Bridging the Information Gap: Legislative Member Organizations as Social Networks in the United States and the European Union* with Jennifer Nicoll Victor (University of Michigan Press 2013) and his research on European Union politics, political parties, and social networks has been published in the *Journal of European Public Policy, Legislative Studies Quarterly, British Journal of Political Science,* and elsewhere.

Jon C. Rogowski holds a Ph.D. in Political Science from the University of Chicago (2012) and is Assistant Professor of Government at Harvard University. He is coauthor of *The Wartime President: Executive Influence and the Nationalizing Politics of Threat* with William G. Howell and Saul P. Jackson (University of Chicago Press 2013) and his research on American politics, electoral politics, and American political institutions has been published in the *American Journal of Political Science, American Political Science Review, Legislative Studies Quarterly,* and elsewhere.

Meredith Rolfe holds a Ph.D. in Political Science from the University of Chicago (2005) and is Associate Professor of Political Science at the University of Massachusetts, Amherst. She is author of *Voter Turnout: A Social Theory of Political Participation* (Cambridge University Press 2012) and her research on decision-making, social networks, and political economy has been published in *Social Networks, Network Science, Public Opinion Quarterly,* and elsewhere.

Derek Ruths holds a Ph.D. in Computer Science from Rice University (2009) and is Associate Professor in the School of Computer Science at McGill University. His research on social informatics, network science, and natural language processing has been published in the *Journal of Computational Biology, BMC Bioinformatics, Science,* and elsewhere.

Lauren Ratliff Santoro holds a Master's in Political Science from the Ohio State University (2013) and is currently a Ph.D. candidate in the Department of Political Science at the Ohio State University.

Manoj Shrestha holds a Ph.D. in Public Administration and Policy from Florida State University (2008) and is Assistant Professor of Public Administration and Policy at the University of Idaho. His research on local government, social-ecological interaction, and community sustainability has been published in *American Politics Review, State and Local Government Review,* and elsewhere.

David A. Siegel holds a Ph.D. in Political Economics from Stanford University (2006) and is Associate Professor of Political Science at Duke University. He is coauthor of *A Mathematics Course for Political and Social Research* with Will H. Moore (Princeton University Press 2013) and his research on collective action, political violence, and elections has been published in the *American Political Science Review, Journal of Politics, Journal of Peace Research,* and elsewhere.

Betsy Sinclair holds a Ph.D. in Social Science from the California Institute of Technology (2007) and is Associate Professor of Political Science at Washington University in St. Louis. She is author of *The Social Citizen* (University of Chicago Press 2012) and her research on American politics and political methodology has been published in the *American Journal of Political Science, PS: Political Science and Politics, Political Research Quarterly,* and elsewhere.

Amy Erica Smith holds a Ph.D. in Political Science from the University of Pittsburgh (2011) and is Assistant Professor of Political Science at Iowa State University. She is coauthor of *Legitimidade e Qualidade da Democracia no Brasil: Uma Visão da Cidadania* with Lucio Rennó, Matthew L. Layton, and Frederico Batista Pereira (Editora Intermeios 2011). Her research on political socialization and Latin American politics has been published in the *American Journal of Political Science, Comparative Political Studies, Journal of Politics in Latin America,* and elsewhere.

Tom A. B. Snijders holds a Ph.D. in Mathematics from the University Groningen (1979) and is Emeritus Fellow of Nuffield College at the University of Oxford. He is coauthor of *Multilevel Analysis: An Introduction to Basic and Advanced Multilevel Modeling* with Roel J. Bosker (Sage Publications 1999) and his research on statistics, social networks, and multilevel analysis has been published in *Social Networks, Sociological Methodology, Journal of the American Statistical Association,* and elsewhere.

Anand Edward Sokhey holds a Ph.D. in Political Science from the Ohio State University (2009) and is Associate Professor of Political Science at the University of Colorado at Boulder. His research on political behavior and American politics has been published in the *American Political Science Review, American Journal of Political Science, Journal of Politics*, and elsewhere.

James M. Strickland holds a Master's in Political Science from the University of Georgia (2014) and is currently a Ph.D. candidate in the Department of Political Science at the University of Michigan.

Paul W. Thurner holds a Ph.D. from the University of Mannheim (1995) and is Professor of Empirical Political Science and Policy Analysis at Ludwig Maximilian University of Munich. He is coauthor of *European Union Intergovernmental Conferences: Domestic Preference Formation, Transgovernmental Networks, and the Dynamics of Compromise* with Franz U. Pappi (Routledge 2009) and his research on European politics has been published in the *Journal of European Public Policy, Energy Policy, Advances in Statistical Analysis*, and elsewhere.

Michael D. Ward holds a Ph.D. in Political Science from Northwestern University (1977) and is professor of Political Science at Duke University. He is coauthor of *Spatial Regression Models* with Kristian S. Gleditsch (Sage Publications 2008) and his research on international relations, political economy, and security has been published in the *American Journal of Political Science, International Organization, Journal of Conflict Resolution*, and elsewhere.

Stanley Wasserman holds a Ph.D. in Statistics from Harvard University (1977) and is Rudy Professor of Statistics, Sociology, and Psychology at the University of Indiana, Bloomington. He is coauthor of the foundational book *Social Network Analysis: Methods and Applications* with Katherine Faust (Cambridge University Press 1994) and his research on applied statistics and network science has been published in the *British Journal of Mathematical and Statistical Psychology, Administrative Science Quarterly, Social Networks*, and elsewhere.

Stefan Wojcik holds a Ph.D. in Political Science from the University of Colorado at Boulder (2014) and is Postdoctoral Fellow at the Lazer Lab of Northeastern University.

Sijia Yang holds a Master's in Communication from the University of Illinois at Urbana-Champaign (2012) and is currently a Ph.D. student in the Annenberg School for Communication at the University of Pennsylvania.

PART I

NETWORK THEORY AND THE STUDY OF POLITICS

CHAPTER 1

....

INTRODUCTION

The Emergence of the Study of Networks in Politics

....

JENNIFER NICOLL VICTOR,
ALEXANDER H. MONTGOMERY, AND
MARK LUBELL

INTRODUCTION

POLITICS is about relationships. Relationships form network structures that shape, enable, and constrain political action. Understanding the properties and consequences of these network structures is a critical part of understanding the political world. Over the past few decades political scientists have increasingly applied network theory and methods to classic questions of governance, decision-making, and political behavior. This has transformed our understanding of political phenomena ranging from legislative cooperation and voter turnout to environmental policy, nuclear proliferation, and terrorism. However, in part due to the dominance of methodological individualism, network analysis has only been taken seriously in a few subject areas within the discipline of political science. Yet it is neither a methodological fad nor a niche concept; indeed, network approaches link political science with a growing movement in other social and natural sciences that use networks to analyze interdependence in complex systems. All of these fields have benefited from increasing cross-disciplinary collaboration, developing techniques and analyzing patterns that span natural and social phenomena. As the cost of computing has dropped and tools have improved, the development and use of network theory and methods have grown significantly in political science. Indeed, political scientists have meaningfully contributed to the overall development of network analysis. Political science must take networks seriously; social relationships are a fundamental component of political systems and must occupy a central place in the discipline.

Network approaches have already advanced our understanding of some of the most pressing questions in political science, such as the following: Why do individuals vote when the costs of voting exceed the benefits? Which members of Congress have the greatest potential to act as bridging agents between divergent coalitions? How do political organizations leverage long-standing relationships to their advantage? How can individuals structure democratic organizations to provide access to new information and innovations? How do governance and policy networks evolve to solve fundamental public policy problems? How can the strength of the relationships among countries encourage peaceful cooperation? Can international networks provide governance under anarchy? What are the most fruitful strategies for disrupting arms trade and violent extremist networks? Recent publications on these and other important topics reveal that answering these questions in the absence of networks results in incomplete or inaccurate conclusions.

Until recently, however, the discipline of political science has not incorporated into its scholarship the basic intuition that relationships are at the heart of politics. This is largely because methodological individualism has been the dominant paradigm in political science during the latter half of the twentieth century and the beginning of the twenty-first. Theories and methods associated with individualism have been extraordinarily productive at advancing our understanding of politics. This paradigm has been a critical force for transforming the study of politics into a discipline that is focused on the logical principles of causal reasoning and hypothesis testing with empirical evidence. Although methodological individualism technically refers to a methodological position, in practice it frequently operates as a paradigm, treating individual units as independent atomistic elements. Relational approaches challenge these assumptions and open the door to alternative epistemological strategies.

Even those who continue to employ methodological individualism can incorporate some of the benefits of relational analysis. After all, the strategic interactions between individuals that are at the heart of rational choice approaches represent a relationship between players; who plays, what moves are allowed, and which payoffs are available can be deeply affected by network structures. More generally, political behavior is a result of an interaction between individual decision-making processes and the social processes that flow on networks. Advances in network models and methods allow a level of empirical rigor that is equivalent to, or higher than, individualist approaches. The authors of this volume shift the disciplinary focus from individualism to network relationships and macro-level political institutions. Collectively, we argue strongly for a fundamental, rather than an incremental, change in perspective, from individual actors to ties between those actors.

In our view, the study of politics stands at a critical juncture. We can choose to shift our thinking, models, and units of analysis to relational approaches, or we can continue to study politics as if political actors are atomistic units only constrained in their behavior by the institutions they create and the behavior of other actors. If we seek to make progress on the important questions of our time, we must consider the contributions of relational perspectives. Network theory and methods have played important roles in and are part of robust research programs across a variety of academic disciplines. The statistical and methodological literature on network analysis encompasses not only social sciences such as sociology, economics, and anthropology, but also natural sciences such as physics, mathematics, and computer science; the humanities; and applied fields such as public health, business, and public policy. Moreover, network analysis is an increasingly prominent area of research in business, communications, and defense.

Contemporary interest in studying relational politics is driven not only by the intuition and evidence that the field provides an important perspective, but also by modern advances in data science. Empirical traces of political and other networks are often captured by information technology, but the quantitative study of such networks demands significant computational memory and processing allowances. Recent advances in the production, storage, management, and analysis of such data have played a critical role in driving engagement in topics on this scale; as personal computers have acquired the capacity to hold and process massive data sets, an increasing number of interested scholars have acquired the capability to enter this field. As a consequence, network studies have gained supporters and practitioners in virtually every area of political study, including but not limited to political institutions, political behavior, public policy, parties and elections, public opinion, interest groups, social movements, political communication, political economy, democratization, transnational actors, international organizations, conflict resolution, peace studies, and security studies. Indeed, few tools of inquiry cut so broadly across the subfields, which is reflected in the depth and breadth of contributions to this volume. In short, we are at a critical moment in the development of a new approach to the study of politics—a moment when new generations of interdisciplinary scholars and graduate students are being exposed to network methods and the new ways of studying politics that they offer.

The study of political networks has also produced important innovations in the methodology of network analysis. Political network analysis requires a fundamental understanding of a variety of theoretical concepts as well as empirical research design and data analysis methods. Political network analysts have generated and adapted numerous methodological innovations, including a generalization of the powerful and popular exponential random graph model (ERGM) as well as a new method of Markov Chain Monte Carlo (MCMC) estimation that allows the model to be applied to networks in which actors can have more than one interaction between them (Cranmer and Desmarais, 2011; Cranmer, Desmarais, and Menninga, 2012; Desmarais and Cranmer, 2012). Furthermore, these and other scholars have developed new techniques for performing unbiased, maximum pseudo-likelihood estimation by bootstrapping across networks in temporal ERGMs (Leifeld, Cranmer, and Desmarais, 2015; Leifeld et al., 2014). Political scientists have also made major contributions to latent space models that estimate the positions of actors in (unobserved) social spaces (Ward, Hoff, and Lofdahl, 2003; Ward and Hoff, 2008; Minhas, Hoff, and Ward, 2016). These methodological innovations from political science are an important part of the overall interdisciplinary dialogue in network science, which is currently undergoing a high rate of methodological development to test relational hypotheses in new ways. This evolution is akin to the transformation in econometrics from basic regression models to more general approaches like maximum likelihood and Bayesian models.

The chapters in this book address three central questions: *What* is political network analysis? *How* does it provide insight into important political phenomena? *Why* is it crucial for all political analysts to engage in network analysis? In this introductory chapter we discuss why networks are crucial for bridging the micro-macro divide; provide a brief history of networks in the discipline; demonstrate the cross-cutting ties among subfields in the study of political networks, highlighting important foundational pieces; give an overview of the chapters in the handbook; and conclude with our thoughts on the future of political network analysis.

We build this handbook on a number of introductory books that describe network methods and theory. For example, Hanneman and Riddle's online textbook (2005) is a great methodological introduction for beginners, although the examples primarily come from sociology. John Scott's textbook on networks is highly accessible, although again it is not specific to political science (Scott 2012). We also build upon political science–focused articles that describe the contributions of network methods to subfields like American politics (Heaney and McClurg, 2009), international relations (Hafner-Burton, Kahler, and Montgomery, 2009; Ward, Stovel, and Sacks, 2011), and comparative politics (Siegel, 2011), as well as broad overviews of the value of network research for political science (Lazer, 2011). This handbook seeks to fill the remaining gap by providing an overview of network analysis specific to political science—and its special set of applications and questions—without being constrained to a limited space in order to tackle a subject and material that have exploded over the last decade.

WHY NETWORKS?

For most people, the importance of networks is clear: social and business network contacts are instrumental to meeting a romantic partner, finding a job, or other social and economic opportunities. More broadly, networks have been fundamental in modern political and economic life to the creation and evolution of social and economic structures (Padgett and Powell, 2012). Large-scale modern societies, with their multiple levels and spheres of social behavior, would not exist without social networks. Social networks are rooted in the evolution of human sociality (Apicella et al., 2012). Yet political analysis has largely been focused on individuals and institutions without considering how relationships constitute both.

Network analysis directly addresses a fundamental and enduring question in political analysis—a problem that has been called variously the "micro-macro divide" (Eulau and Rothenberg, 1986; Eulau, 1963) or individualism-holism (Wendt, 1999). Quite simply, should our understanding of politics be focused on individual actors (i.e., at the micro level) or aggregated social behavior in political institutions (i.e., at the macro level)? Typically, scholars examine either the properties and collective actions of aggregate groups and political institutions or the choices, attitudes, and strategies of individuals. Political scientists also often ask questions about how political institutions influence individual level behavior and vice versa. Neither of these perspectives takes into account how individuals are embedded in social relationships. These relationships, in turn, enable the formation of groups that can ultimately influence the macro-level structure of political institutions. Conversely, the effects of political institutions on individual behavior are also mediated by networks. Hence, networks are an enduring meso-level component of political systems that merits fundamental research.

At the most basic level, this tension is a question of selecting an appropriate unit of analysis for each research question—a lesson included in any introductory course on research design. Since at least the 1960s, political science has been dominated by a focus on methodological individualism, resulting in an increased focus on individuals over systems. This paradigm has led to core discoveries in underlying causal mechanisms at work in many political and social circumstances. For example, without the focus on individuals, we could not have developed the basic theory of re-election motivating legislative action (Mayhew, 2004) or game theoretical concepts of nuclear deterrence (Schelling, 1960, 1966).

At the same time, methodological individualism has sometimes come at a price, eroding the discipline's capacity to richly describe the historical and political processes guiding the evolution and normative consequences of political systems. The analytical challenges posed by methodological individualism have generated numerous theoretical and substantive shortcuts to make analyses tractable by treating groups or organizations as individuals; indeed, methodological individualism is more accurately termed *methodological atomism*, given that it is so frequently applied to units that are not individuals. The state as a unitary actor, the weight of public opinion, the public mood, existence of a political culture, and imposition of structural constraints are inventions constructed, at least in part, as explanatory devices to avoid the unwieldy and sometimes inappropriate apparatus imposed by a reliance on individuals as the unit of political analysis.

More important, when we focus solely on individuals or systems, analyses undertaken at only those levels are likely to provide incomplete or insufficient explanations. Theoretically, the field has been aware for some time that many political outcomes depend on interactions among actors—and that these interactions are in turn constrained by critical institutions (Keohane and Nye, 1977; Shepsle and Weingast, 1987; Padgett and Ansell, 1993; Ostrom, 1995). To offer explanations about such circumstances, scholars must understand not only the incentives of the actors but also the relationships between them and the institutions in which they operate.

Even worse, many empirical estimators rely on statistical assumptions that are grounded in methodological individualism, such as independence of error terms. Social reality violates these types of assumptions, leading to incorrect estimates of population parameters or standard errors. Thus, when we pose questions about politics and consider the appropriate unit of analysis with which to study a particular phenomenon, it becomes impossible to develop an analytical strategy that is wholly individualistic or group oriented. The interdependence between individual and system levels of analysis necessitates an intermediate level. Consequently, a solution to the problem of the micro-macro divide lies in an analytical strategy that accounts for complex interdependence: network analysis.

Beyond bridging the micro-macro divide, network analysis allows for studying meso-level phenomena in and of themselves. Often in network studies the unit of interest is not the individual or the group, but the relationship. The relationship of interest may exist between individuals (e.g., campaign contributions between donors and candidates), organizations (e.g., country-to-country trade or conflict, civil wars), or between the two (e.g., citizen participation in government or nongovernmental organizations). The pattern of relationships is generally hypothesized to reflect a particular social process, such as reciprocity or homophily. Network analysis provides the theoretical framework and tools to engage in analyses at these meso levels that are neither wholly micro nor macro. Adoption of such a perspective provides the analyst with a powerful suite of analytical devices that can account for relational interdependence.

Part of the attraction of this approach is that it allows a scholar to develop models that may more closely resemble reality. Given the complex nature of interdependent relationships in the social and political world, network analysis gives a scholar the freedom to relax assumptions that are necessary in a more constrained framework. Whereas researchers may have previously recognized a trade-off between parsimony and external validity, network approaches offer an analytical strategy that both satisfies the rigorous requirements of scientific reasoning and allows for inference in a complex context.

There are profound implications of a vigorous network focus for the study of politics: the challenges of this approach are observational, theoretical, and methodological and apply to all levels of analysis. First, analysis may occur at the level of individuals, where relations between units are understood to affect the dependent variable under inquiry. Second, inquiry may occur at the level of the relationship between actors. Third, scholars may conduct inquiry at a systemic level using detailed knowledge of an entire network. Regardless of the level of analysis chosen, relations—and therefore networks—must be part of any analysis. Interdependence is both a fundamental theoretical postulate and a social fact that drives politics and political affairs, not a derivative conclusion; without considering the effects of relations, political analysis is necessarily incomplete.

A SHORT HISTORY OF NETWORKS IN POLITICAL SCIENCE

The inclusion of network-oriented perspectives in political science has occurred in three waves over the past century. The first wave appeared around the 1930s and provided descriptions of the importance of relational conceptualizations to sociological questions. Perhaps the first prominent example of this is Jacob Moreno's study of the New York Training School for Girls, which was an attempt to understand why some enrollees in this state-mandated reformatory program were more successful than others. His studies led him to develop the first sociograms, which depicted the relationships between individuals in a defined group. Not only did Moreno controvert then-dominant Freudian theory, but he also pioneered a new form of psychotherapy based on group interactions rather than individual interactions (Moreno, 1934, 1951). His findings spawned an entire field of sociometry, which blossomed into social network theory and analysis. He was not alone; other scholars were making similar observations about the importance of human relationships for understanding the political and social world (Routt, 1938).

The second wave of network applications in political science accompanied the trend toward behavioralism that dominated the discipline in the 1950s and 1960s. During this wave, scholars conceptualized political actors as being driven primarily by psychological characteristics. A handful of researchers recognized that one's psychological approach to a community was affected by one's depth of connectivity in that community (which we would now call *embeddedness*). For example, scholars began to study personal connections of state legislators (Patterson, 1959; Monsma, 1966; Eulau, 1962; Wahlke et al., 1962; Young, 1966). Others focused more on informal communication and strategic cueing as creating connections among political actors (Fiellin, 1962; Matthews, 1959) and on the importance of networks for voters (Lazarsfeld, Berelson, and McPhee, 1968; Berelson, Lazarsfeld, and McPhee, 1986). Ultimately, in the twentieth century this line of inquiry became much less dominant in the discipline than the exclusively individualistic, rational choice approach. Some important network contributions were also made in the public policy realm such as, Hugh Heclo's study of issue networks (Heclo, 1978).

We are currently experiencing the third wave of network study in political science, which is characterized by the development of theoretical and statistical network models of politics. In the 1980s scholars began to focus on the intersection of institutions and public policy. Several groundbreaking studies on representation and lobbying in Washington spawned this third wave (Laumann and Knoke, 1987; Heinz et al., 1990). Scholars also advanced an understanding of socially dependent political decision-making (Matthews and Stimson, 1975; Huckfeldt and Sprague, 1987). Not coincidentally, in the 1990s we saw major advances in computer science and technology as well as scholarship that recognized the importance of context and relationships for understanding all kinds of political behavior and outcomes. The network scholarship in political science is now heavily engaged in the broader dialogue on interdisciplinary methods in network science. The chapters in this volume provide insightful and detailed reviews of the development of literature across many lines of inquiry.

American Political Institutions and Behavior

The study of political networks in American politics has progressed in two related threads that mirror the major topics of this subfield. These threads can be broadly described as institutional politics and behavioral politics.

In the behavioral thread, about seventy years ago scholars recognized the stickiness of political discourse: individuals do not often change their minds (Lazarsfeld et al., 1948; Berelson, 1954). In later research Robert Huckfeldt and John Sprague extended these findings to voters' choices (R. Huckfeldt and Sprague, 1987; R. R. Huckfeldt and Sprague, 1995). More recently, the rational choice model of vote choice has been updated to recognize the importance of voters' contextual and interdependent decision-making (Rolfe, 2012; Sinclair, 2012). Further research has brought nuance to understanding the ways in which social discourse contributes to individual decision-making and behavior (Klofstad, Sokhey, and McClurg, 2013; Klofstad, 2010; McClurg, 2006; Sokhey and McClurg, 2012).

Much of the early research on networks in American political institutions focused on legislative networks. For quite some time scholars have recognized the relevance of social connections between lawmakers (Routt, 1938; Patterson, 1959; Eulau, 1962; Bogue and Marlaire, 1975; Caldeira and Patterson, 1987, 1988; Arnold, Deen, and Patterson, 2000; Peoples, 2008). More recently, scholars have focused on a variety of potential ties between legislators, including cosponsorship (Burkett and Skvoretz, 2001; Crisp, Kanthak, and Leijonhufvud, 2004; Fowler, 2006a, 2006b; Kirkland, 2011; Bratton and Rouse, 2011; Cho and Fowler, 2010), committee assignments (Porter, Mucha, Newman, and Warmbrand, 2005; Porter, Mucha, Newman, and Friend, 2007), campaign contributions (Koger and Victor, 2009; Victor and Koger, 2016), legislative staff (Ringe, Victor, and Gross, 2013), shared workspace and spatial proximity (Masket, 2008; Rogowski and Sinclair, 2012), legislative member organizations (Ringe and Victor, 2013), and "Dear Colleague" letters (Craig, 2015). Further research in political institutions has led to important understandings of the ways that groups interact with the judicial system and the nature of judicial decision-making (Box-Steffensmeier, Christenson, and Hitt, 2013; Box-Steffensmeier and Christenson, 2014).

Policy Studies and Political Institutions

Recent progress in policy studies has been made through building on some of the earliest policy network studies (Heinz et al., 1997). Some of these studies involve the comparative analysis of relationships among political elites across political and policy systems (Laumann and Knoke, 1987; Laumann and Pappi, 1976).

More recent efforts involve network mappings of the policy process (Heaney, 2006; Scholz, Berardo, and Kile, 2008; Berardo and Scholz, 2010; Lubell, Henry, and McCoy, 2010), network impacts on tax compliance (Roch, Scholz, and McGraw, 2000), and the involvement of the public in the supply and consumption of policy benefits (Schneider, Teske, and Marschall, 2002; Schneider et al., 2003). Networks also play a prominent role in public administration research, particularly in the area of network governance (Provan and Kenis, 2008; Jones, Hesterly, and Borgatti, 1997). Recent research also points toward the role of social networks in both the creation and resolution of important public policy problems (Christakis and Fowler, 2011). Moreover, students of institutions have introduced network concepts into the study of cooperation and conflict within and across institutions (Box-Steffensmeier and Christenson, 2014).

Environmental policy and politics have witnessed one of the most robust applications of network theory and methods. Environmental issues are rooted in collective-action problems, an area in which scholars like Elinor Ostrom have long pointed out the importance of networks as a form of social capital (Ostrom, 1995). Environmental policy scholars have advanced theories of the policy process by examining how networks influence the formation of advocacy coalitions (Weible, 2005; Henry, 2011), patterns of policy learning (Berardo, Heikkila, and Gerlak, 2014), capacity for cooperation (Schneider et al., 2003; Berardo and Scholz, 2010), and the structure (Lubell, Robins, and Wang, 2014) and performance (Lubell et al., 2016) of complex and polycentric institutional arrangements.

INTERNATIONAL RELATIONS

Network analysis has a lengthy and often-forgotten tradition in international relations (IR) that until recently followed a different trajectory from the rest of political network analysis. Rather than focusing on connections between individuals or other units, early pioneers worked on examining the emergent structure of the international system resulting from ties derived from trade, international governmental organization (IGO) membership, diplomatic exchanges, and diplomatic visits (Brams, 1966, 1969; Christopherson, 1976; Savage and Deutsch, 1960; Skjelsbaek, 1972). Another group used blockmodeling to determine the socioeconomic structure of the international system (Breiger, 1981; Faber, 1987; Nemeth and Smith, 1985; Peacock, Hoover, and Killian, 1988; Smith and White, 1992; Snyder and Kick, 1979; Van Rossem, 1996). These early works took advantage of then-new techniques commonly used today. Nevertheless, they mostly observed the structure of the networks rather than using network analysis to test structural theories, predict outcomes of interest, or analyze the choices of individual units.

A second wave of research in IR rose when the discipline started showing a renewed interest in networks as a mode of analysis. This wave focused on using network metrics (whether traditional or newly created) in traditional monadic or dyadic regressions. Research in IR focused on IGOs (Dorussen and Ward, 2008; Hafner-Burton and Montgomery, 2006, 2008, 2012; Ward, 2006; Warren, 2010), human rights (Böhmelt, Koubi, and Bernauer, 2014; Carpenter, 2011, 2014; Carpenter et al., 2014; Moore, Eng, and Daniel, 2003; Murdie, 2014; Murdie and Davis, 2012; Murdie, Wilson, and Davis, 2016), conflict (Corbetta, 2010; Corbetta and Dixon, 2005; Maoz, 2006, 2009, 2011; Maoz, Kuperman, et al., 2006; Maoz, Terris, et al. 2007), arms trade (Kinsella, 2006; 2014; Montgomery, 2005, 2008, 2013), and terrorism (Horowitz and Potter, 2013; Asal, Ackerman, and Rethemeyer, 2012; Perliger and Pedahzur, 2011; Eilstrup-Sangiovanni and Jones, 2008; Pedahzur and Perliger, 2006; Brams, Mutlu, and Ramirez, 2006; Sageman, 2004; Krebs, 2002). These approaches were theoretically innovative, taking seriously the idea that complex dependency structures among states were relevant. However, they primarily used network measures and concepts without methodologically challenging the dominant independence assumptions of the discipline. Still, these works blazed a path for more recent work that has questioned methodological individualism directly.

This wave continues to advance a productive research agenda today, and many of the chapters in this volume reflect the gains made in this wave. Yet we are also seeing the beginnings of a third wave of political network analysis in IR, enabled by methodological advances that have allowed researchers to throw out the long-standing assumption that observations (whether monadic or dyadic) are independent of each other (Snijders, 2001; Hoff, Raftery, and Handcock, 2002; Morris, Handcock, and Hunter, 2008; Cranmer and Desmarais, 2011). In exploring interconnectivity, models of geographical and social distance–based spatial networks and their dependencies have also become a topic of interest (Gleditsch and Ward, 2000, 2001; Ward, Hoff, and Lofdahl, 2003; Hoff and Ward, 2004; Plümper and Neumayer, 2010). While the previous wave treated networks seriously as a unit of inquiry, the third has enabled the full implications of network approaches to be realized. These innovations have challenged previously long-held assumptions about the nature of politics, including casting doubt on the democratic peace, diffusion of democracy, alliance structures, preferential trade agreements, and international trade (Cranmer, Desmarais, and Menninga, 2012; Cranmer, Heinrich, and Desmarais, 2014; Gleditsch and Ward, 2006; Hoff and Ward, 2004; Kinne, 2013, 2014; Manger, Pickup, and Snijders, 2012; Ward, Ahlquist, and Rozenas, 2013; Ward and Hoff, 2007; Ward, Siverson, and Cao, 2007).

THE NETWORK STRUCTURE
OF POLITICAL NETWORK RESEARCH

We can observe these general waves of research through an introspective analysis of the network literature. Bibliometric networks provide a useful approach for understanding the relational structure of knowledge within a discipline, typically through examining the strength of relationships between authors, articles, journals, or topics. Here we employ two techniques: co-citation and citation analysis. We start with co-citation analysis, in which the more two works are cited together, the stronger their relationship is (Small, 1973); this metric has been widely used to measure the most important publications in a field of study (Dong and Chen, 2015). We complement this technique with citation analysis, in which two works are connected if one work cites another work.

We have created two co-citation maps and one citation map using the literature in political networks. These maps are based on the same underlying data but analyze different units and relationships. First, we examined a co-citation network of journals, in which two journals are more strongly related the more those journals have both been cited in the same article. Second, we examined a co-citation network of articles, in which articles are more strongly related the more times both have been cited in other articles. Third, since many of the co-cited pieces are outside of the network literature, we also examined which network articles cite each other. These approaches help us understand how the political science network literature has developed by topic and subfield. It also helps us understand where the anchors of the literature are, which can reveal important sources that have made outstanding contributions and perhaps also areas of opportunity for expansion.

To analyze these citation networks, we used the Web of Science search engine and bibliometric graphing software VOSviewer (van Eck and Waltman, 2014). We searched a set of relevant political science and related subfield journals for all articles using the word "network" in the title, abstract, or keywords from 1960 to 2016.[1] The results of the search included 971 input articles from twenty-eight political science journals, which in total cited more than 19,000 (non-unique) sources. In the graphs presented in this chapter, the size of a node and its label indicate its degree centrality (sum of number of ties, weighted by strength) in the network. The layout of items indicates the strength of the relationships between them: items that are more strongly related by being co-cited (or cited, for figure 1.3) are generally closer to each other. The layout thus indicates clusters of highly related groups of sources.

Figure 1.1 shows the co-citation connectivity of journals. Journals are included in the graph if they have been cited a minimum of twenty times in other journals; the graph includes 286 journals. Journals are closer and larger as they receive more co-citations.[2]

There are four distinct clusters apparent in the network. The red cluster on the left is made up of public administration journals, anchored by the flagship journal of that subfield, *Public Administration Review*. This large cluster also includes policy journals. The large green cluster near the bottom of the graph is made up of IR journals, most prominently *International Organization*, along with some comparative politics and economics journals. The blue cluster in the top right contains general political science journals and those focused on American politics. This cluster is dominated by the *American Political Science Review* (APSR), the flagship journal of the discipline.

The small yellow cluster in the center of the graph that bridges the other three clusters includes primarily sociological and methodological journals, showing that many authors have cited sociological research in their political networks analysis. In addition, some books are sufficiently co-cited that they appear in the graph (e.g., Russett and Oneal, 2001, *Triangulating Peace*).

Note that while the source publications all have network content, they frequently cite non-network items as well; hence journals generally prominent in the field will still be quite central even if they have few or no network articles. For example, the APSR ranks first in co-citations *from* network articles in American politics (see table 1.1), but only fifth in citations *to* network articles, and eighth in total network articles published out of the twenty-eight journals surveyed (see table 1.3). The flagship journal of political science has therefore played a modest role in publishing network research, but appears more prominently in the co-citation analysis simply because scholars tend to cite APSR articles.

This visualization demonstrates both bridges and the gaps between political science subfields. First, there are three main subtopics on which political network scholars have published, and these are somewhat related to main subfields of the discipline: American politics, IR and comparative politics, and public administration and policy. There is greater overlap in co-citation between American politics and IR journals than there is between these clusters and the policy and public administration journals. Many of the policy-oriented journals represented here seem to be a bridge between public administration and other subfields. It is somewhat surprising that public administration is not more closely connected to American politics; however, network scholarship in this field has been strong and developed somewhat independently from the rest of political science. Finally, the American politics subfield has heavily cited the sociological journals, demonstrating the main path by which political science has incorporated network studies into the field.

Table 1.1 lists top journals represented in the graph with their respective weights. The algorithm in the bibliometric software calculates the clusters endogenously; we have not imposed clusters or their elements onto the graph. As a result, the graph has outliers such as the *American Sociological Review*, which is a prominent member of the cluster that primarily contains IR and comparative politics journals rather than the cluster that contains many sociological journals. Also, the last and smallest cluster (yellow and central) contains a mix of journals, several of which are sociological, while others are heavy on quantitative methods.

In figure 1.2 we took the same input data set of 971 "network" articles in political science journals and analyzed their bibliographies for co-citations. Again, references are more strongly related if they are both cited by the same source. Using the article as the unit of analysis, we can identify influential items. Articles that have been cited at least eight times are included in the analysis, and then further limited to the top five hundred cited items. Figure 1.2 shows the co-citation network of individual published articles on "networks" published in political science journals.[3]

Table 1.1 Top Journals in Each Co-citation Cluster by Source

Cluster/Subfield	Journal	Weight (Co-citations)
Public Admin	*Public Administration Review*	34,756
	Journal of Public Admin. Research and Theory	32,574
	Policy Studies Journal	12,775
	Administration Science Quarterly	11,913
	Administration & Society	7,882
International Relations	*International Organization*	22,579
	Journal of Conflict Resolution	19,898
	Journal of Peace Research	16,266
	American Sociological Review	14,128
	International Studies Quarterly	12,300
American Politics	*American Political Science Review*	52,154
	American Journal of Political Science	48,650
	Journal of Politics	32,307
	Political Research Quarterly	9,139
	Political Psychology	8,716
Sociology & Methods	*American Journal of Sociology*	19,543
	Social Networks	11,497
	Political Analysis	8,884
	Annual Review of Sociology	6,495
	Legislative Studies Quarterly	6,104

In figure 1.2 we see a dense and tightly connected graph with four major clusters and two minor ones. On the left-hand side of the graph we see a public administration cluster (red) that is prominent and has many highly cited items, but is not at the center of the graph. The network-oriented literature in public administration is strong, but not as well integrated with other threads of political science as some other fields. The public administration cluster includes works that have spawned considerable lines of research (Provan and Milward, 1995; O'Toole, 1997; Agranoff and McGuire, 2003; Granovetter, 1985; Agranoff and McGuire, 2001). This set of articles is the foundation of the idea of network governance and public management of networks: how to organize networks of organizations to pursue policy goals that single organizations cannot independently achieve. As Agranoff and McGuire (2001, 296) note, "networks constitute emergent phenomena that are distinctive managerial vehicles and that offer challenges for the single organization and its management."

Table 1.2 shows the top 5 publications represented in the Figure 1.2, for each cluster or subfield. We display the authors and year of the most heavily weighted sources, with their co-citation weights (NOTE: only a small selection of nodes are labled in Figure 1.2). As with the previous, the clusters are identified endogenously, but here they logically represent the main subfields in political science (e.g., Public Administration, American Politics, Public Policy, Methods, and International Relations).

Table 1.2 Top Articles/Books in Each Co–citation Cluster

Cluster/Subfield	Citation	Weight (Co-citations)
Public Administration	Provan and Milward, 1995	1,105
	O'Toole, 1997	1,073
	Agranoff and McGuire, 2003	954
	Granovetter, 1985	622
	Agranoff and McGuire, 2001	618
American Politics	Huckfeldt and Sprague, 1995	1,501
	Granovetter, 1973	1,175
	Mutz, 2002a	1,029
	Putnam, 2000	960
	Mutz, 2002b	877
Public Policy	Sabatier, 1993	873
	Putnam and Nanetti, 1993	719
	Schneider et al., 2003	695
	Heclo, 1978	534
	Berardo and Scholz, 2010	493
Methods & International Relations	Wasserman and Faust, 1994	979
	Burt, 1992	503
	Beck, Katz, and Tucker, 1998	349
	Cranmer and Desmarais, 2011	326
	Hafner-Burton and Montgomery, 2006	299

Figure 1.2 also includes a large (red) cluster at the top right of the graph that contains predominantly items on American politics. However, toward the middle of the graph but still in this cluster, we see cross-cutting items such as McPherson et al.'s classic work on homophily (McPherson, Smith-Lovin, and Cook, 2001); Putnam's *Bowling Alone* (Putnam, 2000); and sociologist Mark Granovetter's classic piece about the strength of weak ties (Granovetter, 1973), which argues that weak social ties provide an individual with "strength" because they help to connect a single person with disparate others. Deeper in this cluster are classic contributions on American politics by Diana Mutz, Robert Huckfeldt, and John Sprague (Mutz 2002a, 2002b; R. R. Huckfeldt and Sprague, 1995; R. Huckfeldt and Sprague, 1987), who teach us about the importance of listening to countervailing information and the importance of local campaign effects. Bob Huckfeldt and John Sprague's field work in Indiana and Missouri provided a foundational base on which scholars have understood the spread of political information in communication networks. And Diana Mutz's work on persuasion, information, and our choices about how we expose ourselves to confirming and countervailing information has provided a base of understanding on which many scholars have built.

Bridging these two clusters is a public policy group (yellow) that is dominated by foundational pieces that are classics or instrumental in the development of the field (Sabatier, 1993; Putnam and Nanetti, 1993; Schneider et al., 2003; Heclo, 1978; Berardo and Scholz, 2010). The public policy literature has focused on networks as core ingredients of advocacy coalitions, in which policy actors coordinate their behavior on the basis of shared policy beliefs. Public policy research has also deeply investigated the role of networks as social capital that catalyzes cooperation, coordination, and learning in fragmented institutional arrangements. The focus on social capital derives from Elinor Ostrom's Nobel prize–winning research on the evolution of cooperation in the governance of common-pool resources. Interestingly, public policy research spans a structural hole between public administration and other political science subfields, most likely due to an overlap in interest among core ideas like social capital, embeddedness, social influence, and homophily as well as a common origin in network theory and methods from sociology.

The IR cluster (green) also includes critical pieces in political methodology, reflecting both the focus on methods in network analysis in this subfield as well as innovations springing from it (Wasserman and Faust, 1994; Burt, 1992; Beck, Katz, and Tucker, 1998; Cranmer and Desmarais, 2011; Hafner-Burton and Montgomery, 2006). This includes Wasserman and Faust's classic text on social network analysis; Beck, Katz, and Tucker's "Taking Time Seriously"; and Cranmer and Desmarais's work on inference that demonstrated significant third-party effects on the likelihood of conflict, both in terms of piling-on effects and the rarity of two disputants on the same side also fighting each other in international conflicts. This cluster also indicates IR's concern with network theories, including both Burt's structural holes thesis and

Hafner-Burton and Montgomery's hypotheses on centrality and group dynamics in international conflict.

Finally, two smaller clusters emerge that include subfield- or field-spanning works, including research on collective action in networks (Siegel, 2009) and foundational network publications in political science that, though associated with a particular subfield, contain insights that have been applied across such boundaries (Fowler, 2006a). The bibliometric analysis suggests a fair degree of commonality in these threads of research. We are also struck by the relatively weak presence of comparative politics research among these citations. We see applications of network theories and methods to essential questions in comparative politics as a prime area for future research.

Figure 1.3 displays a citation network. While co-citation networks provide an overall picture of how network articles are embedded in the larger discipline, the citation networks seen in figure 1.3 within our sample demonstrate both connections and divisions within the political networks community.[4] While quantitative network analysis in IR is clustered at the bottom (green), a disconnected group of qualitative IR approaches to networks can be seen in the lower left (light blue). Public administration and public policy are in the upper left (red/purple), while American politics is mostly grouped in the upper right (blue), with a few methodological and subject-area-spanning articles in the middle (yellow).

Table 1.3 details the distribution of the number of network articles and citations across the twenty-seven connected journals in our pool of twenty-eight journals (see

Table 1.3 Citation among the Sample Journals

Journal	Network Articles	Network Articles Rank	Citations	Citations Rank
Public Administration Review	126	1	343	3
Journal of Public Administration Research and Theory	91	2	369	2
Policy Studies Journal	80	3	221	6
Journal of Politics	57	4	323	4
Journal of Peace Research	54	5	120	13
American Journal of Political Science	51	6	416	1
International Studies Quarterly	45	7	122	12

(cont.)

Table 1.3 (*continued*)

Journal	Network Articles	Network Articles Rank	Citations	Citations Rank
American Political Science Review	42	8	227	5
Journal of Conflict Resolution	41	9	128	10
Comparative Political Studies	40	10	38	19
Political Behavior	36	11	184	8
American Politics Research	35	12	198	7
Political Research Quarterly	35	13	136	9
International Organization	28	14	60	17
British Journal of Political Science	25	15	115	14
Political Psychology	24	16	126	11
Comparative Politics	21	17	7	26
Journal of Theoretical Politics	19	18	62	16
Party Politics	17	19	16	24
Political Analysis	14	20	88	15
Legislative Studies Quarterly	14	21	40	18
World Politics	14	22	23	21
International Security	14	23	20	22
Perspectives on Politics	14	24	17	23
Polity	12	25	13	25
State Politics & Policy Quarterly	11	26	28	20
European Political Science Review	9	27	6	27

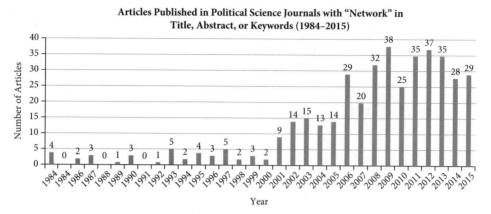

FIGURE 1.4 Frequency of scholarly political science articles on networks.

also note 1 in this chapter). It demonstrates how well-established network analysis is in public administration and public policy journals. As far as general field journals go, network articles in both the *Journal of Politics* and *the American Journal of Political Science* are more frequently published (and are cited) at higher rates than the APSR; similarly, the *Journal of Peace Research, International Studies Quarterly*, and the *Journal of Conflict Resolution* outrank the top IR field journals (*International Organization* and *International Security*).

This handbook is being published at a time of increasing interest in network methods and applications for questions of politics. We calculate that in the ten-year period between 2002 and 2012, the number of scholarly social science articles focused on networks increased by 289 percent. Figure 1.4 shows the distribution of social network–related articles in political science journals over the past thirty years. Around the turn of the twenty-first century a surge occurred in network articles. Our count includes only articles that have the word "network" in the title, abstract, or keywords, excluding those that clearly referenced networks of a nonsocial nature (e.g., computer networks).

We see this increase in popularity as a function of the intuitive nature of studying politics as relational phenomena; the increased technological capacity to gather, manage, and analyze network data; and a multiplier effect that occurs from the coincidence of these events.

STRUCTURE OF THE BOOK

This book is divided into seven parts. Part 1 contains, in addition to the current introductory chapter, five chapters that focus on the theoretical foundations underlying the study of political networks. In chapter 2 John F. Padgett connects the emergence, maintenance, and evolution of formal organizations, markets, and states to the transposition of ties across multiplex networks and the autocatalytic reproduction of networks, reflecting on his recently published book coauthored with Woody Powell (2012). In chapter 3 David Knoke and Tetiana Kostiuchenko describe the power structures present in policy networks. The study of power and political networks has a history that predates the recent rediscovery of network analysis in political science. This chapter connects historical and contemporary notions of structure and power in politics to networks. In chapter 4 David Lazer and Stefan Wojcik provide a general introduction to the intersection of political networks and computational social science. Along with his laboratory partners, postdoctoral fellows, and students, Dr. Lazer has been at the forefront of this young field that is at the cutting edge of harnessing technological innovation and methodological sophistication to engage in inferential modeling on topics as diverse as political communication and socialization and the complex world of political campaign donations. Lazer shows that "thinking big" is both computationally challenging and rewarding. In chapter 5 Jon C. Rogowski and Betsy Sinclair discuss how to engage in causal inference in studies of political networks. Parsing homophilous relationships with causal ones has been a vexing obstacle for scholars of political networks. Sinclair and Rogowski offer concrete advice about how to approach causal inference in the study of political networks. In chapter 6 John W. Patty and Elizabeth Maggie Penn provide an accessible introduction to major theoretical concepts in network analysis. The authors provide a roadmap from useful network concepts, such as centrality and connectivity, to their empirical measurement in political science applications.

Part 2 includes seven chapters that provide an introduction to the primary methodological concepts and approaches used in network analysis. This introduction is intended to be largely nontechnical and accessible; for scholars who seek to enter this field, it provides a useful starting point from which to pursue further study on cutting-edge methodological approaches to questions of politics that involve networks and interdependency. In chapter 7 Justin H. Gross and Joshua M. Jansa provide a primer on introductory network analysis, focusing on instruction in important relational concepts, measurement, and data collection. They address important challenges in research design, such as missing data and sampling, while drawing comparisons with more traditional, frequentist forms of statistical analysis. In chapter 8 Bruce A. Desmarais and Skyler J. Cranmer provide an intermediate introduction to statistical inference in network analysis. They compare a sample of state-of-the-art techniques, including ERGMs, for analyzing network data in ways that will be familiar to students of traditional statistical methods. In chapter 9 Tom A. B. Snijders and Mark Pickup describe stochastic actor oriented models for analyzing dynamic networks. The technique introduced in this chapter is designed for networks in which unbalanced panels can be described as evolving in a Markov process; the chapter also includes an overview of analysis using RSiena software. In chapter 10 Cassy Dorff, Shahryar Minhas, and Michael D. Ward describe methodological approaches for latent and spatial networks. They enumerate the advantages and limitations of the latent space compared with other approaches, including guidance about useful software. In chapter 11 Jürgen Pfeffer provides an instructive introduction to visualization of network data. The authors discuss the principles of visualizing large interrelated data and offer useful and attractive examples. In chapter 12 Philip Leifeld delivers an introduction to discourse analysis using networks. Verbal interactions between political actors provide a rich data source from which to study connections, commonalities, and conflict. Leifeld shows how such exchanges can be analyzed as data, with known properties that allow scholars to draw inferences with the advantage of a temporal component. In chapter 13 Sijia Yang and Sandra González-Bailón describe techniques for analyzing semantic networks. Drawing from the rich literature on natural language processing and machine learning, this chapter introduces readers to essential methodological considerations when extracting and building up semantic networks from textual data.

Parts 3 through 6 are the heart of this volume. They include twenty-four chapters that offer insights on four substantive subfields. These chapters are authored by leading scholars in each of these subfields who have made important contributions to the literature. The chapters provide not only a state-of-the-literature review, but also a sense of how network theories and methods are providing answers to some of the most important questions in each field. Part 3 includes eight chapters on topics of American politics, covering political institutions and political behavior. In chapter 14 Meredith Rolfe and Stephanie Chan provide a summary of the state of modern research that seeks to understand voting and political participation. They describe a variety of methodological approaches to these questions, emphasizing that accounting for social context is critical for understanding these questions. Moving from the question of *whether* to vote to one about *how* to vote, in chapter 15 Lauren Ratliff Santoro and Paul A. Beck explore the effects of social networks on vote choice. They provide an excellent review of the literature in this area, one of the oldest in our discipline, dating back to the behavioral revolution in the mid-twentieth century. This chapter also draws upon useful lessons in comparative politics on this topic and outlines the challenges for making further progress on questions of vote choice. In chapter 16 Paul S. Herrnson and Justin H. Kirkland examine campaign finance networks in American politics. They provide descriptive evidence of large, extended networks in the American parties that include formal and informal components that operate at the national and state levels. In chapter 17 Michael T. Heaney and James M. Strickland discuss the state of networks in the study of organized interests in American politics. They explore the creation, maintenance, and influence of groups in American politics, emphasizing the important role networks play in understanding political organizations. In chapter 18 Greg Koger, Seth Masket, and Hans Noel explain how viewing political parties as extended networks improves our understanding of the role parties play in American electoral and legislative politics. In chapter 19 Nils Ringe, Jennifer Nicoll Victor, and Wendy Tam Cho describe the extensive literature on networks in legislative politics. They outline the variety of ways scholars can think of networks as operating in legislatures and delineate the challenges and opportunities for future study on this topic. In chapter 20 Janet M. Box-Steffensmeier, Dino P. Christenson, and Claire Leavitt describe how networks operate in the American judicial system. Focusing on judicial behavior and decision-making, these scholars provide an overview of the variety of ways to measure connectivity in judicial politics. In chapter 21 Scott D. McClurg, Casey A. Klofstad, and Anand Edward Sokhey provide an overview of the deep literature on political discussion networks. They focus on political behavior as an outcome of interest, giving special attention to "ego-networks" and the theoretical and technical challenges of drawing inferences in this subfield.

Part 4 includes five chapters that touch on leading topics relevant to public administration and public policy. In chapter 22 Richard Feiock and Manoj Shrestha demonstrate how local governments develop formal and informal networks that help them solve collective action problems in a self-organizing framework. In chapter 23 Adam Douglas Henry uses a network framework to describe the process of learning in public policy. He focuses on segregation as an assumed characteristic of policy networks and demonstrates that traditional assumptions about policy networks may be short-sighted. In chapter 24 Paul W. Thurner argues that as a subject of study the European Union is naturally network oriented because of its formal and informal structures, multilevel institutional features, and diverse yet connective components. He highlights how scholars have used, and can use, network perspectives to shed more light on the EU. In chapter 25 Ramiro Berardo, Isabella Alcañiz, Jennifer Hadden, and Lorien Jasny focus on how network structures can inhibit policymakers and advocates to manage preferred outcomes related to environmental policy. Examining the domain of health policy, in chapter 26 Alexandra P. Joosse and H. Brinton Milward show that a network perspective can reveal challenges and potential solutions in health policy formation and implementation.

Part 5 contains six chapters on topics in IR, covering a wide range of relevant topics and network applications, from trade to terrorism and human rights to arms proliferation. In chapter 27 Arie Perliger explains how network analysis can shed light on understanding how terrorist organizations compete, cooperate, merge, and split. A network perspective on terrorism, he argues, can benefit national and international efforts to reduce violence from connected extremist organizations. In chapter 28 Giorgio Fagiolo uses evidence to describe the properties and typologies of international trade networks, which provide a better understanding of extant trade relations and opportunities to predict future trajectories. In chapter 29 Mette Eilstrup-Sangiovanni describes the various types of global governance networks and how they operate. She draws upon the global environmental protection movement to exemplify how these networks operate. In chapter 30 Amanda Murdie and Marc Polizzi describe the network of human rights advocates. These scholars take an empirical approach to understanding the characteristics of human rights advocacy, focusing on network properties to shed light on the conditions under which human rights can be improved around the world. In chapter 31 Zeev Maoz uses an analytical network perspective to explain international cooperation and conflict, arguing that the literature is ripe to move beyond dyadic models and toward systemic network approaches. In chapter 32 David Kinsella and Alexander H. Montgomery detail theories and hypotheses about the factors that enable and constrain international arms trade and proliferation, as well as the potentials and pitfalls of current data sources, suggesting that the field is ripe for further network analyses.

Part 6 includes five chapters on topics in comparative politics, covering both institutions and political behavior. In chapter 33 Armando Razo argues that the subfield of comparative politics has long been focused on relational concepts without fully embracing the benefits of network-oriented theory and analytical approaches. In chapter 34 David A. Siegel details how networks have a direct and indirect effect on the ways in which citizens interact with democratic institutions. He explores the interactive complexity in these relationships, showcasing the value of network perspectives in comparative politics. In chapter 35 Manuel Fischer examines policy networks in Europe, focusing on country-level and sector-level institutions, as well as the connections among state actors. In chapter 36 Barry Ames, Andy Baker, and Amy Erica Smith showcase network analysis, employing the case of the Brazilian electorate to examine egocentric discussion networks from a two-city panel study in 2014. Using the case of global climate change policy networks, in chapter 37 Jeffrey Broadbent shows the value of using network theories and analyses to understand complex cross-national, policy-relevant phenomena.

Part 7 is a somewhat unusual component that we hope readers will find particularly useful and interesting. It includes six short interviews with leading scholars from other disciplines reflecting on the state of network analysis in political science. The study of political networks is inherently interdisciplinary, and as we have already noted, the field has both borrowed heavily from advancement in other disciplines and contributed to advancement in these disciplines. The collective knowledge on these topics is both cumulative and interdependent. We therefore posed a brief set of questions to luminaries in the fields of business (Steven Borgatti), economics (Matthew Jackson), sociology (James Moody), mathematics (Peter Mucha), computer science (Derek Ruths), and statistics and psychology (Stanley Wasserman). We find their insights on the ways in which political science is most likely to make productive contributions highly useful for developing future research plans, and we think the discipline would be wise to heed their advice about potential pitfalls of studying networks in politics.

WHERE DOES THE FIELD GO FROM HERE?

The chapters in this volume demonstrate the benefits of network theory and methods for addressing political puzzles. Over the past century scholars have advanced our collective knowledge of a variety of diverse topics by increasingly recognizing relational, contextual, or interdependent phenomena. Yet the development and application of network theory and analysis to the study of politics is still in its nascent stages. As evidenced by the chapters in this volume, a great deal of advancement has been made on a variety of topics in contemporary social science using network methods, but there are many unanswered questions and productive lines of inquiry to explore with network methods, theories, or perspectives. We view this as a healthy stage of development, and echo Agranoff and MacGuire's (2001, 295) quotation of the mathematician Hilbert (1902), who said that "as long as a branch of science offers an abundance of problems, so long is it alive; a lack of problems foreshadows extinction or the cessation of independent development."

However, we recognize that many political science scholars may remain skeptical of the value of network theory and methods, prognosticating that they will experience the same fate as other intellectual fads. Political network analysis faces a number of important challenges to avoid a "cessation of independent development." Some of these are methodological challenges shared by many disciplines; with the increasing availability of data and improved computing power and algorithms, much headway has already been made. Still, we see six primary challenges and opportunities that we and our transdisciplinary partners are working on to further improve political network analysis.

The first challenge is working on untangling endogenous processes in networked systems. These systems evolve over time according to complex processes, making it difficult to discern different causal or constitutive mechanisms. For example, scholars continue to seek to discern natural homophily from causal peer effects. This is one of the classic challenges of endogeneity that makes it difficult to draw causal inferences from observations of interdependent populations. We know that humans have an innate likelihood to group with those who share their characteristics. Neighborhoods tend to have dominant language and ethnic identities, groups of family members and friends tend to share the same general political preferences, and groups of unrelated people who live together tend to adopt the same habits and natural patterns. But it is difficult to tease apart whether these commonalities arise because one person's attributes or behavior cause others to be the same, or others would have adopted the same patterns even in the absence of observing it from their peers. Political scientists are cleverly using experimental designs as well as longitudinal or panel data to help discriminate between these effects. This challenge is one of the most difficult in our field, and there is a great need for creative, rigorous contributions on this topic.

A second major challenge for political network analysis is sampling and missing data. In frequentist statistics, one can draw an inference about a population by observing a representative sample of that population. When the distributions of data in the population and sample are the same, inference is reasonable, and we can measure its precision. By definition, the nodes or components of a network are interdependent, and it may often be difficult or impossible to find the boundaries of such a population. When the size and attributes of a population are unknown, such that one cannot make reasonable assumptions about its parameters, then drawing a random sample involves making some arbitrary assumptions about network boundaries. Our inability to define whole network populations and draw random samples from these populations is a significant barrier to using social network analysis for causal inference. Furthermore, many network methods assume the researcher observes all existing nodes and relationships, whereas real-world data collection processes are often vulnerable to missing data. This explains, at least in part, why social network analysis was used primarily for descriptive purposes for decades. It also explains the attraction to whole-network data when they are available (e.g., studying all the legislators in a congress, or all the member countries of a treaty agreement). However, scholars have begun to make progress on this challenge (see especially chapter 5), as increasingly creative solutions are developed to help scholars engage in causal inference with network data.

As the third challenge, we see many opportunities for advancement in the area of so-called big data. This topic is discussed in depth in chapter 4. *Big data* is a catch-all term that might not be descriptively useful to distinguish different types of network analysis, insofar as network-based data are often necessarily gathered on a large scale. The digitization of our modern world means that more and more data are being produced; fortunately, at the same time personal computing has also expanded our capacity to store, manage, and analyze data sets measured in terabytes, petabytes, or even exabytes. All of this presents an incredible opportunity for exploration, theory development, and discovery about our social and political world, since now more than ever before we can see, measure, and conceptualize our interconnectivity.

As the fourth challenge, in this same vein, we see great opportunity for progress in the area of analyzing multiplex data. Many areas of study involve units that are connected by many possible ties. For example, members of Congress may be connected by common committee assignments, common policy preferences, shared professional histories, common campaign donors, and many other possibilities. Each set of connections may reveal something different about the relationships among members, and the combination of connections may be more revealing yet. We know that networks have emergent properties that can only be observed at the level of the whole network; additional properties may be revealed as we also come to understand the variety of ways that units or nodes might be tied. Developing better techniques for handling, theorizing, and analyzing complex network data will be an important avenue for future research. Of course the computational demands of this type of data are intense, and political scientists may develop productive coauthoring relationships with computer scientists or others with special technical skills in this area.

The fifth, core challenge for network analysis is dealing with the evolution of networks over time. This is both a theoretical challenge (see in particular chapter 2) and

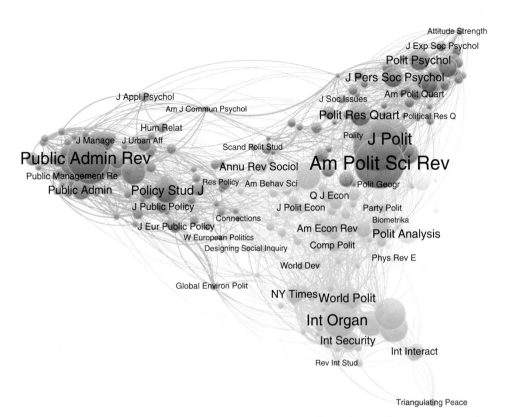

FIGURE 1.1 Co-citation connectivity among the 286 journals cited more than twenty times by articles on political networks

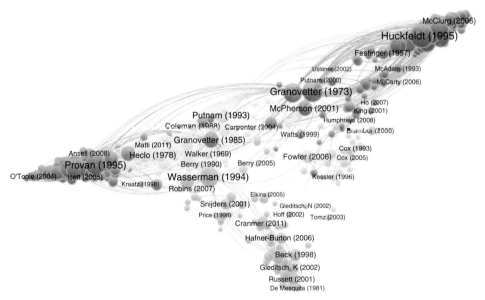

FIGURE 1.2 Co-citations of articles on political network articles, 1960–2016, minimum eight citations, with top five hundred displayed

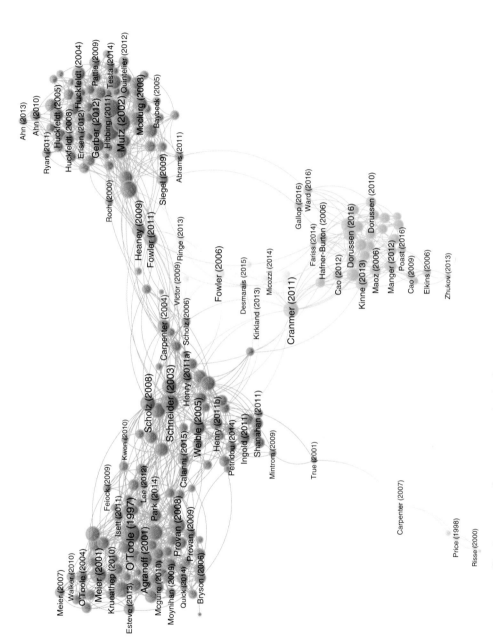

FIGURE 1.3 Citation among the top quarter (243) of our 971 network articles

a methodological one. In this volume alone, we have included three different quantitative approaches to dealing with the complex, time-dependent trajectory of networks (in chapters 8, 9, and 10). Yet these do not exhaust the complexities presented by dynamic networks, which can change functions over time; may respond to shocks differently; and are constantly shaping and being shaped by wider, interlocking sets of institutions. Even if methodological hurdles can be overcome, it is nevertheless even more difficult to collect network data over time (particularly historical data) than it is to collect snapshots, although going forward the increasing collection and availability of data may ease this latter problem.

Finally, the sixth challenge is a strong need for greater theorizing about networks, their properties, and implications for questions of politics (see in particular chapters 2, 3, and 6). From important work done in sociology, we know that some network properties have consistent implications that are relevant for many political questions. For example, we know that triadic closure (when three nodes are connected to one another) occurs under conditions of cooperation and trust. We also know that nodes that are uniquely positioned between two clusters act as brokers and have significant power and control over the interactions between the clusters (Burt 2007, 1995). We know that the emergence, maintenance, and evolution of social and economic structures depend on multiplex connections across networks (Padgett and Powell, 2012). It is also important to understand the extent to which more general mathematical models of networks, such as preferential attachment or small-world processes, are relevant to the study of political networks. Political scientists may have useful insights, beyond what other disciplines have produced, regarding the implications of the unique properties of political networks. For example, a network perspective on policy advocates challenges the basic premise that we can understand political actors' behavior if we know the position of policy preferences in their utility functions (Leifeld and Schneider, 2012). Reconceptualizing or challenging basic theories and assumptions in political science using a network lens may lead us to new insights.

In short, the theoretical and technical development of network analysis and its application to questions of politics presents incredible opportunities. As scholars seek to better understand the complexities of our political world, network approaches fit within an intuitive, relational paradigm and offer a sophisticated set of tools. In the latter half of the twentieth century political science was dominated by a paradigm that was largely borrowed from economics. Methodological individualism was productive, but forced us to accept unrealistic assumptions of independence. We see the relational paradigm as a more realistic and potentially powerful lens through which to study politics. The chapters in this volume are intended to introduce readers to the existing contributions to the literature that fit this description and to encourage curiosity about what contributions may come next. These chapters present the tip of the iceberg of literature on network-relevant topics in the study of politics. We hope readers will find it instructive and motivating.

Appendix A

The table below is a complete list of the source titles that contain the data presented in Figure 1.1. Items in boldface type are not journals (e.g., books, periodicals other than journals).

Label	Full Title
Acad Manage J	Academy of Management Journal
Acad Manage Rev	Academy of Management Review
Activists Borders Ad	**Activists without Borders**
Adm Sci Q	Administrative Science Quarterly
Adm Theory Praxis	Administrative Theory & Praxis
Admin Sci Quart	Administrative Science Quarterly
Admin Soc	Administration & Society
Agendas Alternatives	**Agendas, Alternatives, and Public Policy**
Agendas Instability	**Agendas and Instability in American Politics**
Am Behav Sci	American Behavioral Scientist
Am Econ Rev	American Economic Review
Am J Commun Psychol	American Journal of Community Psychology
Am J Polit Sci	American Journal of Political Science
Am J Public Health	American Journal of Public Health
Am J Sociol	American Journal of Sociology
Am Polit Quart	American Politics Quarterly
Am Polit Res	American Politics Research
Am Polit Sci Rev	American Political Science Review
Am Psychol	American Psychologist
Am Rev Public Adm	American Review of Public Administration
Am Sociol Rev	American Sociological Review
Am Voter	**The American Voter**
Ann Am Acad Polit Ss	Annals of The American Academy of Political And Social Science
Ann Assoc Am Geogr	Annals of The Association of American Geographers

Label	Full Title
Ann M Am Pol Sci Ass	**Annual Meeting of the American Political Science Association**
Ann M Midw Pol Sci A	Annual Meeting of the Midwest Political Science Association
Annu Rev Polit Sci	Annual Review of Political Science, Vol. 13
Annu Rev Psychol	Annual Review of Psychology, Vol. 62
Annu Rev Sociol	Annual Review of Sociology, Vol 36
Asian Surv	Asian Survey
Attitude Strength	**Attitude Strength: Antecedents and Consequences**
Aust J Publ Admin	Australian Journal of Public Administration
Biometrika	Biometrika
Bowling Alone Collap	**Bowling Alone: The Collapse and Revival of American Community**
Brit J Polit Sci	British Journal of Political Science
C Electoral Connecti	**Congress: The Electoral Connection**
Camb Stud Compar	**Cambridge Studies in Comparative Politics: Inside Rebellion**
Case Study Res Desig	**Case Study Research: Design and Methods**
Citizens Politics So	**Citizens, Politics and Social Communication**
Collaborative Public	**Collaborative Public Management**
Commun Res	Communication Research
Communication	Communication
Comp Polit	Comparative Politics (Series)
Comp Polit Stud	Comparative Political Studies
Conflict Manag Peace	Conflict Management And Peace Science
Congressmens Voting	**Congressmen's Voting Decisions**
Connections	Mapping Networks of Terrorist Cells
Democracy Am	**Democracy in America**
Democratization	Democratization
Designing Social Inquiry	**Designing Social Inquiry**
Diffusion Innovation	**Diffusion of Innovations**

Label	Full Title
Ec Theory Democracy	**An Economic Theory of Democracy**
Ecol Soc	Ecology and Society
Econ J	Economic Journal
Econ Polit-Oxford	Economics & Politics
Econometric Anal	**Econometric Analysis**
Econometrica	Econometrica
Economist	Economist
Elect Stud	Electoral Studies
Environ Manage	Environmental Management
Environ Plann C	Environment And Planning C-Government And Policy
Eur J Int Relat	European Journal of International Relations
Eur J Polit Res	European Journal of Political Research
Eur J Soc Psychol	European Journal of Social Psychology
European J Political	European Journal of Political Economy
Europe-Asia Stud	Europe-Asia Studies
Evolution Cooperatio	**The Evolution of Cooperation**
External Control Org	**The External Control of Organizations**
Fdn Social Theory	**Foundations of Social Theory**
Foreign Aff	Foreign Affairs
Foreign Policy	Foreign Policy
Formal Theories Mass	**Formal Theories of Mass Behavior**
Getting Agencies Wor	**Getting Agencies to Work Together**
Getting Results Coll	**Getting Results Through Collaboration: Networks and Network Structures for Public Policy and Management**
Global Environ Polit	Global Environmental Politics
Governance	Governance-An International Journal of Policy Administration And Institutions
Governing Commons Ev	**Governing the Commons: The Evolution of Institutions for Collective Action**
Governing Network Ne	**Governing by Network: The New Shape of the Common Sector**

Label	Full Title
Guardian	**The Guardian of London**
Harvard Bus Rev	Harvard Business Review
Hdb Public Adm	**Handbook of Public Administration**
Hdb Social Psychol	**Handbook of Social Psychology**
Hearing The Other Side: Deliberative Versus Participatory Democracy	**Hearing the Other Side: Deliberative versus Participatory Democracy**
Hum Relat	Human Relations
Hum Rights Quart	Human Rights Quarterly
I I Change Ec Perfor	**Institutions, Institutional Change, and Economic Performance**
Ideology Discontent	**Ideology and Discontent**
Implementation	**Implementation: How Great Expectations in Washington are Dashed in Oakland**
Inform Democratic Pr	Information and Democratic Processes
Int Aff	International Affairs
Int Interact	International Interactions
Int J Public Admin	International Journal of Public Administration
Int J Public Opin R	International Journal of Public Opinion Research
Int Org	International Organization
Int Organ	International Organization
Int Polit Sci Rev	International Political Science Review
Int Public Manag J	International Public Management Journal
Int Security	International Security
Int Stud Quart	International Studies Quarterly
Int Studies Q	International Studies Quarterly
Interorganizational	**Inter-Organizational Networks**
Intro Social Network	**Introduction to Social Network Methods**
J Am Plann Assoc	Journal of The American Planning Association
J Am Stat Assoc	Journal of The American Statistical Association
J Appl Behav Sci	Journal of Applied Behavioral Science
J Appl Psychol	Journal of Applied Psychology

Label	Full Title
J Common Mark Stud	Journal of Common Market Studies
J Commun	Journal of Communication
J Community Psychol	Journal of Community Psychology
J Conflict Resolut	Journal of Conflict Resolution
J Democr	Journal of Democracy
J Econ Behav Organ	Journal of Economic Behavior & Organization
J Econ Lit	Journal of Economic Literature
J Econ Perspect	Journal of Economic Perspectives
J Econ Theory	Journal of Economic Theory
J Econometrics	Journal of Econometrics
J Eur Public Policy	Journal of European Public Policy
J Exp Soc Psychol	Journal of Experimental Social Psychology
J Int Econ	Journal of International Economics
J Law Econ	Journal of Law & Economics
J Law Econ Organ	Journal of Law Economics & Organization
J Manage	Journal of Management
J Manage Stud	Journal of Management Studies
J Math Sociol	Journal of Mathematical Sociology
J Peace Res	Journal of Peace Research
J Pers Soc Psychol	Journal of Personality And Social Psychology
J Plan Educ Res	Journal of Planning Education And Research
J Policy Anal Manag	Journal of Policy Analysis And Management
J Polit	Journal of Politics
J Polit Econ	Journal of Political Economy
J Publ Adm Res Theor	Journal of Public Administration Research And Theory
J Public Econ	Journal of Public Economics
J Public Policy	Journal of Public Policy
J Sci Stud Relig	Journal For The Scientific Study of Religion
J Soc Issues	Journal of Social Issues
J Stat Softw	Journal of Statistical Software
J Strategic Stud	Journal of Strategic Studies

Label	Full Title
J Theor Polit	Journal of Theoretical Politics
J Theoretical Politi	Journal of Theoretical Politics
J Urban Aff	Journal of Urban Affairs
Jama-J Am Med Assoc	Jama—Journal of The American Medical Association
Journalism Quart	Journalism Quarterly
Lat Am Res Rev	Latin American Research Review
Law Soc Rev	Law & Society Review
Leadership Quart	Leadership Quarterly
Legis Stud Quart	Legislative Studies Quarterly
Legislative Studies	Legislative Studies Quarterly
Logic Collective Act	**The Logic of Collective Action**
Making Democracy Wor	**Making Democracy Work**
Manage Sci	Management Science Series A—Theory
Managing Complex Net	**Managing Complex Networks: Strategies for the Public Sector**
Managing Networks Ad	**Managing Within Networks: Adding Value to Public Organizations**
Managing Uncertainti	**Managing Uncertainties in Networks**
Markets Hierarchies	**Markets and Hierarchies: Analysis and Antitrust Implications**
Metropolitan Governa	Metropolitan Governance: Conflict, Competition, and Cooperation
Mobilization	Mobilization
Mobilization Partici	**Mobilization, Participation, and Democracy in America**
Models Methods Socia	**Models and Methods in Social Network Analysis**
Nature	Nature
Nature Origins Mass	**The Nature and Origins of Mass Opinion**
Networked Politics A	**Networked Politics: Agency, Power, and Governance**
New Am Political Sys	The New American Political System
New Engl J Med	New England Journal of Medicine
New I Org Anal	**New Institutionalism in Organizational Analysis**
New Vision	**New Visions for Metropolitan America**

Label	Full Title
Newsweek	Newsweek
Nonprof Volunt Sec Q	Nonprofit And Voluntary Sector Quarterly
Ny Times	The New York Times
Org Working Together	Organizations Working Together
Organ Sci	Organization Science
Organ Stud	Organization Studies
Oxford Econ Pap	Oxford Economic Papers-New Series
Oxford Hdb Political	The Oxford Handbook of Political Psychology
P Natl Acad Sci Usa	Proceedings of The National Academy of Sciences of The United States of America-Physical Sciences
Participation Am Pol	Participation in America: Political Democracy and Social Equality
Party Polit	Party Politics
Peoples Choice	The People's Choice
Peoples Choice Voter	The People's Choice: How the Voter Makes Up His Mind in a Presidential Election
Pers Soc Psychol B	Personality And Social Psychology Bulletin
Perspect Polit	Perspectives On Politics
Perspectives Politic	Perspectives on Politics
Phys Rev E	Physical Review E
Physica A	Physica A—Statistical Mechanics And Its Applications
Plos One	Plos One
Policy Change Learni	Policy Change and Learning: An Advocacy Coalition Approach
Policy Networks Empi	Policy Networks: Empirical Evidence and Theoretical Considerations
Policy Polit	Policy And Politics
Policy Sci	Policy Sciences
Policy Stud J	Policy Studies Journal
Policy Studies Rev	Review of Policy Research
Polit Anal	Political Analysis
Polit Behav	Political Behavior

Label	Full Title
Polit Commun	Political Communication
Polit Geogr	Political Geography
Polit Psychol	Political Psychology
Polit Res Quart	Political Research Quarterly
Polit Sci Quart	Political Science Quarterly
Polit Soc	Politics & Society
Polit Stud-London	Political Studies
Polit Theory	Political Theory
Political Anal	Political Analysis
Political Behav	Political Behavior
Political Behavior	Political Behavior
Political Disagreeme	Political Disagreement: The Survival of Diverse Opinions Within Communication Networks
Political Networks S	Political Networks: The Structural Perspective
Political Res Q	Political Research Quarterly
Political Sci State	**Political Science: The State of the Discipline II**
Politics Context Ass	**Politics in Context: Assimilation and Conflict in Urban Neighborhoods**
Polity	Polity
Polity 4 Project Pol	**The Polity IV Project**
Power Human Rights I	**The Power of Human Rights: International Norms and Domestic Change**
Ps	P S
Ps-Polit Sci Polit	Ps—Political Science & Politics
Psychol Bull	Psychological Bulletin
Psychol Rev	Psychological Review
Psychometrika	Psychometrika
Public Admin	Public Administration
Public Admin Rev	Public Administration Review
Public Budgeting Fin	Public Budgeting and Finance
Public Choice	Public Choice
Public Manag Rev	Public Management Review

Label	Full Title
Public Management	Public Management Review
Public Management Re	Public Management Review
Public Money Manage	Public Money & Management
Public Opin Quart	Public Opinion Quarterly
Public Perform Manag	Public Performance & Management Review
Publius J Federalism	Publius—The Journal of Federalism
Q J Econ	Quarterly Journal of Economics
Q J Polit Sci	Quarterly Journal of Political Science
Ration Soc	Rationality and Society
Regression Models Ca	**Regression Models for Categorical and Limited Dependent Variables.**
Reinventing Govt Ent	**Reinventing Government: How the Entrepreneurial Spirit is Transforming the Public Sector**
Res Organ Behav	Research in Organizational Behavior, Vol. 18, 1996
Res Policy	Research Policy
Rev Econ Stat	Review of Economics And Statistics
Rev Econ Stud	Review of Economic Studies
Rev Int Stud	Review of International Studies
Rev Policy Res	Review of Policy Research
Rev Public Pers Adm	Review of Public Personnel Administration
Scand Polit Stud	Scandinavian Political Studies
Science	Science
Secur Stud	Security Studies
Self Org Federalism	**Self-Organizing Federalism: Collaborative Mechanisms to Mitigate Institutional Collective Action Dilemmas**
Soc Forces	Social Forces
Soc Natur Resour	Society & Natural Resources
Soc Networks	Social Networks
Soc Probl	Social Problems
Soc Psychol Quart	Social Psychology Quarterly
Soc Sci Quart	Social Science Quarterly

Label	Full Title
Social Logic Politic	**The Social Logic of Politics: Personal Networks as Contexts for Political Behavior**
Social Network Anal	**Social Network Analysis: Methods and Applications**
Sociol Forum	Sociological Forum
Sociol Method Res	Sociological Methods & Research
Sociol Methodol	Sociological Methodology 1993, Vol. 23
Sociometry	Sociometry
State Local Govt Rev	State and Local Government Review
State Polit Policy Q	State Politics & Policy Quarterly
Strategic Manage J	Strategic Management Journal
Structural Holes Soc	Structural Holes: The Social Structure of Competition
Stud Comp Int Dev	Studies in Comparative International Development
Stud Confl Terror	Studies in Conflict & Terrorism
Survival	Survival
Terror Polit Violenc	Terrorism and Political Violence
Theor Soc	Theory and Society
Theories Policy Proc	**Theories of the Policy Process**
Theory Cognitive Dis	**A Theory of Cognitive Dissonance**
Theory Int Politics	**Theory of International Politics**
Thesis U California	**Centralizing Principles: How Amnesty International Shaped Human Rights Politics Through its Transnational Network**
Tools Govt Guide New	**The Tools of Government: A Guide to the New Governance**
Triangulating Peace	**Triangulating Peace**
Ucinet Windows Softw	**UCInet software**
Understanding Govern	**Understanding Governance: Ten Years On**
Urban Aff Rev	Urban Affairs Review
Voice Equality Civic	**Voice and Equality: Civic Voluntarism in American Politics**
Voting Study Opinion	**Voting: A Study of Opinion Formation in a Presidential Campaign**
W European Politics	West European Politics

Label	Full Title
Wall Street J	Wall Street Journal
Washington Post	Washington Post
West Eur Polit	West European Politics
Western Polit Quart	Western Political Quarterly
What Am Know Politic	What Americans Know about Politics and Why It Matters
Who Votes	Who Votes?
Working Paper	CESifo Working Paper
World Dev	World Development
World Polit	World Politics
World Politics	World Politics

APPENDIX B

Complete Citations for Labeled Nodes in Figure 1.2

Only the first author's name is used for each source in the figure.

Ansell, C., and Gash, A. (2008). "Collaborative Governance in Theory and Practice." *Journal of Public Administration Research and Theory* 18(4): 543–571. doi:10.1093/jopart/mum032.

Beck, N., Katz, J. N., and Tucker, R. (1998). "Taking Time Seriously: Time-Series-Cross-Section Analysis with a Binary Dependent Variable." *American Journal of Political Science* 42(4): 1260. doi:10.2307/2991857.

Berry, F. S., and Berry, W. D. (1990). "State Lottery Adoptions as Policy Innovations: An Event History Analysis." *American Political Science Review* 84(2): 395. doi:10.2307/1963526.

Berry, W. D., and Baybeck, B. (2005). "Using Geographic Information Systems to Study Interstate Competition." *American Political Science Review* 99(4): 505–519. doi:10.1017/S0003055405051841.

Brambor, T. (2006). "Understanding Interaction Models: Improving Empirical Analyses." *Political Analysis* 14(1): 63–82. doi:10.1093/pan/mpi014.

Carpenter, D. P., Esterling, K. M., and Lazer, D. M. J. (2004). "Friends, Brokers, and Transitivity: Who Informs Whom in Washington Politics?" *Journal of Politics* 66(1): 224–246. doi:10.1046/j.1468-2508.2004.00149.x.

Coleman, J. S. (1988). "Social Capital in the Creation of Human Capital." *American Journal of Sociology* 94(January): S95–S120. doi:10.1086/228943.

Cox, G. W., and McCubbins, M. D. (1993). *Legislative Leviathan: Party Government in the House.* Berkeley: University of California Press.

Cox, G. W., and McCubbins, M. D. (2005). *Setting the Agenda: Responsible Party Government in the U.S. House of Representatives.* Cambridge, UK: Cambridge University Press. http://ebooks.cambridge.org/ref/id/CBO9780511791123.

Cranmer, S. J., and Desmarais, B. A. (2011). "Inferential Network Analysis with Exponential Random Graph Models." *Political Analysis* 19(1): 66–86. doi:10.1093/pan/mpq037.

Elkins, Z. (2005). "On Waves, Clusters, and Diffusion: A Conceptual Framework." *Annals of the American Academy of Political and Social Science* 598(1): 33–51. doi:10.1177/0002716204272516.

Festinger, L. (1957). *A Theory of Cognitive Dissonance.* Stanford, CA: Stanford University Press.

Fowler, J. H. (2006). "Legislative Cosponsorship Networks in the US House and Senate." *Social Networks* 28(4): 454–465. doi:10.1016/j.socnet.2005.11.003.

Gleditsch, K. S. (2002). "Expanded Trade and Gdp Data." *Journal of Conflict Resolution* 46(5): 712–724. doi:10.1177/002200202236171.

Gleditsch, N. P., Wallensteen, P., Eriksson, M., Sollenberg, M., and Strand, H. (2002). "Armed Conflict 1946–2001: A New Dataset." *Journal of Peace Research* 39(5): 615–637. doi:10.1177/0022343302039005007.

Granovetter, M. (1985). "Economic Action and Social Structure: The Problem of Embeddedness." *American Journal of Sociology* 91(3): 481–510. doi:10.1086/228311.

Granovetter, M. S. (1973). "The Strength of Weak Ties." *American Journal of Sociology* 78(6): 1360–1380. doi:10.1086/225469.

Hafner-Burton, E. M., and Montgomery, A. H. (2006). "Power Positions: International Organizations, Social Networks, and Conflict." *Journal of Conflict Resolution* 50(1): 3–27. doi:10.1177/0022002705281669.

Heclo, H. (1978). "Issue networks and the executive establishment." *Public Administartion Concepts Cases* 413: 46–57.

Ho, D. E., Imai, K., King, G., and Stuart, E. A. (2007). "Matching as Nonparametric Preprocessing for Reducing Model Dependence in Parametric Causal Inference." *Political Analysis* 15(3): 199–236. doi:10.1093/pan/mpl013.

Hoff, P. D., Raftery, A. E., and Handcock, M. S. (2002). "Latent Space Approaches to Social Network Analysis." *Journal of the American Statistical Association* 97(460): 1090–1098. doi:10.1198/016214502388618906.

Huckfeldt, R., Beck, P. A., Dalton, R. J., and Levine, J. (1995). "Political Environments, Cohesive Social Groups, and the Communication of Public Opinion." *American Journal of Political Science* 39(4): 1025. doi:10.2307/2111668.

Humphreys, M., and Weinstein, J. M. (2008). "Who Fights? The Determinants of Participation in Civil War." *American Journal of Political Science* 52(2): 436–455. doi:10.1111/j.1540-5907.2008.00322.x.

Isett, K. R. (2005). "The Evolution of Dyadic Interorganizational Relationships in a Network of Publicly Funded Nonprofit Agencies." *Journal of Public Administration Research and Theory* 15(1): 149–165. doi:10.1093/jopart/mui008.

Kessler, D., and Krehbiel, K. (1996). "Dynamics of Cosponsorship." *American Political Science Review* 90(3): 555–566. doi:10.2307/2082608.

King, G., and Zeng, L. (2001). "Logistic Regression in Rare Events Data." *Political Analysis* 9(2): 137–163. doi:10.1093/oxfordjournals.pan.a004868.

Kraatz, M. S. 1998. "Learning by Association? Interorganizational Networks and Adaptation to Environmental Change." *Academy of Management Journal* 41(6): 621–643. doi:10.2307/256961.

Matti, S., and Sandström, A. (2011). "The Rationale Determining Advocacy Coalitions: Examining Coordination Networks and Corresponding Beliefs." *Policy Studies Journal* 39(3): 385–410. doi:10.1111/j.1541-0072.2011.00414.x.

McAdam, D., and Paulsen, R. (1993). "Specifying the Relationship Between Social Ties and Activism." *American Journal of Sociology* 99(3): 640–667. doi:10.1086/230319.

McCarty, N., Poole, K. T., and Rosenthal, H. (2006). *Polarized America: The Dance of Ideology and Unequal Riches.* 1st ed. Cambridge, MA: The MIT Press.

McClurg, S. D. (2006). "Political Disagreement in Context: The Conditional Effect of Neighborhood Context, Disagreement and Political Talk on Electoral Participation." *Political Behavior* 28(4): 349–366. doi:10.1007/s11109-006-9015-4.

McPherson, M., Smith-Lovin, L., and Cook, J. M. (2001). "Birds of a Feather: Homophily in Social Networks." *Annual Review of Sociology* 27(1): 415–444. doi:10.1146/annurev.soc.27.1.415.

Mesquita, B. B. de. (1981). *The War Trap.* New Haven, CT: Yale University Press.

O'Toole, L. J., and Meier, K. J. (2004). "Desperately Seeking Selznick: Cooptation and the Dark Side of Public Management in Networks." *Public Administration Review* 64(6): 681–693. doi:10.1111/j.1540-6210.2004.00415.x.

Price, R. (1998). "Reversing the Gun Sights: Transnational Civil Society Targets Land Mines." *International Organization* 52(3): 613–644. doi:10.1162/002081898550671.

Provan, K. G., and Milward, H. B. (1995). "A Preliminary Theory of Interorganizational Network Effectiveness: A Comparative Study of Four Community Mental Health Systems." *Administrative Science Quarterly* 40(1): 1. doi:10.2307/2393698.

Putnam, R. D. (2000). *Bowling Alone: The Collapse and Revival of American Community.* New York: Simon and Schuster.

Putnam, R. D., Leonardi, R., and Nanetti., R. Y. (1993). *Making Democracy Work: Civic Traditions in Modern Italy.* Princeton, NJ: Princeton University Press.

Robins, G., Snijders, T., Wang, P., Handcock, M., and Pattison, P. (2007). "Recent Developments in Exponential Random Graph (P*) Models for Social Networks." *Social Networks* 29(2): 192–215. doi:10.1016/j.socnet.2006.08.003.

Russett, B. M., and Oneal, J. R. (2001). *Triangulating Peace: Democracy, Interdependence, and International Organizations.* New York: W. W. Norton.

Snijders, T. A. B. (2001). "The Statistical Evaluation of Social Network Dynamics." *Sociological Methodology* 31(1): 361–395. doi:10.1111/0081-1750.00099.

Tomz, M., Wittenberg, J., and King, G. (2003). Clarify: Software for Interpreting and Presenting Statistical Results. 2.1. http://www.stanford.edu/tomz/software/clarify.pdf.

Uslaner, E. M. (2002). *The Moral Foundations of Trust*. New York: Cambridge University Press.

Walker, J. L. (1969). "The Diffusion of Innovations among the American States." *American Political Science Review* 63(3): 880–899. doi:10.2307/1954434.

Wasserman, S., and Faust, K. (1994). *Social Network Analysis: Methods and Applications*. Cambridge, UK: Cambridge University Press. http://www.worldcat.org/oclc/30594217.

Watts, D. J. (1999). *Small Worlds: The Dynamics of Networks between Order and Randomness*. Princeton, NJ: Princeton University Press. http://www.worldcat.org/oclc/40602717.

Appendix C

Complete Citations for Labeled Nodes in Figure 1.3

Only the first author's name is used for each source in the figure.

Abrams, S., Iversen, T., and Soskice, D. (2011). "Informal Social Networks and Rational Voting." *British Journal of Political Science* 41(2): 229–257. doi:10.1017/S0007123410000499.

Agranoff, R., and McGuire, M. (2001). "Big Questions in Public Network Management Research." *Journal of Public Administration Research and Theory* 11(3): 295–326. doi:10.1093/oxfordjournals.jpart.a003504.

Ahn, T. K., Huckfeldt, R., Mayer, A. K., and Ryan, J. B. (2013). "Expertise and Bias in Political Communication Networks." *American Journal of Political Science* 57(2): 357–373. doi:10.1111/j.1540-5907.2012.00625.x.

Ahn, T. K., Huckfeldt, R., and Ryan, J. B. (2010). "Communication, Influence, and Informational Asymmetries among Voters." *Political Psychology* 31(5): 763–787. doi:10.1111/j.1467-9221.2010.00783.x.

Baybeck, B. (2005). "What Do They Know and How Do They Know It? An Examination of Citizen Awareness of Context." *American Politics Research* 33(4): 492–520. doi:10.1177/1532673X04270934.

Bryson, J. M., Crosby, B. C., and Stone, M. M. (2006). "The Design and Implementation of Cross-Sector Collaborations: Propositions from the Literature." *Public Administration Review* 66(s1): 44–55. doi:10.1111/j.1540-6210.2006.00665.x.

Calanni, J. C., Siddiki, S. N., Weible, C. M., and Leach, W. D. (2015). "Explaining Coordination in Collaborative Partnerships and Clarifying the Scope of the Belief Homophily Hypothesis." *Journal of Public Administration Research and Theory* 25(3): 901–927. doi:10.1093/jopart/mut080.

Cao, X. (2009). "Networks of Intergovernmental Organizations and Convergence in Domestic Economic Policies." *International Studies Quarterly* 53(4): 1095–1130. doi:10.1111/j.1468-2478.2009.00570.x.

Cao, X. (2012). "Global Networks and Domestic Policy Convergence: A Network Explanation of Policy Changes." *World Politics* 64(3): 375–425. doi:10.1017/S0043887112000081.

Carpenter, D. P., Esterling, K. M., and Lazer, D. M. J. (2004). "Friends, Brokers, and Transitivity: Who Informs Whom in Washington Politics?" *Journal of Politics* 66(1): 224–246. doi:10.1046/j.1468-2508.2004.00149.x.

Carpenter, R. C. (2007). "Setting the Advocacy Agenda: Theorizing Issue Emergence and Nonemergence in Transnational Advocacy Networks." *International Studies Quarterly* 51(1): 99–120. doi:10.1111/j.1468-2478.2007.00441.x.

Cranmer, S. J., and Desmarais, B. A. (2011). "Inferential Network Analysis with Exponential Random Graph Models." *Political Analysis* 19(1): 66–86. doi:10.1093/pan/mpq037.

Desmarais, B. A., Harden, J. J., and Boehmke, F. J. (2015). "Persistent Policy Pathways: Inferring Diffusion Networks in the American States." *American Political Science Review* 109(2): 392–406. doi:10.1017/S0003055415000040.

Dorussen, H., Gartzke, E. A., and Westerwinter, O. (2016). "Networked International Politics: Complex Interdependence and the Diffusion of Conflict and Peace." *Journal of Peace Research* 53(3): 283–291. doi:10.1177/0022343316637896.

Dorussen, H., and Ward, H. (2010). "Trade Networks and the Kantian Peace." *Journal of Peace Research* 47(1): 29–42. doi:10.1177/0022343309350011.

Elkins, Z., Guzman, A. T., and Simmons, B. A. (2006). "Competing for Capital: The Diffusion of Bilateral Investment Treaties, 1960–2000." *International Organization* 60(4). doi:10.1017/S0020818306060279.

Erisen, E., and Erisen, C. (2012). "The Effect of Social Networks on the Quality of Political Thinking." *Political Psychology* 33(6): 839–865. doi:10.1111/j.1467-9221.2012.00906.x.

Esteve, M., Boyne, G., Sierra, V., and Ysa, T. (2013). "Organizational Collaboration in the Public Sector: Do Chief Executives Make a Difference?" *Journal of Public Administration Research and Theory* 23(4): 927–952. doi:10.1093/jopart/mus035.

Fariss, C. J., and Schnakenberg, K. E. (2014). "Measuring Mutual Dependence between State Repressive Actions." *Journal of Conflict Resolution* 58(6): 1003–1032. doi:10.1177/0022002713487314.

Feiock, R. C., Steinacker, A., and Park, H. J. (2009). "Institutional Collective Action and Economic Development Joint Ventures." *Public Administration Review* 69(2): 256–270. doi:10.1111/j.1540-6210.2008.01972.x.

Fowler, J. H. (2006). "Connecting the Congress: A Study of Cosponsorship Networks." *Political Analysis* 14(4): 456–487. doi:10.1093/pan/mpl002.

Fowler, J. H., Heaney, M. T., Nickerson, D. W., Padgett, J. F., and Sinclair, B. 2011. "Causality in Political Networks." *American Politics Research* 39(2): 437–480. doi:10.1177/1532673X10396310.

Gallop, M. B. (2016). "Endogenous Networks and International Cooperation." *Journal of Peace Research* 53(3): 310–324. doi:10.1177/0022343316631033.

Gerber, A. S., Huber, G. A., Doherty, D., and Dowling, C. M. (2012). "Disagreement and the Avoidance of Political Discussion: Aggregate Relationships and Differences across Personality Traits." *American Journal of Political Science* 56(4): 849–874. doi:10.1111/j.1540-5907.2011.00571.x.

Hafner-Burton, E. M., and Montgomery, A. H. (2006). "Power Positions: International Organizations, Social Networks, and Conflict." *Journal of Conflict Resolution* 50(1): 3–27. doi:10.1177/0022002705281669.

Heaney, M. T., and McClurg, S. D. (2009). "Social Networks and American Politics: Introduction to the Special Issue." *American Politics Research* 37(5): 727–741. doi:10.1177/1532673X09337771.

Henry, A. D. (2011a). "Ideology, Power, and the Structure of Policy Networks." *Policy Studies Journal* 39(3): 361–383. doi:10.1111/j.1541-0072.2011.00413.x.

Henry, A. D., Lubell, M., and McCoy, M. (2011b). "Belief Systems and Social Capital as Drivers of Policy Network Structure: The Case of California Regional Planning." *Journal of Public Administration Research and Theory* 21(3): 419–444. doi:10.1093/jopart/muq042.

Hibbing, M. V., Ritchie, M., and Anderson, M. R. (2011). "Personality and Political Discussion." *Political Behavior* 33(4): 601–624. doi:10.1007/s11109-010-9147-4.

Huckfeldt, R., Ikeda, K., and Pappi, F. U. (2005). "Patterns of Disagreement in Democratic Politics: Comparing Germany, Japan, and the United States." *American Journal of Political Science* 49(3): 497–514. doi:10.1111/j.1540-5907.2005.00138.x.

Huckfeldt, R., and Mendez, J. M. (2008). "Moths, Flames, and Political Engagement: Managing Disagreement within Communication Networks." *Journal of Politics* 70(1): 83–96. doi:10.1017/S0022381607080073.

Huckfeldt, R., Mendez, J. M., and Osborn, T. (2004). "Disagreement, Ambivalence, and Engagement: The Political Consequences of Heterogeneous Networks." *Political Psychology* 25(1): 65–95. doi:10.1111/j.1467-9221.2004.00357.x.

Ingold, K. (2011). "Network Structures within Policy Processes: Coalitions, Power, and Brokerage in Swiss Climate Policy." *Policy Studies Journal* 39(3): 435–459. doi:10.1111/j.1541-0072.2011.00416.x.

Isett, K. R., Mergel, I. A., LeRoux, K., Mischen, P. A., and Rethemeyer, R. K. (2011). "Networks in Public Administration Scholarship: Understanding Where We Are and Where We Need to Go." *Journal of Public Administration Research and Theory* 21 (supp. 1): i157–i173. doi:10.1093/jopart/muq061.

Kinne, B. J. (2013). "Network Dynamics and the Evolution of International Cooperation." *American Political Science Review* 107(4): 766–785. doi:10.1017/S0003055 413 000440.

Kirkland, J. H. (2013). "Hypothesis Testing for Group Structure in Legislative Networks." *State Politics & Policy Quarterly* 13(2): 225–243. doi:10.1177/1532440012473842.

Krueathep, W., Riccucci, N. M., and Suwanmala, C. (2010). "Why Do Agencies Work Together? The Determinants of Network Formation at the Subnational Level of Government in Thailand." *Journal of Public Administration Research and Theory* 20(1): 157–185. doi:10.1093/jopart/mun013.

Kwon, S.-W., and Feiock, R. C. (2010). "Overcoming the Barriers to Cooperation: Intergovernmental Service Agreements." *Public Administration Review* 70(6): 876–884. doi:10.1111/j.1540-6210.2010.02219.x.

Lee, I.-W., Feiock, R. C., and Lee, Y. (2012). "Competitors and Cooperators: A Micro-Level Analysis of Regional Economic Development Collaboration Networks." *Public Administration Review* 72(2): 253–262. doi:10.1111/j.1540-6210.2011.02501.x.

Manger, M. S., Pickup, M. A., and Snijders, T. A. B. (2012). "A Hierarchy of Preferences: A Longitudinal Network Analysis Approach to PTA Formation." *Journal of Conflict Resolution* 56(5): 853–878. doi:10.1177/0022002712438351.

Maoz, Z. (2006). "Network polarization, network interdependence, and international conflict, 1816–2002." *Journal of Peace Research* 43(4): 391–411.

McClurg, S. D. (2003). "Social Networks and Political Participation: The Role of Social Interaction in Explaining Political Participation." *Political Research Quarterly* 56(4): 449. doi:10.2307/3219806.

McGuire, M., and Silvia, C. (2010). "The Effect of Problem Severity, Managerial and Organizational Capacity, and Agency Structure on Intergovernmental Collaboration: Evidence from Local Emergency Management." *Public Administration Review* 70(2): 279–288. doi:10.1111/j.1540-6210.2010.02134.x.

Meier, K. J., O'Toole, L. J., Boyne, G. A., and Walker, R. M. (2006). "Strategic Management and the Performance of Public Organizations: Testing Venerable Ideas against Recent Theories." *Journal of Public Administration Research and Theory* 17(3): 357–377. doi:10.1093/jopart/mul017.

Meier, K. J., and O'toole, L. J. (2001). "Managerial Strategies and Behavior in Networks: A Model with Evidence from U.S. Public Education." *Journal of Public Administration Research and Theory* 11(3): 271–294. doi:10.1093/oxfordjournals.jpart.a003503.

Micozzi, J. P. (2014). "Alliance for Progress? Multilevel Ambition and Patterns of Cosponsorship in the Argentine House." *Comparative Political Studies* 47(8): 1186–1208. doi:10.1177/0010414013488564.

Mintrom, M., and Norman, P. (2009). "Policy Entrepreneurship and Policy Change." *Policy Studies Journal* 37(4): 649–667. doi:10.1111/j.1541-0072.2009.00329.x.

Moynihan, D. P. (2009). "The Network Governance of Crisis Response: Case Studies of Incident Command Systems." *Journal of Public Administration Research and Theory* 19(4): 895–915. doi:10.1093/jopart/mun033.

Mutz, D. C. (2002). "Cross-Cutting Social Networks: Testing Democratic Theory in Practice." *American Political Science Review* 96(1): 111–126. doi:10.1017/S0003055402004264.

O'Toole, L. J. (1997). "Treating Networks Seriously: Practical and Research-Based Agendas in Public Administration." *Public Administration Review* 57(1): 45. doi:10.2307/976691.

O'Toole, L. J., and Meier, K. J. (2004). "Desperately Seeking Selznick: Cooptation and the Dark Side of Public Management in Networks." *Public Administration Review* 64(6): 681–693. doi:10.1111/j.1540-6210.2004.00415.x.

Park, H. H., and Rethemeyer, R. K. (2014). "The Politics of Connections: Assessing the Determinants of Social Structure in Policy Networks." *Journal of Public Administration Research and Theory* 24(2): 349–379. doi:10.1093/jopart/mus021.

Pattie, C. J., and Johnston, R. J. (2009). "Conversation, Disagreement and Political Participation." *Political Behavior* 31(2): 261–285. doi:10.1007/s11109-008-9071-z.

Petridou, E. (2014). "Theories of the Policy Process: Contemporary Scholarship and Future Directions." *Policy Studies Journal* 42(April): S12–S32. doi:10.1111/psj.12054.

Poast, P. (2016). "Dyads Are Dead, Long Live Dyads! The Limits of Dyadic Designs in International Relations Research." *International Studies Quarterly* 60(2): 369–374. doi:10.1093/isq/sqw004.

Price, R. (1998). "Reversing the Gun Sights: Transnational Civil Society Targets Land Mines." *International Organization* 52(3): 613–644. doi:10.1162/002081898550671.

Provan, K. G., Huang, K., and Milward, H. B. (2009). "The Evolution of Structural Embeddedness and Organizational Social Outcomes in a Centrally Governed Health and Human Services Network." *Journal of Public Administration Research and Theory* 19(4): 873–893. doi:10.1093/jopart/mun036.

Provan, K. G., and Kenis, P. (2008). "Modes of Network Governance: Structure, Management, and Effectiveness." *Journal of Public Administration Research and Theory* 18(2): 229–252. doi:10.1093/jopart/mum015.

Quick, K. S., and Feldman, M. S. (2014). "Boundaries as Junctures: Collaborative Boundary Work for Building Efficient Resilience." *Journal of Public Administration Research and Theory* 24(3): 673–695. doi:10.1093/jopart/muto85.

Quintelier, E., Stolle, D., and Harell, A. (2012). "Politics in Peer Groups: Exploring the Causal Relationship between Network Diversity and Political Participation." *Political Research Quarterly* 65(4): 868–881. doi:10.1177/1065912911411099.

Ringe, N., Victor, J. N., and Gross, J. H. (2013). "Keeping Your Friends Close and Your Enemies Closer? Information Networks in Legislative Politics." *British Journal of Political Science* 43(3): 601–628. doi:10.1017/S0007123412000518.

Risse, T. (2000). " 'Let's Argue!' Communicative Action in World Politics." *International Organization* 54(1): 1–39. doi:10.1162/002081800551109.

Roch, C. H., Scholz, J. T., and McGraw, K. M. (2000). "Social Networks and Citizen Response to Legal Change." *American Journal of Political Science* 44(4): 777. doi:10.2307/2669281.

Ryan, J. B. (2011). "Accuracy and Bias in Perceptions of Political Knowledge." *Political Behavior* 33(2): 335–356. doi:10.1007/s11109-010-9130-0.

Schneider, M., Scholz, J., Lubell, M., Mindruta, D., and Edwardsen, M. (2003). "Building Consensual Institutions: Networks and the National Estuary Program." *American Journal of Political Science* 47(1): 143. doi:10.2307/3186098.

Scholz, J. T., Berardo, R., and Kile, B. (2008). "Do Networks Solve Collective Action Problems? Credibility, Search, and Collaboration." *Journal of Politics* 70(2): 393–406. doi:10.1017/S0022381608080389.

Scholz, J. T., and Wang, C.-L. (2006). "Cooptation or Transformation? Local Policy Networks and Federal Regulatory Enforcement." *American Journal of Political Science* 50(1): 81–97. doi:10.1111/j.1540-5907.2006.00171.x.

Shanahan, E. A., Jones, M. D., and McBeth, M. K. (2011). "Policy Narratives and Policy Processes." *Policy Studies Journal* 39(3): 535–561. doi:10.1111/j.1541-0072.2011.00420.x.

Siegel, D. A. (2009). "Social Networks and Collective Action." *American Journal of Political Science* 53(1): 122–138. doi:10.1111/j.1540-5907.2008.00361.x.

Testa, P. F., Hibbing, M. V., and Ritchie, M. (2014). "Orientations toward Conflict and the Conditional Effects of Political Disagreement." *Journal of Politics* 76(3): 770–785. doi:10.1017/S0022381614000255.

True, J., and Mintrom, M. (2001). "Transnational Networks and Policy Diffusion: The Case of Gender Mainstreaming." *International Studies Quarterly* 45(1): 27–57. doi:10.1111/0020-8833.00181.

Victor, J. N., and Ringe, N. (2009). "The Social Utility of Informal Institutions: Caucuses as Networks in the 110th U.S. House of Representatives." *American Politics Research* 37(5): 742–766. doi:10.1177/1532673X09337183.

Walker, R. M., Andrews, R., Boyne, G. A., Meier, K. J., and O'Toole, L. J. 2010. "Wakeup Call: Strategic Management, Network Alarms, and Performance." *Public Administration Review* 70(5): 731–741. doi:10.1111/j.1540-6210.2010.02201.x.

Ward, H., and Dorussen, H. (2016). "Standing alongside Your Friends: Network Centrality and Providing Troops to UN Peacekeeping Operations." *Journal of Peace Research* 53(3): 392–408. doi:10.1177/0022343316628814.

Weible, C. M. (2005). "Beliefs and Perceived Influence in a Natural Resource Conflict: An Advocacy Coalition Approach to Policy Networks." *Political Research Quarterly* 58(3): 461. doi:10.2307/3595615.

Zhukov, Y. M., and Stewart, B. M. (2013). "Choosing Your Neighbors: Networks of Diffusion in International Relations." *International Studies Quarterly* 57(2): 271–287. doi:10.1111/isqu.12008.

NOTES

1. The search included the following journals: *American Political Science Review, American Journal of Political Science, Journal of Politics, British Journal of Political Science, Political Analysis, International Organization, World Politics, Comparative Political Studies, Comparative Politics, Policy Studies Journal, Public Administration Review, Journal of Public Administration Research and Theory, Legislative Studies Quarterly, American Politics Research, Politics & Gender, Party Politics, Perspectives on Politics, State Politics Policy Quarterly, Political Research Quarterly, Journal of Peace Research, Journal of Conflict Resolution, International Studies Quarterly, Political Behavior, Political Theory, Journal of Theoretical Politics, International Security, Polity, Political Psychology, European Political Science Review, Canadian Journal of Political Science*, and *Annals of American Academy of Political and Social Science.* The *Canadian Journal of Political Science* turned out to be an isolate; no other journals cited it.

2. Appendix A in this chapter includes a complete list of titles represented in figure 1.1.

3. Appendix B in this chapter provides the complete citations for the labeled nodes in figure 1.2.

4. Appendix C in this chapter contains the complete citations for labeled nodes in figure 1.3.

References

Agranoff, R., and McGuire, M. (2001). "Big Questions in Public Network Management Research." *Journal of Public Administration Research and Theory* 11(3): 295–326.

Agranoff, R., and McGuire, M. (2003). *Collaborative Public Management: New Strategies for Local Governments*. Washington, DC: Georgetown University Press.

Apicella, C. L., Marlowe, F. W., Fowler, J. H., and Christakis, N. A. (2012). "Social Networks and Cooperation in Hunter-Gatherers." *Nature* 481(7382): 497–501. doi:10.1038/nature10736.

Arnold, L. W., Deen, R. E., and Patterson, S. C. (2000). "Friendship and Votes: The Impact of Interpersonal Ties on Legislative Decision Making." *State & Local Government Review* 32(2): 142–147.

Asal, V. H., Ackerman, G. A., and Rethemeyer, R. K. (2012). "Connections Can Be Toxic: Terrorist Organizational Factors and the Pursuit of CBRN Weapons." *Studies in Conflict & Terrorism* 35(3): 229–254. doi:10.1080/1057610X.2012.648156.

Beck, N., Katz, J. N., and Tucker, R. (1998). "Taking Time Seriously: Time-Series-Cross-Section Analysis with a Binary Dependent Variable." *American Journal of Political Science* 42(4): 1260–1288. doi:10.2307/2991857.

Berardo, R., Heikkila, T., and Gerlak, A. K. (2014). "Interorganizational Engagement in Collaborative Environmental Management: Evidence from the South Florida Ecosystem Restoration Task Force." *Journal of Public Administration Research and Theory* 24: 697–719. doi:10.1093/jopart/muu003.

Berardo, R., and Scholz, J. T. (2010). "Self-Organizing Policy Networks: Risk, Partner Selection, and Cooperation in Estuaries." *American Journal of Political Science* 54(3): 632–649. doi:10.1111/j.1540-5907.2010.00451.x.

Berelson, B. R. (1954). *Voting: A Study of Opinion Formation in a Presidential Campaign*. Chicago: University of Chicago Press.

Berelson, B. R., Lazarsfeld, P. F., and McPhee, W. N. (1986). *Voting: A Study of Opinion Formation in a Presidential Campaign*. Chicago: University of Chicago Press.

Bogue, A. G., and Marlaire, M. P. (1975). "Of Mess and Men: The Boardinghouse and Congressional Voting, 1821–1842." *American Journal of Political Science* 19(2): 207–230. doi:10.2307/2110433.

Böhmelt, T., Koubi, V., and Bernauer, T. (2014). "Civil Society Participation in Global Governance: Insights from Climate Politics." *European Journal of Political Research* 53(1): 18–36. doi:10.1111/1475-6765.12016.

Box-Steffensmeier, J. M., and Christenson, D. P. (2014). "The Evolution and Formation of Amicus Curiae Networks." In "Political Networks," special issue, *Social Networks* 36(January): 82–96. doi:10.1016/j.socnet.2012.07.003.

Box-Steffensmeier, J. M., Christenson, D. P., and Hitt, M. P. (2013). "Quality Over Quantity: Amici Influence and Judicial Decision Making." *American Political Science Review* 107(3): 446–460. doi:10.1017/S000305541300021X.

Brams, S. J. (1966). "Transaction Flows in the International System." *American Political Science Review* 60(4): 880–898. doi:10.2307/1953763.

Brams, S. J. (1969). "The Structure of Influence Relationships in the International System." In *International Politics and Foreign Policy: A Reader in Research and Theory*, 2d ed., edited by J. N. Rosenau, pp. 583–599. New York: Free Press. http://www.worldcat.org/oclc/86035619.

Brams, S. J., Mutlu, H., and Ramirez, S. L. (2006). "Influence in Terrorist Networks: From Undirected to Directed Graphs." *Studies in Conflict and Terrorism* 29(7): 703–718. doi:10.1080/10576100600701982.

Bratton, K. A., and Rouse, S. M. (2011). "Networks in the Legislative Arena: How Group Dynamics Affect Cosponsorship." *Legislative Studies Quarterly* 36(3): 423–460. doi:10.1111/j.1939-9162.2011.00021.x.

Breiger, R. L. (1981). "Structures of Economic Interdependence among Nations." In *Continuities in Structural Inquiry*, edited by P. M. Blau and R. K. Merton, pp. 353–380. London, UK: SAGE Publications.

Burkett, T., and Skvoretz, J. (2001). "Political Support Networks Among US Senators: Stability and Change from 1973 to 1990." Unpublished manuscript, College of Charleston 3123. http://www.researchgate.net/profile/John_Skvoretz/publication/228382999_Political_Support_networks_among_US_Senators_Stability_and_Change_from_1973_to_1990/links/09e415064aba206dc2000000.pdf.

Burt, R. (1992). *Structural Holes: The Social Structure of Competition*. Cambridge, MA: Harvard University Press.

Burt, R. S. (1995). *Structural Holes: The Social Structure of Competition*. 1st paperback ed. Cambridge, MA: Harvard University Press.

Burt, R. S. (2007). *Brokerage and Closure: An Introduction to Social Capital*. Oxford and New York: Oxford University Press.

Caldeira, G. A., and Patterson, S. C. (1987). "Political Friendship in the Legislature." *Journal of Politics* 49(4): 953–975. doi:10.2307/2130779.

Caldeira, G. A., and Patterson, S. C. (1988). "Contours of Friendship and Respect in the Legislature." *American Politics Research* 16(4): 466–485. doi:10.1177/004478088016 004004.

Carpenter, R. C. (2011). "Vetting the Advocacy Agenda: Network Centrality and the Paradox of Weapons Norms." *International Organization* 65(1): 69–102. doi:10.1017/S0020818310000329.

Carpenter, R. C. (2014). *"Lost" Causes: Agenda Vetting in Global Issue Networks and the Shaping of Human Security*. 1st ed. Ithaca, NY, and London: Cornell University Press.

Carpenter, R. C., Duygulu, S., Montgomery, A. H., and Rapp, A. (2014). "Explaining the Advocacy Agenda: Insights from the Human Security Network." *International Organization* 68(2): 449–470. doi:10.1017/S0020818313000453.

Cho, W. K. T., and Fowler, J. H. (2010). "Legislative Success in a Small World: Social Network Analysis and the Dynamics of Congressional Legislation." *Journal of Politics* 72(1): 124–135. doi:10.1017/S002238160999051X.

Christakis, N. A., and Fowler, J. H. (2011). *Connected: The Surprising Power of Our Social Networks and How They Shape Our Lives—How Your Friends' Friends' Friends Affect Everything You Feel, Think, and Do*. New York: Back Bay Books.

Christopherson, J. A. (1976). "Structural Analysis of Transaction Systems: Vertical Fusion or Network Complexity?" *Journal of Conflict Resolution* 20(4): 637–662.

Corbetta, R. (2010). "Determinants of Third Parties' Intervention and Alignment Choices in Ongoing Conflicts, 1946–2001." *Foreign Policy Analysis* 6(1): 61–85. doi:10.1111/j.1743-8594.2009.00102.x.

Corbetta, R., and Dixon, W. J. (2005). "Danger beyond Dyads: Third-Party Participants in Militarized Interstate Disputes." *Conflict Management and Peace Science* 22(1): 39–61. doi:10.1080/07388940590915318.

Craig, A. W. (2015). "Lone Wolves and Team Players: Policy Collaboration Networks and Legislative Effectiveness in the House of Representatives." http://lsvw.org/wp-content/uploads/2014/05/craig-paper.pdf.

Cranmer, S. J., and Desmarais, B. A. (2011). "Inferential Network Analysis with Exponential Random Graph Models." *Political Analysis* 19(1): 66–86. doi:10.1093/pan/mpq037.

Cranmer, S. J., Desmarais, B. A., and Menninga, E. J. (2012). "Complex Dependencies in the Alliance Network." *Conflict Management and Peace Science* 29(3): 279–313. doi:10.1177/0738894212443446.

Cranmer, S. J., Heinrich, T., and Desmarais, B. A. (2014). "Reciprocity and the Structural Determinants of the International Sanctions Network." *Social Networks* 36(January): 5–22. doi:10.1016/j.socnet.2013.01.001.

Crisp, B. F., Kanthak, K., and Leijonhufvud, J. (2004). "The Reputations Legislators Build: With Whom Should Representatives Collaborate?" *American Political Science Review* 98(4): 703–716. doi:10.1017/S0003055404041437.

Desmarais, B. A., and Cranmer, S. J. (2012). "Statistical Inference for Valued-Edge Networks: The Generalized Exponential Random Graph Model." *PLoS One* 7(1). doi:http://dx.doi.org.mutex.gmu.edu/10.1371/journal.pone.0030136.

Dong, D., and Chen, M.-L. (2015). "Publication Trends and Co-Citation Mapping of Translation Studies between 2000 and 2015." *Scientometrics* 105(2): 1111–1128. doi:10.1007/s11192-015-1769-1.

Dorussen, H., and Ward, H. (2008). "Intergovernmental Organizations and the Kantian Peace: A Network Perspective." *Journal of Conflict Resolution* 52(2): 189–212. doi:10.1177/0022002707313688.

Eilstrup-Sangiovanni, M., and Jones, C. (2008). "Assessing the Dangers of Illicit Networks: Why Al-Qaida May Be Less Threatening Than Many Think." *International Security* 33(2): 7–44. doi:10.1162/isec.2008.33.2.7.

Eulau, H. (1962). "Bases of Authority in Legislative Bodies: A Comparative Analysis." *Administrative Science Quarterly* 7(3): 309. doi:10.2307/2390945.

Eulau, H. (1963). *The Behavioral Persuasion in Politics.* 1st ed. New York: Random House.

Eulau, H., and Rothenberg, L. (1986). "Life Space and Social Networks as Political Contexts." *Political Behavior* 8(2): 130–157.

Faber, J. (1987). "Measuring Cooperation, Conflict, and the Social Network of Nations." *Journal of Conflict Resolution* 31(3): 438–464. doi:10.1177/0022002787031003003.

Fiellin, A. (1962). "The Functions of Informal Groups in Legislative Institutions." *Journal of Politics* 24(1): 72. doi:10.2307/2126738.

Fowler, J. H. (2006a). "Connecting the Congress: A Study of Cosponsorship Networks." *Political Analysis* 14(4): 456–487. doi:10.1093/pan/mpl002.

Fowler, J. H. (2006b). "Legislative Cosponsorship Networks in the US House and Senate." *Social Networks* 28(4): 454–465. doi:10.1016/j.socnet.2005.11.003.

Gleditsch, K. S., and Ward, M. D. (2000). "War and Peace in Space and Time: The Role of Democratization." *International Studies Quarterly* 44(1): 1–29. doi:10.1111/0020-8833.00146.

Gleditsch, K. S., and Ward, M. D. (2001). "Measuring Space: A Minimum-Distance Database and Applications to International Studies." *Journal of Peace Research* 38(6): 739–758. doi:10.1177/0022343301038006006.

Gleditsch, K., and Ward, M. D. (2006). "Diffusion and the International Context of Democratization." *International Organization* 60(4): 911–933. doi:10.1017/S0020818306060309.

Granovetter, M. S. (1973). "The Strength of Weak Ties." *American Journal of Sociology* 78(6): 1360–1380.

Granovetter, M. (1985). "Economic Action and Social Structure: The Problem of Embeddedness." *American Journal of Sociology* 91(3): 481–510.

Hafner-Burton, E. M., Kahler, M., and Montgomery, A. H. (2009). "Network Analysis for International Relations." *International Organization* 63(3): 559–592. doi:10.1017/S0020818309090195.

Hafner-Burton, E. M., and Montgomery, A. H. (2006). "Power Positions: International Organizations, Social Networks, and Conflict." *Journal of Conflict Resolution* 50(1): 3–27. doi:10.1177/0022002705281669.

Hafner-Burton, E. M., and Montgomery, A. H. (2008). "Power or Plenty: How Do International Trade Institutions Affect Economic Sanctions?" *Journal of Conflict Resolution* 52(2): 213–242. doi:10.1177/0022002707313689.

Hafner-Burton, E. M., and Montgomery, A. H. (2012). "War, Trade, and Distrust: Why Trade Agreements Don't Always Keep the Peace." *Conflict Management and Peace Science* 29(3): 257–278. doi:10.1177/0738894212443342.

Hanneman, R., and Riddle, M. (2005). *Introduction to Social Network Methods.* Riverside: University of California. http://faculty.ucr.edu/~hanneman/nettext/.

Heaney, M. T. (2006). "Brokering Health Policy: Coalitions, Parties, and Interest Group Influence." *Journal of Health Politics, Policy and Law* 31(5): 887–944. doi:10.1215/03616878-2006-012.

Heaney, M. T., and McClurg, S. D. (2009). "Social Networks and American Politics: Introduction to the Special Issue." *American Politics Research* 37(5): 727–741. doi:10.1177/1532673X09337771.

Heclo, H. (1978.) "Issue Networks and the Executive Establishment." In *The New American Political System*, edited by A. King. pp. 46–57. Washington, DC: American Enterprise Institute. http://goodliffe.byu.edu/310/protect/heclo.pdf.

Heinz, J. P., Laumann, E. O., Nelson, R. L., and Salisbury, R. H. (1997). *The Hollow Core: Private Interests in National Policy Making.* Cambridge, MA: Harvard University Press.

Heinz, J. P., Laumann, E. O., Salisbury, R. H., and Nelson, R. L. (1990). "Inner Circles or Hollow Cores? Elite Networks in National Policy Systems." *Journal of Politics* 52(2): 356–390. doi:10.2307/2131898.

Henry, A. D. (2011). "Ideology, Power, and the Structure of Policy Networks." *Policy Studies Journal* 39(3): 361–383. doi:10.1111/j.1541-0072.2011.00413.x.

Hilbert, D. (1902). "Mathematical Problems: Lecture Delivered Before the International Congress of Mathematicians at Paris in 1900." *Bulletin of The American Mathematical Society* 8: 437–479.

Hoff, P. D., Raftery, A. E., and Handcock, M. S. (2002). "Latent Space Approaches to Social Network Analysis." *Journal of the American Statistical Association* 97(460): 1090–1098. doi:10.1198/016214502388618906.

Hoff, P. D., and Ward, M. D. (2004). "Modeling Dependencies in International Relations Networks." *Political Analysis* 12(2): 160–175. doi:10.1093/pan/mpho12.

Horowitz, M. C., and Potter, P. B. K. (2013). "Allying to Kill Terrorist Intergroup Cooperation and the Consequences for Lethality." *Journal of Conflict Resolution* (January): 22002712468726. doi:10.1177/0022002712468726.

Huckfeldt, R. R., and Sprague, J. (1995.) *Citizens, Politics and Social Communication: Information and Influence in an Election Campaign*. Edited by J. H. Kuklinski, R. S. Wyer, and S. Feldman. Cambridge, UK, and New York: Cambridge University Press.

Huckfeldt, R., and Sprague, J. (1987). "Networks in Context: The Social Flow of Political Information." *American Political Science Review* 81(4): 1197–1216. doi:10.2307/1962585.

Jones, C., Hesterly, W. S., and Borgatti, S. P. (1997). "A General Theory of Network Governance: Exchange Conditions and Social Mechanisms." *Academy of Management Review* 22(4): 911–945. doi:10.5465/AMR.1997.9711022109.

Keohane, R. O., and Nye, J. S. (1977). *Power and Interdependence: World Politics in Transition*. Boston: Little, Brown.

Kinne, B. J. (2013). "Network Dynamics and the Evolution of International Cooperation." *American Political Science Review* 107(4): 766–785. doi:10.1017/S0003055413000440.

Kinne, B. J. (2014). "Dependent Diplomacy: Signaling, Strategy, and Prestige in the Diplomatic Network." *International Studies Quarterly* 58(2): 247–259. doi:10.1111/isqu.12047.

Kinsella, D. (2006). "The Black Market in Small Arms: Examining a Social Network." *Contemporary Security Policy* 27(1): 100–117.

Kinsella, D. (2014). "Illicit Arms Transfers to Africa and the Prominence of the Former Soviet Bloc: A Social Network Analysis." *Crime, Law and Social Change* 62(5): 523–547 doi:10.1007/s10611-014-9531-9.

Kirkland, J. H. (2011). "The Relational Determinants of Legislative Outcomes: Strong and Weak Ties Between Legislators." *Journal of Politics* 73(3): 887–898. doi:10.1017/S0022381611000533.

Klofstad, C. (2010). *Civic Talk: Peers, Politics, and the Future of Democracy*. Philadelphia: Temple University Press.

Klofstad, C. A., Sokhey, A. E., and McClurg, S. D. (2013). "Disagreeing about Disagreement: How Conflict in Social Networks Affects Political Behavior." *American Journal of Political Science* 57(1): 120–134. doi:10.1111/j.1540-5907.2012.00620.x.

Koger, G., and Victor, J. N. (2009). "Polarized Agents: Campaign Contributions by Lobbyists." *PS: Political Science & Politics* 42(3): 485–488. doi:10.1017/S1049096509090805.

Krebs, V. E. (2002). "Mapping Networks of Terrorist Cells." *Mapping Networks of Terrorist Cells* 24(3): 43 52.

Laumann, E. O., and Knoke, D. (1987). *The Organizational State: Social Choice in National Policy Domains*. Madison: University of Wisconsin Press.

Laumann, E. O., and Pappi, F. U. (1976). *Networks of Collective Action: Perspective on Community Influence Systems*. New York: Academic Press.

Lazarsfeld, P. F., Berelson, B. S., and McPhee, W. N. (1968). *Voting A Study of Opinion Formation in a Presidential Campaign*. Chicago: University of Chicago Press.

Lazarsfeld, P. F., Berelson, B., and Gaudet, H. (1948). *The People's Choice: How the Voter Makes Up His Mind in a Presidential Campaign*. New York: Columbia University Press.

Lazer, D. (2011). "Networks in Political Science: Back to the Future." *PS: Political Science & Politics* 44(1): 61–68. doi:10.1017/S1049096510001873.

Leifeld, P., Cranmer, S. J., and Desmarais, B. A. (2015). "Estimating Temporal Exponential Random Graph Models by Bootstrapped Pseudolikelihood." Citeseer. http://citeseerx.ist. psu.edu/viewdoc/download?doi=10.1.1.432.4592&rep=rep1&type=pdf.

Leifeld, P., Cranmer, S. J., Desmarais, B. A., and Leifeld, M. P. (2014). "Package 'xergm.'" http:// cran.revolutionanalytics.com/web/packages/xergm/xergm.pdf.

Leifeld, P., and Schneider, V. (2012). "Information Exchange in Policy Networks." *American Journal of Political Science* 56(3): 731–744. doi:10.1111/j.1540-5907.2011.00580.x.

Lubell, M., Henry, A. D., and McCoy, M. (2010). "Collaborative Institutions in an Ecology of Games." *American Journal of Political Science* 54(2): 287–300. doi:10.1111/ j.1540-5907.2010.00431.x.

Lubell, M., Mewhirter, J. M., Berardo, R., and Scholz, J. T. (2016). "Transaction Costs and the Perceived Effectiveness of Complex Institutional Systems." *Public Administration Review* (September 22). doi:10.1111/puar.12622.

Lubell, M., Robins, G., and Wang, P. (2014). "Network Structure and Institutional Complexity in an Ecology of Water Management Games." *Ecology and Society* 19(4). doi:10.5751/ ES-06880-190423.

Manger, M. S., Pickup, M. A., and Snijders, T. A. B. (2012). "A Hierachy of Preferences: A Longitudinal Network Analysis Approach to PTA Formation." *Journal of Conflict Resolution* 56(5). doi:10.1177/0022002712438351.

Maoz, Z. (2006). "Network Polarization, Network Interdependence and International Conflict, 1816–2002." *Journal of Peace Research* 43(4): 391–411. doi:10.1177/002234330 6065720.

Maoz, Z. (2009). "The Effects of Strategic and Economic Interdependence on International Conflict across Levels of Analysis." *American Journal of Political Science* 53(1): 223–240. doi:10.1111/j.1540-5907.2008.00367.x.

Maoz, Z. (2011). *Networks of Nations: The Evolution, Structure, and Impact of International Networks, 1816–2001.* Structural Analysis in the Social Sciences no. 32. Cambridge, UK, and New York: Cambridge University Press.

Maoz, Z., Kuperman, R. D., Terris, L. G., and Talmud, I. (2006). "Structural Equivalence and International Conflict: A Social Networks Analysis." *Journal of Conflict Resolution* 50 (5): 664–689. doi:10.1177/0022002706291053.

Maoz, Z., Terris, L. G., Kuperman, R. D., and Talmud, I. (2007). "What Is the Enemy of My Enemy? Causes and Consequences of Imbalanced International Relations, 1816–2001." *Journal of Politics* 69(1): 100–115. doi:10.1111/j.1468-2508.2007.00497.x.

Masket, S. E. (2008). "Where You Sit Is Where You Stand: The Impact of Seating Proximity on Legislative Cue-Taking." *Quarterly Journal of Political Science* 3: 301–311.

Matthews, D. R. (1959). "The Folkways of the United States Senate: Conformity to Group Norms and Legislative Effectiveness." *American Political Science Review* 53(4): 1064–1089. doi:10.2307/1952075.

Matthews, D. R., and Stimson, J. A. (1975). *Yeas and Nays: Normal Decision-Making in the U.S. House of Representatives.* New York: Wiley-Interscience.

Mayhew, D. R. (2004). *Congress: The Electoral Connection.* 2d ed. New Haven, CT: Yale University Press.

McClurg, S. D. (2006). "The Electoral Relevance of Political Talk: Examining Disagreement and Expertise Effects in Social Networks on Political Participation." *American Journal of Political Science* 50(3): 737–754. doi:10.1111/j.1540-5907.2006.00213.x.

McPherson, M., Smith-Lovin, L., and Cook, J. M. (2001). "Birds of a Feather: Homophily in Social Networks." *Annual Review of Sociology* 27: 415–444.

Minhas, S., Hoff, P. D., and Ward, M. D. (2016). "A New Approach to Analyzing Coevolving Longitudinal Networks in International Relations." *Journal of Peace Research* 53(3): 491–505. doi:10.1177/0022343316630783.

Monsma, S. V. (1966). "Interpersonal Relations in the Legislative System: A Study of the 1964 Michigan House of Representatives." *Midwest Journal of Political Science* 10(3): 350. doi:10.2307/2108890.

Montgomery, A. H. (2005). "Ringing in Proliferation: How to Dismantle an Atomic Bomb Network." *International Security* 30(2): 153–187.

Montgomery, A. H. (2008). "Proliferation Networks in Theory and Practice." In *Globalization and WMD Proliferation: Terrorism, Transnational Networks, and International Security*, edited by Russell, James A., and James J. Wirtz, pp. 28–39. Routledge. http://www.nps.edu/Academics/centers/ccc/publications/OnlineJournal/2006/Jul/montgomery Jul06.html.

Montgomery, A. H. (2013). "Stop Helping Me: When Nuclear Assistance Impedes Nuclear Programs." In *The Nuclear Renaissance and International Security*, pp. 177–202. Stanford, CA: Stanford University Press.

Moore, S., Eng, E., and Daniel, M. (2003). "International NGOs and the Role of Network Centrality in Humanitarian Aid Operations: A Case Study of Coordination During the 2000 Mozambique Floods." *Disasters* 27(4): 305–318. doi:10.1111/j.0361-3666.2003.00305.x.

Moreno, J. L. (1934). *"Who shall survive?.* Vol. 58. Washington, DC: Nervous and mental disease publishing company.

Moreno, J. L. (1951). *Sociometry, Experimental Method and the Science of Society.* Vol. xiv, 220 pp. Oxford, England: Beacon House, Inc.

Morris, M., Handcock, M. S., and Hunter, D. R. (2008). "Specification of Exponential-Family Random Graph Models: Terms and Computational Aspects." *Journal of Statistical Software* 24(4): 1–24.

Murdie, A. M. (2014). "The Ties That Bind: A Network Analysis of Human Rights International Nongovernmental Organizations." *British Journal of Political Science* 44(1): 1–27. doi:10.1017/S0007123412000683.

Murdie, A. M., and Davis, D. R. (2012). "Looking in the Mirror: Comparing INGO Networks across Issue Areas." *Review of International Organizations* 7(2): 177–202.

Murdie, A. M., Wilson, M., and Davis, D. R. (2016). "The View from the Bottom: Networks of Conflict Resolution Organizations and International Peace." *Journal of Peace Research* 53(3): 442–458.

Mutz, D. C. (2002a). "Cross-Cutting Social Networks: Testing Democratic Theory in Practice." *The American Political Science Review* 96(1): 111–126.

Mutz, D. C. (2002b). "The Consequences of Cross-Cutting Networks for Political Participation." *American Journal of Political Science* 46(4): 838–855. doi:10.2307/3088437.

Nemeth, R. J., and Smith, D. A. (1985). "International Trade and World System Structure: A Multiple-Network Analysis." *Review (Fernand Braudel Center)* 8(4): 517–560.

Ostrom, E. (1995). "Self-Organization and Social Capital." *Industrial and Corporate Change* 4(1): 131–159. doi:10.1093/icc/4.1.131.

O'Toole, L. J. (1997). "Treating Networks Seriously: Practical and Research-Based Agendas in Public Administration." *Public Administration Review* 57(1): 45. doi:10.2307/976691.

Padgett, J. F., and Ansell, C. K. (1993). "Robust Action and the Rise of the Medici, 1400–1434." *American Journal of Sociology* 98(6): 1259–1319.

Padgett, J. F., and Powell, W. W. (2012). *The Emergence of Organizations and Markets*. Princeton, NJ: Princeton University Press.

Patterson, S. C. (1959). "Patterns of Interpersonal Relations in a State Legislative Group: The Wisconsin Assembly." *Public Opinion Quarterly* 23(1): 101–109. doi:10.1086/266850.

Peacock, W. G., Hoover, G. A., and Killian, C. D. (1988). "Divergence and Convergence in International Development: A Decomposition Analysis of Inequality in the World System." *American Sociological Review* 53(6): 838–852. doi:10.2307/2095894.

Pedahzur, A., and Perliger, A. (2006). "The Changing Nature of Suicide Attacks: A Social Network Perspective." *Social Forces* 84(4): 1987–2008. doi:10.1353/sof.2006.0104.

Peoples, C. D. (2008). "Interlegislator Relations and Policy Making: A Sociological Study of Roll-Call Voting in a State Legislature." *Sociological Forum* 23(3): 455–480. doi:10.1111/j.1573-7861.2008.00086.x.

Perliger, A., and Pedahzur, A. (2011). "Social Network Analysis in the Study of Terrorism and Political Violence." *PS: Political Science & Politics* 44(1): 45–50. doi:10.1017/S1049096510001848.

Plümper, T., and Neumayer, E. (2010). "Model Specification in the Analysis of Spatial Dependence." *European Journal of Political Research* 49(3): 418–442. doi:10.1111/j.1475-6765.2009.01900.x.

Porter, M. A., Mucha, P. J., Newman, M. E. J., and Friend, A. J. (2007). "Community Structure in the United States House of Representatives." *Physica A: Statistical Mechanics and Its Applications* 386(1): 414–438. doi:10.1016/j.physa.2007.07.039.

Porter, M. A., Mucha, P. J., Newman, M. E. J., and Warmbrand, C. M. (2005). "A Network Analysis of Committees in the US House of Representatives." *Proceedings of the National Academy of Sciences of the United States of America* 102(20): 7057–7062.

Provan, K. G., and Kenis, P. (2008). "Modes of Network Governance: Structure, Management, and Effectiveness." *Journal of Public Administration Research and Theory* 18(2): 229–252. doi:10.1093/jopart/mum015.

Provan, K. G., and Milward, H. B. (1995). "A Preliminary Theory of Interorganizational Network Effectiveness: A Comparative Study of Four Community Mental Health Systems." *Administrative Science Quarterly* 40(1): 1. doi:10.2307/2393698.

Putnam, R. D. (2000). *Bowling Alone: The Collapse and Revival of American Community*. New York: Simon & Schuster.

Putnam, R. L., and Nanetti, R. Y. (1993). "Making Democracy Work: Civic Traditions in Modern Italy." https://www.amazon.com/Making-Democracy-Work-Traditions-Modern/dp/0691037388/ref=sr_1_1?ie=UTF8&qid=1474338523&sr=8-1&keywords=putnam+making+democracy+work.

Ringe, N., and Victor, J. N. (2013). *Bridging the Information Gap: Legislative Member Organizations as Social Networks in the United States and the European Union*. Ann Arbor: University of Michigan Press.

Ringe, N., Victor, J. N., and Gross, J. H. (2013). "Keeping Your Friends Close and Your Enemies Closer? Information Networks in Legislative Politics." *British Journal of Political Science* 43(3): 601–628. doi:10.1017/S0007123412000518.

Roch, C. H., Scholz, J. T., and McGraw, K. M. (2000). "Social Networks and Citizen Response to Legal Change." *American Journal of Political Science* 44(4): 777. doi:10.2307/2669281.

Rogowski, J. C., and Sinclair, B. (2012). "Estimating the Causal Effects of Social Interaction with Endogenous Networks." *Political Analysis* 20(3): 316–328. doi:10.1093/pan/mps016.

Rolfe, M. (2012). *Voter Turnout: A Social Theory of Political Participation.* Cambridge, UK: Cambridge University Press.

Routt, G. C. (1938). "Interpersonal Relationships and the Legislative Process." *Annals of the American Academy of Political and Social Science* 195(1): 129–136.

Russett, B. M., and Oneal, J. R. (2001). *Triangulating Peace: Democracy, Interdependence, and International Organizations.* New York: Norton.

Sabatier, P. A. (1993). *Policy Change and Learning: An Advocacy Coalition Approach.* Edited by H. C. Jenkins-Smith. Boulder, CO: Westview Press.

Sageman, M. (2004). *Understanding Terror Networks.* Philadelphia: University of Pennsylvania Press. http://www.worldcat.org/oclc/53972026.

Savage, I. R., and Deutsch, K. W. (1960). "A Statistical Model of the Gross Analysis of Transaction Flows." *Econometrica* 28(3): 551–572. doi:10.2307/1910131.

Schelling, T. C. (1960). *The Strategy of Conflict.* Cambridge, MA: Harvard University Press.

Schelling, T. C. (1966). *Arms and Influence.* New Haven, CT: Yale University Press. http://www.jstor.org/stable/j.ctt5vm52s.

Schneider, M., Scholz, J., Lubell, M., Mindruta, D., and Edwardsen, M. (2003). "Building Consensual Institutions: Networks and the National Estuary Program." *American Journal of Political Science* 47(1): 143–158. doi:10.1111/1540-5907.00010.

Schneider, M., Teske, P., and Marschall, M. (2002). *Choosing Schools: Consumer Choice and the Quality of American Schools.* Princeton, NJ: Princeton University Press.

Scholz, J. T., Berardo, R., and Kile, B. (2008). "Do Networks Solve Collective Action Problems? Credibility, Search, and Collaboration." *Journal of Politics* 70(2). doi:10.1017/S0022381608080389.

Scott, J. (2012). *Social Network Analysis.* 3d ed. Los Angeles: Sage Publications.

Shepsle, K. A., and Weingast, B. R. (1987). "The Institutional Foundations of Committee Power." *American Political Science Review* 81(1): 85–104.

Siegel, D. A. (2009). "Social Networks and Collective Action." *American Journal of Political Science* 53(1): 122–138.

Siegel, D. A. (2011). "Social Networks in Comparative Perspective." *PS: Political Science & Politics* 44(1): 51–54. doi:10.1017/S104909651000185X.

Sinclair, B. (2012). *The Social Citizen: Peer Networks and Political Behavior.* Chicago: University of Chicago Press.

Skjelsbaek, K. (1972). "Peace and the Structure of the International Organization Network." *Journal of Peace Research* 9(4): 315–330. doi:10.1177/002234337200900403.

Small, H. (1973). "Co-Citation in the Scientific Literature: A New Measure of the Relationship between Two Documents." *Journal of the American Society for Information Science* 24(4): 265 269. doi:10.1002/asi.4630240406.

Smith, D. A., and White, D. R. (1992). "Structure and Dynamics of the Global Economy: Network Analysis of International Trade 1965–1980." *Social Forces* 70(4): 857–893. doi:10.2307/2580193.

Snijders, T. A. B. (2001). "The Statistical Evaluation of Social Network Dynamics." *Sociological Methodology* 31: 361–395. doi:10.1111/0081-1750.00099.

Snyder, D., and Kick, E. L. (1979). "Structural Position in the World System and Economic Growth, 1955–1970: A Multiple-Network Analysis of Transnational Interactions." *American Journal of Sociology* 84(5): 1096–1126. doi:10.1086/226902.

Sokhey, A. E., and McClurg, S. D. (2012). "Social Networks and Correct Voting." *Journal of Politics* 74(3): 751–764. doi:10.1017/S0022381612000461.

van Eck, N. J., and Waltman, L. (2014). "Visualizing Bibliometric Networks." In *Measuring Scholarly Impact*, edited by Y. Ding, R. Rousseau, and D. Wolfram, pp. 285–320. Cham: Springer International Publishing. http://link.springer.com/10.1007/978-3-319-10377-8_13.

Van Rossem, R. (1996). "The World System Paradigm as General Theory of Development: A Cross-National Test." *American Sociological Review* 61(3): 508–527. doi:10.2307/2096362.

Victor, J. N., and Koger, G. (2016). "Financing Friends: How Lobbyists Create a Web of Relationships among Members of Congress." *Interest Groups & Advocacy* 5(3): 224–262. doi:10.1057/iga.2016.5.

Wahlke, J. C., Eulau, H., Buchanan, W., and Ferguson, L. (1962). *The Legislative System: Explorations in Legislative Behavior*. New York: John Wiley & Sons.

Ward, H. (2006). "International Linkages and Environmental Sustainability: The Effectiveness of the Regime Network." *Journal of Peace Research* 43(2): 149–166. doi:10.1177/0022343306061545.

Ward, M. D., Ahlquist, J. S., and Rozenas, A. (2013). "Gravity's Rainbow: A Dynamic Latent Space Model for the World Trade Network." *Network Science* 1(1): 95–118. doi:10.1017/nws.2013.1.

Ward, M. D., and Hoff, P. D. (2007). "Persistent Patterns of International Commerce." *Journal of Peace Research* 44(2): 157–175. doi:10.1177/0022343307075119.

Ward, M. D., and Hoff, P. D. (2008). "Analyzing Dependencies in Geo-Economics and Geo-Politics." In *Contributions to Conflict Management, Peace Economics, and Development*, vol. 6, *War, Peace, and Security*, edited by Jacques Fontanel and Manas Chatterji, pp. 133–160. Amsterdam: Elsevier.

Ward, M. D., Hoff, P. D., and Lofdahl, C. L. (2003). "Identifying International Networks: Latent Spaces and Imputation." In *Dynamic Social Network Modeling and Analysis: Workshop, Summary and Papers*, edited by Ronald L. Breiger, Kathleen Carley, and Philippa Pattison, pp. 345–360. Washington, DC: Committee on Human Factors, Board on Behavioral, Cognitive, and Sensory Sciences, Division of Behavioral and Social Sciences Education. National Academy of Science/National Research Council, The National Academies Press. https://www.researchgate.net/profile/Michael_Ward12/publication/237440562_Identifying_International_Networks_Latent_Spaces_and_Imputation/links/0046352d055410a170000000.pdf.

Ward, M. D., Siverson, R. M., and Cao, X. (2007). "Disputes, Democracies, and Dependencies: A Reexamination of the Kantian Peace." *American Journal of Political Science* 51(3): 583–601. doi:10.1111/j.1540-5907.2007.00269.x.

Ward, M. D., Stovel, K., and Sacks, A. (2011). "Network Analysis and Political Science." *Annual Review of Political Science* 14(1): 245–264. doi:10.1146/annurev.polisci.12.040907.115949.

Warren, T. C. (2010). "The Geometry of Security: Modeling Interstate Alliances as Evolving Networks." *Journal of Peace Research* 47(6): 697–709. doi:10.1177/0022343310386270.

Wasserman, S., and Faust, K. (1994). *Social Network Analysis: Methods and Applications*. 1st ed. Cambridge, UK, and New York: Cambridge University Press.

Weible, C. M. (2005). "Beliefs and Perceived Influence in a Natural Resource Conflict: An Advocacy Coalition Approach to Policy Networks." *Political Research Quarterly* 58(3): 461–475. doi:10.1177/106591290505800308.

Wendt, A. (1999). *Social Theory of International Politics*. Cambridge Studies in International Relations. Cambridge, UK: Cambridge University Press. http://www.worldcat.org/oclc/40193694.

Young, J. S. (1966). *The Washington Community, 1800–1828*. New York: Columbia University Press.

CHAPTER 2

....

THE EMERGENCE OF
ORGANIZATIONS AND STATES

....

JOHN F. PADGETT[1]

INTRODUCTION

....

UNDERSTANDING the emergence and evolution of political states is a subset of the more general problem of understanding the emergence of organizational novelty, which in turn is a subset of the problem of understanding speciation. This does not mean that the principles of social evolution are the same as the principles of biological evolution.[2] It means that the foundation of human, chemical, or cultural life in general is reproduction, death, and feedback within and among multiple intertwined networks of transformation. These networks (such as those in figure 2.1a) interact through time, coevolving through feedback: sometimes in competition, sometimes in symbiosis, sometimes in contradiction. Networks are in equilibrium if feedback is autocatalytic—that is, if there exists a set of nodes and transformations in which all nodes can be re-created through transformations among other nodes in the set (see figure 2.1b and below).[3] This autocatalytic equilibrium is not static, but dynamic, with change occurring through novelty: the reconfiguration of ways things are done through transpositions and feedback among multiple networks, for example, transposing kinship ties into political networks or vice versa in figure 2.1a through individuals. Equilibrium and change are not different phenomena in this process-oriented view; they are just distinct moments in the same underlying cycle.

Political states are networks of interaction, interwoven with and dependent upon other networks such as economic, kinship, religion, and war, among the same or overlapping set(s) of persons (e.g., figure 2.1a). They are thus subject to selection pressures across multiple network environments simultaneously, even while shaping those environments. What we see as change (such as Deng Xiaoping's reforms, discussed below) at any level of organization or species can be conceptualized as tipping in these underlying networks due to circumstance or perturbation, which can move a system between, for example,

(a)

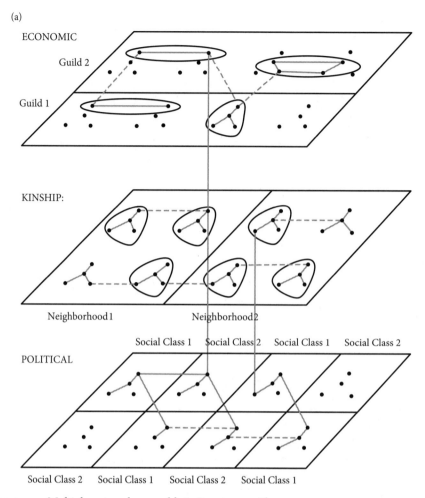

FIGURE 2.1a Multiple-network ensemble in Renaissance Florence.

N.B.: Solid lines are (transformational) constitutive ties, and dotted lines are relational social exchanges. Oblongs are formal organizations (families and firms). People in multiple roles are vertical lines connecting corresponding dots in domains of activity in which people are active. (Only two are shown for illustration.)

(b)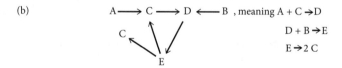

FIGURE 2.1b Example of autocatalytic reaction (Morowitz 1992, 98).

N.B.: C and E are an autocatalytic set, since all nodes can be re-created through transformations among other nodes in the set; if either of these nodes were to be removed, the cycle would continue. A, B, and D are part of the overall autocatalytic cycle, but they cannot be re-created through transformations among other nodes in the set—if D were to be removed, it could not be created with just C and E, but requires B as well, which cannot be created within this cycle. However, A and B may be produced through other autocatalytic cycles.

symbiosis ("regulation") and contradiction ("conflict"). Novelty occurs when ties or networks become transposed across networks, which can lead to innovation. When innovations cascade across an entire network domain (horizontal planes in figure 2.1a), they become inventions. Thus, ties are not simply passive conduits, but rather are transformative, changing products through production rules and information through communication protocols. We as analysts may choose to focus our attention on perturbation ("contingency"), equilibrium ("structure"), individuals ("agency"), or any other part of the elephant we find interesting. But a focus on feedback mechanisms and how they preclude or enable novelty provides a window into organizational- and state-level genesis, evolution, and novelty through time. It is the best bet for understanding how any system (well-functioning or not) lurches in evolution through time. Nodes and ties in social networks are not dots and lines; they are the congealed residues of transformational relations: In the short run, actors make relations; in the long run, relations make actors.

In this chapter I further develop this multiple-network perspective about the emergence of organizational novelty. I then apply this perspective to the comparative analysis of communist reform transitions in the Soviet Union under Stalin and Gorbachev, and in China under Mao and Deng Xiaoping.[4] The communist formal state structure in both cases was a dual-hierarchy interleaving of two coupled interorganizational networks: the Communist Party in the political domain and the central-command economy in the economic domain. Intertwined informal networks grew around these formal hierarchies and were crucial for practical operation of this dual-hierarchy formal structure, in particular, (a) informal top-down networks of mobilization by leaders interested in reform or change (for whatever reason) and (b) informal bottom-up networks of mutual protection or assistance by those resisting leadership pressure. The system exhibited evolutionary feedback; in the short run both (perhaps overlapping) informal networks were structured by the formal networks that they were trying to make work or to subvert, while in the long run the contending informal networks of attempted control altered the formal hierarchy itself. In other words, formal organizational networks induced informal personal networks, which induced political interests and alliances, which then interacted conflictually to reshape the original formal organizational networks in path-dependent iteration across decades. This political reshaping led to biographical consequences: Gorbachev was constructed by the (historical residues of) Stalin he was trying to reform, and Deng Xiaoping was made by the (historical residues of) Mao he was trying to reform. The past shadows through networks that remain.

A radical difference in outcomes between the Soviet Union and China does not mean that underlying dynamics of reform were that different: in both, a knife edge separated symbiosis from contradiction among coevolving multiple networks. In particular, in the Soviet Union top-down mobilization through hyper-centralized formal structures (the legacy of Stalin) induced predominantly horizontal networks of passive resistance, whereas in China top-down mobilization through administratively decentralized formal structures (the legacy of Mao) induced predominantly vertical networks of patron clientage. Both wildly divergent trajectories of communist reform to market socialism in the 1980s were rooted in similar-but-not-identical, endogenous networks iteratively generated by communism itself—not by slavish emulation (and supposed envy) of the West, since reproducing linkages between domestic and foreign (including diaspora) economic networks—one secret to subsequent growth—came after the reforms, not before.

INNOVATION VERSUS INVENTION

Novelty occurs in different degrees. *Innovations* alter existing ways (i.e., activities, conceptions, and purposes) of doing things, whereas *inventions* change the ways things are done.[5] Under this definition, the key to classifying something as an invention is the degree to which it reverberates outward to alter the interacting system of which it is a part and ends up being taken for granted. To some extent we understand micro-logics of innovative combination and recombination. Yet the invention puzzle is that some recombinations cascade out as inventions, reconfiguring entire interlinked ecologies of "ways of doing things," creating new organizational forms and functions (speciation), whereas most innovations do not. The ripeness of a system for reconfiguration by an invention is as equally relevant to be explained as is the system's generation of the invention itself.[6] Inventions are permutations of social context and so cannot be understood in the abstract. But to make progress in understanding discontinuous change, we need to embed our analysis of reconfiguration in the routine dynamics of actively self-reproducing social contexts, where constitutive elements and relations are generated and reinforced.

Figure 2.1a lays the groundwork for understanding this distinction between innovation and invention, viewed through the lens of multiple networks. In a cross-sectional view, all social systems look like this to a social network analyst. Each plane in the figure represents a different domain of activity. In the example of Renaissance Florence illustrated here,[7] these are the economic domain, where goods are produced and exchanged among companies; the kinship domain, where babies are produced through marriage among families; and the political domain, where deals are made among factions within the state. Other domains not shown, such as religion and the military, could be added,[8] depending on the case. Solid within-domain lines represent the "constitutive ties" of cooperation or partnership in production: firms, families, and factions, respectively. Such relations of cooperation constitute people in particular roles because they teach the people participating in them production and communication practices or skills. Circles are placed around these units when they become linguistically corporate or formal, through having collective names. Dotted lines represent exchanges or resource flows between production units: products, wives, and deals, respectively. When resource flows are recurrent and focused, these constitute "relational ties." Markets, for example, are networks of dotted lines within domains. The people participating in organizations and markets can be categorized in various ways, through either personal attributes or institutional memberships, as shown.

Our social science disciplines usually segregate their intellectual activities by analyzing only one domain at a time, as if the other domains and disciplines did not exist. At best, external domains are conceptually black-boxed as reified "environments," without examining their internal structures, even though those intertwine and cross-cut the network structures of focal interest. In contrast, the whole point of a multiple-network perspective is to superimpose multiple domains, with their respective production and exchange networks, and to examine mutual feedback dynamics.

Vertical solid lines in figure 2.1a, connecting dots between planes (domains), are people. Each dot in a plane is a role determined by connections to others within that plane. Figure 2.1a is a snapshot; the trajectories of vertical lines over time are biographies, while the trajectories of dots within a plane over time are careers. In the economic domain, for example, a person may be a businessman; in the kinship domain, he may be a father; in the political domain, he may be a politician—all depending on how he is attached to others in that domain. Properly speaking, individuals don't have goals; roles have goals.[9] Consistency of motivations across roles should in no way be presumed for complicated persons.[10]

Where you sit across multiple networks enables and constrains your agency. It is well recognized by scholars in the social network tradition that the topological overlay created by multiple-network positions can induce cross-domain behavioral effects. At the social psychological level, different ways of nesting various roles in a single person can induce role strain, autonomy, informational access, or even freedom from social control. At the transactional level, a tie in one domain can induce trust, normative reframing, or changes in time horizons in another.

Multiple-network topologies also can shape the dynamics of emergence and evolution of organizational actors over time. Innovation in our usage occurs through recombination of ties or network components across domains, through one of a variety of organizational genesis mechanisms of network folding, discussed below.[11] Invention, then, is the system tipping that might ensue, as a cascade from the original innovation out through the multiple networks that originally induced it.

Network recombinant mechanisms of organizational genesis thus involve transposing social relations from one domain into another. Sometimes this begins as a small-scale transposition, which then reverberates. For example, marriage and economic ties were transposed into the political and social domains by the Medicis.[12] Sometimes this involves larger population transpositions, where entire subsets of new networks from one domain are rewired into old ones in another.[13] Rewiring then reconstructs both sides. Whatever the variant, the resultant topological overlay defines the routes through which innovative relational practices are transported. Transport occurs either via strategically located persons operating in multiple domains (the first case) or via biographies that wend their way across domains (the second case). Where you sit in a multiple-network array affects both whom you can reach and who can reach you. In genetics, this network reachability constraint on recombination has been suggestively labeled "the topology of the possible."[14]

Organizational innovation, whatever its source, must reproduce in order to survive. To reproduce and to grow, organizations must succeed in attracting resource flows (dotted lines) and people flows (solid lines) into their primary fields of activity. For example, economic companies must succeed in product markets. But because companies' component persons and resources are embedded in other domains as well, organizations actually must survive in multiple network selection environments. Politics, kinship, and perhaps even religion, military, or science networks must also reproduce for particular styles of economic entities to exist. Treating multifaceted people as reproducing flows across domains makes the point about multiple selection environments more transparent than does focusing on products and financial flows alone.[15]

In sum, in figure 2.1a organizational innovation is vertical transposition of relational ties and practices across domains. Invention, if it occurs, is horizontal spillover that reorganizes relational and constitutive networks within domains. Organizational innovation becomes systemic invention (if it does) when local network transpositions spill over or cascade throughout a domain through reproductive feedback into the multiple global networks to which local relations are linked. If and when this chain reaction occurs, the selection environment itself for the organizational innovation is altered. This can lead to nonlinear rates of tipping—in other words, to the dynamics of punctuated equilibria. Sometimes (though rarely) invention spillover may even readjust the differentiation of domains themselves, through restructuring vertical lines of multifunctional embeddedness.[16]

The full array of inductively discovered network folding mechanisms that produce organizational invention (Padgett and Powell, 2012) is listed in table 2.1.

Table 2.1 Organizational Genesis (= Multiple–Network Folding) Mechanisms Discovered in Padgett and Powell (2012)

Genesis Mechanism (& Empirical Case)	Definition
Transposition and Refunctionality (Renaissance Florence, chapter 6; Biotechnology firm, chapter 13)	the translation of an old practice to a new purpose, which thrives in new setting (like S.J. Gould's "exaptation")
Incorporation and Detachment (medieval Tuscany, chapter 5)	absorbing old networks into new ones, which hybridize and then leave
Migration and Homology (early-modern Netherlands, chapter 7)	mass migration of people with different practices to new setting, which successfully absorbs them
Purge and Mass Mobilization (Stalin and Mao, chapter 9 [and here])	wholesale elimination of upper layers, to be replaced by social mobility from below
Conflict Displacement and Dual Inclusion (Bismarck in Germany, chapter 8)	attack on third party that splits second party, then absorption of splinter
Robust Action (Cosimo de' Medici, Padgett and Ansell 1993; Deng Xiaoping, chapter 9 [and here])	brokerage between contradictory segments, with multivocal attribution
Anchoring Diversity (Biotech industrial districts, chapters 14, 15; Silicon Valley inventors, chapter 17)	brokerage among overlapping networks, linked through career flows

Other labels for network folding exist in the evolutionary literature. Whereas the selection environment remains fixed in evolution, in coevolution it is altered. When a selection environment is fixed, the performance criterion for any subunit is given, and the concept of optimum becomes well-defined in principle (even if it is impossible to reach or even perceive in practice). When selection environments are endogenously molded by the innovations they select, however, performance criteria migrate, and "optimum" loses the supporting scale upon which it is defined. Coevolution retains notions of "fit" between systems, but it does not retain the notion of an objectively fixed optimum. Social Darwinist fantasies of Panglossian progress thereby usefully vanish into an ethereal mist.

To make these general observations about innovation and invention more systematic requires precision in the motor behind multiple-network feedback. In the research of Padgett and Powell (2012), that engine is primarily autocatalysis. Figure 2.1b is a snapshot from what is actually a movie through time. Autocatalysis brings this otherwise static picture to reproductive life.

AUTOCATALYSIS

In the Padgett and Powell (2012) book and in this chapter, I take the following as my mantra: *In the short run, actors create relations; in the long run, relations create actors.* The difference between methodological individualism and social constructivism is not a matter of religion; it is a matter of time scale. In the short run, all actors—physical, biological, or social—appear fixed, atomic. But in the long run, all actors evolve, that is, emerge, transform, and disappear. To understand their genesis requires a relational and historical turn of mind. In longer time frames, actors congeal out of iterations of transformational relations, which shape ideas and products as they move among nodes. Thus, if actors—organizations, people, or states—are not to be assumed as given, then one must search for some deeper transformational dynamic out of which they emerge. In any domain, without a theory of the dynamics of actor construction, the scientific problem of where novelty comes from remains unsolvable.

The example of the human body may help to fix the idea. Viewed from the perspective of ourselves, we seem solid enough: well bounded and autonomous. But viewed from the perspective of chemistry, we are just a complex set of chemical reactions. Chemicals come into us; chemicals go out of us; chemicals are transformed within us. Solid as we may appear from the outside, no single atom in our body has been there for more than a few years. It is possible (and flattering) to see our physical selves as autonomous bodies exchanging food and other nutrients, but it is also possible to see us as an ensemble of chemicals that flow and interact. Stability of the human body through time does not mean mechanical fixity of parts; it means organic reproduction of parts in flux. Viewed as chemical reactions, we are vortexes in the communicating material of life that wends through us all.

The emergence of new organizational actors operates through analogous mechanisms to the emergence of life in biochemistry. At the theoretical level, this approach is a merger of social network analysis with autocatalysis models from biochemistry.[17] Social network analysis brings an empirical commitment to fine-grained relational data on social and economic interactions through time. The emergence of organizations is grounded in transformations of products and information in social networks, which wend through organizations, bringing them to life. Autocatalysis brings a commitment to discovering and formalizing processual mechanisms of genesis and catalysis (creation and transformation), which generate self-organization in highly interactive systems. Nodes and ties in social networks are not dots and lines; they are the congealed residues of transformational relations derived from iterated production rules and communication protocols in interaction. Learning at the human level is generated by processes analogous to the coevolution of rules and protocols at the "chemical" level. Actors thereby become vehicles through which autocatalytic life self-organizes.

To be more precise, network autocatalysis can be defined as *a set of nodes and transformations in which all nodes can be re-created through transformations among other nodes in the set*. In the context of the biological origins of life in which this concept was originally developed,[18] nodes were chemicals, and transformations were chemical reactions. Chemicals bump into other chemicals, triggering reactions that make new chemicals. If a chemical reaction network contains an autocatalytic set within it, then it reproduces itself through time, given appropriate energy inputs. Positive feedback loops or cycles of self-reinforcing transformations lie at the core of autocatalytic sets. Such cycles are at the foundation of chemical growth.[19]

The implications of autocatalysis, if it emerges, are profound: reproduction can be sustained even in the face of turnover in network components. Destroy a segment of the network, and an autocatalytic network often (not always) can reconstruct its deleted segment. Self-reconstruction and self-repair, in turn, are the crucial dynamic features of autocatalytic sets that gives them continuity through perilous times. Autocatalysis, in other words, allows for an understanding of the generation and reproduction of life across fields. In the context of biological life, the origin-of-life problem is finding prebiotic experimental conditions under which an initial random set of chemicals can self-organize and reproduce itself into an autocatalytic set; similarly, in organizational life, it is finding sets of network ties under which an organization can continually re-create itself. The maintenance-of-life problem is finding conditions that support self-repair and resilience.

The contribution of Padgett (1997), Padgett, Lee, and Collier (2003), and Padgett and Powell (2012, esp. chs. 2–4) was to extend the Eigen-Schuster autocatalysis insight about chemical networks to social networks. In particular, Padgett and Powell propose three nested subtypes of social autocatalysis: (1) *production autocatalysis*, in which rules (or practices or skills) reproduce through products flowing through them in production chains; (2) *biographical autocatalysis*, in which people reproduce sets of roles through rules (or practices or skills) flowing through them via constitutive social interaction such as teaching and learning; and (3) *linguistic autocatalysis*, in which signs and symbols (including corporate names) reproduce through conversations among people. Padgett and Powell (2012) developed the subtypes of production and biographical autocatalysis in considerable modeling and empirical depth, but only pointed to the possible additional significance of linguistic autocatalysis.[20]

Autocatalysis suggests a modification in how social network analysts should conceptualize and measure network ties. Autocatalytic networks are networks of transformations, not networks of mere transmission. Neither products nor information are inert sacks of potatoes passing through passive networks-as-pipes. Products are transformed through production rules, and information is transformed through communication protocols. Either way, social networks don't just pass things; they do transformational work. Under this view, diffusion should be reconceptualized from mimicry or contagion to chain reactions. The autocatalytic self-organization of these chained transformations is emergence.

COMMUNIST ECONOMIC-CUM-POLITICAL TRANSFORMATION IN THE SOVIET UNION AND CHINA

This multiple-network perspective produces considerable insight into the coevolution of economics and politics in communist systems.[21] Whether the innumerable details of the complex cases analyzed below are all accounted for is less important than whether the structure of the logic produces a tractable way of understanding the coevolution of states and markets.

Just to be formulaic, following is the search strategy employed for such a coevolutionary schema:

1. Array political and economic systems or networks next to each other, something like figure 2.1b in the introductory chapter, but rotated 90 degrees such that the planes are vertical instead of horizontal.
2. Pay careful attention to organizational linkages between systems, since these are likely to be loci for dynamic evolutionary feedback and the emergence of new actors. In the context of this chapter, this means looking for the politics induced by economic reforms and for the economics induced by political reforms.
3. Trace historically how intentional change in one system, either in economics or in politics, spilled over (positively or negatively) into often unintentional change in the coupled system. Multiple feedbacks induce chain reactions, possibly contradictory.
4. Induce from these macro histories the micro autocatalytic networks that caused politics or economics to take off (or not) into observed self-reinforcing feedback

loops of new political alliances and/or new economic exchange systems. At their base, these network micro-foundations are reproducing flows of resources and biographies.

5. Find social network data to verify or disconfirm the hypothesized autocatalytic mechanism that induced the observed evolutionary transformation. In my previous research on Renaissance Florence, I had such data (as does Powell for biotech), but in this chapter on communist transitions I do not. This chapter therefore proceeds only through the first four of these research stages—namely, learning and interpretation, but not definitive proof.[22]

To put this theoretical search in didactic terms: to think about economic reform without thinking about the politics that it provokes is to not think very deeply about economic reform. To move from vision to reality, economic reform has to induce the interests that can carry it through. Interests triggered in support of a reform or in deflection of it always emerge on a lattice of prior economic and political networks, which have been laid down in previous iterations. This was the flaw of Western economic advice to Soviet leaders in the 1980s and 1990s and perhaps of Gorbachev himself: to assume that communism could be transformed by decree. Network systems are never designs; they are organic living reproductions and transformations, often turbulent and unintended, of older network systems that have descended into the new. Whatever the fantasies of utopian reformers and leaders, blank slates do not exist in real history. All understanding of innovation must begin with a deep analysis of what was there before.

Dual Hierarchy

I start with a simplification. The Soviet Union, China, and Eastern European states differed in many important respects, but they all shared the dual-hierarchy skeleton sketched in figure 2.2.[23] All communist systems were dual hierarchies in this sense: an economic pillar of centrally planned, state-owned enterprises was paralleled by a political pillar of communist party branches and cells, which interpenetrated, monitored, and attempted to control the economic pillar. One pillar was economics, the other was politics, but they both linked organizationally to each other at multiple levels, like a ladder.

Communist economies, at least at their cores, were central-command economies. The leader (general secretary in the Soviet Union, chairman in China), in consultation with his politburo and council of ministries, established priorities for economic development. Under Stalin and most of his Soviet successors, the economic development of heavy industry and defense was top priority, sometimes almost exclusively so. Central economic ministries developed annual production targets for state-owned enterprises, which implemented the leader's priorities. Lower priority sectors fed into higher priority sectors through mandated supply flows. "Central ministries" included both central

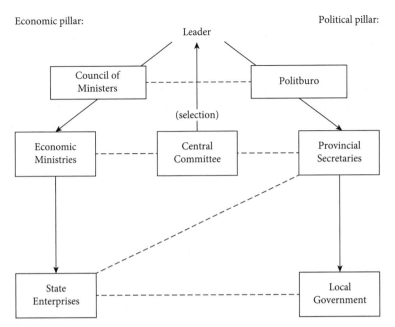

FIGURE 2.2 Communist dual hierarchy.

N.B.: The appointment loop from Leader to Provincial Secretaries to Central Committee to Leader has been called "the circular flow of power" by Daniels (1966, 1971).

planning departments (e.g., Gosplan), charged with designing control figures for input-output material flows by industry, and industry-level ministries, charged with disaggregating the industry control figures into specific production orders for state enterprises. The percentage of the overall economy covered by the plan varied across time and across communist country, with the Soviet Union being almost completely planned, Hungary over half planned, and China fluctuating over time. The detailed content of production orders also varied over time—sometimes with few, sometimes with many, aspects or indicators of production conveyed—but the core command was usually a physical output (e.g., "make x tons of steel this year"). Positive salary and promotion incentives and negative sanctions, sometimes extreme, were attached to the fulfillment of an enterprise's annual production orders.

The second hierarchy was the Communist Party apparatus. This paralleled all levels of the central-command economy, monitoring and enforcing fulfillment of the plan. At the very top, the politburo and the council of ministers overlapped through shared members. The Central Committee formally was the governing body of the Communist Party, in charge of appointing the leader and politburo (albeit usually in a rubber-stamp manner[24]). Meeting only occasionally, it was composed of high-level officials from both of the pillars: provincial secretaries, economic ministers, and the like. The secretariat or bureaucracy of the Central Committee was structured into departments that monitored the work of the Moscow-based economic ministries. Lower down at the provincial level, provincial first secretaries were held responsible for the overall economic performance of enterprises in their region. They, jointly with the industrial ministers, appointed and fired enterprise managers in their region through the *nomenklatura* system.

At the micro level of the economic enterprise or the "firm," dual hierarchy looked like figure 2.3. Communist workers and managers formed party cells at all levels (top management, middle management, and workers) of each plant.[25] The basic organizational ideas of this interlocking, formal structure were not complicated. From the perspective of the economy, dual hierarchy operated to send management orders down the economic hierarchy and to monitor performance (including laxity and corruption) through information feedback, called *kontrol*, up the political hierarchy. The two hierarchies were separated to inhibit lying. From the perspective of politics, dual hierarchy operated to instill communist values (e.g., "the Soviet man" or "the thought of Mao") into the productive personnel of the economy. Economics under communism was never just economics; it was also mass political mobilization of the nation for the future. Needless to say, things rarely worked as smoothly as this organizational chart implies. In subsequent sections I outline actual operations and compare across regimes.

No matter how simplified this starting sketch of dual hierarchy, it is still useful enough to identify constrained trajectories for the politics of communist economic reform, were such a thing to become desired. First of all, it is obvious but worth saying that all reform must come top-down from the leader. The basic dual-hierarchy organizational system had too many cross-checking veto points for political initiative to have been possible from any other quarter. In addition, the "circular flow of power" (see note 25) gave to any communist leader a secure base from which to launch initiatives. But leadership initiative alone was never enough to accomplish reform. For it to become more than just a decree, leadership initiative had to be taken up by others in the system and then achieve self-sustaining reproduction of those interests. The basic dual-hierarchy skeleton

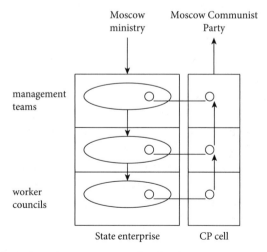

FIGURE 2.3 Dual hierarchy at the enterprise or firm level.

defined the alternative set of potential political allies that communist leaders looked to in order to carry their initiative, whatever that might happen to be. The options within the system were four: to reach down to provincial secretaries, to reach down to local party cadres, to reach down to economic ministries, and to reach down to state enterprises. A leadership initiative that appealed to none of these constituencies was greeted only by silence and obstruction. But if it appealed to at least one, then a sequence of events might ensue, tipping into reform or not.

As a first cut, the various reform drives observed in communist Soviet and Chinese history can be classified according to the primary constituency the leader reached out to. The most tumultuous of such reform drives—Mao's Cultural Revolution and Stalin's Great Purge—involved the leader reaching around provincial party leaders directly down to local party cadres. Such extraordinary mass-mobilization events were not outside of "normal" communist history; they were simply the most dramatic of the inbuilt modalities of reform available to communist leaders. Indeed, seen from the internal perspective of communist reform history, not from our perspective of the West, Gorbachev's revolutionary call for political democracy in 1989 was similar in strategic style to that of the demagogues Stalin and Mao.[26] I demonstrate below that all three of these leaders used "purge and mass mobilization" (wholesale elimination of upper layers, to be replaced by social mobility from below) to attack their own party hierarchy.

A second, less threatening way to mobilize the political pillar for economic reform was for the leader to work through the party hierarchy, not against it. Mao's Great Leap Forward and Stalin's first Five-Year Plan were examples of this.[27] Khruschev's regional economic councils and Deng Xiaoping's fiscal decentralization ("playing to the provinces") were also examples of mobilizing provincial first party secretaries for reform. These cases differed in important details that were consequential for their subsequent evolution, but the point here is that in their constituency politics ("top-down informal network a," in the language above) they are members of a family.

The third political option that dual hierarchy presents to communist leaders interested in reform is mobilization through economic ministries. This modality of reform includes Berliner's categories of Brezhnev-style "conservative" or Andropov-style "reactionary," which is to say, incremental not radical reform. One should not forget, however, that this was the modality that Stalin shifted into, after his Great Purge, in order to build the economy rapidly for war against Hitler. World War II itself shifted Stalin's heavy-industry-defense approach into hyperdrive. Thus economic mobilization through ministries is not only an antireform approach, although in more recent times it was.[28]

Finally there is the fourth, "Hungarian style" of economic reform, which involved leaders reaching around ministries directly down to state enterprises, by loosening ministerial control and increasing enterprise autonomy. Typically this involved not privatization but reorienting central planning away from material flows and toward socially regulated prices and profits. Ministries essentially become state banks in such a transformation. In addition to Hungary as a successful example of this approach to economic reform, the Kosygin reforms of 1965 and the Gorbachev reforms of 1987 stand as unsuccessful Soviet examples of this approach.

I do not list private property as a politically viable route to reform under communism, because a constituency for that did not exist within dual hierarchy. There were noncommunist constituencies for such a reform. Around the consumer margins of the economy—handicrafts, small consumer goods, small plots in agriculture—a private market might become tolerated.[29] But this would always remain marginal, because private property amounts to a dismantlement of dual hierarchy. Any communist leader proposing this would be overthrown.

Deng Xiaoping superficially seems to be the miraculous exception to this political constraint: a communist leader who successfully transformed his central-command economy into a Western-style market. But I show below that actually, Deng employed traditional political strategy number two: the mobilization of provincial and local government cadres to lead his reform.[30] As I explain below, the peculiarly decentralized structure of state ownership in China, bequeathed to Deng by Mao's Great Leap Forward and Cultural Revolution, induced Chinese party cadres to behave as precocious entrepreneurs, without owning private property. While it is fair to hold Deng responsible for successfully managing China's economic transformation,[31] it is less widely appreciated that Mao was responsible over the longer run for rewiring the Soviet version into a party-dominated, decentralized version of dual hierarchy that Deng then could tip into quasi-markets. Mao made accessible what Deng achieved.

On the Soviet side, Gorbachev, like Deng, wanted to be an economic reformer to strengthen communism, not to unravel it. But the dynamics of the reform process turned him into a political revolutionary, more like Stalin and Mao in strategic style than Gorbachev acknowledged. There are many sides to the dynamics of communist economic reform. One is the politics of reform: how leaders' proposals self-organize alliances to support and oppose them. Another is economic feedback: how alliances and policies spill over into the interaction of economic enterprises. But also there is biographical feedback: how reaction from dual hierarchy reconstructs the leader across domains over time. Below I highlight these three interlinked dynamics in the communist-reform cases of Joseph Stalin, Nikita Khrushchev, Mao Zedong, Deng Xiaoping, and Mikhail Gorbachev.

Stalin

The organizational invention of the central-command economy emerged in two stages. The first stage was mobilization of provincial Communist Party officials in the first Five-Year Plan of 1927–1932. The second stage was the purging and mass mobilization of those same Communist Party officials in the Great Terror of 1936–1938.

Given space constraints, I cannot linger on either of these two well-documented episodes of Soviet state formation.[32] I only summarize the core informal network highlights, both on the side of top-down mobilization and on the flip (or "duality") side of bottom-up resistance.

Stalin's first Five-Year Plan is well characterized as a "bacchanalia of planning" because of the astonishingly overoptimistic industrial development goals it set, including the building of entire cities of mass production from scratch.[33] Stalin quite accurately predicted: "We are fifty or a hundred years behind the advanced countries. We must make good this distance in ten years. Either we do it or we shall go under" (Harris 1999, 131). Stalin's economy and his politics were both aggressively built for war—first and foremost war (past and future) with the capitalist West, but as a corollary, war against anyone who stood in his way. The inefficiency of this and subsequent Soviet economic development plans is well known.[34] Less appreciated is the enthusiasm and energy with which the party hierarchy launched itself into this economy-cum-war mobilization task.[35] Measured by the standard of achieving its own absurd targets, the plan was a failure. But measured against the sterner yardstick of defeating Hitler in World War II, the plan was a breathtaking success.[36]

Why did it work at all? The reforms appealed to one of Stalin's constituencies in the two-pillar system: "high up" party officials who were given incentives to maximize production. These incentives in turn created the need for "storming," or seizure of raw material and capital. "The successful Soviet manager during the first Five-Year Plan was less an obedient functionary than a wheeling-and-dealing entrepreneur, ready to cut corners and seize any opportunity to outdo his competitors. The end—fulfilling and overfulfilling the plan—was more important than the means; and there were cases when plants desperate for supplies ambushed freight trains and commandeered their contents, suffering no worse consequences than an aggrieved note of complaint" (Fitzpatrick, 2008, 133). Provincial party officials and the factory directors appointed by them worked together in their hunt for supplies. The infamous mature Soviet informal economy of barter (*blat*) and reciprocity (*tolkach*) was there in spades from the Stalinist beginning, to make the plan actually function. This is not "market" managed by the Communist Party (as the CP itself imagined); this is "market" through the Communist Party—a theme that re-emerges in the case of Communist China. "The economy through politics" need not be the non sequitur that it appears to be in the eyeglasses of neoclassical economics.

The resistance flip side of "storming," however, was "family circles." The penalties for nonfulfillment of the plan included death. Dual-hierarchy horizontal collaboration between party officials and factory managers (see figure 2.3) could easily turn from jointly hunting for supplies to jointly colluding to lie to Moscow superiors, if their factories started to underperform. This was not active resistance in the sense of revolt. This was passive resistance in the sense of sluggish sandbagging. Moreover, the stronger the top-down pressure, the stronger the sandbagging—a problem that continued beyond Stalin to bedevil both Brezhnev and Gorbachev. To complete the vicious-circle feedback: contra Hayek, the core problem with the plan was not the limited cognitive capacity of its linear-programming algorithms to maximize; the core problem was that those algorithms were more or less efficiently maximizing a pile of lies. These family circles of collaboration between political and economic officials were effectively created by Stalin's Five-Year Plan to mobilize the economy through informal networks.

Stalin, given his understanding of the economy as war, labeled sandbagging not a "problem of incentives," but rather "sabotage" and "wrecking"; those who lied to him were "traitors." This recognition of the failures created by reform through party officials led him to switch tactics to reform against party officials through the Great Terror, which I categorize (along with Mao's Cultural Revolution and Gorbachev's aborted democratization) as "Purge and Mass Mobilization" in table 2.1. As illustrated in figure 2.4, 681,692 people were murdered by Stalin in 1937–1938; 70 percent of Stalin's own Central Committee was murdered; only 3.3 percent of delegates to the 27th Party Congress remained from 1934 to 1939; and almost all obkom first secretaries were removed from office in 1937 (Padgett and Powell, 2012, 282).

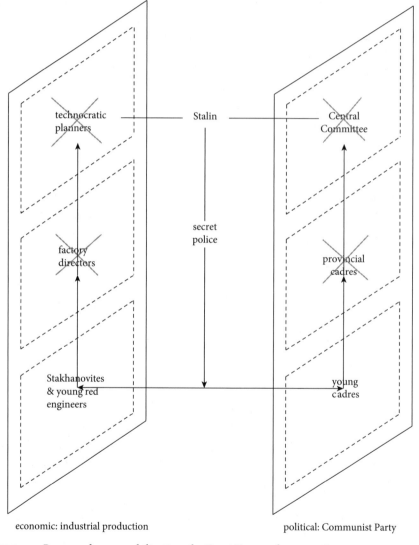

economic: industrial production   political: Communist Party

FIGURE 2.4 Purge and mass mobilization: the Great Terror of 1937–1938.

A bacchanalia of planning in 1927–1932 was followed by a bacchanalia of terror in 1937–1938. It is difficult to dismiss the sense that there was something beyond rationality going on there, but before being too quick to label Stalin insane, never forget that Stalin beat Hitler in World War II.

How did he do it? "Mass mobilization," or as we would say "social mobility"—indeed, astronomically high levels of social mobility given the vacancy rate. Who was left after the murders to run the economic and political machinery? The removal of "high up" party officials could not have occurred if Stalin didn't make the Great Terror appeal to a different constituency, in this case the tens of thousands of communist youths who were beginning to pour out of the engineering training schools that Stalin had set up during his earlier purge of noncommunist technical experts. At thirty years of age, newly minted graduates with no experience whatsoever found themselves summoned to be appointed as new factory directors, ministerial officials, and party secretaries. The job openings above them were enormous in number, so this "generation of '38" experienced the most rapid upward social mobility imaginable. These were the benefi-ciaries of Stalin's murders. Along with glorified Stakhanovite workers and Komsomol teenagers, these young educated cadres, not surprisingly, were grateful and person-ally very loyal to Stalin, even though of course underlying structural contradictions that had led to the lies of the family circles did not go away. This bulging cohort of young engineers—Khrushchev, Brezhnev, Kosygin, Andropov, and their like—aged together, fought a world war together, and eventually ran the country together as eld-erly men, until Gorbachev succeeded them in 1985. For Stalin a crucial advantage of this cohort, besides its zealous personal loyalty to him, was that these were no longer reds *versus* experts; they were reds *and* experts. Structural contradictions were to be solved through personnel. Padgett and Powell (2012) call this "biographical autocataly-sis." The career system that routinized biographical mobilization into autocatalysis was *nomenklatura*.

The organizational consequence of this vast turnover in cadres was a strengthening of the economic pillar of ministries, relative to the political pillar of the party. Almost everybody in administration, ministries and party, was now an engineer. In 1941 the number of ministries grew to forty-three, compared to seventeen in 1933 and nineteen in 1937. Most ministerial proliferation was in the heavy-industry sector. Administrative differentiation implied tighter central supervision and control of industries, even if also greater difficulty in coordination across industries. The portion of the Soviet gross national product devoted directly to military expenditures rose from 7 percent in 1937 to 15 percent in 1940. That was still a far cry from the 55 percent it attained at the height of the war in 1942, but it was a significant escalation in a direction that already had been prepared.

A simplified picture of the autocatalytic economic vision to which Soviet ministries aspired is given in figure 2.5, reproduced from Harrison (1985, 123). Input-output plan-ning in the heavy-industry sector of the Soviet economy was supposed to be like a mod-ern, well-engineered machine, smoothly circulating supplies among gigantic factories that were maximally efficient due to specialized, mass production. Free markets were not required for this circulation because production orders and transfers cleared through state bank accounts at administered prices, reflecting public, not private, demand. This "scientifically designed" economic machine was built primarily for war. Agriculture and consumer goods were squeezed mercilessly to feed it, but success was measured in terms of heavy industry and the military, not in terms of those other sectors.

Ever since Kornai (1980) and even before, it has been fashionable to denigrate the efficiency of the Soviet planned economy; supply bottlenecks, hoarding, and lack of technical innovation were chronic. Without denying that clear reality, it is too easy to overlook the power and efficiency of the military-industrial complex at the core of the Soviet economy. Part of the economic trouble in the Soviet Union was due to informational problems and collusion, as mentioned above. But part of the trouble was due to the intentional diversion of so many resources to war. In a highly concentrated domain like heavy industry, without too many factory nodes, central planning can work. The autocatalytic production and supply economic network feedbacks sketched in figure 2.5 are matters of supply-chain topologies and of balanced input-output volumes, not matters of capitalism. In principle they can be attained either by central command or by private markets. In the Soviet Union, I claim, central command did indeed attain autocatalysis in the military, heavy-industrial core of its economy.

The organizational lock-ins—that is, the emergent actors—for autocatalysis in heavy industry were the centralized economic ministries. Economic concentration in heavy industry reinforced the political power of central ministries, and central ministries protected the centrality of heavy industry in the plan. It is true that the rest of the economy was exploited to serve that military-industrial core, but agriculture and consumer goods were not the goals. Whatever the Soviet citizen thought as a consumer, as a patriotic soldier, he or she could feel proud.

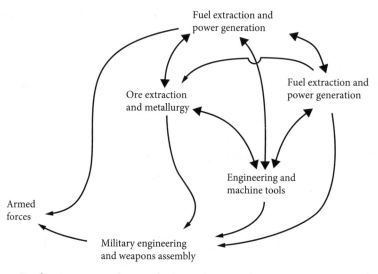

FIGURE 2.5 Production autocatalysis in the Soviet heavy-industry sector (Harrison 1985, 123).

That was the organizational invention of dual hierarchy under Stalin. The original two-pillar formal network enabled Stalin to take two routes toward reform: first through party officials with the Five-Year Plan, and then against party officials through the "purge and mass mobilization" of the Great Terror. Each of the informal networks associated with these reforms led to the creation of new political interests and alliances in response. The plan led to the family circles, while the Great Terror created the new ranks of the class of '38. However, only the latter became "locked in" and was able to redefine the two-pillar system in favor of economic power. World War II provided a powerful stimulus and coevolutionary lock-in to the central-command system that emerged from the terror. Organizational catalysis, which routinized all this, was the *nomenklatura* appointment system of social mobility. This made organizational biographies for the "generation of '38" and also "circular flows of power" for leaders. In contrast, family circles were induced by structural conflict within the system. But they were mitigated by high rates of upward social mobility and returned when rates of mobility slowed down.

Mao

I spend more of my available space on the Soviet Union than I do on China[37] because Stalin was the dual-hierarchy starting point, which established the set of evolutionary trajectories ("topology of the possible") reachable for both cases. Within this range of potential trajectories, variation in degree of administrative centralization (historically rooted in Mao's Great Leap Forward) produced, I argue, divergent developmental paths out of similar organizational and network feedback dynamics. The informal networks generated in China in reaction to Mao's administrative decentralization were predominantly vertical patron-clientage trees, not horizontal family circles of resistance (and storming) as in the Soviet Union.

Given the Soviet framework imported after Mao's victory in 1949, the politics and economics of Mao's Great Leap Forward in 1958–1960 bear a resemblance to the politics and economics of Stalin's collectivization and his first Five-Year Plan in 1928–1932. And the politics of Mao's Cultural Revolution in 1966–1969 bears a resemblance to the politics of Stalin's Great Purge in 1937–1938. Even the temporal gap between their respective stages is similar. The differences are obvious enough: the Chinese Communist Party was rooted in the peasantry, whereas the Soviet Communist Party was rooted in the urban proletariat. And Stalin murdered his opponents, whereas Mao merely "rectified" them. But the broad-scale rhythm of economic-cum-political development in the two communist countries was remarkably similar, with China lagging by thirty years.[38]

The budding planned Chinese industrial economy was subject to the same macroeconomic cycles that the Soviet economy had been: namely, sharp bursts of investment-driven growth, mostly in heavy industry, followed by retrenchments due to subsequent supply imbalances. The first year of such retrenchment and economic confusion in

China was 1956, as new heavy-industry construction and socialist transformation of previously capitalist enterprises ran considerably ahead of the ability of primitive central planning to manage all of that. In addition, 1956 and 1957 were bad harvest years in China, as the first round of collectivization had just been completed. These economic events were ultimately the stimulus to the Great Leap Forward, launched in 1958. But dual hierarchy linked that cause to that particular effect through the medium of politics.

Mao and the Chinese leadership did what Stalin had done in the late 1920s: they turned to the party to mass mobilize. Not only did this mean local cadres at the base, but it also meant provincial secretaries anxious for investment, development, and pork for their regions.

The Great Leap Forward escalated because of an enthusiastic response from the Communist Party, but was initiated in 1956 and 1957 as more incremental reform steps by the central leadership. These empowered the party to engage more deeply in economic management. The first step, in August 1956, was reform at the factory level: a backing away from "dictatorial" management by factory directors toward collective leadership by factory party committees. This was exactly the opposite of what Stalin had done. The second step, in November 1957, was reform at the "ownership" level: factories other than large-scale enterprises in heavy industry would henceforth be administered by governmental planning authorities at the provincial level and below. Mao did not abolish all central ministries—he preserved them for large-scale factories in heavy industry—but he did move 80 percent of the central government's enterprises down to lower governmental levels.

The net effect of Mao's reforms is illustrated in figure 2.6. The Chinese Communist state still owned all of the economy, as in the Soviet Union, but now "the state" no longer meant hypercentralized "Moscow." Huge Soviet-style enterprises were still administered

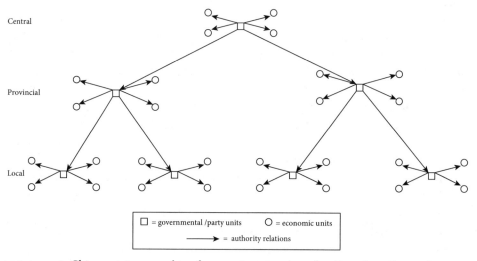

FIGURE 2.6 Chinese state ownership of economic enterprises after Great Leap Forward.

by Beijing, but now administration of medium-sized enterprises was delegated down to provincial capitals, and of small-scale enterprises to county seats.

The reason this system locked in and became autocatalytic in China was the regionalized (almost autarchic) structure of the more underdeveloped Chinese economy at that time. Regional administration fit regional economic clusters (Donnithorne, 1967). This was in sharp contrast to the uber-specialized and regionally interdependent economy that Stalin had bequeathed to the Soviet Union.[39]

Although it began with the same formal network system (two pillar) and choice of constituency to appeal the reform to (party officials), the decentralization of Mao's Great Leap Forward created very different political alliances than the top-down pressure of Stalin's Five-Year Plan. Horizontal family-circle collusion and lying between enterprise managers and party cadres were not as valuable for small- and medium-sized enterprises no longer explicitly part of the central Beijing Plan. Now instead of turning to enterprise managers at the same level, the best route for protection for a local party cadre from top-down pressure from his boss, the principal party secretary, was to end-run that boss with personalized connections to his boss in Beijing. Vertical ties of personal loyalty developed between the top and the bottom to circumvent problematic middle steps in between. If ideology aligned them to mitigate the built-in organizational tension, then vertical ties of "principled particularism" could develop between adjacent levels as well (Walder, 1986).

The net effect of this second-order growth of informal patron-client networks around the trellis of formal economic decentralization is illustrated in figure 2.7. Network trees of clientage grew within regions, culminating at the Central Committee,[40] where contending factions faced off. Bottom-up demands for patronage were met with enthusiastic response from the top, as contending leaders struggled over succession. As long as Mao stood above these "lineage" trees of patronage as charismatic unifier/broker, contending regionally based factions could coexist. But if ever the unifying power of the Chairman weakened (as it did after the Great Leap Forward), the political system splintered automatically into potentially deadly factions.

At that point the weakened CP leader faced the nuclear option of "purge and mass mobilization." As is well known, Mao in fact chose to push exactly this button during the Cultural Revolution, mobilizing the rabid bottom of the party through his Red Guards. Mao's own red faction purged the People's Liberation Army (PLA) after Lin Biao tried to assassinate Mao during an attempted coup; otherwise the PLA might have been able to play a "third-column" control function for Mao during the Cultural Revolution, stabilizing tensions between the political and economic pillars. And thus the Red Guards would not have gotten out of Mao's control. As it was, Mao (like Gorbachev after him) failed to develop Stalin's level of feedback control over the powerful bottom-up forces that he had unleashed. The (now more conservative) PLA was then called in to crush the Cultural Revolution, rather than to manage it.

Call Lin Biao's attempted assassination a "contingency" or "a butterfly effect" if you will. But attempted coups are not exactly surprising given a decapitated version of the

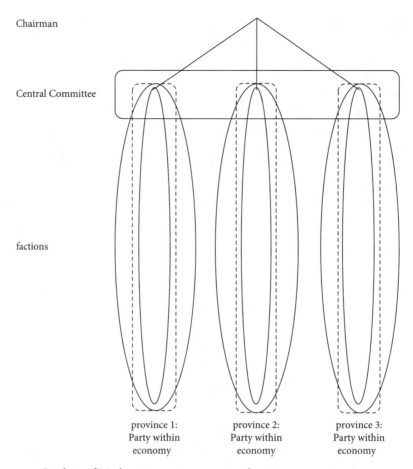

FIGURE 2.7 Catalysis of Mao's communist economy and party.

factional structure in figure 2.7. Just as Stalin turned to "purge and mass mobilization" after witnessing the failures of the political alliances (family circles) created from reform through the party, Mao too changed reform tactics once the disparate factions created by the Great Leap Forward swung out of control.

Deng Xiaoping

Westerners like to think that Deng Xiaoping was a liberal who sensibly repudiated the crazy Mao Tse-tung because he finally understood the superior rationality of the West and its "markets." But this denies that Deng was a communist, trying to strengthen communism, especially after its period of internal troubles, not to weaken it. The path-dependency thesis here, instead, is that socialist "markets" all along were one of the inbuilt trajectories of communist development.[41] There just had to emerge communist politics and networks out of dual hierarchy to push communist economics down that road. The aftermath of the Cultural Revolution generated the prerequisite politics and networks, and it generated the leader to broker those political networks. The political alliances and interests created in reaction to Mao, in the long run, were able to alter the formal network from whence they came. Deng's reforms had nothing to do with imitation of the West.[42] Mao instead made accessible what Deng achieved.

The argument is illustrated in figure 2.8. Factional remnants of the Cultural Revolution were resident in three organizational pillars: (a) the Soviet-style central-command economy, which was the redoubt of Mao's "Gang of Four" radicals; (b) Deng's soon-to-become reform supporters, who were fragmented around this Beijing core, in the decentralized regional provinces; and (c) the chastened PLA, who had cleaned up the Cultural Revolution mess. Deng Xiaoping constructed an alliance between (c) and (b), against Maoist (a), through the multiple-network brokerage mechanism of robust action (brokerage between contradictory segments, with multivocal attribution; see table 2.1 and Padgett and Ansell, 1993).

Deng's original power base was not the decentralization of pillar (b), but rather the PLA of pillar (c). Mao recalled Deng from Cultural Revolution exile in 1974 for two reasons: to substitute for a terminally ill Zhou Enlai in running the economy and to enable the simultaneous rotation of eight commanding officers of PLA military regions, to weaken their collective potential for a new coup.[43] The generals' support for Deng

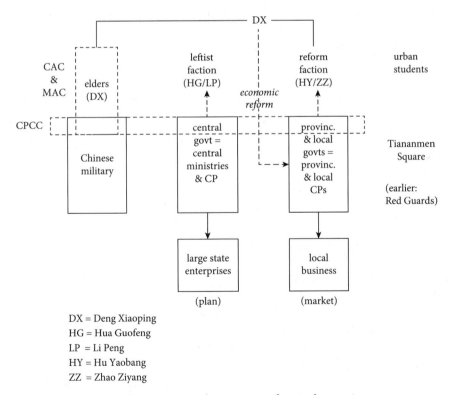

DX = Deng Xiaoping
HG = Hua Guofeng
LP = Li Peng
HY = Hu Yaobang
ZZ = Zhao Ziyang

FIGURE 2.8 The politics of Deng Xiaoping's economic reform: robust action.

(which was not necessarily anti-Maoist) was rooted in their shared Long March days, when Deng himself had been a young general. Struggle for allegiance of the military continued as the inflection point in the interregnum politics between the death of Mao in 1976 and Deng's accession to power in 1978.

Deng's robust-action brokerage emerged through linkage of his old PLA power base with a newly constructed economic-reform leg, assembled out of patronage clusters in the provinces, to build his two-legged political network support structure.[44] This second, more dynamic half of Deng's coalition was his famous sequence of liberalizing economic reforms. Sensibly labeled "playing to the provinces" by Shirk (1993), those economic reforms emerged through standard communist leadership behavior—namely, reaching out and mobilizing local and provincial party cadres through discretionary economic favors directed toward political allies. These famous economic reforms in the late 1970s and early 1980s consisted of three steps: (1) the household responsibility system in agriculture, (2) fiscal decentralization that allowed provinces to keep a negotiable X percent of tax revenue they collected,[45] and finally (3) special economic trading zones in coastal ports. In all three cases, reform benefits were not distributed homogeneously across geography, but were distributed discretionarily to Deng's provincial allies. Economic reform, therefore, was the same as political faction building through patronage, not dissimilar to what it had been in Stalin's first Five-Year Plan. The content of those two economic reforms was rather different, but the politics was similar. Also similar to that first Soviet Five-Year Plan, entrepreneurial storming at a feverish pace ensued among party cadres (Walder, 1995; Oi, 1999).

The main reasons, besides lack of historical perspective, that observers often do not recognize Deng's economic reforms as communist behavior are two twists. The first tactical twist is that usually communist leaders initiated and constituencies responded, whereas with Deng first the constituency responded and then the leader initiated. As a matter of leadership style, this tactic was significant: Deng and his policy goals were inscrutable this way. As a matter of feedback, however, the positive reinforcement that political leaders and party constituencies gave to each other was crucial, whoever initiated the feedback cycle.

The second misleading twist is that CP leader to provincial secretary feedback in communist dual hierarchies usually led to centralization both in the political and in the economic domains. In the case of Deng, it did lead to centralization (or more accurately to re-centralization) in the political domain, but it also led to decentralization in the economic domain. This is because the plan was now constrained to the politically untrustworthy Beijing leg of large factories.

Similar to Cosimo de' Medici in Florence, Deng Xiaoping could plausibly be interpreted as having multiple identities, because of the heterogeneous support structure that he supervised. Because of this structurally enabled multivocality, which Deng did not destroy by uttering words or policies too clearly, he could be seen as a sphinx-like "friend to all" (except the Maoists) and an honest broker. Deng floated above the system, not beholden to any segment. He even imitated his mentor, Mao, by resigning his official offices as chairman ("retreating from the front line"), in order better to rule murkily from behind closed doors. Lest anyone mistake his studied ambiguity for passivity, however, Deng could easily shift back to his original PLA power base, as evidenced by his ruthlessly murdering students in Tiananmen Square.

By Western standards, there can be no doubt that Deng Xiaoping was the most successful communist economic reformer ever. Measured solely by economic criteria, the transformation of China he pulled off was little less than miraculous. The attributional tendency post hoc is to anoint him a genius. But unlike Mao, Deng had no utopian vision. His famous declaration of pragmatism was: "I don't care whether the cat is black or white, as long as it catches mice." While there can be no doubt about Deng's shrewdness, the nature of that shrewdness was not a brilliant plan, skillfully implemented. Chinese economists interviewed by Shirk seem to have captured best his and his allies' leadership style when they reported, "When they found loose stones, they pushed through; when stones would not move, they did not waste energy pushing." Deng, in other words, adapted to what he encountered and to what he inherited. He was not just a leader but an autocatalytic leader, part of the dynamic system he inhabited.

Gorbachev

A brief sketch of Gorbachev serves as a contrast with Deng and demonstrates the path-dependent failure of his sequence of reforms in the 1980s, which led to the collapse of the Soviet Union.[46] Figure 2.9 presents at least the dual-hierarchy, organizational network skeleton of that analysis of Gorbachev and the fall of the Soviet Union.

In the present context, the most important conclusion from that analysis was that dense, "family circle"–style, horizontal informal networks, which were bequeathed to Gorbachev by Stalin, deprived Gorbachev of any Chinese-style, vertical, patron-client networks with which to break through those layers of intentional sandbag resistance within the party. Despite Gorbachev's masterful control of the Kremlin itself, it was the absence of any informal-network leverage to reach outside of the Kremlin[47] that led to his fateful decision to go to war against his own CP, through "democratization." (The right column of figure 2.9 shows the short-lived third pillar that Gorbachev was trying to develop and lead.) Urban liberals, he hoped, would swarm to his charismatic side, giving him the leverage over the party that he needed, without dissolving the CP itself— just as the Stakhanovites had done for Stalin, and just as the Red Guards more problematically had done for Mao. Alas for Gorbachev, those urban liberals chose to swarm to charismatic Yeltsin instead—in the name of nationalist Russia, not Gorbachev's beloved Soviet Union. Gorbachev's high-risk purge and mass mobilization control strategy was hardly beyond the realm of built-in communist evolutionary trajectories. In the end Gorbachev, like Mao, failed to control the powerful feedback dynamics that he himself had unleashed.

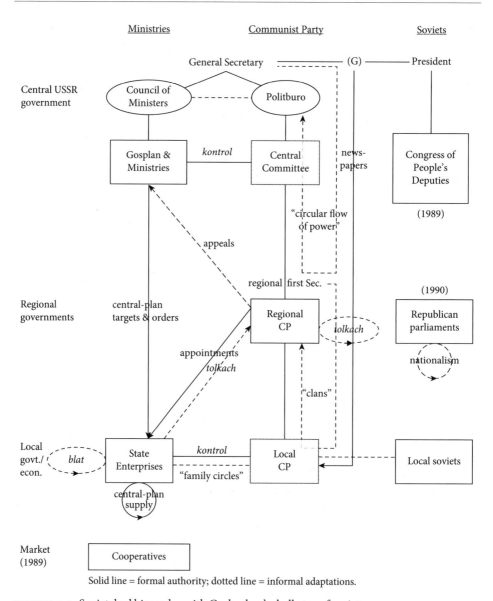

Solid line = formal authority; dotted line = informal adaptations.

FIGURE 2.9 Soviet dual hierarchy, with Gorbachev's challenge of soviets.

Obstreperous horizontal networks within the party drove Gorbachev toward try-ing to create reformist vertical networks for himself outside the party, all in the name (and I think the true goal) of reforming, not abandoning, communism. But even to reproduce, much less to work, political networks have to have autocatalytic reality; they cannot be wished out of thin air. Coevolution and state formation, Gorbachev found out to his dismay, require more than good intentions, a clever mind, and dictatorial power.

Conclusion

This chapter has been the communist illustration of the general mantra of Padgett and Powell: "*In the short run, actors make relations. In the long run, relations make actors*" (2012, 2). There are practical evolutionary and research implications, I argue, of even as general a mantra as this. Social and political coevolutionary history is not a teleological march toward some mythical optimum. It is instead a series of branching trajectories, in which only a finite set of accessible futures are contained within the present multiple-network array. That array, in turn, is the selective memory of its history.

Not unlike the biological evolution of life in general.

Notes

1. I want to thank Alex Montgomery for extremely helpful and thorough suggestions and editing.
2. A conceptual mistake made by social Darwinists of both yesteryear and today.
3. For example, kinship networks raise children to fulfill parenting roles, and guild networks train apprentices to become masters (see figure 2.1a).
4. This chapter draws from chapters 1 and 9 in Padgett and Powell (2012). See those chapters for longer, more thorough analyses of the themes adumbrated in this chapter. Extensive citations are provided there more than here.
5. A distinction developed further in Padgett and Powell (2012).
6. Consider, for example, the meteor that killed the dinosaurs. Yes, it is true that "contingency" did in the dinosaurs. The problem with this analysis, however, is that many similar meteors have struck the earth without ecological catastrophe ensuing. Something about the ecology of the earth at that historical moment made interdependent populations of species vulnerable not just to death, but also to contagions of extinctions. The same logical problem afflicts Tilly's aphorism: "War makes states, and states make war." Yes, there are many examples of this in human history. But there are also cases in which wars make coups, wars make fragmentation, wars make social revolutions, and wars make simple collapse. Looking at "war" as an independent variable, abstracted from the multiple-network feedbacks that both produce it and respond to it, is a conceptually thin approach to understanding evolutionary change. (The real Tilly, by the way, was far more complicated than this cartoon that his antibellicist critics have constructed of him.)
7. This figure is a cartoon of the relational database structure of Padgett's actual Florentine data set. See Padgett (2010) for details.
8. And are in Padgett and Powell (2012)—see especially chapter 6 on early-modern Netherlands during the Dutch Revolt and chapter 7 on nineteenth-century Germany under Bismarck.
9. Profit maximization, for example, might be the goal of a businessman. But that is not the goal of a more complicated businessman-father-politician ensemble person. For this reason, "methodological individualism" is a misnomer. "Methodological role-ism" is a more accurate description of modeling practices in the segregated world of contemporary social science.

10. This caveat makes the imputation of any meta- or cross-role utility function to individuals problematic, because Von Neumann-Morgenstern axioms are likely to be violated. Without a well-defined utility function, the definition of maximization becomes unhinged. Cross-role consistency is of course possible, but that would be quite a social achievement. In this sense, rationality (narrowly conceived as individual maximization) is socially produced.

11. We stick with the word "recombination" because it is so prevalent in the literature. But in our empirical cases the elements being recombined are not atomic entities, decoupled from their context, but rather nodes or ties in some network or other. For that reason, the words "network folding" more accurately describe the phenomena we observe than does the word "recombination," which to our ears has atomistic overtones.

12. See Padgett and Ansell (1993); Padgett and Powell (2012) call this "transposition and refunctionality" (chapters 6 and 13).

13. Padgett and Powell (2012) call this either "incorporation and detachment" (chapter 5) or "migration and homology" (chapter 7), depending upon which half of this process occurs first.

14. Stadler et al. (2001); Fontana (2006).

15. See Padgett, Lee, and Collier (2003).

16. As explained in Padgett and Powell's chapter 1 section on catalysis, if the analyst looks at figure 2.1b from the top down, viewing through superimposed domains, then he or she sees figure 2.1b as a Venn diagram. Patterns of overlaps among domains in the Venn diagram are defined by patterns of multifunctional memberships of people. Change patterns of multifunctional embeddedness, therefore, and one changes patterns of domain differentiation.

17. Autocatalytic theory, described in more detail in chapters 2 and 3 in Padgett and Powell (2012), is a branch (a chemistry branch) of loosely called complexity theory.

18. Eigen and Schuster (1979). See Fontana and Buss (1994) for further development, and Jain and Krishna (1998) for extension of this Eigen-Schuster insight to ecologies of communities of species.

19. This is not to deny, of course, that negative feedback loops are also important to keep such growth in chemical concentrations bounded.

20. Contra the charge of Emirbayer and Goodwin (1994), this postponement of sustained focus on linguistic autocatalysis was not due to some misguided theoretical commitment that "culture is not important." Rather, our particular empirical case studies most often revealed tippings in production and especially biographical autocatalysis to precede in time tippings in linguistic understanding of those tippings. This is not surprising during turbulent periods of punctuated equilibria—often people's consciousness struggles to catch up with huge macro events beyond their control. Since 2012 some limited progress has been made toward understanding and modeling linguistic autocatalysis (Padgett 2015).

21. Success for such an analysis is to be measured not by the vainglorious standard of predicting the future, even in hindsight. It is to be measured instead on the yardstick of whether it can identify finite trajectories of evolutionary economic development, reachable through realistic politics of regimes of the time. The experience of smart but not wise Western economic advisers to Yeltsin should be enough to cure us all of the disease of excessive self-confidence. Interestingly, the impressive success of economic reform under Deng Xiaoping was achieved without any "helpful" advice from Western academics.

22. This is not to apologize. Without the first four research stages, one does not know what to count or where to look for confirmatory data.

23. Schurmann (1968) was the first Western academic, to my knowledge, who analyzed communism explicitly in terms of the concept of dual hierarchy. As for differences, the secret police under Stalin, the people's liberation army under Mao and Deng, and the military under Gorbachev loom large as background third pillars in the histories of those regimes, episodically used as levers on the two primary pillars.

24. Leadership control over the Central Committee was achieved through the "circular flow of power": namely, leaders appointed provincial secretaries and ministers who joined the Central Committee, which voted on the succession and renewal of the leaders.

25. One might consider this political spying, except that the identities of CP members in the firm were not secret.

26. People forget that an important part of Stalin's Great Purge campaign of 1937–1938, which murdered over six hundred thousand party members, was his new constitution, which granted considerable electoral freedom (including the secret ballot) to the lower echelons of the Communist Party. These elections reinforced and fueled denunciations from below.

27. It is interesting that Mao's Cultural Revolution followed soon after his Great Leap Forward, just as Stalin's Great Purge followed soon after his First Five Year Plan. The logic of this sequence is explored below.

28. The developmental states of Japan and South Korea, while not communist, are additional apt examples.

29. The New Economic Policy (NEP) in the 1920s under Lenin was an example, considered by Lenin, however, only as transitional.

30. A more complete description of Deng's strategy will become "robust action" (cf. Padgett and Ansell 1993), once the latent pillar of the People's Liberation Army is taken into consideration.

31. By this language I do not mean to imply that a great man "did it." All any reform leader can do is to perturb autocatalytic processes into self-reorganization. The complexity of changing a country is beyond anyone's intelligence and foresight.

32. For literature and secondary-source evidence behind the brief summaries here, see Padgett, "The Politics of Communist Economic Reform: Soviet Union and China," in Padgett and Powell (2012, ch. 9).

33. Not "from scratch" exactly: on the agrarian-collectivization backs of exploited and murdered peasants.

34. "Building factories today with future bricks," Bukharin scornfully snarled (Cohen 1973, 296).

35. "D.B. Riazanov quite aptly remarked at the sixteenth party conference in April 1929: 'Every speaker from this platform ends with the conclusion: 'Give us a factory in the Urals, and to hell with the Rightists! [*Laughter*] Give us a power station, and to hell with the Rightists! [*Laughter*]'" (Kuromiya 1988, 20).

36. As Gerschenkron (1962), among few others, realized.

37. Again, see chapter 9 in Padgett and Powell (2012) for more details and references.

38. The state of economic development in China after World War II was also roughly similar to the prostrate state of economic development in Russia after World War I.

39. Khrushchev, in other words, was defeated by the organizational ghost of the Stalin that he had denounced.

40. Called Politburo in the Soviet Union.

41. Clear evidence for this was Kádár's Hungary, the model case that most fascinated Gorbachev. Kosygin under Brezhnev and the NEP under Lenin/Bukarin are other examples, albeit ones that did not lock into autocatalysis as in Hungary.

42. Unlike Yeltsin and the East Europeans, for example, Deng never asked Western economists for any advice.

43. "The elements of the bargain were clear. In return for giving up political power, the generals were promised that [the premiership] would be put into the responsible hands of a trusted old comrade" (MacFarquhar 1997, 291).

44. Deng's two-legged political network support structure was structurally similar to Cosimo de' Medici's coupling of old patricians through marriage with new men through business (Padgett and Ansell 1993).

45. Americans of the time period would have called this "revenue sharing."

46. For those interested, please consult chapter 9 of Padgett and Powell (2012, 297–309).

47. "Beginning in 1985 I flew to Moscow three years in a row, immersing myself in the atmosphere of the capital, and met politicians, journalists, artists and writers. What were my impressions? *Perestroika* was going at full speed—a real tidal wave! Then I travelled from the capital into the countryside. Go some hundred or two hundred kilometers away and things were completely different—all quiet, no change" (Report of American researcher Ed Hewitt to Gorbachev in 1991, in Gorbachev 1995, 195–196).

References

Cohen, S. F. (1973). *Bukharin and the Bolshevik Revolution*. New York: Knopf.

Daniels, R. V. (1966). "Stalin's Rise to Dictatorship, 1922-29." In *Politics in the Soviet Union*, edited by A. Dallin and A. Westin, pp. 1–38. New York: Harcourt, Brace & World.

Daniels, R. V. (1971). "Soviet Politics since Khrushchev." In *The Soviet Union under Brezhnev and Kosygin*, edited by J. Strong, pp. 16–25. New York: Van Nostrand-Reinhold.

Donnithorne, A. (1967). *China's Economic System*. New York: Praeger.

Eigen, M., and Schuster, P. (1979). *The Hypercycle: A Principle of Natural Self-Organization*. Berlin: Springre-Verlag.

Emirbayer, M., and Goodwin, J. (1994). "Network Analysis, Culture, and the Problem of Agency." *American Journal of Sociology* 99: 1411–1454.

Fitzpatrick, S. (2008). *The Russian Revolution*. Oxford: Oxford University Press.

Fontana, W. (2006). "The Topology of the Possible." In *Understanding Change: Models, Methodologies, and Metaphors*, edited by A. Wimmer and R. Kössler, pp. 67–84. New York: Palgrave Macmillan.

Fontana, W., and Buss, L. W. (1994). "The Arrival of the Fittest: Toward a Theory of Biological Organization." *Bulletin of Mathematical Biology* 56: 1–64.

Gerschenkron, A. (1962). *Economic Backwardness in Historical Perspective*. Cambridge, MA: Harvard University Press.

Gorbachev, M. (1995). *Memoirs*. New York: Doubleday.

Harrison, M. (1985). *Soviet Planning in Peace and War, 1938–1945*. Cambridge: Cambridge University Press.

Jain, S., and Krishna, S. (1998). "Autocatalytic Sets and the Growth of Complexity in an Evolutionary Model." *Physical Review Letters* 81: 5684–5687.

Kornai, J. (1980). *Economics of Shortage*. Amsterdam: North-Holland.

Kuromiya, H. (1988). *Stalin's Industrial Revolution*. Cambridge, UK: Cambridge University Press.

MacFarquhar, R. (1997). "The Succession to Mao and the End of Maoism, 1969–82." In *The Politics of China: The Eras of Mao and Deng*, edited by R. MacFarquhar, pp. 248–339. Cambridge, UK: Cambridge University Press.

Morowitz, H. J. (1992). *Beginnings of Cellular Life: Metabolism Recapitulates Biogenesis*. New Haven, CT: Yale University Press.

Oi, J. C. (1999). *Rural China Takes Off*. Berkeley: University of California Press.

Padgett, J. (1997). "The Emergence of Simple Ecologies of Skill: A Hypercycle Approach to Economic Organization." In *The Economy as an Evolving Complex System II*, edited by Brian Arthur, Steven Durlauf and David Lane, pp. 199–222. Santa Fe Institute Studies in the Sciences of Complexity, Reading, Mass.: Addison-Wesley.

Padgett, J. F. (2010). "Open Elite? Social Mobility, Marriage, and Family in Florence, 1282-1494," *Renaissance Quarterly* 63: 357–411.

Padgett, J. F. (2015). "The Emergence (or Autocatalysis) of Language." Powerpoint presentation at Computational Social-Science workshop, December 3, 2015.

Padgett, J. F., and Ansell, C. K. (1993). "Robust Action and the Rise of the Medici, 1400–1434." *American Journal of Sociology* 98(6): 1259–1319.

Padgett, J. F., Lee, D., and Collier, N. (2003). "Economic Production as Chemistry." *Industrial and Corporate Change* 12: 843–877.

Padgett, J. F., and Powell, W. W. (2012). *The Emergence of Organizations and Markets*. Princeton, NJ: Princeton University Press.

Schurmann, F. (1968). *Ideology and Organization in Communist China*. Berkeley: University of California Press.

Shirk, S. L. (1993). *The Political Logic of Economic Reform in China*. Berkeley: University of California Press.

Stadler, B., Stadler, P., Wagner, G., and Fontana, W. (2001). "The Topology of the Possible: Formal Spaces Underlying Patterns of Evolutionary Change." *Journal of Theoretical Biology* 213: 241–274.

Walder, A. G. (1986). *Communist Neo-Traditionalism: Work and Authority in Chinese Industry*. Berkeley: University of California Press.

Walder, A. G. (1995). "Local Governments as Industrial Firms." *American Journal of Sociology* 101(2): 263–301.

CHAPTER 3

....

POWER STRUCTURES
OF POLICY NETWORKS

....

DAVID KNOKE AND TETIANA KOSTIUCHENKO

WE trace the origins of policy network analysis to the 1950s, in C. Wright Mills's (1956) depiction of the US national power elite as the interpersonal ties among elite persons occupying the top positions of business, political, and military institutions. Over the following decades, European and North American political sociologists and political scientists theorized and conducted research on policy networks that increasingly integrated numerous features of social network analysis (SNA). Consequently, policy scholars today enjoy a rich gumbo of SNA concepts, propositions, principles, and methodologies that illuminate policymaking structures and power at diverse levels of analysis across a wide range of polities in advanced and developing societies.

This chapter presents an overview of major theoretical policy network developments, disputes and alternative models, and key research results. Taking a chronological approach, the first section identifies the origins of policy network research in studies of power structures and interlocking directorates. The next section examines theories of policy networks constructed on both sides of the Atlantic in the late twentieth century. The third section looks at recent policy network developments, including the emergence of global networks and incorporating new theoretical and methodological paradigms. We conclude that the field has greatly matured as a multidisciplinary specialty and become more institutionalized in recent years. Although it still lacks cohesion around a core set of innovative ideas that could facilitate greater integration, opportunities await for creative analysts to propose paradigms that could take policy network studies in surprising new directions.

THE ORIGINS OF POWER STRUCTURE
ANALYSIS

Policy networks may be defined as "(more or less) stable patterns of social relations between interdependent actors, which take shape around policy problems and/or policy programmes" (Kickert, Klijn, and Koppenjan, 1997, 6). We accept Max Weber's structural definition of power as "the probability that one actor within a social relationship will be in a position to carry out his own will despite resistance, regardless of the basis on which this probability rests" (1947, 152). The actual or potential exercise of power involves asymmetric relations between two or more actors, or groups, that may take varied forms. David Knoke (1990, 3–7) theorized about four pure types of power, based on combinations of influence and domination relations: (1) *coercive power*, in which actors dominate others by "threats and applications of negative sanctions"; (2) *authoritative power*, involving "the issuing of a command with the expectation of uncontested obedience by the recipient"; (3) *persuasive power*, whose basis lies in "the informational content of messages, with no ability to invoke sanctions for refusals to comply"; and (4) *egalitarian power*, in which both domination and influence are largely absent. In formally democratic polities, where most policy network research has been conducted, power tends to blend authoritative and persuasive relations in the legislative and executive organizations of government. Consequently, power structure analysts investigated the patterns of network connections among elite political actors and the outcomes of collective decision-making by these political structures.

This section identifies the origins of policy network analysis in studies of power structures and interlocking directorates beginning in the 1950s. Although these scholars did not draw explicitly on formal SNA principles, they laid the foundation for a subsequent proliferation of such approaches.

Overlapping Circles of the Power Elite

Seven decades ago, American sociologist C. Wright Mills suggested interpreting the social group he called the "power elite" or "ruling class" as highly connected structures with common membership in the power institutions of the political, economic, and military spheres. In *The Power Elite* (1956), he described these densely connected structures, also called "higher circles," as a set of interlocking positions occupied by individuals whose power capacity increases with the number of overlapping positions. Mills's main theoretical claim within the structural approach to studying political groups was that a person's influence on state decision-making increases with an interlocking position during an era of general embeddedness of the political, economic, and military institutional domains.

Although subsequent scholars explored network power structures as horizontal in contrast to hierarchical organizational settings, Mills anticipated the concepts of network hierarchy and power through the interlocks within overlapping elite groups. People who jointly occupy strategic positions in large corporations, political institutions, and armed services constitute the real elite that regularly influences public policymaking. Consequently, large companies might aim to gain access to political authorities to lobby state parliaments or government executives. This basic conceptualization is now widely applied in analyses of the functionality of power elite influences on community power by using network centrality measures. Mills also emphasized that an increasing number of interlocks among economic, political, and military institutions might lead to a reciprocal influence between those actors. Over the next two decades, his concept of overlapping power circles and institutional interlocks was developed and applied in the empirical research discussed in the following subsection.

Interlocking Directorates of Economic Actors and Policymaking

A major theoretical insight of Mills was that overlapping structural positions form interlocks that are more powerful and influential than the broadly defined top positions of separate national institutions. While interlocking positions in Mills's theory were powerful in political, economic, and military spheres—their capacity to provide influence might be higher within one sphere and lower in the other, but they still overlap and can take advantage in all domains—the concepts of "corporate interlocks" and "interlocking directorates" refer only to the sphere of corporate management. According to William Domhoff (1970), interlocks form when the same top managers (nonowners) sit simultaneously on the boards of several companies, chosen not only because of their professional qualities but also because of their interpersonal connections with one another. Further, the business community believes that interorganizational connection is a principal condition for successful company performance. Domhoff argued that interlocked directors foster information flows among members of corporate networks; moreover, they are often invited to the meetings of state committees and are also embedded with lobbies and interest groups.

The ideas and theoretical claims of Mills and Domhoff were later applied by researchers studying interlocking directorates and their role in corporate performance. Their studies examined diverse issues, from mapping the interlocking structures of national-level or political affiliation of corporate interlocks to forecasting how network members may behave in the future. Michael Allen (1974) and Michael Useem (1984) identified the key interlocked directors connecting corporations, banks, and state institutions. Useem revealed the cohesion among political and economic institutions by defining connections that can be examined as interaction structures: corporate donations to political parties or candidates. Useem's findings regarding the "inner circle" (a broader equivalent of Mills's power elite) in the United Kingdom and the United States provided clues to how corporate contributions in political or policymaking domains (party, union, league, think tank, and others) serve as sources of interdependence of corporate and political behavior of power groups within elite networks.

Large companies in the age of "institutional capitalism," as Useem called it, attained unprecedented influence on parliamentary committees and government agencies. Observed more than three decades ago in the United States and the United Kingdom, similar structures emerged in transitional states—that is, the postsocialist countries in Europe and Asia—and therefore merited examination. Former top state managers could obtain parliamentary seats or top governmental positions after the elections, becoming direct advocates for their companies' market interests. For instance, as Vedres (2000) showed in his study of Hungarian corporate and bank affiliations with political actors during the market transition, embeddedness of economic entities in the political sector provided advantages and privileges to firms. Similar effects occurred when Ukrainian banks took advantage of affiliations with state governmental authorities (Baum et al., 2008). Therefore, the mutual interests of political and business actors are implemented through interlocking structures in the form of densely connected policymaking networks. Political actors receive support, including financial contributions, from corporate entities, while the latter obtain opportunities to affect legislation and regulatory policymaking. The main point within this context is that power groups can be studied using the network (structural) perspective, which refers to patterns of financial and communication relations among members of the ruling class.

To summarize, interlocking positions and persons are important for the cohesion of two main institutions: politics and economy. The approaches of Mills, Domhoff, Allen, and Useem differ in that Mills's power elite involves primarily personal attributes, while interlocking directorates treat position as a structural feature of importance for investigation. Moreover, personal characteristics might determine a person's chances of occupying an interlocking position. For example, Domhoff argued that women and ethnic minorities become interlocked more often when corporate boards seek to include such representatives despite perceived shortages of such candidates deemed qualified to serve as directors.

THEORIES OF POLICY NETWORKS

This section reviews policy network studies that, beginning in the 1980s, drew increasingly on formal theories and methodologies of SNA. (Schneider et al. [2007] compiled a structured bibliography of more than 1,100 publications on political networks.) Our recap proceeds in roughly chronological order, necessarily painted with a very broad brush. Recurrent themes are policy networks as metaphors or actual social structures, policy networks as informal relations versus formal governance mechanisms, and qualitative network observations versus rigorous quantitative methods (graphs and matrices).

The Rhodes Way

In a synthesis of interorganizational, resource-dependence, and corporatist theories to explain central-local intergovernmental interactions in UK policy communities, R. A. W. Rhodes (1981, 1985, 1988, 1990) developed a policy network theory, which he and other British political scientists subsequently applied to UK national and European Union (EU) policymaking (e.g., Wilks and Wright, 1987). (For overviews, see Rhodes and Marsh, 1992; Thatcher, 1998; Rhodes, 2008; Börzel, 1998, 2011.) The key theoretical concepts were policy networks, core executive, and the "hollowing out of the state," that is, the privatization of public services. The latter encompasses "the key issues of: the context of policy networks, explaining change and the role of ideas, the decline of that state, rescuing the core executive, and steering networks" (Rhodes, 2007, 1244). Initial characterizations of policy networks as structures for interest group intermediation eventually "mutated into the study of governance, and positivism gave way to an interpretive stance." Rhodes succinctly summarized his theory:

> As used in the analysis of British government, the term "policy network" refers to sets of formal and informal institutional linkages between governmental and other actors structured around shared interests in public policymaking and implementation. These institutions are interdependent. Policies emerge from the bargaining between the networks' members ... The other actors commonly include the professions, trade unions and big business. Central departments need their cooperation because British government rarely delivers services itself. It uses other bodies. Also, there are too many groups to consult so government must aggregate interests. It needs the "legitimated" spokespeople of that policy area. The groups need the money and legislative authority that only government can provide. (Rhodes, 2007, 1244)

A core proposition of the "Rhodes model" (Rhodes, 1990; Börzel, 2011) is that "[p]olicy is not made in the electoral arena or in the gladiatorial confrontation of Parliament, but in the netherworld of committees, civil servants, professions, and interest groups" (Marsh and Rhodes, 1992). The scope conditions of the theory—the limited situations to which its claims apply—require inclusion of all governmental and nongovernmental actors capable of bargaining over and influencing the formation of policy proposals, as well as making collective decisions within a specified policy arena. To illustrate such policy network arenas, a collection of empirical case studies in Marsh and Rhodes's *Policy Networks in British Government* (1992) included agriculture, civil nuclear power, youth employment, smoking, heart diseases, food and health, sea defenses, information technology, and exchange rate policy. David Marsh and Martin Smith (2000) applied a dialectical model of interactions among network structures, agents, contexts, and policy outcomes to explain continuity and change in the British agricultural policy network since the 1930s. The model was also applied to genetically modified foods (Toke and Marsh, 2003) and to the Countryside Alliance, an interest group promoting British rural issues, including farming and hunting with hounds (Marsh et al., 2009).

Rhodes (1986, 1990) classified policy networks along two dimensions: (a) the degree to which a network's members are integrated and (b) which groups belong and how resources are distributed among them. The resulting five types ranged from most to least integrative: (1) *policy communities*, networks with highly restrictive memberships, stable relations, vertical interdependence, and "insulation from other networks and invariably to the general public (including Parliament)" (Rhodes, 1990, 304); (2) *professional networks*, dominated by one profession, such as physicians in the National Health Service; (3) *intergovernmental networks*, "based on the representative organization of local authorities"; (4) *producer networks*, in which public and private sector economic interests dominate policymaking; and (4) *issue networks*, featuring a "large number of participants and their limited degree of interdependence" (1990, 305). Other policy network typologies that deployed multiple dimensions are Wilks and Wright (1987) and Van Waarden (1992).

A major criticism of policy networks theory was its fundamentally metaphorical treatment of networks, promoting primarily descriptive and historical ethnographic research investigations. British political scientists did not apply rigorous SNA concepts and methods, neither in theory construction nor in empirical studies of network structures, processes, and outcomes. Keith Dowding (1995) argued that British political scientists, as well as the US political scientists discussed below, all failed to produce fundamental theories of the policy process because they emphasized the attributes of policy actors. Only formally quantified SNA methods could provide explanations in terms of network properties. "In order to produce a *network* theory, where the properties of the network rather than the properties of its members drives explanation, political science must utilize the sociological network tradition, borrowing and modifying its algebraic methods" (Dowding, 1995, 137). The crucial implication is that network analysts should identify patterns of structural relations among actors occupying key positions in power structures, including their connections within and between governmental institutions. Tanja Börzel (1998, 254) criticized Anglo-Saxon conceptions of policy networks for concentrating on "state/society relations in a given issue area," to the neglect of "the predominantly German understanding of policy networks as an alternative form of governance to hierarchy and market." She subsequently (2011, 49) noted that Rhodes "also pioneered the concept of network governance in the study of British politics," discussed the reflexivity of networks, and advanced the "ethnographic turn" in network studies.

The Organizational State

Around the time that British political scientists were theorizing about policy networks, two American sociologists, Edward O. Laumann and David Knoke, developed

an organizational state model of national policy domains that explicitly incorporated numerous theories, concepts, and methodological tools from SNA (Knoke and
Laumann, 1982; Laumann, Knoke, and Kim, 1985; Laumann and Knoke, 1987; Knoke,
1998). A policy domain is any subsystem "identified by specifying a substantively
defined criterion of mutual relevance or common orientation among a set of consequential actors concerned with formulating, advocating, and selecting courses
of action (i.e., policy options) that are intended to resolve the delimited substantive
problems in question" (Knoke and Laumann, 1982, 256). As the model's name implies,
the relevant actors are all organizations; people appear only as agents acting on behalf
of their organizations, whose interests they represent in policy contests. In policy
domains—such as energy, health, and labor—both private and public sector organizations with interests in specific policy issues and policymaking events exchange political resources and form coalitions to collaborate on lobbying campaigns. These actors
seek to influence the outcomes of policy events in the decision-making institutions of
national governments. Key stipulations (Knoke, 1998, 152–153) of the organizational
state model include the following:

- The state is increasingly an organizational state, whose core actors are organiza-
  tions, not persons.
- The boundaries between public and private sectors are blurred and irrelevant.
- For many events, government organizations are not neutral umpires, but seek to
  promote their own goals.
- Policy preferences of organizations reflect mainly nonideological organizational
  imperatives.
- Major structural changes in both substantive and procedural matters (rules of the
  game) are generally off the agenda.
- Event cleavages reflect the idiosyncratic nature of organizations' interests.
- Most collective decisions involve shifting interorganizational coalitions and influence interactions.
- A crucial dynamic in collective decisions across a series of policy events is the
  exchange of control resources among actors expressing varied interests in specific
  policy outcomes.

In contrast to the British policy network emphasis on qualitative research methods, Laumann and Knoke (1987) developed the organizational state model through
applications of rigorous social network concepts, empirical measures, and analytic
methods to guide their data collection and analyses. Their empirical comparisons of
organizational participation in decision-making events in the US health and energy
policy domains featured multiplex networks of information exchange, resource transactions, and political support, analyzed with block-modeling, hierarchical clustering,
and multidimensional scaling methods. They also applied formal network exchange
models, as discussed below. Similar SNA theories and methods were deployed in a
comparative analysis of US and West German labor policy domains (Knoke and

Pappi, 1991; Pappi and Knoke, 1991) and a three-nation comparison with Japan (Knoke et al., 1996). The organizational state model is a theory of how actors collectively influence policy-event outcomes, but by examining only legislative decisions, it did not try to explain the subsequent implementation of those decisions. Empirical research projects applying an organizational state perspective demonstrated that rigorous applications of social network measures and analytic methods could yield insights into how coalitions form among organizations with similar policy interests, how opposing blocks mobilize political resources, and how policy domain network structures affect the outcomes of collective decisions. These contributions influenced subsequent research away from metaphorical views of policy networks toward greater analytic precision.

German Policy Networks

Neocorporatist theories of interest intermediation—policy bargaining and negotiation among business, labor, and government—were primary sources for policy network analyses of the Federal Republic of Germany during the 1970s and 1980s (Schmitter and Lehmbruch, 1979). Gerhard Lehmbruch (1984, 1989) described the national government's federated structure as a decentralized, interorganizational network in which the states (Länder) preserved important policy powers in relation to the national government. The result was a process of *corporatist concertation*, involving generalized exchanges of power and influence resources among autonomous interest groups such as political parties, state and federal bureaucracies, and private-sector organizations. Intergroup consultation, bargaining, and negotiation supplanted hierarchical domination in federal decision-making. An economic policy network sought national integration, while regional and state policy networks grew in power and influence. Lehmbruch's key proposition was that political institutions constrain and shape the specific structures and dynamics of policy networks. Another German source was the Max Planck Institute for the Study of Societies in Cologne, where scholars such as Fritz Scharpf and Renate Mayntz sought to integrate rational choice, game theory, formal institutions, and informal networks (see volumes edited by Marin and Mayntz [1991] and Scharpf [1993]). Scharpf (1993, 159) argued that "we need to understand the interaction effects between hierarchies and networks in order to explain the importance of institutional structures for the games that real actors could play." Scharpf's actor-centered institutional approach influenced recent developments in modeling policy networks as an ecology of games, discussed below.

Social network theory was an additional source, nurturing Edward Laumann and Franz Pappi's (1976) excavation of decision-making structures among the political elites of "Altneustadt," a small West German city. Applying a structural-functional framework, they discovered shifting coalitions whose members varied with the collective action outcomes at stake. Influence within this community's power structure was intimately tied to the key actors' network centralities. However, an explicit focus on individuals' social and political relations obscured the organizational and institutional bases of political power. Subsequent efforts by German scholars extended the social network analytic approach to national policymaking. Patrick Kenis and Volker Schneider provided a succinct definition:

> A policy network is described by its actors, their linkages and its boundary. It includes a relatively stable set of mainly public and private corporate actors. The linkages between the actors serve as channels for communication and for the exchange of information, expertise, trust and other policy resources. The boundary of a given policy network is not in the first place determined by formal institutions but results from a process of mutual recognition dependent on functional relevance and structural embeddedness. (Kenis and Schneider, 1991, 41–42)

The close affinity between the organizational state's national policy domains and Germanic policy network conceptualizations is not surprising, given the frequent research collaborations among American and German policy network scholars.

In contrast to American and British tendencies to view policy networks as primarily informal structures for mediating state-societal relations, German analysts also treated policy networks as a distinctive form of governance: "Policy network should be seen as integrated hybrid structures of political governance. Their integrative logic cannot be reduced to any single logic such as bureaucracy, market, community or corporatist association, but is characterized by the capacity for mixing different combinations of them" (Kenis and Schneider, 1991, 42). From a public administration perspective, policy networks enable coalition members to coordinate their interests, exchange and pool resources, and negotiate collective decision outcomes with public authorities. As mechanisms for resolving policy disputes, the decentralized corporatist bargaining networks allegedly confer governance advantages over both conventional centralized hierarchies and deregulated markets (Börzel, 1998). Although self-coordinating governance by policy networks avoids both the negative externalities of market failures and the zero-sum solutions of centralized hierarchies, it is "also prone to produce suboptimal outcomes: such bargaining systems tend to be blocked by dissent, preventing the consensus necessary for the realization of common gains" (Börzel, 1998, 261). An empirical example is Volker Schneider's (1986, 1992) research on dangerous chemicals and telecommunications policy networks in Germany and the European Union. He found diverse network governance structures—formal advisory boards, working committees, and informal secretive cabals—that co-opted private-sector organizations in policymaking processes. In the German reunification during the 1990s, policy network governance structures melding public- and private-sector organizations were crucial for the privatization of former East German shipbuilding and steel enterprises (Oschmann and Raab, 2002; Raab, 2002). Formal institutional constraints on the "Treuhandanstalt" agency shaped the informal, dense horizontal and sparser hierarchical communication ties that emerged during negotiations to privatize or shut down outdated industrial properties.

The increasing reliance on policy network governance, particularly in the EU, reflects emergent trends: growing dispersion of policy resources among private- and public-sector organizations; proliferating policy arenas requiring collective action; and governmental overload, which necessitates dependence on private organizations and hence accommodation to their demands during decision-making and policy implementation (Schneider, 1992). Jörg Raab and Patrick Kenis asserted that a complex transnational system of governance emerged, "based on negotiations between national governments, the European Commission, the European parliament, large companies and national or European associations" (2007, 187). Researchers published numerous studies describing these multiplex policy networks, but Raab and Kenis remained skeptical that they constituted a coherent network theory of policymaking. Still lacking were theoretical explanations of how "certain structural features of the policy arrangement"—the macro-level properties of a complete network, such as its density, centralization, and cohesion—influence the effectiveness and democratic quality of its collective policy decisions and outcomes.

Advocacy Coalition Framework

An American political scientist, Paul Sabatier (1987, 1988), developed the advocacy coalition framework (ACF) to investigate the role of scientific and technical information in policy cycles that span a decade or more. (For overviews of this research program, see Weible et al. [2011] and Jenkins-Smith et al. [2014].) An advocacy coalition is a set of potentially hundreds of people and organizations, drawn from diverse institutions—legislatures, government agencies, interest groups, scientific organizations, news media—whose members share a core set of policy beliefs. Coalitions are mechanisms for aggregating the cognitions and behaviors of similar actors. Coordinated action in a coalition of persons and organizations with similar ideologies or policy preferences is more beneficial for producing new public policies than is acting alone. Members of a coalition "show a non-trivial degree of coordinated activity over time," allying with like-minded participants in efforts to influence policies within a policy subsystem (Sabatier, 1988, 139). A subsystem is an issue-specific network, arising when elected officials assign policymaking responsibility to government bureaucrats, who then consult with groups interested in that issue. On the demand side, a coalition needs reliable political or strategic information and timely technical data. The coalition relies on actors believed to be especially well-informed—such as professionals, scientific research organizations, and think tanks—who can supply the technical knowledge that justifies the coalition's policy preferences (Sabatier, 1987, 650). Interest groups also share their technical information—about policy designs, causes and consequences, goal priorities—with opponents in efforts to persuade them to adopt the coalition's preference or to dissuade them from opposing it.

The ACF is grounded in theories about the social psychology of personal beliefs. It emphasizes public policy creation through the convergence of coalition members' ideas about the correct solutions to political controversies. People's beliefs vary in their degree of mutability, with "deep core" and "policy core" normative beliefs unlikely to change. In contrast, narrower "secondary aspect" beliefs about the specific features of a policy are more likely to change as participants learn about policy outcomes and their impacts. Beliefs are generators of policy change. Policy learning occurs as coalitions selectively interpret information and deploy data and persuasive arguments to influence policy outcomes. Technical information may be politicized by coalitions for use against their opponents. Policy change results from competition between coalitions and may be shaped by both stable systemic factors and dynamic external events. The theory assumes that policy participants try to translate their beliefs into policy decisions more swiftly than their opponents can, leading to a "devil shift" or distortion of their opponents' power. Rivals are impugned such that "anyone who disagrees with them must be mistaken about the facts, operating from the wrong value premises, or acting from evil motive" (Sabatier, Hunter, and McLaughlin, 1987, 452).

Sabatier and his colleagues initially applied the ACF in empirical case studies of US environmental policy, such as California water policies. Actors sought to form coalitions either with actors that control formal decision-making authority or that have informal access to such decision makers. A study of the California Marine Protected Area Policy found that "in technical, complex policy subsystems with influential organizational affiliations that control resources, actors have to get some advice/information and coordinate somewhat with influential affiliations—irrespective of beliefs" (Weible and Sabatier, 2005, 471). In a recent revision of the ACF (Sabatier and Weible, 2014), coalition opportunity structures mediate between stable system parameters and policy subsystems. It posits a typology of policy-relevant resources that coalitions can use in attempts to influence public policies (public opinion, information, skillful leadership). Two new paths leading to major policy changes are internal shocks and negotiated agreements. The authors recognized that the framework should be modified for application to collaborative institutions and to corporatist regimes, such as European countries with proportional electoral systems or fewer venues to effect policy changes (e.g., Henry et al., 2014). A key ACF development was empirically linking political similarity of constituents' partisanship and voting behavior to collaboration by local governments in regional planning networks (Henry, 2011; Henry, Lubell, and McCoy, 2011). Political homophily "reduces the political transaction costs of regional collaboration, and network models suggest that political similarity increases the probability of forming network ties" (Gerber et al., 2013, 608). But belief homophily and collaboration do not occur in all collective action situations, so explaining these contingent relationships requires further research comparing diverse contexts.

Exchange Models

Network exchange models treat policy outcomes, such as the passage of legislative bills, as the outcome of resource exchanges among policy actors with varied interests in specific event decisions (for an overview, see Knoke, 2011). The more powerful actors mobilize and deploy their political resources to affect the actions of the less powerful actors, making the latter dependent on the former and thus increasing the powerful actors' ability to achieve their preferred policy outcomes. James Coleman (1973) modeled vote trading as a market in which all legislators possess perfect information about everyone's policy preferences. At market equilibrium, each legislator's power is proportional to his or her control over valued resources for events, that is, the legislator's votes on a set of bills in which the other legislators have high interest. Legislators try to maximize their utilities by exchanging votes, giving up their control of low-interest policy events in return for control over events of greater interest to them.

European policy network analysts elaborated on Coleman's basic exchange model by distinguishing between interest groups and decision-making authorities and assuming that a bargaining process precedes the casting of policy votes. Franz Pappi's institutional access model proposed that interest groups (agents) try to influence decision makers (actors) in the organizational state (Pappi and Kappelhoff, 1984; König, 1993; Pappi, 1993; Pappi, König, and Knoke, 1995). Actor power is derived from gaining access to effective agents. Actors seek to gain control over policy events by deploying their own policy information or by mobilizing the agents' information. A study applying the institutional access model to US, German, and Japanese labor policy domain networks found that an information mobilization process fit the American case, a deployment process fit the German situation, and both models fit the Japanese data (Knoke et al., 1996, 184). In all three countries, the executive and legislative agents became powerful by controlling the policy information sought by interest actors.

Frans Stokman's dynamic access models also posited two-stage decision-making, in which actors try to build winning coalitions by influencing others to support their policy positions (Stokman and Van den Bos, 1992; Stokman and Van Oosten, 1994; Stokman and Zeggelink, 1996). In the first stage, the agent preferences could be influenced by the preferences of actors who have access to them through direct network ties. In the second stage, agents cast their votes based on the set of policy preferences reached during the first stage. In an analysis of ten Amsterdam municipal decisions, a policy maximization model provided the best fit to the observed outcomes (Stokman and Berveling, 1998). Actors unable to access powerful but distant opponents instead tried to influence others who share their policy preferences. This strategy increased their probability of a successful outcome, but avoided having to change their policy preferences when attempting to persuade others to support them.

European Union institutions conduct complex decision-making among member states that are amenable to dynamic access models. Thomson et al. (2006) applied three alternative models of informal bargaining and formal decision-making procedures to EU policy decisions. Interest groups try to influence policy proposals during the European Commission's preparatory stage, or during the subsequent European Council and European Parliament decision-making stage. A simple compromise model made fewer errors in predicting policy adoptions than the more complex challenge model and position exchange model (Arregui et al., 2006, 151). If actors' policy shared interests are higher than their divergent preferences during the informal bargaining stage, some may change their positions due to persuasive information. The policy outcome can then be predicted as a weighted average of the set of actors' most-preferred policies (calculated as the product of actor power times policy salience).

Governance Networks

Some theorists suggested distinguishing between policy networks and governance networks (Blanco, Lowndes, and Pratchett, 2011), while the others tended to consider the latter to be a component of the former (Bevir and Richards, 2009), or just a synonym. For example, Bevir and Richards claimed that "policy networks consist of governmental and societal actors whose interactions with one another give rise to policies" (2009, 3). In their view, policy network analysis focuses on the extent of "continuity in the interactions of interest groups and government departments." Therefore, the governance aspect lies within the policymaking component and is a specific condition for policymaking processes. Moreover, policy networks are a "meso-level concept related to the microlevel of analysis, dealing with the role of interests and government in particular policy decisions, to the macro-level of analysis, dealing with broader questions about the distribution of power" (Bevir and Richards, 2009, 5). The government model is treated as formal structured institutional boundaries, while policy networks move beyond that constraint to encompass sets of interdependent organizations that must exchange resources to realize their goals (Marsh and Rhodes, 1992, 10–11).

Some subsequent works claimed that policy networks lie at the core of governance (e.g., Rhodes, 1997), because governance is a process of service provision that is efficient only when interorganizational connections exist between private organizations and public agencies. Therefore, policy networks are a means of coordinating and allocating resources based on trust, cooperation, and diplomacy. In other words, networks are treated as a specific structural arrangement for efficient governance and for dealing with particular policy problems. Klijn, Edelenbos, and Steijn (2010, 22) used the term governance network to describe "public policy making and implementation through a web of relationships between government, business and civil society actors." Governance networks involve interdependencies, which may not necessarily be equitable, among public, private, and civil society actors.

Other authors (e.g., Blanco et al., 2011) suggested that the concepts "policy network" and "governance network" as research perspectives should be seen as coexisting, offering distinctive interpretations and research strategies that take into account particular empirical context. Blanco and colleagues contrasted the policy and governance network approaches on eight dimensions. For example, the policy network approach focuses on national and sometimes supranational policy domains (agricultural or industrial economic policy), while the governance network approach is focused on modes of governance and on multilevel networks (i.e., modes representing different sectors—public, private, and "third-sector" nongovernmental organizations). Another distinction between the policy and governance network perspectives lies in their conceptualizations of power and politics. Thus, the policy network approach treats networks as restrictive arrangements, limited to actors who possess crucial resources for a given policy area, while governance network theorists are open to a wider range of actors who potentially can contribute to the decision-making process. At present, the dispute over the distinction between governance and policy networks remains unresolved. Theorists would do well to remember Occam's injunction not to multiply entities unnecessarily.

As Blanco et al. (2011, 304) asserted, the policy network approach more closely resembles an elitist model of concentrated power, while the governance perspective is closer to the pluralist tradition of dispersed power. The balance between the two approaches allows for consideration of the impact of national and transnational elites on state-level and global policymaking, as described in the next section.

RECENT POLICY NETWORK DEVELOPMENTS

Theories of corporate interlock networks and policy domains network developed in the 1970s through 1990s, as previously discussed, focused mainly on analyzing power structures and policymaking processes at the national level. These studies provided the analytical foundation for research on global policy networks launched in the twenty-first century.

Global Policy Networks

Globalization, according to Leslie Sklair, "is changing the structure and dynamics of the capitalist class," and therefore analysts must "explore in addition to capitalist classes in separate countries . . . the emergence of a transnational capitalist class" (Sklair, 2001, 12). Transnational refers to "forces, processes, and institutions that cross borders but do not derive their power and authority from the state" (2). Following Domhoff's examination of power networks among corporate interlocks, political actors, and policy-planning specialists, Sklair argued that the global system can also be explored with network concepts such as global power structures consisting of interlocking persons and organizations. His study included analyses of transnational corporations listed as Global 500 by Fortune magazine and how these transnational corporations work effectively through their interaction with bureaucrats in international organizations and politicians in national, or country-level, and international governments. Additional effects of corporate and agenda-setting actors in the global policy network operate through interlocking directorates in the corporate sphere and cross-memberships in such organizations as think tanks, charity foundations, universities, sports, and other nonbusiness entities.

Robinson (2004) presented arguments for a global power class by stressing the distinction between the world economy and global economy—with the formation of globally mobile transnational capital. According to Robinson (2004, 15) "globalization is unifying the world into a single mode of production and a single global system," or global network, to paraphrase this statement. It encompasses international alliances and organizations such as the North American Free Trade Agreement, the Asia Pacific Economic Cooperation regional forum, and the EU, as well as such supranational organizations as the World Trade Organization, the International Monetary Fund, and the World Bank, which foster the integration of national entities into the transnational network and coordinate interactions among countries and corporations (Robinson, 2004, 50, 75). Robinson concluded that politics and policies implemented by the transnational capitalist class—a network of interlocking and interacting agents comprised of transnational corporations, elites and bureaucrats of supranational agencies, and media conglomerates—is conditioned by a logic of global structure of accumulation and production. The network character of the transnational capitalist class also consists of its connections to subcontracting and outsourcing by firms, government agencies, public universities, and other entities.

The empirical structure of the transnational capitalist class was revealed in recent research by William Carroll, who empirically applied network concepts and tools to analyze the transnational corporate community (Carroll, 2010; Carroll and Sapinski, 2010). By mapping global corporate interlocks as of 1976 and 1996, and then from 1996 to 2006, he demonstrated that the largest corporations became more densely integrated into a transnational network with numerous corporate interlocks during the last decade of the twentieth century. The important sites for creating the transnational capitalist class network are policy groups, including five main ones: World Economic Forum at Davos, World Business Council for Sustainable Development, Trilateral Commission, International Chamber of Commerce, and Bilderberg Conferences. In mapping global corporate interlocks, Carroll emphasized persons who sit in multiple corporate boards in two or more Global 500 Fortune corporations and who also occupy seats on policy group boards. The research indicated a core-periphery structure within the transnational corporate-policy network, with a brokerage role played by policy boards and groups.

A major criticism of global policy network studies is their assumption that the transnational corporate community and for-profit organizations are the main actors in the global arena. The national state and the ruling capitalist class are both reified at the global level, without considering the possibilities for emergent social structures. To transform global and transnational public policymaking, Diane Stone (2008) proposed the concept of global agora as a space shaped by the interactions of its actors within the social and political space. It is a domain of relative disorder and uncertainty, where institutions are underdeveloped and political authority lines are unclear and dispersed among proliferating institutions and networks. Like previous theorists, Stone included international institutions (located in Washington, the Hague, Geneva, and Paris) and global financial entities (headquartered in New York, London, Tokyo, and Davos), as well as transnational executive networks, knowledge networks, and other actors into her analysis of a global agora that provides many diffuse opportunities for multimode network analysis.

Other Advances

Other important developments include theories about the ecology of games and self-organizing networks and applications of advanced statistical methodologies to policy networks. Mark Lubell and colleagues revived and updated Norton Long's (1958) ecology of games framework and integrated it with Fritz Scharpf's (1997) actor-centered institutionalization. A policy game "consists of a set of policy actors participating in a rule-governed collective decision making process called a 'policy institution.'" The set of policy institutions that "exist at a particular time and place combine to define the institutional arrangements of governance" (Lubell, 2013, 538). The ecology of games model sought to generate testable hypotheses about complex adaptive governance systems, to analyze the causes of individual behavior and institutional change, and to understand how different institutional arrangements generate policy outputs and outcomes. Explicitly incorporating policy network components (Lubell et al., 2012), the theorists also synthesized concepts from venue shopping, advocacy coalitions, cultural and institutional evolution, agent-based computational models, and other perspectives on policymaking. Bipartite networks connecting actors and institutions provide a method "to usefully represent the EG framework and test some initial hypotheses about the structure of the system" (Lubell, 2013, 553). Empirical applications of the ecology of games included water policymaking in the San Francisco Bay area (Lubell, Henry, and McCoy, 2010; Lubell, Robins, and Wang, 2014) and climate adaptation in Queensland, Australia (McAllister, McCrea, and Lubell, 2014). For example, the SF Bay project identified a bipartite network of 387 persons and policy institutions and displayed a graph of the most central actors and institutions, those having direct ties to sixteen or more other entities (Lubell et al., 2014).

Related to the ecology of games framework, self-organizing networks occur when actor coordination arises from local interactions in the absence of direction or control by a central authority. As a result, the network is decentralized or distributed across all system components and is typically robust against disruption and able to repair and reproduce itself. Informal communication networks among friends typically exhibit self-organizing characteristics, as does the World Wide Web (e.g., Barabási et al., 2002). Self-organizing networks often emerge around common-pool resources (e.g., public grazing lands, fisheries, aquifers), whose users experience diminished benefits when all individuals try to maximize their own self-interests, resulting in resource depletion. Collective action is typically necessary to prevent overuse of the common-pool resource and achieve sustainable production and consumption. Self-organized actors tend to connect with popular actors, creating network structures for efficiently transmitting information and building trust and cohesion. Self-organizing network research included studies of US estuaries (Schneider et al., 2003; Berardo and Scholz, 2010; Berardo, 2013), an Argentine river basin (Berardo, 2014), and a rural water supply and sanitation program in Nepal (Shrestha, 2013).

A third important development is the introduction of advanced statistical methods to policy network research. It reflects the field's evolution away from its earlier meta-phorical and qualitative case methods toward an increasing application of rigorous sta-tistical theory in SNA. Driving this trend were network methodological contributions by mathematicians, physicists, and biologists (Freeman, 2008) and the proliferation of relational "big data" generated by businesses and governments, whose practitio-ners sought solutions for their urgent competitive and governance problems. Notable among these advance methods are quadratic assignment procedures, exponential ran-dom graph models, stochastic actor-oriented models (e.g., Lubell et al., 2012; Robins, Lewis, and Wang, 2012), and eigenspectrum approaches. We lack space to elaborate their technical details, but a few substantive examples illustrate their potential to trans-form policy network research. A stochastic actor-oriented model estimated social capital effects in partner selection for longitudinal data on ten estuaries (Berardo and Scholz, 2010). Lubell et al. (2014) estimated exponential random graph parameters for four nested models of the San Francisco Bay area ecology of water management games. Heaney (2014, 66) demonstrated that "multiple roles of confidant, collaborator, and issue advocate affect how group representatives understand the influence of those with whom they are tied" in the US health policy domain. Melamed, Breiger and West (2013) used spectral partitioning to identify communities within a tripartite network of persons, issues, and games around the construction of a sports stadium in Cincinnati, Ohio. Each study exemplified how the inseparable intertwining of network theories, methods, and substantive data can yield new knowledge and understanding in policy network research.

Looking Forward

The historian of SNA, Linton Freeman, argued that four criteria are essential for an organized research paradigm to emerge:

1. Social network analysis is motivated by a structural intuition based on ties linking social actors,
2. It is grounded in systematic empirical data,
3. It draws heavily on graphic imagery, and
4. It relies on the use of mathematical and/or computational models. (Freeman, 2004, 3)

By those standards, policy network analysis has greatly matured as a multidisciplinary specialty. Within the past decade, it has also become more institutionalized. The signal event was a 2008 conference, "Networks in Political Science," at Harvard University with a grant from a National Science Foundation, which drew two hundred scholars to discuss a wide variety of network topics. Eight of the conference papers were published the following year (Heaney and McClurg, 2009). Also in 2009, a political networks section was formed within the American Political Science Association, which sponsors annual POLNET conferences and this handbook. Other evidence for the subfield's maturation includes proliferating college courses and seminars taught regularly in political science, public administration, sociology, and related disciplines. Policy network analysis is a central element in this renaissance.

At present, contemporary policy network analysis embraces a multitude of theories, frameworks, perspectives, concepts, propositions, and methods. But it lacks cohesion around a core set of innovative ideas that could facilitate greater integration among these components. Divergences in approaches between European and North American scholars, not to speak of developing nations, constrain further progress. In its fragmentation, the field is not so different from many other academic specialties. Nevertheless, opportunities await for creative analysts to propose paradigms that could take policy network studies in surprising new directions.

REFERENCES

Allen, M. P. (1974). "The Structure of Interorganizational Elite Cooptation: Interlocking Corporate Directorates." *American Sociological Review* 39: 393–406.

Arregui, J., Stokman, F. N., and Thomson, R. (2006). "Compromise, Exchange and Challenge in the EU." In *The European Union Decides*, edited by R. Thomson, F. N. Stokman, C. H. Achen, and T. König, pp. 124–152. Cambridge, UK: Cambridge University Press.

Barabási, A.-L., Dezső, Z., Ravasz, E., Yook, S.-H., and Oltvai, Z. (2002). "Scale-Free and Hierarchical Structures in Complex Networks." *AIP Conference Proceedings* 661: 1-16.

Baum, C. F., Caglayan, M., Schäfer, D., and Talavera, O. (2008). "Political Patronage in Ukrainian Banking." *Economics of Transition* 16: 537–557.

Berardo, R. (2013). "The Coevolution of Procedural Fairness and Link Formation in Self-Organizing Policy Networks." *Journal of Politics* 75: 686–700.

Berardo, R. (2014). "The Evolution of Self-Organizing Communication Networks in High-Risk Social-Ecological Systems." *International Journal of the Commons* 8: 236–258.

Berardo, R., and Scholz, J. T. (2010). "Self-Organizing Policy Networks: Risk, Partner Selection, and Cooperation in Estuaries." *American Journal of Political Science* 54: 632–649.

Bevir, M., and Richards, D. (2009). "Decentring Policy Networks: A Theoretical Agenda." *Public Administration* 87: 3–14.

Blanco, I., Lowndes, V., and Pratchett, L. (2011). "Policy Networks and Governance Networks: Towards Greater Conceptual Clarity." *Political Studies Review* 9: 297–308.

Börzel, T. A. (1998). "Organizing Babylon: On the Different Conceptions of Policy Networks." *Public Administration* 76: 253–273.

Börzel, T. A. (2011). "Networks: Reified Metaphor or Governance Panacea?" *Public Administration* 89: 49–63.

Carroll, W. K. (2010). *The Making of a Transnational Capitalist Class: Corporate Power in the Twenty-First Century*. New York: Zed Books.

Carroll, W. K., and Sapinski, J. P. (2010). "The Global Corporate Elite and the Transnational Policy-Planning Network, 1996-2006: A Structural Analysis." *International Sociology* 25: 501–538.

Coleman, J. S. (1973). *The Mathematics of Collective Action*. Chicago: Aldine.

Domhoff, W. G. (1970). *The Higher Circles: The Governing Class in America*. New York: Random House.

Dowding, K. (1995). "Model or Metaphor? A Critical Review of the Network Approach." *Political Studies* 43: 136–158.

Freeman, L. C. (2004). *The Development of Social Network Analysis: A Study in the Sociology of Science*. Vancouver, BC: Empirical Press.

Freeman, L. C. (2008). "Going the Wrong Way on a One-Way Street: Centrality in Physics and Biology." *Journal of Social Structure* 9(2). http://moreno.ss.uci.edu/89.pdf.

Gerber, E. R., Henry, A. D., and Lubell, M. (2013). "Political Homophily and Collaboration in Regional Planning Networks." *American Journal of Political Science* 57: 598–610.

Heaney, M. T. (2014). "Multiplex Networks and Interest Group Influence Reputation: An Exponential Random Graph Model." *Social Networks* 36: 66–81.

Heaney, M. T., and McClurg, S. D. (2009). "Social Networks and American Politics: Introduction to the Special Issue." *American Politics Research* 37: 727–741.

Henry, A. D. (2011). "Ideology, Power, and the Structure of Policy Networks." *Policy Studies Journal* 39: 361–383.

Henry, A. D., Ingold, K., Nohrstedt, D., and Weible, C. M. (2014). "Policy Change in Comparative Contexts: Applying the Advocacy Coalition Framework Outside of Western Europe and North America." *Journal of Comparative Policy Analysis: Research and Practice* 16: 299–312.

Henry, A. D., Lubell, M., and McCoy, M. (2011). "Belief Systems and Social Capital as Drivers of Policy Network Structure: The Case of California Regional Planning." *Journal of Public Administration Research* 21: 419–444.

Jenkins-Smith, H. C., Nohrstedt, D., Weible, C. M., and Sabatier, P. A. (2014). "The Advocacy Coalition Framework: Foundations Evolution, and Ongoing Research." In *Theories of the Policy Process*, 3rd ed., edited by P. A. Sabatier, and C. M. Weible, pp. 183–224. Boulder, CO: Westview Press.

Kenis, P., and Schneider, V. (1991). "Policy Networks and Policy Analysis: Scrutinizing a New Analytical Toolbox." In *Policy Networks: Empirical Evidence and Theoretical Considerations*, edited by B. Marin, and R. Mayntz, pp. 25–62. Boulder, CO/Frankfurt: Campus/Westview.

Kickert, W. J. M., Klijn, E.-H., and Koppenjan, J. F. M. (Eds.). (1997). *Managing Complex Networks: Strategies for the Public Sector*. London: Sage.

Klijn, E. H., Edelenbos, J., and Steijn, B. (2010). "Trust in Governance Networks: Its Impact and Outcomes." *Administration and Society* 42: 193–221.

Knoke, D. (1990). *Political Networks: The Structural Perspective*. New York: Cambridge University Press.

Knoke, D. (1998). "The Organizational State: Origins and Prospects." *Research in Political Sociology* 8: 147–163.

Knoke, D. (2011). "Policy Networks." In *The SAGE Handbook of Social Network Analysis*, edited by J. Scott and P. J. Carrington, pp. 210–222. London: Sage.

Knoke, D., and Laumann, E. O. (1982). "The Social Structure of National Policy Domains: An Exploration of Some Structural Hypotheses." In *Social Structure and Network Analysis*, edited by P. V. Marsden and N. Lin, pp. 255–270. Beverly Hills, CA: Sage.

Knoke, D., and Pappi, F. U. (1991). "Organizational Action Sets in the U.S. and German Labor Policy Domains." *American Sociological Review* 56: 509–523.

Knoke, D., Pappi, F. U., Broadbent, J., and Tsujinaka, Y. (1996). *Comparing Policy Networks: Labor Politics in the U.S., Germany and Japan*. New York: Cambridge University Press.

König, T. (1993). "The Impact of Policy Networks in a Model of Political Decision Making and Public-Private Influence." *Journal für Sozialforschung* 33: 343–367.

Laumann, E. O., and Knoke, D. (1987). *The Organizational State: Social Choice in National Policy Domains*. Madison: University of Wisconsin Press.

Laumann, E. O., Knoke, D., and Kim, Y.-H. (1985). "An Organizational Approach to State Policy Formation: A Comparative Study of Energy and Health Domains." *American Sociological Review* 50: 1–19.

Laumann, E. O., and Pappi, F. U. (1976). *Networks of Collective Action: A Perspective on Community Influence Systems*. New York: Academic Press.

Lehmbruch, G. (1984). "Concertation and the Structure of Corporatist Networks: Order and Conflict in Contemporary Capitalism." In *Order and Conflict in Contemporary Capitalism*, edited by J. Goldthorpe, pp. 60–80. Oxford, UK: Clarendon Press.

Lehmbruch, G. (1989). "Institutional Linkages and Policy Networks in the Federal System of West Germany: A Fortieth Year Appraisal." *Publius* 19: 221–235.

Long, N. E. (1958). "The Local Community as an Ecology of Games." *American Journal of Sociology* 64: 251–261.

Lubell, M. (2013). "Governing Institutional Complexity: The Ecology of Games Framework." *Policy Studies Journal* 41: 537–559.

Lubell, M., Henry, A. D., and McCoy, M. (2010). "Collaborative Institutions in an Ecology of Games." *American Journal of Political Science* 54: 287–300.

Lubell, M., Robins, G., and Wang, P. (2014). "Network Structure and Institutional Complexity in an Ecology of Water Management Games." *Ecology and Society* 19: 23–36.

Lubell, M., Scholz, J., Berardo, R., and Robbins, G. (2012). "Testing Policy Theory with Statistical Models of Networks." *Policy Studies Journal* 40: 351–374.

Marin, B., and Mayntz, R. (Eds.). (1991). *Policy Networks: Empirical Evidence and Theoretical Considerations*. Boulder, CO: Westview Press.

Marsh, D., and Rhodes, R. A. W. (Eds.). (1992). *Policy Networks in British Government*. Oxford, UK: Clarendon Press.

Marsh, D., and Smith, M. (2000). "Understanding Policy Networks: Towards a Dialectical Approach." *Political Studies* 48: 4–21.

Marsh, D., Toke, D., Belfrage, C., Tepe, D. and McGough, S. (2009). "Policy Networks and the Distinction Between Insider and Outsider Groups: The Case of the Countryside Alliance." *Public Administration* 87: 621–638.

McAllister, R., McCrea, R., and Lubell, M. (2014). "Policy Networks, Stakeholder Interactions and Climate Adaptation in the Region of South East Queensland, Australia." *Regional Environmental Change* 14: 527–539.

Melamed, D., Breiger, R. L., and West, A. J. (2013). "Community Structure in Multi-Mode Networks: Applying an Eigenspectrum Approach." *Connections* 33: 18–23.

Mills, C. W. (1956). *The Power Elite*. New York: Oxford University Press.

Oschmann, A., and Raab, J. (2002). "Das institutionelle Erbe des 'Treuhand-Regimes' in Ostdeutschland: Zentralisierung oder Auflösung in der bundesstaatlichen Normalverfassung?" *Politische Vierteljahresschrift* 43: 445–477.

Pappi, F. U. (1993). "Policy-Netze: Erschienungsform moderner Politiksteuerung oder methodischer Ansantz?" *Sonderheft 24 der Politischen Vierteljahresschrift* 1993: 84–94.

Pappi, F. U., and Kappelhoff, P. (1984). "Abhängigkeit, Tausch und kollektive Entscheidung in einer Gemeindeelite." *Zeitschrift für Soziologie* 13: 87–117.

Pappi, F. U., and Knoke, D. (1991). "Political Exchange in the German and American Labor Policy Domain." In *Policy Networks: Structural Analysis of Public Policy*, edited by R. Mayntz and B. Marin, pp. 179–208. Frankfurt am Main: Campus Verlag.

Pappi, F. U., König, T., and Knoke, D. (1995). *Entscheidungsprozesse in der Arbeits- und Sozialpolitik. Der Zugang der Interessengruppen zum Regierungssystem über Politikfeldnetze: Ein deutsch-amerikanischer Vergleich.* Frankfurt/New York: Campus Verlag.

Raab, J. (2002). "Where Do Policy Networks Come From?" *Journal of Public Administration Research and Theory* 12: 581–622.

Raab, J., and Kenis, P. (2007). "Taking Stock of Policy Networks: Do They Matter?" In *Handbook of Public Policy Analysis: Theory, Methods and Politics*, edited by F. Fischer, G. J. Miller, and M. S. Sidney, pp. 187–200. London: Taylor & Francis CRC Press.

Rhodes, R. A. W. (1981). *Control and Power in Central-Local Government Relations.* Aldershot, UK: Ashgate.

Rhodes, R. A. W. (1985). "Power Dependence, Policy Communities and Inter-Governmental Networks." *Public Administration Bulletin* 49: 4–29.

Rhodes, R. A. W. (1986). *The National World of Local Government.* London: Allen & Unwin.

Rhodes, R. A. W. (1988). *Beyond Westminster and Whitehall: The Sub-central Governments of Britain.* London: Unwin-Hyman.

Rhodes, R. A. W. (1990). "Policy Networks: A British Perspective." *Journal of Theoretical Politics* 2: 293–317.

Rhodes, R. A. W. (1997). *Understanding Governance: Policy Networks, Governance, Reflexivity and Accountability.* Buckingham, UK: Open University Press.

Rhodes, R. A. W. (2007). "Understanding Governance: Ten Years On." *Organization Studies* 28: 1243–1264.

Rhodes, R. A. W. (2008). "Policy Network Analysis." In *The Oxford Handbook of Public Policy*, edited by R. E. Goodin, M. Moran, and M. Rein, 423–445. Oxford, UK: University of Oxford Press.

Rhodes, R. A. W., and Marsh, D. (1992). "New Directions in the Study of Policy Networks." *European Journal of Political Research* 21: 181–205.

Robins, G., Lewis, J. M., and Wang, P. (2012). "Statistical Network Analysis for Analyzing Policy Networks." *Policy Studies Journal* 40: 375–401.

Robinson, W. I. (2004). *A Theory of Global Capitalism: Production, Class, and State in a Transnational World.* Baltimore, MD: Johns Hopkins University Press.

Sabatier, P. A. (1987). "Knowledge, Policy Oriented Learning, and Policy Change: An Advocacy Coalition Framework." *Knowledge* 8: 649–692.

Sabatier, P. A. (1988). "An Advocacy Coalition Framework of Policy Change and the Role of Policy-Oriented Learning Therein." *Policy Sciences* 21: 129–168.

Sabatier, P. A., Hunter, S., and McLaughlin, S. (1987). "The Devil Shift: Perceptions and Misperceptions of Opponents." *Western Political Quarterly* 40: 449–476.

Sabatier, P. A., and Weible, C. M. (2014). *Theories of the Policy Process*, 3rd ed. Boulder, CO: Westview Press.

Scharpf, F. W. (Ed.). (1993). *Games in Hierarchies and Networks: Analytical and Empirical Approaches to the Study of Governance Institutions.* Boulder, CO: Westview Press.

Scharpf, F. W. (1997). *Games Real Actors Play: Actor-Centered Institutionalism in Policy Research.* Boulder, CO: Westview Press.

Schmitter, P. C., and Lehmbruch, G. (Eds.). (1979). *Trends Toward Corporatist Intermediation.* Beverly Hills, CA: Sage.

Schneider, M., Scholz, J. T., Lubell, M., Mindruta, D., and Edwardsen, M. (2003). "Building Consensual Institutions: Networks and the National Estuary Program." *American Journal of Political Science* 47: 143–158.

Schneider, V. (1986). "Exchange Networks in the Development of Policy: Regulation of Chemicals in the OECD, EEC, and the Federal Republic of Germany." *Journal für Sozialforschung* 26: 383–416.

Schneider, V. (1992). "The Structure of Policy Networks: A Comparison of the 'Chemicals Control' and 'Telecommunications' Policy Domains in Germany." *European Journal of Political Research* 21: 109–129.

Schneider, V., Land, A., Leifeld, P., and Gundelach, B. (2007). "Political Networks: A Structured Bibliography." http://kops.uni-konstanz.de/handle/123456789/4292

Shrestha, M. K. (2013). "Self-Organizing Network Capital and the Success of Collaborative Public Programs." *Journal of Public Administration Research and Theory* 23: 307–329.

Sklair, L. (2001). *The Transnational Capitalist Class.* Oxford, UK: Blackwell.

Stokman, F. N., and Berveling, J. (1998). "Dynamic Modeling of Policy Networks in Amsterdam." *Journal of Theoretical Politics* 10: 577–601.

Stokman, F. N., and Van den Bos, J. M. M. (1992). "A Two-Stage Model of Policymaking with an Empirical Test in the U.S. Energy-Policy Domain." *Research in Politics and Society* 4: 219–253.

Stokman, F. N., and Oosten, R. V. (1994). "The Exchange of Voting Positions: An Objective-Oriented Model of Policy Networks." In *European Community Decision Making: Models, Applications and Comparisons,* edited by B. Bueno de Mesquita and F. Stokman, pp. 105–127. New Haven, CT: Yale University Press.

Stokman, F. N., and Zeggelink, E. P. H. (1996). "Is Politics Power or Policy Oriented? A Comparative Analysis of Dynamic Access Models in Policy." *Journal of Mathematical Sociology* 21: 77–111.

Stone, D. (2008). "Global Public Policy, Transnational Policy Communities and Their Networks." *Policy Studies Journal* 36: 19–38.

Thatcher, M. (1998). "The Development of Policy Network Analysis: From Modest Origins to Overarching Frameworks." *Journal of Theoretical Politics* 10: 389–446.

Thomson, R., Stokman, F. N., Achen, C. H., and König, T. (Eds.). (2006). *The European Union Decides.* Cambridge, UK: Cambridge University Press.

Toke, D., and Marsh, D. (2003). "Policy Networks and the GM Crops Issue: Assessing the Utility of a Dialectical Model of Policy Networks." *Public Administration* 81: 229–251.

Useem, M. (1984). *The Inner Circle: Large and the Rise of Business Political Activity in the U.S. and U.K.* New York: Oxford University Press.

Van Waarden, F. (1992). "Dimensions and Types of Policy Networks." *European Journal of Political Research* 21: 29–52.

Vedres, B. (2000). "The Constellations of Economic Power: The Position of Political Actors, Banks and Large Corporations in the Network of Directorate Interlocks in Hungary, 1997." *Connections* 23: 44–59.

Weber, M. (1947). *The Theory of Social and Economic Organization.* New York: Free Press.

Weible, C. M., and Sabatier, P. A. (2005). "Comparing Policy Networks: Marine Protected Areas in California." *Policy Studies Journal* 33: 181–202.

Weible, C. M., and Sabatier, P. A., Jenkins-Smith, H. C., Nohrstedt, D., Henry, A. D., and deLeon, P. (2011). "A Quarter Century of the Advocacy Coalition Framework: An Introduction to the Special Issue." *Policy Studies Journal* 39: 349–360.

Wilks, S., and Wright, M. (Eds.). (1987). *Government-Industry Relations: West Europe, U.S. and Japan*. Oxford: Clarendon Press.

CHAPTER 4

POLITICAL NETWORKS AND COMPUTATIONAL SOCIAL SCIENCE

DAVID LAZER AND STEFAN WOJCIK

INTRODUCTION

SOCIAL scientists are witnessing a steep growth of data coming from social media, the Internet, and technological innovations in various forms. The advent of the Internet is responsible for the explosive growth of these data in recent decades, allowing social scientists access to troves of data going forward and backward in time. Because many big data are explicitly or implicitly relational, this digitization of humanity has been vital in the increase in the study of networks. While these data offer considerable opportunities for study, social science is likely to experience some growing pains in adopting computational approaches to data—either in the form of strained talent or computing power. In this chapter, we discuss how this change will cause social scientists to increasingly emphasize relational aspects of human behavior, phenomena at the scale of society rather than just at the level of the individual, and the dynamics of human behavior. We discuss the potential transformation of political science in these directions.

SOURCES OF BIG DATA IN THE STUDY OF POLITICAL NETWORKS

"Big data" is a construction that was coined in a McKinsey report analyzing the rapid growth in importance of large-scale data to business (Manyika et al., 2011). It hit a particular moment in the global zeitgeist, when the issue of large-scale data was having an impact on many sectors, including academia. Within the academy, the term evokes many different phenomena; for example, to a computer scientist it represents the computational challenges of managing large-scale data sets (typically data don't become "big" until they require multiple computers); to biologists it indicates massive scale genomics data; to astronomers it means detailed images of the heavens. The intersection of big data and the social sciences has been called "computational social science" (Lazer et al., 2009). With a few exceptions, big data have yet to make a major impact on the practice of social science—the large majority of big human data research has been done by computer and information scientists and in related fields—which probably reflects the relative paucity of computational talent in the social sciences (see "The Big Challenges of Big Data," below).

The opportunities to use big data to study human behavior are legion. Precise measurement of social behaviors that as few as ten years ago were infrequently recorded and with much effort (and incidentally contained substantial measurement error) is today available by tapping out a few lines of code. The digitization of daily life via platforms such as Twitter and Facebook promises for the social sciences more systematic and high-velocity individual and relational measurements. The daily commute to work, for instance, is automatically collected by Google via your smartphone. Data about social networks, which were particularly costly and inefficient for social scientists to collect, requiring long periods of time in the field and a research team, are today digitally encoded and stored by multiple media as a matter of course (e.g., Twitter, Facebook, web browser, smartphone, the Internet of things). This process creates a large and potentially accurate portrait of one's daily life from multiple angles. The output is exabytes of individual-, relational-, and societal-level data flowing through the web each day.

Political Networks

Political science is at its core the study of networks (Lazer, 2011). Perhaps the foundational concept of political science is power, which should generally be conceived of as a relational construct—for example, who has power over whom. However, historically, with a small but steady stream of exceptions, political science has neglected the study of networks. This has changed dramatically over the last decade. As the chapters in this volume evidence, political science has begun to embrace relational concepts and methods, while graduate training has increasingly emphasized modeling interdependencies rather than treating them as nuisance parameters. Currently, one can find diverse topics covered under political networks, from arms trading networks to rural gossip networks to legislative collaboration networks (see the chapters in this book). Political networks, then, offer useful ways of representing political relationships between individuals, organizations, countries, or other politically relevant entities. These networks are increasingly traceable via digital footprints, which can be harvested to understand societal-level phenomena and relational aspects of human behavior. These trends, combined with better technology and data, have contributed to an upsurge in research on political networks. The availability of big data is likely to accelerate this trend.

What Are the Sources of Big Data about the Relational Dimensions of Politics?

Digitization of human behavior is so ubiquitous that it is difficult to identify moments that might not be somehow digitally memorialized. Even the act of sitting on one's front porch could, in principle, be captured by Google for Google Maps, and movement within your house captured by the Bluetooth capability in your phone (e.g., Eagle et al., 2009). This section examines some of the sources of big data about human behavior (an exhaustive survey is impossible).

The largest driver of the digitization of people's lives is the Internet. Every action a user takes on the web can be, and often is, captured. Just the act of visiting a website is a potentially interesting relational event, establishing a time-stamped link between an individual and a website. Social media activity, including tweets, posts, and various content-sharing platforms, produces terabytes of network information spilling out into the digital world. Personal digital traces that live in the web browser or on Google reveal numerous pieces of data about a person's relationship status, health afflictions, financial obligations, employment, family, religion, and politics (Manber et al., 2000; Hu et al., 2007; Wood, 2014).

Many personal traces of our online and offline social lives are easily recovered simply by downloading a browsing history. Browser cookies are digital fingerprints that are visible to the organizations whose websites we visit every day, such as Google, which tracks searches, clicks, and other web actions for its ad-based revenue. They are inserted into a browser by the websites when they are visited and then act as a digital trace of a person's browsing history. These traces also act like personal fingerprints that can quite easily identify a specific individual while also revealing a person's specific tastes, penchants, curiosities, and interests (Olejnik et al., 2012).

Other observable data visible to the World Wide Web have contributed to a growing trend: "personalizing" web services to users based on the observable data users display through their computers when they visit websites. A large amount of information can be gleaned from a person's computer when he or she logs on to a site. This includes geographic location, third-party tracking data, and the type of computer used. Users are offered various options and even prices for products based on the observable information presented to the site when they log on. These trends outline new opportunities to understand how real-world inequalities manifest on the web (Hannak et al., 2013, 2014). The lesson that the personalization trend teaches us is that automated personalization algorithms may reflect, and possibly even enhance, socially embedded socioeconomic inequalities.

Twitter has rapidly become the most studied corner of the Internet. About half of the research articles presented in 2013 at the International Conference on Web and Social Media (ICWSM), the foremost conference for social media studies, used Twitter data for their analyses (Tufekci, 2014). Studies involving Twitter include everything from methods to infer user locations (Jurgens et al., 2015), to understanding political polarization (Lynch, Freelon, and Aday, 2014), to forecasting the stock market (Bollen et al., 2011). Twitter is a global communication platform whose seeming simplicity and relative transparency make it a tempting focus of study (although see "The Big Challenges of Big Data," below for issues). At its core Twitter allows users to (1) post (or repost) statements up to 140 characters long and (2) follow other users. Tweets typically contain words and sometimes images, as well as occasional "metadata," such as the location where the tweet was posted, the unshortened version of referenced URLs. Tweets also often contain hashtags, such as #politicalnetworks, which allow users to tap into broader, system-wide conversations. Application programming interfaces allow limited scraping of tweets and paid access to 1 percent, 10 percent, and complete samples of tweets.

Twitter offers a variety of rich network data, including who follows whom, who retweets whom, and who uses which hashtags. The information about content, timing, and location adds highly synergistic dimensions to the network information. An example using this synergistic information comes from Gonzalez-Bailon et al. (2011), who harvested Twitter data starting ten days before a large protest and ending a few days after. The authors examine relationships among the size of a user's local network, the amount of exposure of a user to messages regarding the protest, and the timing of each user's activation. Among their insights, the authors reveal that for users who require the same amount of social pressure to become active, the size and composition of local networks shorten or lengthen the time it takes for them to activate. Those with a large number of connections take longer to become active, because social pressure takes longer to build up within large egocentric networks.

However, not even highly detailed data are needed to glean useful insights on Twitter; even basic information on who follows whom can be leveraged to produce highly relevant political information. Barberá (2015) uses information on who follows whom among a subnetwork of politicians, organizations, and citizens on Twitter. The author conceives of the choice of whom to follow on Twitter to be a costly behavior that indicates the willingness of the user to devote some proportion of his or her attention to some legislator, person, organization, or party. The author uses Bayesian ideal point estimation to infer ideal point scores using Twitter follower data. Using samples from various countries, the author shows that the estimates that he derives correlate with ordinary ideal point estimates at $r^2 = .94$.

Facebook

Originally conceived as a social networking site among Harvard University undergraduates, Facebook now hosts over one and a half billion users (Statista, n.d.) and has the potential to study numerous social and political phenomena. Facebook consists not only of "friends," one-mode networks, but also multimodal networks of who engages with what content on the site and who subsequently shares that content. Facebook has much richer stores of data on its users than Twitter does. These data come in the form of real-life user identities; demographics; biographies; and content that is permanently stored, including photos, videos, and posts, which are allowed to be over 63,000 characters long. Unfortunately Facebook data are difficult to access for researchers who do not collaborate directly with the Facebook data team (Tufekci, 2014). Whereas less than 10 percent of Twitter users mark their profiles and posts as private, it is estimated that 50 percent of Facebook user profiles are private (Tufekci, 2014).

Exemplary studies of Facebook include the Bakshy et al. (2015) study of content sharing on Facebook and the Bond et al. (2012) study of political mobilization involving experimental treatments of voting among friends. The former is an observational study of how Facebook users share and consume content and how users behave when content is misaligned with their ideologies, while the latter is an experiment to identify the effect of users' expressed voting behaviors on their peers' real-world verified voting behavior. A further interesting study from Coviello et al. (2014) uses weather patterns to examine the spread of emotions through friend networks on Facebook. These studies exemplify a growing trend toward harnessing big network data to quantify how our online social lives affect our online and offline behavior.

Such research reveals another fascinating aspect of this era: the role of social algorithms in determining the content that we consume on social media (Lazer, 2015). Social networking sites employ content algorithms in an effort to customize feeds to users to make them more likely to engage with content. Users engage with content for various reasons but are more likely to engage with content that is interesting, relevant, and in line with their political leanings. As a result, algorithms pick up on these preferences and cater content that is most likely to be engaged. These algorithms can produce the perverse consequence of filtering out content that is counter to one's own ideology, creating a "filter bubble" effect (Pariser, 2011; Bakshy et al., 2015; Lazer, 2015).

Content-Sharing Platforms

Content-sharing platforms such as YouTube, Flickr, and Instagram offer unprecedented opportunities for candidates and political organizations to communicate with voters outside traditional political channels, often communicating directly to voters using videos and photos without intervention from news media. YouTube videos generated by politicians are often conceived with the intention of going "viral" and setting national political agendas and debates. A handful of studies explore the types of strategies and messaging appeals that are (in)effective in going viral and engaging potential voters (Carlson and Strandberg, 2008; English et al., 2011; Gibson and McAllister, 2011). Opportunities exist for understanding the network structure of content sharing, particularly with regard to political content. These authors note that while we are well into "Web 2.0," there is a paucity of research that leverages content-sharing platforms to understand how such platforms contribute to the dispersion of political messaging, public opinion, and political campaigns across political networks.

News Media, Blogs

Adamic and Glance's (2005) study of the political blogosphere was a preview of the power of big data and networks to reveal insights about political discussions online. This study used links, content, and references of bloggers to understand polarization in political blogs. Political bloggers were tracing a map of information flow and exposure to information in the structure of links they posted to other political blogs. Along a similar line, Siegel (2013) explores patterns of news media flow and response to social networks using computational simulation techniques. He uses a computational model of individuals connected to each other through varying networks, through which they can influence one another (local), be influenced by the media (global), and be influenced by their own biases (internal) to participate in politics or not. He finds that social network structure conditions mass media's impact on opinion, and that social networks can amplify the effects of media bias. The reason is that media bias is better at moving people away from the status quo rather than toward it. These examples illustrate how computational tools in the hands of social scientists can help to resolve complex questions about media and politics that we face in the digital era.

(Other) Textual Data, Like Bills, News Media, and Email

An area with particular room to grow in computational social science is the realm of textual analysis (Grimmer and Stewart, 2013). Digitization of the legislative process is well under way, and the analysis of duplicated text across bills provides a map of legislative ideas, their origins, and their policy destinations (Wilkerson et al., 2015). The study by Wilkerson et al. (2015) uncovers the facts that the source material of legislation comes from far more diverse sources than previously assumed and that the legislative process is one of continuous duplication, iteration, and amalgamation. Legislation is the product of many copy-paste actions across many pieces of source text. Legislative text is produced, mixed, and remixed from many samples before it is etched into law. Other examples of studies using textual tools include examining the flow of information via email (Karsai et al., 2011) and the global network of media coverage (Leetaru and Schrodt, 2013). Analyzing media text appears particularly promising, for example, for forecasting global events (Arva et al., 2013).

One of the major innovations in text analysis, which has led to an explosion of Twitter research, is the development of topic models. Blei et al. (2003) proposed latent Dirichlet allocation (LDA), the standard topic model used in natural language processing. It allows researchers to distinguish topics in a corpus of text that are probabilistically related to specific words. The words *computational, data,* and *politics,* for example, are more probable in this book than in a book about knitting or frankfurters. Latent Dirichlet allocation provides a generative model for distributions of words in documents, which leads to a method to infer distributions of topics in any corpus of text. The LDA topic model assumes "exchangeability," also known as the "bag-of-words" assumption that the ordering of words has no bearing on the dependencies of the words. While this assumption has had its fair share of criticism, LDA remains one of the most commonly used techniques for decoding text. It has been used to analyze text to forecast crime (Wang et al., 2012), to study the topic structure of science in the Proceedings of the National Academy of Science (Griffith and Steyvers, 2004), and to compare Twitter to mainstream media reporting on the same events (Zhao et al., 2011).

The Internet Archive

The Internet Archive is a nonprofit organization whose mission is to preserve the history of the Internet. The organization scrapes and records the hundreds of billions of pages on the World Wide Web, from text content to hyperlinks. These data contain detailed time-stamped link information and original text useful for exploring the paths of different pieces of content across the web or within specific geographic areas such as networks of websites with a common country-specific domain (Hale et al., 2014). The network from the Internet Archive is an evolving tapestry of interwoven organizations that is a growing source of data for scholars of media and communications, but may also have applications well beyond these fields (see, e.g., Weber and Monge, 2014). Scholars have begun to utilize this vast data trove to understand the evolving ecology of organizations online as evidenced by the changing interorganizational linkages between them (Weber, 2012).

Cellular Phones and Smartphones

The uptake of cellular phones promised deep insights to understand network structure on a societal scale. Research in this area has produced many interesting findings, for example regarding how tie strength is affected by local network structure and how mobile phone call patterns can predict interpersonal relationships or employment status (Onnela et al., 2007; Eagle et al., 2009; Toole et al., 2015). Recent work has used mobile phones to understand how citizens migrate following a natural disaster (Bengtsson et al., 2011) and how population densities change over time (Deville et al., 2014). Now this potential has been amplified with the advent of smartphones, possessing increased functions and apps that can act as new sources of highly detailed data. In addition to patterns of movement, migration, reach, and engagement, which can be tapped from any phone, smartphones enable collecting detailed behavioral data, interactive surveys, apps for social experiments, and a variety of GPS-tagged data (e.g., Eagle et al., 2009;

Boase and Ling, 2013). Studies of the impact of mobile phones include nearly everything from credit analysis to curbing violence in the Middle East. While the potential is clear, research has only begun to harness the vast possibilities for social study brought about by smartphones.

Anyone who has stepped inside a subway or bus in the last few years has noticed the tremendous penetration of smartphones into daily life. Smartphones now accompany a person every day, acting as personal assistant, social media liaison, web browser, photo archive, and communication tool. There is little about our daily lives that a smartphone does not witness. This makes smartphones the ideal tool for social research. Because smartphones are fully programmable, relatively cheap, and go nearly everywhere a person goes, they are a flexible and low-cost tool to unobtrusively access highly detailed personal data (Raento et al., 2009). However, ethical concerns arise over who can participate in studies that collect such high-resolution personal data, for what period of time it is appropriate, and for what research questions. Smartphones often possess very intimate information about our daily lives, and therefore social scientists must confront the many ethical implications of using these data.

One important way cellular phone research has contributed to political science is by tackling the question of how changes in communication patterns disrupt violence in highly volatile insurgent areas. Though this area is still in its infancy, Pierskalla and Hollenbach (2013) use cellular data to test for the effects of increased cellular tower coverage in geographical grids on the outbreak of violence in Africa. They find that cell phone coverage has been associated with an uptick in violence across Africa. Along a similar line, but with somewhat contrary findings, Shapiro and Weidmann (2015) explore whether cell phones helped or hindered the occurrence of violence in Iraq between 2004 and 2009. Cell phones reduce violence through two mechanisms, the authors argue: by increasing the ability of counterinsurgents to intercept messages (signal intelligence) and by increasing the ability of people to anonymously report information to counterinsurgents (human intelligence).

Governmental Archival Data

The data on the hundreds of millions of political contributions made by millions of political donors, recorded in the Federal Election Commission's (FEC) official database, are so large and messy as to render it extremely difficult for any researcher to analyze all but a minor subset of them systematically. Recent work on a couple of fronts has surmounted the challenges of cleaning the FEC's data into useable form (Bonica, 2013; Dianati et al., 2015). This research has highlighted just how powerful computational talent can be for political science and the broader social sciences. Problems of "identity resolution," the field of computer science related to determining whether two records in a corpus belong to the same entity, are alien to standard graduate social sciences training. But identity resolution and similar techniques can render large, messy, and complex data sets more directly accessible to social scientists. This issue also highlights the importance of collaboration between the social sciences and fields like computer science and physics.

METHODOLOGICAL OPPORTUNITIES

As noted previously, the distinctive scientific opportunity offered by big data is to study social systems as a system, rather than as a set of individuals who are assumed to be detached from one another. Beyond that, what are the distinct *methodological* opportunities that big data offer? There are some scientific objectives that simply require quantities of data that were heretofore inconceivable. By way of analogy, one application of big data in the medical arena is "personalized medicine": the notion that treatment effects are somehow contingent on factors (e.g., genetic) at the individual level. It is almost certain that most findings in the social sciences represent the average of a set of highly contingent relationships. To identify such contingencies is extremely data hungry, and large-scale data offer a powerful tool for identifying such interactive effects.

By a similar logic, large-scale data offer the opportunity to identify and study small minorities that might be of particular scientific interest (Foucault-Welles, 2014). A special case is when we have existing valuable small data, in which some existing data's power is leveraged by linkage to relevant subsets of the big data. The study by Chetty et al. (2011) is exemplary, linking field experimental data on residential (re)location in the 1970s to IRS data on future incomes of the children in those households and finding dramatic effects contingent on the age of the child.

Many of the sociotechnical systems in which big data are generated offer ripe opportunities for field experiments because of the malleability of those systems. Bond et al. (2012) offer a powerful example, in which an experiment on Facebook involving sixty-two million people manipulated whether individuals could see whether their peers voted. The authors subsequently validated self-reported voting with public voting records.

Computational social science has already begun to show where we might be wrong. For example, the conventional wisdom regarding age and voting is that older people are more likely to be registered to vote because they have a higher propensity to participate in politics generally. However, Ansolabehere et al. (2012) provide evidence, using a large random sample of 1.8 million registered voters in the United States, that the conventional wisdom is faulty. The authors show that voter registration rules in the United States render it more likely that older people will be registered to vote simply because they have a higher likelihood of staying in a place long enough to remain registered, producing a larger cohort of registered voters among older people than younger people.

Others have identified opportunities to improve on existing social research by leveraging the computational power that lives beneath our fingertips. Poast (2010) developed a technique for making inferences about multilateral events, such as the decision of the Allies to unite against the Axis in World War II, which are typically, and sometimes comically, conceived of as many dyadic events (e.g., the Belgium-Turkey alliance in the North Atlantic Treaty Organization). Developed with an eye toward understanding alliances and international treaties, Poast's method infers about k-adic events where the end result is some conglomeration of actors, and it may be useful to reason about how the conglomeration could have been very different. Such computational techniques have many promising applications in understanding group/team formation in political science, communication, and sociology.

THE BIG CHALLENGES OF BIG DATA

Big data present quite a few challenges to current social science methodology. Arguably, the bulk of big data is digital refuse from internal administrative and technical processes. Mobile phones offer a useful example, where each phone call generates a call detail record (CDR), with information on the originating phone number, the destination phone number, the cellular towers involved in transmitting the call, and the timing of the phone call. The purpose of these records is partly for billing, partly for management of the infrastructure, and partly to satisfy legal requirements. These records have been repurposed for academic use, with applications ranging from inferences regarding the structure of society (Onnela et al., 2007), to the prediction of future unemployment reports (Toole, 2015), to modeling human mobility so as to better predict the spread of disease (Wesolowski et al., 2012). However, CDRs pose challenges in interpretation. It is not obvious, for example, whether "who you text" is a deeply meaningful construct for the social sciences; this might be similar, for example, to using how many dollars you spend on groceries as a metric for nutrition. There would likely be a signal there, but the actual measure might be unusably heterogeneous for scientific purposes.

This is reflective of a broader concern about the representativeness of the underlying social mechanisms in big data. Twitter is so popular for research that it has been called the "Drosophila melanogaster" (fruit fly) of media studies (Tufekci, 2014). The platform churns out data rapidly and allows researchers to conduct a study in a matter of days, not weeks or months. Twitter is always on and producing data—data that are easy to collect, store, and analyze because of the simplified platform on which Twitter runs. These traits make it a tantalizing platform for study but introduce some important biases, and not just at the level of users (Tufekci, 2014).

The social processes that lead users to tweet and retweet in 140-character bursts are inherently different from other sources of data with longer life cycles (Tufekci, 2014). If much or most of the research surrounding social media comes from Twitter data, researchers may have the mistaken impression that their findings represent many or most social processes that pertain to social media. Twitter accounts are enormously heterogeneous, including people, organizations, and bots. Who is on Twitter is clearly unreflective of the broader population, and what people are likely and willing to express on Twitter is also probably quite heterogeneous.

As we discuss below, these same concerns plague other sources of data that are easy to retrieve and have quite short life cycles. These are not insurmountable issues, but they need to be addressed carefully.

Big data are also not always *good* data. The widespread availability of data pouring in from the Internet each day is tempting fodder for a bevy of social-scientific questions. However, as mentioned above, much of the available data is digital garbage that can feasibly offer little to social science. One of the major "provocations" that critics of the big data revolution put forth is the confusion of quantity with quality (boyd and Crawford, 2012). Big data do not offer a direct line to knowledge, but require substantial attention to the data-generating process, sampling, cleaning, and interpretation of the results. The social objective of the analysis can easily be lost in the illusion that plentiful data will compensate for other weaknesses. Clever theory, research design, and concern for sampling still remain major considerations in the era of big network data (boyd and Crawford, 2012).

All research relies on measurement to capture some theoretical construct. Reliable measures will produce similar results at different time points. However, many of the measurement strategies that look attractive in the era of big data (e.g., Google queries, Facebook likes, content consumption) rely on complicated, proprietary, and dynamic algorithms produced by staff at companies with different interests in mind. For example, the constant tweaking of the Google search algorithm probably contributed to the persistent overestimation of flu levels by the Google flu team (Lazer et al., 2014). In this case, the underlying measurement strategy of capturing flu-related searches was unstable due to the constant shifting of the Google search algorithm. Such algorithmic instability can occur in similar fashion in any platform that uses algorithms to provide services to clients, as an increasing number of online platforms do. Such instabilities may affect a large number of studies that utilize big data from major companies such as Twitter, Google, and Facebook.

Much disagreement exists about whether the recent incorporation of the tools of big data will lead to a softening of fundamental tenets of statistical and research practice. For instance, some worry that because data are "big," researchers will throw away concerns of sampling and representativeness (see Ardoin and Gronke (2015) on big data). Scholars also disagree about whether the use of big data de-emphasizes theory as a driving force of the research process. Scholars fear that the employment of big data will impel a retreat of theory-driven investigation in favor of data-mining or kitchen-sink models.

Interest in data of high volume, velocity, and variety (i.e., big data) has grown enormously in nearly every corner of the private and public sectors and in nearly every corner of every discipline in academia. Yet many remain highly skeptical of the depth and breadth of their potential. Skeptics argue, often rightly, that research employing big data makes unrealistic assumptions about population properties, makes inferences derived from models, or leverages research designs that would be inappropriate for small data. For example, Patty and Penn (2015) argue that there should be more principled approaches to measurement in the context of big data: researchers should choose measures in an axiomatic fashion in order to properly reduce large data to examine what is interesting and relevant. Nagler and Tucker (2015) rightly argue that data on Twitter and other social media are not representative of any population in particular, and that results from studies on these platforms are unlikely to generalize to data sets that represent specific populations (e.g., likely voters).

Institutional Challenges

Big data present institutional challenges to the social sciences and are bound to stretch social science resources, such as methodological talent, server space, computing power, and time. First, only a tiny fraction of social science faculty and graduate students have the technical skills to work with the infrastructure surrounding big data. Many of the tools that make big data easy to work with are in the domain of computer science: SQL, Python, and distributed computing software. While collaboration with the computer scientists might be the best solution due to the paucity of computational skills in the social sciences, political science has been slow to cultivate such ties. Second, there is essential infrastructure associated with big data to which many faculty do not have access. Scientific computing frequently requires large computers with substantial memory and processing power. Finally, big data take more time to clean, recode, describe, and analyze. Each command on a large data set might take substantial computing costs—even by contemporary standards—to execute, forcing analysts to rethink standard practices and approaches to their analyses.

There is much discussion surrounding the ethics of massive data collection. Public data on Twitter or Instagram are easily accessible by engineering web-scraping tools to suck them up and process them. Passive listening/recording software allows anyone to monitor the public online behavior of users. However, much of the content produced by users (such as Instragram or Tumblr) is not produced with this intent in mind. Users are often unaware that their data are being collected (boyd and Crawford, 2012). The ethical ramifications are worse when data that are apparently anonymous can be de-anonymized (e.g., de Montjoye et al., 2015).

CONCLUSION

Politics is an intrinsically relational phenomenon. How people mobilize and organize, who has power over what and whom, who is allied with and against whom, where people get information from—all of these questions are at their foundation about networks. That is, they should be conceived of as phenomena that should emerge from the connections among people and entities of various types. By happy coincidence for the science of politics, we live in an age of networked technologies, which capture many of these relationships. We can observe who is connected to whom, when, and about what, in ways that just a few years ago would have been the stuff of science fiction. These types of data are just beginning to make an impact across the social sciences, but they should have a particularly important impact in reorienting political science toward analytic frameworks that interrogate the structures of interdependence among people.

REFERENCES

Adamic, L. A., and Glance, N. (2005). "The Political Blogosphere and the 2004 US Election: Divided They Blog." In *Proceedings of the 3rd International Workshop on Link Discovery*, pp. 36–43. New York: ACM.

Ansolabehere, S., Hersh, E., and Shepsle, K. (2012). "Movers, Stayers, and Registration: Why Age Is Correlated with Registration in the US." *Quarterly Journal of Political Science* 7(4): 333–363.

Ardoin, P., and Gronke, P. (Ed). 2015. Symposium: Big Data, Causal Inference, and Formal Theory: Contradictory Trends in Political Science? *PS: Political Science and Politics* 48(1). Cambridge University Press.

Arva, B., Beieler, J., Fisher, B., Lara, G., Schrodt, P. A., Song, W., . . . Stehle, S. (2013). "Improving Forecasts of International Events of Interest." *EPSA 2013 Annual General Conference Papers* 78 (July).

Bakshy, E., Messing, S., and Adamic, L. (2015). "Exposure to Ideologically Diverse News and Opinion on Facebook." *Science* 338(6239): 1130–1132.

Barberá, P. (2015). "Birds of the Same Feather Tweet Together: Bayesian Ideal Point Estimation Using Twitter Data." *Political Analysis* 23(1): 76–91.

Bengtsson, L., Lu, X., Thorson, A., Garfield, R., and Von Schreeb, J. (2011). "Improved Response to Disasters and Outbreaks by Tracking Population Movements with Mobile Phone Network Data: A Post-Earthquake Geospatial Study in Haiti." *PLoS Med* 8(8): e1001083.

Blei, D. M., Ng, A. Y., and Jordan, M. I. (2003). "Latent Dirichlet Allocation." *Journal of Machine Learning Research* 3: 993–1022.

Boase, J., and Ling, R. (2013). "Measuring Mobile Phone Use: Self-Report versus Log Data." *Journal of Computer-Mediated Communication* 18(4): 508–519.

Bollen, J., Mao, H., and Zeng, X. (2011). "Twitter Mood Predicts the Stock Market." *Journal of Computational Science* 2(1): 1–8.

Bond, R. M., Fariss, C. J., Jones, J. J., Kramer, A. D., Marlow, C., Settle, J. E., and Fowler, J. H. (2012). "A 61-Million-Person Experiment in Social Influence and Political Mobilization." *Nature* 489(7415): 295–298.

Bonica, A. (2013). *Database on Ideology, Money in Politics, and Elections: Public Version 1.0.* Stanford, CA: Stanford University Libraries. http://data.stanford.edu/dime.

boyd, danah, and Crawford, K. (2012). "Critical Questions for Big Data." *Information, Communication & Society* 15(5): 662–679. http://doi.org/10.1080/1369118X.2012.678878.

Carlson, T., and Strandberg, K. (2008). "Riding the Web 2.0 Wave: Candidates on YouTube in the 2007 Finnish National Elections." *Journal of Information Technology & Politics* 5(2): 159–174.

Chetty, R., Friedman, J. N., Hilger, N., Saez, E., Schanzenbach, D. W., and Yagan, D. (2011). How Does Your Kindergarten Classroom Affect Your Earnings? Evidence from Project STAR. *The Quarterly Journal of Economics* 126(4): 1593–1660. https://doi.org/10.1093/qje/qjr041.

Coviello, L., Sohn, Y., Kramer, A. D., Marlow, C., Franceschetti, M., Christakis, N. A., and Fowler, J. H. (2014). "Detecting Emotional Contagion in Massive Social Networks." *PloS One* 9(3): e90315.

de Montjoye, Y.-A., Radaelli, L., Singh, V. K., and Pentland, A. S. (2015). "Unique in the Shopping Mall: On the Reidentifiability of Credit Card Metadata." *Science* 347(6221): 536–539. doi.org/10.1126/science.1256297.

Deville, P., Linard, C., Martin, S., Gilbert, M., Stevens, F. R., Gaughan, A. E., . . . Tatem, A. J. (2014). "Dynamic Population Mapping Using Mobile Phone Data." *Proceedings of the National Academy of Sciences* 111(45): 15888–15893.

Dianati, N., Lifshitz, G., Ruths, D., and Lazer, D. (2015). The FEC Campaigns Database Disambiguated. http://www.naviddianati.com/fec.

Eagle, N., Pentland, A. S., and Lazer, D. (2009). "Inferring Friendship Network Structure by Using Mobile Phone Data." *Proceedings of the National Academy of Sciences* 106(36): 15274–15278.

English, K., Sweetser, K. D., and Ancu, M. (2011). "YouTube-ification of Political Talk: An Examination of Persuasion Appeals in Viral video." *American Behavioral Scientist* 55(6).

Gibson, R. K., and McAllister, I. (2011). "Do Online Election Campaigns Win Votes? The 2007 Australian 'YouTube' Election." *Political Communication* 28(2): 227–244.

González-Bailón, S., Borge-Holthoefer, J., Rivero, A., and Moreno, Y. (2011). "The Dynamics of Protest Recruitment Through an Online Network." *Scientific Reports* 1: 197–204.

Griffiths, T. L., and Steyvers, M. (2004). "Finding Scientific Topics." *Proceedings of the National Academy of Sciences* 101(supp. 1): 5228–5235.

Grimmer, J., and Stewart, B. M. (2013). "Text as Data: The Promise and Pitfalls of Automatic Content Analysis Methods for Political Texts." *Political Analysis* 21(3): 267–297.

Hale, S. A., Yasseri, T., Cowls, J., Meyer, E. T., Schroeder, R., and Margetts, H. (2014). "Mapping the UK Webspace: Fifteen Years of British Universities on the Web." In *Proceedings of the 2014 ACM Conference on Web Science*, pp. 62–70. ACM. New York.

Hannak, A., Sapiezynski, P., Molavi Kakhki, A., Krishnamurthy, B., Lazer, D., Mislove, A., and Wilson, C. (2013). "Measuring Personalization of Web Search." In *Proceedings of the 22nd International Conference on World Wide Web*, pp. 527–538. International World Wide Web Conferences Steering Committee. ACM. New York.

Hannak, A., Soeller, G., Lazer, D., Mislove, A., and Wilson, C. (2014). "Measuring Price Discrimination and Steering on E-commerce Web Sites." In *Proceedings of the 2014 Conference on Internet Measurement*, pp. 305–318. ACM. New York.

Hu, J., Zeng, H.-J., Li, H., Niu, C., and Chen, Z. (2007). "Demographic Prediction Based on User's Browsing Behavior." In *Proceedings of the 16th International Conference on World Wide Web*, pp. 151–160. ACM. New York. doi.org/10.1145/1242572.1242594.

Jurgens, D., Finethy, T., McCorriston, J., Xu, Y. T., and Ruths, D. (2015). "Geolocation Prediction in Twitter Using Social Networks: A Critical Analysis and Review of Current Practice." In *Proceedings of the 9th International AAAI Conference on Weblogs and Social Media (ICWSM)*. Cambridge.

Karsai, M., Kivelä, M., Pan, R. K., Kaski, K., Kertész, J., Barabási, A. L., and Saramäki, J. (2011). "Small but Slow World: How Network Topology and Burstiness Slow Down spreading." *Physical Review E* 83(2): 025102.

Lazer, D. (2011). "Networks in Political Science: Back to the Future." *PS: Political Science & Politics* 44(1): 61–68.

Lazer, D. (2015). "The Rise of the Social Algorithm." *Science* 348(6239): 1090–1091.

Lazer, D., Kennedy, R., King, G., and Vespignani, A. (2014). "The Parable of Google Flu: Traps in Big Data Analysis." *Science* 343(14 March): 1203–1205.

Lazer, D., Pentland, A. S., Adamic, L., Aral, S., Barabasi, A. L., Brewer, D., . . . Van Alstyne, M. (2009). "Life in the Network: The Coming Age of Computational Social Science." *Science* 323(5915): 721.

Leetaru, K., and Schrodt, P. A. (2013). "GDELT: Global Data on Events, Location, and Tone, 1979–2012." *ISA Annual Convention* 2(4). http://data.gdeltproject.org/documentation/ISA.2013.GDELT.pdf.

Lynch, M., Freelon, D., and Aday, S. (2014). "Syria's Socially Mediated Civil War." *United States Institute of Peace* 91(1): 1–35.

Manber, U., Patel, A., and Robison, J. (2000). "Experience with Personalization of Yahoo!" *Communications of the ACM* 43(8): 35–39. doi.org/10.1145/345124.345136.

Manyika, J., Chui, M., Brown, B., Bughin, J., Dobbs, R., Roxburgh, C., and Byers, A. H. (2011). "Big Data: The Next Frontier for Innovation, Competition, and Productivity."

Nagler, J., and Tucker, J. (2015). "Drawing Inferences and Testing Theories with Big Data." *PS: Political Science and Politics* 48(1): 84–88.

Olejnik, L., Castelluccia, C., and Janc, A. (2012). "Why Johnny Can't Browse in Peace: On the Uniqueness of Web Browsing History Patterns." In *5th Workshop on Hot Topics in Privacy Enhancing Technologies (HotPETs 2012)*: 48–63. Berlin. https://petsymposium.org/2012/papers/hotpets12_selected_papers.pdf.

Onnela, J.-P., Saramäki, J., Hyvönen, J., Szabó, G., Lazer, D., Kaski, K., . . . Barabási, A.-L. (2007). "Structure and Tie Strengths in Mobile Communication Networks." *Proceedings of the National Academy of Sciences* 104(18): 7332–7336.

Pariser, E. (2011). *The Filter Bubble: How the New Personalized Web Is Changing What We Read and How We Think*. Penguin. London.

Patty, J. W., and Penn, E. M. (2015). "Analyzing Big Data: Social Choice and Measurement." *PS: Political Science and Politics*.

Pierskalla, J. H., and Hollenbach, F. M. (2013). "Technology and Collective Action: The Effect of Cell Phone Coverage on Political Violence in Africa." *American Political Science Review* 107(2): 207–224.

Poast, P. (2010). "(Mis) using Dyadic Data to Analyze Multilateral Events." *Political Analysis* 18(4): 403–425.

Raento, M., Oulasvirta, A., and Eagle, N. (2009). "Smartphones: An Emerging Tool for Social Scientists." *Sociological Methods & Research* 37(3): 426–454.

Shapiro, J. N., and Weidmann, N. B. (2015). "Is the Phone Mightier Than the Sword? Cellphones and Insurgent Violence in Iraq." *International Organization* 69(2): 247–274.

Siegel, D. A. (2013). "Social Networks and the Mass Media." *American Political Science Review* 107: 786–805.

Statista (n.d.). "Number of Monthly Active Facebook Users Worldwide as of 3rd Quarter 2016." http://www.statista.com/statistics/264810/number-of-monthly-active-facebook-users-worldwide.

Toole, J. L., Lin, Y.-R., Muehlegger, E., Shoag, D., González, M. C., and Lazer, D. (2015). "Tracking Employment Shocks Using Mobile Phone Data." *Journal of the Royal Society Interface* 12(107): 20150185.

Tufekci, Z. (2014). "Big Questions for Social Media Big Data: Representativeness, Validity and Other Methodological Pitfalls." In *Eighth International AAAI Conference on Weblogs and Social Media*. n.p.: AAAI Publications. http://www.aaai.org/ocs/index.php/ICWSM/ICWSM14/paper/view/8062.

Wang, X., Gerber, M. S., and Brown, D. E. (2012). "Automatic Crime Prediction Using Events Extracted from Twitter Posts." In *Social Computing, Behavioral-Cultural Modeling and Prediction*, pp. 231–238. Berlin and Heidelberg: Springer.

Weber, M. S. (2012). "Newspapers and the Long-Term Implications of Hyperlinking." *Journal of Computer-Mediated Communication* 17(2): 187–201.

Weber, M. S., and Monge, P. R. (2014). "Industries in Turmoil: Driving Transformation During Periods of Disruption." *Communication Research* (January 13): 93650213514601. doi.org/10.1177/0093650213514601.

Foucault Welles, B. F. (2014). "On Minorities and Outliers: The Case for Making Big Data Small." *Big Data & Society* 1(1): 2053951714540613.

Wesolowski, A., Eagle, N., Tatem, A. J., Smith, D. L., Noor, A. M., Snow, R. W., and Buckee, C. O. (2012). "Quantifying the Impact of Human Mobility on Malaria." *Science* 338(6104): 267–270.

Wilkerson, J., Smith, D., and Stramp, N. (2015). "Tracing the Flow of Policy Ideas in Legislatures: A Text Reuse Approach." *American Journal of Political Science* 59(4): 943–956.

Wood, M. (2014). "Sweeping Away a Search History." *New York Times.* April 3, pp. B9.

Zhao, W. X., Jiang, J., Weng, J., He, J., Lim, E.-P., Yan, H., and Li, X. (2011). "Comparing Twitter and Traditional Media Using Topic Models." In *Advances in Information Retrieval*, edited by P. Clough, C. Foley, C. Gurrin, G. J. F. Jones, W. Kraaij, H. Lee, and V. Mudoch, pp. 338–349. Springer Berlin and Heidelberg: Springer. http://link.springer.com/chapter/10.1007/978-3-642-20161-5_34.

....

CHAPTER 5

CAUSAL INFERENCE
IN POLITICAL NETWORKS

....

JON C. ROGOWSKI AND BETSY SINCLAIR

INTRODUCTION

....

SCHOLARS have developed an increasingly rich set of research findings regarding the structure of political networks. Network approaches have shed new light on the connections among political candidates, donors, and interest groups (see chapters 16 and 17); legal precedents, opinions, and jurists (see chapter 20); terrorist groups (see chapter 28); and actors engaged in weapons trading (see chapter 33). As other chapters in this volume attest, networks such as these affect a wide range of political outcomes. For example, political attitudes and behavior can be shaped by the individuals in their social networks (see chapters 21 and 37), legislative behavior can be influenced by the formal and informal ties that connect legislators (see chapter 19), decision-making by political officials can reflect the policy networks with which they are affiliated (see chapters 26, 27, and 38), and political regimes can be responsive to the structure of interstate relations (see chapter 32). Studying the ways in which influence is transmitted through political networks has enriched our theories of political outcomes in all fields of political science.

However, identifying causal associations between political networks and outcomes of interest presents a range of empirical challenges. These challenges—which include homophily and interference between units—are not unique to the study of political networks, yet addressing these concerns is all the more critical for allowing researchers to draw inferences about the causal effects of political networks. *Homophily* refers to the tendency for connections to form on the basis of shared characteristics. For example, individuals may join social networks that are composed of other individuals with shared interests. *Interference between units* describes a scenario in which administering some treatment to one individual "spills over," so that the treatment is also administered to other people in the individual's network. In some cases, creative research designs will allow scholars to use these identification challenges to their advantage and strengthen their claims about the transmission of influence through networks.

In this chapter we discuss empirical research on political networks using the framework of the Neyman-Rubin causal model and highlight the primary difficulties researchers face when studying the causal effects of networks on political outcomes of interest. Surveying recent literature on the effects of political networks, we show that researchers do not always acknowledge these challenges to identification, and that those who do have taken a wide range of approaches to address these difficulties. We then describe a set of strategies researchers can employ to address these challenges, including suggestions for best practices in both observational and experimental studies.

A GENERAL FRAMEWORK FOR STUDYING NETWORK EFFECTS

We discuss the study of network effects using the potential outcomes framework, also known as the Neyman-Rubin causal model (Rubin, 1974; Holland, 1986). As a running example, we consider how a voter's social network can influence her decision to turn out to vote when some individuals in her network have (and perhaps she also has) received a mobilization message. Much political science research has focused solely on the individual motivations to vote, but this research has overlooked the myriad influences of family, friends, and neighbors. Recent findings from the field of political networks have updated this research, acknowledging the influence of others, with a range of empirical designs (Bond et al., 2012; Sinclair, 2012).

In the Neyman-Rubin causal model, each unit in our study has multiple potential outcomes, but only one observed outcome. Potential outcomes characterize how the units in our study behave in response to the presence or absence of a treatment. For example, suppose we wish to estimate the effect of a treatment on an outcome of interest Y_i, where i indexes the units in our study, $i = 1, 2, \ldots, N$. For simplicity, suppose we have a binary treatment $T_i \in \{0,1\}$, where the value of the variable T_i indicates whether the unit received the treatment. Thus, the two potential outcomes are Y_{i0}, which represents the unit's behavior in the absence of the treatment, and Y_{i1}, which represents the unit's behavior with the treatment. The dependent variable is characterized by $Y_i(1)$ when $T_i = 1$, and $Y_i(0)$ when $T_i = 0$. The observed outcome can be written as $T_i \in \{0,1\}$, and the estimate of the unit-level treatment effect is given by $Y_i = T_i Y_i(1) + (1 - T_i) Y_i(0)$. However, we never observe both outcomes $Y_i(1)$ and $Y_i(0)$ for a given unit i, and thus we cannot estimate the unit-level treatment effect. This is known as the fundamental problem of causal inference. Instead, we focus on identifying other estimands of interest. The most common estimand is the average treatment effect (ATE). The ATE is the average difference between the potential outcomes across the entire population. The ATE is estimated simply using the difference between the mean outcome for treated units and the mean outcome for untreated units, or $\bar{\tau} = \mathbb{E}\,[Y\,|\,T=1] - \mathbb{E}\,[Y\,|\,T=0] = \mathbb{E}\,[Y_{1l} - Y_{10}]$.

Two key assumptions are necessary to generate an unbiased estimate of $\bar{\tau}$: exchangeability (also called unconfoundedness or ignorability) and noninterference (frequently referred to as SUTVA, the stable unit treatment value assumption).[1] Exchangeability requires that treatment assignment be independent of the potential outcomes, or $\left(Y_{i1},\ Y_{i0}\right) \perp T_i$. This assumption allows the researcher to connect unobservable potential outcomes with the observed outcomes. That is, the expected value of the observed outcome for treated units is equal to the expected value of the potential outcome for units that received the treatment, or $\mathbb{E}\,[Y_i\,|\,T=1] = \mathbb{E}\,[Y_{1l}]$ (and defined analogously for untreated units). This assumption is satisfied when treatment assignment is fully randomized. However, satisfying this assumption is more difficult in the context of observational studies, in which researchers might be concerned that units have chosen to receive (or not) a particular treatment due to the perceived benefits of doing so. In these situations, additional assumptions must be satisfied to obtain estimates of causal effects, and satisfying these assumptions is made more challenging in the context of network data.

The noninterference assumption requires that a unit's potential outcomes are influenced only by its own treatment status, not by any other unit's treatment assignment. That is, a J-valued treatment is assumed to result in J potential outcomes. When the noninterference assumption is violated, however, the number of potential outcomes for unit i can increase dramatically. Instead of characterizing a unit's potential outcomes solely as Y_{i1} and Y_{io}, a researcher must consider all the potential outcomes that can result from the combination of administering the treatment to different units through processes such as contagion or spillovers. For instance, consider researchers who are interested in evaluating the efficacy of a new vaccine for reducing the prevalence of an infectious disease (e.g., Hudgens and Halloran, 2008). An experimental participant A, who does not receive the vaccine but is surrounded by other subjects who did receive the vaccine, is likely to have a different outcome from participant B, who also did not receive the vaccine but is surrounded by other subjects who also did not receive the vaccine. Both participants A and B were assigned to receive the same treatment status, but their potential outcomes differ considerably because the treatment status of the individuals with whom they interact also affects the outcome. As the proportion of subjects assigned to receive the treatment increases within a given experimental pool, researchers are likely to underestimate the true efficacy of the vaccine, because the potential outcomes for subjects not assigned to receive the vaccine will more closely resemble the potential outcomes for the subjects who did receive the vaccine.

Failing to satisfy the assumptions of exchangeability and noninterference can result in serious biases in the estimates of causal effects. These challenges are not unique to research on political networks. However, challenges to exchangeability and noninterference can manifest in particular ways in studies of network effects. We now discuss these issues in the context of network research with experimental and observational studies.

Studying Network Effects with Experimental Data

As noted in the previous section, the exchangeability assumption is generally met in experimental studies where treatment status is randomly assigned. Researchers interested in studying network effects are likely to be interested both in studying the direct treatment effect of some intervention and in quantifying the degree of spillover effects. In fact, measuring these spillover effects—which characterize the extent to which the treatment's effect was transmitted through interference—may be the key quantity of interest in some applications (e.g., see Nickerson, 2008; Sinclair, McConnell, and Green, 2012).

Consider a researcher who is interested in studying the effectiveness of public service announcements (PSAs) about recycling that are transmitted through social networks. A researcher may recruit classes of political science majors across different universities and randomly assign one or more students from each class to receive messages about either the importance of recycling or the importance of exercising. The researcher hypothesizes that students in the classes assigned to receive the recycling messages will report higher levels of recycling behavior, because the PSA would have been transmitted through the peer networks in the class. A week later, the researcher may conduct a survey of all the students in each participating class to gauge the extent to which students reported recycling and compare the mean rate of recycling among classes that received the recycling message to the mean rate among classes that received the exercise message.

Suppose that the researcher finds support for her hypothesis: students in classes that received the recycling PSA indeed reported greater rates of recycling behavior than students in classes that received the exercise PSA. What inference can the researcher make in this case? Unfortunately, a simple randomized experiment like this one does not enable the researcher to distinguish the direct effect of the message itself from the message's effects through peer influence. The researcher thus cannot draw any firm conclusions about the effectiveness of peer transmission as a means for communicating messages contained in PSAs. Identifying network effects in experimental research requires that the researcher use a research design that enables her to more precisely differentiate effects that are attributable to interference (or SUTVA violations) from the effects that are directly attributable to the intervention itself.

Studying Network Effects with Observational Data

Observational research presents additional challenges to identification. Unlike randomized experiments, observational studies must take seriously possible threats to exchangeability. Scholars interested in identifying the effects of, for example, social networks on political attitudes, or trade networks on interstate conflict, must think about how those networks formed. Scholarship on networks regularly emphasizes the importance of homophily (e.g., Shalizi and Thomas, 2011; VanderWeele, 2011), in which individuals similar to one another choose to associate with each other. More generally, network relationships may form between members who perceive some benefit from doing so. For example, friendship networks may form because friends share common characteristics or values, and trade networks may form because of the benefits that will accrue to member states as a result of participating in the network. Returning to the notation introduced above, in this situation we are faced with correlation between T_i and (Y_{i1}, Y_{io}). If we were to study the effect of friendship networks on shared political attitudes, we might find that individuals who are part of the same friendship network exhibit substantially more similar attitudes compared with individuals who are not part of the same friendship network. However, because network membership in this case largely may be a function of common values or characteristics, similarity in the political attitudes of members of the friendship network may reflect these commonalities, rather than the effects of network membership—which is the quantity we are interested in estimating. To plausibly attribute this finding to the network's causal effect, we need to account for the vector of characteristic X that determines a unit's treatment assignment. Continuing the running example, this would require including all covariates that influence an individual's choice of social network or a state's decision to join a trade network. In doing so, we can then estimate the effect of the treatment conditional on X. This challenge becomes significantly more difficult to address under the possibility of selection on unobservables. For example, consider a case in which the characteristics that influence an individual's choice to join a social network are unknown to (or unknowable by) the researcher. Because the researcher is unable to condition on these characteristics, the estimated causal effect of network membership on the outcome could in fact reflect these other characteristics rather than network membership itself.

The noninterference assumption is also more difficult to satisfy in observational research than it is in experimental research, for the simple reason that influence patterns cannot easily be separated from the processes we are interested in estimating (see also Morgan and Winship, 2014, section 2.5). For example, if we are interested in studying whether a person is more likely to work for a political campaign if he also has a friend who works for that particular campaign, we run into difficulties when trying to separate the effect of knowing someone who worked for the campaign from the transmission of influence from the campaign worker to the friend.

Empirical challenges such as these are not unique to the study of political networks. Rather, we highlight them to provide illustrations of potential pitfalls in empirical studies of networks. Existing empirical research on political networks, moreover, has not always recognized or addressed these challenges, which thus has implications for the inferences we are able to draw from this body of literature.

IDENTIFYING NETWORK EFFECTS
IN POLITICAL SCIENCE SCHOLARSHIP

Though scholars in political science and related literatures have long been interested in the relevance of social structures for explaining political phenomena, systematic empirical study of these relationships has increased dramatically in recent years. We surveyed nearly one hundred articles published in the discipline's leading journals over the last decade to evaluate how scholars have attempted to address the potential challenges to causal identification outlined in the previous section. We analyzed articles that appeared in the *American Journal of Political Science, American Political Science Review, British Journal of Political Science, Comparative Political Studies, International Organization, Journal of Politics,* and *World Politics.* While we selected these journals for their representation of scholarship across a variety of disciplinary subfields, we do not claim to have identified every article that addresses topics related to networks. Instead, we used a two-step process, in which we first searched each journal database for articles that included the term "network" and either the term "political" or "social." Our decision rule was generous and allowed these terms to appear anywhere in the text of the article. This search yielded several hundred articles. We then perused each article to identify whether it included an empirical study related to transmission of influence through networks. We discarded articles that contained, for example, formal models of network formation or interaction, and empirical studies that were not directly concerned with measuring the effects of a network on an outcome of interest. We further limited our focus to articles that estimated some outcome as a function of a unit's network characteristics. All told, our search revealed eighty-nine articles published between 2005 and 2014.

Table 5.1 presents the summary statistics from our evaluation. To evaluate possible temporal trends in approaches to identifying network effects, articles were divided into groups based on whether they were published between 2005 and 2009 or 2010 and 2014. We then performed a basic content analysis to examine (1) whether the author(s) discussed challenges to causal identification in studies of network effects and (2) what strategy, if any, the author(s) used to address these challenges. We emphasize that our content analysis makes no judgments about the appropriateness or soundness of the approaches used in these papers, but simply evaluates how scholars in political science have studied network effects in recent research.

To address our first query, we examined each article to determine whether the author(s) discussed the difficulties in identifying network effects when a unit's network assignment is not exogenously determined. We used a relaxed standard to evaluate whether the paper addressed this topic. For example, an experimental study of network influence could have simply indicated that the research design was motivated by the desire to avoid homophily and endogeneity, or an observational study could have defended a particular regression specification by citing the need to control for potential confounders related to a unit's selection into a particular network.

Table 5.1   Approaches to Causal Identification in Studies
of Social Influence, 2005–2014

Discuss identification challenges	2005–2009	2010–2014
	24 (51%)	22 (54%)
Identification strategy		
Experiment	5 (10%)	4 (10%)
Natural experiment	0	2 (5%)
Matching	0	1 (2%)
Lagged variables	6 (13%)	4 (10%)
Instrumental variables	2 (4%)	0
Panel design	6 (14%)	3 (8%)
Agent-based models	1 (2%)	0
None of the above	27 (57%)	26 (65%)
Number of articles	47 (100%)	40 (100%)

Entries summarize the contents of articles published between 2005 and 2014 in *American Political Science Review, American Journal of Political Science, Journal of Politics, British Journal of Political Science, Comparative Political Studies, World Politics,* and *International Organization.*

We then classified the identification strategy used in each article into one of the following: "Experiment," "Natural experiment," "Matching," "Lagged variables," "Instrumental variables," "Panel design," "Agent-based models," or "None of the above." Articles placed in the "Experiment" category used a randomization scheme determined by the researcher(s) to manipulate the characteristics or content of a unit's network. "Natural experiment" included articles that studied network effects when network assignment was not assigned by the researcher, but which still could be considered "as-if" random. For example, Urbatsch (2011) studied the transmission of political attitudes among siblings and used the gender of the older sibling as a source of exogenous variation for explaining policy preferences. Urbatsch found that younger siblings with older sisters (or brothers) are much more likely to report the "typical" female (or male) preference on policy items that have a gender gap, which can be plausibly attributed to the quasi-random assignment of the older sibling's sex.

The third category of identification strategy ("Matching") categorizes research that conducted its analyses after using some variant of matching techniques to identify units that were as similar as possible aside from their network assignment. We point out that matching is no panacea for causal inference (see Sekhon, 2009), though it may significantly reduce confoundedness from observables. Only one article in our search fell into this category. Boyd, Epstein, and Martin (2010) studied whether male judges vote differently in the presence of a female judge on US federal appellate panels. After applying matching techniques to identify panels of federal judges who are extremely similar across a range of other variables (including age, ideology, and years of service), across thirteen areas of the law, the authors report evidence that male judges behave significantly differently in the presence of a female judge only in cases that involve sex discrimination.

The fourth category of strategies characterizes research that used some form of lagged variables. Articles in this category generally used regression-based approaches and included at least one (and sometimes multiple) right-hand-side variables that were lagged to account for factors that may be related both to a unit's selection into a network and values of the dependent variable. The fifth category, "Instrumental variables," used an instrument Z to estimate X, unit i's assignment to a particular network, under the assumption that Z and X are strongly correlated, but any association between Z and Y occurs solely through X. (See Sovey and Green, 2011, for a primer on instrumental variables methods.) For example, in an article that appeared in a journal (*Political Analysis*) falling outside of our search parameters, Rogowski and Sinclair (2012) used the lottery number randomly assigned to newly elected members of the U.S. House of Representatives as an instrument for the spatial proximity of legislators' offices. The lottery number (Z) was used to predict whether a spatial tie (X) existed between two legislators, and shared legislative voting patterns (Y) were then regressed on these predicted values.

The sixth category, "Panel designs," includes research that used repeated measures to study how changes in a unit's network contributed to changes in an outcome of interest. The seventh category, "Agent-based models," characterizes research that employs computer simulations to isolate how key network components affect outcomes of interest. The only article we evaluated that used this approach is a study by Scholz and Wang (2006) that examined how the size and connectedness of a population affects learning and cooperation. The final category, "None of the above," indexes articles that do not employ any of the other strategies listed here. Typically, research falling into this category employs traditional regression-based approaches without ancillary attempts to adjust for omitted variables or selection.

As table 5.1 shows, our survey of the literature reveals substantial variation in how recent scholarship has addressed identification challenges in estimating network effects. First, we find that nearly half of the articles we analyzed on network effects did not discuss possible challenges to causal identification. Similar percentages of articles published between 2005 and 2009 (51 percent) and 2010 and 2014 (54 percent) discussed ways in which issues such as self-selection or endogeneity might complicate efforts to identify the effect of network membership on an outcome of interest. We are hesitant to overinterpret these figures since we do not have comparable information on discussions of identification in other empirical literatures. However, the data suggest that empirical scholarship on networks may not have fully recognized the difficulties associated with isolating causal effects attributable to networks or network characteristics. At the same time, our study also indicates that significant opportunities may exist for political methodologists interested in applying innovative research designs or statistical techniques to the study of network effects.

Our analysis also reveals considerable heterogeneity in researchers' approaches to addressing potential challenges to identification. Experiments, lagged variables, and panel designs were the most frequently used identification strategies. We are encouraged by the use of experiments, which represent perhaps the clearest means of addressing concerns about identification. Depending on how they are employed, lagged variables and panel designs may also help mitigate concerns about selection and confoundedness, yet we caution researchers that the strength of these designs ultimately comes down to the assumptions one is willing to make. Perhaps most worrisome is the relatively large proportion of studies that employ none of these identification strategies. Fifty-seven percent of articles published between 2005 and 2009 and 63 percent of those published between 2010 and 2014 did not use any of the identification strategies described here. While this finding itself does not call into question any of the hypotheses or conclusions discussed in these articles, the strength of the evidence increases with the rigor of the identification strategy. For the reasons outlined previously, failing to account for endogeneity or processes such as selection into networks could not only bias the point estimates produced through statistical tests, but also produce altogether incorrect or misleading conclusions. In the next section we provide a substantive example of how researchers can help guard against this possibility even in the context of observational research settings.

Best Practices: Identifying Network Effects in Observational Research

The primary concern with observational research in studies of networks is simply that the network structure does not arise randomly, but rather as a direct consequence of homophily; it is indeed the similarity between individual actors that generates the network. These similarities may, then, also generate similarities in outcomes regardless of differences in treatment assignment.

The fundamental problem of ignorability has been extensively studied, particularly in the context of public health, where randomized trials are deemed unethical. Researchers cannot ethically conduct experiments to evaluate whether smoking causes lung cancer or lead paint exposure causes neurological problems. How then are researchers able to assess causality in these cases? In brief, the appropriate statistical technique is to employ a sensitivity analysis.

Sensitivity analysis allows a researcher to estimate the potential magnitude of a factor that is unmeasured—that is, not observed—and to ascertain the extent to which the unmeasured factor would have to be present in the "treated" population in order to undermine the findings. In the case of smoking and lung cancer, for example, a sensitivity analysis could tell a researcher how prevalent an unobserved factor would need to be within the smoking population to challenge the association between smoking and lung cancer. In the context of network effects, the primary concern is that there are unmeasured causes of homophily that also cause associations in outcomes, distorting the empirical work that purports to document the presence of network effects (Shalizi and Thomas, 2011).

Fortunately, VanderWeele and Arah (2011) have developed a sensitivity analysis approach for network effects. VanderWeele (2011) employs this technique to address the critique that the association between network alters and their obesity, smoking, happiness, and loneliness is driven solely by homophily and not by contagion, as the authors of some studies claim (Christakis and Fowler, 2007, 2008; Cacioppo, Fowler, and Christakis, 2009). The studies by Christakis and Fowler and their colleagues use observational data collected as part of the Framingham Heart Study; in one such study (Christakis and Fowler, 2007), the authors find that the risk of obesity increased by 57 percent for an individual who had a friend who became obese. Though Christakis and Fowler include a series of controls to adjust for homophily, an unmeasured factor that affects both the propensity to become friends and the likelihood of becoming obese could also have seriously biased the results. The sensitivity analysis performed by VanderWeele (2011) evaluates how strong the relationship would have to be between the unmeasured factor and obesity to explain away the results presented by Christakis and Fowler. VanderWeele (2011) finds strong support for the presence of some network effects reported by Christakis and Fowler (particularly those related to obesity and smoking). In particular, to completely explain away the effects of friendship group membership on obesity, the unmeasured factor would have to increase the likelihood of obesity by a factor of three, while also having a much higher prevalence in friendships in which one person was obese than in friendships in which one person was not obese. Results such as these provide an evaluation of how serious threats to identification would need to be to overturn the effects estimated from observational data. We encourage anyone relying on observational data for network analysis to consider employing this technique.

In passing, it should also be noted that some observational studies care about estimation not of an indirect effect per se, but rather of a neighborhood-level effect. In particular, then, no treatment interaction between individuals needs to be explicitly specified.

BEST PRACTICES: IDENTIFYING NETWORK EFFECTS IN EXPERIMENTAL RESEARCH

As discussed previously in this chapter, acknowledging the potential for interference between units dramatically increases the number of potential outcomes. Suppose, for example, there are four individuals in a hypothetical experiment. When there is no interference between units, we need only consider for each person, i, his potential outcomes of having received either treatment or control. When interference is possible, person i could be contacted by person l, person m, or person n, each of whom respectively could have been assigned to treatment or control. Thus the potential outcome space has exploded: not only are there two potential outcomes for i himself, but in each of those outcomes we must consider the two for person l, and again the two for person m, and again for person n ($2 \times 2 \times 2 \times 2$). Indeed, with N subjects in an experiment, if we were to allow for all potential outcomes resulting from interference between all possible subjects, then any kind of statistical inference would quickly become intractable: an individual moves from having two potential outcomes (treated, control) to 2^N potential outcomes. What empirical strategies can be employed to handle this problem?

Researchers have two strategies to reduce the space of potential outcomes and limit the indirect effects from the other individuals in the network. Through clever research design and the deployment of additional substantive information, researchers can constrain the space of potential outcomes such that it is possible to test for the presence of a network effect, and in some cases to infer a network effect. These two strategies require either specific knowledge of the network structure or a theoretical model of network structure. Both strategies enable researchers to constrain the indirect effects between some individuals to zero through either the researcher's substantive knowledge about when this is likely to be true or by deploying a research design that is consistent with the theorized network structure.

First, suppose the network structure is already known. If this is the case, then the researcher can leverage that information to constrain the space of potential outcomes. Based on substantive knowledge of the particular context, the researcher may be able to further constrain the space of potential outcomes by limiting the exposure of individuals to those who, for example, are connected by only one degree of separation across the network. Explicit estimation strategies to marry estimation (or testing) with a known network structure can be found in Aronow and Samii (2012) and Aronow (2012). While much political science research does not have an explicit and known network, a recent example in which the network structure is known is the 61-million-person Bond et al. (2012) Facebook experiment. Some individuals were randomly assigned to receive treatment in the context of a large and known network structure. Given what is known about the network, it is then possible to infer the magnitude of indirect effects. Yet frequently political scientists are in the position of theorizing about the structure of the network as well as hoping to estimate its effects. In this case, our second empirical strategy is the one to follow.

Suppose some component of the network structure is theorized. For example, suppose that voters are believed to be influenced by their housemates. In this case, we have a good theoretical reason to believe that indeed this "network" will influence political choices (e.g., we know people talk about politics!). With an explicit theoretical model of a network, it is then possible to use that model to test for the presence of network effects following the empirical strategies laid out in Bowers,

Fredrickson, and Panagopoulos (2013). There are also cases in which there is additional information known about the network structure, for example that structure is hierarchical. Suppose that we are interested in neighborhood effects (individuals may communicate to other individuals within their neighborhood, but no further) or classroom effects (students may communicate to other individuals within their classroom, but no further). These limitations imposed by geography restrict the space of potential outcomes and thus make inference analytically possible. Essentially, the reduction of potential outcomes relaxes the SUTVA assumption, but only partially. That is, suppose there are simply individual-level and cluster-level potential outcomes. We can then write out four potential outcomes for each individual i in cluster j.

The experimental units can then be organized to receive individual-level or cluster-level treatments, and the potential outcomes for the experimental units will be based on the limitations imposed on the interactions across clusters. In our motivating example about voter turnout, we can imagine that voters live in households and in neighborhoods. We can then proceed with a multistep experimental design in which neighborhoods, then households, then voters are assigned at random to neighborhood-level, then household-level, then individual-level treatments. The probability that an individual will be treated is then based not only on the individual's assignment, but also on the cluster-level assignment. A range of scholars have employed this technique or modifications thereof (Hudgens and Halloran, 2008; Sinclair, McConnell, and Green, 2012). For scholars who wish to conduct multisite experiments, inference in this context frequently requires some model-based assumptions (such as whether the treatment effect of the cluster can be obtained via a linear model, averaging across clusters treated with different intensities, and where we can assume exchangeability across clusters; see Hong and Raudenbush, 2006).

MOVING FORWARD

The study of political networks has flourished over the last decade and has produced a rich set of theoretical insights into how influence is transmitted among individuals, across groups, and between states. Continued progress depends on careful and sustained attention to empirical verification of the theories that animate the field. Though this chapter has highlighted several important challenges that accompany empirical research on political networks, considerable opportunities await scholars working in this area. Here we highlight a few of them.

First, now that scholars have developed strong research designs for analyzing network data, collecting new data is an important task. "Big data" offer significant promise in this regard. Big data often reveal not only social relationships—about how and when people form relationships and interact—but also the structure of entire political networks. Identifying this network structure thus provides a key source of leverage in designing experiments whereby treatments are randomly administered to understand how their effects disseminate through the network. Such processes are much more difficult—if not impossible—to observe in most settings in which indirect effects are largely invisible. In addition, scholars can develop theoretical models of networks to deploy the experimental designs described above, and thus conduct experiments that enable researchers to carefully estimate the effects of network influence. Abundant opportunities for data collection await scholars interested in network processes, and aggressively attending to data collection will help move the field of political networks forward.

Second, recognizing that not all questions of network influence can be studied within an experimental framework, observational studies must be attentive to causal inference. Most observational data are riddled with selection biases and the like, which severely complicates the ability to draw strong causal inferences through traditional modes of data analysis. Scientific progress in this area requires that researchers recognize these limitations and take steps to address them. The strategies we outlined in this chapter for analyzing observational data can help researchers better account for potential biases that arise from homophily, and thus enable scholars to assess when estimates of "network effects" are more or less likely attributable to network processes. Because sensitivity analysis has been deployed relatively infrequently thus far in the study of political networks, scholars might also consider revisiting previous analyses to evaluate the robustness of their conclusions related to unobserved factors like homophily.

As the chapters in this volume attest, political networks is an exciting, vibrant field that touches on every subfield in the discipline. Continued progress in this area requires careful attention to the inferences we draw from our empirical research. In doing so, the field will develop greater insight into the conditions under which networks affect political outcomes of interest and lead us to develop even more nuanced accounts of the transmission of network influence.

Acknowledgments

We gratefully acknowledge Taeyong Park for research assistance and the editors of this volume for helpful feedback on earlier drafts of this chapter.

Note

1. For an especially lucid discussion of causal identification, research design, and statistical analysis, see Keele (2015).

REFERENCES

Aronow, P. M. (2012). "A General Method for Detecting Interference Between Units in Randomized Experiments." *Sociological Methods & Research* 41(3): 3–16.

Aronow, P. M., and Samii, C. (2012). "Estimating Average Causal Effects Under General Interference." Working paper, University of North Carolina.

Bond, R., Fariss, C. J., Jones, J. J., Kramer, A. D. I., Marlow, C., Settle, J. E., and Fowler, J. H. (2012). "A 61-Million-Person Experiment in Social Influence and Political Mobilization." *Nature* 489: 295–298.

Bowers, J., Fredrickson, M., and Panagopoulos, C. (2013). "Reasoning about Interference in Randomized Studies." *Political Analysis* 21(1): 97–124.

Boyd, C. L., Epstein, L., and Martin, A. D. (2010). "Untangling the Causal Effects of Sex on Judging." *American Journal of Political Science* 54: 389–411.

Cacioppo J. T., Fowler, J. H., and Christakis, N. A. (2009). "Alone in the Crowd: The Structure and Spread of Loneliness in a Large Social Network." *Journal of Personality and Social Psychology* 97(6): 977–991.

Christakis, N. A., and Fowler, J. H. (2007). "The Spread of Obesity in a Large Social Network over 32 Years." *New England Journal of Medicine* 357: 370–379.

Christakis, N. A., and Fowler, J. H. (2008). "The Collective Dynamics of Smoking in a Large Social Network." *New England Journal of Medicine* 358: 2249–2258.

Holland, P.W. (1986). "Statistics and Causal Inference." *Journal of the American Statistical Association* 81: 945–960.

Hong, G., and Raudenbush, S. (2006). "Evaluating Kindergarten Retention Policy." *Journal of the American Statistical Association* 202(475): 901–910.

Hudgens, M. G., and Halloran, M. E. (2008). "Toward Causal Inference with Interference." *Journal of the American Statistical Association* 103(482): 832–842.

Keele, L. (2015). "The Statistics of Causal Inference: A View from Political Methodology." *Political Analysis* 23(3): 313–335.

Morgan, S. L., and Winship, C. (2014). *Counterfactuals and Causal Inference.* New York: Cambridge University Press.

Nickerson, D. W. (2008). "Is Voting Contagious? Evidence from Two Field Experiments." *American Political Science Review* 102: 49–57.

Rogowski, J.C., and Sinclair, B. (2012). "Estimating the Causal Effects of Social Interaction with Endogeneous Networks." *Political Analysis* 20: 316–328.

Rubin, D. B. (1974). "Estimating Causal Effects of Treatments in Randomized and Nonrandomized Studies." *Journal of Educational Psychology* 6: 688–701.

Scholz, J. T., and Wang, C.-L. (2006). "Cooptation or Transformation? Local Policy Networks and Regulatory Enforcement." *American Journal of Political Science* 50: 81–97.

Sekhon, J. S. (2009). "Opiates for the Matches: Matching Methods for Causal Inference." *Annual Review of Political Science* 12: 487–508.

Shalizi, C. R., and Thomas, A. C. (2011). "Homophily and Contagion Are Generically Confounded in Observational Social Network Studies." *Sociological Methods and Research* 40: 211–239.

Sinclair, B. 2012. *The Social Citizen.* Chicago: University of Chicago Press.

Sinclair, B., McConnell, M., and Green, D. P. (2012). "Detecting Spillover Effects: Design and Analysis of Multilevel Experiments." *American Journal of Political Science* 56(4): 1055–1069.

Sovey, A. J., and Green, D. P. (2011). "Instrumental Variables Estimation in Political Science: A Reader's Guide." *American Journal of Political Science* 55:188–200.

Urbatsch, R. (2011). "Sibling Ideological Influence: A Natural Experiment." *British Journal of Political Science* 41: 693–712.

VanderWeele, T. J. (2011). "Sensitivity Analysis for Contagion Effects in Social Networks." *Sociology Methods Research* 40(2): 240–255.

VanderWeele T. J., and Arah, O. (2011). "Bias Formulas for Sensitivity Analysis of Unmeasured Confounding for General Outcomes, Treatments and Confounders." *Epidemiology* 22:42–52.

CHAPTER 6

....

NETWORK THEORY AND
POLITICAL SCIENCE

....

JOHN W. PATTY AND ELIZABETH MAGGIE PENN

NETWORK theory is a large tent: from early contributions such as Heider (1946), Harary and Norman (1953), Cartwright and Harary (1956), Davis (1963), and Granovetter (1973) (to list only a few), who worked in a sociological tradition with deep connections to social psychology, the field of "network theory" has grown to encompass all of the social sciences (Borgatti et al., 2009). The fundamental allure of network theory is its ability to describe and analyze the structure of connections between units (individuals, firms, states, parties, etc.) in a rigorous but flexible way. Given that most political phenomena involve collective action and thus interactions between multiple individuals, it is unsurprising that network theory is an active area of research in political science.[1] As indicated by the contents of this handbook, much of the research on political networks to date has been empirically motivated.

In this chapter we consider the role of network theory in the study of political phenomena, by which we mean the analytical theoretical basis of network analysis, as applied in political science.[2] Because the body of theoretical work to date on political networks is much smaller than its empirical complement, our chapter begins with a selection of network concepts around which we frame our discussion of the role of network theory in political science. For reasons of space and focus, we do not discuss applied models in which networks play a role.[3] Partly because there are relatively few such models to date, their commonality with this chapter generally begins and ends with the fact that they include a role for a network.

The main challenge of theoretical research on political networks is that network structures represent in a very literal sense the connective tissue that binds individual decision making and group behavior. Methodological individualism—the belief that the best units of analysis, whenever feasible, are individuals' decisions—is arguably the predominant paradigm in modern, empirical political science research, but the idea that groups may exert one or more forms of independent influences is also at least intuitively relevant for many political phenomena of interest.[4] We discuss the basic building blocks of network theory (nodes, edges, graphs) and their relationship to each other and empirical measurement in the second section.

Reliably measuring classic concepts such as culture, identity, influence, and power—not to mention then attempting to gauge the causal influence of such factors on individual behavior—ultimately requires a theory that can identify these concepts and isolate them from other environmental and individually determined factors. Network theory is particularly well-suited for precisely defining measures of group-based or structurally based concepts. In the third section we consider what we term "measurability" issues that one must confront when attempting to import classical network concepts into the study of political phenomena.

Of course many politically relevant networks are endogenously created from individuals' decisions about with whom to associate. In such situations, an important set of questions arises regarding *why* we observe the network structures that we do. Indeed, many such questions are relevant to identifying the causal impact of network structure. For example, *homophily* (the proclivity of individuals to interact more frequently with other individuals like themselves) is a fundamental issue confronting scholars attempting to identify the independent causal effects of a network. We consider a popular and flexible class of models of network formation in the fourth section.

A roadmap. While network theory is a common framework, the questions that it can be, and has been, applied to are numerous and varied—sometimes so varied as to obscure the common framework linking them. As many scholars in various fields have argued, the idea of a unifying *theory* of networks is both attractive and notoriously slippery; instead of there being a theory of networks, network concepts serve as unifying features of multiple theories in different fields (e.g., Salancik, 1995; Borgatti and Halgin, 2011). Thus in the first section we describe three such concepts: *centrality, community*, and *connectivity*. Applications of centrality rely at least partially on one or more means of ranking the actors within a network in terms of something akin to "power" or "influence." Community, on the other hand, considers the question of how the network indicates differences and commonalities between the actors. Concepts of connectivity link centrality and community by differentiating pairs of actors on the basis of their positions within the network.

In the second section we introduce the basic building blocks of network theory (nodes, edges, and graphs) and discuss the measurement role of these building blocks. Deciding what are (and are not) nodes and edges in a political network is the most fundamental theoretical action an analyst must take. We then use those basic building blocks to discuss how political networks are measured and characterized in the third section. Our discussion of measurement is structured around the concepts of centrality and community, and our focus is on the multiple ways that each of these two concepts have operationalized and employed. We then turn in the fourth section to one of the most active areas of work on network theory in political science: network formation. Finally, we offer some concluding thoughts in the fifth section. With this roadmap in hand, we now discuss the related concepts of centrality and community.

THREE CONCEPTS FROM NETWORK THEORY: CENTRALITY, COMMUNITY, AND CONNECTIVITY

Focusing our attention on two loose categories of network theory–based analysis allows us to speak more directly to the role of formal theory in the study of political networks. This is because, at least in the colloquial sense of the term "theory," analyses falling into either of the two categories are derived from a common theoretical basis. The residual vagueness within each of these categories of analysis illuminates the importance of rigorous, formal linkage between the network theory–based tools and the analyst's foundational theory of how the actors in the network behave.

Such a linkage is fundamental to the validity of any attempts to infer or extrapolate from the results of the empirical analysis. That is, our point is valid regardless of what paradigm of behavior the analyst chooses to work in. For example, our argument is independent of whether the analyst's theory is best described as a "rational choice," "agent-based," "behavioral," or "sociological" model. Rather, every network theory–based empirical tool is based upon multiple assumptions about what types of behaviors it will and will not distinguish between. That is, because all but the most trivial of networks are very high dimensional objects, any practical empirical analysis must aggregate, and hence partially lose some of, the information present in the actual data set. Formal theories of political networks provide the ability to precisely track exactly what information is, and what information isn't, lost in this operation (Patty and Penn, 2015).

Centrality

Perhaps the most common application of network theory in political science is to measure an actor's *centrality* within the group. Centrality has a long history within network theory, particularly as developed within sociology. The degree to which one actor is connected with other actors is broadly accepted—albeit with different interpretations and under varying guises—as one of the principal determinants of an actor's "influence" within a network. We defer a more detailed discussion of centrality measures theories (or, perhaps, arguments) linking centrality with influence, but it is useful to describe a few of the common premises of these theories. We revisit these arguments, and some of the accompanying measures of centrality below.

- *The more people you know, the better.* A fundamental measure of influence is how many people you "know" (or alternatively, how many people "know you"). There are many ways to measure how many people you know (or how many people know you), because there are a variety of ways to define indirect knowledge. As we discuss below, the more complicated measures of centrality along these lines attempt to account for the centralities of the people you know, because arguably people who know important people are more important themselves.

- *The more people you connect, the better.* An important family of centrality measures is derived from the notion of how many actors are connected *by* a particular individual.[5] The basic idea of these, the most widely used of which is known as *betweenness centrality*, is that the centrality of an actor is proportional to the degree that the network structure is more connected (or efficient at transmitting information) with the actor present in the network than it would be if the actor were removed from it.

Community

While a network in a sense presumes a group structure, a powerful application of network theory is detecting subgroups, or "communities," among the actors in the network. *Community detection* is accomplished using various tools, each based on different notions of why or how individuals form groups. A weakness of many of the tools is a lack of rigorous theoretical underpinnings. Jackson (2008) describes the situation as follows:

> [R]esearchers generally start with a simple algorithm for partitioning the nodes of a network, based on some heuristic, without a firm foundation in terms of defining what communities are, how they influence network formation, or why this algorithm is a natural way for uncovering them. Thus communities have tended to be defined as whatever the algorithms find rather than deriving the algorithms based on a well-defined notion of community.[6]

While community detection has many applications in political science,[7] it has not yet been widely implemented. Part of the reason for this is that these techniques are relatively new, made possible only by the fall in price of computational resources. A related (and more interesting) reason for this is that the proper notion of "community," not to mention how to detect it empirically, is an important and challenging theoretical problem that is (or should be) largely application driven. We return to these issues below and now turn to the concept of connectivity.

Connectivity

As discussed above, notions of community attempt to partition actors in a network into subgroups, and notions of centrality attempt to rank these actors according to how well connected they are. These two concepts are related to each other through the concept of *connectivity*, which is a dyadic (or higher order) phenomenon. For example, very central actors will typically be connected to many others, and actors within the same community will tend to be better (or more closely) connected than will actors in different communities. Before discussing the building blocks of network theory, we briefly discuss the concept of connectivity.

When considering two actors within a network, we can ask a number of key questions regarding how they are connected to each other. Three examples of such questions are listed here:

1. Are the actors connected to each other at all—does there exist a *path* of edges between the two actors?[8]
2. How long is the shortest path that connects the two actors?
3. How many independent paths are there between the two actors?

An actor that is connected to many other actors by short paths will both have a high centrality score under most centrality measures and be likely to be in lots of other actors' communities, however defined. Thus, an actor's own "connectivity" is clearly an element of both measures of centrality and notions of community. However, a related, complementary question is how important a given actor is (or would be) to establishing, or strengthening the, *connectivity between other pairs of actors*. A high-profile example of such a notion is that of a *bridge*: edges (or nodes) that, if they were removed from the network, would leave two or more actors no longer connected by any path.[9]

Bridges are very important in network theory whenever one is concerned with the global spread (or "contagion") of influence/action/information, and so forth throughout a network. Space precludes a fuller treatment of this topic, but it is worth mentioning precisely because of its potential applications in political science. Important and obvious examples of topics in which the connectivity of a network—and the sensitivity of this connectivity to "minor" alterations of the network—is of central concern include various security topics such as infiltrating terrorist and criminal networks (Krebs, 2002; Morselli et al., 2007), defending infrastructure networks from attack (Comfort and Haase, 2006; Lewis, 2014), and monitoring and controlling communicable diseases (Christakis and Fowler, 2010; Liu et al., 2012). Less obvious, but no less interesting, topics include the structural integrity of formal and informal organizations (Krackhardt, 1990; Fowler, 2006; Scholz et al., 2008; Grossmann and Dominguez, 2009; Berardo and Sholz, 2010; Leifeld and Schneider, 2012), strategic lobbying (Skinner et al., 2012), and monitoring and/or controlling informational flows in society (Enemark et al., 2014; Song and Eveland Jr., 2015).

THE BASIC BUILDING BLOCKS
OF NETWORK THEORY

A "political network" is simply a network that is somehow relevant to political outcomes, and the basics of any network are usually described with the tools of what we term "classical network theory." The theoretical foundation of classical network theory in the social sciences is *graph theory*,[10] which essentially describes and characterizes how *nodes* (or *vertices*) are connected by *edges*. A *graph*, then, is any collection of nodes, N, and a collection of edges, E, where each edge connects two distinct nodes.[11] Thus, an edge is typically written $e = (n_1, n_2)$, where n_1 and n_2 are distinct nodes in N, and e represents a connection "from" node n_1 "to" node n_2.[12] By distinguishing between the first and second nodes in an edge, this definition describes what are known as *directed* graphs. For any positive integer n, the set of all directed graphs on n nodes is denoted by G_n. This is the set of all possible networks between n actors. As discussed in the third section, it is important to remember from an empirical standpoint that within the confines of classical network theory, this set represents the entire space of "structures" that one can differentiate between.

The Basics of Measurement: Nodes and Edges

Graph theory is abstract and thus agnostic about what nodes and edges represent, but the decision about what they represent is the foundation of any theory of *political* networks. For example, in international relations, nodes are often nations, and edges are interactions such as trade or conflict. In political behavior, nodes are often individuals, and edges denote relationships such as trust or communication. In legislative studies, nodes are often legislators, and edges represent interactions such as cosponsoring legislation or serving on a common committee. In judicial politics, nodes might be written opinions, and edges represent citations. Even in the simplest of studies, the possible assignments of edges and nodes are at least seemingly unbounded.

This vastness becomes even more pronounced once one thinks more broadly and realizes that nodes and/or edges can be quite generally defined. For example, if one is studying legislative politics, one could represent each legislator and each piece of legislation as a separate node, so that there are two "types" of nodes. In such a representation, one can identify sponsorship of a bill by a legislator with an edge. Similarly, one could extend the set of edges to include a second "type" that exists between a legislator and a bill if that legislator voted in favor of the bill. While there are many examples of political networks, we refer to the nodes as individuals, or "actors," but this is only to keep the language simple.

Analysis: Within or Across Networks?

Many scholars have attempted to identify various "network effects" in political settings, and the methodological challenges of such attempts are both well-known and an area of active study (e.g., Fowler et al., 2011; Gentzkow and Shapiro, 2011; Noel and Nyhan, 2011; Klofstad et al., 2013; Campbell, 2013). While we refer the reader to other chapters (e.g., GROSS AND JANSA, ETC.) for discussions of many of the measurement, estimation, and inference challenges inherent to research on political networks, it is useful to note that some network theory concepts compare units such as nodes *within* a network, some allow comparison of two or more different networks, and some can be applied to either type of analysis. It is important to keep this variety in mind when employing network theory concepts: if a concept makes sense only at the network level,[13] then the theoretical underpinnings of a causal linkage between it and individual behaviors is necessarily different than the linkage between such behaviors and a concept that is measured at the node level (as are the concepts of centrality and community discussed in this chapter). Now we turn to what is arguably the most fundamental theoretical challenge facing a social scientist attempting to leverage network theory in empirical research: measuring and characterizing the structure of a network.

Measuring Networks

Measuring, or equivalently, representing networks is an important topic and presents two fundamental (and opposed) challenges for the applied researcher or analyst. The first of these challenges emanates from the fact that networks are "messy," as we describe below. This messiness precipitates the need for measures that impose structure on this messy set. The second challenge is that within the framework of classical network theory, the set of networks can differentiate between connections (i.e., edges) only in the most coarse way. We now discuss each of these challenges in turn.

The Messiness of Networks

We refer to networks as "messy" because, unlike real numbers, they do not have a natural ordering. The set of networks is qualitatively large in the sense that while one can enumerate every possible network structure for a given set of actors, there is no unambiguously correct way to organize or categorize them. Accordingly, a large body of theoretical work on networks focuses on creating functions that organize them, a limited selection of which we discuss in more detail below. Any of these functions eliminates some of the messiness of the relevant set of networks and accordingly loses some of the information contained in the networks' structures (e.g., Patty and Penn, 2015).

This loss of information is necessary in much applied work on networks, because the analyst is typically interested in (one or more) "network effects" that are essentially unidimensional. Just a few examples are Ward (2006) (examining the effect of several network centrality measures on nations' successful pursuit of sustainability practices); Victor and Ringe (2009) (exploring the correlations between legislators' connectedness and centrality measures and other characteristics such as seniority, race, and gender in the US House of Representatives); and Pelc (2014) (utilizing Katz centrality to measure the value assigned to a case as precedent in subsequent disputes in the World Trade Organization). In these applications, an interpretable and portable measure of a node's "location" in the relevant network is needed to advance to empirical analysis. To do this, it is impractical to "shove a network into the regression." These approaches all utilize some form of data reduction.

Many data reduction approaches to measuring and characterizing networks implicitly rely on some notion of *structural equivalence*, due to White (1970). Structural equivalence is an identification concept that posits that a network's "effect" on any of its embedded actors should be measurable with respect to the (local) structure of the network within which that actor is embedded. That is, *ceteris paribus*, if two actors in a network are identical in all individual respects *and* their local neighborhoods within the network are equivalent, then they should behave/choose in identical ways.[14] There is some understandable ambiguity (or perhaps flexibility) in this notion, inherited from the idea of "neighborhood." For example, suppose the two actors are directly connected to similar sets of other individuals, but the actors to whom these "first-order connections" are connected (i.e., the actors' "second-order connections") differ significantly between the two actors: Are the actors structurally equivalent to each other?

Recent work is increasingly bringing multiple aspects of network theory to bear on applied questions. For example, Patty et al. (2013) combine community detection and a new, axiomatically derived scoring algorithm (Schnakenberg and Penn, 2014) to provide estimates of the weight assigned by the US Supreme Court to its own precedents.

Of course, "how big is one's neighborhood?" is a theoretical question, based on a consideration of the phenomena of interest. For example, does interaction between the actors occur in a sequential, or a simultaneous, fashion? If interaction is sequential, how many rounds of interaction occur?[15] The proper answers to these questions depend on the realities at hand: applied network theory is necessarily data-informed theory.

The Coarseness of (Classical) Networks

Classical network theory is based on a binary representation of connections. Between any two actors, an edge either exists or it doesn't. While the notion of a weighted graph—where each edge e is assigned a number, w_e[16]—obviously relaxes this constraint to some degree, this relaxation is not complete, because it assumes that the edges can be ordered by this weight.[17] For reasons of space, we restrict attention to classical, unweighted networks, and now proceed to consider some measures of centrality that are employed in the analysis of political networks.

A Menagerie of Measures: Centrality, Power, and Influence

The notion of centrality is one of the most commonly applied concepts in the study of political networks. This is partly because centrality is often loosely equated with power, an equating that is often justified by the presumption that "links" are desirable or at the very least denote some form of influence.

Unsurprisingly, there are numerous measures of centrality. In line with the focus of this chapter, we discuss some of the more commonly employed measures, but omit a detailed accounting of how they have been used in the empirical study of political networks. Instead, we describe several of the measures so as to illustrate the differences in their theoretical foundations. These foundations have been explored by many scholars (e.g., Freeman, 1979; Bonacich, 1987; Friedkin, 1991; Monsuur and Storcken, 2004; Borgatti and Everett, 2006; and Boldi and Vigna, 2014). Space constraints require our discussion to be simply an introduction to the theoretical connections and distinctions between these measures, so we refer the interested reader to the literature cited here and throughout the chapter for more details.

Degree Centrality. The most fundamental, and most commonly used, measure of centrality is known as *degree centrality*. There are two notions of degree centrality in a directed network: *in-degree* and *out-degree*. In-degree is the number of (other) nodes *from* which an edge extends *to* the node in question, and out-degree is the number of nodes *to* which an edge extends *from* the node in question. The relevance of each these measures of centrality is obvious: a person's in-degree measures how many people "talk to" him or her, and a person's out-degree measures how many "listen to" him or her. Neither in-degree nor out-degree is inherently more relevant than the other, because the definition of "speaker" and "listener" is arbitrary. Nonetheless, the fact that "speaker" and "listener" can represent very different roles is fundamental.

Degree centrality is both incredibly easy to compute and simple to understand. These virtues come at significant costs, of course. In particular, degree centrality is a strictly "local" measure of an actor's centrality. In particular, an actor's degree centrality is completely insensitive to the structure of the network among other actors. That is, whether two other actors j and k are connected does not affect the degree centrality of a third actor i.[18]

Eigenvector Centrality. Almost as obvious as the relevance of degree centrality is its principal weakness: neither notion of degree centrality is responsive to the identities of the other nodes to which a node is connected. This weakness is partially addressed by the notion of *eigenvector centrality*, which is due to Bonacich (1972) (see also Bonacich, 1987, 2007). The basic idea of eigenvector centrality is that the centrality of an actor is positively associated with the centralities of the actors to whom the actor is connected. In other words, eigenvector centrality is *self-referential*—in particular, "important people know important people." More formally, this is one example of a *spectral measure* (e.g., Vigna, 2009), a class of measures that includes several other prominent measures of centrality, including the PageRank algorithm (Page et al., 1999), the hyperlink-induced topic search (HITS) measure (Kleinberg, 1999), Katz centrality (Katz, 1953), and the Kendall-Wei method (Wei, 1952; Kendall, 1955). Though these measures are increasingly being employed in the empirical analysis of networks (e.g., Fowler and

Jeon, 2008; Gray and Potter, 2012), their theoretical foundations in the context of political networks remain unexplored.[19]

Betweenness Centrality. Both degree centrality and eigenvector centrality measure how many actors a given actor is connected to. Betweenness centrality (Freeman, 1977) considers *how many actors are connected to each other by a given actor.* Thus, betweenness centrality partially captures the notion that an actor's centrality is based on how many other actors "need" that actor to communicate or interact with them. An important characteristic of betweenness centrality is that one actor's betweenness centrality can be sensitive to connections between *other* pairs of actors—something that distinguishes this concept from degree centrality. Because of these properties of the measure, it has been used in empirical research on influence in informal policy and issue networks (e.g., Scholz et al., 2008; Skinner et al., 2012).

Closeness Centrality. Closeness centrality (first defined by Bavelas, 1948, 1950) measures, in essence, how many "steps" it would take to get from one actor to every other actor. It is a particularly useful notion of centrality in informational networks, because longer paths require more time to traverse and involve more risk of information loss. Accordingly, it has been employed in some empirical studies of political networks (e.g., Koger et al., 2009). A problem with closeness centrality is that it is ambiguous how to best define it for "unconnected" networks in which there exists some pair of actors for which there is no path of edges connecting the two actors. A second weakness of the measure, shared with degree centrality, is that it assigns all actors equal weight. That is, unlike eigenvector centrality, closeness centrality is not self-referential. That said, closeness centrality does capture more of the structure of the network than does degree centrality.

A Melting Pot of Measures. Each of the measures described above has intuitive appeal, but to be clear, the theoretical foundations in political networks are frequently murky. After all, regardless of the centrality measure one chooses, it is unclear in what types of situations one would seek to maximize one's own centrality when forming a network. For example, focusing on eigenvector centrality for a moment, it is clear that being connected with other "well-connected people" can be advantageous in some situations (e.g., situations involving the exchange of goods or information), undesirable in others (e.g., situations involving the exchange of disease), or ambiguous from an a priori perspective (e.g., situations involving violence or coercion).

Part of this murkiness is due to theoretical incompleteness; a model of the preferences and incentives of, and actions available to, the actors within the network is needed to more precisely adjudicate what the various centrality measures "mean" in the context in which they are being employed. But even with a fully specified theory of the actors' behaviors, the panoply of centrality measures is indicative of a fundamental ambiguity in the notion of centrality that mirrors that of the concept of power (e.g., Bachrach and Baratz, 1962): the different measures vary because centrality is inherently a multifaceted concept. Working through the primitives of the situation being examined is a good first step toward understanding the relative strengths and weaknesses of each of the various measures.

From a purely theoretical angle, work should continue on characterizing what it is that the various centrality measures are actually measuring. Deriving *axiomatic foundations* of existing measures—that is, determining the general properties of the various measures, as well as possibly deriving new ones from desirable properties—will allow a precise and general characterization that can be used to more clearly and reliably choose which measure to use in different applications. In general, we concur with Boldi and Vigna (2014), who describe the value of axiomatic development as follows:

> [E]ven if one does not believe [the axioms] are really so discriminative or necessary, they provide a very specific, formal, provable piece of information about a centrality measure that is much more precise than folklore intuitions such as "this centrality is really correlated to indegree" or "this centrality is really fooled by cliques."[20]

The use of centrality measures (and indeed, many network theory concepts) in empirical work is currently (at least in appearance) based on ad hoc matching of algorithm with theoretical concept or construct. This is a classic issue of measurement: the analyst is typically attempting to ferret out a latent construct from messy and coarse empirical data. This is a difficult job, and it will be rare for a perfect measure to exist. But the current state of theoretical work offers little help in this challenge. Hopefully this will not always be the case. We now turn to a related, but distinct, empirical challenge: measuring and identifying groups within a network.

A Cornucopia of Classifications: Communities, Cliques, and Groups

Whereas centrality is generally equated with power in the study of political networks, the notion of over whom one has power—that is, something like a "group"—is left unaddressed by the centrality measures discussed previously. The problem of identifying the (sub)group structure within a network is one of *classification*, assigning each node to one (or occasionally, more than one) set of nodes. It almost goes without saying that there are many applications for estimating the group structure within a political network.

Cohesion and Structural Equivalence. Two theoretical notions commonly relied on in deriving measures of groups are structural equivalence, mentioned previously, and *cohesion* (e.g., Burt, 1978, 1987; Friedkin, 1984; White and Harary, 2001; Moody and White, 2003). Just as with centrality, there are a variety of formal definitions of each of these concepts. Loosely put, a method of grouping nodes is based on the principle of cohesion, to the degree that two nodes are more likely to be grouped together if there are more paths between them. A grouping method is based on the principle of structural equivalence, insofar as it is more likely to group two nodes together if the nodes occupy similar positions in the network. To make the distinction between these concepts clear, note that two nodes might be grouped together under the principle of structural equivalence even if there exists no path between them, but this would not be the case under a cohesion-based method.

Cliques. The strongest notion of a subgroup within a network, and the heart of cohesion-based measures of groups, is that of a *clique* (Luce and Perry, 1949): a maximally completely connected subgraph within the network or a group of nodes that are directly connected with each other such that there is no other node to which all of the members of the group are each connected as well.[21] Figure 6.1 illustrates this concept.

The notion of a clique is useful as a baseline theoretical standpoint for two reasons. First, a clique is clearly a well-defined group: if a clique within a network is not a group, then it is not clear what structure within the network would constitute a group.[22] Second, the notion can serve as the basis for imputing or estimating latent group structures. This is because the clique is a generalization of the idea of *triadic closure* (Heider, 1946; Granovetter, 1973), a sociological concept that posits that a collection of three individuals will rarely possess exactly two connections.

That said, while representing a clear theoretical baseline, figure 6.1 illustrates why the notion of a clique is arguably too demanding. From a theoretical standpoint, cliques are "fragile," and as a result, large cliques (e.g., containing more than three or four members) are typically rare in empirical networks. Comparing graph (A) in figure 6.1 with graph (B), the removal of a single edge not only destroyed the clique of five nodes, but created two (overlapping) cliques of four nodes. Perhaps more disturbingly from a fragility

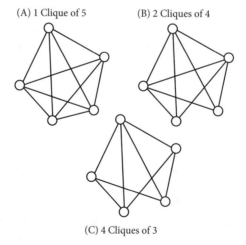

(A) 1 Clique of 5   (B) 2 Cliques of 4

(C) 4 Cliques of 3

FIGURE 6.1 Illustration of a Clique and Its Fragility.

perspective, removal of a second edge, as in graph (C), destroys both cliques of four and results in four overlapping cliques of three nodes.

In addition to their fragility, cliques are arguably of limited interest from a social science perspective because all cliques have identical "internal" structure: every member of any clique is connected to every other member of that clique. Accordingly, using clique as the definition of a "group" leaves nothing to differentiate between groups other than their sizes. Unless one believes that there is only a single dimension along which groups vary, this reality implies that from a networks perspective, the set of groups is richer, and hence larger, than the set of cliques. Because of these weaknesses of the notion of a clique, various relaxations of the notion have been proposed. We now discuss a few of these.

Generalizing Cliques: Clans and Plexes. Any systematic generalization of the notion of a clique requires a choice about how to measure how similar to a clique any given subgraph is. We briefly describe three different notions of similarity and how they are used to define groups in a way that is similar to, but more expansive than that of, a clique.[23]

1. *k-cliques.* A clique of n nodes is a (maximal) subgraph in which each pair of nodes is connected by a shortest path of length 1. Thus, one notion of how similar a subgroup is to a clique is the maximum distance between any pair of nodes in the underlying graph (Luce, 1950). To see the nesting of the notion of a clique within that of a k-clique, note that the set of 1-cliques is identical to the set of cliques.

2. *k-clans.* For $k > 1$, a k-clique can induce a subgraph that is itself disconnected. To correct for this possibility, the notion of a *k-clan* refines the set of k-cliques as follows. A set of nodes is a k-clan if and only if it is a k-clique such that each node in the k-clan has a maximal distance of no more than k *using only nodes within the k-clan* (Alba, 1973). Because every k-clan is a k-clique, it follows that a set of nodes is a 1-clan if and only if it is a clique.

3. *k-plexes.* Note that a clique of n nodes has the following property: each of the n nodes possesses a link with each of the other $n-1$ nodes. Accordingly, one family of subgraphs that is "close" to a clique on n nodes is the family of subgraphs on n nodes, such that each of the nodes is connected to at least $n-2$ of the other nodes. More generally, a *k-plex* consisting of n nodes is a subgraph in which each of the n nodes is connected to at least $n-k$ of the other nodes (Seidman and Foster 1978). As with k-cliques and k-clans, a 1-plex is a clique, and vice versa.[24]

Repeating a common refrain in this chapter, there remains much work to be done in terms of linking community-classification concepts such as cliques, clans, and plexes with various political environments. As with the centrality measures described above, the various approaches to community classification capture different dimensions of a "group," so the proper choice will vary across different political networks, and determining what the proper choice(s) are will be aided by explicitly modeling the individual interactions within the network.

While cliques, clans, and plexes are not yet widely used in political network research, a related approach—latent space models—has attracted some attention.[25]

Latent Spaces. While many community detection algorithms conceive of groups as discrete objects (possibly allowing individuals to have partial, continuous "memberships" in these groups), one can also conceive of actors as being embedded in a space that can then be used to define or infer group structures. These approaches, known as *latent space models* (see Hoff et al., 2002 and Ward et al., 2013 for an application to trade), attempt to describe the nodes as positions in a space such that nodes that are closer to each other in the space are more likely to be connected by an edge.[26]

Communities. Another notion utilized in group classification is that of a *community* (e.g., Radicchi et al., 2004; Clauset, 2005; Porter et al., 2007; Fortunato, 2010). Generally speaking, whereas clique-based approaches to group classification focus almost exclusively on the internal structure of a group,[27] community-based approaches attempt to incorporate information about both the internal structure and external connections of the group. As Radicchi et al. (2004) describe it, "a community is defined as a subset of nodes within the graph such that connections between the nodes are denser than connections with the rest of the network."[28] This type of approach has attracted some attention in political science (e.g., Zhang et al., 2008), but has to date been developed in largely atheoretical ways, focusing on the computational time and complexity of various algorithms more than on the linkage between the algorithms and the underlying nature of the data being examined.

Different Notions, Different Purposes

Historically, approaches to measurement of network concepts such as centrality and groups have been derived from (often informal) theoretical arguments that, owing to the interdisciplinary interest in and origins of network analysis, come from widely varying starting points. An important task for scholars of political networks is to revisit and reconsider preexisting network measures in order to better link them with the scholars' goals and the theoretical underpinnings of the phenomena being studied. In other words, while it is tempting to pull these ready-made measures off the shelf, this temptation should be resisted at least temporarily. While a "kitchen sink" approach that throws many preexisting measures at a data set might be useful in early explorations of *new* data, the productivity of such an approach is directly tied to the degree to which the scholar is aware of the theoretical foundations of the different measures. Uncovering the foundations (i.e., characterizing the properties) of preexisting measures has recently begun attracting attention (e.g., Borgatti, 2005; Borgatti and Everett, 2006; Borgatti et al., 2006; and Lubell et al., 2012). While there remains much to be done, this is particularly true with respect to linking the properties and foundations of network concepts with the incentives and behaviors within political settings.

Models of Network Formation

Scholars have long realized that to the degree that political networks affect outcomes, the formation of such networks will not be completely random. Accordingly, scholars have examined how political networks are formed and sustained (e.g., Chaharbaghi et al., 2005; Rogowski and Sinclair, 2012; Eveland et al., 2013). Similarly, scholars have started to grapple with the reality that many political and social networks are impossible to directly observe, motivating the development of tools to detect or estimate such networks (e.g., Cranmer and Desmarais, 2011; Heaney, 2014; Box-Steffensmeier and Christenson, 2014, 2015). Linking these two strands of work, of course, is the need for a theory of how networks form. This arguably represents the area of work in political networks that is currently experiencing the most active and fertile mixing of theoretical and empirical insights. In this section we discuss the two most prevalent approaches to modeling network formation, random graph theory and exponential random graph models.

Random Graph Theory

Given the unstructured nature of most sets of networks, obtaining and describing general theoretical results about networks was arguably made possible only by the conceptualization of the "random graph" (Erdős and Réyni, 1959). Random graph theory allows one to establish well-defined likelihoods of encountering any given feature in a network. Accordingly, it serves as the theoretical baseline of inference (i.e., the canonical "null hypothesis") when addressing questions about how networks form.

The canonical random graph model is known as the *Poisson random graph model*,[29] which is parameterized by two numbers: the number of nodes, n, and a probability of connection, $p \in (0, 1)$. The model assumes that p represents the probability of any pair of distinct nodes being connected by an edge, and that the realization of any given edge $e = (n_i, n_j)$ is independent of whether any other edge, $e' = (n_k, n_m)$ is realized. This model then induces a probability distribution over the set of all graphs on n nodes, G_n.

From a social science perspective, the Poisson random graph model is best viewed as a starting point. More specifically, for scholars attempting to infer the influence of various factors on the observed structure of political networks, random graph establishes the classic null hypothesis, because the distribution of truly random graphs is arguably the predicted distribution if the network structure is independent of all the factors under consideration.

The pure theory of random graphs is only a "starting point," because one might find that an empirical distribution of network structures that differs from "random" is also independent of any of the factors one is studying, but the fact that one does not necessarily know the distribution of "errors" (i.e., factors outside the model) is generally true in statistical analysis of observational data.

Exponential Random Graph Models (ERGMs)

A popular and tractable family of models of network formation is the exponential random graph model, or ERGM. First described by Frank and Strauss (1986), the ERGM approach refers to a category of random graph models that provide a richer parameterization than, and thus subsumes, the Poisson random graph model. While space precludes an in-depth presentation of the details of the ERGM approach,[30] a brief outline of the structure of this approach is useful when considering how it has been, and can be, applied to political networks.

The parameters of an ERGM can be broken down into two basic categories. The first is *structural parameters*, which characterize the probability of different graph structures without reference to the labels/identities of the actors/nodes themselves. Two classic examples of such parameters in a directed graph are (1) the probability, for any randomly drawn pair of nodes i and j, that i will be connected to j *and* that j will *not* be connected to i; and (2) the probability, for any randomly drawn pair of nodes i and j, that i will be connected to j *and* that j *will* be connected to i. The first probability measures the likelihood of asymmetrical relationships in the network, and the second probability measures the likelihood of symmetrical relationships. One can easily extend this to include additional probabilities for the occurrence of more complicated subgraphs such as "two-in-stars," "two-mixed-stars," and so forth, as displayed in figure 6.2.

The parameters in this category are classically "network-focused" and thus apolitical. Nonetheless, they can be used for exploratory analysis. A common example of this is high-order structures, such as triads: mutual connections among three distinct nodes.[31] Because the triad is the simplest example of higher-order interdependence, examining its impact and emergence is arguably the starting point of true *network* analysis. Thus, while the political theory behind these parameters will often be vague, these parameters can be a useful starting point for establishing a reasonable suspicion that a network analysis (and ultimately, network-based theory) is specifically called for in the application at hand.

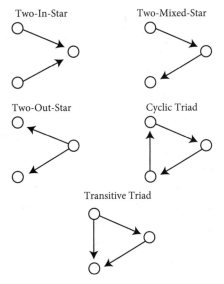

Two-In-Star

Two-Mixed-Star

Two-Out-Star

Cyclic Triad

Transitive Triad

FIGURE 6.2 Some Subgraph Structures.

While the first category differentiates between various network forms, the second category of parameters in an ERGM provides the structure for differential dependence between nodes based on the nodes' characteristics. For example, a social network analysis of cooperative behavior in a partisan legislature might allow the probability of cooperation between copartisans to be different from the probability of cooperation between members of differing parties. Obviously, analogous relationships emerge immediately when considering other political networks: how alliances affect conflict; how resources and factors of production affect trade; how factors such as religion, income, and education affect group membership decisions; and so forth. As always, the principal limitation on the number and complexity of factors that one can include in this category is the amount of data available.

This second category of parameters is arguably the focus of the political science within the political network being examined. Accordingly, it is important to note that these parameters should be derived from an explicit theory. In any event, the decision of which these to include (and how to include them) represents one or more important theoretical choices regarding the phenomenon being studied. In line with the discussion of measures of centrality and group classification, a key need in this area is more work modeling the preferences and behaviors that undergird the formation of political networks, so that explicit linkages between such micro-foundations and statistical models of network formation such as ERGMs can be derived.

Conclusion: One Theory, Many Directions

Network theory is multifaceted and can be applied in many seemingly disparate ways. This is, of course, one of the most powerful appeals of network theory to social scientists. This general applicability represents a challenge as well: the notion of a political network links a menagerie of ancillary concepts and tools, so it is important to remember where these tools come from. Even for the empirically focused researcher, paying attention to "pure network theory" questions is important. Most obviously, such attention helps assure that the assumptions and conditions undergirding the network-based empirical tools being employed are consistent with the researcher's theoretical explanation. More subtly, when multiple network-based empirical tools are employed, paying attention to the network theory undergirding them helps ensure that these tools are consistent with each other.

We have attempted to provide a quick tour through some of the theoretical challenges and opportunities in the study of political networks. Because of space constraints, we have regretfully omitted much that is of interest. In a sense, we have sought to provide a kind of rough roadmap to some of the more widely applied network theory concepts, such as centrality, community, and connectivity. In so doing, we have attempted to illustrate a few directions in which these concepts can be developed. Broadly speaking, we see two areas of work as being particularly important in the coming years.

First, when empirically studying political networks, we need to spend more time considering *how* the data were generated: What do the nodes and edges represent? Why did we collect (or why are we using) *these* data? What are the incentives of the actors within the network? How could the network be altered? If the network is estimated from behavior, the answer to this question—the ultimate goal of policy prescriptions, for example—depends on the incentives of the actors themselves as well as the arsenal of policy levers that can be feasibly altered.

Second, many network concepts and measures are themselves relatively undertheorized, particularly as applied to political settings. That is, aside from intuition and occasionally some computational experimentation, many of the algorithms and approaches to quantifying and classifying concepts such as centrality, power, community, groups, and similarity have poorly understood theoretical foundations and properties. A key challenge is to develop these foundations and articulate the properties in a fashion that can be readily used by the empirically minded scholar of political networks.

Notes

1. Recent reviews of applications of network theory in political science range from the general (e.g., Lazer, 2011; Ward et al., 2011) to more substantively focused reviews such as Huckfeldt (2009) (American politics); Siegel (2011a) (comparative politics); Hafner-Burton et al. (2009) (international relations); and Fowler et al. (2007) (judicial politics).

2. Due to space constraints, we largely omit any discussion of political networks in other disciplines (primarily sociology). This is not intended as a judgment on the quality of such work, much of which is fascinating. Rather, a proper description of the theoretical challenges and opportunities faced by work in the traditions outside of modern political science would have a different focus due to the fields' varying reliance on concepts more closely associated with political science and economics, such as methodological individualism and revealed preference.

3. Some recent examples of such models in political science journals are Volden et al. (2008); Pierskalla (2009); Siegel (2009, 2011b, 2013); Baybeck et al. (2011); and Patty and Penn (2014).

4. A few recent thoughtful considerations of these issues from a variety of perspectives are List and Pettit (2011); Peters (2011); List and Spiekermann (2013); and Zahle and Collin (2014).

5. The most famous popular example of this concept, of course, is the "six degrees of Kevin Bacon."

6. Jackson (2008, 446).

7. A few examples are (1) detecting factions within political parties using legislator behaviors, (2) estimating informal coalitions among interest groups using endorsements, (3) examining linkages between agencies using rule-making and advisory panel collaboration, and (4) detecting issue linkages between campaign contributors using campaign donation data.

8. In a directed network, one can further ask whether there exists a path from each actor to the other.

9. Nearly equivalent is the notion of a *structural hole* (Burt 2009)—an edge that, when present, creates a bridge between two or more actors.

10. We provide the barest of descriptions here, due to space constraints. An excellent textbook treatment of these topics designed for social science applications is provided by Jackson (2008).

11. Technically, an edge could connect more than two nodes; such a graph is sometimes referred to as a *hypergraph*. Similarly, an edge could connect a node to itself, known as a "self-loop." These extensions raise interesting possibilities (and a few challenges), but they are currently relatively infrequently employed in the study of political networks, which is why we exclude them from our notion of "classical network theory."

12. It is not uncommon to assign "weights" to various edges in order to distinguish between ties of varying (say) intensities, frequencies, or importance. We revisit this possibility below, but we generally constrain the discussion to the classical case of unweighted graphs.

13. Examples of such concepts include density and clustering coefficient (e.g., Newman, 2010, 134 and 199).

14. Of course, that might be probabilistically identical.

15. This seemingly simple question can become complicated rather quickly in general networks, because one can vary "rules of interaction" such as whether interaction can occur between a given dyad multiple times.

16. Weights are typically (but not always) between zero and one.

17. Multigraphs—in which two nodes can be connected by multiple connections—are another direction for generalization (not to mention weighted multigraphs), but these have not been commonly employed in political science.

18. This point is discussed in more detail in Patty and Penn (2015), who leverage this property of degree centrality to illustrate the value of taking an axiomatic approach to describing and classifying networks and other examples of "big data."

19. For comparisons between spectral measures and other measures of centrality, see Perra and Fortunato (2008).
20. Boldi and Vigna (2014, 237).
21. For a graph $G = (N, E)$ and any subset of the nodes, $M \subseteq N$, the subgraph induced by M is denoted by G_M and defined as $G_M = (M, E_M)$, where E_M contains exactly those edges $e' \in E$ such that both ends of e' are elements of M. A subgraph G_M is maximally completely connected if it is completely connected (every node in M is connected to every other node in M by an edge in E) and, for any strict superset of M, $M' \supset M$, $G_{M'}$ is not completely connected.
22. This presumes, in line with our discussion in the second section, that the choice of how to represent edges between nodes is sensible. In particular, if edges represent more than one type of connection, then one clique in the resulting network might be very different than another in qualitative terms. But this is not a problem with the notion of a clique, it is a problem with the utilized definition of an edge in the network under examination.
23. For more on these notions, as well as that of a k-club, see Mokken (1979).
24. Closely related to the notion of a k-plex is that of a k-core, which is a maximal subgraph such that each node is connected to at least k of the other nodes in the subgraph (Seidman, 1983).
25. Within the study of political networks, this attention is motivated by at least two facts. First, some kind of latent space model is necessary for the classic visualization of a network as a graph (e.g., Brandes et al., 1999) and, second, the spatial model (e.g., Davis et al., 1970) has a long history in modern political science.
26. Thus, latent space models can be loosely thought of as complementary to approaches such as exponential random graph models (ERGMs), discussed below. While approaches like ERGMs take exogenous attributes of the nodes and attempt to estimate the effect of these attributes on the probability of edges between any pair of nodes, the latent space model takes the edges as given and attempts to construct a set of attributes (coordinates in the latent space) that would be most compatible with an ERGM-style approach based on these estimated locations.
27. Typically, the only "external" requirement is that the subgraph induced by the group be maximal with respect to the desired internal structure property.
28. Radicchi et al. (2004, 2658).
29. See Jackson (2008, 9–14) for an accessible treatment of this framework.
30. And even if space were not a constraint, there are already multiple primers on the ERGM approach. For example, an excellent introduction to this family of models is provided by Robins et al. (2007), who update the primer offered by Anderson et al. (1999).
31. There is one such structure for undirected networks—the triangle—and five for directed networks.

REFERENCES

Alba, R. D. (1973). "A Graph-Theoretic Definition of a Sociometric Clique." *Journal of Mathematical Sociology* 3(1): 113–126.
Anderson, C. J., Wasserman, S., and Crouch, B. (1999). "A p∗ Primer: Logit Models for Social Networks." *Social Networks* 21(1): 37–66.
Bachrach, P., and Baratz, M. S. (1962). "Two Faces of Power." *American Political Science Review* 56(4): 947–952.

Bavelas, A. (1948). "A Mathematical Model for Group Structures." *Human Organization* 7(3): 16–30.

Bavelas, A. (1950). "Communication Patterns in Task-Oriented Groups." *Journal of the Acoustical Society of America* 22: 725–730.

Baybeck, B., Berry, W. D., and Siegel, D. A. (2011). "A Strategic Theory of Policy Diffusion via Intergovernmental Competition." *Journal of Politics* 73(1): 232–247.

Berardo, R., and Scholz, J. T. (2010). "Self-organizing Policy Networks: Risk, Partner Selection, and Cooperation in Estuaries." *American Journal of Political Science* 54(3): 632–649.

Boldi, P., and Vigna, S. (2014). "Axioms for Centrality." *Internet Mathematics* 10(3–4): 222–262.

Bonacich, P. (1972). "Factoring and Weighting Approaches to Status Scores and Clique Identification." *Journal of Mathematical Sociology* 2(1): 113–120.

Bonacich, P. (1987). "Power and Centrality: A Family of Measures." *American Journal of Sociology* 92(5): 1170–1182.

Bonacich, P. (2007). "Some Unique Properties of Eigenvector Centrality." *Social Networks* 29(4): 555–564.

Borgatti, S. P. (2005). "Centrality and Network Flow." *Social Networks* 27(1): 55–71.

Borgatti, S. P., Carley, K. M., and Krackhardt, D. (2006). "On the Robustness of Centrality Measures under Conditions of Imperfect Data." *Social Networks* 28(2): 124–136.

Borgatti, S. P., and Everett, M. G. (2006). "A Graph-Theoretic Perspective on Centrality." *Social Networks* 28(4): 466–484.

Borgatti, S. P., and Halgin, D. S. (2011). "On Network Theory." *Organization Science* 22(5): 1168–1181.

Borgatti, S. P., Mehra, A., Brass, D. J., and Labianca, G. (2009). "Network Analysis in the Social Sciences." *Science* 323(5916): 892.

Box-Steffensmeier, J. M., and Christenson, D. P. (2014). "The Evolution and Formation of Amicus Curiae Networks." *Social Networks* 36: 82–96.

Box-Steffensmeier, J. M., and Christenson, D. P. (2015). "Comparing Membership Interest Group Networks Across Space and Time, Size, Issue, and Industry." *Network Science* 3(1): 78–97.

Brandes, U., Kenis, P., Raab, J., Schneider, V., and Wagner, D. (1999). "Explorations into the Visualization of Policy Networks." *Journal of Theoretical Politics* 11(1): 75–106.

Burt, R. S. (1978). "Cohesion versus Structural Equivalence as a Basis for Network Subgroups." *Sociological Methods & Research* 7(2): 189–212.

Burt, R. S. (1987). "Social Contagion and Innovation: Cohesion versus Structural Equivalence." *American Journal of Sociology* 92(6): 1287–1335.

Burt, R. S. (2009). *Structural Holes: The Social Structure of Competition.* Cambridge, MA: Harvard University Press.

Campbell, D. E. (2013). "Social Networks and Political Participation." *Annual Review of Political Science* 16: 33–48.

Cartwright, D., and Harary, F. (1956). "Structural Balance: A Generalization of Heider's Theory." *Psychological Review* 63(5): 277.

Chaharbaghi, K., Adcroft, A., Willis, R., Todeva, E., and Knoke, D. (2005). "Strategic Alliances and Models of Collaboration." *Management Decision* 43(1): 123–148.

Christakis, N. A., and Fowler, J. H. (2010). "Social Network Sensors for Early Detection of Contagious Outbreaks." *PLOS ONE* 5(9): e12948.

Clauset, A. (2005). "Finding Local Community Structure in Networks." *Physical Review E* 72(2): 026132.

Comfort, L. K., and Haase, T. W. (2006). "Communication, Coherence, and Collective Action: The Impact of Hurricane Katrina on Communications Infrastructure." *Public Works Management & Policy* 10(4): 328–343.

Cranmer, S. J., and Desmarais, B. A. (2011). "Inferential Network Analysis with Exponential Random Graph Models." *Political Analysis* 19(1): 66–86.

Davis, J. A. (1963). "Structural Balance, Mechanical Solidarity, and Interpersonal Relations." *American Journal of Sociology* 68(4): 444–462.

Davis, O., Hinich, M., and Ordeshook, P. (1970). "An Expository Development of a Mathematical Model of the Electoral Process." *American Political Science Review* 64(2): 426–448.

Enemark, D., McCubbins, M. D., and Weller, N. (2014). "Knowledge and Networks: An Experimental Test of How Network Knowledge Affects Coordination." *Social Networks* 36: 122–133.

Erdős, P., and Rényi, A. (1959). "On Random Graphs." *Publicationes Mathematicae Debrecen* 6: 290–297.

Eveland, W. P., Jr., Hutchens, M. J., and Morey, A. C. (2013). "Political Network Size and Its Antecedents and Consequences." *Political Communication* 30(3): 371–394.

Fortunato, S. (2010). "Community Detection in Graphs." *Physics Reports* 486(3–5): 75–174.

Fowler, J. H. (2006). "Connecting the Congress: A Study of Cosponsorship Networks." *Political Analysis* 14(4): 456–487.

Fowler, J. H., Heaney, M. T., Nickerson, D. W., Padgett, J. F., and Sinclair, B. (2011). "Causality in Political Networks." *American Politics Research* 39(2): 437–480.

Fowler, J. H., and Jeon, S. (2008). "The Authority of Supreme Court Precedent." *Social Networks* 30(1): 16–30.

Fowler, J. H., Johnson, T. R., Spriggs, J. F., II, Jeon, S., and Wahlbeck, P. J. (2007). "Network Analysis and the Law: Measuring the Legal Importance of Supreme Court Precedents." *Political Analysis* 15(3): 324–346.

Frank, O., and Strauss, D. (1986). "Markov Graphs." *Journal of the American Statistical Association* 81(395): 832–842.

Freeman, L. C. (1977). "A Set of Measures of Centrality Based on Betweenness." *Sociometry* 40(1): 35–41.

Freeman, L. C. (1979). "Centrality in Social Networks: Conceptual Clarification." *Social Networks* 1(3): 215–239.

Friedkin, N. E. (1984). "Structural Cohesion and Equivalence Explanations of Social Homogeneity." *Sociological Methods & Research* 12(3): 235–261.

Friedkin, N. E. (1991). "Theoretical Foundations for Centrality Measures." *American Journal of Sociology* 96(6): 1478–1504.

Gentzkow, M., and Shapiro, J. M. (2011). "Ideological Segregation Online and Offline." *Quarterly Journal of Economics* 126(4): 1799–1839.

Granovetter, M. S. (1973). "The Strength of Weak Ties." *American Journal of Sociology* 78(6): 1360–1380.

Gray, J., and Potter, P. B. K. (2012). "Trade and Volatility at the Core and Periphery of the Global Economy." *International Studies Quarterly* 56(4): 793–800.

Grossmann, M., and Dominguez, C, B. K. (2009). "Party Coalitions and Interest Group Networks." *American Politics Research* 37(5): 767–800.

Hafner-Burton, E. M., Kahler, M., and Montgomery, A. H. (2009). "Network Analysis for International Relations." *International Organization* 63(3): 559–592.

Harary, F., and Norman, R. Z. (1953). *Graph Theory as a Mathematical Model in Social Science.* Ann Arbor: University of Michigan Press.

Heaney, M. T. (2014). "Multiplex Networks and Interest Group Influence Reputation: An Exponential Random Graph Model." *Social Networks* 36: 66–81.

Heider, F. (1946). "Attitudes and Cognitive Organization." *Journal of Psychology* 21(1): 107–112.

Hoff, P. D., Raftery, A. E., and Handcock, M. S. (2002). "Latent Space Approaches to Social Network Analysis." *Journal of the American Statistical Association* 97(460): 1090–1098.

Huckfeldt, R. (2009). "Interdependence, Density Dependence, and Networks in Politics." *American Politics Research* 37(5): 921–950.

Jackson, M. O. (2008). *Social and Economic Networks.* Princeton, NJ: Princeton University Press.

Katz, L. (1953). "A New Status Index Derived from Sociometric Analysis." *Psychometrika* 18(1): 39–43.

Kendall, M. G. (1955). "Further Contributions to the Theory of Paired Comparisons." *Biometrics* 11(1): 43–62.

Kleinberg, J. M. (1999). "Authoritative Sources in a Hyperlinked Environment." *Journal of the ACM* 46(5): 604–632.

Klofstad, C. A., Sokhey, A. E., and McClurg, S. D. (2013). "Disagreeing about Disagreement: How Conflict in Social Networks Affects Political Behavior." *American Journal of Political Science* 57(1): 120–134.

Koger, G., Masket, S., and Noel, H. (2009). "Partisan Webs: Information Exchange and Party Networks." *British Journal of Political Science* 39(3): 633–653.

Krackhardt, D. (1990). "Assessing the Political Landscape: Structure, Cognition, and Power in Organizations." *Administrative Science Quarterly* 35(2): 342–369.

Krebs, V. E. (2002). "Mapping Networks of Terrorist Cells." *Connections* 24(3): 43–52.

Lazer, D. (2011). "Networks in Political Science: Back to the Future." *PS: Political Science and Politics* 44(1): 61.

Leifeld, P., and Schneider, V. (2012). "Information Exchange in Policy Networks." *American Journal of Political Science* 56(3): 731–744.

Lewis, T. G. (2014). *Critical Infrastructure Protection in Homeland Security: Defending a Networked Nation.* Hoboken, NJ: John Wiley & Sons.

List, C., and Pettit, P. (2011). *Group Agency: The Possibility, Design, and Status of Corporate Agents.* Oxford: Oxford University Press.

List, C., and Spiekermann, K. (2013). "Methodological Individualism and Holism in Political Science: A Reconciliation." *American Political Science Review* 107(4): 629–643

Liu, Y. Y., Slotine, J. J., Barabási, A. L., and Moreno, Y. (2012). "Control Centrality and Hierarchical Structure in Complex Networks." *PLOS ONE* 7(9): e44459.

Lubell, M., Scholz, J., Berardo, R., and Robins, G. (2012). "Testing Policy Theory with Statistical Models of Networks." *Policy Studies Journal* 40(3): 351–374.

Luce, R. D. (1950). "Connectivity and Generalized Cliques in Sociometric Group Structure." *Psychometrika* 15(2): 169–190.

Luce, R. D., and Perry, A. D. (1949). "A Method of Matrix Analysis of Group Structure." *Psychometrika* 14(2): 95–116.

Mokken, R. J. (1979). "Cliques, Clubs and Clans." *Quality & Quantity* 13(2): 161–173.

Monsuur, H., and Storcken, T. (2004). "Centers in Connected Undirected Graphs: An Axiomatic Approach." *Operations Research* 52(1): 54–64.

Moody, J., and White, D. R. (2003). "Structural Cohesion and Embeddedness: A Hierarchical Concept of Social Groups." *American Sociological Review* 68(1): 103–127.

Morselli, C., Giguère, C., and Petit, K. (2007). "The Efficiency/Security Trade-off in Criminal Networks." *Social Networks* 29(1): 143–153.

Newman, M. (2010). *Networks: An Introduction*. New York: Oxford University Press.

Noel, H., and Nyhan, B. (2011). "The 'Unfriending' Problem: The Consequences of Homophily in Friendship Retention for Causal Estimates of Social Influence." *Social Networks* 33(3): 211–218.

Page, L., Brin, S., Motwani, R., and Winograd, T. (1999). "The PageRank Citation Ranking: Bringing Order to the Web." Technical Report SIDL-WP-1999-0120, Stanford Digital Library Technologies Project, Stanford University.

Patty, J. W., and Penn, E. M. (2014). "Sequential Decision-Making & Information Aggregation in Small Networks." *Political Science Research & Methods* 2(2): 249–271.

Patty, J. W., and Penn, E. M. (2015). "Analyzing Big Data: Social Choice & Measurement." *PS: Political Science & Politics* 48(1): 95–101.

Patty, J. W., Penn, E. M., and Schnakenberg, K. E. (2013). "Measuring the Latent Quality of Precedent: Scoring Vertices in a Network." In *Advances in Political Economy: Institutions, Modelling and Empirical Analysis*, edited by Norman Schofield, Gonzalo Caballero, and Daniel Kselman, pp. 249–262. New York: Springer.

Pelc, K. J. (2014). "The Politics of Precedent in International Law: A Social Network Application." *American Political Science Review* 108(3): 547–564.

Perra, N., and Fortunato, S. (2008). "Spectral Centrality Measures in Complex Networks." *Physical Review E* 78(3): 036107.

Peters, B. G. (2011). *Institutional Theory in Political Science: The New Institutionalism*. New York: Bloomsbury Publishing USA.

Pierskalla, J. H. (2009). "Protest, Deterrence, and Escalation: The Strategic Calculus of Government Repression." *Journal of Conflict Resolution* 54(1): 117–145.

Porter, M. A., Mucha, P. J., Newman, M. E. J., and Friend, A. J. (2007). "Community Structure in the United States House of Representatives." *Physica A: Statistical Mechanics and Its Applications* 386(1): 414–438.

Radicchi, F., Castellano, C., Cecconi, F., Loreto, V., and Parisi, D. (2004). "Defining and Identifying Communities in Networks." *Proceedings of the National Academy of Sciences USA* 101(9): 2658–2663.

Robins, G., Pattison, P., Kalish, Y., and Lusher, D. (2007). "An Introduction to Exponential Random Graph (p∗) Models for Social Networks." *Social Networks* 29(2): 173–191.

Rogowski, J. C., and Sinclair, B. (2012). "Estimating the Causal Effects of Social Interaction with Endogenous Networks." *Political Analysis* 20(3): 316–328.

Salancik, G. R. (1995). "WANTED: A Good Network Theory of Organization." *Administrative Science Quarterly* 40: 345–349.

Schnakenberg, K. E., and Penn, E. M. (2014). "Scoring from Contests." *Political Analysis* 22(1): 86–114.

Scholz, J. T., Berardo, R., and Kile, B. (2008). "Do Networks Solve Collective Action Problems? Credibility, Search, and Collaboration." *Journal of Politics* 70(2): 393–406.

Seidman, S. B. (1983). "Network Structure and Minimum Degree." *Social Networks* 5(3): 269–287.

Seidman, S. B., and Foster, B. L. (1978). "A Graph-Theoretic Generalization of the Clique Concept." *Journal of Mathematical Sociology* 6(1): 139–154.

Siegel, D. A. (2009). "Social Networks and Collective Action." *American Journal of Political Science* 53(1): 122–138.

Siegel, D. A. (2011a). "Social Networks in Comparative Perspective." *PS: Political Science & Politics* 44 (1): 51–54.

Siegel, D. A. (2011b). "When Does Repression Work? Collective Action in Social Networks." *Journal of Politics* 73(4): 993–1010.

Siegel, D. A. (2013). "Social Networks and the Mass Media." *American Political Science Review* 107(4): 786–805.

Skinner, R. M., Masket, S. E., and Dulio, D. A. (2012). "527 Committees and the Political Party Network." *American Politics Research* 40(1): 60–84.

Song, H., and Eveland, W. P., Jr. (2015). "The Structure of Communication Networks Matters: How Network Diversity, Centrality, and Context Influence Political Ambivalence, Participation, and Knowledge." *Political Communication* 32(1): 83–108.

Victor, J. N., and Ringe, N. (2009). "The Social Utility of Informal Institutions Caucuses as Networks in the 110th US House of Representatives." *American Politics Research* 37(5): 742–766.

Vigna, S. (2009). "Spectral Ranking." arXiv preprint arXiv:0912.0238.

Volden, C., Ting, M. M., and Carpenter, D. P. (2008). "A Formal Model of Learning and Policy Diffusion." *American Political Science Review* 102(3): 319–332.

Ward, H. (2006). "International Linkages and Environmental Sustainability: The Effectiveness of the Regime Network." *Journal of Peace Research* 43(2): 149–166.

Ward, M. D., Ahlquist, J. S., and Rozenas, A. (2013). "Gravity's Rainbow: A Dynamic Latent Space Model for the World Trade Network." *Network Science* 1(1): 95–118.

Ward, M. D., Stovel, K., and Sacks, A. (2011). "Network Analysis and Political Science." *Annual Review of Political Science* 14: 245–264.

Wei, T.-H. (1952). "*The Algebraic Foundations of Ranking Theory.*" PhD thesis, University of Cambridge.

White, D. R., and Harary, F. (2001). "The Cohesiveness of Blocks in Social Networks: Node Connectivity and Conditional Density." *Sociological Methodology* 31(1): 305–359.

White, H. C. (1970). *Chains of Opportunity: System Models of Mobility in Organizations.* Cambridge, MA: Harvard University Press.

Zahle, J., and Collin, F., eds. (2014). *Rethinking the Individualism-Holism Debate.* New York: Springer.

Zhang, Y., Friend, A. J., Traud, A. L., Porter, M. A., Fowler, J. H., and Mucha, P. J. (2008). "Community Structure in Congressional Cosponsorship Networks." *Physica A: Statistical Mechanics and its Applications* 387(7): 1705–1712.

PART II

POLITICAL NETWORK METHODOLOGIES

CHAPTER 7

....

RELATIONAL CONCEPTS, MEASUREMENT, AND DATA COLLECTION

....

JUSTIN H. GROSS AND JOSHUA M. JANSA

INTRODUCTION

....

POLITICAL life, like social life in general, is fundamentally relational.[1] Politics is the product of relations between humans within institutions and in society, and political outcomes are thus rooted in human relations. As such, scholars study many political phenomena that are relational in nature. Seminal works in political science identify relational concepts such as persuasion, power, interaction, homophily,[2] and trust as critical factors in shaping political phenomena. And yet political science as a field has only recently begun to embrace the theoretical perspectives and empirical techniques known collectively as social network analysis (SNA[3]), approaches specifically tailored to the evaluation of relationships and designed for grappling with the complexity of relational phenomena.

As political scientists become more comfortable with the network analytic perspective broadly defined, we become increasingly conscious of the particular subtleties involved in *political* network analysis; better able to generate and refine network theories of political institutions, behavior, interstate relations, and so forth; and consequently more aware of the shortcomings in our earlier attempts to operationalize and measure political relationships of interest.

Despite the surge of interest in political network analysis over the past decade, several areas of study (e.g., analyses of bureaucracies, inter-organizational power, and relative success of social movements) underutilize network analysis, given the relational concepts central to their most prominent theories. In the areas that have already benefited from a network perspective, increased attention to the discrepancies between latent and observed networks (i.e., the gap between the theoretical network we wish to study and its representation in collected data), greater care in handling the problem of missing data, and more precise specification of units and levels of analysis constitute worthy goals. We begin here by reviewing the use of network analysis in political science since 2000, with an eye toward the relational concepts of existing studies, their research designs, and yet understudied areas.[4] We rely additionally on this recent literature to review common data collection, measurement, and design choices. Most of the chapter deals with common questions scholars must confront when designing political network analyses.

Prominent Relational Concepts in Political Science Studied with Network Techniques

In surveying the literature, we find that SNA of political phenomena has been concentrated in a few main areas of substantive inquiry, including political behavior/political psychology, legislative behavior, interest groups and political parties, and international organizations/trade. Many of the network studies in the realm of behavior/psychology consider the effect of an individual's egocentric or personal network (ego network)—the local subnetwork as provided through the respondent's point of view—on particular political behaviors (Eveland and Hively, 2009; Klofstad, 2007, 2009; Lazer et al., 2010; McClurg, 2006; Bello and Rolfe, 2014). Legislative scholars have taken observable shared behaviors (such as cosponsorship, covoting, and shared membership on committees and in legislative member organizations) to construct and analyze whole networks of federal or state legislators (Porter et al., 2005; Fowler, 2006; Victor and Ringe, 2009; Tam Cho and Fowler, 2010; Bratton and Rouse, 2011; Kirkland, 2011, 2012; Alvarez and Sinclair, 2012; Ringe and Victor, 2013; Kirkland and Gross, 2014; Parigi and Sartori, 2014). Others have relied on shared communication, contributions, and endorsement data to construct and analyze interest group networks and their intersection with party organizations (Carpenter, Esterling, and Lazer, 2004; Grossmann and Dominguez, 2009; Heaney and Lorenz, 2013; Heaney et al., 2012; Koger, Masket, and Noel, 2009, 2010). Box-Steffensmeier and Christenson (2014) use the filing of amicus briefs from 1930 to 2009 as a measure of dynamic relationships between interest groups before the US Supreme Court. In international relations, shared membership in intergovernmental organizations (IGOs), alliances, and the flow of migrants and goods make up the ties that bind states and predict conflict and policy change (Hafner-Burton and Montgomery, 2006; Breunig et al., 2012; Dorussen and Ward, 2008; Manger, Pickup, and Snijders, 2012; Rhue and Sundararajan, 2014). Certain types of relations may be considered "negative," as in the case of economic sanctions linking pairs of countries via negative directional ties (Cranmer et al., 2014).[5] Finally, political scientists in the areas of public administration/public policy have used network analysis to examine the directional flows of innovations and communication between organizations (Desmarais, Harden, and Boehmke, 2015; Provan, Huang, and Milward, 2009; Garrett and Jansa, 2015; Scholz, Berardo, and Kile, 2008). While scholars in this area have played key roles in the development of SNA for organizational behavior (e.g., Krackhardt and Stern, 1988; Krackhardt, 1992), political scientists studying policy processes have been slower to adopt such approaches.

Furthermore, a number of areas in political science are just beginning to incorporate social network perspectives in a systematic manner, opening pathways to new insights. While sociologists have been using network theory and analysis to study the structure and efficacy of movements for decades (e.g., Tilly, 1978; Rosenthal et al., 1985; Tarrow, 1994), political scientists have built a wealth of knowledge about elite responsiveness and the policymaking process; integration of these separate traditions can bring new focus to the processes through which social movements exact political and policy change. We are already seeing some examples of such creative fusion. Heaney and Rojas (2015) examine the effects of the anti-Iraq war movement on the Democratic Party by looking at the mobilization of an antiwar activist network. Similarly, Hadden (2015) studies the internal organization and tactics of the climate change movement and its effects on global policy from a networks perspective. Recent work by Carpenter and Moore (2014) articulates a rich relational theory of social movement institutionalization and political influence in which women's suffrage groups benefited from the social structures female activists built during the antislavery movement.

Common Practices in Designing Political Networks Research

Political network analysts have employed a wide variety of research designs according to their own particular research questions and the obstacles they face. While SNA design options abound, the political scientist intending to incorporate network analysis into a research agenda should be aware of common practices.

A large number of network studies use surveys for data collection. Survey-based data have been used most extensively in political behavior studies, especially investigations of the influence of social ties on knowledge and activity (e.g., Eveland and Kleinman, 2013; McClurg, 2006). A survey instrument may ostensibly allow direct measurement of the relation of interest. For example, one may measure political communication by simply querying individuals about their communication partners. Of course, such surveys do not permit direct measurement per se; unless we legitimately wish to study the network of *recollected* encounters, we will in fact be gathering values on a proxy variable subject to potentially large measurement errors. Moreover, in the mass political behavior setting, the construction of a whole social network is practically impossible; we inevitably sample respondents from the universe of communicators, and surely some communication partners will go unmentioned by any respondents. Thus, survey-based analyses of this sort almost always focus on the effects of one's ego network (ego-net) on personal attributes (see Huckfeldt et al., 2000; Lazer et al., 2010; McClurg, 2006; Klofstad, 2009; Jang, 2009). The advantage of ego-net analyses remains the typical independence of the ego-nets relative to one another, allowing the application of conventional sampling and inferential statistics.[6]

Researchers wishing to examine behavior in elite networks are less likely to find themselves restricted to ego-net analyses. In such cases, the network boundaries are more clearly defined. Within a clearly delineated network, such as relationships among legislators in a single session (e.g., Sarbaugh-Thompson et al., 2006; Ringe, Victor, and Gross, 2013; Leifeld and Schneider, 2012), nonresponse may still plague survey administration, but at least a complete list of nodes is easily obtained and objectively verifiable. A number of articles in the public policy and public administration literature also used survey-based data to analyze information exchange among networks of subgovernments (Huang and Provan, 2007; Provan, Huang, and Milward, 2009) and between public officials and policy advocates (Schloz, Berardo, and Kile, 2008). Although survey based, these studies are able to construct a whole network—or very close to it—because of their focus on a clearly defined elite population.

Observational data more frequently constitute the basis for political network analyses. Unfortunately, the lack of frequency with which we encounter observational data capturing the relational constructs we wish to study means even greater potential slippage between the latent relational concept and operationalization. Consider, for example, the reliance on cosponsorship as proxy for more general social ties between legislators (see Kirkland [2011] and Tam Cho and Fowler [2010] for discussion), covoting as proxy for shared policy agreement (Alvarez and Sinclair, 2012), co-contributing financial support to candidates or ballot initiatives as operationalization of coalition building (Bowler and Hanneman, 2006; Grossmann and Dominguez, 2009), comembership in alliances or IGOs as measure of shared affinity (Maoz et al., 2006), and co-caucus membership as operationalization of capacity for information sharing (Victor and Ringe, 2009). As researchers build on the excellent scholarship of these and other authors, we might wish to reflect on whether we should argue more forcefully for the value of studying these observed behaviors for their own sake (e.g., cosponsorship) or should identify other observable indicators of the latent construct we wish to study (see Kessler and Krehbiel, 1996; Koger, 2003). If one wants to examine the behavior of cosponsorship itself, one can safely assume that data on cosponsorship are indeed capturing the relationship of interest. But if cosponsorship data are used as a proxy for some other relation of interest, a strong argument is needed to justify why this is appropriate, or we need other indicators that—together with cosponsorship—can be used to tap the latent concept.[7]

Although *social* network analysis typically implies the study of connections among individual sentient beings, in network analysis more generally, a node need not always correspond to a person or animal. Indeed, while the phrase *political network analysis* most often refers to a special case of SNA, network analysis applied to political research extends beyond simple interpersonal relations. An increasing number of studies involve the measurement of relations among concepts and other entities. Examples include mapping the path of innovation diffusion (Desmarais, Harden, and Boehmke, 2015; Garrett and Jansa, 2015), proximity of human rights violations (Fariss and Schnakenberg, 2014), and similarity between party platforms (Maoz and Somer-Topcu, 2010). In these studies the nodes are more abstract objects—states, rights, platforms, respectively—and the ties represent particular relations measured on pairs.

KEY RESEARCHER CONSIDERATIONS

As the research process involved in studying networks has its own idiosyncrasies that set it apart from individual attribute-oriented studies, the investigator faces a number of choices that should be considered at the outset. Not all of these are straightforward, and no two researchers investigating the very same phenomenon are apt to make identical choices. We next provide a set of key questions that researchers should ask themselves early on in the research process, as the answers—and indeed the questioning process itself—will shape the research design.[8]

Is a Network Representation Appropriate?

In some cases, it is quite obvious that one is dealing explicitly with a network, such as when relationships are explicit and connections are essential to the research question. In fact, whenever one is interested in relational data observed on a set of individuals, it is generally advisable to conceptualize this as a network, even if the research questions aren't formally network questions and one's theory is not particularly motivated by structural considerations. This is due to the fundamental autocorrelation problem in relational data: unless the researcher is sampling independent dyads (no nodes in common among the sampled dyads and little chance of direct interaction), it is crucial that the dependence structure among dyads be addressed in some way (e.g., Boehmke, 2009; Cranmer and Desmarais, 2011; Bowers et al., 2013). Network representations have become the standard way of modeling the inherent complexity arising from relational data in social science.[9] To see why conventional statistical models are insufficient, one need only consider as an example the relational variable *military belligerence*. For example, it should be obvious that whether Germany has been at war with the United Kingdom during some timeframe is not independent of whether Germany has been at war with the United States during that period. When interdependence is particularly high—that is, it is not likely that the units being studied are behaving independently— there is the potential for bias in model estimates (e.g., Boehmke, 2009). Even if one is not theorizing about such things as network effects or networked concepts such as centrality or connectedness, it is natural to think in network terms in order to take advantage of the inferential machinery that generations of network scholars have assembled. The bottom line is that one must grapple with dyadic interdependence.

Unit of Analysis and Levels of Analysis

An initial, basic question faced in conventional empirical research is that of the appropriate unit of analysis. What sorts of entities have the attributes being measured by the variables of interest? Senators, nations, bills, bureaus, corporations, families? How exactly are data aggregated, or—equivalently—what sorts of objects inhabit each row of the associated rectangular data set? The collection and management of relational data may be more complicated than for individual (nodal) data, but awareness of one's unit of analysis remains crucial to clear thinking about all aspects of the design and measurement process. In general, researchers will be dealing with *dyads*—pairs of nodes—as the basic unit of analysis, although individual nodal attributes will often play a role in analysis as well. At first this may sound like a minor difference from units of analysis typical in non-network studies; after all, we're just shifting from single nodes to pairs of nodes, and it is not unusual to encounter aggregated units of analysis such as households or census tracts in the nonrelational context. The essential difference is that aggregated units of analysis are nonoverlapping in the non-network setting. The complexity inherent in network data arises from the basic fact that dyads overlap and, in fact, can overlap in ways that are not always straightforward (e.g., in two-mode—or bipartite—networks, where the set of nodes is partitioned and each dyad consists of one node drawn from each subset).

An additional related consideration specific to the study of network data is that the researcher may pursue multiple *levels of analysis*[10] potentially within a single study. Just as a biological scientist may study the human body at the systemic level as interactions among systems (nervous, circulation, digestive, etc.), or instead investigate individual organs within these systems, or even drill all the way down to the molecular level, so too may the political scientist study the networked body politic at multiple levels, including—most commonly—nodes, dyads, communities, or the network as a whole.

The research question drives one's choice of level of analysis and determines whether it will be sufficient to confine oneself to a single level. For example, if one seeks to explain dyadic variation (e.g., whether two voters discuss politics, conflict between two nations, or presence of links in a global supply chain), then one will conduct dyad-level analysis. If one is interested in understanding variation at the network level—for example, whether public opinion about Congress predicts the degree to which clusters of legislators cooperate or, alternatively, isolate themselves—then one will need to collect several instances of whole-network data. Often, explanatory and response variables involve measurements taken at different levels of analysis. The researcher should consider whether, for instance, the hypothesis at hand holds that individual-level attributes should predict triad-level outcomes (e.g., if triadic closure is more likely to occur when all three individuals share a particular attribute), that network-level properties predict individual-level outcomes (e.g., density of political conversation network increases probability that each member will turn out to vote), or that dyadic relations predict other dyadic relations (e.g., high level of trade between two nations corresponding to tendency to sign extradition treaties).

Ego-nets constitute yet another possible level of analysis and to some extent represent a distinct analytical approach. Although many have come to associate SNA with whole-network studies, ego-net analysis offers some notable advantages as a form of relational inference. If interest lies in predicting relations from nodal attributes or vice versa, it makes sense to sample individuals and collect data on them and their immediate contacts. This is the one type of network analysis in which the traditional sampling apparatus may be applicable and nonresponse plausibly construed as missing at random (MAR).[11] As long as a researcher is willing to make the assumptions that the individual ego-nets are independent and that the nonresponse mechanism is related only to variables collected, that researcher is on fairly solid methodological ground. For the independence assumption to be reasonable, at the very least it must be true that no alters should appear as egos in the study (Robins, 2015, 52). Borgatti et al. (2013, 270–276) note that the most prominent questions addressed with an ego-net design focus on processes related to social capital or social homogeneity; in either case, the researcher wishes to understand how individuals' interpersonal contexts affect their own attributes and behaviors. Thus, key explanatory values are relational or aggregates of relational variables (e.g., density of one's personal network, tendency toward reciprocity), and the response variable measures some individual attribute. In political research, we might wish to better understand political capital, self-efficacy, political socialization, knowledge, voting behavior, or ideology. In such research, one's direct connections (and the interconnections among those to whom they are connected) are most germane.[12]

Level of Measurement

In nodal (as opposed to relational) variable analysis, we commonly consider what level of measurement is most appropriate—or simply practical for data collection—before we decide which sorts of graphical representations and summary statistics will be well suited to the data. For example, one simple distinction is between categorical (nominal, ordinal) and numerical (ratio-interval), with numerical measurements made on either discrete (countable) or continuous (uncountable) sets. By far the most common choice for relational measurement level is binary nominal, indicating simply whether some relationship is present or absent. Sometimes this choice is justified by theoretical considerations (e.g., a bureaucrat either answers to another person as his or her superior or does not, a potential donor either does or does not donate to a campaign, two members of a legislature serve on a common committee or do not, one nation either does or does not have an extradition treaty with another). Although it may be possible to measure such relations more precisely, presence or absence is often the most important concern; indeed, it may be quite difficult if not impossible to obtain more granular measurements. Furthermore, many of the technical underpinnings of network analysis rest on dichotomous ties. In particular, to take advantage of most common features of mathematical graph theory presumes simple presence or absence of ties in a network. Various configurations—hubs and spokes, closed triads, and so forth—tied to social network theory are inherently discrete.

And yet it is not always clear that this is suitable for political applications. Take, for instance, policy diffusion among states or nations. One might represent the United States as a network in which two states sharing a border are considered linked. Were it the case that policies only diffused geographically, this would be suitable. But states may copy policy innovations from any other state and are not limited to their immediately surrounding neighbors (Karch, 2007). One way to handle this is to assume that links must either be absent or present between each pair of states, but we are unable to directly observe these links. Bill similarity data (Garrett and Jansa, 2015), or repeated measurement of the order of adoption among states (Desmarais, Harden, and Boehmke, 2015), are then taken to be indicators of the hidden network. This is a modeling simplification that may be necessary in order to utilize the usual network toolkit—based in large part on the discrete mathematics and representation derived from graph theory (Barnes and Harary, 1983)—but a more accurate representation might allow for a complete network (ties between every pair of states), where the weight on edge i,j represents the propensity of state j to borrow legislative language from state i and each state has a nonzero probability of adopting legislation from every other state.

An additional question the researcher faces is whether these measurements will be *undirected* or *directed*. Some political relations (e.g., power, donation) are inherently directed, while others are clearly undirected (e.g., shared affiliation, personal contact). Relationships that are inherently directional may be represented as undirected, but not vice versa. Why should one represent an asymmetric relationship as if undirected? Wouldn't that be throwing away information? It depends on the theory driving the research. Although trust is directed, it may be that some outcome is predicted whenever a trust relation in either direction exists, or only when a reciprocated trust relationship exists. Moreover, a number of whole-network analysis procedures are defined only on sets of undirected ties or are more reliable for these types of edges. Whenever calculating, reporting, and attempting to interpret a network statistic, one should always clarify whether it is appropriate for undirected ties, directed ties (*arcs*), or both.

It is especially important to investigate accepted practice, since it is not uncommon for network software packages to carry out calculations even if the results may be nonsensical. Different packages may have different default rules for handling data in such cases (e.g., whether—and how—to transform directed ties into undirected ties or to simply generate an error message), so it is preferable to be proactive and handle any necessary transformations oneself. For example, any statistic—such as betweenness centrality—that relies on *geodesics* (shortest distances) between pairs of nodes does not take direction into account. Suppose the relation of interest is *information sharing*. Whether two individuals should be considered linked if either shares information with the other or only if information flows in both directions is a substantive issue, to be resolved by the researcher based on theoretical considerations. In some cases, it may even be necessary to establish more complicated rules for determining the distance between two nodes (e.g., the shortest path allowing flow of information in either direction via a sequence of arcs arranged tip to tail). The bottom line is that it is essential to think carefully about the research claim being investigated rather than just leaving measurement decisions up to arbitrary software defaults.

Often the focus of a network study is not on properties of relations themselves, predictors of relational outcomes, or consequences of relationships for individual attributes, but instead on some aggregation at the subgroup or whole-network level, or measures associated with each node's position in the whole network. The researcher should clarify at the outset whether the research aim will depend on such aggregation. Whether such aggregate measures as centrality, connectedness, and clique membership are meaningful depends strongly on the nature of the relational variables and measurement error. One should not assume that such aggregate statistics automatically make sense simply because they can be calculated. The better one understands the operationalization of the relation of interest, the better one will be able to assess whether the proposed aggregation of measurements will be edifying or misleading.

Do the Relations Link the Same Types of Nodes?

An observed relational phenomenon of interest may directly connect a pair of actors (or other nodes), but often the connection is indirect, existing by virtue of shared interaction with another sort of node. In some cases, the distinction is left implicit in analyzing a resulting network; in fact, the difference between what SNA scholars term *one-mode* and *two-mode* networks may at times be subtle. Examples of clear one-mode (or unipartite[13]) networks include those based on surveys in which actors identify alters with whom they share some relation (friendship, trust, animosity), while the quintessential two-mode (bipartite) network is one based on shared affiliations (e.g., memberships, attendance at social functions). In the murky middle lie networks easily represented as unipartite, but at least implicitly based on connections via other objects. For example, imagine that we wish to construct a network of politicians based on shared interests. If "shared interest" is kept vague—perhaps by asking members of a parliament to indicate who, among their colleagues, shares interests with them—a unipartite network results. If, on the other hand, we are to use archival data to identify *specific* shared interests, then we are starting from a bipartite network (Ringe and Victor, 2013), with each tie connecting one person and one interest. The researcher must then either choose a strategy for collapsing this into a unipartite network or deal explicitly with the various types of interests each pair shares.

The vast majority of analyses conducted on bipartite networks begin by collapsing their given networks into a single mode (node-type) of interest. To date, the tools available for unipartite network analysis are far more extensive and amenable to interpretation, so this tendency is unsurprising. The rules employed in transforming a bipartite into a unipartite graph, however, should be defended by the researcher, and if they seem too arbitrary, different choices should be attempted to see how measurements are affected. For example, a legislative cosponsorship network looks quite dense if a single act of cosponsorship counts as a tie between two legislators; if we instead only count acts of cosponsorship on bills with fewer than n cosponsors or require repeated instances of collaboration before registering a link, we will wind up with a sparser network indicating stronger ties. In fact, examining different versions of a network representation in this manner can be illuminating.

However one goes about collapsing a multimode network, one should remember that potentially important information will be lost. In the cosponsorship example, we wind up ignoring attributes of the bills and count them as interchangeable. Few studies in political science analyze uncollapsed bipartite network data. Skinner, Masket, and Dulio (2012) are an exception; they explore the influence of tax-exempt political organizations known as 527s within the extended Republican and Democratic Party networks. The authors constructed a two-mode network in which 527s are connected with other party organizations if their staff members used to work for the other organizations. By multiple nodal and network level measures, the authors find that 527s are essential players in party politics, providing coordination within parties and hierarchical structure to the extended party networks. Collapsing the data would not have allowed the authors to analyze the unique contribution of 527s in facilitating the formation of party networks.[14]

Just as network structure and analysis involves various complications absent from conventional unit-by-variable "rectangular" data sets, threats to validity and reliability plague relational analyses. Next we discuss some of these threats, options for dealing with them, and ways in which we have yet to satisfactorily address network measurement problems.

MEASUREMENT ERROR: VALIDITY, RELIABILITY, MISSING DATA

If threats to validity and reliability abound in social science, the difficulties associated with these and other forms of measurement error in network analyses are greater still. Ronald Burt's claim that missing data are "doubly a curse" for social network analysts— due to the special challenges that arise through the greater complexity and sensitivity of such data (1987)—extends to other network measurement issues. Though missing data may be the most vexing problem for analysts, multiple sources of measurement error limit our ability to formulate widely applicable solutions. In this section we consider key threats to accurate measurement; review a few key sensitivity analyses; and discuss different frameworks for addressing these threats through design, modeling, and simulation-based sensitivity analysis conducted on a case-by-case basis.

Within the SNA literature, scholars discussing missing data and other sources of measurement error have approached the topic by demonstrating the particular vulnerabilities of network data to validity and reliability threats. Two authors influential in designing early statistical network models, Holland and Leinhardt (1973), pointed out that the usual notion of observed structure being composed of "true structure plus noise" may not be terribly well suited to networks. They claimed that, in fact, most representations of social networks contain distortions that are far from simple to correct, even with sophisticated modeling. And yet network researchers, at the time the article was written, typically presumed the face validity of their data, treating the error mechanisms as essentially ignorable. Holland and Leinhardt faulted researchers' "inability to distinguish structural complexity from measurement error" and invited them to instead think in terms of the "compatibility" of observed and true networks, a more flexible way of viewing such discrepancies. It is interesting to note that Holland and Leinhardt described the situation as one of a *latent* network, not directly observed, and an *observed* network that consists of imperfect relational indicators. At the time, practical applications of what we now call latent variable modeling—including factor analysis, latent trait analysis, and latent class analysis—were still quite limited by computational constraints, and classical measurement theory continued to dominate, so it should come as no surprise that network researchers did not propose a latent network model formally connected to these other areas of latent structure analysis.

Left unquestioned in this earlier work is whether the relational constructs themselves are well defined. Commonly studied concepts such as friendship, trust, and sexual contact have relatively straightforward meanings, with researcher definitions unlikely to cause much controversy.[15] This is less often the case with concepts such as political influence, political support, adoption of policy innovation, and other phenomena attracting the greatest attention among *political* network analysts. As a consequence, the single most important step we can take to improve the validity of our research is to thoughtfully define and operationalize our relational concepts. The most compelling criticisms of political network analyses often amount to the simple assessment: "I'm not sure you're measuring what you think you're measuring." If we have not clearly defined the relations of interest and made a convincing case that we have chosen a reasonable measurement strategy, no amount of post hoc tinkering or statistical adjustment will help.[16]

Types of Network Measurement Errors

Assuming concepts have been clearly defined and mapped to observable variables, a number of other key hurdles remain. Wang et al. (2012) identify six types of network measurement errors:

- false negative/positive nodes
- false negative/positive edges
- falsely aggregated/disaggregated nodes

These error types include missing data as a special case (yielding false negative nodes or false negative edges), most typically resulting from an incomplete node census, nonresponse, or censored observations. These authors further refine the thinking about network measurement error by identifying *three* levels of interpretation: the *ideal network* (similar to what we call "latent" and Holland and Leinhardt call "true"); the *clean network*, the encoded network data in the absence of measurement error; and the *observed network*, which the researcher actually gets to see. Scholars generally emphasize discrepancies between the clean and observed networks; when they refer to a "true network," they are in fact conflating the ideal and clean networks and ignoring the aforementioned difficulties associated with operationalization.

The likelihood of encountering each of the six errors mentioned above (and listed in table 7.1) depends on the research design employed. In survey-based network research, nonresponse may lead to both *false negative nodes* and *false negative edges*, but not necessarily. In some areas of political science, the *boundary specification* problem—the question of which nodes should be included in the network of interest—is trivial. For example, names of legislators, nations, and lobbyists may be publicly available and accessible with minimal effort, circumventing the risk of incorrectly omitting nodes. In whole-network surveys of elite actors, nonresponse may result in false negative edges, as the nonresponders will not have reported the presence or absence of ties to others, but this does not rule out the use of other sources of information on such ties.[17] In personal

Table 7.1 Types of Network Measurement Errors

Types	Example	Example of Resulting Problems
False Positive Node	Including a Democrat in a Republican fundraising network	Density underestimated; study validity threatened
False Negative Node	Excluding a legislator from the cosponsorship network	Depends on node's importance (e.g., may drastically alter connectivity, centrality scores)
False Positive Edge	Inferring a policy diffusion path that did not really occur	Overestimated density
False Negative Edge	Legislative offices failing to report joint policy meeting	Underestimated density
Falsely Aggregated Node	Counting Bill Nelson (D-FL) and Ben Nelson (D-NE) as the same node	Overestimated degree distribution
Falsely Disaggregated Node	Counting Al Franken and Alfred Stuart Franken as two different nodes	Underestimated degree distribution

network (ego-net) studies, where egos' local networks are assumed to be independent of one another, nonresponse does not pose the same risks as for whole networks. Threats to validity and reliability in these studies bear more resemblance to corresponding ones in non-network designs.

The problem of incorrectly including individual nodes (*false positive nodes*) is analogous to coverage problems in standard surveys (e.g., including a sixteen-year-old on a list of potential voters). This is one of the easier measurement problems to address. In the case of a survey, one may ask qualifying questions at the start and eliminate such nodes from consideration. In many cases, these "errors" involve a judgment call. In such cases, it is incumbent upon the researcher to carefully stipulate the nodes to be included, offer justification, and indicate the measures taken to ensure that those meeting proposed criteria will be included, and no others.

More generally, *boundary specification* issues (Laumann et al., 1983; Kossinets, 2006) are analogous to defining the target population, with the caveat that sloppiness can more easily result in large errors in inference. Even when defining the boundary seems trivial, we often find ourselves with choices to make and defend; if examining the network of cosponsorship support during a given term, shall we include only those who serve a full term? More than half? What if a senator is absent for much of the session while campaigning for president and manages to avoid voting on any controversial bills?

On the other hand, in some newer types of research—on social media, for instance—false positive nodes and edges can more easily slip through unnoticed. For example, if we were to study linking behavior among political blogs, a lack of direct human oversight is likely to promote the inclusion of nonblogs and links to advertisers. A choice must be made between pruning the network back by hand, building automated tools to discern true positives from junk, or acknowledging the likely noise in the observed network.

Reliability troubles abound in self-reported relationships, as the presence or absence of a relationship is rather subjective. Suppose, for example, we are interested in contact between legislative staffers (as in Ringe et al., 2013). We may ask staffers to indicate those with whom they have had a conversation over the past week. Some will misremember and claim interactions that actually took place more than a week ago, while others will forget a conversation that occurred during the past week. These would appear to be cases of false positive and false negative edges, respectively. But are we truly intending to study the network of contact in an arbitrary week? More likely, such a question is intended as a proxy for something not directly observable, such as *frequent contact*. Frequent contact is correlated with *contact in the past week*, but also correlated with *recalled contact in the past week*, even if that recollection is incorrect. Indeed, rather than a network of recent contact, measured with error, we might instead say that we have measured a network of *perceived* recent contact, measured perfectly! Something subtle is at work here, suggesting that what are characterized as "errors" of measurement may in certain cases be better addressed in the operationalization process. The chance of capturing a latent construct such as regular interpersonal contact through a number of different manifest variables suggests the enticing idea of creating network factor or latent trait models, a possibility that has yet to be pursued. Rather than simply choosing a single proxy variable for frequent contact, information sharing, willingness to collaborate, or any other relational concept, we might instead use several correlated measures that all imperfectly capture it.

When Wang et al. (2012) refer to *falsely aggregated* or *disaggregated nodes*, they are referring to disambiguation, a data entry and management issue. For example, we would be falsely aggregating nodes if we conflated Bill Nelson (D-FL) and Ben Nelson (D-NE) in an analysis of the 2003–2004 US Senate. On the other hand, if we somehow managed to count Al Franken and Alfred Stuart Franken as two separate people in the 2013–2014 Senate, we would be falsely disaggregating nodes. Checks on clerical mistakes such as these are easier when dealing with a set of legislators than, say, the linking behavior among thousands of websites. In the latter case, renaming of websites and slight changes in domain names can make such errors more common.

It is impossible to offer an authoritative list of problems resulting from these six errors. Much depends on the underlying generating process of the "true network" being studied. Because network data are interdependent, a single incorrectly measured node or edge may have little importance for characterizing the entire network or inferring parameters of a network model, or it may prove catastrophic. Thus, the principal issue is our inability to confidently quantify uncertainty. We list a few likely estimation problems in table 7.1, but these should be taken with a grain of salt. Some estimation may be more or less robust to errors depending on features of the network. See Wang et al. (2012) for comparisons of difficulties likely to arise from each error type, based on simulations employing a few simple assumptions. In general, they find that networks with low average clustering and node degree distributions not too positively skewed tend to be the most robust to various types of measurement error.

Additional Issues with Aggregation: Persistent vs. Fleeting Ties

Other common problems might also be understood as aggregation or disaggregation issues. Consider, for example, how relational phenomena are aggregated over time; while social network ties are nearly always portrayed as persisting through time,[18] some may more accurately be thought of as fleeting or even instantaneously experienced. Here, the line between conceptual definition and measurement error becomes blurred: two entities may be considered to be at war (persistent), or they may have simply experienced an act of belligerence (fleeting). A senator may be supportive of another's legislative agenda (persistent) or may simply have cosponsored this colleague's bill (fleeting). A presidential candidate may have an acrimonious relationship with an opponent on social media (persistent), or may simply issue an isolated snipe (fleeting) (Gross and Johnson, 2016).

When working with relational event data, one option is to explicitly study these dynamics through longitudinal analysis. Promising new approaches include relational event modeling (Butts, 2008)—a flexible extension to event history (survival) analysis—and other forms of social sequence analysis (Cornwell, 2015). James Kitts (2014) argues that we need to move "beyond networks" in conceptualizing and theorizing about relational interactions, freeing us to look in more detail at the complex dynamics involved. Alternatively, one might consider the relational variable of interest to be a latent propensity toward interaction and treat the fleeting instances as indicators of that underlying tendency.

We face similar choices in individual-oriented research, as we decide among various research designs, based on data availability, theoretical considerations, and our research questions. In network analysis, however, the implications of such choices are—unsurprisingly—more complicated. When we posit network ties based on fleeting events and then analyze the resulting "networks," we take a conceptual leap that, at the very least, should be explicitly mentioned and defended. We may, for example, say that we are analyzing a network of "political information flow" that is operationalized as linking people who have shared an email containing politically relevant content at some point in the past six months. If we wish to make a claim about the shortest path information may take to pass from one node to another and base inferences about who the important conduits for information are, we may have difficulty convincing a critical audience that our operationalization supports such claims. The gap between what has been measured and more general assumptions about information flow becomes more problematic at the whole-network level.

Borgatti et al. (2013, 31) present a typology of common dyadic phenomena in four types to help researchers identify the relationships they are dealing: *co-occurrences* (comembership, coparticipation, physical distance, attribute similarity), *social relations* (kinship, affect, familiarity), *interactions* (transactions and other activity), and *flows* (ideas, information, products, infectious disease). Some types of co-occurrence persist through time (e.g., similarities, shared memberships), while others may be fleeting events (e.g., joint attendance at a convention). Social relations tend to be persistent, in some cases essentially permanent (e.g., familial ties) and in others subject to change (e.g., affection). Interactions and flows may involve isolated incidents connecting nodes (e.g., makes campaign donation, speaks at campaign event), but patterns of such phenomena (e.g., repeated donations, touring with campaign) may constitute persistent ties. Borgatti et al. (2013) point out that certain relational behaviors are "institutionalized," taking on a reality that transcends individual perception. A number of such relations are of interest to political scientists, increasingly accessible through archival data. For instance, if a lobbyist has previously worked for three elected officials, this may be a matter of public record; their relationship may be independently corroborated, sparing us dependence on less reliable self-reporting.

Missing Data

The most serious threat to the measurement integrity of a network study is also the most common: missing data. Modern approaches to handling missing observations in statistical inference rely heavily on the assumption that individual observations are independent. The now standard typology—missing completely at random (MCAR), at random (MAR), and not at random (MNAR)—classifies scenarios according to the broad class of mechanism responsible for the encountered missingness. Accepted methods for grappling with all three situations—even the most problematic one, in which the mechanism responsible for missing data is dependent on unobserved variables (MNAR)—assume that each data point's propensity to be missing is unrelated to that of each other data point. Such an assumption does not hold in full network studies. Worse still, network statistics have the potential to be quite sensitive to even a single missing dyadic observation, so missing data at the levels typically encountered certainly have the potential to wreak havoc.

In most whole-network studies in the social sciences, the goal is to collect a census, rather than a sample of the population. Random sampling of nodes or dyads is not a sensible strategy, since there is no general statistical theory linking a subnetwork's statistics to corresponding parameters for the full network from which it is sampled. In fact, one point of view holds that in a whole network study, there is but a single observation ($n = 1$), so sampling obliterates our only observation. If we wish to describe low-level structures in a network (e.g., particular triads, in-stars, and clusters), we are out of luck, as the sampling process complicates descriptions of particular patterns of interaction beyond what is practical. Thus, the most frequently offered suggestions involve strategies for mitigating nonresponse and advice for proceeding with extreme caution in interpreting results if missing data cannot be avoided. The bottom line is that in contrast to node attribute estimation on independent observations, *no broadly applicable sampling theory for networks exists*. Any such theory requires strong assumptions about the nature of the underlying "true" graph structure from which nodes and edges are being sampled. That said, certain aspects of network topology—density or average degree, for example—may be easier to estimate through sampling than others. Kolaczyk (2009) describes the challenge of network sampling in technical detail, connecting it to the literature on traditional sampling theory. Our own pessimism about the outlook for a general theory for network sampling should not be interpreted as a call to ignore sampling issues or to only analyze completely observed graphs. Rather, applied network analysts will likely always need to argue on a case-by-case basis, demonstrating sensitivity to sampling error via simulations under various plausible assumptions.

Methodological work on the problem of missing data in networks has been rather scarce, not only because of the serious difficulties involved, but also because solutions tend to be narrowly applicable. Authors focusing on this issue in depth have offered three types of contributions: (1) studies aimed at understanding the systematic patterns of missingness and sensitivity analyses to establish the robustness of particular network statistics in the presence of missing data, (2) network imputation strategies, (3) and direct modeling of missingness within broader statistical models. In an early example of the first type, Burt (1987, 67) concentrated on ego networks—generally the least susceptible to the ravages of missingness—and using the 1985 General Social Survey, found that nonreporting of links among alters was correlated with the strength of ties, implying nonignorability. In the context of an example from political communication, this means that if we were to ask a survey respondent to name people with whom he or she has discussed an upcoming election, we would expect the respondent to be less likely to mention actual conversation partners to whom he or she is weakly tied; if asked to indicate pairs of discussion partners who have talked to one another about the election, we would be especially unlikely to name dyads composed of those to whom we are weakly tied.

Three common reasons for units to be missing are unit nonresponse; misspecification of the network boundary; and "vertex degree censoring" due to *fixed-choice designs*, wherein respondents are asked to nominate up to some small number of partners (Kossinets, 2006, 248). Kossinets finds several network level statistics—including assortativity, coefficient mean degree (average ties per node), clustering coefficient, size of the largest component, and mean path in the largest component—to be quite sensitive to vertex degree censoring and/or network boundary misspecification, while these tended to be more robust to unit nonresponse. The article includes exploratory analysis indicating sensitivity as a function of missingness. This article is especially important for the example it provides to researchers of how to go about doing sensitivity analyses for themselves on their own projects.

Whereas imputation strategies have become a matter of best practice in many areas of data analysis, their suitability for networks is less clear. While others (e.g., Robins et al., 2004) have been dismissive of such approaches, Huisman (2009) maintains cautious optimism for network imputation, especially if the missingness remains below 20 or 30 percent. In weighing imputation against simple node deletion (i.e., analyzing the network of respondents and ignoring the nonrespondents), the take-away message is that there is no general preferred solution. As long as the proportion missing was low, bias was found to be limited, and thus imputation was not especially helpful. Different imputation strategies offered a comparative advantage as the proportion missing increased. These included *reconstruction*, random imputation, and *hot deck imputation*, depending on the specific nature of missingness encountered.[19]

Missingness may also be directly modeled. Robins et al. (2004) have adapted the basic ERGM (p*) model to handle nonrespondents as particular types of nodes, so that links from respondent to nonrespondent are distinct from those connecting two respondents.[20] Handcock and Gile (2007, 2010) have also offered a likelihood approach that takes advantage of all information, including partial observations. An examination of goodness of fit, based on likelihood ratio statistics, indicates a much better fit for the all-observation approach (AO) than the respondent-only (RO) approach, though they also discuss the circumstances under which RO may be preferable, such as when arcs are reasonably assumed independent and nonresponse is explained by observed variables only.

The AO approach makes use of information on the size of the full network, as well as the respondent to nonrespondent arcs, and the additional data seem to contain valuable information. Still, Handcock and Gile find that certain parameter estimates are comparable across the two approaches.

Huisman and Steglich (2008) review other methods of dealing with missingness, including modeling nonrespondents separately (Robins et al., 2004) or using Markov-chain Monte Carlo simulation to repeatedly sample the conditional distribution and impute the data (Handcock and Gile, 2006). But these methods (1) assume that you know which nodes are missing and (2) provide no solution for longitudinal network data. To address the first point, in snowball samples the researcher should have some knowledge of which respondents are missing from "nomination" or "outdegree" information. However, missingness can also come from boundary specification or thresholds placed on ties. To address the second point, longitudinal networks can suffer from the usual item or unit nonresponse, but also panel nonresponse. To solve this, Huisman and Steglich (2008) suggest modeling the joining and leaving times as exogenous attributes.

THE FUTURE OF POLITICAL RELATIONAL MEASUREMENT

Many of the complications researchers face in the analysis of political networks stem from the fact that in political science we rarely have the luxury of working with an easily measured relation. Political concepts such as influence and cooperation can be defined and then operationalized as network ties in a variety of ways, and choosing appropriately among these for a given research application is a task not to be treated lightly. Too often, however, we simply make do with a single, readily accessible, relational variable and treat it as synonymous with our concept of interest. During operationalization, there is necessarily slippage between the latent relation and the manifest (observed) relation, just as there is slippage between individual latent attributes and corresponding manifest variables. In conventional nonrelational statistics, best practices leverage the associations among multiple imperfect measurements to tap into the underlying variable of interest, but we have yet to develop comparable techniques suited to network analysis. While SNA has benefited from numerous advances in statistical inference, modeling, and network-level descriptive measures, we have paid relatively little attention to the more basic question of careful relational conceptualization, operationalization, and dyadic measurement. The less confidence we have in dyad-level measurements, the weaker is the foundation on which all other network analysis is based. To paraphrase Gary Robins (2015, 118), network measurement has simply not kept pace with or taken advantage of the breathtaking advances in psychometrics over the past several decades. We agree with Robins that "too many network analysts are too addicted to their analysis and not enough focused on their measurement." And thus we have yet to develop "methods akin to network factor analysis" or even broadly applicable "serious indices of validity and reliability." We believe that these are natural areas of priority for methodological research going forward.

The Latent Relation Measured through Multiplex Networks

Latent variable measurement models were developed primarily within the social and behavioral sciences as a principled means of constructing measures of complex concepts. Bartholomew et al. (2011) offer a unified treatment of such measurement models, which include factor analysis, latent class analysis, and latent trait models (known in educational testing as item response theory). The logic of latent variable modeling and its application to the problem of slippage between operationalized variables and the theoretical concepts they are intended to capture might be further generalized to measurement of relations in political networks. Ideally, one selects potential indicators composed of two sources of variability: the latent concept and the variability unique to the indicator. Some models allow for additional sources of variability, such as multidimensional latent concepts and clusters of indicators with shared idiosyncratic variability. All share a single basic strategy: individually, the measures are imperfect reflections of the latent concept, but together, any common variation shared by them all will serve as more accurate proxy for the latent concept. Technically, this leads to the primary assumption at the heart of all such models, that of *local (conditional) independence*: conditional on a unit's value on the latent variable, the unit's values (or responses) on all indicators will be independent of one another. In other words, the only thing driving correlation among responses should be the concept we intend to measure. If the latent variable is an individual respondent's *political self-efficacy*, for example, we might assume that answers to (1) a question asking whether one feels one's opinion on policy is important and (2) a question on the importance of voting are connected only to the extent that they are partially driven by one's feeling of political self-efficacy. Knowing an individual's answer to one question would help us guess his or her likely answer to the other, but if we could somehow observe the person's level of self-efficacy directly, knowing the answer to one question would offer no additional help in guessing the answer to the other.

What would this look like for a relational concept? One can imagine asking a number of relational questions of respondents, although the respondent burden may be too heavy for full network surveys with many nodes. It is difficult enough to persuade legislative staffers, for instance, to list other staffers with whom they've had a meeting in the past month; how much more difficult it would be to get them to list those with whom they interact socially, those they have emailed, those with whom they have collaborated on getting a bill passed, and so forth. We are starting to see some research that makes use of multiple relational variables, leading to the analysis of *multiplex networks*. Multiplex networks, or multiplex data, are "data that describe multiple relations among the same set of actors" (Hanneman and Riddle, 2005). Applications of multiplex networks in political science are not exactly ubiquitous, but seem to be gaining traction. Heaney (2014) uses three relations to build and analyze an influence-reputation network among interest groups; Shrestha and Feiock (2009) examine contractual agreements between local governments on many different services (and thus many different relations); and Cranmer, Menninga, and Mucha (2015) use multiple relations among countries to detect distinct communities in the international system. Thus far, political network studies have been limited to examining how the different relations in the multiplex relate to one another (Heaney, 2014; Shrestha and Feiock, 2009) and using multiplex networks to answer questions at the subnetwork level (Cranmer, Menninga, and Mucha, 2015). Alternatively, we envision multiplex networks as analogous to multiple indicators used in latent variable models, so that each layer serves as a manifest network for an unobserved latent network. For example, to study the latent network of international belligerence, we might construct a multiplex network with layers devoted to different indicators of tension and use the relationships among the layers to get at the abstract construct of interest.[21]

Why not simply use existing latent variable models for relational variables? The key problem is, of course, the complex interdependence common to all network modeling. Certainly as a first step we might choose to naively assume conditional independence among all indicator relations connecting two nodes, given the latent relationship between them. Latent variable techniques even include goodness-of-fit-indexes to check how well the assumption holds. However, if threats to local independence in individual-level measurement models abound, they surely would pose a far greater threat in a hypothetical latent network model. Interdependence within and across layers of the multiplex would likely wreak havoc on the naïve extension of factor analysis, latent trait analysis, and others. To make progress on such models, we would want to develop some theoretical constraints on the sorts of multiplex interdependence to expect, and then collect evidence of such constraints in the real world and/or indications of robustness to departures from these constraints.

Concluding Comments

In this chapter we have reviewed existing studies that use SNA to study political phenomena and identified the kinds of relations commonly studied. Several relations, such as interest group partnerships, congressional cosponsorship, and international trade and conflict, have enjoyed a flourishing of network analyses focused on the complete network, while studies of various relations within one's ego-net also have long been prominent in political behavior. We have also outlined several points scholars need to consider when designing a network analysis of a political phenomenon. The extant literature has a mixed record of clarity in assumptions about the network design, and potential solutions to some of the challenges (such as missing data) are still evolving. Approaches to research design once seemingly off limits for political network analysis—most notably, experiments (e.g., Bond et al., 2012)—are now possible, if challenging and ethically delicate. Measurement in the context of causal inference brings its own set of considerations (Fowler et al., 2011). Being clear in one's decisions regarding the level of analysis, missing data, aggregation, and even whether a network depiction is appropriate will only strengthen one's work and the field as a whole. A number of relations of interest to political and policy researchers remain understudied, in part because of the uneven diffusion of SNA techniques and lack of confidence in or familiarity with existing methods of network analysis. By developing potential techniques for better measuring the latent relations we care about, network methodologists would go a long way toward bringing relational measurement best practices into line with best practices in individual-level designs. Our goal is for this chapter to provide intrepid political scholars with a blueprint to what has been studied, how it has been studied, what challenges exist for all network designs, and how we might confront these challenges.

NOTES

1. The term *relational* is widely used whenever units of analysis are connected. Its application is indeed broad enough to include abstract relationships—as in the case of *relational databases*, in which data fields are connected in sometimes complex patterns—but in social science, we typically talk of *relational* data whenever individual observations/cases/objects of study are connected to one another, particularly when the connections themselves are of interest. McClurg and Young (2011) argue that *power*, a unifying concept among political scientists, "is, at its very core, *relational*" and consequently call for a "relational political science" as a counterpoint to the prominent individualistic theoretical traditions so prominent in our field (e.g., rational choice, behavioralism, new institutionalism).
2. According to the definition provided by Prell (2012, 129), *homophily* is the tendency for individuals to "prefer to have social relationships with others who are similar to themselves." Homophily is both the product of human interactions and a cause of those interactions: individuals are both drawn to interact with those similar to themselves and tend to become more like those they regularly interact with.
3. We think of political network analysis as most often a special case of social network analysis and so use the common acronym SNA throughout the chapter.
4. We focus on studies that use observational data as opposed to experimental studies. Network experiments have been conducted mostly in the lab (e.g., McCubbins et al., 2009). Bond et al. (2012) conduct a rare network-based field study via Facebook, but this is an exception, as one can almost never ethically manipulate ties in a field study, just signals about node attributes.
5. In international relations, there is also a small but growing body of work using SNA to study terrorist networks (e.g., Krebs, 2002; Pedahzur and Perliger, 2006).
6. More detailed discussion of this point follows the subsections "Is a Network Representation Appropriate?" and "Missing Data" in this chapter.

7. Possible strategies for using multiple measures to represent a latent relation of interest are discussed more thoroughly in the subsection "The Latent Relation Measured through Multiplex Networks" in this chapter.

8. Extended treatments of the research design process for social network analysis may be found in several recent books (e.g., Prell, 2012, ch. 3; Borgatti et al., 2013, chs. 3–5; Robins, 2015, ch. 3). Together with classic treatments such as Wasserman and Faust (1994), these have influenced our thinking on the essential components of political network research design.

9. See Handcock and Gile (2010, 5) for more on the network as convenient device. Other related frameworks have emerged as well, such as the social relations model in psychology (Kenny et al., 2006) and probabilistic/statistical relational models in machine learning (Getoor, 2007; Neville and Jensen, 2007).

10. Note the distinctions among three separate but similarly named terms employed here: unit of analysis, level of analysis, and level of measurement. Further confusing matters, we typically encounter a fourth, related term from grade school: *unit of measurement* refers to the reference unit to be used in interval-level measurements (e.g., kilometers, lbs, hours, thousands of $ GDP per capita, number of emails i sends to j per week).

11. We mean missing at random in the same sense as Little and Rubin (1987).

12. This is true unless one wishes to know how this translates to system-wide dynamics; see Bond et al. (2012) for an example from voter turnout at the whole network level.

13. The terms *unipartite, bipartite*, and *multipartite* apply, strictly speaking, to the graphs used to represent networks rather than the networks themselves. In a bipartite graph, ties occur only between objects of distinct types. For instance, if L is a set of legislators and C is the set of committees on which legislators serve (as in Porter et al., 2005), then a legislative committee network would be a type of affiliation network we might represent with a bipartite graph, edges exclusively connecting pairs of nodes drawn one from each set. We prefer these terms to one-mode, two-mode, etc., to avoid confusion with the unrelated statistical term "mode."

14. More work has been done outside of political science in the modeling of bipartite political networks. For example, in computer science, Akoglu (2014) developed an algorithm for analyzing signed bipartite networks.

15. This is not to say that these terms have universal definitions—they certainly do not—but only that an author's operationalization of such concepts is unlikely to attract theoretically relevant criticism.

16. This is parallel to measurement error in all of statistics. If one is simply measuring a concept completely wrong, say by counting heartbeats to measure lung capacity, estimates will be wrong, and incorrect inferences will be made. We reiterate that no amount of postestimate adjustment will correct for the mismeasurement of the concepts of interest.

17. The ethics of incorporating data on nonrespondents are debatable, though researchers are likely on more solid ground when studying public officials. See Borgatti and Molina (2005) for more on ethical considerations.

18. Persistent ties are elsewhere called "continuous" ties. We eschew this usage to avoid confusion with the sense of continuity in the domain of certain numeric data (continuous vs. discrete).

19. Huisman (2009) finds that imputation by reconstruction works well for undirected networks with low to medium missingness. Imputation by reconstruction does not work as well in directed networks, but still generally outperforms other imputation techniques (ignoring the missingness, preferential attachment, hot decking, imputing zeros).

20. Links between two nonrespondents are necessarily unobserved.
21. See Hanneman and Riddle (2005) for the basics of working with multiplex network data. See also Snijders, Lomi, and Torlo (2013) for modeling unipartite and bipartite multiplex networks.

REFERENCES

Akoglu, Leman. (2014). "Quantifying Political Polarity Based on Bipartite Opinion Networks." Eighth Annual International AAAI Conference on Weblogs and Social Media. http://www.aaai.org/ocs/index.php/ICWSM/ICWSM14/paper/viewFile/8073/8100

Alvarez, R. M., and Sinclair, B. (2012). "Electoral Institutions and Legislative Behavior: The Effects of Primary Processes." *Political Research Quarterly* 65(3): 544–557.

Barnes, J. A., and Harary, F. (1983). "Graph Theory in Network Analysis." *Social Networks* 5(2): 235–244.

Bartholomew, D. J., Knott, M., and Moustaki, I. (2011). *Latent Variable Models and Factor Analysis: A Unified Approach.* 3d ed. West Sussex, UK: John Wiley & Sons.

Bello, J., and Rolfe, M. (2014). "Is Influence Mightier Than Selection? Forging Agreement in Political Discussion Networks During a Campaign." *Social Networks* 36(2014): 134–146.

Boehmke, F. J. (2009). "Policy Emulation or Policy Convergence? Potential Ambiguities in the Dyadic Event History Approach to State Policy Emulation." *Journal of Politics* 71(3): 1125–1140.

Bond, R. M., Fariss, C. J., Jones, J. J., Kramer, A. D. I., Marlow, C., Settle, J. E., and Fowler, J. H. (2012). "A 61-Million-Person Experiment in Social Influence and Political Mobilization." *Nature* 489(7415): 295–298.

Borgatti, S. P., Everett, M. G., and Johnson, J. C. (2013). *Analyzing Social Networks.* Thousand Oaks, CA: Sage Publications.

Borgatti, S. P., and Molina, J. L. (2005). "Toward Ethical Guidelines for Network Research in Organizations." *Social Networks* 27(2): 107–117.

Bowers, J., Fredrickson, M. M., and Panagopoulos, C. (2013). "Reasoning about Interference Between Units: A General Framework." *Political Analysis* 21(1): 97–124.

Bowler, S., and Hanneman, R. (2006). "Just How Pluralist is Direct Democracy? The Structure of Interest Group Participation in Ballot Proposition Elections." *Political Research Quarterly* 59(4): 557–568.

Box-Steffensmeier, J. M., and Christenson, D. P. (2014). "The Evolution and Formation of Amicus Curiae Networks." *Social Networks* 36: 82–96.

Bratton, K. A., and Rouse, S. M. (2011). "Networks in the Legislative Arena: How Group Dynamics Affect Cosponsorship." *Legislative Studies Quarterly* 36(3): 423–460.

Breunig, C., Cao, X., and Ledtke, A. (2012). "Global Migration and Political Regime Type: A Democratic Disadvantage." *British Journal of Political Science* 42(4): 825–854.

Burt, R. S. (1987). "A Note on Missing Network Data in the General Social Survey." *Social Networks* 9: 63–73.

Butts, C. T. (2008). "A Relational Event Framework for Social Action." *Sociological Methodology* 38(1): 155–200.

Carpenter, D. P., Esterling, K. M., and Lazer, D. M. (2004). "Friends, Brokers, and Transitivity: Who Informs Whom in Washington Politics?" *Journal of Politics* 66(1): 224–246.

Cornwell, B. (2015). *Social Sequence Analysis: Methods and Applications.* New York: Cambridge University Press.

Carpenter, D., and Moore, C. D. (2014). "When Canvassers Became Activists: Antislavery Petitioning and the Political Mobilization of American Women." *American Political Science Review* 108(3): 479–498.

Cranmer, S. J., and Desmarais, B. A. (2011). "Inferential Network Analysis with Exponential Random Graph Models." *Political Analysis* 19(1): 66–86.

Cranmer, S. J., Heinrich, T., and Desmarais, B. A. (2014). "Reciprocity and the Structural Determinants of the International Sanctions Network." *Social Networks* 36: 5–22.

Cranmer, S. J., Menninga, E. J., & Mucha, P. J. (2015). "Kantian Fractionalization Predicts the Conflict Propensity of the International System." *Proceedings of the National Academy of Sciences* 112(38): 11812–11816.

Desmarais, B., Harden, J. J., and Boehmke, F. J. (2015). "Persistent Policy Pathways: Inferring Diffusion Networks in the American States." *American Political Science Review* 109(2): 392–406.

Dorussen, H., and Ward, H. (2008). "Intergovernmental Organizations and the Kantian Peace: A Network Perspective." *Journal of Conflict Resolution* 52(2): 189–212.

Eveland, W. P., and Hively, M. H. (2009). "Political Discussion Frequency, Network Size, and Heterogeneity of Discussion as Predictors of Political Knowledge and Participation." *Journal of Communication* 59: 205–224.

Eveland, W. P., and Kleinman, S. B. (2013). "Comparing General and Political Discussion Networks within Voluntary Organizations Using Social Network Analysis." *Political Behavior* 35(1): 65–87.

Fariss, C. J., and Schnakenberg, K. E. (2014). "Measuring Mutual Dependence between State Repressive Actions." *Journal of Conflict Resolution* 58(6): 1003–1032.

Fowler, J. H. (2006). "Legislative cosponsorship networks in the US House and Senate." *Social Networks* 28: 454–465.

Fowler, J. H., et al. (2011). "Causality in Political Networks." *American Politics Research* 39(2): 437–480.

Garrett, K. N., and Jansa, J. M. (2015). "Interest Group Influence in Policy Diffusion Networks." *State Politics and Policy Quarterly* 15(3): 387–417.

Getoor, L. (2007). *Introduction to Statistical Relational Learning*. Cambridge, MA: MIT Press.

Gross, J. H. and Johnson, K. T. (2016). "Twitter Taunts and Tirades: Negative Campaigning in the Age of Trump." *PS: Political Science & Politics*. Forthcoming.

Grossmann, M., and Dominguez, C. B. K. (2009). "Party Coalitions and Interest Group Networks." *American Politics Research* 37(5): 767–800.

Hadden, J. (2015). *Networks in Contention: The Divisive Politics of Climate Change*. New York: Cambridge University Press.

Hafner-Burton, E. M., and Montgomery, A. H. (2006). "International Organizations, Social Networks, and Conflict." *Journal of Conflict Resolution* 50(1): 3–27.

Handcock, M. S., and Gile, K. J. (2006). "Model-based Assessment of the Impact of Missing Data on Inference for Networks." Working Paper 66. Center for Statistics and the Social Sciences. University of Washington.

Handcock, M. S., and Gile, K. J. (2007). "Modeling Social Networks with Sampled or Missing Data." Working Paper 75, Center for Statistics and the Social Sciences, University of Washington.

Handcock, M. S., and Gile, K. J. (2010). "Modeling Social Networks from Sampled Data." *Annals of Applied Statistics* 4: 5–25.

Hanneman, R., and Riddle, M. (2005). *Introduction to Social Network Methods*. Riverside: University of California, Riverside. http://www.faculty.ucr.edu/~hanneman/nettext/.

Heaney, M. T. (2014). "Multiplex Networks and Interest Group Influence Reputation: An Exponential Random Graph Model." *Social Networks* 36: 66–81.

Heaney, M., and Lorenz, G. (2013). "Coalition Portfolios and Interest Group Influence over the Policy Process." *Interest Groups and Advocacy* 2(3): 251–277.

Heaney, M., Masket, S., Miller, J., and Strolovich, D. (2012). "Polarized Networks: The Organizational Affiliations of National Party Convention Delegates." *American Behavioral Scientist* 56(12): 1654–1676.

Heaney, M. T., and Rojas, F. (2015). *Party in the Street: The Anti-war Movement and the Democratic Party after 9/11.* New York: Cambridge University Press.

Holland, P. W., and Leinhardt, S. (1973). "The Structural Implications of Measurement Error in Sociometry." *Journal of Mathematical Sociology* 3(1): 85–111.

Huang, K., and Provan, K. (2007). "Resource Tangibility and Patterns of Interaction in a Publicly Funded Health and Human Services Network." *Journal of Public Administration Research and Theory* 17(3): 435–454.

Huckfeldt, R., Sprague, J., and Levine, J. (2000). "The Dynamics of Collective Deliberation in the 1996 Election: Campaign Effects on Accessibility, Certainty, and Accuracy." *American Political Science Review* 94: 641–651.

Huisman, M. (2009). "Imputation of Missing Network Data: Some Simple Procedures." *Journal of Social Structure* 10(1): 1–29.

Huisman, M., and Steglich, C. (2008). "Treatment of Non-response in Longitudinal Network Studies." *Social Networks* 30: 297–308.

Jang, S.-J. (2009). "Are Diverse Political Networks Always Bad for Participatory Democracy? Indifference, Alienation, and Political Disagreements." *American Politics Research* 37(5): 879–898.

Karch, A. (2007). *Democratic Laboratories: Policy Diffusion Among the American States.* Ann Arbor: University of Michigan Press.

Kenny, D. A., Kashy, D. A., and Cook, W. L. (2006). *Dyadic Data Analysis.* New York: Guilford Press.

Kessler, D., and Krehbiel, K. (1996). "Dynamics of Cosponsorship." *American Political Science Review* 90(3): 555–566.

Kirkland, J. H. (2011). "The Relational Determinants of Legislative Outcomes: Strong and Weak Ties between Legislators." *Journal of Politics* 73(3): 887–898.

Kirkland, J. H. (2012). "Multimember Districts' Effect on Collaboration between US State Legislators." *Legislative Studies Quarterly* 37(3): 329–353.

Kirkland, J. H., and Gross, J. H. (2014). "Measurement and Theory in Legislative Networks: The Evolving Topology of Congressional Collaboration." *Social Networks* 36: 97–109.

Kitts, J. A. (2014). "Beyond Networks in Structural Theories of Exchange: Promises from Computational Social Science." *Advances in Group Processes* 31: 263–298.

Klofstad, C. A. (2007). "Talk Leads to Recruitment: How Discussions about Politics and Current Events Increase Civic Participation." *Political Research Quarterly* 60: 180–191.

Klofstad, C. A. (2009). "Civic Talk and Civic Participation: The Moderating Effect of Individual Predispositions." *American Politics Research* 37(5): 856–878.

Koger, G. (2003). "Position Taking and Cosponsorship in the U.S. House." *Legislative Studies Quarterly* 28(2): 225–246.

Koger, G., Masket, S., and Noel, H. (2009). "Partisan Webs: Information Exchange and Party Networks." *British Journal of Political Science* 39(3): 633–653.

Koger, G., Masket, S., and Noel, H. (2010). "Cooperative Party Factions in American Politics." *American Politics Research* 38: 1.

Kolaczyk, E. D. (2009). *Statistical Analysis of Network Data: Methods and Models*. New York: Springer.

Kossinets, G. (2006). "Effects of Missing Data in Social Networks." *Social Networks* 28: 247–268.

Krackhardt, D. (1992). "The Strength of Strong Ties: The Importance of Philos in Organizations." In *Networks and Organizations: Structure, Form, and Action*, edited by N. Nohira and R. Eccles, pp. 216–239. Boston: Harvard Business School Press.

Krackhardt, D., and Stern, R. (1988). "Informal Networks and Organizational Crises: An Experimental Simulation." *Social Psychology Quarterly* 51: 123–140.

Krebs, V. E. (2002). "Mapping Networks of Terrorist Cells." *Connections* 24(3): 43–52.

Laumann, E. O., Marsden, P. V., and Prensky, D. (1983). "The Boundary Specification Problem in Network Analysis." In *Applied Network Analysis: A Methodological Introduction*, edited by R. S. Burt, M. J. Minor, and R. D. Alba, pp. 18–34. Beverly Hills, CA: Sage Publications.

Lazer, D., Rubineau, B., Chetkovich, C., Katz, N., and Neblo, M. (2010). "The Coevolution of Networks and Political Attitudes." *Political Communication* 27(3): 248–274.

Leifeld, P., and Schneider, V. (2012). "Information Exchange in Policy Networks." *American Journal of Political Science* 56(3): 731–744.

Little, R. J. A., and Rubin, D. B. (1987). *Statistical Analysis with Missing Data*. 2d ed. Hoboken, NJ: John Wiley & Sons.

Manger, M. S., Pickup, M. A., and Snijders, T. A. B. (2012). "A Hierarchy of Preferences: A Longitudinal Network Analysis Approach to PTA Formation." *Journal of Conflict Resolution* 56(5): 853–878.

Maoz, Z., Kuperman, R. D., Terris, L., and Talmud, I. (2006.) "Structural Equivalence and International Conflict: A Social Networks Analysis." *Journal of Conflict Resolution* 50(5): 664–689.

Maoz, Z., and Somer-Topcu, Z. (2010). "Political Polarization and Cabinet Stability in Multiparty Systems: A Social Networks Analysis of European Parliaments, 1945–98." *British Journal of Political Science* 40(4): 805–833.

McClurg, S. D. (2006). "The Electoral Relevance of Political Talk: Examining Disagreement and Expertise Effects in Social Networks on Political Participation." *American Journal of Political Science* 50(3): 737–754.

McClurg, S. D., and Young, J. K. (2011). "Political Networks: Editors' Introduction; A Relational Political Science. *PS: Political Science & Politics* 44(1): 39–43.

McCubbins, M. D., Paturi, R., and Weller, N. (2009). "Connected Coordination: Network Structure and Group Coordination." *American Politics Research* 37(5): 899–920.

Neville, J., and Jensen, D. (2007). "Relational Dependency Networks." *Journal of Machine Learning Research* 8: 653–692.

Parigi, P., and Sartori, L. (2014). "The Political Party as a Network of Cleavages: Disclosing the Inner Structure of Italian Political Parties in the Seventies." *Social Networks* 36: 54–65.

Pedahzur, A., and Perliger, A. (2006). "The Changing Nature of Suicide Attacks: A Social Network Perspective." *Social Forces* 84(4): 1983–2004.

Prell, C. (2012). *Social Network Analysis: History, Theory and Methodology*. Thousand Oaks, CA: Sage Publications.

Provan, K. G., Huang, K., and Milward, H. B. (2009). "The Evolution of Structural Embeddedness and Organizational Social Outcomes in a Centrally Governed Health and Human Services Network." *Journal of Public Administration Research and Theory* 19: 873–893.

Porter, M. A., Mucha, P. J., Newman, M. E., and Warmbrand, C. M. (2005). "A Network Analysis of Committees in the US House of Representatives." *Proceedings of the National Academy of Sciences of the United States of America* 102(20): 7057–7062.

Rhue, L., and Sundararajan, A. (2014). "Digital Access, Political Networks, and the Diffusion of Democracy." *Social Networks* 36: 40–53.

Ringe, N., and Victor, J. N. (2013). *Bridging the Information Gap: Legislative Member Organizations as Social Networks in the United States and the European Union.* Ann Arbor: University of Michigan Press.

Ringe, N., Victor, J. N., and Gross, J. H. (2013). "Keeping Your Friends Close and Your Enemies Closer? Information Networks in Legislative Politics." *British Journal of Political Science* 43(3): 601–628.

Robins, G., Pattison, P., and Woolcock, J. (2004). "Missing Data in Networks: Exponential Random Graph (p*) Models for Networks with Non-respondents." *Social Networks* 26: 257–283.

Robins, G. (2015). *Doing Social Network Research: Network-based Research Design for Social Scientists.* Thousand Oaks, CA: Sage Publications.

Rosenthal, N., Fingrutd, M., Ethier, M., Karant, R., and McDonald, D. (1985). *American Journal of Sociology* 90(5): 1022–1054.

Sarbaugh-Thompson, M., Thompson, L., Elder, C. D., Comins, M., Elling, R. C., and Strate, J. (2006). "Democracy Among Strangers: Term Limits' Effects on Relationships between State Legislators in Michigan." *State Politics and Policy Quarterly* 6(4): 384–409.

Scholz, J. T., Berardo, R., and Kile, B. (2008). "Do Networks Solve Collective Action Problems? Credibility, Search, and Collaboration." *Journal of Politics* 70(2): 393–406.

Shrestha, M. K., and Feiock, R. C. (2009). "Governing U.S. Metropolitan Areas." *American Politics Research* 37(5): 801–823.

Skinner, R. M., Masket, S. E., and Dulio, D. (2012). "527 Committees and the Political Party Network." *American Politics Research* 40(1): 60–84.

Snijders, T. A. B., Lomi, A., and Torlo, V. J. (2013). "A Model for the Multiplex Dynamics of Two-Mode and One-Mode Networks, with an Application to Employment Preference, Friendship, and Advice." *Social Networks* 35(2): 265–276.

Tam Cho, W. K., and Fowler, J. H. (2010). "Legislative Success in a Small World: Social Network Analysis and the Dynamics of Congressional Legislation." *Journal of Politics* 72: 124–135.

Tarrow, S. G. (1994). *Power in Movement: Social Movements, Collective Action, and Politics.* Cambridge, UK: Cambridge University Press.

Tilly, C. (1978). *From Mobilization to Revolution.* Reading, MA: Addison-Wesley.

Victor, J. N., and Ringe, N. (2009). "The Social Utility of Informal Institutions: Caucuses as Networks in the 110th U.S. House of Representatives." *American Politics Research* 37(5): 742–766.

Wang, D. J., Shi, X., McFarland, D. A., and Leskovec, J. (2012). "Measurement Error in Network Data: A Re-classification." *Social Networks* 34: 396–409.

Wasserman, S., and Faust, K. (1994). *Social Network Analysis: Methods and Applications.* New York: Cambridge University Press.

CHAPTER 8

....

STATISTICAL INFERENCE IN POLITICAL NETWORKS RESEARCH

....

BRUCE A. DESMARAIS AND SKYLER J. CRANMER

INTRODUCTION

....

NETWORKS are systems that exhibit complex, interwoven structures. These systems can be illuminating to describe and visualize, but most research agendas eventually arrive at either precise hypotheses regarding endogenous network structures (e.g., the structure of connections within the outcome network of interest) or similarly precise hypotheses regarding exogenous factors but requiring adjustment for endogenous dependencies. The conventional toolkit for statistical inference is poorly suited to evaluating such hypotheses. The core problem is that the classical machinery of hypothesis testing was designed around the assumption that the data set to be used is populated with independent replicates from a datagenerating process. Network data could not be further from this assumption. The observations, which are often organized as dyads, are individual components of a single, broader system. Even if a researcher has several replicates of the system, they are often dependent (e.g., longitudinal network data). Because the interdependencies inherent in networks violate a core assumption upon which standard regression models are built, interest in networks has sparked a wave of methodological innovations aimed at statistical inference, modeling, and hypothesis testing with networks. Here we review the most established of these methods, briefly discuss their structure and capabilities, and highlight selected applications of these tools in political science research. Obviously a review chapter such as this cannot discuss the intricacies of each model exhaustively, but we hope to provide a general orientation to the set of techniques available and point the reader to where further details and examples may be had.

CROSS-SECTIONAL MODELS

The basic approaches to statistical inference with networks are differentiated by the objectives of the researcher vis-à-vis the network structure and dependencies. The approaches that we review here permit researchers to test precise theories of network formation that involve both the effects of covariates on tie formation and relationships among ties themselves. We also present methods that permit inference when the researcher is uncertain about the forms of dependence that underlie tie formation in the network. Here we provide a very brief overview of the three major methods of cross-sectional network analysis and provide some discussion about their use in the political science literature. For a more detailed discussion of how these methods relate to each other and an illustrative application of all three to the same data set, see Cranmer et al. (2016).

The Exponential Random Graph Model (ERGM)

We consider the exponential random graph model (ERGM) (Holland and Leinhardt, 1981; Wasserman and Pattison, 1996) to be the canonical model for network data. The ERGM provides a modeling framework that, just like conventional regression, can accommodate the effects of covariates on the status of relationships, but unlike regression, it can model the prominence and significance of structural dependencies such as reciprocity and transitivity. Furthermore, the ERGM has been extended to accommodate longitudinal relational data (i.e., time series of networks) (Robins and Pattison, 2001; Hanneke, Fu, and Xing, 2010a; Desmarais and Cranmer, 2012b) and networks with edge weights (Wyatt, Choudhury, and Bilmes, 2010; Desmarais and Cranmer, 2011; Krivitsky, 2012).

The mathematical form of the ERGM makes clear its potential as a general framework for statistical inference with networks. The ERGM is a probability model defined on the support of possible adjacency matrices. Let there be n actors/nodes/vertices, among which we represent dichotomous ties as Y; an $n \times n$ matrix with $Y_{ij} = 1$ if there is a tie from i to j and 0 otherwise. The probability of observing Y according to an ERGM is

$$P(Y) = \frac{\exp\left(\sum_{j=1}^{k} \theta_j h_j(Y)\right)}{\sum_{Y^* \in \mathcal{Y}} \exp\left(\sum_{j=1}^{k} \theta_j h_j(Y^*)\right)}. \tag{1}$$

The flexibility of the ERGM for capturing covariate effects and interdependencies in networks arises from the general nature of the h_j. These are statistics—functions applied to the adjacency matrix and optionally covariates—that are theorized to influence the likelihood of observing a configuration of the adjacency matrix (e.g., a network with thirty triangles, one hundred edges, and twenty-five reciprocal dyads). The θ are parameters to be estimated that, similar to regression coefficients, give the effects of the network statistics on the likelihood of observing a particular instance of the adjacency matrix. The larger θ_j, the higher the likelihood of observing subgraph configurations that contribute positively to h_j. The flexibility and grounding in theory come at a cost. An identifying assumption, one also common to the regression framework, is that the model is correctly specified. That is, it is assumed that every feature of a network configuration that is relevant to determining whether we will observe that network configuration is represented by an element of h. Misspecification can result in biased estimates of parameters as well as subpar performance of hypothesis tests. A detailed review of the ERGM is provided by a number of sources, including Goodreau et al. (2008); Hunter et al. (2008); Cranmer and Desmarais (2011); and Lusher, Koskinen, and Robins (2013).

For applications of ERGM in political networks research, see Thurner and Binder (2009); Lazer et al. (2010); Cranmer and Desmarais (2011); Gerber, Henry, and Lubell (2013); Kirkland and Gross (2014); Box-Steffensmeier and Christenson (2014); and Song (2015).

Let us consider the example of Box-Steffensmeier and Christenson (2014) in detail. Recently, scholars have begun to construct networks of interest groups based on cosigning the same amicus curiae brief. Amicus curiae or "friend of the court" legal briefs are written by actors who are not party to a case but believe they can offer information relevant to it. One contribution of this work is that the network measure constructed from amicus curiae briefs is both coordinated and purposive; the process requires negotiation between cosignatories and agreement on the direction, argument, and details of the brief. They find evidence of an increasingly transitive network resembling a host of tightly grouped factions and leadership hub organizations employing mixed coalition strategies. Egocentric networks of organizations show that three major theoretically posited coalition strategies are present in the data: *lone wolves*, who work alone; *teammates*, who work with cliques of varying sizes; and *leaders*, who pull together otherwise disparate groups. They further utilize business directories to gather attribute data on signers from the first decade of the millennium. In doing so, they find a broad range of industries, with the greatest number of signers in the services division of the Standard Industrial Classification (SIC). They also use the attribute data to test homophily hypotheses for various business characteristics in the ERGM. The paper finds that driving the network formation is assortative mixing based on industry area, budget, sales, and membership characteristics.

Substantively, Box-Steffensmeier and Christenson (2014) contribute to the discipline by shedding light on how to measure the networks of the vast expanse of special interests, how the networks have changed over time, and which characteristics are sought out as complements and which are considered threatening to cooperation. In addition, they provide insights into more micro-level considerations about which groups are the most attractive partners and in what capacity.

The Latent Space Model (LSM)

The latent space model, introduced by Hoff, Raftery, and Handcock (2002), is a latent variable model for tie formation in networks that exploits the near ubiquity of homophily in networks: the tendency for nodes to tie to others that are similar on one or more attribute. Nodes are positioned in a k-dimensional latent space, and the probability of a tie between any two nodes is inversely related to the distance between their positions in this latent space. Each dimension in the latent space can be thought of as an unmeasured attribute of nodes. For example, such attributes might be income or age if nodes are people, or level of authoritarianism and unemployment rate if nodes are countries. Under the latent space model, the log odds of a tie between nodes i and j is:

$$\eta_{i,j} = \log \text{odds}(y_{i,j} = 1 \mid z_i, z_j, x_{i,j}, \alpha, \beta) \tag{2}$$

$$= \alpha + \beta' x_{i,j} - |z_i - z_j| \tag{3}$$

where α is an intercept term controlling the overall density of the network, β is a vector of regression coefficients, $x_{i,j}$ is the vector of measured covariates, and $|z_i - z_j|$ is the Euclidean distance between nodes in the latent space. Interpretation of the LSM is similar to interpreting logistic regression. The β is interpreted as the change in the log odds of a tie given a one-unit increase in the value of a covariate.

For applications of LSM in political networks research, see Ward, Siverson and Cao (2007); Kirkland (2012); Krafft et al. (2012); Ward, Ahlquist, and Rozenas (2013); Kirkland and Gross (2014); and Cao and Ward (2014).

To consider an example of such work in detail, let us examine Kirkland (2012). Kirkland was primarily interested in the effect of an exogenous variable, the sharing of a constituency, on the network of cosponsorships in the US Congress. In terms of design, he used a natural experiment. During the 2000–2002 redistricting cycle, North Carolina eliminated its small set of multi-member districts as a result of a court intervention, allowing Kirkland to compare the behavior of legislators in multi-member districts to those in single-member districts (since not all North Carolina districts were multi-member), and to compare legislators from multi-member districts to themselves after the switch. His theory, being about exogenous predictors, did not provide specific hypotheses about the structure of the endogenous network dependencies, making the proper specification of an ERGM difficult. Treating the network dependencies as a nuisance, rather than as an object of interest, he estimated an LSM on each year in the sample. This setup allowed Kirkland to test the effects of the exogenous variable of interest on the network while controlling for the interdependence known to be present. To select the dimensionality of the LSM, Kirkland increased the number of dimensions in the model until the new dimensions stopped producing significant gains in model fit; two dimensions, as should happen.

Substantively, Kirkland (2012) demonstrates that sharing a constituency produces sizable increases in collaboration via cosponsorship. There is some research both in American politics and in the comparative literature that suggests that multi-member districts produce representatives who are likely to compete with one another to build a distinct "brand" from their district partner, and that these districts produce representatives who lack strong geographic ties to their constituents, allowing them to adhere to party lines more frequently. Alternatively, Kirkland hypothesized that the advantages of working together to gain on policy outweighed the potential gains from adhering to party lines and building distinct individual brands and found that multi-member districts provide legislators with natural coalition partners, who stand to gain on policy through collaboration.

The Quadratic Assignment Procedure (QAP)

The quadratic assignment procedure (QAP) (Krackardt, 1987) is a method of hypothesis testing that builds on Mantel's (1967) permutation procedure and computes the statistical significance of parameter estimates when the dependent variable is itself a relational matrix (e.g., distance, correlation, network adjacency matrices). The QAP is a form of nonparametric permutation testing in which row and column shuffles of the dependent and independent variables are used to simulate the null condition, which results in a simulated null distribution of regression coefficients.

To illustrate the basic methodology of QAP, we offer an example of bivariate permutation in figure 8.1. Randomly shuffling rows and columns of the adjacency matrix (Y) maintains the structure of the network right down to the edges, but by shuffling the nodes, the relationship between Y and a hypothetical dyadic covariate X is broken. In the QAP, some measure of relationship (e.g., correlation coefficient, regression) between Y and X is calculated on the unpermuted data, then the same measure is calculated on many permutation-based replications of the data. A two-tailed p-value to assess the null hypothesis that there is no relationship between Y and X can be calculated as the proportion of relationships calculated under permutations that are at least as large, in magnitude, as the value calculated on the observed data.

Using QAP with three or more values is more complicated than using either the Y or the X permutations, which are equivalent in the bivariate case. Suppose there are three relational variables—the dependent network Y, the independent variable of interest X, and a potential confounder Z, for which we would like to control in a regression calculating the effect of X on Y. Figure 8.2 depicts the causal diagram of Z inducing a spurious correlation between X and Y. Consider Y permutation, in which the rows of Y are permuted to reflect the null hypothesis of no relationship between Y and X. Doing this also breaks the relationship between Z and Y, which amounts to assuming away one leg in the confounder diagram. Now consider X permutation, in which just X is shuffled. This would break the relationship between Z and X, also assuming away a leg in the confounding diagram.

	Y		
	A	B	C
A	0	1	1
B	1	0	0
C	0	1	0

	X		
	A	B	C
A	0	3	–2
B	1.2	0	–4
C	0	6	0

⋮

	B	C	A
B	0	0	1
C	1	0	0
A	1	1	0

	A	B	C
A	0	3	–2
B	1.2	0	–4
C	0	6	0

FIGURE 8.1 Illustration of bivariate QAP. Example of dependent network (i.e., Y) permutation.

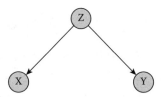

FIGURE 8.2 Causal diagram illustrating the role of a confounder (Z) in creating a spurious correlation between X and Y.

Dekker, Krackhardt, and Snijders (2007) propose an algorithm, termed double semi-partialing, that is intended to balance between X and Y permutations, and they show that it performs better than X or Y permutations. Let $\hat{\delta}Z$ be the estimate from $Y = \delta Z + E$. Define $\hat{\epsilon}_{XZ} = X - \hat{\delta}Z$. Define $\pi(\hat{\epsilon}_{XZ})$ to be a matrix permutation of $\hat{\epsilon}_{XZ}$. The nonparametric null distribution of β is derived by estimating $Y = \pi(\hat{\epsilon}_{XZ})\beta + \delta Z + E$. QAP is a very useful methodology when the researcher is uncertain which dependencies to include in ERGM, or the LSM does not provide a good fit.

For applications of QAP in political networks research, see Mizruchi (1990); Weible and Sabatier (2005); Bochsler (2009); Shrestha and Feiock (2009); Henry (2011); Lee, Feiock, and Lee (2012); Heaney et al. (2012); Desmarais et al. (2015); Andrew et al. (2015); and Chen, Suo, and Ma (2015).

Considering the work of Henry (2011) as an example, the authors were interested in understanding the conditions under which party activists are members of the same associations and particularly the extent to which copartisanship affected this likelihood. Drawing on surveys they had conducted at the 2008 Democratic and Republican National Conventions, Henry (2011) estimated models predicting organizational comembership as a function of copartisanship. They also controlled for ideology, sex/gender, race/ethnicity, age, educational attainment, income, and religious participation. The empirical analysis is particularly interesting given our discussion above, but the authors specified three types of models: logistic regression, the QAP, and an ERGM. Results from all three models showed that being in the same party is a strong positive

predictor of being in the same organization, even after controlling for alternative explanations for comembership. In fact, only 1.78 percent of comemberships crossed party
lines; the association network is strongly polarized by party. The results illustrate one of
the many barriers to partisan cooperation: party activists rarely come into contact with
activists from the other party in their civic and political associations.

Dynamic Models

The statistical analysis of longitudinal networks has a smaller literature than that for
cross-sectional networks. Two models that build on the ERGM, however, have been
applied with some frequency in political science. Here we discuss each model and its
applications to political science briefly. For a direct contrast and comparison of the two
models, see Desmarais and Cranmer (2012a) and Leifeld and Cranmer (2014).

The Temporal ERGM (TERGM)

The temporal exponential random graph model (TERGM) is a straightforward longitudinal extension of the ERGM. The defining feature of the TERGM vis-à-vis the ERGM
is that the statistics in the TERGM model the ways in which past realizations of the network influence the current network.

To modify the ERGM for modeling how the network N at time t, denoted N^t, depends
on previous networks $K \in \{1, \ldots, T-1\}$, we simply introduce the lagged networks
into the $\mathbf{h}$.

$$P(Y^t \mid Y^{t-K}, \ldots, Y^{t-1}, \ \boldsymbol{\theta}) = \frac{\exp(\boldsymbol{\theta}^{\top} \boldsymbol{h}(Y^t, Y^{t-1}, \ldots, Y^{t-K}))}{c(\boldsymbol{\theta}, Y^{t-K}, \ldots, Y^{t-1})}. \quad (4)$$

The specification of K is important because Y^t networks in the time series preceding
time point $K + 1$ cannot be modeled with the correct model.

Equation 4 specifies a TERGM for a single time point, Y^t. The joint likelihood of the
time series of networks spanning times $K + 1$ and T is derived as the product of the conditional probabilities, conditioning on past networks:

$$P(Y^{K+1}, \ldots, Y^T \mid Y^1, \ldots, Y^K, \ \boldsymbol{\theta}) = \prod_{t=K+1}^{T} P(Y^t \mid Y^{t-K}, \ldots, Y^{t-1}, \ \boldsymbol{\theta}). \quad (5)$$

A TERGM can be applied to just a single network, which is equivalent to using ERGM
with statistics involving one or more lagged networks, or a time series of networks with
dozens or even hundreds of networks. For more detailed methodological treatment of
the TERGM, see Hanneke, Fu, and Xing (2010b); Cranmer and Desmarais (2011); and

Desmarais and Cranmer (2012c). The bootstrap pseudo likelihood methods introduced in Desmarais and Cranmer (2012c) permit computationally efficient application to long time series.

Dependence on lagged networks can be incorporated in a fashion similar to including a covariate in a cross-sectional ERGM. For example, reciprocation is a nearly ubiquitous process in social networks. However, in time-stamped data, it is not clear whether the reciprocation of a tie will occur within one time period—especially if ties take a long time to form (e.g., links in an annually measured scientific paper citation network) or if time periods are notably short (e.g., an email network with hourly time stamps). To observe reciprocity, we may need to measure it with a lag. Single-period delayed reciprocity is modeled as

$$h_r(Y^t, Y^{t-1}) = \sum_{ji} Y_{ij}^t Y_{ji}^{t-1}.$$ (6)

The lagged effects in a TERGM specification—the components of **h**—can vary in terms of their order, from 1 to K. For example, if $K = 4$, we could model star-formation processes that aggregate over four periods, but also limit reciprocity effects to a single period. See Morris, Handcock, and Hunter (2008) for an extensive review of endogenous effect specification.

For applications of the TERGM in political networks research, in which myriad examples of lagged endogenous effects can be found, see, for example, Cranmer, Desmarais, and Menninga (2012); Cranmer, Desmarais, and Kirkland (2012); Almquist and Butts (2013); Clark and Caro (2013); Corbetta (2013); Cranmer, Heinrich, and Desmarais (2014); Masket and Shor (2014); and Ingold and Leifeld (2016).

Consider the work of Ingold and Leifeld (2016) as an example. Dozens of policy network case studies in continental Europe have used almost identical survey questionnaires to collect data over the last three decades. In addition to data on collaboration, information exchange, and a variety of actor attributes, respondents were usually asked whom they would judge as particularly important in the rest of the network. While this is obviously a network relation, earlier studies aggregated it into a node attribute in order to measure an actor's overall importance in the policy network. Ingold and Leifeld (2016) exploited the fact that this is a network relation and modeled it using ERGMs for the cross-sectional data sets and TERGMs for the longitudinal data set. Specifically, they used four different data sets from different countries (institutional settings), levels (local to national), and policy stages (implementation and policy formulation decision making) to assure validity of results across context. In terms of specification, they estimated an ERGM of their second temporal observation conditional on the first, thus modeling the changes between periods one and two. The TERGM examined whether changes in the betweenness centrality of actors in the collaboration network could explain their perception as being important at the second time point. In other words, it is not simply collaboration centrality that makes one important, it is not simply collaboration ties with alters that make one regard that other organization as important, and it's not simply one's institutional role that makes one important (e.g., being a decision maker)—it's also that becoming more central over time makes alters perceive an ego as being an important player in the policy process. As the predictor of interest was betweenness centrality, this reflects the ability to tie different communities in the network together.

Stochastic Actor Oriented Models (SAOMs)

The stochastic actor oriented model (SAOM) (Snijders, van de Bunt, and Steglich, 2010) is a statistical model for longitudinal network data that has had considerable application in political networks research and can be considered an alternative to TERGM. The SAOM is a structurally detailed model that is focused on interpretation at the node level. The SAOM and TERGM are similar in many underlying facets. Indeed, the equilibrium distribution of the SAOM is an exponential family random graph (Snijders, 2001). The "actor orientation" in the SAOM begins with an assumption about how the network changes. First, ties change one at a time. An actor is selected at random according to a Poisson process. The actor can then choose to leave its tie profile unchanged or change a single outgoing tie. The rates that parameterize the Poisson processes can be actor specific, modeling how tie volatility varies based on actor-level covariates. Let $Y^{(ij)}$ represent the network in which element ij of the adjacency matrix is toggled (changed from 0 to 1 or from 1 to 0). If selected to consider a tie change, the probability that actor i changes its tie status with j is proportional to $\exp\left(\sum_{h=1}^{k} \theta_h \Gamma_{ih}(Y^{(ij)})\right)$, where $\sum_{h=1}^{k} \theta_h \Gamma_{ih}(Y^{(ij)})$ is the actor "objective function" (Snijders, van de Bunt, and Steglich, 2010). Like the ERGM, the building blocks are regression coefficient style parameters θ and network statistics $\Gamma()$. The SAOM objective function is a dot product of network statistics that change with the ties sent by actor i and real-valued parameters.

An added feature of the SAOM relative to TERGM is that it offers the option of specifying a dynamic model for time-dependent actor attributes termed "behavior." The behavior equation includes both other node covariates and functions of the network designed to evaluate how the network influences behavior. To develop the idea of the behavior model, first consider a regression for a node attribute at time t, which includes as covariates other node attributes as well as node-level statistics calculated on the network at time $t-1$ (e.g., node centrality, the average attribute value of a node's partners in the network). Instead of directly measuring the network at $t-1$ in order to model node attributes at time t, intermediate changes in both the network and behavior are simulated between times t and $t-1$. The model for the change in behavior between times $t-1$ and t includes an iterative process of change between the network and behavior—changes that are simulated/inferred, as they are not observed (Steglich, Snijders, and Pearson, 2010). This simulation of intermediate changes is the modeling feature that differentiates TERGM and SAOM. The canonical form of data for which the SAOM is designed is network snapshot data, in which the ties in a network are sampled at different points in time, and the researcher does not know how the network changed between snapshots. The changes are simulated according to the detailed structural assumptions in the SAOM. Finally, one should also note the widespread misconception that this coevolutionary model can identify separate influences for homophily and influence, two forces that are usually confounded in network research. As Snijders, van de Bunt, and Steglich (2010) point out, the SAOM can only make this differentiation in extremely limited cases, and the model is not generally capable of this differentiation in applied research contexts.

Political science applications of SAOM include Berardo and Scholz (2010), Fischer et al. (2012), Fischer and Sciarini (2013), Berardo (2013), Kinne (2014), and Manger and Pickup (2014).

As a last example from the literature, consider Berardo (2013), who (2013) studied perceptions of procedural fairness in self-organized networks of stakeholders in five US estuaries where environmental problems are common. How members of a group perceive fairness in decision-making processes is a key variable to study for researchers interested in collaborative processes, given that those processes in which procedural fairness is low usually are less likely to be sustained in time. Berardo finds that participation in networks does not alter perceptions of procedural fairness. Instead, perceptions of procedural fairness impact participation in networks, with homophily seeming to drive the process. In other words, similar perceptions of fairness are a strong predictor of the establishment of ties among actors. Berardo claims that this is an important result, because it hints at the fact that in the absence of high levels of procedural fairness, the network is likely to be fragmented into groups of "winners" and "losers" in the decision-making process, which may make long-term collaboration at a systemic level difficult to sustain.

SELECTING AN APPROPRIATE APPROACH

The methods described above differ along a couple of important dimensions, including (1) the role of structural network theory in developing a model specification and (2) the degree to which interdependence is accounted for through the model parameters versus through the hypothesis testing framework. Considering how a given application aligns along these dimensions, the researcher can determine which of these methods is most appropriate.

The first major consideration in selecting a model for a network regards whether one of the objectives of the research is to conduct inference regarding precise patterns of interdependence among the ties in the network. For example, Song (2015) states several hypotheses regarding interdependence between ties in networks of political discussion. These include popularity (the tendency to send ties to nodes with high in-degree), activity (the tendency for nodes with high out-degree to send new ties at a higher rate), and transitivity. When the researcher has formed precise hypotheses regarding dependence among the ties, the only models that we have discussed that can be used are those based on the ERGM—ERGM, TERGM, and SAOM—the latter two in the case of longitudinal networks. The LSM, though useful for the purpose of exploring the structure of the network that is not explained through the use of exogenous node and dyad covariates, cannot be used to test hypotheses regarding the interdependence among ties. The QAP represents a method of hypothesis testing that is robust to the presence of interdependence among the ties in the network, but there is no way to use QAP results in diagnosing the forms of interdependence that exist among the ties.

If the researcher is only interested in testing the effects of covariates, but would like to account for network dependence, the second important consideration is the choice between parametric and nonparametric methods. Both the ERGM and LSM use precise parameterizations to model away the interdependence for which the covariates do not account. In the ERGM, the researcher must specify the exact network statistics that correspond to the forms of interdependence, a process that may sometimes be burdensome. In the LSM, the interdependence is absorbed by a large latent parameter space of unmeasured node attributes, along which nodes are assumed to be homophilous.

With both the LSM and ERGM, it is possible that the researcher will fail to specify a model that results in the good fit required to draw inferences with a parametric model. As noted previously, specification of an ERGM requires precise theory regarding the forms of interdependence in a network. The LSM demands less in terms of precise assumptions regarding structural dependencies, but it does impose some limitations. The dependence structures in the LSM must conform closely to a metric space in which the probability of a tie is inversely proportional to distance in the space. This creates two limitations on the LSM in accounting for dependence. These limitations derive from the properties of metric spaces (Bryant, 1985). The first property is *symmetry*, which means that the distance from i to j is equivalent to the distance from j to i. If the probability of a tie is linked to these symmetrical distances in the latent space, then the LSM implies that ties exhibit a tendency toward reciprocity. Symmetric dependence would be inappropriate for a hierarchical network, for example, in which ties flow along paths that do not loop back (e.g., an organizational chart) (Krackhardt, Carley, and Prietula, 1994). The other relevant property of a metric space is the *triangle inequality*, which indicates that the distance between i and j can be at most the distance between i and k and j and k, where k is any other node in the network. This means that if, according to the latent space, i is very likely to tie with k and j is very likely to tie with k, then i and j will also be likely to tie. The triangle inequality embeds transitivity into the structural assumptions underlying the LSM. Such an assumption would be inappropriate for a conflictual network, in which the enemy of your enemy is likely your friend (Cranmer and Desmarais, 2011). If the researcher's theory of network dependence is not precise enough to specify an ERGM and the structural assumptions associated with the LSM are not suitable in a given application, then QAP is the best option.

Model dependence is the term used to describe the conditions under which the conclusions drawn from a statistical modeling exercise vary across reasonable alternative specifications of the model (Ho et al., 2007). For example, if a test of the hypothesis that nodes in a network exhibit homophily with respect to a given attribute exhibited different results when using LSM and QAP, the test would be model dependent. If the researcher's primary interest lies in testing hypotheses regarding the effects of exogenous covariates, and the researcher has identified plausible specifications of ERGM and/or LSM, it is prudent to also evaluate hypotheses using QAP. If results are consistent across ERGM, LSM, and QAP, that is a strong sign of robustness. If they vary, the researcher should endeavor to understand why and assure that the structural assumptions represented by ERGM and/or LSM are indeed appropriate.

Turning to dynamic models, the literature on political networks presents two modeling options: SAOM and TERGM.[1] Both Desmarais and Cranmer (2012a) and Leifeld and Cranmer (2014) present thorough discussions of the ways in which researchers can draw conceptual and empirical comparisons of SAOM and TERGM. First, in terms of empirical comparison, if the researcher does not have theoretical reasons to prefer either SAOM or TERGM, it is possible to use either in- or out-of-sample comparisons to evaluate which method provides a better fit. Desmarais and Cranmer (2012a) and Leifeld and Cranmer (2014) provide extensive discussion and examples regarding the empirical comparison of SAOM and TERGM.

There are a few considerations that may allow the researcher to select between SAOM and TERGM based on theory. First, is it appropriate to assume that the network changes according to a process in which an actor considers changing one outgoing tie at a time to stochastically optimize its objective function? If the answer to this question is yes, then the SAOM is a favorable option. Through making this assumption about the form of network change, it is possible to identify other features of the network dynamics, such as differentiating between homophily and influence. If the answer to this question is no, then TERGM is favorable, because there are no such assumptions regarding the form of network change. Second, do the ties in the network and behavior coevolve simultaneously? As noted previously, the SAOM consists of two equations: an objective function for tie formation and another for behavior (i.e., node attribute) evolution. The main advantage of using SAOM over estimating these functions separately is that through the structural assumptions regarding change dynamics, it is possible to identify coevolution dynamics that occur at a finer time interval than that at which the data were collected. Third, is there a reason to suspect nonstationarity in the time series of networks? Underlying the TERGM is an assumption that the series of networks under analysis has reached a stationary distribution—a stable time-point-to-time-point process of network generation. In the SAOM it is assumed that change over time follows a stable/stationary process, but it is not assumed that the time series of networks has reached stationarity. Thus, if the network under study has recently come into formation—suggesting that more time may have to pass to reach stationarity, or there is some inexplicable shift in the network's structure over time, use of the SAOM would be favored.

FRONTIERS IN NETWORK MODELING

Scholars of government and politics are in a nearly unique position as far as access to data on ties between the actors they study. In every subfield of political science—from political behavior research on campaign contribution networks of individuals to intra-institutional studies of interaction within legislatures or administrative agencies, to international studies of trade flows, alliances, and migration—data are regularly available and often open by public records mandate. Furthermore, this rich archival data often represent a census of the relevant population that covers several decades or even centuries. Since such varied and rich data are available, it is safe to assume that most established methods for modeling network data could be fruitfully applied to problems in political networks research. Furthermore, as the field of automated text analysis matures, the volume and scope of network data available to political scientists are likely to explode. On the frontier of research we see great promise in the application of network methods to diverse data sets and in the generation of new political networks data.

The frontier of statistical network analysis is also developing quickly. One area in which the field is rapidly evolving is techniques for analyzing weighted (e.g., valued-edge) networks. Wyatt, Choudhury, and Bilmes (2010; Desmarais and Cranmer (2011; and Krivitsky (2012) have proposed methods for approaching this problem, and software is now available to implement these techniques. Other recent developments that show promise and deserve further consideration in political networks research include the mixed membership stochastic blockmodel (Airoldi et al., 2009), exponential family random network models (Fellows and Handcock, 2012), and relational event models for longitudinal data (Butts, 2008), but these methods have yet, as of this writing, to permeate political science.

In sum, political network analysis is developing rapidly in terms of the range of substantive problems to which network analysis is applied, the quality and volume of network data available to political scientists, and the statistical methods themselves. We think it likely that the landscape of political networks will look substantially different ten years after this writing than it does today.

ACKNOWLEDGMENTS

Many thanks to Ramiro Berardo, Jan Box-Steffensmeier, Dino Christenson, Michael Heaney, and Philip Leifeld for their helpful comments This work was supported by National Science Foundation grants SES-1558661, SES-1619644, and CISE-1320219. Any opinions, findings, and conclusions or recommendations are those of the authors and do not necessarily reflect those of the sponsor.

NOTE

1. Ward, Ahlquist, and Rozenas (2013) propose a dynamic extension of the LSM. However, within-dyad autocorrelation is the only form of network dependence for which it accounts. Since it does not account for higher order forms of interdependence, we do not consider it to be a dynamic network model along the same lines as SAOM and TERGM, which both permit the modeling of arbitrary forms of intertemporal dependence.

References

Airoldi, E. M., Blei, D. M., Fienberg, S. E., and Xing, E. P. (2009). "Mixed Membership Stochastic Blockmodels." In *Advances in Neural Information Processing Systems*, edited by Y. Bengio and D. Schuurmans and J. D. Lafferty and C. K. I. Williams, and A. Culotta, pp. 33–40. https://papers.nips.cc/book/advances-in-neural-information-processing-systems-22-2009

Almquist, Z. W., and Butts, C. T. (2013). "Dynamic Network Logistic Regression: A Logistic Choice Analysis of Inter- and Intra-Group Blog Citation Dynamics in the 2004 US Presidential Election." *Political Analysis* 21(4): 430–448.

Andrew, S. A., Short, J. E., Jung, K., and Arlikatti, S. (2015). "Intergovernmental Cooperation in the Provision of Public Safety: Monitoring Mechanisms Embedded in Interlocal Agreements." *Public Administration Review* 75(3): 401–410.

Berardo, R. (2013). "The Coevolution of Perceptions of Procedural Fairness and Link Formation in Self-organizing Policy Networks." *Journal of Politics* 75(3): 686–700.

Berardo, R., and Scholz, J. T. (2010). "Self-Organizing Policy Networks: Risk, Partner Selection, and Cooperation in Estuaries." *American Journal of Political Science* 54(3): 632–649.

Bochsler, D. (2009). "Neighbours or Friends? When Swiss Cantonal Governments Co-operate with Each Other." *Regional and Federal Studies* 19(3): 349–370.

Box-Steffensmeier, J. M., and Christenson, D. P. (2014). "The Evolution and Formation of Amicus Curiae Networks." *Social Networks* 36: 82–96.

Bryant, V. (1985). *Metric Spaces: Iteration and Application.* Cambridge, UK: Cambridge University Press.

Butts, C. T. (2008). "A Relational Event Framework for Social Action." *Sociological Methodology* 38(1): 155–200.

Cao, X., and Ward, M. D. (2014). "Do Democracies Attract Portfolio Investment? Transnational Portfolio Investments Modeled as Dynamic Network." *International Interactions* 40(2): 216–245.

Chen, B., Suo, L., and Ma, J. (2015). "A Network Approach to Interprovincial Agreements A Study of Pan Pearl River Delta in China." *State and Local Government Review* 47(3): 181–191.

Clark, J. H., and Caro, V. (2013). "Multimember Districts and the Substantive Representation of Women: An Analysis of Legislative Cosponsorship Networks." *Politics & Gender* 9(1): 1–30.

Corbetta, R. (2013). "Cooperative and Antagonistic Networks: Multidimensional Affinity and Intervention in Ongoing Conflicts, 1946–2001." *International Studies Quarterly* 57(2): 370–384.

Cranmer, S. J., and Desmarais, B. A. (2011). "Inferential Network Analysis with Exponential Random Graph Models." *Political Analysis* 19(1): 66–86.

Cranmer, S. J., Desmarais, B. A., and Kirkland, J. H. (2012). "Toward a Network Theory of Alliance Formation." *International Interactions* 38(3): 295–324.

Cranmer, S. J., Desmarais, B. A., and Menninga, E. J. (2012). "Complex Dependencies in the Alliance Network." *Conflict Management and Peace Science* 29(3): 279–313.

Cranmer, S. J., Heinrich, T., and Desmarais, B. A. (2014). "Reciprocity and the Structural Determinants of the International Sanctions Network." *Social Networks* 36(January): 5–22.

Cranmer, S. J., Leifeld, P., McClurg, S., and Rolfe, M. (2016). "Navigating the Range of Statistical Tools for Inferential Network Analysis." *American Journal of Political Science*. doi: 10.1111/ajps.12263

Dekker, D., Krackhardt, D., and Snijders, T. A. B. (2007). "Sensitivity of MRQAP Tests to Collinearity and Autocorrelation Conditions." *Psychometrika* 72(4): 563–581.

Desmarais, B. A., and Cranmer, S. J. (2011). "Statistical Inference for Valued-Edge Networks: The Generalized Exponential Random Graph Model." *PLoS ONE* 7(1): e30136.

Desmarais, B. A., and Cranmer, S. J. (2012a). "Micro-Level Interpretation of Exponential Random Graph Models with Application to Estuary Networks." *Policy Studies Journal* 40(3): 402–434.

Desmarais, B. A., and Cranmer, S. J. (2012b). "Statistical Mechanics of Networks: Estimation and Uncertainty." *Physica A: Statistical Mechanics and its Applications* 391(4): 1865–1876.

Desmarais, B. A., and Cranmer, S. J. (2012c). "Statistical Mechanics of Networks: Estimation and Uncertainty." *Physica A: Statistical Mechanics and its Applications* 391(4): 1865–1876.

Desmarais, B. A., Moscardelli, V. G., Schaffner, B. F., and Kowal, M. S. (2015). "Measuring Legislative Collaboration: The Senate Press Events Network." *Social Networks* 40: 43–54.

Fellows, I., and Handcock, M. S. (2012). "Exponential-family Random Network Models." *arXiv:1208.0121.*

Fischer, M., Ingold, K., Sciarini, P., and Varone, F. (2012). "Impacts of Market Liberalization on Regulatory Network: A Longitudinal Analysis of the Swiss Telecommunications Sector." *Policy Studies Journal* 40(3): 435–457.

Fischer, M., and Sciarini, P. (2013). "Europeanization and the Inclusive Strategies of Executive Actors." *Journal of European Public Policy* 20(10): 1482–1498.

Gerber, E. R., Henry, A. D., and Lubell, M. (2013). "Political Homophily and Collaboration in Regional Planning Networks." *American Journal of Political Science* 57(3): 598–610.

Goodreau, S. M., Handcock, M. S., Hunter, D. R., Butts, C. T., and Morris, M. (2008). "A Statnet Tutorial." *Journal of Statistical Software* 24(9): 1–26.

Hanneke, S., Fu, W., and Xing, E. P. (2010a). "Discrete Temporal Models of Social Networks." *Electronic Journal of Statistics* 4: 585–605.

Hanneke, S., Fu, W., and Xing, E. P. (2010b). "Discrete Temporal Models of Social Networks." *Electronic Journal of Statistics* 4: 585–605.

Heaney, M. T., Masket, S. E., Miller, J. M., and Strolovitch, D. Z. (2012). "Polarized Networks: The Organizational Affiliations of National Party Convention Delegates." *American Behavioral Scientist* 56: 1654–1676.

Henry, A. D. (2011). "Ideology, Power, and the Structure of Policy Networks." *Policy Studies Journal* 39(3): 361–383.

Ho, D. E., Imai, K., King, G., and Stuart, E. A. (2007). "Matching as Nonparametric Preprocessing for Reducing Model Dependence in Parametric Causal Inference." *Political Analysis* 15(3): 199–236.

Hoff, P. D., Raftery, A. E., and Handcock, M. S. (2002). "Latent Space Approaches to Social Network Analysis." *Journal of the American Statistical Association* 97(460): 1090–1098. http://www.tandfonline.com/doi/abs/10.1198/016214502388618906.

Holland, P. W., and Leinhardt, S. (1981). "An Exponential Family of Probability Distributions for Directed Graphs." *Journal of the American Statistical Association* 76(373): 33–50.

Hunter, D. R., Handcock, M. S., Butts, C. T., Goodreau, S. M., and Morris, M. (2008). "ERGM: A Package to Fit, Simulate and Diagnose Exponential-Family Models for Networks." *Journal of Statistical Software* 24(3): 1–29. http://www.jstatsoft.org/v24/i03/

Ingold, K. M., and Leifeld, P. (2016). "Structural and Institutional Determinants of Influence Reputation: A Comparison of Collaborative and Adversarial Policy Networks in Decision Making and Implementation." *Journal of Public Administration Research and Theory* 26(1): 1–18. http://dx.doi.org/10.1093/jopart/muu043

Kinne, B. J. (2014). "Dependent Diplomacy: Signaling, Strategy, and Prestige in the Diplomatic Network." *International Studies Quarterly* 58(2): 247–259.

Kirkland, J. H. (2012). "Multimember Districts' Effect on Collaboration between US State Legislators." *Legislative Studies Quarterly* 37(3): 329–353.

Kirkland, J. H., and Gross, J. H. (2014). "Measurement and Theory in Legislative Networks: The Evolving Topology of Congressional Collaboration." *Social Networks* 36:97–109.

Krackardt, D. (1987). "QAP Partialling as a Test of Spuriousness." *Social Networks* 9(2): 171–186.

Krackhardt, D., Carley, K. M., and Prietula, M. J. (1994). "Graph Theoretical Dimensions of Informal Organizations." *Computational Organization Theory* 89(112): 123–140.

Krafft, P., Moore, J., Desmarais, B. A., and Wallach, H. (2012). "Topic-partitioned Multinetwork Embeddings." In *Advances in Neural Information Processing Systems Twenty-Five*, edited by F. Pereira and C. J. C. Burges, L. Bottou, and K. Q. Weinberger. http://machinelearning.wustl.edu/mlpapers/paper_files/NIPS2012_1288.pdf.

Krivitsky, P. N. (2012). "Exponential-Family Random Graph Models for Valued Networks." *Electronic Journal of Statistics* 6: 1100.

Lazer, D., Rubineau, B., Chetkovich, C., Katz, N., and Neblo, M. (2010). "The Coevolution of Networks and Political Attitudes." *Political Communication* 27(3): 248–274.

Lee, I.-W., Feiock, R. C., and Lee, Y. (2012). "Competitors and Cooperators: A Micro-Level Analysis of Regional Economic Development Collaboration Networks." *Public Administration Review* 72(2): 253–262.

Leifeld, P., and Cranmer, S. J. (2014). "Comparing the Temporal Exponential Random Graph Model (TERGM) and the Stochastic Actor-Oriented Model (SAOM)." Paper presented at the 2014 Annual Meeting of the Swiss Political Science Association (SVPW), Bern, Switzerland, January 30.

Lusher, D., Koskinen, J., and Robins, G. (2013). *Exponential Random Graph Models for Social Networks*. New York: Cambridge University Press.

Manger, M. S., and Pickup, M. A. (2014). "The Coevolution of Trade Agreement Networks and Democracy." *Journal of Conflict Resolution* 60(1): 164–191.

Mantel, N. (1967). "The Detection of Disease Clustering and a Generalized Regression Approach." *Cancer Research* 27(2 pt. 1): 209–220.

Masket, S., and Shor, B. (2014). "Polarization without Parties Term Limits and Legislative Partisanship in Nebraska's Unicameral Legislature." *State Politics & Policy Quarterly* 15(1): 67–90.

Mizruchi, M. S. (1990). "Determinants of Political Opposition among Large American Corporations." *Social Forces* 68(4): 1065–1088.

Morris, M., Handcock, M. S., and Hunter, D. R. (2008). "Specification of Exponential-Family Random Graph Models: Terms and Computational Aspects." *Journal of Statistical Software* 24(4): 1–24. http://www.jstatsoft.org/v24/i09/

Robins, G., and Pattison, P. (2001). "Random Graph Models for Temporal Processes in Social Networks." *Journal of Mathematical Sociology* 25(1): 5–41.

Shrestha, M. K., and Feiock, R. C. (2009). "Governing US Metropolitan Areas Self-Organizing and Multiplex Service Networks." *American Politics Research* 37(5): 801–823.

Snijders, T. A. B. (2001). "The Statistical Evaluation of Social Network Dynamics." *Sociological Methodology* 31: 361–395.

Snijders, T. A. B., van de Bunt, G. G., and Steglich, C. E. G. (2010). "Introduction to Stochastic Actor-based Models for Network Dynamics." *Social Networks* 32(1): 44–60.

Song, H. (2015). "Uncovering the Structural Underpinnings of Political Discussion Networks: Evidence from an Exponential Random Graph Model." *Journal of Communication* 65(1): 146–169.

Steglich, C., Snijders, T. A. B., and Pearson, M. (2010). "Dynamic Networks and Behavior: Separating Selection from Influence." *Sociological Methodology* 40(1): 329–393.

Thurner, P. W., and Binder, M. (2009). "European Union Transgovernmental Networks: The Emergence of a New Political Space beyond the Nation-State?" *European Journal of Political Research* 48(1): 80–106.

Ward, M. D., Ahlquist, J. S., and Rozenas, A. (2013). "Gravity's Rainbow: A Dynamic Latent Space Model for the World Trade Network." *Network Science* 1(1): 95–118.

Ward, M. D., Siverson, R. M., and Cao, X. (2007). "Disputes, Democracies, and Dependencies: A Reexamination of the Kantian Peace." *American Journal of Political Science* 51(3): 583–601.

Wasserman, S., and Pattison, P. (1996). "Logit Models and Logistic Regressions for Social Networks: I—An Introduction to Markov Graphs and p*." *Psychometrika* 61(3): 401–425.

Weible, C. M., and Sabatier, P. A. (2005). "Comparing Policy Networks: Marine Protected Areas in California." *Policy Studies Journal* 33(2): 181–201.

Wyatt, D., Choudhury, T., and Bilmes, J. (2010). "Discovering Long Range Properties of Social Networks with Multi-valued Time-Inhomogeneous Models." In *Proceedings of the Twenty-Fourth AAAI Conference on Artificial Intelligence*, edited by M. Fox and D. Poole, pp. 630–636.

CHAPTER 9

STOCHASTIC ACTOR ORIENTED MODELS FOR NETWORK DYNAMICS

TOM A. B. SNIJDERS AND MARK PICKUP

STOCHASTIC ACTOR ORIENTED MODELS: NETWORK PANEL DATA AND COEVOLUTION

THIS chapter, about stochastic actor oriented models (SAOMs), highlights and explicates a statistical model for analyzing network panel data. The data are structured as repeated observations of a network between a given set of nodes that represent political actors of some kind. The set of nodes may be changing now and then, as new actors come in and existing ones drop out, or as actors may combine or split up. At a minimum there are two waves of data, but there might be many more.

The basic idea of SAOMs (Snijders, 2001) is that the panel data are regarded as repeated snapshots of a process that is evolving in continuous time, and this process is a Markov process: probabilities of tie changes are determined by the current state; further, the change is represented as a sequence of changes of single ties. Since each tie change modifies the state of the network, and the later changes will build on this new state, because of path dependence it will change the entire future. The assumption that between the panel observations many tie changes can sequentially take place, each acting on the state that is the result of earlier tie changes, leads to a rich dependence structure for the ties in the observed networks. The phrase "actor oriented" reflects that the tie changes are modeled as being determined by the actors. For the case of directed networks there is no assumption of coordination of tie changes by different actors, so groupwise changes cannot be represented. The Markov chain assumption can be mitigated in two ways: by including covariates from earlier times or by extending the outcome space from a single network to multiple networks—thus leading to the analysis of a multivariate network, as in Snijders et al. (2013)—or with actor-level (i.e., nodal) variables (Steglich et al., 2010). Such an extended outcome space leads to *coevolution models*, representing the interdependent dynamics of several dependent variables. The coevolving network may be a two-mode network, that is, affiliations between the actors who constitute the first mode with some other node set. This offers the possibility of modeling the interdependence of relations between actors and their memberships in organizations, such as the relations between countries through common memberships in nongovernmental organizations (NGOs) or between individuals through common memberships in civic organizations.

This chapter has four main parts. First is a brief overview of applications of this model in political science published to date. Second, we present the model for analyzing dynamics of directed networks with a brief sketch of the associated estimation methods, implemented in the software package RSiena (Simulation Investigation for Empirical Network Analysis; Ripley et al., 2016) of the R statistical system (R Core Team, 2016). A tie change in a directed network requires only the decision of one actor in a dyad, such as the decision of one country to direct hostility at another. Third, this model is extended to nondirected networks, that is, networks in which the ties are by their nature nondirectional (such as trade agreements), which is a type of network often encountered in political science. For nondirected networks it is necessary to take into account the joint decision-making by both actors involved in a given tie. Several models are considered for how these actors coordinate. The definition of this model has not been published before (although some published applications do exist.) The fourth main section sketches the approach to coevolution. The chapter concludes with a discussion of some aspects of this model. For the positioning of this model in the further array of statistical network models, see Snijders (2011) and Desmarais and Cranmer (2016).

APPLICATIONS

The SAOM for network dynamics has been applied in a variety of social science disciplines, including various studies in the political sciences. Other approaches common in political science for the analysis of longitudinal network data include temporal exponential random graph models (ERGMs) (Almquist and Butts, 2013) and dynamic latent space models (Cao and Ward, 2014; Dorff and Ward, 2016).

The use of SAOMs in political science is currently largely limited to the subfields of policy (Berardo and Scholz, 2010; Ingold and Fischer, 2014; Giuliani, 2013), international relations (Kinne, 2013; Rhue and Sundararajan, 2014), and international political economy (Manger and Pickup, 2016; Manger et al., 2012). At least one study has applied SAOMS to political behavior (Liang, 2014). As more and more network data are collected at the level of the individual voter, we might expect an increase in the application of SAOMs to studying political behavior. After all, the social network has been of central importance to the study of political behavior since the subfield's inception (Berelson et al., 1954; Campbell et al., 1960). Further, the application of SAOMs to online networks (well-established outside political science) can be expected to grow within political science, as researchers become increasingly interested in the effects of online social networks on political behavior.

With respect to formal characteristics of the applications, SAOMs in political science have been applied to directed (Rhue and Sundararajan, 2014; Ingold and Fischer, 2014; Liang, 2014; Giuliani, 2013; Fischer et al., 2012; Berardo and Scholz, 2010) as well as nondirected (Manger and Pickup, 2016; Manger et al., 2012; Kinne, 2013) networks. Applications have included networks with anywhere between two and eleven waves, and between 23 and 1,178 nodes. A few have included coevolution models with behavioral dependent variables (Manger and Pickup, 2016; Rhue and Sundararajan, 2014; Berardo and Scholz, 2010), and even fewer have studied coevolution with multiple networks, two-mode networks (Liang, 2014), or multiple behavioral dependent variables (Rhue and Sundararajan, 2014).

Across all subfields within political science, there are methodological innovations that we might increasingly expect researchers to incorporate in their analysis. We can expect an increase in the use of SAOMs to analyze multiple networks as interdependent structures, investigating how changes in one network relate to other networks. This will become increasingly viable as more and more network data are collected. We might expect a greater application of SAOMs to two-mode networks as political scientists apply network analysis to the ties individuals and countries have through organizations. Examples are the ties countries have through treaties, the ties that individuals have through shared media consumption (traditional or online), and shared concept networks (Liang, 2014). As they are evaluated in RSiena, SAOMs allow for arbitrary time lags between observations, facilitating the analysis of longitudinal data that do not have evenly spaced observations in time. RSiena also allows for different rate functions across nodes in the network. This would enable the researcher to account for the differing relevance of the network for the individual or organization. For example, if the network represents social activities or groups, these groups may be more or less salient to different individuals, and those for whom the group is more salient may also change their ties more frequently.

STOCHASTIC ACTOR ORIENTED MODELS FOR NETWORK DYNAMICS

The SAOM (also called Stochastic Actor Based Model) is a statistical model for longitudinal data collected in a network panel design, in which network observations are available for a given set of nodes, for two or more consecutive waves. Some turnover of the nodes is allowed, which is helpful for representing the creation and disappearance of organizations or countries. It represents a network process in which, as time goes by, ties can be added as well as deleted. The model aims to obtain a statistical representation of the influences determining creation and termination of ties; turnover of nodes, if any, is considered an exogenous influence. In this section the fundamental description of the probability model is given, followed by possible ingredients for its detailed specification. Finally, procedures for estimation are briefly described.

Notation

The dependent variable in this section is a sequence of directed networks on a given node set $\{1, \ldots, n\}$. Nodes represent political or other social actors (countries, NGOs, political leaders, voters, etc.). The existence of a tie from node i to node j is indicated by the *tie indicator variable* X_{ij}, having the value 1 or 0 depending on whether there is a tie $i \rightarrow j$. For the tie $i \rightarrow j$, actor i is called the *sender* and j the *receiver*. Self-ties are not considered, so that always $X_{ii} = 0$, for all i. The matrix with elements X_{ij} is the adjacency matrix of a directed graph, or digraph; the adjacency matrix as well as the digraph will be denoted by X. Outcomes (i.e., particular realizations) of digraphs will be denoted by lowercase x. Replacing an index by a plus sign denotes summation over that index; thus, the number of outgoing ties of actor i (the *outdegree* of i) is denoted $X_{i+} = \sum_j X_{ij}$, while the *indegree*, the number of incoming ties, is $X_{i+} = \sum_j X_{ij}$. For the data structure, it is assumed that there are two or more repeated observations of the network. Observation moments are indicated by $t_1, t_2, \ldots, t_M$ with $M \geq 2$. Besides the dependent network, there may be explanatory variables measured at the level of the actors (*monadic* or *actor covariates*) or on pairs of actors (*dyadic covariates*).

Actor Oriented Models

One of the issues for network analysis in the social sciences is the fact that networks by their nature are dyadic—that is, they refer to pairs of actors—whereas the natural theoretical unit is the actor. This issue is discussed more generally by Emirbayer and Goodwin (1994). For modeling network dynamics, a natural combination of network structure and individual agency is possible by basing the model on the postulate that creation and termination of ties are initiated by the actors. In this section the model is presented for binary directed networks, and we postulate that it is meaningful to regard ties as resulting from choices made by the actor sending the tie; in the fourth section we consider nondirected networks, assumed to be based on choices made by both involved actors. The model is explained more fully in Snijders (2001) and Snijders, van de Bunt, and Steglich (2010).

The probability model for network dynamics is based, like other statistical models, on a number of simplifying assumptions:

1. Between observation moments t_1, t_2, etc., time runs on, and changes in the network can and will take place without being directly observed. Thus, while the observation schedule is in discrete time, an unobserved underlying process of network evolution is assumed to take place with a continuous time parameter $t \in [t_1, t_M]$.
2. At any given time point $t \in [t_1, t_M]$ when the network changes, not more than one tie variable X_{ij} can change. In other words, either one tie is created, or one tie is dissolved. The observed change is the net result of all these unobserved changes of single ties.
3. The probability that at time t a particular variable X_{ij} changes depends on the current state $X(t)$ of the network, not on earlier, preceding states.

Assumptions 1 and 3 are expressed mathematically by saying that the network model is a continuous-time Markov process. Assumption 2 simplifies the elements of change to the smallest possible constituent: the creation or termination of a single tie. These assumptions rule out instantaneous coordination or negotiation between actors. They were proposed as basic simplifying postulates by Holland and Leinhardt (1977). In future model developments it may be interesting to allow coordination between actors, but the postulates used here can be regarded as a natural first step to modeling network dynamics.

These three assumptions imply that actors make changes in reaction to each others' changes in between observations. This has strong intuitive validity for many panel observations of networks. Exceptions are situations in which collections of ties are created groupwise, for example, in multilateral alliances. The model is described totally by probabilities of single tie changes, depending on the state of the network. The probability model says nothing about the timing of the observations, and therefore the parameter values are not affected by the frequency of the observations or the time delays between them. It is assumed that the probability function of tie changes, conditional on the current state of the network and covariates, is constant in time; the probability function that a tie exists at any given time may, however, be changing.

The model is actor based in the sense that tie changes are modeled as the result of choices made by the actor sending the tie. The tie change model is split into two components: timing and choice. The timing component is defined in terms of *opportunities for change*, not in terms of actual change. This is to allow the possibility that an actor leaves the current situation unchanged, for example, because he or she is satisfied with it.

4. Consider a given current time point t, $t_m \leq t < t_{m+1}$, and denote the current state of the network by $x = X(t)$. Each actor i has a *rate of change*, denoted $\lambda_i(x; \rho)$, where ρ is a statistical parameter, which may depend on m. The rate of change can depend on actor covariates and on their degrees.

5. The waiting time until the next opportunity for change by any actor has the exponential distribution

$$
\begin{aligned}
&\mathrm{P}\{\text{Next opportunity for change is before } t + \Delta t \mid \text{current time is } t\} \\
&= 1 - \exp(-\lambda \Delta t)
\end{aligned}
\tag{1}
$$

with parameter $\lambda = \lambda_+(x; \rho)$.

6. The probability that the next opportunity for change is for actor i is given by

$$
\mathrm{P}\{\text{Next opportunity for change is by actor } i\} = \frac{\lambda_i(x; \rho)}{\lambda_+(x; \rho)}
\tag{2}
$$

This formula is consistent with a "first past the post" model, where all actors have stochastic waiting times as in item 5, the first one gets the opportunity to make a change, and then everything starts all over again but in a new state.

7. For the choice component, each actor i has an *objective function* $f_i(x^{(0)}, x; \beta)$ defined on the set of all pairs of networks $x^{(0)}$ and x such that $x^{(0)}$ and x differ in no more than one tie variable. The current network is $x^{(0)}$ and the objective function determines the probability that the next tie change by this actor, brings state $x^{(0)}$ into x; β is a statistical parameter. In a utility interpretation, the objective function may be regarded as the net utility that the actor gains from moving from $x^{(0)}$ to x. Since this is the short-term utility from one tie change, it should be regarded as a proximate, not ultimate utility, for example, expressing the advantageous network position that the actor is striving after as a means to obtain further goals.

8. To define this probability, the following notation is used. For a digraph x and $i \neq j$, by $x^{(\pm ij)}$ we define the graph that is identical to x in all tie variables except those for the ordered pair (i,j), and for which the tie variable $i \to j$ is toggled, $x_{ij}^{(\pm ij)} = 1 - x_{ij}$. Further, we define $x^{(\pm ii)} = x$ (just as a convenient formal definition). Assume that at the moment of time $t + \Delta t$ (see item 5) with current network $X(t) = x$, actor i has the opportunity for change. Then the probability that the tie variable changed is X_{ij}, so that the network x changes into $x^{(\pm ij)}$, is given by

$$
\frac{\exp\left(f_i\left(x, x^{(\pm ij)}; \beta\right)\right)}{\sum_{h=1}^{n} \exp\left(f_i\left(x, x^{(\pm ih)}; \beta\right)\right)} = \frac{\exp\left(f_i\left(x, x^{(\pm ij)}; \beta\right) - f_i\left(x, x; \beta\right)\right)}{\sum_{h=1}^{n} \exp\left(f_i\left(x, x^{(\pm ih)}; \beta\right) - f_i\left(x, x; \beta\right)\right)}
\tag{3}
$$

Expression (3) is a multinomial logit form. This can be obtained when it is assumed that i chooses the best j in the set $\{1, \ldots, n\}$ (where $j = i$ formally means "no change"; see above), where the aim is to toggle the variable X_{ij} that maximizes the objective function of the resulting state plus a random residual,

$$
f_i(x, x^{(\pm ij)}; \beta) + R_j
$$

where the variables R_j are independent and have a standard Gumbel distribution (for a proof, see Maddala, 1983). Thus, this model can be regarded as being obtainable as the result of *myopic stochastic optimization*. Game-theoretical models of network formation often use myopic optimization (e.g., Bala and Goyal, 2000). It should be noted, however, that what we assume is the vector of choice probabilities (3), not the myopic optimization—the latter being merely one of the ways in which this expression can be obtained; for the optimization interpretation it should be kept in mind, as suggested above, that the objective functions represent proximate rather than ultimate goals.

For extensions of this model in which different mechanisms or different parameter values may apply for creating new ties and maintaining existing ties, see the treatment in Snijders, van de Bunt, and Steglich (2010) and Ripley et al. (2016) of the endowment or maintenance function.

Transition Rates

The two model components, rate function and objective function, can be put together by considering the so-called transition rates. These give the basic definitions of the continuous-time Markov process resulting from the assumptions formulated above (cf. Norris, 1997, or other textbooks on continuous-time Markov processes) and may be helpful to some for a further understanding. Given that the only permitted transitions between networks are toggles of a single tie variable, the transition rates can be defined as

$$q_{ij}(x) = \lim_{\Delta t \downarrow 0} \frac{P\{X(t+\Delta t) = x^{(\pm ij)} \mid X(t) = x\}}{\Delta t} \tag{4}$$

for $i \neq j$. Note that this definition implies that the probabilities of toggling a particular tie variable X_{ij} in a short time interval are approximated by

$$P\{X(t+\Delta t) = x^{(\pm ij)} \mid X(t) = x\} \approx q_{ij}(x) \Delta t$$

The transition rate can be computed from the assumptions using the basic rules of probability and, denoting (3) by $p_{ij}(x, \beta)$, is given by

$$q_{ij}(x) = \lambda_i(x; \rho) p_{ij}(x, \beta) \tag{5}$$

Specification of the Actor Oriented Model

The specification of the SAOM amounts to the choice of the rate function $\lambda_i(x; \rho)$ and the objective function $f_i(x; \beta)$. This choice will be based on theoretical considerations, knowledge of the subject matter, and the hypotheses to be investigated. The focus of modeling normally is on the objective function, reflecting the choice part of the model.

In many cases, a simple specification of the rate function suffices:

$$\lambda_i(x;\rho) = \rho_m \tag{6}$$

where m is the index of the observation t_m such that the current time point t is between t_m and t_{m+1}. Including the parameter ρ_m allows to fit exactly the observed number of changes between t_m and t_{m+1}. In other cases, the rate of change may also depend on actor covariates or on positional characteristics such as degrees.

The more important part of the model specification is the objective function. As in generalized linear modeling, a linear combination is used:

$$f_i\left(x^{(0)},x;\beta\right) = \sum_{k=1}^{K} \beta_k s_{ki}\left(x^{(0)},x\right), \tag{7}$$

where the $s_{ki}(x^{(0)},x)$ are functions of the network, as seen from the point of view of actor i. These functions are called *effects*. When parameter β_k is positive, tie changes will have a higher probability when they lead to x for which $s_{ki}(x^{(0)},x)$ is higher—and conversely for negative β_k.

The R package RSiena (Ripley et al., 2016) offers a large variety of effects, some of which follow. First we present some effects depending on the network only, which are important for modeling the dependence between network ties. In most cases the effect $s_{ki}(x^{(0)},x)$ depends only on the new state x, not on the old state $x^{(0)}$. This means that the old state plays a role in determining the option set (i.e., which new states are possible), but not the relative evaluation of the various possible new states. To keep notation simple, we use $s_{ki}(x)$ to mean $s_{ki}(x^{(0)},x)$.

1. A basic component is the outdegree, $s_{1i}(x) = \sum_j x_{ij}$. This effect is analogous to a constant term in regression models and will almost always be included. It balances between creation and termination of ties, which can be understood as follows. Equation (3) shows that it is the *change* in the objective function that determines the probability. Given the preceding state $x^{(0)}$, the next state x either has one tie more, or one tie less, than $x^{(0)}$, or the two are identical. If $s_{1i}(x)$ has coefficient β_1, for creating a tie the contribution to (7) is β_1; for dissolving a tie the contribution is $-\beta_1$. Therefore the role of the outdegree effect in the model is the contribution of $2\beta_1$ in favor of tie creation versus tie termination. Usually networks are sparse, so that there are many more opportunities for creating than for terminating ties. Accordingly, in a more or less stable situation, the parameter β_1 will be negative to keep the network sparse (unless this is already determined by other model components).

2. Reciprocation of choice is a fundamental aspect of almost all directed social networks, because there is almost always some kind of exchange or other reciprocal dependence. This is reflected by the reciprocated degree, $s_{2i}(x) = \sum_j x_{ij}x_{ji}$, the number of reciprocal ties in which actor i is involved.

3. The local structure of networks is determined by triads, that is, subgraphs on three nodes (Holland and Leinhardt, 1976). A first type of triadic dependency is transitivity, in which the indirect connection of the pattern $i \rightarrow j \rightarrow h$ tends to imply the direct tie $i \rightarrow h$. This tendency is captured by $s_{3i}(x) = \sum_{j,h} x_{ij} x_{jh} x_{ih}$, the number of transitive triplets originating from actor i.

Theoretical arguments for this effect were formulated by Simmel ([1917] 1950), who discussed the consequences of triadic embeddedness on bargaining power of the social actors and on the possibility of conflicts. Coleman (1988) stressed the importance of triadic closure for social control, where actor i, who has access to j as well as h, has the potential to sanction them in case j behaves opportunistically with respect to h. There is also empirical confirmation of this effect for networks of alliances between firms, for example by Gulati and Gargiulo (1999).

Instead of using triad counts, one may represent tendencies toward transitive closure by weighted counts of structures such as those employed in ERGMs, for example, the geometrically weighted edgewise shared partner (GWESP) statistic (Snijders et al., 2006; Handcock and Hunter, 2006).

Indegrees and outdegrees are fundamental aspects of individual network centrality (Freeman, 1979). They reflect access to other actors and often are linked quite directly to opportunities as well as costs of the network position of the actors. Degrees may be indicators for influence potential, success (de Solla Price, 1976), prestige (Hafner-Burton and Montgomery, 2006), search potential (Scholz et al., 2008), and so forth, depending on the context. Accordingly, probabilities of tie creation and dissolution may depend on the degrees of the actors involved. This is expressed by degree-related effects, such as the following:

4. Indegree popularity, indicating the extent to which those with currently high indegrees are more popular as receivers of new ties. This can be expressed by $s_{5i}(x) = \sum_j x_{ij} x_{+j}$, the sum of the indegrees of those to whom i has a tie. When indegrees are seen as success indicators, this can model the Matthew effect of Merton (1968), which was used by de Solla Price (1976) in his network model of cumulative advantage, rediscovered by Barabasi and Albert (1999) in their "scalefree model." This is an example of an effect with emergent (micro-macro) consequences: if individual actors have a preference for being linked to popular (high-indegree) actors, the result is a network with a high dispersion of indegrees.Since degrees may often have diminishing returns, as argued by Hicklin et al. (2008), alternative specification of this effect could be considered, for example, $s_{5i}'(x) = \sum_j x_{ij} \sqrt{x_{+j}}$.

5. Similarly for outdegrees and for combinations of indegrees and outdegrees (e.g., "assortativity": Are the outgoing ties of actors with high degrees directed disproportionately toward other actors with high degrees?), effects can be defined, linear and nonlinear; see Snijders, van de Bunt, and Steglich (2010).

Depending on the research questions and the type of network under study, many other effects may be considered, and many are available in the software; see Ripley et al. (2016).

In addition to these effects based on the network structure itself, research questions will naturally lead to effects depending on attributes of the actors—indicators of goals, constraints, resources, and so forth—defined externally to the network. Since network ties involve two actors, a monadic actor variable v_i will lead to potentially several effects for the network dynamics, such as the following. Here the word *ego* is used for the focal actor, or sender of the tie, while *alter* is used for the potential candidate for receiving the tie.

6. The *ego effect* $s_{10i}(x) = \sum_j x_{ij} v_i = x_{i+} v_i$, reflecting the effect of this variable on the propensity to send ties and leading to a correlation between v_i and outdegrees.

7. The *alter effect* $s_{11i}(x) = \sum_j x_{ij} v_j$, reflecting the effect of this variable on the popularity of the actor for receiving ties and leading to a correlation between v_i and indegrees.

8. The *similarity (homophily) effect*, which implies that actors who are similar on salient characteristics have a larger probability to become and stay connected, as reviewed in general terms by McPherson, Smith-Lovin, and Cook (2001). An example is the finding by Huckfeldt (2001) that people tend to select political discussion partners who are perceived to have expertise and similar views; this would be reflected by an alter and a similarity effect with respect to (perceived) expertise. Another example is the finding (Manger and Pickup, 2016) that democracies are more likely to form trade agreements with other democracies. Similarity can be represented by the effect

$$s_{12i}(x) = \sum_j x_{ij} \left(1 - \frac{|v_i - v_j|}{Range(v)} \right)$$

where $Range(v) = \max_i (v_i) - \min_i (v_i)$.

9. The *ego-alter interaction effect*, represented like a product interaction, $s_{13i}(x) = \sum_j x_{ij} v_i v_j$, which is a different way to represent how the combination of the values on the covariate of the sender and the receiver of the potential tie may influence tie creation and maintenance.

Further, it is possible to include attributes of pairs of actors, of which one example is how they are related in a different network. Such *dyadic covariates* can express, for example, meeting opportunities (e.g., Huckfeldt, 2009), spatial propinquity (e.g., Baybeck and Huckfeldt, 2002), military alliances, institutional relatedness, competing for the same resources or scarce outcomes, and so forth.

10. The *dyadic covariate effect* of a covariate w_{ij} is defined as $s_{14i}(x) = \sum_j x_{ij} w_{ij}$.

Many other effects that may be used for model specification are mentioned in the RSiena manual (Ripley et al., 2016). Further differences between actors in their objective functions may be represented by interaction effects. Time heterogeneity in the formation probabilities can be incorporated by using time-changing covariates.

PARAMETER ESTIMATION

If a continuous time record is available from the network evolution process as described above, so that for each tie the exact starting and ending times within the observation period are known, and these starting and ending times are all distinct, then the model can be framed as a generalized linear model, and maximum likelihood estimation is possible, in principle, in a straightforward way. It is more usual, however, that only panel data ("snapshots") are available. Sometimes this is at given intervals (e.g., yearly), sometimes at irregular times, depending on what is convenient for data collection. The definition of the model implies that irregular observation times present no problem at all; these will be absorbed in the panel wave-specific parameters ρ_m (see [6]) without affecting the other parameters. For panel data this is a generalized linear model with a lot of missing data (i.e., the unobserved timings of the tie changes). Estimation in this case is possible by a variety of simulation-based methods.

A method of moments estimator was proposed by Snijders (2001). The principle of the method of moments operates by selecting a vector of statistics, one for each parameter coordinate to be estimated, and determining the parameter estimate as the parameter value for which the expected value of this vector of statistics equals the observed value at each observation (wave). For the SAOM, the required expected values cannot be calculated analytically, but they can be approximated by Monte Carlo simulations. These are used in the stochastic approximation developed by Snijders (2001) and implemented in the RSiena package (Ripley et al., 2016). The method simulates the network dynamics many times with trial parameter values, updating them, until the averages of a suitable set of network descriptives, reflecting the estimated parameters, are close enough to the observed values. This method can be called a Markov chain Monte Carlo (MCMC) method, but it is frequentist in nature, not Bayesian, and accordingly does not require the specification of a prior distribution. It is important to check convergence of the algorithm, as discussed in the RSiena manual; sometimes it is necessary to repeat the estimation, using earlier obtained parameters as the new initial values.

The method of moments estimator has proven to be quite reliable and efficient. More recently, other and potentially more efficient estimators have been developed: a Bayesian estimator by Koskinen and Snijders (2007), a maximum likelihood estimator by Snijders, Koskinen, and Schweinberger (2010), and a generalized method of moments estimator by Amati et al. (2015).

Changing Actor Sets

In networks of organizations, voters, countries, or other political actors, changes in composition of the node set are not an exception. Actors may be created or disappear, they may enter or be dropped from the delineation of the data set, and organizations or countries may also merge or split. Often it is reasonable to regard these changes as exogenous. There are several ways in which they can be accommodated. One is to include actors as nodes in the data set for all time points, but for the panel waves where they are absent to specify their incoming and outgoing ties as structural zeros, signifying that these ties are impossible and their absence has no information content. A second way is to use the implementation as a simulation model and to specify for some actors one or more time intervals—which may begin and end at or anywhere between the moments determined by the panel waves—where there cannot be any ties to or from these actors; see Huisman and Snijders (2003). This permits, for example, that simulations for new actors start at some specific time point between the panel waves, if such information is available. Third, one can construct the pairs (t_m, t_{m+1}) of consecutive panel waves each as a separate transition; if the data set is large enough these may be analyzed separately, but if the data set is not so large, in order to obtain an adequate amount of data, several or all of these pairs can be analyzed simultaneously under the assumption of constant parameter values. This is the "multiple group" option of the package (Ripley et al., 2016). If the assumption of constant parameters is doubtful, interactions with time trends (e.g., linear, polynomial, or with dummy variables) may be added. In cases of reconfiguration of the actor set, the third option may be especially useful.

DYNAMICS OF NONDIRECTED NETWORKS

The SAOM as explained above is defined for directed networks, assuming that the actor sending the tie determines its existence. In this section we extend the model to nondirected networks. Such networks occur often in political and organizational studies. There the two actors at either side of the tie have a priori a say in its existence, and assumptions must be made about the negotiation or coordination between the two actors involved in tie creation and termination.

In game-theoretic models of networks, it is usually assumed that for a tie to exist, the consent of both actors is involved. This is the basis of the definition of pairwise stability proposed by Jackson and Wolinsky (1996): a network is pairwise stable if no pair of actors can both gain from creation of a new tie between them, and if no single actor can gain from termination of one of the ties in which that actor is involved. In our statistical approach such a stability concept has no place, but the basic idea that both actors should benefit from the tie is translated to our probabilistic framework. Several models are presented here, all based on a two-step process of opportunity and choice and making different assumptions concerning the combination of choices between the two actors involved in a tie.

Two-Sided Choices

It now is assumed that the network is nondirected; that is, ties have no directionality: $X_{ij} = X_{ji}$ holds by necessity, and the tie variables X_{ij} and X_{ji} are treated as being one and the same variable. Ties now are indicated by $i \leftrightarrow j$.

For the opportunity, or timing, process, two options are considered:

1. *One-sided initiative:* One actor i is randomly (but not necessarily with equal probabilities) selected and gets the opportunity to make a change. This is a multinomial choice about changing one of the ties from i to another actor.
2. *Two-sided opportunity:* An ordered pair of actors (i, j) (with $i \neq j$) is randomly (but not necessarily with equal probabilities) selected and gets the opportunity to make a new decision about the existence of a tie between them. This is a binary choice about the existence of the tie $i \leftrightarrow j$.

The choice process is modeled as one of three options:

D.*Dictatorial:* One actor can impose a decision about a tie on the other.
M.*Mutual:* Both actors have to agree for a tie between them to exist, in line with Jackson and Wolinsky (1996).
C.*Compensatory:* The two actors decide on the basis of their combined objective function, which can represent coming to a joint agreement. The combination with one-sided initiative seems somewhat artificial here, and we only elaborate this option for the two-sided initiative.

Model M.1, one-sided initiative with reciprocal confirmation, is in most cases the most appealing simple representation of the coordination required to create and maintain nondirected ties. An example about preferential trade agreements is given by Manger and Pickup (2016); an example about trade markets in cultural goods is provided by Shore (2015). Models D.1 and D.2 have potential for the modeling of military conflicts, and model C.2 may be of value in a joint bargaining situation.

Mathematical Elaboration

We give a brief elaboration of the formulae involved in these five options, treating first the opportunity element and then the choice process.

1. *One-sided initiative:* For the opportunity to make a change, assumptions 1–6 mentioned above for the directional case are still in place.
2. *Two-sided opportunity:* For the selection of an ordered pair of actors (i, j) $(i \neq j)$, assumptions 1–3 above are maintained, but 4–6 are replaced (in abbreviated description) as follows:

   4.2. Each ordered pair of actors (i, j) has a *rate of change*, denoted $\lambda_{ij}(x; \rho)$.
   5.2. The waiting time until the next opportunity for change by any pair of actors has the exponential distribution with parameter $\lambda_{tot}(x; \rho) = \sum_{i \neq j} \lambda_{ij}(x; \rho)$.
   6.2. The probability that the next opportunity for change is for pair (i, j) is given by

$$
P\{\text{Next opportunity for change is for pair} (i, j)\} = \frac{\lambda_{ij}(x; \rho)}{\lambda_{tot}(x; \rho)} \tag{8}
$$

The choice process has the three options D(ictatorial), M(utual), and C(ompensatory). In all cases assumption 7 as defined for the directed case is retained, and assumption 8 is replaced as follows.

Dictatorial

As in the directed case, actor i selects the change of the single tie variable X_{ij} given the objective function $f_i(x^{(0)}, x; \beta)$ using (3), and actor j just has to accept. Combined with the two opportunity options, this yields the following cases.

8.D.1. For one-sided initiative, the probability that the tie variable changed is X_{ij}, so that the network x changes into $x^{(\pm ij)}$, is given by

$$
p_{ij}(x, \beta) = \frac{\exp\left(f_i\left(x, x^{(\pm ij)}; \beta\right)\right)}{\sum_{h=1}^{n} \exp\left(f_i\left(x, x^{(\pm ih)}; \beta\right)\right)} \tag{9}
$$

just as in the model for directed relations.

8.D.2. For two-sided initiative, actor i makes the binary choice about whether or not tie $i \to j$ should exist. The probability that network x changes into $x(\pm^{ij})$, is given by

$$
p_{ij}(x, \beta) = \frac{\exp\left(f_i\left(x, x^{(\pm ij)}; \beta\right)\right)}{\exp\left(f_i\left(x, x; \beta\right)\right) + \exp\left(f_i\left(x, x^{(\pm ij)}; \beta\right)\right)} \tag{10}
$$

Mutual

8.M.1. In the case of one-sided initiative, actor i selects the tie variable to be changed with probabilities (9) according to i's objective function. If currently $x_{ij} = 0$ so that the change would mean creation of a new tie $i \to j$, this is proposed to actor j, who then accepts according to a binary choice based on j's objective function, with acceptance probability

$$P\{j \text{ accepts tie proposal}\} = \frac{\exp\left(f_j\left(x, x^{(\pm ij)}; \beta\right)\right)}{\exp\left(f_j(x, x; \beta)\right) + \exp\left(f_j\left(x, x^{(\pm ij)}; \beta\right)\right)}$$

If the choice by i means termination of an existing tie, the proposal is always put into effect. Jointly these rules lead to the following probability that the current network x changes into $x^{(\pm ij)}$:

$$p_{ij}(x, \beta) = \frac{\exp\left(f_i\left(x, x^{(\pm ij)}; \beta\right)\right)}{\sum_{h=1}^{n} \exp\left(f_i\left(x, x^{(\pm ij)}; \beta\right)\right)} \left(\frac{\exp\left(f_j\left(x, x^{(\pm ij)}; \beta\right)\right)}{\exp\left(f_j(x, x; \beta)\right) + \exp\left(f_j\left(x, x^{(\pm ij)}; \beta\right)\right)}\right)^{1-x_{ij}} \tag{11}$$

8.M.2. In the case of two-sided opportunity, actors i and j both reconsider the value of the tie variable X_{ij}. Actor i proposes a change (toggle) with probability (10) and actor j similarly. If currently there is no tie, that is, $x_{ij} = 0$, then the tie is created if this is proposed by both actors, which has probability

$$p_{ij}(x, \beta) = \left(\frac{\exp\left(f_i\left(x, x^{(\pm ij)}; \beta\right)\right)}{\exp\left(f_i(x, x; \beta)\right) + \exp\left(f_i\left(x, x^{(\pm ij)}; \beta\right)\right)}\right)$$
$$\times \left(\frac{\exp\left(f_j\left(x, x^{(\pm ij)}; \beta\right)\right)}{\exp\left(f_j(x, x; \beta)\right) + \exp\left(f_j\left(x, x^{(\pm ij)}; \beta\right)\right)}\right) \tag{12a}$$

If currently there is a tie, that is, $x_{ij} = 1$, then the tie is terminated if one or both actors wish to do this, which has probability

$$p_{ij}(x, \beta) = 1 - \left\{\begin{array}{c} \dfrac{\exp\left(f_i(x, x; \beta)\right)}{\exp\left(f_i(x, x; \beta)\right) + \exp\left(f_i\left(x, x^{(\pm ij)}; \beta\right)\right)} \\ \times \dfrac{\exp\left(f_j(x, x; \beta)\right)}{\exp\left(f_j(x, x; \beta)\right) + \exp\left(f_j\left(x, x^{(\pm ij)}; \beta\right)\right)} \end{array}\right\} \tag{12b}$$

Compensatory

The two actors decide on the basis of their combined objective function, which can represent coming to a joint agreement. The combination with one-sided initiative is somewhat artificial here, and we only elaborate this option for the two-sided initiative.

8.C.2. The binary decision about the existence of the tie $i \leftrightarrow j$ is based on the sum of the objective functions of actors i and j. The probability that network x changes into $x^{(\pm ij)}$, now is given by

$$p_{ij}(x,\beta) = \frac{\exp\left(f_i\left(x,x^{(\pm ij)};\beta\right) + f_j\left(x,x^{(\pm ij)};\beta\right)\right)}{\exp\left(f_i\left(x,x;\beta\right) + f_j\left(x,x;\beta\right)\right) + \exp\left(f_i\left(x,x^{(\pm ij)};\beta\right) + f_j\left(x,x^{(\pm ij)};\beta\right)\right)} \quad (13)$$

Putting this together in the transition rates, defined above, gives the following results. Account must be taken of the fact that toggling variable X_{ij} is the same as toggling X_{ji}, and that the rules described above give different roles for the first and the second actor in the pair (i,j). For the models with one-sided initiative, the transition rate is

$$q_{ij}(x) = \lambda_i(x;\rho)p_{ij}(x,\beta) + \lambda_j(x;\rho)p_{ji}(x,\beta) \quad (14)$$

and for the models with two-sided opportunity it is

$$q_{ij}(x) = \lambda_{ij}(x;\rho)p_{ij}(x,\beta) + \lambda_{ji}(x;\rho)p_{ji}(x,\beta) \quad (15)$$

where the functions λ_i, λ_{ij}, and p_{ij} are as defined above.

Model Specification for Undirected Networks

Again, a convenient and flexible class of objective functions can be represented by the linear combination (7). The same effects can be used as for directed networks, but some are redundant, because the ties $i \to j$ and $j \to i$ are now equivalent. For example, the reciprocity effect s_{2i} is the same as the degree effect s_{1i}, for monadic covariates the ego effect s_{10i} is the same as the alter effect s_{11i}, and so forth.

The choice among the five options mentioned above has to be made primarily on theoretical knowledge of how the two actors on both sides of a potential tie act together in deciding about the tie. One-sided initiative with reciprocal confirmation (M.1) often may be the most plausible option, in accordance with Jackson and Wolinsky (1996). Studying the correspondence among the five options may give some insight into which differences to expect when the same data set is subjected to the different model options. Perhaps the clearest example is the following. If all effects s_{ki} included in a model (7) are such that the contributions of ties are the same for both actors involved (which is the case, e.g., for the degree effect s_{1i} and the similarity effect s_{12i}), then the compensatory dyadic model C.2 is identical to the dictatorial dyadic model D.2, except that the parameters β_k are twice as small for C.2 as for D.2., because of the addition of the two objective functions in (13). For general models this identity will not hold, but in a first-order approximation it still may be expected that the β_k parameters in model C.2 are about twice as small as those in D.2, and the ρ_m parameters are quite similar.

Estimation and Examples

Method of moment estimators can be obtained for these models in exactly the same way as described in the previous section for models for directed networks. This is because the algorithm for these estimators is based directly on simulation of the network evolution, and the assumptions in this section can be used straightforwardly for simulating the evolution of a nondirected network.

MODELS FOR COEVOLUTION OF NETWORKS AND NODAL ATTRIBUTES

A major reason for the fruitfulness of a network-oriented research perspective is the entwinement of networks and individual behavior, performance, attitudes, and so forth of political actors. The effect of peers on individual political behavior is a well-studied issue, starting from Lazarsfeld et al. (1948); see, for example, Klofstad (2007). Huckfeldt (2009) argues that since social interaction leads to influence with respect to political behaviors, the composition of the social context of individuals influences their own attitudes and behaviors, and he draws attention to the endogeneity of the network of interaction partners. Interorganizational studies have also drawn attention to the importance of networks for organization-level outcomes. Scholz et al. (2008) show that the position of organizations in general contact networks influences their propensity to collaborate and to perceive agreement between stakeholders. Berardo (2009) shows that cooperation between governmental and nongovernmental organizations enhances organizational performance.

Studying the entwinement of networks and actor-level outcomes is difficult because of the endogeneity of both: the network affects the outcomes, while the outcomes affect the network. One way to get a handle on this is to model these dynamic dependencies both ways in studies of the coevolution of networks and nodal attributes. The combination of network and attributes then is viewed as an evolving system, in which the changes in the network are determined probabilistically by the network itself and also by the attributes, while the same holds for the changes in the attributes. A method for modeling this, using panel data of the network and the attributes, was proposed by Steglich et al. (2010), using an elaboration of the SAOM. This methodology does not pretend to yield causal conclusions by virtue of the statistical analysis; Shalizi and Thomas (2011) argued cogently that this is impossible in panel studies. What is offered by the method, if applied with a well-specified model, is insight in *time sequentiality:* To what extent is there evidence that changes in attributes depend on the state of the network ("first the network, then changes in the attributes"), and to what extent is there evidence that changes in the network depend on the state of the attributes ("first the attributes, then changes in the network")? The idea is similar to Granger causality, but a mathematical elaboration of this similarity has not been made yet. A more elaborate discussion of the severe difficulties in attempts to establish causality in social network research is presented in Robins (2015, ch. 10).

An outline of this model is presented here. When the nodal attributes play the role of dependent variables, we use the term *behavior* as a catchword that also can represent other outcomes such as performance and attitudes.

Dynamics of Networks and Behavior

The modeling framework used above for an evolving network $X(t)$ now is extended by considering a simultaneously and interdependently evolving vector of H behavior variables $Z(t) = (Z_1(t), \ldots, Z_H(t))$. The value of the h'th variable for the i'th actor is denoted $Z_{ih}(t)$. We assume that all components of the behavior vector $Z(t)$ are *ordinal discrete variables* with values coded as an interval of integers; binary variables are the simplest case.

For modeling the joint dynamics of the network and behavior $(X(t), Z(t))$, we follow the same principles as those used to model the development of $X(t)$ alone: time t is a continuous parameter; changes in network and behavior can take place at arbitrary moments between observations; at any single time point, only one variable can change, either a tie variable X_{ij} or a behavior variable Z_{ih}; and the process $(X(t), Z(t))$ evolves as a Markov process—that is, change probabilities depend on the current state of the process, not on earlier states. The principle of decomposing the dynamics in the smallest possible steps is carried further by requiring that a change of a behavior variable at one single moment can only be one step up or down the ladder of ordered values—that is, by +1 or −1—as these variables have integer values.

These principles are elaborated by Snijders, Steglich, and Schweinberger (2007) and Steglich, Snijders, and Pearson (2010) in a model that has the following basic components:

- For the network changes the *network rate function* $\lambda_i^X(x, z; \rho^X)$ indicates the average frequency with which actor i has the opportunity to make changes in one outgoing network variable.
- For each behavior variable Z_h the *behavior rate function* $\lambda_i^{Zh}(x, z; \rho^{Zh})$ indicates the average frequency with which actor i has the opportunity to make changes in this behavior variable.
- The *network objective function* $f_i^X(x^{(0)}, x; z, \beta^X)$ determines the probability of the next tie change by actor i, conditional on i having the opportunity to make a network change.
- The *behavior objective function* $f_i^{Zh}(z^{(0)}, x; z, \beta^{Zh})$ for behavior variable Z_h determines the probability of the next behavior change by actor i, conditional on i having the opportunity to make a change in this behavior.

The network dynamic proceeds just as defined above for the network-only case. The behavior dynamic is analogous. Here the option set for the decision of change is different, however, in the following way. For notational simplicity, we give the formulae only for the case of $H = 1$ dependent behavior variable, dropping index h. In a process driven by the rate functions $\lambda_i^Z(x, z; \rho^Z)$, actor i at stochastic moments gets the opportunity to change the value of his or her behavior Z_i. When this happens, and the current value is denoted $z^{(0)}$, the actor has three options: increase by 1, stay constant, or decrease by 1. If the current value is at the minimum or maximum of the range, one of these options is excluded. The choice probabilities again have a multinomial logit form, the probability of choosing z (with permitted values $z^{(0)} - 1$, $z^{(0)}, z^{(0)} + 1$) being

$$\frac{\exp\left(f_i^Z\left(z^{(0)}, z; x, \beta^Z\right)\right)}{\sum_{d=-1}^{1} \exp\left(f_i^Z\left(z^{(0)}, z^{(0)} + d; x, \beta^Z\right)\right)} \tag{16}$$

with obvious modifications in case z is at the boundary of its range. Again, an interpretation of myopic optimization is possible but not necessary.

This model for the coevolution of networks and behavior permits the expression of both *selection* (e.g., homophilous selection), where the values of Z_{ih} and Z_{jh} influence the probability of creating or of maintaining a tie from i to j, and of *influence*, or contagion, where for actor i the probability of changes in Z_{ih} depends on the behaviors Z_{jh} of those actors j with whom i is tied. More generally, changes in the behavior of actor i may depend on i's network position as well as on the composition of the network neighborhood of i.

Specification of Behavior Dynamics

The main extra component of the model specification regards the objective function for behavior. Here also we use notation just for one single behavior variable, Z. Again, a linear combination is considered:

$$f_i^Z\left(z^{(0)}, z; x, \beta^Z\right) = \sum_k \beta_k^Z s_{ki}^Z\left(z^{(0)}, z; x\right)$$

(17)

where the effects $s_{ki}^Z(z^{(0)}, z; x)$ depend on the network and the behavior. We present effects depending only on the new state z, and accordingly write $s_{ki}^Z(z; x)$ for $s_{ki}^Z(z^{(0)}, z; x)$. A baseline model is a quadratic function of the actor's own behavior as the expression of short-term goals and restrictions. With a negative coefficient for the quadratic term, this represents a unimodal function that could be regarded as a preference function (again, with a myopic interpretation). This includes

1. the linear term $s_{1i}^Z(z; x) = z_i$ and
2. the quadratic term $s_{2i}^Z(z; x) = (z_i)^2$.

Several statistics could be specified to represent social influence (contagion), such as the following two:

3. The similarity between the behavior of actor i and the actors to whom i is tied, measured just like the analogous effect s_{12i} for the network dynamics,

$$s_{3i}^Z(z; x) = \sum_j x_{ij}\left(1 - \frac{|z_i - z_j|}{\text{Range}(z)}\right)$$

4. The product of the own behavior z_i with the average behavior of the other actors to whom i is tied, $s_{4i}^Z(z; x) = z_i\left(\sum_j x_{ij} z_j\right) / \left(\sum_j x_{ij}\right)$ (defined as 0 if this is $0/0$). Together with the two terms s_{1i}^Z and s_{2i}^Z, this yields a quadratic function of which (if the coefficient of s_{2i}^Z is negative) the location of the maximum is a linear function of the average behavior in the "personal network" of i.

The effects s_{3i}^Z and s_{4i}^Z both express the concept of social influence, albeit in different mathematical ways. The choice between them can be based on theoretical grounds, if any theoretical preferences exist—or else on empirical grounds.

The behavior dynamic can also depend on network position directly, for example, on the degrees of the actor. It can depend on, for example,

5. the "popularity" of actor i as measured by the indegree, that is, the number of incoming ties, $s_{5i}^{Z}(z;x)=z_i x_{+i}$, and/or

6. on the "activity" of actor i as measured by the outdegree, that is, the number of outgoing ties, $s_{6i}^{Z}(z;x)=z_i x_{i+}$.

In addition, it will often be important to include effects of other actor-level and contextual variables on z_i, in accordance with the political theories explaining this dependent variable.

The parameter estimation for this model is treated in Snijders et al. (2007). An application to partner selection in policy networks and its coevolution with generalized trust is presented by Berardo and Scholz (2010). Manger and Pickup (2016) and Rhue and Sundararajan (2014) apply this model to the diffusion of democracy.

Coevolution of Multiple Networks

The principle of coevolution can also be applied to the interdependent dynamics of several networks on the same set of actors; one might call this a multivariate network. The elaboration is quite analogous to the coevolution of networks and behavior. Each network has its own rate function and objective function, and the objective function (perhaps also the rate function) for each network will depend on the network itself and the other network(s). It should be noted that the dependence is on the current state of the system, not on the last observed state. The model for coevolution of multiple networks was first presented by Snijders et al. (2013). This extension also allows the representation of networks with ordered tie values (although the number of values must be small).

Liang (2014) applied this method in a study of the coevolution of the discussion network and a semantic interpretation network in an Internet discussion forum about the 2012 US presidential election.

Discussion

Network-related research questions lead to various issues at the interface between theory and methodology—in political as well as other sciences. One issue is how to make the combination of, on the one hand, theories in which individual actors have primacy and that recognize the embeddedness in the social context (cf. DiPrete and Forristal, 1994; Udehn, 2002; Huckfeldt, 2009) and, on the other hand, empirical research with data sets including dyadic as well as monadic variables. Another issue is the fact that hypotheses about dyadic relations between social actors almost by necessity will imply dependence between dyadic tie variables and also between dyadic and monadic variables, which requires novel statistical methods. This dependence often can be regarded as a consequence of endogeneity, that is, resulting from interdependent choices by multiple actors. For example, in studies of how actors are influenced by those actors to whom they are tied it is important to recognize that the network may be endogenous, and in studies of homophilous choice of interaction partners the behavior that is the dimension for homophily may be endogenous. Dropping the assumption of independence implies that the dependence between variables has to be specified in a plausible way in order for the statistical analysis to be reliable. However, our theories mostly give only a very incomplete handle on this specification; statistical models representing dependencies between dyadic variables are recent and still in various stages of development, and as yet we know little about the sensitivity of conclusions for the misspecification of such statistical models.

The three main approaches currently available to statistically analyze network dynamics—the SAOM, temporal ERGMs, and latent Euclidean space models (for an overview see Desmarais and Cranmer, 2016)—employ quite different means to express network and time dependencies, that is, the correlation structure between the tie variables observed at the same and also at different moments. In the SAOM the flow of time is explicitly present, which implies that varying time lags between observations are easily incorporated. If the model is valid for some data set, dropping an observation, or inserting an additional one, or changing the timing of observations, will keep the probability distribution of the rest intact; this is not the case for the other approaches. The fact that the analysis is simulation based allows flexible handling of irregularities in the observation design such as exogenous changes in the node set. The simulation setup is limited, however, in the sense that observed changes are considered as the result of a series of changes of single ties, each of which implies a change—usually small—of the network context for all actors. Sometimes this is reasonable, but this representation of network dependencies may be deficient in cases where groups of actors work in concert to form or rupture ties, especially when the composition of these groups changes endogenously. The SAOM and the various temporal ERGM variants, such as the TERGM (Hanneke et al., 2010), the LERGM (Koskinen and Snijders, 2013) and the StERGM (Krivitsky and Handcock, 2014), are based on explicitly specifying the network dependencies. The latent space models (Sewell and Chen, 2015; Dorff and Ward, 2016), by contrast, assume that network dependencies can be represented by positioning the nodes in a low-dimensional Euclidean space. For some research questions the representation with latent spatial positions will be more natural; for others the representation by differentiated types of network dependencies will be. For example, for directed networks, the SAOM and ERGM representations include separate parameters for reciprocation and for transitive closure, permitting testing of hypotheses about such processes, while in latent space models these are represented together by the spatial configuration. It will be interesting to compare the interpretative value of the spatial representation in latent space models to the value of the dependence aspects represented by the "effects" as explained above for the SAOM, which are used similarly for the temporal ERGMs. The interpretative insights provided by these representations of dependence have not yet been much explored. It should be noted that covariates will "take out" part of the dependence, so that the "remaining" representation of dependence may depend strongly on the covariates used.

The SAOM and temporal ERGM approaches tackle issues of dependence for panel data on "complete networks." This means that the network consists of the pattern of ties among all actors in a well-delineated group, and ties of these actors with others out-side the group may be ignored; the network boundary problem (Marsden, 2005) is assumed to have been solved in an earlier phase of the research. Within these models the wider context outside of this group, to which every group member is exposed, is therefore kept constant, and its influence is not considered. This implies, in terms of the statement by Huckfeldt (2009) that "(p)olitical communication networks are created as the complex product of this intersection between human choices and environmentally imposed options" (p. 928), that the methods treated here focus on the "human choice" component, while the determination of the node set is considered to be "environmentally imposed." The latent space models, on the other hand, are less strict in the assumption of a complete network having been observed; if the data follow a latent space model, after randomly dropping some nodes from the data set what remains still will follow the latent space model. This is a strength with respect to data sets permitted, but it also signals a potential weakness in the representation of network dependencies, because theoretical network "mechanisms" may be sensitive to arbitrary deletions of parts of the network.

Previously we commented on the difficulty of achieving causal interpretations from statistical analyses where networks figure among the dependent variables; briefly stated, the endogeneity of the networks is so strong that statistical methods will be able to estab-lish time sequentiality, but not strict cause-and-effect relationships.

The definition of the SAOM in terms of choices by individual actors means that changing dyadic and monadic variables can be analyzed in a coherent framework according to theories in which the analytical primacy is with structurally embedded individual actors, in line with structural individualism (Udehn, 2002). The inter-pretation of the multinomial logistic model in terms of myopic choices does not exclude strategic considerations, but it does mean that these have to be represented by the short-term goals through which actors attempt to reach their long-term objectives. Theoretical arguments given in the literature for the occurrence of struc-tural effects such as reciprocity and transitivity are indeed mostly based on their importance as intermediate goals serving the purpose of ulterior objectives; this is the case, for example, for the argument proposed by Coleman (1988) that transitiv-ity (triadic closure) gives opportunities for social control and sanctioning, as well as for the theory (Burt, 1992) that structural holes are a means for obtaining positional advantage.

The models presented here are implemented in the program SIENA (Simulation Investigation for Empirical Network Analysis), which is available as the R package

RSiena (Ripley et al., 2016). The associated website http://www.stats.ox.ac.uk/~snijders/siena/ contains substantial tutorial and exemplary material.

References

Almquist, Z. W., and Butts, C. T. (2013). "Dynamic Network Logistic Regression: A Logistic Choice Analysis of Inter- and Intra-Group Blog Citation Dynamics in the 2004 US Presidential Election." *Political Analysis* 21: 430–448.

Amati, V., Schönenberger, F., and Snijders, T. (2015). "Estimation of Stochastic Actor-Oriented Models for the Evolution of Networks by Generalized Method of Moments." *Journal de la Société Française de Statistique* 156: 140–165.

Bala, V., and Goyal, S. (2000). "A Noncooperative Model of Network Formation." *Econometrica* 68: 1181–1229.

Barabási, A.-L., and Albert, R. (1999). "Emergence of Scaling in Random Networks." *Science* 286: 509–512.

Baybeck, B., and Huckfeldt, R. (2002). "Spatially Dispersed Ties among Interdependent Citizens: Connecting Individuals and Aggregates." *Political Analysis* 10: 261–275.

Berardo, R. (2009). "Processing Complexity in Networks: A Study of Informal Collaboration and Its Effect on Organizational Success." *Policy Studies Journal* 37: 521–539.

Berardo, R., and Scholz, J. T. (2010). "Self-Organizing Policy Networks: Risk, Partner Selection and Cooperation in Estuaries." *American Journal of Political Science* 54: 632–649.

Berelson, B. R., Lazarsfeld, P. F., and McPhee, W. N. (1954). *Voting: A Study of Opinion Formation in a Presidential Campaign*. Chicago: University of Chicago Press.

Burt, R. S. (1992). *Structural Holes*. Cambridge, MA: Harvard University Press.

Campbell, A., Converse, P. E., Miller, W. E., and Stokes, D. E. (1960). *The American Voter*. Chicago: University of Chicago Press.

Cao, X., and Ward, M. D. (2014). "Do Democracies Attract Portfolio Investment? Transnational Portfolio Investments Modeled as Dynamic Network." *International Interactions* 40: 216–245.

Coleman, J. S. (1988). "Social Capital in the Creation of Human Capital." *American Journal of Sociology* 94: S95–S120.

de Solla Price, D. J. (1976). "A General Theory of Bibliometric and Other Advantage Processes." *Journal of the American Society for Information Science* 27: 292–306.

Desmarais, B. A., and Cranmer, S. J. (2016). "Statistical Inference in Political Networks Research." In *Oxford Handbook of Political Networks*, edited by J. N. Victor, M. Lubell, and A. H. Montgomery. Oxford: Oxford University Press.

DiPrete, T. A., and Forristal, J. D. (1994). "Multilevel Analysis: Methods and Substance." *Annual Review of Sociology* 20: 331–357.

Dorff, C., and Ward, M. D. (2016). "Latent Networks and Spatial Networks in Politics." In *Oxford Handbook of Political Networks*, edited by J. N. Victor, M. Lubell, and A. H. Montgomery. Oxford: Oxford University Press.

Emirbayer, M., and Goodwin, J. (1994). "Network Analysis, Culture, and the Problem of Agency." *American Journal of Sociology* 99: 1411–1454.

Fischer, M., Ingold, K., Sciarini, P., and Varone, F. (2012). "Impacts of Market Liberalization on Regulatory Network: A Longitudinal Analysis of the Swiss Telecommunications Sector." *Policy Studies Journal* 40: 435–457.

Freeman, L. C. (1979). "Centrality in Networks: I, Conceptual Clarification." *Social Networks* 1: 215–239.

Giuliani, E. (2013). "Network Dynamics in Regional Clusters: Evidence from Chile." *Research Policy* 42: 1406–1419.

Gulati, R., and Gargiulo, M. (1999). "Where Do Interorganizational Networks Come From?" *American Journal of Sociology* 104: 1439–1493.

Hafner-Burton, E. and Montgomery, A. (2006). "Power Positions: International Organizations, Social Networks, and Conflict." *Journal of Conflict Resolution* 50: 3–27.

Handcock, M. S., and Hunter, D. R. (2006). "Inference in Curved Exponential Family Models for Networks." *Journal of Computational and Graphical Statistics* 15: 565–583.

Hanneke, S., Fu, W., and Xing, E. P. (2010). "Discrete Temporal Models for Social Networks." *Electronic Journal of Statistics* 4: 585–605.

Hicklin, A., O'Toole, L., Jr. and Meier, K. (2008). "Serpents in the Sand: Managerial Networking and Nonlinear Influences on Organizational Performance." *Journal of Public Administration Research and Theory* 18: 253–273.

Holland, P. W., and Leinhardt, S. (1976). "Local Structure in Social Networks." *Sociological Methodology* 6: 1–45.

Holland, P. W., and Leinhardt, S. (1977). "A Dynamic Model for Social Networks." *Journal of Mathematical Sociology* 5: 5–20.

Huckfeldt, R. (2001). "The Social Communication of Political Expertise." *American Journal of Political Science* 45: 425–438.

Huckfeldt, R. (2009). "Interdependence, Density Dependence, and Networks in Politics." *American Politics Research* 37: 921–950.

Huisman, M. E., and Snijders, T. A. B. (2003). "Statistical Analysis of Longitudinal Network Data with Changing Composition." *Sociological Methods & Research* 32: 253–287.

Ingold, K., and Fischer, M. (2014). "Drivers of Collaboration to Mitigate Climate Change: An Illustration of Swiss Climate Policy over 15 Years." *Global Environmental Change* 24: 88–98.

Jackson, M. O., and Wolinsky, A. (1996). "A Strategic Model of Social and Economic Networks." *Journal of Economic Theory* 71: 44–74.

Kinne, B. J. (2013). "Network Dynamics and the Evolution of International Cooperation." *American Political Science Review* 107: 766–780.

Klofstad, C. A. (2007). "Participation Talk Leads to Recruitment: How Discussions about Politics and Current Events Increase Civic Participation." *Political Research Quarterly* 60: 180–191.

Koskinen, J. H., and Snijders, T. A. B. (2007). "Bayesian Inference for Dynamic Social Network Data." *Journal of Statistical Planning and Inference* 13: 3930–3938.

Koskinen, J. H., and Snijders, T. A. B. (2013). "Longitudinal Models." In *Exponential Random Graph Models*, edited by D. Lusher, and J. Koskinen and G. Robins, pp. 130–140. New York: Cambridge University Press.

Krivitsky, P. N., and Handcock, M. S. (2014). "A Separable Model for Dynamic Networks." *Journal of the Royal Statistical Society, Series B* 76: 29–46.

Lazarsfeld, P. F., Berelson, B., and Gaudet, H. (1948). *The People's Choice.* New York: Columbia University Press.

Liang, H. (2014). "Coevolution of Political Discussion and Common Ground in Web Discussion Forum." *Social Science Computer Review* 32: 155–169.

Maddala, G. (1983). *Limited-dependent and Qualitative Variables in Econometrics.* 3d ed. Cambridge, UK: Cambridge University Press.

Manger, M. S., and Pickup, M. A. (2016). "The Coevolution of Trade Agreement Networks and Democracy." *Journal of Conflict Resolution* 60: 164–191.

Manger, M. S., Pickup, M., and Snijders, T. A. (2012). "A Hierarchy of Preferences: A Longitudinal Network Analysis Aproach to PTA Formation." *Journal of Conflict Resolution* 56: 852–877.

Marsden, P. V. (2005). "Recent Developments in Network Measurement." In *Models and Methods in Social Network Analysis*, edited by P. Carrington, J. Scott, and S. Wasserman, pp. 8–30. New York: Cambridge University Press.

McPherson, J. M., Smith-Lovin, L., and Cook, J. M. (2001). "Birds of a Feather: Homophily in Social Networks." *Annual Review of Sociology* 27: 415–444.

Merton, R. K. (1968). "The Matthew Effect in Science." *Science* 159(3810): 56–63.

Norris, J. R. (1997). *Markov Chains*. Cambridge, UK: Cambridge University Press.

R Core Team. (2016). *R: A Language and Environment for Statistical Computing*. Vienna: R Foundation for Statistical Computing.

Rhue, L., and Sundararajan, A. (2014). "Digital Access, Political Networks and the Diffusion of Democracy." *Social Networks* 36: 40–53.

Ripley, R. M., Snijders, T. A. B., B´oda, Z., Vörös, A., and Preciado, P. (2016). *Manual for Siena Version 4.0: Technical Report*. Oxford: University of Oxford, Department of Statistics, Nuffield College.

Robins, G. (2015). *Doing Social Network Research: Network-based Research Design for Social Scientists*. London: Sage.

Scholz, J. T., Berardo, R., and Kile, B. (2008). "Do Networks Solve Collective Action Problems? Credibility, Search, and Collaboration." *Journal of Politics* 70: 393–406.

Sewell, D. K., and Chen, Y. (2015). "Latent Space Models for Dynamic Networks." *Journal of the American Statistical Association* 110: 1646–1657.

Shalizi, C. R., and Thomas, A. C. (2011). "Homophily and Contagion Are Generically Confounded in Observational Social Network Studies." *Sociological Methods & Research* 40(2): 211–239.

Shore, J. (2015). "Market Formation as Transitive Closure: The Evolving Pattern of Trade in Music." *World Development* 38: 37–47.

Simmel, G. ([1917] 1950). "Individual and Society." In *The Sociology of Georg Simmel*, edited by K. Wolff, pp. 1–84. New York: The Free Press.

Snijders, T. A. B. (2001). "The Statistical Evaluation of Social Network Dynamics." *Sociological Methodology* 31: 361–395.

Snijders, T. A. B. (2011). "Statistical Models for Social Networks." *Annual Review of Sociology* 37: 131–153.

Snijders, T. A. B., Koskinen, J. H., and Schweinberger, M. (2010). "Maximum Likelihood Estimation for Social Network Dynamics." *Annals of Applied Statistics* 4: 567–588.

Snijders, T. A. B., Lomi, A., and Torló, V. (2013). "A Model for the Multiplex Dynamics of Two-Mode and One-Mode Networks, with an Application to Employment Preference, Friendship, and Advice." *Social Networks* 35: 265–276.

Snijders, T. A. B., Pattison, P. E., Robins, G. L., and Handcock, M. S. (2006). "New Specifications for Exponential Random Graph Models." *Sociological Methodology* 36: 99–153.

Snijders, T. A. B., Steglich, C. E. G., and Schweinberger, M. (2007). "Modeling the Co-evolution of Networks and Behavior." In *Longitudinal Models in the Behavioral and Related Sciences*, edited by K. van Montfort, H. Oud, and A. Satorra, pp. 41–71. Mahwah, NJ: Lawrence Erlbaum.

Snijders, T. A. B., van de Bunt, G. G., and Steglich, C. (2010). "Introduction to Actor-Based Models for Network Dynamics." *Social Networks* 32: 44–60.

Steglich, C. E. G., Snijders, T. A. B., and Pearson, M. A. (2010). "Dynamic Networks and Behavior: Separating Selection from Influence." *Sociological Methodology* 40: 329–393.

Udehn, L. (2002). "The Changing Face of Methodological Individualism." *Annual Review of Sociology* 8: 479–507.

....

CHAPTER 10

LATENT NETWORKS AND SPATIAL NETWORKS IN POLITICS

....

CASSY DORFF, SHAHRYAR MINHAS, AND MICHAEL D. WARD

NETWORK BEGINNINGS

....

IN the 1920s Sigmund Freud developed many incorrect ideas, including the idea that human behavior was largely influenced by the individual human psyche, which in turn was composed of an id, ego, and superego. Freudian psychoanalysis grew in popularity and influence.[1] Psychology was about analyzing individuals.

In the early 1930s, at the height of Freud's influence, a Hungarian researcher had a different idea. Jacob Moreno felt that Freud's approach left out the social context and that the relationships one had with other individuals said a lot about human behavior. He was tasked by New York State to conduct a study on a large number of girls "running away" from the New York Training School for Girls (NYTSG), a court-mandated residence for young women whom the courts found "wayward," typically pregnant or homeless. His approach was to study groups and the interrelationships among the individuals in these groups.

Moreno found that women who were friends with other women who left the NYTSG were quite likely to abandon the facility themselves. This led to Moreno's focus on group dynamics and his recording of linkages among individuals in small groups such as schools and work groups. This so-called sociometry led to the first real network graphs; Jacob Moreno is often thought of as the father of social network analysis. Moreno's ideas also spawned group psychoanalysis in the mid-1930s.

Moreno's map of the relationships among members of a second-grade class is one of the first sociograms (see figure 10.1). It illustrates several classic features of networks. Notice that there are two relatively separate cliques, which represent the males (shown on the left in the figure) and the females in the class. There is only one person in each clique—with a large number of ties to members within the clique—who is connected to the other group. In addition, there is a small, isolated clique of two individuals who only have ties to each other. Moreno's insight served as the basis of a great deal of modern psychology and sociology. Individuals need to be understood in the context of other individuals.

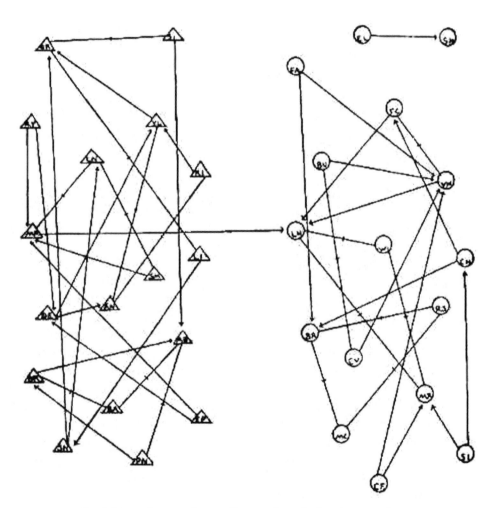

FIGURE 10.1 Jacob Moreno's network map of a second-grade class (ca. ~ 1934).

THREE BARRIERS FACING SOCIOLOGICAL
NETWORK ANALYSIS

The growth of social network analysis advanced sociological research beyond the study of small groups and then beyond simple survey analysis. In early work individual responses and actions are isolated from their broader social context. Social network analysis encouraged researchers to think more carefully about groups, neighborhoods, communities, and other social structures. This approach also allowed analysts to consider the links between groups, shifting the unit of analysis from the individual to the collective group level. As the tools of social network analysis became more familiar to researchers, its application grew to include a wide scope of substantive themes.

One of these major themes is the concept of centrality, which concentrated analysis on the individual. Concerned with understanding which actors in a network were the most "important," measures of centrality multiplied to include degree centrality, eigenvector centrality, betweenness centrality, and closeness centrality (among others). While this focus on measuring power and influence has become foundational to sociological networks, a clear limitation of centrality concepts is that each measure is only applicable to a specific set of questions, and the measures can be difficult to compare. For example, an actor with the highest betweenness centrality is unlikely to also rank highest on degree centrality. This makes it important to carefully choose centrality measures as they relate to the motivating research question.

The focus on measures like centrality highlights an important barrier in sociological network studies: namely, a single missing linkage could conceal the entire structure of the network. Suppose the linkage between the male and female cliques in figure 10.1 was deliberately concealed. The network would appear quite different, and virtually all of the traditional network statistics would be incorrectly calculated. A second barrier complicating the analysis of networks is the idea of dynamics. Suppose the one male in figure 10.1 with a link to a female moved out of town and was no longer in this second-grade class. This would change the network fundamentally, yet researchers' ability to describe that change has been a long-standing challenge for many network studies.

A third barrier is that until recently the focus was on studying networks with binary linkages that simply represented the presence or absence of a relationship. Yet consider the situation wherein one of the males in Moreno's second-grade class occasionally talked to one of the females, but not enough for them to be considered linked. These barriers have meant that the majority of network analysis is binary, is static, and assumes full information. Indeed, these barriers may have prevented some scholars from using network analysis because, for example, they were really interested in the dynamics or nonbinary phenomena. Today, all of these barriers have been largely removed.

Data Dependency as a Solution, not a Problem

The first approaches to modeling and describing networks grew out of the application of the study of graphs to networks. Building on Erdős and Rényi (1959), sociologists and others began studying exponential random graphs as a way to characterize networks based on the absence or presence of linkages between nodes. These models are known as exponential random graph models (ERGMs) and serve as the inspiration for a great deal of sociological, descriptive work.[2] In the ERGM framework, we use a set of attributes $S(Y)$ such as the number of triads or reciprocal pairs to characterize a network; covariates that describe attributes of nodes and dyads can easily be accommodated into this framework as well. Given the set of specified attributes, the probability of observing a particular network can be expressed as

$$\Pr(Y \mid X) = \frac{\exp(\beta^T S_X(Y))}{\sum_{z \in \mathcal{Y}} exp(\beta^T S_X(z))} , \ Y \in \mathcal{Y} \tag{1}$$

where X represents the set of nodal and dyadic attributes, β represents a vector of model coefficients for those attributes, $\mathcal{Y}$ denotes the set of all obtainable networks, and the denominator is used as a normalizing factor that sums across all of the obtainable networks (Hunter et al., 2008). The ERGM approach has proven to be a powerful way to study what characterizes network formation and, in more recent years, network evolution. Underpinning this approach is the Hammersley-Clifford theorem, which states that any probability distribution over networks can be represented through the form shown in equation 1. Though this is a powerful theorem, it brings little actual benefit when it comes to applying ERGMs, as it provides no guidance on the set of statistics necessary to represent the network. In fact, one of the principal challenges anyone using this method faces is developing a theoretical argument for the set of network statistics to be used.[3]

Even after having developed a model specification, actually estimating ERGMs can be quite difficult because of the normalizing factor. Typically, international relations and political economy scholars are dealing with networks that contain well over one hundred actors. If one were to apply an ERGM to studying a directed network of interstate conflict, calculating the normalizing factor would require accounting for and then summing over $2^{n \times (n-1)}$ possible networks. To put this in perspective, let us say that $n = 100$; this means we would need to sum over 2^{9900} networks; the total number of atoms in the universe is approximately $2^{272.4}$. In the undirected case this problem becomes no simpler, as we would still have to sum over $2^{n \times (n-1)/2}$ networks. Strauss and Ikeda (1990) developed a computationally fast pseudolikelihood approach to dealing with this issue that works around the normalizing constant by providing a reconsideration of the problem at the link level. This necessitates rewriting equation 1 as

$$log\left(\frac{\Pr(y_{ij}=1\,|\,X)}{\Pr(y_{ij}=0\,|\,X)}\right) = \beta^{T}\{S_{X}(y_{ij}=1,Y_{-ij})-S_{X}(y_{ij}=0,Y_{-ij})\}$$

$$= \beta^{T}\Delta S_{X}(y_{ij},Y_{-ij}) \tag{2}$$

The revised expression is similar to a standard logistic regression, and to solve it one would use typical maximum likelihood estimation procedures but with the assumption of independent dyadic observations, y_{ij}. By assuming independence here we are effectively ignoring the interdependencies in the data that prompted the utilization of a network-based approach to begin with. Though this approach has seen some use in political science, many argue that due to the independence assumption, the standard errors remain unreliable (Lubbers and Snijders, 2007; Robins et al., 2007; Van Duijn et al., 2009).[4] In addition, under the pseudolikelihood approach, the importance of network terms, such as the number of balanced triads, will be overestimated because of the interrelatedness in the data (Geyer and Thompson, 1992). Finally, both Snijders (2002) and Kolaczyk (2009) make the point that there is no asymptotic theory underlying the pseudolikelihood approach upon which to even base the construction of confidence intervals and conduct hypothesis testing.

As a result of these critiques, a new approach has come into fashion that attempts to approximate the maximum likelihood estimate for equation 1 using Markov Chain Monte Carlo techniques (MCMC-MLE) (Snijders, 2002; Handcock, 2003). This approach is an advancement, but problems remain, as we now again have to address the normalizing constant. As noted previously, estimating an ERGM on a network with over one hundred actors is computationally intensive, and even with MCMC procedures, we can only visit an infinitesimally small portion of the set of possible graphs. Bhamidi et al. (2008) and Chatterjee and Diaconis (2013) have even shown that this procedure can take an exponential time to converge unless the dyadic observations are independent. On top of the computational issues, when fitting an ERGM the model may also end up placing a high probability on a small subset of possible networks that do not at all resemble the observed network (Schweinberger, 2011). For example, most of the probability may be placed on empty graphs, no edges between nodes, or nearly complete graphs; almost every node is connected by an edge. In addition to the computational and estimation issues, ERGMs require that we be observing the full network and not just a subsample (Shalizi and Rinaldo, 2013) and be unable to handle even small levels of missingness (Minhas et al., 2016a); they also require that the exact network structure be correctly specified (Goodreau et al., 2008; Handcock et al., 2008).[5]

Due in part to the computational difficulties associated with ERGMs, a number of other approaches have been developed in recent years to study networks. In part they spring from limitations in how ERGMs rely on the observability of interactions between actors. By focusing only on what can be seen—for example, recording which 2nd second-grade students are outwardly friends with other second graders— these networks do not directly reveal the ways in which *connections* across a network influence one another. Yet relational ties within a given social network are inherently interdependent, a reality that requires further investigation. For example, the probability that one student will develop a friendship with another student is conditional on how many common connections the students share. These interdependencies represent a complex "social space" wherein future social ties are conditional on each actor's previous location within that social space. Accordingly, social space can be defined as a space of unobserved latent characteristics that captures potential transitive tendencies within a network (Hoff et al., 2002). Even though these spaces are not directly observed, they provide a conceptual approach to unraveling the network structures from observed data on networks.

Interdependencies are not unique to a specific range of network phenomena but are relevant across a breadth of cases. The basic idea is straightforward: if network y is composed of $y_{i,j}$ interactions then if i and j interact, it is intuitive that j's characteristics will influence i's actions, and vice versa. Their joint (dyadic) characteristics will also influence their interaction. This is the foundation of Kenny's (1994) social relations model (SRM), a simple approach in social psychology that has been built upon by the latent space network approach. This broad linkage is detailed in Dorff and Ward (2013), and an application of this approach to the study of economic sanctions can be found in Dorff and Minhas (2016b).

In his psychological work, Kenny was motivated to better understand how a person's aggression toward another individual was related to the first person's aggression toward all other actors in the network. This approach allows for a separation of independent and interactive effects across groups and individuals. While a basic sociomatrix captures the direct interactions between i and j, a deeper analysis is required to capture their dependencies via first order (sender and receiver) effects, second order (dyadic) effects, and third order effects (such as clusterability, transitivity, and balance).

In 2002 Hoff, Raftery, and Handcock developed a latent variable approach that would build on these insights to expand the scope of inferential models for social network analyses. While most analyses were based on an analysis of the measured ties among ordered pairs of objects, typically denoted $y_{i,j}$, they proposed looking at linkages probabilistically. The idea that each tie in a network may be probabilistic is important. Typically it is thought that as the similarity of characteristics between individuals increases, the probability of a tie between individuals also increases. Thus, individuals who share similar characteristics are thought to have a high probability of being linked together in a given social context. This leads directly to the idea of a social space in which a group of individuals have similar characteristics, even if they are not physically close. Developed first in the 1970s (McFarland and Brown, 1973), this idea is by now familiar in the modern world of smartphones and omnipresent Internet connections. Suppose, however, that we turn this idea on its head. Let us assume that there is some social space in which each actor is located and that the social space is defined by the probability that any two actors are connected to one another in some meaningful way.

Hoff et al. (2002) defined that space to be a probability space, in which closeness is the probability of a link between individuals. In this way, a latent, unobserved space may be estimated in an approach that builds upon conditional independence:

$$P(Y \mid Z, X, \theta) = \prod_{i \neq j} P\left(y_{i,j} \mid z_i, z_j, x_{i,j}, \theta\right) \tag{3}$$

where X and $x_{i,\,j}$ are observed characteristics and θ and Z are parameters and positions—herein symmetric—in latent space that are to be estimated. The distance metric imposed on the latent space can be Euclidean or take a different form, ideally one that obeys the triangle inequality: $d_{i,j} \leq d_{i,j} + d_{k,j} \ \forall \ \{i,j,k\}$. Distances can also be high dimensional, or more typically of low dimensions. One frequent choice is Euclidean $d_{i,j} = \| z_i - z_j \|$; another is to treat the space in a bilinear manner, similar to the way error covariances are treated in regression models: $d_{i,j} = |z_i \times z_j|$. This approach can be easily estimated and has the advantage of also specifying and estimating the covariances among positions. It works for any type of network data (binary, categorical, or continuous) and can also be specified in a way to capture dynamics. It can be applied to asymmetric networks as well as symmetric ones. An example is using exports as the network characteristic, the asymmetric bilinear mixed effects specification where $Y_{n \times n}$ is an asymmetric matrix of dyadic (log) exports in which y_{ij} is exports that i sends to j. This is formalized thus:

$$(y_{ij}, y_{ji})' \sim \mathrm{MVN}_2((\theta_{ij}, \theta_{ji})', \Sigma_\gamma)$$

$$\Sigma_\gamma = \begin{bmatrix} \sigma_\gamma^2 & \rho\sigma_\gamma^2 \\ \rho\sigma_\gamma^2 & \sigma_\gamma^2 \end{bmatrix}$$

$$\theta_{ij} = \beta' x_{ij} + s_i + r_j + u_i' v_j$$

$$(s_i, r_i)' \sim \mathrm{MVN}_2(0, \Sigma_{sr})$$

$$\Sigma_{sr} = \begin{bmatrix} \sigma_s^2 & \sigma_{sr} \\ \sigma_{sr} & \sigma_r^2 \end{bmatrix} \tag{4}$$

$$u_i \sim \mathrm{MVN}_k(0, \Sigma_u)$$

$$v_i \sim \mathrm{MVN}_k(0, \Sigma_v)$$

$$\Sigma_u = I_k(\sigma_{u_1}^2, \ldots, \sigma_{u_k}^2)'$$

$$\Sigma_v = I_k(\sigma_{v_1}^2, \ldots, \sigma_{v_k}^2)'$$

Each of these terms has a straightforward, substantive interpretation.[6]

First, $y_{i,\,j}$ and $y_{j,\,i}$ are modeled to be bivariate Normal, with capturing the residual covariance within a dyad, that is, reciprocity in network parlance. The $x_{i,\,j}$ are unit or dyadic covariates, and β are estimated regression coefficients. The r_i and s_j are sender and receiver random effects, which can be thought of as rough analogs to indegree and outdegree measures. The σ_r^2 and σ_s^2 represent dependence among dyadic observations having a common receiver and sender, respectively, while $\sigma_{s,r}$ captures the extent to which active receivers are also active senders.

The bilinear term captures the main innovation, $u_i'v_j$, where u_i and v_j describe i's and j's positions in the latent sender and receiver spaces, capturing the hypothesized interdependencies probabilistically. To see that $u_i'v_j$ captures third order dependence, note that $u_i'v_j = |u_i| \; |u_j| \cos \phi$, where ϕ is the angle between the vectors. As the angle approaches zero, there is positive correlation and dependence; as it approaches 180, the correlation approaches -1.

This approach offers a principled way to study dependent data, such as networks and spatially dependent data. It has numerous benefits. First, as should be obvious, the resultant output matrices can be understood as weighted sociomatrices or as a weights matrices in a spatial framework. As such, standard calculations based on eigenvalues—centrality, betweenness, distance, density, and the like—can be meaningfully applied to them. Similarly, they can be used in a wide variety of spatial approaches. This approach offers a variety of additional features:

- It provides an organic way of dealing with missing data: if an edge is missing, then the position in the latent, probability space is estimated for all known nodes, and linkages can be inferred from the model.
- A wide range of data types on networks is admitted: binary, categorical, and continuous.
- This approach explicitly models the extent of dyadic reciprocity within the network, as well as estimating node level random effects.
- The latent space approach also generates estimates of covariances for sender and receiver actions in asymmetric networks.
- Software that implements this flexible approach is available through the $\mathcal{R}$ package amen.[7]

This approach has been applied to the *drosophilia melanogaster* of network analysis: the Medici family intermarriage (Padgett and Ansell, 1993), as well as the data on monks collected by Sampson (1969). Within political science this approach has been used to study a wide variety of phenomena.[8]

By way of illustration, Dorff (2015) applies this approach to study a notoriously opaque concept: criminal networks. Using International Crisis Event Warning System (ICEWS) event data, the study presents a latent space model to capture conflictual (i.e., violent) events between drug trafficking organizations (DTOs) and government actors during the Mexican criminal conflict (2005–2013).[9] This analysis allows one to take into account not only the effects of interesting political covariates, such as the number of protests in the DTO's region of operation in a given year, but also random actor effects and higher order dependencies.

Figure 10.2 compares the network generated from raw data of violent events to the latent space network. Thus, the left panel depicts the empirical network, while the right panel plots the latent space positions for each actor in the network. Nodes closer together in the latent space indicate a high probability of interaction between these two nodes. If there is not a link drawn between two closely positioned nodes in the original network (left panel), then the latent space is likely capturing an unobserved link between actors.

Notably, the latent positions reveal a triadic structure among the Sinaloa cartel, the army, and the federal government. This signals a high probability of interaction among these three actors. This finding indicates that the Mexican army is likely involved in violent events with the Sinaloas, despite the fact that this link is not reported in the raw data. In the context of the Mexican criminal conflict, this is particularly interesting because it suggests that in 2005 federal forces were more involved in managing disputes with the Sinaloas—a rapidly growing, widespread criminal organization—while local level actors such as the state police were frequently engaged with the Gulf cartel, a regionally concentrated organization during this time. The latent space network reveals clusters between actors that would otherwise remain unobserved.

While a standard modeling approach can predict the number of violent events for a given year of the conflict, it cannot predict which events will occur between which actors. Furthermore, a standard approach would proceed by ignoring these interdependencies within the data and essentially treating each group active in each event as *independent*. The latent space approach allows analysts to regard these dependencies as relevant to the development of the conflict rather than ignore them altogether.

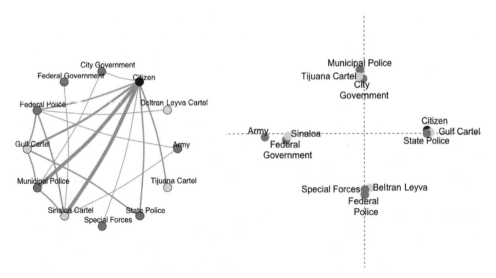

FIGURE 10.2 Latent space analysis of the Mexican drug war (2005).

NETWORKS IN POLITICAL SCIENCE AND THE SO-CALLED DYAD

Latent space approaches contrast with other network models used in political science, though these different approaches are united through similar contestations against traditional dyadic frameworks. In the field of international relations, scholars typically conceptualize political phenomena as they occur between two states. For example, militarized interstate disputes—moments in which military force is employed but full-scale war is avoided—are coded as a singular incident between two states. Motives for these type of events span a wide range of possibilities, including territorial, commercial, religious, and boundary disputes (Mitchell and Prins, 1999). Canonical data sets in international relations thus include multiple rows of data in which many of the same actors appear, since each row captures a singular dispute and multiple disputes contain the same actor.[10] This relates back to a primary concern of Kenny's study on aggression: How do we understand actor-level behavior when one actor is engaged with many other actors in a given context? In international relations studies we violate the assumption that events are independent when we allow for multiple actors to appear across multiple events. Another way to consider independence in this case is to contemplate the role of directionality. In a given network representing conflictual events, a conflict between $i-j$ is not simply a conflict between $i-j$ because there is also the question of what kind of behavior is sent from actor j to actor i. As soon as one adds a third actor into the mix, we must consider whether actor k is tied to i or j and vice versa. In short, to assume that processes *within* dyads are independent *across* dyads leads to bias. Network approaches are the solution to this problem.

While scholars of international relations have begun to acknowledge the importance of network approaches for the study of questions such as whether war is less likely between democracies and whether countries with strong trade relations are more likely to comply to sanctions, many researchers continue to employ biased dyadic approaches to understand international politics. Students in this field thus have a deep literature in which to explore using network tools to better understand influence on a global scale: how do great powers emerge? Why do states fail? Scholars should use the finest tools available to address pressing questions of today relating to political violence. With an increase in the availability of event data via sources such as ICEWS (Lautenschlager et al., 2015) and PHOENIX (http://openeventdata.org/), we have better information linking actors to events. This information allows us to generate accurate data that captures when actors engage violently with others across time and space. Nonstate groups perpetrate violence against civilians, governments, and other nonstate actors, resulting in complex, interdependent contexts wherein predicting peace or violence is conditional on our ability to properly map and access changes in conflict between actors over time.

Previously we detailed a number of the computational and estimation issues associated with ERGMs; however, there are other notable downsides relative to latent space approaches that are worth distinguishing. These models actually require an assumption of homogenous effects across dyads, a strong assumption given the nature of sociopolitical networks that researchers study. As reviewed in the previous section, the latent space model allows for heterogeneous higher order effects between dyads. For example, a concept like reciprocity is seen as having different effects for different actors in the network. Yet though this is a key strength of the latent approach, the way in which we observe the latent space—through an n dimensional space—limits analysts' ability to directly observe the effects of specific types of higher order dependencies. In this sense, while collapsing the latent space into two or three dimensions enhances interpretability of the latent space, it also hinders its utility.

Recent advances in latent space approaches improve these limitations while maintaining the integrity of the model. More recently, Hoff's (2015b) approach allows for a direct parameterization of higher order dependencies; thus concepts like reciprocity and transitivity are now explicitly represented in the model and can be explored directly. This model, known as a multilinear tensor regression (MLTR) model, has been introduced to political science by Minhas et al. (2016b). After a discussion linking these approaches to the study of spatial analysis, we discuss benefits of the MLTR below.

SPATIAL ANALYSIS AND SOCIAL NETWORKS

Wong et al. (2006) cleverly showed that homophily—the idea that birds of a feather flock together—is frequently determined by geographical space. Indeed, they showed that simple networks embedded randomly in geographical space will tend to be characterized by low density, short distances, clustering, and the existence of communities. Although starting with a simple Bernoulli random graph will not lead to such clustering, doing so in the context of some baseline of geographical homophily will lead to many small clusters with a low level of path length. Such networks are typically of the phenomenon known as a small world (Watts and Strogatz, 1998; Watts, 1999).

Indeed, the dependency that exists within a typical spatial model is a type of network. A simple spatial model is given as

$$y = \rho W y + X\beta + \varepsilon \tag{5}$$

with the dependent variable (y) being a function of the network of geographical connections among the observations (W). This network, W, is frequently row-standardized so that each observation has an equivalent number of linkages, but this correction is not necessary. Nor is it necessary that the network be generated by a Bernoulli process. Indeed, the so-called weights matrix W is indeed a type of sociomatrix representation of a network of linkages—herein geographical—among the observations.

Spatial modeling has developed a simple technique (owing to Ord 1975) to solve the interdependency of the data. Note that the full likelihood is given as

$$\ln l = -\frac{n}{2}\ln(\pi\sigma^2) + \ln|I_n - \rho W| - \frac{e^T e}{2\sigma^2}$$

$$e = (I_n - \rho W)y - X\beta \tag{6}$$

This is complicated to evaluate because the determinant must be recalculated for every iteration. Ord's solution was to extract the eigenvalues of the spatial matrix once and to reuse them:

$$\ln|I_n - \rho W| = \ln\prod_{i=1}^{n}(1 - \rho\omega_i) = \sum_{i-1}^{n}\ln(1 - \rho\omega) \tag{7}$$

Hays et al. (2010) have shown that with modern computers, for small enough problems, the inclusion of the eigenvalue calculation in the iterative algorithm is not computationally prohibitive. Indeed, for some problems they propose estimating the values of W along with the other parameters.

The good news is that spatial models can have both networks and geography easily included in them at the same time, if desired, with Z (herein symmetric) for the latent network positions, and W for the geographical network:

$$y = \rho Wy + \rho_2 Zy + X\beta + \varepsilon \tag{8}$$

wherein one sociomatrix is geographical space and the other represents social space. Either can be measured or in some cases estimated. At the same time, latent network approaches can include within them geographical space as a dyadic covariate:

$$P(Y|Z, X, \theta) = \prod_{i \neq j} P(y_{i,j}|z_i, z_j, x_{i,j}, W, \theta). \tag{9}$$

Hence, while networks that represent social behavior allow us to map meaningful connections between actors, an important class of networks is anchored within real space and embodies the physical distance between points. These networks are informed by the physical features of place, space, topography, and geography. These spatial networks are distinct from networks built on the relationships between organizations or actors, but rely on similar principles of connectivity.

Spatial network analysis has been used to study a range of patterns, including traffic flows, commerce, postal service routes, land use, and the spread of water contamination. As technology has developed, global positioning system (GPS) has enabled geocoding for a wide range of phenomena. Spatial analysis is now increasingly applied to assess changes in both physical and immaterial concepts, such as social or political events. Events are inherently constrained and shaped by physical space—such as the way a march is constrained by the size and design of city streets—a process that is very relevant for the use of spatial networks.

Importantly, spatial networks can reveal useful information about the structural environment relevant to social and political life. Take, for example, spatial networks that capture urban street patterns. Crucitti et al. (2006) have studied centrality patterns embedded in the spatial networks of eighteen major cities. The authors consider each urban street sample as an undirected graph in which traffic intersections are nodes and connecting streets are the edges between nodes. Their analysis highlights the ways in which the physical system of roads and traffic intersections correlates with the social system of pedestrian behavior. Gastner and Newman's (2006) study of the US interstate highway network and the Internet offers similar insights into how population density might affect the evolution of these spatial networks over time. We can identify a comparable system when viewing the distribution of criminal events along a spatial plane. Another example is the Denver Crime Map (see figure 10.3), which plots the number of criminal offenses at their precise location within a bounded area.

Just as this example demonstrates, spatial processes can be mapped into graph form, generating a spatial matrix. These criminal data, however, could also be mapped by focusing on the criminal events as ties between actors and relegating spatial considerations into the world of less easily defined characteristics. In this way, spatial and latent processes represent a similar component of network analysis. Relatedly, Ward et al.'s (2012) network analysis of global trade positions uses latent networks to reveal geographical patterns among the dependencies. Figure 10.4 shows latent global trade positions for all countries in the global network for the year 1990. By shading the nodes according to physical proximity (left panel), one can identify the geographical clusterings of trade within latent space.

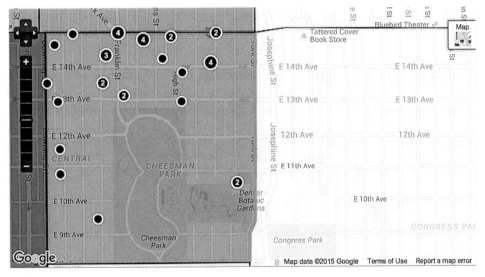

FIGURE 10.3 Crime events for Cheesman Park neighborhood (left panel shown in grey) in Denver, Colorado.

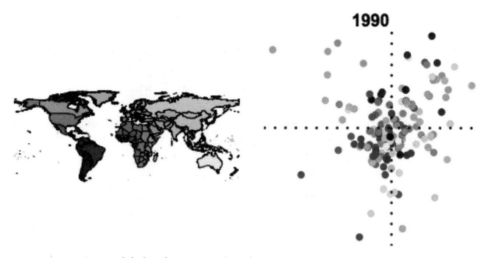

FIGURE 10.4 Latent global trade positions (1990).

In sum, network analyses and spatial analyses are intimately linked. Each approach has been enormously improved by the advance of modern statistics and modern computing so that the barriers once faced are no longer barriers, but opportunities. The approach we have described in this chapter dismantles previous limitations of network analysis. It enables researchers to ask innovative questions about how complicated social dynamics might evolve over time and space. In addition, network studies can now address those phenomena that are often underreported, unobserved, or deeply embedded in complex spatial contexts.

BIPARTITE LATENT SPACE NETWORKS

Most political science studies using networks use a one mode network, in which there is a set of nodes that are linked together in some fashion. But there are different approaches that may serve to enhance inquiry into dependencies deep in social science data. Consider a set of documents, D and a set of words of interest, for example the names of candidates for office, W. These two sets are independent in that no members of one set are in the other, but there may be edges that connect the elements of one set with the elements of the other. One way in which these kinds of graphs or networks have been thought about is a graph of connections for which each end of a given connection is in a separate set (of two possibilities). There are very few studies in political science that explicitly utilize such bipartite networks, but this approach has been widespread in the study of spatial models of voting.[11]

The first attempt to systematically address the relative, ideological positions of politicians from responses to surveys by citizens was made by Aldrich and McKelvey (1977).

This was not conceived as a network problem, but can be thought of as a latent network in one dimension. These studies emerged from a spatial model of party competition. This approach became known as "ideal point" analysis and spawned a long line of productive research. Perhaps most well known is the work of Poole & Rosenthal (1984, 1985), which introduced a scaling procedure to recover latent, unmeasured positions of politicians in a program called NOMINATE.[12] So-called NOMINATE scores have been used in myriad academic studies and have also found a home in media outlets, including the *New York Times* and now popular websites such as fivethirtyeight.com, which use these scores to capture the relative position of institutions and politicians. The fundamental research can be found in Poole and Rosenthal (1991), with an evaluation of it after ten years of use found in Poole and Rosenthal (2001) and an excellent survey done by Clinton et al. (2004). In 2015 the basic ideas were brought into the Bayesian world by Hare et al. (2015), who updated the original Aldrich-McKelvey approach. All of this research can be thought of as a bipartite network in which politicians (or institutions) are linked to votes on legislation (or cosponsorship), so that individuals are linked to documents or other actions. Many have studied this in terms of community identification (Porter et al., 2009).[13]

But for the most part the characteristics of bipartite networks have been ignored. A recent exception is the work of Friel et al. (2016). The changing but interlocking directorate of Irish companies was examined using data over the period 2003–2013. This period covered the 2008 financial crisis, which rerouted Irish economic growth. There were thirty-six company boards in 2003, but only twenty-nine in 2013.

Over the same time period between 250 and 350 individuals who served on these boards, and of those between 15 and 33 individuals served on more than one board; in some years approximately 10% of the board members were *interlocking*. This interlocking nature of the corporate governance in Ireland (and other places) raised the question of whether the degree of "interlockingness" creates an inflexibility of institutions in dealing with systemic shocks such as the financial crisis in 2008.

The latent director positions at time $t \in \{1,\ldots,T\}$ are given as $\mathbf{x}_1^{(t)},\ldots,\mathbf{x}_n^{(t)}$ and the latent positions of companies are represented by $\mathbf{w}_1^{(t)},\ldots,\mathbf{w}_n^{(t)}$. Conditional on these latent positions of directors and companies, the log-odds of director i being a member of board j in year t is

$$\text{logit}\left[p_{ij}^{(t)} \right] = y_{ij}^{(t-1)} \gamma^{(t)} + \left[1 - y_{ij}^{(t-1)}\right]\beta^{(t)} - \| \mathbf{x}_i - \mathbf{w}_j^{(t)} \| \tag{10}$$

where $\gamma^{(t)}$ is an edge persistence parameter and $\beta^{(t)}$ is a non-edge persistence parameter. The likelihood is straightforwardly expressed:

$$\mathcal{L}_y = \prod_{t=1}^{T}\prod_{j\in\beta_t}\prod_{i\in D_t} p_{ij}^{(t)} \tag{11}$$

and this can be estimated as a Bayesian hierarchical model, using a random walk for the latent positions of the boards of directors ($\mathcal{W}$) and a multivariate Gaussian prior for the positions of the directors ($\mathcal{X}$):

$$\pi\left(\mathcal{W}\#\ \tau_w, \tau_w^0\right) = \prod_{j=1}^{M} \prod_{d=1}^{D} f\left(\mathbf{w}_{jd}^1; 0, \frac{1}{\tau_w^0}\right) \times \prod_{t=2}^{T} \prod_{j=1}^{M} \prod_{s=1}^{D} f\left(\mathbf{w}_{jd}^t; \mathbf{w}_{jd}^{t-1}, \frac{1}{\tau_w}\right)$$

$$\pi\left(\mathcal{X}\right) = \prod_{i=1}^{N} \prod_{d=1}^{D} f\left(\mathbf{x}_{id}; 0, \frac{1}{\tau_x}\right) \tag{12}$$

where $f(s, \mu, \nu)$ is a Gaussian density evaluated at s.[14]

Estimating the latent space model in this way shows several things in this study of Irish directorates. First and foremost, the persistency parameters are both important. Perhaps as important is that the latent space contracts until after the 2008 financial crisis but is stabilized thereafter. To our knowledge this is the first application of a bipartite, dynamic latent network and thereby breaks new ground for the latent space approach in the study of political dynamics as well as political institutions.

For example, the network studies of international organizations can be re-conceptualized as bipartite networks consisting of organizations and countries. So far most studies have only examined the unipartite network of comembership (i.e., for a given set of countries, identifying which countries are members of an organization or combined sets of organizations). Representative examples include Wilson et al. (2016), in which the authors present an elaborate argument about the role of conflict resolution organizations (CROs) and how, through networks, such organizations influence states' behaviors toward each other. Data are used for the years 1997 and 2001 from the annual *Yearbook of International Organizations* and begin with the network of CROs in each state. This itself is a bipartite network, that is, a network of organizations (that are not states) and states (that are not networks). Starting with a network of ties among only among CROs in each state, Wilson et al. (2016) count up the number of ties from each state to each CRO and calculate the number of ties from a conflict management organization in each state to every other state *for each dyad*. If there were multiple ties in each state, the sum of these ties was used as an edge weight. This created a dyadic, weighted unipartite network represented in an adjacency matrix (2016, 448). Ironically, while the authors were interested in the conflict resolution network, these organizations do not appear in their network, except implicitly, and their identities are lost. Moreover, interdependency among such organizations is assumed not to be present, and the role of any specific CRO in any specific country is no longer available for analysis in the network model.[15] In a sense, while the authors may have had other goals that dictated their research strategy, they did not take full advantage of the bipartite network data that they created. Such an analysis could have been done in a standard model or by creating a latent space for countries and for CROs. That in itself allows an investigation of a variety of interesting questions that motivated the original article.

In short, not only do latent networks facilitate the study of unipartite, single-layer networks, but they can also be used in multiplex and bipartite models to address more nuanced questions.

DYNAMIC LATENT SPACE NETWORKS

Most network studies begin with a study of a network at a single point in time and then move along to include one or more different time points. Myriad studies adopt this approach. One example is Ward et al. (2007). However, most analysts would like to study the dynamics of networks as they change over time. In general this is complicated, because not only do the edges or linkages change, but the actual members of the network also change. Only five states were considered essential and sovereign at the Congress of Vienna in 1815 (Austria, Prussia, Russia, Great Britain, and France), and a few others were included in the Congress (Italy, Switzerland, Sweden, Denmark, Spain, Portugal), but today there are 195 independent states. Thus, the number of independent states has increased. Not only have some new states been created, but some old states have disappeared. For example, the Holy Roman Empire, East Germany, the Soviet Union, and the United Arab Republic have all disappeared. This ebb and flow of system members means that dynamic analysis of such a network is more complicated, but it is not necessarily less interesting.

Moreover, most network approaches that were developed in the statistical realm did not originally have a way to incorporate time series. But now this problem has been solved, and several different approaches utilize a dynamic network framework. A simplistic solution is to link together the cross sections via the lagged latent positions (Cao and Ward, 2014), but dynamics have also been incorporated directly into the estimation of the latent positions by Ward et al. (2012). More detail on dynamic latent social networks can be found in Sewell and Chen (2015, 2016).

The past few decades have seen the development of a number of network based approaches to dealing with longitudinal network data. One of the more important efforts in this vein is the stochastic actor oriented model (SAOM) developed by Snijders (2001). This approach provides a way to model longitudinal, binary networks that considers the formation of linkages as the result of a myopic utility maximization effort on the part of actors. The temporal exponential random graph model (TERGM) developed by Hanneke and Xing (2007) is a similar approach used to model binary longitudinal relational data.

Another popular approach to modeling longitudinal networks is to specify dynamic latent variables in which a network is modeled as a function of nodal latent variables. The goal of this approach is to collapse information contained in the network about higher order dependencies to a lower dimensional space. As mentioned previously, this approach was first introduced into the political science literature by Ward and Hoff (2007). Common to both the ERGM and latent space approaches is an effort to account for higher order dependencies. Examples of these dependencies include concepts such as reciprocity and transitivity, which are familiar to the international relations literature.

While both the ERGM based and latent space approaches incorporate statistical interdependence among the actors, the ERGM-based approaches assume that this effect is homogeneous among all dyads. The latent variable based approach allows heterogeneity among dyads. The downside, however, of earlier work using the latter approach is that explicit parameterizations of the effect of reciprocity and transitivity could not be calculated due to the simple structure of the latent variables. Instead, all of the information contained within higher order dependencies was collapsed into a lower dimensional latent space. In order to balance the shortcomings and benefits of these approaches, a novel approach, which we refer to as the bilinear autoregression model, has been introduced into the networks and political science literature by Hoff (2015b) and Minhas et al. (2016b). This method provides a way to analyze longitudinal networks and allows for an explicit representation of network dependencies (such as reciprocity and transitivity) between dyads while permitting heterogeneity between dyads. And unlike either the latent space or ERGM based approaches, it enables one to estimate multilayer networks endogenously. Thus, by using this approach we can jointly model the trade network and the conflict network and their interdependence, for example.

CRITICISMS OF LATENT SPACE NETWORKS

Recently there have been a few important criticisms of latent space models (Cranmer et al., forthcoming). They focus on an $\mathcal{R}$ package, latentnet, built around a particular latent space model that employs a Euclidean metric to capture higher order interdependencies (Krivitsky and Handcock, 2015). The approach that has actually been used most often in political science, including by the authors here, has been a latent space model that employs a bilinear term to capture interdependencies.[16] This approach was developed by Hoff (2005) and introduced into political science by Hoff and Ward (2004).[17]

The bilinear approach offers a number of benefits over the Euclidean model. Most important, it avoids confounding the effect of exogenous covariates with nodal actor positions in the latent space. In the undirected version of the bilinear model, the latent space metric, $z_i^T z_j$, is a mean zero random effect that is calculated from the residuals after having taken into account the effect of exogenous covariates. The benefit of this approach is that the parameter estimates for those covariates can be interpreted in a straightforward way that is similar to how one would interpret the output from any generalized linear model (GLM). In the Euclidean approach, on the other hand, interpretation is more difficult, as the latent space metric, $\| z_i - z_j \|$, is incorporated as a fixed effect, where a value of $\| z_i - z_j \| \approx 0$ corresponds to the maximal probability of a link. This is an important distinction to point out, as it directly relates to a critique that Cranmer et al. (forthcoming) have made of latent space models. What is relevant to note is that this critique only applies to latent space models using a fixed effects Euclidean approach. A more detailed discussion and empirical application on this topic can be found in Minhas et al. (2016a).

Cranmer et al. (forthcoming) have asserted a number of other criticisms of latent space models, briefly addressed here in italic text following each criticism:

(1) Latent space models are less flexible than an ERGM because substantive theory related to the dependencies cannot be tested. *Including network statistics in a regression model is not in and of itself testing substantive theory. Substantive theory can be tested with a variety of approaches, but it requires specifying the theory at a very low level. If the researcher has a substantive idea about which actors should be close to one another but cannot measure that either in terms of dyadic or monadic covariates, then he or she can check the results to see if the theory in question is upheld. However, Cranmer et al. (forthcoming) might assume that one cannot include dyadic covariates in the latent space model along with monadic covariates. As suggested herein, we actually can. A dyadic covariate of interest could reflect a substantively interesting aspect of the researcher's argument. For example, many modelers include a distance matrix to capture geographical distance in the covariate part of a latent space model. Moreover, reciprocity is directly estimated, and third order dependencies are also captured directly.*

(2) Latent space models need many more parameters and are therefore less parsimonious. This is especially problematic in situations where few vertices are present because there ultimately may be more parameters than observations. *This is true, but it does not effectively influence the pros and cons of this approach. When iterating through a complicated procedure, such as ERGM—which may be plagued by numerical instability and potential degeneracy—many estimates are used along the way, even if the analyst reports only a select few. All of these methods violate the general idea that statistics reduce the dimensionality in a strict sense. Most important, in Minhas et al. (2016a) we show that latent variable approaches based on the bilinear framework are able to better represent higher order network patterns and can better predict links out-of-sample than alternative network inferential tools such as ERGM. Given that latent space models can better predict out-of-sample, concerns of overfitting are irrelevant.*

(3) Further, latent space models are not useful when the interdependencies are theoretically interesting. *This assessment is inaccurate and ignores the role of dyadic covariates. But even ERGM model requires the researcher to correctly specify the underlying network structure. If the researcher omits a three-star variable and yet the data generating process is dominated by three-starness, then the analysis is severely flawed, even with a (T)(G)ERGM. Moreover, this ignores a serious problem of ERGM models. They not only require that the correct sufficient statistics be included—i.e., that the model is correctly specified—but they also require it to be completely observed. If we sample from an ERGM model, for example, it is very easy to get a resultant network that is degenerate. Degeneracy essentially means that the*

graph structure is destroyed and made sparse by the deletion of nodes. Degenerate graphs cannot be statistically estimated by standard (or even esoteric) statistical procedures. Our experience is that even randomly deleting as few as 3% of the observations in a typical binary graph (network) leads to a resultant graph that is degenerate, with many unconnected nodes (Minhas et al., 2016a). This problem means that even a small amount of missing data can defeat attempts to use ERGM modeling approaches to uncover the structure of a graph.

Though it is important to highlight the differences between the bilinear latent space approach and alternatives, we would be remiss in neglecting to mention the progress that has been made in extending the bilinear approach to account for even more complicated types of dependence patterns. The major type of pattern that both the bilinear and Euclidean approaches capture can broadly be referred to as homophily. Homophily captures the idea that the relationships between actors with similar characteristics in a network are likely to be stronger than nodes with different characteristics. This concept can be used to explain the emergence of patterns such as transitivity ("a friend of a friend is a friend") and balance ("an enemy of a friend is an enemy").[18]

Another major pattern that appears in networks is the concept of stochastic equivalence. This concept refers to the idea that a network can be divided into groups such that members of the same group have similar relational patterns. Typically, assessing stochastic equivalence in a network is only possible through community detection procedures such as stochastic block models. The latent distance model actually confounds stochastic equivalence with homophily by construction. Consider two nodes i and j that are proximate to one another in a two-dimensional latent space. Since these two nodes are proximate, they are predicted to interact with one another at a higher probability as a result of third order dependence patterns. By construction i will then also be more likely to interact with all the other actors that j is likely to interact with. Thus in attempting to account for homophily, the Euclidean model constrains actors to possess similar relational patterns.[19]

To account for stochastic equivalence within the bilinear latent space model, Hoff (2008) shows that we can extend the bilinear effect to a more general asymmetric bilinear effect $z_i^T \Lambda z_j$, where Λ is a diagonal matrix that has rows and columns equal to the number of latent dimensions specified. This approach has been developed into an $\mathcal{R}$ package, amen (Hoff et al., 2015), and Minhas et al. (2016a) introduce the amen package and detail how it differs from earlier latent space models. In addition, Minhas et al. (2016a) also undertake an analysis of the network studied in Cranmer et al. (forthcoming). They suggest that the ERGM offers the most preferred model fit. Our own reanalysis of these data with the approach found in amen suggests otherwise. Table 10.1 illustrates the out-of-sample fit of the various models examined in Cranmer et al. (forthcoming). It shows that while the updated bilinear approach in amen is the best, all the models do pretty well at predicting the overwhelming number of zeros typically found in these sparse political networks. Predicting the absence of a link is pretty easy. However, as shown by the precision recall statistics, the approaches differ markedly at actually predicting the links, and specifically, the amen approach outperforms the alternatives.

Table 10.1 Comparison of Out-of-Sample Fit and Precision Statistics for Network Models Examined in Cranmer et al. (forthcoming)*

Model Type	AUC Score	
	ROC	Precision Recall
Latent distance model (statnet)	0.83	0.64
Logit	0.87	0.64
MRQAP	0.87	0.65
ERGM	0.90	0.68
amen	0.92	0.77

*MRQAP = multiple regression quadratic assignment procedure

CONCLUSION

Latent space models provide a general framework for embracing the interdependencies that exist in the political and social worlds, whether they be binary, ordinal, or continuous, measured at one point in time or longitudinally. The major benefit of these types of models and the reason they were developed is that they provide a modeling framework for dyadic data based on familiar statistical tools such as linear regression, GLM, random effects, and factor models. We have an understanding of how each of these tools work, and they are numerically more stable than ERGM approaches. Further, the dependencies that these approaches capture are explicitly transformed to a multidimensional probability space in which "closer" nodes are more likely to be linked than nodes that are distant from one another.[20] Software and computing power have advanced sufficiently that Bayesian versions of these approaches are relatively straightforward to employ. Surprisingly, however, despite the widespread adoption of latent network approaches in the network sciences (including machine learning, computer science, and Bayesian, applied statistics), these approaches have not yet been widely employed in political science.[21]

The study of international political economy and international organizations broadly conceptualized is a fertile arena for the use of networks, especially latent space and bipartite approaches. In this line of research analysts are often studying both a group of countries that are interdependent and a set of organizations, such as nongovernmental organizations, that are also interdependent. In many instances the organizations are a part of the United Nations or other multilateral organizations, and the members of these organizations are often subsets of the countries in the world. Analysis of the effect of one domain on another is at the heart of policy analysis and should perhaps be at the core of substantive academic research as well. But there is still tremendous upside for the use of network approaches. Following is a short list of topics in this domain:

- multilateral aid and migration, in which the network of recipient nations is a different network than that supporting or causing the migration
- foreign aid, in which the network of recipients is separate from the network of donors
- monetary institutions and the effects of their policies across the world
- terrorist attacks and their prevention, wherein different networks serve as actors and targets
- formation of trade and investment agreements, which can benefit from a network perspective

In addition, scholars of peace and conflict are committed to studying the causes and consequences of violence around the world. To do so, they must employ the most appropriate tools available for their research. While a great number of studies adopt network-like language, using terms such as *linkages* and *fragmentation*, the majority do not also adopt the modeling frameworks most appropriate for addressing these concepts. Network analysis enables us to model how political phenomena move across space, time, and actors, such as the spread of violence between villages or the proliferation of weapon attainment across borders. This applies to regions all over the world, to small arms trades in Central America and localized ethnic violence in the Middle East. Networks are inherent in our study of criminal organizations and pact formation. Violent social movements, whether driven by religious or ethnic violence, are emblematic of network questions: Why do groups fragment? How does shared ethnicity inform or hinder the linkages that drive collective action? The study of inter- and intragroup violence benefits from a network framework, allowing us to consider the role of individuals' influence in the evolution of a group's combined behavior. Social cleavages can drive the formation of new groups, which adopt political strategies opposed to those of their parent groups. All these processes are quintessential network phenomena.

We are not suggesting that latent space networks will be a relevant approach to every problem. But we are suggesting this approach will be useful in addressing many more problems than it is currently used to analyze.

NOTES

1. Many, such as Karl Popper, found Freud's ideas antiscientific, while others—including Herbert Marcuse—drew parallels to grander theories. Today, Freud's ideas are largely relics from an earlier era.
2. A detailed literature review on ERGMs can be found in Freeman (2004).

3. Snijders et al. (2006) have noted the necessity of operationalizing the set of network statistics in a specific and rather complicated way.

4. For example, see Cranmer et al. (2012, 2014).

5. Snijders et al. (2006) note that obtaining the correct model specification is not just a function of incorporating variables to capture network characteristics such as degree or transitivity, but also requires operationalizing those variables carefully to avoid degeneracy.

6. The same cannot be said of the p^* model.

7. A tutorial is available at https://github.com/pdhoff/amen/blob/master/vignettes/amen. pdf. Prior to the release of this package most of the works using latent space approaches in political science relied on software available at http://www.stat.washington.edu/people/pdhoff/Code/hoff_2005_jasa/.

8. See Ward et al. (2003); Hoff and Ward (2004); Ward et al. (2007); Ward and Hoff (2007, 2008); Treier and Jackman (2008); Hafner-Burton et al. (2009); Ward et al. (2012); Cranmer et al. (2012); Cao (2012); Dorff (2015); Greenhill (2015); Metternich et al. (2013); and Barberá (2015)

9. See Boschee et al. (2015) for a description of the ICEWS machine coded event data.

10. Unfortunately, one widely used data generation program—EUGENE (Bennett and Stam, 2000)—enforces this.

11. One exception is Cho and Fowler (2010).

12. Subsequently D-NOMINATE and W-NOMINATE.

13. A recent survey can be found in Kirkland and Gross (2014).

14. Details are found in Friel et al. (2016) and at http://www.pnas.org/content/suppl/2016/05/25/1606295113.DCSupplemental/pnas.1606295113.sapp.pdf. See also Koskinen and Edling (2012). Note that this bipartite specification uses a Euclidean distance metric, not a bilinear one. The latter are available through the amen approach, described in Hoff (2015a) and Minhas et al. (2016a).

15. This article also uses measured aspects of the network—such as eigenvalues—in a regression framework that itself assumes independence of observations. The authors used negative binomial models for the monadic models, and the so-called dyadic analysis used zero-inflated negative binomial regression. Both of these assume independence of observations. This approach also ignores the sender and receiver effects. We don't comment further on the modeling framework beyond the construction of the networks.

16. For example, see Ward et al. (2007); Dorff (2015); and Metternich et al. (2015).

17. Software to estimate this model is available at http://www.stat.washington.edu/people/pdhoff/Code/hoff_2005_jasa/.

18. See Shalizi and Thomas (2011) for a more detailed discussion of the concept of homophily.

19. The only way to effectively address this issue is by increasing the number of latent dimensions to a size equivalent to the number of groups in the network.

20. Defining "closer" in latent space models that use a bilinear metric to capture interdependencies is somewhat more complicated, but feasible using the amen package.

21. Interestingly, some outside of the social sciences are adopting this approach for applied policy problems(Cho et al., 2016).

References

Aldrich, J. H., and McKelvey, R. D. (1977). "A Method of Scaling with Applications to the 1968 and 1972 Presidential Elections." *American Political Science Review* 71(1): 111–130.

Barberá, P. (2015). "Birds of the Same Feather Tweet Together: Bayesian Ideal Point Estimation Using Twitter Data." *Political Analysis* 23(1): 76–91.

Bennett, D. S., and Stam, A. C. (2000). "EUGENE: A Conceptual Manual." *International Interactions* 26: 179–204.

Bhamidi, S., Bresler, G., and Sly, A. (2008). "Mixing Time of Exponential Random Graphs." *Annals of Applied Probability* 21(6): 2146–2170.

Boschee, E., Lautenschlager, J., O'Brien, S., Shellman, S., Starz, J., and Ward, M. D. (2015, March). ICEWS Coded Event Data. Harvard Dataverse Network, version V1. http://dx.doi.org/10.7910/DVN/28075.

Cao, X. (2012). "Global Networks and Domestic Policy Convergence: A Network Explanation of Policy Changes." *World Politics* 64(3): 375–425.

Cao, X., and Ward, M. D. (2014). "Do Democracies Attract Portfolio Investment?" *International Interactions* 40(2): 216–245.

Chatterjee, S., and Diaconis, P. (2013). "Estimating and Understanding Exponential Random Graph Models." *Annals of Statistics* 41(5): 2428–2461.

Cho, W. K. T., and Fowler, J. H. (2010). "Legislative Success in a Small World: Social Network Analysis and the Dynamics of Congressional Legislation." *Journal of Politics* 72(1): 124–135.

Cho, Y.-S., Steeg, G. V., Ferara, E., and Galstyan, A. (2016). "Latent Space Model for Mulit-Modal Social Data." In *Proceedings of the International World Wide Web Conference*, edited by J. Bourdeau, J. Hendler, and R. Nkambou, pp. 447–458. New York: Association for Computing Machinery.

Clinton, J., Jackman, S., and Rivers, D. (2004). "The Statistical Analysis of Roll Call Data." *American Political Science Review* 98(2): 355–370.

Cranmer, S. J., Desmarais, B. A., and Menninga, E. J. (2012). "Complex Dependencies in the Alliance Network." *Conlict Management and Peace Science* 29(3): 279–313.

Cranmer, S. J., Heinrich, T., and Desmarais, B. A. (2014). "Reciprocity and the Structural Determinants of the International Sanctions Network." *Social Networks* 36: 5–22.

Cranmer, S. J., Leifeld, P., McClurg, S. D., and Rolfe, M. (forthcoming). "Navigating the Range of Statistical Tools for Inferential Network Analysis." *American Journal of Political Science*.

Crucitti, P., Latora, V., and Porta, S. (2006). "Centrality Measures in Spatial Networks of Urban Streets." *Physical Review E* 73(3): 1–5.

Dorff, C., and Minhas, S. (August 2016). "When Do States Say Uncle? Network Dependence and Sanction Compliance." *International Interactions*. http://www.tandfonline.com/doi/abs/10.1080/03050629.2016.1221679?journalCode=gini20.

Dorff, C., and Ward, M. D. (2013). "Networks, Dyads, and the Social Relations Model." *Political Science Research and Methods* 1(2): 159–178.

Dorff, C. L. (2015). "Civilian Autonomy and Resilience in the Midst of Armed Conflict." PhD thesis, Duke University.

Erdős, P., and Rényi, A. (1959). "On Random Graphs." *Publicationes Mathematicae* 6: 290–297.

Freeman, L. (2004). "The Development of Social Network Analysis." *A Study in the Sociology of Science*. Vancouver, BC, Canada: Sigma Pi Empirical Press.

Friel, N., Rastelli, R., Wyse, J., and Raftery, A. E. (2016). "Interlocking Directorates in Irish Companies Using a Latent Space Model for Bipartite Networks." *Proceedings of the National Academy of Sciences* 113(24): 6629–6634.

Gastner M. T., and Newman M. E. J. (2006). "The Spatial Structure of Networks." *The European Physical Journal B-Condensed Matter and Complex Systems* 49(2): 247–252.

Geyer, C. J., and Thompson, E. A. 1992. "Constrained Monte Carlo Maximum Likelihood for Dependent Data (with Discussion)." *Journal of the Royal Statistical Society, Series B, Methodological* 54: 657–699.

Goodreau, S. M., Handcock, M. S., Hunter, D. R., Butts, C. T., and Morris, M. (2008). "A statnet Tutorial." *Journal of Statistical Software* 24(9): 1.

Greenhill, B. D. (2015). *Transmitting Rights: International Organizations and the Diffusion of Human Rights Practices.* Oxford: Oxford University Press.

Hafner-Burton, E. M., Kahler, M., and Montgomery, A. H. (2009). "Network Analysis for International Relations." *International Organization* 63(3): 559.

Handcock, M. (2003). "Assessing Degeneracy in Statistical Models of Social Networks." Working Paper 39, Center for Statistics and the Social Sciences, University of Washington.

Handcock, M. S., Hunter, D. R., Butts, C. T., Goodreau, S. M., and Morris, M. (2008). "statnet: Software Tools for the Representation, Visualization, Analysis and Simulation of Network Data." *Journal of Statistical Software* 24(1): 1548.

Hanneke, S., and Xing, E. (2007). "Discrete Temporal Models of Social Networks." In *Statistical Network Analysis: Models, Issues, and New Directions*, edited by Airoldi, E. M., Blei, D. M., Fienberg, S. E., Goldenberg, A., Xing, E. P., Zheng, A. X, pp. 115–125. New York: Springer.

Hare, C., Armstrong, D. A., Bakker, R., Carroll, R., and Poole, K. T. (2015). "Using Bayesian Aldrich-McKelvey Scaling to Study Citizens' Ideological Preferences and Perceptions." *American Journal of Political Science* 59(3): 759–774.

Hays, J. C., Kachi, A., and Franzese, R. J. (2010). "A Spatial Model Incorporating Dynamic, Endogenous Network Interdependence: A Political Science Application." *Statistical Methodology* 7(3): 406–428.

Hoff, P., Fosdick, B., Volfovsky, A., and He, Y. (2015). *amen: Additive and Multiplicative Effects Models for Networks and Relational Data.* R package version 1.1.

Hoff, P. D. (2005). "Bilinear Mixed-Effects Models for Dyadic Data." *Journal of the American Statistical Association* 100(4690): 286–295.

Hoff, P. D. (2008). "Modeling Homophily and Stochastic Equivalence in Symmetric Relational Data." In *Advances in Neural Information Processing Systems 20*, edited by J. C. Platt, D. Koller, Y. Singer, and S. T. Roweis, pp. 657–664. Processing Systems 21. Cambridge, MA: MIT Press.

Hoff, P. D. (2015a). "Dyadic Data Analysis with amen." *arxiv*, arxiv:1506.08237: 1–48.

Hoff, P. D. (2015b). "Multilinear Tensor Regression for Longitudinal Relational Data." *Annals of Applied Statistics* 9(3): 1169–1193.

Hoff, P. D., and Ward, M. D. (2004). "Modeling Dependencies in International Relations Networks." *Political Analysis* 12(2): 160–175.

Hoff, P. D., Raftery, A. E., and Handcock, M. S. (2002). "Latent Space Approaches to Social Network Analysis." *Journal of the American Statistical Association* 97(460): 1090–1098.

Hunter, D., Handcock, M., Butts, C., Goodreau, S. M, and Morris, M. (2008). "ergm: A Package to Fit, Simulate and Diagnose Exponential-Family Models for Networks." *Journal of Statistical Software* 24(3): 1–29.

Kenny, D. A. (1994). *Interpersonal Perception: A Social Relations Analysis.* New York: Guilford Press.

Kirkland, J. H., and Gross, J. H. (2014). "Measurement and Theory in Legislative Networks: The Evolving Topology of Congressional Collaboration." *Social Networks* 36: 97–109.

Kolaczyk, E. D. (2009). *Statistical Analysis of Network Data: Methods and Models.* Berlin: Springer Verlag.

Koskinen, J., and Edling, C. (2012). "Modelling the Evolution of Bipartite Networks: Peer Referral in Interlocking Directorates." *Social Networks* 34(3): 309–322.

Krivitsky, P. N., and Handcock, M. S. (2015). latentnet: Latent Position and Cluster Models for Statistical Networks. The statnet Project. R package version 2.7.1. http://www.statnet.org.

Lautenschlager, J., Shellman, S., and Ward, M. D. (2015, March). *ICEWS Coded Event Aggregations.* Harvard Dataverse Network, version V1. http://dx.doi.org/10.7910/DVN/28117.

Lubbers, M. J., and Snijders, T. A. B. (2007). "A Comparison of Various Approaches to the Exponential Random Graph Model: A Reanalysis of 102 Student Networks in School Classes." *Social Networks* 29(4): 489–507.

McFarland, D. D., and Brown, D. J. (1973). "Social Distance as a Metric: A Systematic Introduction to Smallest Space Analysis." *Bonds of Pluralism: The Form and Substance of Urban Social Networks,* edited by E. O. Laumann, pp. 213–253. New York: Wiley.

Metternich, N., Minhas, S., and Ward, M. (2015). "Firewall? or Wall on Fire? A Unified Framework of Conflict Contagion and the Role of Ethnic Exclusion." *Journal of Conlict Resolution* (September 8): doi:10.1177/0022002715603452.

Metternich, N. W., Dorff, C., Gallop, M., Weschle, S., and Ward, M. D. (2013). "Antigovernment Networks in Civil Conflicts: How Network Structures Affect Conflictual Behavior." *American Journal of Political Science* 57(4): 892–911.

Minhas, S., Hoff, P. D., and Ward, M. D. (2016a, October). "Inferential Approaches for Network Analysis: Amen for Latent Factor Models." Working paper.

Minhas, S., Hoff, P. D., and Ward, M. D. (2016b). "A New Approach to Analyzing Coevolving Longitudinal Networks in International Relations." *Journal of Peace Research* 53(3): 491–505.

Mitchell, S. M., and Prins, B. C. (1999). "Beyond Territorial Contiguity: Issues at Stake in Democratic Militarized Interstate Disputes." *International Studies Quarterly* 43(1): 169–183.

Ord, J. K. (1975). "Estimation Methods for Models of Spatial Interactions." *Journal of the American Statistical Association* 70: 120–126.

Padgett, J. F., and Ansell, C. K. (1993). "Robust Action and the Rise of the Medici, 1400–1434." *American Journal of Sociology* g8(May): 1259–1319.

Poole, K. T., and Rosenthal, H. (1984). "US Presidential Elections 1968–80: A Spatial Analysis." *American Journal of Political Science* 28(2): 282–312.

Poole, K. T., and Rosenthal, H. (1985). "A Spatial Model for Legislative Roll Call Analysis." *American Journal of Political Science* 29(2): 357–384.

Poole, K. T., and Rosenthal, H. (1991). "Patterns of Congressional Voting." *American Journal of Political Science* 35(1): 228–278.

Poole, K. T., and Rosenthal, H. (2001). "D-nominate after 10 Years: A Comparative Update to Congress; A Political-Economic History of Roll-Call Voting." *Legislative Studies Quarterly* 26(1): 5–29.

Porter, M. A., Onnela, J.-P., and Mucha, P. J. (2009). "Communities in Networks." *Notices of the AMS* 56(9): 1082–1097.

Robins, G., Snijders, T., Wang, P., Handcock, M., and Pattison, P. (2007). "Recent Developments in Exponential Random Graph (p*) Models for Social Networks." *Social Networks* 29(2): 192–215.

Sampson, S. F. (1969). "Crisis in a Cloister." PhD thesis. Cornell University.

Schweinberger, M. (2011). "Instability, Sensitivity, and Degeneracy of Discrete Exponential Families." *Journal of the American Statistical Association* 106(496): 1361–1370.

Sewell, D. K., and Chen, Y. (2015). "Latent Space Models for Dynamic Networks." *Journal of the American Statistical Association* 110(512): 1646–1657.

Sewell, D. K., and Chen, Y. (2016). "Latent Space Models for Dynamic Networks with Weighted Edges." *Social Networks* 44: 105–116.

Shalizi, C., and Rinaldo, A. (2013). "Consistency under Sampling of Exponential Random Graph Models." *Annals of Statistics* 41(2): 508.

Shalizi, C. R., and Thomas, A. C. (2011). "Homophily and Contagion Are Generically Confounded in Observational Social Network Studies." *Sociological Methods and Research* 40(2): 211–239.

Snijders, T. A. B. (2001). "The Statistical Evaluation of Social Network Dynamics." *Sociological Methodology* 31: 361–395.

Snijders, T. A. B. (2002). "Markov Chain Monte Carlo Estimation of Exponential Random, Graph Models." *Journal of Social Structure* 3(2): 1–40.

Snijders, T. A. B., Pattison, P. E., Robins, G. L., and Handcock, M. S. (2006). "New Specifications for Exponential Random Graph Models." *Sociological Methodology* 36(1): 99–153.

Strauss, D., and Ikeda, M. (1990). "Pseudolikelihood Estimation for Social Networks." *Journal of the American Statistical Association* 85: 204–212.

Treier, S., and Jackman, S. (2008). "Democracy as a Latent Variable." *American Journal of Political Science* 52(1): 201–217.

Van Duijn, M. A. J., Gile, K. J., and Handcock, M. S. (2009). "A Framework for the Comparison of Maximum Pseudo-Likelihood and Maximum Likelihood Estimation of Exponential Family Random Graph Models." *Social Networks* 31(1): 52–62.

Ward, M. D., Ahlquist, J. S., and Rozenas, A. (2012). "Gravity's Rainbow: A Dynamic Latent Space Model for the World Trade Network." *Network Science* 1(1): 95–118.

Ward, M. D., and Hoff, P. D. (2007). "Persistent Patterns of International Commerce." *Journal of Peace Research* 44(2): 157–175.

Ward, M. D., and Hoff, P. D. (2008). "Analyzing Dependencies in Geo-Politics and Geo-Economics." In *Contributions to Conflict Management, Peace Economics, and Development, vol. 6, War, Peace, and Security*, edited by J. Fontanel and M. Chatterji, pp. 133–160. Amsterdam: Elsevier Science.

Ward, M. D., Hoff, P. D., and Lofdahl, C. L. (2003). "Identifying International Networks: Latent Spaces and Imputation." In *Dynamic Social Network Modeling and Analysis: Workshop, Summary and Papers*, edited by R. Breiger, K. Carley, Kathleen, and P. Pattison, pp. 345–360. Washington, DC: The National Academies Press, for Committee on Human Factors. Board on Behavioral, Cognitive, and Sensory Sciences, Division of Behavioral and Social Sciences Education. National Academy of Science/National Research Council.

Ward, M. D., Siverson, R. M., and Cao, X. (2007). "Disputes, Democracies, and Dependencies: A Reexamination of the Kantian Peace." *American Journal of Political Science* 51(3): 583–601.

Watts, D. J. (1999). *Small Worlds: The Dynamics of Networks between Order and Randomness*. Princeton, NJ: Princeton University Press.

Watts, D. J., and Strogatz, S. H. (1998). "Collective Dynamics of 'Small-World' Networks." *Nature* 393(6684): 440–442.

Wilson, M., Davis, D. R., and Murdie, A. (2016). "The View from the Bottom: Networks of Conflict Resolution Organizations and International Peace." *Journal of Peace Research* 53(3): 442–458.

Wong, L. H., Pattison, P., and Robins, G. (2006). "A Spatial Model for Social Networks." *Physica A: Statistical Mechanics and Its Applications* 360(1): 99–120.

CHAPTER 11

···

VISUALIZATION OF POLITICAL NETWORKS

···

JÜRGEN PFEFFER

INTRODUCTION

···

THE ability to visualize social structures is one of the most obvious advantages of social network analysis. In the context of political networks, researchers are able to use network drawings to visualize in a communicative way the relationships of politicians, parties, and interest groups, as well as political discourses on local, national, and international levels. In "The Development of Social Network Analysis," Freeman (2004) attributes the evolution and growth of network analysis to two factors: the development of metrics and the power of visualizations. This chapter discusses the latter. Visualizations can be very powerful for communicating ideas or research results. Since language and written text require sequential coding, and the amount of information that we can absorb in a given period of time is limited, pictures are an excellent means of communication and are processed *in parallel* at a high *bandwidth* by the human brain. Humans absorb visually thousands of scenes every day. However, we forget most of these visual impressions immediately. The challenge for successful network visualization is therefore twofold. First, one must create network drawings that can be absorbed easily and efficiently and that build on the human ability to process pictures quickly. "The faster the information is understood, the more effective the visualization is" (Krempel, 2005). Second, one must create compelling visualizations that capture the viewer's attention. Even though some network drawings have made it to museums, "efficient communication of information" (Tufte, 2001) with network drawings is not primarily an artistic act. Instead, a better knowledge of visualization algorithms, visual design elements, and human perception can help to create more successful network drawings. This is the motivation for this chapter.

Early network visualizations can be found in medieval times, depicting family trees of biblical figures or of noble families. Early on, visualizations of kin structures were related to policy issues, since they were used to identify possible marriage estoppels. Figure 11.1 shows a similarly motivated network picture from the nineteenth century. Macfarlane visualized the marriage constellations that were prohibited by British law (1883). At the same time, Hobson used network figures to show that the financial system in South Africa is tightly connected and controlled by a few men (figure 11.2). Interestingly, this is a very early representation of two-mode network data—that is, networks that consist of people and connections to affiliations (Borgatti and Everett, 1997). Even though network figures have been used over the course of centuries, modern-day network visualizations are intrinsically tied to Jacob Levy Moreno. Moreno introduced his sociograms in 1934 (figure 11.3), through which he standardized and formalized the drawing of network figures. The focus of this chapter is on sociograms as defined by Moreno, that is, node-and-link diagrams. Other ways of presenting network information, such as matrices (Doreian, Batagelj, and Ferligoj, 2005), are not discussed here. The interested reader is referred to Hennig et al. (2012), as well as Freeman (2000), for an overview of other methods.

Figure 11.4 is a great example of how a network picture actually is worth more than a thousand words. Adamic and Glance (2005) analyzed the links and discussions of political bloggers before the US presidential election of 2004. The gray nodes on the right side (red nodes in online colored version) represent conservative bloggers and the black nodes on the left (blue nodes in online colored version) are their liberal colleagues. The network visualization makes it very clear that these two groups of bloggers actually form two tightly knit communities, with a smaller number of connections among members

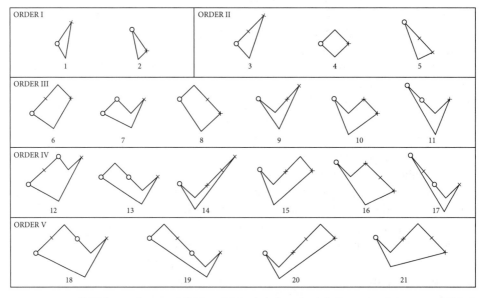

FIGURE 11.1 British marriage prohibition. Males (+), females (o). Lowest points are prohibited offspring.

Reproduced from Macfarlane (1883).

of the two different groups. As a matter of fact, 91 percent of all links in this network stay within the conservative or the liberal community. But just reporting this number would be much less intriguing than the network visualization, which is a perfect representation of a divided blogosphere, or to be more precise, a divided country.

Similar illustrations that demonstrate political polarization can be found in studies that investigate votes in the US House of Representatives. Over time, analysis of changes in voting behavior within the last decades reveals the rise of partisanship (Andris et al., 2015). Other forms of networks of political actors can be social media networks; for example, visualizations are used to communicate the structure of Twitter interactions among politicians (Cherepnalkoski and Mozetic, 2015) or to provide a better understanding of the dynamics of online political communities (Chu, Wipfli, and Valente, 2011). For international politics, network figures can show countries' sanctions against other countries (Cranmer, Heinrich, and Desmarais, 2014), and Flandreau and Jobst (2005) use networks drawn on maps to show the grouping structure of the international monetary system of the late nineteenth century.

In all these examples, network figures are used to present research outcomes (i.e., to show something). However, network visualizations are not used only at the end of a research project. It is also possible to use pictures to explore data (i.e., to find something). Some researchers visualize their network data at a very early stage of the research

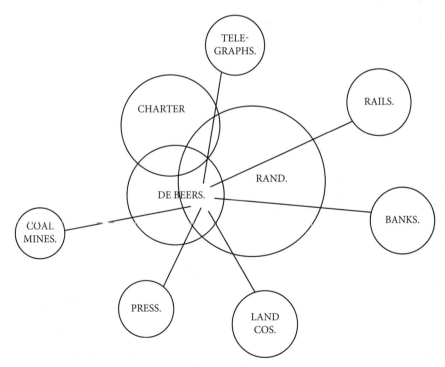

FIGURE 11.2 Interlocking corporate directorates showing the inner ring of South African finance.

Reproduced from Hobson (1884).

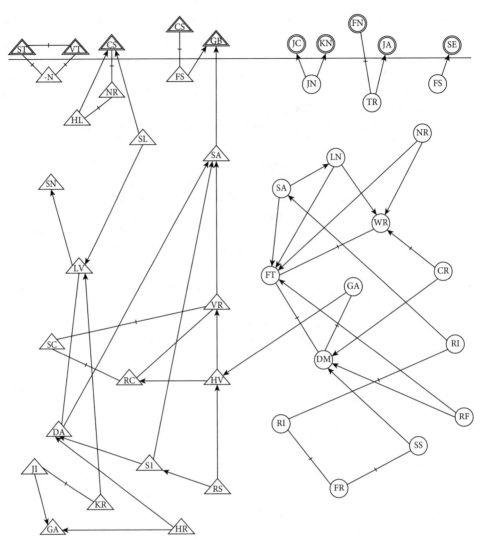

FIGURE 11.3 Girls (circles) and boys (triangles) in a school class. Links represent two best friends. Top line defines group border.

Reproduced from Moreno (1934).

process in order to get a first impression. A good picture of a network can help research-ers gather information about the network data or reveal coding errors. Moreno also used his sociograms in an exploratory manner: "It is first of all a method of exploration" (1953, 96).

Network visualization is often a neglected part of network analytical projects. Yet drawing networks is a more complex act than merely clicking the "Draw" button of social network analysis tools at the end of a project. When drawing a picture of a social network visualization, aspects have to be considered that can be divided into three major components: substance, design, and algorithm (Brandes et al., 1999).

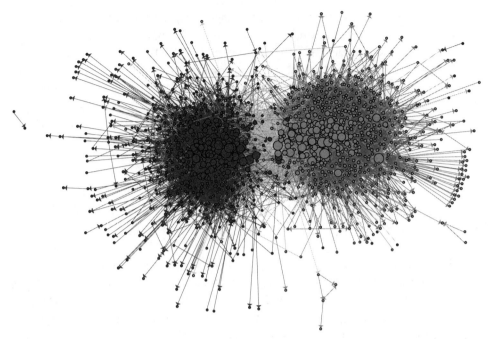

FIGURE 11.4 Political blogs in 2004 US election, red for conservative, blue for liberal. Blue/red links are hyperlinks between blogs within a political camp.

Reprinted with permission from Adamic and Glance (2005).

Substance combines all questions concerning the content of the data. The most interesting substance of network data is the information about the connections among the nodes of a network. But normally there is additional information about the actors of a network. If a network consists of political actors, most likely information such as gender, age, or party affiliation will also be available. If a network consists of companies, the data could be about revenue, profit, or number of employees. The interest groups in Box-Steffensmeier's and Christenson's analysis of the evolution of amicus curiae networks (2014) are coded with twelve industry codes. In addition to these "real-world" data, computed data can be generated for all nodes of a network, for example, centrality measures. When it comes to visualizing networks, it is important to remember that network data are almost always multivariate. Visualizing high-dimensional information "with clarity, precision, and efficiency" is the foundation for "graphical excellence" (Tufte, 2001).

Design is about mapping the substance of a network to graphic elements. Arranging the nodes (layout) to uncover the structure of the network is the most important task of network visualization. Nevertheless, it is also an interesting challenge to enrich the picture with additional information (substance). The major challenge of this chapter—and also of network visualization in general—is dealing with "effective translation of information to a system of visual elements" (Bertin, 1983). The following sections discuss various design elements of network pictures and review them for their suitability to represent different aspects of network data.

Algorithm ultimately deals with the computer-assisted realization of drawing network pictures. Algorithms must be implemented in network analytical tools, and they have to be efficient enough to deal with the size or complexity of the data and ideas. Another aspect is the effectiveness of an algorithm in respect to the substance of the research-er's data and research questions. Is the algorithm helpful, or are distracting visual arti-facts generated? Knowing about the inner workings of visualization algorithms can help in answering this question. Consequently, this chapter also discusses layout algo-rithms. Their development and optimization have been a focus of research for decades (Eades, 1984).

POSITION OF NODES: NETWORK LAYOUT

The layout of a network is the result of the process of positioning the nodes on the surface. This is normally done by layout algorithms that are implemented in network analytical software. Before discussing the concepts of layout algorithms, we must dem-onstrate the difference a *good* layout can make. Figure 11.5 shows three different layouts of "Padgett's Florentine Families Network" (Wasserman and Faust, 1994; Kent, 1978). The nodes represent Florentine families in the fifteenth century; the edges are drawn if there is a marriage relationship between two families. In the first (left) picture the nodes are positioned on a circle. In the second picture the position of the nodes is random. The third picture is drawn by applying a distance scaling layout algorithm (see later in this section). When comparing the righthand picture with the two pictures on the left, the viewer can ask about the differences among the figures and why one of them looks "bet-ter" or even "prettier."

Many criteria exist to judge whether a graph layout is "good" or not (Fleischer and Hirsch, 2001; Battista et al., 1998). These criteria are "technical" but also "aesthetical," because when looking at many graph pictures, it turns out that these aspects often go hand in hand. Increasing the readability and clarity of the image of a network picture often also makes the picture more attractive. The list of criteria for assessing the quality of a network layout can be summarized by the following points:

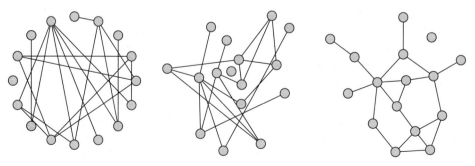

FIGURE 11.5 A circular, a random, and a springlike layout of the same network.

- **Show structure.** If a network has a globally organized structure, the layout should uncover it; for example, if there are two almost separate groups, as in figure 11.4, then the picture should show this structural characteristic. Revealing structural characteristics of networks is the most important reason for applying layout algorithms.
- **Optimize distribution on the surface.** The nodes should be evenly distributed across the whole area and not sit on top of each other. This sounds like a straightforward criterion, but it is all but ignored in most layout algorithms, resulting in areas of the picture with a lot of nodes close to each other (most of the time at the center) surrounded by lots of empty space with almost no nodes.
- **Minimize line crossings, maximize angles, and optimize length of lines.** Line crossing are confusing because they make it more difficult to trace connections. Very acute angles produce overlapping lines, while obtuse angles increase the aesthetics of the layout and also the traceability. If the lines are unweighted, all of them should have approximately the same length in the picture. This is because shorter lines create the impression that nodes are closer to each other than they appear to be when they are connected with a long line.
- **Optimize path distances.** The path distances (how many steps are needed from one node to another one) should be represented in the distances of the nodes in the picture. Therefore, two adjacent nodes should be drawn near each other, while two path-distant nodes should be drawn at a larger distance from one another.

It is all but impossible to meet these criteria perfectly when dealing with complex networks of hundreds or thousands of nodes. Also, the criteria in some respects contradict one another. Nevertheless, they are essential for computer-assisted layout algorithms. As shown in the following discussion, automated algorithms try to optimize one or more of these criteria to create pictures that meet the user's expectation. Layout algorithms can be divided into two groups: distance scaling and classical scaling.

Distance scaling algorithms are very intuitive approaches. The crucial idea of these algorithms is the concept that connected nodes attract each other. That is why these algorithms are called "spring-embedded" (Eades, 1984). The left network (circular) of figure 11.5 can illustrate this idea. There is a node on the top left position of the circle, with a couple of connections that are all in the lower half of the network. These long connections can be seen as stretched out springs that pull the node on top toward its connected nodes. The best known approaches based on the spring idea were developed by Fruchterman and Reingold (1991) and Kamada and Kawai (1989). These two algorithms, or variations of them, are implemented in almost every network analytical tool. A similar algorithm was used by Andris et al. (2015) to show that the rise of partisanship over time based on congressional covoting pulls the members of the two parties apart. The main disadvantage of distance-scaling algorithms is their iterative process for finding an optimized layout. This means that two layouts of the same network will look different and the outcome of a layout calculation will depend on the starting position of the nodes.

Classical scaling approaches are multidimensional scaling (MDS) algorithms based on the classical MDS of Torgerson (1952). These algorithms produce two-dimensional representations of high-dimensional data (e.g., dissimilarities calculated from path distances of nodes). Classical scaling algorithms find a global maximum for every network. Regardless of the starting position of the nodes, different calculations with the same network arrive at the exact same outcome. Porter et al. (2006) use singular valued decomposition (SVD), a closely related method to MDS, to map members of the US Senate to a two-dimensional visualization. The global optimization of the structure implies the disadvantage of these algorithms, which can also be seen in the SVD figure of the senators: structural equivalent nodes (those nodes with connections to the same other nodes) lie exactly on top of each other, reducing the readability of the figure. This is algorithmically correct, but "wrong" from a readability point of view.

A fundamental problem of all traditional layout algorithms is the computational complexity that leads to long calculation times if the networks become larger. If a network consists of more than a few thousand nodes, then these algorithms need too much time to be practicable. However, in recent years new algorithms have been developed that overcome this limitation. For instance, Brandes and Pich (2007) developed Pivot MDS, which creates layouts based on MDS approximations. With this approach it is possible to calculate layouts of networks with millions of nodes. Combining such an efficient method with optimized distance-scaling approaches (Brandes and Pich, 2009) enables the drawing of *good* pictures under the criteria introduced above, even if the network gets very large.

The layout of a network should be assessed carefully, because the position of the nodes is the most dominant visual element for viewers of the figure when it comes to interpreting the picture (see later in this chapter). Certain positions are automatically seen as more important. For example, if a node is in the center of a round-shaped network, or if a node is on top of a hierarchically shaped network, then these nodes are inevitably associated with greater importance. Other interpretation artifacts are rooted in Gestalt theory (Koffka, 1935). Mcgrath, Blythe, and Krackhardt (1997) showed experimentally that people group nodes of the exact same network into different groups depending on the perceived visual grouping of the nodes. In other words, if nodes are combined and separated slightly from the rest of the network, people will see the group and not the details of the links.

Substance-Based Layout

Even though layout is the most important challenge in network visualization, and this challenge is often handed over to a layout algorithm to reveal the structure of the network, there are a couple of other ways to use position to communicate essential content of network data. Following is a discussion of four ways to lay out the nodes of a network, based on the substance of the network data. In all cases, contextual information of the network nodes is used for the positions. Substance-based layouts constrain the possibilities of using the node positions to express the network structure.

Predefined layout. Sometimes the nodes of a network are connected to a physical real-world location. The most obvious location is geographic space. Flandreau and Jobst (2005) illustrate their findings about the continental differences in the international monetary exchange system of the late eighteenth and early nineteenth centuries by mapping the network onto a world map. The existence of many links within Europe and almost none within South America, but many connections from South America to Europe, is an easy concept to grasp without any additional coding or labeling of the nodes (the authors do not even use nodes; links are simply sourced and targeted within country borders). Using real-world locations for positioning nodes has been a common practice since the early days of modern network visualization. Roethlisberger, Dickson, and Wright (1939) observed friendship ties and cliques in a factory, and for their visualizations of the social structure the position of the nodes (workers) reflected the location of their workspaces. The visualization of locations can be helpful in answering questions related to the network data and the underlying social forces that are responsible for creating network ties—for example, that people who are located closer to each other have a higher probability of forming relationships (Festinger, Schachter, and Back, 1950).

Status. In administrations, companies, and other hierarchical organizations, the position of a person on an organizational chart is often used to visualize status. This is a very intuitive way of visualizing the formal hierarchy of an organization, especially because consumers of network figures bring their own experience and "graphical vocabulary," which influence interpretation (McGrath and Blythe, 2004). In Western culture, the most important person is put at the top of a picture. The *importance* of a person as the determinant of his or her position can also be calculated from centrality scores or contextual information. In the illustrations of the famous network study of Sampson (1968) about a novitiate in a period of change, the position of the novices on the y-axis shows the sum of received positive and negative choices—the most liked novices are positioned at the top of the figure. Whyte (1943) used position to show the hierarchies of the social structure in an Italian slum. Krackhardt (1996) impressively showed the differences in importance of people in a company by comparing the formal organization chart with the advice network; both networks were visualized by putting the more important people at the top of the figure.

Centrality. The idea of centrality visualization is similar to the status visualizations introduced in the previous paragraph, but the focus of centrality figures is to put the most important node in the middle of the figure—that is, to put the central nodes at the center (Brandes, Kenis, and Wagner, 2003). This approach can be useful when dealing with centrality metrics (Freeman, 1979), as it makes a lot of sense to put, for example, a node with the highest betweenness centrality[1] (Freeman, 1977) *between* the other nodes of the network. For the rest of the nodes, the centrality score is mapped to the distance from the center (pole) of the circular polar coordinate system. Additional concentric circles, standing for levels of centrality, can help with comparison and interpretation. It is important to notice that this is different from automated layouts, in which the most important nodes are also often in the center of the figure. In these cases, a central position results from the structure. Here, centrality could represent any network or non-network metrics. The first known visualizations in which centrality layouts were used in an elaborate way were created by Northway (1940). She used an acceptability measure to determine importance. Another common use of centrality layout can be found in the visualization drawings of ego networks in which a focal node (ego) is in the center and alter egos are placed around it, often based on emotional closeness. When qualitative network analysists (Hollstein, 2011) collect network data, they often ask their interviewees to manually create such circular layouts of their alters (Kahn and Antonucci, 1980). Related to the idea of centrality layouts is the network representation of Moody and Mucha (2013). They mapped the polarization modularity of the US Senate voting similarity network to the y-axis of a network visualization over time to the increasing polarization of US politics.

Attribute grouping. We can also use attributes of the nodes of the network to structure the layout of the network. This is especially feasible when the network structure is dominated by an attribute; that is, actors are more likely to be connected within the groups and less likely to be connected between the groups. An example for group visualization is the sociogram by Moreno in figure 11.3. Moreno visualized boys on one side and girls on the other side of the picture. By doing so, he communicated the importance of gender for the connections between the actors of the network. This is assisted by the fact that just one line connects the two groups of nodes with each other. Hargittai, Gallo, and Kane (2007) arranged political bloggers on a circle and put liberal bloggers on the left half of the circle and conservative bloggers on the right half in order to analyze linkages between bloggers with different perspectives. In contrast, the visual grouping of bloggers in figure 11.4 is the result of a layout algorithm and was not predetermined by the political orientation attribute.

GRAPHICAL ELEMENTS FOR
MAPPING INFORMATION

Layout algorithms, as discussed in the previous section, are fundamental for drawing networks. However, drawing a network is more than positioning the nodes. The structural information about the nodes and their relationships is just one dimension of network data. If we focus on information about nodes, network variables are vectors of numbers, with one number for each node. Contextual network variables normally come in two different types. In political networks, *quantitative variables* can be percentage points of election results, donation dollars of companies, and so forth.

Quantitative variables can also be the result of centrality calculations, for example, degree centrality (Freeman, 1979) in figure 11.4. *Nominal variables* represent categorical information, such as gender or party affiliation. The result of grouping algorithms (Newman and Girvan, 2004) can also be seen as a nominal variable, since every node is put in a category. Networks are often multivariate; that is, there are a couple of different variables for every node. Mapping these variables successfully and intuitively to a network drawing is key to a compelling network visualization. In order to do that mapping, we need to identify the list of graphical elements that can be used for network drawings.

The properties of an information visualization were defined by the French cartographer Jacques Bertin (1983) as the *retinal variables*: position, size, color value, color saturation, orientation, shape, and texture. These variables can be processed involuntarily by the human brain within a fraction of a second. For example, we are capable of *automatically* identifying the largest or the darkest node. Mackinlay (1986) ordered Bertin's visual variables for different types of statistical data. Subsequently, the visual variables were adapted to network visualization (Pfeffer, 2013). Different visual elements are suitable for visualizing quantitative and nominal variables. Table 11.1 shows the ordering of visual network variables for quantitative and qualitative variables.

These are the elements discussed in this chapter. As mentioned previously, the most important element is position. As position is the strongest visual variable, it is worthwhile questioning whether the result of an automated layout actually shows enough information (e.g., the global structure of the network) to justify using this visualization element, or if substance-based layouts should be applied.

The visual element *shape* is straightforward, especially as the number of different shapes in network visualization tools is often limited to circles, squares, triangles, and other simple geometric figures. Although shape is often used to visualize different types of nodes—for example, people as circles and squares for affiliation in a two-mode network—the visual element *shape* is surprisingly weak in communicating information. People are not as good at distinguishing among different shapes when many nodes are visualized. The other elements of table 11.1, namely hue, saturation, and size, are discussed below.

Table 11.1 Graphical Elements and Their Suitability for Mapping Quantitative and Nominal Variables

Type	Best				Worst
Quantitative	Position	Size	Saturation	Hue	Shape
Nominal	Position	Hue	Saturation	Shape	Size

Size

The graphical element *size* is normally used to mark *important* nodes. In figure 11.4, as well as in most other network visualizations, node size is used to visualize the result of centrality metric calculations. Visually, it is made very obvious that there are larger nodes and smaller nodes and that larger nodes are more important and smaller nodes are less important. However, there are several issues related to mapping a quantitative variable, say a centrality metric, to the size of the node.

Unfortunately, the obvious way to use a quantitative variable to map onto node size is not as straightforward as it might seem. Let us assume that we use circles; we could map a centrality score to the area of a circle. This would be a correct way of doing it. However, human perception puts a spoke in our wheel. It turns out that we are very good at comparing visual information as long as that information is one-dimensional; that is, it is presented as lines. Stevens (1975) defined the psycho-physical power law that describes the inconsistency between actual and perceived differences of two visual (or other) stimuli. Lodge (1981) quantified this perceptual error with experimental studies. Figure 11.6 and table 11.2 illustrate these findings. Node B actually is exactly double the size of node A in terms of circle area. However, most people would say that node B is not that big. Lodge (1981) found that on average, people would estimate the

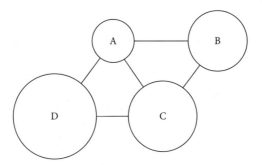

FIGURE 11.6 Node size comparison of different scaling factors.

Table 11.2 Node Sizes with Actual and Perceived Differences in Size and Radius

Node	Actual Size	Perceived Size	Radius
A	100%	100%	100%
B	200%	163%	141%
C	269%	200%	164%
D	400%	263%	200%

scaling factor of these two nodes as about 1.6, while node C, which is actually about 2.7 times larger than node A, is perceived as being only twice the size of node A. Putting the scaling difference not on the area but on the diameter or radius of a node over-emphasizes the differences. The radius and the diameter are both one-dimensional information. Consequently, humans can decide accurately that node D has double the radius of node A, but (without mental arithmetic) would perceive the size difference as smaller than 4:1.

The underlying issue of the size confusion is the fact that network nodes are drawn as two-dimensional objects, while a variable such as degree centrality (Freeman, 1979) is just a one-dimensional variable. As a consequence, some authors (Brandes, Kenis, and Wagner, 2003) suggest using two variables for mapping node size, one for the horizontal and one for the vertical node size, for example, in-degree for the horizontal dimension and out-degree for the vertical dimension of oval-shaped nodes. Using two variables also increases the amount of information that can be communicated with a single network drawing. On the downside, differently shaped ovals take longer to decipher than simple circles or boxes.

Colors

The study of color perception is a small research field, but one with a long tradition (Wyszecki and Stiles, 2000). The human eye has three different color-sensitive photo receptors (cones)—for red, green, and blue (RGB)—that react to different wavelengths of light. The brain analyzes the intensity coming from these three types of receptors and, together with the brightness information coming from a second group of photo receptors (rods), colors are constructed. The famous German writer Johann Wolfgang von Goethe was among the first to be interested in perception of colors. In his "Theory of Colors" (1810), Goethe discussed and criticized Newton's (1704) discovery that all colors come from colorless white light split up in a prism. More important, Goethe was interested in the perception of colors and introduced his color wheel with complementary colors. Even though Goethe's theories were criticized by natural scientists early on, and the colors on his color wheel are not well distributed in terms of perceptual differences, his wheel is widely known and used. However, in the early twentieth century Albert Henry Munsell published a color system that set the standard for modern understanding of colors. Munsell's color system (1912) uses three dimensions: hue (color tint), chroma (saturation), and value (brightness). The great advantage of this system is that it is easy to create perceptually uniform distributed differences in a set of colors and calculate with colors; for example, it is easy to get a color with different saturation levels for color gradients representing quantitative information, which is rather tricky in standard RGB and CMYK (cyan, magenta, yellow, and black) color systems used for monitors and printers. HSL (hue, saturation, lightness) and HSV (hue, saturation, value) are modern color schemes used in graphic tools (e.g., Adobe Photoshop) that are based on Munsell's colors.

For network visualization, it is important to know that there are two different ways of using colors. Following Munsell, color hue represents the different color tints (e.g. red, green, blue). Color saturation is the intensity of the color (e.g. light or dark red). These two different aspects of color are used for two different types of network variables. Color hue is primarily used for ordinal data. In figure 11.4, Democratic and Republican bloggers are drawn in different colors, as are the interest groups based on industry codes from Box-Steffensmeier and Christenson (2014). We could also use hue to mark two groups of nodes in two-mode networks (Borgatti and Everett, 1997), for example, politicians as red and committees as blue circles. If we now assume that we do not want to draw more important bloggers in figure 11.4 with larger nodes, we could use color saturation to represent this quantitative variable; that is, we could draw nodes with high in-degree in dark red/blue and nodes with low in-degree in a very light red/blue. For both parties, we could create a color gradient to cover different in-degree levels.

The use of colors faces a couple of obstacles. For readers of the printed book version of this chapter, the blogger network in figure 11.4 reveals the most obvious limitation of using colors: many journals and books are printed only in black and white, so colors are transformed to grayscales, thus losing most of their communicative power. Even if it is compelling to create network drawings with colors, it is important to be capable of visualizing informative and compelling network drawings without colors. Also, colors often have culturally loaded meanings. One reason figure 11.4 is memorable is the traditional color coding of the nodes and links representing political parties: red for conservatives and blue for liberals. Using colors that are counterintuitive or unfamiliar makes reading and understanding incomparably harder and can easily lead to frustration caused by visually jumping back and forth between the figure and the legend. But colors are globally not unambiguous, and the interpretation of colors is culturally dependent. In most European countries, the color red is used for Social Democratic parties and not for conservatives, as it is in the United States. Comparing the visualizations of the blogger network of Adamic and Glance (2005) with figures of European political networks on Twitter from Ausserhofer and Maireder (2013) can lead to false associations. Or imagine the terms "positive," "negative," "love," "nature," "death," or "money." Certain colors tend to be automatically associated with these terms. But all of these terms are mapped onto different colors in different parts of the world.

Finally, it is important to know that almost 10 percent of people are color-blind—mostly men—and the vast majority of them have problems distinguishing between red and green. Color vision deficiencies are normally inherited and are untreatable. Color-blind people are incapable of seeing the color hue differences of the affected colors.

Links

The above-mentioned graphical elements can also be used to map information about the links of a network to a network figure. In sociograms, links representing connections between pairs of nodes are drawn as lines between those nodes. A simple line connecting two nodes communicates binary univariate information; that is, there is a link between these two nodes. This is sufficient as long as the network is unweighted and undirected. If the network is directed, two bits of information need to be coded with the link, as connections can go in either or both directions of the dyad. Moreno (1934; figure 11.3), Adamic and Glance (2005; figure 11.4), and most other researchers use arrow heads at the end of a line to indicate the target of a directed edge (arc). The case of directed links between a pair of nodes that go in both directions (e.g., blog A links to blog B and blog B links to blog A) can be depicted by different visual elements. In figure 11.4, arrow heads can be found on both ends of the connecting link, while Moreno (1934) omitted the arrow heads for bidirectional links and added a small line at a right angle to the middle of the link. The most straightforward approach to handling bidirectional directed links is to just omit the arrow heads, leaving a simple line.

Layout. In the aforementioned criteria about the quality of network visualization, *minimizing line crossings* was mentioned. However, this criterion was discussed solely from the perspective of rearranging nodes (that are connected to these lines). Lines can also be manipulated directly to optimize a network layout. The most common visual feature in this context is using curved instead of straight lines. While an exclusive usage of curved lines, as seen in many contemporary network visualizations, might be appealing from an aesthetic perspective, it decreases readability and increases visual complexity in most instances. More sophisticated approaches try to optimize a network layout by routing links individually to reduce visual complexity, for example, by avoiding drawing links in a way that they overlap with nodes. For dense networks, link bundling is another approach to increasing the readability of a network figure. This is accomplished by merging links that all go from one area of the network to another area. By removing some level of already hard to read detail from the visualization—that is, which nodes are connected to which other nodes—we render additional macro information to the network, showing areas that are connected.

Size. In weighted networks, links are not just defined by their absence or presence, but by link weights. Link weights can come from two sources. First is direct observations; for example, the link weights in Subramanian and Wei's (2007) represent the volume of trade between pairs of countries. Second is from two-mode network data (Borgatti and Everett, 1997) in the case of shared activities or affiliations. Connections among politicians can be drawn based on the overlap of participation in committees and panels, with the number of shared affiliations as link weight. In any case, handling these different weights is straightforward and can be seen in figure 11.7; larger weights result in stronger lines. However, drawing different-sized links is limited to small and sparse networks. In figure 11.7a no differences in link weights are identifiable.

Color hue. Using colors to mark different types of links was used early on. Moreno (1934) drew red links for positive ("attraction") and black links for negative ("repulsion") relationships. Adamic and Glance (2005) use colors on links to show hyperlinks connecting blogs within political camps (see figure 11.4). The difference between these two examples is that Moreno mapped dyadic information to the links, while Adamic and

Glance derived link colors from source and target nodes of the links. In both cases, link colors can be very useful to help interpretation or to highlight interesting actors or areas of the network. In Moreno's visualization of a football team (1934; not shown in this article), the colored links reveal very clearly one unpopular player. In dense networks, such as in figure 11.4, it is impossible to follow or interpret single links; instead, links can create visual areas that can be important for interpretation of the analysis. In Adamic and Glance's (2005) figure, colored areas consisting of hundreds of links amplify the segregation of the political camps. Another approach of using node information to color links is very similar. The grouping of the nodes is not derived from contextual information, but rather the result of clustering (Newman, 2006). In all these cases, colors for links are used to distinguish among different classes of relations. Along the lines of using different color hues to color different groups of nodes, we applied the same logic to links.

Color saturation. To visualize quantitative information of links, we can turn to color saturation. The thicker links in figures 11.7b and 11.7d can also be drawn in black, while the thinner links are in different scales of gray. This is particularly useful in very dense networks. It is also important to sort the lines so that thicker lines are drawn on top of thinner lines, so that they are actually visible. The network for committees and subcommittees of the House of Representatives in Porter et al. (2006) serves as a good example of using sorted grayscaled links to emphasize important links in a dense and weighted network.

Reducing Visual Complexity

Looking at figure 11.4, but also at many other policy networks—for example, the congressional voting network (Andris et al., 2015) or the world trade network from Subramanian and Wei (2007)—one can see one of the major challenges to visualizing networks: handling dense networks, in other words, a large number of links. On the upside, these links can be used as visualization elements. This is the case in the blogger network in figure 11.4; hundreds of red and blue links create colored regions in the background of the nodes. This *macro* approach is reasonable when, as in the blogger network, the message of the network visualization is also on the macro level. If the level of interest is more detailed on the node level, approaches are needed that reduce the visual complexity of network visualizations.

As a rule of thumb, networks having at most two to three times more links than nodes are favored in terms of readability and aesthetics. This is much less than we find in many empirically collected networks. Consequently, reducing visual complexity is intrinsically tied to removing links (but also nodes). While removing parts of the network can result in a much easier to read network figure, it is important to realize that doing this could change the structure of a network and create visual artifacts.

Comparing different reduction strategies or different removal thresholds can help mitigate this risk.

For the following approaches, we use the world trade network data from Subramanian and Wei (2007). The network (figure 11.7a.) represents 157 countries (nodes) with trade relationships (edges) among them. As one can easily see, there are a lot of lines in this figure, since almost every country has trade relations to a large number of other countries.

Global threshold. When the network is weighted (each line is described by a value), we can remove all lines lower than a defined value (threshold). This threshold can be derived from the data (e.g., more than $1 billion trade volume) or from the readability of the figure (increase threshold until a clear structure is visible). In figure 11.7b the latter has been done. As one can see, the number of nodes is also reduced. This results from the fact that deleting lines with small line values may create isolates (nodes with no remaining links). Normally, such isolates are removed from the network visualization. The focus of such an approach is clearly on the center of the network, since only the most important nodes and links remain in the figure. In a detailed analysis of their blogger network, Adamic and Glance (2005) removed weak links, which made the political separation even clearer.

Local threshold. An alternative approach would be to remove all but the most important lines for each node. With this approach, all nodes are preserved. The disadvantage of this approach is that globally important connections get lost. For example, in figure 11.7c we just show the top two links for each country. However, the third most important link of the United States has a much higher weight than all of the links of most other countries.

Node aggregation. Another approach for reducing the complexity of a network can be used when a grouping attribute of the nodes is available. In our case, countries can be grouped to continents. Consequently, we can merge multiple country nodes (and their links) to a single continent node. In figure 11.7d we did this for all countries except Germany and the United States. Node aggregation can also be applied after calculating communities in networks (Newman, 2006). Porter et al. (2006) identified communities in the US House of Representatives based on common committee memberships. They then aggregated the communities to one node each and showed the connections among the communities. Moreover, as a single group-node now represented multiple politicians, the authors mapped sets of attributes of these actors to pie charts, which replace the nodes in the network visualization.

Focus/context. If the viewer's attention should be directed to a specific part of the network while the rest of the network should still be visible for orientation, a focus/context visualization can be used. Figure 11.7e represents a zoom into a specific area of figure 11.7c, while the overall network is still visible, so that we can see which part of the network is shown. Here we focus on the subnetwork of South American countries and their connections, showing that most of them have their strongest connections within their own continent.

(a)

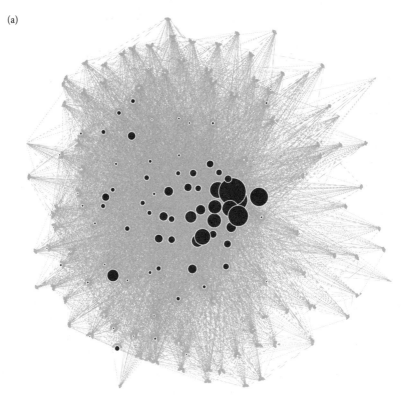

(b)

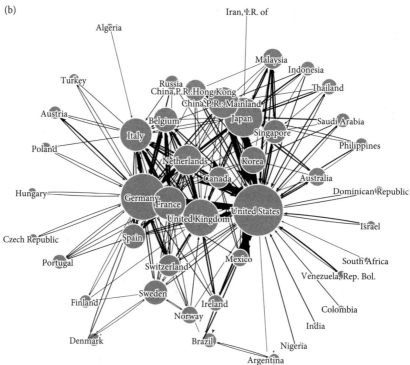

FIGURE 11.7. Different representations of an international trade network. Nodes are countries or continents. Different width of links represents trade volume. a) Original network with all links. b) Global threshold visualization.

Figures created with data from Subramanian and Wei (2007).

(c)

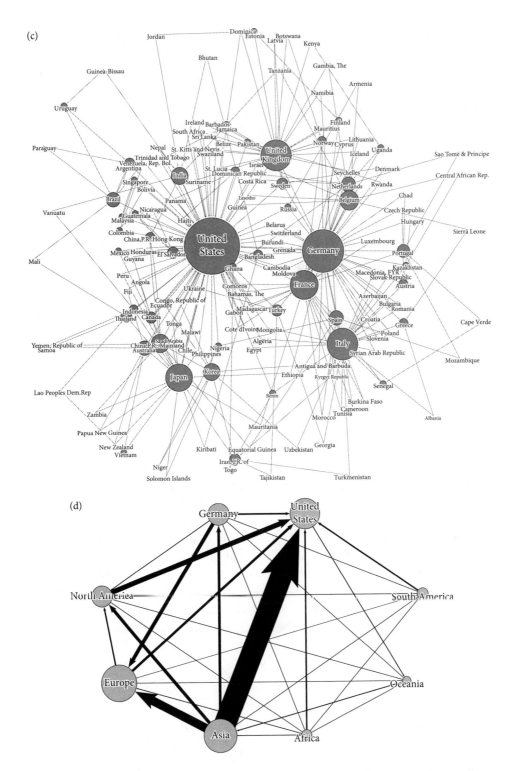

FIGURE 11.7. (continued) c) Local threshold visualization. d) Partially aggregated network.

(e)

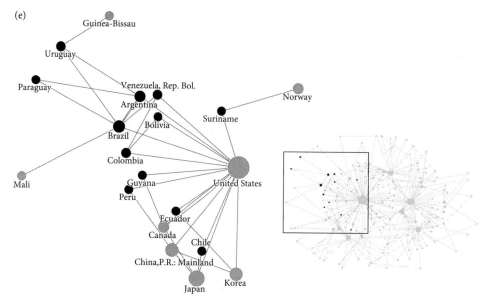

FIGURE 11.7. (continued) e) Focus/context visualization of network.

Summary

This chapter discussed various aspects of visualizing political networks. We discussed layout algorithms, but also argued that visualizing informative networks consists of more steps than optimizing the layout of the network nodes. Being aware of graphical elements such as size, shape, and color and knowing about how to use them to represent different forms of variables in a visualization can create informative network drawings that communicate a large amount of information. Besides the technical and perceptual challenges, the value of a visualization could be evaluated by its narrative quality. A compelling network visualization, like all other information visualizations, tells a story to support scientific findings. Moreover, it is always important to remember that network visualization is about visualizing information, not just data. Excellent network graphics "induce the viewer to think about the substance rather than the methodology" (Tufte, 2001).

Note

1. Betweenness centrality (Freeman 1977) measures the extent to which a node is an intermediate on the shortest path connections between pairs of other nodes.

REFERENCES

Adamic, L. A., and Glance, N. (2005). "The Political Blogosphere and the 2004 U.S. Election: Divided They Blog." In *Proceedings of the 3rd International Workshop on Link Discovery*, pp. 36–43. New York: Association for Computing Machinery. doi:10.1145/1134271.1134277.

Andris, C., Lee, D., Hamilton, M. J., Martino, M., Gunning, C. E., and Selden, J. A. (2015). "The Rise of Partisanship and Super-Cooperators in the U.S. House of Representatives." *PLOS ONE* 10(4): e0123507. doi:10.1371/journal.pone.0123507.

Ausserhofer, J., and Maireder, A. (2013). "National Politics on Twitter: Structures and Topics of a Networked Public Sphere." *Information, Communication & Society* 16(3): 291–314.

Battista, G. D., Eades, P., Tamassia, R., and Tollis, I. G. (1998). *Graph Drawing: Algorithms for the Visualization of Graphs*. 1st ed. Upper Saddle River, NJ: Prentice Hall PTR.

Bertin, J. (1983). *Semiology of Graphics: Diagrams, Networks, Maps*. Madison: University of Wisconsin Press.

Borgatti, S. P., and Everett, M. G. (1997). "Network Analysis of 2-Mode Data." *Social Networks* 19(3): 243–269.

Box-Steffensmeier, J. M., and Christenson, D. P. (2014). "The Evolution and Formation of Amicus Curiae Networks." In "*Political Networks*," special issue, Social Networks 36 (January): 82–96. doi:10.1016/j.socnet.2012.07.003.

Brandes, U., Kenis, P., Raab, J., Schneider, V., and Wagner, D. (1999). "Explorations into the Visualization of Policy Networks." *Journal of Theoretical Politics* 11(1): 75–106.

Brandes, U., Kenis, P., and Wagner, D. (2003). "Communicating Centrality in Policy Network Drawings." In *IEEE Transactions on Visualization and Computer Graphics* 9 (2): 241–253.

Brandes, U., and Pich, C. (2007). "Eigensolver Methods for Progressive Multidimensional Scaling of Large Data." In *Proceedings of the 14th International Symposium on Graph Drawing (GD '06)*, pp. 42–53. Karlsruhe, Germany.

Brandes, U., and Pich, C. (2009). "An Experimental Study on Distance-Based Graph Drawing." In *Graph Drawing*, edited by I. G. Tollis and M. Patrignani, pp. 218–229. Lecture Notes in Computer Science 5417. Berlin, Heidelberg: Springer.

Cherepnalkoski, D., and Mozetic, I. (2015). "A Retweet Network Analysis of the European Parliament." In *Proceedings of the 11th International Conference on Signal-Image Technology & Internet-Based Systems (SITIS)*, pp. 350–357 Bangkok.

Chu, K.-H., Wipfli, H., and Valente, T. W. (2011). "Using Visualizations to Explore Network Dynamics." *Journal of Social Structure: JOSS* 14 (4). https://www.cmu.edu/joss/content/articles/volume14/ChuWipfliValente.pdf.

Cranmer, S. J., Heinrich, T., and Desmarais, B. A. (2014). "Reciprocity and the Structural Determinants of the International Sanctions Network." In *Political Networks*, special issue, Social Networks 36 (January): 5–22. doi:10.1016/j.socnet.2013.01.001.

Doreian, P., Batagelj, V., and Ferligoj, A. (2005). *Generalized Blockmodeling*. Cambridge, UK: Cambridge University Press.

Eades, P. (1984). "A Heuristic for Graph Drawing." *Congressus Numerantium* 42 (11): 149–160.

Festinger, L., Schachter, S., and Back, K. (1950). "The Spatial Ecology of Group Formation." In *Social Pressure in Informal Groups*, edited by L. Festinger, S. Schachter, and K. Back, ch. 4. Cambridge, MA: MIT Press.

Flandreau, M., and Jobst, C. (2005). "The Ties That Divide: A Network Analysis of the International Monetary System, 1890–1910." *Journal of Economic History* 65(4): 977–1007. doi:10.1017/S0022050705000379.

Fleischer, R., and Hirsch, C. (2001). "Graph Drawing and Its Applications." In *Drawing Graphs*, edited by M. Kaufmann and D. Wagner, pp. 1–22. Lecture Notes in Computer Science 2025. Berlin, Heidelberg: Springer. http://link.springer.com/chapter/10.1007/3-540-44969-8_1.

Freeman, L. C. (1977). "A Set of Measures of Centrality Based on Betweenness." *Sociometry* 40: 35–41.

Freeman, L. C. (1979). "Centrality in Social Networks: Conceptual Clarification." *Social Networks* 1(3): 215–239.

Freeman, L. C. (2000). "Visualizing Social Networks." *Journal of Social Structure* 1(1). http://www.cmu.edu/joss/content/articles/volume1/Freeman.html.

Freeman, L. C. (2004). *The Development of Social Network Analysis: A Study in the Sociology of Science*. Vancouver, BC: Empirical Press; North Charleston, SC: BookSurge.

Fruchterman, T. M. J., and Reingold, E. M. (1991). "Graph Drawing by Force-Directed Placement." *Software: Practice and Experience* 21(11): 1129–1164.

Hargittai, E., Gallo, J., and Kane, M. (2007). "Cross-Ideological Discussions among Conservative and Liberal Bloggers." *Public Choice* 134(1–2): 67–86. doi:10.1007/s11127-007-9201-x.

Hennig, M., Brandes, U., Pfeffer, J., and Mergel, I. (2012). *Studying Social Networks: A Guide to Empirical Research*. Frankfurt: Campus Verlag.

Hobson, J. A. (1884). *The Evolution of Modern Capitalism: A Study of Machine Production*. London, New York: Allen & Unwin.

Hollstein, B. (2011). "Qualitative Approaches." In *The SAGE Handbook of Social Network Analysis*, edited by J. Scott, P. J. Carrington, pp. 404–417. London: SAGE Publications.

Kahn, R. L., and Antonucci, T. C. (1980). "Convoys over the Life Course: Attachment, Roles, and Social Support." In *Life-Span Development and Behavior*, edited by Paul B. Baltes and Orville G. Brim, pp. 254–287. New York: Academic.

Kamada, T., and Kawai, S. (1989). "An Algorithm for Drawing General Undirected Graphs." *Information Processing Letters* 31: 7–15.

Kent, D. (1978). *The Rise of the Medici: Faction in Florence, 1426–1434*. Oxford, New York: Oxford University Press.

Koffka, K. (1935). *Principles of Gestalt Psychology*. New York: Harcourt Brace & World.

Krackhardt, D. (1996). "Social Networks and the Liability of Newness for Managers." In *Trends in Organizational Behavior*, edited by C. L. Cooper and D. M. Rousseau, pp. 159–173. Weinheim, Germany: John Wiley & Sons.

Krempel, L. (2005). *Visualisierung komplexer Strukturen: Grundlagen der Darstellung mehrdimensionaler Netzwerke*. Auflage 1. Sonderband Auflage. Frankfurt am Main: Campus Verlag.

Lodge, M. (1981). *Magnitude Scaling, Quantitative Measurement of Opinions*. Beverly Hills, CA: Sage Publications.

Macfarlane, A. (1883). "Analysis of Relationships of Consanguinity and Affinity." *Journal of the Anthropological Institute of Great Britain and Ireland* 12: 46–63. doi:10.2307/2841840.

Mackinlay, J. (1986). "Automating the Design of Graphical Presentations of Relational Information." *ACM Transactions on Graphics* 5(2): 110–141. doi:10.1145/22949.22950.

McGrath, C., and Blythe, J. (2004). "The Effects of Motion and Hierarchical Layout on Viewers' Perceptions of Graph Structure." *Journal of Social Structure* 5(2):. http://www.cmu.edu/joss/content/articles/volume5/McGrathBlythe/.

McGrath, C., Blythe, J., and Krackhardt, D. (1997). "The Effect of Spatial Arrangement on Judgement and Errors in Interpreting Graphs." *Social Networks* 19(3): 223–242.

Moody, J., and Mucha, P. J. (2013). "Portrait of Political Party Polarization." *Network Science* 1(1): 119–121. doi:10.1017/nws.2012.3.

Moreno, J. L. (1934). *Who Shall Survive? A New Approach to the Problem of Human Interrelations*. Washington, DC: Nervous and Mental Disease Publishing Co.

Moreno, J. L. (1953). *Who Shall Survive? Foundations of Sociometry, Group Psychotherapy and Sociodrama*. New York: Beacon House.

Munsell, A. H. (1912). "A Pigment Color System and Notation." *American Journal of Psychology* 23(2): 236–244. doi:10.2307/1412843.

Newman, M. E. J. (2006). "Modularity and Community Structure in Networks." *Proceedings of the National Academy of Sciences of the United States of America* 103(23): 8577–8582. doi:10.1073/pnas.0601602103.

Newman, M. E. J., and Girvan, M. (2004). "Finding and Evaluating Community Structure in Networks." *Physical Review E* 69(2): 026113. doi:10.1103/PhysRevE.69.026113.

Newton, I. (1704). *Opticks: Or, a Treatise of the Reflections, Refractions, Inflections, and Colors of Light*. London: Royal Society.

Northway, M. L. (1940). "A Method for Depicting Social Relationships Obtained by Sociometric Testing." *Sociometry* 3(2): 144–150. doi:10.2307/2785439.

Pfeffer, J. (2013). "Fundamentals of Visualizing Communication Networks." *Communications, China* 10(3): 82–90. doi:10.1109/CC.2013.6488833.

Porter, M. A., Mucha, P. J., Newman, M. E. J., and Friend, A. J. (2006). "Community Structure in the United States House of Representatives." *Chaos: An Interdisciplinary Journal of Nonlinear Science* 16(4): 041106. doi:10.1063/1.2390556.

Roethlisberger, F. J., Dickson, W. J., and Wright, H. A. (1939). *Management and the Worker: An Account of a Research Program Conducted by the Western Electric Company, Hawthorne Works, Chicago*. Cambridge, MA: Harvard University Press.

Sampson, S. F. (1968). "A Novitiate in a Period of Change: An Experimental and Case Study of Social Relationships.", Thesis (Ph.D.), Cornell University.

Stevens, S. S. (1975). *Psychophysics: Introduction to Its Perceptual, Neural, and Social Prospects*. John Wiley & Sons, New York.

Subramanian, A., and Wei, S.-J. (2007). "The WTO Promotes Trade, Strongly but Unevenly." *Journal of International Economics* 72: 151–175.

Torgerson, W. S. (1952). "Multidimensional Scaling." *Theory and Method* 17: 401–419.

Tufte, E. R. (2001). *The Visual Display of Quantitative Informations*. 2d ed. Cheshire, CT: Graphics Press.

Wasserman, S., and Faust, K. (1994). *Social Network Analysis: Methods and Applications*. Cambridge, MA: Cambridge University Press.

Whyte, W. F. (1943). *Street Corner Society: The Social Structure of an Italian Slum*. Chicago: University of Chicago Press.

Wyszecki, G., and Stiles, W. S. (2000). *Color Science: Concepts and Methods, Quantitative Data and Formulae*. 2d ed. New York: Wiley-Interscience.

CHAPTER 12

....

DISCOURSE NETWORK ANALYSIS

Policy Debates as Dynamic Networks

....

PHILIP LEIFELD

INTRODUCTION

....

POLICY debates, or political discourses, are verbal interactions between political actors about a given policy, for example climate or immigration policy. Political actors make public claims about which policy instruments they deem useful and which other measures they reject. Actors participate in policy debates to signal their policy platform to voters or potential allies, convince other actors to adopt their ideal points, or reduce their own uncertainty by learning from other actors in the face of technical complexity.

Policy debates can be highly consequential for political outcomes, for several reasons. First, they determine which policies make it onto the parliamentary agenda and which ones are dropped as a result of preparliamentary agenda setting. Second, they often determine public opinion, which then feeds back into the domain of political decision-making. Third, they also play a role in more private kinds of signaling between actors, for example in discussions and decision-making behind closed doors or in bureaucracies. Finally, they have the potential to translate immediate policy outputs into actual outcomes by altering actors' problem perceptions before policies are implemented. Therefore one should care about how political discourse can be measured and, once this goal has been accomplished, how the structure of empirically observable discourses can be explained by looking at their underlying mechanics.

Political actors comprise legislators, interest groups, agencies, parties, and other organizations or individuals who make public statements about an issue. A *statement* is a verbal or written expression of discontent with a policy or in favor of a policy. Statements must be *public* to qualify as an element of political discourse, because only public claims will be instrumental for the goals actors want to pursue in a discourse. For example, a government agency may voice its concerns about the implementability of a certain policy instrument in a parliamentary hearing, or an interest group may suggest that adoption of a specific policy measure would have positive effects on public welfare, in order to assert their interests. Being public can also mean that statements are visible to an intended target audience, but not necessarily to the broader general public. Therefore discourse network analysis is also applicable to politics behind closed doors.

Political discourse is a network phenomenon because the statements actors are contributing to the discourse are dependent on each other in interesting ways, both temporally and cross-sectionally. In fact, the primary goal of actors is to influence other actors or learn from other actors, which constitutes a relational action. The goal of discourse network analysis is therefore to describe the structures of political discourses and infer their generative processes using techniques from the toolbox of network analysis.

This chapter provides an overview of the theoretical roots of discourse networks, the coding scheme and variables, useful transformations of these data for descriptive discourse network analysis, normalization of discourse network data, some brief empirical examples, a largely nontechnical outlook on inferential statistical methods for modeling discourse networks, and a brief conclusion that summarizes current research frontiers. Although important, this overview does *not* include a discussion of data sources and their validity, as these problems are similar in other types of content analysis. Moreover, this overview does not deal with related kinds of semantic network analysis, which are thoroughly discussed by González-Bailón and Yang in another chapter of this handbook. This chapter rather serves as a primer on descriptive and inferential discourse network analysis from a methodological and theoretical perspective.

The procedures described in this chapter have been implemented in open-source software called Discourse Network Analyzer (Leifeld, 2016a) and the R package rDNA (Leifeld, 2016a). While there are numerous software packages for qualitative content analysis, very few have an explicit functionality for exporting network data, especially when the focus is on actors. Database- or spreadsheet-based solutions do not allow the user to revise earlier statement annotations later on. Discourse Network Analyzer was designed both for the actor-based annotation of statements in text data and for exporting these structured data as networks.

Theory

Several relational characteristics of policy debates have been suggested. The most important one is that debates tend to be structured around competing coalitions. Several prominent public policy frameworks make explicit reference to coalitions that are formed as a consequence of similar ideas, beliefs, arguments, or policy stances within the same policy domain or subsystem:

The advocacy coalition framework (Sabatier, 1988; Sabatier and Weible, 2007) argues that between two and five "advocacy coalitions" of actors are structured around coherent "policy core policy preferences," that is, policy instrument preferences. The framework argues that advocacy coalitions are usually stable over decades. Policy learning takes place within rather than between these coalitions, which leads to policy stability. While current applications of this framework often analyze policy coordination, the original formulation placed a stronger emphasis on beliefs and learning as the "glue" of coalitions (Sabatier and Weible, 2007).

Argumentative discourse analysis (Hajer, 1993, 1995) asserts that conflict over environmental and other policy issues is structured by "discourse coalitions," which primarily serve to defend or propose coherent arguments and narratives as justifications for policy proposals. In this regard, the main difference between advocacy coalitions and discourse coalitions is that advocacy coalitions deal with multiple issues and actors' stances on them, while discourse coalitions are concerned with only one issue at a time but with multiple justifications for a positive versus a negative stance on the issue. If discourse network analysis operationalizes advocacy coalitions by coding statements on different policy instruments, one can expect multiple complex coalitions with different topical foci, while coding arguments for or against a specific issue as an operationalization of discourse coalitions would rather lead to two distinct coalitions and thus a certain degree of bipolarization by design.

Other policy frameworks and theories make implicit reference to the idea of coalitions. For example, punctuated equilibrium theory (Baumgartner and Jones, 1991), the literature on "policy paradigms" and social learning (Hall, 1993), and the notion of epistemic communities (Haas, 1992; Roth and Bourgine, 2005) all deal with groups of actors who share similar beliefs.

The existence of coalitions is an expression of cross-sectional clustering of actors around similar statements. Analyzing the copresence of coalitions in a system of actors permits an evaluation of the overall level of cooperation and conflict within the system and therefore effectively reveals the degree of polarization of actors in the system.

Besides cross-sectional clustering, the policy process and public opinion literature has argued that temporal clustering of topics is at work. Downs (1972) suggests that there is a competition between different issues for attention ("up and down with ecology"). Issues go through an "issue attention cycle," because novel discoveries are valued more highly by public opinion than known policy problems. The consequence is that actors seek to "acquire power in part by trying to influence the political discourse of their day" (Hall, 1993, 290) by jumping on the bandwagon and discussing currently popular topics. Similarly, the notion of "political waves" (Wolfsfeld, 2001; Wolfsfeld and Sheafer, 2006) rests on the observation that actors compete for attention in the news. Due to changing topics in the news media (or other public venues), they have to adapt to changing topics. In other words, discussion topics come and go over time, effectively leading to a temporal clustering of statements.

Two distinct levels are frequently analyzed in relational studies of political discourse: the configuration of actors and the structure of the contents of a debate. While coalitions may be observed at the actor level, the equivalent of clusters of ideas, policy preferences, beliefs, or justifications at the content level is often termed a "frame" (Goffman, 1974; Rein and Schön, 1993). Frames are composed of "concepts," which is a neutral word for policy beliefs, preferences, justifications, and so forth at the content level. A frame can be defined as a congruent set of concepts, where congruence derives from common usage by the same actors and therefore has ideological and intrinsic compatibility (Roth and Bourgine, 2005). According to Steensland (2008, 1030), "few existing studies link frames with the actors who sponsor them, thus presenting an oddly disembodied picture of framing processes." A relationally explicit treatment as in discourse network analysis allows such a joint analysis.

Besides coalition formation (clustering at the actor level), framing (clustering at the level of concepts), and issue attention cycles (temporal clustering of statements), other theoretical mechanisms may guide the development of policy debates. Much abstract theorizing exists and often goes back to classic works in political or social theory, such as critical discourse analysis and deliberative democracy (Foucault, 1991; Habermas, 1981), which paved the way for relating language and verbal interaction to the notion of power. Yet few systematic, empirical, replicable accounts of how these mechanisms shape policy debates as complex systems can be found in print. Discourse network analysis permits studying these mechanisms in such a systematic way in order to facilitate theory building with regard to policy debates.

CODING SCHEME AND VARIABLES

Empirical discourse network analysis is based on a combination of category-based content analysis and network analysis. During the first step, text data are annotated using a coding scheme that is amenable to network analysis. Depending on the type of debate to be analyzed, useful text sources may be newspaper articles, parliamentary testimony, or other types of documents.

Within each document, statements are annotated. They are the basic unit of analysis. A statement may consist of four variables, but this definition can be adjusted to the research purpose or theory.

First, the *actor* $a \in A = \{a_1, a_2, \ldots, a_m\}$ is the person or organization who speaks. Most theories related to the policy process and policy networks assume that organizations are the primary actors in the policy process, and for theoretical clarity, the decision of which kind of actor is analyzed—persons or organizations—should be made before the analysis is conducted.

Second, the *concept* $c \in C = \{c_1, c_2, \ldots, c_n\}$ is an abstract representation of the contents that are discussed. If advocacy coalitions are operationalized, concepts are claims for policy instruments. For example, in the debate over what to do about climate change, concepts could be "we should adopt cap and trade" or "we should replace coal and gas with nuclear power." In contrast, if discourse coalitions in the sense of Hajer (1995) or political claims (Koopmans, 1996; Koopmans and Statham, 1999) are operationalized, concepts would be justifications or narratives. For example, in the debate over whether nuclear energy should be promoted, concepts could be justifications revolving around "health" or "jobs"; some actors may argue that nuclear energy is preferable because it causes fewer cases of lung cancer close to the plant, and other actors may argue that its share should not be increased because it causes more cases of cancer in general due to radiation. In both cases, actors speak about the concept of "health" to justify their position on nuclear energy. When justifications or narratives are used, one can expect by design that two opposing coalitions will emerge. The question then becomes to what extent each coalition argues in a coherent way (i.e., whether different actors use the same set of concepts and whether that pattern is consistent over time) and how polarized the coalitions are (Is there a certain extent of common ground or not?). When policy instruments are used and thus a more encompassing analysis is conducted, one can usually expect more diversity even within groups, and more than two coalitions are possible. For example, in the debate over old-age security, there could be a coalition favoring various privatization measures, another favoring fertility-inducing policy instruments, and another calling for various labor market instruments; depending on the case, there may be more or less overlap among these coalitions.

The third variable in each statement consists of the *agreement* relation $r \in R = \{r_1, r_2, \ldots, r_l\}$. It acts as an edge qualifier and is usually a dichotomous variable (that is, $l = 2$), which captures the sentiment of the statement. It is said to be "positive" (r_1) if the actor refers to the concept in an affirmatory way and "negative" (r_2) if the actor rejects the concept or uses a negative connotation. In the previous example about nuclear power justifications, the first statement was positive and the second one was negative. The distinction between positive and negative statements is important, because competing coalitions may refer to the same concepts in the debate, but with different stances. Ignoring agreement or disagreement and using only "topics" (as is frequently done in other approaches) would connect nodes from competing coalitions, and they would eventually end up in the same coalition despite having opposite opinions. When policy processes are analyzed, it is therefore crucial to move beyond establishing similarity by joint topic affiliation.

Fourth, each statement carries a time or date stamp, for example, the day on which the statement is made. This allows for the temporal analysis of policy debates. Time is actually continuous, but for the sake of simplicity it is modeled here as discrete in the first couple of steps before introducing dynamic methods that make use of time as a continuous variable. Therefore $T = \{t_1, t_2, \ldots, t_k\}$ denotes the set of discrete time steps, for example the set of months or years in which statements are made.

The coding scheme can be adjusted to the problem or theory at hand. For example, the narrative policy framework (Jones and McBeth, 2010; Shanahan, Jones, and McBeth,

2011) requires coding other variables like villains and heroes, and political claims analysis (Koopmans, 1996; Koopmans and Statham, 1999) requires variables like addressee, tone, and location. In these cases or yet other frameworks, the descriptive network models below can be adapted accordingly.

The Descriptive Network Model

Discourse network analysis can be descriptive or inferential. If the goal is to trace a debate over time, visualize competing coalitions, and analyze their characteristics, this can be achieved by employing several descriptive network analysis methods. In particular, six simple transformations of the data are useful for exploring policy debates: an *affiliation* network, an *actor congruence* network, an *actor conflict* network, a *concept* congruence network, a *time window* network, and an *attenuation* network.

The first step is to create an affiliation network (two-mode network or bipartite graph) $G_{r,t}^{aff} = \left(A, C, E_{r,t}^{aff} \right)$ from the statements that have been annotated in the text. In this notation, a *statement* can be understood as an edge from an actor to a concept at a specific point in time in a positive or negative way, in short $e_{r,t}^{aff}(a,c) \in E_{r,t}^{aff}$, where $E_{r,t}^{aff}$ denotes the set of edges in relation r and time slice t. In figure 12.1 (cf. Janning et al., 2009), a simplified illustration without any agreement relation, edges are the broken gray lines (ties)

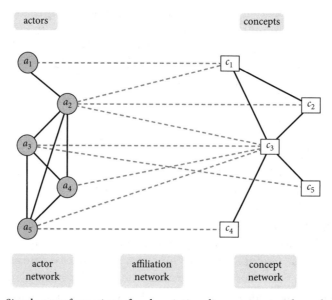

FIGURE 12.1 Simple transformations for descriptive discourse network analysis. Simplified illustration without agreement relation.

Source: Janning et al. (2009) and Leifeld (2016b).

in the middle that connect actors to the concepts they are employing. Note that two separate affiliation networks can be computed: one for positive mentions of concepts and one for negative ones. Each affiliation network usually contains only binary ties within a time step, because the rate at which an actor uses the same concept rarely contains any useful and unbiased information, for example because journalists decide how often an interview partner is asked to report his or her opinion. The profile of ties, that is, which concepts the actor evaluates positively, which ones negatively, and which ones not at all, is usually more important and less biased by external factors than the frequency of each statement. The positive and negative affiliation networks can also be combined into a signed network and visualized with different edge colors, for example, green for agreement and red for rejection. It is possible to define t as the whole time range of a discourse or look at consecutive time slices (e.g., years) separately by setting t accordingly. This allows the user to explore which actors adopt what issue stances and how this changes over time.

However, such a two-mode analysis does not tap the full potential of network analysis. In particular, the visualization may quickly become too complex to infer any systematic meaning from it. Moreover, a more direct operationalization of coalitions would be desirable. For this reason, one can compute one-mode projections $G_t^a = \left(A, E_t^a\right)$ of the affiliation network that preserve the information stored in the agreement variable. Consider the solid lines in figure 12.1 on the left: whenever two actors refer to the same concept, they are directly linked in this co-occurrence network. The weight of the edge between two actors is proportional to the number of different concepts both actors refer to. There are two different ways that one can aggregate ties in the actor network (see figure 12.2): in a congruence network, a tie is established (or its edge weight is increased by 1) every time two actors refer to the same concept both in a positive way or both in a negative way. The edge weight in an actor congruence network is therefore given by

$$w_t\left(a,a\right)= \sum_{r=1}^{l}\left|N_{G_{r,t}^{aff}}\left(a\right)\cap N_{G_{r,t}^{aff}}\left(a'\right)\right|$$

where $N_{G_{r,t}^{aff}}\left(a\right)$ denotes the neighboring nodes of a in the affiliation graph, that is, the concepts used by a, and the vertical bars denote the cardinality of the set. In other words, the similarity between actors a and a' is defined as the number of concept-stances both actors have in common. This definition captures concept agreement between the two actors and prevents actors from ending up in the same coalition just because they are attached to the same concepts but with opposite stances. Actor congruence networks capture important properties of policy debates in an intuitive way. For example, cohesive subgroups in the actor congruence network are a straightforward operationalization of advocacy or discourse coalitions. They can be identified using graph-theoretic community detection algorithms such as community detection based on edge betweenness (Girvan and Newman, 2002), modularity maximization (Newman and Girvan,

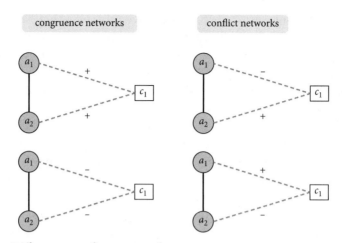

FIGURE 12.2 Different types of actor networks.

2004; Newman, 2006), or other techniques suitable for identifying subgroups in networks. Clusters in the actor congruence network are groups of actors with similar profiles of opinions.

Similarly, one can create a conflict network, in which a tie is established (or its weight is increased) if both actors have opposing agreement patterns (see the right side of figure 12.2). Substantively, this results in a network with negative ties (Labianca and Brass, 2006). The value of an edge indicates the intensity of conflict between two actors. This can be interesting, because a congruence network only captures agreement, whereas disagreement must be inferred from the absence of edges. This may be insufficient in some cases, because it is not possible to distinguish between absent edges due to disagreement and absent edges due to the fact that some actors do not reveal their preferences. Edge weights in the conflict network can be expressed in a similar way as in the congruence network:

$$w_t\left(a,a'\right)=\left|N_{G_{r=1,t}^{aff}}\left(a\right)\cap N_{G_{r=2,t}^{aff}}\left(a'\right)\right|+\left|N_{G_{r=2,t}^{aff}}\left(a\right)\cap N_{G_{r=1,t}^{aff}}\left(a'\right)\right|$$

where the edge weight is the number of concepts actor a agrees on and the other actor a' disagrees on, or vice versa. In the resulting graph, two actors are connected if they have opposing views, and their edge weight indicates the strength of disagreement between them.

One may be tempted to apply the same transformations to the concept level in order to identify frames or ideologies in terms of joint usage by actors. However, this is slightly more complicated, because the direction of agreement may differ across concepts. For example, (positive) agreement with nuclear power in order to curb emissions may be related to (negative) disagreement with subsidies for coal and gas, but it may be at the same time related to (positive) agreement with higher regulatory standards with regard to emissions. In other words, relating concepts only when both of them are used in the same way would be useless, because some concepts are inherently formulated in a reversed way. To rectify the problem, it is possible to redefine each concept node to be intrinsically linked to one of the agreement patterns: $c^* \in C^* = \left\{ c_1^{r=1}, \ldots, c_1^{r=1}, c_2^{r=1}, \ldots, c_2^{r=1}, \ldots c_n^{r=1}, \ldots c_n^{r=1} \right\}$. This yields twice as many concepts as before (if $l = 2$). For example, the node set for concepts would consist of items like "cap and trade—yes" as well as "cap and trade—no" and similar positive and negative pairs of concepts. The agreement qualifier would then no longer matter for the construction of the network. In that case, congruence can be expressed as follows.

$$ w_t \left(c^*, c^* \right) = \left| N_{G_t^{aff}} \left(c^* \right) \cap N_{G_t^{aff}} \left(c^{*\prime} \right) \right| $$

In other words, the more actors use two concept-agreement tuples jointly in the same time period, the greater the similarity between these two items. This is an indicator of ideological fit between the two signed concepts, because they need to be compatible in order to be usable by the same person or organization. Just as the whole congruence network provides an operationalization of coalitions as densely interconnected subgroups, clusters in the concept congruence network can be interpreted as frames or ideologies.

For all of these transformations, it is possible to create versions that take into account the time axis more explicitly. At least two different kinds of transformations may be useful. One of them is based on a time window. The idea is that the meaning of concepts may change over time. If an actor speaks in favor of higher emission standards in a given year, and another actor proposes higher emission standards twelve years later after the standards have in fact been altered in the meantime, should these two actors be connected? The time window approach corrects for this changing context by establishing congruence or conflict ties only within a certain time window of a prespecified number of days. The time window is then moved forward along the time axis, and ties or weights are added to the existing network within each time step. This effectively corrects for problems with changing contexts, and it imposes a temporal restriction in the sense that similarity derives from temporally local interactions.

Yet this method effectively applies a discrete function to time. The weight is added to the network if interaction between two nodes takes place within the time window, and it is not added at all if the interaction spans only one day more than the length of the time window. One may prefer to impose a continuous time function, such that the longer ago the first actor made the same statement, the less a second actor's identical statement at the current time point matters for the edge weight. In such an "attenuation network," edge weights that are added to the network can be weighted by arbitrary functional forms of the number of days that have passed between the two statements, most commonly an exponential decay function with a decay parameter provided by the user. An attenuation network thus values temporally local interactions within a few days much more than congruence or conflict over long time periods. This also makes sense from a conversation perspective, because actors are much more likely to respond to other claims in a debate within a few days.

In principle, either the time window approach or the attenuation approach can be used to create dynamic visualizations of how policy debates and their coalitions and polarization change over time. More details about these time algorithms, including dynamic visualization, are provided by Leifeld (2013, 2016b).

All of the transformations suggested above have their own strengths and weaknesses. Affiliation networks serve to view the full set of information, but may be too complex for meaningful interpretation by means of visual inspection; congruence networks are intuitive operationalizations of coalitions and frames, respectively, but normalization methods may have to be applied due to different levels of activity and diversity of actors (see next section); conflict networks offer a direct operationalization of actor conflict, but are harder to interpret visually; and temporal transformations like the time window approach and the attenuation method serve to correct the actor congruence network by admitting only temporally local interactions. As a starting point for exploring an empirical debate, normalized actor congruence networks and affiliation networks may be the easiest and most intuitive options.

Normalization of Discourse Networks

In most congruence networks, it is important to normalize edge weights. Consider the actor congruence network depicted in the upper panel of figure 12.3. The example shows the German policy debate on the future of the pension system during the first six months of the year 2000. The different node colors indicate actor types. Gray nodes— government actors and political parties—are located at the center of the network. The hyperplanes represent coalitions as identified by edge betweenness community detection (Girvan and Newman, 2002) implemented in the visualization software Visone (Brandes and Wagner, 2004). Clearly, government actors and parties are most central due to their large numbers of statements. This is a typical pattern across many kinds of discourses: some actors are more mediagenic than others because they are officially in charge of a problem (e.g., the Ministry of Social Affairs is in charge of dealing with pension politics), and some actors follow a membership logic according to which they are by definition more diverse than others with regard to opinions (e.g., political parties often have multiple party wings). Their activity and diversity cause these actors to have agreement ties to most other actors in the network at some point. The result is a core-periphery structure in which coalitions cannot be easily identified. Is this an artifact because discursive similarity is confounded by institutional roles of actors, or is this a feature rather than a bug? Both perspectives are defensible, but if the goal is to find coalitions based on the similarity of actors' policy preferences, one may prefer to abate this nuisance.

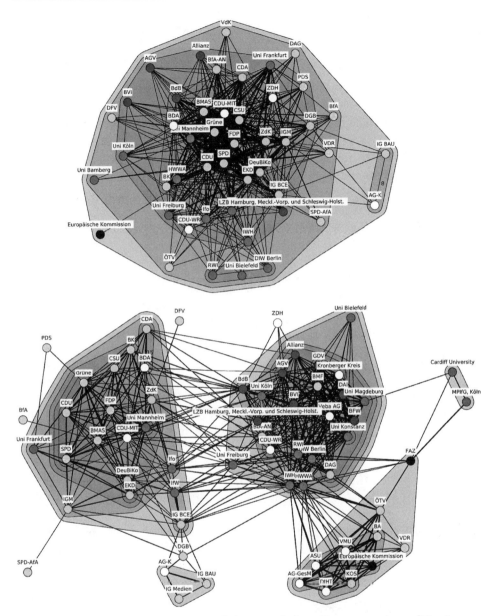

FIGURE 12.3 Normalization. Upper panel: An example from German pension politics, January to June 2000. Lower panel: Same network as before, but with normalization.

Several types of normalization can be applied to an actor congruence network to correct for this "institutional bias." A simple and effective method is to divide each edge weight by the average number of different concepts the two actors use (either in a positive or a negative way):

$$\phi\left(w_{t}\left(a,a'\right)\right)\frac{\sum_{r=1}^{l}\left|N_{G_{r,t}^{aff}}\left(a\right)\cap N_{G_{r,t}^{aff}}\left(a'\right)\right|}{\frac{1}{2}\left|N_{G_{r=1,t}^{aff}}\left(a\right)\cap N_{G_{r=2,t}^{aff}}\left(a\right)\right|+\left|N_{G_{r=2,t}^{aff}}\left(a'\right)\cup N_{G_{r=2,t}^{aff}}\left(a'\right)\right|}$$

For the pension example network, this normalization results in the network shown in the lower panel of figure 12.3. It is easy to see that several distinct coalitions can be identified now.

Two other kinds of normalization are able to minimize this bias. Both are based on vector similarities. Rather than a co-occurrence approach as presented above, one can formulate the concept profile of an actor as a vector $\vec{a}$ of length $\left|C^{*}\right|$ with entries 0 (indicating no statement about a concept-agreement tuple) and 1 (indicating affiliation with a concept-agreement tuple) at a given time step and then compute the similarity between the concept vectors of two actors. At least two similarity measures are known to have normalizing properties when some entries have zeros (Leydesdorff, 2008), a situation that is equivalent to having vectors with unequal lengths. The first one is the Jaccard similarity measure:

$$w_{j}\left(a,a'\right)=1-\frac{M_{11}}{M_{01}+M_{10}+M_{11}}$$

where M_{11} denotes the number of concepts where both actors have a 1, and M_{01} and M_{10} are the numbers of concepts where only one of the two actors have a 1. The second measure with normalizing properties is known as cosine similarity:

$$w_{c}\left(a,a'\right)=\frac{\sum_{i=1}^{n}\vec{a}_{i}\vec{a}_{i}'}{\sqrt{\sum_{i=1}^{n}\left(\vec{a}_{i}\right)^{2}}\sqrt{\sum_{i=1}^{n}\left(\vec{a}_{i}'\right)^{2}}}$$

which is equivalent to dividing the edge weights of the actor congruence network by the square root of the product of the degree centralities of both incident nodes across positive and negative statements (Newman, 2011, 26; compare for the first normalization measure suggested above):

$$\phi\left(w_{t}\left(a,a\right)\right)\frac{\sum_{r=1}^{l}\left|N_{G_{r,t}^{aff}}\left(a\right)\cap N_{G_{r,t}^{aff}}\left(a'\right)\right|}{\sqrt{\left|N_{G_{r=1,t}^{aff}}\left(a\right)\cup N_{G_{r=2,t}^{aff}}\left(a\right)\right|\cdot\left|N_{G_{r=1,t}^{aff}}\left(a'\right)\cup N_{G_{r=2,t}^{aff}}\left(a\right)\right|}}$$

Both metrics, Jaccard similarity and cosine similarity, are standardized between 0 and 1. Besides serving normalization purposes, these vector similarities can also be fed into hierarchical cluster analyses, nonmetric multidimensional scaling, or other clustering techniques that are based on distance or similarity measures in order to identify coalitions in a policy debate as an alternative to community detection in the congruence network.

A fourth normalization measure, the *subtract* method, tackles the problem that actor congruence networks only consider congruence ties, but not conflict. There may be cases in which two coalitions have substantial conflict with regard to some concepts and also substantial agreement on other concepts. A congruence network would only consider the agreement patterns and wrongly identify a single coalition. A simple solution to this problem is to compute both a congruence network and a conflict network and then subtract the conflict edge weights from the corresponding congruence edge weights. The result is a signed, weighted network in which positive ties represent agreement in excess of conflict and where negative ties indicate more conflict than congruence. As in any of the other network types, one can subsequently impose threshold values on the edge weights in order to remove low-intensity (or in this case, negative) ties for purposes of visualizing the network. This will correct the congruence network by removing the bias that may arise because conflict ties are ignored when the congruence network is created. Moreover, if positive and negative usages of concepts have similar frequencies, this type of normalization will effectively remove the institutional bias reported above. For an application, see Nagel (2015).

BRIEF DESCRIPTIVE EXAMPLES

Discourse network analysis has been applied to several policy sectors, such as pension politics (Leifeld, 2013, 2016b), climate politics (Fisher, Leifeld, and Iwaki, 2013; Fisher, Waggle, and Leifeld, 2013; Broadbent and Vaughter, 2014, Gkiouzepas and Botetzagias, 2015; Schneider and Ollmann, 2013; Stoddart and Tindall, 2015; Wagner and Payne, 2015; Yun et al., 2014), software patents and property rights (Leifeld and Haunss, 2012; Herweg, 2013), Internet policy (Breindl, 2013), infrastructure projects (Nagel, 2015), energy policy (Brutschin, 2013; Haunss, Dietz, and Nullmeier, 2013; Mayer, 2015; Rinscheid, 2015; Rinscheid et al., 2015), shooting rampages (Hurka and Nebel, 2013), abortion (Muller, 2014a, 2014b, 2015), outdoor sports (Stoddart, Ramos, and Tindall, 2015), water politics (Brandenberger et al., 2015; Cisneros, 2015), deforestation (Rantala and Di Gregorio, 2014), genetically modified organisms (Tosun and Schaub, 2015), higher education (Nägler, 2015), international financial politics (Werner, 2015), and online deception (Wu and Zhou, 2015), among others.

A simple example of German pension politics between 1993 and 2001 based on newspaper articles illustrates the use of descriptive discourse network analysis. Details about data collection and the study design can be found in Leifeld (2013, 2016b). The study examines the use of sixty-eight solution concepts for fixing the old-age pension system in the face of financial problems and population aging. Some 246 organizations made 7,249 positive or negative statements about these concepts in a newspaper over the course of nine years, culminating in a major policy reform. The new law was adopted in 2001 and introduced privatization measures, although the sixty-eight distinct solution concepts had very different substantive foci, ranging from privatization over labor-market policy instruments to fertility incentives. What dynamics led to the narrowing down of the set of politically feasible concepts? The literature on pension politics argues that there was a single policy coalition until the mid-1990s, and an erosion of this cohesive group of actors and concepts took place between then and 2001 (see Leifeld, 2013 and 2016b for details). The research question is therefore: How is this policy change predated by changing coalitions in the policy debate?

To answer this question, Leifeld (2013, 2016b) computes annual time slices of normalized actor congruence networks for the complete years of 1997, 1998, and 2000 and the five months leading up to the reform in 2001, respectively. Edges with a weight lower than a certain threshold value are removed for clarity. This threshold value for filtering out less intense edges is set individually for each network. The cutoff values are only necessary for easier visual interpretation of the network diagrams. These procedures lead to several consecutive network visualizations similar to the lower panel in figure 12.3. The actual figures can be found in Leifeld (2013, 2016b). The analysis of the development of coalitions over time reveals a strong pattern from one dominant corporatist coalition over a strong bipolarization of two coalitions, some actors leaving the previous coalition and joining the opponent, to an erosion of the corporatist coalition and institutionalization of the new coalition that revolves around privatization ideas. In this case study, the discourse network analysis is able to derive in detail when and how these changes came about.

Figure 12.4 illustrates the consequences of applying a decreasing threshold value to the normalized actor congruence network. The four visualizations are based on the complete time period from 1993 to 2001. In the first panel, a relatively high threshold value of 0.6 retains only the most intense edges and therefore gives a clear picture of the "islands" in the weighted network. In particular, the two competing coalitions are visible, and two smaller coalitions are displayed as well—one of them with financial actors and the other one with a subdiscourse related to employers' associations. While these four core coalitions are visible, their location vis-à-vis each other remains unobservable. Only with a decreasing threshold do more details become gradually visible, among other details the relative location and connectedness between these groups. At the same time, however, zooming in also implies that the structure is less easy to interpret, especially with regard to subgroups. Therefore, setting a threshold value is a tradeoff between too little information and too much complexity. In a sense, one has to filter out the "noise" and retain the "signal" by setting the threshold value in an explorative way. There is no rule of thumb because the distribution of edge weights depends on many factors that are specific to the case study, data source, time period, and so forth. However, imposing a threshold value is only helpful for purposes of visualization; any formal community detection algorithm can be applied to the weighted network matrix.

Finally, figure 12.5 shows a hierarchical cluster analysis of the Jaccard-normalized concept congruence network. Only concept-agreement tuples with at least twelve mentions are retained for this analysis. While the dendrogram on the left shows that there are approximately three clusters or "frames," the different shades of blue in the level plot

w ≥ 0.6   w ≥ 0.5

w ≥ 0.45   w ≥ 0.35

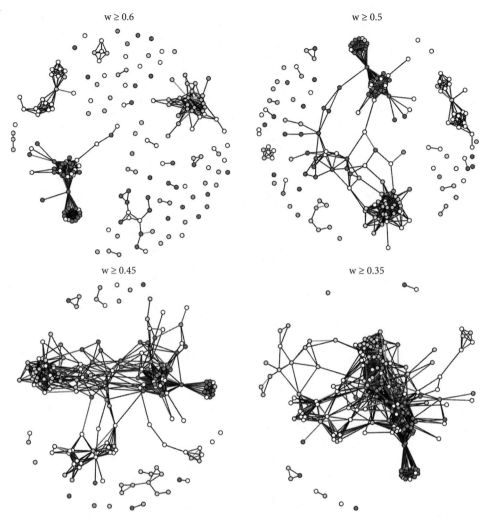

FIGURE 12.4 Threshold values. Whole time period from 1993 to 2001 in the German pension policy debate. Actor congruence network with varying threshold values.

Source: Leifeld (2016b).

provide a micro-level foundation for the frames at the actor level: the darker the color, the more frequently the tuple was mentioned by social interest groups or trade unions (S), interest groups for young people (Y), liberal interest groups and trade unions (L), and financial market actors (F), respectively, with each line showing relative frequencies in a row-standardized distribution. Trade unions have a very coherent frame in the lower third of the plot, which centers around adjustments to the existing pension system, and financial actors and employers' associations share a joint frame in the upper third of the diagram, revolving around privatization and private savings. The frame in the middle is politically moderate and features several subframes. One of them, for example, is concerned with fertility-related measures and is jointly advocated by young

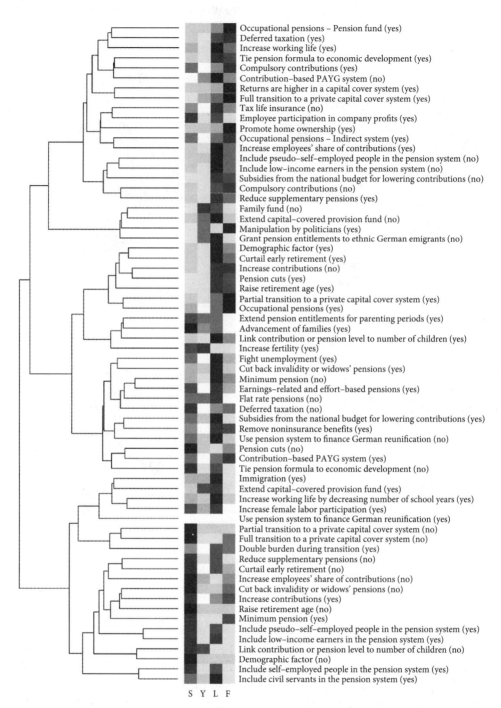

Occupational pensions – Pension fund (yes)
Deferred taxation (yes)
Increase working life (yes)
Tie pension formula to economic development (yes)
Compulsory contributions (yes)
Contribution–based PAYG system (no)
Returns are higher in a capital cover system (yes)
Full transition to a private capital cover system (yes)
Tax life insurance (no)
Employee participation in company profits (yes)
Promote home ownership (yes)
Occupational pensions – Indirect system (yes)
Increase employees' share of contributions (yes)
Include pseudo–self-employed people in the pension system (no)
Include low–income earners in the pension system (no)
Subsidies from the national budget for lowering contributions (no)
Compulsory contributions (no)
Reduce supplementary pensions (yes)
Family fund (no)
Extend capital–covered provision fund (no)
Manipulation by politicians (yes)
Grant pension entitlements to ethnic German emigrants (no)
Demographic factor (yes)
Curtail early retirement (yes)
Increase contributions (no)
Pension cuts (yes)
Raise retirement age (yes)
Partial transition to a private capital cover system (yes)
Occupational pensions (yes)
Extend pension entitlements for parenting periods (yes)
Advancement of families (yes)
Link contribution or pension level to number of children (yes)
Increase fertility (yes)
Fight unemployment (yes)
Cut back invalidity or widows' pensions (yes)
Minimum pension (no)
Earnings–related and effort-based pensions (yes)
Flat rate pensions (no)
Deferred taxation (no)
Subsidies from the national budget for lowering contributions (yes)
Remove noninsurance benefits (yes)
Use pension system to finance German reunification (no)
Pension cuts (no)
Contribution–based PAYG system (yes)
Tie pension formula to economic development (no)
Immigration (yes)
Extend capital–covered provision fund (yes)
Increase working life by decreasing number of school years (yes)
Increase female labor participation (yes)
Use pension system to finance German reunification (yes)
Partial transition to a private capital cover system (no)
Full transition to a private capital cover system (no)
Double burden during transition (yes)
Reduce supplementary pensions (no)
Curtail early retirement (no)
Increase employees' share of contributions (no)
Cut back invalidity or widows' pensions (no)
Increase contributions (yes)
Raise retirement age (no)
Minimum pension (yes)
Include pseudo–self-employed people in the pension system (yes)
Include low–income earners in the pension system (yes)
Link contribution or pension level to number of children (no)
Demographic factor (no)
Include self-employed people in the pension system (yes)
Include civil servants in the pension system (yes)

S Y L F

FIGURE 12.5 Concept network. Hierarchical cluster analysis of the Jaccard-normalized concept congruence network (dendrogram on the left). Partitioning of concept-agreement tuples into actor categories for easier interpretation of the frame clusters at the actor level (level plot in the middle). Darker shades of blue indicate larger relative shares of activity by the actor group denoted at the bottom. S = social interest group or trade union; Y = young interest group; L = liberal interest group or employers' association; F = financial market actor.

Source: Leifeld (2016b).

people's interest groups and employers' associations. Of course, alternative visualizations or analyses based on network layouts and/or other types of subgroup analysis would be possible with the same data.

INFERENTIAL NETWORK ANALYSIS
FOR POLICY DEBATES

Two types of research questions can be answered using discourse network analysis. One relates the macro topology, or aggregate structure, of a discourse network to external variables like policy change or institutional variation between debates. For example: How can coalition dynamics explain a reform? How can the internal structure of competing coalitions explain their policy success or failure? How can the polarization of a debate be explained by events like elections or scientific reports? How far is it possible to relate policy change to shifting coalition memberships of decision-makers? These questions imply a research design at the macro level of debate, which means that at least one of the variables of interest affects the whole network and that descriptive or explorative methods such as subgroup analysis or centrality are employed.

The other fundamental type of research question is concerned with micro-level mechanisms of political discourse. The explanandum is the topology of the network as generated by a sequence of statements. In other words, one would like to understand how discourse works by identifying what behavioral mechanisms and exogenous variables can jointly explain whether any actor a supports or rejects any concept c at any given point in time. Modeling the joint probability of all statements is equivalent to modeling the data-generating process governing political discourse.

Several candidate models for inferential network analysis exist, but most standard models are not ideally suited for inference on policy debates. The exponential random graph model (ERGM) treats time only implicitly and does not discriminate between positive and negative ties (Robins et al., 2007). The temporal exponential random graph model (TERGM) (Hanneke, Fu, and Xing, 2010; Leifeld, Cranmer, and Desmarais, 2016) and the stochastic actor-oriented model (SAOM) (Snijders, van de Bunt, and Steglich, 2010) both assume discrete time periods for measurement purposes, but partitioning a discourse network into arbitrary time slices would likely alter the topology of the network and the statistics to be incorporated. Relational event models as proposed by Butts (2008) permit modeling time and the order of events more explicitly, but the original model and its model terms do not support signed edges (i.e., agreement and disagreement in the case of discourse networks). Lerner et al. (2013) suggest an extension of the relational event model for signed networks, but the model terms are confined to one-mode networks. Brandenberger (2016) and Leifeld and Brandenberger (2016) extend relational event models to the case of bipartite signed graphs with time-stamped edges—that is, actors refer to concepts in a continuous-time setting, and these statements can have complex interactions that lead to coalition formation, the emergence of frames, issue attention cycles, and other properties of empirical debates. These complex interactions are parameterized by modeling the dependencies explicitly as covariates, including them in the regression equation, and estimating their relative importance in the data-generating process.

Relatedly, Leifeld (2014) reports the results of an agent-based simulation of political discourse. The model is not based on any micro-level data but rather proposes several theoretically plausible micro-level mechanisms and tests the implications of combining these effects for the topology (polarization, coalition formation, etc.) of the resulting discourse network. The results indicate that a combination of several relatively simple micro-level dependency statistics like concept popularity, endogenous coalition formation, or the coherence of government actors already produces discourses that are reasonably in line with empirical case studies of discourse networks. Any of the mechanisms specified in the theoretical model can also be formulated as a model term in a relational event model in order to estimate the relative importance of these effects based on real-world observations.

To give a rough nontechnical intuition, relational event models for bipartite signed graphs (Leifeld and Brandenberger, 2016; Brandenberger, 2016; extending Butts, 2008 and Lerner et al., 2013) work as follows. The explanandum is the observed sequence of statements. First, a survival model is used to estimate the probability that actor a refers to concept c at a specific time point or, equivalently, the waiting time until actor a refers to concept c. The probabilities for the different statements are conditionally independent, given some exogenous covariates like actor type or concept type and functions of the statement sequence up to the respective time point. These functions capture endogenous dependencies between observations, for example, recent concept popularity or indirect interactions between actors via concepts. The joint probability of the statement sequence is the product of all individual statement probabilities. A second aspect of the statement sequence is the type of a statement (positive or negative), given that the statement has been observed. This is estimated using a generalized linear model, more specifically a logistic regression model if the sentiment was coded as a binary variable. The odds of observing a positive rather than a negative statement are conditionally independent, given some exogenous covariates and functions of the statement sequence up to the respective point, similar to the previous case. Again, the product of the individual probabilities for each statement type makes up the overall probability of observing the whole sequence of statement types. Both aggregated probabilities, the referral probability/waiting time and the statement type probability, can be multiplied to compute the overall probability of observing the sequence of statements, including frequency and type of statement. The first component of this probability is the *rate component* and the second is the *type component*. Estimation of model parameters for both components can be done separately or jointly via maximum likelihood estimation.

In both cases, the specification of the endogenous dependencies is done by computing network statistics that take into account all previous statements. As previous statements are presumably less relevant the longer ago they took place, each statement's contribution to a statistic is weighted by a function of the time that has passed between the statement and the current time point. The user specifies the functional form of this temporal weighting scheme for the dependencies, for example by setting the "half-life" of statements.

So far, this exposition closely follows Lerner et al. (2013). The task that is specific to discourse network analysis is tailoring the dependency functions to signed two-mode networks as in the following examples. *Actor activity* sums up how often the same actor has issued statements, weighted by time. For example, the more active an actor has been so far, the more likely it is that the actor will make a statement at the upcoming time point. *Concept popularity* is a similar dependency statistic for the number of times a specific concept has been mentioned recently, which captures temporal clustering of concepts. *Inertia* measures the tendency of the actor-concept combination to have appeared before. *Balanced four-cycles* between actors capture the tendency of actors to follow the positive and/or negative concept usage patterns of other actors multiple times. For example, if actor a_1 has supported concept c_1 and rejected c_2 in the past statement sequence, and a_2 has also supported c_1, this increases the probability that a_2 rejects c_2 as well at the current time point if actors 1 and 2 have a positively balanced relationship. To quantify this tendency, cases in which the first three statements of this pattern occur—that is, where a balanced, open four-cycle exists—are counted and weighted temporally. The larger this quantity, the higher the expected probability that a statement is soon made that closes this balanced four-cycle. A similar model term can be designed for *negatively balanced four-cycles*, in which the two actors mention statements in opposing ways more than once. Both model terms operationalize the idea of coalition formation by adopting each other's opinions.

Many more complex endogenous dependency statistics can be defined and added to an empirical model of the discourse at hand. Any count over the previous statements is allowed, possibly in combination with exogenous data. This flexibility allows the researcher to specify any kind of theoretical process that may be potentially responsible for the observed sequence of statements, that is, for the topology of the policy debate. As in an ERGM context, this specification of dependency statistics must be sufficient, in the sense that it covers all endogenous dependencies between statements; otherwise the remaining coefficients cannot be interpreted in a meaningful way. To ensure that this is the case, goodness-of-fit procedures for the endogenous properties of the temporal network are an important tool. These procedures simulate new sequences of statements from the model and compare structural properties of the observed and the simulated statement sequences. If both match up well, the dependencies have been modeled sufficiently. Development of techniques for goodness-of-fit assessment is an ongoing task.

There may be several goals for such an analysis. First, a micro-level explanation of how political discourse works can be informative for the case study at hand. The models suggested here are parametric in the sense that relative weights are estimated for each model term. This permits theory development and testing. Second, inferential network analysis may help to compare the underlying mechanisms across policy debates from different institutional settings. For example, how does newspaper-based political discourse differ from other kinds of arenas, or how does political discourse in one country differ from political discourse in another country? This can be assessed by comparing the coefficients for the different model terms. And third, inferential analysis can be employed to predict the future of a policy debate, at least over a short time period. A software implementation of relational event models for bipartite signed graphs is available in the *rem* package (Brandenberger, 2016), which belongs to the *xergm* suite of *R* packages (Leifeld, Cranmer, and Desmarais, 2016). Currently, a major obstacle to inferential discourse network analysis is the lack of availability of data sets. As many statements are required for such an analysis, semiautomatic statement recognition will be an important tool for generating large data sets.

Conclusion

Discourse network analysis is a versatile methodological approach, which combines qualitative, category-based content analysis with the full array of descriptive and inferential network analysis. It has been used to describe the structure of policy debates and to derive interesting quantities of debates like the degree of polarization, the presence of coalitions, coalition-switching behavior of actors, brokerage, and cohesion or congruence of coalitions, as well as the dynamics of policy debates over time. Such a descriptive mixed-methods approach to the analysis of empirical political discourse is useful for operationalizing important aspects of public policy frameworks like advocacy coalitions, discourse coalitions, policy brokers, issue attention cycles, political waves, or frames. Moreover, in contrast to prevalent empirical approaches to policy networks, it offers a temporally explicit process perspective rather than an analysis of cross-sections of a policy network (e.g., using interview data). The approach comes with its own validity and reliability issues (Leifeld, 2013, 2016b), just like other approaches, but it paves the way for a new array of research questions related to endogenous processes in policy processes, especially with regard to policy beliefs and subsystem dynamics. A promising avenue for future research is the application of specialized inferential network analysis techniques for understanding the data-generating process that governs policy debates and ultimately for predicting political discourse.

Three pertinent problems plague discourse network analysis, and current and future research needs to tackle these issues. First, semiautomatic statement recognition is an active research frontier that has the potential to save a tremendous amount of manual coding efforts and at the same time potentially increase the reliability of the coding. The most promising directions may be a supervised, multistep prediction procedure based on named entity recognition, or syntactic parsing combined with a classification of identified nodes into meta-categories. Second, methods of inferential network analysis for bipartite signed graphs with time-stamped edges need to be implemented and improved to render inference from political debates a routine task (Brandenberger, 2016; Leifeld and Brandenberger, 2016). And third, abstractions from the actor-concept-sentiment coding scheme can offer interesting operationalizations of other policy theories or frameworks. For example, one could devise coding schemes for political claims analysis (Koopmans and Statham, 1999) or the narrative policy framework (Jones and McBeth, 2010) by redefining statements to contain variables such as "addressee" or "hero" and by defining sensible criteria for deriving networks from these structured data. These new developments will greatly facilitate the comparison of empirical discourses across space, time, arena, institutional context, and theoretical framework.

REFERENCES

Baumgartner, F. R., and Jones, B. D. (1991). "Agenda Dynamics and Policy Subsystems." *Journal of Politics* 53(4): 1044–1074.

Brandenberger, L. M. (2016). "rem: Relational Event Models (REM)." R package version 1.1.2. http://CRAN.R-project.org/package=rem.

Brandenberger, L. M., Schläpfer, I., Leifeld, P., and Fischer, M. (2015). "Overlapping Subsystems: Swiss Water Policy across Media and Parliament." Paper presented at the International Conference on Public Policy, Milan, Italy, July 1–4.

Brandes, U., and Wagner, D. (2004). "Visone—Analysis and Visualization of Social Networks." In *Graph Drawing Software*, edited by M. Jünger and P. Mutzel, pp. 321–340. Berlin/Heidelberg: Springer.

Breindl, Y. (2013). "Discourse Networks on State-Mandated Access Blocking in Germany and France." *info* 15(6): 42–62.

Broadbent, J., and Vaughter, P. (2014). "Inter-Disciplinary Analysis of Climate Change and Society: A Network Approach." In *Understanding Society and Natural Resources: Forging New Strands of Integration across the Social Sciences*, edited by M. J. Manfredo, J. J. Vaske, A. Rechkemmer, and E. A. Duke, pp. 203–228. Heidelberg/Berlin: Springer.

Brutschin, E. (2013). "Dynamics in EU Policy-Making: The Liberalization of the European Gas Market." PhD thesis, University of Konstanz, Department of Politics and Public Administration. http://nbn-resolving.de/urn:nbn:de:bsz:352-253135.

Butts, C. (2008). "A Relational Event Framework for Social Action." *Sociological Methodology* 38(1): 155–200.

Cisneros, P. (2015). "Subsystem Interconnectedness as Part of Coalition Strategies for Policy Change: Mining and Water Management in Ecuador between 1991 and 2010." Paper presented at the International Conference on Public Policy (ICPP), Milan, Italy, July 1–4.

Downs, A. (1972). "Up and Down with Ecology—The 'Issue Attention Cycle.'" *The Public Interest* 28(1): 38–50.

Fisher, D. R., Leifeld, P., and Iwaki, Y. (2013). "Mapping the Ideological Networks of American Climate Politics." *Climatic Change* 116(3): 523–545. doi:10.1007/s10584-012-0512-7.

Fisher, D. R., Waggle, J., and Leifeld, P. (2013). "Where Does Political Polarization Come From? Locating Polarization within the U.S. Climate Change Debate." *American Behavioral Scientist* 57(1): 70–92. doi:10.1177/0002764212463360.

Foucault, M. (1991). *Die Ordnung der Diskurse*. Frankfurt am Main: Fischer.

Girvan, M., and Newman, M. E. J. (2002). "Community Structure in Social and Biological Networks." *Proceedings of the National Academy of Sciences* 99(12): 7821–7826.

Gkiouzepas, G., and Botetzagias, I. (2015). "Climate Change Coverage in Greek Newspapers (2001-2008): A 'Polarized Pluralist' Coverage?" *Environmental Communication*. doi:10.1080/17524032.2015.1047888.

Goffman, E. (1974). *Frame Analysis: An Essay on the Organization of Experience*. London: Harper & Row.

Haas, P. (1992). "Introduction: Epistemic Communities and International Policy Coordination." *International Organization* 46(1): 1–35.

Habermas, J. (1981). *Theorie des kommunikativen Handelns*. Frankfurt am Main: Suhrkamp.

Hajer, M. A. (1993). "Discourse Coalitions and the Institutionalization of Practice: The Case of Acid Rain in Britain." In *The Argumentative Turn in Policy Analysis and Planning*, edited by F. Fischer and J. Forester, pp. 43–76. Durham, NC: Duke University Press.

Hajer, M. A. (1995). *The Politics of Environmental Discourse: Ecological Modernization and the Policy Process*. Oxford: Oxford University Press.

Hall, P. A. (1993). "Policy Paradigms, Social Learning, and the State: The Case of Economic Policymaking in Britain." *Comparative Politics* 25(3): 275–296.

Hanneke, S., Fu, W., and Xing, E. P. (2010). "Discrete Temporal Models of Social Networks." *Electronic Journal of Statistics* 4: 585–605.

Haunss, S., Dietz, M., and Nullmeier, F. (2013). "Der Ausstieg aus der Atomenergie: Diskursnetzwerkanalyse als Beitrag zur Erklärung einer radikalen Politikwende." *Zeitschrift für Diskursforschung* 3: 288–315.

Herweg, S. (2013). "Politische Diskursnetzwerke und der Konflikt um das Anti-Piraterie-Abkommen ACTA." Center for International Political Economy at the Free University of Berlin, Papers on International Political Economy (PIPE) 15. http://nbn-resolving.de/urn:nbn:de:101:1-2013072310046.

Hurka, S., and Nebel, K. (2013). "Framing and Policy Change after Shooting Rampages: A Comparative Analysis of Discourse Networks." *Journal of European Public Policy* 20(3): 390–406.

Janning, F., Leifeld, P., Malang, T., and Schneider, V. (2009). "Diskursnetzwerkanalyse. Überlegungen zur Theoriebildung und Methodik." In *Politiknetzwerke: Modelle, Anwendungen und Visualisierungen*, edited by V. Schneider, F. Janning, P. Leifeld, and T. Malang, pp. 59–92. Wiesbaden: VS Verlag.

Jones, M. D., and McBeth, M. K. (2010). "A Narrative Policy Framework: Clear Enough to be Wrong?" *Policy Studies Journal* 38(2): 329–353.

Koopmans, R. (1996). "New Social Movements and Changes in Political Participation in Western Europe." *West European Politics* 19(1): 28–50.

Koopmans, R., and Statham, P. (1999). "Political Claims Analysis: Integrating Protest Event and Political Discourse Approaches." *Mobilization: An International Quarterly* 4(2): 203–221.

Labianca, G., and Brass, D. J. (2006). "Exploring the Social Ledger: Negative Relationships and Negative Asymmetry in Social Networks in Organizations." *Academy of Management Review* 31(3): 596–614.

Leifeld, P. (2013). "Reconceptualizing Major Policy Change in the Advocacy Coalition Framework. A Discourse Network Analysis of German Pension Politics." *Policy Studies Journal* 41(1): 169–198. doi:10.1111/psj.12007.

Leifeld, P. (2014). "Polarization of Coalitions in an Agent-Based Model of Political Discourse." *Computational Social Networks* 1(1): 7. doi:10.1186/s40649-014-0007-y.

Leifeld, P. (2016a). Discourse Network Analyzer (DNA). A Java-Based Software for Qualitative Data Analysis with Network Export. Version 2.0. http://www.github.com/leifeld/dna.

Leifeld, P. (2016b). *Policy Debates as Dynamic Networks: German Pension Politics and Privatization Discourse*. Frankfurt am Main/New York: Campus.

Leifeld, P., and Brandenberger, L. M. (2016). "Endogenous Coalition Formation in Policy Debates." Poster presented at the 9th Annual Political Networks Conference, Washington University in St. Louis, MO, USA, June 23-25, 2016, Working Paper.

Leifeld, P., Cranmer, S. J., and Desmarais B. A. (2016). "Temporal Exponential Random Graph Models with xergm: Estimation and Bootstrap Confidence Intervals." R Package Vignette for the xergm Package Version 1.7.0. http://cran.r-project.org/package=xergm.

Leifeld, P., and Haunss, S. (2012). "Political Discourse Networks and the Conflict over Software Patents in Europe." *European Journal of Political Research* 51(3): 382–409. doi:10.1111/j.1475-6765.2011.02003.x.

Lerner, J., Bussmann, M., Snijders, T. A. B., and Brandes, U. (2013). "Modeling Frequency and Type of Interaction in Event Networks." *Corvinus Journal of Sociology and Social Policy* 1: 3–32.

Leydesdorff, L. (2008). "On the Normalization and Visualization of Author Co-Citation Data: Salton's Cosine versus the Jaccard Index." *Journal of the American Society for Information Science and Technology* 59(1): 77–85.

Mayer, I. (2015). "Fuel Poverty in Germany. An Inquiry into Its Material and Ideational Dimensions." PhD Thesis, University of Konstanz, Department of Politics and Public Administration.

Muller, A. (2014a). "Het meten van beleidscontroverse en polarisatie met discoursnetwerkanalyse: De case van het abortusdebat in de Belgische Kamer (1972–1990)." *Sociologos. Tijdschrift voor Sociologie* 35(3): 159–184.

Muller, A. (2014b). "Het meten van discourscoalities met discoursnetwerkanalyse: Naar een formele analyse van het politieke vertoog." *Res Publica* 56(3): 337–364.

Muller, A. (2015). "Using Discourse Network Analysis to Measure Discourse Coalitions: Towards a Formal Analysis of Political Discourse." *World Political Science* 11(2): 377-404. doi:10.1515/wps-2015-0009.

Nagel, M. (2015). *Polarisierung im politischen Diskurs. Eine Netzwerkanalyse zum Konflikt um "Stuttgart 21"*. Wiesbaden: Springer/VS.

Nägler, R. (2015). "Without a Partner. The Idea of Cooperation in Higher Education Discourses." Paper presented at the International Conference on Public Policy (ICPP), Milan, Italy, July 1–4. http://ssrn.com/abstract=2633108.

Newman, M. E. J. (2006). "Modularity and Community Structure in Networks." *Proceedings of the National Academy of Sciences* 103(23): 8577–8582.

Newman, M. E. J. (2011). "Communities, Modules, and Large-Scale Structure in Networks." *Nature Physics* 8: 25–31.

Newman, M. E. J., and Girvan, M. (2004). "Finding and Evaluating Community Structure in Networks." *Physical Review E* 69(2): 026113.

Rantala, S., and Di Gregorio, M. (2014). "Multistakeholder Environmental Governance in Action: REDD+ Discourse Coalitions in Tanzania." *Ecology and Society* 19(2): 66–76.

Rein, M., and Schön, D. (1993). "Reframing Policy Discourse." In *The Argumentative Turn in Policy Analysis and Planning*, edited by F. Fischer and J. Forester, pp. 145–166. Durham, NC: Duke University Press.

Rinscheid, A. (2015). "Crisis, Policy Discourse, and Major Policy Change: Exploring the Role of Subsystem Polarization in Nuclear Energy Policymaking." *European Policy Analysis* 1(2): 34–70.

Rinscheid, A., Eberlein, B., and Schneider, V. (2015). "Complex Policy Trajectories in Risk Domains: Nuclear Power in Canada, Germany and Japan." Paper presented at the International Conference on Public Policy (ICPP), Milan, Italy, July 1–4.

Robins, G., Pattison, P., Kalish, Y., and Lusher, D. (2007). "An Introduction to Exponential Random Graph (p*) Models for Social Networks." *Social Networks* 29(2): 173–191.

Roth, C., and Bourgine, P. (2005). "Epistemic Communities: Description and Hierarchic Categorization." *Mathematical Population Studies* 12(2): 107–130.

Sabatier, P. A. (1988). "An Advocacy Coalition Framework of Policy Change and the Role of Policy-Oriented Learning Therein." *Policy Sciences* 21: 129–168.

Sabatier, P. A., and Weible, C. M. (2007). "The Advocacy Coalition Framework. Innovations and Clarifications." In *Theories of the Policy Process*, edited by P. A. Sabatier, pp. 189–220. Boulder, CO: Westview Press.

Schneider, V., and Ollmann, J. K. (2013). "Punctuations and Displacements in Policy Discourse: The Climate Change Issue in Germany 2007–2010." In *Environmental Change and Sustainability*, edited by S. Silvern and S. Young, pp. 157–183. Rijeka: InTech.

Shanahan, E. A., Jones, M. D., and McBeth, M. K. (2011). "Policy Narratives and Policy Processes." *Policy Studies Journal* 39(3): 535–561.

Snijders, T. A. B., van de Bunt, G. G., and Steglich, C. E. G. (2010). "Introduction to Stochastic Actor-Based Models for Network Dynamics." *Social Networks* 32(1): 44–66.

Steensland, B. (2008). "Why Do Policy Frames Change? Actor-Idea Coevolution in Debates Over Welfare Reform." *Social Forces* 86(3): 1027–1054.

Stoddart, M. C. J., Ramos, H., and Tindall, D. B.(2015). "Environmentalists' Mediawork for Jumbo Pass and the Tobeatic Wilderness, Canada: Combining Text-Centred and Activist-Centred Approaches to News Media and Social Movements." *Social Movement Studies* 14(1): 75–91.

Stoddart, M. C. J., and Tindall, D. B. (2015). "Canadian News Media and the Cultural Dynamics of Multilevel Climate Governance, 1999–2010." *Environmental Politics* 24(3): 401–422.

Tosun, J., and Schaub, S. (2015): "To Mobilize or Not: Political Attention and the Regulation of GMOs." Paper presented at the Seventh International Conference on Coexistence between Genetically Modified (GM) and non-GM based Agricultural Supply Chains (GMCC-15), Amsterdam, The Netherlands, November 17–20.

Wagner, P., and Payne, D. (2015). "Trends, Frames and Discourse Networks: Analysing the Coverage of Climate Change in Irish Newspapers." *Irish Journal of Sociology*. doi:10.7227/IJS.0011.

Werner, C. (2015). "The Relevance of Left and Right in EU Affairs: A Case Study of German Parliament Debates on the Greek Crisis." Paper presented at the Conference "Democracy: A Citizen Perspective," Turku, Finland, May 27–28.

Wolfsfeld, G. (2001). "Political Waves and Democratic Discourse: Terrorism Waves during the Oslo Peace Process." In *Mediated Politics: Communication in the Future of Democracy*, edited by W. L. Bennett and R. M. Entman, pp. 226–251. Cambridge, UK: Cambridge University Press.

Wolfsfeld, G., and Sheafer, T. (2006). "Competing Actors and the Construction of Political News: The Contest over Waves in Israel." *Political Communication* 23(3): 333–354.

Wu, J., and Zhou, L. (2015). "DOBNet: Exploiting the Discourse of Deception Behaviour to Uncover Online Deception Strategies." *Behaviour & Information Technology* 34(9): 939–948. doi:10.1080/0144929X.2015.1016116.

Yun, S.-J., Dowan, K., Park, N.-B., and Han, J. (2014). "Framing Climate Change as an Economic Opportunity in South Korean Newspapers." *Development and Society* 43(2): 219–238.

CHAPTER 13

....

SEMANTIC NETWORKS AND APPLICATIONS IN PUBLIC OPINION RESEARCH

....

SIJIA YANG AND SANDRA GONZÁLEZ-BAILÓN

INTRODUCTION

....

ON June 26, 2015, the US Supreme Court issued a landmark ruling, granting same-sex couples the constitutional right to marry across states. This court decision was made against the backdrop of already shifting public opinion: while only eleven states plus the District of Columbia recognized the right to same-sex marriage when the ruling was issued, more than half of Americans supported their homosexual peers' right to marry legally (Liptak, 2015). In 2001 the ratio of supporters versus opponents to same-sex marriage was 35 percent versus 57 percent (Pew, 2015); the difference had been as great as 12.6 percent versus 71.9 percent in 1988 (Baunach, 2012). What has happened over the past two and a half decades to reverse the state of public opinion about same-sex marriage? How do people understand the issue of marriage equality, as well as their position on the debate? What are the reasons, beliefs, and values underlying people's aggregated responses to the support/oppose question asked in polls and surveys, the instruments commonly used to measure public opinion? And how are those cognitions connected to each other in public discussions and political debates? Do those associations vary across demographic groups? The analysis of semantic networks can help answer these and related questions.

Semantic network analysis offers a representational framework and a set of modeling strategies to analyze language and the opinions expressed as a relational structure (van Atteveldt, 2008; Baden, 2010; Borge-Holthoefer and Arenas, 2010; Carley and Kaufer, 1993; Carley and Palmquist, 1992; Corman et al., 2002; Danowski, 2009; Diesner and Carley, 2010; Doerfel and Connaughton, 2009; Fisher, Leifeld, and Iwaki, 2012; Popping, 2006; Steyvers and Tenenbaum, 2005). Semantic networks offer a quantitative approach to discourse and language that can also accommodate qualitative tools for data collection, analysis, and interpretation. Semantic networks differ from social network analysis in that the nodes are not social actors (e.g., citizens, nongovernmental organizations [NGOs], political parties), but semantic concepts (e.g., names, places, organizations, policies, values); ties are not social relationships (e.g., friendships) but associations between concepts (e.g., co-occurrence). However, the same metrics and analytical procedures used to analyze social networks can be applied to the study of semantic networks, with the caveat that interpretation will vary depending on the domain of the data.

Since large-scale textual data such as political news coverage, transcripts of politicians' statements and debates, and social media posts and commentary from the public are readily available in today's digital era, the chapter offers an introduction to commonly used natural language processing (NLP) and text mining techniques that can help researchers exploit those data sources. These automated methods can be employed to extract from raw textual data semantic information that is necessary to construct a semantic network, and they complement more traditional approaches like manual coding (now also made more scalable thanks to crowdsourcing platforms; see Benoit et al., 2016). We also offer a discussion of methodological choices that are required to connect research questions with data. These include deciding on the level of data collection (individual, interpersonal, or collective level), the abstraction of the semantic concepts (e.g., words, topics, or themes), the type of association (e.g., based on co-occurrence or other types of semantic relationships, such as causal connections), and the metrics to summarize the structural properties of the network (e.g., centrality scores, community detection).

We start by discussing state-of-the-art techniques for the construction and analysis of semantic networks, paying special attention to this approach's substantive contribution to theory building. We end the chapter with a discussion of potential applications in public opinion research, emphasizing how semantic network analysis is particularly suitable to represent and explain public opinion as conceptualized by discursive and deliberative theories of democracy (Cappella, Price, and Nir, 2002; Carpini, Cook, and Jacobs, 2004; Crespi, 1997; Gutmann and Thompson, 2004; Mendelberg, 2002; Price and Neijens, 1997). Since research on semantic network analysis is still nascent, and studies applying this methodology to public opinion research are just burgeoning, we also gather insights from applications in adjacent domains. Ultimately, our goal is to introduce this methodology to political scientists (and, more generally, social scientists) to showcase its potential to develop public opinion research in new and exciting directions.

What Is a Semantic Network?

Networks offer a general and flexible representational system that captures interdependence among entities and helps model those patterns of interconnection

(Borgatti, Martin, and Johnson, 2013; Newman, Barabási, and Watts, 2006; Scott, 2012; Wasserman and Faust, 1994). In the analysis of semantic networks, the first and most important question is: What semantic units need to be represented? The question that follows is: What relationships need to be mapped? In other words, researchers start by identifying the nodes to be analyzed and operationalizing the definition of a tie. The answer to these questions depends on the research goals and the availability of data. In general, though, there are two main possibilities: to define networks that map relationships between semantic units (e.g., co-occurrence of words in political discourse); and to define networks that map the association of actors with concepts (e.g., policymakers and their statements). Figure 13.1 illustrates these two types of networks.

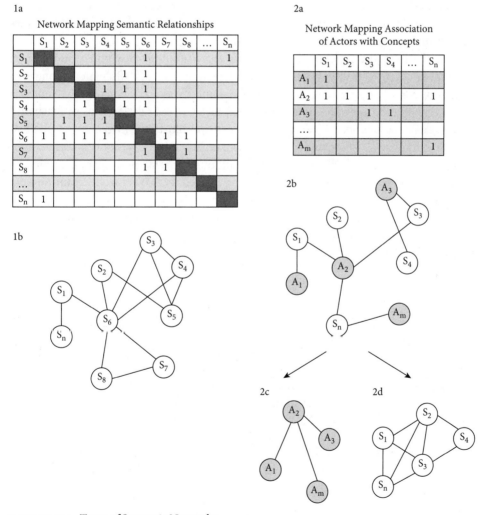

FIGURE 13.1 Types of Semantic Networks.

Panels 1a and 1b in Figure 13.1 show a schematic representation of a network of semantic relationships, both as a square matrix $S_{n \times n}$ and as a graph. Since the matrix is symmetrical (i.e., the upper and lower triangles are identical), the network is undirected. The cell values could indicate a binary semantic relationship (e.g., two concepts co-occur or not) or a continuous count, in which case the network would be weighted and the cell values would indicate to what degree two concepts are semantically related (e.g., the number of times two concepts co-occur). Panels 2a-2b show an actor-concept network, again in its matrix form, $A_{m \times n}$, and as a bipartite graph. Here ties measure an actor's level of endorsement of a semantic unit or concept; again, cell values can either indicate endorsement as a binary relation or give a measure of strength. As with any bipartite network, there are two types of network projections: the actor-to-actor network (panel 2c), in which ties indicate how many concepts any two actors share in their discourses, and the concept-to-concept network (panel 2d), in which ties indicate the number of actors that commonly use any pair of concepts. We expand on each of these representations and illustrate their applications in political science in the following sections.

Since the literature on semantic networks spans multiple disciplines and lacks a coherent theoretical framework, we decided to structure our discussion along two dimensions: the *level of analysis* (i.e., individual, interpersonal, and collective) and the *type of semantic network* (i.e., a network mapping semantic relationships or a network mapping associations between actors and concepts, as illustrated in figure 13.1). To illustrate how the analysis of semantic networks can make a significant contribution to public opinion research, we discuss applications in four of the six possible cells created by the two dimensions we consider, summarized in table 13.1. We introduce and discuss examples drawn from the existing literature and assess their implications for scientific progress in the following domains: cognitive mapping of opinion formation, discourse analysis with concept-to-concept and actor-to-actor network projections, and research on framing and issue salience.

Table 13.1 Examples of Semantic Network Analysis

Level of Analysis	Type of Application	
	Concept-to-Concept	Actor-to-Actor
Individual	cognitive mapping (figure 13.1, panel 1)	
Interpersonal	discourse network analysis—concept congruence/conflict network (figure 13.1, panel 2d)	discourse network analysis—actor congruence/conflict network; discursive fields (figure 13.1, panel 2c)
Collective	salience and framing (figure 13.1, panel 1)	future research

Networks Mapping Sematic Relationships

Cognitive mapping, salience, and framing research relies on networks that only consider relationships among semantic units or concepts; that is, such applications do not consider actor-concept endorsement. While *cognitive mapping* treats the individual as the basic unit of analysis and focuses on the mental representations of external entities (e.g., political issues like same-sex marriage), the other two applications operate on aggregated semantic data produced by a collective of individuals or social actors. For example, by analyzing media coverage of the issue of same-sex marriage rights over time, media frames can be identified from aggregated semantic data of news coverage; similarly, frames adopted by the general public can also be extracted from social media by aggregating the opinions expressed publicly. The distinction between *salience* (e.g., network agenda setting; see Guo, 2012; Vargo et al., 2014) and *framing* (Baden, 2010; Miller, 1997) research at the collective level on the one hand, and *discourse network analysis* (Leifeld, 2013; Leifeld and Haunss, 2012) at the interpersonal level on the other, is that at the interpersonal level, information on who issued what expressions or endorsed what beliefs is retained as a key part of the analysis, but is not explicitly considered in research at the collective level.

Cognitive mapping and its closely related application *mental model mapping* are commonly used by computational linguists and cognitive psychologists. Compared with cognitive mapping, which focuses more on interdependence among lower-level concepts, *mental models* more typically deal with composite cognitions such as causal belief structures (Carley and Palmquist, 1992; Diesner and Carley, 2011; Morgan et al., 2001). However, both applications emphasize the complexities within an individual's cognitive representation and share a common methodological framework. Typically, the matrix S is formed by words directly extracted from some corpus of textual data, and the cell values are typically some type of collocation relationship (e.g., co-occurrence in a size-n moving window, in the same paragraph, sequentially in the same utterance). However, other semantic relationships such as perceived causal relations can also be encoded in the matrix (Morgan et al., 2001; Young, 1996). For computational linguists and cognitive psychologists, collocations in text are assumed to encode semantic affinities that go above and beyond syntactic and grammatical restrictions (Borge-Holthoefer and Arenas, 2010; Steyvers and Tenenbaum, 2005). Frequent collocations extracted from sliced utterances, or "free association tasks,"[1] are taken to represent semantic relatedness (Collins and Loftus, 1975; McRae and Jones, 2013); this includes, but is not limited to, comembership in a same category (e.g., *robin* and *raven* are both *bird*), concepts with similar features (e.g., the geographic contour of *China* and the physical shape of *rooster*), and thematic relations (e.g., *bread* and *butter*).

Associative models of semantic representation emphasize that meanings of words and concepts lie in patterns of word-word associations. Researchers further attempt to link network-level properties of collocation patterns with the evolution and functions of human language, as well as cognitive processes and functions at the individual level. For example, it has been shown that large-scale human lexical semantic networks such as the WordNet and the University of South Florida English Free Association Norms display both small-world properties (high clustering coefficient and low average path length; see Newman, 2000; Watts and Strogatz, 1998) and long-tailed degree distributions (Barabási, 2009; Steyvers, 2005). One study has also shown that more creative people can be distinguished from their "cliché thinking" peers based on the *small-worldness* of free association networks (Kenett, Anaki, and Faust, 2014). Noticeably, small-worldness is a network-level property that cannot be identified by merely counting word frequencies or using conventional methods like self-reported survey; it can only be captured by analyzing the entire semantic network.

Metrics calculated on the basis of individual semantic networks offer another class of individual-level attributes that can be used to predict attitudinal and behavioral changes, which creates a point of connection with persuasion research. For example, cognitions or beliefs occupying more central positions in a mental model are likely to be more consequential for individual behavior than beliefs with similar levels of accessibility but lower centrality scores. A recent study shows that, indeed, the most central cognitions (e.g., goals and values) of farmers correlate better with their adoption of sustainable practices (Hoffman, Lubell, and Hillis, 2014). In the political domain, cognitive mapping has been used to characterize the mental models and belief structures of political leaders as revealed in their public statements; and structural features of these mental models were further found to explain policy initiatives (Kim, 2004).

Since it is usually difficult to gather data on the beliefs and opinions of political elites, their public statements become an important source of data reflecting their psychological states and processes. Crucially, in Kim's (2004) study, the mental models of two political leaders were formed by similar cognitions; it was the way in which those cognitions were structured that seemed to have made a difference in the political initiatives they advocated. Even though this paper analyzed only two mental models, one can expand this line of work by identifying a list of relevant network statistics (e.g., density, centrality, community structure) that are psychologically meaningful and analyze their association with behavioral outcomes in a larger sample of political actors.

Individual-level semantic network has also been used to reveal another dimension of political discourse: persuasiveness. For example, Doerfel and Connaughton (2009) analyzed an archive of speeches made during televised presidential debates from 1960 to 2004 and extracted co-occurrence semantic networks for every candidate. They found that a semantic network characterized by a tightly clustered group of concepts predicted election winning. In this case, semantic network analysis offers an empirical tool to test whether a discourse that is coherently structured along central themes is more persuasive than one with multiple topics. These properties are relatively difficult to unravel using frequency counts of specific words, yet are naturally foregrounded when the entire discourse is viewed as a semantic network.

In research on salience and framing, the analyst aggregates mental models across a collective of individuals but the process excludes the mapping of "who said what" from the analysis. The construction of aggregated semantic networks offers a unique approach to content analysis—a well-established method in the study of political communication (Althaus et al., 2011; Grimmer and Stewart, 2013; Krippendorff, 2012)—and complements frequency-based techniques by emphasizing the structural properties of the corpus under analysis (van Atteveldt, 2008; Carley and Palmquist, 1992; Diesner and Carley, 2011). Researchers adopting the semantic network approach have expanded theories on public opinion formation by highlighting the importance of associations and the relational nature of belief structures. For example, research on agenda setting shows that political elites represented in the media have a persuasive impact on public attitudes, opinions, and policy support (McCombs and Shaw, 1972; Zaller, 1992). A recent study compared the semantic networks of mass media outlets with semantic networks of Obama and Romney supporters during the 2012 presidential election cycle, both constructed from a large corpus of 38 million Twitter messages (Vargo et al., 2014). The findings suggest that media shape not only the salience of issues and issue attributes in public discussions, but also how those issues are coreferenced and linked to each other (i.e., network issue agenda-setting).

The meso-level properties of semantic networks, such as their community structure, offer a different way to operationalize frames. If *frames* are defined as patterns of closely interconnected concepts, semantic networks make it possible to analyze interframe relationships such as how focal frames are associated with other elements of the political discourse (Baden, 2010). For example, for a given policy issue, multiple frames could be put forth to the public without referring to and elaborating upon each other. In a semantic network, this would result in a number of loosely connected communities with few between-community ties. Alternatively, parties could choose to structure their public statements around a few central frames and use other peripheral frames to further explicate these core frames. This would lead to a core-peripheral structure in the semantic network. Treating frames as self-contained semantic entities and analyzing frequency distribution of frames alone will miss these important structural patterns specifying how frames are connected to each other. In the case of the Dutch referendum campaign on the European Union (EU) constitution, parties structured the whole discourse around a few central frames that were often composed of dialectically opposing claims; more important, these central frames did not stand alone but were connected to a series of supportive—though more peripheral—frames (Baden, 2010). Semantic network analysis offers a flexible and systematic tool to identify and compare frames in this context-sensitive way and can reveal nuanced and interesting interframe connection patterns.

Applied to public opinion research, these ideas are useful to reveal the complexities of opinion formation and can provide new information to describe shifts in public opinion as a path-dependent process. At the individual level, semantic networks can reveal the key cognitions (e.g., beliefs and values) that are responsible for the opinions held and provide guidelines to evaluate normative implications and even possible interventions (such as when opinions are based on misconceptions). When aggregated to the group or population level, this type of semantic network can be compared and contrasted, which can help identify groups and demographic segments that employ (dis)similar frames when discussing a political issue; population-level semantic networks (as reconstructed from, say, social media) can be further compared with the networks of political elites, and with the appropriate time resolution, can be used to test temporal models of opinion formation. We discuss these applications further below.

Networks Mapping the Association of Actors with Concepts

At the interpersonal level, discourse network analysis (Fisher, Leifeld, and Iwaki, 2012; Leifeld and Haunss, 2012) and research on *discursive fields* (Bail, 2012) explicitly include the information on how social actors endorse semantic units or concepts in their public discourse. The action of "endorsing" can be captured on a continuous scale (such as the number of times an actor uses a word) or as a binary variable, as represented in figure 13.1, panel 2a, indicating, for example, agreement or disagreement.

There are not many studies that analyze the two-mode network connecting actors with concepts—among other reasons because the range of available tools for analyzing such networks is limited. More often, researchers project the affiliation matrix A into two square matrices: the $m \times m$ matrix of actors represented as a graph in figure 13.1, panel 2c, and the $n \times n$ matrix of concepts represented as a graph in figure 13.1, panel 2d. Ties in panel 2c and 2d are weighted by the number of common concepts two actors co-endorse (panel 2c) and the number of actors a pair of concepts share (panel 2d), respectively. It is important to acknowledge that projections of two-mode networks inherently involve information loss. In projecting the affiliation matrix A into the $m \times m$ one-mode network of actors, information on the set of concepts that link actors is lost. Implicitly, the researcher is making the assumption that all the concepts are equally important and weighted in the same way when determining actor-actor relationships. This choice prevents researchers from directly incorporating nodal attributes of concepts (e.g., whether or not the concept is related to misinformation) in the analysis. Similarly, the concept-concept one-mode projection excludes potentially important information about political actors. These weaknesses can be overcome by applying metrics and statistical methods developed specifically for two-mode networks, which are beginning to appear in the literature (e.g., Agneessens and Everett, 2013); however, in this chapter we focus the discussion on one-mode projections, as they remain the main object of analysis (for an exception, see Kleinnijenhuis and de Nooy [2013]).

The most attractive feature of reconstructing semantic networks while retaining information on actor-concept endorsement is its ability to characterize and model the discourse of specific actors. Researchers can examine how affiliation relationships among actors develop in response to their public statements, which is of relevance in the study of political coalitions and polarization during policy debates. This approach also helps investigate how public discourse becomes more complex or restricted as actors interact with and respond to each other. One exemplary application is the discourse network analysis, developed by Leifeld and colleagues (2012) to simultaneously represent the overall typology of political elites and public political expressions over time. This technique builds up the actor-concept bipartite semantic network by coding political elites' agreement or disagreement (i.e., ties are binary) with policy-related statements from textual archives (e.g., news coverage, congressional testimonials). By analyzing the concept-concept projection (in which ties represent the degree to which a concept is commonly endorsed by multiple political elites, called *concept congruence network*), the authors were able to identify rhetorical patterns of the winning side in the debate. For example, in the case of the software patents controversy in Europe, the prevailing coalition of political actors (including governments, companies, and NGOs) coherently knitted multiple concepts together, a feature missing in opponents' discourse from the other side of the controversy (Leifeld and Haunss, 2012). In the same study, the actor-actor projection whose ties encode the level of shared beliefs and positions (i.e., *actor congruence network*) empirically revealed two competing coalitions with a high degree of within-group consensus and between-group conflicts; this distinction emerged from the construction and analysis of semantic networks, that is, without imposing a grouping criterion based on subjective judgment. This discourse network analysis approach has also been used to track how consensus emerged over time on the issue of climate change in the 110th US Congress, in contrast with the bigroup structure in the 109th Congress (Fisher, Leifeld, and Iwaki, 2012). Chapter 12 in this handbook elaborates in more detail on the methodological and substantive principles behind this analytical approach.

Actor-concept semantic networks can be further complemented by incorporating other types of information. In a study on how the discourse of civil society organizations affected media coverage about Islam after the terrorist attack on September 11, 2001, researchers first positioned these organizations in the discursive field of Muslims and 911 to identify *fringe* organizations, that is, organizations occupying peripheral corners as revealed by patterns of coendorsement of Muslim-related frames (Bail, 2012). Position in the discursive field was found to significantly impact media's mirroring of frames originally adopted by these organizations. More interestingly, these fringe organizations were more likely to influence mass media coverage if their discourse displayed higher levels of emotionality. This example demonstrates that when coupled with other types of information (e.g., content attributes of the text and other characteristics of actors), semantic network analysis can significantly enrich researchers' explanatory repertoire and enable the empirical study of theories (e.g., discursive fields) otherwise difficult to operationalize. Although both the actor congruence/conflict network from discourse network analysis and Bail's (2012) study on discursive fields analyze patterns of endorsing semantic units between individual political actors, it is possible to extend this line of research to groups of actors defined by demographic status, partisanship, or other dimension that is of theoretical significance.

When applied to public opinion research, semantic network analysis is particularly suited to address questions derived from discursive and deliberative theories of opinion formation. These theories aim to analyze the generation, production, and exchange of ideas, arguments, reasons, and even sentiments—all of which can be treated as semantic units in a network. This makes the analysis of semantic networks useful to decode how the collective discourse enriches and is enriched by individuals' cognitive representations of political issues, which is core to much public opinion research (Baek, 2011; Carpini, Cook, and Jacobs, 2004; Dijk, 1995; Gutmann and Thompson, 2004). Semantic network analysis operating at the interpersonal level have so far been applied mostly to political elites, but we foresee nothing preventing researchers from analyzing other types of political actors, especially citizens engaging in political discussion or deliberation, either offline or online.

The analysis of semantic networks differs in important ways from more conventional approaches to text, such as frequency-based content analysis (Krippendorff, 2012). First, content analysis that follows a frequency-based approach focuses exclusively on the counts and distribution of concepts in a corpus; a network approach, on the other hand, adds the additional layer of how concepts are related to each other. The frequency-based approach, in other words, extracts only a text's "fundamental building blocks" but not "the structure in which these blocks are arranged" (Carley and Palmquist, 1992, 605). Second, frequency-based approaches cannot directly incorporate the social aspect of message generation and exchange, that is, the actor-concept relationships captured by the two-mode semantic network. Semantic networks have the additional advantage of being able to represent a variety of semantic units and the ways in which those units are interconnected. This information can be extracted from textual data using NLP and text-mining techniques, as explained in the following section.

BUILDING SEMANTIC NETWORKS

How to Extract Semantic Units (Nodes) from Textual Data

Collecting raw textual data. Raw textual data to construct semantic networks can be collected from various data sources, including but not limited to news coverage, political testimony before the US Congress, social media posts on Twitter and discussion forums, experimentally generated data (e.g., offline and online deliberation studies, free association tasks), recorded and transcribed utterances in natural conversations, and open-ended survey questions. For public opinion research, semantic content generated by political actors is the primary focus.

Typically, researchers interested in user-generated messages from the Internet (e.g., comment boards on news websites, Facebook and Twitter posts, discussion forums) can gain access through scrapping websites, accessing application programming interfaces (APIs), and purchasing data from vendors. Unfortunately, to date there is no single aggregator that offers easy user interface to access the whole body of ever-growing, user-generated texts across social media sites and platforms. Moreover, both ownership issues regarding commercial companies' claim to proprietary data and concerns over user privacy are likely to impact the scope and nature of accessible online semantic data. Which data source to use and through what means to access it need to be evaluated on a case-by-case basis. For instance, tweets posted by average citizens can provide insights into the current state of public opinion (Vargo et al., 2014); however, they are less ideal to examine how public opinion is formed via discursive interactions due to the character limit per tweet and the lack of prolonged discussions among typical Twitter users.

Once the data have been accessed, researchers often need to develop a valid list of keywords to retrieve a corpus that is relevant to the issue being investigated. Compared with news coverage, user-generated content is likely to include nonstandard language, slang terms, and misspellings. The keyword list for data retrieval is thus issue-specific and needs to be developed through trial and error. The performance of the keyword list can be assessed by the criteria of *precision* (i.e., low false positives, the fraction of true fits over the size of the corpus extracted and labeled as relevant) and *recall* (i.e., low false negatives, the proportion of true hits in the extracted corpus over the total set of matched texts, including those not retrieved or mistakenly labeled as irrelevant; see Manning, Raghavan, and Schütze, 2008). For example, assume a researcher wants to retrieve tweets posted in 2015 related to same-sex marriage. Using a test version of a keyword list, the researcher retrieves m tweets in total, out of which j tweets are validated as relevant. Then a point estimate for precision is the simple fraction j/m. To assess recall, the researcher needs to pull out a random sample of tweets of any kind posted during the same time window (say 1 percent of all tweets under Twitter's Firehose retrieval method). In this test sample, the researcher then removes tweets ($n_1 = k$) that are (1) already in the corpus retrieved via keyword matching and (2) classified as true hits. Next, the researcher identifies tweets related to same-sex marriage using a combination of human coding and machine classification ($n_2 = p$). The point estimate of the recall of this retrieving strategy using the particular keyword list will be $\dfrac{k}{k+p}$. Both precision and recall can be improved by adding or deleting keywords to/from the search term list.

Defining the semantic ontology. The first and most important decision prior to analyzing sematic networks is what units to extract from textual data. The primary goal of this step is to define the dimensions of the column space of the two essential matrices introduced in session 2 (i.e., S_n in figure 13.1, panels 1a and 2a). This decision should be guided by the nature and scope of the research. In general, though, two issues should be taken into consideration: first, deciding whether to take a deductive or an inductive approach to the identification of semantic units, that is, derive them from the data or identify them in text according to preconceived categories (Carley and Kaufer, 1993; Carley and Palmquist, 1992); and second, determining the level of abstraction of the semantic units to be analyzed.

The answers will largely determine the methodological techniques to employ, such as whether NLP tools and automatic text processing algorithms are needed. In this section we define an issue-specific collection of texts (e.g., newspaper coverage, public discourse transcribed into texts, testimonials from politicians) as the *corpus*. For the sake of simplicity, we assume $text_i$ is the basic unit of analysis after slicing, binning, or bracketing the corpus based on rules applied to the original documents (e.g., aggregating all the tweets collected on the same day as a single *text*). We focus our discussion primarily on applications related to individual- and collective-level concept-concept semantic networks (e.g., cognitive mapping, salience, and framing research in table 13.1), because procedures to construct political discourse networks at the interpersonal level are discussed in detail in Chapter 12 of this handbook. Methodological considerations discussed below also apply, however, to discourse network analysis, although it typically requires additional layers of complexity—that is, to identify actor-concept mappings from textual data. This additional step poses some unique challenges to the application of automated text-mining techniques, as political actors, semantic units, and pairwise mapping between the elements in these two categories are difficult to automatically extract from unstructured textual data all at once. As a result, current applications of discourse network analysis require human coding to fill in the $A_{m \times n}$ matrix in figure 13.1, panel 2a.

The total set of unique semantic units to be represented in the network creates the *semantic ontology* of a public issue. Often researchers have a predefined set of beliefs, values, themes, or positions they want to analyze. For example, Vargo et al. (2014) identified eight specific policy domains related to the 2012 presidential election judged relevant by researchers (e.g., *economy, foreign policy*). Since categories in a predefined semantic ontology typically represent higher-order concepts or themes that are more abstract than words in raw texts, the deductive approach implicitly poses a double-classification problem that involves determining (1) whether $text_i$ matches or mismatches with each of the categories and (2) if so, in what way (e.g., merely mentioning, positively or negatively endorsing). Both problems can be solved using human coding following standard procedures of content analysis (Krippendorff, 2012); however, if the researcher intends to employ machine learning algorithms with limited human input to achieve more efficiency, the second problem will be much harder to address than the first, especially when the dimensionality of the semantic ontology and ways relating $text_i$ to semantic units grow large. These technical difficulties are likely to be ameliorated in the future, given rapid developments in machine learning and text mining research.

The inductive approach to defining the semantic ontology is exploratory in nature. Researchers identify relevant semantic units after interacting with the raw data. For example, in the study on cognitive networks of farmers around the notion of "sustainable agriculture" and their relationship with sustainable practices, Hoffman, Lubell, and Hillis (2014) elicited unique concepts related to this issue only after inspecting collected data from an open-ended survey question. The inductive approach has the advantage of being more likely to identify novel semantic units and to portray a comprehensive picture of the totality of concepts used by the public when expressing their opinions. For these reasons, this approach is more suitable for early stages of a research project or for more descriptive and exploratory studies.

Lower-order semantic units refer to exact words or phrases used in the text after pre-processing (e.g., stemming and lemmatization; see more details below). On the other hand, higher-order semantic units lack exact one-to-one mapping to the exact words or phrases used and hence require procedures for *inference*, that is to assign meaning (i.e., the word-concept mapping) to lexical symbols used in the text (Corman et al., 2002). Most lexical semantic networks from computational linguistics, networks of association norms from cognitive psychology, and networks constructed using the "moving window" approach (Danowski, 2009; Yuan, Feng, and Danowski, 2013) choose to represent lower-order words, while political discourse networks (Leifeld, 2013; Vargo et al., 2014) tend to use higher-order semantic units. Methodologically, if the researcher is satisfied with lower-order semantic units, directly inspecting the raw text after tokenization and other preprocessing steps will reveal unique semantic units needed to define the dimensionality of the two essential matrices. However, if the researcher chooses to employ automatic textual analytical tools and analyze higher-order semantic units, the text requires more sophisticated algorithms to process, such as topic modeling, or scalable human coding using crowdsourcing platforms (Benoit et al., 2016). To reiterate, the purpose of defining the semantic ontology is to determine the column and row dimensions in matrix S (figure 13.1, panel 1a) and the columns in matrix A (figure 13.1, panel 2a).

Preprocessing of raw textual data. Once raw textual data are collected, they are usually stored as long strings of characters that need to be *tokenized* before further processing. Tokenization breaks the long string down to the smallest unit of semantic content, typically at the word level (Jurafsky and Martin, 2008). Tokenization discards the order by which words appear in the text, although using *n-grams* ($n > 1$) will partially preserve the information on word order. N-grams are contiguous sequences of words of length *n*. For example, bigrams for the short phrase "I love you" would be "I love" and "love you," each treated as a unique token. Discarding word order, known as the bag-of-word approach, is typically found to pose little harm to performance for common NLP tasks such as classification, sentiment analysis, and topic modeling (Grimmer and Stewart, 2013). However, for specific types of one-mode network of semantic relationships, such as causal mapping in the mental models tradition (Carley and Palmquist, 1992; Morgan et al., 2001), word orders convey information about the direction of the causal relationship. For this type of application, more sophisticated NLP techniques such as part-of-speech tagging and semantic role labeling, will be useful to tag tokens with additional attributes (e.g., roles as in agent-predate-patient structure; Jurafsky and Martin, 2008).

A recent study shows that using *n-grams* of different size might reveal different causal mechanisms that lead to similarity in statements produced by US Congressman. While addressing similar topics (i.e., topic similarity) was positively correlated with authors' patterns of using similar words and phrases only when the raw corpus was preprocessed with shorter *n-grams* (n < 3), working in the same chamber was positively correlated with author-author similarity in language use when longer *n-grams* were incorporated as tokens (n > 16) (Lin, Margolin, and Lazer, 2015). This suggests that independently constructing messages is likely to pose a limit on the length of phrases used, but directly copying others' statements poses no such restraint. Therefore, using n-grams of different sizes can be beneficial when the researcher has specific causal mechanisms in mind to test for public opinion formation processes, such as exposure to different media outlets with independent opinion formation (shorter n-gram) versus social learning and persuasion (longer n-gram).

From a data processing perspective, human language is "noisy." The same word can have different forms that are not immediately recognized by a computer (e.g., "U.S."/ "United States"/"U.S.A"/"America"). This issue is addressed by *stemming* and *lemmatizing*, text manipulations that aim to reduce inflectional forms of a word to a common base (Jurafsky and Martin, 2008). Typically preprocessing will also remove punctuation, capitalization, and common functional words that are used to preserve grammatical integrity rather than convey specific meanings (known as "stop-words," typically including prepositions and common verbs like "be").

After preprocessing, the set of unique tokens in the corpus becomes the semantic ontology for the political issue in question (for inductive and lower-order definition of the semantic ontology). Some specific research questions may require extracting a subset of those tokens. For example, Corman et al.'s (2002) *centering resonance analysis* only pays attention to nouns and noun phrases, while discarding verbs, subjectives, and adverbs that might also encode important semantic information about the public issue being analyzed. Decisions like this should be based on the specific application of the semantic network approach and the substantive theoretical question.

Using machine learning to identify higher-order semantic units. For *higher-order* definitions of semantic ontology, the mapping between tokens and categories (defined in the preconceived set or inferred from the data) or latent semantic dimensions (for inductive approach to higher-order semantic units) must be specified. A machine-learning approach would require as input data the term-document matrix with word frequencies after pre-processing, as well as the category labels provided by human coders. For the deductive approach, mapping poses a classification problem to which supervised machine learning algorithms can be applied, such as Naïve Bayesian, Support Vector Machine, Random Forests, Neutral Networks, and the ensemble approach (Aggarwal and Zhai, 2012). However, given the inherent complexities in human language and discourse, good performance of automatic text classification algorithms is not ensured and needs to be evaluated and validated on a case-by-case basis. Current applications (see Vargo et al., 2014) are restricted to higher-order themes (e.g., climate change, terrorist attack) rather than complicated policy statements or positions (e.g., "climate change is real and anthropologenic"). For the latter type of application, human coding remains the primary method (see Fisher, Leifeld, and Iwaki, 2012), but automatic methods are rapidly being developed.

On the other hand, the inductive approach poses a latent dimension extraction problem, in which latent semantic dimensions or topics need to be inferred from the original term-document matrix. One approach is to view this as a matrix factorization problem, in which lower-order n-grams in the original term-document matrix need to be projected into a lower-rank latent semantic space (Dumais, 2004). This is also known as *latent semantic analysis*, and the original term-document matrix can be factorized using singular value decomposition and its variants (Dumais, 2004). The underlying logic is that the latent space is a more parsimonious summarization of observed text-word co-occurrence patterns, and dimensions of this space represent the higher-order semantic themes that the researcher is attempting to uncover. Another approach assumes a probability-based generative model, in which the text is generated from a distribution of topics, which in turn can be derived from distributions of words. Popular probabilistic models such as latent dirichlet allocation (LDA; see Blei, Ng, and Jordan, 2003) is available and can help uncover latent higher-order semantic themes. After iteratively identifying the optimal solution for the topic generative model, the texts' loadings on the latent semantic dimensions can be used to define topic-by-topic relationships—that is, a semantic relationship at a higher level of abstraction than the original tokens. A potential problem with topic modeling, however, is the ambiguity in interpreting the substantive meaning of uncovered latent topics. As a result, once the semantic network is constructed, researchers might benefit from focusing on network-level properties rather than nodal structural attributes, given the node's potentially unclear substantive meaning.

How to Extract Relationships among Semantic Units (Ties) from Textual Data

The strength, sign, and directionality of ties differ in importance as the goal of research changes (Carley and Palmquist, 1992). For example, if the purpose is capturing semantic associations in general, word co-occurrence can be used to assess their strength; directionality does not matter. However, when representing causal relationships, determining the origin and destination of a directed tie is crucial to preserve causal order (Morgan et al., 2001). Ties can also be signed and map positive and negative associations, although in practice researchers tend to favor positive signs and convert semantically negative relationships into a positive number. For example, politicians' *disagreement* with a policy position can be treated as a separate semantic unit in addition to *agreement* (i.e., see Fisher, Leifeld, and Iwaki, 2012).

Ties based on co-occurrence of semantic units. In concept concept semantic networks at the individual and collective levels (e.g., cognitive mapping/mental models, salience and framing research), *ties* typically refer to affinity in a general sense, without a concrete meaning: two concepts can be related because they belong to the same higher-order category; they indicate a causal association; or they are connected in any other way, as long as they "make sense" to message producers such as in free association experiments (Borge-Holthoefer and Arenas, 2010; Marupaka, Iyer, and Minai, 2012; McRae and Jones, 2013; Steyvers and Tenenbaum, 2005). Ties representing this general form of semantic affinity do not impose restrictions on the type of concepts to work with; they can be higher- or lower-order semantic units defined deductively or inductively. In constructing this type of tie from raw textual data, researchers typically rely on counting the frequency of co-occurrence within specified boundaries: words within a moving window of size n (Danowski, 2009, Yuan, Feng, and Danowski, 2013), words within a sentence in transcribed oral speeches from top policymakers (Shim, Park, and Wilding, 2015), predefined issues and names of organizations within the same paragraph in news coverage (Kleinnijenhuis and de Nooy, 2013), predefined issues within the collection of Tweets aggregated by day (Vargo et al., 2014), or inductively derived concepts within the same person's response to open-ended survey questions (Hoffman, Lubell, and Hillis, 2014; Smith and Parrott, 2012). Some texts collected in their original form possess a natural boundary (e.g., Twitter's 140-character limit), while others lack such structure and require researchers to be sensitive to the context in which the text is produced. For example, for orally produced messages such as transcribed political debates, breaks could be placed between shorter passages—turn-takes would serve as the natural break in this context—while the opposite is expected for longer written text such as news coverage.

The obtained co-occurrence matrix based on raw frequencies may require normalization, especially for inductively derived lower-order semantic units, as the raw frequencies are likely to be dominated by a few commonly occurring words that span a great number of texts but convey little substantial meaning (e.g., the pronoun "you"). Normalization can mitigate this problem by comparing the obtained raw frequencies to a null model of expected co-occurrences when no systematic relations exist between pairs of semantic units (Baden, 2010; Griffiths and Steyvers, 2002). Researchers can then threshold or filter out raw frequencies against the distribution derived from the null model.

When applying semantic network analysis to cognitive psychology, the assumption is that mapping concept associations helps uncover how semantic memory is organized in people's minds (Collins and Loftus, 1975; Kenett, Anaki, and Faust, 2014). In this area of research, ties are generated in a lab experiment setting in which participants are asked to provide responses to predefined target words. Responses across participants are then aggregated to define to what extent a pair of target words triggers similar response patterns—the more similar the set of elicited words is, the higher the strength of the tie between two subjects. Rather than using raw counts of frequencies, correlations between pairs of target words are used to adjust for the general tendency for one particular target word to elicit, on average, more responses. In this way, all the target words are placed on the same multidimensional semantic space, spanned by the aggregated set of response words; their pairwise similarity in this space is then used to define tie strength (Kenett, Anaki, and Faust, 2014; McRae et al., 2005).

Some versions of these experiments do not rely on free associations; instead, they supply a full set of predefined concepts to participants and ask them to directly indicate level of perceived association between every pair of concepts (Guo, 2012). This method is more suitable for a smaller set of concepts, as n concepts will require $n(n - 1)/2$ judgments from each participant, which is very demanding for participants when n gets large. The idea of viewing semantic units as situated in a multidimensional space defined by the term-document matrix is particularly useful to define ties between higher-order semantic units uncovered by topic modeling. Metrics such as Euclidean distance or cosine similarity can be used to scale strength of ties.

Ties beyond co-occurrence. Although ties based on co-occurrence are popular in the early stages of semantic network research, scholars are increasingly interested in capturing more specific and substantive semantic meanings, such as cause-effect relationship in research on mental models (Morgan et al., 2001), or actors' agreement/disagreement with policy statements in discourse network analysis (Leifeld and Haunss, 2012). Young (1996) offered a summary of commonly seen categories of semantic relationships, including cause-effect, if-then, entity-attribute, warrant-for, and many more; however, what relationship to extract again depends on specific research goals. For example, researchers can use open-ended interviews and confirmatory questionnaires in an iterative fashion to assess patterns of perceived causal relationships among a set of concepts related to the issue under investigation (Morgan et al., 2001).

When the level of specificity increases, it becomes more difficult to rely on automatic machine learning algorithms. Even extending simple co-occurrence to classify relationships into positive or negative ties is not trivial. Researchers are likely to need more sophisticated NLP techniques, such as named entity recognition and disambiguation, part-of-speech tagging, and syntactic analysis to denote grammatical roles of semantic units (e.g., subject-object pairs) to facilitate the classification task (Atteveldt et al., 2008; Atteveldt, Kleinnijenhuis, and Ruigrok, 2008). This is especially true for actor-concept semantic networks when both (1) the ontology of actors and semantic units and (2) actor-concept association need to be directly extracted from the same raw textual data.

When ties map the association of actors with concepts, their meaning differs depending on the projection analyzed. In the actor-to-actor network (figure 13.1, panel 2c), a tie means that two social actors endorse the same set of semantic units. In the concept-to-concept network (panel 2d), a tie means that two semantic units are endorsed by the same set of social actors. Importantly, ties constructed in this way denote quite distinctive information in contrast to ties in networks mapping semantic relationships (figure 13.1, panel 1). While the former emphasize coendorsement patterns across the population of political actors analyzed, the latter focus on either general semantic affinity or more specific semantic meanings independent of the actor-concept association patterns.

Political scientists have applied this projection method to analyze patterns of political coalition and conflicts among political decision makers and stakeholders (Fisher, Leifeld, and Iwaki, 2012; Leifeld, 2013). When some actors are overrepresented in the data, tie weights in the network need to be normalized. For example, in the actor-policy position network, some actors may contribute disproportionately to the volume of public statements, hence covering a much wider spectrum of policy positions that define the semantic ontology (this is termed "institutional bias" by Leifeld [2013]). If no normalization is done, the analysis of the network and the resulting metrics might reflect this bias and hide meaningful relationships among actors. When original entries are binary, normalization methods such as taking the pairwise correlation coefficient are no longer valid; an alternative is using the family of Jaccard coefficients, which in its simplest form takes the fraction of the intersection between two binary vectors over their union. This coefficient also returns a value that ranges between 0 and 1. More details on this approach, and an expanded discussion of its application, can be found in Chapter 12.

Applications in Public Opinion Research

Classic models treat public opinion as an "emergent product" of interpersonal discussions and social relationships, free and uncensored in procedures, and supported by rational and well-informed arguments (Blumer, 1946; Lazarsfeld, 1957; Price, 1992). Later empirical research found this approach difficult to operationalize, and over time surveys and polls have become the preferred tools to represent the opinion of the public (Converse, 1987). Reflecting on the deficiencies of using surveys to represent public opinion, noticeably because of their disconnection with public discussions, scholars have recently made attempts to refine the measurement tools, including deliberative opinion polls (Fishkin, 1991, 1997). Recent theorists of deliberative democracy place a large weight on citizens' discursive interactions and activities in the political decision-making process (Carpini, Cook, and Jacobs, 2004; Dryzek and Niemeyer, 2008; Fishkin, 1997; Gutmann and Thompson, 2004; Mendelberg, 2002). This involves paying attention to responsiveness to arguments, the extensiveness of the information on which opinions are based, their consistency with values, and the overall stability of opinion—all important dimensions to evaluate the quality of public opinion. The empirical operationalization of these criteria requires a way of representing the full spectrum of arguments, reasons, beliefs, and concepts that are used during discursive interactions; the flexibility to switch between levels of analysis (i.e., from the individual to the collective and population levels); and tools to model changes in the structure of the opinion-related semantic ontology over time. The analysis of semantic networks offers a framework to empirically address these requirements and can serve as a useful tool to study public opinion in its complexity.

In the existing literature, typical applications of semantic network analysis focus on elite political discourse (Baden, 2010; Doerfel and Connaughton, 2009; Fisher, Leifeld, and Iwaki, 2012; Kleinnijenhuis and de Nooy, 2013; Leifeld, 2013; Lin, Margolin, and Lazer, 2015); very few studies have taken advantage of this methodology to study the public's political discourse (for an exception, see Vargo et al. [2014]). Part of the reason is the difficulty of gathering data on political discussions among average citizens in their everyday lives. However, given the explosion of social media and online interactions, in which discursive political exchanges happen naturally, the problem of data access is now considerably mitigated (although issues of representativeness remain). Moreover, semantic network analysis can also handle discussion data generated and collected in more controlled settings, such as online deliberation experiments (Cappella, Price, and Nir, 2002; Price, Nir, and Cappella, 2006) and structured online town hall meetings (Minozzi et al., 2015). Following these developments, we summarize existing and potential applications of semantic networks to the study of public opinion, following the categorization scheme outlined in table 13.1.

A citizen's cognitive representation of a public issue can be mapped out as a semantic network that contains both "cognitions" and "how these cognitions are connected" (Carley and Palmquist, 1992; Johnson-Laird, 2010; Morgan et al., 2001; Popping, 2006), with the nature of ties varying from general associations to specific types like perceived causal relationships. Most public opinion research is concerned with evaluative judgments (e.g., support or oppose); mapping the full range of concepts underlying those judgments can reveal more information about individual issue positions. Carley et al. (1992, 1993) pioneered the methodology to automatically reconstruct mental semantic networks from texts generated by individuals, paving the way for empirical researchers to process large-scale textual data. One potential challenge of this application is the possible discrepancy between written text and genuine thoughts: individuals might generate messages in a biased way for impression management, as a result of social pressure, or to achieve other types of strategic goals.

Another possibility at this level of analysis is to use polls and surveys to reconstruct associations between belief systems and attitudes. This creates a more complex relational account of what underlies political opinions and helps identify types of electorate on the basis of their similarities and differences in the entire system of beliefs (Baldassarri and Goldberg, 2014). More research is needed, however, to appropriately link mental representations with actor networks.

Once a network is constructed, it can be analyzed as any other network object, and researchers can focus on different structural properties in line with the research questions posed. At the node level, a popular measure of a semantic unit's structural importance is its centrality score. Based on betweenness and degree centralities, Shim, Park, and Wilding (2015) offered a typology that classifies nodes into (1) hub for the entire network (high on both centrality measures), (2) hub for the local meaning community (high on degree but low on betweenness centrality), (3) bridges (high on betweenness but low on degree centrality), and (4) peripherals (low on both centrality measures). Interpreting and categorizing nodes in the mental semantic network provides information about *structural* properties, which can be analyzed later along with other nodal attributes the researcher might have data on already. For example, if the researcher knows which cognitions are misconceptions, he or she can identify when misconceptions occupy the hub position in networks and when they are peripheral, then use this structural variation to explain different responses to persuasive attempts, beyond the fact that everyone might hold the same type of misconception.

At the meso level, the community structure of semantic networks can help operationalize concepts such as *schemata* or *frame* popular in political psychology (Lau, Smith, and Fiske, 1991; Scheufele and Tewksbury, 2007). Communities are parts of a network in which connections are denser internally than externally, as compared to what to expect in a random benchmark (e.g., a randomly generated network with the same degree sequence; see Girvan and Newman, 2002). By interpreting what these communities consist of and correspond to, researchers can gain insights into the number of dimensions an individual thinks about when considering a public issue. Methodologically, these community structures can be identified by employing community detection algorithms (Fortunato, 2010; see also Kolaczyk and Csárdi, 2014).

At the global level, even simple metrics such as the size of the semantic network and the overall density tell us how sophisticated an individual is when asked to reflect on an issue. Both the size of the entire semantic network and the number of distinctive communities serve as measures for the degree of cognitive differentiation, though with different resolutions. Compared with size, the number of communities is less likely to be biased by factors like individuals' literacy levels. Larger and more unique communities correspond to a better ability to consider unique dimensions of an issue (i.e., they are proxies for higher levels of cognitive differentiation; for a discussion on cognitive differentiation, see Conway et al. [2014] and Tetlock et al. [2014]). On the other hand, the density of the network measures cognitive integration (i.e., the ability to make connections among unique dimensions), often considered the hallmark for political sophistication (Conway et al., 2014; Tetlock et al., 2014).

When analyzing semantic networks formed by collective actors, such as organizations or groups of people, researchers can focus on identifying rhetorical attractors or disentangling the dynamics of coalition formation. A node with high centrality in the projected concept-to-concept network means that the concept is semantically related to the majority of other concepts also mentioned in the text; these concepts serve as rhetorical attractors around which the discourse converges. A node with high centrality in the projected actor-to-actor network, on the other hand, may play the role of consensus builder and help create a common denominator. In addition to centrality, all the other metrics assessing the local, meso, and macro structure of the network can be applied to characterize discourse and group dynamics. The difference is that at this level, the metrics will reflect properties of the aggregated "group mind" rather than individual mental models. For example, on the issue of energy policies among six countries, a study analyzing semantic networks of speeches made by top-level policymakers found that while Germany emphasizes *clean energy*, the discourse of the United States and Japan was structured by *nuclear safety* and *energy security*, as measured by betweenness centrality of nodes (Shim, Park, and Wilding, 2015). These networks, and their differences, help characterize national policy frames.

Finally, the analysis of semantic networks can zoom out to the population level and model opinion dynamics on a societal scale. Yuan, Feng, and Danowski (2013), for example, applied a modularity-maximization algorithm to identify communities of words in China's Twitter-like social media platform Sina Weibo related to the notion of *privacy*. The analyses helped identify different dimensions underlying the notion privacy, closely related to specific cultural roles. In addition to community detection algorithms, researchers have applied hierarchical clustering analysis to identify groups of words, which offers another way to operationalize frames. After the extraction of clusters of words, Baden (2010) analyzed framing in the interpretation of the EU constitution and concluded that the coherence of the discourse as a whole was determined by how well the core concepts are interconnected.

One application of these ideas attempts to explain public opinion formation from the structure of media coverage. This theoretical approach, dubbed network agenda setting (NAS), argues that the agenda set by news organizations not only concerns how often a specific issue is covered, but also the relationship between different news items (Guo, 2012; Vargo et al., 2014). It follows that overall connection patterns in the semantic network of news coverage should predict connection patterns in the aggregated public mind. Using the quadratic assignment procedure (QAP), the authors found that in the 2012 election, the semantic network of Obama supporters was predicted by vertical media's network agenda (i.e., newspapers and broadcast news networks); the network of Romney supporters, on the other hand, was better accounted for by horizontal media's network agenda (i.e., cable news networks and talk shows).

The longitudinal analysis of those networks can further enrich our understanding of public opinion formation; it provides valuable information on the process by which individuals' cognitive representations evolve as they interact with collective discourse, and it offers metrics to track polarization or convergence over time. So far, however, research using semantic networks to study public opinion formation is rare. Existing literature tends to focus on policy-related elite discourse and on how political coalitions are formed based on actors' responses to each other (Fisher, Leifeld, and Iwaki, 2012; Kleinnijenhuis and de Nooy, 2013; Leifeld, 2013). In the quest to develop this line of research across levels of analysis, researchers can take advantage of powerful techniques to model network dynamics. Although we have not yet seen many studies applying likelihood-based inferential techniques designed specifically for networks, such as the family of exponential random graph modeling (ERGM) methods (for details see Cranmer and Desmarais [2011]; Desmarais and Cranmer [2012]; Ingold and Leifeld [2014]; and Chapter 8), the lack of studies should not prevent researchers from employing such methods—as long as their application complies with the main assumptions made by those techniques. What sets semantic networks apart from social networks is that nodes are not actors having the agency to decide how to form their ties, which is a basic assumption in generative models like ERGMs. Researchers intending to apply ERGMs need to reflect carefully on whether the specific type of semantic network to be analyzed satisfies the analytical assumptions of ERGMs.

Conclusions

Research applying semantic network analysis to the study of politics in general and public opinion in particular is only in its nascent stage. In this chapter we reviewed existing literature analyzing semantic networks on the individual, interpersonal, and collective levels. Semantic networks offer a flexible representational and analytical framework that is particularly well suited to studying public opinion as it forms and evolves, potentially offering new empirical insights to discursive and deliberative theories of democracy. Studies employing this tool in public opinion research are still rare, although significant methodological advances have already been made in other areas, such as computational linguistics, cognitive psychology, political sociology, and policy studies. All of these developments have paved the way for public opinion researchers to apply semantic networks to study issues that have long been neglected due to overreliance on mass opinion polling.

Future research should consider ways to combine and triangulate data sources. For example, the structural information should be combined with other attributes available for actors (e.g., individual's ideological stance, political information consumption, general political knowledge) and semantic units (e.g., values versus factual belief, scientifically valid versus misconceptions). Second, although in this chapter we primarily focus on static semantic networks (i.e., snapshots of evolving structures), their temporal dimension encodes important information that should also be considered. For the networks mapping semantic relationships, a longitudinal view can offer a long-term perspective of public opinion formation. For the networks mapping associations of actors with concepts, the analysis of the processes that lead to differentiation, polarization, and consensus can offer empirically testable hypotheses of discursive and deliberative models of public opinion. Achieving those goals will require solving many challenges that are still open, but we foresee much exciting research rising to the task.

Note

1. In a free association task, subjects are asked to report the first word coming to mind that is related in a specific way (e.g., meaning, rhyme, make words) to the prompted cues. The University of South Florida Word Association Norms is the largest collected free association data set in the United States, covering more than six thousand participants and encompassing nearly three-quarters of a million responses to more than five thousand stimulus words (see Nelson, McEvoy, and Schreiber, 2004).

References

Aggarwal, C. C., and Zhai, C. X. (2012). "A Survey of Text Classification Algorithms." In *Mining Text Data*, edited by C. Aggarwal and C. X. Zhai, pp. 163–222. Springer. http://link.springer.com/chapter/10.1007/978-1-4614-3223-4_6.

Agneessens, F., and Everett, M. G. (2013). "Introduction to the Special Issue on Advances in Two-Mode Social Networks." *Social Networks* 35(2): 145–147.

Althaus, S. L., et al. (2011). "Assumed Transmission in Political Science: A Call for Bringing Description Back In." *Journal of Politics* 73(4): 1065–1080.

Atteveldt, W. v. (2008). *Semantic Network Analysis: Techniques for Extracting, Representing, and Querying Media Content.* Charleston, SC: BookSurge.

Atteveldt, W. v., Kleinnijenhuis, J., and Ruigrok, N. (2008). "Parsing, Semantic Networks, and Political Authority Using Syntactic Analysis to Extract Semantic Relations from Dutch Newspaper Articles." *Political Analysis* 16(4): 428–446.

Atteveldt, W. v., Kleinnijenhuis, J., Ruigrok, N., and Schlobach, S. (2008). "Good News or Bad News? Conducting Sentiment Analysis on Dutch Text to Distinguish Between Positive and Negative Relations." *Journal of Information Technology & Politics* 5(1): 73–94.

Baden, C. (2010). *Communication, Contextualization, & Cognition: Patterns & Processes of Frames' Influence on People's Interpretations of the EU Constitution.* Delft: Eburon Academic Publishers.

Baek, Y. M. (2011). "The Impact of Deliberation on Social and Semantic Networks: Citizens' Mental Models of Bioethical Issues in Genetics Using Automated Textual Analysis." http://repository.upenn.edu/dissertations/AAI3475893.

Bail, C. A. (2012). "The Fringe Effect Civil Society Organizations and the Evolution of Media Discourse about Islam since the September 11th Attacks." *American Sociological Review* 77(6): 855–879.

Baldassarri, D., and Goldberg, A. (2014). "Neither Ideologues nor Agnostics: Alternative Voters' Belief System in an Age of Partisan Politics." *American Journal of Sociology* 120 (1): 45–95. doi:10.1086/676042.

Barabási, A.-L. (2009). "Scale-Free Networks: A Decade and Beyond." *Science* 325(5939): 412–413.

Baunach, D. M. (2012). "Changing Same-Sex Marriage Attitudes in America from 1988 Through 2010." *Public Opinion Quarterly* 76(2): 364–378.

Benoit, K., et al. (2016). "Crowd-Sourced Text Analysis: Reproducible and Agile Production of Political Data." *American Political Science Review: forthcoming.* http://eprints.lse.ac.uk/62242/

Blei, D. M., Ng, A. Y., and Jordan, M. I. (2003). "Latent Dirichlet Allocation." *Journal of Machine Learning Research* 3: 993–1022.

Blumer, H. (1946). "Elementary Collective Behavior." *New Outline of the Principles of Sociology,* 170–177.

Borgatti, S., Martin, E., and Johnson, J. (2013). *Analyzing Social Networks.* Los Angeles, Thousand Oaks, CA, London: Sage Publications.

Borge-Holthoefer, J., and Arenas, A. (2010). "Semantic Networks: Structure and Dynamics." *Entropy* 12(5): 1264–1302.

Cappella, J. N., Price, V., and Nir, L. (2002). "Argument Repertoire as a Reliable and Valid Measure of Opinion Quality: Electronic Dialogue During Campaign 2000." *Political Communication* 19(1): 73–93.

Carley, K., and Kaufer, D. S. (1993). "Semantic Connectivity: An Approach for Analyzing Symbols in Semantic Networks." *Communication Theory* 3(3): 183–213.

Carley, K., and Palmquist, M. (1992). "Extracting, Representing, and Analyzing Mental Models." *Social Forces* 70(3): 601–636.

Carpini, M. X. D., Cook, F. L., and Jacobs, L. R. (2004). "Public Deliberation, Discursive Participation, and Citizen Engagement: A Review of the Empirical Literature." *Annual Review of Political Science* 7(1): 315–344.

Collins, A. M., and Loftus, E. F. (1975). "A Spreading-Activation Theory of Semantic Processing." *Psychological Review* 82(6): 407.

Converse, P. E. (1987). "Changing Conceptions of Public Opinion in the Political Process." *Public Opinion Quarterly 51*: S12–24.

Conway, L. G., Conway, K. R., Gornick, L. J., and Houck, S. C. (2014). "Automated Integrative Complexity: Automated Integrative Complexity." *Political Psychology* 35(5): 603–624.

Corman, S. R., Kuhn, T., Mcphee, R. D., and Dooley, K. J. (2002). "Studying Complex Discursive Systems." *Human Communication Research* 28(2): 157–206.

Cranmer, S. J., and Desmarais, B. A. (2011). "Inferential Network Analysis with Exponential Random Graph Models." *Political Analysis* 19(1): 66–86.

Crespi, I. (1997). *The Public Opinion Process: How the People Speak*. Mahwah, NJ: Routledge.

Danowski, J. A. (2009). "Inferences from Word Networks in Messages." In *The Content Analysis Reader*, ed. Krippendorff, K. and Bock, M., 421–429. Thousand Oaks, CA: Sage publications.

Desmarais, B. A., and Cranmer, S. J. (2012). "Statistical Inference for Valued-Edge Networks: The Generalized Exponential Random Graph Model." *PLOS ONE* 7(1): e30136.

Diesner, J., and Carley, K. M. (2010). "A Methodology for Integrating Network Theory and Topic Modeling and Its Application to Innovation Diffusion." In *2010 IEEE Second International Conference on Social Computing*, pp. 687–692. http://ieeexplore.ieee.org/lpdocs/epic03/wrapper.htm?arnumber=5591514.

Diesner, J., and Carley, K. M. (2011). "Semantic Networks." In *Encyclopedia of Social Networking*, ed. Barnett, G., 766–769. Thousand Oaks, CA: Sage publications.

Dijk, T. A. v. (1995). "Discourse Semantics and Ideology." *Discourse & Society* 6(2): 243–289.

Doerfel, M. L., and Connaughton, S. L. (2009). "Semantic Networks and Competition: Election Year Winners and Losers in U.S. Televised Presidential Debates, 1960–2004." *Journal of the American Society for Information Science and Technology* 60(1): 201–218.

Dryzek, J. S., and Niemeyer, S. (2008). "Discursive Representation." *American Political Science Review* 102(4): 481–493.

Dumais, S. T. (2004). "Latent Semantic Analysis." *Annual Review of Information Science and Technology* 38(1): 188–230.

Fisher, D. R., Leifeld, P., and Iwaki, Y. (2012). "Mapping the Ideological Networks of American Climate Politics." *Climatic Change* 116(3–4): 523–545.

Fishkin, J. S. (1991). *Democracy and Deliberation: New Directions for Democratic Reform*. New Haven, CT: Yale University Press.

Fishkin, J. S. (1997). *The Voice of the People: Public Opinion and Democracy*. New Haven, CT: Yale University Press.

Fortunato, S. (2010). "Community Detection in Graphs." *Physics Reports* 486(3–5): 75–174.

Girvan, M., and Newman, M. E. J. (2002). "Community Structure in Social and Biological Networks." *Proceedings of the National Academy of Sciences* 99(12): 7821–7826.

Griffiths, T., and Steyvers, M. (2002). "A Probabilistic Approach to Semantic Representation." In *Proceedings of the 24th Annual Conference of the Cognitive Science Society*, pp. 381–386. Citeseer. http://citeseerx.ist.psu.edu/viewdoc/download?doi=10.1.1.9.5961&rep=rep1&type=pdf.

Grimmer, J., and Stewart, B. M. (2013). "Text as Data: The Promise and Pitfalls of Automatic Content Analysis Methods for Political Texts." *Political Analysis* 21(3): 1–31. doi:10.1093/pan/mps028.

Guo, L. (2012). "The Application of Social Network Analysis in Agenda Setting Research: A Methodological Exploration." *Journal of Broadcasting & Electronic Media* 56(4): 616–631.

Gutmann, A., and Thompson, D. (2004). *Why Deliberative Democracy?* Princeton, NJ: Princeton University Press.

Hoffman, M., Lubell, M., and Hillis, V. (2014). "Linking Knowledge and Action through Mental Models of Sustainable Agriculture." *Proceedings of the National Academy of Sciences* 111(36): 13016–13021.

Ingold, K., and Leifeld, P. (2014). "Structural and Institutional Determinants of Influence Reputation: A Comparison of Collaborative and Adversarial Policy Networks in Decision Making and Implementation." *Journal of Public Administration Research and Theory* 26 (1): 1–18. doi:10.1093/jopart/muu043.

Johnson-Laird, P. N. (2010). "Mental Models and Human Reasoning." *Proceedings of the National Academy of Sciences* 107(43): 18243–18250.

Jurafsky, D., and Martin, J. H. (2008). *Speech and Language Processing*. 2d ed. Upper Saddle River, NJ: Prentice Hall.

Kenett, Y. N., Anaki, D., and Faust, M. (2014). "Investigating the Structure of Semantic Networks in Low and High Creative Persons." *Frontiers in Human Neuroscience* 8. http://www.ncbi.nlm.nih.gov/pmc/articles/PMC4051268/.

Kim, D.-H. (2004). "Cognitive Maps of Policy Makers on Financial Crises of South Korea and Malaysia: A Comparative Study." *International Review of Public Administration* 9(2): 31–38.

Kleinnijenhuis, J., and de Nooy, W. (2013). "Adjustment of Issue Positions Based on Network Strategies in an Election Campaign: A Two-Mode Network Autoregression Model with Cross-Nested Random Effects." *Social Networks* 35(2): 168–177.

Kolaczyk, E. D., and Csárdi, G. (2014). *65 Statistical Analysis of Network Data with R*. New York: Springer New York. http://link.springer.com/10.1007/978-1-4939-0983-4.

Krippendorff, K. H. (2012). *Content Analysis: An Introduction to Its Methodology*. 3d ed. Los Angeles, London: Sage Publications.

Lau, R. R., Smith, R. A. and Fiske, S. T. (1991). "Political Beliefs, Policy Interpretations, and Political Persuasion." *Journal of Politics* 53(3): 646–675.

Lazarsfeld, P. F. (1957). "Public Opinion and the Classical Tradition." *Public Opinion Quarterly* 21(1): 39–53.

Leifeld, P. (2013). "Reconceptualizing Major Policy Change in the Advocacy Coalition Framework: A Discourse Network Analysis of German Pension Politics." *Policy Studies Journal* 41(1): 169–198.

Leifeld, P., and Haunss, S. (2012). "Political Discourse Networks and the Conflict over Software Patents in Europe." *European Journal of Political Research* 51(3): 382–409.

Lin, Y.-R., Margolin, D., and Lazer, D. (2015). "Uncovering Social Semantics from Textual Traces: A Theory-Driven Approach and Evidence from Public Statements of U.S. Members of Congress." *Journal of the Association for Information Science and Technology* June 2. doi:10.1002/asi.23540.

Liptak, A. (2015). "Supreme Court Ruling Makes Same-Sex Marriage a Right Nationwide." *New York Times*, June 26. http://www.nytimes.com/2015/06/27/us/supreme-court-same-sex-marriage.html.

Manning, C. D., Raghavan, P., and Schütze, H. (2008). *Introduction to Information Retrieval*. New York: Cambridge University Press.

Marupaka, N., Iyer, L. R., and Minai, A. A. (2012). "Connectivity and Thought: The Influence of Semantic Network Structure in a Neurodynamical Model of Thinking." *Neural Networks* 32: 147–158.

McCombs, M. E., and Shaw, D. L. (1972). "The Agenda-Setting Function of Mass Media." *Public Opinion Quarterly* 36(2): 176–187.

McRae, K., Cree, G. S., Seidenberg, M. S., and Mcnorgan, C. (2005). "Semantic Feature Production Norms for a Large Set of Living and Nonliving Things." *Behavior Research Methods* 37(4): 547–559.

McRae, K., and Jones, M. N. (2013). "Semantic Memory." In *The Oxford Handbook of Cognitive Psychology*, pp. 206–219. Oxford University Press.

Mendelberg, T. (2002). "The Deliberative Citizen: Theory and Evidence." *Political Decision Making, Deliberation and Participation* 6(1): 151–193.

Miller, M. M. (1997). "Frame Mapping and Analysis of News Coverage of Contentious Issues." *Social Science Computer Review* 15(4): 367–378.

Minozzi, W., Neblo, M. A., Esterling, K. M., and Lazer, D. M. J. (2015). "Field Experiment Evidence of Substantive, Attributional, and Behavioral Persuasion by Members of Congress in Online Town Halls." *Proceedings of the National Academy of Sciences* 112(13): 3937–3942.

Morgan, M. G., Fischhoff, B., Bostrom, A., and Atman, C. J. (2001). *Risk Communication: A Mental Models Approach.* Cambridge, UK, and New York: Cambridge University Press.

Nelson, D. L., McEvoy, C. L., and Schreiber, T. A. (2004). "The University of South Florida Free Association, Rhyme, and Word Fragment Norms." *Behavior Research Methods, Instruments & Computers* 36(3): 402–407.

Newman, M., Barabási, A.-L., and Watts, D. J. (2006). *The Structure and Dynamics of Networks.* Princeton, NJ: Princeton University Press.

Newman, M. E. J. (2000). "Models of the Small World." *Journal of Statistical Physics* 101(3–4): 819–841.

Pew Research Center. (2015). *"Changing Attitudes on Gay Marriage."* http://www.pewforum.org/2015/06/08/graphics-slideshow-changing-attitudes-on-gay-marriage/.

Popping, R. (2006). "Text Analysis for Knowledge Graphs." *Quality & Quantity* 41(5): 691–709.

Price, V. (1992). *4 Public Opinion.* Newbury Park, CA: Sage Publications.

Price, V., and Neijens, P. (1997). "Opinion Quality in Public Opinion Research." *International Journal of Public Opinion Research* 9(4): 336–360.

Price, V., Nir, L., and Cappella, J. N. (2006). "Normative and Informational Influences in Online Political Discussions." *Communication Theory* 16(1): 47–74.

Scheufele, D. A., and Tewksbury, D. (2007). "Framing, Agenda Setting, and Priming: The Evolution of Three Media Effects Models." *Journal of Communication* 57(1): 9–20.

Scott, J. (2012). *Social Network Analysis.* 3d ed. Los Angeles: Sage Publications.

Shim, J., Park, C., and Wilding, M. (2015). "Identifying Policy Frames through Semantic Network Analysis: An Examination of Nuclear Energy Policy across Six Countries." *Policy Sciences* 48(1): 51–83.

Smith, R. A., and Parrott, R. L. (2012). "Mental Representations of HPV in Appalachia: Gender, Semantic Network Analysis, and Knowledge Gaps." *Journal of Health Psychology* 17(6): 917–928.

Steyvers, M., and Tenenbaum, J. B. (2005). "The Large-Scale Structure of Semantic Networks: Statistical Analyses and a Model of Semantic Growth." *Cognitive Science* 29(1): 41–78.

Tetlock, P. E., Metz, S. E., Scott, S. E., and Suedfeld, P. (2014). "Integrative Complexity Coding Raises Integratively Complex Issues: Complexities of Integrative Complexity Coding." *Political Psychology* 35(5): 625–634.

Vargo, C. J., Guo, L., McCombs, M., and Shaw, D. L. (2014). "Network Issue Agendas on Twitter During the 2012 U.S. Presidential Election: Network Issue Agendas on Twitter." *Journal of Communication* 64(2): 296–316.

Wasserman, S., and Faust, K. (1994). *Social Network Analysis: Methods and Applications*. Cambridge, UK, and New York: Cambridge University Press.

Watts, D. J., and Strogatz, S. H. (1998). "Collective Dynamics of 'Small-World' Networks." *Nature* 393(6684): 440–442.

Young, M. D. (1996). "Cognitive Mapping Meets Semantic Networks." *Journal of Conflict Resolution* 40(3): 395–414.

Yuan, E. J., Feng, M., and Danowski, J. A. (2013). " 'Privacy' in Semantic Networks on Chinese Social Media: The Case of Sina Weibo: Privacy in Semantic Networks on Sina Weibo." *Journal of Communication* 63(6): 1011–1031.

Zaller, J R. (1992). *The Nature and Origins of Mass Opinion*. Cambridge, UK, and New York: Cambridge University Press.

PART III

NETWORKS AND
AMERICAN POLITICS

CHAPTER 14

......

VOTING AND POLITICAL PARTICIPATION

......

MEREDITH ROLFE AND STEPHANIE CHAN

INTRODUCTION

......

THE question of why some citizens participate in the electoral process, or rather why some citizens don't participate, is one of the oldest empirical questions in political science (Merriam and Gosnell, 1924). Perhaps surprisingly, however, the classic Columbia School studies of voting behavior devoted scant attention to providing an explanation of political participation (Lazarsfeld, Berelson, and Gaudet, 1944; Berelson, Lazarsfeld, and McPhee, 1954), focusing instead on the impact of discussion on partisanship, electoral choice, and opinion change during a campaign. Any mention of turnout in either book is brief, and the authors suggest that turnout is embedded in the process of campaign-generated discussion and mobilization: "Real involvement in politics is characteristic of only the minority. . . . But with the temporary campaign excitement and increase in partisanship . . . the majority take some part in the discussion and even more register their preferences on election day" (Berelson, Lazarsfeld, and McPhee, 1954, 33).

Although these early studies took for granted that political participation was affected by social interaction, more recent research has used a range of methodological approaches to demonstrate the existence of network effects on voter turnout and other forms of political participation. People are affected by the participation decisions of those around them, regardless of whether those relationships are with intimates, neighbors, or even strangers. There is a long-standing debate in the literature over whether exposure to cross-pressures or political disagreement has a positive or negative impact on participation, but an emergent consensus finds that disagreement has a nonlinear impact on participation that is moderated by individual characteristics. In recent years, significant strides have been made in the use of methods designed to address concerns about the role of selection and influence in network studies of participation, and there is a growing interest in identifying the structural and psychological mechanisms that link social networks and political behavior.

Sources of Influence

Political discussion networks are widely agreed to have an impact on turnout and participation, but the extent of the influence varies depending on who does the influencing and the exact mechanisms through which this influence occurs (for a more extensive discussion of mechanisms, see Emerging Area: Mechanisms of Influence). There is general agreement that political discussion networks lead to increased turnout and participation. The strength of influence, however, varies according to who does the influencing: a housemate, a spouse, an assigned roommate, a discussant of the same race and religion, or a stranger who is canvassing.

Spouses

Spouses have long been seen as important motivators of participation. Spouses are almost always named as core political discussants (Klofstad, McClurg, and Rolfe, 2009) and are also the most likely to try to persuade one another to vote (Stoker and Jennings, 1995). It is well established that married individuals vote more often than those who have never been married or who are no longer married (Campbell et al., 1960; Stoker and Jennings, 1995), particularly after controlling for the negative impact on participation of having children at home (Wolfinger and Wolfinger, 2008.) Spousal turnout decisions can cut both ways, however, as spouses who turn out can encourage voting, while turnout among people married to nonvoting spouses is significantly depressed (Schmitt-Beck and Mackenrodt, 2010).

Much of the earlier research establishing that married people vote at higher rates than nonmarried people was based on cross-sectional surveys and could not control for the effects of self-selection or any omitted factors that affected both the propensity to marry and the propensity to participate. More recent experimental work addresses these potential objections by looking at what happens when an exogenous shock affects only one member of a partnership. Field experiment results show that voting is "contagious" within households; when one voter in a two-voter household is contacted by a canvasser as part of a field experiment, the likelihood of increased turnout is passed on to the spouse or partner who did not have any direct contact with the canvasser (Nickerson, 2008). Hobbs, Christakis, and Fowler (2014) take another approach to identifying an exogenous shock, using a combined data set of California voting records and death records to compare voting participation before and after a spouse has died. Analyzing this quasi-natural experiment using statistical matching techniques to control for alternative explanations, they find that widowed individuals are still 9 percentage points less likely to vote after the grieving period than they would have been if their spouses had still been living.

Families

Families have also been seen as an important source of socialization into politics and participation (Verba, Schlozman, and Burns, 2005), and family members are frequently named as core political discussants (Klofstad, McClurg, and Rolfe, 2009). Young adults with politically active parents are more likely to be politically active (Jennings and Niemi, 1974). Politics in the home can have a persistent effect on adult political participation, although some (but not all) of this effect may be moderated by parents passing down their political knowledge, interest, and other relevant resources to their children (Verba, Schlozman, and Brady, 1995). In a reanalysis of the Jennings and Niemi Parent-Student Socialization Study, Plutzer (2002) finds that whether or not a young adult participates in the first election in which he or she is eligible to vote is most strongly predicted by whether or not his or her parents voted in the same election. Parental turnout is the only factor that significantly affects whether or not a young person in the study initially voted, and these young adults continue to vote at a higher rate for two to three additional elections before the differences mostly level off over time. Interestingly, the impact of strength of parental partisanship did not decline over time, with young adults whose parents were strong partisans remaining significantly more likely to vote long after they left home (Plutzer, 2002). Most respondents participating in a survey prior to a local election in Germany reported that their family expected them to vote and would object if they failed to do so (Schmitt-Beck and Mackenrodt, 2010). Family norms had a significant impact on an individual's likelihood of voting, even after controlling for a range of variables including education, political interest, internal voting norms, political discussion, and spousal turnout.

Close Friends and Discussants

Interpersonal discussion is the main mechanism through which influence travels in a network, and therefore an obvious source of potential influence is anyone with whom one has regular political discussion outside of the family. Political talk is often embedded into informal, everyday conversation (Walsh, 2004; McClurg, 2003), and there is little difference between the more specialized political discussion networks and core discussion networks (Klofstad, McClurg, and Rolfe, 2009). More generally, we would therefore expect to find that any regular interaction partner might impact political participation. The literature confirms that close friends, or those who are core network discussants, have a significant impact on turnout probability.[1]

Knack's (1992) analysis of the 1987 General Social Survey (GSS) political networks module finds that people who report more frequent political discussion with up to three named political discussants also had higher levels of political interest and participation. Kenny (1992) reanalyzed the 1984 South Bend data using an instrumental variables approach to control for endogeneity and found that all five forms of political participation included in the study were affected by discussants' political activity.[2] German citizens were more likely to vote (or not vote) when they expected one or both of their other named political discussants to vote (or not vote) in the upcoming election (Schmitt-Beck and Mackenrodt, 2010). The impact of the voting decisions of friends was much greater than the impact of media consumption on turnout. Furthermore, the impact of the turnout decisions of friends was independent of both political discussion frequency and normative expectations of turnout. Many of these studies are based on cross-sectional survey data, but their findings have been confirmed by more recent studies that have taken advantage of random assignment to university classes and residential dorms to demonstrate that regular discussion partners can and do have a significant causal impact on turnout and participation.

Klofstad (2011) studied freshmen who were randomly assigned to dorms at the University of Wisconsin–Madison, surveying them three times: at the start and end of their first academic year and again just before graduation. In general, freshmen whose roommates engaged them in discussion about politics and civic interests became more involved in civic and political activities. Participation in civic voluntary organizations increased by around 40 percent after exposure to civic talk. Engaging in civic talk with roommates increased turnout in the 2004 presidential election by around 10 percentage points (with a slightly lower but still significant estimate obtained using matching to control for other factors that might have influenced roommate assignments). Interestingly, the effects of political discussion were most pronounced for those who were already politically active, whose parents were interested in politics, and who already had stronger ideological preferences. In other words, students did not respond in a linear way to cumulative social influence, but instead social effects on participation compounded as students were exposed to additional active political discussion partners.

College students are not just meeting new roommates, but entering into entirely new friendship groups. Lazer et al. (2015) collected information about a larger set of social connections: members of fellowship dorms at one of fourteen different universities in the United States. Two waves of surveys (one prior to the start of school and one just after the election) were administered surrounding each of the four national elections between 2008 and 2014. Voting intent and party ID were measured in August, and information was collected on actual turnout and social network ties of dormitory residents after the election. Like other studies of college students, this study of a "nascent" network in formation allowed the authors to control for whether or not students self-selected partners based on their voting intentions. The impact of the voting intent of all named alters on actual turnout was estimated using network autoregression, and the impact was significant even after controlling for both political interest and ego intent. Substantively, the estimated effects are in line with predictions of analytical models of contagion (Rolfe, 2012), ranging from little chance of voting if few or no associates are planning to vote to a nearly 100 percent expected probability of participation if friends all definitely plan to vote.

Campos, Heap, and de Leon (2017) find that influence occurs even without cohabitation. Students at the Universidade de São Paulo, the majority of whom commuted to school, were randomly assigned to introductory classes. Some 635 students participated in both waves of a two-wave survey that bookended the 2010 presidential campaign in Brazil, and students were not asked questions about their friendships or discussion partners. Instead, the authors looked at the impact of average peer characteristics in the randomly assigned class section during the initial wave on right-wing preferences, turnout intention, political identification, and political knowledge measured just after the first round of presidential elections. In contrast to earlier results, peer effects on voting intention were more significant for students who started out with lower levels of political engagement. The article's focus on average peer effects in a large classroom instead of actual networks of discussion is a departure from much of the literature and may account for the difference in results. The dynamics of political discussion within a group such as a class section can reflect the average distribution of opinions within that group, with students holding less common political attitudes being less centrally engaged in the student political discussion network (Lazer et al., 2010). Thus, measuring only average peer effects may provide a misleading picture of the actual patterns of discussion engaged in by students in the class.

Friends and Acquaintances

There is a long-standing distinction between "strong" ties and "weak" ties in the social networks literature (Granovetter, 1973), and many authors assume that strong tie discussants such as family and close friends are most likely to have an effect on political behavior. However, weak ties have traditionally been seen as crucial to providing access to new and diverse information, and thus weak ties might shape political participation by providing information about campaigns and candidates. Furthermore, Putnam (1995) has argued that "social capital" based in weak ties formed by joint membership in civic organizations, neighborhood associations, and the like is crucial to maintaining healthy attitudes and participation patterns among democratic citizens. An emerging literature on weak tie networks, including weak ties that are created or sustained online, finds that people do discuss politics with weak tie associates and that weak tie interactions can have a positive effect on participation.

Several studies have documented that political discussions are not uncommon among members of less close-knit friendship groups. Eveland and Kleinman (2011) collected surveys from members of twenty-five student groups at a large university and found that significant levels of political discussion took place between these weak tie acquaintances, although noticeably less than more general discussion topics. Political discussion is also common among online discussion partners, although people are less likely to be exposed to political disagreement when participating in groups dedicated to political discussion (Wojcieszak and Mutz, 2009).

Zúñiga and Valenzuela (2011) used an online survey of the general American population to estimate the impact of social media usage and online social network size and discussion frequency on various forms of political participation. They asked respondents to estimate the number of people with whom they had discussed public affairs, differentiating between discussions taking place offline (face to face or over the phone) and those taking place online (email, chat rooms, etc.) People with larger discussion networks both online and offline were more likely to be engaged in civic activity, and much of the effect of network size on activity was mediated by the frequency of weak tie political discussion with coworkers and acquaintances.

Studies of political discussion networks have traditionally looked at the impact of variation in personal network (or egonet) size and found that people who have larger networks were more likely to participate than those who had smaller personal networks (Leighley, 1990; La Due Lake and Huckfeldt, 1998; Mutz, 2002; Eveland and Hively, 2009). Rolfe (2012) provides an analytical theory of the relationship between the size of weak tie networks and political participation. Building on a mathematical model of conditional decision making (or contagion) in social networks, she shows that participation is not directly affected by personal network size but by the average size of the personal networks of one's friends (and the friends of their friends, etc.). Rolfe's model of the impact of network size produces test implications that are consistent with a range of empirical findings, including individual level turnout variation in a national election and precinct level variation in smaller local elections and primaries.

Bond et al. (2012) reports the results of one of the largest field experiments focusing on the impact of social networks on turnout. The authors worked with Facebook to expose sixty-one million American Facebook users to one of two different experimental messages during the 2010 US election. Some users were shown a clickable button that said "I Voted" and information such as their polling place, along with photos and a count of their other Facebook friends who had already voted at the top of their newsfeed. Other users were also shown the button at the top of the newsfeed, but only given information such as the closet polling location, while nothing was added to the control group's newsfeed. Subjects who received a message about their friends voting were more likely to vote themselves than those who received only information or nothing. In contrast, information alone did not increase turnout. These results were found for both self-reported vote and validated vote. Interestingly, however, weak ties were not necessarily the primary source of the influence; the strongest effects were found among those who were most likely to also be friends outside of Facebook (Bond et al., 2012).

Mobilization

Historically, face to face mobilization or canvassing has been a significant aspect of election campaigns, with candidates or volunteers going door to door to contact residents and encourage them to vote. In the second half of the twentieth century, face to face canvassing was slowly replaced by other forms of mobilization such as direct mail and phone calls. However, research has shown clearly that face to face social contact is far more effective than mediated forms of social contact. Gerber and Green (2000) conducted a large-scale field experiment of 30,000 voters in New Haven, Connecticut, during the November 1998 election. They found that face to face mobilization had a strong and significant impact on turnout probability, with those who had been contacted personally turning out at a rate from 8 to 14 percentage points higher than the control group.[3] Direct mail had only a small positive effect, and telephone calls had no significant impact on turnout rate.

The effectiveness of face to face mobilization doesn't necessarily mean that political participation is easily influenced by strangers or weaker social ties. Instead, the literature suggests that shared social identity is a crucial mediator of the impact of face to face mobilization. The canvassers in Green and Gerber's original study were student volunteers not likely to be socially connected to most New Haven residents, but were chosen to reflect the racial and ethnic neighborhoods that they canvassed when possible. More recent research confirms that face to face contact is particularly effective when canvassers are from the community in which they canvass, as compared to nonlocal canvassers (Sinclair, McConnell, and Michelson, 2013). Davenport (2010) also finds a particularly large effect size of 15 to 18 percentage points in a study that involves local canvassers: all canvassers were either current or former residents of Boston Public Housing, and they went door to door in the public housing areas. However, there were no nonlocal canvassers involved in the study, so it is difficult to say whether shared social identity contributed significantly to the particularly effective mobilization attempt (Davenport, 2010).

Related mobilization studies have used direct mail to investigate the impact of various social mechanisms on turnout. Gerber, Green, and Larimer (2010) compare the effect of publicizing neighbor voting records (the "neighbors" treatment) to the effect of other direct mail messages such as civic duty or simply reporting the resident's own past voting history. They find that publicizing the voting records of neighbors increases turnout in the treated group by 8.1 percentage points as compared to the control, and around 3.2 percentage points of this increase can be attributed to the inclusion of neighbors' voting records (as compared to the other elements in the treatment). Panagopoulos (2010) tried to disentangle potential affective motivations underlying the "neighbors" treatment effect by distinguishing between "shame" (telling subjects that the names of nonvoters would be printed in the local paper) and "pride" (telling subjects that the names of voters would be printed in the local paper). He found that pride motivated high-propensity voters to turn out, while shame motivated everyone (Panagopoulos, 2010). Similarly, Panagopoulos (2011b) found that a reminder mailer thanking people for their previous election participation was more effective at stimulating turnout among previous voters than a simple reminder mailer without gratitude. Study subjects who received a mailing that included their voting history and indicated their community's turnout was high were the most likely to turn out (Panagopoulos, Larimer, and Condon, 2013).

Interestingly, the impact of treatments that increase awareness of publicly available voting records can last beyond a single election. Davenport et al. (2010) followed up and collected information on up to two years of subsequent turnout behavior of over a million people who had been involved in one of six separate experimental studies of mobilization. Subjects who were made aware that turnout decisions were available in the public record (including both the "neighbors" treatment and the related "self" treatment, in which subjects were shown their own past voting turnout) continued to participate at significantly higher rates up to two years after they were initially mobilized. Even those who hadn't voted immediately after the treatment were more likely to turn out in future elections.

Neighborhoods and Social Context

If one were to look at a map color-coded by the turnout rate at a set geographic level such as a neighborhood (or precinct, census tract, city, state, country, etc.), it would be easy to spot the existence of contextual effects. Turnout varies systematically across social units and is higher in some and lower in others. The existence of variation in turnout at the neighborhood level is well known within political science and was described in one of the earliest empirical studies of participation (Merriam and Gosnell, 1924). While the mere existence of contextual level variation in participation does not necessarily mean that social influence is affecting participation decisions, the findings of the contextual effects literature are generally in line with research that studies more direct forms of social influence.

Contextual variation is not necessarily attributable to social influence alone. Some of the observed contextual variation in participation can be attributed to the aggregation of individual level factors within the context. For example, turnout is generally higher in neighborhoods where most residents are from a high status, college-educated background, and is lower in low-SES neighborhoods (Huckfeldt, 1979). Likewise, some of this contextual variation can be attributed to institutional variation. For example, turnout is generally lower in states with difficult or onerous registration laws (Rosenstone and Hansen, 1993) and higher in precincts with more accessible ballot locations (Gimpel and Schuknecht 2003). However, existing research has shown that contextual effects on political participation cannot be reduced to aggregated individual characteristics or shared institutional variation and confirms that social interaction is likely still playing an important role in driving shared contextual variation.

If contextual effects work at least in part via the mechanism of social interaction, we would expect to find stronger contextual effects in social contexts with more regular interaction. Huckfeldt (1980) argues that one cannot avoid members of the neighborhood in the course of daily life, and that neighbors are therefore a potentially powerful source of contextual influence on political behavior. But neighborhood effects are still heavily dependent on social interaction, as turnout is lower in suburban neighborhoods where a large proportion of community members commute to work alone—and presumably interact less often as a result of the commute (Hopkins and Williamson, 2010).

In one of the earliest contextual studies of political participation, Huckfeldt (1979) merges sample survey data on white adults in Buffalo, New York, with aggregate census tract data. Survey respondents were asked whether or not they had engaged in eleven different political actions (e.g., vote in elections, write letters to public officials), and the socioeconomic status of neighborhoods was proxied by the proportion of adults living in the area with at least twelve years of education. The effect of individual characteristics on turnout was strongly moderated by social context: individual education had a fairly small impact on participation when the individual lived in a low-SES neighborhood, while there was a much larger correlation between individual education and partici-pation in high-SES neighborhoods. Further analysis suggests that interaction is likely to underlie these contextual effects. Smaller parishes, for example, are found to have a greater contextual influence than neighborhoods as a whole (Huckfeldt, 1979).

Neighborhood partisanship can also have a significant impact on individual political participation. Democrats are more likely to display a yard sign when they are part of the partisan majority in the neighborhood, while Republicans are more likely to display a yard sign if they are in a neighborhood with heavy mobilization by the Republican Party (Huckfeldt and Sprague, 1992). Gimpel, Dyck, and Shaw (2004) found that turnout was generally depressed among Republicans living in majority Democratic neighborhoods, while the converse was not true for Democrats living in majority Republican neighbor-hoods. Partisan contextual effects on turnout may in part be attributable to mobilization efforts by candidates and local parties. Potential Republican (Democratic) voters living in majority Republican (Democratic) neighborhoods are more likely to be contacted by the party prior to an election than those who are part of a partisan minority (Huckfeldt and Sprague, 1992.) While it is most likely that these partisan contextual effects are medi-ated by social interactions with neighbors, social communication and influence may exist even without direct contact. Community members are able to accurately describe the political preferences of their local communities, even if they report that they rarely interact with neighbors or read local newspapers (Baybeck and McClurg, 2005).

The ethnic composition of a community can also affect political participation, with increasing levels of ethnic diversity generally leading to lower levels of participation for members of both minority and majority ethnic groups (Alesina and Ferrara, 2000). Barber and Imai (2014) analyzed more than fifty million voter records from three states and found that people were less likely to turn out in neighborhoods of mixed ethnicity. This effect cannot be explained by differences in candidate-driven mobilization efforts, as it persists even in noncompetitive electoral districts. Cho, Gimpel, and Dyck (2006) also used voter registration records to document the negative impact of increasing eth-nic diversity, but found neighborhoods in California where increasing ethnic diversity can actually improve participation for both minority and majority group members. They argue that the critical mass of immigrants can increase the benefits of mobiliza-tion of minority group members, particularly in the Japanese and Asian Indian neigh-borhoods that show evidence of the positive impact of diversity. Gimpel, Cho, and Wu

(2007) found some evidence of active registration and mobilization of Arab Americans after 9/11 in neighborhoods with a greater proportion of Arab American residents.

Recent studies have tried to identify more precisely how mobilization and other mechanisms work to shape aggregate level participation. Rolfe (2012) used voter roll data to demonstrate the importance of candidate mobilization strategies on turnout in low salience elections. Precinct level variation in turnout during primaries and mayoral races can be attributed almost exclusively to candidate mobilization efforts in conjunction with local social institutions. White candidates campaigned by reaching out to friends and neighbors who lived nearby and went to the same churches and neighborhood clubs, while black candidates were more likely to frequently travel to neighborhoods with strong black social institutions to campaign regardless of where they lived. Candidates from newer neighborhoods with fewer social institutions reported extreme difficulty campaigning in local elections (a claim supported by lower turnout in these neighborhoods), although turnout during national elections was not adversely affected.

Candidate-driven mobilization is not the only mechanism that might inspire higher levels of political discussion within a community and thus underlie observed contextual effects. In the original Columbia School studies, the media-driven campaign was assumed to underlie campaign effects via the two-step flow of political information and discussion. Recent studies have found that media-driven variation in campaign salience does stimulate increased political discussion and thus can increase the chance that contextual effects will emerge. Communities that receive more political ads are more likely to discuss politics and to pay more attention to news (Cho, 2011). During election campaigns in both the United Kingdom and the United States, respondents reported increases in both the size of political discussion networks and the volume of political discussion (Rolfe and Bello, 2013).

CONTROVERSIES: POLITICAL DISAGREEMENT

One long-standing debate within the political networks literature has been whether or not exposure to political disagreement has a demobilizing or suppressive effect on participation and turnout. The Columbia School studies followed Simmel ([1908] 1958) in treating cross-pressures as a result of being located at the intersection of politically significant social cleavages. Thus, if a potential voter was both middle class and Catholic, he or she would be subject to cross-pressures because Catholics in the United States were likely to vote Democratic and midde-class voters leaned Republican. Cross-pressures had a significant impact on both the timing of the vote decision and the likelihood of participating, with cross-pressured individuals deciding which candidate they would vote for much later in the election, if they participated at all (Lazarsfeld et al., 1944; Berelson et al., 1954).

By the 1970s, however, these findings were largely dismissed as a statistical artifact (Knoke, 1990; Mutz, 2002). The past few decades have a seen a revival of interest in the issue of political disagreement and cross-pressures, with multiple studies arriving at seemingly contradictory conclusions (Klofstad, Sokhey, and McClurg 2013; Nir, 2011). A review of the literature suggests that there is an emerging consensus that disagreement can have an impact on participation, but the extent and direction of the impact depends on how the disagreement is measured and how widespread the disagreement is. Exposure to isolated or sporadic disagreement is rarely demotivating and can even prove stimulating for some citizens, while others may be more sensitive to the experience of political conflict among alters. Political isolation, or the experience of being surrounded by those with different viewpoints, can dampen the desire to participate unless a person can form a protective discussion group of like-minded others.

After methodological debates over the original measurement of cross-pressures, recent studies have adopted one or more measures of political disagreement based on a survey respondent providing details about his or her political discussion network. Respondents name several political discussants and then provide further details on each of the discussants. Follow-up questions might include the respondent's self-report of (1) *egocentric political disagreement* with the alter, or how often the respondent (ego) and his or her named alter tend to disagree when they discuss political issues; and/or (2) the partisan identity or vote choice of the named alter, which can then be compared to ego's party ID or vote choice to create a measure of *egocentric partisan disagreement*. The same questions used to understand egocentric disagreement can also be used to measure individual level contextual effects in the form of *network partisan disagreement* or *network homogeneity/heterogeneity*. Measures of network homogeneity compare the party ID or vote choice of all named alters to calculate what proportion of alters hold the same political views as each other, ranging from complete agreement to more balanced opinion. Network composition measures can also be compared to the vote choice or party ID of ego to create measures of oppositional or supportive discussion networks. Aggregate level contextual measures of disagreement are usually based on averages of party ID or vote choice within a local context instead of on a diffuse sense of political disagreement. Contextual measures can be constructed to measure *isolation* (similar to egocentric partisan disagreement), *contextual conflict* (similar to network partisan disagreement), or *cross-pressures*.

Disagreement or Political Isolation

Mutz (2002) analyzed data from two large national survey studies, the 1996 Spencer Study and the 1992 Cross-National Election Project (CNEP). Disagreement was measured using a hybrid index of questions tapping into both general and partisan disagreement within egocentric networks. People who disagree with their alters are less likely to turn out to vote and more likely to delay making a decision about whom to vote for. The experience of disagreement works in part by increasing psychological ambivalence toward candidates among those exposed to it. Furthermore, disagreement does not have a negative impact on explicitly partisan forms of participation, such as working on a campaign or attending a fundraiser. In other words, people who don't agree with their discussants may still seek out and find like-minded others with whom they can become politically engaged.

Later work has clarified that Mutz's original findings do not demonstrate the negative impact of disagreement in general, but instead reflect the specific negative impact of political isolation. So-called hostile or oppositional networks exist when no alters share the same opinion as the focal citizen (ego). This political isolation can have a negative effect on turnout and other forms of political participation (Nir, 2011; Bello, 2012). Bello (2012) reanalyzed the CNEP, Spencer, and South Bend studies, and distinguished cases in which an ego is politically isolated (i.e., none of his or her alters agrees with him) from cases in which discussion networks are more heterogeneous in terms of disagreement. Only respondents who are politically isolated are less likely to vote, while respondents in politically diverse environments are not affected by disagreement. Nir (2011) found a similar pattern of response to political isolation among respondents on the 2000 American National Election Study (ANES). Political isolation can depress turnout and delay the turnout decision, particularly when compared to the effect of discussion networks with at least some degree of political heterogeneity.

Studies that do not specifically distinguish the nonlinear impact of political isolation from the (largely inconsequential) effect of variation in the level of egocentric network disagreement continue to find that exposure to disagreement can have a negative impact on participation. For example, Parsons (2009) split the 2008–2009 ANES sample to create a measure of egocentric political disagreement: separating those who disagreed with fewer of their discussants than average from those who disagreed with more than average. He found that respondents exposed to higher levels of disagreement were more likely to experience conflicting emotional considerations with respect to presidential candidates and thus were less interested in politics, less likely to vote, and less accurate when identifying candidates' positions on issues. Unfortunately, it is not clear whether the negative effect of disagreement is limited to those who are political isolated, or if there is also a negative impact on respondents who agree with at least one member of their discussion network.

In line with the claim of a nonlinear relationship between disagreement and participation, multiple studies have shown that exposure to moderate levels of disagreement can have a positive effect on participation (Ikeda and Boase, 2011; Quintelier, Stolle, and Harell 2012; Nir, 2011), subsequent engagement in political discussion (Bello and Rolfe, 2014), use of political news media (Scheufele et al., 2004), political knowledge (Eveland and Hively, 2009), and the ability to understand the other side in a political debate (Capella, Price, and Nir 2002; Huckfeldt, Mendez, and Osborn, 2004; Mutz, 2006). Studies that find a positive impact of disagreement have not been limited to the United States (Nir, 2011), but have utilized national survey data from Japan (Ikeda and Boase, 2011), Belgium (Quintelier, Stolle, and Harell, 2012), and the United Kingdom (Bello and Rolfe, 2014). In general, whether disagreement will have a positive impact on political activity depends not only on whether the experience of disagreement is completely isolating, as discussed above, but also on individual responses to disagreement and the nature of the relationship in which disagreement is expressed.

Individual Differences in Response to Disagreement

Individuals may vary in their response to moderate forms of disagreement. Mutz (2002) found that only individuals who had a higher than average desire to avoid political conflict (as measured by a four-item political avoidance scale) were negatively impacted by disagreement. Individuals with less of a desire to avoid conflict were unaffected by disagreement. Previous research has found that women are on average more conflict avoidant and agreeable than men, and a reanalysis of the CNEP data found that gender may serve as a proxy for conflict avoidance, with women potentially more affected by disagreement than men (Djupe, McClurg, and Sokhey, 2016). One reason people seek to avoid conflict is that they wish to avoid social disapproval for their views or actions. Hopmann (2012) used national survey data from Germany and Denmark, finding that individual differences in the belief that one's peers will disapprove of one's vote choice mediate response to disagreement. Concrete measures of egocentric partisan disagreement have no impact on turnout or delay in vote choice once beliefs about social disapproval have been taken into account. A fear that one's friends and family will disapprove of one's intended vote choice makes it more difficult for the ego to decide whom to vote for, indirectly lowering turnout, although this effect can be offset somewhat by having peers who would disapprove of not turning out to vote (Hopmann, 2012).

An alternative approach to understanding individual variation in responses to disagreement emphasizes the role of trust and closeness in social relationships. Using an index of egocentric political disagreement, Matthes (2013) also found that individual factors mediate response to disagreement. Only individuals with low levels of trust in others (as measured by a three-item index) are less likely to participate in a range of political activities when exposed to political disagreement; more trusting individuals are immune to the negative impact of disagreement. These results were replicated in a smaller online survey that explicitly controlled for the individual factor of conflict avoidance introduced by Mutz (2002).

Trust can also vary at the relationship level, and higher levels of trust and intimacy in a relationship can lower uncertainty avoidance by providing some protection against the potentially stressful introduction of political disagreement into everyday conversation (Morey, Eveland, and Hutchens 2012). For example, Bello and Rolfe (2014) found that during an election cycle, people were more likely to continue to discuss politics with a spouse with whom they disagreed, but less likely to continue to discuss politics with other family members. On the other hand, political disagreement with weak tie acquaintances may be safer, as it is less likely to become emotional and heated. Torcal and Maldonado (2014) analyzed CNEP data from twenty-one countries, finding that

while disagreement with family members and close friends can decrease political interest and activity, disagreement with weaker social ties has no negative impact.

Finally, it is likely that politically relevant individual differences may also moderate
the impact of disagreement, much as differences in political knowledge and attention
moderate the impact of media exposure (Zaller, 1992). Across a range of countries, political engagement by respondents who are high in political knowledge is less likely to be
negatively impacted by disagreement (Torcal and Maldonado, 2014). The moderating
impact of higher levels of political knowledge may be attributable in part to confidence
in one's own political opinions. Kim, Scheufele, and Han (2011) found that a willingness
to express a differing opinion significantly increased political participation. Somewhat
surprisingly, Torcal and Maldonado (2014) also found that strong partisans were more
likely to be negatively affected by disagreement, although other studies suggest that
those with stronger and more extreme views are positively affected by disagreement
(e.g., Wojcieszak 2011). If we assume, as in the case of media exposure, that political
knowledge and partisan strength have a nonlinear relationship with political discussion
and political activity, then inconsistencies along these lines likely reflect the complications introduced by measuring and modeling a nonlinear relationship. Indeed, there is
some evidence that this is the case: Bello and Rolfe (2014) found that during an election
cycle, moderate partisans were more likely than either weak or strong partisans to continue discussing politics with discussants holding opposing political views, while strong
partisans and those with very high levels of political interest were more likely to drop
discussants with whom they disagreed.

Given the fairly strong evidence that individuals vary in their response to political
disagreement, there has been increased interest in what exactly is being captured in
the various measures of disagreement that are available. The 1984 South Bend and 1996
Indianapolis-St. Louis (ISL) surveys (Huckfeldt and Sprague, 1991; Huckfeldt, Sprague,
and Levine, 2000) included a "snowball" component, wherein a follow-up survey was
conducted with some of the discussants (or alters) named by the original survey respondents. Comparisons revealed that people were generally accurate in their perceptions
of discussant partisanship and vote choice preferences, but when they made mistakes
they were likely to overestimate agreement. Overestimation effects were particularly
pronounced when the discussant held views in the minority based on the surrounding neighborhood (Huckfeldt and Sprague, 1991; Huckfeldt, Sprague, and Levine, 2000),
and a similar pattern of inaccuracy was also found among Japanese respondents (Ikeda
and Huckfeldt, 2001). A recent Facebook study confirmed that people often underestimate the amount of disagreement in their networks (Goel, Mason, and Watts, 2010).

Given this general pattern of misperception, it is likely that all self-reported survey
measures of agreement with discussion partners may confound individual sensitivity
to conflict (whether rooted in personality or the experience of social and political cross-
pressures and isolation) with actual exposure to differences of opinion. Furthermore,
more diffuse measures of political disagreement measures are particularly likely to blur
this distinction, while the impacts of individual differences in sensitivity are likely to be
somewhat attenuated by measures that capture (potentially) observable differences in

partisan identity, vote choice, or even specific issue attitudes. Because these measures blur the line between individual sensitivity to conflict and actual exposure to disagreement, studies using general disagreement measures are more likely to find evidence of the negative impact of disagreement. Klofstad, Sokhey, and McClurg (2013) used the 2008–2009 ANES to compare the effects of general perceptions of disagreement to more concrete measures of partisan difference. Even though they did not control for political isolation, they still found that specific measures of partisan disagreement had a smaller impact than more general perceptions of diffuse political disagreement. The negative impact of partisan disagreement on vote certainty is about half the size of the estimated impact of general political disagreement, and unlike political disagreement, partisan disagreement does not appear to decrease strength of partisanship or ideology.

Cross-Pressures and Structural Position

Regardless of which measure is used, measures of egocentric network properties are still imperfect proxies for the structural network features that were originally hypothesized to underlie the relationship between network disagreement and participation. Traditionally, cross-pressures were believed to result from a structural position between two or more identity groups, not mere exposure to a difference of opinion. Individuals who occupied this structural brokerage role might be freed from social constraint and able to make political choices in accordance with their own preferences (Burt, 1992), but they could also feel rudderless and torn between allegiances to two or more social identities. There was no way to vote such that one could both be a good Catholic and a good member of the middle class. It was this identity-related stress induced by structural position—not the everyday experience of disagreement, although the two are likely related—that was hypothesized to delay vote decisions and even decrease the probability of participating in an election.

Studies that look at the impact of contextual level disagreement on political participation are therefore closer in spirit to the original notion of cross-pressures operating via structural position. Several of the studies of neighborhood and social context discussed above speak directly to the question of whether daily experience with disagreement affects participation, and results generally confirm that the experience of being politically isolated (i.e., in the political minority when compared to neighbors) can depress participation. Although the reasons that a Democrat might end up in a majority Republican neighborhood (or vice versa) are rarely explored, it is plausible that individuals who fall into these categories are cross-pressured in the traditional sense (e.g., a wealthy black doctor living in a neighborhood with similarly wealthy whites).

The negative impact of conflicting political cleavages is also evident in studies of the impact of ethnic diversity and fragmentation on political engagement. Communities with higher degrees of ethnic fragmentation show evidence of lower levels of turnout, civic engagement, and community goods provision at the aggregate level, and this general association has been found in many countries around the world. If we consider the impact of structural cleavages on individual level behavior, however, the relationship is not so clear-cut. Individuals located in structurally diverse communities were more likely to report heterogeneous political discussions, and respondents with heterogeneous networks were more likely to report high levels of political engagement as measured by an index of participation in nine different political activities such as fundraising, writing a letter to the editor, or attending a town meeting (Scheufele et al., 2006). Individuals who lived in diverse communities and reported engaging with diverse political viewpoints were actually more likely to participate politically, even though the aggregate trend runs in the opposite direction.

More generally, it may be that individuals who don't "fit" with others within their immediate social context are less likely to engage in prosocial activities such as political participation. Using the 2010 Cooperative Congressional Election Study (CCES), Karpowitz et al. (2014) found that those who felt like outsiders were less likely to turn out. Moreover, this sense of being an outsider was related to partisanship within the broader social context, as people who were of a different partisanship than the rest of the community were more likely to report feeling like outsiders. The blending of individual level and contextual data holds significant promise for exploring the impact of network structure on individual behavior. For example, McClurg (2006) found that disagreement with personal network discussants only had a negative impact on participation if ego was also in the political minority in his or her local neighborhood. Survey-based measures of disagreement that capture more general patterns of discussion with copartisans (or non-copartisans) or other politically relevant demographic groups have the potential to capture contextual variation in structural access to discussion partners within the survey context (e.g., Scheufele et al., 2006; Eveland and Hively, 2009). Brader, Tucker, and Therriault (2014) have proposed an updated version of a survey-based cross-pressures measure that also may better tap into the concept of structural location.

Two additional trends in network research have particular promise for helping move along research on the impact of network disagreement on participation. One is the use of full network data of the sort gathered by Song and Eveland (2015). The study collected sociometric data from 502 students who were members of twenty-five groups at a midwestern university, and thus it was possible to compare survey responses to full information about the political preferences of peers and the structural location of students within the groups. This data collection approach highlights some of the inherent tensions in structural logic. For example, while reported ambivalence was lower on average for members of highly diverse and political groups, individuals who were in the political minority in their group were more ambivalent. Conversely, individual group members who occupied highly constrained positions within the group (i.e., high in closeness centrality) were also more likely to express political ambivalence. Belonging "too much" and "too little" both had negative impacts on ambivalence and subsequent political participation.

Another promising approach to the study of disagreement builds on a long tradition of research on small group experiments (e.g., Stasser and Titus, 1985) and political deliberation (Delli Carpini, Cook and Jacobs 2004). In small group experiments, the researcher can manipulate experience with disagreement by providing participants with information intended to shift their opinion on a political issue or choosing partici- pants in a discussion on the basis of their preexisting political views. It is then possible to analyze how different configurations of disagreement affect participation patterns within the experiment itself, as well as (realized) intentions to participate in the future. For example, Wojcieszak (2011) assigned participants to moderated discussion groups with six group members: four participants holding extreme views on rights for sexual minorities (two for and two against) and two members with more moderate views. She found that participants holding more extreme initial views were both more active dur- ing the discussion and more likely to express a desire to continue participating in the future than subjects with more moderate initial views.

New Directions: Selection versus Influence

Methodological innovations have also been used to address another long-standing controversy in the study of networks and political behavior: whether people select sim- ilar others to associate with or influence makes them become more like their friends as they interact. While the issue of selection versus influence has traditionally been cited as a concern primarily with regard to studies of social effects on contested political behaviors such as vote choice or issue attitude change, scholars interested in political participation are highly aware of the issues and continue to find innovative approaches to research that can address any lingering concerns. Approaches that have been used to isolate the causal direction of network effects include longitudinal and panel stud- ies, experiments (often field experiments), analytical models of network dynamics, and collection of "whole network" data in combination with advanced statistical meth- ods such as network autocorrelation models and exponential random graph models (ERGMs).

Longitudinal and panel surveys are a popular approach to studying social networks, as measuring the same behavior(s) repeatedly over time allows us to isolate the direc- tion of change for two measures that are correlated in cross-sectional data. Although panel surveys have been a part of the political network research since its inception, more recent panel studies have included repeated measures of political networks to enable researchers to study the coevolution of network and political choices. These panel sur- veys may also be planned around a period of time with significant change and flux in social activity, such as during an election (Bello and Rolfe, 2014) or soon after starting at a new university (Lazer et al., 2010), to allow researchers to observe and control for self-selection of friends and group activities. In other studies, panel survey designs take advantage of the natural quasi-experiment created when universities randomly assign students to dorms or classrooms (Klofstad, 2011; Campos, Heap, and de Leon, 2017).

Field experiments have also been used to great effect in studies of mobilization and turnout (Gerber and Green, 2000) and to demonstrate how the effects of mobilization can spill over onto spouses and partners (Nickerson, 2008).

While scholars often discuss the importance of theoretical clarity, the use of analytical models of network dynamics can play a particularly significant role in helping to identify network effects (Huckfeldt, Johnson, and Sprague, 2004; Rolfe, 2012). Although it is possible that some network effects might be identified merely by inspecting the correlation of attitudes or turnout patterns among alters, mathematical models of network-based diffusion or contagion suggest that direct influence is unlikely to be directly observable; instead, the traces of network dynamics may be uncovered in cross-sectional data. For example, Rolfe (2012) shows that mathematical models of turnout predict that the range of precinct level variation in turnout rate will remain essentially constant in high and low salience elections, while the average turnout rate will change substantially. This prediction is at odds with the predictions of a resource-based interpretation of the turnout decision and can be confirmed using precinct level variation in turnout without the usual concerns about direction of causality.

Finally, although the sample survey has long been the workhorse of research on political behavior, there is increased interest in trying to bring together survey data with better measures of contextual and structural variation in networks. One approach has been to collect "whole network" data on well-defined populations (e.g., college students or members of social or political organizations). Whole network data can then be analyzed using advanced statistical techniques such as multiple regression quadratic assignment process or MRQAP (Lazer et al., 2010; Song and Eveland, 2015) and ERGMs (Lazer et al., 2010; Song, 2015). Another approach has been to try to tie together sample survey data with better measures of local social context (Scheufele et al., 2006), an approach that allows the incorporation of sophistical geospatial analysis techniques (Makse, Minkoff, and Sokhey, 2014).

Emerging Area: Mechanisms
of Influence

In response to mounting evidence that participation decisions do reflect interpersonal influence or network effects, increasing attention is being given to the issue of mechanism: the question of *how* social interaction affects an individual's participation decision. We identify here three basic approaches to identifying mechanisms that may be at work in network studies of political behavior and reflect briefly upon the limits and promise of each approach.

In discussions of mechanism, many researchers have tried to fit network influences back into the standard framework of instrumental decision making or individual rationality. Network effects are boiled down to an ill-defined sense of social pressure (Gerber, Green, and Larimer, 2008) or a rational response to the existence of social norms that reward voting and punish nonvoting (Gerber et al., 2014). At the aggregate level, this appears somewhat plausible. For example, county level variation in norms is strongly correlated to county level variation in turnout (Gerber et al., 2014). Contextual variation in normative salience can also lead to behavioral changes that on the surface appear rational, such as citizens making larger campaign donations when giving is highly visible (Sinclair, 2012). While this approach is appealing and fits the dominant academic folk theory of political behavior, simply tacking on a "D-term" of social norms and social pressure does not address long-standing criticisms of a rational choice explanation of the individual decision to participate. Furthermore, critical implications of the individual rationality mechanism have not been empirically confirmed, such as the expectation that social pressure would be more pronounced in smaller communities (Panagopoulos, 2011a).

There is also a significant tradition of treating networks as the "pipes" of political behavior: the structural platform over which ideas, preferences, and fads spread out and do battle. Structural network logic can be used to identify network-based mechanisms associated with contagion or the spread of information through network structures. For example, mobilization efforts by candidates and politicians may take advantage of existing network ties, and observed contextual level differences in turnout may be the direct result of candidate- or activist-led mobilization (Rosenstone and Hansen, 1993; Cox, Rosenbluth, and Thies, 1998; Rolfe, 2012; Cho, Gimpel, and Dyck, 2006). A network model of behavioral diffusion underlies theories of how network density (or the average size of personal networks) affects voter turnout and thus can provide an account of why college-educated Americans vote at higher rates than those without a college degree (Rolfe, 2012). Recent studies of political disagreement and participation have gone even further with a structural logic, emphasizing the explanatory potential of structural concepts such as structural isolation and network constraint.

One of the benefits of analytical approaches to understanding structural network effects is that it is possible to make sense of what might appear to be conflicting findings within the literature. An analytical approach to network dynamics allows us to identify conditions under which the same network structure—for example, network density—is expected to have different effects on the political behavior to be explained. Research on political disagreement, and the link between political disagreement and participation, has traditionally emphasized how dense networks can constrain behavior and put greater pressure on individuals to conform with local norms. This would seem to contradict research on political participation that argues that low density networks promote the diffusion of norms of participation, but the apparent contradiction is resolved by the fact that one model is intended to capture diverse local opinion norms while the other is a model of diffusion of global norms of participation. Thus, Huckfeldt et al. (2004) find that members of denser personal networks are less likely to be exposed to political disagreement than citizens whose personal networks are less constrained. Although a great deal of empirical evidence on political participation is better accounted for by a structural approach to network effects, this approach is still somewhat limited, as it cannot easily incorporate explanations that invoke motivated individual differences and individual choice.

Rolfe (2012) argues that network effects can be linked to a social psychological micro-foundations, which points to a fertile area for research at the junction of networks, social psychology and studies of social and ethnic identity. Scholars interested in the political behavior of minorities cannot explain the distinctive behavior patterns of minority group members in purely instrumental terms. Since the civil rights movement of the 1960s, African Americans have continued to vote almost exclusively along Democratic lines even though there has been a tremendous growth in the number of middle-class and professional blacks. Dawson (1994) proposes that a sense of collective identity, or linked fate, helps shape the political choices of blacks. Blacks make political choices that reflect their social identities, even when they do not share the same economic circumstances. This sense of linked fate or shared group consciousness has been shown to influence rates of political activity among minorities (Calhoun-Brown, 1996; Stokes, 2003). This shared identity is cultivated by regular social interaction between minority group members (Mehra, Kilduff, and Brass, 1998).

An identity-based mechanism has particularly significant implications for network-based approaches, because so many of the demographic "usual suspects" of survey research serve as important network cleavages due to network-based homophily. For example, sharing a race and religion predicts the formation of a tie, while political leanings do not (Lazer et al., 2010). However, the potential applicability of an identity-based psychological mechanism is not limited to explaining the behavior of those who belong to the "marked categories" of survey research. Identification with one's community has a significant effect upon one's likelihood to participate in civic and political events (Huddy and Khatib, 2007; Karpowitz et al., 2014). Rolfe (2012) shows that voting is one of the most salient acts of an American citizen and argues that most potential voters understand and react to the turnout decision as the act of a citizen.

Significant opportunities exist for studying the active construction of the content and meaning of social network–based political identities. For example, studies of immigrants and immigrant communities (Klofstad and Bishin, 2014) may be able to take advantage of the same types of regular shifts in population and social networks associated with panel studies of college students. Studies of political discussion and participation in new democracies and democratizing nations would also add to our understanding of the links among participation, networks, and identity. In order for this literature to make truly robust claims about the effects of networks on turnout and other forms of political participation, studies in a broad range of social contexts are essential.

NOTES

1. It is difficult to accurately measure the intimacy of relationships, as the network name generators used on most surveys limit the sources of influence to only a few of the named associates. These issues are explored in more detail in Klofstad, McClurg and Sokhey's chapter on "Political Discussion."
2. These include turnout, displaying a sign or sticker, working for a candidate, donating money, and attending a political rally.

3. This range reflects different ways to calculate the treatment effect, as not everyone in the treatment group was contacted by the canvassers.

REFERENCES

Alesina, A., and La Ferrara, E. (2000). "Participation in Heterogeneous Communities." *The Quarterly Journal of Economics* 115(3): 847–904.

Barber, M., and Imai, K. (2014). "Estimating Neighborhood Effects on Turnout from Geocoded Voter Registration Records." Working paper. http://imai.princeton.edu/research/neighbor.html.

Baybeck, B., and McClurg, S. (2005). "What Do They Know and How Do They Know It?" *American Politics Research* 33(4): 492–520.

Bello, J. (2012). "The Dark Side of Disagreement? Revisiting the Effect of Disagreement on Political Participation." *Electoral Studies* 31(4): 782–795.

Bello, J., and Rolfe, M. (2014). "Is Influence Mightier Than Selection? Forging Agreement in Political Discussion Networks during a Campaign." *Social Networks* 36 (January): 134–146.

Berelson, B., Lazarsfeld, P. F., and McPhee, W. N. (1954). *Voting: A Study of Opinion Formation in a Presidential Campaign*. Chicago: University of Chicago Press.

Bond, R. M., Fariss, C. J., Jones, J. J., Kramer, A. D. I, Marlow, C., Settle, J. E., and Fowler, J. H. (2012). "A 61-Million-Person Experiment in Social Influence and Political Mobilization." *Nature* 489(7415): 295–298.

Brader, T., Tucker, J. A., and Therriault, A. (2014). "Cross Pressure Scores: An Individual-Level Measure of Cumulative Partisan Pressures Arising from Social Group Memberships." *Political Behavior* 36(1): 23–51.

Burt, R. S. (1992). *Structural Holes: The Social Structure of Competition*. Cambridge, MA: Harvard University Press.

Calhoun-Brown, A. (1996). "African American Churches and Political Mobilization: The Psychological Impact of Organizational Resources." *Journal of Politics* 58(4): 935–953.

Campbell, A., Converse, P., Miller, W. E., and Stokes, D. (1960). *The American Voter*. New York: John Wiley.

Campos, C., Hargreaves-Heap, S., and de Leo, F. L. L. (2017). "The Political Influence of Peer Groups: Experimental Evidence in the Classroom," *Oxford Economic Working papers*, forthcoming.

Capella, J. N., Price, V., and Nir, L. (2002). "Argument Repertoire as a Reliable and Valid Measure of Opinion Quality: Electronic Dialogue during Campaign 2000." *Peace Research Abstracts* 39(6): 763–957.

Cho, J. (2011). "The Geography of Political Communication: Effects of Regional Variations in Campaign Advertising on Citizen Communication." *Human Communication Research* 37(3): 434–462.

Cho, W. K. T., Gimpel, J. G., and Dyck, J. J. (2006). "Residential Concentration, Political Socialization, and Voter Turnout." *Journal of Politics* 68(01): 156–167.

Cox, G. W., Rosenbluth, F. M., and Thies, M. F. (1998). "Mobilization, Social Networks, and Turnout: Evidence from Japan." *World Politics* 50(03): 447–474.

Davenport, T. C. (2010). "Public Accountability and Political Participation: Effects of a Face-to-Face Feedback Intervention on Voter Turnout of Public Housing Residents." *Political Behavior* 32(3): 337–368.

Davenport, T. C., Gerber, A. S., Green, D. P., Larimer, C. W., Mann, C. B., and Panagopoulos, C. (2010). "The Enduring Effects of Social Pressure: Tracking Campaign Experiments Over a Series of Elections." *Political Behavior* 32(3): 423–430.

Dawson, M. C. (1994). *Behind the Mule: Race and Class in African-American Politics.* Princeton, NJ: Princeton University Press.

Delli Carpini, M. X., Cook, F. L., & Jacobs, L. R. (2004). "Public deliberation, discursive participation, and citizen engagement: A review of the empirical literature." *Annual Review of Political Science* 7: 315–344.

Djupe, P., Mcclurg, S., & Sokhey, A. E. (2016). "The political consequences of gender in social networks." *British Journal of Political Science*, 1–22.

Eveland, W. P., and Hively, M. H. 2009. "Political Discussion Frequency, Network Size, and 'Heterogeneity' of Discussion as Predictors of Political Knowledge and Participation." *Journal of Communication* 59(2): 205.

Eveland, W. P., and Kleinman, S. B. (2011). "Comparing General and Political Discussion Networks Within Voluntary Organizations Using Social Network Analysis." *Political Behavior* 35(1): 65–87.

Gerber, A. S., and Green, D. P. (2000). "The Effects of Canvassing, Telephone Calls, and Direct Mail on Voter Turnout: A Field Experiment." *American Political Science Review* 94(03): 653–663.

Gerber, A. S., Green, D. P. and Larimer, C. W. (2008). "Social Pressure and Voter Turnout: Evidence from a Large-Scale Field Experiment." *American Political Science Review* 102(1): 33–48.

Gerber, A. S., Green, D. P., and Larimer, C. W. (2010). "An Experiment Testing the Relative Effectiveness of Encouraging Voter Participation by Inducing Feelings of Pride or Shame." *Political Behavior* 32(3): 409–422.

Gerber, A. S., Huber, G. A., Doherty, D., and Dowling, C. M. (2014). "Why People Vote: Estimating the Social Returns to Voting." *British Journal of Political Science* (October): 1–24.

Gimpel, J. G., Cho, W. K. T., and Wu, T. (2007). "Spatial Dimensions of Arab American Voter Mobilization after September 11." *Political Geography* 26(3): 330–351.

Gimpel, J., Dyck, J., and Shaw, D. (2004). "Registrants, Voters, and Turnout Variability Across Neighborhoods." *Political Behavior* 26(4): 343–375.

Gimpel, J. G, and Schuknecht, J. E. (2003). "Political Participation and the Accessibility of the Ballot Box." *Political Geography* 22(5): 471–488.

Goel, S., Mason, W., and Watts, D. J. (2010). "Real and Perceived Attitude Agreement in Social Networks." *Journal of Personality and Social Psychology* 99(4): 611–621.

Granovetter, M. S. (1973). "The Strength of Weak Ties." *American Journal of Sociology* 78(6): 1360–1380.

Hopkins, D. J., and Williamson, T. (2010). "Inactive by Design? Neighborhood Design and Political Participation." *Political Behavior* 34(1): 79–101.

Hobbs, W. R., Christakis, N. A., and Fowler, J. H. (2014). "Widowhood Effects in Voter Participation." *American Journal of Political Science* 58(1): 1–16.

Hopmann, D. N. (2012). "The Consequences of Political Disagreement in Interpersonal Communication: New Insights from a Comparative Perspective." *European Journal of Political Research* 51(2): 265–287.

Huckfeldt, R. (1979). "Political Participation and the Neighborhood Social Context." *American Journal of Political Science* 23(3): 579–592.

Huckfeldt, R. (1980). "Variable Responses to Neighborhood Social Contexts: Assimilation, Conflict, and Tipping Points." *Political Behavior* 2(3): 231–257.

Huckfeldt, R., Johnson, P. E., and Sprague, J. (2004). *Political Disagreement: The Survival of Diverse Opinions Within Communication Networks.* Cambridge: Cambridge University Press.

Huckfeldt, R., Mendez, J. M., and Osborn, T. (2004). "Disagreement, Ambivalence, and Engagement: The Political Consequences of Heterogeneous Networks." *Political Psychology* 25(1): 65–95. doi:10.1111/j.1467-9221.2004.00357.x.

Huckfeldt, R., and Sprague, J. (1991). "Discussant Effects on Vote Choice: Intimacy, Structure, and Interdependence." *Journal of Politics* 53(1): 122–158.

Huckfeldt, R., and Sprague, J. (1992). "Political Parties and Electoral Mobilization: Political Structure, Social Structure, and the Party Canvass." *American Political Science Review* 86(1): 70.

Huckfeldt, R., Sprague, J., and Levine, J. (2000). "The Dynamics of Collective Deliberation in the 1996 Election: Campaign Effects on Accessibility, Certainty, and Accuracy." *American Political Science Review* 94(3): 641–651.

Huddy, L., and Khatib, N. (2007). "American Patriotism, National Identity, and Political Involvement." *American Journal of Political Science* 51(1): 63–77.

Ikeda, K., and Boase, J. (2011). "Multiple Discussion Networks and Their Consequence for Political Participation." *Communication Research* 38(5): 660–683.

Ikeda, K., and Huckfeldt, R. (2001). "Political Communication and Disagreement Among Citizens in Japan and the United States." *Political Behavior* 23(1): 23–51.

Jennings, M. K., and Niemi, R. G. (1974). *Political Character of Adolescence: The Influence of Families and Schools.* Princeton, NJ: Princeton University Press.

Karpowitz, C. F., Monson, J. Q., Nielson, L., Patterson, K. D., and Snell, S. A. (2014). "The People in Your Neighborhood: How Political Minority Status Affects Political Participation." Paper presented at American Political Science Association, Washington, D.C., 2014.

Kenny, C. B. (1992). "Political Participation and Effects from the Social Environment." *American Journal of Political Science* 36(1): 259.

Kim, E., Scheufele, D., and Han, J. Y. (2011). "Structure or Predisposition? Exploring the Interaction Effect of Discussion Orientation and Discussion Heterogeneity on Political Participation." *Mass Communication and Society* 14(4): 502–526.

Klofstad, C. A. (2011). *Civic Talk Peers, Politics, and the Future of Democracy.* Philadelphia: Temple University Press.

Klofstad, C. A., and Bishin, B. G. (2014). "Do Social Ties Encourage Immigrant Voters to Participate in Other Campaign Activities?" *Social Science Quarterly* 95(2): 295–310.

Klofstad, C. A., McClurg, S. C., and Rolfe, M. (2009). "Measurement of Political Discussion Networks: A Comparison of Two 'Name Generator' Procedures." *Public Opinion Quarterly* 73(3): 462–483.

Klofstad, C. A., Sokhey, A. E., and McClurg, S. D. (2013). "Disagreeing about Disagreement: How Conflict in Social Networks Affects Political Behavior." *American Journal of Political Science* 57(1): 120–134.

Knack, S. (1992). "Civic Norms, Social Sanctions, and Voter Turnout." *Rationality & Society* 4(2): 133–156.

Knoke, David. (1990). "Networks of Political Action: Toward Theory Construction." *Social Forces* 68(4): 1041–1063.

La Due Lake, R., and Huckfeldt, R. (1998). "Social Capital, Social Networks, and Political Participation." *Political Psychology* 19(3): 567–584.

Lazarsfeld, P. F., Berelson, B., and Gaudet, H. (1944). *The People's Choice; How the Voter Makes Up His Mind in a Presidential Campaign.* New York: Columbia University Press.

Lazer, D., Rubineau, B., Chetkovich, C., Katz, N., and Neblo, M. (2010). "The Coevolution of Networks and Political Attitudes." *Political Communication* 27(3): 248–274.

Lazer, D., Ognyanova, K., Minozzi, W., and Neblo, M. "The Social Control of Political Participation: Conflict and Contagion as Processes (De)mobilizing Voting." Paper presented at American Political Science Association, San Francisco, California, 2015.

Leighley, J. E. (1990). "Social Interaction and Contextual Influences on Political Participation." *American Politics Quarterly* 18(4): 459–475.

Makse, T., Minkoff, S. L., and Sokhey, A. E. (2014). "Networks, Context, and the Use of Spatially Weighted Survey Metrics." *Political Geography* 42(September): 79–91.

Matthes, J. (2013). "Do Hostile Opinion Environments Harm Political Participation? The Moderating Role of Generalized Social Trust." *International Journal of Public Opinion Research* 25(1): 23–42.

McClurg, S. D. (2003). "Social Networks and Political Participation: The Role of Social Interaction in Explaining Political Participation." *Political Research Quarterly* 56(4): 449–464.

McClurg, S. D. (2006). "Political Disagreement in Context: The Conditional Effect of Neighborhood Context, Disagreement and Political Talk on Electoral Participation." *Political Behavior* 28(4): 349–366.

Mehra, A., Kilduff, M., and Brass, D. J. (1998). "At the Margins: A Distinctiveness Approach to the Social Identity and Social Networks of Underrepresented Groups." *Academy of Management Journal* 41(4): 441–452.

Merriam, C. E., and Gosnell, H. F. (1924). *Non-Voting: Causes and Methods of Control.* Chicago: University of Chicago Press.

Morey, A. C., Eveland, W. P., Jr, and Hutchens, M. J. (2012). "The 'Who' Matters: Types of Interpersonal Relationships and Avoidance of Political Disagreement." *Political Communication* 29(1): 86–103.

Mutz, D. C. (2002). "The Consequences of Cross-Cutting Networks for Political Participation." *American Journal of Political Science* 46(4): 838–855.

Mutz, D. C. (2006). *Hearing the Other Side: Deliberative versus Participatory Democracy.* Cambridge, UK, and New York: Cambridge University Press.

Nickerson, D. W. (2008). "Is Voting Contagious? Evidence from Two Field Experiments." *American Political Science Review* 102(1): 49–57.

Nir, L. (2011). "Disagreement and Opposition in Social Networks: Does Disagreement Discourage Turnout?" *Political Studies* 59(3): 674–692.

Panagopoulos, C. (2010). "Affect, Social Pressure and Prosocial Motivation: Field Experimental Evidence of the Mobilizing Effects of Pride, Shame and Publicizing Voting Behavior." *Political Behavior* 32(3): 369–386.

Panagopoulos, C. (2011a). "Social Pressure, Surveillance and Community Size: Evidence from Field Experiments on Voter Turnout." In "Electoral Forecasting Symposium," special issue, *Electoral Studies* 30(2): 353–357.

Panagopoulos, C. (2011b). "Thank You for Voting: Gratitude Expression and Voter Mobilization." *Journal of Politics* 73(03): 707–717.

Panagopoulos, C., Larimer, C. W., and Condon, M. (2013). "Social Pressure, Descriptive Norms, and Voter Mobilization." *Political Behavior* 36(2): 451–469.

Parsons, B. M. (2009). "Social Networks and the Affective Impact of Political Disagreement." *Political Behavior* 32(2): 181–204.

Plutzer, E. (2002). "Becoming a Habitual Voter: Inertia, Resources, and Growth in Young Adulthood." *American Political Science Review* 96(1): 41–56.

Putnam, R. D. (1995). "Bowling Alone: America's Declining Social Capital." *Journal of Democracy* 6(1): 65.

Quintelier, E., Stolle, D., and Harell, A. (2012). "Politics in Peer Groups Exploring the Causal Relationship between Network Diversity and Political Participation." *Political Research Quarterly* 65(4): 868–881.

Rolfe, M. (2012). *Voter Turnout: A Social Theory of Political Participation.* New York: Cambridge University Press.

Rolfe, M., and Bello, J. (2013). "Campaign Driven Increases in Political Discussion." Paper presented at the 2013 Political Networks Conference, Bloomington, Indiana.

Rosenstone, S. J., and Hansen, J. M. (1993). *Mobilization, Participation, and Democracy in America.* New York: Macmillan.

Scheufele, D. A., Hardy, B. W., Brossard, D., Waismel-Manor, I. S., and Nisbet, E. (2006). "Democracy Based on Difference: Examining the Links Between Structural Heterogeneity, Heterogeneity of Discussion Networks, and Democratic Citizenship." *Journal of Communication* 56(4): 728–753.

Scheufele, D. A., Nisbet, M. C., Brossard, D., and Nesbet, E. C. (2004). "Social Structure and Citizenship: Examining the Impacts of Social Setting, Network Heterogeneity, and Informational Variables on Political Participation." *Political Communication* 21(3): 315–338.

Schmitt-Beck, R., and Mackenrodt, C. (2010). "Social Networks and Mass Media as Mobilizers and Demobilizers: A Study of Turnout at a German Local Election." In "Voters and Coalition Governments," special issue, *Electoral Studies* 29(3): 392–404.

Simmel, Georg. [1908] 1958. *Soziologie: Untersuchungen über die Formen der Vergesellschaftung* [Sociology: Inquiries into the Construction of Social Forms]. Berlin: Duncker & Humblot.

Sinclair, Betsy. 2012. *The Social Citizen: Peer Networks and Political Behavior.* Chicago: University of Chicago Press.

Sinclair, Betsy, Margaret McConnell, and Melissa R. Michelson. 2013. "Local Canvassing: The Efficacy of Grassroots Voter Mobilization." *Political Communication* 30 (1): 42–57.

Song, Hyunjin. 2015. "Uncovering the Structural Underpinnings of Political Discussion Networks: Evidence From an Exponential Random Graph Model." *Journal of Communication* 65 (1). 146–169.

Song, H., and Eveland, W. P., Jr. (2015). "The Structure of Communication Networks Matters: How Network Diversity, Centrality, and Context Influence Political Ambivalence, Participation, and Knowledge." *Political Communication* 32(1): 83–108.

Stasser, G., and Titus, W. (1985). "Pooling of Unshared Information in Group Decision Making: Biased Information Sampling during Discussion." *Journal of Personality and Social Psychology* 48(6): 1467–1478.

Stoker, L., and Jennings, M. K. (1995). "Life-cycle Transitions and Political Participation: The Case of Marriage." *American Political Science Review* 89(2): 421–433.

Stokes, A. K. (2003). "Latino Group Consciousness and Political Participation." *American Politics Research* 31(4): 361–378.

Torcal, M., and Maldonado, G. (2014). "Revisiting the Dark Side of Political Deliberation: The Effects of Media and Political Discussion on Political Interest." *Public Opinion Quarterly* 78(3): 679–706.

Verba, S., Schlozman, K. L., and Brady, H. E. (1995). *Voice and Equality: Civic Voluntarism in American Politics.* Cambridge, MA: Harvard University Press.

Verba, S., Schlozman, K., and Burns, N. (2005). "Family Ties: Understanding the Intergenerational Transmission of Participation." In *The Social Logic of Politics*, edited by Alan Zuckerman, pp. 95–114. Philadelphia: Temple University Press.

Walsh, K. C. (2004). *Talking about Politics: Informal Groups and Social Identity in American Life.* Chicago: University of Chicago Press.

Wojcieszak, M. (2011). "Pulling Toward or Pulling Away: Deliberation, Disagreement, and Opinion Extremity in Political Participation." *Social Science Quarterly* 92(1): 207–225.

Wojcieszak, M. E., and Mutz, D. C. (2009). "Online Groups and Political Discourse: Do Online Discussion Spaces Facilitate Exposure to Political Disagreement?" *Journal of Communication* 59(1): 40.

Wolfinger, N. H., and Wolfinger, R. E. (2008). "Family Structure and Voter Turnout." *Social Forces* 86(4): 1513–1528.

Zaller, J. (1992). *The Nature and Origins of Mass Opinion.* Cambridge, UK and New York: Cambridge University Press.

Zúñiga, H. G. de, and Valenzuela, S. (2011). "The Mediating Path to a Stronger Citizenship: Online and Offline Networks, Weak Ties, and Civic Engagement." *Communication Research* 38(3): 397–421.

CHAPTER 15

SOCIAL NETWORKS AND VOTE CHOICE

LAUREN RATLIFF SANTORO AND PAUL A. BECK

CENTRAL to the study of citizen political behavior is the understanding of who participates in politics and toward what ends. While the previous chapter by Rolfe and Chan
addressed how attention to social networks aids our understanding of *who* participates,
the current chapter demonstrates that social networks also influence the *content* of that
participation. Our focus is on if and how social networks influence candidate or party
choice in elections. Because many aspects of the social environment or context can act
upon these individual voting choices, we limit the discussion in this chapter to the influence of *social* networks. Social networks are distinguished from social contexts in that
they are individually constructed, whereas contexts typically are structurally imposed.
Specifically, we define social networks as the places where informal conversation with
social intimates, such as family, friends, and coworkers, occurs and occasionally where
"everyday political disagreement" may take place (Klofstad, Sokhey, and McClurg,
2013). With the increase in Internet and social media use in recent years, these conversations are increasingly not the face-to-face conversations of old, but rather encompass
"arm's-length" tweets, messages, and snapchats via electronic media such as computers
and cell phones. Most studies of social networks that we review here predate the explosion of these forms of conversation, which will need to be an important focus in the
years to come.

A crucial debate in the literature, which Rolfe and Chan also address in Chapter 14,
involves the question of whether people *select* their political discussants during a campaign, quite likely choosing those who agree with them and shunning those who do not,
or whether their discussants may come, sometimes inadvertently, from non-agreeing
groups, opening up more possibilities for *influence* on their own choices. These alternative possibilities are likely to be even more prominent for vote choices than for turnout. It is difficult to conceive of people who have voted or plan to vote choosing their
political discussants based on that decision, but it is not at all difficult to think of people
with particular vote preferences selecting discussants with those preferences in mind.

Determining the direction of causality, in short, is a thorny issue for studies of the effects of social networks on vote choice. It can be addressed, as we shall see, by embedding the partisanship of the social network in a more comprehensive model of the vote decision, by utilizing panel studies over the course of the campaign, or through experimental randomization, but it cannot be satisfactorily resolved.

We would also be remiss if we did not express the following caveats before engaging with the literature on social networks and vote choice. First, it should be expected that not very many people change their minds about politics; in support of results from the path-breaking studies by Lazarsfeld and his colleagues (Lazarsfeld, Berelson, and Gaudet, 1948; Berelson, Lazarsfeld, and McPhee, 1954), most often social networks serve to reinforce preexisting political beliefs. Those individuals who do change their minds are expected to be exposed to more cross-pressures, or disagreement, in their social environment. Thus, a majority of the time social networks serve to reinforce political beliefs, not to change them outright. In competitive electoral politics, however, even limited conversions can be consequential in changing the outcomes of elections.

Second, it is likely that influence on voting choices from our social networks is episodic rather than continuous, especially in its dependence on electoral campaigns. Outside of election season, few people seem likely to change their minds about politics or even to think about specific vote choices (Lazarsfeld, Berelson, and Gaudet, 1948; Berelson, Lazarsfeld, and McPhee, 1954; Huckfeldt and Sprague, 1995), which is why most research has not considered non-election campaign periods. For those who have already made up their minds to give their support to a particular party, the campaign often serves to reinforce their vote choice once its candidates are determined. For those who have not reached a vote decision, the greater media attention, interest, and discussion that the campaign stimulates are important factors in helping them to come to a vote decision, either through the added information they gain about the particular parties and candidates (Huckfeldt and Sprague, 1995) or in response to the social pressure they feel (Sinclair, 2012). And yet while the decision to turn out to vote is primarily activated within the bounds of a political campaign resulting from discussion and increased interest, the choice of whom to vote for may outrun the bounds of a single political campaign, resulting more from the passive absorption of cues from parents, family, and friends over the course of time. In other words, "vote choices and opinions appear to be formed less by discussion and more by passive absorption of cues from the network and environment" (Sokhey and Djupe, 2011, 56)—and these cues often may be long-standing and consequently difficult to observe in a single election.

Third, as will become readily apparent, much of the research on social networks and vote choice has been conducted on particular elections and in the United States. This raises questions about the generalizability of its findings across elections and across countries. As we attempt to build broad understandings of how social networks affect vote choices, replications across elections and across countries (with different features of their political systems) are important. Therefore, we pay special attention to how the findings on particular elections and in the United States square with the research that has been conducted in other countries.

Finally, social networks are not the sole influencers of vote choice, or even the primary one. Political socialization, social identities, personality, values, the party identifications they foster, and the more immediate issues and candidates of a particular campaign are important components of vote choice (Jennings and Niemi, 1981; Campbell et al., 1960; Green, Palmquist, and Schickler, 2002). We contend that social networks are an important, and often missing, component of understanding what shapes individual voting choices. In short, as Beck et al. (2002, 69) have put it, "voters' enduring personal characteristics interact with the messages they are receiving from the established social context in which they operate."

Our review of the research literature of social networks and voting proceeds as follows. First we reach back to some of the first studies of voters in the 1940s, which have served as a foundation for subsequent work. Then we examine more recent work in the United States and other countries. We conclude with a discussion of challenges and opportunities facing the field.

FOUNDATIONAL WORK

The study of if and how social networks influence the vote decision has a long-standing history. Perhaps the first evidence of the social environment's influence on political attitudes and beliefs stems from Theodore Newcomb's study in the 1930s. Young women from well-to-do and mostly conservative households entered the notoriously liberal setting of Bennington College. If they remained in attendance there, the women became more liberal during their years at Bennington, and these effects persisted across twenty-five years, influencing even their choice of spouses and careers (Newcomb, 1943; Newcomb et al., 1967). Interactions in the social environment were found to have a profound influence on the political views of these young women, moving them away from the views and voting preferences most had held when they entered Bennington.

Not long afterward Paul Lazarsfeld and his colleagues at Columbia University took the study of opinion formation further through their panel studies of voters during the 1940 and 1948 election campaigns for president. Their work in first Erie County, Ohio (Lazarsfeld, Berelson, and Gaudet, 1948) and then Elmira, New York (Berelson, Lazarsfeld, and McPhee, 1954) pioneered the study of the effects of social processes on voting behavior. Although it emphasized the effects of social cross-pressures that figured prominently in studies of turnout (as discussed in the Rolfe and Chan chapter of this handbook), its primary focus was on vote choice. Their results became the "conventional wisdom" on social network influences on the vote, even as studies of voting behavior left their study behind, turning in a more autonomous-individual-decision-maker direction for the next several decades.

Perhaps most important, these foundational works established face-to-face contacts as the most important influences on the stimulation of opinion change (Eulau, 1980). Lazarsfeld and his colleagues argued that voting is a "group experience" in which individuals are influenced by the group with which they live from day to day. In their words, "people vote not only with their social group, but also for it" (Lazarsfeld, Berelson, and Gaudet, 1948, 148). Lazarsfeld and his colleagues went on to elaborate a "two-step flow of communications," in which ideas from media and political elites flow from elite opinion leaders to the mass public, sometimes through nonelite opinion leaders in the individual's discussion network. Campaigns *activate* preexisting political beliefs, and the media and discussion increase interest in the campaign. This interest was seen to lead to the crystallization of political opinions through selective exposure and, in some cases, persuasion (Lazarsfeld, Berelson, and Gaudet, 1948).

For individuals whose minds were made up before the campaign began, the campaign was shown to *reinforce* those decisions, with stronger partisans insulating themselves from contrary points of view. Accordingly, only a few people were converted, or convinced by the 1940 presidential campaign, which resulted in the re-election of the familiar Franklin D. Roosevelt to a third term in office. Those who were converted were exposed to an increased amount of cross-pressures: "the conflicts and inconsistencies among the factors which influence the vote decision . . . drive him [the voter] in opposite directions" (Lazarsfeld, Berelson, and Gaudet, 1948, 53). The more cross-pressures an individual was exposed to, the later the vote decision was crystalized. However, the vote intentions of 88 percent of voters in the Erie County, Ohio, study remained steadfast with one party. The remaining 12 percent of voters who switched parties were less interested in the campaign and were exposed to more conflicting pressures; accordingly, they were more open to persuasion from a personal contact or, ultimately, to not voting.

In their study of residents in Elmira, New York, during the 1948 presidential campaign, Berelson, Lazarsfeld, and McPhee (1954, 19) concurred that "votes do not change easily, at least during a campaign" and found that cross-pressured individuals were the ones most likely to change. However, most of this instability occurred *within* political parties and not *across* them. These "molecular" changes polarized the electorate at the expense of moderation: the "ordinary campaign is characterized by numerous shifts over short distances of the political spectrum" (Berelson, Lazarsfeld, and McPhee, 1954, 22).[1]

In both the 1940 and 1948 presidential elections, campaigns were dominated by candidates of the two major parties, a regular feature of American elections, which raises questions about how much even these foundational studies could be generalized to the common multiparty races beyond American shores. Even the challenge from a third-party candidate in 1948, who received 9 percent of the vote in New York State, was not conspicuous in Elmira.

Despite limited opportunities for social influence on vote choice within the bounds of a political campaign, social influence on partisan views may best be illuminated through one's standing, primary relationships with other people, such as family, spouse, and friends (Jennings and Niemi, 1974, 1978, 1981; Jennings, Stoker, and Bowers, 2009; see also Rolfe and Chan, this volume). When discord is present in these primary groups, the impact of the broader social context can be more clearly seen. However, disagreement in these groups is not widespread; "most of the political talk that went on in the living

rooms of Elmira, over the back fences, at the bars, on the job, and in similar places—
the everyday, informal, grassroots discussion on public affairs that serves as a base of
democratic judgment—involved the exchange of mutually agreeable points of view"
(Berelson, Lazarsfeld, and McPhee, 1954, 108). Thus, initial evidence suggested that the
decision of whom to vote for results from the absorption of cues from individuals' networks and contexts over time, where close and strong ties are of more importance than
weak ones (Granovetter, 1973; see also Sinclair, 2012).

Drawing on his involvement in the Columbia studies and expanding the "two-step
communication model," McPhee (1963) conceptualized individual vote choice as resulting from three processes: stimulation, discussion, and learning. Individuals bring their
individual (psychological) dispositions and their external (political) stimuli into the
stimulation process. Here, individuals sample the distributions of the external stimuli;
the weaker (stronger) the internal disposition toward a party, the stronger (weaker) the
stimulus required to elicit a "yes" choice for that party. The output of the stimulation
process is an initial preference for or against an issue or candidate. In the discussion
process, individuals put their initial preferences through "social reality testing" (Lewin,
1947). In this process, individuals cross-check their preferences with the preferences
of others in their networks. When the individual's initial preference agrees with that of
his or her social intimate, the initial reaction is confirmed and doubts are put to rest.
However, when the individual's initial preference disagrees with that of his or her social
intimates, the individual seeks renewed exposure to the external stimuli, or objective
reality. This recheck results in either a confirmation or rejection of the advice from the
social environment. In the learning process, the surviving convictions from the stimulation and discussion processes inform future political choices. McPhee's (1963) model
remains one of the most comprehensive. Though it has been tested in part, a complete
test of the model remains to be done (Sokhey and Djupe, 2011).

From these early, foundational works, principally those of Lazarsfeld and his colleagues, a few key themes emerge. First, voters do not make political decisions independently, or in isolation; their choices are constrained by the social environment in which
they live. Second, outright conversion of individual political attitudes is rare; social
networks most often reinforce individual partisan views during the course of a campaign. Third, preference change most often results from the presence of disagreement,
or cross-pressures, in the immediate, or primary, groups. This discordant information
leads individuals to check and recheck their initial preferences against other preferences
and against the external context, resulting in a continual process of preference updating
in the presence of new information filtered by the social environment. And finally, the
influence of the social network on individual political attitudes is more heavily influenced by our relationships with close social ties than by our discussions with weak ties.
McPhee sums these observations up nicely:

> (A) fundamental reorientation, a reversal of a previous disposition, is rare in real
> life.... It occurs only in the extreme example, where not only a sustained social
> influence is consistently contrary over a substantial period, but the influence is also

always supported by the objective reality of external events.... [A]fter socialization or other causes have started dispositions in one direction ... social influence alone cannot reverse that direction. (McPhee, 1963, 94)

THE RECENT PHASE OF US RESEARCH ON NETWORKS AND VOTING

We have devoted so much attention to the foundational Columbia studies because for several decades they dominated thinking about the role of social networks in voting behavior, and they remain important to this day. Three decades after their publication, voting behavior scholars returned to a focus on social networks. The interim period was dominated by a conceptualization of voters as autonomous decision makers, influenced most by their social-psychological identifications and evaluations (Campbell et al., 1960) or their rational choice retrospective and prospective judgments of parties and candidates (Downs, 1957; Fiorina, 1981).[2]

The return to social influences is best epitomized by the work of Huckfeldt and Sprague (1987, 1991, 1995), who first studied the dynamics of opinion change throughout the course of the 1984 presidential election in South Bend, Indiana. They too demonstrated that disagreement, once again, is a key ingredient in social influence: "[W]hen citizens encounter political information that disagrees with their own viewpoints, they may rationally reassess their positions, and herein lies the potential for influence" (Huckfeldt and Sprague, 1995, 20). However, social influence on individual political behavior may not result from traditional learning after all (McPhee, 1963); rather, information from the social environment may provide efficient shortcuts to the high cost of gathering political information (Downs, 1957; Huckfeldt and Sprague, 1995). The social environment is influential primarily because of shared intimacy (social cohesion) and/ or shared social position (structural equivalence) between respondent and discussant (Burt, 1987; Huckfeldt and Sprague, 1991; Kenny, 1998). Spousal and other family discussants primarily influence vote choice because of shared intimacy, respect, and experience, whereas shared social positions may account for influence among nonrelatives (but see Kenny [1998]). Furthermore, nonrelative discussants are most influential when perceptions of their beliefs are accurate and agreement is perceived (Huckfeldt and Sprague, 1991; Kenny, 1998).

Following the return to a focus on social influences on the vote decision, many studies demonstrated correlation, and even plausibly showed causation, between the candidate choice of respondents and their discussants. Beck et al. (2002) analyzed the effects of partisan cues from the social network within a comprehensive model of the vote decision in the 1992 presidential election. They found that information from individual social networks that is biased toward one candidate or another was significantly related to individual vote choice. Individuals whose personal discussants supported the Democratic

(Republican) candidate were more likely to vote for the Democrat (Republican). While these effects persisted across high and low levels of interest in politics, personal discussants were more important for less politicized individuals. Moreover, the effect of perceived and actual discussant bias on vote choice survived controls for other influences on the vote choice, including party identification, ideology, and organizational and media bias. Drawing on the same national survey, Levine (2005) echoed these results and went on to suggest that both intimate (family and friends) and nonintimate discussants impact people's political views, again after controls.

There is one American study that provides insight into how social networks may influence the vote in multiparty systems, thus anticipating the cross-national research considered below. The 1992 US presidential election turned out to be a three-candidate contest, with independent Ross Perot winning about 19 percent of the vote nationwide. The interesting question his candidacy raised was how a third choice under plurality (the candidate with the most votes wins, even if it falls short of a majority) rules complicates the vote decision. With only two viable candidates, voters can be expected to vote sincerely for their first choice. With three, and Perot was perceived as viable especially early in the campaign, they can vote sincerely or they can vote strategically for their second choice if they think that their first choice cannot win. How do they gauge the prospects of their preferred candidate? Certainly public opinion polls and public commentary can indicate candidate standings, and voters may pay attention to them. But voters may also take their cues from their social networks. Beck (2002) examined the ultimate votes of respondents who said that they had preferred Perot at some point during the long campaign in relationship to the preferences that they perceived their discussion partners held. The more people in their discussion network were perceived to support Perot, the more likely the voter was to vote for Perot. The "reality" testing in their immediate social network led those who favored Perot to vote sincerely if they found reinforcement or strategically if they did not.

More generally, Huckfeldt, Johnson, and Sprague (2004) demonstrated that vote choice correspondence between respondent and discussant is conditional on the distribution of candidate preferences in the rest of the network, especially among weaker partisans.[3] In other words, the more discussants in an individual's network support the same presidential candidate, the more likely the respondent is to vote for that candidate. This occurs, they contend, according to a process of autoregressive influence, in which individuals weigh every incoming message against other messages. Messages that agree with each other are accepted, while discordant messages are discarded. This autoregressive process can explain opinion change resulting from the social environment.

Evidence of this distributional network effect has been replicated in other recent work. Sinclair (2012) demonstrated that as the percentage of Republicans (Democrats) in a discussion network increases, the likelihood of a respondent voting for the Republican (Democratic) candidate increases, even when variables influencing the choice of those discussants are controlled for. Using panel data, she showed that agreement increases over the course of the campaign. Using the 2000 American National Election Study survey, Ryan (2010) demonstrated that individuals support the candidate who is supported by the majority of their discussion partners. Dominant signals from the social network win out, even when these signals come from less politically knowledgeable discussants. Social networks provide crucial information shortcuts for citizens, and these shortcuts sometimes lead individuals to make "correct" (in the sense of voting for the candidate who best aligns with their interests) voting decisions (Ryan, 2010, 2011). Where disagreement in these networks is present, social networks provide ambiguous political signals, resulting in less "correct" voting decisions (Sokhey and McClurg, 2012).

The Social Citizen provides perhaps the most direct evidence that social networks influence vote choice and even partisan identification (Sinclair, 2012). While previous work demonstrated correlations between individuals' party identification and the party identification of their respondents (Huckfeldt, Johnson, and Sprague, 2004; Mutz, 2006), Sinclair argued that an individual's closest ties, more likely to be stable over the course of time, drove party identification. Using longitudinal analysis and propensity score matching, she demonstrated that the "partisanship of an individual's discussion network appears to affect not only the probability that the individual will change party identification but also the party to which the individual will change" (Sinclair, 2012, 138). Importantly, these ties go above and beyond ties to parents and family members, to include close friends and more expansive social influence units. Whereas weak ties are important for the introduction of new information, the decision to turn out, and exposure to diverse political views (Granovetter, 1973; Rolfe, 2012; Mutz, 2002), strong ties are more important for influencing long-term political beliefs, especially with more frequent interaction among individuals who are geographically proximate (Sinclair, 2012). Similarly, Ryan and Milazzo (2015) demonstrated that Catholics identified as Republicans in greater numbers over time as a result of their movement into social contexts with pro-Republican and anti-Democratic messages.[4]

These findings, based entirely on survey evidence, have found some confirmation in experimental work. Klar (2014) demonstrated that social settings play an important role in the formation of political preferences. She embedded experimental subjects in groups with contrasting homogenous or heterogeneous political preferences. Participants were asked to discuss two issues (healthcare and energy policy) as a group. Partisans were found to engage in more partisan motivated reasoning in ideologically homogeneous groups, but to pursue more accuracy-driven information when their settings were diverse, providing experimental evidence that the partisan makeup of a social network is consequential for the vote decision.

Other recent work with implications for voting choice has emphasized the dynamic nature of network influence on attitudes about politics. Lazer (2001) conducted a two-wave study with whole-network data of individuals who worked in the Office of Information and Regulatory Affairs (OIRA). He found that while individuals' policy attitudes conformed to the attitudes of other members of their organization at a single point in time, these policy attitudes appeared to stabilize across time. Individuals who changed their attitudes changed in a direction that was consistent with the attitudes of individuals in their network. Building on this work in the political science context, Lazer et al. (2010) demonstrated that individuals' political attitudes become more similar to the attitudes of those they are connected to over time, and this influence is especially powerful among friends in contrast to coworkers.

In summary, recent work in the American context echoes the foundational research of Lazarsfeld and his colleagues in pointing to the consistent influence of social networks on candidate choice in an election. Homogeneously partisan social networks foster agreeing vote choices. More heterogeneous networks, on the other hand, lead to indecision in coming to a vote decision and disagreement with at least some members of the network. Homogeneous networks are far more common than heterogeneous ones. How much network homophily varies across elections is less clear, however, with the tantalizing suggestion that when the candidate choices are broadened beyond the usual two in America's two-party system, network influences may become more important in reinforcing choices or challenging them.

NETWORKS AND VOTING BEHAVIOR FROM A NON-AMERICAN PERSPECTIVE

Both the foundational studies by the Columbia scholars in the 1940s and early 1950s and the recent resurgence in research on the role of social networks in voting discussed so far are entirely rooted in the United States. Where voting choice is concerned, however, the United States is an unusual case on which to base understandings of the role of social networks in general. First, with its dominant two-party system, network heterogeneity means having discussants who support a party opposed to one's own or no party at all. This necessarily precludes understanding the role social networks play in the more common multiparty systems, in which a voter may be shopping for different alternatives within a governing or opposition coalition, a "minor" party standing on its own, or a strategic choice in a second-round election. In most political systems beyond the American, in short, social network heterogeneity may be more common, or even where it is not, more important in guiding voting choices. There is a second, cultural consideration in casting the net more widely than the United States. Discussion via social networks, especially involving politics, is more common in some countries than others. The legacies of divisive civil wars (e.g., in Spain) or authoritarian repression (e.g., in Eastern Europe) may make citizens hesitant to discuss controversial matters with others, particularly people who may be on the other side politically. Studies of other countries promise to broaden our understanding of the role of social networks, especially in multiparty settings and less discussion-oriented political cultures.

There are a considerable number of studies of social networks and vote choices in democracies beyond the United States.[5] In most cases, like the American studies, they focus on a single election in a single country, and they are most common in the advanced industrialized democracies with traditions of academically oriented election surveys. National election surveys that included network batteries have been conducted in Britain, Germany, and Japan in particular. Studies of those elections broaden the picture of social network influence on vote choice. Interestingly, some of these studies were published before the recent turn to social network research in the United States after a long period of neglect following the pioneering Columbia studies and the sociodemographic tradition of European voting research.

Japan has long been thought of as a culture in which interpersonal relations and social network influences are particularly strong. Flanagan (1991) examined the role social networks played as the mechanism connecting geographic and associational contexts to the vote, especially drawing on empirical evidence from the 1976 election. He depicted Japanese voters as deeply embedded in homogeneously partisan networks, guided and mobilized in their partisan choices by opinion leaders from that network. Drawing mostly from the same election, Richardson (1991) went beyond a narrower emphasis on opinion leaders to include a variety of other interpersonal influences, including family, friends, neighbors, and coworkers, on voter choice. Candidates for the national parliament in multimember districts who sought to build personal connections to voters by drawing on their interpersonal network ties made networks especially important in sending voting signals.

More recent studies of Japanese politics have used more directly focused measures of discussion networks to reach similar conclusions, even during a period of upheaval in the post–World War II party system. Huckfeldt, Ikeda, and Pappi (2005) found that few Japanese voters in the 1993 election had discussants with whom they perceived disagreement in voting preferences—far fewer than in American and German elections around the same time. However, just half of Japanese voters that year had agreeing discussants (far less than in those comparison countries), while a third of them reported not being able to determine their discussants' vote. With the defeat of the long-standing governing party, 1993 was a particularly turbulent time in Japanese politics and understandably fostered greater indeterminacy in the partisan preferences of network discussion partners. Even so, many Japanese voters in this contest were embedded in reinforcing partisan networks and voted in concert with their discussion partners, as was reported in a follow-up 1993–1995 national panel study (Liu, Ikeda, and Wilson, 1998). Supporters of the major parties found more reinforcement in their networks, while minor party supporters were more exposed to challenging messages from their discussion networks, a result that was echoed in a 1997 local study (Ikeda and Huckfeldt, 2001). However, the finding (Ikeda et al., 2005) that respondent party identifications were more stable than discussant partisanship should give pause to anyone who might assume that network partisanship is more or less constant across elections in the same country.

Great Britain is another place in which some studies of voting behavior have included a social networks approach. Drawing on a panel study of the 1992–1997 British general elections, Pattie and Johnson (1999) showed that most people were exposed to political discussions, and many had conversations across partisan lines. They also found that vote changes from 1992 to 1997 moved in the direction of voting for a particular party when people had had conversations with supporters of that party, paralleling similar changes in the 1987 to 1992 elections (Pattie and Johnson, 2001).

In their study of political interactions within the family, Zuckerman, Dasovic, and Fitzgerald (2007) drew on panel data over the decade 1991–2001 to show how partisan allegiances and votes were influenced by the most intimate members of their social networks. They depicted partisan ties for most Britons as "bounded" rather than strict loyalties: never supporting one of the parties steadfastly across elections, but not supporting one of the others. Bounded partisanship was shown to be rooted in their family; they were responsive to the partisan choices of their partners, parents, and children, especially wives and mothers. By contrast, partisanship was not likely to be bounded when the partisan choices of these intimates were not themselves bounded. In voting, about two-thirds of Britons were found to be bounded partisans whose family favored the same party. They voted for that party or did not vote in a particular election, but rarely crossed over to the "other side." That left about a third of the electorate in more heterogeneous partisan families, and they responded with less constancy in their votes. Zuckerman and colleagues concluded with a discussion of how bounded partisanship could apply to other political systems, with most voters not crossing the gulf between parties in their own bloc and the ideological opposition. This supports our previous suggestion that the partisan heterogeneity of the social network may appear to be higher in multiparty systems even if it is limited in its reach.

Germany is another country outside of the United States where scholars have systematically examined the connection between social networks and voting behavior. Faas and Schmitt-Beck (2010) found that election-focused discussion within primary networks made people more likely to vote in the 2005 election, but it could make their vote choice more difficult, perhaps because 2005 was a particularly confusing election. The impact of partisan disagreement within their social network on difficulty in the vote decision, paradoxically, was different between primary (family, friends) and secondary (neighbors, coworkers) networks. Disagreement with intimates decreased certainty about vote direction, but it was increased when the discussion was with discordant neighbors and coworkers, suggesting that "weak" ties (Granovetter, 1973) might not be so strong after all. Using the 2009 German election study to examine Sinclair's (2012) distinction between social pressure and information provision as mechanisms of influence, Schmitt-Beck and Partheymüller (2014) developed a two-stage explanation of social network influences directly on voting behavior in multiparty systems like Germany's. They found unequivocal evidence that social pressure first pushed voters to support parties from the same ideological "camp." Then, through their provision of information about choices within that camp, discussants influenced the ultimate party chosen. The closer the relationship to the discussant, the greater the influence on choice of camp, with spouses and relatives being especially important and friends less so. At the second stage, though, discussant knowledge and trustworthiness emerged as important moderators. This two-stage process differentiates Germany and other multiparty systems from the two-party focus on network influences in the United States.

Two German studies relying on longitudinal surveys from 1985 to 2001 showed that the family had a strong impact on the development of partisan attitudes. First, the Zuckerman et al. (2007) study of bounded partisanship focused on Germany as well as Britain, albeit without a vote variable. Couples became more alike in their partisanship across the course of their marriages, with husbands more influential than wives, in contrast to the British pattern. And in Germany, like Britain, mothers tended to have more direct influence on their children. All in all, though, this longitudinal evidence supports the conclusion that the partisanship of the social network is important for voting choices. Second, Schmitt-Beck, Weick, and Christoph (2006) showed high year-to-year fluctuations in partisan loyalties, especially movements out of partisanship into independence and from smaller to larger parties, echoing the notion of bounded partisanship rather than a strict single-party identification. Partisan changes were the product of, among other factors, changes in family relationships as people moved through the life cycle—especially leaving their childhood home or marrying someone from another party or no party at all—even as the family remained an important "anchor" for partisanship.

Two additional single-country studies further inform our consideration of social network effects beyond the United States. Baker, Ames, and Renno (2006) employed a three-wave panel study to examine the dynamics of political discussion and voting preferences during the volatile 2002 Brazilian presidential election campaign (also see Ames et al. in this volume). Partisan ties in this election were especially weak, and voters relied on cues from their interpersonal discussions to help them navigate through a particularly complicated multiparty and multicandidate system. Conversations across lines of political disagreement were found to be common and consequential in influencing voters to change their preferences in a campaign that witnessed the electoral collapse of a leading candidate. Heterogeneity in the number of different candidates supported in the network seemed to discourage preference changes, however, while those with homogeneously disagreeing networks were inclined to bring their preferences into line with the network by election day.

A comparison of the realigning 2013 Italian election, characterized by record levels of volatility and fragmentation, and its 2008 predecessor provides another perspective on how discussion networks can help voters make their choices amid uncertainty. Campus, Ceccarini, and Vaccari (2015) found that discussion increased dramatically from 2008 to 2013, especially among those who were critical of the political system, its traditional parties, and leaders and were embedded in homogeneous social networks with people holding similar "disenchanted" views. Although vote preference is not brought into the analysis, there seems little doubt that the protest Five-Star Movement (which obtained a quarter of the popular vote), like the Perot candidacy in the 1992 US election, benefited from the reinforcing social support found in many discussion networks.

Since the early 1990s, the Comparative National Election Project (CNEP) has employed the same network questions in multiple election surveys, enabling cross-national comparisons to be made throughout the democratic world.[6] This research addresses three questions about social networks and voting. First, how much is politics discussed within networks? Second, how politically homogenous or heterogeneous are these networks? That is, to what extent do people discuss politics with people who hold views similar to or different from theirs? Third, and most relevant to this chapter, how much do the partisan preferences of the discussion network relate to a person's vote?

Several studies draw on multiple CNEP surveys to compare discussion networks across some of the advanced industrial democracies that have been the scenes of the individual country studies reviewed above. In a comparison of East and West Germany (voting together for the first time since World War II), Japan, and the United States in the early 1990s, Huckfeldt et al. (2005) found that Japanese respondents had considerably smaller discussion networks and faced less disagreement as well as more indeterminacy regarding the partisan preferences of their discussants. In all four places, having only discussants who agreed with them (half or more of the discussants in each) was common. With the exception of Japan, though, as many as one-quarter to one-third of respondents reported having at least one discussant supporting a different party than theirs. Minority party supporters in all four cases were less likely to have politically homogeneous personal networks, especially those with smaller networks overall. But Japanese who supported minority parties that were deeply embedded in a social or ideological milieu were insulated from this effect, which implies that supporters of certain minority parties may find reinforcement for their deviance in their social networks.

Some cross-national studies using the CNEP data have gone a step further, estimating the effects of discussion networks within a comprehensive model of voting behavior. Schmitt-Beck (2004) found that the partisan direction of interpersonal communications was significantly related to the vote in early 1990s elections in Britain, Germany (East and West), Spain, and the United States, even after controlling for political predispositions and exposure to partisan messages in the media. Interpersonal discussion, especially with relatives and friends and in countries where political predispositions were weaker overall, proved to be more important than the media.

A major advantage of the CNEP surveys is that they include many recently formed and non-Western democracies. Not only are the United States, Japan, Britain, and Germany similar in the at least half-century longevity of their party systems, but they also are free societies in which there are few constraints on political conversations. The CNEP includes surveys from democracies that recently emerged from long periods of civil war, like Mozambique, or from one-party repressive authoritarian rule, like Bulgaria, Chile, Hungary, Indonesia, Mexico, Portugal, South Africa, and Spain. It also includes countries in which cultural norms may stifle reciprocal discussions between genders even in the same family and more generally outside the family where politics is concerned. And it includes political systems in which as many as a dozen parties (e.g., South Africa) compete in elections, parties themselves are barely developed and transient (Indonesia), or democratic elections are at best thinly rooted (China, at the local level). Examining elections within this diverse set of country cases allows us to take another step toward developing a general theory of social networks and voting behavior.

In an early study, Magalhães (2007) assessed the homogeneity of discussion networks in eleven CNEP surveys conducted prior to 2004 and found a significant relationship between the respondents' own partisanship and the vote preferences of their discussion network. Interestingly, and attesting to the importance of cross-national comparisons, two of the three strongest relationships were found in Great Britain (1992) and the United States (even in 1992!). This suggests that the role of discussion networks in voting behavior may be more pronounced in places where it happens that the most research has been conducted. Using these same CNEP data, Richardson and Beck (2007) reported considerable variation in exposure to discussion with family, friends, neighbors, and coworkers, with Western nations leading the way and Asian nations falling far behind— a possible cultural difference in interpersonal talk, especially when politics is involved.

Drawing on an expanded set of CNEP country surveys through 2008 (twenty elections in fourteen political systems), Beck and Gunther (2016) chronicled wide variations in reported discussion with family, friends, neighbors, and coworkers, with discussion with family members being most frequent everywhere. Gunther et al. (2016a) moved beyond sheer exposure to discussion, using this expanded set of CNEP surveys, to estimate the net effects of discussion network partisanship on the vote in a comprehensive model of voting behavior. In twelve of these cases, the partisanship of discussion networks and the mass media together and separately had no net impact on the vote. The other variables in the model, including party identification, demographics, and short-term attitudes toward party leaders, accounted for significant variance in the vote. But in a disparate set of seven cases, the partisanship of the discussion network was found to be a significant predictor of vote choice, in most cases eclipsing the relationship for the partisanship of the media to which the individual is exposed. These elections occurred in Argentina (2007), Bulgaria (1996), Mexico (2006), Mozambique (2004), Portugal (1995), Spain (1993), and the United States (1992).[7] Although discussion networks are not significant influences on voting choices everywhere, their importance extends well beyond the Western nations that have been the focus of most comparative research on political discussion. This is complex modeling to be sure, and more focused specification of network effects is in order, but it is promising that the influence of networks holds up even when subjected to the most stringent of multivariate analyses.[8]

Another data set has supported cross-national analysis of the relationship between social networks and vote choices: the World Values surveys. Anderson and Paskeviciute (2005) examined differences between majority and minority party supporters and also ideological outliers in the frequency of political conversations with friends across fifteen Western nations. Contrary to the conventional wisdom that being in the minority can silence political expression (Noelle-Neumann, 1984), they found that supporters of the opposition parties were more likely to engage in political discussions, a result that is replicated across twenty CNEP country elections for family, friends, and coworkers by Beck and Gunther (2016). Being in the minority may expose people to more discrepant messages, but it also seems to lead them to engage in more political conversations, perhaps in defense of their views. Moreover, countries with greater political heterogeneity showed higher levels of political discussion overall in the Anderson and Paskeviciute study.

The results from American studies typically square with those in other countries, with one exception. First, most citizens in modern democracies are exposed to partisan discussant networks. Second, these networks typically are consistent with people's own partisan inclinations; that is, they are decidedly homophilous, even after allowing for the understandable inflation in the extent to which agreement is perceived. Third, nonetheless, many citizens throughout the democratic world are embedded in discussion networks that contain voices discordant with their own preferences, especially if they have partisan preferences that favor the opposition or are embedded in multiparty systems that offer multiple opportunities for partisan heterogeneity even if within the same ideological family. Fourth, the partisanship of the discussion network is significantly related to the individual's vote. Notably, it is supporters of the minor parties who are most exposed to challenging partisanship in their social networks, with the possible consequence that support for those parties can fall below "sincere" levels for their candidates when they are not supported by minor-party discussion partners. This exception to the general patterns returns us full circle to the American studies, where a minor or third-party option typically is absent, and demonstrates the importance of broadening the focus to include multiparty systems in any theory of social network effects on voting, such as in the United States in its 1992 presidential contest.

Concluding Thoughts

An appreciation of the role social networks can play has enhanced our understanding of voting behavior. The chapter by Rolfe and Chan in this volume demonstrates this role where turnout is concerned. The current chapter shows it for vote choices in elections. There is no doubt that voters throughout the democratic world are embedded in social networks that support their own partisan choices. Even partial social support seems important for those who lean toward opposition or minor party candidates, but such social support surely provides strong bindings for major party supporters to their parties. Moreover, the research results suggest that multiparty, multicandidate situations can reduce social network homogeneity, but probably only within a "family" of parties on one side or another of the ideological divide. Nonetheless, voters in a variety of elections across countries are exposed to political discussants who have different political views. Sometimes these differences can be valuable in helping them to navigate through complicated electorate choices, such as in Brazil's 2002 contest, but ordinarily they make it more difficult for them to reach electoral decisions.

Inadequacies in Studies of Social Networks and Voting

Based on this wide-ranging review of the research literature, there can be no doubt that our understanding of how and how much social networks affect voting decisions is thinly based on empirical evidence. There are too few studies of different electoral conditions or country characteristics for us to develop much sense of what moderates social network influences on the vote. How much does the size of the party system matter? What is the role of social networks in changing, even volatile, electoral situations? How much are supporters of minority parties silenced by overwhelmingly majority political conversations, or are they able to carve out their own supportive networks? In his comprehensive review of voting behavior research, Heath (2007, 613) laments the absence of social network analysis in studies of voting behavior, concluding that the " 'absence of evidence does not imply the evidence of absence.' Lack of data on the role of social networks, either nationally or internationally, does not imply that such social processes do not operate." Even to this day, the failure to incorporate adequate discussion network questions in leading national election studies remains an imposing barrier to progress in understanding the role of social networks in voting.

The study of social networks more generally is also plagued by variations in measurement. Some studies define social networks as "n" persons with whom the ego initially discusses "important matters" rather than politics per se, while others use an explicitly political discussant name generator.[9] And in survey studies, given the difficulties of administering network batteries, "n" is necessarily limited. The heterogeneity of the network surely increases as we reach beyond the first one or two discussants mentioned and include what Granovetter (1973) has called the "weak" ties (Eveland, Appiah, and Beck, 2016). How much such weak ties influence voters, therefore, is difficult to determine based on the limited empirical evidence. Still other studies define social networks' homogeneity or heterogeneity more through what might be referred to as "summary" measures (i.e., what the partisan leanings of family, friends, neighbors, coworkers, etc., are), which are more subject to perceptual distortion and casual averaging.

Along the same lines, scholars need to be clearer about the aspect of the social network that does the influencing (Hopmann, Matthes, and Nir, 2015). Is it the number of ties to other individuals in the network? Is it the passive absorption of cues? Is it informal political conversation? Is it the network structure itself? There are many ways to measure the partisanship of a network, including even decisions about how to count partisan indifference. How it is measured surely affects its connection to the vote (as in Klofstad, Sokhey, and McClurg, 2013).

In addition, our knowledge is built on an unstable foundation of studies of particular countries in particular elections. There is evidence of considerable variation in the role of social networks even in one country, as some of the multiyear election studies show. The evidence from Brazil in 1992, Germany in the 1990s, Italy in 2015, and even the United States in 1992 (and possibly 2016) warns us that social networks may play a different role in exceptional elections than they do in more routine contests, not to mention across countries with different electoral and party systems and different cultures. We cannot gain a strong purchase on the role of social networks in voting behavior until we can begin to round out the various election and country conditions that may affect it.

The Causal Conundrum: Influence versus Selection

Probably the major challenge to research on networks and voting behavior is distinguishing between prior selection of discussion partners for political reasons and influence from those discussion partners. As Rolfe and Chan (this volume) address, researchers' ability to causally link social networks to political behavior is hampered by the reality that citizens construct their own social worlds. Because citizens choose with whom they discuss politics (Huckfeldt and Sprague, 1995; Walsh, 2004; Sinclair, 2012), it is difficult to establish whether social networks act on political behaviors independently or if they do so by (other) shared, and perhaps unobservable, characteristics that predict the formation of a tie. Homophily, likes associating with likes, is a robust and consistent finding across multiple disciplines (see McPherson, Smith-Lovin, and Cook [2001] for a summary). This question of causality is probably an even greater challenge for voting choice than when the behavior to be explained involves turnout. Indeed, it can be conjectured that the small number of studies of social network influences on voting choices is the result of the inability to make clear causal statements, a failure that more experiments and small network studies might remedy.

It follows that for social networks to affect vote choice, one must presume that individuals do not form relationships with others for explicitly political reasons. And in fact, most of the literature suggests that this is the case. Individuals primarily establish ties for nonpolitical reasons, though political attitudes are often shared among ties (Huckfeldt and Sprague, 1995; McPherson, Smith-Lovin, and Cook, 2001; Walsh, 2004; Sinclair, 2012), and both general and political networks have similar levels of political homophily (Eveland and Kleinman, 2013). However, more recent work suggests that politics may be directly involved in the selection of social alters. In their analysis of an online dating community, Huber and Malhotra (2013) demonstrated that individuals use information about a potential match's political affiliation to select mates. The potential mate's political affiliation rivals other consequential predictors of selection, such as educational level (but see Klofstad, McDermott, and Hatemi [2012]). Similarly, in a comparison of the United States and West Germany using CNEP data, Wolf (2010) found that minority partisans in an environment dominated by the majority party sought out reinforcement in forming their discussion networks, just as Republican auto workers did in Finifter's (1974) study.[10] This suggests that voters in the minority may be more assiduous than their majority counterparts in trying to build a social network that supports their "deviance." Of course, if individuals do select discussants for primarily political reasons, then "shared political preferences precede relationship formation rather than follow from it," further confounding efforts to separate homophily and contagion (Huber and Malhotra, 2013, 33).

Responses to this selection problem are often shortsighted and incomplete. Most work aims to statistically control for the factors that might influence discussant selection, such as race, gender, social class, and even party identification. In fact, many of the findings discussed above can only hold up under the explicit assumption that controlling for characteristics about the respondent and his or her discussants effectively eliminates the selection problem (Sinclair, 2012). While controlling for shared characteristics is important, the possibility that other, unobserved factors are causing the increased similarity in political attitudes cannot be definitively ruled out. Simulations, propensity scoring, and other matching techniques have been utilized to overcome these limitations in observational settings (Sinclair, 2012); however, there are unique limitations and problems with employing these techniques as well.

An alternative approach returns us to the pioneering work of Lazarsfeld and his Columbia University colleagues. They studied voter decision making in several panel waves during the course of an election campaign. The key to such an approach is to establish a baseline before voters have even begun to think about the election campaign and their vote decisions and then to follow voters across the campaign period. The problem with this approach is finding the "before" baseline. Voters develop partisan preferences early in their lives, most often during childhood or early adulthood, and carry them from election to election, often predetermining their selection of discussion partners and their ultimate vote. Nonetheless, panel studies have advantages that single-shot election surveys, especially post-election surveys, do not.

Some purchase on the causality question may be gained by the choice of discussant name generators. If asked to identify with whom they discussed politics or the campaign, respondents already may be reporting on the selection process. If asked instead to identify those with whom they discuss important matters, then asked whether politics or the campaign was discussed with them, researchers are able to monitor the selection process *within* their study rather than have it be beyond their reach. While this approach almost necessarily expands the number of discussants asked about, it does offer some insight into selection versus influence.

We recommend that researchers take selection more seriously, by designing research in light of this reality. This includes designing research that occurs across time (longitudinally) and space (comparatively) (Hopmann, Matthes, and Nir, 2015). Creative experimental work, such as that by Klar (2014), provides a path forward. Experimental work, however, can be difficult given the realities of the social world; researchers cannot randomly assign individuals to interact with each other in meaningful ways in the real world, for example. Small group studies may also provide a way forward. We believe that the sacrifice of external validity in exchange for depth in understanding of how networks influence political attitudes will be worthwhile (Mendelberg, 2005; Sokhey and Djupe, 2011; Eveland and Kleinman, 2013). There is no perfect or complete solution to the selection problems that plague social network research, however. The most innovative work will seek to draw inferences from a variety of data sources and clever research designs, using triangulation to provide leverage on causality.

New Developments in Network Studies: Online Social Networks

In closing, we need to acknowledge that our review of the extent research literature on social networks and voting behavior ignores important recent developments in social networking. In addition to face-to-face conversations, "communication about politics can take place by phone, Internet, and other technologies" (Sinclair, 2012, 83), which seem to be expanding rapidly. These networking possibilities are too new to be represented in all but the most recent research, and they may not be widely available to voters across the democratic world.[11] While research on face-to-face conversations may still be limited by the challenges and costs of such observation (but see work in the deliberative context, such as Karpowitz and Mendelberg [2014]), research on online networks provides a great opportunity for growth through measurement of its use in survey reports (for examples, see Brundidge [2010] on the direct capture of interaction data). Most Twitter data, for example, can be obtained for free, requiring only some knowledge of statistical software, such as Python or R, although Facebook data are increasingly harder to obtain in the aftermath of a controversial experiment that manipulated Facebook feeds to elicit emotion (Kramer, Guillory, and Hancock, 2014).[12] Research using online social network data has demonstrated the importance of social networks in the turnout decision (Bond et al., 2012), individual political ideology (Bond and Messing, 2015), and the likelihood of changing someone's mind (the Reddit platform, ChangeMyView, described in Tan et al., 2016). While the explosion of work in this area primarily focuses on turnout, opportunities exist to explore how these online networks influence individual political choice.

Notes

1. This work also demonstrated that in some circumstances, personal contacts were more influential on the vote choice than the media (see also Katz and Lazarsfeld 1955).
2. On this shift in the focus of voting studies, see Schmitt-Beck and Lup (2013).
3. Huckfeldt et al. (2004, 63) do demonstrate, however, that "strong partisans are not immune to the political messages that are filtered through networks of political communication".
4. Occasionally, research results show little support for a linkage between political discussions in social networks and partisan views. Klofstad (2011), for example, studied students who lived on campus at the University of Wisconsin, Madison, throughout their first year. His findings demonstrated that civic talk, or discussion about politics and current events, affects individual's participation in politics (as Rolfe and Chan note in the previous chapter). However, he found *no* support that civic talk affects individual partisan strength or direction. This research result, though, is a lone outlier and may be restricted to partisanship without generalizing to voting choice.
5. This review focuses only on research published in English. There may be studies of network influences on vote choices outside of the United States that have received less attention because they are published in that particular country's language.
6. Most CNEP surveys used both a "discuss important matters" egocentric discussant generator, often including spouse specifically, and summaries of the extent of discussion with family, friends, neighbors, and coworkers.
7. In comparison with three early CNEP countries, Morales (2010) showed that Spaniards were most likely to have discussion partners who shared their voting choices.
8. These CNEP surveys are now in the public domain (u.osu.edu/cnep) and are fertile ground for cross-national explorations of discussion networks.
9. Some research, however, has indicated that there is little difference between political and important discussant batteries—or that they generally lead to the same discussants (Klofstad, McClurg, and Rolfe, 2009).

10. Finifter (1974) found that Republicans in the United Auto Workers union had developed a friendship network of like-minded Republicans as a protective environment for their deviance from the overwhelmingly Democratic orientations of their union colleagues. Finifter's results also mesh with the findings reported for other countries on how opposition party supporters are inclined to discuss politics more often, presumably in search of support for their minority views within their social networks.

11. In an examination of the CNEP surveys through 2008, for example, only the most recent ten surveys were found to have any Internet activity, and its use had included more than 15 percent of survey respondents only in the United States in 2004 (Beck and Gunther, 2016). Internet use and other forms of non-face-to-face "electronic interactions" have expanded greatly since these studies were conducted.

12. For a review of Facebook work see Wilson, Gosling, and Graham (2012).

REFERENCES

Anderson, C. J., and Paskeviciute, A. (2005). "Macro-Politics and Micro-Behavior: Mainstream Politics and the Frequency of Political Discussion in Contemporary Democracies." In *The Social Logic of Politics: Personal Networks as Contexts for Political Behavior*, edited by A. S. Zuckerman, pp. 228–248. Philadelphia: Temple University Press.

Baker, A., Ames, B., and Renno, L. R. (2006). "Social Context and Campaign Volatility in New Democracies: Networks and Neighborhoods in Brazil's 2002 Elections." *American Journal of Political Science* 50: 382–399.

Beck, P. A. (2002). "Encouraging Political Defection: The Role of Personal Discussion Networks in Partisan Desertions to the Opposition Party and Perot Votes in 1992." *Political Behavior* 24: 309–337.

Beck, P. A., Dalton, R. J., Greene, S., and Huckfeldt, R. (2002). "The Social Calculus of Voting: Interpersonal, Media, and Organizational Influences on Presidential Choices." *American Political Science Review* 96: 57–73.

Beck, P. A., and Gunther, R. (2016). "Global Patterns of Exposure to Political Intermediaries." In *Voting in Old and New Democracies*, edited by R. Gunther, P. A. Beck, P. Magalhães, and A. Moreno, pp. 20–63. New York: Routledge.

Berelson, B. R., Lazarsfeld, P. F., and McPhee, W. N. (1954). *Voting: A Study of Opinion Formation in a Presidential Campaign*. Chicago: University of Chicago Press.

Bond, R., Fariss, C., Jones, J., Kramer, A., Marlow, C., Settle, J., and Fowler, J. (2012). "A 61-Million-Person Experiment in Social Influence and Political Mobilization." *Nature* 489: 295–298.

Bond, R., and Messing, S. (2015). "Quantifying Social Media's Political Space: Estimating Ideology from Publicly Revealed Preferences on Facebook." *American Political Science Review* 109: 62–78.

Brundidge, J. (2010). "Encountering 'Difference' in the Contemporary Public Sphere: The Contribution of the Internet to the Heterogeneity of Political Discussion Networks." *Journal of Communication* 60: 680–700.

Burt, R. (1987). "Social Contagion and Innovation: Cohesion Versus Structural Equivalence." *American Journal of Sociology* 92: 1287–1335.

Campbell, A., Converse, P., Miller, W. E., and Stokes, D. E. (1960). *The American Voter*. New York and London: John Wiley & Sons.

Campus, D., Ceccarini, L., and Vaccari, C. (2015). "What a Difference a Critical Election Makes: Social Networks and Political Discussion in Italy Between 2008 and 2013." *International Journal of Public Opinion Research* 27: 588–601.

Downs, A. (1957). *An Economic Theory of Democracy.* New York: Harper.

Esser, F., and Pfetsch, B. (Eds.). (2004). *Comparing Political Communication: Theories, Cases, and Challenges.* Cambridge, UK: Cambridge University Press.

Eulau, H. (1980). "The Columbia Studies of Personal Influence: Social Network Analysis." *Social Science History* 4: 207–228.

Eveland, W. P., and Kleinman, S. B. (2013). "Comparing General and Political Discussion Networks within Voluntary Organizations using Social Network Analysis." *Political Behavior* 35: 65–87.

Eveland, William, Ossei Appiah, and Paul A. Beck (2016). "Scratching Below the Core Network Surface: Capturing Hidden Exposure to Political Disagreement and Difference." Paper presented at the PolNet Conference, St. Louis, MO.

Faas, T., and Schmitt-Beck, R. (2010). "Voters' Political Conversations during the 2005 German Parliamentary Election Campaign." In *Political Discussion in Modern Democracies: A Comparative Perspective*, edited by M. R. Wolf, L. Morales, and K. Ikeda, pp. 99–116. London: Routledge.

Finifter, A. W. (1974). "The Friendship Group as a Protective Environment for Political Deviants." *American Political Science Review* 68: 607–625.

Fiorina, M. P. (1981). *Retrospective Voting in American National Elections.* New Haven, CT: Yale University Press.

Flanagan, S. C. (1991). "Mechanisms of Social Network Influence in Japanese Voting Behavior." In *The Japanese Voter*, edited by S. C. Flanagan, S. Kohei, I. Miyake, B. M. Richardson, and J. Watanuki, pp. 143–197. New Haven, CT: Yale University Press.

Flanagan, S. C., Kohei, S., Miyake, I., Richardson, B. M., and Watanuki, J. (Eds.). (1991). *The Japanese Voter.* New Haven, CT: Yale University Press.

Granovetter, M. S. (1973). "The Strength of Weak Ties." *American Journal of Sociology* 78: 1360–1380.

Green, D. P., Palmquist, B., and Schickler, E. (2002). *Partisan Hearts and Minds: Political Parties and the Social Identities of Voters.* New Haven, CT, and London: Yale University Press.

Gunther, R., Beck, P. A., Magalhães, P., and Moreno, A. (Eds.). (2016). *Voting in Old and New Democracies.* New York: Routledge.

Gunther, R., Lobo, M. C., Bellucci, P., and Lisi, M. (2016a). "The Changing Determinants of the Vote." In *Voting in Old and New Democracies*, edited by R. Gunther, P. A. Beck, P. Magalhães, and A. Moreno, pp. 150–192. New York: Routledge.

Gunther, R., Montero, J. R., and Puhle, H.-J. (Eds.). (2007). *Democracy, Intermediation, and Voting on Four Continents.* New York: Oxford University Press.

Heath, A. (2007). "Perspectives on Electoral Behavior." In *The Oxford Handbook of Political Behavior*, edited by R. J. Dalton and H.-D. Klingemann, pp. 610–618. New York: Oxford University Press.

Hopmann, D. N., Matthes, J., and Nir, L. (2015). "Informal Political Conversation Across Time and Space: Setting the Research Agenda." *International Journal of Public Opinion Research* 27: 448–460.

Huber, G., and Malhotra, N. (2013). "Dimensions of Political Homophily: Isolating Choice Homophily along Political Characteristics." Unpublished manuscript.

Huckfeldt, R., Ikeda, K., and Pappi, F. U. (2005). "Patterns of Disagreement in Democratic Politics: Comparing Germany, Japan, and the United States." *American Journal of Political Science* 49: 497–514.

Huckfeldt, R., and Sprague, J. (1991). "Discussant Effects on Vote Choice: Intimacy, Structure, and Interdependence." *Journal of Politics* 53: 122–158.

Huckfeldt, R., Johnson, P., and Sprague, J. (2004). *Political Disagreement: The Survival of Diverse Opinions within Communication Networks*. Cambridge, UK, and New York: Cambridge University Press.

Huckfeldt, R. and Sprague, J. (1987). "Networks in Context: The Social Flow of Political Information." *American Political Science Review* 81: 1197–1216.

Huckfeldt, R., and Sprague, J. (1995). *Citizens, Politics, and Social Communication: Information and Influence in an Election Campaign*. Cambridge, UK, and New York: Cambridge University Press.

Ikeda, K., and Huckfeldt, R. (2001). "Political Communication and Disagreement among Citizens in Japan and the United States." *Political Behavior* 23: 23–51.

Ikeda, K., Liu, J. H., Aida, M., and Wilson, M. (2005). "Dynamics of Interpersonal Political Environment and Party Identification: Longitudinal Studies of Voting in Japan and New Zealand." *Political Psychology* 26: 517–542.

Jennings, K., and Niemi, R. G. (1974). *The Political Character of Adolescence: The Influence of Families and Schools*. Princeton, NJ: Princeton University Press.

Jennings, K., and Niemi, R. G. (1978). "The Persistence of Political Orientations: An Over-Time Analysis of Two Generations." *British Journal of Political Science* 8: 333–363.

Jennings, K., and Niemi, R. G. (1981). *Generations and Politics: A Panel Study of Young Adults and Their Parents*. Princeton, NJ: Princeton University Press.

Jennings, K., Stoker, L., and Bowers, J. (2009). "Politics Across Generations: Family Transmission Reexamined." *Journal of Politics* 71: 782–799.

Karpowitz, C., and Mendelberg, T. (2014). *The Silent Sex: Gender, Deliberation, and Institutions*. Princeton, NJ: Princeton University Press.

Katz, E., and Lazarsfeld, P. F. (1955). *Personal Influence: The Part Played by People in the Flow of Mass Communications*. Glencoe, IL: Free Press.

Kenny, C. (1998). "The Behavioral Consequences of Political Discussion: Another Look at Discussant Effects on Vote Choice." *Journal of Politics* 60: 231–244.

Klar, S. (2014). "Partisanship in a Social Setting." *American Journal of Political Science* 58: 687–704.

Klofstad, C. (2011). *Civic Talk: Peers, Politics, and the Future of Democracy*. Philadelphia: Temple University Press.

Klofstad, C., McClurg, S., and Rolfe, M. (2009). "Measurement of Political Discussion Networks." *Public Opinion Quarterly* 73: 462–483.

Klofstad, C., McDermott, R., and Hatemi, P. K. (2012). "Do Bedroom Eyes Wear Political Glasses? The Role of Politics in Human Mate Attraction." *Evolution and Human Behavior* 33: 100–108.

Klofstad, C., Sokhey, A., and McClurg, S. (2013). "Disagreeing about Disagreement: How Conflict in Social Networks Affects Political Behavior." *American Journal of Political Science* 57: 120–134.

Kramer, A., Guillory, J., and Hancock, J. (2014). "Experimental Evidence of Massive-Scale Emotional Contagion through Social Networks." *Proceedings of the National Academy of Sciences of the United States of America* 111: 8788–8790.

Lazarsfeld, P. F., Berelson, B., and Gaudet, H. (1948). *The People's Choice: How the Voter Makes Up His Mind in a Presidential Campaign*. New York: Columbia University Press.

Lazer, D. (2001). "The Co-Evolution of Individual and Network." *Journal of Mathematical Sociology* 25: 69–108.

Lazer, D., Rubineau, B., Chetkovich, C., Katz, N., and Neblo, M. (2010). "The Coevolution of Networks and Political Attitudes." *Political Communication* 27: 248–274.

Levine, J. (2005). "Choosing Alone? The Network Basis of Modern Political Choice." In *The Social Logic of Politics: Personal Networks as Contexts for Political Behavior*, edited by A. S. Zuckerman, pp. 132–151. Philadelphia: Temple University Press.

Lewin, K. (1947). "Frontiers in Group Dynamics: Concept, Method and Reality in Social Science; Social Equilibria and Social Change." *Human Relations* 1: 5–41.

Liu, J. H., Ikeda, K., and Wilson, M. S. (1998). "Interpersonal Environment Effects on Political Preferences: The 'Middle Path' for Conceptualizing Social Structure in New Zealand and Japan." *Political Behavior* 20: 183–212.

Magalhães, P. C. (2007). "Voting and Intermediation: Informational Biases and Electoral Choices in Comparative Perspective." In *Democracy, Intermediation, and Voting on Four Continents*, edited by R. Gunther, J. R. Montero, and H.-J. Puhle, pp. 208–254. New York: Oxford.

McPhee, W. N. (1963). *Formal Theories of Mass Behavior*. New York: Free Press of Glencoe.

McPherson, M., Smith-Lovin, L., and Cook, J. M. (2001). "Birds of a Feather: Homophily in Social Networks." *Annual Review of Sociology* 27: 415–444.

Mendelberg, T. (2005). "Bringing the Group Back into Political Psychology: Erik H. Erikson Early Career Award Address." *Political Psychology* 26: 637–650.

Morales, L. (2010). "Getting a Single Message? The Impact of Homogeneous Political Communication Contests in Spain in a Comparative Perspective." In *Political Discussion in Modern Democracies: A Comparative Perspective*, edited by M. R. Wolf, L. Morales, and K. Ikeda, pp. 201–222. London: Routledge.

Mutz, D. C. (2002). "Cross-Cutting Social Networks: Testing Democratic Theory in Practice." *American Political Science Review* 96: 111–126.

Mutz, D. C. (2006). *Hearing the Other Side: Deliberative Versus Participatory Democracy*. New York: Cambridge University Press.

Newcomb, T. (1943). *Personality & Social Change: Attitude and Social Formation in a Student Community*. New York: Dryden Press.

Newcomb, T., Koenig, K. E., Flacks, R., and Warwick, D. P. (1967). *Persistence and Change: Bennington College and its Students After Twenty-Five Years*. New York: Wiley.

Noelle-Neumann, E. (1984). *The Spiral of Silence: Public Opinion—Our Social Skin*. Chicago: University of Chicago Press.

Pattie, C., and Johnston, R. (1999). "Context, Conversation and Conviction: Social Networks and Voting at the 1992 British General Election." *Political Studies* 47: 877–889.

Pattie, C., and Johnston, R. (2001). "Talk as a Political Context: Conversation and Electoral Change in British Elections." *Electoral Studies* 20: 17–40.

Richardson, B. M. (1991). "Social Networks, Influence Communications, and the Vote." In *The Japanese Voter*, edited by S. C. Flanagan, S. Kohei, I. Miyake, B. M. Richardson, and J. Watanuki, pp. 332–366. New Haven, CT: Yale University Press.

Richardson, B., and Beck, P. A. (2007). "The Flow of Political Information: Personal Discussants, the Media, and Partisans." In *Democracy, Intermediation, and Voting on Four Continents*, edited by R. Gunther, J. R. Montero, and H.-J. Puhle, pp. 182–207. New York: Oxford.

Rolfe, M. (2012). *Voter Turnout: A Social Theory of Political Participation*. New York: Cambridge University Press.

Ryan, J. B. (2010). "The Effects of Network Expertise and Biases on Vote Choice." *Political Communication* 27: 44–58.

Ryan, J. B. (2011). "Social Networks as a Shortcut to Correct Voting." *American Journal of Political Science* 55: 753–766.

Ryan, J. B., and Milazzo, C. (2015). "The South, the Suburbs, and the Vatican Too: Explaining Partisan Change among Catholics." *Political Behavior* 37: 441–463.

Schmitt-Beck, R. (2004). "Political Communication Effects; The Impact of Mass media and Personal Conversations on Voting." In *Comparing Political Communication: Theories, Cases, and Challenges*, edited by F. Esser and B. Pfetsch, pp. 293–324. Cambridge, UK: Cambridge University Press.

Schmitt-Beck, R., and Lup, O. (2013). "Seeking the Soul of Democracy: A Review of Recent Research into Citizens' Political Talk Culture." *Swiss Political Science Review* 19: 513–538.

Schmitt-Beck, R., and Partheymüller, J. (2014). "A Two-Stage Theory of Discussant Influence on Vote Choice in Multiparty Systems." *British Journal of Political Science* 21: 1–28.

Schmitt-Beck, R., Weick, S., and Christoph, B. (2006). "Shaky Attachments: Individual-level Stability and Change of Partisanship among West German Voters, 1984–2001." *European Journal of Political Research* 45: 581–608.

Sinclair, B. (2012). *The Social Citizen: Peer Networks and Political Behavior*. Chicago: The University of Chicago Press.

Sokhey, A., and Djupe, P. (2011). "Interpersonal Networks and Democratic Politics." *PS— Political Science and Politics* 44: 55–59.

Sokhey, A., and McClurg, S. (2012). "Social Networks and Correct Voting." *Journal of Politics the Journal of Politics* 74: 751–764.

Tan, C., Niculae, V., Danescu-Niculescu-Mizil, C., and Lee, L. (2016). "Winning Arguments: Interaction Dynamics and Persuasion Strategies in Good-faith Online Discussions." *arXiv (February)*. doi:10.1145/2872427.2883081.

Walsh, K. C. (2004). *Talking about Politics: Informal Groups and Social Identity in American Life*. Chicago: University of Chicago Press.

Wilson, R., Gosling, S., and Graham, L. (2012). "A Review of Facebook Research in the Social Sciences." *Perspectives on Psychological Science* 7: 203–220.

Wolf, M. R. (2010). "Local Partisan Context and Political Discussion Network Construction: Minority Party Loyalty Under Challenge." In *Political Discussion in Modern Democracies: A Comparative Perspective*, edited by M. R. Wolf, L. Morales, and K. Ikeda, pp. 79–98. London: Routledge.

Wolf, M. R., Morales, L., and Ikeda, K. (Eds.). (2010). *Political Discussion in Modern Democracies: A Comparative Perspective*. London: Routledge.

Zuckerman, A. S. (Ed.). (2005). *The Social Logic of Politics: Personal Networks as Contexts for Political Behavior*. Philadelphia: Temple University Press.

Zuckerman, A. S., Dasovic, J., and Fitzgerald, J. (2007). *Partisan Families: The Social Logic of Bounded Partisanship in Germany and Great Britain*. Cambridge, UK: Cambridge University Press.

CHAPTER 16

....

POLITICAL PARTIES AND CAMPAIGN FINANCE NETWORKS

....

PAUL S. HERRNSON AND JUSTIN H. KIRKLAND

GIVEN the increasing importance of money in elections, it is surprising that there are so few studies of transactions among parties, candidates, and interest groups from a network perspective. The world of campaign finance contains social networks that comprise many individuals and groups that belong to the same organizations, routinely interact with each other, and consult with one another before making a contribution. Members of campaign finance networks exchange donor lists (Koger, Masket, and Noel, 2009), cosponsor fundraising events (Herrnson, 2012), and share political intelligence (Francia et al., 2003). These are important activities in the current era of cash-driven elections. Network analysis techniques are useful for identifying associations among campaign donors and recipients and establishing the boundaries of party activities in campaign finance networks.

We begin this chapter by reviewing the literature on campaign finance and party networks. We then provide an empirical overview of the structure of campaign finance networks, in particular the place of formal party organizations within those networks.[1] Party organizations have coordinated campaigns across simultaneously occurring elections for most of US history, and there are theoretical and practical reasons to believe they continue to do so. After briefly reviewing the literature and providing the basis for our expectations, we use data from the 2006 elections for the House of Representatives and network-based statistics to present descriptive and inferential evidence regarding the structure of campaign finance networks. Our findings demonstrate the existence of separate Democratic and Republican networks. These networks are hierarchical in nature. Located at the core of each is the party's congressional campaign committee. The network's next layer mainly consists of candidates' principal campaign committees and leadership political action committees (PACs), and its outer layer is mostly made up of PACs that predominantly support one party's candidates.[2] Our findings furnish insights into the relationships among parties, interest groups, congressional candidates, and members of Congress.

THE EXTENDED PARTY NETWORK

Recent research on the parties' influence on the flow of money in elections emphasizes the importance of the "extended party network," which includes formal party organizations and traditional party allies. It presents compelling challenges to theories that have dominated research on political parties and electoral politics for more than half a century. Extended party research has demonstrated that some of the distinctions Schattschneider (1960) and others drew between parties and organized interests have blurred because these groups carry out similar activities (e.g., Heaney, 2010). Similarly, the increased campaign roles of nonparty groups associated with members of Congress, such as leadership PACs, raise questions about Key's (1958) conceptualization of political parties as the "party in government," the "party as organization," and the "party in the electorate" (Herrnson, 2009, 2012; Koger, Masket, and Noel, 2009, 2010).

Extended party network studies have used social network analysis to identify actors associated with each party and their relations within (or outside) a party's network. They highlight the increasing interdependence among formal parties and nonparty actors. Fowler's (2006) analysis of bill cosponsorships shows that party affiliation and personal friendships rank highly among the determinants of legislative influence. Heaney and Rojas's (2007) study of antiwar activist networks indicates that partisanship affects activists' tactics and access to members of Congress. Koger, Masket, and Noel's (2009, 2010) research on the circulation of donor and subscriber lists indicates that parties turn to interest group and media outlets in their respective networks for information about likely supporters. Grossmann and Dominguez (2003, 2009), Heaney et al. (2012), and Skinner, Masket, and Dulio (2012) demonstrate that partisan divisions structure the behavior of political activists, interest groups, voluntary organizations, and political consultants. Robbins and Tsvetovat's (2009) analysis of PAC contributions and expenditures demonstrates the centrality of the parties' presidential candidates and national committees in the financing of the 2000 elections.

Aldrich's (1995) and Herrnson's (2009) theories of parties are good starting points for thinking about how conceptions of the extended party might structure campaign financing. Building on theories of political ambition (e.g., Schlesinger, 1966), Aldrich's theory explains why elites would participate in the creation or augmentation of party committees. At the institutional level, it encompasses explanations for changes in the organizational, governing, and electoral segments of the party (Schlesinger, 1985), and it is consistent with findings about the integration of party organizations and their transformation into campaign service providers (e.g., Cotter et al., 1984; Herrnson, 1988). At the elite level, the theory complements explanations for the increased participation of political activists and organized interests in elections (e.g., Shafer, 1983) and embraces theories of party change that focus on interest groups (e.g., Karol, 2009) and party insiders (e.g., Ware, 2002). At the system level, its arguments about issues, interests, and politicians are reminiscent of those discussed in the political realignment literature (e.g., Clubb, Flanigan, and Zingale, 1990).

Herrnson's (2009) theory of political parties as enduring, multilayered coalitions focuses on relations among contemporary partisan actors. It emphasizes that a party's strength is largely determined by its ability to meet the needs of its officeholders, candidates, and supporters. The theory underscores the importance of looking beyond institutionally defined party organizations when assessing the roles of parties. It posits that the roles of parties have changed as a result of internal developments, such as the establishment of campaign service programs, and external changes, including a reliance on consultants, PACs, 527 committees, and most recently 501(c) organizations (see also Kolodny and Dulio, 2003; Skinner, Masket, and Dulio, 2012).

The theory presupposes a hierarchy among partisan actors. It posits that *formal party organizations* are at the center of each extended party network. Because of their national leadership roles, the parties' congressional, senatorial, and national campaign committees are the most influential of all formal party organizations that participate in congressional elections. The formal party organizations' power is derived from their leaders' ability to manipulate the political agenda (Petrocik, 1996; Damore, 2005), collect and redistribute political money, and influence the campaign spending of other donors. Formal parties' training and hiring of political operatives employed by party leaders, candidates, political consulting firms, and other partisan nonparty groups also increases their political influence (Skinner, Masket, and Dulio, 2012). Especially important are the parties' electoral surveillance and outreach efforts, which enable them to act as gatekeepers for the behind-the-scenes information others use to formulate their political strategies. Interest groups and political activists may assume substantial roles in party nominations (Cohen et al., 2008; Bawn et al., 2012), but most of those who spend money in elections lack the research capabilities to develop an overall contribution strategy or select specific candidates for support. As a result, many PACs and other donors turn to parties for decision-making cues (Biersack, Herrnson, and Wilcox, 1994, 1999; Francia et al., 2003). Recent variations of the methods the parties historically have used to channel contributions and media attention to candidates in competitive races, such as the Democratic Congressional Campaign Committee (DCCC)'s Red to Blue and Jumpstart programs and the National Republican Congressional Committee (NTCC)'s Young Guns Program, have helped designated congressional challengers raise significantly more funds than others (Herrnson, 2012). Another reason for formal party organizations' centrality in campaign networks is nonparty actors' awareness that they cannot compete with parties to place their candidates on the ballot or win control over government (e.g., Schattshneider, 1960). These factors combine to enable formal party organizations to raise large sums and influence the campaign spending of others.

Party-connected committees, consisting of party members' principal campaign committees and leadership PACs, form an extended party network's next layer. Many congressional leaders use both types of organizations to advance their individual objectives and their party's collective goals. Principal campaign committees are simply candidates' campaign organizations. Leadership PACs, once used by a small group of powerful legislators to contribute to candidates, numbered 338 in 2006. Each organizational form offers advantages. Leadership PACs, like PACs in general, are permitted to contribute $5,000 to a candidate in each phase of an election (primary, general, and runoff), but may contribute a maximum of only $15,000 to all national party committees and $5,000 to each state party committee per year. Principal campaign committees, on the other hand, are permitted to contribute only $2,000 per candidate in each phase of the election, but they can make unlimited transfers to party committees.

Party-connected committees are receptive to decision-making cues disseminated by formal party organizations. The principal-agent relationship between members of Congress and the leaders of their party's congressional campaign committee is an important explanation for the similarities in the distribution of their funds (Herrnson, 2009); others are based on the activities and relationships described above. Differences in spending patterns can be attributed largely to party-connected committee sponsors' pursuit of congressional leadership posts and other selective benefits. These pursuits lead them to distribute some contributions to safe incumbents and candidates in contested primaries (Currinder, 2003; Cann, 2008; Heberlig and Larson, 2012). The overall differences in the funds that party-connected committees and formal party organizations receive are due to similar factors. Party-connected committees are able to raise funds from donors that share some of their goals, but are disinclined to support a formal party organization and its broader agenda. Because candidates are the ultimate targets of most contributions and expenditures, party-connected committees raise money from more sources than do formal party organizations.

Party allies constitute an extended party network's next layer. Exemplified by ideological groups and labor unions, they include actors that give most of their support to one party. Party allies are receptive to election information disseminated by their preferred party, but because most party allies seek to advance a few salient issues or an ideological agenda it is rare for them to simply follow party cues. Rather, allied PACs make some contributions and independent expenditures to help primary and general election contestants who are not party priorities, including a few affiliated with the opposing party (Cann, 2008; Heberlig and Larson, 2012). This leads to the expectation that the distribution of allied PAC expenditures will have fewer similarities to those of formal party organizations than does the distribution of party-connected committee expenditures. Allied PACs' goals, lack of sponsorship by a candidate, and limited policymaking influence (they cannot cast congressional votes) make it more challenging for them to raise contributions from other groups than for party-connected committees and formal party organizations to do so.

Outside the parties' extended networks, but part of the larger campaign finance network, are *nonaligned actors*. These include PACs that do not consistently support candidates or organizations associated with one party. Most nonaligned PACs are concerned with advancing a particular economic interest. Their contribution strategies are designed to gain access to incumbents in a position to affect the group's goal achievement (e.g., Hall and Wayman, 1990). In some cases, nonaligned PACs coordinate efforts and form bipartisan networks (Robbins and Tsvetovat, 2009). For this reason, the contributions and expenditures of nonaligned PACs should have the fewest similarities to those of formal party organizations. Like party allies, nonaligned PACs' goals and lack of ballot status make them unlikely recipients of contributions from other groups.

This conceptualization of extended party networks suggests that campaign finance networks include many actors with a variety of associations. In place of the bilateral party-candidate ties that characterized the parties' golden age (when formal party organizations dominated most aspects of politics) are multilateral relationships among members of Congress, congressional candidates, party committees, and interest groups. Based on our review of the literature, we hypothesize that formal party organizations are the most centrally located actor type within a web of ties that connect partisan actors in both the full campaign finance network and their extended party network. We also hypothesize that party-connected committees form the next layer, as they are directly linked to many actors in one direction (receiving funds), but a limited subset, mostly incumbents, are connected to actors in another direction (distributing funds). Finally, we expect that the final layer of each party's campaign finance network consists of allied PACs (which provide virtually all of their support to one party's candidates).

DATA AND METHODS

The flow of political money results from decisions made by actors that possess different resources and objectives. Their choices have a relational component in that they collectively determine the ties that exist among actors. This makes social network analysis an appropriate lens through which to view campaign finance activity. Within the parlance of social network analysis, degree centrality forms the basis for most network summary statistics. Degree centrality refers to the number of direct ties (or edges) an actor has with all others. More complex centrality indexes extend degree by indicating the relative importance of actors based on both their direct and indirect connections to one another. Betweenness centrality is the most useful index to identify which actors constitute a focal point of activity. Betweenness is based on the *geodesic*, or shortest path, across a network between two actors. The betweenness centrality of each network actor is defined as the number of shortest paths (or geodesics) between other actor-pairs on which a particular actor is located, divided by the other actors' total number of shortest paths (Freeman, 1977). Actors with the highest betweenness centrality have the fewest degrees of separation from others. The theoretical framework described previously leads us to expect that the substantial heterogeneity in betweenness centrality within campaign finance networks is a function of actor type. That is, because formal party organizations are postulated to constitute the major hubs of the campaign finance network, they should exhibit the most betweenness centrality. Allied PACs ought to exhibit the least betweenness centrality, because they wield less influence over the distribution of a party coalition's resources.[3] Party-connected committees should lie somewhere in between formal party organizations and allied PACs.

The first step in determining whether formal party organizations are the most central actors in campaign finance networks involves the construction of the networks themselves. We consider two actors in this network linked if they are connected by a financial transaction. We do not consider the directionality of transactions because in some cases, such as party-connected committee and PAC contributions to formal party organizations and congressional incumbents, the beneficiary of the spending is as important in initiating the transaction as the benefactor (e.g., McChesney, 1997). In other cases, however, the benefactor clearly initiates the transaction. This is particularly the case for independent expenditures, which prohibit any direct coordination among these actors. The data used to construct our network are more inclusive than those used in many previous studies of campaign finance, which usually incorporate only some subset of contributions, expenditures, and, occasionally, interest group communications made in connection with general election campaigns. Our study includes these transactions plus those involving primary candidates or exchanges not directly associated with a candidate's election campaign, such as a transfer from a party-connected committee or an allied PAC to a formal party organization. Although routinely ignored, these transactions provide important information about ongoing relationships among parties, interest groups, and candidates.

Because of the importance of strategic considerations in theories of campaign finance, our analysis focuses on elections for one office (the House) and a single election (2006). This enables us to take into account the strategic environment in which donors responded. The analysis relies on a network constructed from data provided by the Federal Election Commission and the Center for Responsive Politics. It consists of the receipts and disbursements of all political organizations and all major-party candidates who contested a House primary or general election in 2006.

The 2006 election cycle was similar to many elections held since the early 1990s. Partisan polarization and the majority party's slim margin of control in both chambers of Congress led to a campaign season defined by heavy spending and negative advertising. Almost $3 billion was spent, including roughly $850 million by House candidates, $537 million by Senate candidates, $457 million by PACs, and $1.1 billion by formal party organizations. In addition to contributions, coordinated expenditures, and independent expenditures, large sums were transferred among political organizations.[4] For example, party-connected committees transferred $50.7 million to Democratic formal party organizations and $37.9 million to their Republican counterparts. Allied and non-aligned PACs transferred substantially more.[5] Consistent with other recent elections, House incumbents spent, on average, roughly three times more than the typical House challenger. Party leaders, in cooperation with others, undertook extraordinary efforts to collect, redistribute, and channel campaign money to competitive races. The 2006 cycle also was the first of three nationalized elections to take place since 1994. Both this election and the one held four years later resulted in a change in party control of the House. Moreover, because the 2006 election was the last midterm held prior to the *Citizens United* (*Citizens United v. Federal Election Commission*, 129 S. Ct. 2893, 557 U.S. (2009))

ruling, it provides a baseline for assessing the impact of the deregulation of campaign spending. It also furnishes a reference point for assessing the impact of the Bipartisan Campaign Reform Act (BCRA), which went into effect in 2004.

After building the full network, we designate each network member as a formal party organization, party-connected committee, party ally, or nonaligned actor. Party allies are defined as PACs that donate at least 90 percent of their donations to one party's candidates. Some may consider this threshold low, and others may consider it high, but it is consistent with what one might expect of a shadow party (Skinner, 2006). Varying the cutoff point has little impact on the results; when allied PACs are defined using an 80 percent cutoff, the findings are virtually identical (see tables 16.A4 and 16.A5 in the chapter appendix).

After providing an overview of the data in the full campaign finance network, we use a community detection algorithm, which uncovers the existence of separate Democratic and Republican campaign finance networks.[6] Next, we evaluate the structure of the full campaign finance network by examining the centrality of different types or categories of actors. Finally, we examine these differences in centrality within each party's campaign finance network. Because network data usually violate assumptions of independent observations, we pair our network summary statistics with permutation-based regressions and a difference of means test in order to facilitate statistical inferences (Cranmer and Desmarais, 2011; Kirkland, 2013).

The first step in a network permutation difference of means test for the centrality of different types of groups is to calculate the differences between means based on the "true" (original) network. Next, we create a reference distribution by scrambling (or rewiring) each of the connections in the network with some probability (Watts and Strogatz, 1998).[7] This creates a new, randomly generated network. We repeat this random generation thousands of times. We then compare the differences among means from the true network to the reference distribution of means created from the rewired network data. The standard deviations calculated from the reference distributions are used to test whether the true differences of means are statistically significant.[8] The procedure for network permutation regression proceeds along similar lines. First, we regress the betweenness centrality from the true network data on the dummy variables for each type of actor. Next, using a rewired network, we recalculate the betweenness centrality scores and regress them on the dummy variables for actor types. We repeat this process to produce a distribution of coefficients likely to be observed due to random chance. The standard deviations calculated from this distribution are used to determine whether the coefficients generated from the true network data are statistically significant.

THE FULL CAMPAIGN FINANCE NETWORK

The full campaign finance network has 6,383 actors and 372,188 direct connections out of a possible 40,736,306. The range for the number of connections per actor is 1 to 2,127. The network's clustering coefficient is 0.074, indicating that only 7.4 percent of potentially closable triads are actually closed.[9] Its average path length is 3.344, which is relatively short. The distribution of connections in the network is also highly skewed: only 20 percent of its actors have 100 or more direct connections to others, and this group is responsible for 76.5 percent of all network connections. The network also conforms to a power law distribution (alpha = 1.299, p < .05). These statistics indicate that the network has a strong core-periphery structure. This is typical of hierarchical networks, which are characterized by "the rich get richer" effects, wherein a few actors account for most network connections (Barabasi and Albert, 1999).[10] Our findings for the dynamics of the full congressional campaign finance network are consistent with Vonnahme's (2012) findings for donations to state legislative candidates.

The most powerful hierarchies involve partisan actors. Figure 16.1 presents a visualization of the full campaign finance network created using the Fruchterman-Reingold algorithm, which plots actors that have more connections to one another closer together and scales actors based on their total number of connections. Formal party organizations are represented by squares, party-connected committees by triangles, and allied PACs by circles. Members of the Democratic network are depicted in black; members of the Republican network are depicted in grey; nonaligned PACs are depicted as white squares.[11] The anticipated patterns are easily visible: the actors associated with the Democratic Party are on the left, those associated with the Republican Party are on the right, and the nonaligned actors are in the center or spread across the network. The full campaign finance network is defined by two unique financial coalitions that have limited overlap.

While the visual patterns in figure 16.1 make it easy to spot the partisan structure of campaign finance, a more rigorous deconstruction of the network is possible using community detection. We rely on the fast-greedy method of community detection, one of a number of algorithms whose primary purpose is to take a complex network and break it apart into "communities," where communities are clusters of actors in the network with dense connections among each other and sparse connections to others (Clauset, Newman, and Moore, 2004; Newman, 2006a). Community detection algorithms are unsupervised data reduction techniques that help researchers identify relevant clusters in networks for a variety of purposes, ranging from combating the spread of epidemics (Liu and Hu, 2005) to uncovering relevant dimensions of consumer choices in online networks (Newman, 2006b). Most community detection algorithms focus on maximizing a mathematical function called modularity, which describes how well partitioned a network is, with high modularity values symbolizing a well-partitioned network.

The community detection analysis (CDA) divides the campaign finance network actors into two large, three small, and several minuscule communities (see figure 16.2).[12] The first two communities are based largely on partisan ties and account for slightly more than 83 percent of all actors in the campaign finance network. This is a nontrivial result, given that 71.7 percent of the network actors, comprising all the PACs except for leadership PACs, have no official party affiliation. Theoretically, organizational sponsorship (whether by a corporation, labor union, trade association, member of Congress, or no group, in the case of nonconnected PACs) or strategic objectives (seat maximization

FIGURE 16.1 The full campaign finance network.

Source: Constructed from Center for Responsive Politics and Federal Election Commission data.

Notes: FPOs are represented by squares, PCCs by triangles, and allied PACs by circles. Members of the Democratic party network are depicted in black; members of the Republican party network are depicted in grey; nonaligned PACs are depicted as white squares. Node sizes are scaled by the number of network connections. Created using Fructermain-Reingold force based algorithm. N = 6,383.

or access) could have played a greater role in the optimal partition of PACs and other network actors. The remaining three communities account for an additional 10.6 percent of the actors. The 6.4 percent of the actors excluded from the five communities include many small, isolated groups.

The results demonstrate that more than 1,200 (88 percent) of the formal party organizations, party-connected committees, and allied PACs affiliated with the Democratic Party are assigned to community 1. Similarly, the community detection algorithm assigns more than 1,000 (79 percent) of the organizations affiliated with the Republican Party to

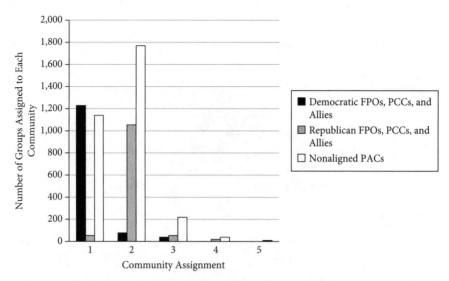

FIGURE 16.2 The distribution of community memberships within the network resulting from unsupervised network partitioning.

Source: Compiled from Center for Responsive Politics and Federal Election Commission data.

Notes: Only the first five communities are presented. The modularity of the network partitioning = 0.2355. N = 6383.

community 2. In addition, it places few (less than 5 percent) groups associated with one party into the community dominated by its opposition. The largest number of nonaligned PACs is assigned to community 2. The Republicans' control of Congress prior to the 2006 elections probably strengthened their connections with nonaligned groups. Although they are relatively small, the fact that communities 3 and 4 are primarily made up of nonaligned PACs corroborates the existence of bipartisan PAC networks. In sum, the results from the CDA and the plot in figure 16.1 suggest that the full network, comprising thousands of groups with no formal party affiliation, is strongly characterized by partisan divisions.

Having established the importance of partisanship to the overall network, the next step is to assess the impact of organization type on the centrality of different network actors. Formal party organizations constitute the smallest group of actors (see table 16.1). Numbering 291, less than 5 percent of the network's membership, they are responsible for less than 4 percent of its direct connections. These figures contrast sharply with the 3,563 nonaligned PACs, which account for almost 56.9 percent of all network members and are a party to more than 184,000 transactions—almost half of the total. Democratic party-connected committees significantly outnumber Democratic Party allies and have substantially more connections. The same is true of party-connected committees and allied PACs affiliated with the Republicans.

Despite their small numbers, party organizations are fairly active in the campaign finance network. The 161 Democratic and 130 Republican formal party organizations averaged 46.2 and 51.4 direct connections, respectively. Moreover, some formal party organizations have an abundance of direct connections. Foremost among them are the

Table 16.1 The Connectivity of Actors in the Full Campaign Finance
Network

	Number of Groups	Direct Network Connections				
		Average	Standard Deviation	Min.	Max.	Total
Democratic formal party organizations	161	46.21	162.35	1	1,640	7,440
Democratic Party-connected committees	858	86.95	119.12	1	756	74,603
Democratic Party allies	478	11.89	38.62	1	306	5,683
Republican formal party organizations	130	51.42	214.31	1	2,127	6,685
Republican Party-connected committees	723	128.76	164.03	1	1,074	93,093
Republican Party allies	470	9.5	30.88	1	324	4,465
Nonaligned PACs	3,563	51.71	92.13	1	854	184,243

Source: Compiled from Center for Responsive Politics and Federal Election Commission data.
N = 6,386.

DCCC, with 1,640, and the NRCC, with 2,127. This is of little surprise given the prominent roles of these organizations in congressional elections (Herrnson, 1988, 2012). As anticipated, party-connected committees exhibit more overall connectivity than formal party organizations (p < .001 for each party). Nevertheless, no one party-connected committee has as many connections as either party's congressional campaign committee, suggesting that the congressional campaign committees are the major hubs of activity among the financiers of congressional elections.

Allied PACs have significantly fewer average direct network connections than formal party organizations (p < .001 for each party). This supports our contention that allied PACs' primary role as sources, rather than recipients, of campaign funds limits their connectivity. Finally, nonaligned PACs average 5.5 more direct network connections than Democratic formal party organizations (p < .001), but roughly equal to the number for Republican formal party organizations (p < .583). The diversity of their objectives, their role as suppliers rather than recipients of funds, their membership in bipartisan networks, and their lack of candidate sponsorship all influence nonaligned groups' levels of connectivity.

A cross-party comparison of the statistics for the formal party organizations, party-connected committees, and allied PACs suggests there is a stronger hierarchy among actors associated with the Republican than with the Democratic Party. More Democratic than Republican formal party organizations and party-connected committees were financially involved in the election, but the Republican groups appear to have compensated for their lesser numbers by participating, on average, in a larger number of financial exchanges.

We present the results of our permutation-based regressions for the betweenness centrality in table 16.2. The coefficients represent the differences for each type of actor compared to the base category (nonaligned PACs) represented by the intercept. The coefficients for Democratic and Republican formal party organizations demonstrate that both sets of formal party organizations represent the shortest route between two different groups for 85 percent more network actors than nonaligned PACs.[13] Party-connected committees have many network connections, but not as many as formal party organizations. The coefficient for Democratic party-connected committees indicates that they represent the shortest path between network members 83 percent fewer times than Democratic formal party organizations. Democratic allies represent the shortest path almost 117.4 percent fewer times than Democratic formal party organizations.

Table 16.2 The Betweenness Centrality of Different Types of Actors in the Full Campaign Finance Network

	Coefficients	Standard Deviations
Intercept	6,908.91***	741.32
Democratic formal party organizations	49,131.78***	4,471.18
Democratic Party–connected committees	8,262.66***	2,277.55
Democratic Party allies	−8,538.61***	3,073.26
Republican formal party organizations	49,047.14***	5,052.70
Republican Party–connected committees	8,234.77***	2,382.37
Republican Party allies	−9,347.41***	2,829.77
N = 6,383		

Source: Compiled from Center for Responsive Politics and Federal Election Commission data.

Note: The larger the coefficient, the more influence a type of organization has in its party's network. The comparison group (represented by the intercept) is nonaligned PACs.

*p < .05, **p < .01, ***p < .001 one-tail test.

The differences in the coefficients for actors associated with the GOP indicate that Republican party-connected committees and allied PACs represent the shortest path between network actors almost 83.2 percent and 119.1 percent fewer times, respectively, than Republican formal party organizations. Overall, these results suggest that formal party organizations have greater reach and are likely to have more influence over the full campaign finance network than any other type of actor, and that they are located at the top of a hierarchical structure defined by a large array of actors that pursue diverse goals.

The results also suggest the Republican network is more hierarchical than the Democratic network. This is supported by a formal hypothesis that shows that the effect of being a formal party organization on betweenness centrality is larger for Republicans than it is for Democrats, and the effect of being a party-connected committee or party ally on betweenness centrality is smaller for Republicans than it is for Democrats (see table 16.A3 in the appendix).

DEMOCRATIC AND REPUBLICAN PARTY FINANCIAL NETWORKS

While an examination of the full campaign finance confirms the existence of two distinctive extended party networks and allows for some comparisons between them, understanding the hierarchies in campaign finance requires us to examine each party's campaign finance network separately. Bipartisan campaign activity influences the relationships among different types of actors, including their betweenness centrality, and thus furnishes only limited information about the relationships within each extended party. That is, an organization may be identified as having high connectivity or high betweenness centrality in the full network because it is located between the two parties rather than because it is centrally located within one. Figure 16.3 provides a visualization of the positioning of the actors in the Democratic Party's extended financial network.[14] The DCCC, represented by the largest square in the figure, clearly has more centrality than any other member of the Democratic extended party network. The Democratic National Committee and the Democratic Senatorial Campaign Committee also exhibit high degrees of centrality. Many party-connected committees also are located near the middle of the network. Among the largest and most central are AmeriPAC: The Fund for a Greater America, affiliated with Rep. Steny Hoyer, the second-ranking House Democrat, and Forward Together PAC, sponsored by Democratic Senator Mark Warner. Several recognizable party allies also figure prominently in the Democratic extended party network, including the Association of Trial Lawyers of America (also referred to as the American Association for Justice) PAC, and the United Steel Workers Political Action Fund. Some less recognizable actors are located near the periphery of the network. They include challenger Wendy Wilde's principal campaign committee, which raised less than $68,000 and suffered a landslide defeat to then eight-term incumbent Jim Ramstad (R-MN).

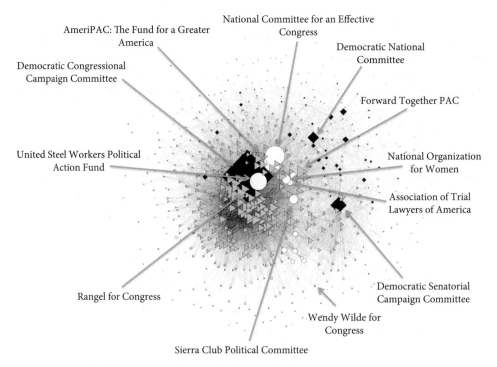

National Committee for an Effective
Congress

AmeriPAC: The Fund for a Greater
America

Democratic National
Committee

Democratic Congressional
Campaign Committee

Forward Together PAC

United Steel Workers Political
Action Fund

National Organization
for Women

Association of Trial
Lawyers of America

Rangel for Congress

Democratic Senatorial
Campaign Committee

Wendy Wilde for
Congress

Sierra Club Political Committee

FIGURE 16.3 The democratic campaign finance network.

Source: Compiled from Center for Responsive Politics and Federal Election Commission data.

Notes: Black squares, grey triangles, and white circles represent FPOs, PCCs, and allied PACs.
Actor size reflects degree centrality. N = 1497.

The Republican extended network bears many similarities to the Democratic network (see figure 16.4). The party's congressional campaign committee (the NRCC) is its most central actor, and its national and senatorial committees are prominent. Its most influential party-connected committees are associated with party leaders, including Keep Our Majority PAC (then-House Speaker Dennis Hastert) and Straight Talk America PAC (Senator John McCain). The National Federation of Independent Business/Save America's Free Enterprise Trust PAC, the National Pro-Life Alliance PAC, and other groups associated with the Republican Party also stand out. Among the most peripheral actors is Jose Sandoval's principal campaign committee. Sandoval spent $225,000 against then six-term incumbent Bill Pascrell (D-NJ) and was defeated by a 43 percent margin.

Table 16.3 presents information about the connectivity of formal party organizations, party-connected committees, and allied PACs within the separate extended party networks. Because each extended party network possesses fewer actors than are present in the full campaign finance network, the actors have fewer direct connections. As expected, the largest reductions in the size of the averages for an actor type are among the party-connected committees, which we theorized would have the highest levels of direct connectivity. The smallest drop-offs are among party allies, which were posited to have the least connectivity.

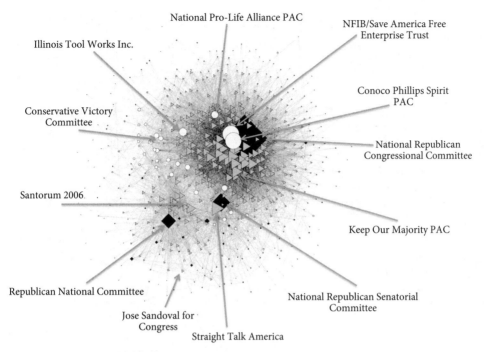

National Pro-Life Alliance PAC

NFIB/Save America Free
Enterprise Trust

Illinois Tool Works Inc.

Conoco Phillips Spirit
PAC

Conservative Victory
Committee

National Republican
Congressional Committee

Santorum 2006

Keep Our Majority PAC

Republican National Committee

National Republican Senatorial
Committee

Jose Sandoval for
Congress

Straight Talk America

FIGURE 16.4 The republican campaign finance network.

Source: Compiled from Center for Responsive Politics and Federal Election Commission data.

Notes: Black squares, grey triangles, and white circles represent FPOs, PCCs, and allied PACs.
Actor size reflects degree centrality. N = 1323.

Table 16.4 presents the results for the permutation regressions for each extended party network. The intercept for each model represents formal party organizations, which we suspected would have the highest level of betweenness centrality. As expected, the coefficients representing formal party organizations are substantially larger than the others, indicating that traditional party organizations have the highest levels of betweenness centrality in each extended party network. The coefficients for Democratic party-connected committees and allied PACs indicate that they represent the most efficient routes between actors for 34.7 percent and 75.8 percent fewer network members than Democratic formal party organizations. The Republican extended party network is characterized by even larger differences: party-connected committees and allied PACs provide the shortest paths between actors for 59.7 percent and 85.5 percent fewer organizations than formal party organizations.[15] In addition to supporting our hypothesis about each party's extended network, the results further suggest that Republican formal party organizations exhibit a higher level of network centrality than Democratic formal party organizations.

What accounts for the more hierarchical nature of the Republican extended party network? There are several possible explanations. Republican members of Congress are somewhat more ideologically homogeneous (e.g., Theriault, 2006). The GOP traditionally has focused more on strengthening its party's campaign infrastructure, while

Table 16.3 The Connectivity of Actors in the Democratic and
Republican Campaign Finance Networks

	Number of Groups	Direct Network Connections				
		Average	Standard Deviation	Min.	Max.	Total
Democratic formal party organizations	161	17.78	53.11	1	610	2,864
Democratic Party-connected committees	858	22.08	31.16	1	178	18,949
Democratic Party allies	478	8.28	24.32	1	287	3,961
Republican formal party organizations	130	17.26	54.56	1	553	2,244
Republican Party-connected committees	723	24.51	24.51	1	187	17,723
Republican Party allies	470	7.18	7.18	1	193	3,377

N = 2,820

Source: Compiled from Center for Responsive Politics and Federal Election Commission data.

the Democrats have been concerned with enhancing demographic representation (e.g., Klinkner, 1994). Moreover, Democratic candidates have relied on unions and other groups for campaign support, while Republicans have turned primarily to their party for campaign assistance (Cotter et al., 1984; Herrnson, 1988, 2012). The differences between the perspectives of party operatives and activists, and other aspects of party culture, probably are also relevant (Dulio, 2004; Freeman, 1986). The Republican network also may be more hierarchical because its members raise larger amounts from fewer sources than do their Democratic counterparts. Another explanation concerns the impact of control over Congress on the distribution of campaign money. Members of the majority party (the Republicans in 2006) give more support to candidates in marginal districts, in part to maintain the benefits of majority control (Heberlig and Larson, 2012). Presumably, PACs allied with the majority party also respond to this logic (Cox and Magar, 1999).

Although network analysis does not lend itself to isolating the impact of party organizations on the spending of other actors, campaign finance data can furnish insights into the influence of formal party organizations, party-connected committees, and

Table 16.4 The Betweenness Centrality of Different Types of Actors in the Democratic and Republican Campaign Finance Networks

	Democratic Network	Republican Network
Intercept	2,692.49*	4,048.99***
	(488.62)	(421.42)
Party-connected committees	−934.66*	−2,417.39***
	(521.02)	(445.28)
Party allies	−2,042.32***	−3,463.39***
	(501.15)	(473.26)
N	1,497	1,323

Source: Compiled from Center for Responsive Politics and Federal Election Commission data.

Note: The larger the coefficient, the more influence a type of organization has in its party's network. Standard deviations are in parentheses. The comparison group (represented by the intercept) is formal party committees. *p < .05, **p < .01, ***p < .001 one-tail test.

allied PACs on the candidate-focused spending of members of different subnetworks. During the 2006 elections, Democratic Party organizations had direct connections to 905 Democratic party-connected committees and allied PACs and the highest level of betweenness centrality of all actors in their extended party network.[16] The members of the subnetwork that had direct connections to Democratic formal party organizations made approximately $101.7 million in contributions and independent expenditures in support of Democratic House candidates, and subnetwork members that had indirect connections to Democratic formal party organizations spent an additional $188.6 million (see table 16.5.) The $290.3 million total, which excludes the $242 million in spending by Democratic formal party organizations themselves, is 460 percent larger than the total expenditures made by members of subnetworks organized around party-connected committees and 876 percent larger than the expenditures of subnetworks organized around allied PACs. The figures for Republicans similarly demonstrate that extended party network members connected to Republican formal party organizations spent considerably more on the campaigns of GOP candidates than did extended party network members connected to Republican party-connected committees or allied PACs. While it would be wrong to credit parties with determining the flow of contributions from every extended party network member that is directly or indirectly connected to them, the literature on party strategy, spending, and campaign activities (cited previously) reinforces the notion that formal party organizations are well-positioned to influence the spending of partisan nonparty groups within network.

Table 16.5 The Campaign Contributions and Expenditures of Network Members Connected to Formal Party Organizations, Party-Connected Committees, or Allied PACs (in $ Millions)

	Democrats		
	Directly Connected	Indirectly Connected	Total
Formal party organizations	101.7	188.6	290.3
Party-connected committees	21.5	30.3	51.8
Allied PACs	18.3	11.4	30.0
Formal party organizations	810.7	890.5	170.1
Party-connected committees	27.7	19.3	47.0
Allied PACs	11.7	74.5	19.2

Source: Compiled from Center for Responsive Politics and Federal Election Commission data.
Note: Figures are for millions of dollars in spending made directly or indirectly by groups of actors.

CONCLUSION

This study has used campaign finance data and social network analysis to examine hierarchies in the extended party campaign finance network. The findings buttress arguments suggesting that an actor's strategic objectives, resources, and sponsorship by a candidate influence its position within financial networks. These factors, in turn, have an impact on the actor's direct and indirect connections to others, its location within a campaign finance network, and the overall structure of that network. More specifically, we find that formal party organizations are optimally positioned to wield the greatest influence across both the full finance network and their respective extended party networks despite the fact that they have fewer direct connections to other actors than party-connected committees; party-connected committees have the most direct connections within their extended party network and the full network, but they rank second in terms of indirect connections. Finally, allied PACs, which pursue narrow partisan goals, average the fewest direct and indirect connections to other actors and are thus positioned to exercise the least influence within their extended party network and the full campaign finance network. These results are precisely what we would expect to find in a campaign finance network that is structured like a hierarchical, multilayered party coalition.

These results have several implications for the study of political parties. First, they add to the literature demonstrating that despite various attempts to reform parties, party organizations continue to play a central role in contemporary campaign finance activities. Second, they support the conceptualization of party networks as coalitions of different types of actors connected by overlapping collective and individual goals, shared information and personnel, and a web of financial exchanges. Third, the findings build on theories based on the premise that a party's influence is largely determined by its ability to meet its politicians' needs, and they demonstrate that formal parties are positioned to be redistributive actors between party allies and party-connected committees. Fourth, the differences in the hierarchies of the Democratic and Republican extended party networks provide additional support for generalizations developed from studies of congressional organization, campaign conduct, and the organization of the party apparatus itself. Finally, our dependent variables, network connectivity and centrality, have the potential to serve as independent variables that provide insights into other aspects of politics, including legislators' responsiveness to party pressure and interest group lobbying and the impact of campaign money on the polarization of American politics.

In summary, this study has demonstrated the existence of distinctive Democratic and Republican party campaign finance networks which, like the full network, are defined by hierarchies among different types of actors. Nevertheless, more research is needed. Given that individuals typically account for about 56 percent of the funds raised by House candidates, 68 percent of the funds raised by Senate candidates, and most of the monies collected by national party organizations and PACs, it would be interesting to extend the analysis to include individual donors. It also would be instructive to move beyond the presence (or absence) of nodes based on financial transactions to include information about the directionality and amounts of these exchanges. Campaign contributions and expenditures range from a few dollars to millions of dollars. Including the actual sums involved could alter the structure of campaign finance networks and the relationships among their members. Combined with the unweighted results presented in this study, the new findings would offer a more complete picture of campaign financing and extended party networks. In addition, the findings from this study provide a baseline for studying other election cycles, particularly 2012, the first full presidential election cycle in which super PACs, 527 committees, 501(c) groups, and their sponsors could spend general treasury monies in federal elections. Finally, given that Senate candidates rely less on contributions from interest groups and that the Senate is the least hierarchical of Congress's chambers, future research should compare the structure of House and Senate campaign finance networks.

Regardless of the outcomes of additional research, the findings of this study demonstrate that to fully understand the roles of political parties in elections, one must look beyond the organizations that the law and most academic studies formally recognize as party committees. They also should consider the actors that routinely support a party and coordinate activities with it. Formal party organizations, party-connected committees, party allies, and the other groups and individuals that inhabit extended party networks play important roles in orchestrated bids for power.

NOTES

1. Formal party organizations are campaign committees directly tied to a political party and, in this case, that registered with the Federal Election Commission.

2. In this context, "layer" refers to clear differences in the core-periphery structure of a network. The core constitutes one layer, the periphery another. We expect there to be a clear and identifiable middle layer between the core formal party organizations and the periphery party allies. Thus, we expect the network to have a series of concentric rings constituting layers of increasingly pivotal actors.

3. It is important to emphasize that actors with high betweenness centrality may have relatively few direct connections to others (Freeman, Roeder, and Mulholland 1980).

4. Monies also were used for fundraising, overhead, and transactions not associated with any specific campaign, such as agenda-setting ads and voter mobilization.

5. They contributed $233.6 million to Democratic formal party organizations and $262.6 million to Republican formal party organizations. Center for Responsive Politics, http://www.opensecrets.org/.

6. It is worth noting at this point that we use the term "network" when referring both to the full network of campaign finance activities and to the subnetworks associated with each party. Technically, each party's network is a subgraph of the full network, but we retain the use of the term "network" in order to cohere with literature focusing on each party's *extended party network*.

7. We scramble the network ten thousand times and rewire the connections so that each connection is redrawn between a different set of actors with a probability of 0.95.

8. We report standard deviations across the reference distribution because standard errors for such a test have not yet been developed. In a traditional hypothesis test, standard errors, and thus p-values, decrease as sample size increases even when effects sizes do not change. It is not clear that this increase in certainty is applicable to network effects, because the number of possible network configurations increases exponentially as the number of network actors increases. By contrast, standard deviations do not decrease as the size of the network increases.

9. The density and clustering coefficient are unusually low, probably because many allies possess only one connection, leaving many unrealized connections.

10. Network statistics are calculated using the igraph package in R (Csardi and Nepusz 2006).

11. Other network studies of extended party networks focus heavily on the interest group allies of extended party networks (Grossman and Dominguez 2009). Excluding formal party organizations and party-connected committees has the potential to exaggerate the centrality of some groups while ignoring the importance of formally affiliated groups.

12. The network's modularity is .2365. Virtually identical results were generated using the walktrap, leading eigenvector, and edge betweenness community detection algorithms.

13. Altering the comparison group in the regression demonstrates that the coefficients for formal party organizations are statistically larger than those for the other types of organizations.

14. For better visualizations of the actors, see the plots at https://dl.dropboxusercontent.com/u/19453819/DemsWebPageST.htm.

15. As noted, changing the cut-points used to define allied PACs produces virtually identical results (see the appendix).

16. The figure for direct connections is less than the 2,864 in Table 16.3 because it excludes connections among Democratic formal party organizations.

Appendix

We further test the connectivity hypotheses using permutation-based differences of means tests. This approach allows us to combine our hypotheses tests with the descriptive overviews of the data provided in tables 16.1 and 16.3. An alternative approach is to use permutation regressions to assess the impact of organization type on direct centrality. The results, presented in table 16.A1 for the full network and table 16.A2 for each Extended Party Network (EPN), corroborate the findings presented in the study.

Table 16.A3 presents a formal test of the hypothesis that the Republican extended campaign finance network is more hierarchical than the Democratic extended campaign finance network. The positive coefficient for Republican negative (the dummy variable) indicates that the Republican actors have greater betweenness centrality than the Democratic actors. The negative coefficients for Republican*Party allies and Republican*Party-connected committees indicates they have less betweenness centrality than Republican formal party organizations.

It is possible that the results in tables 16.3 and 16.4 are sensitive to the decision rule we used to categorize interest groups as allied or nonaligned PACs. That is, because we examine party-specific subnetworks, our choices about inclusion in those subnetworks, based on an a priori definition of party allies, could potentially influence the results. To check for this possibility, we repeat our analysis using a different cut-point to define allied and nonaligned PACs. Recall that the decision rule used in the analysis presented in table 16.4 defined allied PACs as those that make 90 percent or more of their contributions to candidates of one party. The results in tables 16.A4 and 16.A5 are based on analyses that use an 80 percent threshold to distinguish between allied and nonaligned PACs. As the tables show, the results for the 80 percent cutoff point are very similar to those based on the 90 percent cutoff.

Table 16.A1 The Degree Centrality of Different Types of Actors in the Full Campaign Finance Network

	Coefficients	Standard Deviations
Intercept	57.96*	1.20
Democratic formal party organizations	−8.82	8.76
Democratic Party–connected committees	50.44***	3.98
Democratic Party allies	−58.76***	5.06
Republican formal party organizations	−8.64	9.03
Republican Party–connected committees	82.85***	4.14
Republican Party allies	−63.67***	5.28
N = 6,383		

Source: Compiled from Center for Responsive Politics and Federal Election Commission data. The larger the coefficient, the more connections an actor-type has in a network. The comparison group (represented by the intercept) is nonaligned PACs.

*p < .05, ***p < .001 one-tail test.

Table 16.A2 The Direct Centrality of Different Types of Actors in the Democratic and Republican Campaign Finance Networks

	Democratic Network	Republican Network
Intercept	2.83	3.19
	(0.10)	(0.11)
Party-connected committees	0.40***	0.27**
	(0.11)	(0.11)
Party allies	−0.88***	−1.35***
	(0.12)	(0.13)
N	1,497	1,323

Source: Compiled from Center for Responsive Politics and Federal Election Commission data. The larger the coefficient, the more connections an actor-type has in a network. The comparison group (represented by the intercept) is nonaligned PACs. **$p < .01$, ***$p < .001$.

Table 16.A3 An Interactive Model of Betweenness Centrality

	Coefficients	Standard Deviations
Intercept	27,297***	3,914
Party-connected committees	−8,129***	3,967
Party allies	−23,326***	4,070
Republican*Party allies	−20,231***	5,954
Republican*Party–connected committees	−21,075***	5,779
Republican (dummy variable)	22,018***	5,064
N		2,820

Source: Compiled from Center for Responsive Politics and Federal Election Commission data. The interaction terms indicate the difference between the betweenness centrality of a type of actor in the Democratic network and the Republican network. Standard deviations are in parentheses. The comparison group (represented by the intercept) is Democratic formal party committees. ***$p < .001$ one-tail test.

Table 16.A4 The Direct Centrality of Different Types of Actors in the Full Campaign Finance Network Using an 80 Percent Cutoff Point

	Democratic Network	Republican Network
Intercept	3.29***	3.37***
	(0.10)	(0.11)
Party-connected committees	0.18***	0.23**
	(0.10)	(0.11)
Party allies	−0.51***	−1.02***
	(0.10)	(0.11)
N	1,506	1,468

Standard deviations are in parentheses. The comparison group (represented by the intercept) is Democratic formal party committees.

*p < .01, **p < .001 one-tail test.

Table 16.A5 The Betweenness Centrality of Different Types of Actors in the Democratic and Republican Campaign Finance Networks Using an 80 Percent Cutoff Point

	Democratic Network	Republican Network
Intercept	2.86***	4.60***
	(0.46)	(0.45)
Party-connected committees	-0.78***	-2.54**
	(0.47)	(0.48)
Party allies	-1.84***	-3.92***
	(0.46)	(0.47)
N	1,506	1,468

Source: Compiled from Center for Responsive Politics and Federal Election Commission data. The larger the coefficient, the more connections an actor-type has in a network. The comparison group (represented by the intercept) is nonaligned PACs.

**p < .01, ***p < .001 one-tail test.

REFERENCES

Aldrich, J. H. (1995). *Why Parties? The Origin and Transformation of Political Parties in America*. Chicago: University of Chicago Press.

Barabasi, A.-L., and Albert, R. (1999). "Emergence of Scaling in Random Networks." *Science* 286: 509–512.

Bawn, K., Cohen, M., Karol, D., Masket, S., Noal, h., and Zaller, J. (2012). "A Theory of Political Parties: Groups, Policy Demands, and Nomination in American Politics." *Perspectives on Politics* 10(3): 271–597.

Biersack, R., Herrnson, P. S., and Wilcox, C. (1994). *Risky Business? PAC Decisionmaking in Congressional Elections*. Armonk, NY: M. E. Sharpe.

Biersack, R., Herrnson, P. S., and Wilcox, C. (1999). *After the Revolution: PACs and Lobbies in the Republican Congress*. Boston: Allyn and Bacon.

Cann, D. M. (2008). *Sharing the Wealth: Member Contributions and the Exchange Theory of Party Influence in the U.S. House of Representatives*. Albany: State University of New York Press.

Cohen, M., Karol, D., Noel, H., and Zaller, J. (2008). *The Party Decides: Presidential Nominations Before and After Reform*. Chicago: University of Chicago Press.

Clauset, A., Newman, M. E. J., and Moore, C. (2004). "Finding Community Structure in Very Large Networks." *Physical Review E* 70(6): 066111.

Clubb, J. M., Flanigan, W. H., and Zingale, N. H. (1990). *Partisan Realignment: Voters, Parties, and Government in American History*. Boulder, CO: Westview Press.

Cox, G. W., and Magar, E. (1999). "How Much Is Majority Status in the U.S. Congress Worth?" *American Political Science Review* 93: 299–309.

Cotter, C. C., Gibson, J. L., Bibby, J. F., Huckshorn, R. J. (1984). *Party Organizations in American Politics*. New York: Praeger.

Cranmer, S. J., and Desmarais, B. D. (2011). "Inferential Network Analysis with Exponential Random Graph Models." *Political Analysis* 19: 66–86.

Csardi, G., and Nepusz, T. (2006). "The igraph Software Package for Complex Networks Research." *InterJournal, Complex Systems* 1695(38).

Currinder, M. L. (2003). "Leadership PAC Contribution Strategies and House Member Ambitions." *Legislative Studies Quarterly* 28(4): 551–577.

Damore, D. F. (2005). "The Dynamics of Issue Ownership in Presidential Campaigns." *Political Research Quarterly* 57(3): 391–397.

Dulio, D. A. (2004). *For Better or Worse? How Political Consultants Are Changing Elections in the United States*. Albany: State University of New York Press.

Fowler, J. H. (2006). "Connecting the Congress: A Study of Cosponsorship Networks." *Political Analysis* 14(4): 456–487.

Francia, P. L., Green, J. C., Herrnson, P. S., Powell, L. W., and Wilcox, C. (2003). *The Financers of Congressional Elections*. New York: Columbia University Press.

Freeman, J. (1986). "The Political Culture of the Democratic and Republican Parties." *Political Science Quarterly* 101(3): 327–356.

Freeman, L. C. (1977). "A Set of Measures of Centrality Based on Betweenness." *Sociometry* 40(1): 35–41.

Grossmann, M., and Dominguez, C. B. K. (2003). "Candidates and Candidacies in the Extended Party." *PS: Political Science and Politics* 36: 165–169.

Grossmann, M., and Dominguez, C. B. K. (2009). "Party Coalitions and Interest Group Networks." *American Politics Research* 37: 767–800.

Hall, R. L., and Wayman, F. W. (1990). "Buying Time: Moneyed Interests and the Mobilization of Bias in Congressional Committees." *American Political Science Review* 84: 797–820.

Heaney, M. T., Masket, S. E., Miller, J. M., and Strolovitch, D. Z. (2012). "Polarized Networks: The Organizational Affiliations of National Party Convention Delegates." *American Behavioral Scientist* 56: 1654–1676.

Heaney, M. T. (2010). "Linking Political Parties and Interest Groups." In *The Oxford Handbook of American Political Parties and Interest Groups*, ed. L. S. Maisel and J. M. Berry, pp. 568–587. New York: Oxford University Press.

Heaney, M., and Rojas, F. (2007). "Partisans, Nonpartisans, and the Antiwar Movement in the United States." *American Politics Research* 34(4): 431–464.

Heberlig, E. S., and Larson, B. A. (2012). *Congressional Parties, Institutional Ambition, and the Financing of Majority Control*. Ann Arbor: University of Michigan Press.

Herrnson, P. S. (1988). *Party Campaigning in the 1980s*. Cambridge, MA: Harvard University Press.

Herrnson, P. S. (2009). "The Roles of Party Organizations, Party-Connected Committees, and Party Allies in Elections." *Journal of Politics* 71(4): 1207–1224.

Herrnson, P. S. (2012). *Congressional Elections*. Washington, DC: CQ Press.

Karol, D. (2009). *Party Position Change in American Politics: Coalition Management*. New York: Cambridge University Press.

Key, V. O. (1958). *Politics, Parties, and Pressure Groups*. New York: Thomas Y. Crowell.

Kirkland, J. H. (2013). "Hypothesis Testing for Group Structure in Legislative Networks." *State Politics and Policy Quarterly* 13(2): 225–243.

Klinkner, P. A. (1994). *The Losing Parties*. New Haven, CT: Yale University Press.

Koger, G., Masket, S., and Noel, H. (2009). "Partisan Webs: Information Exchange and Party Networks." *British Journal of Political Science* 39: 633–653.

Koger, G., Masket, S., and Noel, H. (2010). "Cooperative Party Factions in American Politics." *American Politics Research* 38(1): 33–53.

Kolodny, R., and Dulio, D. A. (2003). "Political Party Adaptation in US Congressional Campaigns: Why Political Parties Use Coordinated Expenditures to Hire Political Consultants." *Party Politics* 9(6): 729–746.

Liu, Z., and Hu, B. (2005). "Epidemic Spreading in Community Networks." *Eurphysics Letters* 72(2): 315–321.

McChesney, F. S. (1997). *Money for Nothing: Politicians, Rent Extraction, and Political Extortion*. Cambridge, MA: Harvard University Press.

Newman, M. E. J. (2006a). "Finding Community Structure in Networks Using the Eigenvectors of Matrices." *Physical Review E* 74(3): 036104.

Newman, M. E. J. (2006b). "Modularity and Community Structures in Social Networks." *Proceedings of the National Academy of Sciences* 103: 8577–8582.

Petrocik, J. R. (1996). "Issue Ownership in Presidential Elections, with a 1980 Case Study." *American Journal of Political Science* 40(3): 825–850.

Robbins, S. M., and Tsvetovat, M. (2009). "Follow the Money." In *Interest Groups & Lobbying*, edited by C. McGrath, pp. 21–43. Lewiston, NY: Edwin Mellen Press.

Schattschneider, E. E. (1960). *The Semi-Sovereign People*. New York: Holt, Rinehart and Winston.

Schlesinger, J. A. (1966). *Ambition and Politics*. Chicago: Rand McNally.

Schlesinger, J. A. (1985). "The New American Political Party." *American Political Science Review* 79(4): 1152–1169.

Shafer, B. E. (1983). *Quiet Revolution: The Struggle for the Democratic Party and the Shaping of Post-Reform Politics*. New York: Russell Sage Foundation.

Skinner, R. M. (2006). "Do 527's Add Up to a Party? Thinking about the 'Shadows' of Politics." *The Forum* 3(3). http://www.degruyter.com/view/j/for.2005.3.3_20120105083450/for.2005.3.3/for.2005.3.3.1098/for.2005.3.3.1098.xml

Skinner, R. M., Masket, S. E., and Dulio, D. A. (2012). "527 Committees and the Political Party Network." *American Politics Research* 40: 60–84.

Theriault, S. M. (2006). "Party Polarization in the U.S. Congress: Member Replacement and Member Adaptation." *Party Politics* 12(4): 483–503.

Vonnahme, G. (2012). "A Preferential Attachment Model of Campaign Contributions in State Legislative Elections." *Public Choice* 1: 1–15.

Watts, D., and Strogatz, S. (1998). "Collective Dynamics of Small World Networks." *Nature* 393(6684): 440–442.

Ware, A. (2002). *The American Direct Primary*. New York: Cambridge University Press.

CHAPTER 17

A NETWORK APPROACH TO INTEREST GROUP POLITICS

MICHAEL T. HEANEY AND JAMES M. STRICKLAND

INTRODUCTION

An "interest group" is a nongovernmental organization for which a core part of its mission is to advocate its visions of the public interest to various governmental bodies—such as legislatures, commissions, courts, or state agencies—and/or private-sector institutions. Interest groups participate in politics at the local, state, regional, national, and international levels. Interest groups can assume a wide array of organizational forms, which are adapted to their heterogeneous political objectives. Some of the most common types of interest groups are citizen advocacy organizations (e.g., Greenpeace), professional societies (e.g., British Medical Association), labor unions (e.g., Industrial Workers of the World), and trade associations (e.g., Association of the German Trade Fair Industry).

While interest groups differ markedly in their political purposes and organizational forms, what they have in common is that as *intermediary institutions* they attempt to mediate between formal decision-making institutions and other organized subgroups of society. Thus, a key feature of interest groups is their position in networks: they are located between those with interests and those with the authority to make decisions. As a result, interest groups act as *brokers* in many different political situations; that is, they help to facilitate relationships between actors that would otherwise have difficulty relating to one another. At the same time, groups can connect individuals by stimulating the formation of ties among members, thereby serving as brokers between individuals. In doing so, they sometimes help citizens, firms, nonprofit organizations, and other actors obtain the policy changes they seek. At other times, interest groups may use their brokerage roles in service to the status quo by blocking changes from taking place.

In the process of brokering among decision makers and other actors, interest groups build, use, and transform networks. They build networks by envisioning new ways to represent interests, such as through setting up ad hoc coalitions or permanent advocacy organizations. They use networks by distributing campaign contributions, seeking advice, and spreading gossip. They transform networks by framing issues in ways that force realignments of interests or inspire bystanders to join the political fray.

Given the fundamental relationship between interest groups and networks, it is reasonable to expect that key aspects of interest group politics ought to be understandable in network terms. Prior scholarship has investigated some of these aspects but neglected others. The purpose of this chapter is to further elucidate the politics of interest groups using a network approach. We address five central questions about interest groups to consider how network analysis has or could offer potential answers:

(1) Where do interest groups come from? What is their genesis?
(2) How do interest groups develop, maintain, and change their identities over time?
(3) Under what conditions do interest groups work together? How do they do so?
(4) How do interest groups relate to other kinds of political institutions?
(5) What influence do interest groups have on democratic politics generally?

In addressing these questions, we review the previous work of scholars, but we also point to gaps or opportunities where prior research has revealed less than it might have. Our discussion of these topics is uneven, as network scholars have given greater attention to questions of how interest groups work together (question 3) and their broader effects on democratic politics (question 5), since these are areas in which network theories and methods have appeared most readily applicable. Yet questions of interest group origins (question 1), identities (question 2), and interinstitutional relationships (question 4) are also areas in which a network approach is likely to be fruitfully extended.

We view the fields of interest group politics and network analysis as mutually informative. Network analysis has answered—and has the potential to answer—important questions about interest groups that are not answered as satisfactorily using other approaches (e.g., How do interest groups develop reputations for policy influence?). At the same time, the study of interest group politics provides a laboratory to develop and expand the study of networks, such as by exploring the ways that organizations are embedded in dynamic, multiplex networks. This chapter aspires to help set the agenda for both fields by explicating their relevance to one another.

WHERE DO INTEREST GROUPS COME FROM? WHAT IS THEIR GENESIS?

The question of where interest groups come from has long been at the center of the study of interest group politics (Halpin, 2014). In his seminal book *The Governmental Process*, David Truman (1951) developed a "wave theory" for the emergence of interest groups. For Truman, new interest groups, such as trade associations and labor unions, emerged in waves as disturbances in society (e.g., economic growth, economic depression, war, technological innovation) called for new forms of political organization. In *The Logic of Collective Action*, Mancur Olson (1965) disputed Truman's claim that interest groups would arise naturally as a result of disturbances. Instead, he saw interests in society as limited by the self-interests of their members, who would prefer to free-ride on the efforts of others rather than contribute personally to a public good. Olson argued that new organizations were possible when their leaders devised ways to offer material incentives to their members (such as group benefits on insurance), which had the potential to incentivize their contributions to the public good.

As part of a new generation of scholars working on these questions, Elisabeth Clemens (1997) explained in *The People's Lobby* that citizens' interest groups were originally forged through the recombination of other successful organizational forms, including business lobbies, women's organizations, churches, and fraternal organizations. Clemens argued that strategic actors crafted interest groups as a new form of organization to deal with the inadequacy of political parties in addressing people's problems. Another stream of work on the growth of interest groups modeled it as a function of competition for limited resources within well-defined geographic areas. Virginia Gray and David Lowery's (1996a) book *The Population Ecology of Interest Representation* inspired a spate of studies on the dynamics of interest group populations in the US states and in other nations.

The extant literature on the emergence of interest groups devotes relatively little attention to the role that networks might play in the rise of new interest organizations. An important exception is a recent book by Jennifer Hadden (2015), *Networks in Contention*, which chronicled the growth of the international movement to stop climate change. She focused on the composition of new coalitions from among existing networks of environmental and other progressive organizations. At the same time, she documented how events and networks within political coalitions create the conditions for the rise of new advocacy organizations, such as "climate camps," which built grass-roots infrastructure for the climate change movement. Nevertheless, the formation of new organizations was a peripheral—rather than focal—element of Hadden's study.

Network analysis offers the potential to shed light on how interest groups emerge over time. In their work on organizational emergence, Padgett and Powell (2012) considered how a wide range of organizations—from early states and markets to communist economies and modern capitalistic enterprises—can be understood as developing through the dynamic concatenation of multiple networks. Padgett and Powell suggested that the formation of organizations can be likened to a biological process whereby subsets of elements break apart during catalysis to create new life. Analogously, Padgett and Powell demonstrated that new organizations arise from folding multiple networks onto one another through processes such as refunctionality, agglomeration, mass mobilization, and robust action.

Akin to Padgett and Powell, we argue that interest group emergence could be better understood by modeling new organizations as the networked product of prior interest

groups or other strategic actors. Perhaps the most obvious place to start is with the surprisingly underexamined subject of interest group mergers and splits. "New" interest
groups are often a renegotiation of political arrangements by more fundamental actors.
For example, the most powerful organization advocating for the interest of the health
insurance industry in the United States is America's Health Insurance Plans (AHIP),
which was born in 2002 from a merger between the Health Insurance Association of
America (HIAA) and American Association of Health Plans (AAHP) when the overlapping member companies decided that there was too much redundancy between the two
associations (Heaney, 2006, 921).

In contrast, some organizations may split from one another when organizational
leaders see opportunities for autonomous entities to achieve more than a unified effort
could. For example, in 1997 the Sierra Club Legal Defense Fund broke its formal ties to
the Sierra Club when it reconstituted itself as "Earthjustice" (Heaney, 2007). In both of
these examples, there is a stable, underlying network of organizational elites who strategically draw the boundaries of organizations to modify the way that they pursue their
political interests. Indeed, there is evidence that lobbyists themselves may encourage the
formation of new groups by persuading members of associations to become independent, at both the state (Gray and Lowery, 1996b) and national levels (Drutman, 2015) in
the United States. Scholars could potentially demystify these processes by identifying
the key actors and interests below the organizational level. A study of board interlocks
or coaffiliation by member organizations could provide insights in this area, much as
similar studies have done in the field of business (cf. Mizruchi, 1992).

More could be learned about the creation of new interest groups by closely examining the networks of the political entrepreneurs who founded them. Except for cases
of highly prominent interest group founders (such as Ralph Nader), scholars of interest groups and networks have not collected data on the individuals who found interest groups. Much network data could be derived from where these individuals went to
school, where they worked before founding interest groups, and sources of funding for
new organizations. Such analysis would likely reveal unlikely players in interest group
politics, including members of Congress, executive branch officials, foundations, and
privately wealthy individuals (though see Walker [1991] for research on patronage of
interest groups).

The essence of the network approach to interest group genesis is to envision networks
as part of the raw materials that bring interest groups into existence. Interest groups
do not spring up mechanically from the mere availability of resources or lack of representation of significant interests. Rather, they enter the political arena when strategic
actors draw upon their networks to secure resources, build staff, and articulate agendas.
Formal analysis of these networks among individuals promises to broaden the range of
interests that are seen as contributing to group formation and bring to light the implications of interest group connectedness. Research along these lines could further the
understanding of how organizations develop from networks, as interest groups represent an important, dynamic, and underexamined field using this type of analysis.

How Do Interest Groups Develop, Maintain, and Change Their Identities over Time?

When a new interest group forms, it joins a community of thousands of other interest groups. Amid this sea of competing advocates, one of its key challenges is to craft a distinctive identity. Identity is what an interest group is known for. Having a well-defined identity reduces the transaction costs for other actors that wish to do business with the group (Browne, 1990). Thus, a clear identity is generally advantageous when an interest group seeks to attract members or other supporters, extract resources from its environment, and establish a demand from policymakers for its advocacy.

Browne (1990) developed the first detailed theory of how interest groups craft their identities. Drawing on evidence from the agricultural policy domain, he argued that interest groups differentiate themselves from other groups by forming increasingly narrow issue niches. According to Browne, each group is motivated by the desire to have a monopoly over some issue area in order to be the one, unique group working on a topic. As more groups crowd into a policy domain, interest groups mutually accommodate one another by forming—and accepting—a narrower scope of control. Browne (1990, 480) referred to this process of identity formation as "balkanization" (see also Laumann and Knoke, 1987). Browne's work was a major advance for the field of interest group studies, providing a theoretical connection among how groups define themselves, the issues that they work on, and their standing among their peers.

Building on Browne's insights, Heaney (2004, 2007) sought to generalize the theory of interest group identity. Where Browne saw identity as focused on issues, Heaney argued that identities are created in multiple dimensions, including representation, issues, issue positions, ideology, and tactics (see also Jacobson, 2011). For example, the American-Israel Public Affairs Committee (AIPAC) has an identity based on working on US-Israeli foreign policy (an issue niche), but is also identified based on the idea that it takes a specific issue position in this niche (which is pro-Israel). Similarly, the rise of J Street as another interest group in the US-Israeli foreign policy niche has reconfigured identities in this area based on ideology, such that J Street occupies the relatively liberal/progressive position, and AIPAC occupies the relatively conservative position. Seeing Browne's study of agricultural policy as a special case, Heaney further claimed that groups may sometimes prefer to establish broad issue identities rather than narrow ones. In general, Heaney's work validated Browne's emphasis on identity as a key concept in interest group politics, but suggested that the processes of identity formation are broader and more complex than Browne proposed.

Over the past decade, interest group scholars have explored the implications of identity in a wider range of group behaviors. Most notably, Engel (2007) demonstrated how interest groups' identities can shape their selection of the venues in which they pursue their policy objectives. Jacobson (2011) showed how organizational identities guide the way that the AFL-CIO, the Sierra Club, and the Christian Coalition have shifted their positions on immigration issues, thus reinforcing the view that interest group identities may be prior to—and not necessarily derivative of—issue positions. Halpin and Jordan (2009) pointed to identity as a guiding principle that interest groups use in adapting their organizational forms in the wake of threats to their survival (see also Halpin and Daugbjerg, 2015).

Political scientists investigating interest group identities have generally ignored or deemphasized the potential connections between identities and intergroup networks. Yet there are numerous ways in which these phenomena might plausibly be connected. Networks might guide groups to identify potential competitors and therefore the dimensions on which they define their groups' identities. As a group chooses to emphasize representation, issues, ideology, tactics, or other dimensions of its identity, it may look to other groups to which it is connected in making this decision. For example, a group may explicitly seek to differentiate itself from its close network contacts—especially on the dimensions on which they most readily identify—if the group's leadership believes that external audiences may conflate the groups because of their network ties. For example, the US Chamber of Commerce and the National Association of Manufacturers (NAM) have close network ties and often work together in coalitions. Because they represent business interests broadly, their identities are sometimes confused; in fact, in 1976 the two organizations seriously considered merging (Waterhouse, 2014, 86). Since the failed merger, they have been especially careful to differentiate their identities, with NAM representing only manufacturers and the Chamber representing all classes of business interests. Under such conditions, interest group identities would be, in part, a function of preexisting social networks.

Conversely, a group may choose its network contacts in part based on alignment or dealignment with their identities, as Anand, Joshi, and O'Leary-Kelly (2013) established in a nonpolitical context. For example, an interest group may wish to create a portfolio of network contacts with a particular identity configuration. In making such choices, the group may prefer to have contacts with homophilous identities on some dimensions (e.g., partisanship or ideology) and with heterophilous identities on other dimensions (e.g., industry or geography). Under these conditions, interest group identities would be, in part, a function of preexisting social networks. Thus, the causation from identity to networks may run in either or both directions.

In light of possible bidirectional causation, empirical evaluation of the possible links between interest group networks and identities would require careful, longitudinal observations of interest group tie formation. It would be critical to observe the choices that groups made when forming new relationships with groups with which they did not have previously existing ties. The network structure of existing coalitions should also factor into such an analysis, as groups would likely be influenced by the preexisting alignments of their potential new partners. When a new interest group connects to a preexisting coalition of groups, are there conditions under which members of the coalition need to adjust their identities in response to the presence of the new partner? For example, if the new partner is very similar along some dimension, does that prompt the group to further differentiate itself based on that dimension? Information to evaluate these possibilities could be gathered from coalition web pages and online membership lists, which could be mined for data on identities and interorganizational ties.

Examining the relationship between interest group identities and networks could potentially yield insights valuable for the study of political networks more generally. Scholars of social network analysis have neglected questions of network *content* in favor of examination of network *structure*. Yet the types of alters that an actor chooses may be just as consequential as the structure of the relationships between those alters. Interest group identity in networks is a good example of a type of network content that is politically important and would afford the opportunity to weigh the relative contributions of structure and content to the effects of social networks. For example, examining what roles particular groups may fulfill within coalitions of multiple interest groups might shed light on which coalitions groups choose to join (or not).

Under What Conditions Do Interest Groups Work Together? How Do They Do So?

As the population of interest groups has grown steadily over time, the nature of cooperation among groups has become correspondingly more important, both substantively and theoretically. When there were only a few peak interest groups representing broad sectors of society (e.g., agriculture, medicine, labor, and manufacturing), each group could plausibly stand on its own vis-à-vis the government, at least for most matters. As groups in each sector proliferated—agriculture divided its representation into wheat, corn, soybeans, sugar, and so forth—the ability of groups to collaborate formally through advocacy coalitions and to work together informally by sharing information and resources became all the more critical to the success of their advocacy. Thus, questions of which groups worked with one another, who shared information with whom, and to what effect, became more integral to understanding the activities of interest groups. These questions are, at their heart, about the operation of political networks. Research on these questions has factored not only into the development of interest group studies, but also into the modeling of interorganizational networks of all types.

The first study to offer a systematic network analysis of interest group cooperation was *The Organizational State* by Edward Laumann and David Knoke (1987). It examined multiple networks (i.e., communication, influence, events, and issues) that connect interest groups in the health and energy policy domains. In doing so, it revealed the dominant role that nongovernmental organizations play in national policymaking in the United States relative to policy experts and other ephemeral actors. It elucidated the relevance of networks to how groups worked together to identify problems, share information, exchange resources, and exercise influence. While these findings represented a critical advance in interest group studies, Laumann and Knoke also provided an exemplar of how to study interorganizational relations among complex institutions.

Numerous scholars continued to pursue the trail blazed by Laumann and Knoke. Most notably, a series of articles by Carpenter, Esterling, and Lazer (1998, 2003, 2004) reanalyzed Laumann and Knoke's data. Carpenter et al. (1998) showed how interest groups that formed weak ties with many groups tended to have an informational advantage over groups with fewer weak ties. Carpenter et al. (2003) revealed, however, that groups tend to place a greater emphasis on forming strong ties rather than weak ties, since each tie is costly to maintain (i.e., the bandwidth constraint), they have more precise information about their strong ties, and they are more likely to derive the type of asymmetric information that produces political advantages from strong ties. Carpenter et al. (2004) demonstrated that sharing information in these networks is a function of preference similarity (i.e., homophily) and third-party brokerage. Collectively, these studies were essential in uncovering the strategic political behavior latent in the ways that interest groups communicate with one another when working together.

With the rise of exponential random graph models (ERGMs) as an approach to network analysis (Lusher et al., 2012), scholars have become increasingly interested in how interest groups choose specific network partners. The ERGMs have the advantage of allowing the researcher to model the formation of ties as a function of endogenous network structures, as well as actor-level independent variables that are traditionally included in regression models. An excellent example of work in this vein is Leifeld and Schneider's (2012) investigation of thirty advocates in the German toxic chemicals policy domain. They asked whether similarity in policy preferences determined which advocates share information with one another. They found that transaction costs and the opportunity to have contact in social settings had a greater impact on information sharing than did preferences.

Moving beyond information sharing, two recent studies by Box-Steffensmeier and Christenson (2014, 2015) focused on how groups worked together on common policy goals. In particular, they looked at how interest groups collaborate on the authorship of amicus curiae briefs before the US Supreme Court. Amicus briefs are statements that advocate for a particular outcome in a case, filed by outside parties with a stake in the court's decision. They found a dominant pattern of brief authorship in which large, well-endowed groups tend to coauthor with a large number of smaller groups. They also found that political homophily among groups based on industry area, budget, sales, and membership was critical in determining which groups worked together. In comparing networks across organizational types, they found that religious, labor, and political organizations tended to differ from business, civic, and professional groups.

The extant literature on cooperation is rich with respect to questions of information exchange. We know a great deal about who communicates with whom and why. However, we know relatively little about the substance of what is communicated among groups. What explains variations in the level of sensitivity of information that is communicated? Why does information sometimes get transferred quickly and at other times experience significant delays? Does information transfer depend on the subject at hand? Making significant advances in this area is challenging, because it would require the collection of new types of data that are more fine-grained and detailed. If such information were to be collected through traditional interview and survey techniques, it would place substantially increased burdens on informants when reporting data. Extracting data from email and social media databases may be an alternative solution to this problem. In the short term, data from such sources are likely to be unrepresentative of the population of groups, due to the limited number of organizations that might be willing to share such data. In the longer term, possible advances seem much more promising as suitable data become more widely available, provided that logistical and ethical concerns can be addressed satisfactorily.

Published research on the determinants of coalition formation among groups is much less developed than is the case for information exchange. This gap exists partly because of heterogeneity in the nature of interest group coalitions. First, there is considerable variation in the level of formality attached to coalitions. Some coalitions are merely ad hoc assemblies of groups, while others erect elaborate formal institutions. Second, coalitions differ in the scope of their objectives and, concomitantly, on their intended permanence; some coalitions have targeted goals, leading them to exist only for a short period of time, while other tackle more enduring policy issues, leading them to persist for decades. Third, coalitions vary in the extent of their public visibility, with some broadcasting their existence on the web and others lurking only in the subterranean worlds of elite lobbyists.

Advancing the analysis of coalition networks would require addressing the heterogeneity in what constitutes a network tie. Indeed, scholars may benefit from focusing added attention on the theoretical justifications for studying the particular types of ties they choose to observe (Krackhardt, 1992). For example, how is analysis to be conducted when different groups are united by different *types* of coalitions that involve different forms of relationships between members? This issue could be viewed as a problem for analysis, or it could be approached as central to what we would like to know about interest group coalitions. Network analysis could prove to be especially valuable if it not only uncovered who allied with whom, but also what did or did not happen within these coalitions.

Clearer analysis of how interest groups work together is needed to present a more complete picture of how these institutions engage in advocacy. Progress in this area will require better theoretical integration of the formal sides of collaboration (e.g., coalitions) with the informal sides (e.g., communication, trust). Research that illuminated how formal and informal ties among interest groups are compatible or incompatible could distill the mechanisms through which interest groups convert their loose affiliations into collective action.

Further network analyses of interest group cooperation could prove relevant for understanding interorganizational cooperation beyond advocacy organizations. Although interest group cooperation differs from cooperation among other types of organizations (e.g., firms, nonprofit organizations, government agencies), it shares many of the same features, such as the uncertainty attached to which partners may be good collaborators and which may not. Thus, analysis of interest group cooperation may yield findings that are of general interest to network scholars, such as about how alliances evolve over time. Such information may be more readily available about interest groups than about other types of organizations, to the extent that the public-interest dimension of interest groups makes them more likely than other types of organizations to disclose to scholars details about their collaborative behavior. As a result, the world of interest group politics likely will continue to be a desirable laboratory for the study of interorganizational collaboration.

How Do Interest Groups Relate to Other Kinds of Political Institutions?

Interest groups develop relationships not only with one another, but also with actors in the myriad types of institutions that they attempt to influence. These relationships may yield intelligence, trust, and resources that are critical to the ways that interest groups do their work. Relationships may be manifest by the transfer of staff through the revolving door between government and the private sector, the sharing of expertise and policy consultations, and the direct exchange of resources through political contributions. Although networks are a crucial part of these activities, scholars have only occasionally approached these topics from the perspective of network analysis. In this section we discuss applications of network analysis to interest group relationships with legislatures, bureaucratic agencies, and political parties.

Lobbying the legislature is perhaps the most common, as well as the most studied, aspect of interest group behavior. Classic texts in this area include works by Herring (1929), Milbrath (1963), and Baumgartner and Leech (1998). This tradition has focused on questions such as (1) How do interest groups choose their lobbying strategies and what strategies do they choose?; (2) Whom do interest groups choose to lobby?; and (3) What tactics do interest groups use when lobbying? These studies tended to place a greater emphasis on the groups or their targets, without seeing these patterns as part of a larger network.

Recent studies have articulated a rationale for viewing network position as a critical variable in modeling lobbying activity. Mahoney and Baumgartner (2014, 205, 214) explained: "Lobbyists are not lone actors trying to influence officials in a vacuum; they are embedded in an issue context that involves other actors who agree with them and still others who do not. . . . Rather than pick an individual lobbying organization and count up its resources, we need to recognize that lobbyists, like wolves, work in packs" (see also DeGregorio, 1997). Fully implementing these issues in empirical analysis would require a shift in the way that political scientists typically study lobbying.

An exemplar of work in this new tradition is LaPira and Thomas's (2014) analysis of "revolving door" lobbyists. Drawing on data disclosed pursuant to the requirements of the Lobbying Disclosure Act of 1995, they investigated lobbyists that have moved between staff positions on Capitol Hill and lobbying (i.e., "revolvers"). Among current lobbyists, they found that former congressional staff members who were promoted up the hierarchy of Congress tended to attract a more economically diverse set of lobbying clients than did those who left Congress before moving up the ladder. This research hints that the movement of actors between government and the private sector may correspond with building networks rich in "structural holes"; that is, when contacts are drawn from distant parts of a network rather than forming redundant contacts that are closely connected with one another (Burt, 1992).

While LaPira and Thomas's (2014) work represents a notable advance in the field, it only scratches the surface of network analysis that could possibly be conducted using data derived from the Lobbying Disclosure Act and other sources, such as congressional staff directories. The ability to track the movement of employees over time from Congress to the private sector—and back—raises a number of intriguing possibilities for network analysis. The careers of lobbyists and congressional staff bring them in contact with multiple networks based on the different groups of people and organizations they work with, such as other lobbyists, other congressional staff members, members of Congress, congressional offices, and lobbying firms. From following the movements of individuals through the revolving door, it is easy to imagine mapping networks among lobbying firms, congressional offices, and lobbyists/staff themselves. Analyses of these networks could, for example, prove invaluable in following the diffusion of lobbying tactics, cooperation among lobbyists, and the flow of sensitive information. Such research could borrow from related work by Nyhan and Montgomery (2015), which deals with diffusion of campaign tactics.

Relationships matter in the ways that interest groups relate to other kinds of institutions, too. One of the most promising areas for formal network analysis is the study of group interactions with the bureaucracy. Although they do not include formal network models, Daniel Carpenter's (2001, 2010) books on the political development of federal bureaucratic agencies, such as the Department of Agriculture and the Food and Drug Administration, narrated elaborate patterns of network formation and decay among interest groups attempting to influence policies in these areas. Similarly, research on interest group involvement in regulatory rule-making has suggested the value of formal network analysis, but has not undertaken it. For example, the analysis in Nelson and Webb Yackee's (2012) article on coalitions of interest groups active in rule-making could have been adapted using a network approach by examining how the membership composition of coalitions working on rule-making overlap with one another. Such an approach might reveal which interest groups exert influence across debates on numerous rules through their coalition involvement.

Perhaps the greatest barriers to conducting network analyses of interest group-bureaucratic interactions are the organizational complexity of the bureaucratic agencies and their insularity from public view. Organizational complexity presents a conceptual challenge to network analysis, because it may be difficult to specify what nodes and links should be included in an analysis. For example, it may be insufficiently specific to say that an interest group has a tie with "the US Department of Education" without also stating something about the office within which the contact is made (e.g., Civil Rights, Postsecondary Education). But naming an office may also be misleading, since the contact may be more meaningfully with a *person* than with an *office*. In short, the analyst may have trouble specifying the proper unit of analysis. Moreover, the insularity of agencies from the public may make it difficult for researchers to contact and interview the key players that make contacts and forge networks. The real decision makers may be buried under layers of bureaucracy that are difficult for an outside researcher to penetrate.

Even accounting for common obstacles, there are many unexplored possibilities for investigating interest group-bureaucratic networks. The presence of interest groups on advisory commissions, comments by groups on regulations, and the revolving door of staff from interest groups to the bureaucracy (and back) present ways to identify and measure nodes and links in a manner that is amenable to formal analysis. Analysis of these ties could help to disentangle how variations in the content of network ties matter to political relationships by combining content analysis with network analysis. For example, the texts of regulatory comments could be content-analyzed for the level of expertise that they convey, thus allowing for comparison of the relative effects of expertise and network position on their influence over policymaking. Examination of the long-term movement of staff between groups and agencies could trace out long-term patterns of influence that are not apparent in analysis conducted over shorter time periods. Finally, network analysis allows the investigator to capture the nonuniformity and multilayered nature of bureaucratic organization in ways that other types of analysis are unable to do, thus allowing for studies reflecting greater realism in how interest groups intersect with agencies.

Examining interactions between interest groups and political parties is another area in which a network approach holds some unexplored promise (Fraussen and Halpin, 2016), though there have already been notable network studies on this topic. Grossmann and Dominguez (2009) mapped out multiplex party-group ties that cross-cut legislative and electoral politics, drawing on data from networks of campaign endorsements, legislative coalitions, and financial contributions. They found that interest group ties mirror party coalitions in electoral—but not legislative—arenas. Heaney et al. (2012) also found isomorphism between the structure of party coalitions and interest group comembership among party activists. In the area of social movements, Heaney and Rojas (2007, 2015) pointed out that activist networks similarly are closely aligned with partisan coalitions.

A promising next direction for understanding interest group-party networks is to pay closer attention to how they affect the unfolding of political processes. Heaney and Rojas

(2015) suggested that these connections tend to serve parties to a greater extent than they serve social movements. Does the same advantage hold for parties over interest groups in legislative debates? How do partisan ties among interests groups affect their ability to exert leverage over policy outcomes? One way to understand the effects of these networks may be to look at how interest groups work together in coalitions (Heaney and Lorenz, 2013). For example, how is the strength of an interest group coalition affected by the strength of its networks with political parties? Coalitions with strong partisan ties may be able to marshal the procedural might of the party on their behalf, but may also be beholden to the party's fickle nature. In contrast, coalitions with weak ties to parties may find it harder to obtain access to the legislative agenda, but may also be able to sustain the coherence of their positions over longer periods of time. Research along these lines could provide insights into the extent to which group-party interrelationships matter to legislative outcomes.

Studies on interest group relationships with other types of institutions may be informative for interinstitutional network analysis more generally. Interest groups connect with myriad organizations in society, thus raising the possibility that interest group networks reveal aspects of how these organizations operate. For example, Lee Drutman's (2015) book *The Business of America Is Lobbying* documented how many corporations become members of a panoply of trade associations; the overall patterns in these relationships could be examined as two-mode networks. Given the breadth of institutions with which interest groups connect, analysis of their networks presents significant potential for appreciating interorganization networks generally.

What Influence Do Interest Groups Have on Democratic Politics Generally?

Political scientists and sociologists have long sought to understand what types of actors influence the outcomes of government decisions. Early writings by scholars such as Dahl (1961) analyzed which elites exerted the most influence (see also Hunter, 1953; Laumann and Pappi, 1973; Polsby, 1960). Schattschneider (1960) argued that under some conditions, interest groups were among the influential elites—especially when the issue was narrow in scope and not very visible to the public. As this tradition continues, recent research by Gilens and Page (2014) found that interest groups that represent businesses are likely to have a substantial, independent impact on policy over time, although interest groups representing citizens and other mass-based interests have little detectible influence.

Network studies have made major contributions to deciphering which interest groups exert influence and how they do so. The extant literature on interest group networks demonstrates convincingly that the ability to influence policy outcomes is at least partly a function of their ability to exploit connections and positions in networks. This conclusion is supported by studies conducted in various nations, examining different types of policymaking institutions and employing diverse approaches to network analysis (Varone, Ingold, and Jourdain, 2016).

The seminal study on this topic, by Laumann and Knoke (1987), examined the development and distribution of networked reputations for influence based on in-depth interviews with elites in the health and energy policy domains. Laumann and Knoke found that interest group influence depends, in part, on the nature of the issues at the top of the agenda in the policy domain, the presence or absence of government decision-making elites, the degree of consensus among those elites, and the closeness of their positions to the center of the network. Importantly, they observed the presence of a "hollow core" within the networks of policymaking elites, meaning that there are no "core" actors that uniquely broker among the issues of a policy domain. This finding cemented their image of the organizational state as fragmented and balkanized. This key result was verified in *The Hollow Core*, a related book by John Heinz, Edward Laumann, Robert Nelson, and Robert Salisbury (1993), which similarly found hollow cores among networks of advocates in the agriculture, health, labor, and energy policy domains (although research by Heaney [2006] and Grossmann [2014] has questioned the persistence of hollow cores).

Research that followed in the Laumann-Knoke tradition focused on how the influence of interest groups depends on their ability to leverage positions in networks. Of particular interest is the extent to which network structures might enable interest groups to act as brokers among other competing interests. Fernandez and Gould (1994) concentrated on brokerage between groups and government actors. They found that the capacity to exert influence depends on the type of brokerage role played, such as whether the organization is a representative, a liaison, or an itinerant broker (see also Gould and Fernandez, 1989). Heaney's (2006) study of health policy elites investigated the capacity of groups to broker across party lines. He found that crossing party lines in communication networks is associated with stronger reputations for policy influence among congressional staff and other lobbyists. However, crossing party lines in coalition networks was associated with stronger influence reputations among other lobbyists, but not among congressional staff.

A new direction for this work has been to parse the micro-components of influence. Along these lines, Heaney (2014) argued that interest group reputations for influence are formed as they interact with one another in multiplex networks. That is, representatives of groups form opinions about who is influential in part through their direct communication with other groups, comembership in coalitions, and coinvolvement in issues. Drawing on data extracted from interviews in ten Swiss policy arenas, Fischer and Sciarini (2015) raised the concern that these reputations may be inflated by efforts of interest groups to engage in self-promotion and from misperceptions formed in personal relationships among informants in network studies.

Other recent studies of network influence have broken out of the Laumann-Knoke tradition by introducing new approaches to measuring networks and their influence.

Grossmann (2014) derived the structure of policy networks (which included interest groups) from a massive content analysis of scholarly books written about policy change. His measure of interest group influence was based on the attributions that the books' authors made about who shaped legislative outcomes. He found that networks of interest group influence are highly centralized, with some ideological polarization. According to Grossmann, interest group networks vary considerably in structure and influence over the policy process, with interest groups recognized as especially relevant in the areas of civil rights and liberties, criminal justice, labor, and immigration.

Moving outside the legislative arena, Box-Steffensmeier, Christenson, and Hitt (2013) transferred the investigation of interest group networks to influence over the US Supreme Court by considering the impact of amicus curiae briefs filed by interest groups. In examining *amicus* briefs from 1946 to 2001, Box-Steffensmeier and her colleagues found that in competitive cases (i.e., where brief totals were similarly matched for each side), amicus briefs were powerful signals for judges. Groups that were more connected with other groups via amicus briefs, and groups that were connected with well-connected groups, were more successful in influencing court decisions.

The insights accumulated by recent research on this topic suggest the need for a deeper and more varied approach to understanding interest group influence in future research. Approaches that rely on reputation-based measures of influence have become standard. Yet reputations for influence may differ in significant ways from actual influence, as reputations may persist long after real capacities change. Alternatively, the Box-Steffensmeier et al. (2013) and Grossmann (2014) studies demonstrated the utility of approaches that rely on content analysis. Still, content analysis may neglect to incorporate inside information from elites that is intrinsically a part of the reputational approach. Balancing these considerations suggests that future work may benefit from attempting to triangulate on estimates of influence by combining the reputational and content-based approaches. Future work that utilized both approaches would be more labor intensive for scholars, but could also generate evidence on the conditions under which the two approaches confirmed or contradicted one another.

Accumulated knowledge in this area points to the benefits of looking further at the implications of multiple, interacting networks. Heaney (2014) modeled interactions among four networks (influence, communication, coalition comembership, and issue coactivity), yet the Box-Steffensmeier et al. (2013) and Grossmann and Dominguez (2009) articles suggested the relevance of still other networks, such as legislative endorsements and amicus curiae cosigning. As the availability of data on diverse, interlinked networks expands—and as statistical methods for looking at the simultaneous interaction of networks improve (Lusher, Koskinen, and Robins, 2013)—new projects would be well-served to pay greater attention to modeling the interaction of multiple networks. Such analysis should extend beyond seeing different networks as having separate causal effects on influence—analogous to independent variables in a regression model—to seeing them as genuinely interactive with one another. That is, an effect of a tie between two interest groups in network A may be greater if they are also tied in network B. Previous empirical research has made only modest efforts to look for such effects when studying influence, but deeper analysis along these lines could contribute richly to unpacking the mechanisms of influence.

While interest group influence is in some ways unique to the political universe, researchers in many areas of study—public health, information sharing, and business, to name a few—are concerned about how network structures matter to institutional decision making. Thus, analyses on interest group politics that combine multiple ways to measure this type of outcome could also be suggestive of approaches to assessing the consequences of networks in nonpolitical contexts.

Conclusion

Interest group action is embedded in social contexts that are rich in multiple, overlapping, and interacting social networks. Networks reflect the underlying political coalitions that support and oppose interest groups, patterns of information flow, and access to information. Thus, viewing interest group politics through the lens of social network analysis has produced important insights into the ways that interest groups and networks work. For example, from Hadden (2015) we see how new interest groups are born out of preexisting political networks. From Laumann and Knoke (1987) and the scholars who followed in their footsteps we learn how interest groups use interorganizational networks to access reliable information and influence the policy process, as well how their efforts map onto larger patterns of relationships among political elites. From Box-Steffensmeier et al. (2013, 2014, 2015) we discover how interest groups work together on amicus curiae briefs and what effects they have on judicial decision making. From LaPira and Thomas (2014) we see how the revolving door affects which clients lobbyists choose to work with. From Heaney (2006, 2014) we appreciate the consequences of multiple, intersecting networks for legislative and policy outcomes.

At the same time, there is more to learn from and about interest group networks. A first strategy for doing so would be to pay greater attention to the many ways that interest group networks are linked to one another, including through communication, coalition comembership, event coparticipation, campaign contributions, cosigning amicus curiae briefs, board comemberships, and regulatory comments. Toward this end, it would be valuable for researchers to consider the ties between networks that exist at different levels of analysis. For example, it could be valuable to explore the interpersonal networks that underlie interorganizational networks. Scholars should examine not only how these networks matter separately, but also how they operate in conjunction with one another.

A second strategy would be to explore new kinds of data, especially texts that are amenable to content analysis. Grossmann's (2014) innovative content analysis of books on policy change is an excellent example of how new sources of information can be mined to extract relational data. Another potentially fruitful source of data is state-level lobbying disclosure records, which have yet to be fully examined for insight on lobbyist-client dyads and dynamics. In general, the study of social networks could benefit by seeking more synergy with advances in content analysis (cf. Grimmer and Stewart, 2013).

A third strategy would be to lengthen the period of time over which interest group networks are investigated. Interest group network studies have typically relied on surveys or interviews, which have been conducted over short periods of time, usually not more than a few years. Scholars may have planned research designs with these limited time horizons because of the high financial costs associated with using these methods. However, it is conceivable to conduct longitudinal studies of interest groups or lobbyists that are analogous to the National Longitudinal Study of Youth (Bureau of Labor Statistics, 2016). Work in this vein may allow scholars to uncover network effects on phenomena such as interest group emergence and identity development, which have been difficult to assess in studies with shorter time periods. This strategy may also help to more clearly address questions of causality, which are endemic to network studies (Fowler et al., 2011).

Given that the politics of interest groups are inextricably bound to their positions in networks, the study of networks and interest groups ought to be closely integrated. This chapter reviews much of the excellent scholarship that has striven toward this goal and points to opportunities for future research to expand upon it. An expanded agenda for the study of interest group networks could provide deeper insight into the emergence and evolution of interest groups, as well as their collaboration, communication, and influence over political processes. New research may be able to achieve these goals by combining network analysis with content analysis and expanding the timeframe over which networks are examined.

References

Anand, V., Joshi, M., and O'Leary-Kelly, A. M. (2013). "An Organizational Identity Approach to Strategic Groups." *Organization Science* 24(2): 571–590.

Baumgartner, F. R., and Leech, B. L. (1998). *Basic Interests: The Importance of Groups in Politics and in Political Science*. Princeton, NJ: Princeton University Press.

Box-Steffensmeier, J. M., Christenson, D. P., and Hitt, M. P. (2013). "Quality over Quantity: Amici Influence and Judicial Decision Making." *American Political Science Review* 107(3): 446–460.

Box-Steffensmeier, J. M., and Christenson, D. P. (2014). "The Evolution and Formation of Amicus Curiae Networks." *Social Networks* 36(1): 82–96.

Box-Steffensmeier, J. M., and Christenson, D. P. (2015). "Comparing Membership Interest Group Networks across Space and Time, Size, Issue and Industry." *Network Science* 3(1): 78–97.

Browne, W. P. (1990). "Organized Interests and Their Issue Niches: A Search for Pluralism in a Policy Domain." *Journal of Politics* 52(2): 477–509.

Bureau of Labor Statistics. (2016). "National Longitudinal Surveys." http://www.bls.gov/nls/.

Burt, R. S. (1992). *Structural Holes: The Social Structure of Competition*. Cambridge, MA: Harvard University Press.

Carpenter, D. P. (2001). *The Forging of Bureaucratic Autonomy: Reputations, Networks, and Policy Innovation in Executive Agencies, 1862–1928*. Princeton, NJ: Princeton University Press.

Carpenter, D. P. (2010). *Reputation and Power: Organizational Image and Pharmaceutical Regulation at the FDA*. Princeton, NJ: Princeton University Press.

Carpenter, D. P., Esterling, K. M., and Lazer, D. M. J. (1998). "The Strength of Weak Ties in Lobbying Networks: Evidence from Health-Care Politics in the United States." *Journal of Theoretical Politics* 10(4): 417–444.

Carpenter, D. P., Esterling, K. M., and Lazer, D. M. J. (2003). "The Strength of Strong Ties: A Model of Contact-Making in Policy Networks with Evidence from U.S. Health Politics." *Rationality and Society* 15(4): 411–440.

Carpenter, D. P., Esterling, K. M., and Lazer, D. M. J. (2004). "Friends, Brokers, and Transitivity: Who Informs Whom in Washington Politics?" *Journal of Politics* 66(1): 224–246.

Clemens, E. S. (1997). *The People's Lobby: Organizational Innovation and the Rise of Interest Group Politics in the United States, 1890–1925*. Chicago: University of Chicago Press.

Dahl, R. A. (1961). *Who Governs? Democracy and Power in an American City*. New Haven, CT: Yale University Press.

DeGregorio, C. A. (1997). *Networks of Champions: Leadership, Access, and Advocacy in the U.S. House of Representatives*. Ann Arbor: University of Michigan Press.

Drutman, L. (2015). *The Business of America Is Lobbying: How Corporations Became Politicized and Politics Became More Corporate*. New York: Oxford University Press.

Engel, S. M. (2007). "Organizational Identity as a Constraint on Strategic Action: A Comparative Analysis of Gay and Lesbian Interest Groups." *Studies in American Political Development* 21(1): 66–91.

Fernandez, R. M., and Gould, R. V. (1994). "A Dilemma of State Power: Brokerage and Influence in the National Health Policy Domain." *American Journal of Sociology* 99(6): 1455–1491.

Fischer, M., and Sciarini, P. (2015). "Unpacking Reputational Power: Intended and Unintended Determinants of the Assessment of Actors' Power." *Social Networks* 42: 60–71.

Fowler, J. H., Heaney, M. T., Nickerson, D. W., Padgett, J. F., and Sinclair, B. (2011). "Causality in Political Networks." *American Politics Research* 39(2): 437–480.

Fraussen, B., and Halpin, D. (2016). "Political Parties and Interest Organizations at the Crossroads: Perspectives on the Transformation of Political Organizations." *Political Studies Review* 14(Online First): 1–13.

Gilens, M., and Page, B. I. (2014). "Testing Theories of American Politics: Elites, Interest Groups, and Average Citizens." *Perspectives on Politics* 12(3): 564–581.

Gould, R. V., and Fernandez, R. M. (1989). "Structures of Mediation: A Formal Approach to Brokerage in Transaction Networks." *Sociological Methodology* 19: 89–126.

Gray, V., and Lowery, D. (1996a). *The Population Ecology of Interest Representation: Lobbying Communities in the American States*. Ann Arbor: University of Michigan Press.

Gray, V., and Lowery, D. (1996b). "The World of Contract Lobbying." *Comparative State Politics* 17(5): 31–40.

Grimmer, J., and Stewart, B. M. (2013). "Text as Data: The Promise and Pitfalls of Automatic Content Analysis Methods for Political Texts." *Political Analysis* 21(3): 267–297.

Grossmann, M. (2014). *Artists of the Possible: Governing Networks and American Policy Change since 1945*. New York: Oxford University Press.

Grossmann, M., and Dominguez, C. B. K. (2009). "Party Coalitions and Interest Group Networks." *American Politics Research* 37(5): 767–800.

Hadden, J. (2015). *Networks in Contention: The Divisive Politics of Climate Change.* New York: Cambridge University Press.

Halpin, D. (2014). *The Organization of Political Interest Groups: Designing Advocacy.* New York: Routledge.

Halpin, D., and Jordan, G. (2009). "Interpreting Environments: Interest Group Response to Population Ecology Pressures." *British Journal of Political Science* 39(2): 243–265.

Halpin, D., and Daugbjerg, C. (2015). "Identity as Constraint and Resource in Interest Group Evolution: A Case of Radical Organizational Change." *British Journal of Politics and International Relations* 17(1): 31–48.

Heaney, M. T. (2004). "Outside the Issue Niche: The Multidimensionality of Interest Group Identity." *American Politics Research* 32(6): 611–651.

Heaney, M. T. (2006). "Brokering Health Policy: Coalitions, Parties, and Interest Group Influence." *Journal of Health Politics, Policy and Law* 31(5): 887–944.

Heaney, M. T. (2007). "Identity Crisis: How Interest Groups Struggle to Define Themselves in Washington." In *Interest Group Politics*, 7th ed., edited by A. J. Cigler and B. A. Loomis, pp. 279–300. Washington, DC: CQ Press.

Heaney, M. T. (2014). "Multiplex Networks and Interest Group Influence Reputation: An Exponential Random Graph Model." *Social Networks* 36(1): 66–81.

Heaney, M. T., Masket, S. E., Miller, J. M., and Strolovitch, D. Z. (2012). "Polarized Networks: The Organizational Affiliations of National Party Convention Delegates." *American Behavioral Scientist* 56(12): 1654–1676.

Heaney, M. T., and Lorenz, G. M. (2013). "Coalition Portfolios and Interest Group Influence over the Policy Process." *Interest Groups & Advocacy* 2(3): 251–271.

Heaney, M. T., and Rojas, F. (2007). "Partisans, Nonpartisans, and the Antiwar Movement in the United States." *American Politics Research* 35(4): 431–464.

Heaney, M. T., and Rojas, F. (2015). *Party in the Street: The Antiwar Movement and the Democratic Party after 9/11.* New York: Cambridge University Press.

Heinz, J. P., Laumann, E. O., Nelson, R. L., and Robert, H., Salisbury, R. L. (1993). *The Hollow Core: Private Interests in National Policy Making.* Cambridge, MA: Harvard University Press.

Herring, P. (1929). *Group Representation before Congress.* Baltimore, MD: Johns Hopkins Press.

Hunter, F. (1953). *Community Power Structure: A Study of Decision Makers.* Chapel Hill: University of North Carolina Press.

Jacobson, R. D. (2011). "The Politics of Belonging: Interest Group Identity and Agenda Setting on Immigration." *American Politics Research* 39(6): 993–1018.

Krackhardt, D. (1992). "The Strength of Strong Ties: The Importance of Philos in Organizations." In *Networks and Organizations: Structure, Form, and Action*, edited by N. Nohria and R. Eccles, pp. 216–239. Boston: Harvard Business School Press.

LaPira, T. M., and Thomas, H. F., III. (2014). "Revolving Door Lobbyists and Interest Representation." *Interest Groups & Advocacy* 3(1): 4–29.

Laumann, E. O., and Knoke, D. (1987). *The Organizational State: Social Choice in National Policy Domains.* Madison: University of Wisconsin Press.

Laumann, E. O., and Pappi, F. U. (1973). "New Directions in the Study of Community Elites." *American Sociological Review* 38(2): 212–223.

Leifeld, P., and Schneider, V. (2012). "Information Exchange in Policy Networks." *American Journal of Political Science* 56(3): 731–744.

Lusher, D., Koskinen, J., and Robins, G.(Eds.). (2013). *Exponential Random Graph Models for Social Networks: Theory, Methods, and Applications.* New York: Cambridge University Press.

Mahoney, C., and Baumgartner, F. R. (2014). "Partners in Advocacy: Lobbyists and Government Officials in Washington." *Journal of Politics* 77(1): 202–215.

Milbrath, L. (1963). *The Washington Lobbyists*. Chicago: Rand McNally.

Mizruchi, M. (1992). *The Structure of Corporate Political Action: Interfirm Relations and Their Consequences*. Cambridge, MA: Harvard University Press.

Nelson, D., and Webb Yackee, S. (2012). "Lobbying Coalitions and Government Policy Change." *Journal of Politics* 74(2): 339–353.

Nyhan, B., and Montgomery, J. M. (2015). "Connecting the Candidates: Consultant Networks and the Diffusion of Campaign Strategy in American Congressional Elections." *American Journal of Political Science* 59(2): 292–308.

Olson, M. (1965). *The Logic of Collective Action: Public Goods and the Theory of Groups*. Cambridge, MA: Harvard University Press.

Padgett, J. F., and Powell, W. W. (2012). *The Emergence of Organizations and Markets*. Princeton, NJ: Princeton University Press.

Polsby, N. W. (1960). "How to Study Community Power: The Pluralist Alternative". *Midwest Journal of Political Science* 22(3): 474–484.

Schattschneider, E. E. (1960). *The Semisovereign People: A Realist's View of Democracy in America*. Fort Worth, TX: Harcourt Brace Jovanovich College Publishers.

Truman, D. B. (1951). *The Governmental Process: Political Interests and Public Opinion*. New York: Knopf.

Varone, F., Ingold, K., and Jourdain, C. (2016). "Studying Advocacy through Social Network Analysis." *European Political Science* 15(Online First): 1–13.

Walker, J. L. (1991). *Mobilizing Interest Groups in America: Patrons, Professions, and Social Movements*. Ann Arbor: University of Michigan Press.

Waterhouse, B. C. (2014). *Lobbying America: The Politics of Business from Nixon to NAFTA*. Princeton, NJ: Princeton University Press.

CHAPTER 18

···

NO DISCIPLINED ARMY

American Political Parties as Networks

···

GREGORY KOGER, SETH MASKET, AND HANS NOEL

> Viewed over the entire nation, the party organization constitutes no dis-
> ciplined army. It consists rather of many state and local points of power,
> each with its own local following and each comparatively independent of
> external control.
>
> Key (1964)

INTRODUCTION

···

FOR at least a decade, one of the most salient fights between Democrats and Republicans has been over healthcare reform.[1] The Democratic Party successfully passed the Patient Protection and Affordable Care Act in 2010, after years of debate, drafting, and deliberation. Since the act, commonly called Obamacare, was passed, it has remained a focal point of criticism from the Republican Party, which would like to repeal or replace it.

We say the "Democratic Party" passed the legislation, and that the "Republican Party" opposes it. Even though some House Democrats voted against the legislation, and not all Republican candidates advocate repeal, it is fair to characterize the conflict as between the parties. But who, exactly, is competing? The parties were marshaling forces in the legislature, but they also drew on policy expertise from think tanks and activist groups. Promises to "repeal Obamacare" are made in electoral campaigns and resonate with some voters and donors. Activists have been speaking out on the legislation at least since the wave of town hall meetings in the summer of 2009. Partisan media have traded interpretations of the act's success or failure in the years since its implementation. We want to speak of all of these actions as the collective efforts of the partisans on either side. But whom are we talking about?

This chapter discusses a relatively new conceptualization of political parties: a political party is a *network* of organizations and actors collaborating to win elections and enact policies. This includes elected officials and formal party organizations like the Republican and Democratic national committees, but also party-aligned media, interest groups, activists, donors, and think tanks. The nodes in these networks retain autonomy, cooperate by choice, and may choose to leave one party's network to join an opposing party network or to become independent of any party.

We have three goals. The first is to explain why a network model is especially useful for understanding modern American parties. Second, we provide a critical analysis of the extant literature on political parties utilizing a network approach. Finally, we suggest further directions for network studies of political parties, including both topics for future studies and methodological improvements.

Toward a Network Theory
of Political Parties

However we think of them, political parties are complicated things. When we speak of "the Democrats" or "the Republicans,"[2] there are many different actors we could be referring to. We might be talking about your neighbor with his yard sign, or maybe the folks who knock on your door to encourage you to vote. We might be talking about people who hold office in your city or your state capital. We might be talking about officials in the party, and we might be talking about the president of the United States. Parties are teams, and there is a lot of room on the roster.

Of the many ways political scientists think about these players, one of the most enduring is a taxonomy that is now more than seventy years old. In 1942 political scientist V. O. Key organized his textbook *Politics, Parties and Pressure Groups* around three aspects of a political party. After introducing "The Party System," Key discussed the party in these parts: "Party Structure and Procedure," then "Party and the Electorate," and finally "Party and the Government." The shorthand for these categories that we now use is party as organization, the party in the electorate,[3] and the party in government (or "PaO," "PiE," and "PiG," for those taking notes for comps).

There's nothing inherently wrong with dividing parties in this way. Indeed, this three-party model has been so enduring because it is profoundly useful and reasonably accurate for much of party scholarship. Party activity among voters is definitely different from party activity among members of the US Congress. Scholars need to divide the world into manageable bites, and there are excellent literatures on each domain of parties in the United States. But most of the interesting things about political parties happen *among* those three worlds. Party leaders in Congress (PiG) work with outside party leaders (PaO) to choose agendas to help their members win reelection (PiE) (e.g., Koger and Lebo 2017; Sinclair, 1995, 2006). Ambitious officeholders across the country run their states (PiG) in a way that will improve their stature in the party so that they might win nomination (PaO) for the presidency (e.g., Cohen et al., 2008). Informal party organization (PaO) makes some issues salient for those in government (PiG) and those aspiring to win government office (PiE), as we saw in the introduction.

At no time in these actions that bridge the parts of the party do leaders from the PiG actually convene with a delegation from the PiE. The coordination is informal and dispersed. It may occur at the same time, place, or manner as coordination within one part of the party.

Party activity also often involves actors who are not clearly part of one of Key's three components. Partisan media, less salient in the middle of the twentieth century when Key and others were developing party theory, but very important both before and since, don't appear to fit anywhere. But when partisan talking points start spreading on blogs, this might be the party acting. And informal organizations have always been hard to square with formal party organizations. Are super PACs part of the party, or not? Are the Koch brothers part of the Republican organization, or just unusually enthusiastic fans with their own tools and agenda? We could ask the same question of a host of informal organizations that have built parties throughout American history.[4]

Thus in recent years some political scientists have begun thinking of other ways of conceptualizing the pieces of political parties. Instead of focusing on three domains, we might note that there are a large number of partisan actors and organizations committed to some part of the party's mission. These actors are connected to other partisan actors, but not according to some hierarchical organizational chart. They have ties to actors who are in their same domain as well as to those in others. In this model, the party is the whole network of partisan actors, motivated broadly by a common set of goals, with each trying to do its part. It is a decentralized structure, but it is still a structure.

Thinking of parties as a network of actors addresses two other distinctions that scholars have drawn since at least Key's textbook. The first is the difference between the party and "pressure groups." Parties differ from pressure groups in that parties seek control of elected offices. Parties also often care about a broader agenda, because that agenda is part of a coalition needed to win office. Pressure groups have no need of a broad coalition, so they may have no need for a broader agenda.

Like Key's tripartite model, this is a useful distinction. But many important partisan actions bridge this divide as well.[5] The politics of health policy brought together interest groups and think tanks as well as formal party leaders. And those organizations didn't just operate as isolated actors, advocating for what they wanted. They weighed in on partisan plans and acknowledged compromises necessary for the parties to enact legislation. The relationship of ostensibly nonpartisan interest groups like the National Rifle Association or National Organization for Women to one party is not the same as to the other.

Thinking of parties as networks also allows us to bridge the divisions in the US federal system. Parties mirror the institutions around which they operate, and so they also have a federal structure. Key weighed in on this as well: "In a sense, no nationwide party exists, though each party, to be sure, has its own national organs. Rather, each party consists of a working coalition of state and local organizations" (Key, 1964, 315). He elaborated:

Viewed over the entire nation, the party organization constitutes no disciplined army. It consists rather of many state and local points of power, each with its own local following and each comparatively independent of external control. Each of the dispersed clusters of party professionals has its own concerns with state and local nominations and elections. Each has a base of existence independent of national politics. Each in fact enjoys such independence that more than a tinge of truth colors the observation that there are no national parties, only state and local parties. (329)

Part of this perspective is less and less true, as national party organs, both formal and especially informal, have become much more significant and as elections have grown more nationalized. But what has not changed is the way in which the party is the aggregation of many independent "points of power." National parties rarely dictate orders to the state parties. Again, they relate informally, via a network structure. The national party's formal organizations, such as the Republican National Committee and the Democratic National Committee, are not as important as the informal actors who increasingly concentrate power at the national level.

The network approach can thus not only reunite Key's tripartite party, it can reunite other separated elements of the party as well. There may well be reasons to focus on one part of the party, or on one level of the federal structure, even when using a network approach. All research needs to focus on something, and much of the work we discuss here follows these distinctions. But the network approach provides a framework for uniting them, if still often conceptually.

The Concept of the Party as a Network

The idea that a party should be viewed as an informal connection of players, rather than as having any hierarchical or formal structure, is not new. As we have seen, even Key understood that the party was best understood as a coalition of different actors, rather than a formal structure. But it is one thing to note that the party has a decentralized structure, and another to treat that structure as a network, to put that framework at the center of scholarship, and to seek to measure it.

The first attempt we are aware of to treat a political party as a network is Mildred A. Schwartz's *The Party Network* (1990). Schwartz conducts a case study of the Illinois Republican Party using social network analysis (SNA) concepts and methods. Schwartz takes as her unit of analysis specific offices or positions, such as "governor," "senator," "local committeeman," and "interest group." She interviewed actors across these various positions and asked them about the contacts they themselves had, and in some cases, that they knew about. This allowed her to create a matrix of contacts among the different kinds of actors, which forms the basis of much of her analysis.

Figure 18.1 shows a visualization of the relationships that Schwartz reported in her figure 18.1.[6] One thing to note in the figure is the apparent centrality of "financial contributor" and "interest group." Indeed, Schwartz reports that they have the highest centrality

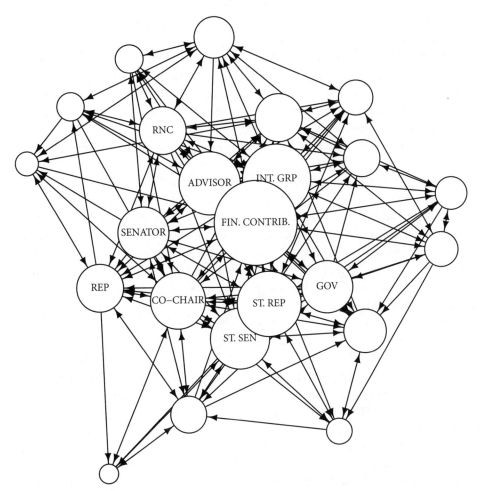

FIGURE 18.1 Graphical representation of the network matrix, from Schwartz (1990, 53). Nodes are sized in proportion to their degree of centrality.

measures. But this is probably because, rather than identifying different contributors or groups, Schwartz treated them as one. Similarly, state Senate and House leaders are less central than regular senators and representatives, but that's because all legislators in each chamber are treated as one. Presumably many actors have contact with at least one legislator, but the legislators with the most connections might well be the leaders that this analysis does not show as particularly central.

For Schwartz's purposes, this may have been a useful simplification, but it obscures much of the informal party structure. We prefer to think of the nodes in the network as being the specific actors, rather than the type of actor. Part of what makes the network approach valuable is precisely that it seamlessly integrates intra-domain contact with inter-domain contact. So we would want to see connections between the different interest groups and financial contributors, as well as their independent connections to other actors that are not interest groups. There are probably important within-type networks.

The other early effort to conceptualize parties as networks is J. P. Monroe's *The Political Party Matrix* (2001). Monroe also relies on interviews, mostly of party staff leaders in Los Angeles. Monroe stops short of using formal network methods, however; the analysis features nothing like centrality measures or adjacency matrices. But Monroe establishes that the various party offices he studies interact with one another in an informal way, and argues that the structure that connects them is important, even if he does not have quantitative measures of the structure itself.

This tendency to think in terms of network concepts but not network measures characterizes another set of works that borders on a network model of parties. This work argues that we should think of parties as largely the creatures of policy-demanding activists, not merely those of office-seeking politicians (Cohen et al., 2008; Masket, 2009; Karol, 2009; Bawn et al., 2012; Noel, 2013). This approach, sometimes called the UCLA school, is not the same as a network theory, but it shares some considerations. The main argument of the UCLA authors is that parties are made up of groups of "intense policy demanders," who in turn pressure politicians to coordinate so as to accomplish policy goals. When politicians are isolated from these policy demanders, they may not organize parties at all (Masket, 2009).

However, once we shift our attention to policy demanders, the informal actors become at least as important as the formal officeholders. And their relationships to each other and to the formal party are exactly the kinds of informal relationships that a network model claims are important. Thus the policy-demander approach implies an interest in networks. But a networks model of parties is consistent with approaches that do not place policy demanders at the center of the party.

In our own earlier work (Koger et al., 2009, 2010) we sought to track some of this informal coordination across a wide range of party actors. We approached this by making donations and paying membership and subscription fees to federal candidates, interest groups, and political magazines and newspapers, then tracking the solicitations we received from related organizations that used an identical return address. These studies were highly revealing about the nature of party networks, showing them to be large and insular, with little sharing of information across party lines. However, by its nature the study only captured the behavior of specific types of organizations.

This same approach has been applied to other kinds of partisan actors, notably political consultants. Often depicted as hired guns or mercenaries, independent of partisan loyalties, several strains of research show them to be not only extremely loyal to political parties, but also integral parts of the larger party network structure. Bernstein (1999) and Doherty (2006) examine the range of activities in which campaign consultants engage and the clients they take on. They find that consultants ultimately end up facilitating coordination among candidates within a broader party network. Montgomery and Nyhan (2010) find that consultants aid in the dissemination of campaign techniques among a party's candidates, helping to advantage the party network in the next election cycle.

Another valuable strain of party network research has focused on campaign finance patterns. Over the past two decades, campaign donors have developed new ways to channel funds to candidates indirectly, largely due to new campaign finance rules such as the Bipartisan Campaign Finance Reform Act of 2002 (BCRA) and the US Supreme Court's decision in *Citizens United v. F.E.C.* (2010). A substantial percentage of spending on state and federal candidates, that is, no longer exists in the form of direct donations from donors to candidates, but rather involves intermediary groups with fewer restrictions on how much they can spend and on what they can spend it.

Skinner et al. (2011, 2012), in a series of pieces, examine the composition of so-called 527s active in the 2004 and 2006 election cycles through the use of Internal Revenue Service personnel records. Their findings suggest that 527s are not "loose cannons," but rather are closely tied to party networks; many of their employees have also worked for national party organizations and in presidential campaigns and administrations. An important implication of this is that parties may use 527s for their own purposes, helping to transfer funds to candidates in service of party goals but in excess of what the law would otherwise allow. In another series of pieces, Masket (2011, 2016) examines elite donation patterns in the California gubernatorial recall election of 2003. The election to replace Governor Gray Davis had no primary or other official means by which a party could pick its nominee. But party endorsements and funding patterns showed clear preferences for certain candidates (Arnold Schwarzenegger and Cruz Bustamante) and pressured many other high-quality candidates to drop out of the race. Meanwhile, research on Nebraska's nonpartisan elections finds an important role for partisan donors in inducing polarization in the legislature (Masket and Shor, 2015).

Dowdle et al. (2013) trace donors who gave to multiple presidential candidates in the 2012 Republican invisible primary. They treat these multiple givers as more central in the party network, since they are not merely attracted to one candidate. Such donors coalesced around eventual winner Mitt Romney. Their analysis shows the decentralized network making a decision in real time.

Interest groups also align in a partisan manner. Heaney et al. (2012) conducted a survey of the delegates to the 2008 Democratic and Republican presidential nominating conventions, asking delegates about, among other things, their interest group memberships. The results chart out a network of interest groups, connected via party delegates, and demonstrate intriguing differences between the party networks, such as the diversity of interest groups on the Democratic side and the concentration of Republicans in just a few key groups.

Grossmann and Dominguez (2009) examine links between interest groups, including their ties in terms of campaign endorsements, campaign donations, and legislative alliances. This network study reveals some important facets of interest group behavior; while they do band together as part of expanded party networks, they also sometime pursue bipartisan legislative coalitions to advance their policy goals. Heaney (2006) similarly examines links between health policy interest groups, based on interviews with policy elites, and finds these groups to be playing the role of brokers among dispersed actors in a decentralized system, rather than mediators on a broad range of issues in a centralized one. Blum (2016) studies the organizational structures and language of local Tea Party chapters to examine how that movement has taken over the broader Republican Party. These studies have offered important insights on the place of interest groups in the broader party system, and some of this work illuminates the collaboration between interest groups and political parties.

Network approaches may also be used to examine partisan structures within a legislature. Kettler (2015), for example, examines monetary transfer patterns between state legislative candidates and finds that those with high "brokerage" scores (those who are connected to many other legislators) have a good chance of ending up as chamber leaders in the coming years. Parigi and Sartori (2014) show that the structure of cleavages in Italian society in the 1970s determines the structure of cleavages in the legislature. Nyhan (2009) uses a network approach to examine the use of Clinton-era scandal references in floor speeches by congressional Republicans. This work nicely maps the contours of what Hillary Clinton dubbed the "vast right wing conspiracy" in 1998 (Squitieri, 1998).

Examining a Political Party as a Network

Social versus Political Networks

Social network analysis has flourished in a variety of disciplines, but the social science discipline in which it has had the largest impact is sociology. Sociologists using network methods are interested in the spread of behavior, the context of social interactions, and the like. Social networks have thus been fruitfully applied to such cases as the development of a schism within a karate club (Zachary, 1977), the friendship patterns among high school students (Resnick et al., 1997), and success in the job market (Granovetter, 1973).

Sociology and political science are cognate disciplines, and many of the theories that explain behavior among these social phenomena might also explain political phenomena. But political phenomena also have their unique characteristics, as evidenced by the other chapters in this volume. At least some of the forces that govern the development and maintenance of a political party, in our case, are probably not the same as those that govern the high school cafeteria.[7] For this reason, it is important that political scientists interested in importing network methods develop their own theories about the microprocesses that generate networks, rather than adopting those developed for other kinds of social phenomena.

The primary difference is that political networks are purposive, rather than natural. As a result, social networks might not behave quite like political ones. Social theorists usually explain social networks with reference to processes like preferential attachment (in which the most popular nodes attract more nodes), homophily (in which like actors will form ties with one another), or triadic closure (in which two nodes which are connected to a third node will tend to be connected to each other as well).

These social tendencies probably also exist in political networks, which are of course made up of people, who also have social natures. But other, politically oriented incentives might also be at play, possibly overwhelming these social tendencies. From the point of view of a political party, the need to manage a coalition ought to loom large.

And building and maintaining a coalition involves a number of incentives (discussed in the next few paragraphs) at odds with the above.

A winning coalition: The main thing a party must do is win, either an election or votes in a legislature. This requires, in most settings, building a coalition that is 50 percent of the voting base, plus one (Riker, 1962; Schwartz, 1989; Aldrich, 1995). Some circumstances might require slightly larger coalitions, but there is a winning threshold, and something meaningful happens at that threshold.

Most network formation algorithms don't pay attention to these thresholds. If connection to only those who are similar to you (homophily) or whom you have been introduced to (triadic closure) does not get you to 50 percent, you have to keep building the coalition. This may involve tradeoffs, in that one set of coalition partners may not be willing to be in a coalition that includes another set. This simple dynamic of coalition management (Karol, 2009) is probably different in light of a network, but it doesn't mean it doesn't happen.

A minimal winning coalition: An oversized coalition can be as much trouble as an undersized one, if it requires dividing the spoils too extensively (Riker, 1962), or if it brings together too many actors who disagree with one another and so cannot work together (Rohde, 1991; Aldrich and Rohde, 2000). Most network formation algorithms do not account for those incentives.

It may well be exactly the network nature of coalitions that explains why we often form oversized coalitions. It may not be possible to cut out a few excess members, because those members have connections to still others. At the same time, party leaders do face incentives to keep coalitions from growing too large, and a network theory that ignores this incentive would be misleading.

A united front: Holding together a party requires that groups with potentially different goals set aside those differences for the sake of the party (Aldrich, 1995; Cohen et al. 2008). To maintain this, actors within the party will have to work with those they disagree with to cement the coalition. Successful presidential candidates have to appeal to all groups. Successful legislation has to accommodate all their needs.

It is not entirely clear what these incentives look like in network data, especially when both parties are struggling with these different incentives, and one is at least temporarily more successful than another. Existing research on coalition formation, size, and maintenance all tends to treat the coalition partners atomistically. There may be some reasons that some partners will want to work together or others will have tensions, but the idea that they are connected by social ties is not usually present. A network theory of parties should address these issues.

Identifying Party Networks

Attempting to actually measure party networks can be a challenging but revealing scholarly pursuit. Theoretically, what we want is to identify every party organ or actor and the other organs or actors to which each is "connected." But the need to operationalize this means we must immediately start thinking about what kinds of actors really make up the party. And we must think about what kinds of connections really constitute party ties.

We suggest a few guiding principles. First, nodes should consist of actors who make autonomous and unitary decisions. So it is less helpful to think of "Congress" as a node, since most of the interesting party dynamics happen among members of Congress. This also allows different members of Congress to have a different relationship to other actors outside the institution. After all, one member may be focused on building a power base within their state, while another may seek to rise in the House, and another may seek to enact a certain type of policy; different goals will yield different network ties.

Second, ties should consist of connections that indicate a meaningful relationship. This includes *strategic cooperation*, such as sharing information, coordinating at the same meetings, or adhering to the same set of talking points. It can also mean sharing and allocating *resources*, such as staff, money, or time. The distinction between meaningful and superficial relationships is usually difficult to observe, but researchers should be mindful of whether they are measuring substantive connections or incidental similarities.

This advice is, we think, appropriate for most studies of political networks. Indeed, some of the work that we characterize as studies of party networks is really an analysis of political networks broadly, and parties then emerge from the analysis. With those thoughts in mind, we note two important considerations. First, political parties are political networks, not merely social networks. And second, it may be difficult to distinguish party-driven networks from networks that are determined by other forces.

Future Directions in Party Networks Research

Why Networks?

One challenge for future research is explaining *why* American political parties take the form of networks. A party's structure is the result of choices made by political party leaders and by those who would seek to regulate those parties. Parties might take on a variety of forms, such as a strong, centralized, and hierarchical party, which we might associate with some European parliamentary parties. Or politicians might be only nominally partisan, instead working for their own ends at the expense of the party's collective fate. A network organization is neither rigid and hierarchical nor atomized and uncoordinated. Why do parties take this form?

Do party leaders desire to organize as networks? What are the costs and benefits associated with a network structure? For example, are party networks more adaptable to changing technological and legal developments than formal party institutions are? Are networks better able to balance disagreements between actors than a formalized party is? Like recent celebrity businessmen for the presidency if they reasserted direct control over the nomination process? Is it a problem if parts of a party network legally can't speak to each other? What kind of candidates does a party nominate if key decisions are made within advocacy groups rather than within formal party organizations?

What role do antiparty rules play in forcing parties to become more decentralized? Progressive-era reforms sought to curb the influence of parties, and American law tends to ignore parties (Masket, 2009; Mowry, 1951; Ranney, 1975; Rosenblum, 2008). Campaign finance rules tend not to empower political parties. For example, allied organizations are sometimes legally barred from coordinating with candidates, but such coordination is exactly what political parties are about. The informal network structure may be the only way for a party to operate in such a hostile legal environment.

While we think something like this is what is driving modern party network structure, we may be wrong. Maybe networks are inherent in parties. Even in the most hierarchical party machine era, political parties were built on informal relationships. Political bosses were rarely elected officials, and they often did not hold official leadership positions in the formal party structures. Their power was built through networks of reciprocal patronage, albeit networks with a more hierarchical structure, with the boss in a position of more influence than almost anyone is in modern political parties.

To pursue these questions, scholars would need a clear theory to test and a metric of centralization across political units.[8] Social network theory, with an understanding of the role and importance of network position and network structure, can provide a framework for generating hypotheses about why networks should form. And social network methods, with sophisticated measures of centrality and network-based power, could be very helpful in testing them.

How Party Networks Think

In our view, party networks make big decisions. They choose candidates, set policy agendas, formulate ideologies, and build coalitions. Obviously, though, networks lacking centralized leadership or decision-making rules usually do not "make" these decisions by fiat or vote counting, but rather through communication and mutual consent. This creates opportunities for dissent, factionalism, or exit. Both the process of making decisions and the responses of dissenting actors deserve further study. If party actors are playing a signaling games, which signals are most influential within a network, and why? How are party actors rewarded or punished for the signals they send? Under what conditions will party-affiliated interest groups, media, and activists "leave" a party network?

Subjects

Since the network model of political parties is relatively new, there are ample opportunities to study little-understood sectors of the party network. One example is the evolution of staff and lobbying networks. While there are ample studies of lobbyists and a few works on legislative and presidential staff, it would be possible and fruitful to study these actors as a single network of politicos who move from government jobs to lobbying to campaigns. This network is presumably highly polarized into Republicans and Democrats, but more interestingly, there may be substantial variation in the career paths of staffers within each party. To what extent are party staff networks subdivided by geography and factions? What happens to staffers whose employers (or former employers) experience a significant career milestone, such as election to a new party leadership post, selection as a committee chair, or resignation in disgrace?

Second, recent developments in technology and campaign finance provide an opportunity to study how party networks evolve. The Internet makes it possible for average citizens to communicate and coordinate across the country or the globe. And it makes it economical for campaigns to raise funds from small donors. In both cases, technology potentially acts as a centrifugal force, dispersing power from party elites to activists and voters. Has this diminished the ability of party elites to influence nominations and achieve policy change?

On the other hand, recent developments in campaign finance law may have shifted the balance of power within party networks toward extremely wealthy super donors—individuals who can give millions of their own funds to their favorite candidates. Super donors have long had a role in the political system, but the new regulatory regime has increased their ability to influence campaigns on their own. In a sense, these reforms have had a centripetal effect, increasing the influence of a small number of actors. On the other hand, the changes in campaign law may weaken the influence of other party elites (broadly defined) over nominations while allowing the personal preferences of a few donors to influence the agenda and outcome of elections. Further research could illuminate whether super donors cooperate with the rest of the party elites or inject their idiosyncratic preferences into campaigns.

Causal Inference and Party Networks

The mechanisms by which a party network might coordinate have many features in common with the dissemination of other traits through a network. For example, some scholars think that political attitudes among voters spread through a network (Sinclair, 2012). This, in turn, reflects the very large literature attempting to estimate the "contagion" of everything from obesity to smoking to depression to divorce in a network (Christakis and Fowler, 2007, 2008; Fowler and Christakis, 2008a, 2008b; Cacioppo, Fowler, and Christakis, 2009; Rosenquist et al., 2010; Rosenquist, Fowler, and Christakis, 2010; see also Manski, 1993; Shalizi and Thomas, 2011; Noel and Nyhan, 2011). This research notes that for all of these traits, those with connections tend to be more alike than those who are not, and that pattern might be due to the "spread" of the trait through the network.

But all of this research faces serious difficulties in establishing causal inference. There are three reasons that actors who are connected might be similar (Manski, 1993):

- **Contagion or influence:** One actor might have influenced the other actor to change on that trait, perhaps even subconsciously. In the case of obesity, one actor sees the example set by another in exercising, or in overeating, and decides it is acceptable for himself or herself.

- **Homophily**: The two actors might have established their ties in the first place because they were similar. In the obesity case, two actors who have similar interests in physical activity, or similar tastes in food, might be more likely to meet and become friends.
- **Environment**: The two actors might have similar experiences. In the obesity case, the opening or closing of a gym or a fast-food restaurant near where two friends live might affect them both similarly.

All three of these explanations also might relate to attempts to understand parties. Actual party coordination is akin to contagion or influence. It posits that the reason actors connect with one another is that they are trying to form a united front behind a coalition they hope will win. Thus the connections cause the actors to behave differently than they would have in the absence of the connections. Without the connections, the coalition would not hold together, or would end up supporting different policies, or something. At the same time, party coordination might cause ties that the contagion hypothesis doesn't account for.

But the other two explanations might also explain connections. Homophily, for example, may be behind party networks. Since similar actors will join the same network—and might even be closely related within that network—we definitely expect to observe homophily within a party. But if homophily is the only reason the network ties form, then the network is not doing much. This argument matches almost exactly the widely known argument about the role of parties in the legislature. Keith Krehbiel (1993, 2000) has argued that legislative voting behavior is driven not by parties but by underlying preferences, and that parties don't matter if they do not change the behavior of partisan actors. Many scholars have since demonstrated that parties do seem to affect legislative behavior (Aldrich and Rohde, 2000; Ansolabehere et al., 2001; Bawn, 1998; Brady and Epstein, 1997; Cox and McCubbins, 1993, 2005; Cox and Magar, 1999; Koger and Lebo, 2017; Lawrence, et al., 2006; Sinclair, 1995, 2006; Snyder and Groseclose, 2000; Lebo et al., 2007). Similarly, we think that the party network matters, but it may often be observationally equivalent to a model in which preferences alone determine ties. Similar work is needed to demonstrate its independent influence.

Common environmental factors might also explain party ties. Two politicians from the same state or with similar district demographics might end up connected to the same campaign consultants. So if we observe that politicians who represent similar districts are all connected by their common employment of the same survey firm, this might just mean they face the same issues.

Nevertheless, we believe that actual coordination occurs with party networks. At this early stage of research, it may not be possible to always rule out the alternative explanations. But scholars working on party networks need to begin grappling with this problem.

Two-Mode, Multiactor, Multistage Analysis

Another methodological challenge is grappling with the complexity of party networks. So far, most work on this topic has dealt with tractable subsets of actors or bounded systems. As this literature progresses, however, it may be useful to combine data sets to obtain a broad view of the party network. For example, eventually scholars may combine data on campaign contributions, endorsements, legislative debates, and staff contacts to portray a network of candidates, interest groups, donors, and staff, with overlapping directed ties.

Finally, a partial solution to the problem of causality is to use more temporal network data to assess how changes in independent variables affect the same actors over time. This may be especially effective when there are major events (such as the *Citizens United* [2010] decision, or a switch in party control of Congress) that lend themselves to clear before-and-after comparisons. Even better, an event may only affect a portion of a network, allowing a clear baseline for an entire network and then a comparison between the treated network and the untreated control network.

Conclusion

In our view, political parties—particularly today and particularly in the United States—are best understood as networks of cooperating actors. As such, they suggests potentially a rich opportunity to apply the concepts and methods of SNA to shed new light on contemporary politics. The range of actors involved in these networks—including politicians, party organizations, donors, and interest groups—provides rich data sets of behavior to analyze. Scholars have already made some progress in describing and explaining party networks, but much more theoretical and empirical work remains to be done. We encourage scholars working in this area to focus on the purposive behavior of political actors and to strive to identify causal relationships.

Notes

1. The authors would like to thank participants at the 2015 Political Networks Conference for their useful comments.
2. We constrain our discussion in this chapter to the United States. Most of the concepts we raise here may apply in other countries as well, but differences in party systems, governmental systems, electoral rules, and party rules all imply significant considerations that we do not address.
3. John Aldrich (1995) prefers "party in elections" to argue that this part of the party is created and shaped by campaigns, rather than being an independent force.
4. See, for example, Klinghard (2010) and Galvin (2010).
5. Key himself noted that the boundaries between interest groups and parties were not sharp, observing that party machines sometimes behaved like interest groups.
6. Figure 18.1 in Schwartz is the adjacency matrix, but we represent it here graphically.

7. The reader may now take a moment to chuckle at their own joke about Congress.
8. Mayhew (1986) is a classic version of such a project.

REFERENCES

Aldrich, J. (1995). *Why Parties? The Origin and Transformation of Political Parties in America.* Chicago: University of Chicago Press.

Aldrich, J. H., and Rohde, D. W. (2000). "The Consequences of Party Organization in the House: The Role of the Majority and Minority Parties in Conditional Party Government." In *Polarized Politics: Congress and the President in a Partisan Era*, edited by J. R. Bond and R. Fleisher, pp. 31–72. Washington, DC: CQ Press.

Ansolabehere, S., Snyder, J. M., and Stewart, C., III (2001). "The Effects of Party and Preferences on Congressional Roll-Call Voting." *Legislative Studies Quarterly* 26: 533–572.

Bawn, K. (1998). "Congressional Party Leadership: Utilitarian versus Majoritarian Incentives." *Legislative Studies Quarterly* 23: 219–243.

Bawn, K., Cohen, M., Karol, D., Masket, S., Noel, H., and Zaller, J. (2012). "A Theory of Parties: Groups, Policy Demanders and Nominations in American Politics." *Perspectives on Politics.* 10: 571–597.

Bernstein, J. (1999). "The Expanded Party in American Politics." Phd diss., University of California.

Blum, R. (2016). "The Tea Party: A Party Within a Party." Phd diss., Georgetown University.

Brady, D., and Epstein, D. (1997). "Intraparty Preferences, Heterogeneity, and the Origins of the Modern Congress: Progressive Reformers in the House and Senate, 1890–1920." *Journal of Law, Economics and Organization* 13(1): 26–49.

Cacioppo, J. T., Fowler, J. H., and Christakis, N. A. (2009). "Alone in the Crowd: The Structure and Spread of Loneliness in a Large Social Network." *Journal of Personality and Social Psychology* 97(6): 977.

Christakis, N. A., and Fowler, J. H. (2007). "The Spread of Obesity in a Large Social Network over 32 Years." *New England Journal of Medicine* 357(4): 370–379.

Christakis, N. A., and Fowler, J. H. (2008). "The Collective Dynamics of Smoking in a Large Social Network." *New England Journal of Medicine* 358(21): 2249–2258.

Cohen, M., Karol, D., Noel, H., and Zaller, J. (2008). *The Party Decides: Presidential Nominations before and after Reform.* Chicago Studies in American Politics. Chicago: University of Chicago Press.

Cox, G. W., and Magar, E. (1999). "How Much Is Majority Status in the U.S. Congress Worth?" *American Political Science Review* 93(2): 299–309.

Cox, G. W., and McCubbins, M. D. (1993). *Legislative Leviathan.* Los Angeles: University of California Press.

Cox, G., and McCubbins, M. (2005). *Setting the Agenda.* Cambridge, UK: Cambridge University Press.

Doherty, J. W. (2006). "The Candidate-Consultant Network in California Legislative Campaigns: A Social Network Analysis of Informal Party Organization." Phd diss., University of California.

Dowdle, A., Limbocker, S., Yang, S., Sebold, K., and Stewart, P. (2013). *Invisible Hands of Political Parties in Presidential Elections: Party Activists and Political Aggregation from 2004–2012.* New York: Palgrave Pivot.

Fowler, J. H. and Christakis, N. A. (2008a). "The Collective Dynamics of Smoking in a Large Social Network." *New England Journal of Medicine* 358: 2249–2258.

Fowler, J. H., and Christakis, N. A. (2008b). "Dynamic Spread of Happiness in a Large Social Network: Longitudinal Analysis Over 20 Years in the Framingham Heart Study." *British Medical Journal* 337: a2338.

Galvin, D. J. (2010). *Presidential Party Building: Dwight D. Eisenhower to George W. Bush.* Princeton, NJ: Princeton University Press.

Granovetter, M. S. (1973). "The Strength of Weak Ties." *American Journal of Sociology* 78: 1360–1380.

Grossmann, M., and Dominguez, C. B. K. (2009). "Party Coalitions and Interest Group Networks." *American Politics Research* 37: 767–800.

Heaney, M. T. (2006). "Brokering Health Policy: Coalitions, Parties, and Interest Group Influence." *Journal of Health Politics, Policy and Law* 31: 887–944.

Heaney, M., Masket, S., Miller, J., and Strolovitch, D. (2012). "Polarized Networks: The Organizational Affiliations of National Party Convention Delegates." *American Behavioral Scientist* 56: 1654–1676.

Karol, D. (2009). *Party Position Change in American Politics: Coalition Management.* New York: Cambridge University Press

Kettler, J. (2015). "The Season for Giving: Candidate Contributions and the Path to Leadership." Paper presented at the 15th Annual State Politics and Policy Conference, Sacramento, CA, May 30.

Key, V. O. (1964). *Politics, Parties, and Pressure Groups, Crowell,* 5th edition.

Klinghard, D. P. (2010). *The Nationalization of American Party Organizations, 1880–1896.* New York: Cambridge University Press.

Koger, G., and Lebo, M. J. (2017). *Strategic Party Government.* Chicago: University of Chicago Press.

Koger, G., Masket, S. E., and Noel, H. (2009). "Partisan Webs: Information Exchange and Party Networks." *British Journal of Political Science* 39: 633–653.

Koger, G., Masket, S., and Noel, H. (2010). "Cooperative Party Factions in American Politics." *American Politics Research* 38: 33–53.

Krehbiel, K. (1993). "Where's the Party?" *British Journal of Political Science* 23(2): 235–266.

Krehbiel, K. (2000). "Party Discipline and Measures of Partisanship." *American Journal of Political Science* 44(2): 212–227.

Lawrence, E. D., Maltzman, F., and Smith, S. S. (2006). "Who Wins? Party Effects in Legislative Voting." *Legislative Studies Quarterly* 31(1): 33–69.

Lebo, M., Adam, J, McGlynn, J., and Koger, G. (2007). "Strategic Party Government: Party Influence in Congress, 1789–2000." *American Journal of Political Science* 51: 464–481.

Manski, C. F. (1993). "Identification of Endogenous Social Effects: The Reflection Problem." *The Review of Economic Studies* 60(3): 531–542.

Masket, S. E. (2009). *No Middle Ground: How Informal Party Organizations Control Nominations and Polarize Legislatures.* Ann Arbor: University of Michigan Press.

Masket, S. E. (2011). "The Circus That Wasn't: The Republican Party's Quest for Order in the 2003 California Gubernatorial Recall." *State Politics and Policy Quarterly* 11: 124–148.

Masket, S. E. (2016). *The Inevitable Party.* Oxford: Oxford University Press.

Masket, S. E., and Shor, B. (2015). "Polarization without Parties: Term Limits and Legislative Partisanship in Nebraska's Unicameral Legislature." *State Politics and Policy Quarterly* 15: 67–90.

Monroe, J. P. (2001). *The Political Party Matrix: The Persistence of Organization*. Albany: State University of New York Press.

Montgomery, J., and Nyhan, B. (2010). "The Party Edge: Consultant-Candidate Networks in American Political Parties." Paper presented at the Third Annual Political Networks Conference, Durham, NC.

Mowry, G. E. (1951). *The California Progressives*. Chicago: Quadrangle.

Noel, H. (2013). *Political Ideologies and Political Parties in America*. New York: Cambridge University Press.

Noel, H., and Nyhan, B. (2011). The "Unfriending" Problem: The Consequences of Homophily in Friendship Retention for Causal Estimates of Social Influence. *Social Networks* 33: 211–218.

Nyhan, B. (2009). "Strategic Outrage: The Politics of Presidential Scandal." Duke University, Working Paper.

Paolo, P., and Sartori, L. (2014). "The Political Party as a Network of Cleavages: Disclosing the Inner Structure of Italian Political Parties in the Seventies." *Social Networks* 36(January): 54–65. http://dx.doi.org/10.1016/j.socnet.2012.07.005.

Ranney, A. (1975). *Curing the Mischiefs of Faction: Party Reform in America*. Jefferson Memorial Lectures. Berkeley: University of California Press.

Resnick, M. D., Bearman, P. S., Blum, R. W., Bauman, K. E., Harris, K. M., Jones, J., Tabor, J., Beuhring, T., Sieving, R. E., Shew, M., Ireland, M., Bearinger, L. H., Udry, J. R. (1997). "Protecting Adolescents from Harm. Findings from the National Longitudinal Study on Adolescent Health." *Journal of the American Medical Association* 278: 823-832.

Riker, W. H. (1962). *The Theory of Political Coalitions*. New Haven: Yale University Press.

Rohde, D. W. (1991). *Parties and Leaders in the Post-reform House*. Chicago: University of Chicago Press.

Rosenblum, N. L. (2008). *On the Side of the Angels: An Appreciation of Parties and Partisanship*. Princeton, NJ: Princeton University Press.

Rosenquist, J. N., Fowler, J. H., and Christakis, N. A. (2010). "Social Network Determinants of Depression." *Molecular Psychiatry* 16: 273-281.

Rosenquist, J. N., Murabito, J., Fowler, J. H., and Christakis, N. A. (2010). "The Spread of Alcohol Consumption Behavior in a Large Social Network." *Annals of Internal Medicine* 152(7):426–433.

Schwartz, M. A. (1990). *The Party Network: The Robust Organization of Illinois Republicans*. Madison: University of Wisconsin Press.

Schwartz, T. (1989). Why Parties?. Research memorandum, 1–17.

Shalizi, C. R. and Thomas, A. C. (2011). "Homophily and Contagion Are Generically Confounded in Observational Social Network Studies." *Sociological Methods and Research* 40: 211-239.

Sinclair, B. (1995). *Legislators, Leaders and Lawmaking*. Baltimore, MD: Johns Hopkins University Press.

Sinclair, B. (2006). *Party Wars: Polarization and the Politics of National Policy Making*. Norman: University of Oklahoma Press.

Sinclair, B. (2012). *The Social Citizen: Peer Networks and Political Behavior*. Chicago: University of Chicago Press.

Skinner, R., Masket, S. E., and Dulio, D. (2011). "527 Committees, Formal Parties, and the Party Networks." Paper presented at the Annual Conference of the Midwest Political Science Association, Chicago, IL, April 2.

Skinner, R. M., Masket, S. E., and Dulio, D. A. (2012). "527s and the Political Party Network." *American Politics Research* 40: 60–84.

Snyder, J. M., Jr., and Groseclose, T. (2000). "Estimating Party Influence in Congressional Roll-Call Voting." *American Journal of Political Science* 44: 193–211.

Squitieri, T. (1998). "First Lady: Prosecutor Part of Plot." *U.S.A. Today*, January 28. 1A.

Zachary, W. W. (1977) "An Information Flow Model for Conflict and Fission in Small Groups." *Journal of Anthropological Research* 33: 452–473.

CHAPTER 19

....

LEGISLATIVE NETWORKS

....

NILS RINGE, JENNIFER NICOLL VICTOR, AND WENDY K. TAM CHO

INTRODUCTION

....

STUDIES of lawmaking have been dominated by examinations of individual lawmakers (e.g., their behavior, incentives, characteristics) and research on legislatures (or parliaments) themselves (e.g., the role of a legislature vis-à-vis other institutions of government, policymaking). In this chapter we seek to emphasize the importance of studying legislatures with a relational lens. Legislators are inherently connected in a variety of ways, and studying these connections can help us to better understand legislative behavior and processes.

Social networks in legislatures differ from those in many other contexts in that the participants in the network are selected by an external force: elections. This means that unlike in many other political networks, legislators have not necessarily connected to one another because of some shared characteristic. But over time, many of them develop personal relationships and friendships with one another that may affect their politically relevant behavior. As Baker puts it, "[F]riendships among U.S. Senators are at one and the same time political and personal" (1999, 6).

Legislatures are not mere social clubs, however, but an environment in which formal rules, informal institutions, and social networks interact. In this context, strategic considerations directly counteract the impulse of individuals to associate themselves with those who share their preferences or attributes. How do lawmakers choose to connect themselves to others, given the institutional structures they find themselves in? And how do other features of legislatures, like their size or the number of legislative parties, shape those patterns? Existing institutions directly influence network structures (e.g., because they group subsets of lawmakers in legislative committees or other forums), making social networks partly exogenous, but they also impact with whom individual lawmakers (endogenously) choose to establish social ties. Those different types of social ties in legislative politics are measured in a variety of ways, including cosponsorship of legislation, comembership in various internal institutions, covoting, campaign contributions from the same donors, spatial proximity and shared workspace, as well as direct measures of social ties through interviews or surveys. Legislative scholars have relied on such indicators, both as outcomes to be explained and as variables to explain a variety of political processes and outcomes: the creation and diffusion of information, collaboration between (groups of) lawmakers, policy coordination, coalition building, and voting behavior.

In this chapter, we explore the variety of ways legislators are tied to one another and how those ties may affect their legislative behavior. This effort is confined to studies that are explicitly about legislative politics and that employ a social network approach.[1] We start with the early beginnings of studying legislatures as social networks and the various difficulties associated with studying them in this way, noting which challenges scholars have and have not yet overcome. We describe some of the most common applications of networks in legislatures and the most common methods used. Then we examine the ways in which legislative institutions both encourage and limit the creation and maintenance of social networks. The chapter highlights the fact that legislative networks can be conceived of as something to be explained (as a dependent variable), or networks can help us understand common legislative behavior (as independent variables). We also look at some of the most common applications of network methods in legislatures, on questions such as the exchange of legislative information, roll-call voting, and partisan polarization.

We close by exploring avenues for future research on legislative networks, highlighting in particular how consideration of incentives, institutions, and interdependencies affects network creation and network effects, within legislatures and beyond. Possibilities for new research on legislative networks are also rich, because of the vast amount of data not yet collected, processed, and analyzed. Finally, the great majority of research on networks in legislatures is focused on either the Congress or state legislatures in the United States, with some notable exceptions that are discussed in this chapter. Taking a comparative perspective, however, would greatly enhance our understanding of networks in legislatures and legislative politics in general.

EARLY APPLICATIONS

The idea that relationships and social networks play an important role in legislative politics is not only intuitive, but has also been recognized for a long time. Routt made an early case that "personal contacts between human beings lie at the very heart of all problems of government and society," and described human relationships as the "basic political prerequisite . . . necessary for survival in public life" (1938, 129–130). Following this premise, he observed, recorded, counted, and classified who talked to whom on the floor of the Illinois Senate and found that personal contacts centered on legislative leaders (especially those of the majority Democratic party).

Building on this classic study, other scholars sought to investigate the nature of social relationships between lawmakers. Particularly influential is the work by Samuel Patterson, who made his first mark with his 1959 article on interpersonal contacts between members of the Wisconsin Assembly (Patterson, 1959), investigating friendship ties between lawmakers and the friendship cliques they formed. Apparently the first to have applied sociometric methods to the study of a legislature (Kirkland and Gross, 2014), Patterson identified as the determinants of friendship choices leadership positions, geography, seniority, previous alliances, and seating arrangements on the floor.

Friendship ties, self-identified by legislators from multiple US state assemblies in interviews and surveys, would remain the focus of additional research by Patterson and others. Eulau (1962), for example, considered the relationship between two types of political "authority" in four state legislatures, namely between authority derived from interpersonal sentiments like friendship and respect and from formal sources of authority, like legislative leadership. He found that formal authority correlates positively with interpersonal relations, but that leaders differ most from rank-and-file legislators in the degree to which they are respected, as opposed to being perceived as close personal friends.

Monsma (1966) also considered different "types" of social ties between lawmakers, in the Michigan House of Representatives. Rather than focusing on differences between ties built on friendship and respect, however, his focus was on the intensity of the relationship, as he distinguished between primary ties ("Who are your closest personal friends?") and secondary ties ("With whom do you frequently discuss legislation?"). He found this to be a meaningful distinction in explaining the legislature's social structure, in that secondary relations were more likely to cut across party lines, were more likely to be reciprocated, and tended to be more clustered.

Monsma found relatively few primary relations, or close friendship ties, between lawmakers of opposite parties, a finding that mirrored those of Patterson (1959) and a more extensive study of four state legislatures by Wahlke et al. (1962). This finding connects the research agenda on the social foundations of legislative politics to broader questions in the field, such as the determinants of intraparty unity and interparty competition. As Wahlke and colleagues put it, friendship ties "are more likely to reinforce team spirit and party competition" (1962, 225); indeed, they find a positive relationship between friendship ties and agreement on roll-call votes, above and beyond shared partisanship.

The relationship between social ties and political parties as formal legislative institutions was at the heart of a second strand of inquiry during this period, which focused on social ties established in congressional boardinghouses (or messes) in the first half of the nineteenth century, voting behavior in the US Congress, and the origins of political parties. These considerations were a key component of James Sterling Young's book, which identified the mess as a crucial determinant of legislative behavior in the Congress and the emerging US political system. Importantly, residents of the same boardinghouse tended to vote alike (Young, 1966). While this last finding would be challenged and qualified by Bogue and Marlaire (1975) after controlling for geographic region, they did not challenge the broader interpretation of boardinghouses as "the basic social units of the Capitol Hill community" (Young, 1966) and as the foundation of important informal group structures in legislative politics.

Such informal groups were the focus of Fiellin (1962), who was particularly interested in informal social groups as communication networks that allow lawmakers to exchange information, advice, and voting cues (see especially Matthews and Stimson, 1975). Such informal groups and networks, Fiellin argued, are not only of value to individual legislators, but also aid the efficiency and effectiveness of the chamber as a whole by, for example, contributing to successful coalition formation and the negotiation of compromises. While formal institutions like parties and committees satisfy some of the individual and collective needs of legislators, "informal groups supplement and fill in the remaining gaps" (Fiellin, 1962). For example, even the relatively few cross-partisan ties identified in other research have the potential to bridge partisan boundaries, facilitate information exchange and coordination, and mitigate gridlock. As Caldeira and Patterson (1988, 482) later put it, "friendship provides the oil that lubricates the legislative process."

Patterson and his collaborators remained especially notable contributors to the body of research on legislative networks that predates the surge of the last decade or two. In 1972, Patterson returned to questions raised in his earlier work, namely how spatial proximity and friendship ties affect important outcomes like shared attitudes, party cohesion, and partisan polarization. Both, he argued, matter greatly in that they tend to reinforce partisan loyalties and feelings of intraparty unity. Finally, in the late 1980s and early 1990s, Patterson pursued productive collaborations with Gregory Caldeira and John Clark, using data from the Iowa State Assembly and focusing on the differentiation between friendship and respect made earlier by Eulau (1962). Their articles found friendship and respect to be independent bases of legislative power (Caldeira and Patterson, 1987, 1988; Caldeira, Clark, and Patterson, 1993). While the foundations of friendship are shared partisanship, geography, and age, the bases of respect are less affective; it is driven by education, legislative work, leadership, and experience, and accorded to only a small number of lawmakers. Unlike friendship, respect follows largely from performance, achievement, and formal leadership, and both Democrats and Republicans and freshmen and senior members accord respect based on different criteria.

Even though most of this earlier body of work focused on explaining interpersonal relations rather than examining their impact on legislative processes and outcomes, it previewed many of the major themes that have been picked up in more recent legislative networks research. Important examples are the relationships among formal legislative institutions, lawmakers' personal attributes, and social networks (Routt, 1938; Patterson, 1959, 1972; Eulau, 1962; Fiellin, 1962; Wahlke et al., 1962; Young, 1966; Caldeira and Patterson, 1987, 1988; Caldeira, Clark, and Patterson, 1993); communication and information exchange, including voting cues (Fiellin, 1962; Caldeira and Patterson, 1987; Caldeira, Clark, and Patterson, 1993); and the role of spatial proximity and shared workspace (Rustow, 1957; Patterson, 1959, 1972; Caldeira and Patterson, 1987; Caldeira, Clark, and Patterson, 1993). This research also considered the relationship between social networks and floor voting (Fiellin, 1962; Wahlke et al., 1962; Young 1966; Bogue and Marlaire 1975; Patterson 1972) and how networks may affect internal party cohesion (Wahlke et al., 1962; Young, 1966; Bogue and Marlaire, 1975; Patterson, 1972; Caldeira and Patterson, 1988), as well as ideological polarization and competition between legislative parties (Wahlke et al., 1962; Patterson, 1972; Caldeira and Patterson, 1988). As such, it provided a strong basis for future theorizing and applications. This work also illustrates some of the difficulties associated with investigating legislative networks, a topic we turn to next.

CHALLENGES

There are numerous challenges associated with studying social networks in legislative politics, some of which plague all network research, while others are more pronounced in the legislative context than in others. Among the former is the trade-off associated with analyzing one-mode or two-mode (or bipartite) networks. Most legislative network data are collected in two-mode fashion, where some object or actor, i, is connected with some other object or actor, j (e.g., sponsors to bills, staff to offices, bills to topics, donors to candidates), but scholars have to make the choice of analyzing the two-mode data themselves or projecting them as one-mode (e.g., number of common cosponsored bills between legislators, number of common staffers between legislators, number of common topics in bills, number of common donors to candidates). The latter can be conceptualized as converting an $M \times N$ matrix into an $N \times N$ matrix by multiplying the former by its inverse. The projection can be done by rows or by columns, and depending on the weighting of ties, there may be many different one-mode networks that can be derived from a bipartite network. This conversion has the advantage of offering the researcher a greater number of analytical approaches and tools to work with, because the descriptive and inferential statistics that can be computed from two-mode data are limited. However, two-mode data can be useful for visualization or discovering general properties of a network; more important, converting a two-mode to a one-mode network necessarily discards information and may impose artificial connectivity on a network.

Among the challenges that are more pronounced in the legislative context than in others is the difficulty of measuring social ties directly, as opposed to relying on proxies for interpersonal relationships. Given that much of the data used in the older studies discussed in the previous section measured friendship, respect, or other interpersonal ties directly through self-reporting in interviews or surveys, this statement may seem a bit curious. It has, however, become more difficult to gain direct access to large numbers of lawmakers as legislatures have become increasingly professionalized, and information is guarded more carefully by legislators and their offices than by other types of respondents at a time when it may spread rapidly through online channels and social networks. As a case in point, two of the authors of this article at one time sought to conduct a survey and interviews to measure ties between legislative offices in the US Congress and received not a single response. They were more successful in another legislative context, the European Parliament (EP) (Ringe, Victor, and Gross, 2013), but even then it was evident that political elites are reluctant to discuss or identify their social networks. The result is that it is difficult, if not impossible, to garner the kind of response rates (of all lawmakers or above 90 percent) that the early studies of US state assemblies feature. Sampling, therefore, becomes a major concern, including the various challenges associated with sampling and network data.

On the upside, legislative networks have an important advantage relative to many other social networks: they have a clearly defined number of members, which has three important advantages. First, there is a finite total population of members to be captured, rather than an indeterminate and often much greater number of potential nodes. Second, it allows for the a priori identification of distinct subnetworks, such as members of particular legislative parties or committees, that can productively be investigated as networks in and of their own; this, in turn, may alleviate some concerns associated with sampling from a larger total population of actors (Ringe, Victor, and Gross, 2013, 613–614). Finally, if investigating a sample of legislators is inevitable, dealing with an identifiable population of all potential nodes gives researchers some leverage in gauging the extent of sampling bias, as it allows them to compare subgroups of legislators not included in the sample to those who are (Ringe, Victor, and Gross, 2013, 614–615).

Yet even if sampling is not a problem, data collection efforts based on self-reporting of ties can be problematic given respondents' cognitive constraints and biases, and the possibility that answers are strategic rather than reflective of actual social relations. The method also suffers from reproducibility and replicability problems, for three reasons. First, the data are likely considered so sensitive that sharing them with other researchers may be inappropriate, thereby making replicability impossible.[2] Second, reproducing data collection across legislatures is exceedingly difficult because of inherent differences in legislative institutions. Finally, reproducing data collection in the same chamber may produce different results, because data collected at different points in time may be inconsistent.

The difficulty of capturing longitudinal networks is quite pronounced when relying on directly measured social ties in legislative politics. Along with the difficulty of collecting such data in the first place, this is one of the reasons that some proxies for social connectedness have been quite popular. Cosponsorship data, which are available across time, are a notable example. Any proxy for interpersonal ties has its own problems, however. The most important challenge is to establish the validity of the measure, or that the proxy reflects the social relationship it intends to capture. Joint membership in a legislative committee, for example, may suggest that two members have a social tie; it is possible, however, that the two never exchanged a single word or glance. Similarly, while there are good reasons to treat cosponsorship as a social tie (see our discussion below), it may well be endogenous.

Indeed, a final major challenge for legislative network scholars lies in the possibility that the observed ties and networks are endogenous. Put another way, studies of legislative networks are particularly vulnerable to a classic dilemma of network studies: whether an observed commonality between actors is the product of shared characteristics (homophily) or because of some causal peer effect. For example, what we may identify as the impact of friendship, respect, communication, cosponsorship, or collaborative ties may not actually capture the "network effect" of one (or more) actor(s) affecting the behavior of others; rather, the observed tie may reflect those factors that determine network structures in the first place. It may be that lawmakers' choices about whom to exchange information with are a function of their preferences and strategies, and any outcome associated with communication networks can ultimately be traced back to these determinants of the network structure. Similarly, cohabitation in a boarding house may be associated with like voting, but like voting may simply be reflective of lawmakers with shared preferences, attitudes, and backgrounds choosing to live together. This challenge is an important one, but not often made explicit in research on networks in legislative politics or other context.

The Social Legislator: What Connects Lawmakers?

Due to data limitations, legislative scholars often have to proxy social ties between legislators by measuring observable behaviors or characteristics. None of those proxies are perfect, but many are reasonable substitutes for social interaction. For example, one study assumes that legislators who simultaneously serve as party or committee leaders are likely to share a social connection (Arnold, Deen, and Patterson, 2000) and shows that those who are tied by leadership roles are more likely to vote the same way. Likewise, serving on the same committees renders legislators liable to exhibit common behavior (Porter et al., 2005, 2007). In a direct study of the relationship between social interaction and legislative voting, Peoples (2008) shows a strong effect arising from shared characteristics, social ties, and spatial proximity on voting behavior (see also Masket, 2008 and Rogowski and Sinclair, 2012).

Alternatively, Ringe and Victor use comembership in legislative organizations, such as caucuses in the US Congress or intergroups in the EP, to indicate connections between legislators (Victor and Ringe, 2009; Ringe and Victor, 2013). This research shows that legislators gain information and solidify relationships through legislative member organizations (LMOs), and these, in turn, can impact their legislative behavior. Another take on measuring social connection is to examine cases in which legislators attended the same schools. Cohen and Malloy (2014) show that alumni networks among legislators positively affect their legislative roll-call behavior, especially with respect to logrolling and earmarks. In addition, scholars have observed that legislators engage in other common, observable events that can be used to proxy social relationships. For example,

Desmarais et al. (2015) show that legislators who participate in joint press events have a positive correlation in their voting behavior.

A particularly popular way to define relationships or links between legislators is via legislative cosponsorship. The development of studies on legislative cosponsorship has occurred in part due to data convenience, since information about the bills sponsored and cosponsored by members of Congress (and also other legislatures) is readily available. Apart from the convenience factor, however, support for using cosponsorship as an indicator for relationships has a strong history in the institutions literature. Campbell (1982), for example, notes that legislators expend considerable effort recruiting cosponsors with personal contacts and "Dear Colleague" letters (see also Craig, 2015). Moreover, legislators frequently refer to these cosponsorships in floor debate, public discussion, letters to constituents, and campaigns. In a hearing of the House Ways and Means Committee, Representative Wally Herger touted both the number of cosponsors as well as the bipartisanship of the cosponsors for the Marriage Penalty Relief Act (Herger, 1967). These examples give credence to the notion that cosponsorship is meaningful and a signal of relationship between legislators, even though the cosponsorship literature is sometimes criticized for overstating the potential network connection provided by common cosponsorship (Kirkland and Gross, 2014).

Beginning with Kessler and Krehbiel (1996), scholars have used cosponsorship as an indication of relationships between legislators. Kessler and Krehbiel show that legislators use cosponsorship as a signaling device to their colleagues, rather than as a low-cost position-taking mechanism. Scholars have also used cosponsorship to document links between legislators defined by expertise and budgetary preferences (Gilligan and Krehbiel, 1987; Krehbiel, 1995). In this way, cosponsorship came to be thought of as signaling strategic behavior between legislative actors, rather than as "cheap talk" that might be considered less significant. A number of follow-up studies on cosponsorship continued this trend without being explicit about the networks formed by cosponsorship (Pellegrini and Grant, 1999; Burkett and Skvoretz, 2001; Koger, 2003; Goodliffe et al., 2005).

The social network literature has capitalized on both data availability and the conceptualization of cosponsorship as a measure of connectedness by demonstrating an empirical link between cosponsorship and other legislative behavior. Fowler (2006a, 2006b) examines basic descriptive features of the social network when cosponsorship is used to define the links, computing connectedness and centrality scores for legislators. Cho and Fowler (2010) use cosponsorship links to understand the small-world properties of various US Congresses and the relationship of that social structure with the ability of Congress to pass important legislation. Indeed, the structure induced by cosponsorship links has garnered significant interest (Fowler, 2006a, 2006b; Gross, 2008; Zhang et al., 2008; Bernhard and Sulkin, 2009; Cho and Fowler, 2010), and cosponsorship has been shown to be a correlate of numerous variables that are of crucial interest and relevance in legislative studies. To offer several examples, Alemán et al. (2009) demonstrate that ideal-point estimates derived from cosponsorship and roll-call vote data, respectively, are strongly associated with each other. Bratton and Rouse (2011) explore the determinants of cosponsorship and how group dynamics affect legislative agenda set-ting. Kirkland (2011) shows that weak, bridging cosponsorship ties are associated with greater legislative success. Kirkland and Williams (2014) find that collaboration across chambers is important in developing bipartisanship and norms of reciprocity. Kirkland (2012) examines cosponsorship networks in four states that use a combination of single-member and multimember districts and finds that multimember systems generate or strengthen relationships between actors with shared constituencies. In addition, schol-ars have leveraged the massive amounts of newly available data on voting in a variety of legislatures and parliaments to provide highly useful and stimulating databases and visualizations of such data. A good recent example is from François Briatte, who pro-vides cosponsorship data and visualizations for twenty-seven parliamentary chambers in Europe, providing insights about parliamentary politics (Briatte n.d., Briatte 2016).

In addition to offering descriptive statistics about cosponsorship networks and their properties (such as centrality, connectedness, and density), scholars have also been exploring cosponsorship networks via exponential random graph models (ERGMs, also known as p^* or p-star models), which allow one to examine the process that might underlie network formation (see chapter by Bruce Desmarais and Skyler Cranmer in this volume). Indeed, cosponsorship has been a defining measure for ERGMs of leg-islative networks. For example, Kirkland and Williams (2014) examine cross-chamber collaborative networks in the Texas, Maine, Oklahoma, and Colorado legislatures. In addition to legislator characteristics such as partisanship, leadership, and committee membership, they examine the process of reciprocity, out-stars, in-stars, and edges. Their analysis indicates that exogenous characteristics (partisanship, committee mem-bership) as well as endogenous characteristics (reciprocity both within and between parties) are the basis of tie formations across chambers. In a similar study of state leg-islatures in Arizona, California, Colorado, Florida, Illinois, Maryland, Michigan, South Carolina, and Texas, with cosponsorship defining ties, Bratton and Rouse (2011) find that while network formation varies somewhat across states, the results generally indi-cate that ideological distance, district proximity, homophily (race, gender, ideology, dis-trict location), and transitivity are important factors leading toward cosponsorship ties and network formation. With data from policy networks in the Chilean and Argentinian congresses, Alemán and Calvo (2013) again use cosponsorship to define ties and find similar results. They examine edges, triangles, and two-stars and find that partisan, ter-ritorial, and committee effects have a significant impact on tie formation.

Cosponsorship will continue to be a staple of legislative network studies, but we see two important routes for advancing this research agenda. First, cosponsorship data have been drawn primarily from US legislatures, with only a few exceptions, such as Calvo and Leiras (2012) and Alemán et al. (2009), who examine cosponsorship networks in the Argentine congress; Alemán and Calvo (2013), who look at both Argentina and Chile; a study of the Chilean cosponsorship networks (Lee, Magallanes, and Porter, 2015); and Parigi and Sartori (2014), who use bill consponsorship in the Italian par-liament in the 1970s. There is, accordingly, much to be learned from cases outside the United States. Second, since cosponsorship is not the only way in which ties or edges may be operationalized, we may find that nuances in legislative behavior are illuminated by different data conceptualizations. As data are curated, they would be usefully supplemented with information on other types of legislator ties to offer greater richness in understanding legislative networks in general—even if it may become difficult to cut through the noise and density of such measures to glean insights that cannot be understood with a single measure of social connectedness (Victor, Haptonstahl, and Ringe, 2014).

INFORMATION

Information is an important currency in legislative politics, of course, and it would put lawmakers at a major disadvantage not to maintain any social contacts that provide access to information on the goals, policy positions, and strategies of their colleagues—whether friend or foe. Lawmakers cannot afford to ignore dissonance-producing information by interacting only with political allies with whom they tend to agree, as that would put them at a distinct strategic disadvantage. In other words, while there are important reasons (including strategic ones) to build social ties with trusted colleagues who pursue the same goals, there are also sound strategic incentives for including political "enemies" in one's social networks. This makes legislatures a fruitful venue for investigating social networks and the motivations that drive the creation of interpersonal ties and broader network structures (Ringe, Victor, and Gross, 2013).

The value of social networks as venues for the exchange and diffusion of information in legislative politics has long been recognized. Fiellin (1962, 78) discusses informal groups in legislative politics as communication networks that facilitate the provision and dissemination of "trustworthy" information, contribute to the development of legislative strategy, aid negotiation and coalition formation, and provide the basis of voting cues. The informational benefits of interpersonal ties—based on friendship, respect, or trust—are also highlighted by Eulau (1962) and Patterson and his collaborators (Patterson, 1972; Caldeira and Patterson, 1988; Caldeira, Clark, and Patterson, 1993; Arnold, Deen, and Patterson, 2000). Notably, Fiellin implies already in the early 1960s that legislative network structures affect information flow, when he suggests that informal groups facilitate communication across party and committee lines (1962, 82). His observation touches on two important themes that would be picked up in later work: the importance of weak, cross-cutting ties for information exchange and the relationship between social networks and formal legislative institutions.

The concept of weak (Granovetter, 1973), cross-cutting ties that bridge structural holes (Burt, 1995) is a staple of social network research. In the study of legislative politics, Kirkland (2011) demonstrates that weak ties between legislators are most useful in increasing legislative success. Ringe and Victor (2013) show how LMOs—such as caucuses in the US Congress and intergroups in the EP—allow lawmakers to establish social relationships with colleagues with whom they share a common interest in a particular political issue or policy theme. The social networks composed of these relationships, in turn, offer valuable opportunity structures for the efficient exchange of policy-relevant information, because LMO ties cut across party and committee lines and provide lawmakers with access to otherwise unattainable information. Moreover, because LMOs often maintain close relationships with outside actors, such as interest groups or lobbyists, they facilitate the flow of policy-relevant information into the legislature (see also Fiellin, 1962). Another structural characteristic of legislative networks is considered by Cho and Fowler (2010), who identify congressional cosponsorship networks as "small worlds," where actors are densely interconnected with few intermediaries, which they suggest may affect the efficiency and speed of information flow.

Network structures between legislators or legislative offices are not independent of the broader institutional environment in which they are formed and maintained, however, which underscores the promise of extending the focus of research on legislative networks beyond the United States. Institutions and networks interact in several ways that have been investigated by legislative scholars. First, attributes of legislatures such as their overall size and the number of parties affect lawmakers' informational needs and, by extension, the social networks they build and maintain. Ringe and Victor (2013), for example, find that LMOs (and the cross-cutting social ties they provide) are more likely to be established in legislatures with a larger total number of members and greater number of parties, since it is in those contexts that legislators have a greater need for both "political intelligence" about the positions of other actors and cross-party coalitions to pass legislation. Looking at collaboration networks, Kirkland (2014b) demonstrates that large legislatures tend to have low-density, highly partisan networks, and that larger legislative committees mitigate these effects. Second, resources available to lawmakers shape their informational needs. An extensive, in-house research service, for example, decreases their dependence on the expertise of their colleagues or actors outside the legislature, such as interest groups, and a large personal staff allows lawmakers to establish policy positions more autonomously (Ringe, 2010; Ringe, Victor, and Gross, 2013). Variation in available resources thus helps shape whom lawmakers choose to establish interpersonal ties with, and thereby a legislature's social structure. Third, legislative rules (and changes thereto) impact network structures directly. For example, Sarbaugh-Thompson et al. (2006) show that term limits create information networks with more prominent hubs able to control the flow of information and entail a decrease in cross-party ties. Also, evidence shows that so-called legislative knowledge networks have distinct network properties that can be leveraged to understand the likelihood of adopting particular policy proposals (Bonvecchi, Calvo, and Stein, 2016).

Legislative rules also affect information flow in the context of voting cues (Matthews and Stimson, 1975; Kingdon, 1981). Masket (2008), for example, investigates the impact of rules that determine seating arrangements in the California Assembly, where lawmakers (often from opposite parties) share desks, on voting behavior. He finds that spatial proximity increases the likelihood that two legislators cast like-votes because, he argues, lawmakers take cues from those closest to them geographically. In contrast, Rogowski and Sinclair (2012) use the US House of Representatives office lottery (whereby new members select their offices in a random order) to investigate the relationship between spatial proximity and legislative behavior; unlike other studies, however, they do not find an effect. Finally, Ringe, Victor, and Gross (2013) consider the possibility that lawmakers purposely establish social ties with political allies for the sake of *positive* cueing and with political enemies for the sake of *negative* cueing. Measuring actual social ties between legislative offices through surveys and interviews of legislative staff in the EP (rather than relying on a proxy measure), they maintain that lawmakers build social ties and exchange information with both political friends and enemies in order to increase the confidence they have in their own policy positions. Specifically, if a lawmaker expects to agree with a colleague, their actual rate of voting agreement increases as the level of social connectedness goes up, while the rate of voting agreement declines as levels of social connectedness increase if a legislator anticipates that he or she is unlikely to agree with a colleague.

LEGISLATIVE VOTING AND POLARIZATION

The idea of voting cues combines an explicitly relational conceptualization of legislative politics with the outcome most commonly investigated and explained by legislative scholars: roll-call voting. Roll-call votes are not only intrinsically interesting to students of lawmaking institutions because they represent the final outcome of the legislative process; they also have the advantage of being widely and increasingly available for many legislatures.

When legislators cast votes, they express a preference on a proposal. Whether such an expression represents a legislator's "true" policy preference may be a matter of some debate, but by and large, roll-call voting is widely accepted in the academic world and beyond as an indicator of preferences. Beginning with Bogue and Marlaire (1975), scholars interested in examining the social nature of legislative behavior have focused on roll-call agreement, or some aggregation of roll calls (Arnold, Deen, and Patterson, 2000; Masket, 2008; Peoples, 2008, 2010; Rogowski and Sinclair, 2012; Ringe, Victor, and Gross, 2013; Cohen and Malloy, 2014; Craig, 2015).

Studying roll-call voting in the context of social network analysis comes with significant challenges, however. As a dyadic, or network, measure, roll-call voting is typically described as "co-voting" or "agreement scores." These represent mathematical aggregations of individual roll-call votes that provide a descriptive indicator for each pair of legislators, which describes how often they vote the same way. The process of creating such scores is relatively straightforward and familiar to legislative scholars, because of the conceptual and mathematical similarities to NOMINATE scores. NOMINATE scores, developed by Poole and Rosenthal, also aggregate roll-call votes; however, their algorithm takes an inferential step further than agreement scores, because the outcome of NOMINATE provides a numerical measurement of ideology (Poole and Rosenthal, 1991, 2011; Cox and Poole, 2002). By comparison, agreement scores are a nonparametric description of roll-call voting activity, whereas NOMINATE scores map the behavior to a scale that is both comparable across time and venues and allows scholars to infer relative ideological placement in two-dimensional space. NOMINATE scores have been criticized for methodological reasons (Londregan, 1999) that do not apply to agreement scores, despite the underlying similarities in their creation. This is because agreement scores simply provide descriptive information about behavior, whereas NOMINATE scores draw an inference about the substantive interpretation of that behavior. This difference represents a strength and a weakness of agreement scores, because it means they can be applied without consideration to identification or standard errors; however, they cannot be used to infer ideological placement or some other indicator. On the other hand, there is some question as to whether agreement scores represent a true network. As we have described, these scores are simply a description of a behavior; however, it is a behavior that legislators are more or less compelled to engage in and therefore does not represent a voluntary choice to make a connection with a counterpart. Covoting networks are networks in the sense that they describe a behavior that can be measured as a network because of a shared experience, but does not necessarily represent a tie between legislators in the same way that, say, being from the same state does. However, covoting may be interpreted as a *reflection* of an underlying social process. For example, in a recent application, Ringe and Wilson (2016) conceptualize legislative vote choice as the result of a cueing dynamic that can be captured using (co-)voting data. They show that legislators' centrality in covoting networks can be used as a measure of what they call "signaling influence," in which the most influential legislators are those who influence the votes of the greatest number of colleagues. Notably, this network measure travels easily across legislative arenas, since it is derived from often readily available roll-call vote data.

Voting data can also be used to investigate partisan polarization (Porter et al., 2007; Poole and Rosenthal, 2011), along with committee assignments (Porter et al., 2005, 2007), cosponsorship (Zhang et al., 2008), campaign donations (Koger and Victor, 2009), the aforementioned agreement scores (Andris et al., 2015), and other measures. The literature on political polarization includes a number of controversies and existing puzzles, especially with respect to the sources of polarization. Recently, scholars have begun to apply network-based theories and techniques to this ripe area of research, and that has proved fruitful and enlightening. Kirkland examines ideology and voting agreement in state legislatures to determine that ideological moderates are less likely to support their parties in roll-call votes compared to ideological extremists (Kirkland, 2014a). Moreover, the study shows that states with ideologically heterogeneous populations are more likely to have political parties comprised of ideological extremists. Using networks of campaign donations, Masket and Shor (2011) find that political parties constrained by an institutional unicameral legislature and strict term limits can overcome their limitations by capitalizing on campaign finance networks. In general, the network approach has been useful in describing the robust nature of political parties both within the legislature and outside of it (Masket, 2002; Cohen et al., 2008; Karol, 2009; Koger, Masket, and Noel, 2009; Waugh et al., 2009; Bawn et al., 2012). Network analysis has also led to hypotheses that the social ties created by some networks may help offset the stagnating effects of polarization (Victor, Haptonstahl, and Ringe, 2014).

Conclusion

The maxim that politics is inherently relational rings particularly true in the context of legislative decision-making, making legislatures a particularly fruitful venue to study politics from the relational perspective. Yet while the evolution of literature on legislative politics was strongly informed by networks in its early years, it became somewhat disassociated with network analysis during the behavioral and rational choice periods in political science from the 1960s to the late 1990s. Only recently have we seen a resurgence of social network theories, ideas, methods, and insights.

Legislating is a naturally interactive process. For many, the strong assumptions of independence required by many of the most prominent methodological and statistical approaches in the study of legislatures were a convenient untruth, easily accepted. The recent reintroduction of dependency into our understanding of legislative behavior, structures, and outcomes ushers into the social sciences a vast opportunity to capitalize on the best that our prior paradigms have offered. That is, one does not need to divorce rational choice theory in order to adopt a network-based view of the legislature. Game theoretic models have natural dependencies built into them (e.g., extensive form games) and have helped advance our knowledge of legislative interactions (Calvert and Fenno, 1994); therefore, our understanding of the political world can be simultaneously informed by actors' incentives, the constraining institutions in which they operate, and the interdependencies between actors and institutions. It is at this nexus where we expect to see some of the most productive legislative network research being produced in the coming decade.

A second key to future research on legislative networks lies in the collection of data on social ties between lawmakers. Legislators create and maintain a multitude of social connections, and one could imagine plotting a variety of networks on a single legislative body (e.g., networks based on covoting, cosponsorship, cocommittee membership, colegislative member organization membership, common lobbyist contacts, common donors, common leadership roles, etc.), including actual friendships or social connections. Much of these data are freely available, or scrapable, and can be analyzed from a relational perspective. As they are collected and digitized, and as our personal computers have an increasing capacity to store, manage, and analyze them, we may see the creation of vast databases that help reveal network structures and how they affect legislative processes and outcomes. Even though the availability of data today often exceeds our capacity to process and analyze them statistically, scholars are already showing increasing creativity in capturing and collecting both qualitative and quantitative data that will help us better understand the relational process of lawmaking and its place in politics and government. Among the most exciting of these possibilities in our imagined future awash in data is the potential to better understand global properties of networks.

Theoretically, all networks have graph-level properties that can only be observed if all data (nodes and edges) are present, and if the relations capture meaningful properties. When (or if) such networks can be observed, scholars can understand properties such as centrality, density, the presence of brokers, or triangles, each of which carries its own implications about the network. For instance, centrality can be measured on a graph-level network and may provide inferential information about power structures in a network. Networks that exhibit a greater number of triads are known to exhibit greater trust and reciprocity. If we can reliably observe such features in legislative networks, we will expand our understanding of the properties, behaviors, and potential in them.

The third major opportunity for future research on legislative networks lies in extending its theoretical and empirical focus beyond the United States. A comparative perspective offers institutional variation—at both the macro-institutional level of the political system as a whole and at the level of the legislature itself—well beyond what can be found in a single-country case. While social networks surely matter in every legislature, there is bound to be notable and consequential variation in their structures, the roles they play, and their relative importance in shaping legislative processes and outcomes. How does the balance of power between legislature and executive impact network patterns? How do electoral rules affect the networks between legislators once they are in office? Does the internal organization of the legislature structure social networks? Does the strength of parties strengthen or weaken social ties? Are social relations inside legislatures of greater importance when party systems are unconsolidated? How do legislative networks differ between democratic legislatures and those in authoritarian countries? Such questions warrant a comparativist turn in the study of legislative networks, with existing research on the United States poised to serve as a major reference point.

NOTES

1. For example, we disregard research that focuses on legislative elections without connecting them to politics inside the legislature and studies that broadly conceptualize legislative politics as relational without, however, investigating social *networks*.
2. In the aforementioned EP study by Ringe, Victor, and Gross (2013), for example, all respondents were assured complete anonymity, and the small sample of (actual and potential) respondents prevented the release of data even if proper names had been replaced by general attributes such as party affiliation and nationality.

REFERENCES

Alemán, E., and Calvo, E. (2013). "Explaining Policy Ties in Presidential Congresses: A Network Analysis of Bill Initiation Data: Policy Ties in Presidential Congresses." *Political Studies* 61(2): 356–377. doi:10.1111/j.1467-9248.2012.00964.x.

Alemán, E., Calvo, E., Jones, M. P., and Kaplan, N. (2009). "Comparing Cosponsorship and Roll-Call Ideal Points." *Legislative Studies Quarterly* 34(1): 87–116.

Andris, C., Lee, D., Hamilton, M. J., Martino, M., Gunning, C. E., and Selden, J. A. (2015). "The Rise of Partisanship and Super-Cooperators in the U.S. House of Representatives." *PLoS ONE* 10(4): e0123507. doi:10.1371/journal.pone.0123507.

Arnold, L. W., Deen, R. E., and Patterson, S. C. (2000). "Friendship and Votes: The Impact of Interpersonal Ties on Legislative Decision Making." *State & Local Government Review* 32(2): 142–147.

Baker, R. K. (1999). *Friend & Foe in the U.S. Senate*. Acton, MA: Copley Editions.

Bawn, K., Cohen, M., Karol, D., Masket, S., Noel, H., and Zaller, J. (2012). "A Theory of Political Parties: Groups, Policy Demands and Nominations in American Politics." *Perspectives on Politics* 10(3): 571–597. doi:10.1017/S1537592712001624.

Bernhard, W. T., and Sulkin, T. (2009). "Cosponsorship and Coalition-Building in the US House." Paper presented at the American Political Science Association 2009 Annual Meeting. http://papers.ssrn.com/Sol3/papers.cfm?abstract_id=1452258.

Bogue, A. G., and Marlaire, M. P. (1975). "Of Mess and Men: The Boardinghouse and Congressional Voting, 1821–1842." *American Journal of Political Science* 19(2): 207–230. doi:10.2307/2110433.

Bonvecchi, A., Calvo, E., and Stein, E. (2016). "Legislative Knowledge Networks, Status Quo Complexity, and the Approval of Law Initiatives." *Legislative Studies Quarterly* 41(1): 89–117. doi:10.1111/lsq.12107.

Bratton, K. A., and Rouse, S. M. (2011). "Networks in the Legislative Arena: How Group Dynamics Affect Cosponsorship: Networks in the Legislative Arena." *Legislative Studies Quarterly* 36(3): 423–460. doi:10.1111/j.1939-9162.2011.00021.x.

Briatte, F. (n.d.). "Legislative Cosponsorship Networks." http://f.briatte.org/parlviz/.

Briatte, F. (2016). "Network patterns of legislative collaboration in twenty parliaments." *Network Science* 4(2): 266–271.

Burkett, T., and Skvoretz, J. (2001). "Political Support Networks Among US Senators: Stability and Change from 1973 to 1990." Unpublished manuscript, College of Charleston, 3123. http://www.researchgate.net/profile/John_Skvoretz/publication/228382999_Political_Support_networks_among_US_Senators_Stability_and_Change_from_1973_to_1990/links/09e415064aba206dc2000000.pdf.

Burt, R. (1995). *Structural Holes: The Social Structure of Competition*. Cambridge, MA: Harvard University Press.

Caldeira, G. A., Clark, J. A., and Patterson, S. C. (1993). "Political Respect in the Legislature." *Legislative Studies Quarterly* 18(1): 3–28.

Caldeira, G. A., and Patterson, S. C. (1987). "Political Friendship in the Legislature." *Journal of Politics* 49(4): 953–975. doi:10.2307/2130779.

Caldeira, G. A., and Patterson, S. C. (1988). "Contours of Friendship and Respect in the Legislature." *American Politics Research* 16(4): 466–485. doi:10.1177/004478088016004004.

Calvert, R. L., and Fenno, R. F. (1994). "Strategy and Sophisticated Voting in the Senate." *Journal of Politics* 56(2): 349–376.

Calvo, E., and Leiras, M. (2012). "The Nationalization of Legislative Collaboration: Territory, Partisanship, and Policymaking in Argentina." *Revista Ibero-Americana de Estudos Legislativos* 1(2): 2–19.

Campbell, J. E. (1982). "Cosponsoring Legislation in the U. S. Congress." *Legislative Studies Quarterly* 7(3): 415. doi:10.2307/439366.

Cho, W. K. T., and Fowler, J. H. (2010). "Legislative Success in a Small World: Social Network Analysis and the Dynamics of Congressional Legislation." *Journal of Politics* 72(1): 124–135. doi:10.1017/S002238160999051X.

Cohen, L., and Malloy, C. J. (2014). "Friends in High Places†." *American Economic Journal: Economic Policy* 6(3): 63–91. doi:10.1257/pol.6.3.63.

Cohen, M., Karol, D., Noel, H., and Zaller, J. (2008). *The Party Decides: Presidential Nominations Before and After Reform.* Chicago: University of Chicago Press.

Cox, G. W., and Poole, K. T. (2002). "On Measuring Partisanship in Roll-Call Voting: The U.S. House of Representatives, 1877–1999." *American Journal of Political Science* 46(3): 477–489. doi:10.2307/3088393.

Craig, A. W. (2015). "Lone Wolves and Team Players: Policy Collaboration Networks and Legislative Effectiveness in the House of Representatives." http://lsvw.org/wp-content/uploads/2014/05/Craig-Lone-Wolves-and-Team-Players.pdf.

Desmarais, B. A., Moscardelli, V. G., Schaffner, B. F., and Kowal, M. S. (2015). "Measuring Legislative Collaboration: The Senate Press Events Network." *Social Networks* 40(January): 43–54. doi:10.1016/j.socnet.2014.07.006.

Eulau, H. (1962). "Bases of Authority in Legislative Bodies: A Comparative Analysis." *Administrative Science Quarterly* 7(3): 309–321.

Fiellin, A. (1962). "The Functions of Informal Groups in Legislative Institutions." *Journal of Politics* 24(1): 72. doi:10.2307/2126738.

Fowler, J. H. (2006a). "Connecting the Congress: A Study of Cosponsorship Networks." *Political Analysis* 14(4): 456–487. doi:10.1093/pan/mpl002.

Fowler, J. H. (2006b). "Legislative Cosponsorship Networks in the US House and Senate." *Social Networks* 28(4): 454–465. doi:10.1016/j.socnet.2005.11.003.

Gilligan, T. W., and Krehbiel, K. (1987). "Collective Decisionmaking and Standing Committees: An Informational Rationale for Restrictive Amendment Procedures." *Journal of Law, Economics, & Organization* 3(2): 287–335. doi:10.2307/764831.

Goodliffe, J., Rothenberg, L. S., Sanders, M. S., and Harris Interactive. (2005). "From Goals to Actions: The Dynamics of Cosponsorship Reconsidered." Unpublished manuscript. http://front.cc.nctu.edu.tw/Richfiles/15827-rothenberg_s05.pdf.

Granovetter, M. S. (1973). "The Strength of Weak Ties." *American Journal of Sociology* 78(6): 1360–1380.

Gross, J. H. (2008). "Cosponsorship in the U.S. Senate: A Multilevel Approach to Detecting the Subtle Influence of Social Relational Factors on Legislative Behavior." Unpublished manuscript, H. John Heinz III School of Public Policy & Management and Department of Statistics, Carnegie Mellon University. http://polmeth.wustl.edu/media/Paper/GrossJustin%20-%20Cosponsorship%20in%20the%20US%20Senate%20-%20Sep%2008.pdf.

Herger, W. (1967). Marriage Penalty Relief Act. *Congressional Record* 10710

Karol, D. (2009). *Party Position Change in American Politics: Coalition Management.* Cambridge, UK, and New York: Cambridge University Press.

Kessler, D., and Krehbiel, K. (1996). "Dynamics of Cosponsorship." *American Political Science Review* 90(3): 555–566. doi:10.2307/2082608.

Kingdon, J. W. (1981). *Congressmen's Voting Decisions.* 2d ed. New York: Harper & Row.

Kirkland, J. H. (2011). "The Relational Determinants of Legislative Outcomes: Strong and Weak Ties Between Legislators." *Journal of Politics* 73(3): 887–898. doi:10.1017/S0022381611000533.

Kirkland, J. H. (2012). "Multimember Districts' Effect on Collaboration between U.S. State Legislators: Multimember Districts." *Legislative Studies Quarterly* 37(3): 329–353. doi:10.1111/j.1939-9162.2012.00050.x.

Kirkland, J. H. (2014a). "Ideological Heterogeneity and Legislative Polarization in the United States." *Political Research Quarterly* 67(3): 533–546.

Kirkland, J. H. (2014b). "Chamber Size Effects on the Collaborative Structure of Legislatures: Chamber Size Effects." *Legislative Studies Quarterly* 39(2): 169–198. doi:10.1111/lsq.12041.

Kirkland, J. H., and Gross, J. H. (2014). "Measurement and Theory in Legislative Networks: The Evolving Topology of Congressional Cooperation." *Social Networks* 36: 97-109

Kirkland, J. H., and Williams, R. L. (2014). "Partisanship and Reciprocity in Cross-Chamber Legislative Interactions." *Journal of Politics* 76(3): 754–769. doi:10.1017/S0022381614000097.

Koger, G. (2003). "Position Taking and Cosponsorship in the U.S. House." *Legislative Studies Quarterly* 28(2): 225–246.

Koger, G., Masket, S., and Noel, H. (2009). "Partisan Webs: Information Exchange and Party Networks." *British Journal of Political Science* 39(3): 633–653. doi:10.1017/S0007123409000659.

Koger, G., and Victor, J. N. (2009). "Polarized Agents: Campaign Contributions by Lobbyists." *PS: Political Science & Politics* 42(3): 485–488. doi:10.1017/S1049096509090805.

Krehbiel, K. (1995). "Cosponsors and Wafflers from A to Z." *American Journal of Political Science* 39(4): 906–923. doi:10.2307/2111662.

Lee, S. H., Magallanes, J. M., and Porter, M. A. (2015). "Time-Dependent Community Structure in Legislation Cosponsorship Networks in the Congress of the Republic of Peru." *arXiv* (October). http://arxiv.org/abs/1510.01002.

Londregan, J. (1999). "Estimating Legislators' Preferred Points." *Political Analysis* 8(1): 35–56.

Masket, S. E. (2002). "The Emergence of Unofficial Party Organizations in California." *Spectrum: The Journal of State Government* 75(4): 29–33.

Masket, S. E. (2008). "Where You Sit Is Where You Stand: The Impact of Seating Proximity on Legislative Cue-Taking." *Quarterly Journal of Political Science* 3: 301–311.

Masket, S. E., and Shor, B. (2011). "Polarization without Parties: The Rise of Legislative Partisanship in Nebraska's Unicameral Legislature." *SSRN Electronic Journal* (August). http://www.researchgate.net/profile/Boris_Shor/publication/228152628_Polarization_Without_Parties_The_Rise_of_Legislative_Partisanship_in_Nebraskas_Unicameral_Legislature/links/0deec5316046ee3175000000.pdf.

Matthews, D. R., and Stimson, J. A. (1975). *Yeas and Nays: Normal Decision-Making in the U.S. House of Representatives.* New York: Wiley-Interscience.

Monsma, S. V. (1966). "Interpersonal Relations in the Legislative System: A Study of the 1964 Michigan House of Representatives." *Midwest Journal of Political Science* 10(3): 350. doi:10.2307/2108890.

Parigi, P., and Sartori, L. (2014). "The Political Party as a Network of Cleavages: Disclosing the Inner Structure of Italian Political Parties in the Seventies." Special issue on political networks, *Social Networks* 36 (January): 54–65. doi:10.1016/j.socnet.2012.07.005.

Patterson, S. C. (1959). "Patterns of Interpersonal Relations in a State Legislative Group: The Wisconsin Assembly." *Public Opinion Quarterly* 23(1): 101–109. doi:10.1086/266850.

Patterson, S. C. (1972). "Party Opposition in the Legislature: The Ecology of Legislative Institutionalization." *Polity* 4(3): 344. doi:10.2307/3233966.

Pellegrini, P. A., and Grant, J. T. (1999). "Policy Coalitions in the U.S. Congress: A Spatial Duration Modeling Approach." *Geographical Analysis* 31(1): 45–66. doi:10.1111/j.1538-4632.1999.tb00410.x.

Peoples, C. D. (2008). "Interlegislator Relations and Policy Making: A Sociological Study of Roll-Call Voting in a State Legislature." *Sociological Forum* 23(3): 455–480. doi:10.1111/j.1573-7861.2008.00086.x.

Peoples, C. D. (2010). "Contributor Influence in Congress: Social Ties and PAC Effects on US House Policymaking." *Sociological Quarterly* 51(4): 649–677.

Poole, K. T., and Rosenthal, H. (1991). "Patterns of Congressional Voting." *American Journal of Political Science* 35(1): 228–278. doi:10.2307/2111445.

Poole, K. T., and Rosenthal, H. L. (2011). *Ideology and Congress.* New Brunswick, New Jersey: Transaction Publishers.

Porter, M. A., Mucha, P. J., Newman, M. E. J., and Warmbrand, C. M. (2005). "A Network Analysis of Committees in the US House of Representatives." *Proceedings of the National Academy of Sciences of the United States of America* 102(20): 7057–7062.

Porter, M. A., Mucha, P. J., Newman, M. E. J., and Friend, A. J. (2007). "Community Structure in the United States House of Representatives." *Physica A: Statistical Mechanics and Its Applications* 386(1): 414–438. doi:10.1016/j.physa.2007.07.039.

Ringe, Nils. (2010). *Who Decides, and How? Preferences, Uncertainty, and Policy Choice in the European Parliament.* Oxford: Oxford University Press.

Ringe, N. and Victor, J. N. (2013). *Bridging the Information Gap: Legislative Member Organizations as Social Networks in the United States and the European Union.* Ann Arbor: University of Michigan Press.

Ringe, N., Victor, J. N., and Gross, J. H. (2013). "Keeping Your Friends Close and Your Enemies Closer? Information Networks in Legislative Politics." *British Journal of Political Science* 43(3): 601–628. doi:10.1017/S0007123412000518.

Ringe, N., and Wilson, S. L. (2016). "Pinpointing the Powerful: Co-Voting Network Centrality as a Measure of Political Influence." *Legislative Studies Quarterly, Early View.* doi:10.1111/lsq.12129

Rogowski, J. C., and Sinclair, B. (2012). "Estimating the Causal Effects of Social Interaction with Endogenous Networks." *Political Analysis* 20(3): 316–328. doi:10.1093/pan/mps016.

Routt, G. C. (1938). "Interpersonal Relationships and the Legislative Process." *Annals of the American Academy of Political and Social Science* 195: 129–136.

Rustow, D. A. (1957). *The Politics of Compromise.* 2d ed. Princeton, NJ: Princeton University Press.

Sarbaugh-Thompson, M., Thompson, L., Elder, C. D., Comins, M., Elling, R. C., and Strate, J. (2006). "Democracy among Strangers: Term Limits' Effects on Relationships between State Legislators in Michigan." *State Politics & Policy Quarterly* 6(4): 384–409. doi:10.1177/153244000600600402.

Victor, J. N., Haptonstahl, S., and Ringe, N. (2014). "Can Caucuses Alleviate Partisan Polarization in the U.S. Congress?" In Paper presented at the 2014 Annual Meeting of the American Political Science Association, August 27–31, Washington, DC.

Victor, J. N., and Ringe, N. (2009). "The Social Utility of Informal Institutions Caucuses as Networks in the 110th U.S. House of Representatives." *American Politics Research* 37(5): 742–766. doi:10.1177/1532673X09337183.

Wahlke, J. C., Eulau, H., Buchanan, W., and Ferguson, L. (1962). *The Legislative System: Explorations in Legislative Behavior.* New York: John Wiley & Sons.

Waugh, A. S., Pei, L., Fowler, J. H., Mucha, P. J., and Porter, M. A. (2009). "Party Polarization in Congress: A Network Science Approach." http://papers.ssrn.com/sol3/papers.cfm?abstract_id=1437055.

Young, J. S. (1966). *The Washington Community, 1800–1828.* New York: Columbia University Press.

Zhang, Y., Friend, A. J., Traud, A. L., Porter, M. A., Fowler, J. H., and Mucha, P. J. (2008). "Community Structure in Congressional Cosponsorship Networks." *Physica A: Statistical Mechanics and Its Applications* 387(7): 1705–1712. doi:10.1016/j.physa.2007.11.004.

CHAPTER 20

JUDICIAL NETWORKS

JANET M. BOX-STEFFENSMEIER,
DINO P. CHRISTENSON, AND CLAIRE LEAVITT

INTRODUCTION

THIS chapter presents a comprehensive summary of the literatures that benefit from the study of judicial networks. We pay particular attention to networks in which exciting scholarly advances are concentrated and those that show great promise in contributing to the literature on judicial behavior and extant decision-making models. Throughout the discussion, we identify the necessary tools and measures to study these networks and describe the varying processes of data collection while highlighting the strengths and weaknesses of both the classic and most recent literatures.

In what follows, we classify judicial networks into three broad types. First, we explore the literature on *citation networks*, or networks of judicial opinions linked by references to one another. Citation networks provide crucial insights into the foundations of judicial decision-making by exposing the opinions judges believe to be most significant. Second, we look at the networks created by considering the interactions among judges, law clerks, lawyers, and other relevant figures, which we call *prestige networks*. Such networks have the potential to reveal possible peer effects among judges and the roles of social and professional relationships in determining judicial outcomes. Finally, the developing literature on *amicus curiae networks*, which map connections among signatories of "friend of the court" legal briefs, helps identify which extralegal actors enjoy the greatest influence on the courts. More importantly, perhaps, these networks expose the often secretive relationships among organized interests that are potentially relevant across branches of government and in a host of democracies.

CITATION NETWORKS

Citation networks are the most commonly studied networks in the judicial literature. They map connections among judicial opinions, as measured by references and citations (Caldeira, 1985; Post and Eisen, 2000; Fowler et al., 2007; Fowler and Jeon, 2008; Bommarito et al., 2010; Cross et al., 2010; Lupu and Voeten, 2012). These citations represent the traditional legal principle of stare decisis in action. Literally meaning "to stand by things decided," stare decisis mandates the reliance on "legal doctrines, principles or rules established by prior court opinions" (Hansford and Spriggs, 2006, 5)—that is, precedent—to inform judicial rulings. The social network analysis of these citation patterns offers unique insights into debates within and among the three traditional jurisprudential models.

Legal or formalist models of judicial decision-making are strictly apolitical and conceive of justices as independent actors who make their decisions based on legal precedent (Leiter, 1999; Richards and Kritzer, 2002). In other words, judicial actors do not make law in a substantive sense; rather, justices operate in a highly constrained, rule-dominated environment and solidify laws that "in some Platonic sense, already exist" (Gilmore, 1977, 62). However, strictly mechanical theories of jurisprudence are largely dead, at least at the US Supreme Court (Kritzer and Richards, 2010), and judicial scholars have offered alternative models that allow for varying degrees of influence of preferences on citation behavior (Lupu and Fowler, 2013; Choi and Gulati, 2008; Bartels, 2009).

Attitudinal models, in almost perfect opposition to legal models, claim that justices base their rulings on sincere ideological preferences alone (Rohde and Spaeth, 1976; Banks, 1992; Segal and Spaeth, 1993, 2002; Brenner and Spaeth, 1995). Strategic models offer an alternative paradigm of judicial behavior that emphasizes judges' roles as sophisticated, strategic actors who base their decisions on fealty to precedent as well as a number of extralegal factors, including but not limited to ideological preferences, consideration and anticipation of others' preferences and choices, and the institutional and political contexts in which they operate (Epstein and Knight, 1998; see also George and Epstein, 1992). In short, judges make calculated decisions based on assessments of long-term consequences and implications for the political system as a whole (Baum, 2006), and thus judicial behavior cannot be assessed solely through individual-level attributes.

Though the strategic model explicitly accounts for contextual influences on judicial behavior, over the last two decades both attitudinal and legal models have slowly made room for the relevance of political and social (as opposed to ideological) considerations that may themselves help construct individual preferences and notions of the correct way to interpret the law (Baum, 2006; see also Segal and Spaeth, 2002; Kornhauser and Sager, 1993). After all, judges do not operate in isolation. Many of the judicial actors who cross paths professionally have been socially acquainted for years, and judges do—indeed, are encouraged to—communicate with their state-level and international counterparts in order to exchange perspectives, judicial philosophies, and information

(Slaughter, 2004; Katz and Stafford, 2010). Judges also frequently argue with one another over the content of opinions and circulate drafts for comment and revision (Maltzman and Wahlbeck, 1996), and since judges and lawyers are taught to argue and reason by analogy, citation to precedent is the single most important rhetorical device they possess (Levi, 1949).

However, even fealty to judicial precedent is far less straightforward than it appears at first glance: "There are many techniques . . . judges may use to evade precedents they do not wish to follow" (Lee, 2005, 5). Judges must often sort through a variety of similar and contradictory preceding opinions when making a decision (Spaeth, 1979) and in many instances rely on abstract argumentation (Dworkin, 1978) rather than existing precedent to construct an opinion on a novel case. Nor are interpretations of preceding opinions set in stone; Hansford and Spriggs (2006) show that judges may revisit and reinterpret prior noteworthy opinions as either positive or negative in order to institutionalize their own ideological preferences, so precedent both constrains and galvanizes present judicial decision-making. The reputation and prestige of certain courts also may prove directly or implicitly influential on judges' citation decisions. Certain courts are indubitably more highly regarded than others (Mott, 1936; Caldeira, 1983; Gleason and Comparato, 2014), and seats on certain courts are more highly coveted by jurists (e.g., the US Court of Appeals for the District of Columbia). However, the hypothesis that the "prestige factor" has an independent effect on how frequently a court's opinions are cited is more controversial, especially when applied to horizontal citations (citations between opinions that are issued by courts at the same level). When a court's opinion includes vertical citations (citations of opinions that are issued by a higher court), the court is likely either adhering to the requirement of mandatory or binding precedent—the rule, under stare decisis, that a court must abide by the precedents issued by higher-ranking courts with the requisite appellate jurisdictional power—or conforming to the expectation that lower courts should take their judicial cues from all courts that outrank them. But many horizontal citations have multiple interpretations with implications for strategic models of judicial behavior and may indicate that a court confers greater legitimacy upon the opinions of certain peer courts over others. Given the variation in reputational esteem within the state and federal court systems, studying the citation practices of prestigious courts may help illuminate the effects of prestige on a court's citation counts and thus may help reconstitute legal/formalist models as more political than previously believed.

Each jurisprudential model permits and has already helped pave the way for the applicability of network methods to the study of the judiciary. The ubiquity of judicial interactions, among and across all court systems, justifies the assessment of common law as a complex, adaptive system—in other words, as a network (Post and Eisen, 2000; Katz, Stafford, and Provins, 2008; Katz et al., 2011). Yet citation networks are somewhat ill-equipped for causal analysis. For example, is it the legal validity of the opinions themselves or the social connections between the opinions' authors (judges) that drive frequent citations? While authors have offered opposing perspectives on this question (Hinkle, 2015; Choi and Gulati, 2008), the undisputed value of citation networks lies in their use for identifying the opinions that judges themselves, as opposed to third-party legal scholars, deem the most influential or the most relevant. The opinions that emerge in central positions within citation networks perform well against qualitative scholarly rankings of the most important decisions (Fowler and Jeon, 2008; Gerhardt, 2008; Cross et al., 2010). Furthermore, certain centrality measures indicate the opinions that judges may deem the most strategically relevant. Hitt and Kassow (2015) argue that precedents that are cited frequently by both conservative and liberal opinions—so-called broker-age precedents—are less constrained by the application of stare decisis. Since brokerage precedents are used to justify decisions that span the ideological gamut, they may serve as post hoc rationalizations for decisions made "in an attitudinal manner" (Hitt and Kassow, 2015, 2). Nevertheless, even conceding that judges may choose to cite certain prior opinions to advance ideological or political purposes (Lupu and Fowler, 2013; Hitt and Kassow, 2015), citation networks underscore that reliance on precedent still drives the practice of constitutional law (Gerhardt, 2008), since citations remain the most effective way for a judge to confer instant legitimacy upon an opinion (Segal and Spaeth, 1993; Cross et al., 2010; Cross, 2012; Lupu and Voeten, 2012).

While invaluable, judicial networks are arduous to construct. Fowler and Jeon (2008) and Fowler et al. (2007) have ambitiously mapped complete networks of majority Supreme Court opinions from the eighteenth century to the early 2000s. Bommarito et al. (2010) have constructed an early-stage historical network of Supreme Court deci-sions, before stare decisis was institutionalized. Lupu and Voeten (2012) have turned their attention to the relevance of precedent in international courts, mapping a complete network of European Court of Human Rights decisions from the court's formation until 2006. Hitt and Kassow (2015) have mapped a network of all US circuit court citations from 1947 to 2007 that refer to Supreme Court precedents, in order to identify the deci-sions that bridge ideological divides—that is, the Supreme Court opinions that are most frequently cited by both liberal and conservative circuit court opinions. Hinkle (2015) has compiled a data set of all Fourth Amendment–related circuit court decisions over a fifty-seven-year period. This recent attention to the lower courts is a harbinger of the construction of further and more expansive lower-court networks as well as a schol-arly focus on how court systems' hierarchical positions may affect judicial behavior. In all types of citation networks, nodes represent judicial opinions and vertices represent citations and references between opinions. In most cases, networks have a clear direc-tion: either a case is cited by other judicial opinions or a case cites other opinions. Most networks are structured chronologically, with an arc (a directed edge) directing the head node, the opinion that cites others, to the tail node, the opinion that is being cited (Bonmarito et al., 2009).

The centrality score(s) of each opinion often serves as a proxy for assessing the power or influence of a given opinion. Thanks to Kleinberg (1998) and his work distinguishing inward and outward directed edges, citation networks literature has relied on author-ity and hub centrality scores to distinguish between two types of influence. Authority scores, measured as eigenvector centrality, are calculated as quality-weighted functions of the number of edges leading to a particular node—in other words, they measure the number of times an opinion is cited, weighted according to the quality of cases that cite the opinion (Fowler et al., 2007; Fowler and Jeon, 2008). Opinions with high authority scores are most likely to be considered significant, and an opinion that achieves the maximum authority score increases its probability of being cited by the Supreme Court to a greater extent than an opinion deemed significant by third-party legal scholars or media outlets (Fowler et al., 2007).

One-directional authority, as denoted by eigenvector centrality scores, however, has been shown to be insufficient for measuring the true relevance of a judicial opinion. For example, if a recently issued opinion cites a large number of precedents, but has not yet itself been cited by other opinions, its eigenvector centrality score would be zero and the opinion would be (unfairly) dismissed as insignificant (Fowler et al., 2007). Reliance on authority scores alone risks discounting the importance of nodes that may become central as the network continues to evolve. Hub scores, by contrast, measure the number of important cases that an opinion cites, also weighted according to quality. A high hub score indicates an opinion that is well grounded in common law. These scores are particularly valuable for analyzing changes in courts' priorities, cases' relevance, and legal rubrics over time. Fowler and Jeon (2008) show that opinions that were later overturned tend to have higher hub centrality scores; in addition, the hub centrality scores of opinions that overturn precedent are even higher. In other words, cases that overturn previous decisions are more grounded in precedent than cases that are later overturned.

Relationships between nodes, and thus nodal positions, change as more opinions are issued and more and more citations enter the network. Because new nodes and edges frequently enter a citation network, the number of possible relationships that can be formed over time is, in theory, infinite. Measuring citation networks over time is crucial for isolating genuine influence within a network from the effects of selection (Burk, Steglich, and Snijders, 2007): In other words, when Opinion A cites Opinion B, does this citation tell us something valuable about the inherent legal significance of Opinion B, or merely about the practical and legal constraints facing the author of Opinion A? Longitudinal analyses that assess network properties and nodal attributes observed at various points in time present an appealing solution, but due to the dynamic nature of citation networks, any method would have to account for the continuous evolution of the network. Snijders (2001) has used continuous-time Markov chain models to get around this problem, a methodological approach that estimates the probability distribution of relational changes in future networks according to the properties of the current network (as opposed to based on past configurations). For example, Burk, Steglich, and Snijders (2007) devised an actor-oriented model that predicts the probability of independent actors' behavioral changes based on the current state of the network at any selected point in time.

While there is a growing literature exploring methods for network dynamics, much of the previous scholarship has opted to assess networks at discrete points in time—for example, to map and assess citation networks for each decade across a court's entire history. For almost any given time period, citation networks in American federal and state-level judiciaries are organized around several clusters of important opinions that are cited by a large number of others as well as a far greater number of unimportant opinions that are cited by only a few others, or by none at all (Albert and Barabasi, 2002; Fowler, 2006; Fowler et al., 2007; Fowler and Jeon, 2008). This pattern also occurs in younger constitutional court systems, such as the European Court of Human Rights (Lupu and Voeten, 2012). Any complex citation network will naturally contain at least one case that is not cited by another judicial opinion (i.e., an authority score of 0), as well as at least one case that does not cite another judicial opinion (a hub score of 0). Cases that do not cite any others are known as "sinks" (Bommarito et al., 2010) and are valuable because they exemplify entirely new elements of judicial thinking—legalistic philosophies and protocols that are not explicitly indebted to any previous judicial decision.

Sinks are crucial to our understanding of historical citation networks. Networks of opinions issued in the first quarter century of the American republic, for example, will naturally contain a lot of sinks due to the absence of a large, preexisting body of rulings. To establish a clear pattern of judicial precedent, then, courts must go through a "loading phase" (Bommarito et al., 2010), during which the norm of stare decisis is constructed. Goodhart (1930) argues that stare decisis did not become institutionalized in the United States until around 1900, although Bommarito et al. (2010) maintain that US citation networks began exhibiting a clear structure in the 1820s. During the inchoate years of the American federal court system, however, there was a noticeable lack of meaningful clustering in citation networks—and thus scholars may expect the same structure in networks for recently established courts. Bommarito et al. (2010) devised a measure of centrality specifically for assessing early-stage networks characterized by an abundance of sinks. The authors' sink-based distance measure is inspired by betweenness centrality[1] and measures the shortest path between two sinks in a given network. Opinions with high sink-based scores thus represent the decisions responsible for connecting isolated opinions with one another—the very process that ensured the emergence of complex citation networks.

Hitt and Kassow (2015) have utilized a less common centrality measure, introduced by Burt (2004) and closely related to betweenness, to assess the ability of certain opinions to bridge "structural holes" in a larger citation network (i.e., the ability of certain opinions to directly connect distinct clusters of subnetworks). Constraint scores measure the ability of an opinion to connect clusters of nodes with one another, particularly if the nodes in each cluster are not themselves highly connected (Hitt and Kassow, 2015). Constraint scores thus offer an alternative to betweenness measures for larger, more complex networks; Burt (2005) suggests that betweenness is best suited for smaller, more compact networks, since betweenness scores do not account for whether an opinion brokers between two close connections or two distant connections.

Citation networks are crucial for understanding the full extent of judicial decision-making. For legal/formalist models in particular, these networks help clarify not just whether judges rely heavily on precedent to inform their decisions, but rather on *which* cases and opinions judges base their rulings. Thus, the most heavily cited opinions in an increasingly large legal corpus should help to clarify one of the central questions of judicial decision-making: whether judges rely on opinions purely for their legal value or for their comportment with those judges' own ideological or political preferences. Opinions with consistently high authority scores over time are more likely to represent legal arguments that span the ideological divide and are more widely respected. In addition, the foray into textual analysis of court decisions and the construction of text/semantic networks (see, e.g., Kok and Domingos, 2008) may shed some light on whether and how judicial actors distinguish their ideological and legal rationales in written opinions. For example, Hinkle et al. (2012) have shown that district court judges use so-called hedging, or ideologically equivocal, language when their preferences are not aligned with the majority of the judges on the requisite circuit court that is empowered to reverse district court rulings.

Continued study of historical networks should aid in illuminating the opinions that remain consistently relevant over long periods versus *flash in the pan* decisions, which do not stand the test of time. However, citation networks are unable to distinguish between highly central opinions that are cited as brilliant precedent and those that are consistently cited as cautionary tales (i.e., examples of what not to do). Positive citations explicitly commend the legal authority and/or reasoning of a prior opinion, while negative citations question or denounce a previous ruling (Hansford and Spriggs, 2006), but citation networks have no clear method for separating the two. Notorious opinions (e.g., *Plessy v. Ferguson* or *Dred Scott v. Sandford*) thus may have high centrality scores, but do not provide much help in identifying new foundations of judicial legitimacy. Clark and Lauderdale (2012) have developed a genealogical model that identifies antecedents in a particular case's doctrinal trajectory, which may help distinguish substantively novel opinions from those that simply pay lip service to a particular legal tradition and thus help correct for inflated significance due to citation counts. In order to tease out these nuances, network centrality cannot be studied in isolation; future analyses will likely rely on supplemental empirical measures (e.g., measures of judicial ideology, public opinion, or discourse quantifiers).

PRESTIGE NETWORKS

Jurisprudential models that permit judges to make strategic decisions based on social, political, and institutional factors require, among other things, a broader frame for analyzing judges' conceptions of legitimacy—that is, how judges (and other legal and political actors) confer authority upon a decision (Gibson, 2007). Neither precedent nor ideological preferences can fully explain historical and contemporary examples of judges' amending their behavior in response to other political actors (Clark, 2009); in the midst of President Franklin Roosevelt's notorious "court-packing" scheme in 1937, for instance, the Supreme Court strategically reversed course on its opposition to Roosevelt's New Deal legislative package. The Court overturned its own precedent to uphold labor and minimum-wage protections in an effort both to combat Roosevelt's attempted power grab and to retain the Court's legitimacy in the eyes of the Congress and a public that overwhelmingly supported the president's priorities (Caldeira, 1987). In 2012, political analysts and news reports suggested that Chief Justice John Roberts switched his vote on the constitutionality of the Affordable Care Act's (ACA) individual-mandate requirement at the eleventh hour, speculating that Roberts ultimately chose to uphold the act in a 5–4 decision due neither to legalistic considerations nor to political ideology, but rather to concern for his and the Court's reputation (Crawford, 2012); this rationale has been shown to magnify the effect of the public's perceived ideological proximity to the Court on their diffuse support for it (Christenson and Glick, 2015a).[2]

These examples are part of a long legal tradition of voting fluidity that suggests the need to incorporate the relationships among various political actors in all types of institutions in order to explain puzzling judicial behavior. Maltzman and Wahlbeck (1996) suggest that the context of the decision-making process is relevant to explaining judicial behavior, because ideological preferences are not always strict, and judges' assessments of possible legal outcomes and the effects on their court's institutional legitimacy evolve over the course of a case's consideration. This suggests that judges may be susceptible to new and understudied pathways of influence, such as peer effects and socially constructed norms (e.g., the perceived power of a particular court, judge, legal actor, or opinion). Thus, formally mapping social communities of judicial actors should prove exceedingly valuable for illuminating the entire context in which judges operate and possibly for refining strategic models of judicial decision-making to account for these effects.

Prestige networks, or purely social networks, compromise a burgeoning arena of judicial network analysis that promises significant reconceptualization of how power and legitimacy are constructed in the judiciary. While analyses of citation networks and most amicus curiae networks are also predicated on the hypothesis that definitions of legal legitimacy may be at least in part socially constructed and thus constitute an independent influence on judicial decision-making, both judicial opinions and amicus briefs are prima facie founded in logically compelling legal arguments. Not so for prestige networks, which evaluate the authority and the legitimacy of judicial actors[3] based wholly on social status and reputational esteem. The implicit hypothesis of prestige network analyses is that peer effects may play a role in the decision-making process of judges. Given that Judge A enjoys a particular degree of esteem or prestige (she is well respected, and her merit is deemed of superior quality by her colleagues), will Judges B, C, and D be more likely to imbue an opinion penned by Judge A with authority and legitimacy and, as a result, cite Judge A's opinions more often? If so, we may concede that Judge A enjoys a certain degree of prestige relative to her peers.

However, it is extremely difficult to divine a causal relationship between the frequency of the citations of a judge's opinions and that judge's level of relative esteem, thanks to a significant endogeneity problem: Are more prestigious judges more frequently cited by their peers, or do more frequent citations of their opinions confer prestige upon judges? In addition, all peer citations are not necessarily created equal; if a judge cites a particular opinion that is outside of her court's appellate jurisdictional path, that citation may exist for a multitude of extralegal reasons, including ideological bias toward or against other judges (Gulati and Choi, 2007). Finally, citations of particular opinions are extricable from the judges who wrote those opinions; many citations do not mention judges by name, and as a result, "citations are not connected clearly enough to individual judges . . . to be fully satisfactory measures of those judges' prestige" (Klein and Morrisroe, 1999, 375). Thus, while analyzing the degree to which prestige may influence citations is an important and preeminent goal of judicial scholarship, defining and measuring prestige itself—via social networks—is a necessary prelude to determining its influence.

Prestige networks distinguish between institutional prestige, a concept substantively comparable with legitimacy, and social prestige, since "institutional authority alone does not explain the prestige and influence across judges" (Katz and Stafford, 2010, 460). However, operationalizing prestige separately from the context of institutional legitimacy is challenging. Until recently, surveys were the most frequently employed method for measuring prestige (McGuire, 1993; Wasserman and Faust, 1994), along with the assessments of judicial scholars and other observers (Blaustein and Mersky, 1972, 1978). However, due to the systemic biases (including nonresponse) inherent in survey measurements and the intellectual value of defining peer prestige according to the assessments of judges themselves, scholars have devised creative proxies for reputational esteem.

Among judges, prestige may be operationalized as the flow of law clerks from one judge to another (Katz and Stafford, 2010; Baum, 2014), since the hiring process for federal judicial clerks is notoriously selective. Judges want to hire the best clerks in order to maximize their effectiveness, and the best clerks seek to work with the best judges in order to maximize their career prospects (Wald, 1990). The professional benefits of a prestigious clerkship for a recent law school graduate are obvious, while the intellectual quality and management styles of law clerks have been shown to have a significant impact on federal judges' workloads and final rulings (Peppers, 2006; Ward and Weiden, 2006). In other words, clerks and judges need each other and mutually benefit one another. Katz and Stafford (2010) suggest that there is a natural selection process through which the highest-quality clerks are hired by the most prestigious judges, making the movement of law clerks a credible measure of social prestige. Katz and Stafford (2010) find that the distribution of degree centrality scores,[4] the raw number of connections enjoyed by each node or judge in the network of approximately nineteen thousand clerks hired by federal courts during the Rehnquist era (1995–2004), is highly skewed; only 1.7 percent of the judges in the network enjoy ten or more clerk-fueled connections to other judges. These results suggest that there is high inequality in social power, at least among judges.

Measuring judges' prestige via the movement of law clerks alone, however, neglects the fact that clerks are selected not simply according to academic merit but also according to ideological preferences; a conservative judge is not likely to hire a liberal law clerk, no matter how impeccable the prospective clerk's law school transcript. Since the 1990s ideological ties between judges and clerks have remained consistently strong (Baum,

2014), likely thanks in tandem to increased polarization among judicial elites (Lazarus, 2005; Baum and Ditslear, 2001) and to the fact that—due to the increase in applications for federal clerkships and for lack of a more effective signaling mechanism—judges are likely to assess the ideological tenor of a prospective hire according to the preferences of judges the applicant previously clerked for (Baum, 2014).

The use of clerk movement as a heuristic for social prestige among judges suggests that judicial actors *other than judges* may be relevant in assessments of judicial decision-making. In other words, judges' opinions may be susceptible to the influence of reputable private lawyers, law professors, attorneys general, or solicitors general, particularly when drafting opinions that are not heavily constrained by precedent and particularly when the actor enjoys a high level of social prestige. McGuire (1993) finds that the most socially powerful private lawyers in a network of approximately seven hundred litigators who have argued before the Supreme Court are overwhelmingly former law clerks, former staffers in the Office of the US Solicitor General, former law professors at elite universities, and employed by the largest and most famous Washington, DC, private firms. Katz et al. (2011) measure the prestige of law professors in a network of all tenured or tenure-track law faculty at American Bar Association–accredited American universities according to the flow of faculty members between universities. Professors with high outward-directed degree scores[5] work at universities that hire faculty from the most prestigious law schools, while professors with high hub scores work at law schools that place their graduates in the most prestigious tenure-track jobs. The authors also calculate closeness centrality, which controls for a node's position within the network itself (see Wasserman and Faust, 1994) and thus for a professor's (and the professor's law school's) overall influence on the structure of an institutional community.[6] Professors with the highest degree and hub centrality scores enjoy the highest levels of social prestige and authority. While these findings may seem intuitive, their implications are important: The existence of peer effects within the judicial system has the potential to create an intellectual echo chamber in which the most influential actors all hail from the same narrow experiential sphere.

The validity of prestige networks, of course, depends on the credibility of the available proxy for network power. For example, while the law clerk market may appear to naturally select for quality, critics have pointed out the "rapidity with which clerkship matches are made" (Avery et al., 2007, 452) and the first-mover advantage granted to well-known judges who snap up the most in-demand students before these students have the chance to consider other, possibly more compelling, offers (Priest, 2003). Thus, the reality of law clerks' hiring might compromise the integrity of the selection process and thus the network as a reliable indicator of prestige. The practical realities of any prestigious industry or institution for which networks can be constructed are likely to engender the same problem. Thus, the value of prestige networks in assessing possible peer effects among judges will likely emerge from a corpus of work rather than from making the case for the reliability of a particular type of network.

AMICUS CURIAE NETWORKS

Nonjudicial actors—such as private citizens, official legal actors, and organized interest groups—may interact with the judicial system by indicating their political preferences to federal and state judges via amicus curiae briefs. These "friend of the court" legal briefs are written by actors who are not parties to a case but believe they can offer information relevant to it. Amicus briefs are thought to be one of the most effective (and cost-effective) methods of legal advocacy available to nonjudicial actors (Krislov, 1963); indeed, the presence of these briefs has been shown to affect judicial decision-making (Collins, 2008; Box-Steffensmeier, Christenson, and Hitt, 2013).

Recently scholars have begun to construct networks based on amicus briefs. The richness of the data allows for a number of possible network constructions. Most simply, ties might be drawn between actors that have signed onto the same case, creating an issue network in which shared interest about an issue in a particular case joins actors. More pointedly, perhaps, network ties might be drawn only between those who are arguing for the same decision in the same case; that is, tying all those in support of or in opposition to the petitioner/respondent. This outcome network would then indicate not merely that the issue was of interest to both parties, but also that they wanted a similar outcome. However, while interesting in their own right, these constructions provide little clue as to who works with whom. The actors in these network constructions do not need to know one another, let alone communicate, in order to be tied together. Indeed, groups filing separate briefs may be advocating for distinct legal and social issues, which begs the question of how best to construct a social network from amicus briefs.

Amicus briefs are frequently co-signed by multiple parties. That is, organizations and/or individuals often choose to join forces and share resources by constructing and signing briefs together, indicating their shared political priorities in an attempt to affect judicial outcomes (Hojnacki, 1997; Clark and Wilson, 1961). This process requires negotiation between co-signatories and agreement on the argument and details of the brief, which can be costly (Caldeira and Wright, 1988) and difficult (Wasby, 1995). As such, it is natural to use the act of co-signing to construct ties between actors before the courts. Contrary to the other constructions, networks built on co-signing are both "purposive" and "coordinated," providing leverage on which actors work together and to what ends (Box-Steffensmeier and Christenson, 2014).

These networks are by nature nondirected networks. That is, one cannot consistently and objectively distinguish co-signers of Supreme Court amicus briefs in terms of senders and receivers or leaders and followers. Despite the fact that one of the organizations may be listed first as the filer of the amicus brief, to give more weight to such an organization would be inappropriate. Often the reports are filed alphabetically or in some other manner that gives no indication of a lead signatory (Gibson, 1997; Box-Steffensmeier and Christenson, 2014). Amicus networks have been considered primarily in terms of one-mode projections from a two-mode or bipartite graph. Despite the fact that interest groups are tied by virtue of signing the same brief, a one-mode projection has been justified based on the process of creating the brief, which requires coordinated action and denotes a deliberate link between organizations. While interest groups undoubtedly interact broadly, an interest group network based on amicus briefs suggests that the interests draw one another together to create the brief, not the other way around, with the brief drawing the interests together. In sum, the brief is simply a physical manifestation of a true social network. Having said that, the one-mode projection does throw away some information on the briefs and thus suggests a potential pathway for future scholarship.[7]

While both individuals and organized groups sign amicus briefs, the networks literature has focused primarily on groups. In the study of judicial decision-making it has become common practice, beginning with Gibson (1997),[8] to focus on the effect of amicus briefs from organized interest groups, corporations, and associations rather than from individuals and governments (see also Collins, 2008; Box-Steffensmeier, Christenson, and Hitt, 2013). Indeed, Collins (2008) notes that a preponderance of amicus signers are interest groups. Thus, this work dovetails with that of interest group scholars (see Chapter 17 of this book) and is poised to play a role well beyond the judicial branch. In addition to legally defined interest groups and lobbies—a weak definition that misses almost 50 percent of actual interest groups (LaPira and Thomas, 2013)—all of the organized groups, corporations, and associations in the amicus network have political stakes and objectives. Moreover, they participate in the political process by virtue of constructing a brief. As such, amicus briefs may help expand the compendium of interest groups far beyond what the literature is frequently able to study.

Indeed, the comprehensiveness of the amicus data is one of its strongest features. In addition to the broad collection of organizations that act as amici, amicus briefs have been collected by Box-Steffensmeier and Christenson (2014) from the 1930s onward, though they have a longer history (see Krislov, 1963). There were large periods of growth in amicus brief filers in the 1960s and 1970s, leading to the massive involvement of today, with around five thousand organizations signing briefs in each of the most recent decades (Box-Steffensmeier and Christenson, 2014). These conditions provide the opportunity to make comparisons over time and to dynamically model the network. In addition, these organizations span a host of issues and industries, as well as sizes. Box-Steffensmeier and Christenson (2014, 2015) utilize business directories to gather attribute data on signers from the first decade of the millennium. In doing so, they find a broad range of industries, with the greatest number of signers in the services division, according to the Standard Industrial Classification (SIC).

The breadth of these data stands in stark contrast to collecting interest group networks based on mass surveys or small sample interviews. Traditionally, scholars have relied on one method or the other. In the former, scholars might ask respondents to recall their major partners via egocentric network batteries (see, e.g., Huckfeldt, Johnson, and Sprague, 2002, 2004; Huckfeldt and Sprague, 1987, 1991; Mutz and Mondak, 2006). In the latter, they might conduct interviews that ask respondents to identify their partners and may even follow that by interviewing the partners named in the first interview, that is, snowball sampling (see, e.g., Heaney, 2004, 2006). Both approaches may suffer from relatively high costs and nonresponsiveness. Moreover, responses are likely to suffer from weak and selective memories, wherein organizations only (choose to) remember certain other organizations (e.g., friends over enemies, major over minor players, ethical over unethical behavior). However, there are of course limits to the amicus data that these approaches do not suffer, including the ability to ask precisely the questions of interest and confirm the division of labor among partners.

The aforementioned purposive and coordinated nature of these briefs also provides some improvement over various other data used to construct networks of interest groups. Consider, for example, the collections of data offered by the Lobbying Disclosure Act of 1995 (LDA) and the Federal Elections Committee (FEC). The LDA filings disclose who lobbies whom and on which issues and bills. Networks that employ LDA data link lobbyists and/or organizations based on their lobbying the same member of Congress or for the same bill or issue (see, e.g., Scott, 2007; Koger and Victor, 2009; LaPira, Thomas, and Baumgartner, 2014). The network is therefore based on a shared interest or policy domain. The FEC filings contain information on who contributes to campaigns, including lobbyists and organizations, from which ties are drawn between interest groups that contribute to the same candidate. While both approaches offer important insights, especially pertaining to individual lobbyist behavior (see, e.g., LaPira, Thomas, and Baumgartner, 2014), neither provides indications of coordination and shared purpose on the part of the linked interest groups. In both cases, interest groups may be drawn together that neither worked together nor wanted to see the same political outcomes. In contrast, using amici networks is attractive because scholars can distinguish the polarity of advocacy. In sum, studying interest group networks based on amicus briefs has the potential to deepen the study of interest group networks by focusing on interest groups' collaborative behavior in pursuit of a specific political outcome.

Interest groups often coordinate to share resources, disseminate information, and signal broad support (Hula, 1999). Less understood are how to measure the networks of the vast expanse of special interests, how network strategies compare across policy domains, and how networks have changed over time. These general questions motivate more micro-level considerations about which groups are the most attractive partners, which characteristics are sought out as complements, and which are considered threatening to cooperation. To these ends, Box-Steffensmeier and Christenson (2014) present evidence of an increasingly transitive network resembling a host of tightly grouped factions and leadership hub organizations employing mixed coalition strategies. Egocentric networks of organizations show that three major theoretically posited coalition strategies are present in the data: "lone wolves," who work alone; "teammates," who work with cliques of varying sizes; and "leaders," who pull together otherwise disparate groups. Driving these network strategies is assortative mixing based on industry area, budget, sales, and membership. In a related piece, Box-Steffensmeier and Christenson (2015) dig deeper into the different network strategies employed across industry and issue areas. They focus on membership interest groups, which, by virtue of representing the interests of voluntary members, face particular organizational and maintenance constraints.

Coupling exponential random graph models (ERGMs) and multidimensional scaling provides a compact spatial representation in which religious, labor, and political organizations do not share the same network structure as each other or as the business, civic, and professional groups.

Scholars have begun to explore these naturally occurring networks of signatories to assess which actors enjoy the most influence on the courts. Kearney and Merrill (2000) call for quantitative studies on the influence of amicus briefs that stem from the aforementioned theoretical models of judicial behavior. In their comprehensive study they find that briefs drafted by more experienced lawyers are more likely to be filed under the successful party, briefs supporting respondents have a higher success rate than those supporting petitioners, and briefs cited by the justices' opinions are not associated with being on the winning side. Ultimately, they find that the number of briefs filed on behalf of either party is limited and thus argue that there is little evidence that greater disparities in brief numbers equate to greater chances of success. Collins (2008), however, finds that justices will be more likely to make liberal (conservative) decisions when there is a greater number of liberal (conservative) briefs. In evaluating the case and related arguments, one might also wonder whether judges take into account the relative power of interest groups, above and beyond the sheer number of supporters for the liberal and conservative positions. Box-Steffensmeier, Christenson, and Hitt (2013) find that when the two sides of a case have similar numbers of briefs, the social network power of an interest group—as measured by its eigenvector centrality in the network—is a valuable signal to judges. The results provide insights into the conditions under which the quality of interest groups may matter as much if not more than the quantity.

These papers are only the tip of the proverbial iceberg for research focused on any of the branches of government that may benefit from an understanding of interest groups' social networks. There are works in progress exploring the effects of interest group power—frequently construed as a measure of social network centrality—on the progress of bills through the legislative process (Box-Steffensmeier, Christenson, and Craig, 2013) and on the duration of executive nominations (Box-Steffensmeier, Christenson, and Ratliff, 2013). For organizations that have lobbied over several years, one can investigate the effect of their networks on their life spans (Box-Steffensmeier, Christenson, and Leavitt, 2015), as well as how different factors affect network formation and dissolution over time (Box-Steffensmeier and Christenson, 2016). In addition, scholars can divide the data into subsets to focus on types of groups and/or cases. Kawai and Iida (2011) examine whether having cross-cutting brokerage positions across different types of groups has an impact on the success of patent cases, while Box-Steffensmeier et al. (2016) focus on the networks of groups interested in environmental cases.

Delving into this network has also motivated the development of promising new measures and methodologies. Hansford (2012), for example, classifies relationships between groups as positive if they co-sign a brief and includes an obliquely derived negative tie between groups who sign ideologically opposing briefs in order to calculate a measure of ideological scores for Supreme Court cases over time. Relatedly, Christenson et al. (2015) offer an approach to measure the political ideology of each interest group based on the directions of their briefs. Moreover, the intricacies of the amicus network data have inspired research on new methodologies that can be used to explore the network. As a response to the difficulties of detecting communities with these data, Peng et al. (2015) offer a flexible, group-corrected stochastic block model under a Bayesian framework. Likewise, the network has led to modifying the frequently employed ERGM to account for unobserved heterogeneity, which is both pervasive and damaging in these models. In particular, Box-Steffensmeier et al. (forthcoming) have proposed a solution in the form of an ERGM that includes a frailty or random effect term.

Opportunities also exist for making use of amicus curiae briefs beyond the US Supreme Court. Amici interests may file briefs in federal circuit courts, districts courts, and state courts under certain conditions and at the judges' discretion (Gidiere, 2012).[9] Indeed, recently attention has been paid to the US Court of Appeals, where amicus briefs have been shown to occur in great numbers (Collins and Martinek, 2010) and influence the decision-making of appeals court judges, contingent on a judge's ideology (Collins and Martinek, 2015). However, there is a relative dearth of scholarship on amicus coalitional activity in the lower courts. One exception is Gleason (2013), who argues that powerful state actors—specifically, state attorneys general—are able to mobilize their like-minded counterparts and engage in coalitional advocacy via amicus briefs before the Supreme Court. This suggests that the successful political efforts of state actors at the federal level might be replicable via amici activity at the state level.

Outside of the United States, the study of amici advocacy in civil and mixed-law systems is rare due to practical constraints; amici activity is a relatively recent phenomenon in nations outside of the British common law tradition. The gradual acceptance of amici participation in civil law systems in Europe is arguably a direct result of European Council regulations mandating that the court systems of all EU member states permit some amici access. This usually occurs in antitrust cases (see Kochevar, 2013); however, France began permitting formal amicus brief submissions in 1989 (Duncan, 1994), and the Israel Supreme Court accepted its first amicus brief in 1996 (Doron and Totry-Jubran, 2005). In addition, since 2000 Latin American courts—particularly in Argentina and Colombia—have ruled that they will allow amici to not only submit written briefs but also participate in oral arguments according to "fairly broad" protocols (Johnson and Amerasinghe, 2009).

The increasing legitimacy of amici participation in nationally based civil law courts has paved the way for third-party interests to advocate in international courts and adjudicatory bodies structurally modeled after civil law regimes (Johnson and Amerasinghe, 2009), galvanizing the political and social advocacy of nonstate actors (particularly nongovernmental organizations). Kochevar (2013) suggests that NGOs itching for policy influence pushed for the acceptance of amici participation in non-common-law systems and built on domestic successes to increase amici advocacy before international courts. Third-party interests are permitted conditional representation before international courts and tribunals, such as the UN's International Court of Justice and the European Court of Human Rights (Bartholomeusz, 2005), while since the late 1990s the World Trade Organization's Dispute Panels and Appellate Body has permitted NGOs and global civil society organizations to submit formal briefs in trade disputes (Eckersley, 2007). In some instances, supranational organizations like the European Commission, in addition to NGOs, have been permitted to advocate as amici in investment arbitration disputes that occur through interstate trade-based institutions such as the International Centre for the Settlement of Investment Disputes (ICSID) and the North American Free Trade Agreement (NAFTA) (Levine, 2011). And as the practice of amici participation before international courts and tribunals increases, as trends suggest it will (Shelton, 1994; Ala'i, 2000; Hollis, 2002; Howse, 2003; Bartholomeusz, 2005; Eckersley, 2007), assessments of early-stage international amici networks will be able to provide insights into the social power of nonstate actors on the global stage, an area of global governance that remains understudied. In sum, there is great potential to use amicus curiae to better understand special interest behavior and political outcomes across various levels and countries.

FUTURE DIRECTIONS

A review of judicial networks highlights the progress made in this area of study and promising routes for future empirical and theoretical advancements. Within the citation networks literature, for example, identifying positive and negative citations will be crucial to advance the field. Likewise, a consideration of a myriad of alternative measures for prestige in the complex network of judges, clerks, and lawyers will likely to lead to advances. Amicus networks at any level of the courts offer exciting advances for both judicial and interest group scholars, but progress here will require greater attention to the context of the cases that organizations act on, as well as the frequency of cosigning.

More generally, further work comparing network configurations as well as the implications of particular actors within it is needed. Exploring whether alternative networks are more effective or better suited for the purpose of the individual nodes and/or the collective network, for example, deserves more scholarly attention. Empirically and theoretically examining the role of certain nodes in an egocentric network is also a promising route to better understanding various judicial networks. This agenda also blends with methodological advancements, namely the development of egocentric ERGMs. These models take potential covariates as predictors for whether or not a given node belongs to a particular role or group (Krivitsky, Handcock and Morris, 2011; Salter-Townshend and Murphy, 2015). Frailty ERGMs (FERGMs) are also likely to be helpful to judicial scholars, as these models take into account unmeasured, unmeasurable, and unimagined covariates—which we take to be the rule, not the exception—in the formation of various judicial networks. In other words, the FERGM adds a random effect to relax the assumption of a perfectly specified model for the often used ERGM. This methodological advancement seems especially useful for human behavioral networks (Box-Steffensmeier et al., 2014). Another recent methodological advancement that holds promise for greater substantive understanding is longitudinal or dynamic network analysis, which allows scholars to examine the evolution of judicial networks over time. Thus, one can examine not just the formation, but also the dissolution of ties, as in temporal ERGMs (TERGMs) (Hanneke et al., 2010; Desmarais and Cranmer 2010, 2012; Leifeld et al. 2016) and separable temporal ERGMs (STERGMs) (Krivitsky and Handcock, 2014). Related advances in stochastic actor-oriented network dynamics allow researchers to test a variety of hypotheses on the influences of network change (Snijders, 2001, 2005; Snijders et al., 2010).

Jones (2008) urges judicial scholars to use complex systems and network analysis to "identify and understand individual human behaviors that result in dramatic human group behavior and use this understanding to optimally design institutions that constrain this behavior in ways that promise social welfare"—a lofty but critical goal. The judicial branch is replete with network data, and the works we have discussed here have already made invaluable contributions to our understanding of social, political, and economic behavior. Still, it should be clear that we have only scratched the surface, which makes it an exciting time to study judicial networks.

Acknowledgments

We thank Larry Baum, Rebecca Hinkle, Matthew Hitt, Laura Moyer, Sahar Abi-Hassan, and Benjamin Campbell for helpful comments and discussions.

Notes

1. Betweenness centrality scores calculate the number of times a node appears on the shortest path between an edge and all other edges in a network. Nodes with high betweenness scores are the actors/entities that are crucial to maintaining overall network connectivity; these are the nodes that indirectly connect non-associated clusters with one another.
2. Relatedly, Christenson, and Glick (2015b) show that while the ACA decision had little to no effect on the public's support for general healthcare reform, it bumped up public opinion on the individual mandate provision.
3. These actors include judges on the bench; litigants; and advocates, who make the arguments before the court and write and sign amicus briefs.
4. Degree centrality scores, unlike eigenvector centrality, are not weighted according to the quality of ties.
5. An outdegree score simply measures the number of connections coming from a node.
6. Closeness centrality is calculated as the sum of the distance—the length of the shortest path from one node in the network to another—of one node to all other nodes, distinguishing closeness measures from betweenness, which accounts for the number of times a node appears on the shortest path between two other nodes. See Freeman (1979).
7. For a brief bipartite exploration of these data, see the appendix in Box-Steffensmeier and Christenson (2014).
8. Gibson (1997) was among the first to compile systematic data on amicus participation, but there was a lot of research on amicus briefs prior to that time; inclusion of the amicus data in the database reflected the long-standing interest in amici.
9. Even the Supreme Court has rules about who can file amicus briefs, though in practice almost nobody gets barred.

References

Ala'i, P. (2000). "Judicial Lobbying at the WTO: The Debate Over the Use of Amicus Curiae Briefs and the US Experience." *Fordham International Law Journal* 24(62): 62–94.

Albert, R., and Barabasi, A. L. (2002). "Statistical Mechanics of Complex Networks." *Reviews of Modern Physics* 74(1): 47–97.

Avery, C., Jolls, C., Posner, R. A., and Roth, A. E. (2007). "The New Market for Federal Judicial Law Clerks." *University of Chicago Law Review* 74: 447–486.

Banks, C. P. (1992). "The Supreme Court and Precedent: An Analysis of Natural Courts and Reversal Trends." *Judicature* 75(5): 262–268.

Bartels, B. L. (2009). "The Constraining Capacity of Legal Doctrine on the US Supreme Court." *American Political Science Review* 103(3): 474–495.

Bartholomeusz, L. (2005). "The Amicus Curiae before International Courts and Tribunals." *Non-State Actors and International Law* 5: 209–286.

Baum, L. (2006). *Judges and Their Audiences: A Perspective on Judicial Behavior*. Princeton, NJ: Princeton University Press.

Baum, L. (2014). "Hiring Supreme Court Law Clerks: Probing the Ideological Linkage Between Judges and Justices." *Marquette Law Review* 98: 333.

Baum, L., and Ditslear, C. (2001). "Selection of Law Clerks and Polarization in the U.S. Supreme Court." *Journal of Politics* 63(3): 869–885.

Blaustein, A. P., and Mersky, R. M. (1972). "Rating Supreme Court Justices." *American Bar Association Journal* 58: 1183–1190.

Blaustein, A. P., and Mersky, R. M. (1978). *The First One Hundred Justices*. Hamden, CT: Archon Books.

Bommarito, M., Katz, D. M., Zelner, J., and Fowler, J. (2010). "Distance Measures for Dynamic Citation Networks." *Physica A* 389: 4201–4208.

Bommarito, M.J., II, Katz, D. and Zelner, J., (2009, June 14). Law as a seamless web?: comparison of various network representations of the united states supreme court corpus (1791–2005). In Proceedings of the 12th international conference on artificial intelligence and law, pp. 234–235. Association for Comuting Machinery.

Box-Steffensmeier, J. M., and Christenson, D. P. (2014). "The Evolution and Formation of Amicus Curiae Networks." *Social Networks* 36: 82–96.

Box-Steffensmeier, J. M., and Christenson, D. P. (2015). "Comparing Membership Interest Group Networks Across Space and Time, Size, Issue and Industry." *Network Science* 3(1): 78–97.

Box-Steffensmeier, J. M., Christenson, D. P., and Craig, A. (2013). "Interest Group Signals from Dear Colleague Letters." Paper presented at the Annual Meeting of the American Political Science Association, Chicago, IL, August 29–31.

Box-Steffensmeier, J. M., Christenson, D. P., and Hitt, M. P. (2013). "Quality Over Quantity: Amici Influence and Judicial Decision Making." *American Political Science Review* 107(3): 1–15.

Box-Steffensmeier, J. M., Christenson, D. P., and Leavitt, C. (2015). "The Consequences of Connectivity: How Networks Help Interest Groups Survive." Paper presented at the Annual Meeting of the Midwest Political Science Association, Chicago, IL, April 16–19.

Box-Steffensmeier, J. M., Christenson, D. P., and Morgan, J. W. (Forthcoming). "The Frailty Exponential Random Graph Model." *Political Analysis*.

Box-Steffensmeier, J. M., Campbell, B., Christenson, D. P., and Navabi, Z. (2016). "Role Analysis and Environmental Interest Group Coalitions." Paper presented at the Annual Meeting of the Midwest Political Science Association, Chicago, IL, April 7–10.

Box-Steffensmeier, J. M., Christenson, D. P., and Ratliff, L. (2013). "The Role of Interest Group Networks in Executive Branch Nominations." Paper presented at the Annual Meeting of the Midwest Political Science Association, Chicago, IL, April 11–14.

Box-Steffensmeier, Janet M., and Christenson, D. P. (2016). "Why Amicus Curiae Cosigners Come and Go: A Dynamic Model of Interest Group Networks." Proceedings of the International Workshop on Complex Networks and their Applications. *Studies in Computational Intelligence* 349–360.

Brenner, S., and Spaeth, H. J. (1995). *Stare Indecisis: The Alteration of Precedetnt on the US Supreme Court, 1946–1992.* Cambridge, UK: Cambridge University Press.

Burk, W. J., Steglich, C. E.G., and Snijders, T. A.B. (2007). "Beyond Dyadic Interdependence: Actor-Oriented Models for Co-Evolving Social Networks and Individual Behaviors." *International Journal of Behavioral Development* 31(4): 397–404.

Burt, R. S. (2004). "Structural Holes and Good Ideas." *American Journal of Sociology* 110(2): 349–399.

Burt, R. S. (2005). *Brokerage and Closure: An Introduction to Social Capital.* Oxford: Oxford University Press.

Caldeira, G. A. (1983). "On the Reputation of State Supreme Courts." *Political Behavior* 5(1): 83–108.

Caldeira, G. A. (1985). "The Transmission of Legal Precedent: A Study of State Supreme Courts." *American Political Science Review* 79(1): 178–194.

Caldeira, G. A. (1987). "Public Opinion and The U.S. Supreme Court: FDR's Court-Packing Plan." *American Political Science Review* 81(4): 1139–1153.

Caldeira, G. A., and Wright, J. R. (1988). "Organized Interests and Agenda Setting in the U.S. Supreme Court." *American Political Science Review* 82(4): 1109–1127.

Choi, S. J., and Gulati, G. M. (2008). "Bias in Judicial Citations: A Window into the Behavior of Judges?" *Journal of Legal Studies* 37(1): 87–130.

Christenson, D. P., Carvalho, L., Peng, L., and Box-Steffensmeier, J. (2015). "An Ideological Mapping of Interest Groups by Amicus Curiae Behavior." Working Paper.

Christenson, D. P., and Glick, D. M. (2015a). "Chief Justice Roberts's Health Care Decision Disrobed: The Microfoundations of the Court's Legitimacy." *American Journal of Political Science* 59(2): 403–418.

Christenson, D. P., and Glick, D. M. (2015b). "Issue-Specific Opinion Change: The Supreme Court and Health Care Reform." *Public Opinion Quarterly* 79(4): 881–905.

Clark, P. B., and Wilson, J. Q. (1961). "Incentive Systems: A Theory of Organizations." *Administrative Science Quarterly* 6(2): 129–166.

Clark, T. S. (2009). "The Separation of Powers, Court Curbing, and Judicial Legitimacy." *American Journal of Political Science* 53(4): 971–989.

Clark, T. S., and Lauderdale, B. E. (2012). "The Genealogy of Law." *Political Analysis* 20(3): 329–350.

Collins, P. M. (2008). *Friends of the Supreme Court: Interest Groups and Judicial Decision Making.* Oxford: Oxford University Press.

Collins, P. M., and Martinek, W. L. (2010). "Friends of the Circuits: Interest Group Influence on Decision Making in the U.S. Courts of Appeals." *Social Science Quarterly* 91(2): 397–414.

Collins, P. M., and Martinek, W. L. (2015). "Judges and Friends: The Influence of Amici Curiae on U.S. Court of Appeals Judges." *American Politics Research* 43: 255.

Crawford, J. (2012). "Roberts Switched Views to Uphold Health Care Law." *CBS News, July 2*. http://www.cbsnews.com/news/roberts-switched-views-to-uphold-health-care-law/.

Cross, F. B. (2012). "The Ideology of Supreme Court Opinions and Citations." *Iowa Law Review* 97(3): 693–751.

Cross, F. B., Spriggs, J. F., II, Johnson, T. R., and Wahlbeck, P. J. (2010). "Citations in the U.S. Supreme Court: An Empirical Study of their Use and Significance." *University of Illinois Law Review* 2010(2): 489–576.

Desmarais, B. A. and Cranmer, S. J. (2010). "Consistent Confidence Intervals for Maximum Pseudolikelihood Estimators. In Proceedings of the Neural Information Processing Systems 2010 Workshop on Computational Social Science and the Wisdom of Crowds.

Desmarais, B. A. and Cranmer, S. J. (2012). "Statistical Mechanics of Networks: Estimation and Uncertainty." *Physica A* 391(4):1865–1876.

Doron, I., and Totry-Jubran, M. (2005). "Too Little, Too Late? An American Amicus in an Israeli Court." *Temple International and Comparative Law Journal* 19(1): 105–131.

Duncan, D. W. (1994). "A Little Tour in France: Surrogate Motherhood and Amici Curiae in the French Legal System." *Western State University Law Review* 21(2): 447–465

Dworkin, R. (1978). *Taking Rights Seriously*. Cambridge, MA: Harvard University Press.

Eckersley, R. (2007). "A Green Public Sphere in the WTO?: The Amicus Curiae Interventions in the Transatlantic Biotech Dispute." *European Journal of International Relations* 13(3): 329–356.

Epstein, L., and Knight, J. (1998). *The Choices Justices Make*. Washington, DC: CQ Press.

Fowler, J. H. (2006). "Connecting the Congress: A Study of Cosponsorship Networks." *Political Analysis* 14(4): 456–487.

Fowler, J. H., and Jeon, S. (2008). "The Authority of Supreme Court Precedent." *Social Networks* 30(1): 16–30.

Fowler, J. H., Johnson, T. R., Spriggs, J. F., II, Jeon, S., and Wahlbeck, P. J. (2007). "Network Analysis and the Law: Measuring the Legal Importance of Precedents at the U.S. Supreme Court." *Political Analysis* 15(3): 324–346.

Freeman, L. C. (1979). "Centrality in Social Networks I: Conceptual Clarification." *Social Networks* 1(3): 215–239.

George, T. E., and Epstein, L. (1992). "On the Nature of Supreme Court Decision Making." *American Political Science Review* 86(2): 323–337.

Gerhardt, M. J. (2008). "The Irrepressibility of Precedent." *North Carolina Law Review* 86(5): 1280–1297.

Gibson, J. L. (1997). UNITED STATES SUPREME COURT JUDICIAL DATABASE, PHASE II: 1953-1993. ICPSR version. Houston, TX: University of Houston [producer], 1996. Interuniversity Consortium for Political and Social Research, Ann Arbor, MI [distributor]. http://doi.org/10.3886/ICPSR06987.v1

Gibson, J. L. (2007). "The Legitimacy of the U.S. Supreme Court in a Polarized Polity." *Journal of Empirical Legal Studies* 4(3): 507–538.

Gidiere, P. S., III. (2012). "The Facts and Fictions of Amicus Curiae Practice in the Eleventh Circuit Court of Appeals." *Seton Hall Circuit Review* 5(1): 1–18.

Gilmore, G. (1977). *The Ages of American Law*. New Haven, CT: Yale University Press.

Gleason, S. (2013). "Lobbying Together: State Attorney General Amicus Curiae Coalitions." Paper presented at the Annual Meeting of the Political Networks Section of the American Political Science Association, Bloomington, IN, June 26–29.

Gleason, S. A., and Comparato, S. A. (2014). "The Importance of Context and Opinion Author Identity in State Supreme Court Citation Networks." Paper presented at the Annual Meeting of the Midwest Political Science Association, Chicago, IL, April 3–6.

Goodhart, A. L. (1930). "Determining the Ratio Decidendi of a Case." *Yale Law Journal* 40: 161–183.

Gulati, M., and Choi, S. J. (2007). "Ranking Judges According to Citation Bias." *Notre Dame Law Review* 82: 1279–1309.

Hanneke, Steve, Wenjie Fu and Eric P. Xing. (2010). "Discrete Temporal Models of Social Networks." *The Electronic Journal of Statistics* 4: 585–605.

Hansford, T. (2012). "Using the Amici Network to Measure the Ex Ante Ideological Loading of Supreme Court Cases." Paper presented at the Annual Meeting of the Midwest Political Science Association, Chicago, IL April 12–15.

Hansford, T. G., and Spriggs, J. F., II. (2006). *The Politics of Precedent on the U.S. Supreme Court.* Princeton, NJ: Princeton University Press.

Heaney, M. T. (2004). "Reputation and Leadership inside Interest Group Coalitions." Paper presented at the annual meetings of the American Political Science Association, Chicago, IL, April 15–18.

Heaney, Michael T. (2006). "Brokering Health Policy: Coalitions, Parties, and Interest Group Influence." *Journal of Health Politics, Policy and Law* 31(5): 887–944.

Hinkle, R. K. (2015). "Legal Constraint in the U.S. Courts of Appeals." *The Journal of Politics* 77(3): 721–735.

Hinkle, R. K., Martin, A. D., Shaub, J., and Tiller, E. H. (2012). "A Positive Theory and Empirical Analysis of Strategic Word Choice in District Court Opinions." *Journal of Legal Analysis* 40: 407–444.

Hitt, M. P., and Kassow, B. J. (2015). "Uncovering Attitudinal Treatments of Precedent in Judicial Opinions." Paper presented at the Annual Meeting of the Midwest Political Science Association, Chicago, IL, April 16–19.

Hojnacki, M. (1997). "Interest Groups' Decisions to Join Alliances or Work Alone." *American Journal of Political Science* 41(1): 61–87.

Hollis, D. B. (2002). "Private Actors in Public International Law: Amicus Curiae and the Case for the Retention of State Sovereignty." *Boston College International and Comparative Law Review* 25: 235–255.

Howse, R. (2003). "Membership and Its Privileges: The WTO, Civil Society, and the Amicus Brief Controversy." *European Law Journal* 9(4): 496–510.

Huckfeldt, R., Johnson, P. E., and Sprague, J. (2002). "Political Environments, Political Dynamics, and the Survival of Disagreement." *Journal of Politics* 64(1): 1–21.

Huckfeldt, R. R., Johnson, P. E., and Sprague, J. D. (2004). *Political Disagreement: The Survival of Diverse Opinions within Communication Networks.* Cambridge, UK: Cambridge University Press.

Huckfeldt, R., and Sprague, J. (1987). "Networks in Context: The Social Flow of Political Information." *American Political Science Review* 81(4): 1197–1216.

Huckfeldt, R., and Sprague, J. (1991). "Discussant Effects on Vote Choice: Intimacy, Structure, and Interdependence." *Journal of Politics* 53(1): 122–158.

Hula, K. W. (1999). *Lobbying Together: Interest Group Coalitions in Legislative Politics.* Washington DC: Georgetown University Press.

Johnson, L., and Amerasinghe, N. (2009). "Protecting the Public International Dispute Settlement: The Amicus Curiae Phenomenon. Center for International Environmental Law. http://www.ciel.org/Publications/Protecting_ACP_Dec09.pdf

Jones, G. T. (2008). "Dynamical Jurisprudence: Law as a Complex System." *Georgia State Law Review* 24(4): 873–883.

Katz, D. M., and Stafford, D. K. (2010). "Hustle and Flow: A Social Network Analysis of the American Federal Judiciary." *Ohio State Law Journal* 71(3):457–509.

Katz, D. M., Stafford, D. K., and Provins, E. A. (2008). "Social Architecture, Judicial Peer Effects and the 'Evolution' of the Law: Toward a Positive Theory of Judicial Social Structure." *Georgia State Law Review* 24(4): 975–1000.

Katz, D. M., Gubler, J. R., Zelner, J., Bommarito, M. J., Provins, E., and Ingall, E. (2011). "Reproduction of Hierarchy? A Social Network Analysis of the American Law Professoriate." *Journal of Legal Education* 61(1): 16–30.

Kawai, R., and Iida, R. (2011). "The Legal Issue Network: Network Analysis of Patent-Related Amicus Briefs at the Court of Appeals for the Federal Circuit." Paper presented at the Annual Conference on Political Networks, Ann Arbor, MI, June 14–18.

Kearney, J. D., and Merrill, T. W. (2000). "The Influence of Amicus Curiae Briefs on the Supreme Court." *University of Pennsylvania Law Review* 148(3): 743–855.

Klein, D., and Morrisroe, D. (1999). "The Prestige and Influence of Individual Judges on the U.S. Courts of Appeals." *Journal of Legal Studies* 28(2): 371–391.

Kleinberg, J. M. (1998). "Authoritative Sources in a Hyperlinked Environment." *Journal of the ACM (JACM)* 46(5): 604–632.

Kochevar, S. (2013). "Amici Curiae in Civil Law Jurisdictions." *Yale Law Journal* 122(6): 1653.

Koger, G., and Victor, J. N. (2009). "The Beltway Network: A Network Analysis of Lobbyists Donations to Members of Congress." Paper presented at the Midwest Political Science Association Meetings in Chicago, IL, April 2–5.

Kok, S., and Domingos, P. (2008). "Extracting Semantic Networks from Text Via Relational Clustering." In *Proceedings of the Nineteenth European Conference on Machine Learning (ECML 2008)*, 624–639.

Kornhauser, L. A., and Sager, L. G. (1993). "The One and the Many: Adjudication in Collegial Courts." *California Law Review* 81(1): 1–59.

Krislov, S. (1963). "The Amicus Curiae Brief: From Friendship to Advocacy." *Yale Law Journal* 72: 694–721.

Kritzer, H. M., and Richards, M. J. (2010). "Taking and Testing Jurisprudential Regimes Seriously: A Response to Lax and Rader." *Journal of Politics* 72(2): 285–288.

Krivitsky, P. N., and Handcock, M. S. (2014). "A Separable Model for Dynamic Networks." *Journal of the Royal Statistical Society: Series B (Statistical Methodology)* 76(1): 29–46.

Krivitsky, P. N., Handcock, M. S., and Morris, M. (2011). "Adjusting for Network Size and Composition Effects in Exponential-Family Random Graph Models." *Statistical Methodology* 8(4): 319–339.

LaPira, T. M., Thomas, H.F., III. (2013). "Just How Many Newt Gingrich's Are There on K Street? Estimating the True Size and Shape of Washington's Revolving Door." Paper presented at the annual meeting of the Midwest Political Science Association, Chicago, IL, April 11.

LaPira, T. M., Thomas, H. F., and Baumgartner, F. R. (2014). "The Two Worlds of Lobbying: Washington Lobbyists in the Core and on the Periphery." *Interest Groups & Advocacy* 3(3): 219–245.

Lazarus, R. J. (2005). *Closed Chambers: The Rise, Fall, and Future of the Modern Supreme Court.* New York: Penguin Books.

Lee, E. G., III. (2005). "Precedent Direction and Compliance: Horizontal Stare Decisis on the U.S. Court of Appeals for the Sixth Circuit." *Seton Hall Circuit Review* 1(1): 5–26.

Leifeld, Philip, Skyler J. Cranmer and Bruce A. Desmarais. (2016). "Temporal Exponential Random Graph Models with btergm: Estimation and Bootstrap Confidence Intervals." Working Paper.

Leiter, B. (1999). "Legal Realism." In *The Philosophy of Law: An Encyclopedia*, edited by C. B. Gray, pp. 720–725. New York: Garland.

Levi, E. H. (1949). *An Introduction to Legal Reasoning*. Chicago: University of Chicago Press.

Levine, E. (2011). "Amicus Curiae in International Investment Arbitration: The Implications of an Increase in Third-Party Participation." *Berkeley Journal of International Law* 29(1): 200–225.

Lupu, Y., and Fowler,J. H. (2013). "Strategic Citations to Precedent on the US Supreme Court." *Journal of Legal Studies* 42(1): 151–186.

Lupu, Y., and Voeten, E. (2012). "Precedent in International Courts: A Network Analysis of Case Citations by the European Court of Human Rights." *British Journal of Political Science* 42(2): 413–439.

Maltzman, F., and Wahlbeck, P. J. (1996). "Strategic Policy Considerations and Voting Fluidity on the Burger Court." *American Political Science Review* 90(3): 581–592.

McGuire, K. T. (1993). "Repeat Players in the Supreme Court: The Role of Experienced Lawyers in Litigation Success." *Journal of Politics* 57(1): 187–196.

Mott, R. L. (1936). "Judicial Influence." *American Political Science Review* 30(2): 295–315.

Mutz, D. C., and Mondak, J. J. (2006). "The Workplace as a Context for Cross-Cutting Political Discourse." *Journal of Politics* 68(1): 140–155.

Peng, L., Carvalho, L., Christenson, D. P., Box-Steffensmeier, J. M. (2015). Bayesian Group-Corrected Stochastic Blockmodels for Communicty Detection in Amicus Curiae Networks." Working Paper.

Peppers, T. C. (2006). *Courtiers of the Marble Palace: The Rise and Influence of the Supreme Court Law Clerk*. Stanford, CA: Stanford University Press.

Post, D. G., and Eisen, M. B. (2000). "How Long Is the Coastline of Law? Thoughts on the Fractal Nature of Legal Systems." *Journal of Legal Studies* 29(2): 545–584.

Priest, G. L. (2003). "Reexamining the Market for Judicial Clerks and Other Assortative Matching Markets." Yale Law and Economics Research Paper No. 286.

Richards, M. J., and Kritzer, H. M. (2002). "Jurisprudential Regimes in Supreme Court Decision Making." *American Political Science Review* 96(2): 305–320.

Rohde, D. W., and Spaeth, H. J. (1976). *Supreme Court Decision Making*. San Francisco: W.H. Freeman.

Salter-Townshend, M., & Murphy, T. B. (2015). Role analysis in networks using mixtures of exponential random graph models. *Journal of Computational and Graphical Statistics* 24(2): 520–538.

Scott, J. C. (2007). "The Social Embeddedness of Lobbying." Paper presented at the Annual Meeting of the American Political Science Association, Chicago, IL, August 30–September 2.

Segal, J. A., and Spaeth, H. J. (1993). *The Supreme Court and the Attitudinal Model*. New York: Cambridge University Press.

Segal, J. A., and Spaeth, H. J. (2002). *The Supreme Court and the Attitudinal Model Revisited*. Cambridge University Press.

Shelton, D. (1994). "The Participation of Nongovernmental Organizations in International Judicial Proceedings." *American Journal of International Law* 88(4): 611–642.

Slaughter, A.-M. (2004). *A New World Order*. Washington, DC: Brookings Institution Press.

Snijders, T. A. B. (2001). "The Statistical Evaluation of Social Network Dynamics." *Sociological Methodology* 31(1): 361–395.

Snijders, T. A. B. (2005). "Models for Longitudinal Network Data." *Models and Methods in Social Network Analysis* 1: 215–247.

Snijders, T. A. B., Van de Bunt, G. G., and Steglich, C. E. G. (2010). "Introduction to Stochastic Actor-Based Models for Network Dynamics." *Social Networks* 32(1): 44–60.

Spaeth, H. J. (1979). *Supreme Court Policy Making: Explanation and Prediction*. San Francisco: W.H. Freeman.

Wald, P. M. (1990). "Selecting Law Clerks." *Michigan Law Review* 89(1990–1991): 152–163.

Ward, A., and Weiden, D. L. (2006). *Sorcerers' Apprentices: 100 Years of Law Clerks at the United States Supreme Court*. New York: New York University Press.

Wasby, S. L. (1995). *Race Relations Litigation in an Age of Complexity*. Charlottesville: University of Virginia Press.

Wasserman, S., and Faust, K. (1994). *Social Network Analysis: Methods and Applications*. New York: Cambridge University Press.

....

CHAPTER 21

DISCUSSION NETWORKS

....

SCOTT D. McCLURG, CASEY A. KLOFSTAD, AND
ANAND EDWARD SOKHEY

INTRODUCTION

....

A takeaway message of this handbook might be summarized as "Networks matter in politics." If that is the case, then a takeaway message of this chapter might be "Networks matter in politics at multiple levels of analysis." Most of the chapters in this volume focus on what we would call the "whole network" approach, which entails measurement of social ties and analysis of their resultant structures, all in order to understand political phenomena. Here we concern ourselves with another tradition that is generally not centered on larger structures; it is more focused on (1) "egocentric" networks[1]—that is, the small group of individuals to which a person is (often closely) connected—and (2) the impacts of such networks on individuals' attitudes and behaviors. Because the unit of analysis (usually individuals rather than whole networks, network components, or network ties) is different here, the problems, theories, and questions addressed in this area of research also tend to be different.

The principal concerns of this research tradition have generally been organized around two points. First, work in this vein argues that individuals' political choices are a product of both their own traits and their surroundings (e.g., Huckfeldt and Sprague, 1987, 1988). While it is still presumed that individuals have agency in their political choices, this perspective assumes that information is constrained by social context. Those constraints can come from a number of sources, such as institutions and laws. However, what is of most interest to us is that they can also come from the social networks in which people are embedded.

Second, work in this tradition has tended to assume that observed network influences are indeed causal (a concern we return to in subsequent sections). Given such a perspective, researchers have considered the micro-social processes that explain how networks shape individual political behavior. While some research has considered the role of social norms, most has focused on the role of communication of political information. This has led to research on the content of discussions, such as whether discussion partners tend to agree or disagree with each other about issues, candidates, and the like.

While we can discuss egocentric networks solely as a theoretical issue,[2] this approach to studying political phenomena is motivated by important substantive and normative questions. For example, it is often remarked that political science's core concept is power—something that is developed and exercised as people struggle with others over political goods like policy outcomes. We note that such a struggle can only be understood in the context of people interacting with each other. Thus, networks are not just an intuitive and useful tool for understanding such processes, but almost a necessity.

More specific to the egocentric (or "egonet") approach are questions about how political discussion affects political decisions (e.g., Sokhey and McClurg, 2012). Mutz and Martin (2001) note that "[e]xposure to dissimilar views has been deemed a central element—if not the sine qua non—of the kind of political dialogue that is needed to maintain a democratic citizenry" (97). This quote is a helpful starting point in a review of the research on political discussion, as it acknowledges the normative roots (e.g., Gutmann and Thompson, 1996; Habermas, 1989) of studies of interpersonal interaction. This in turn focuses our attention on the extent to which one's politics is intertwined with those of others in complicated ways.

In this chapter we begin by tracing the development of political network research on the masses, a tradition largely formed around the study of elections in the United States, which now covers myriad topics, including vote choice, opinion formation and persuasion, and political participation (among other outcomes of interest). We then focus on how scholars have captured person-to-person political discussion through the implementation of "egocentric" network name generator techniques (i.e., as opposed to the "whole"/complete-graph data commonly used in other network studies). Next we outline a series of challenges to this research paradigm that involve questions of (1) causal inference, (2) measurement, and (3) mechanisms of influence. Finally, we conclude by reviewing some promising answers to these challenges and propose some next steps for this research agenda.

History

Although the foundations of the egocentric network tradition are well documented (for helpful reviews, see Huckfeldt and Sprague, 1993, 1995; Mutz, 2006; Sokhey and Djupe, 2011; Zuckerman, 2005), a brief review helps elucidate subsequent directions and the current state of this area of inquiry. This line of scholarship traces its origins to the seminal works of the Columbia school of political behavior (e.g., Berelson et al., 1954; Lazarsfeld et al., 1944). The Columbia researchers popularized the study of mass communication and helped advance the use of survey research techniques for studying opinion dynamics. Although they did not study networks in the same way that later scholars would conceptualize and operationalize them, they were notable for pushing a vision of relational politics; they used measures of demographic characteristics and group identities to study the role of social pressures/social interactions in explaining voting behavior. Simply put, their work provided the foundation for modern research on networks by suggesting that groups affect political behavior through interpersonal connections.

The American Voter (Campbell et al., 1960)—and the concomitant rise of the more individualistic, social-psychological approach of the Michigan school—relegated queries into the "social logic of politics" (Zuckerman, 2005) to the back pages of journals for several decades. Although scholars continued to study the social foundations of political behavior during this time,[3] that research tended to focus more on the role of social context (e.g., Huckfeldt, 1979, 1983; MacKuen and Brown, 1987; Putnam, 1966), rather than on explicit patterns of interaction and discussion taking place in interpersonal networks. This distinction is important, as networks and contexts are overlapping and interdependent, but are by no means equivalent concepts (e.g., Huckfeldt and Sprague, 1995; McClurg, 2006a, b, 2011).

Fortunately, by the 1980s scholars had not only firmly refocused their attention on the social components of political behavior, but had also drawn clearer distinctions between these ideas. Indeed, important breakthroughs for political network research occurred in the efforts of Huckfeldt and Sprague (e.g., Huckfeldt, 1979, 1983; Huckfeldt and Sprague, 1987, 1988, 1995; Sprague, 1976), whose examinations of communities produced a series of major contributions that set the stage for contemporary research on discussion networks.[4] First, these scholars found a relationship between network formation (i.e., discussant selection) and social context (i.e., the supply of possible discussion partners in an environment). Second, they demonstrated that political preferences communicated via discussion networks were related to observed variance in political behavior. Third—and as we detail in the following section—they adapted the name generator methodology developed by sociologists for use in political science. This method has become the standard for collecting data on interpersonal political discussion and consequently is an essential component of the discussion network literature's past, present, and future.

The transition and dialogue between these areas of inquiry define the contemporary study of political networks using egocentric data. From the Columbia school came an interest in communication, particularly in the character of discussion. Contextual research then sustained the field by providing evidence that political behaviors were strongly related to local patterns (e.g., the number of people in an area with certain traits), rather than just those things specific to an individual (e.g., a person's age). Finally, the scholarship of Huckfeldt and Sprague demonstrated that context and networks were related—but distinct—concepts. This last step was crucial, for it connected discussion in networks to contexts (whether defined in terms of organizations or geographic boundaries), all while incorporating other behavioral variables.

NAME GENERATORS AND
THE MEASUREMENT OF INTERPERSONAL
NETWORKS

Much of what social scientists have learned about political discussion networks has come from "name generator" batteries embedded in public opinion studies (for a review, see Sokhey and Djupe, 2014). In line with the Michigan school, early social surveys such as the American National Election Study (ANES) were largely focused on studying the influence of individual-level characteristics on political behavior, such as income, education, and partisanship (e.g., Campbell et al., 1960). However, starting in the 1970s sociologists began pushing to add measures of social context to nationally representative surveys (e.g., Laumann, 1973; McCallister and Fischer, 1978; Fischer, 1982; Burt, 1984, 1985). In 1985 a standard set of discussion network questions based on interaction was adopted by sociologists for inclusion in the General Social Survey (GSS). More specifically, respondents were asked the following:

> From time to time, most people discuss important matters with other people. Looking back over the last six months—who are the people with whom you discussed matters important to you. Just tell me their first names or initials.
>
> (Burt, 1985, 119)

After completing this roster of discussants (or "alters"), the respondent was then prompted to provide information on each of these individuals (e.g., demographics, how often they discuss politics, and the like). The result of this and similar procedures used since is data on a subsample of an individual's larger (i.e., "global") social network (Marin and Hampton, 2007), which is often comprised of social intimates who might be considered a person's "core" network of alters (Marsden, 1987). Reports by respondents on their alters are commonly referred to as "egocentric" network data structures. Unlike whole network studies, information on the structure of an individual's entire social network is generally not obtained using name generator techniques. Instead, this approach is used to collect more detailed information on a smaller subset of the person's broader social network.[5]

In their 1984 South Bend Study, Huckfeldt and Sprague (1985, 1987, 1988, 1995) adapted this methodology for studying political discussion networks during that year's presidential election. Specifically, they designed a "compound" name generator (Sokhey and Djupe, 2014) that combined approaches based on interaction, exchange, and role:

> We are interested in the sort of political information and opinions people get from each other. Can you give me the FIRST names of the three people you talked with most about the events of the past election cycle? These people might be from your family, from work, from the neighborhood, from church, from some other organization you belong to, or they might be from somewhere else.

Since its inception, many have followed Huckfeldt and Sprague's (e.g., 1995: 105) lead in using political name generators; variants of this wording have been used in studies affiliated with the ANES.

While the two main approaches to the name generator procedure described above might appear to capture information on different types of social networks, Klofstad et al. (2009) show that the types of discussants generated by the "important matters" and "political matters" question wordings are largely comparable. That is, they find that we discuss politics with the same type of people with whom we discuss other important matters: our "core" network of family, friends, and acquaintances (also see Huckfeldt and Sprague, 1995; Mutz, 2002a; Walsh, 2004; McClurg, 2006a). In a series of question wording survey experiments conducted with political name generators, Sokhey and Djupe (2014) reinforce this finding with respect to the political name approach. More specifically, they find that the standard "compound" political name generator generally performs well when it comes to sampling individuals' political networks.

One concern that has been raised about these types of generators involves measurement validity. For example, in a now famous piece, Bearman and Parigi (2004) examine what constitutes "important matters" to respondents. Their inquiries revealed apparently trivial conversational topics such as "cloning headless frogs." Likewise, Sokhey and Djupe (2014) find evidence that the egocentric networks generated by political name generators often underreport disagreement about politics. When individuals are asked to generate names based on disagreeable interactions, they produce more disagreeable discussants than when the standard compound political network generator is used. Accordingly, Sokhey and Djupe suggest that researchers may want to consider using specific prompts to increase measurement validity and avoid problems with generation commands that allow respondents to report WIMTY, or "whatever it means to you" (Moore, 2004).[6]

CHALLENGES TO THE RESEARCH PARADIGM

As noted previously, egocentric political discussion network studies (i.e., studies incorporating data resulting from the name generator methodologies) have added—and continue to add—much to our understanding of how interpersonal interactions influence political behavior. However, there are several challenges to this line of research, all of which should be considered by scholars analyzing existing data or designing similar studies.

Questions of Causality

The first challenge is identifying causal effects. Because they are time-consuming for respondents to complete, network batteries have rarely been included in multiple waves of longitudinal surveys. And more often than not, information on network discussion items has been collected in a cross-section and at the same time as the political outcome of interest (e.g., a vote in an election). This standard research design, combined with other factors, poses problems for making causal inferences.

One of the main arguments made by network scholars studying political behavior is that exposure to political discussion leads individuals to become more active in politics (e.g., Campbell and Wolbrecht, 2006; Huckfeldt and Sprague, 1991, 1995; Huckfeldt et al., 1995; Kenny, 1992, 1994; Klofstad, 2007, 2009, 2010, 2011; Lake and Huckfeldt, 1998; McClurg, 2003, 2004; Mutz, 2002a; Rolfe, 2012; Sinclair, 2012; Zuckerman, 2005).[7] But while this argument is relatively straightforward—and correlations in survey data support it—demonstrating causal effects of political discussion is challenging for three reasons: (1) rather than discussion leading to participation, participating in politics may cause one to talk about politics (i.e., reciprocal causation); (2) individuals who choose to be politically active might also choose to associate with people who are also politically active and thus interested in talking about politics (i.e., selection bias or homophily); and (3) a factor that has yet to be accounted for, or that cannot be accounted for, may explain the relationship between discussion and participation (i.e., endogeneity or omitted variable bias). In the context of the present example, the question is whether the relationship between political discussion and political participation is spurious (e.g., Klofstad 2011; Laver, 2005; Lazer et al., 2010). More generally, these problems of reciprocal causation, selection bias/homophily, and endogeneity/omitted variable bias always pose challenges for researchers studying political discussion networks and social influence processes.

Debates over Conceptualization and Measurement of the Content of Communication in Networks

Building on the name generator approach, existing research on discussion networks has tended to emphasize communication (as interaction is central to the typical, "compound" prompt). Accordingly, a natural question to ask is: "What are the salient characteristics of discussions in networks?" Previous research has tended to focus on two concepts: political disagreement and political sophistication. More specifically, in the context of discussion networks scholars have generally been interested in the degree to which egos are exposed to different political preferences and different levels of political expertise via their named alters.

Following the lead of Huckfeldt and Sprague (e.g., 1987, 1995), there has been a great deal of interest in the field on interpersonal political disagreement. That is, do Democrats (Republicans) talk politics with Republicans (Democrats), and if so, what are the consequences? There is an ongoing debate in the literature over the extent to which individuals are exposed to disagreement and over the effect that exposure to dissonant points of view has on political discussants. While some scholars focus on the fact that many of us choose to surround ourselves with like-minded discussants (e.g., Mutz, 2006), others make the case that it is also rare for a person to not be exposed to at least some dissonant points of view in his or her social network (Huckfeldt et al., 2004). Further, Mutz's work (2002a, 2002b, 2006) suggests that while disagreement leads to better understanding of other viewpoints and higher levels of political tolerance, it simultaneously leads to lower levels of political participation through the dual mechanisms of social accountability pressures and ambivalence. Taken together, these findings stand as a bit of a "democratic dilemma," one that pits models of deliberative and participatory democracy against one another and that continues to stimulate further research as scholars attempt to figure out the role that political discussion networks play in our understanding of how democracy works.

Most research following Mutz (2002a, 2002b, 2006) has generally qualified her rather stark conclusions regarding disagreement, tolerance, and political participation. On the one hand, it has been suggested that the negative effects of disagreement on political participation are sometimes overstated or even nonexistent (Djupe et al., 2007; Huckfeldt et al., 2004; Klofstad et al., 2013; McClurg, 2006a; Nir, 2005; Noelle-Neumann, 1993). For example, Klofstad et al. (2013) suggest that this debate over the effect of exposure to disagreeable points of view is predicated on how the concept is measured. Using data from the 2008–2009 ANES Panel Study, they find that respondents' general perceptions of how disagreeable the members of their social network are negatively correlated with the frequency of political discussion in the network. In contrast, the relationship between disagreement over partisan identification in the network and political discussion in the network is statistically insignificant.

On the other hand, a growing body of research on political disagreement also points to heterogeneity and conditionality in terms of individual predispositions. A common argument is that individuals' psychological traits limit the impact of disagreement for many people and that they may, for those who enjoy conflict, actually encourage political engagement (Bloom and Levitan, 2011; Bloom and Bango-Moldavsky, 2014; Gerber et al., 2012; Klar, 2014; Lyons et al., 2016; Lyons and Sokhey, 2014; Parsons, 2010; Testa et al., 2014). Other research focuses on the network conditions that affect how and when disagreement demobilizes political engagement. Here some studies suggest that disagreement is only harmful when all alters are disagreeable (Bello, 2012; Nir, 2011; McClurg, 2006b). And a variant of network-based arguments examines different types of groups, usually focusing on those defined by ascribed traits such as sex (Djupe and Calfano, 2012; Quintelier et al., 2012; Osborn and Morehouse Mendez, 2011; Morehouse Mendez and Osborn, 2010; Lyons, 2011), or different types of social contexts, such as the workplace (Mutz and Mondak, 2006; Brundidge, 2010; Fitzgerald and Curtis, 2012).

Another area of inquiry has focused on the extent to which political discussion networks serve as a source of political expertise. Socially supplied political expertise is defined as information relevant to politics held by alters that could be shared with an ego. Huckfeldt (2001) studied egos' perceptions of their alters' political knowledge using the 1996 Indianapolis-St. Louis study and found that individuals were able to reliably identify the experts in their networks. McClurg (2006a) argued that social expertise is important for motivating political participation, and more specifically, that it potentially counters the negative impact of disagreement. More recently, through a series of laboratory experiments, Ahn and colleagues have provided insights into the social dynamics and aggregate consequences of socially supplied expertise (e.g., Ahn et al. 2010; Ahn et al., 2013; Ahn, Huckfeldt, and Ryan 2014; Ahn and Ryan, 2015). Among other findings, their research suggests that network-based expertise may not always be a good thing, as it can potentially lead citizens away from their own true preferences.

Unfortunately, with the notable exception of these laboratory experiments, there have been fewer extensions of political expertise relative to work on political disagreement. For example, Leighley and Matsubayashi (2009) look at differences in social expertise among different ethnic groups, while Sokhey and Djupe (2014) and Djupe et al. (2016) touch on gender differences. However, considerably more research is needed on what constitutes political expertise, its conditionality, and how it matters for different types of civic and political activities.

Debates over Mechanisms of Influence

A third challenge involves the question of how discussion networks influence political outcomes such as opinion formation, vote choice, and political participation. This point is motivated by two challenges already discussed: concerns about causality and questions about the roles played by the communication of disagreement and expertise. Recognizing that networks can cause behaviors (despite inferential hurdles)—and that there are strong observed relationships between discussion networks and conversational content—provokes questions about underlying models of social influence. While mechanisms are at the heart of social science (e.g., Falleti and Lynch, 2009), this question has received less attention or has too often been assumed away.

In part, mechanisms have likely been understudied because of the aforementioned concerns about causality. However, the field's lack of focus on this point surely also reflects problems involving conceptualization—most notably, the absence of a clear definition for what might be called "socially supplied (political) information." That is, exactly what is it that people are taking away from their political discussion networks? The default in the interpersonal influence literature has been to define content obtained in terms of information about others' political opinions about issues, or their preferences concerning candidates. Such an approach blends early communication and rational choice theories. For example, McPhee et al. (1963) provided an elegant model of social communication: when confronted by new political information, people "check" their initial opinions against their network partners'. Such a process of social interaction and feedback emerges as the mechanism by which networks provide information that then comes to influence political behavior. Downs (1957) helps explain why such information has an impact: because it is rational for individuals to draw upon their associates when making a political decision versus paying the cognitive and other potential costs of solely informing themselves. In this sense, networks are heuristics that are grounded in the political preferences of network members (see also Huckfeldt and Sprague, 1995).

This information-based model of social influence is consistent with a great deal of research. Most notably, it underlies the research on disagreement summarized previously (though not for the purposes of explaining the micro-foundations of said work). Of perhaps more direct interest, however, is research that demonstrates how and when the political preferences in a network affect decisions, or put differently, when it is that exposure to discussion translates into influence. Some work indicates that the influence of alters' preferences depends on how clearly egos perceive them (Huckfeldt et al. 1999, 2000, 2002). This theory has received some support from experimental studies. For example, the behavioral economic experiments of Huckfeldt, Ahn, and colleagues explore the confluence of incentives and (biased) social information on the quality of individuals' decision-making (e.g., Ahn et al., 2014; Ryan 2011, 2013).

Despite the utility of such approaches, there are indications that such ways of thinking about social influence have limits with respect to the mass public and may in fact be inadequate when it comes to explaining some behaviors. Recent treatments have speculated that there may be several potential routes through which networks exert influence on individuals (for discussions of different possible mechanisms, see, e.g., Rolfe, 2012; Sinclair, 2012). As scholars continue to give attention to these questions, we suggest organizing approaches to this line of research into two broad camps and using labels that clarify the mechanism tying socially supplied information to individual political behavior. On the one hand, "learning models" (much of what we describe above) focus on explicit information exchange; the idea is that information can change choices and behaviors, and that individuals are influenced by the network providing such resources via interpersonal interaction. On the other hand, "information shortcut models" need not involve explicit interaction processes. Rather, an individual may perceive the network and adjust his or her behavior in response (something more akin to receiving cues or picking up norms). Specific categorizations aside, the more important point is that additional work is needed on this front, and we encourage scholars to continue to theorize carefully and to design their research in ways that can parse mechanisms effectively.

AN AGENDA FOR POLITICAL DISCUSSION RESEARCH

The previous sections note the historical development and current state of the literature on political discussion networks. But where are things headed next? In this penultimate section we speculate on the future of the field, offering some thoughts on the topics and ideas that are growing and/or that we think are particularly important. We organize this discussion into three broad sections: methodology, theory, and data.

Advancing Methodology

We have pointed out several challenges facing research on political discussion. Fortunately these problems have produced a variety of methodological responses and design innovations. Notably, a growing number of studies make use of experimental methods to demonstrate evidence of causal effects, and we expect this trend to continue. For example, laboratory experiments have found evidence that political discussion partners influence each other's preferences (e.g., Klar, 2014; Visser and Mirabile, 2004). Large-scale "get out the vote" (GOTV) field experiments (for a summary, see Gerber and Green, 2012) show that individuals who are recruited to vote also influence the other members of their household to vote (e.g., Nickerson, 2008), presumably through political discussion precipitated by GOTV treatments (Sinclair, 2012). Quasi-experimental designs (e.g., Klofstad, 2011) have leveraged natural instances of random assignment to social settings (e.g., college dormitory roommates) to help identify causal effects from exposure to political discussion. Random assignment, of course, helps to address the threats to inference we discussed in previous sections.

While not experimental in nature, panel surveys (e.g., ANES 2009; Lazer et al., 2010) allow for temporal separation between the measurement of cause (i.e., political discussion) and effect (i.e., political behavior); this increases the validity of causal inferences and allows researchers to consider changes in the network alongside the observation of the outcome of interest (e.g., Sokhey et al., 2015).

Advancing Theory

Although extant research on disagreement and expertise represents a significant step forward in understanding the content of communication in political discussion networks, there are (at least) three clear questions that should guide development of discussion network theory going forward. First (and as mentioned previously), there has been little attention given to basic/underlying concepts. Klofstad et al. (2013) make this point in comparing two different observational measures of disagreement within a single data set; they find that otherwise identical specifications yield different results across multiple dependent variables. Their results suggest that disagreement is not a simple, one-dimensional concept, and that more theory is needed on what types of interpersonal political disagreements should be connected to different political behaviors of interest. The same observation could be made about the other concepts that we have discussed (e.g., political expertise), as well as those that we have not but that hold a significant place in the history and development of network analysis in the social sciences (e.g., multiplex social ties, different types of social relationships, and the like). Our take on previous research is that there has simply been too little attention given to definitions. Without better consensus about objects of study—for example, what constitutes a meaningful ego-alter link—it will be difficult to fully understand the implications of current results for theories and hypotheses.

A second issue also pertains to theory and measurement. Most of the aforementioned research tends to be concerned with broad measures of disagreement and expertise. However, these represent only a very narrow band of the total range of possibilities when it comes to interpersonal interaction. For example, there is relatively little work that examines the differences between an ego's perceptions of the network and the actual information being exchanged between egos and alters (Eveland and Kleinman, 2011; Huckfeldt and Sprague, 1995). Moreover, researchers have been constrained by fairly nonspecific pieces of information collected in social surveys, such as "the number of Democrats in the network." Such broad definitions potentially miss important aspects of communication and therefore fail to fully capture the complete range of effects that discussion networks have on behavior. For example, some Democrats disagree with some Democrats, and some Republicans with other Republicans. However, the nature of those intra-party disagreements may not have the same character or behavior effects as cross-party disagreements. To the extent that we want to better understand the roles that discussion networks play in democratic politics, such issues are of utmost importance.

One last observation is that only minimal attention has been given to structural considerations, even as parts of the core conceptual vocabulary have been borrowed from work on full network data. With a few exceptions (e.g., Huckfeldt et al., 2005; Lazer et al., 2010; Eveland and Hively, 2009), the field has not included structural characteristics in thinking about the information contained in—and consequences of—political discussions. While this is understandable given the trade-offs and limitations imposed by name generator methods, it is unfortunate given the volumes of full social network analysis theory on network structure and the roles that such structures play in explaining the messages (not) heard by members of the mass public.

Advancing Discussion Network Data

A final important area for future research involves thinking seriously about the array of data used in the field. When we say this we are referring not just to methodological issues or research designs, but to different types of data that could enrich our understanding of discussion networks. Here an obvious candidate would be the incorporation of digital discussion. Most of the data that we have referenced up to this point have come from surveys or experiments focused on face-to-face interactions (even if much of the information contains only main-respondent reports on networks). However, an obvious point is that many of the mass public's discussions take place online, via computers, smartphones, and other electronic platforms. While there is a rich literature on computer-mediated communication (e.g., Walther, 1996), less attention has been given to the overlap with interpersonal discussion of politics (though see, e.g., Bond et al., 2012; Brundidge, 2010; Gonzalez-Bailon, Kaltenbrunner, and Banchs, 2010; Valenzuela, Kim, and Gil de Zuniga, 2012). Exploring these kinds of data could lead to a number of interesting questions: Are online versus in-person interactions in competition? Is the social information that people acquire offline more diverse than that which they acquire online? Are people more active in searching for political information when they interact online? Though some potential answers to these questions are emerging, there is clearly much work to be done.

Another way to improve practice through attention to data would be for scholars to give more consideration to the overlap between networks and contexts. Although we intend to apply this comment to all different types of contexts (e.g., organizations, communities, time periods, etc.), we especially wish to highlight countries. From our point of view, there has been an artificial boundary between American studies and similar research done in other countries. Perhaps this simply reflects the organization of fields in political science or the fact that many political behavior literatures developed primarily in the United States. Whatever the cause, this is a missed opportunity. For example, what is the role of disagreement in multiparty systems? The logic of voting in such systems is different, but is the role of discussion networks as well? Some work has considered these questions (e.g., see Wolf et al., 2010, for discussions), but the findings have generally not entered back into the America literature, which in turn has slowed broader theoretical development. The same logic (and critique) could be extended to consider things such as historical legacy and political culture.

Conclusion

Political discussion is an essential part of democratic politics, and egocentric approaches to the study of mass behavior are important, whether viewed from empirical or theoretical angles. On the empirical side, the techniques we have discussed in this chapter are uniquely tailored to the (difficult, but worthwhile) objective of studying the constant influence that individuals have on each other through their daily interactions. With regard to theory, it is clear that citizens' social context matters a great deal to their politics, and one's immediate network of social intimates is arguably the most influential component of that context. If we are to have a full understanding of how politics works, we must adopt a relational perspective, and that means considering roles played by micro-social processes.

Keeping this in mind, we conclude by returning to some brief comments we made at the outset about how the present research agenda fits into the bigger picture of the handbook. Our chapter represents perhaps one of the broadest takes on the idea of political networks, for the questions are almost entirely driven by individual outcomes, and the methods are often based on random population surveys or experiments. Methodologically, then, the study of discussion networks actually looks more like the rest of the discipline of political science: measures are probed for their content rather than what they say about network structure. Theory-wise, the literature we have reviewed is less about the whole network than it is about how individuals benefit (or are constrained) by their local connections. Still, we argue that this work fits well with the other chapters and is perhaps most illuminating when viewed against them (young researchers interested in studying political communication and social influence should be mindful of this point). The scholarship of this volume argues that networks matter in politics, which is to say that it shares a common interest in understanding how individual units combine in complicated ways. Tackling such a topic requires attention not only to aggregate outcomes and middle-level network structures, but also to microprocesses, and that is where this chapter comes into play.

In our view, there has not been enough attention given to combining the insights gleaned from different levels of analysis and from different approaches. This can be seen, for example, in the paucity of work that combines traditional network measures (i.e., that are typical of whole/complete network data) with detailed measures of interaction (i.e., that have seen more progress on the egocentric data side). Methodological advances suggest one way forward, as the use of sophisticated statistical models (e.g., exponential random graph model techniques) points to estimation and interpretation strategies that effectively combine individual and structural characteristics. On the other side of things, the research highlighted in this chapter could be used to seed theoretical models that help scholars explore society-wide processes of aggregation (e.g., Fowler, 2006). Indeed, understanding the aggregate implications of individual findings—like those summarized here—should stimulate more questions, and ultimately advances, at both levels. As work on political discussion networks continues to mature alongside the more general study of political networks, we anticipate that the advances in data and methodology on both sides will yield more unity in our theories of social influence.

Notes

1. This can also be thought of as the portion of the larger graph/network to which a person is directly connected—thus, ego-nets are sometimes called "personal" or "neighborhood" networks (e.g., Borgatti et al., 2013).
2. Specifically, we might think of egocentric techniques as "bottom-up"—or more micro—perspectives on/approaches to the study of networks (Hanneman and Riddle, 2005).
3. A number of these works drew inspiration from Key's (e.g., 1949) seminal examinations of local politics and political context.
4. Early study sites included Buffalo, New York (e.g., Huckfeldt, 1986) and South Bend, Indiana (e.g., Huckfeldt and Sprague, 1987, 1988, 1995).
5. Because all observations on the network are tied to a main respondent, such data have a familiar structure; as is the case for typical survey data, analysis is often conducted using general purpose software such as SPSS, R, or Stata. Routines for calculating ego-network measures within whole network data (i.e., for focusing on specific nodes' networks within the larger graph) are available in specialized software packages such as UCINET (Borgatti et al. 2002) and embedded in popular R network analysis packages such as "statnet" (Handcock et al., 2003).
6. Such prompts could also address concerns over the potential overreporting of *the absence* of core networks (i.e., having zero discussants), a subject of ongoing debate in light of McPherson et al.'s (2006) claim that Americans' core discussion networks have decreased in size over the past twenty-five years (for a rebuttal, see Fischer, 2009).

7. A number of mechanisms are thought to underlie the relationship between discussion and participation: discussants transfer information about politics to each other (Downs, 1957; McClurg, 2003), increase each other's civic engagement (Klofstad 2007, 2011), and mobilize each other to engage in political activities (Klofstad, 2007, 2011; Rolfe, 2012). Questions of mechanisms are discussed more fully in a subsequent section of this chapter.

References

Ahn, T., Huckfeldt, R., and Ryan, J. (2010). "Communication, Influence, and Informational Asymmetries among Voters." *Political Psychology* 31: 763–787.

Ahn, T., Huckfeldt, R., Mayer, A., and Ryan, J. (2013). "Expertise and Bias in Political Communication Networks." *American Journal of Political Science* 57: 357–373.

Ahn, T. K., Huckfeldt, R., and Ryan, J. B. (2014). *Experts, Activists, and Interdependent Citizens: Are Electorates Self-Educating?* Cambridge, UK: Cambridge University Press.

Ahn, T., and Ryan, J. (2015). "The Overvaluing of Expertise in Discussion Partner Choice." *Journal of Theoretical Politics* 27(3): 380–400.

American National Election Study (ANES). (2009). Advance Release of the 2008–2009 ANES Panel Study Dataset. www.electionstudies.org.

Bearman, P, and Parigi, P. (2004). "Cloning Headless Frogs and Other Important Matters: Conversation Topics and Network Structure." *Social Forces* 83: 535–557.

Bello, J. (2012). "The Dark Side of Disagreement? Revisiting the Effect of Disagreement on Political Participation." *Electoral Studies* 31: 782–795.

Berelson, B., Lazarsfeld, P., and McPhee, W. (1954). *Voting.* Chicago: Chicago University Press.

Bloom, P., and Bagno-Moldavsky, O. (2014). "The Conditional Effect of Network Diversity and Values on Tolerance." *Political Behavior* (August 10): doi: 10.1007/s11109-014-9284-2.

Bloom, P., and Levitan, J. (2011). "We're Closer Than I Thought: Social Network Heterogeneity, Morality, and Political Persuasion." *Political Psychology* 32: 643–665.

Bond, R. M., Fariss, C., Jones, J., Kramer, A. Marlow, C., Settle, J., and Fowler, J. (2012). "A 61-Million Person Experiment in Social Influence and Political Mobilization." *Nature* 489: 295–298.

Borgatti, S. P., Everett, M. G., and Freeman, L. C. (2002). *UCINET for Windows: Software for Social Network Analysis.* Harvard, MA: Analytic Technologies.

Borgatti, S., Everett, M., and Johnson, J. (2013). *Analyzing Social Networks.* London: Sage.

Brundidge, J. (2010). "Encountering 'Difference' in the Contemporary Public Sphere: The Contribution of the Internet to the Heterogeneity of Political Discussion Networks." *Journal of Communication* 60: 680–700.

Burt, R. S. (1984). "Network Items and the General Social Survey." *Social Networks* 6: 293–339.

Burt, R. S. (1985). "General Social Survey Network Items." *Connections* 8: 119–123.

Campbell, A., Converse, P. E., Miller, W. E., and Stokes, D. E. (1960). *The American Voter.* New York: Wiley.

Campbell, D. E., and Wolbrecht, C. (2006). "See Jane Run: Women Politicians as Role Models for Adolescents." *Journal of Politics* 68: 233–247.

Djupe, P., and Calfano, B. (2012). "American Muslim Investment in Civil Society: Political Discussion, Disagreement, and Tolerance." *Political Research Quarterly* 65: 516–528.

Djupe, P., McClurg, S., and Sokhey, A. E. (2016). "The Political Consequences of Gender in Social Networks." *British Journal of Political Science.* Online First View: 1–22.

Djupe, P. A., Sokhey, A. E., and Gilbert, C. P. (2007). "Presented but Not Accounted For? Gender Differences in Civic Resource Acquisition." *American Journal of Political Science* 51: 906–920.

Downs, A. (1957). *An Economic Theory of Democracy*. New York: Harper and Row.

Eveland, W. and Hively, M. H. (2009). "Political Discussion Frequency, Network Size and 'Heterogeneity' of Disvcussion as Predictors of Political Knowledge and Participation." *Journal of Communication* 59(2): 205–224.

Eveland, W., Jr., and Kleinman, S. (2011). "Comparing General and Political Discussion Networks Within Voluntary Organizations Using Social Network Analysis." *Political Behavior* 35: 65–87.

Falleti, T., and Lynch, J. (2009). "Context and Causal Mechanisms in Political Analysis." *Comparative Political Studies* 42(9): 1143–1166.

Fischer, C. (1982). *To Dwell among Friends*. Chicago: University of Chicago Press.

Fischer, C. (2009). "The 2004 GSS Finding of Shrunken Networks: An Artifact?" *American Sociological Review*. 74: 657–669.

Fitzgerald, J., and Curtis, K. (2012). "Partisan Discord in the Family and Political Engagement: A Comparative Behavioral Analysis." *Journal of Politics* 74: 129–141.

Fowler, J. (2006). "Turnout in a Small World." In *The Social Logic of Politics*, edited by A. Zuckerman, pp. 269–287. Philadelphia: Temple University Press.

Gerber, A. S., and Green, D. P. (2012). *Field Experiments: Design, Analysis, and Interpretation*. New York: W. W. Norton.

Gerber, A., Huber, G., Doherty, D., and Dowling, C. (2012). "Disagreement and the Avoidance of Political Discussion: Aggregate Relationships and Differences across Personality Traits." *American Journal of Political Science* 56: 849–84l.

Gonzalez-Bailon, S., Kaltenbrunner, A., and Banchs, R. E. (2010). "The Structure of Political Discussion Networks: A Model for the Analysis of Online Deliberation." *Journal of Information Technology* 25 (2): 230–243.

Gutmann, A., and Thompson, D. (1996). *Democracy and Disagreement*. Cambridge, UK: Cambridge University Press.

Habermas, J. (1989). *The Structural Transformation of the Public Sphere*. Cambridge, MA: MIT Press.

Handcock, M. S., Hunter, D. R., Butts, C. T., Goodreau, S. M., and Morris, M. (2003). *statnet: Software Tools for the Statistical Modeling of Network Data*. Seattle, WA: Statnet Project. R package version 2.0. http://CRAN.R-project.org/package=statnet.

Hanneman, R., and Riddle, M. (2005). *Introduction to Social Network Methods*. Riverside: University of California.

Huckfeldt, R. (1979). "Political Participation and The Neighborhood Social Context." *American Journal of Political Science* 23: 579–592.

Huckfeldt, R. (1983). "Social Contexts, Social Networks, and Urban Neighborhoods: Environmental Constraints on Friendship Choice." *American Journal of Sociology* 89: 651–669.

Huckfeldt, R. (1986). *Politics in Context: Assimiation and Conflict in Urban Neighborhoods*. Agathon Press.

Huckfeldt, R. (2001). "The Social Communication of Political Expertise." *American Journal of Political Science* 45(2): 425–438.

Huckfeldt, R., Beck, P. A., Dalton, R. J., and Levine, J. (1995). "Political Environments, Cohesive Social Groups, and the Communication of Public Opinion." *American Journal of Political Science* 39: 1025–1054.

Huckfeldt, R., Johnson, P. E., and Sprague, J. (2002). "Political Environments, Political Dynamics, and the Survival of Disagreement." *Journal of Politics* 64: 1–21.

Huckfeldt, R., Johnson, P. E., and Sprague, J. (2004). *The Survival of Diverse Opinions Within Communication Networks*. Cambridge, UK: Cambridge University Press.

Huckfeldt, R., Levine, J., Morgan, W., and Sprague, J. (1999). "Accessibility and the Political Utility of Partisan and Ideological Orientations." *American Journal of Political Science* 43: 888–911.

Huckfeldt, R., and Sprague, J. (1985). Presidential Election Campaign Study, 1984 [Computer file]. ICPSR version. Bloomington: Center for Survey Research, Indiana University [producer], 1985; Ann Arbor, MI: Inter-university Consortium for Political and Social Research [distributor], 1995.

Huckfeldt, R., and Sprague, J. (1987). "Networks in Context: The Social Flow of Political Information." *American Political Science Review* 81: 1197–1216.

Huckfeldt, R., and Sprague, J. (1988). "Choice, Social Structure, and Political Information: The Informational Coercion of Minorities." *American Journal of Political Science* 32 (2): 467–482.

Huckfeldt, R., and Sprague, J. (1991). "Discussant Effects on Vote Choice: Intimacy, Structure, and Interdependence." *Journal of Politics* 53: 122–158.

Huckfeldt, R., and Sprague, J. (1993). "Citizens, Contexts, and Politics." In *Political Science: The State of the Discipline II*, edited by A. W. Finifter, pp. 281–303. Washington, DC: American Political Science Association.

Huckfeldt, R., and Sprague, J. (1995). *Citizens, Politics, and Social Communication: Information and Influence in an Election Campaign*. Cambridge, UK: Cambridge University Press.

Huckfeldt, R., Sprague, J., and Levine, J. (2000). "The Dynamics of Collective Deliberation in the 1996 Election: Campaign Effects on Accessibility, Certainty, and Accuracy." *American Political Science Review* 94: 641–651.

Kenny, C. (1992). "Political Participation and Effects from the Social Environment." *American Journal of Political Science* 36: 259–267.

Kenny, C. (1994). "The Microenvironment of Attitude Change." *Journal of Politics* 56: 715–728.

Key, V. O., Jr. (1949). *Southern Politics*. New York: Alfred A. Knopf Press.

Klar, S. (2014). "Partisanship in a Social Setting." *American Journal of Political Science* 58: 687–704.

Klofstad, C. A. (2007). "Talk Leads to Recruitment: How Discussions about Politics and Current Events Increase Civic Participation." *Political Research Quarterly* 60: 180–191.

Klofstad, C. A. (2009). "Civic Talk and Civic Participation: The Moderating Effect of Individual Predispositions." *American Politics Research* 37: 856–878.

Klofstad, C. A. (2010). "The Lasting Effect of Civic Talk on Civic Participation: Evidence from a Panel Study." *Social Forces* 88: 2353–2375.

Klofstad, C. A. (2011). *Civic Talk: Peers, Politics, and the Future of Democracy*. Philadelphia, PA: Temple University Press.

Klofstad, C. A., McClurg, S. D., and Rolfe, M. (2009). "Measurement of Political Discussion Networks: A Comparison of Two 'Name Generator' Procedures." *Public Opinion Quarterly* 73: 462–483.

Klofstad, C. A., Sokhey, A., and McClurg, S. D. (2013). "Disagreeing About Disagreement: How Conflict in Social Networks Affects Political Behavior." *American Journal of Political Science* 57: 120–134.

Lake, R. L. D., and Huckfeldt, R. (1998). "Social Capital, Social Networks, and Political Participation." *Political Psychology* 19: 567–583.

Laumann, E. O. (1973). *Bonds of Pluralism: The Form and Substance of Urban Social Networks*. New York: Wiley.

Laver, M. (2005). Review of *The Social Logic of Politics*. *Perspectives on Politics* 3: 933–934.

Lazarsfeld, P., Berelson, B., and Gaudet, H. (1944). *The People's Choice: How the Voter Makes Up His Mind in a Presidential Campaign*. New York: Duell, Sloan, and Pearce.

Lazer, D., Rubineau, B., Chetkovich, C., Katz, K., and Neblo, M. (2010). "The Coevolution of Networks and Political Attitudes." *Political Communication* 27: 248–274.

Leighley, J., and Matsubayashi, T. (2009). "The Implications of Class, Race, and Ethnicity for Political Networks." *American Politics Research* 37: 824–855.

Lyons, J. (2011). "Where You Live and Who You Know: Political Environments, Social Pressures, and Partisan Stability." *American Politics Research* 39: 963–992.

Lyons, J., McClurg, S., Seib, D. and Sokhey A. E. (2016). "Personality, Interpesonal Disagreement, and Electoral Information." *Journal of Politics* 78(3): 806–821.

Lyons, J., and Sokhey, A. (2014). "Emotion, Motivation, and Social Information Seeking about Politics." *Political Communication* 31: 237–258.

MacKuen, M., and Brown, C. (1987). "Political Context and Attitude Change." *American Political Science Review* 81: 471–490.

Marin, A., and Hampton, K. (2007). "Simplifying the Personal Network Name Generator: Alternatives to Traditional Multiple and Single Name Generators." *Field Methods* 19: 163–193.

Marsden, P. (1987). "Core Discussion Networks of Americans." *American Sociological Review* 52: 122–131.

McCallister, L., and Fischer, C. S. (1978). "A Procedure for Surveying Personal Networks." *Sociological Methods and Research* 7: 131–148.

McClurg, S. (2011). "Porous Networks and Overlapping Contexts: Methodological Problems in the Study of Social Communication and Political Behavior." In *Sourcebook of Political Communication Research: Methods, Measures, and Analytical Techniques*, edited by L. Holbert and E. Bucy, pp. 346–364. London: Routledge.

McClurg, S. D. (2003). "Social Networks and Political Participation: The Role of Social Interaction in Explaining Political Participation." *Political Research Quarterly* 56: 449–464.

McClurg, S. D. (2004). "Indirect Mobilization: The Social Consequences of Party Contacts in an Election Campaign." *American Politics Research* 32: 406–443.

McClurg, S. D. (2006a). "The Electoral Relevance of Political Talk: Examining Disagreement and Expertise Effects in Social Networks on Political Participation." *American Journal of Political Science* 50: 737–754.

McClurg, S. D. (2006b). "Political Disagreement in Context: The Conditional Effect of Neighborhood Context, Disagreement, and Political Talk on Electoral Participation." *Political Behavior* 28: 349–366.

McPhee, W., Ferguson, J., and Smith, R. (1963). "A Theory of Informal Social Influence." In William McPhee, ed., *Formal Theories of Mass Behavior*. London: Collier-Macmillan.

McPherson, M., Smith-Lovin, L., and Brashears, M. (2006). "Social Isolation in America: Changes in Core Discussion Networks over Two Decades." *American Sociological Review* 71(3): 353–375.

Moore, R. J. (2004). "Managing Troubles in Answering Survey Questions: Respondents' Uses of Projective Reporting." *Social Psychology Quarterly* 67: 50–69.

Morehouse Mendez, J., and Osborn, T. (2010). "Gender and the Perception of Knowledge in Political Discussion." *Political Research Quarterly* 63: 269–279.

Mutz, D., and Mondak, J. (2006). "The Workplace as a Context for Cross-Cutting Political Discourse." *Journal of Politics* 68: 140–155.

Mutz, D. C. (2002a). "The Consequences of Cross-Cutting Networks for Political Participation." *American Journal of Political Science* 46: 838–855.

Mutz, D. C. (2002b). "Cross-Cutting Social Networks: Testing Democratic Theory in Practice." *American Political Science Review* 96: 111–126.

Mutz, D. C. (2006). *Hearing the Other Side: Deliberative versus Participatory Democracy.* Cambridge, UK: Cambridge University Press.

Mutz, D. C., and Martin, P. (2001). "Facilitating Communication Across Lines of Political Difference: The Role of Mass Media." *American Political Science Association* 95(1): 97–114.

Nickerson, D. (2008). "Is Voting Contagious? Evidence from Two Field Experiments." *American Political Science Review* 102(1): 49–57.

Nir, L. (2005). "Ambivalent Social Networks and Their Consequences for Participation." *International Journal for Public Opinion Research* 17: 422–442.

Nir, L. (2011). "Disagreement and Opposition in Social Networks: Does Disagreement Discourage Turnout?" *Political Studies* 59: 674–692.

Noelle-Neumann, E. (1993). *The Spiral of Silence: Public Opinion—Our Social Skin.* Chicago: University of Chicago Press.

Osborn, T., and Morehouse Mendez, J. (2011). "Two Become One? Spouses and Agreement in Political Opinions." *American Politics Research* 39: 783–803.

Parsons, B. (2010). "Social Networks and the Affective Impact of Political Disagreement." *Political Behavior.* 32: 181–204.

Putnam, R. D. (1966). "Political Attitudes and the Local Community." *American Political Science Review* 60: 640–654.

Quintelier, E., Stolle, D., and Harell, A. (2012). "Politics in Peer Groups: Exploring the Causal Relationship between Network Diversity and Political Participation." *Political Research Quarterly* 65: 868–881.

Rolfe, M. (2012). *Voter Turnout: A Social Theory of Political Participation.* Cambridge, UK: Cambridge University Press.

Ryan, J. (2011). "Social Networks as a Shortcut to Correct Voting." *American Journal of Political Science* 55: 752–765.

Ryan, J. (2013). "An Experimental Study of Persuasive Social Communication." *Political Communication* 30: 100–116.

Sinclair, B. (2012). *The Social Citizen: Political Networks and Political Behavior.* Chicago: University of Chicago Press.

Sokhey, A., Baker, A., and Djupe, P. (2015). "The Dynamics of Socially Supplied Information: Examining Discussion Network Stability Over Time." *International Journal of Public Opinion Research* 27(4): 565–587.

Sokhey, A., and Djupe, P. (2011). "Interpersonal Networks and Democratic Politics." *PS: Political Science and Politics* 44: 55–59.

Sokhey, A., and Djupe, P. (2014). "Name Generation in Interpersonal Political Network Data: Results from a Series of Experiments." *Social Networks* 36: 147–161.

Sokhey, A., and McClurg, S. (2012). "Social Networks and Correct Voting." *Journal of Politics* 74: 751–764.

Sprague, J. (1976). "Estimating a Boudon Type Contextual Model: Some Practical and Theoretical Problems of Measurement." *Political Methodology* 3: 333–353.

Testa, P., Hibbing, M., and Ritchie, M. (2014). "Orientations toward Conflict and the Conditional Effects of Political Disagreement." *Journal of Politics* 76: 770–785.

Valenzuela, S., Kim, Y., and Gil de Zuniga, H. (2012). "Social Networks that Matter: Exploring the Role of Political Discussion for Online Political Particiaption." *International Journal of Public Opinion Research* 24(2): 163–184.

Visser, P., and Mirabile, R. (2004). "Attitudes in the Social Context: The Impact of Social Network Composition on Individual-Level Attitude Strength." *Journal of Pesonality and Social Psychology* 87(6): 779–795.

Walsh, K. K. (2004). *Talking about Politics: Informal Groups and Social Identity in American Life*. Chicago: University of Chicago Press.

Walther, J. (1996). "Computer-Mediated Communication: Impersonal, Interpersonal, and Hyperpersonal Interaction." *Communication Research* 23(1): 3–43.

Wolf, M., Morales, L., and Ikeda, K., eds. (2010). *Political Discussion in Modern Democracies: A Comparative Perspective*. New York: Routledge.

Zuckerman, A. S. (2005). *The Social Logic of Politics: Personal Networks as Contexts for Political Behavior*. Philadelphia, PA: Temple University Press.

PART IV

NETWORKS
IN PUBLIC POLICY
AND PUBLIC
ADMINISTRATION

CHAPTER 22

....

LOCAL GOVERNMENT NETWORKS

....

MANOJ K. SHRESTHA AND RICHARD C. FEIOCK

INTRODUCTION

....

IN any multilevel political system, local governments are fundamental to everyday life. They provide a wide variety of services to residents, ranging from basic services like police, fire, and trash collection to economic development and quality-of-life services. However, local governments cannot operate independently from other local actors, and local provision of these services does not occur in isolation. The scope of many of these services often crosses local government boundaries and can encompass multiple communities. Provision of these services requires coordination among affected juris-dictions, which involves sharing of information, expertise, or resources.

A defining feature of local government affairs is the dynamic interdependence among local governments or between local governments and a wide variety of gov-ernmental, civic, and business organizations acting to improve local conditions. For example, local governments work with federal and state agencies in a host of policy areas, including water quality, air quality, transportation, and public safety. They work with peer governments for the provision of critical services like emergency, solid waste, and airport services that are often regional in nature. They also work with busi-nesses and civic organizations to enhance economic development and human services. These webs of interactions are an integral part of the daily life of local governments and are considered essential for creating vibrant communities for residents and businesses. One can envisage widespread prevalence of such webs of interactions in metropolitan areas consisting of numerous local governments and other governmental, as well as nongovernmental, entities.

Defining Local Government Networks

We define local government networks (LGNs) as structures of interdependent relationships between local governments or between local governments and other actors that help fulfill their functions. We distinguish LGNs from policy networks in general; LGNs are distinct in the types of actors, the specific exchange relationships, and the high degree of knowledge and resource interdependence involved. Policy networks encompass a large variety of state and societal actors involved in influencing the policymaking process and policy outcomes. Local governments are the primary actors or nodes in LGNs; they create exchange relationships within their own set or with other governmental or nongovernmental actors.

Local government networks can take the form of "shared governance" or they can be led by a "lead organization," in which a local government acts as the primary actor. The nature of the issues dealt with in LGNs is also somewhat unique, in that they are defined by specialized services the local governments are responsible for providing to their residents. The number and type of actors involved in LGNs depend on the nature and scope of the public services they deal with. What is critical for theories of LGNs is to understand what factors give rise to particular network structures and how those structures influence individual and collective outcomes.

Interdependency in the provision of services is at the core of LGNs and is central to our conceptualization of them. One of the conditions that creates interdependency in service provision is political fragmentation of local governments. Political fragmentation results numerous local governments and scale mismatch, with complexity in the governance and management of services of local concern (Ostrom, Tiebout, and Warren, 1961). Marble-cake-like overlap of authorities across federal, state, and local governments in almost every policy area adds another layer of governance complexity. Interconnectedness between different functional areas or policies creates additional complexity. For example, economic development policy is not independent from land use, natural resources, or infrastructure development. Multiplicity of local governments with overlapping jurisdictions creates externalities and diseconomies of scale, resulting in the need for joint problem solving. Externalities occur when decisions made by one local government affect other local governments. Diseconomies of scale occur when smaller local governments are unable to produce services at lower average cost.

Another condition that creates interdependency in service provision is the local governments' operating environment, in which knowledge and resources are unevenly distributed at different scales across fragmented jurisdictions. Asymmetry in fiscal capacity across jurisdictions and the need for fiscal equalization are widely discussed in the literature on fiscal federalism (Oates, 1999). Unequal distribution of capacity is also true of information, knowledge, technical and managerial expertise, and political and social capital. Administrative partition of functions within local governments by specialized agencies and the growing number, scope, and influence of nonprofits and civic organizations in local affairs reflect this phenomenon.

Interdependency in service provision produces institutional collective action (ICA) dilemmas for local actors—situations in which decisions made by individual actors based on their short-term interests lead to collectively inefficient outcomes (Feiock, 2013). While solutions imposed by higher level governments, including manufactured networks with a designated lead agency (Provan and Kenis, 2008), are not uncommon to overcome highly conflictual ICA dilemmas, local governments, motivated by a strong desire to maintain their autonomy, prefer collaborative solutions for addressing these dilemmas (Feiock and Scholz, 2010). Collaborative solutions can range from informal relationships to contractual agreements to creating joint partnerships and authorities, depending on the extent of the risks collaboration imposes and the ability of these mechanisms to mitigate those risks (Shrestha, 2010; Feiock, 2013). Local government networks represent collaborative mechanisms that are founded on relational structures, with the potential to overcome the risks the local actors face in pursing collaborative solutions.

Collaboration requires local governments working with peers and/or other actors in the environment—a necessary condition for the existence of relational ties. Accordingly, numerous dyadic ties that exist among local governments or between local governments and other actors emerge as an LGN consisting of various configurations of ties. The presence of a particular configuration of ties in an LGN should reflect the actions by local actors in response to specific collective action problems they wish to solve, given the opportunities and constraints that the distribution of ties in the network presents. Local government networks can also be conceptualized as a local governance system in which the actors are the elements of the system, interconnected by various ties or relationships. By extension, LGNs are amenable to a system-based analysis where structural patterns are of central interest, both for their emergence as well as for their effects on individual and systemic outcomes.

The scope or boundary of an LGN depends on the function or policy in question. With different functions of varying scope, one can conceive of LGNs with different boundaries. Service delivery networks, economic development networks, and emergency management networks are examples of function-specific networks with different boundaries. These networks could overlap, as the same actors are often part of two or more such networks. When they do, actors in LGNs can be considered to be embedded in multiple networks, which can create different sets of opportunities or constraints for them in addressing the problems in collaboration that they encounter.

Another key aspect of any LGN is network connectivity or ties. Network paths or the sequence of ties provides avenues for local government actors to access resources or social capital. A local government's access to a particular resource depends on what problems this actor encounters, which in turn determines whom to connect to given the opportunities and constraints the network ties offer. The nature of these interdependencies is considered critical to the formation and structure of collaboration networks among local governments (Feiock, 2009, 2013). Connectivity is about creating, maintaining, or breaking ties with valuable actors in the network that facilitate the access to specific resources to overcome the collective problems. These problems determine connectivity needs. Varying connectivity needs thus lead to different network structures.

We build on the foundation of the ICA framework to identify how interdependency in service provision creates local governance dilemmas across policy arenas and what role LGNs play in mitigating those dilemmas. Next, we review the type of ICA dilemmas that the interdependencies in service provision produce and the range of collaboration mechanisms suitable for overcoming them. While networks can be facilitated by a central authority or a third party,[1] we focus on self-organizing LGNs and review the theory and empirical evidence regarding what factors shape these network structures. In this regard, we discuss the motivations, incentives, and risks local governments face in collaboration. We argue that collaboration risks pose significant barriers to collaboration and explain how local governments seek partners that structure relationships to reduce those risks. Finally, we explore the state of scholarship on LGNs and conclude with a discussion of important gaps in and the future direction of LGN scholarship.

The Institutional Collective Action Framework and Local Government Networks

The ICA framework captures the nature and contexts of local policy problems, the actors affected, and their motivations to engage in network exchanges. As noted, ICA dilemmas arise from fragmentation of service responsibilities and asymmetrical distribution of knowledge and resources among a multitude of local actors. The framework extends Ostrom's (1990) theory of individual collective action to cities, counties, and other collective entities (Feiock, 2008; Feiock and Scholz, 2010). Individual collective action theory posits that individuals communicate, resolve differences, and build mutual trust and norms to overcome coordination and defection problems. The ICA framework builds on agency and social network theories to identify benefits and transaction costs of organizational collaboration (Lubell et al., 2002; Schneider et al., 2003; Feiock and Scholz, 2010). The ICA framework focuses on solutions to dilemmas of fragmented authority. It has proven particularly useful for diagnosing local and regional dilemmas and for understanding network strategies of local actors to resolve those dilemmas.

This framework compares alternative mechanisms to mitigate horizontal, vertical, and functional dilemmas. Horizontal dilemmas can arise when jurisdictional boundaries of the governmental units are too small to effectively solve the problem individually, and/or the actions of one government actor create externalities for neighboring governments (Mitchell, 2005). Vertical ICA dilemmas arise when different levels of government pursue similar or overlapping policy objectives. Functional ICA dilemmas are defined by the connectedness of functions, policies, and resource systems. They can also arise from fragmentation of authority among agencies within a single government (Feiock and Krause, 2015). For example, land use decisions made by a city's planning department have consequences for the city's infrastructure maintenance, administered by the public works department; its natural resources, overseen by the environment division; its transportation system, managed by the infrastructure division; and its open space, managed by the parks and recreation division, all of which have indirect inputs into the policy decision. It is not uncommon for elements of each to be present in complex policy systems.

The traditional response to ICA dilemmas has been a call for centralized coordination. A higher level government with authority to change the geographic boundaries or functional jurisdiction can address diseconomies of scale and internalize externalities. For example, city-county consolidation and consolidation of cities can internalize unconsidered impacts within a larger consolidated government. Special districts rely on consolidated authority to address scale diseconomies and externalities over a broad geographic area for specific functions. Centralized coordination can also take the form of a mandated network in which a higher level authority provides funding and directs relations among local actors or designates a lead agency to manage and coordinate intergovernmental service provision (Provan and Kenis, 2008). The political and administrative costs of relying on a centralized authority as a regional integration mechanism often limit the scope of its use. Government units generally resist their loss of authority. Even if a centralized coordination mechanism produces efficiencies, they are achieved at the cost of reducing the ability of local units to vary the provision of services to reflect differences in local preferences.

Local government networks offer self-organizing alternatives to centralized coordination. They encompass everything from informal communications to more formal exchanges to complex interlocal agreements and service contracts. These exchanges can occur bilaterally or multilaterally. Because of the involvement of multiple actors, multilateral exchanges become more complex than bilateral exchanges. Figure 22.1 displays four distinct relational exchanges, whether they are bilateral or multilateral in scope and whether they involve primarily informal commitments or legally binding exchanges.[2]

Dyadic informal interactions among local actors are the basis for the informal networks in the left bottom cell in figure 22.1. Informal networks can coordinate complex decisions independently. These informal exchanges preserve local autonomy, although federal and state programs can influence their development (Schneider et al., 2003). Similarly, cities routinely engage in bilateral agreements with other local units for the supply of services (Warner and Hefetz, 2001; Shrestha and Feiock, 2009; Krueger and Bernick, 2010; Shrestha, 2010). While interlocal cooperation through service contracts and agreements has existed for a long time, these agreements have gained popularity in the United States and other Western countries in recent years (Thurmaier and Wood, 2002; Tavares and Feiock, 2014).

Multilateral	Deliberative forums/venues	Multilateral agreements/contracts
Bilateral	Informal exchanges	Bilateral agreements/contracts
	Informal	Formal

FIGURE 22.1 Four types of relational exchanges.

Local actors also participate in deliberative forums or venues such as community meetings or professional conferences. These affiliations provide valuable opportunities for informal communication and networks. Local actors also enter into multilateral agreements. For example, regional emergency dispatch and regional planning are often organized through multilateral agreements involving local governments and other local actors. Multilateral agreements also provide venues for local actors to create regional economic development partnerships to exchange resources and to coordinate economic development decisions (Chen, Feiock, and Hseih; 2015). These informal and formal multilateral venues provide pathways for local actors to know each other and expand networks for shared understanding and actions crucial for collaborative solutions. It is noteworthy that some of these voluntary choices leading up to formation of LGNs in different functional areas are also shaped by the rules, conditions, or incentives created by higher level governments. For example, enabling state laws create conditions for local governments to engage in interlocal contracting networks. Similarly, federal or state grants awarded for collaborative solutions incentivize local actors to work together to address a local collective action, be it regional planning, transportation, or environmental issues.

Local Government Functions, Institutional Collective Action Dilemmas, and Problems in Collaboration

Local governments exist for the provision of essential services to their residents. These services or functions can be categorized into functions that do not pose problems of scale and/or externalities and functions that are prone to problems of scale and/or externalities. The former does not pose ICA problems so long as a local government is unconstrained by information and resources in performing a function. But when the local government requires information and other resources to perform a function and is able to assemble a group of supporting partners, then the need for coordination and development of operating norms among the partners can be conceived of as a joint (ICA) problem.

Local functions that pose problems of scale and/or externalities represent a general form of ICA dilemma for local governments. When the affected actors perceive these problems as threats, they begin conversations about addressing them. The participating actors may disagree about the strategies and actions to confront a threat. These actors may find coordination difficult if they come up with a diverse array of responses (Maser, 1985). They may be unaware of available strategies or have no information about what other actors plan to do, what resources will be needed, or what resources other actors have to address the problems. When the actors lack adequate information for coordination, they face a *coordination search problem*. Overcoming a search problem creates an avenue for developing collective norms or rules involving who does what and how benefits and costs are divided among the actors, defined as a *division problem*. Division problems are distinguished from coordination in that although actors may agree on the joint action, difficulties could arise in dividing its benefits and costs (Steinacker, 2004). Unfair distribution of responsibilities, benefits, or costs among the partners or an unfair process followed for such a distribution can inhibit collaboration. Both search and division problems relate to coordination of resources and strategies essential for developing an agreed upon collective norm.

Even if a collective norm is defined and agreed upon, compliance remains uncertain. The participating actors may not follow through on the commitment. They may withdraw or defect when they find that the gains from defection are greater than the costs of defection. At the root of the *defection problem* is opportunistic behavior of actors encouraged by the possibility to freeride, low probability of spotting reneging, and lack of penalty or reputational loss. For example, two local governments may enter into an interlocal service contract, but the difficulty of monitoring the quality or quantity of a service can provide an incentive for a supplier local government to cheat the buyer government (Shrestha, 2010).

Linking Risks in Collaboration and Network Structures

Collaboration is risky because coordination may fail, and cooperation is subject to potential defections. Within the ICA framework, collaboration risks reflect certain behavioral dispositions that serve as barriers to resolving search, division, and defection problems in collaboration (Feiock, 2004, 2013; Carr and Hawkins, 2013). The ability to overcome search problems is constrained if actors withhold information.

Heavy reliance on a single source of information is not only risky, it also limits the potential for verification of the received information. When the information-seeking actor is part of a closely tied group, groupthink may prevent the actor from reaching out for new ideas or information. The development literature suggests that communities are often rich in their close-knit ties but lack bridging ties outside their communities for new ideas and resources considered essential for advancement (Woolcook, 1998).

Perceptions of uneven distribution of benefits and costs of collaboration among the actors can prevent them from resolving division problems. Division problems involve an unfair decision process as well as unfair distribution of gains and responsibilities. One of the key outputs of the division process is the development of collective norms or rules agreed upon by the participating actors (Ostrom, 1990). A credible division process leading to establishment of a credible collective norm is crucial to overcome unfair division.

Defection is a posterior behavior. A pledge to collaborate does not guarantee effective compliance unless actors are committed to faithfully follow through. The risk of defection increases with situational uncertainty, limited information, and the possibility of others behaving opportunistically (Brown and Potoski, 2005). With changing circumstances and limited information, actors may find the original division of benefits and costs unfavorable for continuing to be a part of the collaboration. The possibility of freeriding and lack of collective enforcement or the threat of reputational loss can also increase defection risk. Defection risks are especially high for the implementation of programs and services that are new to the organization and for which there is no history of collaboration.

Local actors respond to these risks in collaboration by seeking specific network structures through their choices of partners. Collaboration risks determine the need for connecting to collaborating partners. Local actors can adopt one or more of the relational exchanges illustrated in figure 22.1 for choosing partners (Shrestha, Berardo, and Feiock, 2014). They can even enter into multiple service contracts and create interlocking service networks to guard the terms of collaboration from potential defection (Shrestha and Feiock, 2011). It is not uncommon for local governments to take part in multiple venues or to maintain both bilateral contacts and multilateral venues for managing collaboration risks.

Choosing the right collaborating partner is crucial for building specific networks in order to overcome the risks of collaboration. Actors' positions in the existing network and their attributes provide signals or clues about the available opportunities and constraints to an actor seeking collaborators. Potential collaborators occupy certain positions in the network depending on how ties are interwoven, resulting from the process of creating, breaking, or maintaining ties. If the position of a potential partner signals that its commitments may not be credible, fewer local governments will be willing to collaborate with that partner (Carr, Gerber, and Lupher, 2009). Likewise, a city seeking contractual supply of police services, for example, might be more attracted to a county with greater capacity to provide such services rather than to another city with less capacity. Connectivity needs, together with the right choice of collaborating partner, determine the specific configuration of ties, which in turn helps overcome the risks of collaboration.

In the following subsections we discuss the link between collaboration risks and the structure of networks. For simplicity, we discuss this link in a simplex network setting, which considers a single relationship between the actors. We focus on how a particular collaboration problem encourages local governments to create a specific network structure. Local governments can face these risks simultaneously, forming combinations of networks to address them.

Coordination Problems and Bridging Networks

Even when interests are shared, actors in LGNs can face search and division problems. Actors can create a wider network and bridging ties to address search problems, while seeking network centrality, or a popularity network, to resolve division problems. These networks are bridging structures. Creating a wider network involve network activity or directly reaching out to diverse actors in the network. Bridging ties involve indirectly reaching out to other actors through intermediate contacts to access new information. Network centrality entails utilizing the popular (central) actor in the network.

Network activity: Local governments are hardly self-sufficient. They require information and a variety of other resources (e.g., funding, expertise, political support) to deliver programs and services. A common network strategy that a local government can utilize for efficient access of these resources is to seek direct ties with multiple partners that offer those resources. This is akin to the resource dependency theory of organization, which suggests that organizations seek resources from other organizations in the environment to achieve success (Pfeffer and Salancik, 1978). For example, a city develops ties with various public, nonprofit, and business organizations to access the information, funds, expertise, and even political support needed to effectively implement its economic development plan (Agranoff and McGuire, 2003; Hawkins, 2010; Feiock, Lee, and Park, 2012). Communities develop partnerships with a wide range of organizations for successful implementation of their projects that require diverse resources (Shrestha, 2013). In network terms, forming direct ties with multiple partners, called *network activity*, produces a wider (broad-based) network. Network activity represents the degree centrality of an actor, simply measured by the number of ties of that actor. These networks are efficient in accessing information and resources because the partners are only one step away, and no redundant ties exist between the partners. Wider networks are considered boundary-spanning networks, as they offer choices for accessing various resources from a variety of sources and thereby reduce the risk of dependency on any single partner.

Bridging ties: Another network strategy is the open path or weak ties. This type of bridging network is particularly valuable for accessing information that is available to distant actors in the network. Weak ties help bridge distant actors through direct partners, a mechanism often referred to as "friends of my friend are my friends." According to Granovetter (1973), bridging ties provide connectivity between regions of strong or closed ties in a network. The "strength of weak ties" rests on the idea that weak ties transmit new information across the network. The finding that successful job seekers utilize weak ties or open paths to connect to individuals outside of their own circle for new job information shows the critical value of weak ties in a network (Granovetter, 1973).[3] The resulting open, two-or-more-path network could serve as a conduit for novel information for the actors. Actors occupying the bridging position enable others to gain new knowledge not available within a closed network. Structural holes theory (Burt, 1992) suggests that the unconnected parts of a network produce structural holes, and actors that bridge these structural holes are in a position to gain advantage as network entrepreneurs or brokers. Regardless of their degree centrality, actors in structural holes have higher betweenness centrality (Robins, 2015). However, being the bridging partner can be a double-edged sword unless another mechanism, such as reciprocal ties, is in place to curb the partner's potential opportunism.

Network centrality: Establishing credible norms or rules for equitable distribution of responsibilities, benefits, and costs is essential for overcoming the division problem. For a set of local governments facing a division problem, the emergence of a central actor in the network is one pathway to address the problem. A central figure emerges within a network when many local actors seek exchanges with a particular actor. The most popular actor occupies the central position in the network by attracting ties from many other actors. The endorsement provided by these incoming ties implies credibility and competence. This signal is crucial information for other actors looking for potential partners that can be trusted to address the division problem in a fair manner (Gulati and Gargiulo, 1999).

A central coordinator reduces negotiation costs by being efficiently positioned to receive and transmit information as well as to function as a mediator among the partners. The popular actor in the network is also a depository of information influential enough to coordinate resources or activities for collective benefit. For example, in metropolitan service delivery, cities can gain economies of scale in production by entering into service contracts with a county in the network. Attracting many service contracts means that the county as the central provider can consolidate the demand and coordinate the use of production and managerial inputs in service production, leading to economies of scale gains for all cities involved. Similarly, in metropolitan areas where multiple local governments coexist, shared interests in managing traffic flow to avoid congestion and gridlock can encourage cities to follow the lead of a trusted actor in the network to coordinate road construction, lane closures, and the timing of traffic signals.

Defection Problems and Bonding Networks

Upholding the credibility of commitment made by members in LGNs is essential to overcome defection problems. Actors facing credibility of commitment problems can address them by creating bonding networks represented by reciprocity and network closure. The former is a simple form of bonding involving two actors, whereas the latter is a more complex form of bonding involving three or more of actors. Both structures facilitate the flow of overlapping information among the actors in a network, enabling them to resolve differences, build trust, and even detect and punish defective behavior, thereby ensuring credibility of commitment.

Reciprocity: Harnessing the norm of reciprocity is one way to ensure credibility of commitment. Reciprocity occurs when two actors are tied to each other through a reciprocal relationship. Even the informal exchange of information and advice can follow norms of reciprocity. In contractual service delivery, reciprocity occurs when, for example, city A supplies police services to city B, and city B supplies fire services to city A. Reciprocity creates mutual commitment by both parties and thereby reduces the risk of defection. Reciprocity also helps parties to know each other better, which develops into mutual trust and improves collaboration by reducing behavioral uncertainties (Uzzi, 1997). It also builds or strengthens social capital, manifested in expectations of taking turns in fulfilling mutual obligation and of trusting each other in exchange (Coleman, 1988; Putnam, 2000). Reciprocity can also function as "mutual deterrence" (Williamson, 1981), as actors can punish each other by declining to cooperate in the next round. In this way, reciprocity incentivizes both parties to build credible ties based on the verification of commitments. The observed prevalence of reciprocity across services in service delivery between cities in Florida provides evidence that the reciprocal service arrangement provided mutual assurance to both the recipient and the supplier jurisdictions of their credibility of commitment (Shrestha and Feiock, 2009).

Network closure: Network closure is another strategy that actors can use to prevent defection. While reciprocity is dyadic, network closure is a group feature with tendencies toward triangulation or social closure (Davis, 1970). The idea that two actors have a higher tendency to connect with each other when they share a common third actor underlies social closure (Snijders et al., 2006; Robins, Pattison, and Wang, 2009). Formed by path-shortening strategies or direct ties between unconnected actors, social closure prevents defection because the parties can better monitor each other's behavior, resolve conflicts through consultations, and impose sanctions on wrongdoers (Coleman, 1988). Network closure reduces uncertainty and creates conditions for sustaining cooperation.

The possibility of shirking imposes costs on those who have already invested their time and resources. A tightly clustered network structure is advantageous in reducing the transaction costs of enforcing and monitoring the relational obligations, since any actions taken or not taken by a locality are made public (Feiock and Scholz, 2010). Network closure also promotes credible commitment and helps build trust and group norms (Putnam, 2000). Groups with a high degree of network closure are more cohesive. In project implementation networks, community projects supported by a more cohesive group of organizations are more successful than projects that are supported by a less cohesive group of organizations (Shrestha, 2013).

Network closure takes various forms. Two common ones are transitive closure and three-cycles (Robins, 2015). Transitive closure or transitivity in social networks occurs when actors have a tendency to close an open two-path configuration because of potential defection by an intermediary. For example, even when federal dollars to local governments pass through state agencies, local governments maintain direct lobbying ties with federal agencies because of the fear that states may seek to manipulate the transfer. Cyclic closure is another form of network closure. When every actor in a group is interlocked with its partner through at least 1 in-coming (in-degree) and out-going (out-degree) tie, a local configuration with cyclic closure is formed. A cyclic closure (three-cycles) can be seen as a triadic version of reciprocity facilitating exchange and cooperation, sometimes referred to as generalized exchange (Robins, 2015). These closure mechanisms ensure speedy flow of information in the group to detect and punish actions that deviate from the agreed upon norms. These mechanisms also contribute to building trust and group norms essential for restraining potential defection.

State of the Scholarship on Local Government Networks

What do we know about LGNs? How does empirical evidence match up to theoretical expectations about the workings of LGNs? Considerable work has been done in the area of local service delivery (Andrew, 2009, 2010; Shrestha, 2008, 2010), economic development (Agranoff and McGuire, 2003; Feiock, Lee, and Park, 2010; Hawkins and Feiock, 2011; Lee, Lee, and Feiock, 2012; Hawkins et al., 2015; Hawkins et al., 2016; Kwak et al., 2016), emergency management (Andrew and Carr, 2013; Andrew et al., 2016; Jung and Song, 2015; Song and Jung, 2015), water governance (Shrestha, 2013), and local sustainability (Bae, Feiock, and Kwon, 2012; Bae and Feiock, 2013; Feiock and Krause, 2015). These works examine structural configurations that are linked to minimizing risks in collaboration. We begin with research on egocentric LGNs, followed by works that focus on whole LGNs. Our survey of LGN studies is brief and is by no means exhaustive.

Egocentric Local Government Networks

An egocentric LGN consists of a network neighborhood formed around a local government actor (ego) and network partners of the ego, referred to as alters. An ego's network neighborhood contains ties from the ego to each alter, including alters' ties with their partners (Robins, 2015). One stream of LGN research treats an observed network as a dependent variable, where the focus is to explain the formation of the network (Lee, Lee, and Feiock, 2012; Carr, Gerber, and Lupher, 2009; Feiock, Lee, and Park, 2012; Gerber, Henry, and Lubell, 2013; Kwak et al., 2016). Another emerging stream of LGN research treats network relationships as independent variables affecting outcomes (Andrew 2010; Feiock, Lee, and Park 2012; Hawkins 2010; Meier and O'Toole 2003; Song and Jung 2015; Kwak 2016).

Local Government Networks as Dependent Variable

Studies interested in explaining networks focus on understanding the endogenous processes that lead to particular configurations of ties in a network. As discussed previously, network activity, indirect ties, preferential attachment, reciprocity, and closure are examples of endogenous processes. In each case, the existence of certain ties encourages the presence or maintenance of other ties, leading to a particular network configuration. Since these processes are latent, the presence of particular configurations of ties provides clues about the structural processes that produce certain networks (Robins, 2015).

Feiock et al. (2010, 2012) extensively studied these structural processes in the context of local economic development in the Orlando and Tampa Bay metropolitan areas in Florida to explain the presence of bridging and bonding networks that local governments create to address coordination and defection problems. They found that risk-averse local government officials looking for valuable information not only seek wider sources of information (network activity) for cross-verification but also utilize reciprocity and closure to prevent obtaining misleading information. While there was no evidence of a popularity network, they found that elected officials avoided intermediaries (open two-path) to access information. Lee (2011) and Lee, Lee, and Feiock (2012) found similar network strategies adopted by local governments in the Tampa Bay metropolitan area, Florida, engaged in local economic development, with an exception of no evidence for reciprocity. In a study of eight metropolitan areas in the United States, Hawkins (2010) found network activity to be associated with cities' formation of joint venture partnerships.

A comparative analysis of the communication networks between local elected and appointed officials relating to economic development found strikingly similar network patterns between the two when they faced similar coordination and cooperation problems (Feiock, Lee, and Park, 2012). Like appointed officials, elected officials are risk averse, in that the fragility of electoral support makes them sensitive to the political costs of their actions (Steinacker, 2004). Even if there are joint benefits to sharing information with other jurisdictions, elected officials are unwilling to subject themselves to political risks or the potential to be misled. Therefore, they not only use reciprocity and closure to prevent obtaining misleading information, but also seek diverse sources with an ability to verify the credibility of the information.

Dyadic attributes can also influence formation of ties between actors. One such widely studied attribute-based selection, or social selection, process is homophily. Local government units can form ties because they are members of the same association, or attend the same professional meeting, or share the same form of government. Similar actors face lower transaction costs of creating ties than do dissimilar actors. It is easier for a local jurisdiction to bargain and negotiate with other jurisdictions when they have a similar demographic composition, because their preferences and motives are likely to be similar. Studies of formal and informal networks confirm the salience of homophily. Similarity among communities, reflected in socioeconomic characteristics, partisan ideological composition, and forms of government, increases the likelihood of collaborative relationships (Feiock, 2008, 2009; Gerber, Henry, and Lubell, 2013).

Local governments with certain attributes can have a greater tendency to acquire a particular network position. For example, in a local service delivery network, counties were found to occupy a central position, as they were able to attract smaller cities because of the capacity and size to offer services cost-effectively (Shrestha, 2010). Similarly, studies have found that cities with greater fiscal capacity, independent executive authority, and strong organizational commitments, evidenced by dedication of organizational resources, are influential in resolving coordination problems (Hawkins et al., 2015; Terman and Feiock, 2014). Transaction costs to potential partners and their willingness to collaborate are also shaped by how successful a focal city is in signaling the credibility of its commitments to potential partners. Studies of collaborative networks in economic development demonstrate that a city is able to attract a collaborating partner by projecting a greater degree of certainty in successfully implementing economic development programs (Hawkins and Carr, 2015).

Local Government Networks as Independent Variables

The issue here is to determine how networks shape outcomes (Provan and Milward, 2001; O'Toole, 2015). A small number of studies have examined the link between network structures and nodal outcomes. Meier and O'Toole (2003) found a positive association between school superintendents' wider networking and higher school performance. Shrestha's (2013) study of an implementation network between beneficiary communities and organizational partners in Nepal showed that communities that were able to create a wider network, greater indirect reach, and greater network closure among the partner organizations were more successful in getting agency funding for their water supply projects than their counterparts that were not able to build these networks. In a national study of economic development partnerships for cities with a population over 50,000, Feiock, Steinacker, and Park (2009) found that cities with strong ties with their partners and weak ties across members of different groups were more likely to form joint ventures with other local governments. Andrew and Carr (2013), in their study of the communication network among local government managers in the Dallas-Fort Worth-Denton metropolitan area, found that a closed network among these actors increased their participation in disaster preparedness, as closeness breeds familiarity, trust, and confidence among the actors. Feiock and Krause (2015) reported that the number of functional units involved in city sustainability decision-making was related to green job creation and reduced greenhouse gas emissions.

Contextual factors also affect performance and are generally used as controls in the studies examining impact of networks. For example, political context (consensual political environment) and managerial talent (capacity) were found to influence the effect of school superintendents' networking on the performance of their school districts (Hicklin, O'Toole, and Meier, 2008; O'Toole and Meier, 2004; Swann, 2015). In Shrestha's (2013) study, important community attributes affecting outcomes were the time (hours) saved due to water supply projects and geographic distance. Remote communities were less successful in securing agency funding. On the other hand, projects that saved more time for the families were more successful in securing agency funds.

Whole Local Government Networks

A whole LGN comprises a fixed set of local government actors and relations among them. A small but important literature examines exchange relations among entire sets of local governments or between local governments and other local actors. Similar to egocentric network studies, the questions for whole network analysis are what rules govern network emergence and how networks influence outcomes at the network level. The majority of whole LGN studies so far have focused on local service delivery networks. In these studies, the nodes are the sets of all relevant local governments (cities and counties) tied through service contracts and/or mutual aid agreements. Here too, the interest has been in explaining the observed networks based on endogenous network and social selection processes. For example, recent work has compared network centrality across metropolitan regions in Florida to examine relationships between whole network structure and sustainability actions (Bae, Feiock, and Kwon, 2012) and green economic development (Kwak, 2016).

Interlocal service contracts and mutual aid agreements are formal ties. These formal ties reflect an attempt by the participating local governments to minimize risks in service exchange by defining provisions for legal redress if the parties to the agreement renege. Nevertheless, formal service agreements do not completely eliminate possible opportunism in contracts. Service agreements are not only incomplete because of the inability of the parties to ascertain all future contingencies; they also create dependencies (Andrew, 2009; Shrestha, 2008, 2010).

Drawing from Williamson (1981), the primary sources of opportunism that these works examine are the asset specificity and measurement difficulty of services considered for interlocal service contracts. Asset specificity implies large investments by a supplier to produce a specific contracted service, limiting alterative use of the investment. Thus, asset-specific investment creates limited suppliers in the public service market, creating greater dependency on one or a few suppliers. In contrast, less asset-specific service means less dependency. Faced with greater dependency, a government would prefer a broad-based supplier network to reduce dependency on any single supplier local government. Measurement difficulty complicates monitoring the quality or quantity of the delivered service—a situation prone to defection by the supplier from the commitment made in the agreement. Here, the buyer local government would prefer closed network structures based on reciprocity or transitive triads (triangle-like structures) to prevent defection. Cross-section and longitudinal research on service delivery network among local governments finds support for the predicted emergence of these network structures (Andrew, 2009, 2010; Shrestha, 2008, 2010; Shrestha and Feiock, 2013).

With regard to the influence of local government attributes on the formation of network ties, form of government is frequently cited as important. For example, cities with the council-manager form of government more often form ties with other similar cities, because professional public managers inherit a common set of professional norms and disciplinary values, what Frederickson (1999) calls administrative conjunction ties. In Florida, Andrew (2009) found that pairs of local governments are more likely to enter into a law enforcement agreement when both have accredited law enforcement credentials. LeRoux, Brandenburger, and Pandey (2010) observed that cities attending common venues such as regional associations or councils of government enter into interlocal agreements more frequently. Other attributes commonly used in determining collaborative service arrangements are size of the jurisdiction, geographic proximity, and income level of the population (Andrew, 2009; Shrestha, 2008, 2010; Shrestha and Feiock, 2013). These attributes reflect a jurisdiction's capacity for extending or attracting ties. For example, a large jurisdiction with potential for generating economies of scale is more attractive to small jurisdictions facing diseconomies of scale in the provision of services.

FUTURE ISSUES

Research on LGNs has made great progress, particularly in the study of egocentric networks and how those networks are linked to responses to ICA dilemma and collaboration risks. However, much work remains to be done. There is an urgent need to know more about how networks influence performance for individual nodes and for the collective at the network level. Some progress has been made in identifying how network structure relates to node level performance, but we know little about the link between networks and collective outcomes. Of course, network level outcome research will require a large number of network cases, which also means greater demand on resources and time to map the structures of multiple networks. Nevertheless, this is well worth pursuing given the theoretical and practical contributions that are possible.

Most LGN research has focused on cross-section networks, limiting our understanding of dynamic social processes that drive network emergence. A move toward longitudinal network analysis of LGNs (e.g., Andrew, 2009), as well as coevolutionary analysis of network and influence, will be crucial for the future development of LGN scholarship. In addition, current LGN scholarship focuses primarily on the functional areas of service delivery, economic development, emergency management, and local sustainability and has done so individually. Future studies should investigate systematic patterns in forming networks across different functional areas when local governments face similar ICA dilemmas and collaboration risks.

Another important question that demands greater attention is what role multiple networks play in addressing the risks in collaboration, given that local governments are embedded in multiple formal and informal networks. For example, for the provision of local services, local governments not only maintain multiple formal service contracts with their peers (Shrestha and Feiock, 2009; Shrestha, 2010; Hawkins et al., 2016), they also form informal ties through sharing information or meeting one another in regional decision-making venues (Feiock, Lee, and Park, 2012). Network research based on a single relation is an oversimplification of the real-world networks, and the conclusions drawn from such a study could be overgeneralized (Bae and Feiock, 2013; Shrestha, Berardo, and Feiock, 2014). The question here is how local government actors shape both their formal and informal relations to overcome ICA dilemmas (Shrestha, Berardo, and Feiock, 2014; Hawkins et al., 2016). Compared to a single network, a multiplex network can provide improved opportunities for the local actors in the network to form multiplex bridging and bonding networks like multiplex reciprocity (Shrestha and Feiock, 2009) to address such dilemmas.

Another layer of complexity that local governments face is that these governments frequently operate in bipartite and multilevel network contexts. A bipartite network occurs when a set of local governments engage with another set of actors, but have no relationships within their own sets. For example, in the case of a collaborative rural water supply program in Nepal, the beneficiary communities built ties with a variety of external organizations for successful implementation of their projects (Shrestha, 2013). Multilevel networks exist when an LGN is nested in larger networks such as a regional or statewide network in a hierarchical manner in which one network level influences others. Although there has been some progress on bipartite network analysis (Shrestha, 2013), less progress has been made on multilevel analysis of LGNs. Research advancement in this direction will help move toward developing a more realistic portrayal of the complex realities within which LGNs operate.

Given the enormous complexity of LGNs involving multiple, bipartite, and multilevel relationships, the larger question is not only who governs, which Robert A. Dahl (1961) sought to answer more than fifty years ago, but also *how* local governments and other actors organize these relationships to govern, and *what* network structures emerge in a metropolitan area, to overcome the ICA dilemmas in self-organizing governance. These questions can be answered by scholarship, guided by a network science perspective that involves comprehensive network analysis of all local governments in a metropolitan area. Network mapping and analysis of the emergent multiple, overlapping, and nested webs of relationships of a grand community structure would tremendously advance our understanding of the underlying organizing principles of metropolitan governance and network governance more generally.

Finally, this stream of research can have practical implications for public policy and management if we can modify the network ties in a community to reproduce ideal-type networks to overcome ICA dilemmas. Progress in this direction would significantly increase the practical value of LGN scholarship for managers and policymakers. As O'Toole (2015) suggests, combining network science with agent-based modeling-type simulation could provide a way forward for a more systematic understanding of the implications of manipulating certain network ties or positions on network behavior and outcomes. If so, scenario-based network analyses would be helpful in optimizing the link between networks and outcomes.

NOTES

1. Provan and Kenis (2008) discuss two forms of centralized networks, called lead organization-governed networks and network administration organization model.
2. Figure 22.1 is a modified version of the typology of ICA mitigation mechanisms advanced by Feiock (2013). It illustrates relation-based exchanges relevant to local governments.
3. When the node of interest is a group or a community, a broad-based network for this node could be considered a bridging network as it creates open paths to outside world for this group or community.

REFERENCES

Agranoff, R., and McGuire, M. (2003). "Inside the Matrix: Integrating the Paradigms of Intergovernmental and Network Management." *International Journal of Public Administration* 26(12): 1401–1422.

Andrew, S. A. (2009). "Regional Integration through Contracting Networks: An Empirical Analysis of Institutional Collection Action Framework." *Urban Affairs Review* 44(3): 378–402.

Andrew, S. A. (2010). "Adaptive versus Restrictive Contracts: Can They Resolve Different Risk Problems?" In *Self-Organizing Federalism: Collaborative Mechanisms to Mitigate Institutional Collective Action Dilemmas*, edited by R. C. Feiock and J. T. Scholz, pp. 91–113. New York: Cambridge University Press.

Andrew, S. A., Arlikatti, S., Siebeneck, L., Pongponrat, K., Jaikampan, K. (2016). "Sources of Organizational Resiliency during the Thailand Floods of 2011: A Test of Bonding and Bridging Hypotheses." *Disasters* 40(1): 65–84.

Andrew, S. A, and Carr, J. B. (2013). "Mitigating Uncertainty and Risk in Planning for Regional Preparedness: The Role of Bonding and Bridging Relationships." *Urban Studies* 40(4): 709–724.

Bae, J., and Feiock, R. C. (2013). "Forms of Government and Climate Change Policies in U.S. Cities." *Urban Studies* 50(4): 776–788.

Bae, J. R., Feiock, R. C., and Kwon, S. (2012). "Regional Network Centrality and Local Government Sustainability Policy." Paper presented at the Political Networks Conference, Boulder, CO, March.

Brown, T., and Potaski, M. (2005). "Transaction Costs and Contracting: The Practitioner Perspective." *Public Performance and Management Review* 28(3): 326–351.

Burt, R. S. (1992). *Structural Holes*. Cambridge, MA: Harvard University Press.

Carr, J. B., Gerber, E. R., and Lupher, E. R. (2009). "Local Fiscal Capacity and Intergovernmental Contracting: Horizontal and Vertical Cooperation in Michigan." In *Sustaining Michigan: Metropolitan Policies and Strategies*, edited by R. Jelier, S. Adelaja, and G. Sands, pp. 207–235. East Lancing: Michigan State University Press.

Carr, J. B., and Hawkins, C. V. (2013). "The Costs of Cooperation: What Research tells us about Managing the Risks of Service Collaborations in the U.S." *State and Local Government Review* 45(4): 224–239.

Chen, S., Feiock, R. C., and Hsieh, J. (2015). "Regional Partnerships and Metropolitan Economic Development." *Journal of Urban Affairs* 38(2): 196–213.

Coleman, J. (1988). "Social Capital in the Creation of Human Capital." *American Journal of Sociology* 94(S): 95–121.

Dahl, R. A. (1961). *Who Governs? Democracy and Power in an American City*. New Haven, CT: Yale University Press.

Davis, J. (1970). "Clustering and Hierarchy in Interpersonal Relations: Testing Two Graph Theoretical Models on 742 Sociomatirces." *American Sociological Review* 35(5): 843–851.

Feiock, R. C. (Ed.). (2004). *Metropolitan Governance: Conflict, Competition and Cooperation*. Washington, DC: Georgetown University Press.

Feiock, R. C. (2008). "A Transaction Cost Theory of Federalism." Local Governance Research Laboratory working paper, Florida State University. http://localgov.fsu.edu/research_projects/service_delivery.htm.

Feiock, R. C. (2009). "Metropolitan Governance and Institutional Collective Action." *Urban Affairs Review* 45(3): 357–377.

Feiock, R. C. (2013). "The Institutional Collective Action Framework." *Policy Studies Journal* 41(3): 397–425.

Feiock, R. C., and Krause, R. (2015). "Integrating Climate and Energy Efficiency Efforts to Overcome Functional Institutional Collective Action Dilemmas within City Governments." Paper presented at the Association for Public Policy Analysis and Management 2015 Fall Research Conference, November 12–14.

Feiock, R. C., Lee, I. W., and Park, H. J. (2010). "Collaboration Network among Local Elected Officials: Information, Commitment, and Risk Aversion." *Urban Affairs Review* 46(2): 241–262.

Feiock, R. C., Lee, I. W., and Park, H. J. (2012). "Administrators and Elected Officials' Collaboration Networks: Selecting Partners to Reduce Risk in Economic Development." *Public Administration Review* 72(S1): 58–68.

Feiock, R. C., and Scholz, J. T. (Eds.). (2010). *Self-Organizing Federalism: Collaborative Mechanisms to Mitigate Institutional Collective Action Dilemmas*. New York: Cambridge University Press.

Feiock, R. C., Steinacker, A., and Park, H. J. (2009). "Institutional Collective Action and Economic Development Joint Ventures." *Public Administration Review* 69(2): 256–270.

Frederickson, H. G. (1999). "The Repositioning of American Public Administration." *PS: Political Science & Politics* 32: 701–711.

Gerber, E., Henry, A., and Lubell, M. (2013). "Political Homophily and Collaboration in Regional Planning Networks." *American Journal of Political Science* 57(3): 598–610.

Granovetter, M. S. (1973). "The Strength of Weak Ties." *American Journal of Sociology* 78(6): 1360–1380.

Gulati, R., and Gargiulo, M. (1999). "Where Do Interorganizational Networks Come From?" *American Journal of Sociology* 104(5): 1439–1493.

Hawkins, C. V. (2010). "Competition and Cooperation: Local Government Joint Ventures for Economic Development." *Journal of Urban Affairs* 32(2): 253–275.

Hawkins, C. V., and Carr, J. B. (2015). "Collaboration Risk in Joint Venturing among Governments: Understanding the Risk Perception of Economic Development Officials." Paper presented at the Annual Meeting of the American Society for Public Administration Association.

Hawkins, C. V., and Feiock, R. C. (2011). "Joint Ventures, Economic Development Policy, and the Role of Local Governing Institutions." *American Review of Public Administration* 41: 329–347.

Hawkins, C. V., Feiock, R. C., Hu, Q., and Lee, Y. (2016). "Self-Organizing Governance of local economic development: Informal policy networks and regional institutions." *Journal of Urban Affairs* doi:10.1111/juaf.12280.

Hawkins, C. V., Krause, R., Feiock, R., and Curley, C. (2015). "Administrative Capacity and Collaboration in Local Sustainability Initiatives." Paper presented at the Association for Public Policy Analysis and Management 2015 Fall Research Conference, November 12–14.

Hicklin, A. O'Toole, L. J., and Meier, K. J. (2008). "Serpents in the Sand: Managerial Networking and Nonlinear Influences on Organizational Performance." *Journal of Public Administration Research and Theory* 18(2): 253–273.

Jung, K., and Song, M. (2015). "Linking Emergency Management Networks to Disaster Resilience: Bonding and Bridging Strategy in Hierarchical or Horizontal Collaboration Networks." *Quality & Quantity* 49: 1465–1483. doi:10.1007/s11135-014-0092-x.

Kwak, C. (2016). "Exogenously Driven Network Change and Its Impact on Policy Performance: The Impact of Federal EECBG Programs on Metropolitan Green Economies." PhD diss., Askew School of Public Administration, Florida State University.

Kwak, C., Feiock, R. C., Hawkins, C., and Lee, Y. (2016). "Impacts of Federal Stimulus Funding on Economic Development Policy Networks among Local Governments." *Review of Policy Research* 33(2): 140–159.

Kreuger, S., and Bernick, E. (2010). "State Rules and Local Governance Choices." *Publius: The Journal of Federalism* 40(4): 697–718.

Lee, Y. (2011). "Economic Development Networks among Local Governments: The Structure of Collaboration Networks in the Tampa Bay Metropolitan Area." *International Review of Public Administration* 16(1): 113–134.

Lee, Y, Lee, I. W., and Feiock, R. C. (2012). "Interorganizational Collaboration in Economic Development Networks: An Exponential Random Graph Analysis." *Policy Studies Journal* 40(3): 547–573.

LeRoux, K., Brandenburger, P. W., and Pandey, S. K. (2010). "Interlocal Service Cooperation in U.S. Cities: A Social Network Explanation." *Public Administration Review* 70(2): 268–278.

Lubell, M., Schneider, M., Scholz, J. T., and Mete, M. (2002). "Watershed Partnerships and the Emergence of Collective Action Institutions." *American Journal of Political Science* 46(1): 148–163.

Maser, S. (1985). "Demographic Factors Affecting Constitutional Decisions: The Case of Municipal Charters." *Public Choice* 47: 121–162.

Meier, K. J., and O'Toole, L. J. (2003). "Public Management and Educational Performance: The Impact of Managerial Networking." *Public Administration Review* 63(6): 689–699.

Mitchell, B. (2005). "Integrated Water resource Management, Institutional Arrangements, and Land-Use Planning." *Environment and Planning A* 37: 1335–1352.

Oates, W. E. (1999). "An Essay on Fiscal Federalism." *Journal of Economic Literature* 37(3): 1120–1149.

Ostrom, E. (1990). *Governing the Commons: The Evolution of Institutions for Collective Action.* Cambridge, UK: Cambridge University Press.

Ostrom, V., Tiebout, C. M., and Warren, R. (1961). "The Organization of Government in Metropolitan Areas: A Theoretical Inquiry." *American Political Science Review* 55: 831–842.

O'Toole, L. J., Jr. (2015). "Networks and Networking: The Public Administrative Agendas." *Public Administration Review* 75(3): 361–371.

O'Toole, L. J., Jr., and Meier, K. J. (2004). "Public Management in Intergovernmental Networks: Matching Structural Networks and Managerial Networking." *Journal of Public Administration Research and Theory* 14(4): 469–494.

Pfeffer, J., and Salancik, G. R. (1978). *The External Control of Organizations: A Resource Dependence Perspective.* Stanford, CA: Stanford University Press.

Provan, K. G., and Kenis, P. (2008). "Modes of Network Governance: Structure, Management, and Effectiveness." *Journal of Public Administration Research and Theory* 18(2): 229–252.

Provan, K. G., and Milward, H. B. (2001). "Do Networks Really Work? A Framework for Evaluating Public-Sector Organizational Networks." *Public Administration Review* 61(4): 414–423.

Putnam, R. (2000). *Bowling Alone: The Collapse and Revival of American Community.* New York: Simon & Schuster Paperbacks.

Robins, G. (2015). *Doing Social Network Research—Network-Based Research Design for Social Scientists.* Los Angeles: Sage.

Robins, G., Pattison, P., and Wang, P. (2009). "Closure, Connectivity and Degrees: New Specifications for Exponential Random Graph (p*) Models for Directed Social Networks." *Social Networks* 31: 105–117.

Schneider, M., Scholz, J. T., Lubell, M., Mindruta, D., and Edwardsen, M. (2003). "Building Consensual Institutions: Networks and the National Estuary Program." *American Journal of Political Science* 47(1): 143–158.

Shrestha, M. (2008). "Decentralized Governments, Networks and Interlocal Cooperation in Public Goods Supply." PhD diss., Florida State University.

Shrestha, M. (2010). "Do Risk Profiles of Services Alter Contractual Patterns? A Comparison across Multiple Metropolitan Services." In *Self-Organizing Federalism: Collaborative Mechanisms to Mitigate Institutional Collective Action,* edited by R. C. Feiock, and J. T. Scholz, pp. 114–141. Cambridge, UK: Cambridge University Press.

Shrestha, M., and Feiock, R. (2009). "Governing U.S. Metropolitan Areas: Self-Organizing and Multiplex Service Networks." *American Politics Research* 37: 801–823.

Shrestha, M. K. (2013). "Self-Organizing Network Capital and the Success of Collaborative Public Programs." *Journal of Public Administration Research and Theory* 23(2): 307–329.

Shrestha, M. K., Berardo, R., and Feiock, R. C. (2014). "Solving Institutional Collective Action Problems in Multiplex Networks." *Complexity, Governance & Networks* 1: 49–60.

Shrestha, M. K., Feiock, R. C. (2011). "Transaction Cost, Exchange Embeddedness, and Interlocal Cooperation in Local Public Goods Supply." *Political Research Quarterly* 63(3): 573–587.

Shrestha, M. K., and Feiock, R. C. (2013). "Institutional Collective Action Dilemmas in Service Delivery: Exchange Risks and Contracting Networks among Local Governments." Paper presented at the Public Management Research Association Conference, Madison, WI, June 20–22.

Snijders, T. A. B., Pattison, P. E., Robins, G. L., and Handcock, M. S. (2006). "New Specifications for Exponential Random Graph Models." *Sociology Methodology* 36(1): 99–153.

Song, M., and Jung, K. (2015). "Filling the Gap between Disaster Preparedness and Response Networks of Urban Emergency Management: Following the 2013 Seoul Floods." *Journal of Emergency Management* 13(4): 327–338

Steinacker, A. (2004). "Game Theoretic Models of Metropolitan Cooperation." In *Metropolitan Governance: Conflict, Competition and Cooperation*, edited by R. C. Feiock, pp. 67–94. Washington, DC: Georgetown University Press.

Swann, W. L. (2015). "Examining the Impact of Local Collaborative Tools on Urban Sustainability Efforts: Does the Managerial Environment Matter?" *American Review of Public Administration* (August). doi:10.1177/0275074015598576.

Tavares, A. F., and Feiock, R. C. (2014). "Intermunicipal Cooperation and Regional Governance in Europe: An Institutional Collective Action Framework." Paper presented at the Annual Meeting of the European Consortium for Political Research in Glasgow, Scotland, September 3–6.

Terman, J. N., and Feiock, R. C. (2014). "Improving Outcomes in Fiscal Federalism: Local Political Leadership and Administrative Capacity." *Journal of Public Administration Research and Theory* 25(4): 1059–1080.

Thurmaier, K., and Wood, C. (2002). "Interlocal Agreements as Overlapping Social Network: Picket-fence Regionalism in Metropolitan Kansas City." *Public Administration Review* 62(5): 585–598.

Uzzi, B. (1997). "Social Structure and Competition in Interfirm Networks: The Paradox of Embeddedness." *Administrative Science Quarterly* 42(1): 35–67.

Warner, M. E., and Hefetz, A. (2001). "Local Government Restructuring: Privatization and Its Alternatives." *Journal of Policy Analysis and Management* 20(2): 315–336.

Williamson, O. (1981). "The Economics of Organization: The Transaction Cost Approach." *American Journal of Sociology* 87(3): 548–577.

Woolcock, M. (1998). "Social Capital and Economic Development: Toward a Theoretical Synthesis and Policy Framework." *Theory and Society* 27(2): 151–208.

CHAPTER 23

NETWORK SEGREGATION AND POLICY LEARNING

ADAM DOUGLAS HENRY

INTRODUCTION

MANY public policy issues are characterized by a gap between technical knowledge about what can and should be done about a problem and political actions that translate this knowledge into practical solutions (Cash et al., 2003; McNie, 2007; Mitchell et al., 2006). Closing this gap between knowledge and action is a matter of promoting *learning* among participants of the policy process. Learning is a multiplex concept that involves increasing the ability of policy participants to manage complex problems by drawing on scientific or technical information, developing common understandings of problems to be addressed, and collectively producing innovative policy solutions (Henry, 2009). There is long-standing interest in understanding learning in the policy process (Bennett and Howlett, 1992; May, 1992; Parson and Clark, 2005), and there are many different treatments of this concept by policy scholars. In general, however, "learning" implies some degree of evidence-based policymaking involving the use of data to define and monitor problems, understand the causes of these problems, assess the efficacy of possible solutions, and then take action based on this knowledge.

Scholarship on learning often focuses on the critical role that policy networks play in enabling actors to successfully learn and manage shared policy problems. One of the major challenges that we face in terms of promoting learning is the problem of network segregation (Fagiolo, Valente, and Vriend, 2007; Freeman, 1978; Henry, Prałat, and Zhang, 2011; Takács, 2007)—that is, when individuals with shared or similar attributes also tend to be connected through policy-relevant relationships important to learning, such as collaboration and trust. Similarly, in a segregated network, those with different traits tend to not be connected with one another. This inhibits diverse, boundary-spanning networks, which are commonly thought to be a prerequisite for policy learning to occur (Bidwell, Dietz, and Scavia, 2013). These are central ideas in the emerging literature on collaborative policy regimes (e.g., Emerson, Nabatchi, and Balogh, 2011; Pretty, 2003; Sabatier et al., 2005). This literature emphasizes the need to form networks across diverse groups of actors; such networks are hypothesized to maximize the collective ability of policy participants to synthesize information and coordinate policy actions. At the same time, much remains unknown about the effectiveness of collaborative regimes (Lubell, 2004), particularly how they influence the structure of networks (Schneider et al., 2003).

The idea of network segregation is not only central to studies of collaborative governance, but also pervades the more general literature on policy process and policy change. There is, however, relatively little systematic research on segregation in policy networks: why it emerges, the effects of network segregation on learning, and the influence of institutions meant to promote more effective network structures. This chapter explores these issues by considering three commonly assumed propositions about segregation, learning, and policy networks:

> Proposition 1: Policy networks exhibit network segregation.
> Proposition 2: Network segregation tends to inhibit learning.
> Proposition 3: Network segregation emerges as a result of homophily.

As discussed in greater detail below, these propositions represent assumptions that are often made in scholarship on learning and networks. These assumptions have had a powerful effect on the study of learning and the types of solutions that scholars and practitioners look to in order to manage emerging, complex, and high-stakes problems. By treating these assumptions as empirical questions, we see that there is a complicated relationship between networks and learning, and that a more broad theoretical discussion is needed to understand this relationship. Each proposition has mixed support, and proposition 2 has been subject to almost no systematic research. Reviewing the evidence for each proposition and clarifying future research needs is an important step toward developing a comprehensive theory of policy learning.

This chapter begins with an overview of concepts of learning as they are commonly used in policy research, with a particular emphasis on the importance of networks and the perceived problem of segregation. The varied treatments of network segregation in theories of the policy process are then reviewed. Finally, each of the three propositions about network segregation is considered—including their theoretical foundations as well as the empirical evidence in support of each proposition. A deeper understanding of the logic of and evidence for these propositions is of theoretical interest, but can also inform practical strategies that may be used to enhance learning outcomes in the policy process.

Learning and the Importance
of Networks

The concept of learning is frequently used in the policy literature (Adger, 2005; Bennett and Howlett, 1992; Gerlak and Heikkila, 2011; Henry, 2009; Hoverman et al., 2011; Parson and Clark, 2005) and the social sciences in general (Feldman, Aoki, and Kumm, 1996; Rendell et al., 2010). Broadly speaking, "learning" refers to shifts in the behavior or cognition of social agents due to information gained through direct experience (in what may be referred to as "individual learning") or from other social agents (in what may be referred to as "social learning"), as depicted schematically in figure 23.1.

This broad categorization of individual and social learning does conceal diversity in scholarly treatments of the concept. One aspect of this diversity is that "social agents" may mean different things, including people or aggregates of people such as formal organizations (Busenberg, 2001), collaborative groups or teams (Gerlak and Heikkila, 2011; Heikkila and Gerlak, 2013), policy subsystems (May, 1992; Sabatier and Jenkins-Smith, 1993), or even entire societies (Parson and Clark, 2005; Social Learning Group, 2001). Depending on the definition of these social agents, the outcomes that constitute behavioral or cognitive changes may vary greatly. At the level of individuals, we may be interested in cognitive changes such as shifts in belief systems, culture, or political ideology. Shifts in individual behaviors may include the strategies that one uses in social dilemmas, consumption choices, or voting behavior. At the level of organizations, scholars may study organizational cultures or innovative practices. Groups of individuals and organizations, such as participants in collaborative governance processes, may learn by synthesizing information, solving problems, or reaching consensus on key issues. At an even higher scale, entire governments or

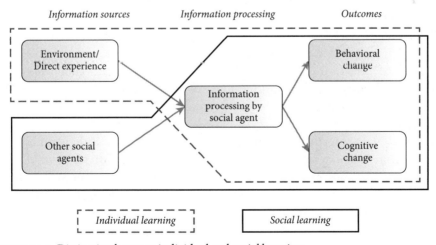

FIGURE 23.1 Distinction between individual and social learning.

policy systems might formulate and implement new policies (a behavioral change) based in part on shifting beliefs and values that underpin policy choices (a cognitive change).

The use of learning concepts in the social sciences, and the policy literature in particular, are highly varied. These include positive approaches focused on better theoretical understandings of belief systems and cognitive change (Henry and Dietz, 2012), how policies and innovations diffuse across governments and organizations (Berry and Berry, 2007; O'Neill, Pouder, and Buchholtz, 1998; Strang and Soule, 1998), and the use of experience to update policy (Birkland, 2004). More normative perspectives on learning emphasize the need for decisionmaking tools that are based on systematic evidence about problems and the likely efficacy of solutions—this is the major focus of the policy analysis and program evaluation literatures (Bardach, 2012; Weiss, 1972, 1977).

Two important features distinguish learning (in particular) from behavioral and cognitive change (in general). The first, as illustrated in figure 23.1, is that learning is change based on new information made available to a learning agent. This is opposed to changes based on random shifts resulting from some set of exogenous factors. For instance, a city might implement water conservation measures as a response to new information about future water supply pressures. This would be a form of learning. On the other hand, water conservation measures that are implemented to meet state-level requirements would count as change, but not learning (although the changing requirements might be considered learning by agents at the state level).

The second feature of policy learning is that the changes in question further one or more goals of the learning agent. Learning is meant to further an outcome of interest; this is an important criterion, because the existence of desired outcomes provides a basis for an agent to assess the efficacy of its behaviors, as well as the need for further adjustments over time. Following the water conservation example, a city might implement conservation measures to accomplish a number of goals, such as reducing the city's reliance on external water supplies, incentivizing more water-smart development, or replenishing groundwater reserves. The idea that learning is goal-oriented distinguishes policy learning from learning as it is traditionally thought of in education. In education, "learning" is limited to the accumulation of knowledge, regardless of how this knowledge is used for the furtherance of the learner's goals. Knowledge accumulation entails gathering information and processing this information to produce cognitive shifts. Learning, on the other hand, involves using accumulated knowledge to solve problems of interest.

Some scholars assert that certain types of policy change, such as mimicry, do not constitute learning (e.g., May, 1992). This would suggest that innovation models are not truly models of learning, since they focus on how an individual agent's behavior is conditioned on the behaviors of those with whom it has contact (or shares a social space). But this would depend on the goals of the agent and the rationale for change. Mimicry is an important mechanism of social learning, in that copying others can be a way of acquiring skills—for example, survival skills of human and nonhuman animals or governance practices that effectively respond to public opinion—without bearing the costs of trial-and-error experimentation (Rendell et al., 2010).

Despite this great variety in perspectives, they all share a common focus on how we—as societies, governments, organizations, or people—can make better decisions that help us to solve complex problems and increase our overall well-being. It can be difficult to navigate the many concepts of learning as they are used in the policy literature. And yet, the attention that scholars pay to learning is evidence of its great practical importance in understanding policy change and, most importantly, policy change that leads to improvement in wrenching social and environmental problems.

CHALLENGES OF LEARNING: WHY NETWORKS MATTER

A common theme in the learning literature is that networks matter, and therefore network influences should take center stage in any comprehensive theory of learning (Henry, 2009). This is because the existence (or absense) of certain relationships helps to explain the ability of policy participants to deal with multiple challenges of learning. To illustrate these challenges, consider one type of learning: climate change adaptation as defined by the Intergovernmental Panel on Climate Change (IPCC). According to the IPCC's Third Assessment Report, climate adaptation is *adjustment in natural or human systems in response to actual or expected climactic stimuli or their effects, which moderates harm or exploits beneficial opportunities.*

In this definition, "adjustment in natural or human systems" may include some combination of behavioral or cognitive changes, such as the migration of populations vulnerable to sea level rise (a behavioral change) or the inclusion of sea level rise as an evaluative criterion for planning national policies for climate change adaptation (a cognitive change). This may happen at the level of an individual, such as a single person who migrates from a coastal area, or at the level of a government that implements a program to relocate an entire island population.

The IPCC definition of climate change adaptation underscores the myriad challenges that accompany learning in any complex, uncertain, and polarized issue. These challenges are discussed below.

Understanding complex systems. Many policy issues are technically complex, meaning that the causes of problems and the efficacy of potential solutions are not fully understood. Moreover, for many issues, scientific uncertainty will be endemic to any policy decision. Given the complexity of many issues, a better understanding of the underlying systems is necessary to formulate effectual policy solutions.

Translating knowledge from those who produce information to those who take action. Understanding what is possible is different from implementing change. A major challenge of learning is therefore to move information from those who hold knowledge that informs better policy to those with the power and authority to act on this knowledge.

Learning common goals, beliefs, and values. Not all stakeholders in a policy issue have a common understanding of what constitutes a "problem," and indeed conflict over normative aspects of policy is common. Belief change that leads to convergence in normative perspectives on an issue—or at least that reduces the negative effects of belief polarization—is an important challenge of learning (Lackey, 2007).

These challenges are especially salient in issues of sustainability (Henry and Vollan, 2014), but apply broadly to other policy issues as well. Networks both constrain and enable the types of social interactions that are needed to meet these cross-cutting challenges of learning. A social agent's collaborative relationships, for example, shape the resources they have access to, such as information about problems and varied beliefs about the causes of problems.

The idea that social environments matter for learning is broadly recognized in the literature, even when networks and network dynamics do not take center stage. Heikkila and Gerlak's (2013) theoretical treatment of learning in collaborative processes provides an illustration. These authors frequently invoke network concepts in their treatment of the process by which one moves from learning by individuals to learning by collectives of individuals. In particular, this process involves (1) the acquisition of information, in part from "active dialogue or deliberation among organizational members or across networks of actors with diverse bases of knowledge"; (2) the translation of raw information through mechanisms such as seeking the assistance of "expert knowledge" or "trusted advisers" to help interpret and understand raw information; and (3) the dissemination of knowledge throughout the collective through mechanisms such as communication and dialogue (Heikkila and Gerlak, 2013, 488–491).

Not only do networks matter for the aggregation and processing of information, but they are also an important part of the contextual factors that influence social agents' ability to work together to solve or manage shared problems (Dietz and Henry, 2008). For example, network structures may influence power structures, conflict, and the perceived legitimacy of learning processes (Booher and Innes, 2002), for example through the centralization of relationships around a single group of influential actors or through the marginalization of some peripheral groups (Bodin and Crona, 2009; Henry and Vollan, 2014).

THE (PERCEIVED) PROBLEM OF NETWORK SEGREGATION

If the structure of networks influences the capacity of social agents to learn, it is natural to ask: What types of network structures are desirable? There is a common assumption that diversity in one's networks is important for addressing the learning challenges described above. It is hypothesized that, for instance, that diverse teams of problem solvers are better able to solve complex problems (Hong and Page, 2004); this is reflected in strategies of organizations to promote interdisciplinary research efforts and science centers. Regarding the challenge of moving information from communities of knowledge to communities of action, networks are important for creating pathways through which decision makers gain access to scientists, as well as promoting the engagement of scientists and other technical professionals in the policy process (Booher and Innes, 2002; Frank et al., 2012). Regarding the challenge of resolving belief and value conflict, diverse networks are thought to reduce the tendency toward the creation of "echo chambers," in which information and arguments are exchanged among those with high propensity to agree, without influencing larger-scale debates.

But while the ideal structure of networks resembles a "complex web" that promotes diverse and boundary-spanning interactions (Feldman and Ingram, 2009; Laird-Benner and Ingram, 2010), in many policy systems those who *should* work together to meet learning challenges *do not* work together. In other words, real-world policy networks tend to inhibit diversity, in that they predominantly connect individuals with shared or similar traits.

This feature of networks is called *network segregation*. This term is drawn from Freeman's (1978) paper, which extends intuitive notions of spatial segregation to the more generic context of social networks. This work offers a quantitative measure of segregation that captures the degree to which the diversity of connected actors compares to the global diversity of actors in a system. According to Freeman, "a social network displays an extreme of segregation when all the members of one class of persons are cut off from all relationships with all members of other classes" (414). Given that the "class" of a network actor could mean anything—ranging from static, observable traits such as gender, to unobserved, malleable traits such as a person's beliefs—the concept of network segregation allows us to measure fragmentation of networks along any arbitrary set of dimensions. When the diversity of a social agent's local network is lower than the diversity of the network as a whole, then the network is said to be segregated.

Network scholars have long known that many real-world networks exhibit segregation—that is, that one tends to observe ties between individuals with shared or similar traits more frequently than ties between individuals who are very different

(Jackson, 2008, 2014). Many networks exhibit segregation along a wide spectrum of traits—this is one of the most robust empirical findings in the social network literature. For instance, segregation has been observed in terms of socioeconomic variables such as race (Currarini, Jackson, and Pin, 2009, 2010), nationality (Girard, Hett, and Schunk, 2015), and gender (Kleinbaum, Stuart, and Tushman, 2013); cognitive and behavioral traits such as personal tastes (Lewis, Gonzalez, and Kaufman, 2012) and one's propensity to cooperate with others (Girard, Hett, and Schunk, 2015); as well as genetic traits (Boardman, Domingue, and Fletcher, 2012).

Given such widespread evidence of network segregation, it is curious that this term appears relatively infrequently in the network literature. This is because two related terms have, for the most part, replaced the concept of network segregation: homophily and community structure. While both are closely related to concepts of segregation, neither is precisely the same thing.

First, consider the term *homophily*—referring to the tendency of people who are similar to form connections with one another (Kossinets and Watts, 2009; McPherson, Smith-Lovin, and Cook, 2001). Much of the literature cited above as evidence of network segregation empirically describes segregation, but is theoretically oriented toward finding evidence of homophily.

A few different concepts of homophily have emerged to parse the theoretical mechanisms at play in the tendency for actors to form ties on the basis of attribute similarity. For example, one persistent question in understanding homophily is whether this phenomenon is due to a systematic bias for ties with similar individuals (a phenomenon known as *choice homophily*) or due to the increased opportunities for forming ties with similar individuals because people select themselves into social contexts—such as schools, clubs, or residential neighborhoods—based on certain traits (a phenomenon known as *structural homophily*). Clearly distinguishing between these effects—and making clear inferences about whether observed correlations between network ties and attribute similarity are due to choice or structural homophily—is an important area of research (Boucher, 2015; Bramoullé et al., 2012; Currarini, Jackson, and Pin, 2010; Kleinbaum, Stuart, and Tushman, 2013; Kossinets and Watts, 2009).

In either case, a fundamental difference between both forms of homophily and network segregation is that homophily concepts refer to *processes that determine tie formation*, whereas segregation refers to an *observed characteristic of social networks*. Many studies of network structure focus on identifying homophily as a force behind the structure of networks; however in studies of cross-sectional networks, this is done by identifying network segregation. And while network segregation by itself is suggestive of homophily, segregated networks do not necessarily imply that homophily was responsible for generating observed structures—a point that is returned to below.

Second, community structure is also closely related to segregation. Many networked systems are *modular*, in that nodes may be naturally partitioned into two or more groups with many within-group linkages, but relatively few linkages across groups (Girvan and Newman, 2002; Newman, 2006; Palla et al., 2005; Porter, Onnela, and Mucha, 2009).

These groups, or the "communities" within a network, often map onto a natural definition of groups based on clusters of nodal attributes such as scientific discipline within
co-citation networks of scientific papers (Kajikawa et al., 2007) or compartmentaliza-
tion in the structure of food webs (Krause et al., 2003). In this way, community structure
is often a strong form of network segregation. However, modularity refers to a concentration of linkages among certain groups of nodes, whereas network segregation refers
to a situation in which the existence of links is correlated with the similarity of nodal
attributes. It is possible to have networks that exhibit both segregation and community structure, but modularity is also possible without network segregation, and network
segregation is possible without modularity.

The distinction between the modularity of networks and network segregation is
illustrated in figure 23.2, which depicts four idealized network structures that vary
in both dimensions. In all cases, network actors have some arbitrary, binary attribute
signified by the shading of the node (either closed or open circles). In these diagrams,
networks A and C are both highly segregated, in the sense that nearly all of the network links exist between actors of the same group; in network A there is only one
link connecting nodes belonging to different groups, and in network C there are only
two such cross-group linkages. Networks B and D, on the other hand, exhibit low levels of segregation. In these networks, every link is a cross-group link. This situation
yields a perfectly *integrated* network (Freeman, 1978), such that the levels of segregation are actually lower than what one would expect if ties among actors were formed
at random.

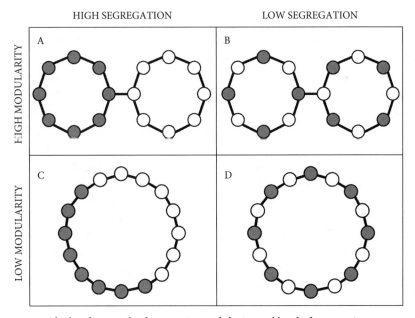

FIGURE 23.2 Idealized networks that vary in modularity and level of segregation.

In terms of modularity, networks A and B both exhibit high levels of modularity—or an intuitive community structure—because one need only cut one link (the linkage joining the two cycles) in order to create a network with two (disconnected) components. Moreover, in networks A and B only one link exists that will, once removed, yield two disconnected components. On the other hand, one must remove two linkages from networks C and D to create a disconnected network. In these networks it is arbitrary which links should be removed to create two disconnected components, making it unclear which nodes in networks C and D should be naturally grouped together. This demonstrates that segregation and community structure are different, and need to be treated as such.

NETWORK SEGREGATION IN POLICY THEORY

Up to this point, the problem of network segregation has been considered in rather generic terms. Segregation is such a prolific characteristic of networks that one must be careful to apply the concept in ways that make it meaningful to the learning challenges outlined above. To this end, let us consider a few theoretical perspectives on public policy that give network segregation a prominent role, in either explicit or implicit terms. This leads to particular hypotheses about the types of segregation one expects to observe and why this feature of networks is expected to pose a barrier to policy learning.

Advocacy coalition framework (ACF). The ACF is a relatively long-standing perspective on the policy process that seeks to understand why major policy changes occur—or more frequently, do not occur—in the context of policy issues characterized by high scientific or technical complexity and high levels of conflict over normative beliefs, values, and ideologies (Henry et al., 2014; Sabatier and Jenkins-Smith, 1993, 1999; Sabatier and Weible, 2007; Weible et al., 2011). The ACF begins with the observation that much of what constitutes public policy is the translation of a particular belief system that specifies, among other things, which problems are important enough to take action on, why problems persist over time, and the potential efficacy of different policy solutions. Crucially, belief systems are viewed as integrating both positive and normative dimensions. So, for example, while climate change policy might be based on established facts, such as the famous IPCC statement *there exists a discernible human impact on the global climate*, it is also based on normative ideas or beliefs, such as *it is (or is not) acceptable for humans to interfere with natural systems* (Henry and Dietz, 2012). As a result, many policy debates about objective, scientific issues become proxies for unresolvable debates over normative beliefs and values—a widespread problem in environmental policy (Lackey, 2006), a policy realm to which the ACF has been widely applied.

Network segregation is a central concept in the ACF. In particular, the ACF argues that policy elites—those individuals who are both engaged in a policy subsystem and specialists in a particular policy issue—tend to organize themselves into two or more "advocacy coalitions" that share fundamental belief systems about the policy issue. An advocacy coalition is defined as a group of policy elites who engage in nontrivial degrees of coordination and share fundamental belief systems (Sabatier and Weible, 2007). In other words, networks of coordination among policy elites are hypothesized to exhibit segregation in policy beliefs. This belief-oriented segregation of policy networks is hypothesized to emerge and be maintained by social psychological factors such as biased assimilation, which causes individuals to trust primarily information that conforms their prior beliefs (Lord, Ross, and Lepper, 1979), and devil shift, which causes individuals to view opponents (e.g., individuals or organizations in competing coalitions) as more powerful and nefarious than they really are (Sabatier, Hunter, and McLaughlin, 1987). So in the ACF, network segregation is viewed as a primary mechanism that creates and sustains political conflict and inhibits policy learning.

Agenda setting and multiple streams. The multiple-streams framework is a widely used perspective on the policy process developed originally by Kingdon (1995). This theoretical perspective seeks to explain agenda setting; that is, why some issues become prominent on governmental agendas for potential action, and other issues do not. One important starting point is the recognition that our collective focus on certain policy issues is not necessarily a function of the importance of the issue. Rather, attention to issues is a function of unpredictable, external factors such as catastrophic events (or "focusing events") that bring an issue to the forefront of public or political attention, as well as the presence of well-connected individuals who work to shape governmental agendas.

To explain why agenda setting occurs, this perspective views policy processes as unfolding within three independent "streams," known as the policy stream, the politics stream, and the problem stream. The problem stream consists of information about problems, including indicators of problem severity, such as data on global mean temperatures and storm intensity, in the case of climate change. The policy stream consists of options for problem improvement (known as policy alternatives) that are researched and developed by technical experts, such as the potential efficacy of carbon taxes or emissions trading. The politics stream includes factors of more immediate and direct relevance to political outcomes, such as shifts in public opinion (often as a result of focusing events, such as catastrophic storms) or interest group lobbying efforts. The reason a particular issue does not typically make the agenda is that one needs a coupling of these streams, however the streams typically operate independently of one another. Thus, for a problem to rise to the immediate attention of decision makers, one must have information about severity and trends (problem stream), a set of viable policy alternatives to deal with the problem (policy stream), and a favorable political climate (politics stream). Couplings of these streams becomes possible when an individual known as a "policy entrepreneur" links independent streams during a window of opportunity, such as a major focusing event that makes a situation ripe for political action. The multiple streams perspective has been applied to many different types of issues, including climate change (Pralle, 2009; Shibuya, 1996), education policy (McLendon, 2003), international trade and regulation (Ackrill and Kay, 2011; Brunner, 2008), criminal justice (Saint-Germain and Calamia, 1996), and transportation (Khayesi and Amekudzi, 2011).

While the multiple streams literature does not describe streams as networks, nor even as collections of policy actors, network concepts are easily applied here. In particular, each of these streams is in fact the result of a community of people and organizations that are professionally engaged in a particular policy issue—such as the lab or field scientists who describe a problem and accumulate information about it (i.e., those contributing to the problem stream); the policy professionals, including academics and agency bureaucrats, who define alternatives (i.e., those contributing to the policy stream); and the interest groups and media organizations that respond to public opinion and the elected officials who respond to these trends (i.e., those contributing to the politics stream). The conjecture that each of the streams operates independently suggests that policy participants—including scientists, academics, agency bureaucrats, media professionals, and elected officials—generally contribute to only one stream, and thus coordination among actors contributing to distinct streams should be relatively rare. In other words, typical networks of coordination among policy professionals should be segregated in terms of politics, policy, and problem stream contributions. When a policy entrepreneur couples streams within a window of opportunity, they create linkages that span these fragmentations, thereby increasing the likelihood of an issue being put on the national agenda.

Institutional collective action (ICA). ICA is an emerging framework that argues that inefficiencies in decision-making result primarily from fragmentation within policy systems. In local or regional decision-making, one often observes a lack of coordination on common policy issues across individual local governments, different vertical scales of political authority, and fragmentation across functional domains. These fragmentations create inefficiencies and collective action problems in the public policy process, particularly in the coordination of regional governance processes. As an example, consider transportation and land use policy in the United States, where transportation policy is primarily the responsibility of metropolitan planning organizations, which are regional entities often covering multiple cities and counties within large metro regions. In more rural areas, state governments take primary responsibility to plan and spend federal transportation funds. On the other hand, land use authority tends to be the domain of local town or city governments. Having an integrated land use and transportation planning process creates more efficient policies, given the large impact transportation infrastructure has on land use and the effect of land use patterns on transportation demand and transportation choices (Cervero, 2003). But integrated planning also means that local governments must give up some policymaking authority in the interests of regional planning, creating collective action problems in the distribution and use of political power. This typically results in the continuance of traditional, fragmented decision-making.

This fragmentation of local and regional decision-making is also a story of network segregation. In terms of the types of "typical" policy networks one should expect to see, networks of collaboration should be observed among governments, organizations, and individuals working in a given functional domain, local jurisdiction, or vertical level of government. Thus, policy networks are expected to be segregated in at least three dimensions; consistent with the ACF, this perspective has also been expanded to include the expectation that networks will be segregated along ideological dimensions as well (Schneider et al., 2003). Given the ICA's focus on transaction costs as a barrier to the formation and maintenance of collaborative ties, solutions to this problem of network segregation include the formation of institutions that will reduce the transaction costs of collaborating with actors who are very different—for example, through a collaborative process emphasizing cross-boundary coordination.

It should be noted that this is not an exhaustive account of network segregation concepts as they appear in the policy process literature. Several additional theories, most notably theories of social capital and collaborative governance, cut across these perspectives and provide a basis for understanding why segregation persists, why it matters for learning, and what can be done about it. When we once again widen our view to network segregation as a general feature of policy networks—which may be realized in specific terms, such as the formation of coalitions around shared beliefs, independence of streams within the policy process, or fragmentation in local decision-making—three propositions about network segregation emerge. These are generally treated as assumptions but are in fact testable hypotheses: (1) policy networks exhibit segregation, (2) network segregation inhibits learning, and (3) network segregation is a result of homophily. Let us critically examine the evidence surrounding each of these propositions.

Proposition 1: Policy Networks Exhibit Segregation

As noted above, network segregation is a common characteristic of real-world social networks (e.g., Boardman, Domingue, and Fletcher, 2012; Jackson, 2014; Kossinets and Watts, 2009; McPherson, Smith-Lovin, and Cook, 2001). Yet one must be careful in generalizing this claim to the context of policy networks. In addition, a network may exhibit segregation in one trait and not others; we must therefore ask not only whether policy networks are segregated, but whether they are segregated in the traits that matter for learning.

The three policy process theories outlined above provide guidance in the relevant types of segregation to be examined. Consider first the question of whether policy networks are segregated around shared belief systems, a proposition drawn from the ACF. Figure 23.3 shows a network linking organizations involved in climate change policy in Switzerland over a ten-year period from 1995 to 2005, measured through a series of face-to-face interviews with representatives of these organizations (Ingold, 2011). Organizational representatives were asked to nominate other organizations they view as allies and opponents in climate policy. These individuals were then asked about beliefs concerning various policy instruments to mitigate climate change. The shading of network nodes represents subscription to a common belief system, as defined by a k-means clustering algorithm that assigns all individuals to one of two clusters of policy beliefs.

A casual examination of the network of reported alliances in this Swiss climate policy system (dark black links in figure 23.3) shows a high degree of modularity. When the belief system "membership" of each of these nodes is superimposed on the modular network (symbolized by node shading), one also observes a fairly strong pattern of segregation in terms of belief systems—making this network an example of one displaying high modularity and high segregation, similar to network A in figure 23.2. This intuitive conclusion is supported by a statistical test correlating shared belief system membership (where dyads are coded zero if two nodes belong to different belief system clusters and coded as one, otherwise) with reported alliances (coded as one) and reported

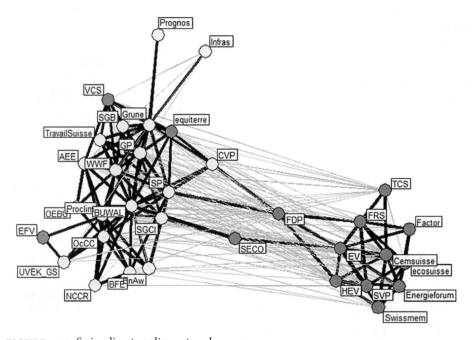

FIGURE 23.3 Swiss climate policy network, 1995–2005.

Note: Network vertices represent organizations involved in climate policy. Black links represent reported alliances; grey links represent reported oppositional relations. Vertex color represents cluster membership in terms of belief system, using a k-means clustering algorithm. Data used to generate this network diagram are discussed further in Ingold (2011).

oppositions (coded as negative one). This observed graph correlation statistic is both positive and significantly different from zero based on a quadratic assignment procedure (QAP; Krackardt, 1987) test of significance (graph correlation = 0.355; QAP p-value < 0.001 in 1,000 permutations).

While the Swiss climate policy network exhibits network segregation based on policy belief, other policy networks display more subtle levels of belief-oriented segregation that are difficult to identify through casual examination of the network structure. For example, figure 23.4 depicts a network of contact relations among organizations involved in environmental risk policy in the United States around 1984, a time when risk assessment and risk analysis were emerging techniques for better understanding and formulating policies related to environmental issues (Dietz and Rycroft, 1987).

The high density of this network prevents us from seeing a clean community structure; however, this is a segregated network. One can test empirically for segregation by correlating contact ties with the beliefs of individual policy organizations as measured by a survey. When the difference of organizations in terms of beliefs about a wide spectrum of environmental risk issues is calculated, there is a strong negative correlation between contact linkages and belief distance (graph correlation = −0.20; QAP test p-value < 0.05 over 1,000 iterations). This suggests that although the network is not strongly modular, it is strongly segregated in terms of policy beliefs, similar to network C in figure 23.2.

Many other research studies in the ACF tradition support the notion that policy networks—variously conceptualized as alliances, collaboration, and information exchange relations—exhibit segregation along critical types of policy beliefs. For example, belief-oriented network segregation has been observed in the context of regional transportation and land use planning (Henry, Lubell, and McCoy, 2011; Henry, 2011), marine protected areas (Weible and Sabatier, 2005; Weible, 2005), and wildlife management (Matti and Sandström, 2011).

What about segregation in other dimensions? As noted previously, the ICA tradition points to the existence of segregation across functional domains, vertical levels of government, and horizontal jurisdictions. In their study of organizations involved in watershed policy, Schneider et al. (2003) provide empirical evidence of these fragmentations and add a fourth type of segregation (along ideological lines) to the list. To illustrate further the empirical evidence, consider a study of how local governments collaborate on land use and transportation issues in five regions of California (Gerber, Henry, and Lubell, 2013). Using exponential random graph models (EGRMs), these authors show that collaborations among local governments exhibit segregation in terms of socioeconomic factors such as the affluence and racial composition of the city's population, as well as political ideology as measured by the political party registration of city residents. Additional factors predicting the existence of collaborations are geographic proximity and the sharing of a common border. Collaborations across vertical levels of government (at least between city and county governments) were relatively frequent, indicating a lack of segregation across vertical levels of government, at least in this particular empirical context.

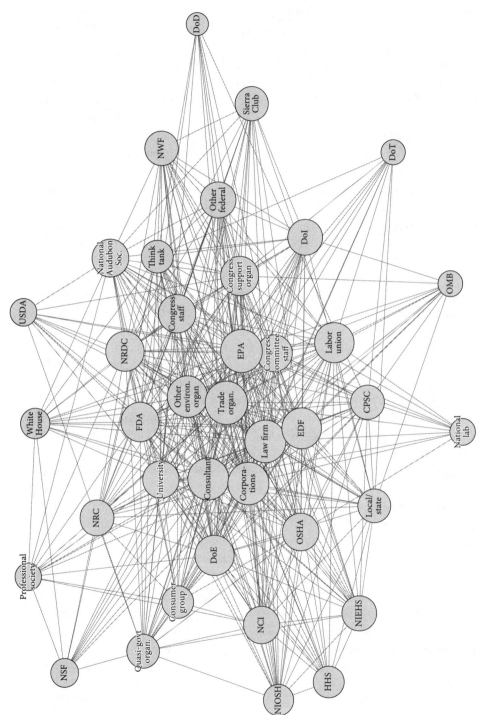

FIGURE 23.4 U.S. Environmental Risk Policy network, circa 1984.

Note: Network vertices represent organizations involved in the scientific of political aspects of environmental risk policy in the United States, circa 1984. Nodes represent organizations involved in environmental risk policy. Links represent contact between organizations to coordinate or share information about environmental risk issues. Data used to generate this network diagram are discussed further in Dietz & Rycroft (1987).

Overall, while more work is needed to assess the proposition that policy networks are segregated along a wide spectrum of network types and actor attributes, there is a large amount of support for this general proposition.

PROPOSITION 2: NETWORK SEGREGATION INHIBITS LEARNING

In sharp contrast to the research identifying segregation within policy networks, the claim that network segregation inhibits learning is generally made on theoretical, rather than empirical, grounds. As previously noted, these arguments generally emphasize the importance of diversity for several reasons, including (1) to increase one's exposure to information, thereby giving social agents better information about problems; (2) to enable face-to-face communication between people, increasing trust, cooperation, and allowing for a more effective communication of ideas; and (3) to enable social agents to manage policy issues that are not appropriately managed at a single scale or by a single class of institutions.

There is relatively strong theory and empirical evidence that local diversity of a network—that is, a more integrated network exhibiting lower segregation levels—will improve the situation of individuals embedded within a network, whether or not these outcomes may be counted as "learning." Based on the analysis of communications networks, for example, locations where people have more diverse social networks also have higher levels of economic development (Eagle, Macy, and Claxton, 2010). These findings are in line with the well-known perspective of brokerage in networks, claiming that those individuals who span disparate communities are more likely to innovate because of their unique ability to couple together different types of knowledge and skills (Burt, 2004).

The literature on the benefits of diversity in one's network is closely related to the idea of social capital, the subject of a vast theoretical and empirical literature (Burt, 2000; Coleman, 1988; Lin, 1999; Portes, 2000; Putnam, 2000). Social capital is thought to be embodied by one's social connections (i.e., engagement with and investments in network ties), trust, and norms of reciprocity. Social capital provides a basis for cooperation among individuals even in the presence of social dilemmas in which one has incentives to act in a self-interested manner. It is hypothesized that barriers to learning, such as trust in information, ideological conflict, and collective action problems, can be overcome through the development of two types of social capital, known as bridging and bonding forms of social capital.

Bridging social capital is reflected in network structures in which individuals maintain connections with multiple disparate communities—that is, structures that are more integrated and less segregated. Consistent with the ICA perspective, bridging structures are thought to lead to more coordinated and efficient policy outcomes, because they link together actors from disparate levels of government, institutional affiliations, and functional domains. One way in which bridging structures are thought to enhance learning is that they enable certain critical actors to become more engaged in the policy process. For example, organizations occupying bridging structures in regional estuary policy in the United States also participate in more collaborative policy activities (Scholz, Berardo, and Kile, 2008). Organizations and individuals that occupy bridging positions between belief systems—"policy brokers"—are able to broker deals and promote policy change on contentious issues such as climate change (Ingold and Varone, 2012). Scientists occupying bridging positions tend to have higher levels of engagement in policy, leading to a more effective use of science in the policy process (Frank et al., 2012).

The benefits of bridging structures are thought to derive also from the accessibility they afford network actors to diverse resources, such as information, that are necessary inputs to learning. In a segregated network, knowledge systems existing in one community are likely to stay in that community (e.g., indigenous populations may have information about local climate changes that is different from the information available to outside scientists), which may exacerbate misunderstandings and mistrust of information from outside one's own community (Lebel et al., 2016). Among natural resource users, ecological knowledge (e.g., knowledge about the extent and quality of fish stocks) tends to be higher when networks among resource users exhibit low levels of segregation in terms of personal background and worldviews (Sandström and Rova, 2010), and when networks exhibit lower segregation in professions and the access that resource users have to different types of physical resources (Crona and Bodin, 2006). Horizontal fragmentations in a network are thought to inhibit the ability of local actors to organize grass-roots efforts to advocate for political actions such as environmental protection (Marín and Berkes, 2010).

Bonding social capital, on the other hand, is reflected in network structures in which individuals maintain in-group ties, as well as ties embedded within triadic structures—meaning that individuals in bonding structures tend to be linked through both direct and multiple indirect connections. These structures are consistent with network segregation. Indeed, research on bonding structures highlights some possible benefits of network segregation to learning. Bonding structures tend to enhance trust and propensity to cooperate based on shared group identity (Sherif, 1966; Tajfel et al., 1971), meaning that actors connected in a segregated network may be in better positions to efficiently share and synthesize policy-relevant information. Related to this, Berardo and Scholz (2010) advance the "risk hypothesis," arguing that policy organizations will generally prefer bridging (nonsegregated) structures for the greater access they provide to diverse information and resources. But in situations where there is a substantial risk of uncooperative behavior, policy organizations will instead seek out bonding (segregated) structures that better support trust and collective action.

Overall, the proposition that network segregation inhibits learning has inconclusive support. It seems that the answer is very sensitive to the outcomes of interest—such as enhanced trust, engagement of policy actors, or the ability to synthesize information— all of which are preconditions for policy learning. Crucially, the answer is also sensitive to the context in which policy processes unfold. The riskiness of cooperation, the complexity of the issue, and the extent to which ideology clouds interpretations of science will all help to determine the effects of network segregation on learning.

PROPOSITION 3: NETWORK SEGREGATION IS A RESULT OF HOMOPHILY

Policy networks evolve as a result of network self-organization—that is, the decisions of individual policy actors to form and delete ties over time. Understanding how networks self-organize as a result of individual attributes (e.g., though homophily), as well as structural factors (e.g., through transitivity, or the creation of linkages with those one is indirectly connected to), is the subject of an emerging literature that has been enabled in part by advances in the statistical modeling of networks (Robins et al., 2007; Snijders et al., 2006; Snijders, van de Bunt, and Steglich, 2010).

The idea that networks self-organize is important to learning because it suggests that one cannot simply mandate a desired network structure. If segregation across political beliefs is undesirable, for example, one might institute programs meant to create connections across these segregated communities, such as a deliberative, collaborative process that brings parties together to discuss competing points of view. But this process may not create the desired linkages, for a variety of reasons—for example, if the process serves only as a way to magnify conflicts rather than points of common interest, or if participants do not have a strong incentive to cooperate with the process. The most important types of linkages in a policy network—such as collaboration and trust—are voluntary. For this reason, institutions meant to promote learning by creating the "right connections" are interventions in an evolving system; these interventions may change an evolutionary trajectory, but will not necessarily create the desired output. Thus, to design better interventions, a better understanding of network self-organization is needed.

The assumption that network segregation is a result of homophily is understandable but limited, for a number of important reasons explored below. For the moment let us consider the power of homophily in generating segregated network structures.

In an early and influential example of an agent-based model, Thomas Schelling (1971) reported an exercise in which a relatively simple decision rule produced an aggregate pattern of behavior that was typically attributed to a different decision rule. In particular, Schelling was interested in modeling the emergence of racial segregation—that is, the tendency of people to live within racially homogenous communities. The standard assumption is that people live in homogenous communities because they prefer to; that is, people have a strict preference for racial segregation. But Schelling's model did not assume such a preference. Instead, Schelling's model assumed only a slight preference against being a minority in one's local neighborhood. So if a particular agent was surrounded by other agents who were different on average, then with some small probability, the minority agent would move to another random point in space. In time, this process produces stark patterns of segregation without the need to assume that individual agents are systematically attracted to homogenous neighborhoods.

On the one hand, this model demonstrates the extreme power of homophily in generating segregated structures. The notion of spatial closeness explored in the Schelling segregation model easily applies to other types of social relations, such as friendship, collaboration, or trust. Thus network segregation is just a more generalized form of the residential segregation that Schelling focused on. And without assuming strict preferences for segregation (a strong form of homophily that may be called *attraction homophily*), a slight aversion from maintaining ties with others who are dissimilar (a weaker form of homophily that may be called *aversion homophily*) is sufficient to produce global patterns of network segregation. Henry, Prałat, and Zhang (2011) show this mathematically and prove that an aversion to maintaining network ties with others who are different is sufficient to produce network segregation given any initial network structure, no matter how small this level of aversion is. These dynamics are illustrated in figure 23.5, which depicts an agent-based model of the emergence of segregation out of an integrated network as a result of a slight level of aversion homophily.

On the other hand, the Schelling segregation model and derivative work illustrate why we need to treat with caution the proposition that network segregation is produced through homophily. Consider first how homophily is commonly conceptualized in the literature. The literal meaning of *homophily*—"love of the same"—suggests that homophily is about attraction to those who are similar, rather than aversion to those who are different. And indeed, as the Schelling model demonstrates, the phenomenon of attraction homophily is conceptually distinct from the phenomenon of aversion homophily. These processes are not just two sides of the same coin, and either form of homophily may independently lead to network segregation.

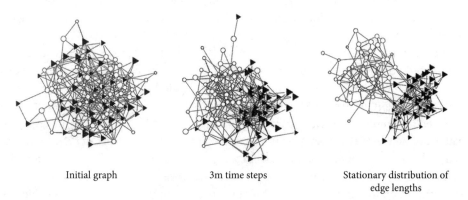

| Initial graph | 3m time steps | Stationary distribution of edge lengths |

FIGURE 23.5 Emergence of network segregation as a result of aversion homophily.

Note: Graphics depict the transition from a random integrated network (left panel) to a segregated network, when the stationary distribution of cross- and within-group ties has been reached (right panel). Given a network with *m* ties, one begins to see segregation emerge after approximately 3m time steps (center panel).

Source: Henry, Prałat, & Zhang, (2011).

The ACF proposition that policy actors form ties on the basis of belief similarity (i.e., that individuals and organizations coordinate as a result of homophily) provides an illustration. The engine driving this phenomenon is biased assimilation, or the tendency for actors to interpret policy-relevant information in a way that tends to confirm their prior belief systems. This is hypothesized to create mistrust between actors with divergent belief systems, which in turn causes those who have very different belief systems to not form networks. In other words, biased assimilation is a mechanism of aversion homophily. But the further assumption that policy actors systematically form ties with those who share their beliefs (attraction homophily) is a different hypothesis. It may be that policy organizations avoid collaboration with others that hold very different beliefs, but shared beliefs may not provide a sufficient basis for actors to coordinate with one another, especially in risky environments that make collective action difficult (Schlager, 1995). And indeed, given that aversion homophily is sufficient to produce network segregation, one cannot distinguish between these mechanisms simply by identifying network segregation.

Finally, there is an important problem in applying the Schelling segregation model to a network context. In the original research context, segregation was studied in terms of attributes that are static over time (race and ethnicity). In policy networks, however, we care about segregation in terms of attributes that are, at least in theory, malleable. Foremost among these are policy-relevant belief systems, including normative values and worldviews, as well as positive understandings of the science that underpins policy issues. It should be the case that belief systems are potentially updated as a result of communication and collaboration with other policy actors. Our theories of network self-organization should therefore consider the possibility that network structures coevolve with the attributes—such as beliefs—of actors within the network (Lazer, 2001).

The realization that network actors potentially adopt the attributes of those they are connected to provides yet another potential pathway other than choice homophily to produce network segregation. Indeed, some network researchers pay primary attention to the diffusion of attributes rather than homophily as an explanation for network segregation (Aral, Muchnik, and Sundararajan, 2009).

Paths Forward

The literature on policy learning is vast, and there will continue to be scholarly discussions on how to best define and study learning. There is broad recognition that policy networks are a key ingredient in the learning process, even though promoting learning through networks is a nontrivial task. Not only is it unknown exactly what structures we should aim to create, but there is also no single lever that may be pulled to realize such a structure. Policy actors, for the most part, choose their trusted collaborators; they are not chosen by others.

Thus, it is crucial for us to ask a fourth question about policy networks: *How do external factors influence network structure and network segregation?* The literature on collaborative governance is relevant to this question. Complex policy problems—particularly those existing on local or regional scales—are increasingly being addressed through collaborative institutions (Emerson, Nabatchi, and Balogh, 2011; Sabatier et al., 2005). These collaborative processes seek to bring together (and promote cooperation among) diverse groups of stakeholders who collectively desire a solution to shared problems, but no single actors can address the problem on their own. Following an ICA perspective on network segregation, collaborative institutions are thought to promote more integrated networks because they reduce the transaction costs involved in creating and maintaining network ties among diverse actors, thus reducing the tendency toward choice homophily. This may be accomplished through mechanisms such as the provision of professional forums, trained facilitators, and opportunities for informal and face-to-face dialogue, which may not be present in more traditional, and more adversarial, policy venues.

The evidence that collaborative institutions produce more integrated networks is still emerging. While participation in collaborative institutions is known to change perceptions of conflict and cooperation (Lubell, 2004), the effect on networks and network segregation is less clear. If a collaborative institution is imposed on policy participants by an external actor, it can be very difficult to create trust and cooperation (Ostrom, 2000), and it is possible that an externally imposed institution will even lower the propensity of individuals to cooperate with one another through a "crowding out" effect of cooperation (Vollan, 2008).

At the same time, we are starting to learn more about the effects of collaborative institutions on networks and learning outcomes. There is evidence that collaborative participants do tend to form more linkages with one another (Schneider et al., 2003; Scott, 2016; Scott and Thomas, 2015); however it is also possible that collaborative institutions may have negative effects on relationships policy actors maintain in other policy venues (Lubell, Henry, and McCoy, 2010; Lubell, 2013; Scott, 2015).

Collectively, this research demonstrates that the networked systems underpinning policy learning are extremely complex, and there will be no single solution to address the varied challenges of policy learning. Comprehensive treatments of learning should give a prominent role to network factors: how they are structured, how they evolve over time, and crucially, how external interventions shape structure. Understanding these factors will help us develop strategies to promote learning, an essential goal that is relevant to many complex and polarized issues of public policy.

Acknowledgments

This essay is based on two talks delivered in spring 2015 at the University of Southern California Sol Price School of Public Policy and the Evans School of Public Policy and Governance at the University of Washington. Both talks were generously supported by the Consortium on Collaborative Governance.

REFERENCES

Ackrill, R., and Kay, A. (2011). "Multiple Streams in EU Policy-Making: The Case of the 2005 Sugar Reform." *Journal of European Public Policy* 18(1): 72–89. http://doi.org/10.1080/13501763.2011.520879.

Adger, W. N. (2005). "Social-Ecological Resilience to Coastal Disasters." *Science* 309(5737): 1036–1039. http://doi.org/10.1126/science.1112122.

Aral, S., Muchnik, L., and Sundararajan, A. (2009). "Distinguishing Influence-Based Contagion from Homophily-Driven Diffusion in Dynamic Networks." *Proceedings of the National Academy of Sciences* 106(51): 21544–21549. http://doi.org/10.1073/pnas.0908800106.

Bardach, E. (2012). *A Practical Guide for Policy Analysis: The Eightfold Path to More Effective Problem Solving.* 4th ed. Los Angeles: Sage; Thousand Oaks, CA: CQ Press.

Bennett, C. J., and Howlett, M. (1992). "The Lessons of Learning: Reconciling Theories of Policy Learning and Policy Change." *Policy Sciences* 25: 275–294.

Berardo, R., and Scholz, J. T. (2010). "Self-Organizing Policy Networks: Risk, Partner Selection, and Cooperation in Estuaries." *American Journal of Political Science* 54(3): 632–649. http://doi.org/10.1111/j.1540-5907.2010.00451.x.

Berry, F. S., and Berry, W. D. (2007). "Innovation and Diffusion Models in Policy Research." In *Theories of the Policy Process*, edited by Paul A. Sabatier, 2d ed., pp. 223–260. Boulder, CO: Westview Press.

Bidwell, D., Dietz, T., and Scavia, D. (2013). "Fostering Knowledge Networks for Climate Adaptation." *Nature Climate Change* 3: 610–611.

Birkland, T. A. (2004). "Learning and Policy Improvement after Disaster: The Case of Aviation Security." *American Behavioral Scientist* 48(3): 341–364. http://doi.org/10.1177/0002764204268990.

Boardman, J. D., Domingue, B. W., and Fletcher, J. M. (2012). "How Social and Genetic Factors Predict Friendship Networks." *Proceedings of the National Academy of Sciences* 109(43): 17377–17381. http://doi.org/10.1073/pnas.1208975109.

Bodin, Ö., and Crona, B. I. (2009). "The Role of Social Networks in Natural Resource Governance: What Relational Patterns Make a Difference?" *Global Environmental Change* 19(3): 366–374. http://doi.org/10.1016/j.gloenvcha.2009.05.002.

Booher, D. E., and Innes, J. E. (2002). "Network Power in Collaborative Planning." *Journal of Planning Education and Research* 21(3): 221–236. http://doi.org/10.1177/0739456X0202100301.

Boucher, V. (2015). "Structural Homophily." *International Economic Review* 56(1): 235–264. http://doi.org/10.1111/iere.12101.

Bramoullé, Y., Currarini, S., Jackson, M. O., Pin, P., and Rogers, B. W. (2012). "Homophily and Long-Run Integration in Social Networks." *Journal of Economic Theory* 147(5): 1754–1786. http://doi.org/10.1016/j.jet.2012.05.007.

Brunner, S. (2008). "Understanding Policy Change: Multiple Streams and Emissions Trading in Germany." *Global Environmental Change* 18(3): 501–507. http://doi.org/10.1016/j.gloenvcha.2008.05.003.

Burt, R. S. (2000). "The Network Structure of Social Capital." *Research in Organizational Behavior* 22: 345–423. http://doi.org/10.1016/S0191-3085(00)22009-1.

Burt, R. S. (2004). "Structural Holes and Good Ideas." *American Journal of Sociology* 110(2): 349–399. http://doi.org/10.1086/421787.

Busenberg, G. J. (2001). "Learning in Organizations and Public Policy." *Journal of Public Policy* 21(2): 173–189.

Cash, D. W., Clark, W. C., Alcock, F., Dickson, N. M., Eckley, N., Guston, D. H., . . . Mitchell, R. B. (2003). "Knowledge Systems for Sustainable Development." *Proceedings of the National Academy of Sciences* 100(14): 8086–8091. http://doi.org/10.1073/pnas.1231332100.

Cervero, R. (2003). "Road Expansion, Urban Growth, and Induced Travel: A Path Analysis." *Journal of the American Planning Association* 69(2): 145–163. http://doi.org/10.1080/01944360308976303.

Coleman, J. S. (1988). "Social Capital in the Creation of Human Capital." *American Journal of Sociology* 94: S95–S120.

Crona, B., and Bodin, Ö. (2006). "What You Know Is Who You Know? Communication Patterns Among Resource Users as a Prerequisite for Co-management." *Ecology and Society* 11(2): 7.

Currarini, S., Jackson, M. O., and Pin, P. (2009). "An Economic Model of Friendship: Homophily, Minorities and Segregation." *Econometrica* 77(4): 1003–1045. http://doi.org/10.2139/ssrn.1021650.

Currarini, S., Jackson, M. O., and Pin, P. (2010). "Identifying the Roles of Race-Based Choice and Chance in High School Friendship Network Formation." *Proceedings of the National Academy of Sciences* 107(11): 4857–4861. http://doi.org/10.1073/pnas.0911793107.

Dietz, T., and Henry, A. D. (2008). "Context and the Commons." *Proceedings of the National Academy of Sciences* 105(36): 13189–13190. http://doi.org/10.1073/pnas.0806876105.

Dietz, T., and Rycroft, R. W. (1987). *The Risk Professionals*. New York: Russell Sage Foundation.

Eagle, N., Macy, M., and Claxton, R. (2010). "Network Diversity and Economic Development." *Science* 328(5981): 1029–1031. http://doi.org/10.1126/science.1186605.

Emerson, K., Nabatchi, T., and Balogh, S. (2011). "An Integrative Framework for Collaborative Governance." *Journal of Public Administration Research and Theory* 22(1): 1–29. http://doi.org/10.1093/jopart/mur011.

Fagiolo, G., Valente, M., and Vriend, N. J. (2007). "Segregation in Networks." *Journal of Economic Behavior & Organization* 64(3–4): 316–336. http://doi.org/10.1016/j.jebo.2006.09.003.

Feldman, D. L., and Ingram, H. M. (2009). "Making Science Useful to Decision Makers: Climate Forecasts, Water Management, and Knowledge Networks." *Weather, Climate, and Society* 1(1): 9–21. http://doi.org/10.1175/2009WCAS1007.1.

Feldman, M. W., Aoki, K., and Kumm, J. (1996). "Individual Versus Social Learning: Evolutionary Analysis in a Fluctuating Environment." *Anthropological Science* 104(3): 209–231. http://doi.org/10.1537/ase.104.209.

Frank, K., Chen, I.-C., Lee, Y., Kalafatis, S., Chen, T., Lo, Y.-J., and Lemos, M. C. (2012). "Network Location and Policy-Oriented Behavior: An Analysis of Two-Mode Networks of Coauthored Documents Concerning Climate Change in the Great Lakes Region." *Policy Studies Journal* 40(3): 492–515. http://doi.org/10.1111/j.1541-0072.2012.00462.x.

Freeman, L. C. (1978). "Segregation in Social Networks." *Sociological Methods & Research* 6(4): 411–429. http://doi.org/10.1177/004912417800600401.

Gerber, E. R., Henry, A. D., and Lubell, M. (2013). "Political Homophily and Collaboration in Regional Planning Networks." *American Journal of Political Science* 57(3): 598–610. http://doi.org/10.1111/ajps.12011.

Gerlak, A. K., and Heikkila, T. (2011). "Building a Theory of Learning in Collaboratives: Evidence from the Everglades Restoration Program." *Journal of Public Administration Research & Theory* 21(4): 619–644.

Girard, Y., Hett, F., and Schunk, D. (2015). "How Individual Characteristics Shape the Structure of Social Networks." *Journal of Economic Behavior & Organization* 115: 197–216. http://doi.org/10.1016/j.jebo.2014.12.005.

Girvan, M., and Newman, M. E. J. (2002). "Community Structure in Social and Biological Networks." *Proceedings of the National Academy of Sciences of the United States of America* 99(12): 7821–7826. http://doi.org/10.1073/pnas.122653799.

Heikkila, T., and Gerlak, A. K. (2013). "Building a Conceptual Approach to Collective Learning: Lessons for Public Policy Scholars: Lessons for Public Policy Scholars." *Policy Studies Journal* 41(3): 484–512. http://doi.org/10.1111/psj.12026.

Henry, A. D. (2009). "The Challenge of Learning for Sustainability: A Prolegomenon to Theory." *Human Ecology Review* 16(2): 131–140.

Henry, A. D. (2011). "Ideology, Power, and the Structure of Policy Networks." *Policy Studies Journal* 39(3): 361–383.

Henry, A. D., and Dietz, T. (2012). "Understanding Environmental Cognition." *Organization & Environment* 25(3): 238–258. http://doi.org/10.1177/1086026612456538.

Henry, A. D., Ingold, K., Nohrstedt, D., and Weible, C. M. (2014). "Policy Change in Comparative Contexts: Applying the Advocacy Coalition Framework Outside of Western Europe and North America." *Journal of Comparative Policy Analysis: Research and Practice* 16(4): 299–312. http://doi.org/10.1080/13876988.2014.941200.

Henry, A. D., Lubell, M., and McCoy, M. (2011). "Belief Systems and Social Capital as Drivers of Policy Network Structure: The Case of California Regional Planning." *Journal of Public Administration Research and Theory* 21(3): 419–444. http://doi.org/10.1093/jopart/muq042.

Henry, A. D., Prałat, P., and Zhang, C.-Q. (2011). "Emergence of Segregation in Evolving Social Networks." *Proceedings of the National Academy of Sciences* 108(21): 8605–8610. http://doi.org/10.1073/pnas.1014486108.

Henry, A. D., and Vollan, B. (2014). "Networks and the Challenge of Sustainable Development." *Annual Review of Environment and Resources* 39(1): 583–610. http://doi.org/10.1146/annurev-environ-101813-013246.

Hong, L., and Page, S. E. (2004). "Groups of Diverse Problem Solvers Can Outperform Groups of High-Ability Problem Solvers." *Proceedings of the National Academy of Sciences* 101(46): 16385–16389. http://doi.org/10.1073/pnas.0403723101.

Hoverman, S., Ross, H., Chan, T., and Powell, B. (2011). "Social Learning through Participatory Integrated Catchment Risk Assessment in the Solomon Islands." *Ecology and Society* 16(2): 17.

Ingold, K. (2011). "Network Structures within Policy Processes: Coalitions, Power, and Brokerage in Swiss Climate Policy: Ingold: Network Structures within Policy Processes." *Policy Studies Journal* 39(3): 435–459. http://doi.org/10.1111/j.1541-0072.2011.00416.x.

Ingold, K., and Varone, F. (2012). "Treating Policy Brokers Seriously: Evidence from the Climate Policy." *Journal of Public Administration Research and Theory* 22(2): 319–346. http://doi.org/10.1093/jopart/mur035.

Jackson, M. O. (2008). *Social and Economic Networks*. Princeton, NJ: Princeton University Press.

Jackson, M. O. (2014). "Networks in the Understanding of Economic Behaviors." *Journal of Economic Perspectives* 28(4): 3–22. http://doi.org/10.1257/jep.28.4.3.

Kajikawa, Y., Ohno, J., Takeda, Y., Matsushima, K., and Komiyama, H. (2007). "Creating an Academic Landscape of Sustainability Science: An Analysis of the Citation Network." *Sustainability Science* 2(2): 221–231. http://doi.org/10.1007/s11625-007-0027-8.

Khayesi, M., and Amekudzi, A. A. (2011). "Kingdon's Multiple Streams Model and Automobile Dependence Reversal Path: The Case of Curitiba, Brazil." *Journal of Transport Geography* 19(6): 1547–1552. http://doi.org/10.1016/j.jtrangeo.2011.06.012.

Kingdon, J. W. (1995). *Agendas, Alternatives, and Public Policies.* 2d ed. New York: Longman.

Kleinbaum, A. M., Stuart, T. E., and Tushman, M. L. (2013). "Discretion Within Constraint: Homophily and Structure in a Formal Organization." *Organization Science* 24(5): 1316–1336. http://doi.org/10.1287/orsc.1120.0804.

Kossinets, G., and Watts, D. J. (2009). "Origins of Homophily in an Evolving Social Network." *American Journal of Sociology* 115(2): 405–450. http://doi.org/10.1086/599247.

Krackardt, D. (1987). "QAP Partialling as a Test of Spuriousness." *Social Networks* 9(2): 171–186. http://doi.org/10.1016/0378-8733(87)90012-8.

Krause, A. E., Frank, K. A., Mason, D. M., Ulanowicz, R. E., and Taylor, W. W. (2003). "Compartments Revealed in Food-Web Structure." *Nature* 426(6964): 282–285. http://doi.org/10.1038/nature02115.

Lackey, R. T. (2006). "Axioms of Ecological Policy." *Fisheries* 31(6): 286–290.

Lackey, R. T. (2007). "Science, Scientists, and Policy Advocacy." *Conservation Biology* 21(1): 12–17. http://doi.org/10.1111/j.1523-1739.2006.00639.x.

Laird-Benner, W. (G.), and Ingram, H. (2010). "Sonoran Desert Network Weavers: Surprising Environmental Successes on the U.S./Mexico Border." *Environment: Science and Policy for Sustainable Development* 53(1): 6–17. http://doi.org/10.1080/00139157.2011.539943.

Lazer, D. (2001). "The Co-Evolution of Individual and Network." *Journal of Mathematical Sociology* 25(1): 69–108. http://doi.org/10.1080/0022250X.2001.9990245.

Lebel, L., Garden, P., Luers, A., Manuel-Navarrete, D., and Giap, D. H. (2016). "Knowledge and Innovation Relationships in the Shrimp Industry in Thailand and Mexico." *Proceedings of the National Academy of Sciences* November 5. 113(17): 4585–4590. http://doi.org/10.1073/pnas.0900555106.

Lewis, K., Gonzalez, M., and Kaufman, J. (2012). "Social Selection and Peer Influence in an Online Social Network." *Proceedings of the National Academy of Sciences* 109(1): 68–72. http://doi.org/10.1073/pnas.1109739109.

Lin, N. (1999). "Building a Network Theory of Social Capital." *Connections* 22(1): 28–51.

Lord, C. G., Ross, L., and Lepper, M. R. (1979). "Biased Assimilation and Attitude Polarization: The Effects of Prior Theories on Subsequently Considered Evidence." *Journal of Personality and Social Psychology* 37(11): 2098–2109. http://doi.org/10.1037/0022-3514.37.11.2098.

Lubell, M. (2004). "Collaborative Environmental Institutions: All Talk and No Action?" *Journal of Policy Analysis and Management* 23(3): 549–573. http://doi.org/10.1002/pam.20026.

Lubell, M. (2013). "Governing Institutional Complexity: The Ecology of Games Framework." *Policy Studies Journal* 41(3): 537–559. http://doi.org/10.1111/psj.12028.

Lubell, M., Henry, A. D., and McCoy, M. (2010). "Collaborative Institutions in an Ecology of Games." *American Journal of Political Science* 54(2): 287–300. http://doi.org/10.1111/j.1540-5907.2010.00431.x.

Marín, A., and Berkes, F. (2010). "Network Approach for Understanding Small-Scale Fisheries Governance: The Case of the Chilean Coastal Co-Management System." *Marine Policy* 34(5): 851–858. http://doi.org/10.1016/j.marpol.2010.01.007.

Matti, S., and Sandström, A. (2011). "The Rationale Determining Advocacy Coalitions: Examining Coordination Networks and Corresponding Beliefs." *Policy Studies Journal* 39(3): 385–410. http://doi.org/10.1111/j.1541-0072.2011.00414.x.

May, P. J. (1992). "Policy Learning and Failure." *Journal of Public Policy* 12(4): 331. http://doi.org/10.1017/S0143814X00005602.

McLendon, M. K. (2003). "Setting the Governmental Agenda for State Decentralization of Higher Education." *Journal of Higher Education* 74(5): 479–515. http://doi.org/10.1353/jhe.2003.0038.

McNie, E. C. (2007). "Reconciling the Supply of Scientific Information with User Demands: An Analysis of the Problem and Review of the Literature." *Environmental Science & Policy* 10(1): 17–38. http://doi.org/10.1016/j.envsci.2006.10.004.

McPherson, M., Smith-Lovin, L., and Cook, J. M. (2001). "Birds of a Feather: Homophily in Social Networks." *Annual Review of Sociology* 27: 415–444.

Mitchell, R. B., Clark, W. C., Cash, D. W., and Dickson, N. M. (Eds.). (2006). *Global Environmental Assessments: Information and Influence.* Cambridge, MA: MIT Press.

Newman, M. E. J. (2006). "Modularity and Community Structure in Networks." *Proceedings of the National Academy of Sciences* 103(23): 8577–8582. http://doi.org/10.1073/pnas.0601602103.

O'Neill, H. M., Pouder, R. W., and Buchholtz, A. K. (1998). "Patterns in the Diffusion of Strategies across Organizations: Insights from the Innovation Diffusion Literature." *Academy of Management Review* 23(1): 98–114.

Ostrom, E. (2000). "Collective Action and the Evolution of Social Norms." *Journal of Economic Perspectives* 14(3): 137–158.

Palla, G., Derényi, I., Farkas, I., and Vicsek, T. (2005). "Uncovering the Overlapping Community Structure of Complex Networks in Nature and Society." *Nature* 435(7043): 814–818. http://doi.org/10.1038/nature03607.

Parson, E. A., and Clark, W. C. (2005). "Sustainable Development as Social Learning: Theoretical Perspectives and Practical Challenges for the Design of a Research Program." In *Barriers and Bridges to the Renewal of Ecosystems and Institutions*, Lance H. Gunderson, C. S. Holling, and Stephen S. Light, pp. 428–460. New York: Columbia University Press.

Porter, M. A., Onnela, J.-P., and Mucha, P. J. (2009). "Communities in Networks." *Notices of the American Mathematical Society* 56(9): 1082–1097.

Portes, A. (2000). "The Two Meanings of Social Capital." *Sociological Forum* 15(1): 1–12.

Pralle, S. B. (2009). "Agenda-setting and Climate Change." *Environmental Politics* 18(5): 781–799. http://doi.org/10.1080/09644010903157115.

Pretty, J. (2003). "Social Capital and the Collective Management of Resources." *Science* 302(5652): 1912–1914. http://doi.org/10.1126/science.1090847.

Putnam, R. D. (2000). *Bowling Alone: The Collapse and Revival of American Community.* New York: Simon and Schuster.

Rendell, L., Boyd, R., Cownden, D., Enquist, M., Eriksson, K., Feldman, M. W., . . . Laland, K. N. (2010). "Why Copy Others? Insights from the Social Learning Strategies Tournament." *Science* 328(5975): 208–213. http://doi.org/10.1126/science.1184719.

Robins, G., Snijders, T., Wang, P., Handcock, M., and Pattison, P. (2007). "Recent Developments in Exponential Random Graph (p*) Models for Social Networks." *Social Networks* 29(2): 192–215. http://doi.org/10.1016/j.socnet.2006.08.003.

Sabatier, P., Hunter, S., and McLaughlin, S. (1987). "The Devil Shift: Perceptions and Misperceptions of Opponents." *Western Political Quarterly* 40(3): 449–476. http://doi.org/10.2307/448385.

Sabatier, P. A., Focht, W., Lubell, M., Trachtenberg, Z., Vedlitz, A., and Matlock, M. (Eds.). (2005). *Swimming Upstream: Collaborative Approaches to Watershed Management.* Cambridge, MA: MIT Press.

Sabatier, P. A., and Jenkins-Smith, H. C. (Eds.). (1993). *Policy Change and Learning: An Advocacy Coalition Approach*. Boulder, CO: Westview Press.

Sabatier, P. A., and Jenkins-Smith, H. C. (1999). "The Advocacy Coalition Framework: An Assessment." In *Theories of the Policy Process*, edited by Paul A. Sabatier, pp. 117–166. Boulder, CO: Westview Press.

Sabatier, P. A., and Weible, C. M. (2007). "The Advocacy Coalition Framework: Innovations and Clarifications." In *Theories of the Policy Process*, edited by Paul A. Sabatier, 2d ed., vol. 1, pp. 189–220. Boulder, CO: Westview Press.

Saint-Germain, M. A., and Calamia, R. A. (1996). "Three Strikes and You're In: A Streams and Windows Model of Incremental Policy Change." *Journal of Criminal Justice* 24(1): 57–70. http://doi.org/10.1016/0047-2352(95)00052-6.

Sandström, A., and Rova, C. (2010). "Adaptive Co-Management Networks: A Comparative Analysis of Two Fishery Conservation Areas in Sweden." *Ecology and Society* 15(3): 14.

Schelling, T. C. (1971). "Dynamic Models of Segregation." *Journal of Mathematical Sociology* 1(2): 143–186. http://doi.org/10.1080/0022250X.1971.9989794.

Schlager, E. (1995). "Policy Making and Collective Action: Defining Coalitions Within the Advocacy Coalition Framework." *Policy Sciences* 28(3): 243–270.

Schneider, M., Scholz, J., Lubell, M., Mindruta, D., and Edwardsen, M. (2003). "Building Consensual Institutions: Networks and the National Estuary Program." *American Journal of Political Science* 47(1): 143–158. http://doi.org/10.1111/1540-5907.00010.

Scholz, J. T., Berardo, R., and Kile, B. (2008). "Do Networks Solve Collective Action Problems? Credibility, Search, and Collaboration." *Journal of Politics* 70(2): 393–406. http://doi.org/10.1017/S0022381608080389.

Scott, T. A. (2016). "Analyzing Policy Networks Using Valued Exponential Random Graph Models: Do Government-Sponsored Collaborative Groups Enhance Organizational Networks?" *Policy Studies Journal* 44(2): 215–244. http://doi.org/10.1111/psj.12118.

Scott, T., and Thomas, C. (2015). "Do Collaborative Groups Enhance Interorganizational Networks?" *Public Performance & Management Review* 38(4): 654–683. http://doi.org/10.1080/15309576.2015.1031008.

Sherif, M. (1966). *In Common Predicament: Social Psychology of Intergroup Conflict and Cooperation*. Boston: Houghton Mifflin.

Shibuya, E. (1996). "'Roaring Mice Against the Tide': The South Pacific Islands and Agenda-Building on Global Warming." *Pacific Affairs* 69(4): 541. http://doi.org/10.2307/2761186.

Snijders, T. A. B., Pattison, P. E., Robins, G. L., and Handcock, M. S. (2006). "New Specifications for Exponential Random Graph Models." *Sociological Methodology* 36: 99–153. http://doi.org/10.1111/j.1467-9531.2006.00176.x.

Snijders, T. A. B., van de Bunt, G. G., and Steglich, C. E. G. (2010). "Introduction to Stochastic Actor-Based Models for Network Dynamics." *Social Networks* 32(1): 44–60. http://doi.org/10.1016/j.socnet.2009.02.004.

Social Learning Group (Ed.). (2001). *Learning to Manage Global Environmental Risks*. Cambridge, MA: MIT Press.

Strang, D., and Soule, S. A. (1998). "Diffusion in Organizations and Social Movements: From Hybrid Corn to Poison Pills." *Annual Review of Sociology* 24: 265–290.

Tajfel, H., Billig, M. G., Bundy, R. P., and Flament, C. (1971). "Social Categorization and Intergroup Behaviour." *European Journal of Social Psychology* 1(2): 149–178. http://doi.org/10.1002/ejsp.2420010202.

Takács, K. (2007). "Effects of Network Segregation in Intergroup Conflict: An Experimental Analysis." *Connections* 27(2): 59–76.

Vollan, B. (2008). "Socio-Ecological Explanations for Crowding-Out Effects from Economic Field Experiments in Southern Africa." *Ecological Economics* 67(4): 560–573. http://doi.org/10.1016/j.ecolecon.2008.01.015.

Weible, C. M. (2005). "Beliefs and Perceived Influence in a Natural Resource Conflict: An Advocacy Coalition Approach to Policy Networks." *Political Research Quarterly* 58(3): 461–475.

Weible, C. M., and Sabatier, P. A. (2005). "Comparing Policy Networks: Marine Protected Areas in California." *Policy Studies Journal* 33(2): 181–201. http://doi.org/10.1111/j.1541-0072.2005.00101.x.

Weible, C. M., Sabatier, P. A., Jenkins-Smith, H. C., Nohrstedt, D., Henry, A. D., and deLeon, P. (2011). "A Quarter Century of the Advocacy Coalition Framework: An Introduction to the Special Issue." *Policy Studies Journal* 39(3): 349–360. http://doi.org/10.1111/j.1541-0072.2011.00412.x.

Weiss, C. H. (1972). *Evaluation Research: Methods for Assessing Program Effectiveness.* Englewood Cliffs, NJ: Prentice-Hall.

Weiss, C. H. (1977). "Research for Policy's Sake: The Enlightenment Function of Social Research." *Policy Analysis* 3(4): 531–545.

CHAPTER 24

....

NETWORKS AND EUROPEAN UNION POLITICS

....

PAUL W. THURNER

INTRODUCTION

....

THIS chapter begins with a short introduction to the peculiarities of the political system of the European Union (EU). Then it clarifies the usefulness of the network approach for investigating markets, hierarchies, and all kinds of hybrid governance systems. This is followed by a presentation of quantitative empirical studies in the EU context. I concentrate on practical relevance, theoretical intention, and research design. Finally, I outline several new strands of theorizing and applications.

The EU is a regional cooperation regime among sovereign member states. It exhibits a very specific and still fluid governance structure.[1] Its institutional predecessor, the European Community (EC), was the result of a merger in 1965 of three organizations, themselves based on intergovernmental treaties. This fusion led to a pooling of executive structures and initiated an increase in power and autonomy for the European Commission. From its foundation by six signatory member states, the system has successively evolved and now includes twenty-eight countries. It constitutes not only the world's largest but also its most deeply integrated system of international relations combined with supranational features of collective decision-making, conflict resolution, and administrative structures. Despite many constitutional modifications over time, the main decision-making structure of the political system has remained relatively constant. The legislative process comprises one bureaucratic agenda setter (the European Commission) and two legislative chambers: the European Parliament (EP), with directly elected members, and the Council of Ministers. Note that the latter consists of constantly varying compositions of sectoral ministries deployed by the national governments. Thus, the chain of democratic delegation is longer in this case. The members of the EP are directly elected but face the dilemma of having two principals: the national party and the party group in parliament (see Hix and Hoyland, 2011, 54). There are two legislative chambers and a "dual executive" (Hix and Hoyland, 2011, 46), as the heads of member states select and propose the Commission president, and the EP has the right to support and remove the Commission as a whole. Consequently, the system is a quite complex mixture of components usually incorporated in parliamentary or presidential systems. Moreover, the institutional architecture of the EU is policy specific (Hix and Hoyland, 2011, 3); that is, for each type of policy (regulatory, expenditure, macroeconomic, interior, foreign) under consideration, different institutional rules apply, with different actors who have varying influence potentials and decision-making competences.

The increasing number of states and policy fields in which decision-making competencies have been transferred to the EU has led to the creation of additional actors, like the Court of Justice, the Court of Finance, a Committee of the Regions, and more than forty agencies (see http://europa.eu/about-eu/agencies/). The multitude of actors and the vertical and horizontal interdependence between actors with varying decision-making and implementation competencies are further complicated by the fact that rules of policymaking vary across policy fields (e.g., common foreign and security policies is still the least Europeanized policy field, whereas common agricultural policy is one of the most Europeanized ones). All this makes the EU admittedly an extremely difficult research object for political scientists.

Beginning in the 1990s, political scientists have increasingly raised the question of whether the institutional reforms of the EC (as reflected in the Single European Act [1987] and in the Maastricht Treaty [1991]) were actually indicating an ever-deepening integration, that is, the move toward a majority system resembling domestic decision-making of democracies,[2] rather than consensus and unanimity-seeking systems. The latter are supposed to be the predominant rules of decision-making in the international sphere. The question is not only how member states can decide on policies in the face of conflicts under unanimity voting, but also whether the formal introduction of (qualified) majority voting had actually an impact on the practice of legislative decision-making—or whether unanimity continued to be the informal rule.

More specifically, political scientists discussed whether the formation of an institutionalized majority system, with the EP becoming more and more an effective legislative second chamber, was under way. A major impulse was provided by George Tsebelis's suggestion that, with the cooperation procedure in the Single European Act, the EP was on the (latent) path to becoming a conditional agenda setter soon (see Hix and Hoyland, 2011, ch. 3 for a résumé of the discussion) and an powerful second chamber eventually. This induced an intense debate on the impact of procedural rules (see also the respective debate in Thomsen et al., 2006). Another thread of the scientific discussion culminated in the fierce intergovernmentalism versus neofunctionalism debate triggered by Andrew Moravcsik (1998), who concluded that the EU continued to be an intergovernmental system of nation-states.

Due to the hybrid and transient character of the system, the EU literature accentuates informal aspects of policymaking (see, e.g., Farrell and Heritier, 2003) and its complex, multilevel character (see, e.g., Hooghe and Marks, 2003). Others emphasize the "network character" of this institutionalized policymaking system or designate the in essence whole system as "network governance."[3] Wessels (1997) and Trondal and Peters (2013) highlight the emergence of a new administrative space.

Instead of relying on these new designations, I follow the argument by Hix and Hoyland (2011) that the political system of the EU is amenable to established and standard concepts and theories of positive political science. More specifically, I argue that network theory and network analysis constitute an appropriate approach to conceive of both formal as well as informal political institutions[4] and to potentially forecast which parts may be converted from informal leadership into future formal hierarchies. Carpenter's (2001) study of the processes leading to bureaucratic autonomy in the nineteenth-century US administrative system is an insightful example, teaching us that the interplay between formal and informal institutional development of political systems is omnipresent in history, and not at all specific to the EU. Sociological studies have time and again shown that formal and informal structures can be theoretically captured by network analysis (see Blau, 1955; Krackhardt, 1987).[5] More recently, in their reconstruction of Max Weber's relational theory of authority, Aghion and Tirole (1997) distinguish between the allocation of formal competencies with regard to specific issues/policies toward persons and the cognitive ascription of authority reputations (with regard to specific issues/policies) toward persons. In short, formal and informal authority systems imply relational concepts. These forms of authority may match or diverge. The advantage of a strictly relational (i.e., graph-theoretically understood) network approach is that it enables us to compare formal and informal structures systematically.

QUANTITATIVE NETWORK STUDIES RELATED TO EUROPEAN UNION POLITICS

With the following synopsis (see Table 24.1) I provide a first overview of the literature in summary. I focus exclusively on quantitative empirical research. I characterize the existing studies using the following criteria: (1) Which policy field or area does the contribution investigate, or/and how many issues are considered? (2) Which and how many actors are involved, and which institutional context is relevant (member states, the European Commission, the Council of Ministers, the EP, domestic actors, interest groups, parties, agencies, etc.)? (3) Which data collection procedures and network analysis methods are used? Table 24.1 summarizes the results of the extant EU network studies, both with regard to the specific network perspective on the substantial topic and with regard to their methodical contribution, ordering the contributions chronologically and thematically.

Table 24.1 Synopsis of Contributions with Empirical Network Analyses

Authors/Year	Policy Field/Issues	(Number of) Actors	Method
Stokman and van Oosten 1994	Limits on car emissions; radiation contamination; air transport liberalization	Council, EC members N = 12 (B, DK, F, Ger, GR, IR, I, L, NL, P, E, UK)	Formal modeling of logrolling, no measurement of real networks.
König 1997	Labor and social policy (6 issue areas, N = 122 issues).	Council, EC members N = 12 (B, DK, F, Ger, GR, IR, I, L, NL, P, E, UK) EP, Commission	Expert survey on information exchange networks (issue-area-specific). Methods: centralities; visualization; block models.
Pappi and Henning 1998	Formal model of collective decision-making including interest groups.		Formal modeling.
Pappi and Henning 1999	Common Agricultural Policy EU-15. Distribution of power/control in a market of control exchange	Interest groups, committees in the Commission, domestic ministries, party groups in the EP N = 124 actors	Extensive survey of complete system on information exchange, support; reputation network. Methods: block models.
Henning and Wald 2000 Henning 2000	Common Agricultural Policy EU-15. Derivation of fine-grained typologies of interest mediation transcending traditional types (pluralism, neocorporatism)	Interest groups, committees in the Commission, domestic ministries, party groups in the EP N = 124 actors	Extensive survey of complete system on information exchange, support; reputation network. Methods: block models.
Krause 2005 Henning 2009	Common Agricultural Policy EU-27.	Interest groups, committees in the Commission, domestic ministries, party groups in the EP N = 124 Interest groups, N = 18 supranational organizations and N = 127 national organizations	Extensive survey of complete system on information exchange. Derivation of exchange equilibria.

Table 24.1 (Continued)

Authors/Year	Policy Field/Issues	(Number of) Actors	Method
Thurner et al. 2002	Intergovernmental conference, constitutional negotiations, (Amsterdam Treaty). N = 46 issues. Data handbook.	N = 15 member states, N = 140 ministries.	Extensive elite survey of complete system; domestic and transgovernmental communication; reputation network; allocation of formal decision-making competencies as network.
Thurner and Stoiber 2002	Interministerial coordination of negotiation positions in Germany.	N = 15 member states, N = 140 ministries	Centralities; block models.
Stoiber 2003	Prediction of negotiation positions. N = 46 constitutional issues (Amsterdam Treaty).	N = 15 member states, N = 140 ministries.	Centralities; block models; exchange models.
Thurner et al. 2005	Transgovernmental communication between ministries during IGC 1996.	N = 140 ministries of N = 15 member states	Centralities; block models.
Thurner 2006 and Thurner and Pappi 2009	Monographs on domestic ministerial coordination and international negotiations.	N = 140 ministries of N = 15 member states, N = 46 issues	Centralities as predictors in regressions; random p2 model for the explanation of transgovernmental network choice.
Thurner and Binder 2009	Explaining transgovernmental network choice.	N = 140 ministries of N = 15 member states, N = 46 issues	Exponential random graph model (ERGM).
Binder 2010	Determinants of national position taking.	N = 140 ministries of N = 15 member states, N = 46 issues	Multilevel models including network measures.
Thurner 2010	Team formation based on different rules and network behavior.	N = 140 ministries of N = 15 member states, N = 46 issues	Counterfactual thought experiment based on network centralities.
Thurner and Binder 2012	Explaining performance of domestic ministries in getting their positions contracted in the international treaty.	N = 140 ministries of N = 15 member states, N = 46 issues	Multilevel models including network measures.

(cont.)

Table 24.1 (Continued)

Authors/Year	Policy Field/Issues	(Number of) Actors	Method
Ringe, Victor, and Carman 2013	Environmental policy and consumer protection Covoting of MEPs on N = 40 bills.	N = 30 Assistants to MEPs of the Committee on Environment	Web-Based Survey. Methods: Centralities; Multi-Level-Model.
Ringe, Victor, and Gross 2013	Intergroups in the EP as an example of legislative member organizations (LMOs).	N = 24 in the period 2004-2009 N = 27 in the period 2009-2014	Centralities, Densities.
Jensen and Winzen 2012	Directive on Ambient Air Quality and Cleaner Air for Europe.	N = 55 MEPs	Snowball design. Methods: centralities; correspondence analysis, ERGM.
Maggetti and Gilardi 2011	Committee of European Securities Regulators.	N = 29 member regulatory authorities	Affiliation membership. Methods: degree of centrality in regression (N = 29).
Maggetti 2014a	Communication of regulatory networks—energy.	All members of the CEER and ERGEG (68% response rate)	Survey-based. Methods: centralities as predictors in regressions (N= 21, N = 23).
Beyers and Donas 2014	Information exchange among European regions.	N = 127 regional offices	Visualization, degree index, ERGM
Merand et al. 2011	EU common security and defense policy, information exchange.	N = 100 target actors, N = 47 interviews	Centralities.
Leifeld and Haunns 2012	Directive on the patentability of computer-implemented invention.	N = 124 newspaper articles, N = 338 signed claims	Affiliation networks, centralities.
Weishar et al. 2015	EU antismoking policy, cooperation networks of organizations	N = 176 statements by pro and con organizations	Densities, centralities.
Koniaris et al. (2015)	Legal corpus of the EU 1951–2013; cross-citations.	N = 249,690 legal documents	Power-law features, small-worldness.

In the follow-up sections I discuss these contributions in more detail. According to the incidence and frequency of topics, I distinguish research that is mainly inspired by the network-extended exchange model of James Coleman, studies on the networks in the EP, common security and defense, the Committee of the Regions, regulatory agencies, and discourse networks.

COLLECTIVE DECISION MAKING AS EXCHANGE OF INFLUENCE RESOURCES

Against the background of ongoing institutional transformations, network analysts began to contribute their own perspective. Note that this first wave of studies (Stokman and van Oosten, 1994; König, 1997; Pappi and Henning, 1998, 1999; Thurner and Pappi, 2006) was heavily influenced by Lauman and Knoke's (1987) research design, and more fundamentally by Coleman's mathematical system of action (1990, 1972).

Coleman (1972, 1990) provided a fully fledged, formal mathematical model of collective decision-making. It has been extended to conceive of actors as embedded in network relations where the nodes consist of a mixture of private and public actors exchanging influence resources (see Marsden and Lauman, 1977; Stokman et al., 2013; Stokman, 2014). This general model has been applied in a now-classic network study of policy-making in the field of energy and healthcare in the US Congress (Lauman and Knoke, 1987) and to policymaking in the field of social policies in Germany, Japan, and the United States (see Knoke et al., 1996). Simplified, the Coleman model assumes a bounded action system in which actors are deciding on multiple issues of a policy. They assign different relative weights (aka salience) to these issues. Therefore, asymmetrical placement of issue salience permits logrolling or any other type of mutual adjustment. In addition, actors are endowed with resources to control the outcome of the collective decision. Public actors (government, parliament, administrations) usually have formal decision-making rights as a resource. Private actors may have differential access to and influence over the deciders and therefore also hold parts of decision-making control. Both private and public actors may benefit from social capital arising from their positions in informal relations. This parsimonious and quite general model has also inspired studies applied to EU policymaking.

Stokman and van den Bos (1994) initiated a powerful program of formally modeling informal logrolling processes with regard to collective decision-making on multiple issues under varying context conditions (decision-making rules, institutions, actors, networks). A fundamental assumption and innovative extension of this new model[6] as applied to the EU is the spatial representation of issues and preferences, that is, single peaked preferences over a geometrical line, including the location of the current status quo and the observation of an outcome position after the collective decision stage has been reached. Thus, the Coleman model of collective decision-making, originally developed for binary decisions only, was made compatible with the spatial theory of voting, another important approach in positive political theory.

So-called procedural approaches (see Steunenberg and Selck, 2006) argue that formal institutional rules are actually determining the result, given the position of a rational agenda setter, a decision rule, and the distribution of preferences. The unanimity rule or the (super-) majority rule then applies mechanistically without communication. Contrary to this position, the bargaining-based approach emphasizes effective communication at the preplay stage (see Stokman and van den Bos, 1994; Arregui et al., 2006; and Thurner and Pappi, 2009 for an overview). If unanimity is the formal decision rule, but we observe an outcome despite conflict, then some exchange over multiple issues (or external side payments) should have been bargained informally. Moreover, if we observe a deviation from outcomes predicted by procedural models (e.g., from the majority position), this indicates again some norm of cooperative consensus building, that is, the continuation of consensus seeking despite the availability of a majority rule.

A farsighted book (Mesquita and Stokman, 1994) both anticipated and stimulated this ongoing controversy. The authors provide a scrupulous quantitative policy analysis of the decision-making within the EC in the late 1980s and early 1990s. Applied to twenty-three legislative issues on banking, nuclear energy, air pollution, and transport liberalization, with some decided under unanimity and others under qualified majority, Stokman and van Oosten (1994) put forward a model of mutual adjustment of positions. Without understanding the background of network exchange theory and especially without understanding the exact algorithm behind this model, readers may be surprised that the Stokman and van Oosten (1994; see also Arregui, Stokman, and Thomson, 2006) model is considered a network approach, since there are no observed and measured networks. However, communication networks are assumed to be formed in the first stage of a collective decision-making game. The formal decision in the second stage follows an informal bargaining process, with the objective of involved actors (potentially including those with no formal voting power) being to influence others to compromise, that is, to modify their position as measured on the issue scales. The model assumes bilateral sequential exchanges of voting positions instead of the instantaneous exchange of control based on a spot market equilibrium in the Coleman model. Bilateral exchange networks are a function of the actors' issue positions and the relative weight they attach to an issue when calculating the value trade-offs for binary comparisons of issues. These are the basis for determining a sequence of position adjustments. The algorithm of this model has been criticized for leading to externalities. Follow-up studies by Dijkstra et al. (2008) and Dijkstra (2009) account for externalities and propose to bring in real, that is, actually observed, exchange networks. The model predictions of the original model outperformed the Bueno de Mesquita noncooperative challenge model in the 1994 book and the procedural approach in the 2006 book. Stokman (2014) considers that these results indicate a still-prevalent norm of consensus seeking in the EU, despite the formal possibility of supermajority voting. His conclusion from the analyses of the project in Thomson et al. (2006) is that so-called persuasion networks predominate in legislative decision-making in the EU and that formal voting procedures just constitute the boundaries within which these networks produce collectively binding decisions. It remains to be seen in future applications whether such preplay networks actually exist and how they are structured for given decisions.

König (1997) is another important contributor to this research program. As the title of his book (in English: Europe on the way toward a majority system) already indicates, the starting point here is again whether European collective decision-making still acknowledges the veto power of nation-states, or the (qualified) majority system is actually effective. The results positively affirm the real existence and effectiveness of a majority system. Moreover, the author extends the concept of voting by combining formal (voting power) and informal control resources (favorable position in a communication network). A central aspect of this contribution is again a spatial extension of the Coleman exchange model, in which expectation formation is guided now with regard to an expected outcome in order to realistically build exchange prices (see also Pappi and Henning, 1998, for a similar argument, but a different formal setup). As in Laumann and Knoke (1987), the control of actors is partitioned into, first, a matrix of voting rights over issues, and second, a position in the informal information exchange network, where the latter is considered a social capital and a fungible control resource. The major methodical advance here is the real measurement of issue-area-specific information exchange networks in the field of social policies in the EU.[7] König selects six representative issue areas (including protection of pregnant women, labor time, the European Working Council, mass dismissals, posting of workers in the framework of the provision of services, and workforce mobility) based on six directives and one ordinance (see König, 1997, 119), where different voting rules in the Council of Ministers (qualified majority, unanimity) applied. In sum, he collects data on ninety-nine spatial issues decided in the period between 1989–1991, that is, positions of fourteen involved actors (European Commission, EP, and twelve member states). For the generation of the network of directed information exchange, the author relies on top officials in the Council of Ministers (see König, 1997, 135). The author aggregates issue-area-specific networks resulting in a valued network. This allows him to determine the relative informal social power (information provision and information dependence) and to combine it with the formal voting power. The author shows that the exchange models specified this way perform best in predicting the outcomes. In addition, a COBLOC block model analysis is carried out to identify the underlying structure, which is composed of a core group and a periphery. A major finding of his application is that Europe was indeed on its way toward a majority regime even at the cost of enforcement against the losing minority. This is an interesting complementary interpretation to Stokman and van Oosten (1994) and Arregui et al. (2006).

Whereas Stokman and collaborators proposed to make explicit the trajectory of exchange of policy positions between dyads without actually measuring the network component, König (1997) and Pappi and Henning (1998, 1999) remain in the tradition of the original Coleman (1972, 1990) exchange model. They assume a Walrasian spot market in which the predicted equilibrium avoids negative externalities and optimization occurs simultaneously over all actors and all issues.[8] Pappi and Henning (1998) propose to conceive of the relevant network structure as exhibiting different types of exchange resources (e.g., information, support) and to reflect varying transaction costs. The latter have to be taken into account in the formation of prices and for the prediction of collective decisions. Empirically, this new theoretical approach is applied to one of the largest network data collection projects ever undertaken (see also Krause, 2005; Henning, 2009)—at least with regard to survey-based network studies! Their application case is the most important policy area in the EC/EU for decades: the Common Agricultural Policy (see Hix and Hoyland, 2011, 224ff.). Given the enormous budget shares for agriculture in European expenditures—more than 50 percent until the early 1990s—numerous new concepts, conjectures, and assertions were put forward by political scientists and pundits: supranational corporatism, transnational and supranational pluralism, and ongoing national clientelism were major "explanatory concepts" at that time. Pappi and Henning (1998, 1999) proposed to turn these concepts into measurable variables and delineated the universe of possible influence channels in the given policy field. This resulted in a theoretically inspired typology based on the combination of operational variables.

In the first wave of data collection, the authors intended to reconstruct the collective decision leading to the so-called McSharry reform in 1992, when the EU still consisted of fifteen member states. Surveys of issue positions and saliencies, as well as network generators, were carried out from 1993 to 1997. Interviews were conducted with national ministers of agriculture and the respective permanent representatives at the Council of Ministers, Directorate-General VI of the Commission, and the parties of the EP, resulting in thirty-three institutional public actors. Second, from the identified 214 interest groups (national and European), 53 proved to be relevant and were considered for interviews. Note that the authors investigated several networks, that is, the provision of expertise, support, and perceived reputation. For the empirical analysis, the authors restricted the actor set to the farmers' associations only.

More generally, Pappi and Henning provide a theory of interest mediation in multilevel systems. Comparing the network densities across different possible channels (national interest groups targeting national ministries, European peak organizations, the commission, the EP, the Council of Ministers, etc.) allowed them to reconstruct the real organization of interest mediation for the case of the 1992 reform. Already the large number of existing interest groups involved precluded the frequent characterization as a corporatist system. The authors characterize it as a mixture of transnational and supranational targeting strategies, clearly determining the overall macrostructure. At the same time, there continued to be a strong collaboration between national ministries and national interest groups, which was obviously quite segmented because French interest groups naturally didn't seek access to German ministries. Based on block models on the reputation question, Henning and Wald (2000) identify the macrostructure of this system of interest mediation, which turned out to be highly transnational and supranational, at the same time exhibiting a highly segmented and clientelistic structure at the national level.

In a follow-up study, Krause (2005) and Henning (2009) investigate the agricultural policymaking of the EU-27, with a major focus on the system of interest mediation in Eastern Europe in the context of the Mid-Term Review (MTR) of the Common Agricultural Policy (CAP) of July 2002. Based on extensive interviews carried out in the period 2003–2007, including 18 supranational public organizations, 127 national public organizations, and 145 national and European interest groups, they are able not only to compare Eastern and Western European systems of interest mediation and lobbying strategies, but also to compare intertemporal network formation and developments in the West European system of agricultural interest mediation. A major result is that Eastern European organizations still targeted nearly exclusively the national agricultural ministries, whereas in Western Europe a mixture between supranational pluralism and national clientelism persisted. Methodically, Krause (2005) and Henning (2009) are using input-output techniques to identify central actors and to determine network-based transactions costs in a segmented exchange system comprising public and private actors.

In sum, this is the most extensive empirical study on policymaking in the EC/EU with network components focusing on lobbying strategies. The data set is very large. Both waves started with the complete set of actors based on a positional approach. In a second stage, only those actors considered irrelevant by the system itself are no more taken into account. This data set would offer itself for further systematic analyses of lobbying strategies in the EU by using different techniques of prediction.

A parallel project was initiated in 1996 by Thurner and Pappi on the occasion of the European Intergovernmental Conference in 1996–1997. These negotiations led to the Amsterdam Treaty, which constituted an important step in the sequence of constitutional reforms. Thus, the project was not on policymaking but rather on constitution building by the European member states. It was called International Negotiations and Interministerial Coordination (INNIC). The main objective of this project was again the conceptualization and operationalization of a prominent term at that time, the notion of two-level games, which was inspired by Putnam (1988). In order to reconstruct the discretionary leeways—that is, the win sets of governments and their impact on negotiation results—it was necessary to identify the relevant domestic actors. In this case, diverse national ministries proved to be the relevant participants. Thus, the focus in this project was on "administrative interest groups" rather than on private interest groups. This gave rise to including another perspective introduced earlier by Scharpf (1977): interministerial coordination from a network perspective. As in its predecessor projects, a complete identification of the action system was carried out. Based on insider information during the negotiations (i.e., the availability of the full set of issues and issue options on the negotiation table), it was possible to promptly construct a standardized questionnaire including questions on preferences with regard to forty-six spatial issues, issue saliencies, intranational and transgovernmental communication networks, and reputation networks with regard to nine homogenous groups of issues. In sum, 140 representatives of ministries in fifteen countries were interviewed, giving rise to 690 cases at the level of the nation-states, and more than 2,000 unbalanced observations at the ministerial level.[9] Thus, statistical analysis proved to be possible in this quantitative case study. Boundary specification followed a two-stage procedure. In the first stage, national delegation members were asked during or right after the negotiations which national ministries were involved in the preparation of negotiation positions. "Involved" was defined as having provided written proposals. All these ministries were contacted. Provided that two involved ministries considered other ministries as important according to the reputation generator, these ministries were also interviewed face to face. A detailed description and comparison of the formal coordination structures and informal communication behavior in the fifteen member states was provided by Stoiber (2003). A case study focusing on the coordination of the negotiating positions of Germany (see Thurner and Stoiber 2002) demonstrated deviations of informal authority structures from formal ones. Based on a block model analysis with regard to the issue-area-specific reputation networks, four different types of actors in the core executive can be identified: the externally leading actors based on their formal power, those ministries having accumulated responsibilities with regard to multiple issues, those actors coordinating a set of homogenous issues, and finally those ministries responsible for single issues.

A book-length investigation of the structure, determinants, and impact of transgovernmental network is provided by Thurner (2006) and Thurner and Pappi (2009). The authors use random p2 models for the explanation of transgovernmental network formation based on a concatenation of nine ministerial subnetworks. They show that the incentive of bypassing one's own government had no effect; rather, economic interdependencies structure the communication networks. The impact of network positions of the ministries in the transgovernmental communication network is also taken into account with regard to the negotiation performance of nation-states in each of the forty-six issues (measured as the utility income of governments with regard to each of the issues). It turned out that transgovernmental betweenness centrality (indicating a broker quality) based on the valued overall network improved the negotiation performance of countries. In the first political science application of exponential random graph models (see chapter by Desmarais and Cranmer, this volume), Thurner and Binder (2009) explain transgovernmental network formation in nine separate sectoral ministerial networks and corroborate the main findings of Thurner (2006): economic interdependence crucially impacts the selectivity of transgovernmental network formation.

Binder (2010) compares formal and informal coordination structures at the ministerial level and relates them to countries' position taking prior to international negotiations. Predicting also the informally perceived authority of ministries with regard to issue areas, he finds that formal structure predominantly determines such perceptions. Thurner and Binder (2012) investigate the negotiation performance or negotiation return again at the ministerial level, controlling for formal and informal governmental structures as well as for the negotiation system as surrounding context factors. With regard to network positions, the authors are able to show that the endowment of formal authority has a major impact on negotiation returns. Transgovernmental networking pays only when carried out by central foreign ministries. In a counterfactual thought experiment, Thurner (2010) illustrates that the application of a different management concept (i.e., process management instead of project management) would have led to a different composition of the national delegations. The criteria for the composition of process management teams are constructed on the basis of within-governmental authority and informal transgovernmental authority networks.

EUROPEAN PARLIAMENT

The EP has been the object of several network analyses (Jensen and Winzen, 2012; Ringe, Victor, and Gross, 2013; and Ringe, Victor, and Carman, 2013). A further application of exponential random graph models was provided by Jensen and Winzen (2012) to explain the network of collaboration networks during the production of a policy in the EP. The collective decision they investigate is the Directive on Ambient Air Quality and Cleaner Air for Europe, initiated by the Commission in 2005 and entering into force in June 2008. The main objective of their study is explaining the structure and causes of legislative negotiations, more specifically of relations of cooperation in the EP under procedural conditions in which the EP has the highest involvement, that is, under codecision. Their boundary specification starts by interviewing the rapporteurs and shadow rapporteurs of a legislative act of the Environment Committee. This step is followed by a relational approach based on a snowball sampling over several rounds until no more new names are generated.[10] Based on fifty-five identified actors, the authors first propose a center-periphery analysis. The results are interpreted as showing the rapporteurs and shadow rapporteurs in the center of the action system. Interestingly, not only members of the committee are involved, but also outsiders who prove to be even more active networkers. Both the overall system and informal party groups are highly centralized, with actors formally endowed with positions (rapporteurs and shadow rapporteurs) being the most central actors in the cooperation network. However, there is no perfect match between formal and informal authority positions: for example, the committee chair is not part of the negotiations, and there are additional core members. The authors derive a series of hypotheses inspired by theories formulated for the context of the US Congress (distributional, informational, and partisan approaches) about why actors form specific ties. A major finding is that tie formation follows party groups.

In-depth studies on the EP are also provided by Ringe, Victor, and Gross (2013) and Ringe, Victor, and Carman (2013). In Ringe, Victor, and Gross (2013), the authors accentuate the fact that voting patterns in the EP are not as constrained as in parliamentary systems, and therefore the social organization of voting patterns constitutes a scientific puzzle. The authors intend to contribute to the explanation of bilateral co-voting patterns by accounting for the social embeddedness of members of the EP (MEPs). They also focus on environmental policy, but consider the whole legislative output for the period 2004–2009, that is, forty floor votes on legislative proposals that were under the jurisdictional responsibility of the Committee on Environment. The objective here is to reconstruct the relations behind the scenes, that is, the "interoffice communication" of the MEPs' assistants. For their boundary specification, Ringe and colleagues start with a positional approach, including all members of the respective committees. However, the real target persons are the assistants of the MEPs, considered to be the carrying infrastructure of working relations of MEPs. Interviewing was based on web questionnaires and, if necessary, on personal interviews. The participation rate of 47 percent (target population 65) is attributable to the sensitive information. Symmetrizing those relations indicated by participants yields a dyadic response rate of 71.4 percent. The dependent variable is the co-voting rate of each dyad. For the operationalization of the social connectedness, the authors decided to select the point-connectivity measure. A major finding is that those disagreeing on issues but nevertheless being highly connected are covoting to a statistically significant lower degree. This counterintuitive result is argued to result from the necessity to strategically seek dissonant information.

Ringe, Victor, and Carmann (2013) compare the EP's so-called intergroups with the Congress's member organizations. Both are categorized as legislative member organizations (LMOs) that are informal and voluntary. Nevertheless, they seem to have some function for their members, which is, at least for the EP case, unknown due to the lack of research so far. Thus, the contribution of the authors is novel. They advance a new theory of LMOs and empirically scrutinize twenty-four intergroups in the 2004–2009 period and twenty-seven in the 2009–2014 period, reconstructing their membership. Using complementary data, they are able to show that these LMOs provide platforms for exchanging information and to enable candidates to have direct contact and mutual access otherwise not available given their committee and party group memberships.

Common Security and Defense Networks

Merand et al. (2011) analyze the field of common security and defense policy (CSDP) from 2007 to 2009. Note that CSDP continues to be the least integrated policy field—at least with regard to formal decision rules. The authors raise the question of whether it is possible to observe an institutionalization of cooperation beyond the nation-state. Based on a combined and consecutive position approach and reputation approach for the boundary specification, the authors identified one hundred target actors for the UK, French, German, North Atlantic Treaty Organization (NATO), and EU-related public, private, and intergovernmental organizations. Defining "cooperation" as the intensive exchange of important information and joint work toward the development of common positions, they carried out forty-three interviews. Symmetrizing resulted in 117 actors within the defined boundaries. Based on centrality measures (indegree, betweenness) and density scores, they came to the conclusion that, despite exhibiting two-level characteristics, the system is still heavily state-centered—as we would expect from the formal rules.

The Committee of Regions

The establishment of the Committee of Regions in 1994 naturally attracted scientific interest and paved the way to transcend the focus on two-level games to "three-level governance," addressing the increasing activities of especially wealthy regions to coordinate their interests. Kohler-Koch (1998), in a large-scale project, "Regions as Political Actors in the Process of European Integration," investigated the changing role of regions and intended to discover whether there was a convergence of (cooperative) policy styles visible in patterns of interactions and especially in an expansion of transnational networks. The research group selected eight regions (Baden-Württemberg, Lower Saxony, Andalusia, Catalonia Lombardy, Sicily, Languedoc-Roussillon, Rhone-Alpes, and Wales) from the five larger EU member states (France, Germany, Italy, Spain, and the United Kingdom) at that time with a target population of about 3,000 public, private, and semipublic organizations and achieved a response rate of 42 percent, that is, 1,264 participants (see Grote, 1998). The survey questionnaire included network questions (reputation, regular relations) on relevant partners at the domestic regional and national levels as well as at the European level. The analyses compared especially densities of relations and centralities and used block modeling approaches. A major finding, according to the authors, is that cognitive convergence on concepts and ideas conflicted with interaction structures due to varying predominant national styles of policymaking. Knodt (1998) provides a book-length, in-depth study of the two German regions, coming to a similar conclusion.

Nearly twenty years later, Beyers and Donas (2014) take a different perspective and investigate exclusively the horizontal relations of information exchange between regional representations in Brussels. They consider these representations as a sign of territorial lobbying and focus—similar to Kohler-Koch and collaborators—on whether there are proactive and cooperative regional efforts with regard to supranational funding. The authors identified a target population of 180 representations and achieved a participation in their telephone survey of 127 participants. The network generator elicited the sharing and exchange of information. A major finding based on an exponential random graph model is that horizontal exchange at the Brussels level proceeds mainly between regions of the same country, depends on endowment with resources (staff), and declines with geographical distance. Again, this study seems to indicate that there is no convergence or integration of regional strategies, but rather an institutionalized, international competition and segmentation.

Regulatory Agencies

There are three contributions investigating the phenomenon of so-called European regulatory networks by Maggetti and Gilardi (2011) and Maggetti (2014a, 2014b). Whereas European agencies are formalized institutions (i.e., legal entities), European regulatory networks are informal platforms. Participation and implementation of negotiated standards are voluntary. They are induced and created by national regulatory agencies or by the European Commission. Consequently, they constitute another highly interesting research object, because some of these networks of regulatory agencies eventually become formalized agencies.

The major research objective of Maggetti and Gilardi (2011) is (1) to identify the relevant network structure and (2) to determine its impact on the domestic adoption of rules. They focus on the Council of European Energy Regulators/European Regulators' Group for Electricity and Gas (CEER/ERGEG) and Independent Regulators Group/Body of European Regulators for Electronic Communications (IRG/BEREC), a group of utilities regulators. The issues under investigation are three standards and a set of guidelines adopted in the period 2002–2006. The number of observed participating organizations is twenty-nine (including Iceland and Norway). The identification of the network structure is based on documents in which "coparticipation in (1) the network, (2) the board, (3) permanent groups, (4)working groups" (see Maggetti and Gilardi 2011, 839) is assumed to constitute distinct ties. The sum of degrees of an actor is then Ordinary Least Square (OLS)-regressed (twenty-nine) on a variety of independent variables showing, inter alia, that regulators of countries with larger financial industries have more ties; that is, they are assumed to participate more. More participation, derived from higher centralities, is then used in an OLS regression to explain the adoption of standards and guidelines until the year 2006. Results indicate that higher participation leads to faster adoption.

Maggetti (2014a) extends this perspective for the same regulatory network, but this time by using an expert survey focusing on collaboration networks. Again, collaboration centrality for the reduced set of responding countries (68% response rate) speeds up the domestic adoption of soft standards. The focus in this study is on the Guidelines for Information Management and Transparency in Electricity Markets as the issue spanning the boundaries of the action system. Maggetti (2014b) investigates four European regulatory networks, in the fields of finance, energy, telecommunications, and competition in Europe. Based on a panel analysis design, he is able to show that network membership leads to staff growth and enhanced competencies of domestic regulators. The findings of Maggetti and his collaborators are instructive because by definition, they focus on informal cooperation regimes and their structure, evolution, and impact. Thus they contribute to the understanding of the relevance of independent regulatory agencies (IRAs)—and could be reanalyzed in the future by comparing the structural preconditions of those that became formal institutions from those remaining informal associations.

Discourse Networks

The investigation of discourse networks is a more recent phenomenon in the study of the EU. It is inspired by the increasing public politicization of European policies and relies on new data collection methods.

Weishaar et al. (2015) trace the EU's antismoking policy since the issuance of the European Commission's Green Paper "Towards a Europe Free from Tobacco Smoke: Policy Options at EU Level," followed by a public consultation process on smoke-free policy initiated by the Directorate General for Health and Consumer Affairs. The authors identified statements by 176 organizations. For the identification of pro- and antismoking stakeholder networks, the authors chose the following approach. Submitted documents by the actors were content-analyzed with regard to the occurrence of social relations between submitting organizations. A relationship between two organizations was assumed to exist (1) if organization B was referred to as a partner in the document or on the website, and/or (2) a match of three or more cited references was detected, and/or (3) 40 percent match of wording of the submitted text was discovered. First, based on descriptive network analysis, the authors show a clear polarization and bipartition of the network. Second, it turns out that density and centralization are higher in the opposing prosmoking stakeholder coalition.

Leifeld and Haunss (2012) reconstruct the discourse induced by the directive "on the patentability of computer-implemented invention," which was rejected by the EP in 2005 in the second reading of a codecision process. Their article provides a useful network operationalization of a series of core concepts proposed in the discourse literature—stability of coalitions over time, competition, hegemony, etc.— allowing them to measure these concepts. A major objective beyond description is to explain the spectacular rejection of a legislative proposal that was originally backed by the Commission, the Council, and many powerful multinational companies. The authors are proposing to conceive discourse networks relationally as positive or negative claims by actors with regard to topics, that is, as a signed affiliation network evolving over time. Simple matrix multiplication allows them to identify, on the one hand, clusters or coalitions of actors (in an actor congruence network) using concepts identically. On the other hand, reverse matrix multiplication produces a concept congruence network indicating similarly used concepts or coherent storylines, as interpreted by the authors. The respective dynamic data can be generated using the software Discourse Network Analyzer produced by Leifeld. The database is 124 newspaper articles from four key countries (Germany, the United Kingdom, France, and Poland) that appeared in the period 1997–2005. Coding of mostly verbal statements was carried out manually, producing 338 signed claims. The authors show that the opposed discourse coalition proved to generate the hegemonic discourse in terms of higher numbers of actors mobilized, a higher density of realized connections, and a more cohesive clustering of relations. This application shows again, intriguingly, the potential of network analysis to offer hard operational variables for heuristically valuable but often still vague concepts in political science theories.

Koniaris et al. (2015) provide a fascinating new approach to all legal sources of the EU, including primary, secondary, and complementary law (the case law of the Court of Justice, international law). Based on the EUR-Lex database, they automatically extracted 249,690 documents for the period 1951–2013. Whereas previous research on legislation network was based on citation references only, the authors proposed for the first time to rely on metadata of legal documents in which different types of references are made, such as "amended by," "amendment to," "legal bases," and "instruments cited." The consideration of the multirelational embeddedness of individual legal instruments opens a much richer insight into the latent pattern of legislative discourses. The authors show that the resulting network exhibits well-known properties such as small-world-ness, high resilience, and power-law features.

CONCLUSIONS AND FUTURE DEVELOPMENTS

"The method is the content" (King, Keohane, and Verba, 1994). This insight applies also to network studies on the EU. Concepts, labels, and metaphors may be heuristically valuable. In the end, it is empirical propositions and their testing that contribute to the accumulation of knowledge. The EU is without doubt a new and hybrid developing institution. The system's complexity has triggered a series of insightful studies. A major argument illustrated by most of these reviewed contributions is that network analysis allows researchers to operationalize heuristically valuable theoretical concepts through operationally sound network concepts and mechanisms. An essential claim of this review, uncontested in the sociological network literature, is that network concepts allow researchers to capture and compare both formal and informal features of political systems.

The existing studies illustrate the differentiated institutional architecture of the EU and its dynamic development. Most analyses still use descriptive network-analytic tools like centralities and visualization. A minority of the studies have begun to apply more advanced models, such as exponential random graph models. The "statistical and the computational turn in network analysis" will increasingly also impact EU studies. As network analysis—like any quantitative analysis—hinges crucially on sound data collection, this aspect has to be given greater attention in future applications. Process-produced data (by administrations, social media, etc.) should especially be given more consideration as actors are becoming more and more familiar with the network perspective and are hesitating to provide interview-based answers. The increasing availability of large data sets will allow researchers to investigate multiple theoretical questions in the future by doing focused secondary analyses. The research program inspired by the mathematical conception of collective decision-making as initiated by James Coleman still waits for multiple applications in order to get a better understanding of the admittedly high degrees of freedom in specifying these models. In addition, more fresh research questions originating from the specific system features of the EU (e.g., its two-chamber system, the varying composition of the Council along sectoral and functional lines) are required to study the evolution of this fascinating political system.

Acknowledgments

Comments by Franz U. Pappi, Frans Stokman, Manuel Fischer and by the editors are gratefully acknowledged.

Notes

1. For textbook introductions, see Hix and Hoyland (2011) and Wallace et al. (2010).
2. See, however, the relativization of this aspect in consensus democracies.
3. Börzel and Heard-Lauréote (2009) provide extensive references to the literature qualitatively analyzing networks (in the EU).
4. See Kenis and Schneider (1991); Pappi (1993); and Thurner (2010).
5. The author investigates the following relations: informal, "Who would you go to for advice at work?" and "Who are your friends?"; formal, "Who reports to whom?" (according to the formal organizational chart).
6. As compared to the setup in Laumann and Knoke (1987) and Knoke et al. (1996).
7. This book can be considered an important extension of the comparison in Knoke et al. (1996).
8. See Pappi and Henning (1998); Krause (2005); and Henning (2009) for a theoretical clarification of the model including interest groups. A discussion of these exchange models is not possible here due to space limitations. For a detailed description and application, see Pappi and Henning (1998) and Thurner and Linhart (2004).
9. The resulting extensive data set is documented in Thurner et al. (2002) and available at http://www.mzes.uni-mannheim.de/publications/misc/thurner/ for secondary analysis of new research questions.
10. The name generator is the following: "With whom in the European Parliament did you cooperate on the Directive on Ambient Air Quality and Cleaner Air for Europe?"

References

Aghion, P., and Tirole, J. (1997). "Formal and Real Authority in Organizations." *Journal of Political Economy* 105: 1–29.
Arregui, J., Stokman, F. N., and Thomson, R. (2006). "Compromise, Exchange and Challenge in the European Union." In *The European Union Decides*, edited by R. Thomson et al., pp. 124–152. Cambridge, UK: Cambridge University Press.
Beyers, J., and Donas, T. (2014). "Inter-regional Networks in Brussels: Analyzing the Information Exchanges Among Regional Offices." *European Union Politics* 15(4): 547–571.
Binder, M. (2010). *National Position Taking Prior to EU Intergovernmental Negotiations: The Impact of Formal and Informal Governmental Structures in the Member States of the EU-15.* Mannheim: Mannheim University Press.
Blau, P. M. (1955). *The Dynamics of Bureaucracy: A Study of Interpersonal Relations in Two Government Agencies.* Chicago: University of Chicago Press.
Börzel, T. A., and Heard-Lauréote, K. (2009). "Networks in EU Multi-level Governance: Concepts and Contributions." *Journal of Public Policy* 29(2): 135–151.

Bueno de Mesquita, B., and Stokman, F. N. (1994). *European Community Decision Making: Models, Applications, and Comparisons.* New Haven, CT: Yale University Press.

Carpenter, D. P. (2001). *The Forging of Bureaucratic Autonomy: Reputations, Networks, and Policy Innovation in Executive Agencies, 1862–1928.* Princeton, NJ: Princeton University Press.

Coleman, J. S. (1972). "Systems of Social Exchange." *Journal of Mathematical Sociology* 2(2): 145–163.

Coleman, J. S. (1990). *Foundations of Social Theory.* Cambridge, MA: Belknap Press.

Dijkstra, J. (2009). "Externalities in Exchange Networks: An Adaptation of Existing Theories of Exchange Networks." *Rationality and Society* 21(4): 395–427.

Dijkstra, J., Van Assen, M. A. L. M., and Stokman, F. N. (2008). "Outcomes of Collective Decisions With Externalities Predicted." *Journal of Theoretical Politics* 20(4): 415–441.

Farrell H., and Héritier, A. (2003). "Formal and Informal Institutions under Codecision: Continuous Constitution Building in Europe." *Governance* 16(4): 577–600.

Grote, J. (1998). "Regionale Vernetzung: Interorganisatorische Strukturdifferenzen regionaler Politikgestaltung." In *Interaktive Politik in Europa: Regionen im Netzwerk der Integration*, edited by B. Kohler-Koch, pp. 62-96. Opladen: Leske + Budrich.

Henning, C. H. C. A. (2000). *Macht und Tausch in der europäischen Agrarpolitik: Eine positive politische Entscheidungstheorie.* Frankfurt am Main: Campus.

Henning, C. H. C. A. (2009). "Networks of Power in the CAP System of the EU-15 and EU-27." *Journal of Public Policy* 29(2): 153–177.

Henning, C. H. C. A., and Wald, A. (2000). "Zur Theorie der Interessenvermittlung: Ein Netzwerkansatz dargestellt am Beispiel der Gemeinsamen Europäischen Agrarpolitik." *Politische Vierteljahresschrift* 41(4): 647–676.

Hix, S., and Høyland, B. K. (2011). *The Political System of the European Union. The European Union series.* Basingstoke: Palgrave Macmillan.

Hooghe, L., and Marks, G. (2003). "Unraveling the Central State. But How? Types of Multi-level Governance." *American Political Science Review* 97(2): 233–243.

Jensen, T., and Winzen, T. (2012). "Legislative Negotiations in the European Parliament." *European Union Politics* 13(1): 118–149.

Kenis, P., and Schneider, V. (1991). "Policy Networks and Policy Analysis: Scrutinizing a New Analytical Toolbox." In *Policy Networks: Empirical Evidence and Theoretical Considerations*, edited by B. Marin and R. Mayntz, pp. 25–59. Frankfurt am Main: Campus.

King, G., Keohane, R. O., and Verba, S. (1994). *Designing Social Inquiry: Scientific Inference in Qualitative Research.* Princeton, NJ: Princeton University Press.

Knodt, M. (1998). *Tiefenwirkung europäischer Politik: Eigesinn oder Anpassung regionalen Regierens?* Baden-Baden: Nomos.

Knoke, David, Franz U. Pappi, Jeffrey Broadbent, and Yutaka Tsujinaka. (1996). *Comparing Policy Networks: Labor Politics in the U.S., Germany and Japan. Cambridge studies in comparative politics.* Cambridge, UK: Cambridge University Press.

Kohler-Koch, B. (Ed.). (1998). *Interaktive Politik in Europa: Regionen im Netzwerk der Integration.* Opladen: Leske + Budrich.

Koniaris, M., Ioannis A., and Vassiliou, Y. (2015). "Network Analysis in the Legal Domain: A Complex Model for European Union Legal Sources." http://arxiv.org/pdf/1501.05237.pdf.

König, T. (1997). *Europa auf dem Weg zum Mehrheitssystem: Gründe und Konsequenzen nationaler und parlamentarischer Integration.* Opladen: Westdeutscher Verlag.

Krackhardt, D. (1987) "Cognitive Social Structures." *Social Networks* 9(2): 109–134.

Krause, K. C. (2005). *Lobbying in der Gemeinsamen Europäischen Agrarpolitik einer erweiterten EU-25: Theorie und empirische Messung.* Göttingen: Cuvillier.

Laumann, E. O., and Knoke, D. (1987). *The Organizational State: Social Choice in National Policy Domains.* Madison: The University of Wisconsin Press.

Leifeld, P., and Haunss, S. (2012) "Political Discourse Networks and the Conflict over Software Patents in Europe." *European Journal of Political Research* 51(3): 382–409.

Maggetti, M. (2014a). "The Politics of Network Governance in Europe: The Case of Energy Regulation." *West European Politics* 37(3): 497–514.

Maggetti, M. (2014b). "The Rewards of Cooperation: The Effects of Membership in European Regulatory Networks." *European Journal of Political Research* 53(3): 480–499.

Maggetti, M., and Gilardi, F. (2011). "The Policy-making Structure of European Regulatory Networks and the Domestic Adoption of Standards." *Journal of European Public Policy* 18(6): 830–847.

Marsden, P. V., and Laumann, E. O. (1977). "Collective Action in a Community Elite: Exchange, Influence Resources and Issue Resolution." In *Power, Paradigms, and Community Research*, edited by R. J. Liebert and A. W. Imershein, pp. 199–250. Beverly Hills: Sage.

Mérand, F., Hofmann S. C., and Irondelle, B. (2011). "Governance and State Power: A Network Analysis of European Security." *Journal of Common Market Studies* 49(1): 121–147.

Moravcsik, A. (1998). *The Choice for Europe: Social Purpose and State Power from Messina to Maastricht.* Ithaca, NY: Cornell University Press.

Pappi, F. U. (1993). "Policy-Netze: Erscheinungsform moderner Politiksteuerung oder methodischer Ansatz?" In *Policy-Analyse*, edited by Adrienne Héritier, pp. 84–94. Opladen: Westdeutscher Verlag.

Pappi, F. U., and Henning, C. H. C. A. (1998). "Policy Networks. More Than a Metaphor?" *Journal of Theoretical Politics* 10(4): 553–575.

Pappi, F. U., and Henning, C. H. C. A. (1999). "The Organisation of Influence in the EC's Agricultural Policy: A Network Approach." *European Journal of Political Science Research* 36(2): 257–281.

Putnam, R. (1988). "Diplomacy and Domestic Politics: The Logic of Two-Level Games." *International Organization* 42(3): 427–460.

Ringe, N., Victor, J. N., and Carman, C. J. (2013). *Bridging the Information Gap: Legislative Member Organizations as Social Networks in the United States and the European Union.* Ann Arbor: University of Michigan Press.

Ringe, N., Victor, J. N., and Gross, J. (2013). "Keeping Your Friends Close and Your Enemies Closer? Information Networks in Legislative Politics." *British Journal of Political Science* 43(3): 601–628.

Scharpf, F. (1977). "Does Organization Matter? Task Structure and Interaction in the Ministerial Bureaucracy." *Organization and Administrative Sciences* 8: 149–167.

Steunenberg, B., and Selck, T. (2006). "Testing Procedural Models of EU Legislative Decision-making." In *The European Union Decides*, edited by R. Thomson et al., pp. 54–85. Cambridge, UK: Cambridge University Press.

Stoiber, M. (2003). *Die Vorbereitung auf EU-Regierungskonferenzen: Interministerielle Koordination und kollektive Entscheidung.* Frankfurt am Main: Campus.

Stokman, F. N. (2014). "Policy Networks: History." In *Encyclopedia of Social Network Analysis and Mining*, edited by R. Alhajj and J. Rokne, pp 1291–1310. New York: Springer.

Stokman, F. N., et al. (2013). "Modeling Collective Decision-making." In *Handbook of Rational Choice*, edited by V. Nee et al., pp. 151–181. Stanford, CA: Stanford University Press.

Stokman, F. N., and Van den Bos, J. M. M. (1994). "The Exchange of Voting Positions in the EC Council." In *European Community Decision Making: Models, Applications, and Comparisons*, edited by B. Bueno de Mesquita and F. N. Stokman, pp. 161–84. New Haven, CT: Yale University Press.

Stokman, F. N., and van Oosten, R. (1994). "The Exchange of Voting Positions: An Object-oriented Model of Policy Networks." In *European Community Decision Making: Models, Comparisons, and Applications*, edited by B. Bueno de Mesquita and F. N. Stokman, pp. 105–127. New Haven, CT: Yale University Press.

Thomson, R., et al. (2006). *The European Union Decides*. Cambridge, UK: Cambridge University Press.

Thurner, P. W. (2006). *Die graduelle Konstitutionalisierung der Europäischen Union: Eine quantitative Fallstudie am Beispiel der Regierungskonferenz 1996*. Tübingen: Mohr Siebeck.

Thurner, P. W. (2010). "Enhancing Horizontal and Vertical Self-Organization: Harnessing Informal Networks to Integrate Policies Within and Between Governments in the European Union." In *Self-organizing Federalism: Collaborative Mechanisms to Mitigate Institutional Collective Action*, edited by R. Feiock and J. T. Scholz, pp. 261–282. Cambridge, UK: Cambridge University Press.

Thurner, P. W., and Binder, M. (2009). "EU Transgovernmental Networks: The Emergence of a New Political Space beyond the Nation State?" *European Journal of Political Research* 48(1): 80–106.

Thurner, P. W., and Binder, M. (2012). "Formal and Real Authority of Ministerial Jurisdictions in Semi-Open States: The Comparative Value of Inside and Outside Networking." *Journal of European Public Policy* 19(6): 817–843.

Thurner, P. W., and Linhart, E. (2004). "Political Multilevel Negotiations and Issue Linkage during an EU Intergovernmental Conference: An Empirical Application." *Computational and Mathematical Organization Theory* 10(3): 243–266

Thurner, P. W., and Pappi, F. U. (2006). "Domestic and International Politics during EU Intergovernmental Conferences: Bridging the Gap between Negotiation Theory and Practice." *Negotiation Journal* 22(2): 167–185.

Thurner, P. W., and Pappi, F. U. (2009). *European Union Intergovernmental Conferences: Domestic Preference Formation, Transgovernmental Networks, and the Dynamics of Compromise*. New York, London: Routledge.

Thurner, P. W., Pappi, F. U., and Stoiber, M. (2002). "EU Intergovernmental Conferences: A Quantitative Analytical Reconstruction and Data-Handbook of Domestic Preference Formation, Transnational Networks and Dynamics of Compromise during the Amsterdam Treaty Negotiations." Arbeitspapiere Mannheimer Zentrum für Europäische Sozialforschung Nr. 60/IINS Research Paper No. 15.

Thurner, P. W., and Stoiber, M. (2002). "Interministerielle Netzwerke: Formale und informelle Koordinationsstrukturen bei der Vorbereitung der deutschen Verhandlungspositionen zur Regierungskonferenz 1996." *Politische Vierteljahresschrift* 42(4): 561–605.

Thurner, P. W., Stoiber M., and Weinmann, C. (2005). "Informelle Transgouvernementale Koordinationsnetzwerke der Ministerialbürokratie der EU-Mitgliedstaaten bei einer Regierungskonferenz." *Politische Vierteljahresschrift* 43(4): 552–574.

Trondal, J., and Peters, B. G. (2013). "The Rise of European Administrative Space: Lessons Learned." *Journal of European Public Policy* 20(2): 295–307.

Wallace, H., Pollack, M. A., and Young, A. (Eds.). (2010). *Policy-Making in the European Union*. Oxford: Oxford University Press.

Weishaar, H., Amos, A., and Collin, J. (2015). "Best of Enemies: Using Social Network Analysis to Exlore a Policy Network in European Smoke-free Policy." *Social Science & Medicine* (133): 84–95.

Wessels, W. (1997). "An Ever Closer Fusion: A Dynamic Macro-political View of Integration Processes." *Journal of Common Market Studies* 35: 267–299.

CHAPTER 25

NETWORKS AND THE POLITICS OF THE ENVIRONMENT

RAMIRO BERARDO, ISABELLA ALCAÑIZ,
JENNIFER HADDEN, AND LORIEN JASNY

INTRODUCTION

SOCIAL scientists have made significant progress in the last three decades in understanding how societies tackle critical environmental problems. This progress has been facilitated by the development of behavioral models that recognize that the networks of interactions in which actors are embedded affect the way those actors respond to environmental problems.

Studies of networks in environmental policy and politics ask critical questions regarding how networks form and evolve and, in turn, how the interactions between networks and individual-level variables shape socio-environmental outcomes. Do networks transmit information and promote learning, ultimately altering attitudes and behavior? Do they provide social structures through which actors can overcome collective action problems and affect the governance of the environment and the management of natural resources on local, national, and supranational scales?

A rich body of research has emerged to answer these questions across multiple scales of political activity. A sustained stream of literature has demonstrated how the links between components of social-ecological systems can be carefully analyzed through the application of social network analysis (SNA) techniques (Bodin and Tengö, 2012; Bodin et al., 2014; McAllister et al., 2015). At the local level, studies have shown how relational ties that configure local and regional networks play an important role in averting conflict among users of common-pool resources[1] (Ostrom, 1990; Schneider et al., 2003;

Betsill and Bulkeley, 2006; Marshall, 2007; Ostrom, 2008). At the international level, scholars use SNA to examine how environmental global governance is shaped by the interaction of a wide range of actors, including transgovernmental organizations (Cao et al., 2014), independent experts (Andonova, Betsill, and Bulkeley, 2009; Stephens et al,. 2011), state experts (Alcañiz, 2016a, 2016b), and social movements and NGOs (Hadden, 2015; Hadden and Jasny, 2017).

In this chapter we review some of the main themes tackled by scholars who study environmental policy and management of natural resources through the use of SNA. While this is a diverse field, the members of this scholarly community share an interest in what we term the "politics of the environment," a moniker that encompasses a wide variety of human decision-making processes that may affect the likelihood of successfully responding to environmental problems on different scales. Since it is beyond the scope of this chapter to provide a comprehensive review of all the literature loosely connected under this rubric, we focus our discussion on contributions that employ SNA measures and techniques to connect actor-level behavior, network-level activity, and socio-environmental outcomes. We start by proposing a simplified model of how these relationships take place, then offer a review of some of the research that has zoomed in on these relationships. We end our chapter by discussing potential avenues for future research.

A MODEL OF NETWORKS, ACTOR BEHAVIOR, AND SOCIO-ENVIRONMENTAL OUTCOMES

Figure 25.1 illustrates a basic, general model of the relationship among the key themes in our discussion. The figure portrays a connection between activity that takes place in networks and micro-level behavior, which social network analysts usually view as intertwined in a coevolving relationship. We focus on three network characteristics that have been well explored with regard to their effect on individual behavior and group-level performance: density and fragmentation, bridging and bonding social capital realized in network structures, and structural role performance (e.g., brokerage and leadership).[2]

The coevolving relationship between network-level activity and micro-level behavior affects the likelihood of groups achieving adaptive governance and/or adaptive co-management in the environmental realm. The terms *adaptive governance* and *adaptive co-management* explicitly acknowledge the role of collective learning processes in sustainable practice and thus replace other concepts such as management or adaptive management, which referred purely to implementation of management actions on individual natural resources or whole ecosystems without paying much attention to the social-political environments in which those management actions took place (Dietz, Ostrom, and Stern, 2003; Bodin and Tengö, 2012).[3] Both terms evoke a continuous

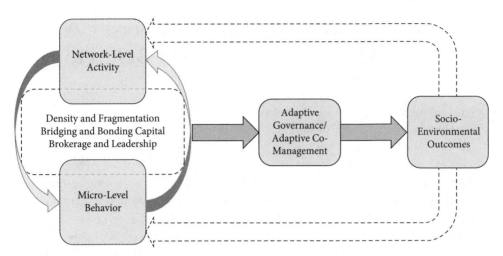

FIGURE 25.1 Network processes in environmental policy and politics.

problem-solving process that is realized through collaborative work by a rich variety of actors coupled by sociopolitical relationships.

We argue, along with many others, that the focus on complexity and facilitation of cooperation among decentralized actors lends itself to a network perspective. The network structures that contribute to the ability of actors to coordinate their actions, cooperate with each other, share information, and adapt in their decision-making process are more likely to facilitate social-environmental outcomes valued by a majority of involved stakeholders (Ostrom, 1990; Folke et al., 2005; Plummer and Armitage, 2007; Newman and Dale, 2007; Armitage et al., 2008; Bodin and Crona, 2008, 2009; Berkes, 2009). The achievement of an adaptive governance or adaptive co-management outcome, in turn, shapes socio-environmental outcomes such as rate of conservation of specific natural resources or the resilience of social-ecological systems.

In a final stage, as socio-environmental outcomes occur, our model proposes that they have a feedback effect on both network-level activity and micro-level behavior. Examples of this feedback process abound. For instance, Dell'Apa et al. (2013) use regular equivalence analysis to study the network of trade of spiny dogfish to the European Union before and after the introduction of regulations in the United States to protect the species. They show that the regulations, prompted by a decision by the U.S. National Marine Fisheries Service to declare the stock as overfished in 1998, led to changes in the structure of the trade network, in which the United States was the main exporter of the species prior to the introduction of the regulations. After the regulations were enacted, the main exporter role went to Canada, while other countries also became more central as exports from the United States dwindled. Thus a decision made in response to the level of network activity by one node led to network-level rearrangement and subsequent change in a global socio-environmental system.

THE COEVOLUTION OF NETWORK-LEVEL ACTIVITY AND MICRO-LEVEL BEHAVIOR

Scholars interested in the study of environmental policy and natural resource management from a network perspective have identified (a) ways in which networks can affect the behavior of the actors that form them and (b) how the behavioral patterns of actors can in turn produce changes in the network. This coevolving relationship can be studied in a myriad of ways. Here, we focus on reviewing research that examines how certain network characteristics—their density and fragmentation, the bridging and bonding capital structures that form in them, and the brokerage and leadership positions that certain nodes occupy—affect governance processes and socio-environmental outcomes. We note that these network characteristics often co-vary; for example, denser networks typically have more bonding capital, while less dense networks facilitate the emergence of central actors occupying brokering positions that are more likely to produce higher levels of bridging capital. However, we analytically separate these concepts in order to review the ways in which, according to the specialized literature, they connect with our outcomes of interest for this chapter.

Network density and fragmentation. Network density and fragmentation are the two most widely used indicators of network cohesion. Density is simply the proportion of possible ties in a network that actually exist. Fragmentation, on the other hand, is the proportion of pairs of nodes in a network that cannot reach each other, either directly or indirectly (through others).[4] Both of these measures correlate with network activity. The greater the level of activity in the network (i.e., the greater the number of links), the higher the density and the lower the chances of fragmentation.[5]

As noted by various scholars, a common expectation among students of environmental policy and natural resource management is that more cohesive networks—denser, less fragmented—should be able to facilitate better, more adaptive responses to environmental problems (Bodin, Crona, and Ernstson, 2006; Sandström and Rova, 2009). Scholars generally expect that higher level of activity and lower levels of network fragmentation facilitate the exchange of information and reduce bargaining costs, thereby leading to better coordination of different individual views and positions and thus to greater collective learning (Scholz et al., 2008). This, in turn, facilitates the emergence of adaptive management practices that are conducive to the solution of environmental problems (Newig, Günther, and Pahl-Wostl, 2010).

Schneider et al. (2003) provide a good example of the relationship between network cohesion and governance outcomes in their research on the National Estuary Program (NEP). The NEP was created by the 1987 amendments to the Clean Water Act (Section 320) and allowed state governors in the United States to identify

estuaries of significant importance that require protection against pollution resulting from human activities. According to directives contained in Section 320, in each
of the selected estuaries a Comprehensive Conservation and Management Plan was
to be developed by a management conference attended by multiple stakeholders
from both governmental and nongovernmental sectors, with support from the US
Environmental Protection Agency.[6] Schneider et al. collected data on twenty-two
estuaries (ten with NEP status, twelve without it) and found that stakeholder networks in estuaries with NEP status were significantly denser than networks in non-
NEP-status estuaries. In addition, actors participating in the former had more faith in
the results of collaborative processes, nurtured stronger interpersonal ties with other
stakeholders, and exhibited higher levels of faith in the procedural fairness of local
policies (Schneider et al., 2003), all variables thought to facilitate adaptive governance on a regional scale (Scholz and Stiftel, 2005). Scholz et al. (2008) then used parts
of the same data set to extend these findings, reporting that actors participating in
denser networks were more likely to exhibit higher levels of agreement on the causes
of environmental problems in the estuaries, which they ascribe to the fact that denser
networks facilitate redundancy of information and heightened levels of trust among
the network participants.[7]

Bodin and Crona (2008) provide another example of the relationship between density and fragmentation in networks and responses to management problems that might
result when multiple users access a common-pool resource. In their study of a rural
coastal fishing village in Kenya, they link the low level of fragmentation in the network
of exchange of information among fishermen with a higher ability to generate useful
social capital that may help avoid the problem of resource overuse.

Despite the evidence that has shown the positive effects that activity levels in networks may have in realizing adaptive governance and adaptive co-management, it bears
keeping in mind that this positive relationship is by no means ubiquitous. For example, some research shows that excessive density can impede, instead of facilitate, collective action (Oh et al., 2004) and lead to a homogenization of knowledge that can
inhibit innovative solutions to existing problems (Bodin and Norberg, 2005). Smythe,
Thompson, and Garcia-Quijano (2014) examine two cases of collaborative marine
ecosystem-based management (EBM) planning in Rhode Island and New York. The
authors find that a lower-density network is more effective for collaborative marine
EBM planning, because this type of network is more likely to remain diverse and provide decision makers with non-redundant information that can help tackle problems in
a more innovative way.

In general, studies that question the value of high density in networks to achieve
desirable environmental outcomes point to the fact that denser networks face two problems. First, they may result in the excessive homogenization of positions or visions held
by network participants. Second, and as a result of the first problem, denser networks
might be less able to adapt to exogenous shocks simply because the members are more
likely to become locked in a form of "groupthink" that is calcified by the lack of informational diversity (Crona et al., 2011). Thus, research points to a "middle ground" between

excessive and insufficient density, although what this ideal middle point might be is difficult to determine ex ante.

Bridging and bonding capital. Existing scholarship often outlines a positive relationship between successful collaboration and management of natural resources and high levels of social capital among users (Folke et al., 2005; Plummer and Armitage, 2007). Bourdieu defines social capital as "the aggregate of the actual or potential resources which are linked to possession of a durable network of more or less institutionalized relationships of mutual acquaintance and recognition" (1986, 248–249; see also Coleman, 1988).[8] Social capital is valuable for adaptive co-management because it lowers the vulnerability of actors embedded in networks by improving their chances of detecting and punishing uncooperative behavior, facilitates learning, and aids communities in generating better responses to environmentally risky situations (Adger, 2010). Social capital does all these things by helping lower transaction costs, increase trust, and trigger the adoption of norms at the group level that facilitate cooperation (Pretty and Ward, 2001).

Network researchers often brand social capital in networks as either bonding or bridging capital. Bonding capital emerges when connections among members of a network (or a subgroup in it) create structures that favor closeness in relationships. Specifically, bonding capital results when the members of a network tend to build their connections to others in a way that increases their ability to exert influence or control over their ego network. In this regard, bonding structures promote cooperation by providing assurance against behavior that might be deemed undesirable. Bridging capital, on the other hand, results when nodes build ties in ways that facilitate access to more distant parts of the network. This kind of capital is more likely to produce nonredundant information, making it valuable in generating innovation or learning.

In addition, which type of capital dominates in a network may have a critical effect on the resilience of the network to external threats. According to Newman and Dale (2005), bonding social capital can hinder innovation by cutting off actors from novel sources of information, in turn reducing adaptability and resilience. Networks characterized by a wide availability of bridging social capital can provide links to a diverse web of resources, making the community more adaptable in the face of change (Newman and Dale, 2007; Ernstson, Sörlin, and Elmqvist, 2008). This expectation has been supported by considerable empirical evidence. For example, in their study of adoption of farming management practices in cocoa agroforestry systems in Ghana, Isaac et al. (2007) find that certain producers provide bridging social capital in their communities by connecting local groups of producers to outside experts through informal networks of advice, resulting in more adaptive management practices. Further probing into the relationship between bridging social capital and individual performance of natural resource users, Isaac (2012) shows a positive and significant correlation between the bridging capacity of farmers in communication networks and the agrodiversity in their farms (measured as "richness of tress species"), which contributes to sustainable agrarian management. Another example of the importance of bridging relationships in the management of natural resources is contained in a study on the management of wetlands in Sweden, where the authors found that bridging relationships among stakeholders allowed for the increase in levels of trust that serves as a catalyst for the implementation of better management actions (Hahn et al., 2006).

Research has also found that actors' tendency toward bonding modes and homophily—whereby similar groups are more likely to engage than diverse ones (McPherson et al., 2001)—may impede the development of bridging organizations (Newman and Dale, 2007). This in turn affects social learning in the network, as new information, skills, and ideas are less likely to emerge among homogenous actors. The rather pessimistic view of bonding social capital presented here must be taken with a grain of salt. Bonding capital might not be particularly conducive to the spread of information that can be used for solving problems in an innovative way, but it is beneficial in promoting trust and reciprocity among members of a group. This facilitates the detection and quick punishment of uncooperative behavior (Bodin and Crona, 2008) and thus contributes to a sustained use of shared resources.

Recent scholarship has moved from a static analysis of social capital in networks and has started to examine how social capital emerges and evolves. Conducting research in a set of ten US estuaries, Berardo and Scholz (2010) analyzed how networks self-organize by testing the "risk hypothesis." According to the hypothesis, when actors face high-risk situations, they tend to form bonding structures that generate overlapping information more likely to help detect and punish freeriding behavior in the use of common-pool resources. On the other hand, when actors face low-risk situations, assurance against defection is not a priority, and thus actors tend to form bridging structures that facilitate access to nonoverlapping information that comes from more distant parts of the network, a type of information that is more useful to solve coordination problems.

Findings showed that there was a predominant tendency among the actors in the networks toward the formation of bridging structures in which a central stakeholder had the potential to fulfill a coordination role. Berardo and Scholz (2010) claimed that this tendency was explained at least in part by the fact that the regional governance systems in the estuaries were not characterized by high risks of defection among stakeholders, which lowered the likelihood of cooperation dilemmas. This low level of risk, in turn, allowed stakeholders to not have to focus on the formation of bonding structures, instead forming structures that could be valuable to solve coordination problems, which resulted in the appearance of star-like configurations, in which a central node bridged otherwise separated actors. This research thus suggested that low-risk situations are indeed associated with the emergence of bridging structures in networks.

Since then, other research in environmental policy and natural resources management has found additional support for the risk hypotheses (Henry and Vollan, 2012; Lubell, Robins, and Wang, 2014), though more work is needed to create richer models of the coevolving relationship between risk perception and network behavior and to gauge whether and how participation in networks affects individual perceptions of risk. Fortunately, ongoing efforts tackle this limitation. In a recent article on efforts to manage the Swiss landscape, Angst and Hirschi (2016) examine the evolution of a network of actors involved in the governance of natural resources in a regional nature park project in Switzerland. They test two hypotheses based on Berardo and Scholz's risk hypothesis using separable temporal exponential random graph modeling (STERGM) and find that the network evolves (as they expect given the conditions the network actors face) toward bonding capital. But interestingly enough, they also find that the generation of bonding capital does not mean that the network becomes less hierarchical over time. This is an important finding, because it hints that the relationship between bonding and bridging in networks is not necessarily antagonistic, something that previous work has also established. In fact, Berardo and Scholz (2010) observed that, regardless of the fact that bridging structures were dominant in the networks they examined, bonding structures were also present, although to a lesser extent. Based on this result, they contended that stakeholders in complex social-ecological systems might form relational structures that address both coordination and cooperation problems simultaneously, a finding that has been replicated since (Berardo, 2014a; McAllister, McCrea, and Lubell, 2013).

Finally, it is worth noting that other recent scholarship is beginning to extend the study of social capital beyond the familiar confines of one-mode networks, where almost all of the research has been produced. For instance, Berardo (2014b) has proposed utilizing some of the structural configurations available in software packages for fitting exponential random graph models to two-mode networks as good proxies for the social capital that actors generate when they interact with each other through their participation in certain events. For instance, Berardo claims that actors might generate "weak" forms of bonding capital when they participate in few activities together and "stronger" forms of bonding when they participate in many activities. This approach to the study of social capital in two-mode networks continues to evolve as researchers further investigate how policy stakeholders create bonding and bridging structures through their participation in policy venues or forums in which decisions are made that affect the sustainability of common-pool resources (Berardo and Lubell, 2016).[9]

Brokerage and leadership. The literature on environmental policy and management of natural resources stresses that in order to achieve adaptive governance in complex social-ecological systems, individual actors need to be able to steer decision-making processes toward the production of collaborative outcomes (Ostrom, 2009). How leaders and policy brokers shape change has been a central preoccupation of policy scholars since Kingdon's Multiple Streams theory posited that leaders can help open policy windows to address specific problems of interest. In their review of adaptive governance scholarship, Folke et al. contend that "leadership is essential in shaping change and reorganization by providing innovation in order to achieve the flexibility needed to deal with ecosystem dynamics" and support this assertion on work on forest and water management (2005, 451). Armitage et al. (2008), in turn, claim that "key individuals" can help maintain a focus on collaboration and create conditions that are conducive to learning and the avoidance of conflict, while Crona et al. (2011) assert that key players can facilitate a move from unsustainable to more sustainable regimes. In a study of four social-ecological systems in Australia, Sweden, Thailand, and the United States, Olsson et al. (2006) examined how key leaders in networks can prepare a system for change by using or creating windows of opportunity to integrate and communicate how actors view a problem, thus helping the system navigate toward adaptive governance.

Most network studies identify the "leaders" in networks by relying on simple degree centrality measures (see Bodin and Crona, 2008; Bono and Anderson, 2005; Friedkin and Slater, 1994 for examples). Central actors are more likely to fulfill a coordinating role in networks (Berardo and Scholz, 2010), which is a particularly important social function in periods of rapid change that demand adaptive behavior at a systemic level (Bodin, Crona, and Ernstson, 2006).[10] Such measures can also be employed to identify "brokers" in networks, who serve a similar function (Diani, 2003). Scholarship on leadership, brokerage, and bridging capital usually overlaps considerably, even if these concepts are not synonymous.[11] Both leaders and bridging actors are seen as key to the successful co-management of natural resources, as they both transmit relevant information and knowledge among actors that operate across different geographies, ideologies, or scales (Berkes, 2009; Cohen, Evans, and Mills, 2012). Problem-solving and governance in socio-ecological networks rest on the capacity of these actors to learn and share knowledge (Armitage, Marschke, and Plummer, 2008; Newig, Günther, and Pahl-Wostl, 2010).

It is important to note, however, that leaders and brokers are not necessarily experts, even though expert knowledge is useful in dealing with environmental problems and has garnered the attention of students of environmental networks (Conca, 2006; Kamelarczyk and Smith-Hall, 2014; Weible, Sabatier, and McQueen 2009; to name a few). Research shows that both expert and nonexpert knowledge can play a role in problem identification and analysis, contributing to the successful implementation of adaptive co-management (Davidson-Hunt, 2006; Berardo, Olivier, and Lavers, 2015).

Other work has identified the importance of brokers in institution building to reach adaptive governance. Jasny and Lubell (2015) explored the complex system of organizations and institutions engaged in water resources management in California and concluded that brokerage emerges as a result of an evolutionary process in which those who bridge political, geological, and technological divides reap benefits. Interestingly, by extending Gould and Fernandez's (1989) classic work on brokerage to two-mode networks, Jasny and Lubell show that brokerage is not only provided by individual actors, but also by the policy venues in which the former interact to advance their agendas. Many of those venues have the goal of spanning various types of boundaries to increase cooperation, bringing together stakeholders that would otherwise be isolated.

We should not assume that actors in positions of leadership, or those who can bridge distant parts of the network, automatically exercise a positive influence in the network or even improve their chances of reaching their own goals.[12] In an article that describes the participation of governmental and nongovernmental organizations in a cooperative program implemented by the South West Florida Water Management District, Berardo (2009) shows that project managers who include more collaborative partners in a project increase their chances of getting their projects funded, but that those chances actually decrease when more of those collaborative partners occupy positions of leadership in the network, measured by their capacity to reach distant parts of the network through their bridging ties. In other words, organizations perform better by adding more partners, as long as this addition does not result in an excessive influx of novel information brought into the project by the bridging partners. Indeed, as the saying goes, too many cooks can spoil the soup.

Even when leaders or brokers are not constrained in their information-processing capacity, they may be more focused on retaining their status and influence than on achieving collective goals. In related work concerning entrepreneurs, Meijernik and Huitema (2010) review sixteen case studies around the globe on policy entrepreneurs in water transitions, finding that real-life entrepreneurs are often more interested in institutionalizing their policy ideas than in promoting social learning based on the flow of high-quality information. Research with a more explicit focus on social network measurement of leadership finds similar results. For instance, scholars have found that excessive centralization can obstruct learning when the central actor controls information and prevents others from accessing it (Bodin, Crona, and Ernstson, 2006; Scholz et al., 2008), or when centralization is associated with less deliberation even in the process of undisrupted information flows (Newig, Günther, and Pahl-Wostl, 2010).

DIRECTIONS FOR FUTURE RESEARCH

Our review of the uses of SNA in the fields of environmental policy and natural resources management has revealed a keen interest by scholars in linking network analytic tools to the examination of variables that are thought to lead to successful adaptive co-management in complex social-ecological systems. Such adaptive co-management practices are in turn critical to improving social-ecological resilience and contributing to the use of natural resources in a sustainable manner.

Social network theory and methods have come a long way from the days of relying on small, binary networks and descriptive statistics. In general, until the early 2000s advances were tentative in a majority of cases, with a profusion of studies utilizing the term "network" as a metaphor for complex social interactions that were rarely measured exhaustively. But as theoretical perspectives have come to incorporate more explicitly the role that social relationships play in affecting environmental outcomes, network methods have made crucial strides in more accurately capturing this reality. Recent work suggests that researchers are finding innovative ways to examine these relationships (Angst and Hirschi, 2016; Berardo and Lubell, 2016; Bodin et al., 2014; Kininmonth, Bergsten, and Bodin, 2015; Guerrero et al., 2015). We highlight here three particularly compelling directions for future research in this area.

First, scholars need to move more decisively toward the production of research that explores in greater detail how activity in social networks impacts specific environmental indicators of interest. Some teams of researchers are already committed to this vision and have begun to examine the interaction between ecological and social networks in ways that can inform public policy. For example, Bergsten, Galafassi, and Bodin (2014) study a collaborative wetland management network formed by twenty-six municipalities in the Stockholm county in Sweden and examine how this collaborative network "fits" with an ecologically defined network of ecologically interconnected wetlands. Using multiple regression quadratic assignment procedure (MRQAP), the authors test whether observed collaborations among municipalities are explained by spatial adjacency and/or shared ecological connectivity to wetlands that cross jurisdictional boundaries. Findings show that spatial nearness explains collaboration, but ecological connectivity to wetlands does not. This type of research has important implications for policy practitioners, since it reveals the disconnect between ecological linkages and the collaborative behavior upon which successful management of the natural resources depends.

Multilevel models may have an important role to play in this area, since they allow for the simultaneous modeling of both social relationships and the linkages that may take place between human users and certain natural resources of interest. For example, it would be possible to model one network of information exchange among fishermen, a second ecological relationship among the fish themselves (predator-prey relationships, coexistence in habitat niches, dependence on food sources, etc.), along with a bipartite network relating the members of the first to the second (Hollway and Koskinen, 2016). Guerrero et al. (2015) provide another example of the use of the modeling of multiplex networks. Using data collected from participants of a biodiversity conservation initiative in Australia, the authors fit multilevel exponential random graph models and find that individual parcels of native vegetation are the object of more collaborative activities among stakeholders in comparison to parcels that are interconnected from an ecological standpoint. Based on this finding, Guerrero et al. contend that SNA can help improve the capacity of stakeholders to assess the obstacles to improved management of natural resources. More work like this is needed if scholars want to make meaningful contributions to the debates on how adaptive management and governance are to be achieved.

Second, many studies in this area explicitly acknowledge a temporal dimension, in which governance and socioecological outcomes affect one another sequentially. To explicitly examine this topic, we need to model how networks evolve. Modeling network evolution would allow us to tackle critical questions about how governance initiatives affect socio-environmental outcomes and vice versa. Even though work has already been done on network evolution to explain how specific network configurations are formed (see Angst and Hirschi, 2016; Berardo and Scholz, 2010; Berardo, 2014a for examples) and how nodal attributes affect network behavior (Berardo, 2013), longitudinal work remains greatly undersupplied. The reasons are obvious. Longitudinal analyses demand the investment of considerable resources (i.e., time and money) on the part of researchers. Yet it is only with this type of work that scholars will be able to fully understand the evolution of many of the variables and processes of interest discussed in this chapter, which are thought to facilitate adaptive management and governance, such as the availability of social capital, proper leadership, and a minimum of group cohesion to facilitate collaborative behavior.

Finally, this area of research would benefit from greater availability of explicitly comparative work. As mentioned in previous sections, similar network features—like density and bonding capital—appear to have different levels of importance for how networks operate in different settings. Bonding capital tightly connecting stakeholders in a network, for instance, might yield more positive results in contributing to the sustainable use of natural resources in situations in which formal rules to regulate behavior are either absent of ineffective, as is often the case in developing countries with weak bureaucracies (Berardo and Lubell, 2016). Bridging capital, on the other hand, might render more benefits in networks in which the actors face a deficit of innovative responses to local problems while still socially embedded in societies where interpersonal trust is high. To reveal the benefits and costs of different network structures for the adaptive management and governance of natural resources and the environment, comparative work is key. Through this approach, researchers can expand the knowledge base regarding which network structures work under specific conditions rather than providing generalizations from findings collected from nonrepresentative cases.

Acknowledgments

We thank Alex Montgomery for valuable comments on an earlier draft of this chapter. The usual caveats apply.

Notes

1. Common-pool resources (CPRs) are goods that are nonexcludable (i.e., they are open access and thus can be used by multiple users) yet are subject to rivalrous consumption (i.e., a unit of the good used by a user is not available to other users), which leads to problems of congestion in use and the associated cooperation dilemmas that may end up resulting in the exhaustion of the resource.
2. As would be the case with any schematic representation of how networks affect individual behavior and systemic variables, Figure 25.1 contains a simplified depiction of the relationships among these variables. For instance, the figure does not incorporate the effect that macroculture (a system of widely shared assumptions and values that guides actions) has on the behavior of the network actors. A strong macroculture may promote shared understandings of the need for cooperative behavior, which in turn positively affects governance processes (Robins, Bates, and Pattison 2011).
3. Specifically, *adaptive governance* describes the evolution of institutions capable of generating sustainable policy solutions to environmental problems through the coordinated

actions of previously independent systems of users, knowledge, authorities, and organized interests (Scholz and Stiftel 2005, 5). *Adaptive co-management,* on the other hand, also describes situations in which actors explicitly cooperate in order to achieve common goals, but places a less explicit emphasis on the role of institutions in the process. The term "institution" has historically been difficult to define. North (1990) provided perhaps the most widely used definition, seeing institutions as "rules of the game" that are used to coordinate human activities. Hodgson (2006) extends that definition, noticing that institutions should not only include formally designed rules, but also self-organizing emergent strategies around coordination problems that are rarely studied in detail. Ostrom (2009) picks up the baton and devises a more comprehensive definition, which describes institutions as rules, norms, or strategies that people derive to coordinate or cooperate more successfully in collective endeavors.

4. In other words, for the network to be fragmented, more than one component has to exist. A component is a subgraph in the network that is connected; that is, there is a path between all pairs of nodes that form it (Wasserman and Faust 1994, 109).

5. There is a linear, positive relationship between activity and density. Any new link in a network will increase its density by the same amount, regardless of how many links already exist. However, there is no such linear relationship between level of activity and level of fragmentation in a network. A link that connects two nodes that could have reached each other through intermediaries in the absence of the new link will not reduce fragmentation. This will only happen if the new link connects two nodes that are members of different components (i.e., different connected subgraphs). Of course, as new links are created the likelihood of separated components drops, so eventually a network with high levels of activity is more likely to see less fragmentation.

6. Altogether twenty-eight estuaries were identified through this process in the country. For a list of these estuaries go to http://www.epa.gov/nep.

7. Other research shows that activity level in networks is in turn affected by the types of actors and issues discussed in networks. Berardo and colleagues have studied meetings of the South Florida Ecosystem Restoration Task Force over a five-year period. The task force is a collaborative partnership of fourteen federal, tribal, state, and local agencies, whose goal is to restore the Florida Everglades. Using the discussion on each agenda item in a meeting as a separate "network of engagement," where a link between two nodes indicates that both actors participate in the same discussion, the authors find that the level of technical complexity of issues being discussed, as well as the types of actors that voice their opinions in the discussions, have an effect on the overall level of engagement (Berardo, Heikkila, and Gerlak 2014).

8. As a concept, social capital has been problematic, but engaging in a discussion of the merits of different definitions is clearly beyond the scope of this chapter. For a more detailed discussion of different definitions and meanings of the term "social capital," see Pretty and Ward (2001).

9. The study of bonding and bridging capital in two-mode networks is not restricted to networks concerned with the management of CPRs. McAllister, Taylor, and Harman (2015), for example, analyze the formation of bridging and bonding capital in partnership networks for urban development in Australia, where stakeholders participate in policy venues in which the topic of development is discussed.

10. Measures of centrality have also been used in international relations scholarship to study how countries perform environmentally. Ward (2006) examines the network of nations

linked to each other through joint participation in international governmental organizations and finds that measures of network centrality positively impact a nation's performance on different sustainability indicators.

11. We treat brokers and leaders as similar in nature for the sake of simplicity, though differences between the two concepts exist. See Diani (2003) for a detailed examination of those differences.

12. This contradicts well-ingrained assumptions in the literature about "networks as actors" concerning the more democratic nature of networks (vis-à-vis hierarchical organizations and competitive markets).

References

Adger, W. N. (2010). "Social Capital, Collective Action, and Adaptation to Climate Change." In *Der Klimawandel*, edited by Martin Voss, pp. 327–345. Springer. http://link.springer.com/chapter/10.1007/978-3-531-92258-4_19.

Alcañiz, I. (2016a). *Environmental and Nuclear Networks in the Global South: How Skills Shape International Cooperation.* New York: Cambridge University Press.

Alcañiz, I. (2016b). "Partner Selection in International Environmental Networks: The Effect of Skills and Money on Cooperation in the Global South." *Environmental Science & Policy* 55: 107–115.

Andonova, L. B., Betsill, M. M., and Bulkeley, H. (2009). "Transnational Climate Governance." *Global Environmental Politics* 9(2): 52–73.

Angst, M., and Hirschi, C. (2016). "Network Dynamics in Natural Resource Governance: A Case Study of Swiss Landscape Management." *Policy Studies Journal* 45(2): 315–336.

Armitage, D. R., Plummer, R., Berkes, F., Arthur, R. I., Charles, A. T., Davidson-Hunt, I. J., . . . Wollenberg, E. K. (2008). "Adaptive Co-Management for Social-Ecological Complexity." *Frontiers in Ecology and the Environment* 7(2): 95–102.

Armitage, D., Marschke, M., and Plummer, R. (2008). "Adaptive Co-management and the Paradox of Learning." *Global Environmental Change* 18(1): 86–98.

Berardo, R. (2009). "Processing Complexity in Networks: A Study of Informal Collaboration and Its Effect on Organizational Success." *Policy Studies Journal* 37(3): 521–539.

Berardo, R. (2013). "The Coevolution of Perceptions of Procedural Fairness and Link Formation in Self-organizing Policy Networks." *Journal of Politics* 75(3): 686–700.

Berardo, R. (2014a). "The Evolution of Self-Organizing Communication Networks in High-Risk Social-Ecological Systems." *International Journal of the Commons* 8(1): 236–258.

Berardo, R. (2014b). "Bridging and Bonding Capital in Two-Mode Collaboration Networks." *Policy Studies Journal* 42(2): 197–225.

Berardo, R., Heikkila, T., and Gerlak, A. K. (2014). "Interorganizational Engagement in Collaborative Environmental Management: Evidence from the South Florida Ecosystem Restoration Task Force." *Journal of Public Administration Research and Theory* 24(3): 697–719.

Berardo, R., and Lubell, M. (2016). "Understanding What Shapes a Polycentric Governance System." *Public Administration Review* 76(5): 738–751.

Berardo, R., Olivier, T., and Lavers, A. (2015). "Environmental Crises as Shocks to an Ecology of Policy Games: Evidence from the Parana River Delta." *Review of Policy Research* 76(5): 738–751.

Berardo, R., and Scholz, J. T. (2010). "Self-Organizing Policy Networks: Risk, Partner Selection, and Cooperation in Estuaries." *American Journal of Political Science* 54(3): 632–649.

Bergsten, A., Galafassi, D., and Bodin, Ö. (2014). "The Problem of Spatial Fit in Social-Ecological Systems: Detecting Mismatches between Ecological Connectivity and Land Management in an Urban Region." *Ecology and Society* 19(4): 6.

Berkes, F. (2009). "Evolution of Co-Management: Role of Knowledge Generation, Bridging Organizations and Social Learning." *Journal of Environmental Management* 90(5): 1692–1702.

Betsill, M. M., and Bulkeley, H. (2006). "Cities and the Multilevel Governance of Global Climate Change." *Global Governance: A Review of Multilateralism and International Organizations* 12(2): 141–159.

Bodin, Ö., Crona, B., and Ernstson, H. (2006). "Social Networks in Natural Resource Management: What Is There to Learn from a Structural Perspective." *Ecology and Society* 11(2): r2.

Bodin, Ö., Crona, B., Thyresson, M., Golz, A.-L., and Tengö, M. (2014). "Conservation Success as a Function of Good Alignment of Social and Ecological Structures and Processes." *Conservation Biology* 28(5): 1371–1379.

Bodin, Ö., and Crona, B. I. (2008). "Management of Natural Resources at the Community Level: Exploring the Role of Social Capital and Leadership in a Rural Fishing Community." *World Development* 36(12): 2763–2779.

Bodin, Ö., and Norberg, J. (2005). "Information Network Topologies for Enhanced Local Adaptive Management." *Environmental Management* 35(2): 175–193.

Bodin, Ö., and Crona, B. I. (2009). "The Role of Social Networks in Natural Resource Governance: What relational patterns make a difference?" *Global Environmental Change* 19(3): 366–374.

Bodin, Ö., and Tengö, M. (2012). "Disentangling Intangible Social-ecological Systems." *Global Environmental Change* 22(2): 430–439.

Bono, J. E., and Anderson, M. H. (2005). "The Advice and Influence Networks of Transformational Leaders." *Journal of Applied Psychology* 90(6): 1306–1314.

Bourdieu, P. (1986). "The Forms of Capital." In *Handbook of Theory and Research for the Sociology of Education*, edited by John G. Richardson, pp. 241–258. New York: Greenwood Press.

Cao, X., Milner, H. V., Prakash, A., and Ward, H. (2013). "Research Frontiers in Comparative and International Environmental Politics An Introduction." *Comparative Political Studies* 47(3): 291–308.

Cohen, P. J., Evans, L. S., and Mills, M. (2012). "Social Networks Supporting Governance of Coastal Ecosystems in Solomon Islands." *Conservation Letters* 5(5): 376–386.

Coleman, J. S. (1988). "Social Capital in the Creation of Human Capital." *American Journal of Sociology* 94(1): 95–120.

Conca, K. (2006). *Governing Water: Contentious Transnational Politics and Global Institution Building*. Cambridge, MA: MIT Press.

Crona, B., Ernstson, H., Prell, C., and Hubacek, K. (2011). "Combining Social Network Approaches with Social Theories to Improve Understanding of Natural Resource Governance." In *Social Networks and Natural Resource Management*, edited by Örjan Bodin and Christina Prell, pp. 44–71. Cambridge, UK: Cambridge University Press.

Davidson-Hunt, I. J. (2006). "Adaptive Learning Networks: Developing Resource Management Knowledge through Social Learning Forums." *Human Ecology* 34(4): 593–614.

Dell'Apa, A., Johnson, J. C., Kimmel, D. G., and Rulifson, R. A. (2013). "The International Trade and Fishery Management of Spiny Dogfish: A Social Network Approach." *Ocean & Coastal Management* 80: 65–72.

Diani, M. (2003). "Leaders or Brokers? Positions and Influence in Social Movement Networks." In *Social Movements and Networks: Relational Approaches to Collective Action*, edited by Mario Diani and Doug McAdam 105–122. New York, NY: Oxford University Press.

Dietz, T., Ostrom, E., and Stern, P. C. (2003). "The Struggle to Govern the Commons." *Science* 302(5652): 1907–1912.

Ernstson, H, Sörlin, S., and Elmqvist, T. (2008). "Social Movements and Ecosystem services— The Role of Social Network Structure in Protecting and Managing Urban Green Areas in Stockholm." *Ecology and Society* 13(2): 39.

Folke, C., Hahn, T., Olsson, P., and Norberg, J. (2005). "Adaptive Governance of Social-Ecological Systems." *Annual Review of Environmental Resources* 30: 441–473.

Friedkin, N. E., and Slater, M. R. (1994). "School Leadership and Performance: A Social Network Approach." *Sociology of Education* 67(2): 139–157.

Gould, R. V., and Fernandez, R. M. (1989). "Structures of Mediation: A Formal Approach to Brokerage in Transactions Networks." *Sociological Methodology* 19: 89–126.

Guerrero, A. M., Bodin, Ö, McAllister, R. R. J., and Wilson, K. A. (2015). "Achieving Social-ecological Fit through Bottom-up Collaborative Governance: An Empirical Investigation." *Ecology and Society* 20(4): 41.

Hadden, J. (2015). *Networks in Contention: The Divisive Politics of Climate Change.* New York: Cambridge University Press.

Hadden, J., and Jasny, L. (2017). "The Power of Peers: How Transnational Advocacy Networks Shape NGO Strategies on Climate Change." British Journal of Political Science https://doi.org/doi:10.1017/S0007123416000582.

Hahn, T., Olsson, P., Folke, C., and Johansson, K. (2006). "Trust-Building, Knowledge Generation and Organizational Innovations: The Role of a Bridging Organization for Adaptive Comanagement of a Wetland Landscape around Kristianstad, Sweden." *Human Ecology* 34(4): 573–592.

Henry, A. D., and Vollan, B. (2012). "Risk, Networks, and Ecological Explanations for the Emergence of Cooperation in Commons Governance." *Rationality, Markets and Morals* 3(59): 130–147.

Hodgson, G. (2006). "What Are Institutions?" *Journal of Economic Issues* 40(1): 1–25.

Hollway, J., and Koskinen, J. (2016). "Multilevel Embeddedness: The Case of the Global Fisheries Governance Complex." *Social Networks* 44: 281–294.

Isaac, M. E. (2012). "Agricultural Information Exchange and Organizational Ties: The Effect of Network Topology on Managing Agrodiversity." *Agricultural Systems* 109(June): 9–15.

Isaac, M. E., Erickson, B. H., Quashie-Sam, S. J., and Timmer, V. R. (2007). "Transfer of Knowledge on Agroforestry Management Practices: The Structure of Farmer Advice Networks." *Ecology and Society* 12(2): 32.

Jasny, L., and Lubell, M. (2015). "Two-Mode Brokerage in Policy Networks." *Social Networks* 41(May): 36–47.

Kamelarczyk, K. B. F., and Smith-Hall, C. (2014). "REDD Herring: Epistemic Community Control of the Production, Circulation and Application of Deforestation Knowledge in Zambia." *Forest Policy and Economics* 46: 19–29.

Kininmonth, S., Bergsten, A., and Bodin, Ö. (2015). "Closing the Collaborative Gap: Aligning Social and Ecological Connectivity for Better Management of Interconnected Wetlands." *Ambio* 44(1): 138–148.

Lubell, M., Robins, G., and Wang, P. (2014). "Network Structure and Institutional Complexity in an Ecology of Water Management Games." *Ecology and Society* 19(4): 23.

Marshall, G. (2007). "Nesting, Subsidiarity, and Community-based Environmental Governance beyond the Local Scale." *International Journal of the Commons* 2(1): 75–97.

McAllister, R. R. J., McCrea, R., and Lubell, M. N. (2013). "Policy Networks, Stakeholder Interactions and Climate Adaptation in the Region of South East Queensland, Australia." *Regional Environmental Change* 14(2): 527–539.

McAllister, R. R. J., Robinson, C. J., Maclean, K., Guerrero, A. M., Collins, K., Taylor, B. M., and De Barro, P. J. (2015). "From Local to Central: A Network Analysis of Who Manages Plant Pest and Disease Outbreaks across Scales." *Ecology and Society* 20(1): 67.

McAllister, R. R., Taylor, B. M., and Harman, B. P. (2015). "Partnership Networks for Urban Development: How Structure is Shaped by Risk. *Policy Studies Journal* 43(3): 379–398.

McPherson, M., Smith-Lovin, L., and Cook, J. M. (2001). "Birds of a Feather: Homophily in Social Networks." *Annual Review of Sociology* 27: 415–444.

Meijerink, S., and Huitema, D. (2010). "Policy Entrepreneurs and Change Strategies: Lessons from Sixteen Case Studies of Water Transitions around the Globe." *Ecology and Society* 15(2): 21.

Newig, J., Günther, D., and Pahl-Wostl, C. (2010). "Synapses in the Network: Learning in Governance Networks in the Context of Environmental Management." *Ecology and Society* 15(4): 24.

Newman, L., and Dale, A. (2005). "Network Structure, Diversity, and Proactive Resilience Building: A Response to Tompkins and Adger." *Ecology and Society* 10(1): r2.

Newman, L., and Dale, A. (2007). "Homophily and Agency: Creating Effective Sustainable Development Networks." *Environment, Development and Sustainability* 9(1): 79–90.

North, D. C. (1990). *Institutions, Institutional Change and Economic Performance*. Cambridge, UK: Cambridge University Press.

Oh, H., Chung, M. H., and Labianca, G. (2004). "Group Social Capital and Group Effectiveness: The Role of Informal Socializing Ties". *Academy of Management Journal* 47(6): 860–875.

Olsson, P., Gunderson, L. H., Carpenter, S. R., Ryan, P., Lebel, L., Folke, C., and Holling, C. S. (2006). "Shooting the Rapids: Navigating Transitions to Adaptive Governance of Social-Ecological Systems." *Ecology and Society* 11(1): 18.

Ostrom, E. (1990). *Governing the Commons: The Evolution of Institutions for Collective Action*. New York, NY: Cambridge University Press.

Ostrom, E. (2008). "The Challenge of Common-pool Resources." *Environment: Science and Policy for Sustainable Development* 50(4): 8–21.

Ostrom, E. (2009). *Understanding Institutional Diversity*. Princeton, NJ: Princeton University Press.

Plummer, R., and Armitage, D. (2007). "A Resilience-based Framework for Evaluating Adaptive Co-management: Linking Ecology, Economics and Society in a Complex World." *Ecological Economics* 61(1): 62–74.

Pretty, J., and Ward, H. (2001). "Social Capital and the Environment." *World Development* 29(2): 209–227.

Robins, G., Bates, L., and Pattison, P. (2011). "Network Governance and Environmental Management: Conflict and Cooperation." *Public Administration* 89(4): 1293–1313.

Scholz, J. T., and Stiftel, B. (Eds.). (2005). *Adaptive Governance and Water Conflict: New Institutions for Collaborative Planning*. Washington, DC: Resources for the Future.

Sandström, A. C., and Rova, C. V. (2009). "The Network Structure of Adaptive Governance: A Single Case Study of a Fish Management Area." *International Journal of the Commons* 4(1): 528–551.

Schneider, M., Scholz, J., Lubell, M., Mindruta, D., and Edwardsen, M. (2003). "Building Consensual Institutions: Networks and the National Estuary Program." *American Journal of Political Science* 47(1): 143–158.

Scholz, J. T., Berardo, R., and Kile, B. (2008). "Do Networks Solve Collective Action Problems? Credibility, Search, and Collaboration." *Journal of Politics* 70(2): 393–406.

Smythe, T. C., Thompson, R., and Garcia-Quijano, C. (2014). "The Inner Workings of Collaboration in Marine Ecosystem-Based Management: A Social Network Analysis Approach." *Marine Policy* 50, pt. A (December): 117–125.

Stephens, J. C., Hansson, A., Liu, Y., de Coninck, H., and Vajjhala, S. (2011). "Characterizing the International Carbon Capture and Storage Community." *Global Environmental Change* 21(2): 379–390.

Ward, H. (2006). "International Linkages and Environmental Sustainability: The Effectiveness of the Regime Network." *Journal of Peace Research* 43(2): 149–166.

Wasserman, S., and Faust, K. (1994). *Social Network Analysis. Methods and Applications.* New York: Cambridge University Press.

Weible, C. M., Sabatier, P. A., and McQueen, K. (2009). Themes and Variations: Taking Stock of the Advocacy Coalition Framework. *Policy Studies Journal* 37(1): 121–140.

CHAPTER 26

....

HEALTH POLICY NETWORKS

....

ALEXANDRA P. JOOSSE AND H. BRINTON MILWARD

INTRODUCTION

NETWORKS, an organizational form in which independent actors come together to address a mutual goal, exist in a variety of domains, including environmental policy (Berardo, 2014), education policy (Meier and O'Toole, 2001), transportation policy (Henry et al., 2010), and health policy (Provan and Milward, 1995). Their increasing prevalence can largely be attributed to the belief that they present a different, more collaborative way to solve complex collective action problems that no single actor has the resources, capacity, or incentive to adequately address on its own (Milward and Provan, 2006).

Many similarities exist in the research on different types of policy networks with regard to the analysis tools used, the challenges faced, and the lessons learned; however, reviewing this literature in general has been done before (Adams and Kriesi, 2007; Kickert et al., 1997; Rhodes, 2008). Therefore, this chapter takes a different approach. Namely, it focuses on the research in one particular policy domain: health policy networks.

The obvious benefit of this narrow focus is that it highlights the challenges and lessons that are most pertinent to this domain. Perhaps more important, though, it serves as a primer for scholars interested in health policy more generally to explore how networks can be used to learn more about how policy is formed and implemented in this domain. With that said, this chapter also draws parallels to other policy domains where appropriate to demonstrate the areas in which the learnings reported here can be more broadly applied, as well as point to areas in which health policy network research can learn from other policy domains.

This chapter is organized around three main questions. First, what types of networks exist in the health policy domain, and how have scholars used them to learn more about health policy? Second, what are the main challenges that scholarship has highlighted about health policy networks, and how have those challenges been addressed by scholars? Finally, where is the field of health policy research heading?

TYPES OF NETWORKS IN THE HEALTH POLICY DOMAIN

To begin with, it is useful to understand how scholars have used networks to better understand health policy. Given the fragmented nature of health policy network research across a variety of interest areas, scholarship from the following academic disciplines was reviewed: organization theory, public management, nonprofit management, global governance, community organization, and sociology.

While networks can be found throughout the policymaking process (Thatcher, 1998), the research on health policy networks tends to fall into two categories that focus on different stages of that process. The first examines networks of actors that influence how policies are formed and is referred to hereafter as *policy formation* studies. The second focuses on networks whose function is to implement policies that have already been adopted and is referred to hereafter as *policy implementation* studies.[1] By and large, these categories of health policy research have developed independently of one another and reside in different literatures. Thus, one of the main goals of this chapter is to put the policy formation and policy implementation research into dialogue with one another. By doing so, a more complete picture emerges of the state of research on health policy networks today, a picture that highlights not only the knowledge that has been accumulated, but also the areas in which more research is needed.

Along with the distinction between research on policy formation versus policy implementation networks, the scholarship can be further classified according to whether it uses the method of social network analysis (SNA) to study the networks of interest. Social network analysis is a method of visualizing and measuring social structure, or the regular and persistent relations among individual or collective actors (Scott, 1998). It does so by examining the relations, or ties, between the set of actors in some bounded network defined by the researcher.[2] To collect these data, researchers generally ask all members of a network to report on their ties with other network members. Because it is time-intensive to collect such data, SNA methodology is not suitable for all research interests; however, it is very useful insofar as it allows researchers to quantify and compare structural characteristics of networks.

Other methods are also used to observe and examine health policy networks. In particular, scholars also rely on observations and interviews to describe a network.[3] These techniques are less quantitative, but they are nonetheless useful because of the descriptive nuance they add to the understanding of issues facing health policy networks. Moreover, they are more accessible to researchers when network data are difficult to collect. Despite the differences between SNA and non-SNA methods, scholars should be careful not to make too strong a distinction between the two. Many studies utilize both to very good effect, using interviews of participants to understand the context and meaning of the structural measures (Provan and Milward, 1995).

The studies included in this chapter are listed in table 26.1. A quick inspection makes clear that the two categories of health policy network research tend to employ different methodologies. Researchers examining policy implementation networks by and large use SNA. On the other hand, scholarship on policy formation networks in health policy—especially the more recent work—relies primarily on more descriptive analysis techniques. As discussed in greater detail in the sections that follow, the choice of method can be attributed to two main factors. First, some networks are so large that SNA becomes less feasible. Second, SNA is simply not known or not widely used in all literatures that study health policy networks.

Table 26.1 Classification of Health Policy Network Studies

Type of Health Policy Network	Social Network Analysis	Observations/Interviews
Policy formation	Laumann and Knoke (1987)	Wistow (1992)
	Carpenter et al. (1998)	Boase (1996)
	Fernandez and Gould (1994)	Wheeler and Berkley (2001)
		Buse and Walts (2002)
		Buse (2003)
		Buse and Harmer (2004)
		Ramiah and Reich (2005)
		Nikolic and Maikisch (2006)
		Buckup (2008)
		Sorenson (2009)
		Mays and Scutchfield (2010)
Policy implementation	Morrissey and Tausig (1985)	Grusky et al. (1985)
	Provan and Milward (1991)	Lynn Jr. (1996)
	Morrissey et al. (1994)	Mitchell and Shortell (2000)
	Provan and Milward (1995)	Banek et al. (2014)
	Morrissey et al. (1997)	van Raaij (2006)
	Provan et al. (2003)	
	Provan et al. (2004)	
	Isett and Provan (2005)	
	Huang and Provan (2007)	
	Valente et al. (2007)	
	Provan et al. (2009)	
	Milward et al. (2010)	

Networks in Health Policy Formation

Research on the formation of policy networks comes out of the pluralist tradition of policy subsystems in political science (Adam and Kriesi, 2007). Across different policy domains, network research became a way to study the nexus between the state and society as nongovernmental actors became increasingly involved in policy formation alongside their governmental counterparts (Boase, 1996). The scholarship in this category of policy network studies is thus largely driven by a desire to understand how policy is created by a diverse set of actors. With regard to policy formation networks in the health domain in particular, the research developed in two waves: the early literature focused on health policymaking at the national level, but more recent scholarship has shifted health policy to the global stage.

The first significant use of networks to understand health policy was undertaken by Laumann and Knoke (1987), two sociologists. Their research was focused on understanding how national policy was created in two policy domains during the 1970s: health and energy. Recognizing that a variety of governmental and nongovernmental actors influence policy formation, they collected extensive network data about the information ties linking the most politically active organizations in each domain. Using SNA methods, they then examined the structure of the resultant network and its implications for the policy formation process.

Laumann and Knoke (1987) found the health domain to be concentrated and dominated more by governmental agencies than the energy domain. In fact, in the list of the top ten organizations most influential for health policy formation in the 1970s, only two were not governmental agencies or committees: the American Medical Association (number 1) and the American Hospital Association (number 8) (174–175). Moreover, the authors found that this structure had remained largely unchanged since World War I, when the basic framework of the US healthcare system and its major players was established. With that said, their research revealed a complex network of information sharing among the key actors that in part determined the degree to which each actor was influential in shaping policy decisions. This is helpful, for example, in adding nuance to the explanation and prediction of why certain policies are or are not adopted. Their research also suggested that the degree to which a domain is dominated by one or a few interests is also likely linked to its life-cycle stage, with the health domain at a much later stage of its life cycle than the relatively new (at the time) energy domain.

Unfortunately, Laumann and Knoke's approach of mapping the structure of the entire health policy domain, while groundbreaking, is limited by two factors: it is both time-intensive and time-sensitive. As a result, while some scholars have discussed the institutional structure of the health policy domain (Boase, 1996; Carpenter, Esterling, and Lazer, 1998; Fernandez and Gould, 1994; Wistow, 1992), no new data have been collected. Thus, the influence structure of the health policy domain produced in such detail by Laumann and Knoke remains a static view. Given the authors' own conclusions about the importance of a domain's stage in its life cycle, the structure of any domain is likely to be dynamic.

Future research can examine what if anything has changed, especially in light of the passage of the Affordable Care Act in 2010, a feat that Boase (1996) argued would be difficult to achieve given the domain's institutional structure as described by Laumann and Knoke. In a fast-changing policy environment, however, the utility of such analysis may be called into question unless a way can be developed to map these domains over their life cycles in a timely manner. One potential way to make such a study of the health domain more feasible for SNA methods is to look at smaller subnetworks within the health policy domain, rather than attempting to say something more generally about its overall structure. The smaller the network examined, the more plausible SNA methods become.

The second wave of research on policy formation networks is situated in a different literature: the global governance literature. As health issues have become more global in nature, these scholars have begun to recognize the importance of networks for understanding how governmental and nongovernmental actors can work together to form policy. The recent Ebola epidemic demonstrated, for example, that infectious disease outbreaks can have widespread impacts. Responses that traditionally came primarily from the affected governments and intergovernmental agencies like the World Health Organization (WHO) are being increasingly crafted through networks involving governments from multiple countries as well as for-profit companies and nonprofit organizations (Buse, 2003).[4] In addition to addressing the spread of infectious diseases, research shows that these networks are a useful way to address neglected diseases like malaria and tuberculosis, diseases not considered to be lucrative investments from a commercial standpoint (Buckup, 2008; Ramiah and Reich, 2005; Sorenson, 2009). The research suggests one of the main benefits of networks in this area of health policy is that they enable the cost and risk associated with addressing complex problems to be shared (Nikolic and Maikisch, 2006; Sorenson, 2009).

Using observations and interviews with network participants as the primary method of analysis, this line of research seeks to understand how networks of organizations and nation-states—often referred to in the global governance literature as public-private partnerships—work collaboratively to craft solutions to complex global health problems. Similar to the national policy formation literature, one of the recurring themes in this literature is the shifting locus of power from governmental actors to for-profit and, to a lesser extent, nonprofit actors. Buse and Walt (2002), for example, question whether the WHO can maintain its commitment to neutrality and ethical behavior as it becomes increasingly influenced by nongovernmental parties that may have an agenda. Buse and Harmer (2004) point out that despite these networks' attempts to include all relevant stakeholders, many still lack representation, and thus the voice of some of the poorer countries.

The other main topic on which scholars in this area have focused deals with the criteria that lead to the success of global health policy networks. Buckup (2008), for example, finds that the most appropriate ownership structure of the network—whether it is privately, publicly, or jointly owned—depends on several factors, including the degree to which the parties value the outcome that is produced by the network. Other studies present in-depth examinations of the successes and failures of single networks, like Ramiah and Reich's (2005) study of an HIV/AIDs partnership among Merck, the Bill and Melinda Gates Foundation, and the government of Botswana, in an effort contribute to the knowledge of the factors that lead to effectiveness.

In sum, the policy formation approach uses networks to better understand how health policy is created and, specifically, who has influence in that process. Fittingly, then, one of the main themes in both the national and global literature is the distribution of power among participants in these networks. Unfortunately the SNA methods that Laumann and Knoke (1987) used have not carried over into the more recent global health policy formation literature. This is likely due to the more recent wave of policy formation research emerging from a literature that traditionally has not used SNA methodology. The absence of network analysis in this literature opens a big area for future research, discussed in greater detail in the section on future research directions below.

The other main area of growth for research on networks in health policy formation is in linking it to existing frameworks about the policymaking process. In particular, the research would benefit from drawing parallels to the advocacy coalitions framework (ACF), a framework and several constituent theories focused on explaining policy change by advocacy coalitions of like-minded policy actors, or policy networks (Sabatier and Weible, 2007). While the main focus of ACF scholars has been examining how changes in policy actors' belief systems lead to policy change over time, more recent research looks to issues like power distribution to explain how and why policy actors coordinate their actions to bring about policy change (Henry, 2011). Thus, the research described above can both contribute to and learn from this line of research.

Networks in Health Policy Implementation

The second main category of research on health policy networks examines the networks of organizations that develop to implement public policies. This type of research emerged first and foremost due to the issues related to the fragmentation of service delivery. Specifically, one of the leading problems of implementation is how to coordinate a more seamless provision of public service when multiple agencies, multiple jurisdictions, and different levels of government are involved. This issue is not specific to the health policy domain; in fact, the institutional collective action (ICA) framework is principally concerned with understanding this issue from the perspective of local government policy networks (Feiock, 2008). With that said, research on implementation networks in the health policy domain is at the forefront of understanding the challenges and implications of networks in this area of policy studies.

The implementation networks research in the health policy domain has by and large focused on a very particular type of health policy: delivery of services to the severely mentally ill (SMI). Following the deinstitutionalization of the SMI population in the

1960s and 1970s, the National Institute of Mental Health (NIMH) recognized that service delivery was fragmented across organizations at the community level, making it difficult for the SMI population to obtain quality care. In response, it established the Community Support Program initiative in 1977, which encouraged the coordination of services between organizations at the community level for the SMI population. This initiative caused what became known as "service delivery networks" to emerge all over the United States and prompted researchers interested in networks to study them, often with funding from the NIMH. The vast majority of the research on policy implementation networks uses SNA, which has resulted in arguably the clearest understanding of the implementation of certain network structures in all of the policy implementation literature, including how they are governed (Milward and Provan, 2000; Provan and Kenis, 2008). The pervasiveness of SNA in this category of health policy can be attributed to the research coming largely from a single research program as well as networks that are limited in size and thus more suitable for this type of analysis.

A number of scholars have added to research in this area (Banek et al., 2014; Morrissey and Tausig, 1985; Morrissey et al., 1994; Morrissey, Johnsen, and Calloway, 1997; Lynn, 1996; Valente, Chou, and Pentz, 2007; van Raaij, 2006). Much of the scholarship, though, comes from a research program originally funded by the NIMH and undertaken by Provan, Milward, and their colleagues. Beginning in the early 1990s and continuing to this day, this research program has used and still uses SNA to study mental health policy implementation networks (Huang and Provan, 2007; Isett and Provan, 2005; Milward et al., 2010; Provan and Milward, 1991, 1995; Provan et al., 2003; Provan, Isett, and Milward, 2004; Provan, Huang, and Milward, 2009). It includes examinations of single networks, cross-network comparisons, and networks over time. Moreover, these scholars have examined a broad range of ties connecting organizational participants in implementation networks, including information, service contract, referrals, and influence ties. The use of SNA on a variety of ties across multiple networks as well as across time is notable because it increases the reliability of scholars' findings.

Generally speaking, the scholars in this category of health policy network research seek to understand the implications of different network structures, both formally (i.e., how the network is governed) as well as informally (i.e., the structure of resource flows among participants in the network). From a formal governance standpoint, scholars have found that centralized structures, in which administrative duties are assigned to one actor or a few actors, are widespread (cf. Grusky et al., 1985; Isett and Provan, 2005; and Provan et al., 2009). Informally speaking, one of the main foci for scholars is how participants in these networks establish and grow trusting relationships with one another. Huang and Provan (2007), for example, find that trust is very important for implementation networks, but that it takes time to establish. Finally, like the policy formation scholars, scholars in this category of health policy have been devoted to understanding the criteria associated with network effectiveness (cf. Morrissey et al., 1997; and Provan and Milward, 1995).

In summary, the research concerning policy implementation networks in the health policy domain highlights the utility of networks to coordinate service delivery.

The complex nature of services for the SMI population has provided fertile ground for scholars seeking to learn more about how to effectively coordinate the communication and behavior of multiple, independent organizations at the local level. The research has demonstrated that the structure of a network—both how it is governed and administered, as well as how resources flow through it—affects its sustainability and effectiveness.

While the research described above is concerned with policy implementation networks in the health policy domain in particular, much of the research is likely generalizable to other policy domains and issues. Researchers using the institutional analysis and development framework (IAD),[5] for example, can benefit from the findings on formal and informal structure of policy domains. In particular, findings from the health policy implementation scholarship could shed light on how the structure of a domain affects the incentives that participants of these networks rely on to overcome collective action problems, an area of interest for IAD scholars.

CHALLENGES FOR HEALTH POLICY NETWORKS

With a better understanding of how scholars are using networks to inform health policy, the findings from these studies can now be put into dialogue with one another. In particular, this section is organized around four common challenges that have emerged with respect to health policy networks as well as how those challenges have been addressed by scholars studying both policy formation and policy implementation networks. In focusing on these common challenges, overlap between the two categories of health policy networks emerges that creates potential for mutual learning. It should be noted that these challenges are not unique to health policy networks, nor are they the only challenges faced by these networks; rather, they are the challenges that were mentioned most frequently and consistently in the studies that were reviewed.

Challenge 1: Coordination

Coordination is perhaps the single most pervasive challenge for all networks, including health policy networks, due largely to the absence of hierarchical structure in networked forms of governance (Gray, 1989). Without hierarchy, the task of coordinating the actions of multiple, independent actors is likely to impose high transaction costs in time and energy on the participants. In turn, these costs may deter actors from participating (Lynn, 1996).

The difficulties of coordination are evident in a number of health policy network studies concerned with both policy formation and policy implementation. For example, Banek et al.'s (2014) study of an implementation network of community-based care for children suffering from malaria found that the lack of coordination in this network undermined the goals of the policy. In particular, the results suggest that the success of community health workers in delivering services was hampered by a lack of coordination by the local health system. Studying networks of service delivery for the SMI population, Provan et al. (2003) found that coordination is especially difficult when network participants hail from different sectors and professions, due to conflicting norms and values that develop over time within each. Likewise, in their examination of nine global health policy networks in Europe, Nikolic and Maikisch (2006) found coordination to be a recurring problem.

Health policy networks have addressed coordination issues in various ways. The first category of responses deals with governance structure. Governance structures can be classified into one of three ideal types: shared governance, the most simple governing arrangement, in which all participants govern equally; lead agency, a brokered arrangement in which one organization within the network takes on administrative duties; and network administrative organization (NAO), another brokered arrangement, in which an external, dedicated administrative agency is created (Provan and Kenis, 2008). The research on policy implementation networks reveals that in response to the difficulties of coordination, the governance of these networks occurs almost exclusively via one of the brokered forms because they assign responsibility to a single party. Several networks chose a lead agency structure (Isett and Provan, 2005; Lynn, 1996; Provan and Milward, 1991, 1995), while others used an NAO-led structure (Grusky et al., 1985; Huang and Provan, 2007; Milward et al., 2010; Morrissey et al., 1994; Morrissey, Johnsen, and Calloway, 1997; Provan, Isett, and Milward, 2004; Provan, Huang, and Milward, 2009). Buse's (2003) research on infectious disease networks suggests that a similar response occurs in global health policy formation networks. He suggests that as networks grow to include more partners, more complex governing arrangements prevail in order to better deal with coordination problems.

Aside from network governance structure, policy implementation studies find that coordination problems can also be eased by increasing the level of trust among participants, as trust is thought to induce more cooperative behavior (Isett and Provan, 2005). High levels of trust are, of course, difficult to achieve, but scholars have found that trust does tend to be higher under certain conditions. For example, trust is often higher in networks in which members have a history of previous collaboration (Mitchell and Shortell, 2000), as well as those in which participants are linked by multiplex ties, or a number of different types of ties, such as information sharing *and* referrals (Provan and Milward, 1991; Isett and Provan, 2005).

The policy formation literature also offers solutions to coordination problems. Using Laumann and Knoke's data on the US health policy domain, Fernandez and Gould (1994) suggest that the strategic placement of key individuals in the structure of the network can ease problems of coordination. Specifically, they suggest that the existence of brokers, or "organizational actors linking otherwise unconnected pairs of actors" (1460) is critical, because situations arise in which diverse, unconnected actors may share a similar interest in a particular policy. In these situations, brokers are positioned to coordinate efforts to formulate policy.

Carpenter et al. (1998) also use Laumann and Knoke's data to suggest a solution to coordination problems. In studying how lobbyists obtain access in policymaking, they find that weak ties, which arise between acquaintances, allow for coordinated policy action more than strong ties, which arise between close contacts. The authors explain this finding by saying that new information typically flows through weak-tie as opposed to strong-tie networks. This in turn enables a shared understanding of policy issues to spread more quickly and allows for more coordinated policy action between the participants of an issue network.

Challenge 2: Accountability

Diffuse accountability is problematic for all public sector networks because of the difficulty of assigning responsibility in a structure that lacks formal hierarchy. In addition, different constituencies hold networks to account, which exacerbates the problem when their demands do not overlap (Rhodes, 2008). The accountability issue is especially prevalent in health policy networks in light of the research on health policy formation. In particular, because the institutional structure of the US health domain is such that there exist multiple human services agencies that contribute to and oversee health policy, networks in this field often struggle to discern to whom they are accountable (Boase, 1996). The accountability issue becomes even more complex when dealing with policymaking on the global stage. In studying seventeen infectious disease networks, Buse (2003) finds that in nearly all of them, multiple layers of accountability exist, as participants are often governments, which have their own systems of accountability.

Responses to this challenge have been proposed by both categories of health policy network studies. Policy implementation scholars offer two solutions. First, brokered governance structures are proposed, once again, as a solution. Provan et al. (2004) and Huang and Provan (2007) find that having an NAO-governed network, in particular, helps to allay some of the accountability fears of network funders. Second, Mitchell and Shortell (2000) suggest that participant satisfaction ratings can also be used to bolster external accountability.

Solutions for accountability issues take a different tack in the policy formation literature. Researching global health policy networks, Wheeler and Berkley (2001) suggest that the accountability of a network as a whole will increase with greater transparency. To increase transparency, they argue that these networks need to invest more time and energy in external communication; in particular, communication must include an explanation of the methods by which the network functions. In doing so, networks will enable the public to increasingly hold them to account for their actions.

Challenge 3: Assessment

Assessing effectiveness or general performance is another perennial issue for all policy networks. Ideally, networks measure results that a variety of stakeholders then use to assess them; however, this endeavor has proven to be challenging for many networks (Mitchell and Shortell, 2000). Two main problems plague network assessment. The first problem is the difficulty of defining and measuring what it is that a network produces. Particularly in health policy implementation networks, it is often individual organizations, not the network, that produce outcomes like psychotherapy for the SMI population. The network facilitates this process by making it more likely that clients will get all of the services they need, but it generally does not produce its own outcomes. In these situations, a tension between assessing the network and assessing the individual organizations that comprise the network exists. Furthermore, assessing the network as a whole creates complications that arise when goals are more intangible in nature, like the creation of relationships among participants (Provan et al., 2009), or broader in scope, like the improved health of a particular population (Mays and Scutchfield, 2010).

A second assessment issue is the fact that different stakeholders may value outcomes differently. Provan and Milward (1995) assessed the four SMI networks they studied by gathering data from SMI adults ("clients"), their families, and their case managers. What they discovered was that clients and their families held very similar views of the network's effectiveness, while case managers' views were very different. Formalizing this finding in a later paper, Provan and Milward (2001) suggest that three sets of stakeholders are likely to assess the same network in different ways: the network as a unit (i.e., the funders and the network administrative organizations), the community (i.e., those receiving services from the network), and the organization/participants. How, then, are network managers to determine which stakeholders it is most important to satisfy?

Scholars from the health policy implementation literature have used three main approaches to assess networks. In their study, Provan and Milward (1995) ultimately focused on the perspective of one stakeholder: the community (defined as clients and their families). In particular, they used network survey data to develop a measure that assessed client well-being. Namely, they asked clients receiving SMI services about their quality of life, adjustment to community-based care, psychopathy, and satisfaction with services provided. Their study found that no one single factor determines the effectiveness of a network. Rather, the authors find that effectiveness in these types of networks is likely to be maximized when the network is centralized, has nonfragmented external control, and exists in a stable environment in which resources are relatively abundant.

Second, Huang and Provan (2007) suggest that reputation can often be relied upon as a proxy for effectiveness. This, they find, is especially true when nonprofits are involved in the networks, as this form of organization commonly struggles to measure performance and outcomes:[6]

> A good reputation generates goodwill and is key to success in fundraising, volunteer recruitment, staff retention, and overall organizational health. A bad reputation, often the result of a scandal involving malfeasance or widely publicized client injury, can often create irreversible damage to an agency. (438)

Finally, both Provan et al. (2004) and van Raaij (2006) suggest that an examination of the prevailing norms in a network may provide some information on its effectiveness. In particular, the degree to which these participants conform to professional norms may be a proxy for effectiveness (Provan, Isett, and Milward, 2004). Similarly, van Raaij (2006) provides evidence that norms are used by participants to assess the success of the network. In particular, she finds the norms of network legitimacy, network climate, and activating capacity to be particularly relevant for participant-based assessments.

The health policy formation literature has struggled with assessment issues as well, but has not come as far in addressing them as has the policy implementation literature. Buse (2003) recognizes that network assessment is complex and must be approached from multiple perspectives. He proposes five criteria by which global health policy networks should be judged: legitimacy, representation/participation, accountability, transparency, and effectiveness/efficiency/sustainability of the governing arrangements. Other studies have focused exclusively on measuring progress toward observable outcomes. In their review of health networks geared toward finding solutions for chronic diseases, for example, Mays and Scutchfield (2010) find that many networks measure their impact either by selecting the most pertinent population indicators or by assessing the changes in policies or programs caused by network actions. The problem with these methods, as the authors point out, is that confounding factors exist that may obscure the true effect of the network. In addition, they do not capture other, less tangible successes of networks, like the relationships that are built among participants.

Challenge 4: Uneven Distribution of Power

Uneven distribution of power among participants is a natural occurrence in all networks and thus can never be completely eliminated (Buse and Harmer, 2004). The various streams of health policy network research, however, have dealt with the issue of power in different ways, with the policy formation stream most openly addressing it.

Understanding which actors hold the most power in national health policymaking was Laumann and Knoke's (1987) main focus. They found that health policy is concentrated and dominated more by governmental agencies, although those agencies do not necessarily coordinate with one another. Boase's (1996) study relies on this description of a silo-esque structure to explain why the United States (at the time of the study) did not have a national healthcare system, arguing that a fragmented government response in which agencies have a monopoly on knowledge has prevented cohesive action in this area. This research was the last major effort to directly investigate power distribution until the global health policy literature more recently turned its attention to it.

In particular, scholars studying global health policy networks highlight power as a problem that has largely been ignored, but one that deserves attention. As Sorenson (2009, 4) notes:

> [S]tudies of global governance forms have been inattentive to the totality of power. This is somewhat surprising given that the inclusion of a plurality of actors in

partnerships undoubtedly reshapes power relations, and that distributed governance forms, such as PDPs [product development partnerships], are considered (in principal) a model of more complex and presumably sophisticated power-sharing. It is important that the normative problem-solving bias frequently attached to public–private partnerships does not obstruct a realistic view on power relations when assessing these governance forms.

Buse and Walt (2002) are among the few who do concentrate on the problems posed by uneven distribution of power among network participants, focusing their discussion on the global health networks involving the United Nations. They describe a power shift away from the traditional loci of power—governments and intergovernmental agencies—to for-profit and, to a lesser extent, nonprofit organizations. This shift has caused some to question about whether the government, the voice of those traditionally responsible for protecting and furthering the public's well-being, is being muted. If it is, there is a potential for for-profit participants in positions of power to enable these organizations to further their own business interests and to be in conflict with the main goal of the network (Buse, 2003).

The policy implementation literature, on the other hand, examines the effects of power distribution in a more implicit manner. One of the most frequently used measures in network analysis is a set of centrality measures, which involve locating participants who are important in the flow of resources in a network (Freeman, 1978). A common finding in network research is that central actors are powerful (cf. Brass, 1984; Fernandez and Gould, 1994; Galaskiewicz, 1979; Ibarra and Andrews, 1993; Krackhardt, 1990; Milward and Provan, 2006; and Padgett and Ansell, 1993). Therefore, studies that examine the degree of centralization of networks are by default measuring how concentrated power is in the hands of one or a few participants. Several studies have hinted at the challenge surrounding power: namely, that some level of power centralization is needed for networks to function effectively (Morrissey et al., 1994; Provan and Milward, 1995), but that overcentralization can be a liability because it can lead to lower commitment among noncentral participants (Valente, Chou, and Pentz, 2007).

The responses to the challenges posed by uneven distribution of power have been few and far between. An exception is Buse and Harmer's (2004) focus on power in global health policy networks. They suggest that different types of "hosting arrangements"—meaning whether the network is independent or is housed within another organization—will affect the distribution of decision-making power. Specifically, networks hosted in other organizations, like the WHO, may not give participants as much power to make decisions as would a network that is independent. Regardless of where networks are hosted, though, the authors discuss two main ways that networks deal with certain actors having undue influence, both of which deal with governance structure. Some networks use consensus decision-making to ensure equality of voice. Others have simply excluded representatives from the for-profit sector from certain decision-making bodies. They note that exclusion may have negative ramifications for the willingness of for-profits to engage, however.

In addition, the dissertation research of one of the coauthors of this chapter, Joosse (2015), takes a first step into conceptualizing and measuring the effects of uneven distributions of power on the processes and outcomes of health policy formation networks. She focuses on a particular type of power that is especially salient for these types of networks: structural power, or the power that resides in the dependence relationships that are a natural part of collaborative efforts. Using original survey data from three collaborative networks working toward improving the Food and Drug Administration's pharmaceutical drug development process, she examines the relationship between structural power and two variables: the degree to which participants of collaborative networks behave cohesively and how satisfied they are with the process and outcomes of collaboration. The findings suggest that the effects of structural power are not as pervasively negative as is assumed in the literature. In particular, uneven distribution of power affects cohesive behavior less in working groups than in the overall governance structure of these networks. Furthermore, the negative effects of uneven distribution of power only affect one dimension of participants' satisfaction: how satisfied they are with the process of collaboration. This research represents an initial foray into issues of power in networks; however, as expounded on more in the next section, the authors see issues surrounding power as one of the frontiers for health policy network research.

Future Research Directions

Putting the two categories of networks in the health policy domain in dialogue with one another highlights several directions for future research. First and foremost, scholars in both categories of health policy network studies need to be more aware of one another. Research on health policy networks is published in a variety of journals. In particular, those using SNA methodology tend to be published in general public administration and policy journals such as the *Journal of Public Administration, Research and Theory* and *Administrative Science Quarterly*. On the other hand, research on global policy networks is published more in journals focused on health policy, such as *Health Policy and Planning* and *Health Economics, Policy, and Law*. This division is natural, but it often means that learning is generally not shared across the two categories of studies.

As this chapter attempts to communicate, there are several areas in which policy formation research and policy implementation research can learn from one another. To begin with, the policy formation literature has much room to grow and learn from the methodology used by policy implementation scholars. Laumann and Knoke's (1987) use of SNA stands as the only study that collected network data in the policy formation category. Scholars of global health policy, on the other hand, rely primarily on observations and interviews. Although this type of research design provides rich detail about the successes and failures of global health policy networks, much remains to be to learned about how global health networks function. For instance, a recurring finding in the literature is that influence over the direction of global health policy has been shifting to the private sector (Buse, 2003; Buse and Harmer, 2004; Sorenson, 2009). Future research could use SNA tools to more rigorously investigate this observation as well as trace its implications. Social network analysis provides a more quantitative way to report on this. To reduce the challenges of collecting network data, however, researchers should concentrate on defining distinct global policy networks, rather than on attempting to gather data on the global health policy domain in general.

On the other hand, scholars studying policy implementation networks in the health policy domain have been focused primarily on the structural features of these networks. Their research contributes to a much clearer understanding of the implications of different governance structures, as well as the informal structure of resource flows through a network. However, this area of research could take their findings a step further by examining the implications of structure on the process of collaboration that takes place within these networks. This is where learning from the policy formation studies can be of use. The rich case study data on global health policy networks provide a look into how collaboration actually functions. It focuses, for example, on how nonrepresentative decision-making bodies affect perceptions of fairness in how the network functions (Buse, 2003). Research on the development of trust in the policy implementation category is a step in the right direction, but future research could examine the implications of certain network structures on process like perceptions of fairness, which are so integral to the network form of organizations.

An area of research that both categories of health policy networks need to make progress in is issues of power. As mentioned previously, both policy formation and policy implementation scholars have found that uneven distributions of power pose challenges to health policy networks. The policy formation literature has been more forthright in highlighting why the lack of study of power is problematic, but has not made much progress in addressing this challenge.

To begin to better understand issues surrounding power, it first must be better conceptualized. What kinds of power are particularly salient for health policy networks? How can these types of power be measured and compared? What are the effects of uneven distribution of power on the processes and outcome of health policy networks? While the concept of power can be daunting due to its complexity, it is a problem that is both important and pervasive enough that researchers must begin to address it in a more rigorous manner.

Another area of research for both categories of health policy networks is sector differences. In policy formation and policy implementation networks alike, cross-sector collaboration is common. In fact, it is *because* differences exist among the government, nonprofit, and for-profit sectors that health policy networks often involve members from all three. These differences mean that organizations have different ideas and perspectives, all of which contribute to the innovativeness of the network form of organization. The effects of sector differences are not clear at this time. Milward et al. (2010) find that organizations from different sectors actually behave similarly when in a network governed by a similar structure; however, Buse (2003) finds that there are variations in the interests, needs, and concerns of participants hailing from different sectors. More research is thus needed to determine when, if ever, sector differences matter in the functioning and success of health policy networks.

One last major area of research involves studying areas of overlap between the main challenges facing health policy networks. For instance, is there a connection between the challenges of uneven distribution of power and coordination? If so, what is it? Moreover, there are likely to be interesting synergies between the challenges of accountability and effectiveness. To what degree are health policy networks connected to the institutions of overhead democracy—legislatures, executive agencies, and courts—and is their effectiveness related to their degree of autonomy?

Conclusion

This chapter discussed the main types of networks in the health policy domain and what researchers have learned about health policy from them. A review of the literature found that there are two main types of networks—policy formation networks and policy implementation networks—which differ in that they focus on two different stages of the policy process. The review also revealed different methodologies used to examine the networks: policy formation studies largely rely on observations and interviews, while policy implementation studies primarily use SNA.

The policy formation approach uses networks to better understand how health policy is created and, specifically, who has influence in that process. Laumann and Knoke's (1987) innovative approach shed light on these issues. Unfortunately, given the dynamic nature of the health domain, their analysis is now dated. While network methods and analysis have gotten much better and easier to work with since the 1980s, the health policy domain has grown in terms of its share of US GDP (World Bank, 2015). In addition, it has become more complex, with major expansions of federal health programs, including both the addition of prescription drug coverage to Medicare under George W. Bush and the passage of the Affordable Care Act under Barack Obama. This increase in scope and scale accentuated the problem of mapping a national policy domain like health. Thus, research at the national policy level akin to that of Laumann and Knoke will likely have to await significant increases in efficiency in the collection and the analysis of network data or until researchers concentrate on smaller subnetworks within the health policy domain.

More recently, research on health policy formation networks has shifted focus from mapping to a concern with governance, specifically the global governance of health. Using a case-study-based methodology, this research seeks to understand how networks of organizations and nation-states—often referred to in the global governance literature as public-private partnerships—work collaboratively to create solutions to complex global health problems. Similar to the national policy formation literature, one of the recurring themes in this literature is the shifting locus of power from governmental actors to for-profit and nonprofit actors. Especially in the case of less-developed states, there is a concern that international nongovernmental organizations may subsume the efforts of national governments and that, rather than viewing this as a task in which cost and risk are shared, the international actors almost constitute a health para-state that relieves host country governments of the responsibility of building stronger national healthcare systems.

The second main category of research on health policy networks is policy implementation networks that consist largely of organizations that emerge to implement healthcare policies. It has by and large focused on a very particular type of health policy: delivery of services to the SMI adult population. The reason for this focus is that there was a major change in the United States, from providing mental healthcare in institutions to providing it in communities. Communities were encouraged by the federal government to coordinate these services in partnerships, alliances, and systems—in other words, networks. This provided a very interesting natural experiment for those funding community mental health networks and those studying them. This is the area of health policy network research in which SNA has most consistently been used. Scholars in this area have produced a wealth of knowledge about the implications of network governance structure for the outcomes of health policy implementation networks.

The rest of this chapter focused on four common challenges from both categories of health policy network research: coordination, accountability, assessment, and uneven distribution of power. Examining these challenges from the perspectives of both policy formation and policy implementation studies revealed two important conclusions. First, scholars can and should learn from one another how to best address these challenges. Rather than reinventing the wheel, these lessons could have a much broader impact if scholars and practitioners recognize the synergies between the two categories of health policy network studies. Second, the analysis revealed some holes in our understanding of health policy networks that scholars across both categories need to address. Addressing these areas, including the implications of uneven distribution of power and sector differences, will lead to a better understanding of how networks function in the health policy domain.

NOTES

1. Several studies on health networks do not fit into this classification because they are not directly relevant to public policy; rather, they are more sociological in nature, in that they seek to understand individual behavior. These studies include Coleman et al.'s (1966) study of the diffusion of drug prescribing behavior (and Burt's [1987] reanalysis of the data), as well as Fattore et al.'s (2009) study of the prescribing behavior of doctors in Italy. These studies are not included in this chapter.
2. For a primer on social network analysis, see Knoke and Yang (2008) or Wasserman and Faust (1994).
3. Research that uses networks as a metaphor or that develops frameworks to classify styles of policymaking are excluded from this review.

4. Social network analysis has also been used in this area of health policy to determine the trajectory of a disease as it spreads through a population. For an example, see http://www.nytimes.com/2014/12/30/health/how-ebola-roared-back.html?_r=0.
5. The Institutional Analysis and Development Framework focuses on understanding how institutions—defined as norms, rules, and strategies—affect the outcomes that some group of actors is trying to achieve (Ostrom, 2005).
6. Salamon (2012) cites the striving for and measuring of effectiveness as one of the main challenges facing the nonprofit sector. He argues that the increased competition with for profits has resulted in the need for nonprofits to not only perform more effectively, but also demonstrate this performance. This trend is problematic for many nonprofits that do not have the resources to devote to this task. Moreover, nonprofits must respond to multiple bottom lines, meaning the performance measures that are most commonly used by for profits are not necessarily suitable for measuring nonprofit performance.

REFERENCES

Adam, S., and Kriesi, H. (2007). "The Network Approach." In *Theories of the Policy Process*, edited by P. A. Sabatier II, pp. 129-154. Boulder, CO: Westview Press.

Banek, K., Nankabirwa, J., Maiteki-Sebuguzi, C., DiLiberto, D., Taaka, L., Chandler, C. I. R., and Staedke, S. G. (2014). "Community Case Management of Malaria: Exploring Support, Capacity and Motivation of Community Medicine Distributors in Uganda." *Health Policy and Planning* 30(May): 451-461.

Berardo, R. (2014). "The Evolution of Self-Organizing Communication Networks in High-Risk Social-Ecological Systems." *International Journal of the Commons* 8(1): 236–258.

Boase, J. P. (1996). "Institutions, Institutionalized Networks and Policy Choices: Health Policy in the US and Canada." *Governance* 9(3): 287–310.

Brass, D. J. (1984). "Being in the Right Place: A Structural Analysis of Individual Influence in an Organization." *Administrative Science Quarterly* 29(4): 518–539.

Buckup, S. (2008). "Global Public-Private Partnerships against Neglected Diseases: Building Governance Structures for Effective Outcomes." *Health Economics, Policy, and Law* 3(1): 31–50.

Burt, R. S. (1987). "Social Contagion and Innovation: Cohesion versus Structural Equivalence." *American Journal of Sociology* 92(6): 1287–1335.

Buse, K. (2003). "Governing Public-Private Infectious Disease Partnerships." *Brown Journal of World Affairs* 10(2): 225–242.

Buse, K., and Harmer, A. (2004). "Power to the Partners? The Politics of Public-Private Health Partnerships." *Development* 47(2): 49–56.

Buse, K., and Walt, G. (2002). "The World Health Organization and Global Public-Private Health Partnerships: In Search of 'Good' Global Governance." In *Public-Private Partnerships for Public Health*, edited by M. R. Reich, pp. 169–195. Cambridge, MA: Harvard Center for Population and Development Studies.

Carpenter, D. P., Esterling, K. M., and Lazer, D. M. J. (1998). "The Strength of Weak Ties in Lobbying Networks Evidence from Health-Care Politics in the United States." *Journal of Theoretical Politics* 10(4): 417–444.

Coleman, J. S., Katz, E., and Menzel, H. (1966). *Medical Innovation: A Diffusion Study*. New York: Bobbs-Merrill Co.

Fattore, G., Frosini, F., Salvatore, D., and Tozzi, V. (2009). "Social Network Analysis in Primary Care: The Impact of Interactions on Prescribing Behaviour." *Health Policy (Amsterdam, Netherlands)* 92(2–3): 141–148.

Feiock, R. C. (2008). "Institutional Collective Action and Local Government Collaboration." In *Big Ideas in Collaborative Public Management*, edited by L. Bingham and R. O'Leary. London and New York: M.E. Sharpe.

Fernandez, R. M., and Gould, R. V. (1994). "A Dilemma of State Power: Brokerage and Influence in the National Health Policy Domain." *American Journal of Sociology* 99(6): 1455–1491.

Freeman, L. C. (1978). "Centrality in Social Networks Conceptual Clarification." *Social Networks* 1(3): 215–239.

Galaskiewicz, J. (1979). *Exchange Networks and Community Politics*. Beverly Hills, CA: Sage Publications.

Gray, B. (1989). *Collaborating: Finding Common Ground for Multiparty Problems*. San Francisco: Jossey-Bass.

Grusky, O., Tierney, K., Holstein, J., Anspach, R., Davis, D., Unruh, D., Webster, S., Vandewater, S., and Allen, H. (1985). "Models of Local Mental Health Delivery Systems." *American Behavioral Scientist* 28(5): 685–703.

Henry, A. D. (2011). "Ideology, Power, and the Structure of Policy Networks." *Policy Studies Journal* 39(3): 361–383.

Henry, A. D., Lubell, M., and McCoy, M. (2010). "Belief Systems and Social Capital as Drivers of Policy Network Structure: The Case of California Regional Planning." *Journal of Public Administration Research and Theory* 21(3): 419-444.

Huang, K., and Provan, K. G. (2007). "Resource Tangibility and Patterns of Interaction in a Publicly Funded Health and Human Services Network." *Journal of Public Administration Research and Theory* 17(3): 435–454.

Ibarra, H., and Andrews, S. B. (1993). "Power, Social Influence, and Sense Making: Effects of Network Centrality and Proximity on Employee Perceptions." *Administrative Science Quarterly* 38(2): 277–303.

Isett, K. R., and Provan, K. G. (2005). "The Evolution of Dyadic Interorganizational Relationships in a Network of Publicly Funded Nonprofit Agencies." *Journal of Public Administration Research and Theory* 15(1): 149–165.

Joosse, A. P. (2015). "Power in Collaborative Networks." PhD diss., University of Arizona.

Kickert, W. J. M., Klijn, E.-H., and Koppenjan, J. F. M. (Eds.). (1997). *Managing Complex Networks: Strategies for the Public Sector*. London: Sage Publications.

Knoke, D., and Yang, S. (2008). *Social Network Analysis*. 2d ed. Los Angeles: Sage Publications.

Krackhardt, D. (1990). "Assessing the Political Landscape: Structure, Cognition, and Power in Organizations." *Administrative Science Quarterly* 35(2): 342–369.

Laumann, E. O., and Knoke, D. (1987). *The Organizational State: Social Choice in National Policy Domains*. Madison: University of Wisconsin Press.

Lynn, L. E., Jr. (1996). "Assume a Network: Reforming Mental Health Services in Illinois." *Journal of Public Administration Research and Theory: J-PART* 6(2): 297–314.

Mays, G. P., and Scutchfield, F. D. (2010). "Improving Public Health System Performance through Multiorganizational Partnerships." *Preventing Chronic Disease* 7(6): 1–8.

Meier, K. J., and O'Toole, L. J., Jr. (2001). "Managerial Strategies and Behavior in Networks: A Model with Evidence from U.S. Public Education." *Journal of Public Administration Research and Theory* 11(3): 271–294.

Milward, H. B., and Provan, K. G. (2000). "Governing the Hollow State." *Journal of Public Administration Research and Theory* 10(2): 359–380.

Milward, H. B., and Provan, K. G. (2006). *A Manager's Guide to Choosing and Using Collaborative Networks*. Washington, DC: IBM Center for The Business of Government.

Milward, H. B., Provan, K. G., Fish, A., Isett, K. R., and Huang, K. (2010). "Governance and Collaboration: An Evolutionary Study of Two Mental Health Networks." *Journal of Public Administration Research and Theory* 20 (supp. 1): i125–i141.

Mitchell, S. M., and Shortell, S. M. (2000). "The Governance and Management of Effective Community Health Partnerships: A Typology for Research, Policy, and Practice." *Milbank Quarterly* 78(2): 241–289.

Morrissey, J. P., Calloway, M., Bartko, W. T., Ridgely, M. S., Goldman, H. H., and Paulson, R. I. (1994). "Local Mental Health Authorities and Service System Change: Evidence from the Robert Wood Johnson Foundation Program on Chronic Mental Illness." *Milbank Quarterly* 72(1): 49–80.

Morrissey, J. P., Johnsen, M. C., and Calloway, M. O. (1997). "Evaluating Performance and Change in Mental Health Systems Serving Children and Youth: An Interorganizational Network Approach." *Journal of Mental Health Administration* 24(1): 4–22.

Morrissey, J. P., and Tausig, M. (1985). "Community Mental Health Delivery Systems: A Network Perspective." *American Behavioral Scientist* 28(5): 704–720.

Nikolic, I. A., and Maikisch, H. (2006). "Public-Private Partnerships and Collaboration in the Health Sector: An Overview with Case Studies from Recent European Experience." The World Bank report no. 37807. http://documents.worldbank.org/curated/en/2006/10/7171601/public-private-partnerships-collaboration-health-sector-overview-case-studies-recent-european-experience.

Ostrom, E. (2005). *Understanding Institutional Diversity*. Princeton, NJ, and Oxford: Princeton University Press.

Padgett, J. F., and Ansell, C. K. (1993). "Robust Action and the Rise of the Medici, 1400-1434." *American Journal of Sociology* 98(6): 1259–1319.

Provan, K. G., Huang, K., and Milward, H. B. (2009). "The Evolution of Structural Embeddedness and Organizational Social Outcomes in a Centrally Governed Health and Human Services Network." *Journal of Public Administration Research and Theory* 19(4): 873–893.

Provan, K. G., Isett, K. R., and Milward, H. B. (2004). "Cooperation and Compromise: A Network Response to Conflicting Institutional Pressures in Community Mental Health." *Nonprofit and Voluntary Sector Quarterly* 33(3): 489–514.

Provan, K. G., and Kenis, P. (2008). "Modes of Network Governance: Structure, Management, and Effectiveness." *Journal of Public Administration Research and Theory* 18(2): 229–252.

Provan, K. G., and Milward, H. B. (1991). "Institutional-Level Norms and Organizational Involvement in a Service-Implementation Network." *Journal of Public Administration Research and Theory: J-PART* 1(4): 391–417.

Provan, K. G., and Milward, H. B. (1995). "A Preliminary Theory of Interorganizational Network Effectiveness: A Comparative Study of Four Community Mental Health Systems." *Administrative Science Quarterly* 40(1): 1–33.

Provan, K. G., and Milward, H. B. (2001). "Do Networks Really Work? A Framework for Evaluating Public-Sector Organizational Networks" *Public Administration Review* 61(4): 414–423.

Provan, K. G., Nakama, L., Veazie, M. A., Teufel-Shone, N. I., and Huddleston, C. (2003). "Building Community Capacity around Chronic Disease Services through a Collaborative Interorganizational Network." *Health Education & Behavior: The Official Publication of the Society for Public Health Education* 30(6): 646–662.

Ramiah, I., and Reich, M. R. (2005). "Public-Private Partnerships and Antiretroviral Drugs for HIV/AIDS: Lessons from Botswana." *Health Affairs (Project Hope)* 24(2): 545–551.

Rhodes, R. A. W. (2008). "Policy Network Analysis." In *The Oxford Handbook of Public Policy*, edited by R. E. Goodin, M. Moran, and M. Rein, pp. 425–447. Oxford: Oxford University Press.

Sabatier, P. A., and Weible, C. M. (2007). "The Advocacy Coalition Framework: Innovations and Clarifications." In *Theories of the Policy Process*, 2nd ed., edited by P. A. Sabatier, pp.189–220. Boulder, CO: Westview Press.

Salamon, L. M. (2012). "The Resilient Sector: The Future of Nonprofit America." In *The State of Nonprofit America*, 2nd ed., edited by L. M. Salamon, pp. 3-86, Washington, DC: Brookings Institute Press.

Scott, W. R. (1998). *Organizations: Rational, Natural, and Open Systems.* Upper Saddle River, NJ: Prentice Hall.

Sorenson, C. (2009). "Product Development Partnerships (PDPs) for Neglected Diseases: Considerations on Governance." *Health Economics, Policy and Law* 4(01): 1–10.

Thatcher, M. (1998). "The Development of Policy Network Analyses: From Modest Origins to Overarching Frameworks." *Journal of Theoretical Politics* 10(4): 389–416.

Valente, T. W., Chou, C. P., and Pentz, M. A. (2007). "Community Coalitions as a System: Effects of Network Change on Adoption of Evidence-Based Substance Abuse Prevention." *American Journal of Public Health* 97(5): 880–886.

van Raaij, D. P. A. M. (2006). "Norms Network Members Use: An Alternative Perspective for Indicating Network Success or Failure." *International Public Management Journal* 9(3): 249–270.

Wasserman, S., and Faust, K. (1994). *Social Network Analysis: Methods and Applications.* Cambridge, UK, and New York: Cambridge University Press.

Wheeler, C., and Berkley, S. (2001). "Initial Lessons from Public-Private Partnerships in Drug and Vaccine Development." *Bulletin of the World Health Organization* 79(8): 728–734.

Wistow, G. (1992). "The Health Service Policy Community." In *Policy Networks in British Government*, edited by D. Marsh and R. A. W. Rhodes, pp. 51-74. Oxford: Oxford University Press.

The World Bank. (2015). "Health Expenditure, Total (% of GDP)." http://data.worldbank.org/indicator/SH.XPD.TOTL.ZS.

PART V

NETWORKS IN INTERNATIONAL RELATIONS

CHAPTER 27

TERRORISM NETWORKS

ARIE PERLIGER

INTRODUCTION

In the first half of 2003, in the midst of the suicide attack campaigns that character-ized the early stages of the second Palestinian Intifada (uprising), a growing number of policy experts and scholars identified unique patterns in the violent Palestinian struggle. More specifically, as a result of the intensive Israeli response, which included the reoccupation of the West Bank, most of the Palestinian groups, mainly Hamas and the Palestinian Islamic Jihad, increased their reliance on informal or alternative social frameworks to maintain their operational capabilities. Probably the most well-known illustration of this trend was the case of the A-Rabat Mosque soccer team from the Abu Katila neighborhood of Hebron. No fewer than six members of the soccer team perpetrated suicide attacks in a short time, and other members became Hamas activ-ists as well. In other words, the social framework of the soccer team, which combined both religious and leisure activities, was incorporated by the Hebron Hamas chapter (Regular, 2003). Systematic studies further confirmed that the violent campaign of the Palestinian groups was based on the utilization of preexisting social networks, which were structured by ties formed in various social frameworks such as extended families, student unions, and workplaces (Pedahzur and Perliger, 2006). As similar patterns were observed in other areas of conflict (Parkinson, 2013), an increasing number of scholars acknowledged that the task of understanding the nature of violent groups and processes of radicalization demands, among other things, a rigorous exploration of the groups' social structure, the social ties between their members and the way these are related to specific roles and functions, and the overall groups' decision-making processes (Carley et al., 2002; Qin et al., 2005; Brams et al., 2006; Koschade, 2006; Asal and Rethemeyer, 2008; Helfstein and Wright, 2011; Perliger and Pedahzur, 2011; Sageman, 2011).

The dynamics of the Israeli-Palestinian conflict in the last three decades reveal an additional complexity that is shared by other arenas of contemporary terrorism. To illustrate, since the late 1980s most of the Palestinian groups have cooperated and coordinated their efforts with other actors in the region, in many ways becoming part of a network of entities; this has influenced the Palestinians' strategic and tactical decisions. Hamas, initially a branch of the Muslim Brotherhood in Palestine has since the 1990s developed strong linkages to Iran and Hezbollah, which in many ways facilitated its transition to suicide attacks in the early to mid-1990s and helped it to develop more conventional "military" capabilities in the last decade.[1] The landscape of the Syrian civil war further confirms that terrorist groups have a growing tendency to operate within a broader system of networks. The various coalitions of military forces fighting in Syria and Iraq include multiple entities, both state and substate actors, which promote specific ideological/political objectives. Hence, it seems that as more and more violent substate groups and movements assume a global capacity, our ability to understand their rationale and behavior depends on our capacity to effectively analyze their interactions with other entities, that is, the networks that are formed and facilitate cooperation among multiple violent substate/state actors.

Finally, studying counterterrorism policies reveals a complex system of networks that include various legal, operational, political, and diplomatic actors. Whereas all these actors are interested in limiting the potential impact of the terrorist threat, they define the threat differently, address it with their unique tools, and use different metrics to measure their success. We can improve our understanding of the nature of counterterrorism policies by looking into the interactions among the various actors that are shaping these policies.

From the preceding discussion it is evident that research into all three dimensions of the terrorism phenomenon and the responses to it can benefit greatly from the implementation of network science. The following sections provide a more detailed description of the relevant networks at play, suggest methodological approaches to analyze these networks, and address the way they can help us decipher new dimensions in existing conflicts. There are several reasons for using mainly case studies from the Middle Eastern arena. First, it is one of the most active hubs of contemporary substate violence and is thus rich with examples of the current dynamics that characterize terrorist networks. Second, since Middle Eastern terrorism is not a new phenomenon, significant data are available on the structure and, more important, evolution of the region's terrorist entities. Finally, many of the characteristics of modern terrorism originally appeared in the Middle Eastern arena, so examining Middle Eastern terrorism can provide important insights into potential future developments in terrorism's landscape.

Networks of Terrorists

The most systematic use of network science in the study of terrorism so far has been manifested in studies that map ties between members of terrorist groups and strive to identify relations between the structure of terrorist groups and their behavior, as well as how the relations between the group's members affect various aspects of the group.

In retrospect, this corpus of literature evolved in several distinct phases. The first phase was related to the growing prominence of a new analytical framework—"the new terrorism"—among students of terrorism since the mid-1980s. Simply put, it reflected an acknowledgment that terrorism is going through significant changes, as modern/new groups have a higher tendency to operate globally, promote religious agendas, use especially lethal tactics, and adopt a flat/network structure (Hoffman, 1999; Laqueur, 1999; Kurz, 2003). Focusing on the latter, various scholars were seeking to explain the implications of this new structure and the challenges it represents for states' counterterrorism efforts (Arquilla and Ronfeld, 1999; Jones et al., 2003; Mishal, 2003; McAllister, 2004; Sageman, 2004; Stohl and Stohl, 2007). Nonetheless, despite the important conceptual and analytical contributions of these studies, they did not include systematic empirical analysis of terrorist groups' structure or attempt to utilize methods of network analysis. In the tradition of terrorism studies of the 1970s and 1980s, they mainly focused on the use of anecdotal evidence or specific case studies to provide an inside look into the changing organizational structure of terrorist groups.

The second phase, shortly after September 11, 2001, comprised studies that utilized the growing coverage of the various manifestations of al-Qaeda, in order to try to map some of its networks/cells and provide basic insights regarding the evolution, structure, and type of relations between members of jihadi networks (Krebs, 2002; Rodríguez, 2005; Carley et al., 2006; Koschade, 2006). The major contribution of these studies was not made particularly in the theoretical realm, as most did not attempt to utilize social network analysis to support or reject a theoretical framework; rather, they exemplified the feasibility of mapping the social structure of terrorist networks with acceptable levels of accuracy and the potential theoretical insights that such mapping can provide.

The third phase, which began around the mid-2000s, included two types of studies, each using network science to develop nuanced theoretical frameworks related to a specific level of the terrorism phenomenon. The first type of studies focused on the individual level, attempting to decipher processes of radicalization and recruitment, as well as the possible association between the social status of the individual within the terrorist network and his operational role and influence (Pedahzur and Perliger, 2006; Helfstein and Wright, 2011). The second type of studies focused on the group level and attempted to use social network analysis (SNA) to identify the structural characteristics that determine durability and stability of terrorist networks. While some of these studies focused on real-life case studies (Carley et al., 2003; Helfstein and Wright, 2011; Cale and Horgan, 2012; Perliger, 2014), others used simulated network models (Tsvetovat and Carley, 2005; Carley et al., 2006; Jackson, 2006).

An overview of the three phases helps to identify some clear patterns in which the network-oriented approach facilitated progress in our understanding of the terrorism phenomenon. From a conceptual perspective, the network approach anchored the notion that many terrorist attacks are not the product of vast organizational entities, but of a small social framework, whose dynamics and behaviors can be investigated primarily via the collection of data regarding the interpersonal relations of their members (i.e., social climate). Moreover, in some cases it seems that the social climate is a better predictor of the group's behavior than organizational cost-benefit analysis. Finally, after many years of unsuccessful attempts to construct an effective sociodemographic profile of members of terrorist groups, the network approach seems to provide some solutions, as various studies have exemplified how the sociodemographic profile may be associated with the members' in-group social status and roles within the group (Pedahzur and Perliger, 2006; Helfstein and Wright, 2011).

From a theoretical perspective, it seems that the network approach can potentially help in the development of explanations related to the radicalization of the social networks, by analyzing paths of recruitment and socialization within the specific structures of the terrorist network. Perliger and Pedahzur (2014), for example, illustrated how subgroups/cliques within the networks are essential for the radicalization of the group's members, and how specific members operate as recruitment hubs for the entire network. In addition, the network approach has helped to develop a more nuanced understanding of the factors determining terrorist group durability and stability by correlating between various structural characteristics and the groups' lifespan and effectiveness.

The utilization of the network approach also provided the study of terrorism with a boost from a methodological perspective. To begin with, the need to map ties and interactions among members of terrorist groups led to a significant improvement in information-gathering techniques, many of which are now used widely. To illustrate, the most current and comprehensive attempts to collect information about networks of foreign fighters, a worrying phenomenon that has recently attracted the attention of both academics and law enforcement, rely largely on data gathered from social media platforms and similar digital data sets (mainly from the financial realm; see, for example the King's College ICSR relevant data set at http://icsr.info/projects/western-foreign-fighters-syria/). In many ways these are extensions of efforts by earlier scholars who introduced new techniques to identify potential covert networks (see, for example, Diesner and Carley's [2008] usage of software for advanced textual analyses to identify and plot clandestine networks). These new techniques have also facilitated the expansion of data collected about the members of terrorist groups and have exposed students of terrorism to a new set of concepts for describing the role and influence of members of terrorist groups. In addition, the use of SNA has allowed the creation of effective typologies of terrorist groups based on their structure and the nature of ties between their members (Jackson, 2006). These distinctions (e.g., between small worlds' networks and star networks) have exposed researchers to a new and growing array of opportunities for examining the relations between terrorist groups' structural characteristics and their behavior. Finally, the growing use of SNA has further illustrated the dynamic nature of terrorist groups and their tendency to change over time; hence, the adoption of the network approach fosters attempts to address the evolving and dynamic nature of terrorist groups through a rigorous and empirically based lense (Rodríguez, 2005; Perliger and Pedahzur, 2014).

Despite these advances, some important challenges are still apparent in the attempts to use network science in the study of terrorism. Some are methodological and seem inherent to the study of clandestine or covert networks, such as the inevitability of gaps in the data and the inability to validate the completeness or complete accuracy of the data, the difficulties in ascertaining the boundaries of the network, and potential reliance on a small number of sources of information. Other challenges are conceptual in nature; despite great efforts, there is still a lack of clarity regarding the applicability of a network approach to the study of more paramilitary or hierarchical organizations, as the behavior of such organizations seems to be more suited to analysis via organizational theories. Another conceptual issue is the categorization or metric of ties, as to date there is still no consensus on how to distinguish between different types of ties or between different strengths of ties. Finally, it seems that beyond some preliminary theories related to the association between structure and durability/productivity, students of terrorism are still finding it difficult to identify additional areas where SNA can help validate/reject theoretical frameworks. The concluding section of this chapter tries to provide some ideas in this regard.

NETWORKS OF GROUPS

In September 2014 a small group of jihadists, former members of Al-Qaeda in the Islamic Maghreb (AQIM) declared an alliance with Islamic State in Iraq and Syria (ISIS) (Porter, 2015). In the following months other groups in North Africa followed suit. Nevertheless, their declarations attracted very little attention, as many of these groups were unknown until that time (Porter, 2015). This dismissive response changed quickly when, in early March 2015, Abibakar Shekau, the leader of the Nigerian terrorist group Boko Haram, pledged allegiance to ISIS (Zenn, 2015). This time, a highly capable organization had associated itself with the most prominent group in the jihadi landscape. At that point, policymakers and experts expressed concerns about the spread of Islamic State influence in regions outside the core Middle East. Many also indicated that the spread of ISIS's influence was not too different from the global expansion of al-Qaeda following the 9/11 attacks. The increase in the number of violent campaigns that are a product of "coalitions" of groups that share similar ideological sentiments indicates that a network approach may be highly suitable for understanding relevant patterns of ties and cooperation among terrorist groups, as well as how these impact the operational behavior of the relevant groups. But before discussing the potential of the network approach for improving our understanding of interactions among terrorist groups, it is important first to provide conceptual and historical context for the phenomenon of terrorist groups' cooperation.

Cooperation and alliances among terrorist groups are not new, but as with many other characteristics of modern terrorism, one can identify some significant changes in the last couple of decades in the nature of their cooperative relations. As mentioned recently by Moghadam (2015), interactions among terrorist groups can be divided into two major categories. *High-end cooperation*, which is manifested via mergers or strategic alliances (extensive sharing of resources, human power, and knowledge), usually demands ideological proximity. In other words, the groups are part of a wider ideological movement. *Low-end cooperation* is manifested by short-term, tactical cooperation, in order to execute specific operations or ongoing transactional relations for (the most part) narrow logistical objectives. While the latter type of cooperation can effectively describe most interactions among groups in the 1960s and the 1970s—as groups such as the Palestinian Liberation Organization (PLO), Euskadi Ta Askatasuna (ETA), Red Army Faction (RAF), Japanese Red Army (JRA), and Irish Republican Army (IRA) cooperated sporadically to facilitate specific campaigns or to utilize each other's specific resources (the use of PLO training camps in Lebanon by the European organizations is a case in point; see McKinley, 1984)—since the early 1980s it seems that a growing number of terrorist organizations are developing more long-term strategic relations with both state and nonstate entities and thus fit the first category of cooperation.

Even though the typology above allows us to identify some aspects of cooperation (mainly regarding length, scope, and level of resource sharing), a more network approach–oriented typology may be a more effective mechanism for distinguishing among contemporary networks of terrorist groups. Specifically, four types of networks seem to populate the contemporary terrorism landscape. The first can be designated a state star network (SSN). This kind of network includes multiple nodes (substate violent entities) that are connected to a single hub, which in this case is a state actor. While some of the nodes maintain some level of interaction, this is in many cases weak and sporadic and is usually monitored or facilitated by the state actor (the only hub of the network). A case in point is the network of violent groups that are affiliated with Iran. Since the mid-1980s, a few years after the establishment of the Islamic Republic of Iran, the Iranian Revolutionary Guards Corps (IRGC) has been developing proxies and networks that were supposed to enable the export of revolutionary ideas to neighboring Middle Eastern countries, as well as to serve security and military purposes. The proxy organizations, in most cases, represented a local Shiite community, in many cases marginalized and oppressed by a Sunni majority, which saw the Iranian Grand Ayatollah as its supreme spiritual leader. The first group that became part of this network was Hezbollah, which was founded in the early 1980s, when Iranian forces exploited the sectarian civil war in Lebanon to create a new organization that represented Shiite interests and, while devoted to the ideals of the Islamic revolution, also incorporated Lebanese nationalistic sentiments into its ideological platform (Harik, 2004). With the ongoing support of Iran, Hezbollah is still considered by many to be the most capable terrorist group in the world. Over the years the Iranian network has continued to expand. In the late 1990s Hamas was gradually incorporated as well, as it started to receive significant military and financial support from Iran (Coughlin, 2015). An indication of the strength of the relations between these two actors is the fact that they have survived both disagreements related to the civil war in Syria and objections to these relations by some high-profile members of Hamas (Cafiero and Certo, 2014). Other noteworthy Palestinian members of the Iranian network are the Islamic Palestinian Jihad (IPJ) and the Popular Front for the Liberation of Palestine-General Command (PFLP-GC). The Palestinian groups are the only Sunni organizations to become part of the network. Other groups that are part of the network and that are gaining attention are Houthi rebel groups in Yemen and various Shiite militia groups in Iraq. In both cases, these groups are perceived as promoting Iranian interests in their respective countries and adopting tactics that in the past were developed and effectively implemented by other organizations in the network (mainly Hezbollah). Hence, it seems that the network effectively promotes sharing of operational knowledge, which has facilitated the success of its members. In some cases, this sharing is being done directly, as indicated by the presence of Hezbollah's mentors in Yemen, assisting Houthi rebels.[2]

In addition to the proxy organizations mentioned above, there are indications that IRGC cells, located outside Iran, are also part of the Iranian network. For example, in July 2012 it was reported that a network comprising IRGC members was responsible for the attempted attack against Israeli diplomats in New Delhi (Momatz, 2012). The failed assassination attempt on the Saudi Ambassador to the United States in October 2011 is another indication that the IRGC is maintaining and developing operational networks outside Iran (Savage and Shane, 2011). To conclude, the Iranian network seems to include two types of nodes, proxy organizations and IRGC cells, which are incorporated differently, serve different strategic objectives, and differ in terms of the nature of their ties to the hub (Iran). A rigorous SNA can probably provide important insights regarding the nature of ties between different types of nodes and the hub, the association between the type of nodes and the stability and strength of the ties, as well as the dynamics related to the level of centralization and density of the entire network. Simply put, a network approach may be able to expose a new layer of knowledge regarding the behavior of such a network.

The second type of networks can be designated a substate star network (SSSN). While these networks also have one major hub, they differ in several aspects from the SSN discussed above. First, the hub is usually a substate actor (rather than a state), such as ISIS or al-Qaeda, and it is usually the most prominent group within an ideological movement. Second, while the relations between the hub and the other nodes in an SSN are extremely asymmetrical in terms of influence and transition of resources, in an SSSN the relations are more symmetrical and voluntary, and as a result less stable. Finally, an SSSN has lower levels of centralization and density. In other words, we will see more ties between members of the network (and not just between the hub and other nodes) than we usually find in a classic star network. These characteristics seem to fit the growing network of groups affiliated with, or that pledge allegiance to, ISIS in the last couple of years. The examination of this network, which currently includes twenty-three nodes/actors, uncovers several interesting insights.[3] First, it is important to note that both groups and individuals pledge allegiance (*Bay`a*) to ISIS. Hence the network includes both violent groups and ideological figures, each providing a different type of resources to the network (operational capabilities versus ideological or religious legitimacy). Second, most of the groups that pledge allegiance to ISIS are new or unknown groups (except for Boko Haram), reflecting that a major incentive for joining the network is the logistical and operational resources that ISIS can provide, as well as public legitimacy. Third, the expansion of the network has occurred in waves (four *Bay`as* were offered in early July 2014, then another five on the same day, November 10, 2014; then another four on December 14, 2014), which may indicate that there is some contingency effect at play, as well as that specific external factors can explain the expansion of the network. Finally, while the first fifteen or so groups that joined the network never fought against or criticized ISIS, four out of the last five groups to join have had hostile relations with ISIS in the past. This may indicate that as the influence of ISIS grows, it is more successful in incorporating former foes and eliminating potential competition. Another reason for the quick expansion of ISIS's network is the organization's nonelitist and inclusive nature, most definitely in comparison to al-Qaeda (Milton and Al-Ubaydi, 2015). To conclude, it is important to note that such a network is not exclusive to the international arena, nor to the Islamic realm. For example, in many ways the network of branches that was associated with the Ku Klux Klan (KKK) in the 1950s and 1960s (after the collapse of the organization's central leadership in the late 1940s) espoused similar characteristics (Perliger, 2013). To conclude, a network approach can be extremely useful in tracking the trends of expansion of an SSSN and how the various characteristics of the network may impact the strength and durability of its hub. Thus, for example, understanding ISIS's relationships with other actors in its network can eventually teach us a lot about the factors that may strengthen or weaken ISIS.

The third type of network tends to evolve in domestic contexts and is compatible with the structure of "scale-free networks" (see Laszlo-Barabasi and Bonabeau, 2003). Thus, this type of network tends to be less centralized and includes a small number of actors (hubs) with a large number of ties, while the majority of the actors' number of ties is around the average for the network. Moreover, since there is no centralized authority (as in the previous two networks), which determines which groups will be included or excluded from the network, its borders are more vague and less stable, as some of the groups in the network may prefer to opt out and directly challenge the network. The less centralized nature of the network also provides more flexibility and room for ideological maneuvering. Finally, the division of power within the network is more dynamic and less structured; hence the central actors (groups) of today may become the marginal actors of tomorrow. The characteristics elaborated above could be effectively exemplified in the case of the violent American Far Right.

Far-Right violence in the United States was traditionally linked with the militant activism of the KKK. However, other types of ideological groups have begun to populate the American Far Right in recent decades. Among them are militias, Christian identity groups, skinheads, and neo-Nazis. Thus, the American Far Right has become more vibrant and more ideologically and structurally diverse than ever before. Moreover, its boundaries have become vaguer, as many of the new groups have occasionally been inspired by ideas and practices that originated from outside the Far-Right universe. These new developments, as well as developments in technology, facilitate greater interaction among the various groups that comprise the American Far Right, and that in turn has resulted in more mergers, splits, and joint activism, as well as competition. In the current situation it is difficult to identify prominent actors, as most of the leading actors of the past eventually collapsed or lost much of their influence. This was the case with the KKK, the Aryan Nations (which dominated the Christian identity movement), the National Alliance (which dominated the neo-Nazi movement) and the Hammerskin Nations (which dominated the skinhead subculture) (Perliger, 2013). Thus, any attempt to understand the violent components of the contemporary American Far Right will be served by using a network approach. This approach can potentially help identify how ideological differences affect interactions among different group actors, if we can identify unique locations and ties associated with the more violent groups, and can help in trying to identify emerging leading groups from within this diverse and complicated landscape.

The last type of network seems to be a combination of the first two, in the sense that it combines both prominent state and substate hubs. It also reflects the growing tendency of sovereign polities to join coalitions that also include substate actors. In the Syrian civil war, for example, most of the fighting sides are a coalition of both substate and state actors, merging their resources and efforts. To illustrate, the Syrian Revolutionary Command Council (SRCC) is an alliance of a few dozen groups (such as the Free Syrian Army or the Authenticity and Development Front) and state actors (United States, France, Saudi Arabia), which are cooperating against both ISIS and the Syrian government. A similar dynamic was visible in the early stages of the operation that was led by the US-led coalition in Afghanistan during the early 2000s. And while these networks may be perceived as ad hoc in nature, intending to provide an answer to a specific, time-restricted security issue, they still reflect the growing tendency of leading international powers to rely on coalitions that include local substate groups.

To conclude, in the complicated and rapidly changing landscape of asymmetrical conflicts, in which many violent campaigns are a product of cooperation among multiple groups, a network approach can provide important theoretical and analytical insights. First, by identifying how ties between groups are formed and who initiates them, it is possible to gain better clarity regarding the factors that facilitate joint violent campaigns. Second, by mapping and analyzing the power division within the network, it may be possible to understand the variables that determine patterns of cooperation, how a group's strength impacts its role within a specific coalition of groups, and how that eventually shapes the group's effectiveness and durability. Third, understanding the structure of these coalitions of groups may also help us understand changes in other dimensions of terrorism, such as ideological shifts (how groups that cooperate influence each other's ideological tendencies) or adaptations of new organizational structures and tactics (Do groups belonging to the same coalitions tend to imitate each other?). Finally, we can learn more about processes that are related to the end, or collapse, of such coalitions. This naturally is also of significant interest to agencies responsible for mitigating the threat of terrorism. How the utilization of the network approach can help us understand the operational effectiveness of these agencies is at the center of the following section.

NETWORKS OF COUNTERTERRORISM

On July 31, 2002, a powerful bomb, hidden in a bag and composed of explosives and nails, was activated by remote control at one of the major cafeterias of the Mount Scopus campus of the Hebrew University in Jerusalem. The fact that the bomb was activated during lunchtime led to devastating results. Nine people were killed, and close to ninety were wounded (Perliger, Pedahzur and Zalmanovitch, 2005). It was later revealed that a local cell of a Palestinian organization, Hamas, based in East Jerusalem, had perpetrated the attack. In the minutes following the event, the most seriously injured were taken to an evacuation point near the cafeteria, while those who were less seriously injured were taken to a farther location that was more accessible to rescue vehicles. Unfortunately, during the initial stages of the evacuation the medical forces were not informed about the existence of a second evacuation point; hence, in the first crucial minutes after the attack, first responders evacuated mainly the lightly injured (Perliger, Pedahzur and Zalmanovitch, 2005). As a result, the evacuation took significantly longer than evacuations in previous terrorist attacks (Perliger, Pedahzur, and Zalmanovitch, 2005).

Several factors contributed to the imperfect response to the attack at the Hebrew University, including the unfamiliarity of the medical forces with the site of the attack, lack of a command post at the scene, and lack of coordination among the various units of first responders (Perliger, Pedahzur, and Zalmanovitch, 2005). The latter is especially crucial, considering that the number of actors who take part in the response to acts of terrorism. In the Israeli case, for example, more than two dozen organizations usually take part in the crisis management stage (immediately following the attack) and in the pre- and post-attack response. These include the national/municipal police, the Israeli Defense Forces (IDF), Israel's border patrol units, MADA (the Israeli national medical evacuation organization), the fire department ZAKA (the national organization of volunteers who assist in evacuating human remains at sites of attacks), the Israeli General Security Service (the Israeli equivalent of the US Federal Bureau of Investigation), Israel's social security institute, the Israeli Taxes Authority, local hospitals, the Israel Electric Corporation, and private contractors. If we also take into consideration the organizations that are engaged in the offensive dimensions of the response to terrorism, it is clear that we are dealing with a complex set of organizational networks, which are composed of entities with unique organizational cultures, history, and leadership styles, that have to find effective ways to cooperate and share institutional knowledge while operating together at a high tempo and in a stressful environment. Analyzing the characteristics of these networks can potentially help us better understand the factors that determine success or failure in the context of the response to terrorist campaigns.

Despite the fact that all of the above-mentioned networks are engaged at some level in the response to terrorism, they differ in some cardinal ways. The network of organizations that is active in what can be described as the "crisis management" stage (the immediate response after the attack, mostly at the site of the attack) includes actors for which the response to terrorist attacks is only a small part of their overall activities; hence, they have had to develop specific mechanisms and routines for such situations (these include, among others, medical forces, police units, social services, municipal departments, and fire departments). Moreover, while in most of their activities these actors enjoy significant autonomy, when responding to terrorist attacks they must operate under a more rigid command structure, as they are subordinate to other actors at the site of the attack. Finally, during a response to a terrorist attack, security concerns are more than usually influential in shaping their operational routines and protocols. For example, after a few cases in which suicide attacks were followed by a second suicide bomber or the activation of a remote control bomb aimed at generating casualties among first responders, the Israeli police decided to prevent access to the site of the attack, including for medical forces, until a bomb squad can ensure that the site of the attack is safe. Another example is related to the necessity to prevent the contamination of potential evidence at the site of the attack that might be useful in the investigation. In both cases, security considerations, which are under the control of other actors such as the police or intelligence agencies, shape the activities of first responders. This of course can elevate tension among the various actors, especially in such a stressful environment. The tools of network analysis can provide important insights into the way specific network structure and implementation of a specific type of ties and communication procedures, as well as other network characteristics, can help overcome these challenges.

In the network that focuses on the prevention of terrorist attacks, most of the ties are formed to facilitate information flow and sharing. In general, the organizations in these networks can be divided into two types: those focusing on the gathering and analysis of information that may help prevent future terrorist attacks (intelligence agencies and relevant ancillaries) and those who are on the receiving end and hope to utilize this information for operational activities. This embedded asymmetry naturally affects the division of power/influence within the network, as the latter (organizations focusing on active prevention of terrorism) are mostly dependent on the former (organizations gathering and analyzing information). Moreover, since occasionally operational intelligence can be contradictory or inconsistent (e.g., multiple intelligence agencies that are part of the network can provide differing assessments), the overall network needs to develop a mechanism that will ensure that the operational organizations on the receiving end obtain a coherent assessment regarding potential threats. In addition, communications must be quick and effective in order to prevent a potential attack; hence, redundant ties are important in such networks and are usually encouraged. In the United States, for example, in order to ensure this redundancy, the government has created both regional (the various regional Joint Terrorism Task Forces) and national (National Counter Terrorism Center) hubs, where members of the various organizations operate together. Here again, it seems that the utilization of network science could help policymakers in devising effective structures to maximize these necessary characteristics of the networks operating in the pre-attack stage.

Networks that focus on the offensive response against terrorist entities usually include a significant number of actors; however, unlike the previous networks, most of these actors are affiliated with a small number of organizational frameworks, usually the military and intelligence agencies, as well as relevant political frameworks. This produces more structured and hierarchical networks and a more defined division of labor/responsibilities (which creates fewer tensions within the network). Hence, these networks are in many ways better equipped to solidify effective coordination.

The study of counterterrorism within the academic community has focused so far on several distinct issues, including the need to balance civil liberties and security needs (Wilkinson, 2000; Schmid, 1992; Chalk, 1998; Cerlinsten and Schmid, 1992; Groenewold, 1992); the association between the state's social and political characteristics and the counterterrorism measures it adopts (Katzenstein, 2003; Omelicheva, 2007; Perliger, 2012); and specific types of counterterrorism tactics, such as targeted killings, military intervention, or specific types of legislation (Bowen, 2000; Hoyt, 2004; Hafez and Hatfield, 2006). Less attention has been given to the examination of the possible association between the characteristics of the organizational networks that are responsible for the implementation of counterterrorism policies and the nature and effectiveness of the struggle against terrorism. This section has tried to provide some analytical seeds that will highlight the potential of network science in clarifying some gaps in our understanding of the factors shaping the formulation and effectiveness of counterterrorism policies.

Concluding Remarks

The chapter has tried to provide new ideas on how network science can be implemented to improve our understanding of the complexities of the terrorism phenomenon. More specifically, it has focused on how groups operate, compete, cooperate and merge, or split, as well as the dilemmas and challenges involved in the contemporary response to terrorism, which is based mostly on coordination and cooperation both on the international and the national levels among various actors. In order to do so, it was first vital to illustrate the various networks at play, by outlining effective typologies of relevant networks and showing that these typologies can provide substantial insights about the current landscape of terrorism and counterterrorism. These typologies are preliminary and must be subjected to a more strict empirical analysis; nonetheless, they serve as an important illustration of how the contemporary security environment is shaped by interactions and interdependency among multiple actors.

But can we also identify potential contributions on the theoretical level, such as theories of terrorism that are anchored in a network perspective? It seems that while from a conceptual and analytical perspective, students of terrorism have acknowledged the relevance and utility of network science, this is not necessarily the case when we focus on the theoretical level. As mentioned previously, theories of terrorism based on a network perspective are mostly found in an individual-level analysis of the terrorism phenomenon, but much less so when trying to explain group-level behavior, and almost not at all when studying various dimensions of counterterrorism. Hence, it seems like the obvious next step. But what exactly should we strive to explain?

In terms of group behavior, the immense diversity in terms of structural characteristics should push scholars to try to understand if, beyond questions of durability, the network approach and the structure and interactions within substate violent groups can help us understand routines of decision-making processes; how information related to ideological/operational/social developments outside the network is interpreted, processed, and eventually translated into group behavior; and how a group's interactions with external actors are managed and developed (recruitment, training, discharge of members, creating alliances with other groups, etc.). And while there are some encouraging signs for the utilization of the network approach to studying these issues, it seems that there are still many gaps awaiting exploration. Finally, as counterterrorism policies are gradually becoming a central component of the foreign and domestic policy framework in most polities, we should expect a growing push to utilize new methodologies for the development of a network-oriented theoretical framework that can explain various facets of those polities' struggles with terrorism, especially issues related to short- and long-term effectiveness.

NOTES

1. To illustrate, the US State Department's foreign terrorist organizations (FTO) list from 2013 states that Iran is supporting Hezbollah, Hamas, Palestinian Islamic Jihad, and the Popular Front for the Liberation of Palestine—General Command. See http://www.state.gov/j/ct/rls/crt/2013/224826.htm.
2. This claim is supported by various reports, mainly in the Arab media, in newspapers such as Lebanon's *al-Mustaqbal* and the pan-Arab news outlet *Asharq al-Awsat*. The Saudi Ambassador to the United States also attested to that; see http://www.arabnews.com/saudi-arabia/news/724391.
3. I would like to thank Dr. Dan Milton from the Combating Terrorism Center at the US Military Academy for sharing his data set of ISIS's allegiance network.

REFERENCES

Arquilla, J., and Ronfeld, D. (1999). *Networks and Netwar, the Future of Terror, Crime, and Militancy*. Washington, DC: Rand Corporation.

Asal, V., and Rethemeyer, R. K. (2008). "The Nature of the Beast: Organizational Structures and the Lethality of Terrorist Attacks." *Journal of Politics* 70: 437–449.

Bowen, D. (2000). "Something Must Be Done—Military Intervention." *Studies in Conflict and Terrorism* 23(1): 1–19.

Brams, J. S., Mutlu, H., and Ramirez, S. L. (2006). "Influence in Terrorist Networks: From Undirected to Directed Graphs." *Studies in Conflict & Terrorism* 29(7): 703–718.

Cafiero, G., and Certo, P. (2014). "Hamas and Hezbollah Agree to Disagree on Syria." *Atlantic Council*, January 30 http://www.atlanticcouncil.org/blogs/menasource/hamas-and-hezbollah-agree-to-disagree-on-syria.

Cale, H., and Horgan, J. (2012). "Methodological Triangulation in the Analysis of Terrorist Networks." *Studies in Conflict & Terrorism* 35(2): 182–192.

Carley, M. K., Diesner, K., Reminga, J., and Tsevetovat, M. (2006). "Towards an Interoperable Dynamic of Network Analysis Toolkit." *Decisions Support System* 43(4): 1324–1347.

Carley, K., Dombroski, M., Tsvetovat, M., Reminga, J., and Kamneva, N. (2003). "Destabilizing Dynamic Covert Networks." In *Proceedings of the 8th International Command and Control Research and Technology Symposium*, Washington, DC: National Defense War College. http://www.casos.cs.cmu.edu/publications/papers/a2c2_carley_2003_destabilizing.pdf.

Carley, M. K., Ju-Sung, L., and Krackhardt, D. (2002). "Destabilizing Network." *Connections* 24: 79–92.

Cerlinsten, D. R., and Schmid, A. (1992). "Western Response to Terrorism: A Twenty Five Year Balance Sheet." *Terrorism and Political Violence* 4(4): 307–340.

Chalk, P. (1998). "The Response to Terrorism as a Threat to Liberal Democracy." *Australian Journal of Politics and History* 44(3): 373–388.

Coughlin, C. (2015). "Iran Is Intensifying Efforts to Support Hamas in Gaza." *The Telegraph*, April 4. http://www.telegraph.co.uk/news/worldnews/middleeast/iran/11515603/Iran-is-intensifying-efforts-to-support-Hamas-in-Gaza.html.

Diesner, J., and Carley, M. K. (2008). "Conditional Random Fields for Entity Extraction and Ontological Text Coding." *Computational and Mathematical Organization Theory*, 14(3): 248–262.

Groenewold, K. (1992). "The German Federal Republic's Response and Civil Liberties." *Terrorism and Political Violence* 4(4): 136–150.

Hafez, M. M., and Hatfield, M. J. (2006). "Do Targeted Assassinations Work? A Multivariate Analysis of Israel's Controversial Tactic during Al-Aqsa Uprising." *Studies in Conflict & Terrorism* 29(4): 359–382.

Harik, P. J. (2004). *Hezbollah: The Changing Face of Terrorism*. London: Tauris.

Helfstein, S., and Wright, D. (2011). "Covert or Convenient? Evolution of Terror Attack Networks," *Journal of Conflict Resolution* 55(5): 785–813.

Hoffman, B. (1999). "Terrorism Trends and Prospects." In *Countering the New Terrorism*, edited by I. Lesser, pp. 7–38. Santa Monica, CA: RAND.

Hoyt, D. T. (2004). "Military Force." In *Attacking Terrorism*, edited by J. M. Ludes and A. K. Cronin, pp. 162–185. Washington, DC: Georgetown University Press.

Jackson, A. B. (2006). "Groups, Networks, or Movements: A Command-and-Control-Driven Approach to Classifying Terrorist Organizations and Its Application to Al Qaeda." *Studies in Conflict & Terrorism* 29(3): 241–262.

Jones, D., Smith, L. R. M., and Wedding, M. (2003). "Looking for the Pattern: Al Qaeda in South East Asia—The Genealogy of a Terror Network." *Studies in Conflict and Terrorism* 26(6): 443–457.

Katzenstein, J. P. (2003). "Same War-Different Views: Germany, Japan, and Counterterrorism." *International Organization* 57(4): 731–760.

Koschade, S. (2006). "A Social Network Analysis of Jemaah Islamiyah: The Applications to Counterterrorism and Intelligence." *Studies in Conflict & Terrorism* 29(6): 559–575.

Krebs, E. V. (2002). "Mapping Network of Terrorist Cells," *Connections* 24: 43–52.

Kurz, A. (2003) "New Terrorism: New Challenges, Old Dilemmas." *Strategic Assessment* 6. http://www.inss.org.il/uploadImages/systemFiles/New%20Terrorism%20New%20Challenges%20Old%20Dilemmas.pdf

Laqueur, W. (1999). *The New Terrorism. Fanaticism and the Arms of Mass Destruction*. New York: Oxford University Press.

Laszlo-Barabasi, A., and Bonabeau, E. (2003). "Scale-Free Networks." *Scientific American* 288(5): 60–69.

McAllister, B. (2004). "Al Qaeda and the Innovative Firm: Demythologizing the Network," *Studies in Conflict and Terrorism* 27: 297–319.

McKinley, M. (1984). "The International Dimensions of Terrorism in Ireland." In *Terrorism in Ireland*, edited by Y. Alexander and A. O'Day, pp. 3–30. New York: Routledge.

Milton, D., and Al-Ubaydi, M. (2015). "Pledging Bay`a: A Benefit or a Burden to the Islamic State?" *CTC Sentinel* 8(3). https://www.ctc.usma.edu/posts/march-2015-baya-special-issue.

Mishal, S. (2003). "The Pragmatic Dimension of the Palestinian Hamas: A Network Perspective." *Armed Forces and Society* 29(4): 569–589.

Moghadam, A. (2015). "Terrorist Affiliations in Context: A Typology of Terrorist Inter-Group Cooperation." *CTC Sentinel* 8(3). https://www.ctc.usma.edu/posts/terrorist-affiliations-in-context-a-typology-of-terrorist-inter-group-cooperation.

Momatz, R. (2012). "Iran's Revolutionary Guard Accused in Israeli Embassy Bombing: Report." *ABC News*, July 30. http://abcnews.go.com/Blotter/irans-revolutionary-guard-accused-israeli-embassy-bombing-report/story?id=16888481.

Omelicheva, Y. M. (2007). "Combating Terrorism in Central Asia: Explaining Differences in States' Responses to Terror." *Terrorism and Political Violence* 19(3): 369–393.

Pedahzur, A., and Perliger, A. (2006). "The Changing Nature of Suicide Attacks—A Social Network Perspective." *Social Forces* 84(4): 1983–2004.

Perliger, A. (2012). "How Democracies Respond to Terrorism: Regime Characteristics, Symbolic Power, and Counter-Terrorism." *Security Studies* 21(3): 490–528.

Perliger, A. (2013). *Challengers from the Sidelines, Understanding the American Violent Far Right*. West Point, NY: Combating Terrorism Center.

Perliger, A. (2014). "Terrorist Networks' Productivity and Durability—A Comparative Multi-level Analysis." *Perspectives on Terrorism* 8(4): 36–52.

Perliger, A., and Pedahzur, A. (2011). "Social Network Analysis in the Study of Terrorism and Political Violence." *PS: Political Science and Politics* 44(1): 45–50.

Perliger, A., and Pedahzur, A. (2014). "Political Violence and Counter-Culture Communities—An Alternative Outlook on Religious Terrorism," *Political Studies*, 10. doi:10.1111/1467-9248.12182

Perliger A., Pedahzur, A., and Zalmanovitch, Y. (2005). "The Defensive Dimension of the Battle against Terrorism—An Analysis of Management of Terror Incidents in Jerusalem." *Journal of Contingencies and Crisis Management* 13(2): 79–91.

Porter, Geoff. (2015). "What to Make of the Bay`a in North Africa?" *CTC Sentinel* 8(3). https://www.ctc.usma.edu/posts/what-to-make-of-the-baya-in-north-africa.

Qin, J., Xu, J. J., Hu, D., Sageman, M., and Chen, H. (2005). "Analyzing Terrorist Networks: A Case Study of the Global Salafi Jihad Network." *Intelligence and Security Informatics* 3495: 287–304.

Regular, A. (2003). "Hebron's Playing, and Plotting Field." *Haaretz Daily*, May 3. http://www.haarctz.com/print edition/news/hebron-s-playing-and-plotting-field-1 89861 (Hebrew).

Rodríguez, J. (2005). "The March 11th Terrorist Network: In Its Weakness Lies Its Strength." Paper presented at XXV International Sunbelt Conference, Los Angeles, February 16–20.

Sageman, M. (2004). *Understanding Terror Networks*. Philadelphia: University of Pennsylvania Press.

Sageman, M. (2011). *Leaderless Jihad: Terror Networks in The Twenty-First Century*. Philadelphia: University of Pennsylvania Press.

Parkinson, S. (2013). "Organizing Rebellion: Rethinking High-Risk Mobilization and Social Networks in War." *American Political Science Review* 107(3): 418–432.

Savage, C., and Shane, S. (2011). "Iranians Accused of a Plot to Kill Saudies' US Envoy." *New York Times*, October 11. http://www.nytimes.com/2011/10/12/us/us-accuses-iranians-of-plotting-to-kill-saudi-envoy.html?_r=0.

Schmid, P. A. (1992). "Terrorism and Democracy." *Terrorism and Political Violence* 4(4): 14–15.

Stohl, C., and Stohl, M. (2007). "Networks of Terror: Theoretical Assumptions and Pragmatic Consequences." *Communication Theory* 17(2): 93–124.

Tsvetovat, M., and Carley, M. K. (2005). "Structural Knowledge and Success of Anti-Terrorist Activity: The Downside of Structural Equivalence." *Journal of Social Structure* 6. http://repository.cmu.edu/isr/43/.

Wilkinson, P. (2000). *Terrorism Versus Democracy: The Liberal State Response*. New York: Routledge.

Zenn, J. (2015). "A Biography of Boko Haram and the Bay`a to al-Baghdadi." *CTC Sentinel* 8(3). https://www.ctc.usma.edu/posts/pledging-baya-a-benefit-or-burden-to-the-islamic-state.

CHAPTER 28

THE INTERNATIONAL TRADE NETWORK

Empirics and Modeling

GIORGIO FAGIOLO

INTRODUCTION

IN the second half of the last century, the volume and value generated by the exchange of goods and services across international borders (aka international trade) boomed. During the "second wave of globalization"[1] the share of world trade to gross domestic product (GDP) has more than doubled, increasing from 25 to 60 percent.[2] Such a spectacular trend has been achieved not only *intensively* (i.e., through increases in trade flows between countries already trading in the past), but also *extensively* (i.e., via newly created trade relationships). Indeed, according to the estimates in Felbermayr and Kohler (2006), about 40 percent of world trade growth after 1950 has come from newly established bilateral trading relationships.

This process has generated an intricate web of trade linkages, which currently tightly connects the great majority of world countries, channels a huge economic value, and facilitates cross-border technological differences (Keller, 2004) and global human mobility (Egger et al., 2012). It is therefore of paramount importance to quantitatively understand its structure, as well as its socioeconomic, political, and geographical determinants.

If one thinks of countries as nodes and yearly trade flows as links connecting exporter to importer countries, the web of international trade relationships observed in a given year can be naturally described in terms of a network. If such an exercise is repeated year by year, one ends up with a time sequence of network snapshots. Each snapshot network may be directed (insofar as only import or export relations are considered) and possibly weighted (if the value of import or export flows is associated to the correspondent links to appreciate the heterogeneity of trade intensities).

This idea has a long tradition in economics and political sciences, independent of the development of graph theory in mathematics (West, 2001) and social network analysis (Scott, 2000). For example, Hilgerdt (1943) and Saul (1954) both provide pictorial descriptions of the major flows in international trade and export balances in the form of a static network. Furthermore, in the introduction of the volume by the League of Nations (1942, 7), it is clearly stated: "International trade is much more than the exchange of goods between one country and another; it is an intricate network that cannot be rent without loss" (see also the discussion in De Benedictis and Tajoli, 2011).

Despite such a promising starting point, economists have subsequently been employing network representations of international trade only for descriptive and visualization purposes.[3] Indeed, economic theory traditionally approaches the study of international trade and its determinants with simple theoretical and empirical models, aiming at explaining why and how much a country trades and how geography and country-specific characteristics shape bilateral trade flows between any two countries (van Bergeijk and Brakman, 2010), thus de facto abstracting from consideration about the deep structure of the network of trading relationships. Only recently, with the development of the interdisciplinary research field labeled "network science" (Barabási, 2015), have economists begun to acknowledge the positive and normative relevance of a network approach to international trade. Several contributions have stressed how the detailed structure of trade networks acquires a fundamental importance in explaining issues such as economic globalization and internationalization, the spreading of international crises, and the transmission of economic shocks (Helliwell and Padmore, 1985; Forbes, 2002; Artis et al., 2003). Furthermore, although direct bilateral trade (i.e., dyadic) linkages are known to be one of the most important channels of interaction between world countries (Krugman, 1995), recent studies have suggested that they can only explain a small fraction of the impact that an economic shock originating in a given country can have on another one that is not among its trade partners (Abeysinghe and Forbes, 2005).

All this empirical evidence supports the conjecture that in order to understand international trade and its consequences for macroeconomic dynamics, it is not sufficient to look at each single country in isolation or to the dyadic linkages it has with its trade partners. What is needed instead is a more holistic perspective, in which countries are seen as embedded in the whole web of trade relationships. In such a systemic view of international trade, countries are characterized by not only how much they trade, but also with whom they trade; whether they are systemically important (or central) in the whole web of trade relationships; whether they trade with countries that trade a lot, or trade with pairs of countries that are themselves trade partners; if they are embedded in tightly connected groups (or communities) of countries, relatively disconnected from others; and so forth. Similarly, the importance of a particular dyadic trade relationship cannot be related only to the quantity or value traded and to the properties of the importer and the exporter. Rather, a bilateral trade relationship may acquire relevance insofar it plays an important role in linking groups of countries that otherwise would have been disconnected.

This chapter critically reviews the recent literature quantitatively studying international trade issues from a complex network perspective. We survey three interrelated lines of research.[4] First, after having formally defined what we mean by international trade networks (ITNs) and what the main data sources one can employ are, we discuss the empirical evidence on the topological properties of trade networks. This body of literature is mostly descriptive and aims at providing a deep knowledge of what trade networks look like and where world countries are located within the networks, borrowing methods from statistical physics and social network analysis. Second, we explore some simple models that are able to reproduce some of those empirical properties. We cover both stochastic models of network formation and econometric (micro-founded) formalizations based on gravity models. Finally, we ask whether the way international trade networks are shaped influences macroeconomic dynamics, for example, the spreading of crises or the patterns of country growth and development. We shall see that the answer to this question is firmly positive. On the one hand, this hints at the relevance of international trade linkages in channeling shocks and mediating externalities across world countries. On the other hand, this result suggests that a detailed knowledge of the structure of ITNs is necessary to understand the past and future evolution of its building blocks.

THE INTERNATIONAL TRADE NETWORK

The ITN, also known as the world trade web (WTW) or world trade network (WTN), is a graphic representation of bilateral trade flows among world countries across the years.[5] More formally, consider a set of countries $C^t = \{1, 2, \ldots, N^t\}$ observed at year $t \in \{t_0, \ldots, t_1\}$ and let $e_{ij}^t > 0$ be the value (e.g., in real USD) of total exports from country i to country j in year t. The weighted directed ITN at year t is defined as the network whose set of nodes is C^t, and the list of weighted directed links is given by $E^t = \left\{ e_{ij}^t, \forall (i,j) \in C^t \times C^t, i \neq j \text{ s.t. } e_{ij}^t > 0 \right\}$.

Empirical data to build the time sequence of ITN snapshots are easily available.[6] When possible, aggregate trade values can be broken down in commodity-specific export flows $e_{ij}^t (h)$, where $h = 1, \ldots, H$ is a specific commodity defined at some level of a given hierarchical product classification (e.g., HS or SITC). In such a case, for any year t, one ends up with H different weighted-directed networks. Each network represents the web of international trade linkages among our N^t countries for a particular commodity $h = 1, \ldots, H$. In network jargon, the time sequence of the H product-specific snapshots is called a multilayer network (Kivelä et al., 2014) and can be studied to get insights about the heterogeneity of network structures among traded commodities.

Depending on the specific research questions one is interested in, any given weighted-directed snapshot of the (aggregate or commodity-specific) ITN can be simplified, disregarding either the directed or weighted nature of trade links (or both). For example, if the researcher is interested only in the existence/absence of trade linkages, and not so much in the heterogeneity of their intensities, the ITN can be projected on its binary counterpart, by replacing all existing link weights with 1. This operation generates binary directed graphs, where a link $i \to j$ is present only if country i exports to j. Furthermore, if possible asymmetries between exports from i to j ($i \to j$) and imports of i from j ($j \to i$) are not a key factor in the analysis, one might consider symmetrizing the networks. If the original network is weighted, this might be done by replacing each link weight e^t_{ij} with $\frac{1}{2}(e^t_{ij} + e^t_{ji})$, that is, the arithmetic average of imports and exports. If the network is binary, every time a directed link $i \to j$ does not have its counterpart $j \to i$, the latter may just be added to the edge list. In either cases, one ends up with a symmetrical network.

EMPIRICAL EVIDENCE

The investigation of the topological properties of the ITN and their evolution over time have attracted much attention in the last years. Here we discuss some of the most relevant regularities observed in the data, organized under five topical issues.

Connectivity and Assortativity

The ITN is a very dense graph compared to other real-world networks; its density is close to $\frac{1}{2}$, meaning that half of all possible bilateral relations are not exploited. In other words, most countries do not trade with all the others, but rather select their partners. In the period 1950–2000, the ITN showed a marked increase in the number of directed linkages and a (weak) positive trend in density (Garlaschelli and Loffredo, 2005; De Benedictis and Tajoli, 2011). This occurs irrespective of whether one does or does not factor in any increase in the number of countries in the sample, due, for example, to improvements in data collection or newborn countries. Therefore, trade globalization has not only increased the connections among countries that were already trading back in 1950, but also, by embedding in the trade web the newcomers over the years, has induced a stronger trade integration.

The ITN is also a very heterogenous network. For example, the distribution of the number of export and import partners of each country (i.e., in-degree and out-degree in network jargon) has become more and more bimodal over the years, with a group of very tightly connected countries coexisting with another group holding a smaller number of inward and outward links, thus preventing reference to a representative country in terms of trade patterns. Note also that the distribution of country imports, exports, and total trade all follow log-normal densities (Fagiolo et al., 2008), implying that a few countries exporting and importing a great deal exist side by side with many countries characterized by very low trade levels.

Furthermore, the ITN exhibits a disassortative nature: countries that have many trade partners typically trade with countries having a few links (Fagiolo et al., 2010). This is relatively less true from a weighted perspective: countries that import or export a lot tend to do so from and to countries characterized by low export and import levels, but there is a small number of very intensively connected countries trading with very similar partners.

Modularity

Despite trade globalization, the ITN is still a strongly modular network. For geographic, economic, and political reasons, over time countries have been forming relatively stable modular patterns of multilateral trade relations, possibly interacting among them, which can be easily identified through network analysis. A first interesting property is that countries that trade more tend to form intense trade triangles in their neighborhoods (i.e., clustering patterns; cf. Fagiolo, 2007). This hints at the presence of a core of tightly connected countries in the ITN (Fan et al., 2014). Indeed, at least in the year 2000, the ten richest countries in terms of total trade were responsible for about 40 percent of the total trade flows, a strong indication in favor of the existence of a rich club in the weighted ITN. More generally, community-detection techniques (Fortunato, 2010) allow us to identify several clusters of countries forming tightly connected trade groups, each relatively disconnected from the others (Barigozzi et al., 2011; Piccardi and Tajoli, 2015). These groups tend to mimic geographical partitions of the world in macro areas but have less overlap with existing preferential trade agreements (PTAs), confirming previous findings hinting at an ambiguous role of PTAs in explaining trade (Rose, 2004). Despite communities of countries in the ITN being easy to identify, their statistical significance is still an open issue (Piccardi and Tajoli, 2012). Indeed, intercommunity linkages are far from being irrelevant, providing support for the ITN as a globalized trading system.

Aggregate versus Commodity-Specific Networks

Do commodity-specific trade networks display properties similar to the aggregate ITN? Putting it in another way, are the network properties observed for total trade due to aggregation of heterogeneous commodity-specific networks? To answer this question, Barigozzi et al. (2010) have analyzed the ITNs for ninety-seven commodities in the period 1992 to 2003. Focusing on the fourteen most-traded commodities, which make up almost 60 percent of total trade, they find that commodity-specific networks are strongly heterogeneous and statistically different from the aggregate one. For example, country import and export distributions are almost never log-normally distributed, suggesting that their observed shapes in the aggregate ITN are generated as a sheer outcome of aggregation. Commodity-specific networks also display average connectivity and clustering patterns very different from their aggregate counterpart. Interestingly, many commodity-specific layers of the ITN are not even fully connected.[7] This means that when considering trade for specific commodities, there are disconnected islands of countries trading in them. Connectivity at the aggregate level is mainly achieved through the presence of many weak links that keep commodity-specific networks together. More recently, the properties of commodity-specific trade networks have been explored in the context of certain important families of products (e.g., food and water-intensive commodities; see Dalin et al., 2012; D'Odorico et al., 2014). Using data on international trade of food products, links between countries in the global food network can be weighted either by their caloric content or by the virtual transfer of water used for their production. These studies show that in the period 1986–2009, both the total amount of food calories and the volume of virtual water traded internationally (which is about one-fourth of total food production for human consumption) more than doubled. This increase in trade volumes went hand in hand with increases in water use efficiency of food trade (i.e., food calories produced per unit volume of water used), especially for the richest countries, possibly due to the use of more efficient technologies. Overall, the recent dynamics of international food trade seem to have been beneficial for regional and global food security, despite the huge geographic reorganizations that food trade networks have been undergoing in the last decades (e.g., Asia switching from North America to South America as its main partner; North America increasingly orienting itself toward more intraregional trade patterns; the increase in China's virtual water imports). However, the overall implications of such changes are difficult to predict on a global scale, as they can impact very different spheres of the socioeconomic and environmental fabric of the planet (e.g., increase in food imports may require higher production rates to be concentrated in environmentally fragile ecosystems).

Network Evolution

As mentioned above, the ITN experienced some structural changes over the second decade of the twentieth century. Trade globalization occurred through intensive and extensive processes, leading to a denser but more bimodal network, with a stronger core. This does not mean, however, that the periphery of the network has become more and more marginal (De Benedictis and Tajoli, 2011). Indeed, both the overall betweenness centralization of the network (Vega Redondo, 2007) and the average path length between the countries (Albert and Barabási, 2002) have been decreasing over time, meaning that hubs have become less important and countries formerly located in the periphery have moved closer to the core, not necessarily through exclusive trade connections made with the hubs.

Interestingly, He and Deem (2010) connect these changes with the ability of the ITN to recover after worldwide crises, such as the 2007–2008 global financial crisis. Their model shows that the modular structure induced by trade globalization in the ITN is responsible for the fact that the ITN is more sensitive nowadays to shocks than it was forty years ago. Furthermore, its ability to recover after the crisis has been greatly reduced, hinting at a higher sensitivity to trade costs associated with long-distance links or a tendency toward protectionism.

Even though trade globalization induced structural changes in the ITN in the period 1950–2000, one can still hope to learn from the past evolution of the network to project its future evolution. Indeed, as shown in Fagiolo et al. (2009), the Markovian nature of the ITN dynamics allows us to predict its long-run state. Their analysis suggests that the architecture of the ITN will probably evolve toward a more polarized (Pareto) distribution for link weights (i.e., export flows), implying an increasingly large majority of links carrying moderate trade flows and a small bulk of very intense trade linkages.

Trade Imbalances

A network approach to international trade may be applied not only to the network of import/export relationships between countries, but also to their patterns of bilateral imbalances (Serrano et al., 2007). A way to do this is to replace link weights e^t_{ij} in the ITN with the absolute value of the difference between exports and imports, that is, $t^t_{ij} = \left| e^t_{ij} - e^t_{ji} \right|$. The resulting network, also known as the trade imbalance network (TIN), is symmetrical by construction. To remove any country-size effect (i.e., higher trade imbalances for larger countries), one may consider dividing t^t_{ij} by total bilateral trade $(e^t_{ij} + e^t_{ji})$ and weight the links by this quantity. The resulting network is known as the relative TIN (or RTIN). Comparing the properties of the TIN and RTIN reveals interesting regularities (Dueñas and Fagiolo, 2014). For example, the TIN is characterized by a hierarchical arrangement wherein a few developed economies display high clustering and carry an important amount of global-trade imbalances. In contrast, the RTIN exhibits a fragmented topology, with poorly concentrated clustering that is particularly high for developing countries. More generally, developing economies have more asymmetrical relationships with other developing countries, implying that they might face higher volatility. Conversely, developed economies have on average more symmetrical relationships. While this may result in more stability, developed economies may still be subject to volatility through their connections with developing economies, which turn out to be a major driver for the asymmetries in world trade.

This analysis, however, does not take into account that many countries have aggregate surpluses only because they serve as middlemen. For example, the Netherlands has an aggregate trade surplus because it serves as a hub in the trade network, importing from the rest of the world and exporting to many other countries, with most of the import value just transiting toward the final importer. To clean these indirect effects from the network, Krings et al. (2014) developed an indicator that is able to reveal the ultimate trade debtors and creditors of a country and applied it to the study of trade imbalances in the European Union. As expected, they have found that final surpluses (net of the effect of countries such as the Netherlands) are typically more concentrated than original ones. For example, only France, Spain, and the United Kingdom have an ultimate deficit toward Germany. This is important to identify the portfolio of countries with which to discuss possible adjustment plans.

Models

The huge body of descriptive contributions investigating the emergence of statistical regularities in the topology of the ITN has spurred a parallel literature that explores the theoretical roots of such stylized facts. There are three main approaches to the quest for models explaining the properties and evolution of the ITN. The first one draws from probability theory and aims at fitting null statistical models to the data. The second one employs econometric models of bilateral trade (e.g., the gravity model, cf. Anderson, 2011) to fit the structure of the ITN. Finally, the third one develops theoretical models of (stochastic) network dynamics to understand if their limit properties can reproduce the observed ones.

Null Models

The first stream of theoretical research on the ITN aims at identifying observed statistical properties that cannot be produced by sheer randomness. This approach develops "null" statistical models that generate, for each yearly snapshot of the ITN, an ensemble of binary and weighted networks that only preserve some features of the observed ITN and are otherwise purely random (Squartini et al., 2011a, 2011b; Fronczak and Fronczak, 2012). By comparing the observed ITN snapshot to the distribution of ITN instances generated by the null model, one may infer which properties are significantly different from what the null model would have predicted, and which ones instead cannot be discriminated from noise. A key ingredient of null models concerns the features of the observed ITN that are to be preserved. Indeed, one may be increasingly demanding in picking these features and require the null model to preserve only the density of the graph (as in the Erdos-Renyi model; cf. Erdős and Rényi, 1960), the distribution or exact sequence of node degrees (Maslov and Sneppen, 2002) or node strengths (Squartini and Garlaschelli, 2011), all the way to the exact binary topology. Of course, as the constraints on the null model become more stringent, the role of randomness becomes weaker, as the degree of freedom in generating a graph satisfying all the constraints decreases. For the sake of economic interpretation, constraints should provide some minimal realism to the null model, as they prevent the null hypothesis allowing for economically unrealistic trade networks. For example, if in the undirected ITN one does not constrain for the exact node strength sequence (i.e., total country imports plus exports), it may well be the case that, among all possible null instances, there would be a graph in which the flow of trade between the United States and Canada (i.e., the largest in the world) is randomly assigned to a trading relationship between Vanuatu and Iceland, quite an unlikely match! A null-model analysis of the ITN provides interesting insights. For example, Squartini et al. (2013) show that most of the properties of the binary ITN (e.g., disassortativity) can be easily replicated by a null model preserving only country degrees. This means that knowing the number of country trade partners is sufficient to explain why countries trading with more partners trade with countries that instead trade with fewer countries. Conversely, the exact sequence of country total imports and exports (i.e., node strengths) is not enough to reproduce the properties of the network at the weighted level, as knowledge of the binary structure is also required (Mastrandrea et al., 2014a; Almog et al., 2015). This points to the importance of explaining why countries begin to trade among each other, rather than how much they trade given that a trade relationship has been established (Felbermayr and Kohler, 2006; Mastrandrea et al., 2014b).

Gravity Models and Trade Networks

The gravity model (GM) is the workhorse for much empirical research in international trade (Head and Mayer, 2013). The GM is extremely successful in explaining variation in bilateral trade flows due to country-specific characteristics, as well as bilateral and multilateral factors. Furthermore, it is backed up by solid theoretical micro-foundations: a gravity-like equation can be derived starting from trade specialization models, monopolistic-competition frameworks with intra-industry trade, or Hecksher-Ohlin models (De Benedictis and Taglioni, 2011). In its simplest formulation, the GM states that bilateral trade flows are proportional to the product of origin and destination country GDP, divided by geographical distance between the two countries, where the latter proxies for all trade frictions impeding free trade (e.g., tariffs). This simple idea can be complicated by adding more covariates (e.g., country population and landlocking effects, common language and religion, past colonial ties, existence of preferential trade agreements, synthetic measures accounting for country remoteness) and making more sophisticated the econometric specification that is applied to the data (e.g., testing the model with panel data allowing for fixed country and bilateral effects, using nonlinear estimators, allowing for zero-trade flows in the estimation).

The GM typically attains a very high goodness of fit, both cross-sectionally and longitudinally and therefore configures itself as *the* natural candidate to model the ITN structure. This idea has been explored in Fagiolo (2010) and Dueñas and Fagiolo (2013). They fit to bilateral trade data a gravity model and used both predicted trade flows and residuals to weight the links. This allowed the authors to build a predicted ITN (in which links are weighted using predicted trade flows from the GM) and a residual ITN (in which links are weighted using the residuals from the GM regressions). Results indicate that the GM is a good model for the ITN only when the binary structure is known and kept coincident with the observed one. In this case, the structures of predicted and observed weighted ITNs are highly similar. However, the GM is not able to satisfactorily predict the binary structure of the ITN, that is, the probability that a link is present. Note that the binary structure is indeed the ITN feature that research on null models has found to be central in explaining the weighted structure of the ITN (see above).

Furthermore, when one removes the variance in bilateral flows and weights the existing ITN links with the residual from a GM fit, the resulting network is far from being random. On the contrary, it displays marked signatures of a complex system and is characterized by a topological architecture very different from the observed one (Fagiolo, 2010). For example, whereas the original ITN displays a structure with a few large-sized country hubs and a relatively strong connectivity among nearby countries (either geographically, socially, politically, or economically), the residual ITN is organized around many relatively small-sized but trade-oriented countries that, independently of their geographical position, either play the role of local hubs or attract large and rich countries in complex trade interaction patterns. To get a feel for this result, note that standard regression theory only requires residual link weights to be uncorrelated between them. In other words, the residuals from exports from country A to country B will be uncorrelated with residuals from C to A trade. Such a dyadic-level requirement does not prevent residuals from exhibiting some nontrivial higher-order patterns, for example at the level of triads and higher-order node groups. This explains why after having removed from link weights the effects of country GDP, geographical distance, and many other possible explanatory variables, significant nontrivial network structure still exists, a further indication that network structure matters in explaining trade incidence, values, and volumes. This intuition was applied to the data by Ward et al. (2013), who expanded a standard gravity model with "latent space" networks in order to account for higher-order dependencies in trade flows, such as reciprocity (i.e., exports from A to B can be correlated with exports from B to A) and clustering (i.e., the fact that A exports to both B and C increases the probability that B and C trade between them). Results strongly indicate that taking into account higher-order network effects in gravity models allows for a substantial improvement in both their in-sample and out-of-sample predictive performance.

Stochastic Models of Trade Network Dynamics

In addition to statistical null models and econometric gravity specifications, a third stream of theoretical research has employed theoretical models of network dynamics in order to reproduce and explain the structure and evolution of the ITN. Being rooted in the econophysics literature (see Sinha et al., 2010, for an introduction), such models are based on simple (and often economically unrealistic) assumptions about the trading behavior of firms and countries and their interactions. Nonetheless, they have been typically successful in deriving long-run (limit) implications for the distributions of the main network statistics, which are in line with observed regularities. An example of this approach is the model developed by Riccaboni and Schiavo (2010). They describe the evolution of the ITN as a set of (stochastic) transactions of different magnitude occurring among countries. They decouple the processes of link formation and weight growth by assuming that the first follows a preferential-attachment mechanism (Barabási and Albert, 1999),[8] whereas the second is governed by an independent geometric Brownian motion, much in the spirit of the law of proportionate effects in the firm-growth literature (Ijiri and Simon, 1977). Despite its simplicity, the model is able to correctly predict several statistical regularities pertaining to the ITN, including the intensity and growth distribution of links, the relationship between the size of link weights and the variance of their growth rates, and the correlation between country degrees and strengths.

Impact on Macroeconomic Dynamics

In the previous sections we have discussed the empirical literature uncovering the structure and evolution of the ITN, as well as some work addressing from a theoretical perspective the issue of reproduction and explanation of the observed statistical regularities that characterize the ITN. Here we ask whether the structure of the ITN can affect macroeconomic dynamics. More precisely, we are interested in investigating if the way countries are directly and indirectly connected in the ITN, their overall position and embeddedness in the network, and more generally the binary and weighted topology of the ITN, can constrain and influence the processes going on *over* the ITN. These may include, for example, economic growth and development of countries and macro-regions, as well as diffusion of shocks that originate locally and possibly percolate globally.

Although the answers to these questions are in general positive, indicating that networks matter in explaining macroeconomic dynamics, the identification of causal linkages going from network structure to dynamic processes over the network can be strongly limited by endogeneity issues. Indeed, network structure can affect macroeconomic dynamics, but the latter is likely in turn to change the network structure over time. For example, the level of country integration in the ITN may well affect future development, but countries growing more may also become more embedded in the ITN as a result of economic development.

Diffusion of Shocks in the International Trade Network

Since international trade is one of the most important channels of interaction among world countries, and data are easily available at a sufficient level of commodity disaggregation for a long time span, the ITN has often been used as a testing ground to understand how locally originated shocks differ throughout the system. The idea is very simple. Suppose that countries are connected via weighted trade links, as proxied by a time snapshot of the ITN, and that a negative shock hits a given country. Assume a set of rules that govern the way in which this initial shock is transmitted to the neighbors of the shocked country, to the neighbors of neighbors, and so on. By shocking one after the other to reach all world countries and observing each time how shock diffusion evolves, impacts other countries, and possibly dies away, one may understand the relative importance of each country as a crisis propagator. Following this intuition, Lee et al. (2011) studied a simple dynamic model of shock diffusion over the ITN. In the model, countries are characterized by their capacity (proxied by their GDP). Every time a negative shock hits a country, all its incoming and outgoing link weights are decreased by a certain percentage. If the decrease in total country trade exceeds some fraction of its capacity, the shock is transmitted to all its trade neighbors. This may initiate an avalanche of shocks, as some of the neighbors can then transmit the shock to their neighbors. The process terminates when all countries hit by the shock do not transmit it to any other additional country. An interesting statistic describing the diffusion process is the number of countries that are eventually hit by an initial shock that originated in a given country (call it "avalanche size"). Interestingly, the authors show that there is a certain range of model parameters that allow the avalanche-size distribution to become a power law (i.e., a Pareto distribution). This implies that countries play very heterogeneous roles in their ability to propagate local crises through the system, and there is a small but not irrelevant number of countries that, once hit by a shock, are able to diffuse it worldwide. Big countries (in terms of GDP) tend to be the most disruptive, but this is not the end of the story. Indeed, the position of the country in the ITN and its local embeddedness in the web of indirect connections play a very crucial role in explaining avalanche size. This is because the way in which countries may be hit by a shock and transmit it to their neighbors may be either direct or indirect. It is direct if the link with the neighbor that has transmitted the shock is so strong, as compared to its GDP, that the capacity threshold is exceeded right away. Conversely, the shock transmission may be indirect if, for example, country A withstands a first shock transmitted by neighbor B, but then it is hit by a second shock transmitted by neighbor C, who is also a neighbor of B, which was hit by the shock transmitted by B and did not withstand it, thus transmitting it to its neighbors, among which is A. All countries belonging to any single avalanche can then be associated with a direct versus indirect chain of diffusion. By repeating this exercise for all major avalanches generated in the simulations, Lee et al. (2011) show that indirect patterns account for a very large percentage of chains of reaction. This confirms that second- and third-order effects in the ITN are crucial to understand how shocks propagate in the system (Abeysinghe and Forbes, 2005).

A shock that reduces country size or capacity is not the only type of negative distress that can impact the ITN. For example, one may consider shocks that reduce bilateral exports from one country to another by a certain fraction; terminate bilateral trade between any two countries (e.g., caused by wars or trade embargoes); or a worst-case scenario, in which a country ceases to trade with all other countries (i.e., as if the node were removed from the network). To assess the vulnerability of the ITN to these different types of distress, Foti et al. (2013) studied a simple model of diffusion in which, after the system is shocked, a local rebalancing of supply and demand is assumed to occur in order to mitigate the effects of the shock. In the model, shocks may occur randomly or can be targeted according to the importance of nodes (e.g., in terms of their degree). Overall, the ITN is found to be quite a robust network for random attacks, but very fragile if the shock is more likely to target nodes that are among the most connected. This robust-yet-fragile feature also characterizes financial networks (Haldane, 2013). Furthermore, higher connectivity (e.g., density) is shown to be beneficial when the shock is small, but very dangerous in the face of a large distress, when stronger connectivity leads to broader contagion. This ability of the ITN to absorb a shock up to a given size casts some doubts on the positive effects of globalization. On the one hand, a more connected ITN can allow less developed countries to better cope with weak, regional shocks. On the other hand, a more interdependent trade system can favor a quicker and ampler propagation of large shocks, potentially leading to worldwide trade crises. In fact, there is considerable empirical evidence showing that the ITN, especially at a commodity-specific level, is becoming more and more vulnerable to systemic disruptions. For example, consider the staple-food trade network, that is, bilateral trade links and flows concerning food commodities such as wheat and rice. As Puma et al. (2015) show, over the period 1992–2009 the number of links in the wheat and rice trade networks grew by 42 percent and 90 percent, respectively. This increased connectivity makes both networks more exposed to systemic, large-scale disruptions. Indeed, simulations superimposing continental-scale shocks on the wheat and rice trade networks lead to extremely discouraging results. Very large losses in global wheat and rice exports at both the extensive and intensive level are to be expected. Even more worrying, the least developed countries are expected to suffer the greatest import losses, since large-scale shocks make them more dependent on imports for staple food.

Trade Networks, Economic Growth, and Development

It is well-known that trade is one of the potential explanatory factors of the variation in economic performance across countries (Frankel and Romer, 1999; Alcalá and Ciccone, 2004). Traditionally, the empirical strategy employed to elicit the trade-performance link was to regress measures of country income or growth against openness to trade (defined as the ratio of country imports and exports to GDP), after taking care of potential endogeneity biases. In network jargon, openness to trade is just country total strength in the ITN divided by GDP, that is, an indicator of one-step connectivity or local node centrality. To take this idea one step further, one might ask whether the overall integration of a country in the ITN, for example in terms of global centrality, can explain its performance, beyond what local measures of connectivity like trade openness can do. This is a natural question in light of the empirical and theoretical evidence stressing the relevance of indirect connections in the ITN and the importance of higher-order structure in channeling cascading events (see above). Kali and Reyes (2007) and Duernecker et al. (2012) address this issue, employing standard panel-regression frameworks—in which country growth rates are regressed against trade openness and a set of other controls concerning, for example, human and physical capital endowment, institutional quality, and geography—and augmenting them with network-related, country-specific measures of local and global node connectivity and centrality. These studies find that network-based country measures are in general statistically and economically significant and increase the power of the regression above that obtained using only the traditional covariates. Furthermore, net of the effect of trade openness and potential endogeneity caused by omitted-variable biases and reverse-causation effects, the overall embeddedness of a country in the ITN, and therefore its integration in the network of global trade, appears to significantly boost country performance and has substantial implications for economic development. A similar insight also comes from Reyes et al. (2010), who have compared the development patterns of high-performing Asian economies (HPAEs) and Latin American (LATAM) countries over the last decades. They suggest that the observed differences in the economic performance of these regions are mirrored by the evolution of their international economic integration process in the global trade web, as characterized from a network perspective, and not so much by their trade openness. Indeed, HPAEs have been moving from the periphery of the network toward its core, thus becoming more and more integrated into the world economy through the years. Conversely, LATAM countries have increased their degree of trade openness without attaining a higher degree of international economic integration in the ITN. Therefore, the benefits from integration (i.e., technology spillovers and diversification of economic activity) have not materialized.

The position of world countries in the ITN has also been shown to potentially explain the differences in financial crises, as well as stock market synchronicity. In an influential paper, Kali and Reyes (2010) studied how country stock market performance over a certain crisis window depends on both its centrality in the ITN and centrality in the ITN of the epicenter of the crisis (in addition to standard macroeconomic determinants of currency, banking, and financial crises). They show that the more the epicenter is central in the ITN, the more a crisis is amplified. However, when a country is hit by a crisis, a higher centrality is beneficial, as idue to a diversification effect, it allows for a better and wider dissipation of the impact. Furthermore, Adarov et al. (2009) show that country centrality in the ITN is associated with greater stock market synchronicity for the majority of world countries, typically the most peripheral. However, those at the top of centrality ranks (i.e., the United Kingdom, Germany, France, Italy, China, and Japan) experience uniformly less synchronicity in their financial markets than noncore countries, suggesting a "decoupling" that may have implications in terms of susceptibility to global financial shocks.

Concluding Remarks

In this chapter we have discussed complex-network approaches to the study of international trade. We have argued that describing international trade flows using graph-like representations is not only useful from a visualization purpose, but also offers several empirical and theoretical insights. Overall, moving from the traditional approach, focusing only on bilateral relationships, to a new, more holistic one, in which countries and trade are seen as embedded in a complex web of relationships, allows us to (1) identify a wealth of additional and nontrivial empirical properties concerning higher-order structures in the ITN; and (2) show that these higher-order structures, and more generally the relative positions of countries in the ITN, have substantial implications for country performance and shock diffusion.

The main take-home message is therefore that networks do matter in international trade: direct and indirect connections among countries, as well as modular structures in the web of bilateral trade flows, are indeed relevant to understanding not only international trade issues, but more generally macroeconomic dynamics.

Since bilateral trade is one of the most important (and best measured) channels of interactions among countries, the ITN has been extensively used as a testing ground to study the extent to which the structure of the network affects the change in country economic profiles over time.

From a complex-network perspective, considering all these interaction dimensions together means building a time sequence of multilayer networks (Kivelä et al., 2014). In other words, every time snapshot of a multilayer network is composed of a finite number of nodes (i.e., countries) that may be connected by several different types of links, each representing a different interaction channel (i.e., trade, finance, migration, etc.).

Studying how multilayer macroeconomic networks evolve over time represents a challenging research line and a natural extension of the work surveyed in this chapter. Indeed, the properties of all these interaction layers have been explored independently of each other, with a few exceptions regarding the investigation of the causal links between migration and trade networks (Fagiolo and Mastrorillo, 2014; Sgrignoli et al., 2015). More generally, a multilayer approach to macroeconomic networks would allow us to better understand how different interaction channels correlate among them and cause each other. Furthermore, one might extend standard network indicators of node importance (e.g., centrality) to the case of a multilayer network (Boccaletti et al., 2014) and thus characterize the position of a country in the whole multilayer, and not only in each separate layer. This would allow one to dig deeper into the relationship between the role of a country in the network and its economic performance.

Notes

1. By "second wave of globalization" we mean the period from 1945 onward, as opposed to the "first wave of globalization" (1800–1914). The two waves are separated by a slump in international trade that occurred between the two world wars.
2. World Development Indicators Online (WDI) database, http://data.worldbank.org/datacatalog/world-development-indicators.
3. A more quantitative approach to the study of trade in terms of networks has been followed in sociology and political science. For example, the seminal paper by Snyder and Kick (1979) triggered a fruitful literature mostly aimed at testing some flavor of "world system" or "dependency" theories using social network analysis techniques; see, for example, Nemeth and Smith (1985), Sacks et al. (2001), Breiger (1981), Smith and White (1992), Kim and Shin (2002), and Mahutga (2006), and the discussion in Fagiolo et al. (2010, section 3).
4. Due to space constraints, our survey is necessarily limited and largely nonexhaustive. For example, we are not able to properly account for the vast literature on trade networks and international relations (Wilkinson, 2002; Hafner-Burton et al., 2009), including conflict (Polachek, 1980; Dorussen and Ward, 2010; Kinne, 2012), as well as for the literature on input-output networks (Alatriste Contreras and Fagiolo, 2014; Cerina et al., 2015) and global commodity chains (Gereffi, 1999), among others.
5. In this chapter we deal mostly with trade of goods and commodities. Service trade is still poorly analyzed from a complex-network perspective (De Benedictis et al., 2013), mostly because of a lack of reliable data that cover a large number of countries for a sufficiently long period of time.
6. See, for example, COMTRADE (comtrade.un.org), the BACI data set at CEPII (cepii.fr), or data on trade in goods and services at UNCTAD (unctadstat.unctad.org). Additional data are available from individual researchers, such as Andrew Rose (http://faculty.haas.berkeley.edu/arose/), Kristian Gleditsch (privatewww.essex.ac.uk/~ksg/, Robert Feenstra (cid.econ.ucdavis.edu), and Arvind Subramanian and Shang-Jin Wei (users.nber.org/~wei/data.html).
7. A network is said to be connected if any two of its nodes are linked by a path of directed or undirected edges.
8. In other words, they assume that for each country, the probability of exporting a new product/destination increases in the number of existing relationships.

References

Abeysinghe, T., and Forbes, K. (2005). "Trade Linkages and Output-Multiplier Effects: A Structural VAR Approach with a Focus on Asia." *Review of International Economics* 13: 356–375.

Adarov, A., Kali, R., and Reyes, J. (2009). "Stock Market Synchronicity and the Global Trade Network: A Random-Walk Approach." Working paper, Department of Economics, Sam M. Walton College of Business, University of Arkansas, Fayetteville.

Alatriste Contreras, M. G., and Fagiolo, G. (2014). "Propagation of Economic Shocks in Input-Output Networks: A Cross-Country Analysis." *Physical Review E* 90(December): 062812.

Albert, R., and Barabási, A.-L. (2002). "Statistical Mechanics of Complex Networks." *Review of Modern Physics* 74: 47–97.

Alcalá, F., and Ciccone, A. (2004). "Trade and Productivity." *Quarterly Journal of Economics* 119: 612–645.

Almog, A., Squartini, T., and Garlaschelli, D. (2015). "A GDP-Driven Model for the Binary and Weighted Structure of the International Trade Network." *New Journal of Physics* 17: 013009.

Anderson, J. E. (2011). "The Gravity Model." *Annual Review of Economics* 3: 133–160.

Artis, M., Galvão, A.-B., and Marcellino, M. (2003). "The Transmission Mechanism in a Changing World." Economics Working Papers ECO2003/18. European University Institute.

Barabási, A.-L. (2015). *Network Science*. Cambridge, UK: Cambridge University Press.

Barabási, A.-L., and Albert, R. (1999). "Emergence of Scaling in Random Networks." *Science* 286: 509–512.

Barigozzi, M., Fagiolo, G., and Garlaschelli, D. (2010). "The Multi-Network of International Trade: A Commodity-Specific Analysis." *Physical Review E* 81: 046104.

Barigozzi, M., Fagiolo, G., and Mangioni, G. (2011). "Identifying the Community Structure of the International-Trade Multi Network." *Physica A* 390: 2051–2066.

Boccaletti, S., Bianconi, G., Criado, R., del Genio, C., Gómez-Gardeñes, J., Romance, M., Sendiña-Nadal, I., Wang, Z., and Zanin, M. (2014). "The Structure and Dynamics of Multilayer Networks." *Physics Reports* 544: 1–122.

Breiger, R. (1981). "Structure of Economic Interdependence among Nations." In *Continuities in Structural Inquiry*, edited by P. M. Blau and R. K. Merton, pp. 353–380. Newbury Park, CA: Sage.

Cerina, F., Zhu, Z., Chessa, A., and Riccaboni, M. (2015). "World Input-Output Network." *PLOS ONE* 10: e0134025.

Dalin, C., Konar, M., Hanasaki, N., Rinaldo, A., and Rodriguez-Iturbe, I. (2012). "Evolution of the Global Virtual Water Trade Network." *Proceedings of the National Academy of Sciences* 109: 5989–5994.

De Benedictis, L., Nenci, S., Santoni, G., Tajoli, L., and Vicarelli, C. (2013). "Network Analysis of World Trade Using the BACI-CEPII Dataset." Working Papers 2013–24. CEPII.

De Benedictis, L., and Taglioni, D. (2011). "The Gravity Model in International Trade." In *The Trade Impact of European Union Preferential Policies*, edited by L. De Benedictis and L. Salvatici, pp. 55–89. Berlin and Heidelberg: Springer.

De Benedictis, L., and Tajoli, L. (2011). "The World Trade Network." *The World Economy* 34: 1417–1454.

D'Odorico, P., Carr, J. A., Laio, F., Ridolfi, L., and Vandoni, S. (2014). "Feeding Humanity Through Global Food Trade." *Earth's Future* 2: 458–469.

Dorussen, H., and Ward, H. (2010). "Trade Networks and the Kantian Peace." *Journal of Peace Research* 47: 29 42.

Dueñas, M., and Fagiolo, G. (2013). "Modeling the International-Trade Network: A Gravity Approach." *Journal of Economic Interaction and Coordination* 8(1): 155–178.

Dueñas, M., and Fagiolo, G. (2014). "Global Trade Imbalances: A Network Approach." *Advances in Complex System* 17: 1–19.

Duernecker, G., Meyer, M., and Vega-Redondo, F. (2012). "Being Close to Grow Faster: A Network-Based Empirical Analysis of Economic Globalization." Economics Working Papers ECO2012/05. European University Institute.

Egger, P. H., von Ehrlich, M., and Nelson, D. R. (2012). "Migration and Trade." *The World Economy* 35: 216–241.

Erdős, P., and Rényi, A. (1960). "On the Evolution of Random Graphs." *Publication of the Mathematical Institute of the Hungarian Academy of Sciences* 5: 17–61.

Fagiolo, G. (2007). "Clustering in Complex Directed Networks." *Physical Review E* 76: 026107.

Fagiolo, G. (2010). "The International-Trade Network: Gravity Equations and Topological Properties." *Journal of Economic Interaction and Coordination* 5: 1–25.

Fagiolo, G., and Mastrorillo, M. (2014). "Does Human Migration Affect International Trade? A Complex-Network Perspective." *PLOS ONE* 9: 1–11.

Fagiolo, G., Schiavo, S., and Reyes, J. (2008). "On the Topological Properties of the World Trade Web: A Weighted Network Analysis." *Physica A* 387: 3868–3873.

Fagiolo, G., Schiavo, S., and Reyes, J. (2009). "World-trade Web: Topological Properties, Dynamics, and Evolution." *Physical Review E* 79: 036115.

Fagiolo, G., Schiavo, S., and Reyes, J. (2010). "The Evolution of the World Trade Web: A Weighted-Network Approach." *Journal of Evolutionary Economics* 20: 479–514.

Fan, Y., Ren, S., Cai, H., and Cui, X. (2014). "The State's Role and Position in International Trade: A Complex Network Perspective." *Economic Modelling* 39: 71–81.

Felbermayr, G. J., and Kohler, W. (2006). "Exploring the Intensive and Extensive Margins of World Trade." *Review of World Economics (Weltwirtschaftliches Archiv)* 142: 642–674.

Forbes, K. (2002). "Are Trade Linkages Important Determinants of Country Vulnerability to Crises?" In *Preventing Currency Crises in Emerging Markets*, edited by S. Edwards and J. A. Frankel, pp. 77–132, Chicago: University of Chicago Press.

Fortunato, S. (2010). "Community Detection in Graphs." *Physics Reports* 486: 75–174.

Foti, N. J., Pauls, S., and Rockmore, D. N. (2013). "Stability of the World Trade Web Over Time—An Extinction Analysis." *Journal of Economic Dynamics and Control* 37: 1889–1910.

Frankel, J. A., and Romer, D. H. (1999). "Does Trade Cause Growth?" *American Economic Review* 89: 379–399.

Fronczak, A., and Fronczak, P. (2012). "Statistical Mechanics of the International Trade Network." *Physical Review E* 85: 056113.

Garlaschelli, D., and Loffredo, M. (2005). "Structure and Evolution of the World Trade Network." *Physica A* 355: 138–144.

Gereffi, G. (1999). "International Trade and Industrial Upgrading in the Apparel Commodity Chain." *Journal of International Economics* 48: 37–70.

Hafner-Burton, E. M., Kahler, M., and Montgomery, A. H. (2009). "Network Analysis for International Relations." *International Organization* 63(July): 559–592.

Haldane, A. G. (2013). "Rethinking the financial Network." In *Fragile Stabilität—stabile Fragilität*, edited by S. A. Jansen, E. Schröter and N. Stehr, pp. 243–278. Wiesbaden: Springer Fachmedien.

He, J., and Deem, M. W. (2010). "Structure and Response in the World Trade Network." *Physical Review Letters* 105: 198701.

Head, K., and Mayer, T. (2013). "Gravity Equations: Workhorse, Toolkit, and Cookbook." CEPR Discussion Papers 9322. C.E.P.R.

Helliwell, J. F., and Padmore, T. (1985). "Empirical Studies of Macroeconomic Interdependence." In *Handbook of International Economies*, edited by R. Jones and P. Kenen, pp. 1107–1151, Elsevier Science Publishers B.V.

Hilgerdt, F. (1943). "The Case for Multilateral Trade." *American Economic Review* 33: 393–407.

Ijiri, Y., and Simon, H. A. (1977). *Skew Distributions and Sizes of Business Firms. Studies in Mathematical and Managerial Economics* 24. New York: North-Holland.

Kali, R., and Reyes, J. (2007). "The Architecture of Globalization: A Network Approach to International Economic Integration." *Journal of International Business Studies* 38: 595–620.

Kali, R., and Reyes, J. (2010). "Financial Contagion on the International Trade Network." *Economic Inquiry* 48: 1072–1101.

Keller, W. (2004). "International Technology Diffusion." *Journal of Economic Literature* 42: 752–782.

Kim, S., and Shin, E.-H. (2002). "A Longitudinal Analysis of Globalization and Regionalization in International Trade: A Social Network Approach." *Social Forces* 81: 445–471.

Kinne, B. J. (2012). "Multilateral Trade and Militarized Conflict: Centrality, Openness, and Asymmetry in the Global Trade Network." *Journal of Politics* 74: 308–322.

Kivelä, M., Arenas, A., Barthelemy, M., Gleeson, J. P., Moreno, Y., and Porter, M. A. (2014). "Multilayer Networks." *Journal of Complex Networks* 2: 203–271.

Krings, G. M., Carpantier, J.-F., and Delvenne, J.-C. (2014). "Trade Integration and Trade Imbalances in the European Union: A Network Perspective." *PLOS ONE* 9: e83448.

Krugman, P. (1995). "Growing World Trade: Causes and Consequences." *Brookings Papers on Economic Activity* 26: 327–377.

League of Nations. (1942). *The World Trade Network*. Princeton, NJ: Princeton University Press.

Lee, K.-M., Yang, J.-S., Kim, G., Lee, J., Goh, K.-I., and Kim, I.-M. (2011). "Impact of the Topology of Global Macroeconomic Network on the Spreading of Economic Crises." *PLOS ONE* 6: e18443.

Mahutga, M. C. (2006). "The Persistence of Structural Inequality? A Network Analysis of International Trade, 1965–2000." *Social Forces* 84: 1863–89.

Maslov, S., and Sneppen, K. (2002). "Specificity and Stability in Topology of Protein Networks." *Science* 296: 910–913.

Mastrandrea, R., Squartini, T., Fagiolo, G., and Garlaschelli, D. (2014a). "Enhanced Network Reconstruction from Irreducible Local Information." *New Journal of Physics* 16: 1–16.

Mastrandrea, R., Squartini, T., Fagiolo, G., and Garlaschelli, D. (2014b). "Reconstructing the World Trade Multiplex: The Role of Intensive and Extensive Biases." *Physical Review E, Statistical, Nonlinear, and Soft Matter Physics* 90.

Nemeth, R., and Smith, D. (1985). "International Trade and World-System Structure: A Multiple Network Analysis." *Review: A Journal of the Fernand Braudel Center* 8: 517–560.

Piccardi, C., and Tajoli, L. (2012). "Existence and Significance of Communities in the World Trade Web." *Physical Review E* 85: 066119.

Piccardi, C., and Tajoli, L. (2015). "Are Preferential Agreements Significant for the World Trade Structure? A Network Community Analysis." *Kyklos* 68: 220–239.

Polachek, S. W. (1980). "Conflict and Trade." *Journal of Conflict Resolution* 24: 55–78.

Puma, M. J., Bose, S., Chon, S. Y., and Cook, B. I. (2015). "Assessing the Evolving Fragility of the Global Food System." *Environmental Research Letters* 10: 024007.

Reyes, J., Schiavo, S., and Fagiolo, G. (2010). "Using Complex Networks Analysis to Assess the Evolution of International Economic Integration: The Cases of East Asia and Latin America." *Journal of International Trade & Economic Development* 19: 215–239.

Riccaboni, M., and Schiavo, S. (2010). "Structure and Growth of Weighted Networks." *New Journal of Physics* 12: 023003+.

Rose, A. K. (2004). "Do We Really Know That the WTO Increases Trade?" *American Economic Review* 94: 98–114.

Sacks, M., Ventresca, M., and Uzzi, B. (2001). "Global Institutions and Networks: Contingent Change in the Structure of World Trade Advantage, 1965–1980." *American Behavioral Scientist* 44: 1579–1601.

Saul, S. B. (1954). "Britain and World Trade, 1870–1914." *Economic History Review* 7: 49–66.

Scott, J. (2000). *Social Network Analysis*. London: Sage.

Serrano, A., Boguñá, M., and Vespignani, A. (2007). "Patterns of Dominant Flows in the World Trade Web." *Journal of Economic and Coordination* 2: 111–124.

Sgrignoli, P., Metulini, R., Schiavo, S., and Riccaboni, M. (2015). "The Relation between Global Migration and Trade Networks." *Physica A: Statistical Mechanics and Its Applications* 417: 245–260.

Sinha, S., Chatterjee, A., Chakraborti, A., and Chakrabarti, B. (2010). *Econophysics: An Introduction*. Hoboken, NJ: John Wiley & Sons.

Smith, D., and White, D. (1992). "Structure and Dynamics of the Global Economy: Network Analysis of International Trade, 1965–1980." *Social Forces* 70: 857–893.

Snyder, D., and Kick, E. (1979). "Structural Position in the World System and Economic Growth 1955–70: A Multiple Network Analysis of Transnational Interactions." *American Journal of Sociology* 84: 1096–1126.

Squartini, T., Fagiolo, G., and Garlaschelli, D. (2011a). "Randomizing World Trade, I: A Binary Network Analysis." *Physical Review E* 84: 046117.

Squartini, T., Fagiolo, G., and Garlaschelli, D. (2011b). "Randomizing World Trade, II: A Weighted Network Analysis." *Physical Review E* 84: 046118.

Squartini, T., Fagiolo, G., and Garlaschelli, D. (2013). "Null Models of Economic Networks: The Case of the World Trade Web." *Journal of Economic Interaction and Coordination* 8: 75–107.

Squartini, T., and Garlaschelli, D. (2011). "Analytical Maximum-Likelihood Method to Detect Patterns in Real Networks." *New Journal of Physics* 13: 083001.

van Bergeijk, P., and Brakman, S. (Eds.). (2010). *The Gravity Model in International Trade*. Cambridge, UK: Cambridge University Press.

Vega Redondo, F. (2007). *Complex Social Networks*. New York: Cambridge University Press.

Ward, M. D., Ahlquist, J. S., and Rozenas, A. (2013). "Gravity's Rainbow: A Dynamic Latent Space Model for the World Trade Network." *Network Science* 1: 95–118.

West, D. B. (2001). *Introduction to Graph Theory*. New York: Prentice Hall.

Wilkinson, D. (2002). "Civilizations as Networks: Trade, War, Diplomacy, and Command-Control." *Complexity* 8: 82–86.

CHAPTER 29

....

GLOBAL GOVERNANCE NETWORKS

....

METTE EILSTRUP-SANGIOVANNI

INTRODUCTION

....

SINCE the 1990s a growing literature in politics and international relations has depicted a shift from government-centered, interstate relations to a more complex system of global governance. The cross-border, cross-sectoral, and multi-stakeholder nature of many global governance initiatives has in turn meant that global governance has become increasingly synonymous with "networked politics." It is not only political scientists who appear enamored of the idea of governance networks. Major intergovernmental organizations (IGOs), such as the European Union, the United Nations Development Programme (UNDP), the International Monetary Fund (IMF), and the World Bank, have launched extensive partnership projects, bringing together IGOs, nongovernmental organizations (NGOs), and private sector actors in bring so-called 'multi-stakeholder networks'. The goal of these networks is to harness the resources and expertise of NGOs and other civil society organizations (CSOs)[1] in designing, planning, and implementing global policy programs, thereby ensuring more effective and responsive governance.[2]

In this chapter I seek to clarify the concept of networked governance and probe deeper into the dynamics and consequences of an apparent proliferation of global governance networks (GGNs). I have two main aims. The first is to bring the theoretical concept of *networked governance* into sharper focus. Despite growing scholarly interest in governance networks, significant ambiguity remains about how to define them, how actors within networks relate to one another, and how different types of GGNs differ from one another. My second aim is to urge a more critical perspective on network performance and outputs. As I discuss later in this chapter GGNs are often assumed—on theoretical grounds—to offer innovative and effective solutions to complex global problems. However, it is often unclear what the expected production outputs of GGNs are, and attempts to empirically verify and measure network output performance are relatively rare.

Throughout the chapter I illustrate my discussion with reference to GGNs in the fields of sustainable development and environmental protection. There is growing consensus among scholars and practitioners that the complexities of global development and environmental problems call for networked solutions: connecting international policymakers with local stakeholders across different sectors and across geographical and jurisdictional boundaries. The last few decades have seen a rapid proliferation of new GGNs, which bring together IGOs, government agencies, social and environmental international (I)NGOs, and multinational and local businesses to promote environmental protection and sustainable development goals. Yet beyond facilitating regular contract and information exchange, it is often unclear what concrete benefits these initiatives produce and for whom. Before uncritically endorsing the ideal of "a globally networked politics," we therefore need a better grasp of the political dynamics of GGNs and of what results they deliver on the ground.

The first section of the chapter seeks to define the conceptual boundaries of the governance network paradigm. The next section reviews some of the main theoretical benefits (and pitfalls) of networked governance. The third section outlines a bare-bones model of network effectiveness. It begins with a critical look at current notions of network effectiveness. I then offer some hypotheses regarding structural and agent-specific properties, which may influence the effectiveness of governance networks. While it is beyond the scope of this chapter to offer an empirical test of these hypotheses, I illustrate my argument with reference to recent global governance initiatives in the realm of sustainable development and environmental protection. The fourth section concludes the discussion.

DEFINING GOVERNANCE NETWORKS

As explained elsewhere in this volume, the term "network" is a structural concept denoting an unspecified system of interconnected entities or nodes. Nodes could be individuals, groups, organizations, or states, and ties between them could be channels for exchange of both material and nonmaterial resources (money, goods, technology, information, knowledge, reputation, ideas, etc.) (Emirbayer, 1997; Hafner-Burton et al., 2009). This open-ended definition implies that—in structural terms—most systems of political coordination (whether hierarchical or market-based, formal or informal) can be defined as networks and analyzed as such. However, in a global governance context, most scholars have followed Walter Powell in conceiving of networks as a particular way of organizing collective action. In this view, networks are a specific form of social organization, distinct from both hierarchies and markets, but incorporating elements of both (Powell, 1990).

A central premise of the literature on global governance is that globalization processes have exposed limitations to both pure hierarchies and pure markets as means for coordinating global political and economic activities and have prompted a shift toward more inclusive and flexible policy networks (Castells, 2008; Ansell and Gash, 2007; Newig et al., 2010). This process has been driven by two underlying dynamics. First, states have for several decades been decentralizing power and resources, ceding authority over essential governance functions to local, regional, and international institutions (Castells, 2008). Second, there has been a proliferation of new global political actors—including NGOs, multinational corporations (MNCs), and civil society actors—whose political influence and capacity for collective action continue to grow (Young, 2008; Castells, 2008). The result has been a general diffusion of governance capacity away from central government toward new political actors. In this context, GGNs can be viewed as an attempt to (re-)integrate dispersed governance capacities and to unite the resources of governments, NGOs, and private actors in pursuit of shared goals.

Against this backdrop how, precisely, can we best define GGNs? Webber et al. define governance as "the coordinated management and regulation of issues by multiple and separate authorities, the interventions of both public and private actors, . . . formal and informal arrangements, in turn structured by discourse and norms, and purposefully directed toward particular policy outcomes" (Webber et al., 2004). In a similar vein, Sørensen and Torfing define a governance network as

> a relatively stable horizontal articulation of interdependent, but operationally autonomous actors who interact through negotiations that involve bargaining, deliberation and intense power struggles, which take place within a relatively institutionalized framework of contingently articulated rules, norms, knowledge and social imaginaries, that is self-regulating within limits set by external agencies and which contribute to the production of public purpose in the broad sense of visions, ideas, plans and regulations.
>
> (Sørensen and Torfing, 2005)

Together, these definitions highlight five essential aspects of global networked governance (see also Ansell and Gash, 2007):

- GGNs bring together different kinds of actors, spanning the public and private spheres, who all participate directly in decision-making (Ansell and Gash, 2007: 544).
- GGNs have a degree of endurance or "institutionalization" that sets them apart from more ad hoc forms of coordination, such as markets.
- Although they engage in continuing cooperation, participants in GGNs remain formally independent and operationally autonomous.
- GGNs embody deliberate (and voluntary) processes of coordination and negotiation, aimed at achieving specific policy outcomes (Kirchner, 2006).
- GGNs contribute to the production of some notion of public good (Ansell and Gash, 2007, Huppé, Creech, and Knoblauch, 2012, p. 2).

On these points most scholars seem to agree. There is less agreement on how to define the structural properties of GGNs. Many scholars view governance as entailing exclusively *informal, nonauthoritative* and *nonhierarchical* relationships (see, e.g., Webber et al., 2004). In this view, governance contrasts sharply with government, which implies the exercise of formal, rule-based authority through top-down command. Others take a broader view, suggesting that governance "can be formal or informal and can involve flat, hierarchical or heterarchical patterns of interaction" (Kirchner and Sperling, 2007, p. 43). This second definition is more aligned with the understanding among social network theorists that networks are not necessarily void of hierarchy or formal relationships. What unites both views, however, is the recognition that governance networks often lack a legally constituted point of central command. Crucially, this also implies that most GGNs lack a legitimate organizational authority to settle any disputes that may arise among participants (Podolny and Page, 1998).[3]

In this chapter I take a broad view of governance networks as entailing both formal and informal, vertical and horizontal relationships. Broadening our definition of governance networks to encompass horizontal, hierarchical, and heterarchical interrelationships clarifies a seeming ambiguity in the literature on networked organizations. Although networks are often described as fundamentally flat and decentralized, in reality many social networks entail elements of both centralization and de facto hierarchy. Indeed, most formal network studies use a variety of centralization measures to describe and analyze the structure of individual networks. But how can networks be at once horizontally distributed and centralized, flat but with elements of hierarchy? To resolve this seeming contradiction, we must distinguish between formal and informal hierarchy, as well as between hierarchy and centralization. Centralization in network terms can imply either (1) a de facto concentration of certain powers or resources within a subset of the network or (2) the consolidation and standardization of specific organizing functions that are carried out by some subset of node(s) on behalf of (but typically in consultation with) the network as a whole. Importantly, network centralization does not concentrate formal authority in a single location, nor does it vest authority in a single actor that is empowered to define or enforce collective rules. If that were the case, we would be looking at an organizational hierarchy.[4] Similarly, while concentrations of power and resources may introduce elements of de facto hierarchy, organizational networks lack an overarching structure of formal (or de jure) authority that locks participants into permanent relations of superiority and subordination. Rather, social rankings remain informal and fluid, and concentrations of power and/or functional tasks may give rise to several "network centers." GGNs can thus be conceptualized as "pluri-centric" forms of governance, as opposed to the "uni-centric" systems associated with top-down, state-led rule.[5]

Several implications follow from this mode of organization. First, unlike formal hierarchies that can rely on authoritative rules and legal arbitration to govern relations, networks are fundamentally self-enforcing governance structures disciplined mainly by reputation and norms of reciprocity (see Powell, 1990; Thompson, 2003; Podolny and

Page, 1998). This places a high premium on interpersonal trust as the primary currency sustaining cooperation (Powell 1990, p. 304).

Second, a lack of centralized authority implies that decision-making and coordination in governance networks tend to be based on mutual adjustment and consensus seeking, rather than top-down command (Zaring, 1998; Thompson, 2003, p. 43; Ansell and Gash, 2007).

Third, the voluntary nature of policy coordination within GGNs implies a notional equality among participants, who are considered jointly responsible for decisions and outcomes (Thompson, 2003). Indeed, while GGNs may feature a lopsided distribution of power and resources, it is widely assumed that there is a strong ethos of equality in such networks. This is particularly important in the context of networks that are orchestrated by government agencies or other public actors endowed with formal policymaking authority. Here the norms of networked governance are seen to dictate that nonstate participants must be included directly in decision-making processes, as opposed to merely being "consulted" by public agencies (see Ansell and Gash, 2007). This ethos is clearly illustrated by UNDP's "Policy of Engagement with Civil Society Organizations," which states:

> Partnership with CSOs is founded on the principle of a horizontal relationship between parties which, while institutionally different, are of equal standing in promoting the same development objectives, especially poverty reduction through sustainable human development. The relationship is premised on mutual trust that must be earned by both sides.
>
> (UNDP, 2001)

Beyond these shared features, GGNs differ widely in size, shape, substantive focus, and mode of operation. Before exploring these differences in greater detail, it is however useful to briefly distinguish GGNs from other types of transnational policy networks, such as transnational advocacy networks (TANs) and private regulatory initiatives. Margaret Keck and Kathryn Sikkink in their seminal book Activists Beyond Borders defined TANs as "networks of activists, distinguishable largely by the centrality of principled ideas or values in motivating their formation" (1998, p. 1). They argued that TANs are "organized to promote causes, principled ideas, and norms, and they often involve individuals advocating policy changes that cannot be easily linked to a rationalist understanding of their interests" (Keck and Sikkink, 1998, pp. 8–9). Although TANs and GGNs share many features (and may engage in similar and overlapping activities), this definition sets them apart in several respects. First, as defined by Keck and Sikkink, TANs are distinguished by a primary focus on *principled* causes. By contrast, participants in GGNs often advance both principled and self-interested goals, and *for-profit* activities may form an integral part of actors' contribution to a governance network. Second, whereas participants in TANs seek to influence policymaking through *advocacy* (e.g., by promoting new norms or policies or by seeking national or international legislative change), GGNs often focus on improving delivery of existing policies. Thus, policy implementation and policy evaluation are often equally as important goals for GGNs as normatively driven policy change.

The understanding of GGNs I propose here also sets GGNs apart from private transnational regulatory organizations (PTROs). As defined in this chapter, GGNs link actors across the public and private sectors. This definition excludes a host of mainly private initiatives that rely on market-based incentives to develop and promulgate international standards and that have no direct involvement by governments or other public actors. Sometimes referred to as "private governance," such initiatives may involve cooperation among firms to develop international codes of conduct, set standards, or introduce private product certification and labelling systems (see Young, 2008, Vandenbergh 2013; Abbott, Green and Keohane, 2016). Examples from the environmental realm include the London-based Marine Stewardship Council (MSC), founded in 1997 by Unilever and the World Wildlife Fund, which seeks to improve the sustainability of fisheries through a voluntary certification system, and the Forest Stewardship Council (FSC), which sets standards for responsible forest management. As mainly private enterprises, these initiatives fall outside the scope of this chapter.

Dynamics of Networked Governance

A large swathe of literature in IR is dedicated to exploring the theoretical benefits of governance networks. Here I briefly review some of the main advantages (and drawbacks) attributed to governance networks, before discussing the potential value-added of different network configurations. Most of these theoretical advantages and disadvantages apply to organizational networks in general, while some are specific to GGNs.

Benefits of Organizational Networks

Perhaps the most important advantage claimed for governance networks vis-à-vis traditional state-led hierarchies is that they assimilate knowledge, resources, information, and expertise from diverse sets of actors. By integrating capacities across different segments and levels of society, governance networks are said to be well suited to solving complex problems, which transcend the boundaries of existing political systems or administrative sectors (Huppé, Creech, and Knoblauch, 2012). Governance networks do not merely aggregate dispersed resources. According to Huppé et al., they are specifically structured to take advantage of the fact that participants bring different *kinds* of resources and expertise to the table by creating synergies. In their words, GGNs "combine the voluntary energy and legitimacy of the civil-society sector with the financial muscle and interest of businesses and the enforcement and rule-making power . . . of states and international organizations" (Huppé, Creech, and Knoblauch, 2012, p. 2).

The theoretical capacity of GGNs to integrate diverse resources is confirmed by many practitioners. For example, the Sustainable Trade Initiative cites the value created by "the public and private partners we work with who bring in funds, entrepreneurship, procurement power, legislation, laws, regulations, know-how, local expertise and credibility" (IDH, n.d.). Similarly, UNDP (2016) highlights the capacity of civil society actors for enhancing the effectiveness and legitimacy of development interventions through broad-based mobilization of marginalized and vulnerable groups. According to the UNDP CSO-Division, CSOs "have vital roles to play as participants, legitimizers and endorsers of government policy and action, as watchdogs of the behaviour of regimes and public agencies, and as collaborators in the national development effort" (UNDP, 2001). At the same time, the coordinating role of UNDP within the United Nations system implies that UNDP acts as an important source of financial and administrative support for many CSO initiatives.

A second theoretical advantage of organizational networks is fast and efficient communication and information exchange. In traditional hierarchical organizations, information must typically pass through a centralized processing unit, creating risks of bottlenecks and delay (Watts, 2003). It may also be difficult to transmit useful information on local problems to central decision makers who lack field expertise. By contrast, the decentralized yet tightly interconnected structure of organizational networks implies that communication can flow directly between local stakeholders. Theoretically, this enables actors to acquire new and diverse information faster than in centralized, hierarchical organizations (Scharpf, 1993; Powell, 1990).

Third, as a result of their capacity for information-sharing, organizational networks are widely held to promote learning and innovation (Podolny and Page, 1998, Newig et al., 2010). By facilitating rapid exchange of information and knowledge, a networked organization allows participants to learn about new events, challenges and opportunities. For example, participants in the European Commission's Sixth Environmental Action Program report that network participation has enabled collective identification and discussion of emerging environmental problems. Horizontal interactions based on peer-to-peer deliberation and exchange of ideas are also said to engender more creative and innovative policy solutions than when actors make decisions in relative isolation, or when they are locked into fixed routines within formal hierarchies (Newig et al., 2010; Klijn et al., 2016). Finally, the flat decision-making structure associated with networked cooperation allows new ideas and methods to be tested locally without having to await central authorization, thereby encouraging learning through experimentation. These dynamics of networked cooperation are particularly important in the context of many global governance initiatives. GGNs often bring together actors with different priorities, values, mandates, and resources. In this context, the direct peer-to-peer communication enabled by a networked organization allows representatives of local communities, (I)NGOs, and government agencies to share knowledge and experience across functional and geographic divides, and to identify successful local practices that may be replicated elsewhere.

A fourth, and related, advantage of networked organizations is the potential for strengthening local initiative. By decentralizing policy initiative and implementation, governance networks promote diverse solutions to local problems as opposed to centrally dictated, "one-size-fits-all" policies. The practice of designing and implementing policies "close to the ground" is held to reduce transaction costs and increase efficiency by facilitating customized policies that are directly responsive to people's needs (Paris, 2009). In a global governance context, local initiative is also seen to enhance accountability and legitimacy. For example, the IMF (2016) highlights direct engagement with local NGOs and CSOs as a way to demonstrate its accountability to recipient countries and their citizens.

A final alleged advantage of a networked organization is flexibility and adaptability. Because the structure and boundaries of networked organizations are generally easier to adjust than those of formal hierarchies, the composition of governance networks can be more easily modified to respond to changing needs. This organizational flexibility may be particularly valuable in the context of global governance initiatives, where stakeholders often join collaborative projects with little prior knowledge of one another's mode of operation, competence, accountability, or reputation. In this context, the informal nature of network ties allows different actors to collaborate on specific problems according to the nature of the problems rather than according to predetermined divisions of responsibility or jurisdiction (Podolny and Page, 1998). Importantly, it also means that links between stakeholders can be severed and unrewarding collaborations abandoned with relative ease.

Drawbacks of Organizational Networks

The theoretical advantages of governance networks are easy to grasp. These theoretical benefits may not always be easy to realize in practice, however.[6] Consider the simple aspect of information exchange. Theoretical models hold that networked organizations provide easy access to information. Yet in practice, searching for relevant information in a decentralized network may be complicated and time-consuming, insofar as individual nodes often produce duplicate information, and insofar as organizational networks often lack a central point of contact tasked with collecting and distributing information. As a result, although the network notionally provides access to a wide range of information, in practice each new piece of information may be subject to higher transaction costs than in a more centralized system (see Watts, 2003; Eilstrup-Sangiovanni and Jones, 2008; Agranoff and McGuire, 2011). Over time, participants in networks may therefore develop information "shortcuts" whereby they primarily source information from partners they know and trust to possess relevant expertise (Ward, Stovel, and Sacks, 2011; Eilstrup-Sangiovanni, 2014).[7] For example, Amanda Murdie, in her study of collaboration among international human rights organizations (HROs), finds that northern HROs tend to form more and closer ties to other northern HROs than to HROs in the global South (Murdie, 2014). Moira Faul similarly documents a high degree of *homophily* (i.e., a tendency for actors to link to other actors that are similar to themselves) in global networks dedicated to improving the delivery of development education aid (Faul, 2015). Such homophilous tie-formation may have the effect of fragmenting a network, cutting off participants from new sources of information and ideas, and excluding potentially valuable input from actors on the network's periphery.

A loose, horizontal structure may also undermine capacity for strategic decision-making. In their efforts to reach common goals, partners in GGNs must sometimes prioritize different objectives and decide how to allocate scarce resources. Yet given a commitment to consensus-oriented decision-making by nominally equal partners, decision-making in GGNs can be a slow process and involve high transaction costs (Powell, 1990; Meyer and Baltes, 2004). The voluntary nature of cooperation further implies that collective decisions may not be respected by all participants. The UNDP's "Policy of Engagement with CSOs" stresses, "Neither UNDP nor CSOs are required to accept or endorse each other's agendas, interpretations of events or methods. Each party is individually accountable for its behaviour to its owners or constituencies" (2006). While this principle ensures local autonomy, it also means that organizational networks such as GGNs may lack clear collective purpose and allocation of responsibility for promoting joint goals (Powell, 1990; Thompson, 2003; Eilstrup-Sangiovanni and Jones, 2008).

Collective learning presents another challenge for networked organizations. Organizations typically learn by distilling lessons and storing them in ways that are easily accessible to others, despite turnover of staff (Levitt and March, 1988). However, lack of central authority in organizational networks often implies that no single actor is responsible for consolidating information and distilling practical knowledge so as to build organizational memory (see, e.g., Eilstrup-Sangiovanni and Jones, 2008). Lack of centralized authority may also prevent proper evaluation of local projects. As a result, actors may be unable to translate the lessons learned through local experimentation into collective improvements of practice.

Finally, network functionality may be undermined by reliance on trust and direct reciprocity (as opposed to contractual rules and legal arbitration) to govern exchanges. Network scholars widely identify trust as a prerequisite for the smooth performance of social networks (Gulati et al., 2011; Provan and Kenis, 2008; Klijn et al., 2016; Powell, 1990; Thompson, 2003; Agranoff and McGuire, 2011). Scholars note that given the voluntary nature of networking, trust is needed both to persuade actors to invest time and resources in cooperation and to restrain subsequent opportunistic behavior (Klijn et al., 2016). But while interpersonal trust may successfully substitute for contractual provisions among individuals or groups that share a common cultural, social or professional background (as has been found by many sociological network studies), it may be more difficult to invoke in a global context where the geographical, cultural, and professional distance among actors is often wide. In this context, building and sustaining trust may require significant investments of time and resources devoted to face-to-face dialogue and other trust-building actions (Ansell and Gash, 2007). Thus, conclude Meyer and Baltes, "governance through networks . . . is rather inefficient because of the amount of informal and non-task-related communication necessary for the production of trust" (2004, p. 44).

The benefits and drawbacks highlighted here may not pertain equally to all organizational networks. Below I discuss structural aspects of particular network configurations (such as their size, geographic span, and homogeneity), which may lessen or aggravate particular benefits or dysfunctions. Practical steps can also be taken by network members to reduce the drawbacks associated with an informal, distributed forms of organization. Many GGNs have institutionalized arrangements to help members coordinate activities, share information, identify joint priorities, and engage in collective learning (see Betsill, 2014). For example, the UNDP's CSO-Division has established a specific Learning Grant Facility to support peer-to-peer learning among community participants. Participants first convene in so-called learning workshops, where they share experiences and ideas and identify best practices. Based on this initial exchange, a learning agreement is drawn up, outlining a detailed proposal, timeline, and budget for further learning exchanges. Decisions about which learning agreements to fund are made by a steering committee made up of UNDP staff and CSO representatives (UNDP, 2006). In other words, there is an element of centralized orchestration.

Initiatives such as the UNDP Learning Grant Facility aim to enhance collective learning. At the same time, however, they can introduce an element of central steering and gatekeeping that may reinforce existing power inequalities and thereby reduce a network's capacity for bottom-up articulation of needs and ideas. In the case of the UNDP learning grant facility, the power of the steering committee to reject or approve particular learning agreements implies that it is effectively able to "vet" the agenda for exchange of ideas and practices and to restrict access to network resources. This may exclude some ideas and reduce some actors to a marginal position within the network. In the next section I consider this and other trade-offs related to network management in more detail.

A MODEL OF GOVERNANCE NETWORK PERFORMANCE

The preceding review of strengths and weaknesses of organizational networks suggests that the effectiveness of networked global governance cannot be taken for granted. It also raises the question of what concrete benefits are generated by different types of governance networks. Yet whereas the structural features of GGNs and their theoretical benefits have been subjects of extensive research, the practical *outputs* of networked governance have been less studied. After reviewing 137 case studies of collaborative governance across different policy sectors, Ansell and Gash (2007) found that few studies actually evaluated governance outcomes.[8] Instead most studies treated the network itself as the main output or variable of interest. This problem is aptly illustrated by a 2014 report from the IOB (the Policy and Operations Evaluation Department of the Ministry of Foreign Affairs of the Netherlands) that evaluates the impact of the International Trade Initiative (Initiatief Duurzame Handel, IDH), a flagship development network founded in 2008 by the Dutch Ministries of Development

Cooperation, Economic Affairs, and Agriculture in cooperation with private companies, trade unions, and NGOs, with the aim of enhancing sustainable sourcing from developing countries. While the IOB report praises IDH for linking global investors and local smallholders, it concludes with that "good impact studies of the [IDH] programmes are lacking. Most remain strongly process . . . oriented, but they say little about anticipated impact such as improved incomes or poverty reduction" (Ministry of Foreign Affairs, Netherlands, 2014).

In this section I briefly discuss the production logic and output measures of GGNs. Drawing on studies in public policy and public administration, I first consider how one might devise simple metrics for evaluating GGN outputs. I then outline a preliminary model of network effectiveness, which highlights both structural and agent-specific features that are likely to impact on the performance of GGNs. This model is not intenteded as a full-fledged theory of governance network performance. Rather, my aim is to highlight some basic factors that may influence network performance and to suggest some avenues for further research.

Conceptualizing Network Effectiveness

When conceptualizing network effectiveness, the first point to consider is, what concrete results do we expect GGNs to deliver? As Agranoff notes, different GGNs are created with different goals in mind and should be evaluated accordingly (Agranoff, 2007; Agranoff and McGuire, 2011). As a starting point, Agranoff distinguishes among networks that aim to facilitate information exchange, networks that combine information exchange with attempts to build problem-solving capacities, and networks that seek to facilitate collective action (Agranoff, 2007; Agranoff and McGuire, 2011). A network that aims mainly to facilitate information exchange may not be expected to generate collective action, but may nonetheless have a demonstrable impact on policy outcomes downstream.

A model of GGN effectiveness must consider not only the results but also the costs of networking (Agranoff, 2007; Agranoff and McGuire, 2011). As discussed, network-based decision-making may be subject to high transaction costs. Endless hours may be spent in conferences or focus groups that wind up producing little more than joint statements. As Voets et al. (2008) argue insofar as the time and resources devoted to participation in GGNs may be taken away from other organizational tasks, networking through GGNs may entail significant opportunity costs, which must be factored into assessments of network effectiveness (see also Vandenbergh 2013).

In addition to asking whether GGNs have a visible impact on the problems they seek to address, we ideally also want to know how well they perform compared to organizational alternatives. So far, scholars have rarely sought to evaluate governance networks against organizational alternatives (see Kahler, 2009; Eilstrup-Sangiovanni 2009, Eilstrup-Sangiovanni and Jones, 2008). Indeed, much literature on GGNs appears to implicitly assume that networked governance solutions are driven by earlier failures to address a problem through other organizational means (see, e.g., Ansell and Gash, 2007). The superiority of a networked solution is thus effectively presupposed. A better understanding of the value-added of GGNs would require scholars to undertake more explicit and systematic comparisons of the strengths and weaknesses of GGNs vis-à-vis alternative organizational responses (such as top-down, state-led governance or market-based solutions).

As these points suggest, proper evaluations of the effectiveness of governance networks involve must an assessment of the output of a network as well as of network's relative efficiency. It also raises the question, efficiency for whom (Head, 2008)? Who are the primary intended beneficiaries of specific global governance initiatives?

With a focus on administrative governance networks in a domestic context, Voets et al. (2008, pp. 777) suggest that network performance can be assessed at three main levels:

- single participants
- the network as a whole
- the wider community

The first level assesses network benefits from the perspective of individual participants. Do they gain access to valuable information or other resources? Does participation in the network increase their visibility or reputation? The second level measures the combined goal attainment of individual participants. Does the network produce new knowledge or collective problem-solving capacity? Does it give rise to synergies so that the combined effects of actors' activities exceed the sum of their separate actions? The third level captures benefits to target groups or community stakeholders outside the network (Voets et al., 2008, 779). Does the network produce concrete benefits for a target population? As Voets et al. argue, goal attainment at one level does not imply goal attainment at another. Network participants may consider that the network performs well because it serves their individual interests, while community stakeholders "outside" the network reap few gains or may even suffer adverse side effects (Voets et al., 2008, 779). Moreover, benefits at each level may be unevenly spread across participants.

The value-added of GGNs may be most straightforward to gauge at the level of single participants. At this level, it is relatively easy to learn from individual participants whether they view a network as providing access to useful information or resources. Nonetheless, if we wish to evaluate GGNs as tools for solving complex global problems, the network and community levels seem to offer more relevant measures of the benefits of networked governance. After all, most GGNs aim to supply some notion of public goods (Ibid.). At these levels, evaluating network performance would require us to consider the following questions:

- *Does the network facilitate sharing of information, knowledge or resources that would not otherwise be available to participants?*
- *Has the network led to adoption of new or improved practices by participants?*
- *Has the network led to implementation of joint projects? (Does it facilitate collective action?)*
- Has the network expanded its membership or become involved in a broader set of issues?

- *Do participants report satisfaction with results of joint projects?*
- *Do stakeholders in the wider community report satisfaction with the results of joint network projects?*
- *Is network participation and decision-making open to all relevant stakeholders. That is, is the network inclusive?*

Clearly these questions are not always easy to answer, and accurate evaluations of network effectiveness will require scholars to develop specific methods for quantifying and measuring outputs such as information exchange or sharing of resources. Yet given that most empirical studies of governance network are case study based, broad measures of effectiveness should be achievable through use of simple techniques such as questionnaires, interviews, content analysis of reports from individual organizations, and counterfactual analysis.

A Model of Network Effectiveness

As discussed above, GGNs are widely celebrated for offering flexible and innovative solutions to complex global problems. In particular, GGNs are said to be well suited to tackling problems that transcend sectoral and/or geographic boundaries (Klijn et al., 2016). Yet not all governance networks are equally likely to generate effective responses to transboundary problems. Literature in public policy and public administration highlight a number of variables that may be critical in determining whether GGNs can successfully deliver desired policy outcomes. Mainly, these variables group into categories of structural design features (e.g., centrality, density, heterogeneity), quality of leadership, and distribution of power and resources among nodes (Huppe et. al, 2012, p. 11, Ansell and Gash, 2007). I briefly discuss each category below in order to derive some preliminary hypotheses about GGN effectiveness. My analysis does not constitute a comprehensive model of network effectiveness. My aim is merely to highlight some basic properties of GGNs that are likely to affect their operation. While space does not allow me to offer an empirical test of my hypotheses, I draw on several empirical examples to illustrate the argument.

Structural Network Features as Determinants of Network Effectiveness

A core insight of social network theory is that the structure of relationships among social actors (rather than just features of the actors themselves) is a crucial determinant of the quality and outcome of social interactions. First, and most obviously, a network's capacity for fostering productive exchange may be a function of network *size*. The ability of GGNs to address complex problems chiefly hinges on their ability to integrate diverse resources—information, financial resources, knowledge, and legitimacy—across different actors, sectors, and jurisdictions. Since networks with wide participation provide access (in principle) to a wider range of resources and knowledge, it is often assumed that network performance increases with growing membership (Voets et al., 2008, Huppe et al. 2012).

The capacity of GGNs for information exchange and joint problem-solving may also be a function of network *density*. Structurally dense networks (i.e., networks that feature multiple and strong links among individual nodes) are assumed on theoretical grounds to facilitate greater exchange of information and other resources than sparsely connected ones (Smith-Doerr and Powell, 2005; Provan and Milward, 2001). The extensive face-to-face dialogue associated with densely connected networks enables "thick communication," which allows stakeholders to discover opportunities for joint projects across a range of issues and also helps to build trust (Carlsson and Sandströem, 2008; Ansell and Gash, 2007).

Network functionality may also be influenced by network homogeneity and homophily. Homogeneity refers to the degree to which a network connects participants that are highly similar in terms of some attributes (e.g., geographic or professional background, values, beliefs, or resources). Homophily captures the extent to which pairs of individuals who interact within the network are similar with respect to certain attributes. In principle, networks that comprise many diverse actors are likely to provide access to wider capabilities, knowledge, expertise, and resources than networks connecting highly similar actors (Carlsson and Sandströem, 2008). As such, heterogeneous networks may generate more opportunities for productive exchange. However, this will only be the case if these networks are also characterized by heterophily—that is, if actors in the network communicate and exchange ideas with other actors that are not closely similar to themselves. Heterophilous interactions serve to expose actors to new ideas and knowledge and facilitate the integration of dispersed resources. Whereas homophily may serve to reinforce existing patterns of cooperation, network heterophily may open up new opportunities for collaboration that would not otherwise have been available.

From a purely theoretical perspective, then, the ideal network is large and densely connected with high levels of heterophilous interactions which are in turn underpinned by high levels of interpersonal trust. But while optimal in theory, in practice such structural conditions may be close to impossible to achieve. Consider that as a network increases in size, so do the costs of maintaining dense connections and of sustaining the "thick" communication required to identify opportunities for productive exchange (Meyer and Baltes, 2004). This is especially true in heterogeneous networks, in which participants may need to devote considerable resources to face-to-face communication in order to build trust and arrive at a common viewpoint. Also, whereas densely connected networks facilitate 'thick communication', they may also lead to unnecessary duplication of exchanges, which drive up overall costs of interaction—especially where large numbers are involved. These dilemmas suggest that a degree of centralization is needed to ensure effective cooperation across large social networks. In particular, large networks may benefit from institutionalizing central mechanisms for information exchange and project evaluation. Due to the inherent difficulty of reaching agreement among large numbers, large, heterogeneous GGNs may also benefit from clear operating procedures regarding how joint decisions will be made. Importantly, such centralization does not imply traditional organizational hierarchy. As already discussed, networks may centralize certain organizing functions without thereby concentrating authority in a single actor.

The high transaction costs associated with coordination and exchange in large distributed systems should promt us to ask whether—at least in some contexts—smaller GGNs may be more productive better than larger ones. It is generally easier to establish trust and stabilize expectations of reciprocity among small groups, where mutual actions can be easily monitored. The transaction costs associated with joint decision-making and action also tend to be lower in small groups, where all participants can be effectively included in face-to-face deliberation. Finally, the difficulty of achieving jointness of purpose among heterogeneous actors may be more easily overcome with small numbers. Although small networks may lack access to the array of resources that networks with large membership have, "smallness" may be partially offset by heterogeneous membership and heterophilous interactions, which allow participants to exploit synergies among different resources and capacities.

The ideal size of a GGN will of course be largely dictated by the nature of the problem(s) it seeks to address. However, the pros and cons of different structural network properties suggest that large and small GGNs may benefit from different configurations of relationships. Whereas the main challenge in small networks is to ensure access to diverse resources (favoring heterogeneity and heterophily), the chief challenges in large networks are to build trust among participants and to ensure efficient information exchange. This suggests that a relatively homogeneous membership and homophilous tie-formation may enhance productivity. There are two reasons for this. First, since direct, face-to-face communication among all participants in a large network may be impossible, having a homogeneous membership means that fewer resources must be devoted to building trust and defining joint goals. Second, although the network as a whole may be sparsely connected, homophilous interactions enable 'thick' communication among subsets of participants, allowing smaller groups to identify opportunities for joint projects while at the same time benefiting from "thinner" interaction with the wider network.

Summing up, while it is unlikely that theoretical analysis can uncover an ideal network design, theory suggests that some structural network configurations will tend to perform better than others. Specifically, I propose that high-performing GGNs will tend to feature *either*

(a) a relatively small and heterogeneous membership that is densely integrated, and features a high degree of heterophilous interactions, or
(b) a large and homogenous membership, sparsely connected at the global level but with dense local interactions enabled by homoplilous tie-formation, and with some centralization of basic "organizing functions."

Networks with these traits combine access to diverse resources with a high capacity for building (or sustaining) trust, stabilizing expectations of reciprocity and enabling collective action and learning through rapid information exchange, while at the same time keeping transaction costs low.

Structural Network Features: Two Models of Success?

Network Size	Nature of Membership	Links Among Nodes	Network Density	Network Management
Large	Homogeneous	Homophilous	Sparse overall but locally dense	Centralized
Small	Heterogeneous	Heterophilous	Densely connected	Decentralized

A good illustration of how small size and limited access to resources can be partially offset by the formation of heterophilous links between diverse actors is provided by a small environmentalist network working to combat illegal fishing in the Mediterranean. The network centers around Black Fish, a Dutch-based environmental grassroots organization founded in 2010. With fewer than thirty staff members spread across five countries and no major donors or fee-paying members, Black Fish is a minor player among international environmental groups. Nonetheless, creative collaboration with other private and public actors has enabled it to launch several highly effective and visible projects. The key to Black Fish's success appears to be an innovative approach to building partnerships. Rather than focusing on lobbying and political advocacy—activities that tend to require either privileged political access, strength in numbers, and/or access to significant campaigning resources—the group trains ordinary people as "citizen fishing inspectors." Citizen inspectors pay for their own training and travel costs and generally operate in local ports, where—posing as tourists—they take photographs of illegal fishing gear and suspect landings. Evidence is then collected by Black Fish and passed on to local authorities. As the group itself has no capacity—legal or physical—to follow up on infringements, it has signed a memorandum of understanding with the Italian Coast Guard, whereby the two actors agree to share intelligence and resources. The basis for this agreement is a degree of mutual trust established over several years, during which Black Fish has consistently supplied the Coast Guard with reliable evidence. As a result of this evidence, Italian authorities have been able to confiscate large quantities of illegal fish and to initiate prosecutions against a illegal traders. In sum, the project links a small number of highly dissimilar actors—a public authority, a grassroots organization, and varying numbers of part-time volunteers from all walks of life—who each contribute a unique set of complementary resources.

Black Fish's innovative approach to networking with other actors is also evident in other projects. While citizen inspectors operate in local ports, much illegal fishing takes place far out at sea. "Lacking larger donors and the funds to buy a ship, there was no way we could keep an eye on what happens offshore," explains Wietse van der Werf, founder of Black Fish (interview with author, June 16, 2015). But then he discovered an untapped resource: trainee pilots. Trainee or newly licensed pilots often struggle to get commercial jobs due to a lack of prior flying experience. They may not be passionate about conservation, but they are passionate about flying and need to build their flight hours, explains Wietse. "Many are already flying in areas where we are working, so all we needed to do was to persuade them to take our Citizen Inspectors on board. It's a win-win!" (interview with author, June 16, 2015). As a result of this simple idea, a new network-based partnership—the Wildlife Air Service—has been launched, which provides aerial surveillance capacity not only for Black Fish but also for other environmental NGOs and grassroots organizations on a project-by-project basis.[9]

The network that has emerged around Black Fish may be small (at the time of writing it links less than a dozen organizations), but it provides a good example of how dense connections among heterophilius actors—that is, actors that are highly diverse in terms of organization, resources, and goals—can generate added value. It also illustrates the importance of face-to-face communication for building trust among diverse actors. Each partnership in the network has grown out of intense dialogue and face-to-face meetings at which ideas have been exchanged and opportunities for joint projects examined and fine-tuned. Wietse summarizes Black Fish's strategy of linking to other actors as follows: "As we cannot afford to pay people, we instead get them to donate their time and skill. We try to 'repurpose' what people are already doing for conservation purposes." Importantly, this means that partners in the network do not have to share the same vision or goals. "The groups we work with–we are connecting less on *issues* but rather on skills and capacity; we try to provide a new purpose to what people already do and enjoy doing." As an example, Black Fish has partnered with diving schools in Holland and the United Kingdom that help train citizen inspectors in underwater investigation of fishing crimes. The diving instructors agree to work one week per year for free, training volunteer inspectors. "They already have the facilities and instructors, so from their perspective they are not giving much. But it's of great value to us", explains Wietse (interview with author, June 16, 2015).

At the opposite end of the spectrum in terms of network size and structure is the UN Global Compact (UNGC), which seeks to build partnerships among private companies, UN agencies, and CSOs in support of UN sustainable development goals. With more than eight thousand companies, eight UN agencies, and four hundred CSOs from 170 countries participating,[10] the compact is the world's largest corporate sustainability initiative. In 2004—five years after being established—it organized the largest meeting of business, labor, and civil society leaders in the history of the UN (see Thérien and Pouliot, 2006). But while the Global Compact in principle offers opportunities for collaboration between businesses and CSOs at a vast scale, practical results have been modest (see UN Joint Inspection Unit, 2010; Arevalo and Aravind, 2010, and Hoemen 2013), and major NGOs, including Amnesty International, Oxfam, and Human Rights Watch, have openly threatened to leave the UNGC due to "lack of tangible evidence of progress" (see, e.g,. Amnesty International, 2003; Thérien and Pouliot, 2006; Rasche, 2009, Arevalo and Aravind, 2010).

Among the chief problems cited by critics of the UNGC is a lack of a clearly defined mandate which has led to a weak focus and reduced impact (UN Joint Inspection Unit, 2010). Another problem is a lack of centralized monitoring of implementation. The compact invites the private sector "to embrace, support and enact . . . a set of core values in the areas of human rights, labor standards, the environment, and anti-corruption."[11] Companies that join the UNGC commit to voluntarily applying ten principles designed to advance these values. There are, however, no clear mechanisms for holding companies to account for respecting these non-binding principles and low rates of compliance have drawn repeated criticism from external observers (UN Joint Inspection Unit, 2010, Arevalo and Aravind, 2010, Thérien and Pouliot, 2006). Critics also cite lack of reporting on progress as undermining collective learning and building of trust. A crucial aim of the UNGC is to facilitate exchange of ideas and best-practices and thereby encourage collective learning.[12] To this end, companies are required to supply regular "Communication on Progress Reports" detailing their activities and efforts to comply with the compact's principles. However, lack of reporting on progress has been a persistent problem since the birth of the Compact (UN JIU 2010). According to Therien and Pouliot, in 2006 fewer than 60 percent of participating companies reported taking at least one action to implement UNGC principles in their annual reports, and among those that declared having undertaken policy change, 40 percent openly admitted that participation in the compact had no significant impact on their decisions (Thérien and Pouliot, 2006. It appears, therefore, that the compact offers a way for some companies to improve their corporate image while making few meaningful changes to their practice (so-called 'green-washing') (UN JIU, 2010). These problems appear to be the result of a very large and heterogeneous membership, which makes jointness of purpose and direct peer-to-peer monitoring difficult to achieve. A 2010 Report by the UN Joint Inspection Unit found that the Global Compact lacked effective screening and monitoring of members so as to ensure that those who joined were truly committed to its principles, and called for stricter criteria for participation and expulsion (UN JIU 2010). The report also critized weak provisions for centralized information exchange or evaluation of initiatives, which could facilitate collective learning and improvement of practice, labelling the compact an example of "costly and questionably effective governance". Again, these problems appear to stem from the large size and great heterogeneity of the network combined with a lack centralized network steering, although establishing whether this is the case would require further empirical research.

Perhaps the most damning criticism of the UNGC is that its focus on getting partners to sign up to a set of vague and non-binding principles whilst doing little to stimulate joint projects or monitor implementation undermines efforts to establish more effective governance measures. As Plaul Hoemen (2013) observes, "as with all voluntary corporate responsibility initiatives, the Global Compact is open to charges that it slows progress towards mandatory measures by giving the impression that laws on corporate accountability and reporting are not needed." This highlights an important factor in assessing the overall impact of GGNs, namely their impact on existing governance structures and on the likelihood of other governance solutions emerging (Vandenbergh

2013, p. 184). While GGNs may fill gaps in state-led, public governance or complement mandatory regulatory frameworks they may also risk undermining or delaying government action or undermine support for more effective regulatory measures (ibid).

Quality of Leadership

In addition to structural network features, productivity may also be influenced by the quality of leadership in a network. Literature in public policy has broadly concluded that governance networks require an element of central leadership to operate effectively (Klijn et al., 2016; Agranoff, 2007; Meyer and Baltes, 2004). Although GGNs may weakly link actors with complementary goals and resources, active brokerage is often needed to facilitate collaboration. In particular, leadership may be required to carry out the following operational functions:

- bringing stakeholders to the table (Ansell and Gash, 2007),
- problem definition and prioritization (Carlsson and Sandströem, 2008),
- identifying opportunities for mutual gain,
- integrating the resources of different partners to create synergy (Gulati et al., 2011),
- helping to resolve potential conflicts among stakeholders (brokering) (Huppe et al. 2012), and
- distributing gains from cooperation.

Against this background, I propose that productivity is enhanced when a network contains one or more nodes whose structural position between other nodes (or issues) puts them in a position to connect otherwise separate agendas and to combine the resources of different actors in ways that enhance opportunities for joint gains. I call this "facilitative" leadership. To play a facilitative role, a node must enjoy a high degree of trust from other participants. However, there is no presumption that facilitators are formally empowered to define the rules of interaction or to decide who gets to participate in a network on what terms. In contrast to leadership in an organizational hierarchy, which typically rests on formal allocation of voting rights or veto powers, facilitative leadership merely entails providing an element of steering to otherwise decentralized, voluntary actions. Nonetheless, it is important to acknowledge that a position as network facilitator may endow nodes with structural or 'relational' power to keep particular problems off the agenda or to prioritize some types of collaborative solutions over others.[13]

Returning to my previous example, the role of Black Fish within the small network working to combat illegal fishing in the Mediterranean illustrates the value of facilitative leadership. Although there is no centralized information exchange, official schedule of meetings, or even a clear set of shared goals or common agendas, the entrepreneurship of Black Fish has played an instrumental role in bringing other actors together, encouraging them to share information and ideas and identifying opportunities for mutual gains. This facilitative leadership has been exercised in large part through personal relationships built through face-to-face communication. By contrast, whereas the UN Secretariat provides an element of central coordination to the UNGC by defining sustainable development principles and acting as a depository for companies' individual reports on implementation, it does not appear to play an active role in facilitating joint projects among participants.

Distribution of Resources

A third feature that may determine the productivity of GGNs is the distribution of power among actors. Although they are notionally equal stakeholders, participants in GGNs often vary greatly in the resources they bring to a network and in the time they are able to devote to joint deliberation processes (Ansell and Gash, 2007). If resource imbalances are stark, governance processes may be prone to manipulation by stronger actors. This may in turn reduce incentives for other stakeholders to participate (Ansell and Gash, 2007; see also McGuire and Agranoff, 2007). In the specific context of sustainable development, there are often significant resource inequalities between large MNCs and smaller CSOs, which may undermine direct CSO-industry collaboration. For example, a study by McCloskey finds that American environmental groups are often skeptical of collaborative governance at the domestic level because they feel it advantages stronger, organized industry groups (McCloskey, 2000, cited in Ansell and Gash, 2007). Similarly, many scholars and CSO representatives have voiced concern that the UNGC aggravates inequalities and widens the gulf between global North and South by "privatizing sustainable development." Critics object that the transnational corporations that make up the bulk of the membership have access to human and financial resources unavailable to other members, including UN agencies, to defend their views (UN JIU, 2010 and Therien and Pouliot, 2006). A related criticism is that the norm of consensus deliberation favors the private sector, because it leads inescapably to a "minimalist agenda of corporate social and environmental responsibility" and thereby rules out options that would involve redistributive policies or binding codes of conduct (Fomerand, 2003; CorpWatch, 2000).

Inequality of power and influence may also be a result of the participation of government agencies that occupy a powerful central position in governance networks. As Agranoff and McGuire (2011) argue, governments have unique resources, including formal decision-making authority, budgets, personnel, and democratic legitimacy, which may enable them to dictate the activities of other actors in ways that further their own goals. The same is true of many IGOs, whose regulatory power may enable them to shape the activities of CSOs and other private participants. In a recent study, Abbott and Snidal explore ways in which governments and international organizations (IOs) seek to enhance their own performance by collaborating with private actors and institutions. States and IOs, they argue, frequently 'orchestrate' the creation and operation of private and "mixed" regulatory standard–setting schemes (e.g., by convening and facilitating private collaborations or persuading and inducing firms and industries to self-regulate) in order to achieve their regulatory policy goals (Abbott and Snidal, 2010). Klijn and Skelcher (2013) label this the "instrumental conjecture" on networks: powerful governmental actors seek to enhance their own capacity to deliver public policy through instrumental use of governance networks.

The instrumental conjecture is not of purely academic interest. A 2001 evaluation of the UNDP's global program for mainstreaming collaboration with CSOs, undertaken by the UNDP itself, concluded that the program was "impeded by incentives and procedures that push staff to a utilitarian approach towards CSOs to achieve UNDP goals" (UNDP, 2001). An obvious danger of orchestration and instrumentalization of GGNs by governmental actors is that it may lead to the exclusion of resource-poor actors or actors whose agendas deviate from official government policy. This may in turn reduce the inclusiveness, innovative capacity, and overall value of a network. A 2006 report on the UNDP's "Policy on Engagement with CSOs" noted that "in the past, country offices have limited their partners to well known and established NGOs, overlooking the potential of other civil society actors to contribute to achieving their development goals." (UNDP, 2006) Similarly, the orchestration of private regulatory responses by government agencies that are de facto empowered to withhold support for specific initiatives may lead to the exclusion of ideas, perspectives, and demands from peripheral nodes. These concerns have led some analysts to suggest that "self-organizing" or "bottom-up" governance networks in which governments play only a minimal role and resources are relatively evenly distributed are likely to be the most productive (Huppé, Creech, and Knoblauch, 2012).

CONCLUSION

Global governance networks are increasingly cited by scholars, policymakers, business leaders, and NGO representatives as instrumental in enabling communities worldwide to respond to the challenges of globalization. They are seen as particularly useful for handling complex problems that transcend the boundaries of different countries and sectors and where uncoordinated actions may produce perverse outcomes. In this chapter I have examined some of the main benefits and drawbacks of networked governance and offered some general hypotheses concerning structural network features that may enhance GGN effectiveness. I have sought to demonstrate that different structural network configurations may lead to different dynamics of cooperation. It is unlikely that one can identify an "ideal" network structure on theoretical grounds. Different types of problems call for different collaborative solutions, and most structural network features involve trade-offs. For example, a degree of centralization may be necessary to ensure efficient information exchange in large networks, but may at the same time reduce a network's inclusivity and ability to generate new ideas. Decentralization, on the other hand, may enhance inclusivity and facilitate access to a greater diversity of resources and knowledge from different groups. However, decentralization may also impede consensus building and reduce a network's capacity for collective learning, due to a lack of centralized interpretation and dissemination of lessons. A skewed distribution of power among participants may under some conditions provide a basis for effective leadership, while in other circumstances it can create a disincentive for participation by resource-poor actors. While such trade-offs may be unavoidable, attention to the pros- and cons of different structural network configurations may help actors to take remedial actions.

The effects of structural network features such as centralization/decentralization and homogeneity/heterogeneity on network performance need further study. But while there is a growing literature examining the dynamics of different network configurations from a theoretical perspective, empirical studies of network performance are still lagging behind. Future conceptual and empirical research should pay careful attention to how the outputs of GGNs can be conceptualized, measured, and compared against the outputs of other forms of institutionalized collaboration.

Notes

1. According to UNDP (2006), the term "civil society organization" (CSO) comprises the full range of formal and informal organizations within civil society, including NGOs, community-based organizations, indigenous peoples' organizations, academia, journalists' associations, faith-based organizations, trade unions, and trade associations.
2. See, e.g., World Bank, "Defining Civil Society," http://web.worldbank.org/WBSITE/EXTERNAL/TOPICS/CSO/0,,contentMDK:20101499~menuPK:244752~pagePK:220503~piPK:220476~theSitePK:228717,00.html; UNDP (2016).
3. Most conceptions of governance networks align with Podolny and Page's (1998) definition of an organizational network as "any collection of actors (N>2) that pursue repeated, enduring exchange relations with one another and at the same time lack a legitimate organizational authority to arbitrate and resolve disputes that may arise during the exchange."
4. I build here on Lake's (2015) definition of hierarchy.
5. I borrow these terms from Kersbergen and Waarden (2004, 151).
6. For a detailed discussion of the limitations of organizational networks, see Eilstrup-Sangiovanni and Jones (2008).
7. For example, Ward, Stovel and Sacks (2011) find that large networks are often characterized by localized homophily—that is, the tendency for nodes to associate with other nodes that share similar attributes. See also Eilstrup-Sangiovanni (2014).
8. On the dearth of empirical evaluations of governance networks, see also Arevalo and Aravind (2010); Newig et al. (2010); and Klijn et al. (2016).
9. See http://www.wildlifeair.org.
10. Besides private corporations and the UN Secretariat, the Compact involves six UN specialized agencies (ILO, UNDP, UNEP, OHCHR, UNIDO, and UNODC) as well as a number of NGOs, labor associations, business associations, and think tanks.
11. http://globalcompactfoundation.org/about-ungc.php and https://www.unglobalcompact.org.
12. Ibid.
13. For an in-depth discussion of social or "network power" see Hafner-Burton et al. (2009).

References

Abbott, Kenneth W. and Snidal, D. (2010). "International regulation without international government: Improving IO performance through orchestration." *The Review of International Organizations* 5(3): 315–344.

Agranoff, R. (2007). *Managing Within Networks: Adding Value to Public Organizations.* Washington, DC: Georgetown University Press.

Agranoff, R., and McGuire, M. (2011). "The Limitations of Public Management Networks." *Public Administration* 89(2): 265–284.

Amnesty International. (2003). "Letter to Louise Fréchette Raising Concerns on UN Global Compact," April 7. https://www.globalpolicy.org/component/content/article/177/31749.html (accessed March 22, 2015).

Ansell, C., and Gash, A. (2007). "Collaborative Governance in Theory and Practice." *Journal of Public Administration Research and Theory* 18(4): 543–571.

Arevalo, J. A., and Aravind, D. (2010). "The Impact of the Crisis on Corporate Responsibility: The Case of UN Global Compact Participants in the USA." *Corporate Governance* 10(4): 406–420.

Betsill, M. M. (2014). "Transnational Actors in International Environmental Politics." In *Advances in International Environmental Politics*, edited by Michelle M. Betsill, Kathryn Hockstetler, Dimitries Stevis (UK: Palgrave Macmillan), pp. 185–210.

Carlsson, L., and Sandström, A. (2008). "Network Governance of the Commons." *International Journal of the Commons* 2(1): 33–54.

Castells, M. (2008). "The New Public Sphere: Global Civil Society, Communication Networks, and Global Governance." *Annals of the American Academy of Political and Social Science* 616(1): 78–93.

CorpWatch. (2000). "Letters to Kofi Annan Blasting the Global Compact Corporations," July 25. http://www.corpwatch.org/article.php?id=961#july20 (accessed September 25, 2015).

Eilstrup-Sangiovanni, M. (2014). "Network Theory and Security Governance." In *Handbook of Governance and Security*, edited by J. Sperling (Cheltenham, UK: E. Elgar Publishing), pp. 41–63.

Eilstrup-Sangiovanni, M., and Jones, C. (2008). "Assessing the Dangers of Illicit Networks: Why Al-Qaeda May Be Less Dangerous Than Many Think." *International Security* 33(2): 7–44.

Emirbayer, M. (1997). "Manifesto for a Relational Sociology." *American Journal of Sociology* 103: 281–317.

Faul, M. V. (2015). "Networks and Power: Why Networks Are Hierarchical Not Flat, and What to Do about It." *Global Policy Journal.* doi: 10.1111/1758-5899.12270

Fomerand, J. (2003). "Mirror Tool, or Linchpin for Change? The UN and Development." International Relations Studies and UN Occasional Papers no. 2.

Gulati, R., Lavie, D., and Madhavan, R. (2011). "How Do Networks Matter? The Performance Effects of Interorganizational Networks." *Research in Organizational Behavior* 31: 207–224.

Hafner-Burton, E., Kahler, M., and Montgomery, A. H. (2009). "Network Analysis for International Relations." *International Organization* 63(2): 559–592.

Head, B. W. (2008). "Assessing Network-based Collaborations: Effectiveness for Whom?" *Public Management Review* 10(6): 733–749.

Hoemen, P. (2013). "Is the UN Global Compact Leadership Summit an Effective Forum for Change?" *Guardian*, Friday 6 September 2013.

Huppé, G., Creech, H., and Knoblauch, D. (2012). *The Frontiers of Networked Governance.* International Institute for Sustainable Development. http://www.iisd.org/pdf/2012/frontiers_networked_gov.pdf.

Initiatief Duurzame Handel (IDH): Sustainable Trade Initiative. (n.d.). "What We Do." http://www.idhsustainabletrade.com/what-we-do.

International Monetary Fund (IMF). (2016). "The IMF and Civil Society Organizations." http://www.imf.org/en/About/Factsheets/The-IMF-and-Civil-Society-Organizations.

Kahler, M., ed. (2009). *Networked Politics: Agency, Power, and Governance*. Ithaca, NY: Cornell University Press.

Keck, M. E., and Sikkink, K. (1998). *Activists beyond Borders: Advocacy Networks in International Politics*. Ithaca, NY: Cornell University Press.

Kersbergen, K. van, and Waarden, F. van. (2004). "Governance as a Bridge between Disciplines: Cross-disciplinary Inspiration Regarding Shifts in Governance and Problems of Governability, Accountability and Legitimacy." *European Journal of Political Research* 43(2): 143–171.

Kirchner, E. J. (2006). "The Challenge of European Union Security Governance." *Journal of Common Market Studies* 44(5): 945–966.

Kirchner, E., and Sperling, J. (2007). *EU Security Governance*. Manchester, UK: Manchester University Press.

Klijn, E. H., Ysa, T., Sierra, V., Berman, E., Edelenbos, J., and Chen, D. Y. (2016)."The Influence of Trust on Network Performance in Taiwan, Spain, and the Netherlands: A Cross-Country Comparison." *International Public Management Journal* 19(1): 111–139.

Lake, D. (2015). "Origins of Hierarchies: Laws, Norms, and Sovereignty." Paper prepared for the workshop Hierarchies in World Politics, University of Cambridge, June 21–22, 2015.

Levitt, B., and March, J. G. (1988). "Organizational Learning." *Annual Review of Sociology* 14: 319–338.

McCloskey, M. (2000). "Problems with using collaboration to shape environmental public policy." *Valparaiso University Law Review* 34: 423.

McGuire, M., and Agranoff, R. (2007). "Answering the Big Questions, Asking the Bigger Questions: Expanding the Public Network Management Empirical Research Agenda." Paper presented at the 9th Public Management Research Conference, Tucson, AZ, October 25–27.

Meyer, W., and Baltes, K. (2004). "Network Failures—How Realistic Is Durable Cooperation in Global Governance?" In *Governance for Industrial Transformation: Proceedings of the 2003 Berlin Conference on the Human Dimensions of Global Environmental Change*, edited by K. Jacob, M. Binder, and A. Wieczorek, pp. 31–51. http://userpage.fu-berlin.de/ffu/akumwelt/bc2003/proceedings/032%20-%20051%20meyer.pdf.

Ministry of Foreign Affairs, Netherlands. (2014). "IOB Review: Riding the Wave of Sustainable Commodity Sourcing." August. Review of the Sustainable Trade Initiative IDH 2008-2013, IOB Review no. 397. (https://www.rijksoverheid.nl/documenten/rapporten/2014/10/31/iob-review-riding-the-wave-of-sustainable-commodity-sourcing-engels).

Murdie, A. (2014). "The Ties That Bind: A Network Analysis of Human Rights INGOs." *British Journal of Political Science* 44(1): 1–27.

Newig, J., Günther, D., and Pahl-Wostl, C. (2010). "Synapses in the Network: Learning in Governance Networks in the Context of Environmental Management." *Ecology and Society* 15(4): 24. http://www.ecologyandsociety.org/vol15/iss4/art24/.

Paris, R. (2009). "Understanding the 'Coordination Problem' in Postwar Statebuilding." In *The Dilemmas of Statebuilding*, edited by R. Paris and T. D. Sisk, pp. 53–77 London: Routledge.

Podolny, J. M., and Page, K. L. (1998). "Network Forms of Organization." *Annual Review of Sociology* 24: 57–76.

Powell, W. (1990). "Neither Market nor Hierarchy: Network Forms of Organization." *Research in Organizational Behavior* 12: 295–336.

Provan, K., and Kenis, P. (2008). "Modes of Network Governance: Structure, Management, and Effectiveness." *Journal of Public Administration Research and Theory* 18(2): 229–252.

Provan, K., and Milward, B. (2001). "Do Networks Really Work? A Framework for Evaluating Public-Sector Organizational Networks." *Public Administration Review* 61(4): 414–423.

Rasche, A. (2009). "'A Necessary Supplement'—What the United Nations Global Compact Is and Is Not." *Business and Society* 48(4): 511–537.

Reinicke, W., Deng, F., Witte, J. M., Benner, T., Whitaker, B., and Gershman, J. (2000). *Critical Choices: The United Nations, Networks, and the Future of Global Governance.* Ottawa: International Development Research Centre.

Scharpf, F. W. (1993). "Coordination in Hierarchies and Networks." In *Games in Hierarchies and Networks: Analytical and Empirical Approaches to the Study of Governance Institutions,* edited by F. Scharpf, pp. 125–165. Boulder, CO: Westview.

Smith-Doerr, L., and Powell, W. W. (2005). "Networks and Economic Life." In *Handbook of Economic Sociology,* 2d ed., edited by N. Smelser and R. Swedberg, p. 384. Princeton, NJ: Princeton University Press.

Sørensen, E., and Torfing, J. (2005). "The Democratic Anchorage of Governance Networks." *Scandinavian Political Studies* 28(3): 195–218.

Thérien, J.-P., and Pouliot, V. (2006). "The Global Compact: Shifting the Politics of International Development?" *Global Governance* 12(1): 55–75.

Thompson, G. F. (2003). *Between Hierarchies and Markets: The Logic and Limits of Network Forms of Organization.* New York: Oxford University Press.

United Nations Development Programme (UNDP). (2001). *UNDP and Civil Society Organizations: A Policy of Engagement.* http://www.undp.org/content/dam/undp/documents/partners/civil_society/publications/2001_UNDP-and-Civil-Society-Organizations-A-Policy-of-Engagement_EN.pdf.

United Nations Development Programme (UNDP). (2006). "UNDP and Civil Society Organizations: A Toolkit for Strengthening Partnerships." https://sustainabledevelopment.un.org/content/documents/2141UNDP%20and%20Civil%20Society%20Organizations%20a%20Toolkit%20for%20Strengthening%20Partnerships.pdf.

United Nations Development Programme (UNDP). (2016). "Civil Society Organizations." http://www.undp.org/content/undp/en/home/ourwork/funding/partners/civil_society_organizations.html.

UN Joint Inspection Unit (2010). "United Nations corporate partnerships: The role and functioning of the Global Compact". Report prepared by Papa Louis Fall Mohamed Mounir Zahran, Geneva, 2010. JIU/REP/2010/9.

Vandenbergh, M. P. (2013). "Private Environmental Governance." *Cornell Law Review* 99(1): 129–200.

Voets, J., van Dooren, W. and de Rynck, F. (2008). "A Framework for Assessing the Performance of Policy Networks." *Public Management Review* 6(10): 773–790.

Ward, M. D., Stovel, K., and Sacks, A. (2011). "Network Analysis and Political Science." *Annual Review of Political Science* 14: 245–262.

Watts, D. J. (2003). *Six Dgrees: The Science of a Connected Age.* London: William Heinemann.

Webber, M., Croft, S., Howorth, J., Terriff, T., and Krahmann, E. (2004). "The Governance of European Security." *Review of International Studies* 30: 3–26.

Young, O. R. (2008). "The Architecture of Global Environmental Governance: Bringing Science to Bear on Policy." *Global Environmental Politics* 8(1): 14–32.

CHAPTER 30

....

HUMAN RIGHTS AND TRANSNATIONAL ADVOCACY NETWORKS

....

AMANDA MURDIE AND MARC POLIZZI

INTRODUCTION

....

DURING the Arab Spring of 2011, Bahraini citizens protested to demand an expansion of their political and civil rights, ultimately calling for an end to the monarchy. In response to the uprising, a royal decree declared a state of emergency. Security forces took to the streets, often with deadly consequences to peaceful protesters. Restrictions on civil liberties were coupled with widespread violations of physical integrity rights, including political killings, imprisonment, and torture.

During and in the aftermath of the uprisings, multiple human rights organizations have worked to try to improve the human rights situation. Within Bahrain, the ability of local human rights organizations, like the Bahrain Centre for Human Rights (BCHR), to work unencumbered for change is severely restricted. Even before 2011, the organization had been banned for speaking out against the government.[1] In response to protests in 2011, many of the organization's leadership were imprisoned and tortured. Some of the leadership remains behind bars.

Luckily, at the time of the uprising the BCHR was already well-connected to the larger human rights community. Leaders of BCHR were involved in other human rights organizations, including sitting on the board of advisers for the large, New York–based organization Human Rights Watch and a prominent umbrella group of human rights organizations, the International Federation for Human Rights.[2] The BCHR had also set up an office in Denmark after it was banned in Bahrain, allowing it to continue to spread its message internationally as the situation in Bahrain deteriorated.

Because of the connections the BCHR maintains, the plight of the people of Bahrain has not been forgotten. The larger human rights movement has ensured that the detention of the BCHR leadership and the human rights situation in Bahrain are international issues. In 2012, for example, the United Nations Working Group on Arbitrary Detention called for the immediate release of BCHR's founder, Abdulhadi Al-Khawaja, calling his imprisonment "arbitrary" and demanding the Bahraini government remedy the situation by ensuring Al-Khawaja's "immediate release" with compensation (UN A/HRC/WGAD/2012/6). In April 2015 Nabeel Rajab, the current president of BCHR, issued an open letter to US president Barack Obama from prison on the *New York Times*' website.[3] The letter thanked Obama for calling for his release and requested that Obama make the human rights situation in Bahrain a foreign policy concern in future interactions with the Bahraini government and other countries in the Middle East. The *New York Times* letter came after a joint statement in March 2015 by over two dozen human rights organizations that called for the release of Al-Khawaja, who was still in a Bahraini prison on hunger strike.[4] The current push for improvement in Bahraini human rights has not yet come to fruition; however, advocates hope that the attention the country received in the spring of 2015, which was heightened during the Grand Prix, will finally bring about lasting change.[5]

Sadly, the case of the BCHR and its struggle to support human rights is not unique. The pathway to human rights improvement is often very long and deadly (Risse, Ropp, and Sikkink, 2013). However, as the BCHR example illustrates, work by human rights advocates is not done in isolation. Advocates often formally organize and become part of larger movements for human rights improvements. In a very basic sense, human rights advocacy is *networked* advocacy. It often involves actions taken by actors that are interdependent, forging connections across borders (Keck and Sikkink, 1998). Through their connections, advocates are often able to influence the flow of information and resources in the support of certain human rights norms.

This chapter outlines the academic study of human rights and advocacy networks, mainly within international relations. For more than two decades, scholars have focused on the interactive and interdependent nature of activists with human rights goals (Brysk, 1993). Keck and Sikkink (1998) canonically referred to the work of many human rights activists as part of a "transnational advocacy network" (TAN). This term has become part of the human rights vernacular, routinely used by both governmental and nongovernmental actors to describe civil society's push for the realization of human rights principles.[6]

In addition to the terminology of the "network" within the study of human rights improvement, there is much more that network theory and network methods can add to this research area. After reviewing the extant literature, we illustrate how recent network studies in this area can be expanded and how more focus on the larger network literature can add to our understanding of human rights promotion.

THE TRANSNATIONAL ADVOCACY NETWORK

As mentioned, the study of human rights advocacy owes much to the work of Keck and Sikkink (1998) and their discussion of the TAN. According to this work, local organizations often become involved with a large number of like-minded groups and individuals outside of their state. These actors, which can include international nongovernmental organizations (NGOs) like Amnesty International and Human Rights Watch, UN officials, members of the clergy, donor foundations, third-party states, the media, and international celebrities, help local organizations in their push for human rights change. Keck and Sikkink (1998, 9) refer to these connected organizations and actors collectively as an actor in its own right: a TAN. Although TANs are not new, prior to Keck and Sikkink (1998), attention to TANs was rather limited within international relations (IR), in which many scholars focused solely on states as the only type of actor that can be effective at policy and behavior change in the international arena (Waltz, 1979).

Keck and Sikkink's (1998) discussion of TANs focuses on how information, goods, and ultimately power, are conveyed through the network. Although local organizations may be ineffective at bringing about human rights change by themselves, through the "dense web of connections" between organizations in the TAN, human rights improvement is possible (27).[7] According to Keck and Sikkink (1998), TANs are likely to emerge on issues that have some preexisting resonance, in which the effectiveness of purely domestic collective action is limited, but international contact is possible (12, 27).

Keck and Sikkink (1998) discuss one of the main processes of how TANs form and how they influence political outcomes as a "boomerang" pattern (12).[8] Within the boomerang model, a local organization that has been thwarted in its efforts to achieve political change sends out a call to the international community for help. The international community, typically through international NGOs located in democracies in the global North, responds to this call, working to increase both domestic pressure on and international attention to the repressive government (Brysk, 1993). Through the strategic use of information (often referred to as "naming and shaming") about human rights abuses, INGOs are able to get the attention of the international media, intergovernmental organizations (IGOs), and like-minded third-party governments. These international actors then put pressure on the repressive state to change its human rights practices. As Rodríguez Garavito (2015) recently remarked, with the rise of social media and the growth of organizations in the global South, it is now possible for there to be "multiple boomerang[s]," with "political pressure for human rights change com[ing] from different geographic locations, and is simultaneously mobilized and directed towards different and multiple targets" (n.p.). Risse, Ropp, and Sikkink (1999, 2013) later expanded on the boomerang model, outlining the stages a repressive government goes through as it is faced with increased advocacy network pressure. Although Keck and Sikkink (1998) do not argue that TANs are likely to be effective in all areas, their work outlines how TANs have influenced human rights improvement on issues of "bodily harm" and "legal equality" in states vulnerable to international pressure, as occurred in Mexico in the 1990s (26–29).

The study of networks is often divided into two approaches: "network-as-structure" and "network-as-actor" (Elkins, 2009).[9] Elkins (2009) calls Keck and Sikkink's (1998) work the "paradigmatic case of the network-as-actor" approach, in which "the network is no longer just a way of describing relationships among actors, but an actor unto itself"

(55–56). This might have been the case among the first wave of studies that focused on TANs, whose focus was often on case studies in which TANs had been successful in bringing about human rights change (Risse, 2002).

However, we cannot simply explore advocacy network outcomes without understanding both the variation in these network structures and how those differences can be consequential to the effects of TANs. Much recent work has used the framework of Keck and Sikkink (1998) as a springboard for looking within the TAN, both on how actors are connected and how these relationships can influence a whole host of outcomes critical to the study of human rights improvement (Bob, 2002; DeMars, 2005; Carpenter, 2007; Lake and Wong, 2009; Hughes et al., 2009; Paxton et al., 2015; von Bulow, 2009; Murdie and Davis, 2012a; Wong, 2012; Murdie, 2014; Bush, 2015).

The "networks-as-structures" approach has shifted the debate in an effort to develop a more complete picture of how these networks vary. Simply because two networks have the same general goal in mind, that does not necessarily mean that they have the same ability to achieve that goal. For example, the invisible children movement aims to end the use of child soldiers by Joseph Kony and his rebel army in war-torn Uganda. Amnesty International has long pursued this same agenda. While the latter is an international operation, pursuing multiple human rights agendas and holding organized operations resembling those of a corporation, beginning in 2004, less than a decade after it formed, there were questions about the stamina of the invisible children campaign.[10]

While the invisible children movement was successful in generating buzz on a worthy issue through a savvy social media campaign, it ultimately lacked the structures and clout that the more established Amnesty International possessed. This is not to say that the efforts of one group are "morally superior" to another. It simply means that the structures of these networks vary greatly due to the makeup of the actors, and the resources and technological expertise that some actors bring to the debate can drastically change the ability to see real human rights changes. As Wong (2012) notes, these internal network structures affect the tools and strategies that these networks can use, ultimately influencing their ability to make human rights issues politically salient on the world stage. How salient these issues become then determines the density of networks.

Many of these studies draw on network theory and methods. Due to lack of data, much of this work focuses only on networks of formal human rights organizations. The following sections outline some of this work and the research questions this work addresses, all of which draws on the canonical Keck and Sikkink study of TANs (1998).

The Benefits of Network Connections to Human Rights Actors

At the heart of the TAN approach is the idea that the connections between the actors that make up TANs help improve advocacy outcomes. In this sense, the network provides resources for the actors involved that they would not have if they had not been connected. In line with their principled motivations, these resources are then used to heighten the push for human rights improvement.

What resources does the network provide? The cross-disciplinary literature on TANs sees the resources from the network as a public good (Shumate and Dewitt, 2008; Shumate and Lipp, 2008; Murdie, 2014). DeMars (2005) contends that the advocacy network facilitates the transfer of "normative frames, material resources, political responsibility and information" between the organizations involved (51). By normative frames and political responsibility, DeMars is referring to the diffusion of specific tactics and advocacy approaches that can come from interactions among advocacy actors. One example here may be the expansion of the "rights-based" approaches to health and development; as organizations began to see positive results in framing what used to be humanitarian goals within the human rights framework, those that were part of this network reframed their work using this rights-based approach (Uvin, 2007). Normative framing can also be critical to expanding the overall size of the network.

Normative frames play an important role in connecting even seemingly unrelated organizations. As these organizations come together, local marginalized actors are able to sustain mobilization through increased associational and collective power against a more powerful rival (Arce, 2014). For example, in the early 2000s, in the small agricultural town of Tambogrande, Peru, local farmers worked alongside national and international NGOs in an effort to expel foreign mining companies from the community. Diverse frames were used for each level, forming a network of interrelated, but distinct, organizations (Arce, 2014). At the local level, the issue was one of economic livelihood. Mineral extraction threatened the local economy by consuming mass quantities of water, threatening their predominantly agricultural livelihood. At the national level, organizations framed resource extraction as a threat to the national culture of Peru. Tambogrande primarily grows lemons, an important ingredient in the national dish *ceviche*. Demonstrations at the local level revolved around the mantra "save the ceviche" (*salvemos el ceviche*) in order to garner support from regional and national NGOs (Paredes, 2008, 296). These regional organizations formed the Mesa Ténica, which provided legal and technical assistance to the local resistance. At the international level, a completely different frame was utilized, one of democratic rights for the people of Tambogrande. Shortly thereafter, Oxfam International and Oxfam UK funded and formally oversaw a local referendum, providing approximately US $20,000 (Paredes, 2008, 295).[11] These frames aided in successfully organizing a diverse, but interrelated, network of actors, using frames ranging from economic opportunities to democratic ideals.

There is also a plethora of examples of the material resources that flow between connected actors within TANs. Donors and donor organizations, like the Ford Foundation's Global Human Rights Fund or George Soros, fund NGOs that they know of or have worked with, like Human Rights Watch, which may then provide resources to local advocates or to human rights victims. Critics have often commented that there is North–South division in the amount of resources within many TANs and a sort of "benevolent colonialism" in the flow of resources (Sampson, 2002, 4). Donor funds mainly flow from the global North to the global South through a few powerful northern NGOs (Dieng, 2001; Fowler, 1992; Smith and Wiest, 2005; Shumate and Dewitt, 2008). Many organizations and donors have tried to respond to this criticism, increasing South–South NGO dialogue and learning (Keeney, 2012). This issue remains problematic for TANs and a fruitful area for more network research, as discussed in more depth below.

The TANs often criticize powerful state actors for egregious human rights violations. As actors that lack traditional military power, TANs "must use the power of their information, ideas, and strategies" to alter behavior (Keck and Sikkink, 1998, 16). Information flows in many directions within the network and can draw additional actors into the network, as occurred in the Bahraini example. Meernik et al. (2012) and Ron, Ramos, and Rodgers (2005) show that the existence of international NGOs within a state can increase the international media attention and international advocacy about human rights concerns that a state receives. Davis, Steinmetz, and Murdie (2012) show that information about human rights can alter opinions about human rights conditions. This information can ultimately influence foreign policy (Murdie and Peksen, 2013, 2014).

Reiterating DeMars's (2005) argument for the role of the network in increasing information about human rights, Murdie (2014) examines how network connections matter for information production. Murdie (2014) looks at the connections among 481 human rights organizations, as provided in the 2001/2002 edition of the *Yearbook of International Organizations*, a sourcebook for NGOs created by the Union of International Organizations. She finds that organizations that are more central to the overall human rights network have more stories attributed to them in Reuters Global News Service. In line with arguments that the human rights network is akin to a public good, Murdie (2014) also finds evidence of a "free-rider effect," wherein organizations with more unreciprocated ties (i.e., claiming to be connected to an organization that does not also claim a tie) receive less international press coverage because their benefits from the network in terms of information and resources could be limited.

Are these network resources ultimately successful for the goal of TANs? Under the network-as-actor approach, evidence of successful human rights change as a result of TANs does exist, albeit with some issues of case selection on the dependent variable (Risse, 2002). Using a large-scale cross-national approach, Wilson, Davis, and Murdie (2016) examine how characteristics of the network created by internationally connected conflict resolution organizations reduce the likelihood of conflict. It must be noted that this study, like most studies that attempt to examine the advocacy TAN, focuses only on the connections among international NGOs. This may be due to the difficulty in data connection in this area (Hafner-Burton, Kahler, and Montgomery, 2009).

Other non-network research has also found outcomes consistent with the TAN approach. For example, Murdie and Davis (2012b) find that the human rights information produced about a country ("shaming" reports) is only effective in bringing about human rights change when coupled with an increased presence of international human rights organizations within the state. Similarly, Neumeyer (2005) found that the UN human rights regime is only associated with an improvement in human rights when it is coupled with more international NGOs within a state.

This existing evidence, although incomplete, for the role of TANs in ultimately improving basic human rights is somewhat surprising, given what Keck and Sikkink (1998) termed the "information paradox." As Fariss (2014) explains, "the paradox occurs when an increase in information leads to difficulties in assessing the efficacy of advocacy campaigns over time because of the very success in collecting and aggregating accounts of repressive actions in the first place" (299). Since empirical data on human rights practices often rely on information produced by TANs, the very work of TANs may make it more difficult to assess their ultimate effectiveness. Fariss (2014) outlines a statistical procedure to account for the changing "standard of accountability" over time; the empirical work outlined above all finds evidence consistent with the basic boomerang model of human rights improvement even without this statistical fix.

The Effects of the Network on Human Rights Advocacy

Some have contended that Keck and Sikkink's (1998) portrayal of TANs downplayed the possible inequalities and hierarchies within the networks and among the organizations in TANs (Landolt, 2004; Bob, 2005; Carpenter, 2011). According to Carpenter et al. (2014), early work often saw TANs as composed of "homogeneous actors or a mass of dense, reciprocal ties that lead to collaborative outcomes" (5). Unlike the idea of TANs as horizontal and reciprocal, much recent work has stressed that there are often just a few central actors in the human rights network, and that hierarchy in the network can be linked to certain pathologies or idiosyncrasies in human rights advocacy (Bob, 2005; Carpenter, 2007, 2011; Lake and Wong, 2009; Murdie, 2014).

As Carpenter (2011) states, TANs "are less like road systems with many pathways between nodes and more like airlines, where the route between any two small cities generally depends on passing through a major hub" (73). Focusing on human rights international NGOs, Murdie (2014) finds Amnesty International is a major hub; its number of incoming ties from other organizations is almost double all others in the network. Murdie's (2014) analysis of the network of 481 human rights organizations in the 2001/ 2002 *Yearbook* shows that "many organizations are only connected to the overall network through a small number of organizations," and that the majority of human rights organizations have no connections to the larger network (15). Similarly, Carpenter (2011), in looking at the hyperlink-created network of human security organizations that focus on weapons bans, finds that a very small handful of organizations is central to the network, having the most connections to others.

In a qualitative study of Amnesty International, Lake and Wong (2009) and Wong (2012) discuss human rights TANs as scale-free networks, a common term in network science for a network structure dominated by a few central nodes that a steady stream of new actors want to be connected to, leading to a structure that resembles a hub and spoke (Barabási and Albert, 1999; Barabási, 2009). Bush's (2015) analysis of the hyperlink-created democracy promotion network also uses this scale-free terminology. Looking at a network beyond just NGOs, Bush finds that

> the inner core of the democracy establishment mostly consists of donor governments, multilateral organizations, and large Western NGOs, such as Freedom House and the National Democratic Institute, which themselves act as donors. (136)

What are the consequences of the scale-free nature of the human rights TAN? The extant literature has identified at least three consequences of the hub-and-spoke structure. Often the discussion of these consequences of the scale-free structure of the human rights TAN is negative, implying that the scale-free structure creates some problems in the promotion of human rights that might have been missing from the more idealistic view of TANs in Keck and Sikkink (1998). Our own reading of this literature, coupled with the overall network science literature on scale-free networks, does support the idea that the scale-free structure, although great for the quick dispersion of information from a central node, does create some limitations in global human rights promotion.

First, many scholars have stressed how a few powerful gatekeepers in the network control which human rights issues get advocacy attention (Bob, 2005; Carpenter, 2007, 2011; Lake and Wong, 2009; Wong, 2012; Carpenter et al., 2014). For example, Lake and Wong's (2009) and Wong's (2012) analysis of Amnesty International focuses on how the internal structure of Amnesty, which is itself organized as a scale-free network, together with its role as a central hub in the overall network, gave it a unique gatekeeping role in deciding which human rights norms would receive the most attention. Carpenter's many works on issue-emergence and nonemergence in various human security networks also indicates that organizational relationships and central organizations matter for both which issues get adopted and the timing of issue adoption in the larger network (2007, 2011; Carpenter et al., 2014).

Bob's (2005) work on issue adoption also highlights how gatekeeper organizations can pick human rights issues from the plethora presented to them by domestic groups and human rights victims, all of whom are trying to market themselves to these gatekeepers. Gatekeepers pick issues that fit their specific needs and that they think will be the most effective for their organizational goals. Bob's (2005) work stresses that actors in TANs have very different resources at their disposal. The ability to get the attention and support of the powerful gatekeepers varies by the savviness of the various domestic groups. Unlike Keck and Sikkink (1998), Bob's (2005) discussion of TANs centers on the "mutual but unequal value and need" that "underlie[s] network operation[s]." Bob's (2005) case studies reiterate how connections in TANs follow a preferential attachment property, with new domestic groups wanting to be attached to those already central to the network. Bob's (2005) qualitative analysis, however, does differ from the classical idea of growth in scale-free networks (Barabási and Albert, 1999): although new domestic groups and advocates are continually being created, they often lack the resources to become part of the overall network. We return to this dynamic in our discussion of the inequalities within TANs below.

The gatekeeping role has demonstrated the long-term power of these central actors in effectively controlling the nature of the debate. Less established, more isolated actors may be able to serve important functions within a network, such as increasing the salience of a particular issue, but this effect only occurs in the short term. As demonstrated in Meriläinen and Vos (2014), these actors can increase the salience of particular issues by bringing them to the attention of larger and more central NGOs. In their exploration of the grass-roots, social media–driven Kony 2012 campaign, Invisible Children (IC), a relatively unestablished NGO, was able to temporarily change the agenda. The campaign was able to garner the attention of predominant actors within the human rights network, including Amnesty International and Human Rights Watch. As previous scholars have noted, the more dominant actors within the network still serve a gatekeeping role, thereby applying dominant pressure on the network to change the agenda back. This case points to two important points about the modern network. New technologies presented by social media may be able to lower the threshold for new actors to make significant changes in the network, but this also demonstrates that gatekeepers still exert a great deal of power in what the final agenda will look like (Meriläinen and Vos, 2014).

A second consequence of the scale-free network structure of TANs is that the tactics and managerial practices of central organizations, especially when they are donor organizations, can permeate the network quickly and be adopted by those in "spoke" positions. Although the scale-free network may be an asset in the diffusion of best practices among actors in a TAN (Appe, 2015), this network structure could also limit innovation. As an example, Bush (2015) points out that there has been "taming" of democracy promotion in NGOs in the last few decades. Instead of a diversity of programs that seek regime change, central nodes in the democracy promotion network encouraged "technical programs that do not confront dictators" (i). Organizations that wanted to continue to be part of the network and receive the financial benefits of the network adopted these tactics. Although Bush (2015) remains agnostic about the overall effect of this change in tactic on democratization, it is clear that the structure of the network influenced the choice of tactics in these organizations.

A third implication of the scale-free network structure is best summed up by Barabási's (2009) statement that the creation of scale-free networks allow for a "rich-gets-richer process [to be] observed" (412). A number of studies have pointed out severe disparities in resources between organizations in the global North and those in the global South (Fowler, 1992; Dieng, 2001; Smith, 2002). A lack of resources can make it difficult for southern organizations to attend the international conferences where networking often occurs. It can also limit the communication technology through which southern organizations can become connected to other organizations. As a result, organizations in the global South are less likely to be connected to the overall human rights TAN (Murdie, 2014). For example, landless movements in South America fail to garner the international attention necessary for complex TANs to form (Bob, 2005). Even when they are connected, the preferential attachment property of scale-free networks may imply that other human rights actors are more likely to pass them over when forging new network ties in favor of the already established northern organizations that make up the core of the TAN.

What does this dynamic imply for human rights promotion? In addition to potentially limiting the issues and tactics that could flow from organizations in the global South, this disparity between organizations in the global North and the global South in the network could limit the legitimacy of the overall human rights movement in the global South. To the extent that the human rights issues covered are seen as "Western" or northern instead of reflecting the needs and desires of the global South, the overall movement loses potential advocacy actors and allies (Leech 2013). This exclusion leads to impotence within the network, as diverse perspectives, resources, frames, and labor are left out of the system.

The rosy view of technological advancements generated excitement that the proliferation of NGOs would be able to cross borders unimpeded (Falk, 1995). However, many groups employing these tools still fail to reach a wider audience. Moses Werror, the leader of Indonesia's Free West Papua Movement, writes, "We have struggled for more than 30 years, and the world has ignored our cause" (quoted in Bob, 2005, 3). The frame these groups employ matters a great deal for the connections they can create with northern NGOs. Bob (2005) notes the success that the Tibetan independence movement has in reaching out to a global community of activists, while its northwest neighbors, the Uyghurs, have been unable to reach the same audience, despite the use of domestic and international protests.

Moreover, as previously mentioned, the human rights network is a public good, providing resources to those who are part of the network (Murdie, 2014). To the extent that the scale-free structure and North–South disparities make it difficult for some organizations to be part of the network and expand their network connections, the potential benefits of the network for newly formed organizations in the global South may be somewhat limited. In addition, the need for forging network connections and expanding resources with northern organizations can also create dependence among organizations, complicating relationships and "often leading to a loss of domestic accountability for the Southern" organization (Murdie, 2014, 8).

Efforts to form South–South network connections have expanded; the idea here is to try to combat some of these issues in the existing network structure and the disparities in resources among organizations (Hill, 1996; Keeney, 2012). For example, as Lim and Kong (2013) remarked:

> Korean human rights groups have realized the necessity of developing solidarity among Asian human rights groups, thus strengthening South-South NGO cooperation, because they have grown tired of the over-representation of a few star North NGOs in the transnational public sphere. (53)

Despite these attempts, many southern NGOs simply get steamrolled out of the debate. Even though this has real consequences in disadvantaging human rights networks, empirical data demonstrate that these groups simply are unable to have to their voices heard over those in the global North (Carpenter et al., 2014; Murdie, 2014).

MOVING THE TAN LITERATURE FORWARD

Like Hafner-Burton, Kahler, and Montgomery (2009), we think that "analysts of transnational activist networks and nongovernmental organizations (NGOs) have only begun to apply network analysis" to this research area (576). The works discussed above show the promise of applying network theory and methods to the rigorous study of TANs. Network theory and network methodology provide at least two major contributions to existing literature on TANs. First, these tools leverage methodological rigor on existing theoretical research. Some existing studies have assumed networks as given without analyzing the structure or characteristics of such a network. As discussed, this structure can have drastic consequences for how the agenda is set and what tactics are used, and could exasperate existing disparities in resources among actors within the network. A hierarchical network type can be necessary for quick information flows throughout the network; it may help organizations respond quickly to urgent human rights abuses. However, a more hierarchical network—revolving around a small set of actors with high centrality—can ignore the perspectives of the global South, denying resources and information to some and marginalizing some actors in favor of others. When these structures are more consensus-based, decision-making may be more egalitarian, which allows the structure to incorporate the perspectives of a more diverse set of actors.

Second, and related, these methodologies open the door for previously unasked questions to be presented and analyzed. For example, we know that human rights organizations from the global South are less likely to be part of the overall human rights network of international NGOs (Murdie, 2014). What we do not know a lot about, however, is whether there is variation in the propensity of global South organizations to be part of the network. A key assumption in Keck and Sikkink (1998) is that TANs are likely to form about a specific repressive state when that state allows international contact (27). Future work could test whether organizations and actors from countries that severely restrict association rights are less likely to be part of the overall network. Given recent pushes by some repressive governments to limit the presence of foreign NGOs, empirically examining how country of origin matters for the ability of a human rights actor to be part of the larger network is definitely necessary. This would expand upon work by Stroup (2012) examining differences within organizations in the global North.

Murdie (2014) also outlines how other characteristics of organizations, like their connections to UN actors and whether they are religious or secular, matter for their likelihood to tie to certain organizations in the network. The larger literature on networks lays out the idea that homophilious actors are more likely to tie to each other (McPherson and Smith-Lovin, 1987). In this vein, future work looking at the attributes of the actors in TANs and how these attributes influence their propensity to tie would be incredibly useful to understand how TANs develop and which actors are likely to become an integral part of a TAN. For example, Murdie and Davis (2012a) look at a sample of over four thousand human rights, development, environmental, and health organizations and find that organizations with mission statements that include more than one issue area ("hybrids") are more likely to tie both to each other and to other organizations in the network; they are also more likely to fill a role as a "bridge" in the overall international NGO network. Within the human rights TAN area, it would be interesting to examine whether hybridity matters for an organization's position within the human rights TAN. Does being a hybrid bring about negative consequences for the organization within a specific issue area? Does it spread its resources thin, diluting the group's effectiveness in setting the agenda of either network?

One key limitation in the application of network analysis to the study of TANs is the availability of data (Hafner-Burton, Kahler, and Montgomery, 2009). This appears to be quickly changing, however, in many exciting ways. As mentioned, most of the extant work on TANs only focuses on formal NGOs, often using the *Yearbook of International Organizations* as its source for organizational information. Although this data source is not without its limitations, even existing data from the *Yearbook* could be expanded upon in looking at human rights TANs. For example, many projects on IGO networks within IR make use of data from the *Yearbook* to create country-level measures of embeddedness in the overall network (Dorussen and Ward, 2008). Similar analyses are currently being conducted within human rights (Wilson, Davis, and Murdie, 2016). Another interesting use of *Yearbook* network data that could be extended to focus solely on human rights organizations has been carried out in sociology by Paxton et al. (2015) in their focus on the INGO Network Country Score.

A major criticism raised against quantitative human rights research is the potential bias of the data utilized, particularly when they come from human rights organizations themselves (Fariss, 2014). New improvements in how these data are obtained and the detail of information provided can help overcome some of these criticisms. Amnesty International, for example, has recently been using satellite imaging to show on-the-ground abuse. Rather than figures coming from secondhand accounts and reports, these visual data help us clearly see the consequences of human rights organization shaming campaigns. For example, in early January 2015 the *New York Times* reported that Amnesty International and Human Rights Watch had used satellite imaging to report on the destruction caused by Boko Haram in northern Nigeria.[12] Original figures of the devastation could not be verified due to difficulties in reaching conflict areas controlled by the militia group. This is not an issue unique to the case of Boko Haram. Many human right organizations find it difficult to obtain information in such locales, where gunmen can come in at anytime, targeting civilians indiscriminately. Satellite images provide more accurate and safer access to sensitive information, and data from satellite images could be very useful for human rights research in the future (Min, 2015).

Many TAN data collection projects are making use of Issue Crawler[13] and related techniques to create network data using hyperlinks across organizations and actors (Carpenter, 2007, 2011; Bush, 2015). Possibilities exist, of course, for examining networks created by Facebook or Twitter addressing human rights issues. As Hennicke (2014)'s work on Eurpean Union NGOs indicates, hyperlink methods can be used to create non-binary network data, which may be useful at expanding our understanding of networking dynamics in human rights. The great thing about these techniques is that they can be used on samples of actors that are expanded beyond the traditional focus on just formal international NGOs. Another related technique that could be useful for human rights researchers is to focus on network analysis from texts and narrative (Franzosi, 2010). This could be especially useful for understanding how networks develop and change in response to a specific repressive event or uprising. Another data source that could be incredibly useful for network analysis is the Transnational NGO Interview Project and its survey of US organizational leaders about their networking partners (Hermann et al., 2010; Mitchell, 2014).

CONCLUSION

This chapter has outlined the importance of applying network theory and methodologies to existing studies of human rights transnational advocacy. The seminal work of Keck and Sikkink (1998) laid the groundwork for our understanding of human rights advocacy using a "networks-as-actors" approach, highlighting how nonstate actors can play a large role in improving human rights conditions. This work has since expanded into examining how TANs can inform our understanding of the process of human rights change beyond the state level. Now, as network theories and methodologies have evolved into the international relations discipline, and as data on these networks become more available, scholars can ask new and exciting questions about how the structure of the network itself can influence human rights outcomes.

We have outlined a few important areas in which these methodologies and theories have made a significant contribution to the literature. As demonstrated, the scale-free network of TANs, with strong central actors, has played an important role in forming the human rights agenda, as well as influencing the distribution of resources, information, and financing. Previous work has demonstrated massive disparities in available resources between the global North and the global South (Fowler, 1992; James, 1994; Dieng, 2001; Smith, 2002). Actors in the global South are largely left out of the agenda-setting process by the more powerful gatekeepers and receive fewer resources and less international attention to alleviate human rights abuses. This can ultimately lead to distrust and a bias within human rights advocacy. Network analysis has afforded us the ability to understand not only how the TAN structure has generated this disparity, but also how some of these negative consequences can be overcome.

Future studies can explore how network characteristics and structures can influence human rights outcomes. For example, a network's decision-making style can foment a more efficient use of resources and division of labor, having real consequences for human rights outcomes. Further, focusing on the connections among various groups of actors, like NGOs and IGOs, can help us understand the nuisances of the boomerang model of Keck and Sikkink (1998), analyzing the causal processes behind human rights improvement and why some attempts by certain TANs are more effective than others.

Human rights literature has only recently adopted network methodologies and has already developed a rich understanding of the consequences of these structures. The possibilities presented by increased data collection and evolving knowledge of network methodologies not only present the opportunity for empirical rigor to existing studies, but also illuminate a whole new line of questions that previously could not be asked. Given the ever-increasing connectedness of the international community, these networks can have real implications for human rights conditions around the world.

Notes

1. http://www.bahrainrights.org/en/about-us.
2. See https://www.fidh.org/International-Federation-for-Human-Rights/north-africa-middle-east/bahrain/bahrain-end-reprisals-against-leading-human-rights-defender-nabeel.
3. http://kristof.blogs.nytimes.com/2015/04/10/open-letter-from-nabeel-rajab-to-president-obama/?_r=0.
4. https://www.fidh.org/International-Federation-for-Human-Rights/north-africa-middle-east/bahrain/bahrain-human-rights-groups-express-grave-concern-as-imprisoned.
5. https://www.amnesty.org/en/articles/news/2015/04/bahrain-hopes-of-reform-crushed-amid-chilling-crackdown-on-dissent/.
6. For example, Keck and Sikkink (1998) was referenced in a recent preliminary text of a UN declaration on the rights of people to international solidarity (UN General Assembly 2014, A/HRC/26/34/Add.1). Dejusticia, a Columbian human rights organization, has also referred to Keck and Sikkink (1998) in the discussion of its prior campaigns (Rodríguez Garavito 2015).
7. Although the focus here is on TANs within the realm of human rights, Keck and Sikkink (1998) also outlined examples from environmental politics. More recently, scholars have also extended the study of environmental advocacy networks (Hadden 2015).
8. It is worth noting that a recent lecture on the fifteenth anniversary of Keck and Sikkink (1998) at Brown University reiterated that the boomerang model is just one model of transnational advocacy. See http://watson.brown.edu/events/2015/15-years-transnational-activism-what-difference-has-it-made.
9. Sikkink (2009), in a chapter in the same volume as Elkins (2009), sees these two approaches as more of a continuum.
10. The *Washington Post* ran an article on December 30, 2014, entitled "Why did Invisible Children Dissolve?" While the founders of the organization stated that they were "going through a transition," questions about the accuracy of the data provided by the group raise concerns about the effectiveness that such a group can have. In addition, their social media

campaign reaches tens of thousands of individuals, but many of these individuals fit within the same demographic of American teenagers of middle- and upper-class socioeconomic backgrounds.

11. As Arce (2014) notes, despite the legality of the referendum being debated at the national level, it is important to realize that this democratic mechanism would not have been possible without the infrastructure of an international network.

12. Nossiter (2015).

13. www.issuecrawler.net.

REFERENCES

Appe, S. (2015). "NGO Networks, the Diffusion and Adaptation of NGO Managerialism, and NGO Legitimacy in Latin America." *Voluntas: International Journal of Voluntary and Nonprofit Organizations* 26(1): 122.

Arce, M. (2014). *Resource Extraction and Protest in Peru*. Pittsburgh, PA: University of Pittsburgh Press.

Barabási, A.-L. (2009). "Scale-Free Networks: A Decade and Beyond." *Science* 325(5939): 412.

Barabási, A.-L., and Albert, R. (1999). "Emergence of Scaling in Random Networks." *Science* 286(5439): 509–512.

Bob, C. (2002). "Globalization and the Social Construction of Human Rights Campaigns." In *Globalization and Human Rights*, edited by A. Brysk, pp. 133–147. Berkeley and Los Angeles, CA: University of California Press.

Bob, C. (2005). *The Marketing of Rebellion: Insurgents, Media, and International Activism*. Cambridge, UK: Cambridge University Press.

Brysk, A. (1993). "From Above and Below Social Movements, the International System, and Human Rights in Argentina." *Comparative Political Studies* 26(3): 259–285.

Bush, S. (2015). *The Taming of Democracy Assistance*. Cambridge, UK: Cambridge University Press.

Carpenter, C. (2007). "Setting the Advocacy Agenda: Theorizing Issue Emergence and Non-emergence in Transnational Advocacy Networks." *International Studies Quarterly* 51: 99–120.

Carpenter, C. (2011). "Vetting the Advocacy Agenda: Network Centrality and the Paradox of Weapons Norms." *International Organization* 65(1): 69–102.

Carpenter, C., Duygulu, S., Montgomery, A. H., and Rapp, A. (2014). "Explaining the Advocacy Agenda: Insights From the Human Security Network." *International Organization* 68(2): 449–470.

Davis, D., Steinmetz, C. G., and Murdie, A. (2012). "'Makers and Shapers': Human Rights INGOs and Public Opinion." *Human Rights Quarterly* 34(1): 199–224.

DeMars, W. E. (2005). *NGOs and Transnational Networks: Wild Cards in World Politics*. London: Pluto Press.

Dieng, A. (2001). "The Contribution of NGOs to the Prevention of Human Rights Violations." In *The Prevention of Human Rights Violations*, edited by L.-A. Sicilianos, pp. 259–268. The Hague: Kluwer Law International.

Dorussen, H., and Ward, H. (2008). "Intergovernmental Organizations and the Kantian Peace A Network Perspective." *Journal of Conflict Resolution* 52(2): 189–212.

Elkins, Z. (2009). "Constitutional Networks." In *Networked Politics: Agency, Power, and, Governance*, edited by M. Kahler, pp. 43–66. Ithaca, NY: Cornell University Press.

Falk, R. A. (1995). *On Humane Governance: Toward a New Global Politics; The World Order Project Report of the Global Civilization Initiative*. University Park: Pennsylvania State University Press.

Fariss, C. J. (2014). "Respect for Human Rights Has Improved over time: Modeling the Changing Standard of Accountability." *American Political Science Review* 108(2): 297–318.

Fowler, A. (1992). "Distant Obligations: Speculations on NGO Funding and the Global Market." *Review of African Political Economy* 19: 9–29.

Franzosi, R. (Ed.). (2010). *Quantitative Narrative Analysis*. No. 162. Sage.

Hadden, J. (2015). *Networks in Contention: The Divisive Politics of Climate Change*. Cambridge: Cambridge University Press.

Hafner-Burton, E., Kahler, M., and Montgomery, A. H. (2009). "Network Analysis for International Relations." *International Organization* 63(3): 559–592.

Hennicke, M. (2014). "Birds of a Feather, Stronger Together? Network Externalities in NGO Cooperation." http://federation.ens.fr/ydepot/semin/texte1314/HEN2014BIR.pdf.

Hermann, M. G., Lecy, J. D., Mitchell, G. E., Pagé, C., Raggo, P., Schmitz, H. P., and Viñuela, L. (2010). "Transnational NGO: A Cross-Sectorial Analysis of Leadership Perspectives." http://www.maxwell.syr.edu/uploadedFiles/moynihan/tngo/Abridged_white_paper_19_APR_2010.pdf.

Hill, T. (Ed.). (1996). *United Nations, Ngos and Global Governance: Challenges for the 21st Century*. Darby, PA: DIANE Publishing.

Hughes, M. M., Peterson, L., Harrison, J. A. and Paxton, P., 2009. "Power and relation in the world polity: the INGO network country score, 1978–1998." *Social Forces* 87(4): 1711–1742.

Keck, M. E., and Sikkink, K. (1998). *Activists Beyond Borders: Advocacy Networks in International Politics*. Ithaca, NY: Cornell University Press.

Keeney, G. (2012). "Knowledge Management and Collaboration Effects: South-South Ngo Collaboration: A Case Study on the Brazilian Interdisciplinary Aids Association." *Future Studies Research Journal: Trends and Strategies* 4(1): 159–201.

Lake, D., and Wong, W. (2009). "The Politics of Networks: Interests, Power, and Human Rights Norms." In *Networked Politics: Agency, Power, and Governance*, edited by M. Kahler, pp. 127–150. Ithaca, NY: Cornell University Press.

Landolt, L. K. (2004). "(Mis) constructing the Third World? Constructivist Analysis of Norm Diffusion: Feature Review." *Third World Quarterly* 25(3): 579–591.

Leech, G. (2013). "Promoting Injustice: The Bias of Human Rights Watch." CounterPunch, March 14. http://www.counterpunch.org/2013/03/14/the-bias-of-human-rights-watch/.

Lim, H.-C., and Kong, S.-K. (2013). "Threats or Leverage for Korean Civil Society in Contesting Globalization." In *Citizenship and Migration in the Era of Globalization*, edited by M. Pohmann, J. Yang, and J.-H. Lee, pp. 39–58. New York: Springer.

McPherson, J. M., and Smith-Lovin, L. (1987). "Homophily in Voluntary Organizations: Status Distance and the Composition of Face-to-Face Groups." *American Sociological Review* 52: 370–379.

Meernik, J., Aloisi, R., Sowell, M., and Nichols, A. (2012). "The Impact of Human Rights Organizations on Naming and Shaming Campaigns." *Journal of Conflict Resolution* 56(2): 233–256.

Meriläinen, N., and Vos, M. (2014). "Framing by Actors in the Human Rights Debate: The Kony 2012 Campaign." *Nordic Journal of Human Rights* 32(3): 238–257.

Min, B. (2015). *Power and the Vote: Elections and Electricity in the Developing World*. New York: Cambridge University Press.

Mitchell, G. E. (2014). "Collaborative Propensities among Transnational NGOs Registered in the United States." *American Review of Public Administration* 44(5): 575–599.

Murdie, A. (2014). "The Ties That Bind: A Network Analysis of Human Rights International Nongovernmental Organizations." *British Journal of Political Science* 44: 1–27.

Murdie, A., and Davis, D. R. (2012a). "Looking in the Mirror: Comparing INGO Networks Across Issue Areas." *Review of International Organizations* 7: 177–202.

Murdie, A. M., and Davis, D. R. (2012b). "Shaming and Blaming: Using Events Data to Assess the Impact of Human Rights INGOs." *International Studies Quarterly* 56(1): 1–16.

Murdie, A. and Peksen, D. (2013). "The impact of human rights INGO activities on economic sanctions." *Review of International Organizations* 8(1): 33–53.

Murdie, A. and Peksen, D. (2014). "The Impact of Human Rights INGO Shaming On Humanitarian Interventions." *Journal of Politics* 76(1): 215–228.

Neumeyer, E. (2005). "Do International Human Rights Treaties Improve Respect for Human Rights?" *Journal of Conflict Resolution* 49(6): 925.

Nossiter, A. (2015). "Satellite Images Show Ruin Left by Boko Haram, Groups Say." *New York Times*, January 15. http://www.nytimes.com/2015/01/16/world/africa/boko-haram-rampage-in-nigeria-is-shown-in-satellite-images-groups-say.html?_r=0. Accessed September 3, 2015.

Paredes, M. (2008). "El caso de Tambogrande." In *Defendiendo derechos y promoviendo cambias: El Estado, las empresas extractivas y las comunidades locales en el Perú*, edited by M. Scurrah, pp. 268–300. Lima: Instituto de Estudios Peruanos.

Paxton, P., Hughes, M. M., and Reith, N. (2015). "Extending the INGO Network Country Score, 1950–2008." *Sociological Science* 2: 287–307.

Risse, T. (2002). "Transnational Actors and World Politics." In *The Handbook of International Relations*, edited by T. Risse, W. Carlsenaes, and B. Simmons, pp. 255–274. Thousand Oaks, CA: Sage Publications.

Risse T., Ropp, S. C., and Sikkink, K. (Eds) (1999). *The Power of Human Rights: International Norms and Domestic Change*. Cambridge, UK: Cambridge University Press.

Risse, T., Ropp, S. C., and Sikkink, K. (Eds.). (2013). *The Persistent Power of Human Rights: From Commitment to Compliance*. Cambridge, UK: Cambridge University Press.

Rodríguez Garavito, C. (2015). "Multiple Boomerangs: New Models of Global Human Rights Advocacy." https://www.opendemocracy.net/openglobalrights/c%C3%A9sar-rodr%C3%ADguezgaravito/multiple-boomerangs-new-models-of-global-human-rights-advocy.

Ron, J., Ramos, H., and Rodgers, K. (2005). "Transnational Information Politics: NGO Human Rights Reporting, 1986–2000." *International Studies Quarterly* 49(3): 557–588.

Sampson, S. (2002). "Weak States, Uncivil Societies and Thousands of NGOs: Benevolent Colonialism in the Balkans." In *The Balkans in Focus: Cultural Boundaries in Europe*, edited by S. Resic and B. Tornquist-Plewa, pp. 27–44. Sweden: Nordic Academic Press.

Shumate, M., and Dewitt, L. (2008). "The North/South Divide in NGO Hyperlink Networks." *Journal of Computer-Mediated Communication* 13: 405–428.

Shumate, M., and Lipp, J. (2008). "Connection Collective Action Online: An Examination of the Hyperlink Network Structure of an NGO Issue Network." *Journal of Computer-Mediated Communication* 14: 178–201.

Sikkink, K. (2009). "The Power of Networks in International Politics." In *Networked Politics: Agency, Power, and Governance*, edited by M. Kahler, pp. 228–250. Ithaca, NY: Cornell University Press.

Smith, J. (2002). "Bridging Global Divides? Strategic Framing and Solidarity in Transnational Social Movement Organizations." *International Sociology* 17(4): 505–528.

Smith, J., and Wiest, D. (2005). "The Uneven Geography of Global Civil Society: National and Global Influences on Transnational Association." *Social Forces* 84: 621–652.

Stroup, S. S. (2012). *Borders among Activists: International NGOs in the United States, Britain, and France*. Ithaca, NY: Cornell University Press.

Uvin, P. (2007). "From the Right to Development to the Rights-based Approach: How 'Human Rights' Entered Development." *Development in Practice* 17(4–5): 597–606.

Von Bülow, M. (2009). "Networks of Trade Protest in the Americas: Toward a New Labor Internationalism?" *Latin American Politics and Society* 51(2): 1–28.

Waltz, K. (1979). *Theory of International Politics*. Reading, MA: Addison-Wesley.

Wilson, M., Davis, D. R. and Murdie, A., (2016). "The View from the Bottom Networks of Conflict Resolution Organizations And International Peace." *Journal of Peace Research* 53(3): 442–458.

Wong, W. H. (2012). *Internal Affairs: How the Structure of NGOs Transforms Human Rights*. Ithaca, NY: Cornell University Press.

CHAPTER 31

···

DEMOCRACY AND COOPERATIVE NETWORKS

···

ZEEV MAOZ

INTRODUCTION

···

NATION-STATES interact along a large number of dimensions. Some of these interactions are cooperative; some are conflictual. Two states may engage in both conflictual and cooperative interaction simultaneously. The frequency and degree of cooperation, however, outpaces the frequency and degree of conflict. Just as an illustration, consider figure 31.1, which provides a stream of conflict and cooperation events throughout the globe over the period of June 2014 to February 2015.

As can be seen from this figure, conflict and cooperation events are strongly and negatively correlated (r = −0.931), suggesting that fast-news days are those with a lot of reports on both conflict and cooperation. Conversely, slow-news days are typically slow on both. However, the rate of cooperation on most days averages about 1.5 times the rate of conflict events. This is a conservative estimate of the cooperation-to-conflict ratio. This inequality is especially significant given the strong bias toward reporting of conflict events compared to cooperative ones in the source media for such event data sets. Importantly, it vindicates persistent complaints by scholars of international cooperation that cooperative behavior receives far less attention in the scholarly literature than conflictual behavior (Mansbach and Vasquez, 1981; Blainey, 1988).[1]

Cooperation happens all the time and with relatively high frequency. Some aspects of cooperative international behavior are institutionalized by agreements, treaties, or organizations. Such formalized activity may be governed or regulated by policies of national governments. Other forms of cooperation are largely informal and entail little or no government control or intervention. These may involve cooperative interactions by individuals, groups, or institutions across national borders without official intrusion. My focus in this review is on institutionalized cooperation. Because these cooperative behaviors take place due to governmental decisions or with the consent and approval of

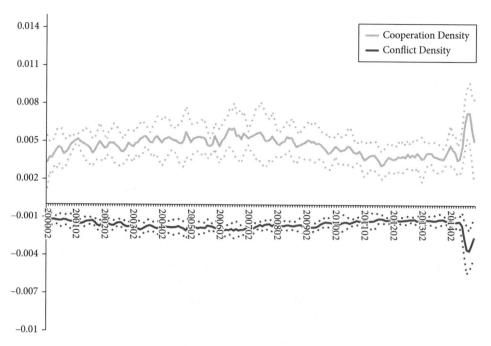

FIGURE 31.1 Fluctuation of Global Patterns of Conflict and Cooperation, 2000–2015 Data are three-month moving averages of mean densities of conflict and cooperation networks. Dotted lines are 95% confidence intervals.

Source: Original data combine two events data sets: the Integrated Crisis Early Warning System (ICEWS—https://dataverse.harvard.edu/dataverse/ICEWS) and the Phoenix Events Data Set (http://phoenixdata.org/).

national governments, a key question in the literature concerns the factors that affect the emergence, persistence, and termination of cooperative arrangements.

The aim of this brief review is to assess the contribution of network analysis to the study of international cooperation. To do so, I focus on the key theories of international cooperation that are not formally linked to network analysis. Although the concept of network may be used quite often in such studies, the key insights of network analysis have not been part of much of the work on international cooperation. The study of international cooperation from a network analytic perspective is a relatively new enterprise, and as such the contributions of this approach are only beginning to influence the field.

The key theme of this review is threefold.

1. Studies of cooperative behavior that have not relied on the fundamental assumptions of network analysis have suffered from significant substantive and methodological issues. The key contribution of network analytic studies to our understanding of the causes and processes of international cooperation is that they identified these inherent issues in previous research and made important strides to fix many of these problems.

2. Network analytic studies of cooperation worked pretty much within the general theoretical frameworks of previous studies; they have not developed new theories of cooperation. However, the methodological and conceptual advances provided by network analytic studies help clarify (and in some cases settle) some of the key controversies in the field and corroborate other results on the determinants of international cooperation.

3. However, the network analysis of cooperation has yet to harness the full potential of this approach. There are important lacunae that both traditional studies and more recent network analytic studies of cooperation have yet to fill. I point out some of these and demonstrate the future potential of employing network analytic approaches to the study of cooperation.

The Conventional Wisdom on International Cooperation

A key argument in the traditional literature on international cooperation is that the factors that determine cooperation in one domain may be different from those that determine cooperation in other domains. For example, models of alliance behavior focus on security-related factors such as the need to balance against threats or power (e.g., Walt, 1988), while the common model of trade cooperation—the gravity model—focuses on the structure of economic systems (e.g., Helpman, Melitz, and Rubinstein, 2008). Several studies suggest that there exists a—potentially causal—relationship between different cooperative domains (e.g., between trade and alliances). However, regarding the existence of such a linkage or the direction of the causal arrow, the jury is still out.[2]

Theories of international cooperation are typically associated with the liberal paradigm of international relations (Keohane and Nye, 1987; Keohane, 1984, 1986; Moravcsik, 1997). This paradigm is based on a number of key assumptions (Maoz, 2010, 158–159; Moravcsik, 1997, 516–521):

- *Political actors—individuals, groups, organizations—are rational, utility maximizers.* Liberals agree with realists that political actors are rational, seeking to maximize their interests. However, liberals—unlike offensive realists, who argue that states are relative-gains maximizers—claim that these actors are absolute-gains maximizers. The implication of this is that most international interactions reflect mixed-motive games rather than fixed-sum games.
- *Domestic structures and processes affect states' foreign policies.* States are not unitary actors; the choices that political leaders make vis-à-vis external actors are the net result of processes of interest representation of several societal sectors.[3]

- *States' international behavior is driven by multiple motivations.* Unlike realist theorists, who claim that states' international behavior is driven primarily (or exclusively) by security concerns or by the pursuit of power, liberals suggest that states' behavior is driven by multiple goals, including economic, social, and even personal ambitions of political leaders.
- *State behavior is determined (at least in part) by international interdependence.* One state's preferences interact with the preferences of others. This implies that a state cannot accomplish desirable outcomes without taking into account other states' preferences. It also means that in many settings, international coordination is instrumental for accomplishing national goals.
- *Institutions are designed to overcome collective good dilemmas.* Due to the inherent structure of interdependence in international relations, collective good problems are bound to arise. Consequently, states have designed institutions to mitigate these problems, by increasing transparency and managing distributional issues.

Several sets of testable ideas stem from these assumptions. The first has to do with differences between states' foreign policy strategies due to differences in the makeup of their domestic political systems or societal processes. Perhaps the key set of insights in this context concerns systematic differences between democracies and authoritarian states when it comes to conflict and cooperation. The general propositions in this context suggest that democracies are less prone to fight and more prone to cooperate—especially with one another—than are autocracies. This insight was corroborated across a wide array of studies. The most robust set of results concerns the so-called democratic peace proposition. The finding that democracies do not fight each other in full-scale wars and are far less likely to fight each other in lower-level militarized disputes has received overwhelming support and corroboration in empirical studies (Small and Singer, 1976; Maoz and Abdolali, 1989; Maoz and Russett, 1992, 1993; Russett, 1993; Russett and O'neal, 2001). Although this has been challenged from a number of different perspectives (e.g., Spiro, 1994; Farber and Gowa, 1995; Oren, 1995; Rosato, 2003; Gartzke, 2007; Mousseau, 2013; Gibler, 2012), it generally seems to hold as one of the most robust results in international relations (IR) research (Maoz, 1998; Dafoe, O'neal, and Russett, 2013; Ray, 2013).

The differences between democracies and other states extend to other forms of "positive," that is, cooperative, interactions. Siverson and Emmons (1991) and Maoz (2000, 2002) show that democracies are far more likely to form alliances with each other than are other regime combinations. Here too, the causal arrow between democracies and alliances has been challenged (Gibler and Wolford, 2006), but the general result seems to be fairly robust.

In the area of international trade, joint democracy also seems to feature as a strong determinant of the presence and magnitude of trade (Mansfield and Milner, 2012; Mansfield, Milner, and Rosendorf, 2000; 2002; Rosendorff and Milner, 2001). Finally, there is significant evidence that democracy is a strong motivator for participation in international organizations (Mansfield and Pevehouse, 2006).

Another important implication of these arguments is the relationship between interdependence and conflict. Here too a significant debate exists in the literature. O'neal et al., (1996); Russett, Oneal, and Davis (1998); and Russett and O'neal (2001) showed, in the spirit of such economic and political philosophers as August Comte, Adam Smith, and Emmanuel Kant, that economic interdependence has a significant negative impact on the probability of conflict. The literature on the "capitalist peace" (Gartzke, 2007; Mousseau, 2013), while questioning the validity of the democratic peace proposition, also suggests that economic ties tend to promote peaceful relations between states.

A third element in the "Kantian Tripod" (Russett and O'neal, 2001) is the effect of international organizations on peace. Here the evidence is less robust (e.g., Russett, Oneal, and Davis, 1998; Pevehouse and Russett, 2006), but it is nonetheless suggestive of a potential relationship. This relationship, however, has been challenged by evidence of selection effects: states select themselves to the same international organizations because they do not have reason (and therefore are unlikely) to fight each other.

All in all, there seems to be compelling evidence that some of the key propositions of the liberal paradigm about the relationship between domestic political structures and international cooperation, as well about the relationship between indicators of political and economic cooperation and peace are supported by empirical evidence. On the face of it, this research appears to be quite convincing. So the key question here is how network analysis can contribute to these insights.

To answer this question, we first have to ascertain to what extent empirical analyses of liberal theories of cooperation—in particular those that focus on the effects of democracy and cooperation—have dealt with potential biases, both substantive and methodological. This is the key line of attack of network analysts on traditional studies of conflict and cooperation. Specifically, most analyses of the determinants and consequences of international cooperation assume—implicitly or explicitly—that dyads are independent of each other. Methodologically, most analyses discussed above use the dyad-year as the unit of analysis, and the estimation methods rely on assumptions of independent identically distributed (IID) errors. However, as numerous analyses suggest (Cranmer and Desmarais, 2011; Cranmer, Desmarais, and Menninga, 2012; Ward, Siverson, and Cao, 2007; Cranmer and Desmarais, 2016), the probability and magnitude of cooperation between two states is affected by the extent to which each of these states cooperates with third parties. It may also be affected by the degree and nature of cooperation in the system as a whole. This suggests that dyadic observations are not independent of each other. Rather, they may be subject to "network effects." The key argument here is that once we estimate the way in which the structure of network ties affects dyadic cooperation, our inferences about the way in which such exogenous variables as democracy or interdependence affect the level of cooperation or the level of conflict between states are apt to change significantly.

Beyond controlling for network effects, understanding how and which specific aspects of network structure affect cooperation is substantively important regardless of the need to provide meaningful statistical inference. This is important because the structure of networks might not only affect dyadic choices about finding or sustaining partners for cooperative ventures. It might also affect spillover processes from one network to another. It might affect the emergence of cooperative structures beyond the dyad. Finally, it may affect overall degrees of conflict and cooperation in the system.

Dyadic interaction between states is interesting to understand and model. However, the interaction within a dyad does not occur in a vacuum; it is both influenced by and influences the interaction between dyad members and other states. The choice of partners for interaction in one domain (e.g., security) may also be influenced by the choice of partners for interaction in other domains (e.g., trade, environment). Finally, the implications of the interactive choices of states go beyond the selection of individual partners for cooperation or the targets of conflict actions. Specifically, these choices have both higher-order and emergent consequences. These are key insights of network analysis and—until recently—vastly under-researched areas in IR.

These two insights form the key contributions of network analytic studies to the understanding of the causes and consequences of international cooperation. This is what we turn to next.

Network Analytic Studies of Conflict and Cooperation

To facilitate the review, I focus first on network-related determinants of international cooperation. Next, I examine the network-related implications of international cooperation on behavior—principally on the occurrence and magnitude of international conflict.

Network Determinants of International Cooperation

The first group of network studies of cooperation focused on the manner in which different types of network dependencies affected cooperative behavior. The work of Ward and Hoff (Hoff and Ward, 2004; Ward, Hoff, and Lofdhall, 2003) examined the effect of second- and third-order effects on conflict and cooperation events. They find remarkable similarity of network (first-, second-, and third-order) effects on both dyadic conflict and dyadic cooperation.

Maoz (2010) explored the relationship between intrinsic nodal attributes and cooperative network position. He found that a state's regime score was one of the most robust predictors of its centrality across a number of cooperative networks—including alliances and trade—and across different indicators of network prestige. Joint democracy (measured on a continuous scale ranging from -100 to +100) was also a significant predictor of joint clique membership across these cooperative networks.

Several network analytic studies focused on the determinants of alliances emphasizing network effects, in addition to the more traditional determinants such as joint democracy, major power status, distance, and the like. Warren (2010, 2016) used stochastic actor oriented models (SAOMs; Snijders, 2001, 2005) to examine alliance formation patterns. He found that triadic closure and common enemies have a strong impact on dyadic alliance cooperation. The latter result corroborates Maoz et al (2007). However, this is only a partial aspect of the latter study (more on that below). Warren (2016) extended this analysis to study the coevolution of alliances, conflict, and democracy. He found a significant tendency of democracies to select other democracies as allies. He also found that states with alliance ties to states that have democratic allies significantly increase the likelihood of becoming democracies or retaining their democratic institutions.

Cranmer et al. (2012) found that a generalization of the closed triangle network statistic, the geometrically weighted edgewise shared partner (GWESP), has a significant effect on alliance formation. They also confirmed, controlling for network effects via an exponential random graph model (ERGM), that joint democracy has a robust effect on alliance ties. Kinne (2014), examining bilateral cooperation agreements—principally on defense matters—also found a strong tendency for triadic closure in these agreements. However, both Kinne and Warren also found significant tendencies for preferential attachment (popularity effects) in security cooperation networks.

Ward et al. (2013) offer a strong critique of traditional gravity models of international trade. They show that trade relations are affected significantly by reciprocity and clusterability (akin to triadic closure) beyond the traditional factors of economy size and distance that are used as key predictors of trade by economists.

No significant network-related studies focused on the determinants of intergovernmental organization (IGO) membership beyond Maoz's (2010) analysis of IGO clique comembership. Accordingly, we have still to establish the extent to which endogenous network structure affects the degree of shared IGO membership.

A key result in network analytic studies of international cooperation is the existence of spillover across networks. This was one of the key results of the many analyses in Maoz (2010). However, these analyses were based on strict correlational indicators of spillover. Maoz found a reciprocal effect of alliance ties on trade ties and of trade ties on alliance ties. He also found system-level spillover effects between these networks. A similar result emerges in more recent studies of network coevolution (Warren, 2016; Haim, 2016), with the latter also finding cross-community spillover. Vijayaraghavan et al. (2015) developed a multiplex Markov chain model to detect over-time transition between or among layers of a multiplex network. Using this model, they found significant spillover from alliances to trade and—to a lesser extent—from trade to alliances. They found that dyads that have both alliance and trade ties are less likely to break either of them than would be expected by chance alone. This suggests a significant corroboration of the strategic nature of trade relations over the period 1950–2000. Warren's (2016) study of network coevolution also found significant evidence for the effect of conflict on alliance formation, supporting earlier results by Maoz (2010).

Taken together, several observations emerge from network analytic studies of cooperative dynamics in world politics. First, and most important, the key contribution of these studies to our understanding of the factors that affect cooperative ties is the fact that important endogenous processes—primarily triadic closure and, to a lesser extent, preferential attachment—have a significant impact on cooperative behavior. Most of the evidence of such endogeneity uses the dyad level of analysis, which somewhat limits the generalizability of these results.

Second, these analyses corroborate results of non-network studies of cooperation, but they also help resolve some of the key disputes in the discipline. For the most part, the network analytic studies support the key result of the prenetwork studies of cooperation: democracy increases the centrality of states across cooperative networks; joint democracy is the most robust determinant of cooperation in security, economic, and institutional networks. Third, network studies help resolve important debates in the literature on the spillover effects of cooperative ties. Specifically, they demonstrate quite convincingly that security cooperation breeds economic and institutional cooperation, but the inverse processes, whereby economic or institutional cooperation induce security cooperation, are less robust.

A key weakness of these studies is that while they criticize the focus on dyadic analysis and make a strong case for abandoning the assumption of independence between dyads within a network in favor of explicitly modeling endogenous network effects, they also perform overwhelmingly dyadic analyses. The few analyses of cooperation at the network level (Maoz, 2012, 2010; Cranmer et al., 2015; Haim, 2016) suggest that there is much to study beyond the dyad, and the results of these few analyses offer interesting insights into the evolution of IR.

The studies that focus on dyadic interactions, which essentially retest existing hypotheses about specific factors that promote cooperation from a network perspective. By contrast, network analytic studies that focus on systemic processes add insights that have not been captured in the more conventional literature on cooperation. Maoz (2012) finds significant evidence for a homophily model of alliances at the network level. The homophily model of network formation (McPherson et al., 2001) suggests that similarity attracts. Nodes that have similar attributes are more likely to form ties than nodes of different attributes. Consequently, there is fairly strong evidence that alliance networks are likely formed by a tendency of states that (a) have common enemies, (b) are jointly democratic, and (c) are culturally similar (cf. Maoz and Joyce, 2016). Haim (2016) finds that alliance and trade ties tend to form coherent communities. Maoz (2012) also finds significant evidence of preferential attachment processes, suggesting a strong popularity effect in the formation of trade ties. The important insight from these results is that we can connect the attributes of individual states—both those attributes that are exogenous to the network of interstate relations and those that are endogenous to such networks—to structures that go well beyond the dyadic level of analysis. More on that below. I now turn to a discussion of the implications of network structures for conflict behavior.

A study by Maoz and Joyce (2016) is one of the first attempts to examine how shocks affect international networks. Combining agent-based modeling (ABM) techniques with empirical analyses of alliance networks, they investigate the ways in which shocks—defined as dramatic changes in the identity of shared enemies (a key determinant of alliance ties) due to international conflict—affect changes in the structure of alliance networks. They distinguish between positive shocks, such as an increase in the number of states with shared enemies, which presumably increases the degree of common interests, and negative shocks, such as a significant decline in shared enmities, which presumably reduces the degree of common interests. They find significant parallels between the results of the ABM with random network data and changes in the structures of real-world networks. Specifically, the connectivity and consistency (transitivity) of alliance ego nets (and networks in general) increase following positive shocks and following positive shocks operating on states' allies (neighbors), and decrease following negative shocks. A significant result is that states change alliances not only in response to shocks that they themselves experience, but also in response to shocks that their neighbors (and potentially the neighbors of neighbors) experience. Here too, results seem to be generalizable across network levels: from the individual egonet of a given state to the system as a whole.

Network Determinants of International Conflict

As noted, prenetwork (or non-network) studies of conflict tended to focus on national, dyadic, or systemic attributes that either increase or decrease the probability or magnitude of interstate conflict. As in the case of the study of cooperative networks, the key contribution of network analytic frameworks to the study of international conflict is in providing insight about the relationship between the structure of various (typically cooperative) networks and conflict behavior. Some of the more central examples illustrate this contribution.

Hafner-Burton and Montgomery (2006) examine the effects of IGO-related centrality and IGO clustering on dyadic conflict behavior. They find that the presence of structurally equivalent dyads in such clusters increases the probability of conflict, while disparity between dyad members in terms of centrality reduces the probability of conflict. Their analysis continues to corroborate the democratic peace result, suggesting that joint democracy is robust with respect to the structural effects of clustering on conflict.

Embracing the Kantian peace notion, Dorussen and Ward (2008) extend the linkages between IGO comembership and peace by focusing on the effect of indirect IGO ties on dyadic conflict. They find that such ties significantly reduce the propensity of dyadic conflict, and these effects go beyond security-related IGOs; they apply to economic and administrative IGO membership as well.

Hafner-Burton and Montgomery extend the result about power (centrality) disparities and sanctions behavior (2008). They also find that the sender's regime score increases the propensity to sanction, whereas the target's regime score (democracy) reduces the propensity of sanctions. This suggests that preferential trade agreements (PTAs) between states create power dependencies that increase the probability of sanctions between dyad members. Building on the latter finding, these authors (Hafner-Burton and Montgomery, 2012) find that PTAs tend to create power hierarchies, which increase the probability of conflict due to growing distrust between states. Here too, their results continue to provide support to the democratic peace propositions even when controlling for network-related variables such as dependence, centrality, and shared PTA membership. This result challenges previous results suggesting that PTA membership tends to reduce the probability of dyadic conflict (Mansfield, Pevehouse, and Bearce, 1999, Mansfield and Pevehouse, 2000).

Maoz (2010) also performed a major test of the democratic peace proposition within a network framework. Extending the normative model of the democratic peace into a network framework, he argued that this model can be extended into multiple levels of analysis by focusing on the concept of "democratic networks," that is, endogenously defined groups dominated by democratic states. The focus of this modal was a concept he termed "strategic reference groups" (SRGs). An SRG is defined for each state as "the set of states that has an immediate, direct, and profound impact on its national security." Operationally the SRG of a state consists of its present and past enemies, as well as the allies of these enemies. This concept enabled him to develop an SRG network, wherein each edge denotes an actual or potential rivalry between pairs of states. Maoz showed that when the SRG of democratic states democratizes, the level of conflict involvement of the focal state drops significantly. Likewise, as more SRG cliques democratize, the level of conflict in the system as a whole also drops significantly. This research is the first to establish a consistent link between democracy and peace across levels of analysis.

Network analysis also helps clarify the work on interdependence and conflict. Maoz (2009) developed a network theoretic index of interdependence that applies to the nodal, dyadic, and network levels of analysis and is generalizable across different networks. Using these measures, Maoz tested the extent to which interdependence in different networks affects conflict behavior. He found that strategic interdependence—measured by combining alliance networks with national capabilities—has inconsistent effects on peace. While strategic interdependence reduces rates of national conflict, it does not have significant impact on dyadic conflict. By contrast, strategic interdependence reduces systemic conflict. Economic interdependence, on the other hand, appears to have significant dampening effects on conflict at the national, dyadic, and systemic levels of analysis.

Dorussen and Ward (2010) also tackle the linkage between economic interdependence and peace, extending their argument on the effect of indirect trade ties on dyadic peace. Here too, they find support for the argument that economic interdependence has a consistently dampening effect on dyadic conflict. However, they find that while the effect of indirect trade ties on conflict diminishes as the density of the trade network increases, the embeddedness of dyads in that network has increasingly pacifying effects. This converges with another network-related result: namely that shared economic group membership (e.g., clique comembership or community comembership) has a consistent dampening effect on dyadic conflict (Maoz, 2010). These results seem to add considerable credence to the economic aspect of the Kantian Tripod. Both the work of Maoz

(2009, 2006) and that of Cranmer et al. (2015) suggest that systemic interdependence (measured by the concept of Kantian factionalism—a combined modularity coefficient across several (multiplex) networks)—has a considerable dampening effect on the level of systemic conflict. However, they find that systemic democracy adds little if at all to the dampening effects of trade and international organizations.

Several studies focus on the relationship between signed networks (composed of juxtaposing cooperative and conflict networks) and both cooperative and conflictual relations. Maoz et al. (2007) used network analysis to examine the extent to which balanced relations (the ally of my ally is my ally, the enemy of my enemy is my ally, the ally of my enemy is my enemy) affect alliance ties and conflict relations. They found that balanced relations of the enemy of my enemy type tend to affect alliance formation (thus closing a balanced triangle: the enemy of my enemy is my ally). However, contrary to the intuition stemming from realist perspectives of IR, they also found that two states having one or more common enemies are more likely to be enemies themselves than would be expected by chance alone (thus creating an imbalanced triangle: the enemy of my enemy is my enemy). They found that imbalanced relations of various types significantly increase the probability of dyadic conflict.

By contrast, Lerner (2015) argued that testing for balance and imbalance in such networks requires adjustment for the probability of interaction. He finds that once controls are introduced for network effect that may determine the probability of balance or imbalance, balanced relations tend to reduce the probability of conflict. Lerner's analysis also provides support to some of the key results of other network analytic studies—principally the dampening effects of democracy on conflict even when controlling for interaction probability and network effects.

Using novel measures of balance and imbalance, Maoz and San-Akca (2015) find that relational imbalances in the Middle East are far more common and extensive than in any other region. They also find significant evidence for the effect of relational imbalances on subsequent conflict levels in that region.

Overall, the contribution of network analytic studies to our understanding of conflict and cooperation is similar to the contribution of these studies to cooperative international behavior. The key significance of network analytic studies of international conflict lies in corroborating some of the key results of prenetwork studies—primarily of the relative robustness of the democratic peace result. In the case of conflict research too, network analytic studies have helped clarify some of the key debates, such as the "interdependence reduces conflict" argument.

Yet the network analytic literature adds an important layer to our understanding of the sources and processes of international interactions, one that is not present in the more traditional literature: the focus on relational imbalances and its effects on conflict and cooperation. While this work is still in its infancy and—common to such emerging interests—has still to produce consistent findings, it offers a new dimension to modeling international interactions. This is the focus on combinations of friendship and enmity relations, the extent to which they break down into specific and consistent regimes (friends flock together against common enemies) or whether they entail significant inconsistencies (friends that have both positive and negative ties at the same time, or imbalanced triads such as "the friend of my friend is an enemy"). Maoz and San-Akca (2015) show that some regions are significantly more prone to the rise of relational imbalances, and these are also the regions in which conflict is a recurrent and significant phenomenon. This is an important result that sheds new light on the relationship between conflict and cooperation in world politics.

The failure to move away from dyadic analyses of conflict is also a weakness of both the network-analytic and non-network literature. The few studies that focus on endogenous groups show important patterns. For example, Maoz's (2010) study of the democratic peace focuses on strategic reference networks (SRNs), which are networks of actual or potential enemies. He shows that when such networks democratize, the traditionally high level of within-group conflict declines significantly. Likewise, the evidence suggests that when the proportion of SRN cliques that democratize increases, systemic levels of conflict decline. This is consistent with and reinforces other studies that found some evidence of a systemic democratic peace (Kadera, Crescenzi, and Shannon, 2003; Kadera and Mitchell, 2005).[4]

In the next section I illustrate some of the potential for employing network analysis to examine conflict- and peace-related issues beyond the dyadic level of analysis.

Cooperative International Communities

In contrast to formal institutional structures that entail cooperative agreements between and among states, cooperative communities are emergent structures. They arise out of the pattern of relations between states. Communities may—but do not necessarily—correspond to formal institutional structures that imply collective cooperation. To illustrate this, figure 31.2 presents alliance communities in 2010. In this figure, green squares are community identifiers. Circles are states with Correlates of War (COW) state numbers: light circles are democratic states, and dark circles are nondemocratic states. The quality of the community detection solution, as measured by the modularity coefficient (Girvan and Newman, 2004, discussed in the appendix) is quite good ($Q = 0.721$; $T = 68.04$; $p < 10^{-15}$). Note that some states (e.g., number 20, Canada, and number 625, Sudan) overlap over two communities. There also seems to be strong democratic clustering in community R4 (primarily, but not exclusively, NATO members) and authoritarian clustering in community R3 (primarily, but not exclusively, the Arab League). Note also that communities tend to overlap with geographic proximity, but some communities contain states from different regions.

Community detection is completely endogenous; the structure of alliance ties between states determines community membership. However, can we say something meaningful about exogenous factors that determine community membership? One

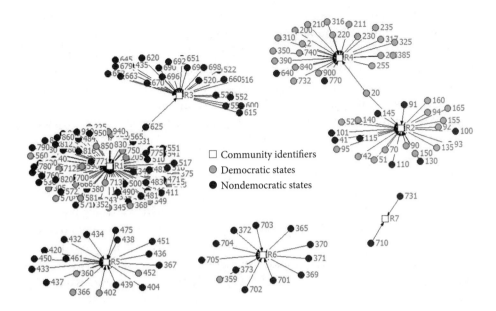

FIGURE 31.2 Alliance Networks and Alliance communities 2010.

Source: Alliances, COW alliance data set (Gibler, 2008). Democracy, POLITY IV (Marshall et al., 2014). Numbers are COW country codes.

way to answer the question is to ask about community cohesion. Specifically, we can ask questions such as: Are democracies more likely—than what can be expected by chance alone—to cluster together in cooperative communities? Are culturally similar states more likely—than might be expected by chance—to cluster in cooperative communities?

Answers to such questions involve a more rigorous and demanding set of empirical tests than the ones suggested by both traditional non-network studies of democracy and cooperation and network analytic studies of democracy and cooperation. This is so because we move from a strictly dyadic level to a level that is clearly emergent. Dyads are defined exogenously as units of analysis. Communities are defined by the structure of dyadic ties. If we find a strong tendency for clustering by such attributes as joint democracy or religious similarity, this has important substantive implications for the study of international cooperation. It would suggest that beyond endogenous determinants of tie-formation such as reciprocity (built in to the definition of alliance), popularity (k-stars), and triadic closure typically identified by network analysts, there are important factors that define clustering.

To determine the effect of exogenous factors in the emergence of cooperative communities, I developed a cohesion coefficient. I discuss the derivation of the cohesion coefficient in the appendix to this chapter. Here I present the general intuition of this statistic. The cohesion coefficient focuses on community membership as the unit of analysis. It measures the degree to which the within-community cohesion (or similarity among members making up a given community) in terms of some attribute is higher than the between-community cohesion (or the similarity between members in one community and members in other communities) in terms of that attribute. For example, in figure 31.2 we can see clustering of democracies in community R4 and—to a lesser extent—in community R2. Likewise, we can see significant clustering of autocracies in community R3. By contrast, communities R1 and R5 are quite mixed. As noted, the cohesion coefficient measures the differences between within- and between-community clustering of a given exogenous attribute. It can be estimated in terms of whether it is significantly different from chance, using an ordinary difference-of-means T-test. To illustrate some patterns of community cohesion, I show in figure 31.3 the cohesion coefficients and T-scores of alliance communities over the period 1946–2010. The exogenous factors examined are democracy and religious similarity.

As can be seen, there is significant clustering of both democracy and religious similarity in alliance communities. Religious clustering is much higher than democratic clustering. This is so in spite of the fact that democratic attributes are binary (and therefore entail limited variability), while religious similarity is measured in continuous terms (Maoz and Henderson, 2013). The level of statistical significance, however, is quite high. Democratic clustering is more remarkable, given that the proportion of democracies in the system over the period varied between 0.21 and 0.40 (mean democracy = .268), which means that the probability of a pair of states being jointly democratic is 0.07. There also appears to be a slight upward trend in the statistical significance of democratic cohesion of security cooperation networks; however, this trend is not detectable from the actual size of the coefficient. This is due to the fact that the probability of two democracies ending up in the same community actually declines as a function of the number of communities.

Religious similarity clustering of alliance communities is even more remarkable. This suggests a homophily pattern of cultural similarity. Alliance communities are significantly more similar in terms of the religious characteristics of members than other pair combinations (between-community religious similarity).

CONCLUSION

A common criticism of network analytic studies of international conflict and cooperation is the "so what" question: What is the marginal contribution of network analysis to the substantive understanding of these phenomena? The answer to this question is not straightforward. On a theoretical level, network analytic studies have not developed new theoretical insights on the structure of conflict and cooperation. As noted, the key contribution of such studies is in drawing our attention to the complex dependence of dyadic cooperative and conflict behavior on the structure of the network as a whole.

The notion that network structure affects individual and dyadic choices about conflict and cooperation is an important one. The way it is modeled, however, leaves a lot to be desired from a substantive point of view. The ERGMs (Cranmer and Desmarais, 2011) or SAOMs (Snijders, 2005; Warren, 2016) are useful statistical tools, but results stemming from these models do not offer any meaningful substantive insights into the dynamics of conflict and cooperation. For example, the finding that security cooperation is a function of triadic closure dynamics seems appealing, but from a substantive perspective it doesn't tell us much. Triadic closure may be a function of homophily. If states that share similar attributes, such as a similar regime or cultural/religious similarity, or if they have common interests, and if these similarities or interests drive them to form collective security structures such as NATO, the Warsaw Pact, or the Arab League, then we will find that alliances are affected by triadic closure. So that triadic closure is due to some exogenous factor and does not have an independent effect on alliance formation.

Likewise, popularity effects that result in strong impact of the k-star statistic on dyadic ties may be due to specific attributes of some nodes (e.g., capabilities) that make them popular alliance partners. The fact that we find popularity effects in ERGM or SAOM estimations means very little in terms of improving our substantive understanding of network formation and network evolution processes.

Network analytic studies of conflict and cooperation may offer important new insights if they move beyond the dyadic analysis (which they criticize but do not abandon) to explain the structure and nature of emergent units, such as international communities and network characteristics. The few studies that focus on these units of analysis (Maoz, 2006, 2009, 2010; Cranmer et al., 2015; Haim, 2016) suggest that this is the area in which network analytic studies can contribute the most.

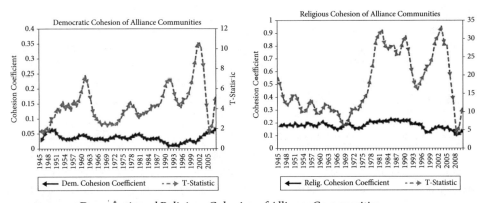

FIGURE 31.3 Democratic and Religious Cohesion of Alliance Communities.
Left panel shows the democratic cohesion of alliance communities and right panel shows the religious cohesion of alliance communities.

Very little attention has been given in the empirical IR literature in general to issues of balance and imbalance. By contrast, the theoretical literature devotes a lot of attention to these matters (e.g., neorealist focus on balancing—Waltz, 1979; Mearsheimer, 2001). The distinction between the balancing conception in realist theories and the concept of relational balance in network analysis offers important theoretical avenues and interesting empirical patterns. More work is needed to understand the relationship between friendship and enmity in IR, because a number of studies suggest that this relationship is far from simple (Barbieri and Levy, 1999; Maoz et al., 2007; Maoz and San-Akca, 2015).

Overall, network analytic studies have made some important contributions to our understanding of international conflict and cooperation. However, the potential of this approach is far from being fully exploited. The opportunities for applying network analysis to leverage important theoretical generalizations about such processes are immense. The data revolution in the field offers many opportunities for research that did not exist fifteen or twenty years ago, when network analysis started making (or remaking) inroads into IR. The growing community of network scholars in IR suggests that the basic framework has already attracted the attention of the scholarly community, beyond political science. Collaborations between IR scholars and mathematicians or physicists (e.g., Macon et al., 2012; Vijayaraghavan et al., 2015; Cranmer et al., 2015) open up important avenues of modeling and empirical insights. The conditions for significant leaps of knowledge and understanding are quite ripe. We need to wait and see whether they are realized.

DEMOCRACY AND COOPERATIVE NETWORKS: METHODS APPENDIX

Data Sources

The following data sources were used in the article. Events data were combined from two sources: Integrated Crisis Early Warning System (ICEWS—https://dataverse.harvard.edu/dataverse/ICEWS) and Phoenix Events Data Set (http://phoenixdata.org/). The ICEWS data set covers 2000–2014. The Phoenix data cover 2014–2016.

Raw data and R-algorithms for recovery of networks are available on http://spins.faculty.ucdavis.edu.

Nodes in the networks are states. Edges in the networks are defined as the sum of interactions corresponding to the Goldstein conflict-cooperation scale between state i and state j over a week. Conflict data aggregate all conflictual interactions, and cooperation networks aggregate all cooperative interactions. This forms two sets of longitudinal, weighted, and directed networks. Each network captures all weekly interactions in the international system.

Data used for the community section came from the following sources:

Alliances: Data combine the ATOP (Leeds, 2005) data set, which goes up to 2004, with the COW alliance data set (Gibler, 2008), which goes up to 2010. Both data sets are highly correlated (Chi-squared = 4.7e + 05; tau-b = 0.824; Yule's Q = 0.999). An edge on the alliance network is assigned a score of 1 if two states have an alliance at year t, and zero otherwise. This is an unweighted and undirected network.

Democracy: Data are derived from the POLITY IV data set (Marshall et al., 2014). Democracy is defined as 1 if the Maoz-Russett (1993) democracy score is equal to or higher than 30 and zero otherwise.

Politically relevant dyad: Data are derived from the COW contiguity data set (COW, 2006; Stinnett et al., 2002). A dyad is politically relevant (Maoz and Russett, 1993) if it is directly contiguous, is separated by a body of water of 150 nautical miles or less, or is contiguous through colonial possession of members, or if one state is a regional power or major power.

Religious similarity: Data are based on the World Religion Dataset (Maoz and Henderson, 2013). The religious similarity score is a two-mode to one-mode conversion of the religion data set. This score varies from 0 (two states contain completely different religious groups) to 1 (the distribution of religious groups in one state's population is exactly equal to the distribution of religious groups in another state's population).

Methods

Derivation of Communities: I use a modified community detection algorithm based on the Girvan and Newman (2004) fast and greedy algorithm and on the Leicht and Newman (2008) modularity maximization procedure for directed networks. As in the case of these algorithms, the process of community detection is based on modularity maximization. The modularity coefficient is a measure of the extent to which a given partition of a network into communities maximize within-community density and minimize between-community density. Furthermore, this partition is maximally different from what we would have expected by chance alone. Specifically,

$$Q = \frac{1}{2m} \Sigma \left(A_{ij} - \frac{d_{out(i)} d_{in(j)}}{2m} \right) \delta c_i c_j \qquad [1]$$

Where A_{ij} is the adjacency score of nodes i and j; $d_{out(i)}, d_{in(j)}$ and in-degrees of these nodes, respectively; m is the number of edges in the networks; and $\delta c_i c_j$ is the Kronecker delta, defined as

$$\delta c_i c_j = \begin{cases} 1 & if \ c_i = c_j \\ 0 & otherwise \end{cases} \qquad [2]$$

Note that the quantity $\dfrac{d_{out(i)} d_{in(j)}}{2m}$ is the expected value of an edge by chance.

This community detection algorithm iterates until Q is maximized. It then produces a partition of the network into discrete communities. However, as quite a few scholars have pointed out (e.g., Lancichinetti et al., 2011; Shen et al., 2009; Macon et al., 2012), it might be possible to improve on the modularity of communities—and make these partitions more realistic—when cross-community overlap is allowed. Consequently, the procedure I use is the following.

First, I use a modified measure of modularity that I call the separation coefficient (S). This is given by generating community density (CD) matrix of size k (where k is the number of communities), with entries defined as $cd_{qr} = \dfrac{\sum_{i \in q, j \in r} A_{ij}}{n_q n_r - n_{qr}}$, where n_q, n_r are the number of nodes in communities q and r, respectively, and n_{qr} are the number of nodes that are common to both communities. Note that the diagonal of the CD matrix reflects the within-community density and the off-diagonal entries reflect the edges between the nodes in community q and the nodes in community r. From here we derive S as

$$S = \frac{\sum_q \sum_r \left(cd_{qq} - cd_{qr} \right)}{k(k-1)} \qquad [3]$$

Second, I generate a community structure based on the maximization of modularity as discussed above. From this community structure I calculate the out-density and in-density between each node and each of the communities, such that

$$d_{iq} = \frac{\sum_{j \in q} A_{ij}}{n_q^*}, \quad d_{qi} = \frac{\sum_{j \in q} A_{ji}}{n_q^*} \qquad [4]$$

Where $n_q^* = n_q - 1 \, if \, i \in q, \, and \, n_q \, if \, i \notin q$. This avoids counting self-ties.

Third, if there exists a node that satisfies (1) $i \notin q, \, and$ (2) $\min\left(d_{iq}, d_{qi} \right) > cd_q$, we add the node to community q (while maintaining that node's membership in its previous community as well). We recalculate Q and S. We retain the new community structure if it meets both following conditions, (1) $Q_t \geq Q_{t-1}$, and (2) $S_t > S_{t-1}$ (where t indexes iterations in the detection process).

In other words, a node's overlap across two communities is justified if (1) it does not reduce modularity,[5] and (2) it strictly increases separation. This process iterates until condition 2 is maximized (subject to satisfaction of condition (1)).

The advantage of this procedure over the discrete community detection process is that it allows some overlap of nodes over several communities. By doing so it increases within-community density while maximizing separation between communities. At the same time, it preserves the maximal modularity score.

I use the alliance network to generate security communities for the period 1946–2010. Each year is a network; thus I derive a community structure for each year. The community structure for each year allows for a new unit of analysis wherein we can detect the effects of exogenous variables on the endogenous process of community formation.

Estimating Cohesion: To what extent do the attributes of nodes or of dyads affect community structure? To answer this question, we need to examine the extent to which communities are internally homogenous with respect to some exogenous variable. If a given exogenous variable, such as democracy, affects the type of communities that emerge, then we would expect that the density of democracies within communities—that is, between states that belong to the same community—is significantly higher than the density of democracies between communities (i.e., a grouping that is formed by the states making up one community and the states making up another community).

The following network illustrates the calculation of the separation and cohesion coefficients. Consider the hypothetical network in figure 31.4. This network partitions into three communities (these happen to be discrete). We partition the network into a community-ordered matrix, shown by table 31.1.

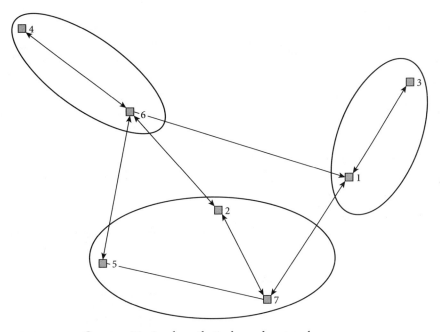

FIGURE 31.4 Communities in a hypothetical 7-node network.

The leftmost matrix—the partitioned adjacency matrix—is the original network ordered by community. Community I is composed of nodes 2, 5, and 7; community II is composed of nodes 1 and 3; and so forth.[6]

The central matrix, the CD matrix, measures the density of these blocks. We calculate the separation coefficient S as in equation 3 above (see the between-community difference matrix). In this case the score is quite high. However, to evaluate whether this difference between within- and between-community densities is significant, we use the following procedure.

First we calculate the weighted within- and between-community mean densities. The within-community mean is given by

$$w_m = \frac{\sum_{qq} g d_{qq} n_{qq}^2}{\sum_{qq} n_{qq}^2} \qquad [5]$$

Table 31.1 Community–Partitioned Adjacency Matrix and Community Density Matrix

Partitioned Adjacency Matrix

Node	2	5	7	1	3	4	6
2	1	0	1	0	0	0	1
5	0	1	1	0	0	0	1
7	1	1	1	1	0	0	0
1	0	0	1	1	1	0	1
3	0	0	0	1	1	0	0
4	0	0	0	0	0	1	1
6	1	1	0	1	0	1	1

Community Density Matrix (CD)

	COM I	COM II	COM III
COM I	0.777	0.167	0.333
COM II	0.167	1	0.25
COM III	0.333	0.25	1

Between-Community Differences

	COM I	COM II	COM III	Sum
COM I	0	0.61	0.444	1.054
COM II	0.833	0	0.75	1.583
COM III	0.667	0.75	0	1.417
				3.833

S = 0.676

Q = 0.148

Table 31.2 Community Variance Matrix (CV)

	COM I	COM II	COM III
COM I	0.17284	0.138889	0.222222
COM II	0.138889	0	0.1875
COM III	0.222222	0.1875	0

and the between-community mean is given by

$$b_m = \frac{\sum_{q \neq r} g d_{qr} n_q n_r}{\sum_{qr} n_q n_r}$$

[6]

Next we calculate the community variance matrix based on the partitioned adjacency matrix. This matrix is shown in table 31.2.

We derive weighted within- and between-community variances by

$$w_v = \frac{\sum_{qq} g v_{qq} n_{qq}^2}{\sum_{qq} n_{qq}^2}$$

[7]

$$b_v = \frac{\sum_{q \neq r} g v_{qr} n_q n_r}{\sum_{qr} n_q n_r}$$

Finally, we calculate a difference of means test as

$$T = \frac{w_m - b_m}{\sqrt{\dfrac{w_v}{\sum_{q=r} n_{qq}^2} + \dfrac{b_v}{\sum_{q \neq r} n_q n_r}}}$$

[8]

Now suppose there is some property that characterizes the dyads in this network. This could be some ideological similarity score. Suppose this similarity attribute is given by the matrix shown in table 31.3. The entries of this matrix reflect the extent to which two nodes are ideologically similar.[7]

Table 31.3 Dyadic Similarity (Hypothetical)

Dyadic Ideological Similarity Score

Node	1	2	3	4	5	6	7
1	1	0.857	0.429	0.714	0.857	0	0.143
2	0.857	1	0.571	0.857	1	0.143	0.286
3	0.429	0.571	1	0.714	0.571	0.571	0.714
4	0.714	0.857	0.714	1	0.857	0.286	0.429
5	0.857	1	0.571	0.857	1	0.143	0.286
6	0	0.143	0.571	0.286	0.143	1	0.857
7	0.143	0.286	0.714	0.429	0.286	0.857	1

Table 31.4 Community Cohesion Coefficient

Partitioned Cohesion Matrix

	2	5	7	1	3	4	6
2	1	1	0.286	0.857	0.571	0.857	0.143
5	1	1	0.286	0.857	0.571	0.857	0.143
7	0.286	0.286	1	0.143	0.714	0.429	0.857
1	0.857	0.857	0.143	1	0.429	0.714	0
3	0.571	0.571	0.714	0.429	1	0.714	0.571
4	0.857	0.857	0.429	0.714	0.714	1	0.286
6	0.143	0.143	0.857	0	0.571	0.286	1

Community Cohesion Matrix (CD)

	COM I	COM II	COM III
COM I	0.683	0.619	0.548
COM II	0.619	0.714	0.5
COM III	0.548	0.5	0.643

	COM I	COM II	COM III	Sum
COM I	0	0.063	0.135	0.198
COM II	0.095	0	0.214	0.31
COM III	0.095	0.143	0	0.238
				0.746
			C =	0.124

Again, we partition the similarity matrix into a community-based similarity and calculate the C score. This is shown in tables 31.4 and 31.5. The calculation of the cohesion coefficient and its significance are the same as for the separation coefficient. In this case, $T = 1.22$, which is not statistically significant.

This approach works well for both small and very large networks. Note that so far most of the work on community detection stopped once communities were detected. Discussion of the properties of such communities stopped at a descriptive level. Analytic measures of community characteristics were missing, so it was difficult to make out any meaningful sense of the attributes of communities in terms of the nodal (or dyadic) properties. For example, Macon et al. (2012) spent a great deal of effort detecting international communities based on UN General Assembly voting. However, they did not examine whether these communities were cohesive in terms of economic development. Zhang et al. (2008) examined the modularity of cosponsorship networks in the US Senate. To examine polarization in the Senate, they calculated modularity based on a leading eigenvector of the cosponsorship matrix, then re-examined modularity based on party IDs. However, they did not enable an analytic way of distinguishing between the two.

Table 31.5 Community Variance Matrix (CV)

	COM1	COM2	COM3
COM1	*0.125876*	0.058916	0.104776
COM2	0.058916	*0.08151*	0.086658
COM3	0.104776	0.086658	*0.127449*

The advantage of the method discussed above is that we can now examine the structure of communities in terms of the attributes of nodes or dyads, in order to inspect whether nodes cluster in communities based on similar attributes. The cohesion coefficient reflects a more demanding test of community attributes than the modularity method. This is because the former coefficient subtracts intercommunity cohesion from intracommunity cohesion. By contrast, modularity-based cohesion (e.g., Girvan and Newman, 2004; Zhang et al., 2008) focuses only on the intracommunity cohesion.

NOTES

1. Blainey's (1988, 3) observation that "for every thousand pages published on the causes of war, there is less than one page on directly the causes of peace" is particularly telling.

2. Gowa (1995); Mansfield and Bronson (1997); Gowa and Mansfield (2004); and Long and Leeds (2006) find that alliance ties between pairs of states increase the level of trade flows between them. Keshk et al. (2004) find that trade "follows the flag"; that is, trade flows are predicated on both economic and security factors. However, Morrow, Siverson, and Tabares (1998) do not find a robust effect of alliance on trade. By contrast, Fordham (2010) Maoz (2010), and Vijayaraghavan *et al.* (2015) find that trade and alliances mutually affect each other.

3. This assumption is also consistent with the fundamental assumption of the political survival theory (Bueno de Mesquita et al., 2003) that political leaders need to provide public or private goods so that the winning coalition that sustains them in power can continue to do so.

4. One of the problems of these studies is that they refer to "democratic communities" but derive these communities exogenously. By contrast, Maoz focuses on endogenously derived groupings that are ex ante likely to have high levels of conflict and examines what happens to them when they democratize.

5. Note that modularity may have several local maxima, not all of which maximize separation. In other words, there may exist several different partitions of a network into a set of communities that generate the same modularity score. So if we can find some cross-community overlap that increases separation but does not reduce modularity, this solution is preferable over the discrete partition.

6. Note that the original network does not have self-ties, but the partitioned adjacency matrix has self-ties for all nodes. The purpose for this is to generate a random community structure against which the actual community structure is compared and that has a degree distribution that is the same as the degree distribution of the original network. This is possible only if we assume self-ties.

7. Those familiar with the IR literature can think of these as alliance portfolio similarity scores measured as S (Signorino and Ritter, 1999), or tau-b (Bueno de Mesquita, 1981), or structural equivalence (Maoz et al., 2006).

References

Barbieri, K., and Levy, J. S. (1999). "Sleeping with the Enemy: The Impact of War on Trade." *Journal of Peace Research* 36(4): 463–479.

Blainey, G. (1988). *The Causes of War*. New York: Free Press.

Bueno de Mesquita, Bruce. (1981). *The War Trap*. New Haven, CT: Yale University Press.

Bueno de Mesquita, B., Smith, A., Siverson, R. M., and Morrow, J. D. (2003). *The Logic of Political Survival*. Cambridge, MA: MIT Press.

Correlates of War (COW) Project 2006. Direct Contiguity Dataset, Version 3.1. http://correlatesofwar.org.

Cranmer, S. J., and Desmarais, B. A. (2011). "Inferential Network Analysis with Exponential Random Graph Models." *Political Analysis* 19(1): 66–86.

Cranmer, S. J., and Desmarais, B. (2016). "A Critique of Dyadic Design." *International Studies Quarterly* 60 (3): 355–362.

Cranmer, S. J., Desmarais, B. A., and Menninga, E. J. (2012). "Complex Dependencies in the Alliance Network." *Conflict Management and Peace Science* 29(3): 279–313.

Cranmer, S. J., Menninga, E. J., and Mucha, P. J. (2015). "Kantian Fractionalization Predicts the Conflict Propensity of the International System." *Proceedings of the National Academy of Sciences* 112(38): 11812–11816.

Dafoe, A., Oneal, J. R., and Russett, B. (2013). "The democratic peace: Weighing the evidence and cautious inference". *International Studies Quarterly* 57(1): 201–214.

Dorussen, H., and Ward, H. (2008). "Intergovernmental Organizations and the Kantian Peace: A Network Perspective." *Journal of Conflict Resolution* 52(2): 189–212.

Dorussen, H., and Ward, H. (2010). "Trade Networks and the Kantian Peace." *Journal of Peace Research* 47(1): 29–42.

Farber, H.S., and Gowa, J. (1995). Polities and Peace. *International Security* 20(2): 123–145.

Fordham, B. O. (2010). Trade and asymmetric alliances. *Journal of Peace Research* 47(6):685–696.

Gartzke, E. (2007). "The Capitalist Peace." *American Journal of Political Science* 51(1): 166–191.

Gibler, D. M. (2008). *International Military Alliances, 1648–2008*. Washington, DC: CQ Press.

Gibler, D. M. (2012). *The Territorial Peace*. New York: Cambridge University Press.

Gibler, D. M., and Wolford, S. (2006). "Alliances, Then Democracy: An Examination of the Relationship between Regime Type and Alliance Formation." *Journal of Conflict Resolution* 50(1): 129–153.

Girvan, M., and Newman, M. E. J. (2004). "Community Structure in Social and Biological Networks." *Proceedings of the National Academy of Sciences* 99(12): 7821–7826.

Gowa, J. (1995). *Allies, Adversaries, and International Trade*. Princeton, NJ: Princeton University Press.

Gowa, J., and Mansfield, E. D. (2004). "Alliances, Imperfect Markets, and Major-power Trade." *International Organization* 58(4): 775–805.

Haim, D. A. (2016). "Alliance networks and trade The effect of indirect political alliances on bilateral trade flows". *Journal of Peace Research* 53(3): 472–490.

Hafner-Burton, E. M., and Montgomery, A. H. (2006). "Power Positions: International Organization, Social Networks, and Conflict." *Journal of Conflict Resolution* 51(1): 3–27.

Hafner-Burton, E. M., and Montgomery, A. H. (2008). "Power or Plenty How Do International Trade Institutions Affect Economic Sanctions?" *Journal of Conflict Resolution* 52(2): 213–242.

Hafner-Burton, E. M., and Montgomery, A. H. (2012). "War, Trade, and Distrust: Why Trade Agreements Don't Always Keep the Peace." *Conflict Management and Peace Science* 29(3): 257–278.

Helpman, E., Melitz, E., and Rubinstein, Y. (2008). "Estimating Trade Flows: Trading Partners and Trading Volumes." *Quarterly Journal of Economics* 123(2): 441–487.

Hoff, P. D., and Ward, M. D. (2004). "Modeling Dependencies in International Relations Networks." *Political Analysis* 12(2): 160–175.

Kadera, K. M., Crescenzi, M. J. C., and Shannon, M. L. (2003). "Democratic Survival, Peace, and War in the International System." *American Journal of Political Science* 47(2): 234–247.

Kadera, K. M., and Mitchell, S. M. (2005). "Heeding Ray's Advice: An Exegesis on Control Variables in Systemic Democratic Peace Research." *Conflict Management and Peace Science* 22(4): 311–326.

Keohane, R. O. (1984). *After Hegemony: Cooperation and Discord in the World Political Economy*. Princeton, NJ: Princeton University Press.

Keohane, R. O. (1986). *Neorealism and Its Critics*. New York: Columbia University Press.

Keohane, R. O., and Nye, J. S. (1987). *Power and Interdependence*. 2d ed. New York: Random House.

Keshk, O. G., Pollins, B. M., and Reuveny, R. (2004). "Trade Still Follows the Flag: The Primacy of Politics in a Simultaneous Model of Interdependence and Armed Conflict." *Journal of Politics* 66(4): 1155–1179.

Kinne, B. J. (2014). "Network Dynamics and the Evolution of International Cooperation." *American Political Science Review* 107(4): 766–785.

Lancichinetti, A., Radicchi, P. Ramasco J. J., and Fortunato, S. (2011). Finding Statistically Significant Communities in Networks. *PLoS One* 6(4): 1–18.

Leeds, B. A. (2005). *Alliance Treaty and Obligations Provisions (ATOP) Codebook*. Rice University. http://atop.rice.edu/download/ATOPcdbk.pdf.

Leicht, E., and Newman, M. J. (2008). "Community Structure in Directed Networks." *Physical Review Letters* 100(118703): 1–4.

Lerner, J. (2015). "Structural Balance in Signed Networks: Separating the Probability to Interact from the Tendency to Fight." *Social Networks* 45(1): 66–77.

Long, A. G., and Leeds, A. (2006). "Trading for: Military Alliances and Economic Agreements." *Journal of Peace Research* 43(4): 433–451.

Macon, K. T., Mucha, P. J., and Porter, M. A. (2012). "Community Structure in the United Nations General Assembly." *Physica A: Statistical Mechanics and Its Applications* 391(1): 343–361.

Mansbach, R. W., and Vasquez, J. A. (1981). *In Search of Theory: A New Paradigm for Global Politics*. New York: Columbia University Press.

Mansfield, E., and Bronson, R. (1997). "Preferential Trading Arrangements, and International Trade." *American Political Science Review* 91(1): 94–107.

Mansfield, E., Pevehouse, J., and Bearce, D. H. (1999). "Preferential Trading Arrangements and Military Disputes." *Security Studies* 9(1–2): 92–118.

Mansfield, E. D., and Milner, H. V. (2012). *Votes, Vetoes, and the Political Economy of International Trade Agreements*. Princeton, NJ: Princeton University Press.

Mansfield, E. D., Milner, H. V., and Rosendorff, B. P. (2000). "Free to Trade: Democracies, Autocracies, and International Trade." *American Political Science Review* 94(2): 305–321.

Mansfield, E. D., Milner, H. V., and Rosendorff, B. P. (2002). "Why Democracies Cooperate More: Electoral Control and International Trade Agreements." *International Organization* 56(3): 477–513.

Mansfield, E. D., and Pevehouse, J. C. (2000). "Trade Blocs, Trade Flows, and International Conflict." *International Organization* 54(4): 775–808.

Mansfield, E. D., and Pevehouse, J. C. (2006). "Democratization and International Organizations." *International Organization* 60(1): 137–167.

Maoz, Z. (1998). "Realist and Cultural Critiques of the Democratic Peace: A Theoretical and Empirical Reassessment". *International Interactions* 24(1): 3–89.

Maoz, Z. (2000). "The Street-Gangs of World Politics: The Origins, Management, and Termination of International Alliances." In *What Do We Know About War*, ed. J. A. Vasquez. New York: Rowman and Littlefield.

Maoz, Z. (2002). "Paradoxical Functions of International Alliances: Security and Other Dilemmas." In *Balancing of Power*, ed. J. A. Vasquez and C. Elman. Boston: Rowman and Littlefield.

Maoz, Z. (2006). "Network Polarization, Network Interdependence, and International Conflict, 1816–2002." *Journal of Peace Research* 43(4): 391–411.

Maoz, Z. (2009). "The Effects of Strategic and Economic Interdependence on International Conflict Across Levels of Analysis." *American Journal of Political Science* 53(1): 223–240.

Maoz, Z. (2010). *Networks of Nations: The Evolution, Structure, and Impact of International Networks, 1816–2001*. New York: Cambridge University Press.

Maoz, Z. (2012). "Preferential Attachment, Homophily, and the Structure of International Networks, 1816–2003." *Conflict Management and Peace Science* 29(3): 341–369.

Maoz, Zeev, and Nasrin Abdolali. (1989). "Regime Types and International Conflict, 1816–1976". *Journal of Conflict Resolution* 33(1): 3–35.

Maoz, Z., and Henderson, E. A. (2013). "The World Religion Dataset 1945–2010: Logic, Estimates, and Trends." *International Interactions* 39(3): 265–291.

Maoz, Z. and Joyce, K. A. (2016). "The Effects of Shocks on International Networks: Changes in the Attributes of States and the Structure of International Alliance Networks". *Journal of Peace Research* 57(3): 292–309.

Maoz, Z. and Russett, B. (1992). "Alliance, Wealth Contiguity, and Political Stability: Is the Lack of Conflict between Democracies a Statistical Artifact?" *International Interactions* 17(4): 245–267.

Maoz, Z., and Russett, B. (1993). "Normative and Structural Causes of Democratic Peace, 1946–1986." *American Political Science Review* 87(3): 624–638.

Maoz, Z., and San-Akca, B. (2015). "Causes and Consequences of Unbalanced Relations in the International Politics of the Middle East, 1946-2010." In *The Israeli Conflict System: Analytic Approaches*, edited by H. Starr and S. Dubinsky, pp. 51–88. New York: Routledge.

Maoz, Z., Terris, L. G., Kuperman, R. D., and Talmud, I. (2006). "Structural Equivalence and International Conflict, 1816–2001: A Network Analysis of Affinities and Conflict." *Journal of Conflict Resolution* 50(5): 664–689.

Maoz, Z., Terris, L. G., Kuperman, R. D., and Talmud, I. (2007). "What Is the Enemy of My Enemy: Causes and Consequences of Imbalanced International Relations, 1816–2001." *Journal of Politics* 69(1): 100–115.

Marshall, M., Jaggers, K., and Gurr, T. R. (2014). "POLITY™ IV Project: Political Regime Characteristics and Transitions, 1800–2013." Center for Systemic Peace. www.systemic-peace.org/polity/polity4.htm.

McPherson, M. J., Smith-Lovin, L., and Cook, J. M. (2001). "Birds of a Feather: Homophily in Social Networks." *Annual Review of Sociology* 27: 415–444.

Mearsheimer, J. J. (2001). *The Tragedy of Great Power Politics*. New York: W. W. Norton.

Moravcsik, A. (1997). "Taking Preferences Seriously: A Liberal Theory of International Politics." *International Organization* 51(4): 513–553.

Morrow, J. D., Siverson, R. M., and Tabares, T. E. (1998). "The Political Determinants of International Trade: The Major Powers, 1907–90." *American Political Science Review* 92(3): 649–661.

Mousseau, M. (2013). "The Democratic Peace Unravels: It's the Economy." *International Studies Quarterly* 57(2): 186–197.

Oneal, J. Oneal, F. H., Maoz, Z. and Russett, B. (1996). "The liberal peace: Interdependence, democracy, and international conflict, 1950-85." *Journal of Peace Research* 33(1): 11–28.

Oren, I. (1995). "The Subjectivity of the "Democratic" Peace." *International Security*, 20(2): 147–184.

Pevehouse, J., and Russett, B. (2006). "Democratic International Governmental Organizations Promote Peace." *International Organization* 60(4): 969–1000.

Ray, J. L. (2013). "War on democratic peace". *International Studies Quarterly* 57(1): 198–200.

Rosato, S. (2003). "The flawed logic of democratic peace theory." *American Political Science Review* 97(4): 585–602.

Rosendorff, B. P., and Milner, H. (2001). "The Optimal Design of International Trade Institutions: Uncertainty and Escape." *International Organization* 55(4): 829–857.

Russett, B. (1993). *Grasping the Democratic Peace*. Princeton NJ: Princeton University Press.

Russett, B. and Oneal, J. (2001). *Triangulating Peace: Democracy, Interdependence, and International Organization*. New York: W. W. Norton.

Russett, B., Oneal, J. and Davis, D. R. (1998). "The Third Leg of the Kantian Tripod for Peace: International Organizations and Militarized Disputes, 1950-85." *International Organization* 52(3): 441–467.

Shen, H. W., X. Q. Cheng, K. Cai, and M. B. Hu. (2009). Detect overlapping and hierarchical community structure in networks. *Physica a-Statistical Mechanics and Its Applications* 388(8): 1706–1712.

Signorino, C. S., and Ritter, J. M. 1999. Tau-b or Not Tau-b: Measuring the Similarity of Foreign Policy Positions. *International Studies Quarterly* 43(1): 115–144.

Siverson, R. M., and Emmons, J. (1991). "Birds of a Feather: Democratic Political Systems and Alliance Choices in the 20th Century." *Journal of Conflict Resolution* 53(2): 285–306.

Small, M., and Singer, D. J. (1976). "The War Proneness of Democratic Regimes." *Jerusalem Journal of International Relations* 1(1): 41–64.

Snijders, T. A. B. (2001). "The statistical evaluation of social network dynamics." *Sociological Methodology* 31: 361–395.

Snijders, T. A. B. (2005). "Models for Longitudinal Network Data." In *Models and Methods in Social Networks Analysis*, edited by P. J. Carrington, J. Scott, and S. Wasserman, pp. 215–247. New York: Cambridge University Press.

Spiro, D. (1994). "The Insignificance of the Liberal Peace." *International Security* 19(2): 50–86.

Stinnett, Douglas M., Jaroslav Tir, Philip Schafer, Paul F. Diehl, and Charles Gochman. (2002). The Correlates of War Project Direct Contiguity Data, Version 3. *Conflict Management and Peace Science* 19(2): 58–66.

Vijayaraghavan, V., Noell, P-A., Maoz, Z., and D'Souza, R. M. (2015). "Quantifying Dynamic Spillover in Co-Evolving Multiplex Networks". *Scientific Reports* 5(15442): 1–10. doi: 10.1038/srep15142

Walt, S. (1988). *The Origins of Alliance*. Ithaca, NY: Cornell University Press.

Waltz, K. N. (1979). *Theory of International Politics*. New York: Random House.

Ward, M. D., Ahlquist, J. S., and Rozenas, A. (2013). "Gravity's Rainbow: A Dynamic Latent Space Model for the World Trade Network." *Network Science* 1(1): 95–118.

Ward, M. D., Hoff, P. D., and Lofdhall, C. L. (2003). "Identifying International Networks: Latent Spaces and Imputations." In *Dynamic Social Network: Modeling and Analysis*, edited by R. Breiger, C. Carley, and P. Pattison, pp. 345–362. Washington, DC: Committee on Human Values.

Ward, M. D., Siverson, R. M., and Cao X. (2007). "Disputes, Democracies, and Dependencies: A Reexamination of the Kantian Peace." *American Jounral of Political Science* 51(3): 583–601.

Warren, T. C. (2010). "The Geometry of Security: Modeling Interstate Alliances as Evolving Networks." *Journal of Peace Research* 47(6): 697–709.

Warren, T. C. (2016). "Modeling the Co-Evolution of International and Domestic Institutions: Alliances, Democracy, and the Complex Path to Peace." *Journal of Peace Research* 52(3): 424–441.

Zhang, Y., Friend, A. J., Amanda, L. Traud., Mason, A. Porter., James, H. Fowler., and Peter, J. Mucha. (2008). Community structure in Congressional cosponsorship networks. *Physica A: Statistical Mechanics and its Applications* 387(7): 1705–1712.

....

CHAPTER 32

ARMS SUPPLY AND PROLIFERATION NETWORKS

....

DAVID KINSELLA AND
ALEXANDER H. MONTGOMERY

INTRODUCTION

....

THE transfer of small arms and light weapons (SALW), major conventional weapons (MCW), and weapons of mass destruction (WMD)—as well as the components used in their production—remains a central scholarly focus in the field of security studies and a pressing matter for policymakers and political activists.[1] Despite this, network-analytic approaches to arms transfers are surprisingly infrequent. Network language and imagery are frequently invoked by those who investigate the transfer of weapons and related contraband, but neither social network theory nor the tools of social network analysis (SNA) presently feature prominently in the literature. Yet questions pertaining to global and regional arms flows, proliferation of WMD, and the related matters of international insecurity and criminality should lend themselves quite well to this mode of analysis.

Although network analytic methods are now widely used in political science, some of the main challenges for their application to these questions derive from the limited availability of data. Information on the mostly legal interstate trade in MCW is well developed. But data are often missing or distorted for the trafficking of SALW and WMD, which are restricted in interstate commerce by law or policy.[2] Naturally, clandestine networks of actors (both individuals and organizational entities) are defining characteristics of much of this weapons flow, which also means that their activities and connections are not easy to trace. Describing even the structural features of these networks is therefore a significant challenge.

Nonetheless, the extant literature contains a number of implicit or explicit hypotheses that could be explored or tested using network analysis. Claims that clandestine actors use network forms of organization, for example, have observable implications for the network structures of arms transfers. Similarly, arguments that social or cultural networks facilitate illicit transfers can be tested by comparing these underlying structures with actual arms networks. Hypotheses that brokerage positions are particularly valuable should be reflected in the behavior of middlemen seeking to maintain or expand their influence by preventing competing intermediaries from closing structural holes. And network structures should reflect the varying hostility of the legal and political environment as well as the technical requirements for transfers.

This chapter first provides an overview of the main factors shaping these networks through supply and demand, examining the illicit and/or clandestine nature of many of these ties and the immense variance across levels of analysis and technologies in the arms trade. It then discusses these networks' structural characteristics, focusing on the trade-offs between security and efficiency embodied in them, the pressures on networks to adopt more or less centralized forms, and how different layers in networks relate to each other and adapt to different constraints such as geography. Finally, it reviews some existing data sets and network analyses (surprisingly few at present) and concludes with a discussion of the potential for network analysis to inform the study of arms transfer networks.

Supply and Demand

The analysis of supply and demand factors driving arms transfers tends to start with monadic and dyadic considerations rather than network ones. Nevertheless, these considerations hint at possible network mechanisms. Weapons and military-technology transfers ought to be understood as both economic and political transactions; consequently, transfers should correlate with economic and political networks. State-sanctioned transfers, especially those involving MCW systems, are often elements in an ongoing political-military relationship between governments. They are undertaken for the purpose of enhancing the military capability of the receiving state, but they may also afford the supplier some degree of political influence over the recipient (although frequently less than expected) and signal to third parties that the supplier has some interest in the military security of the recipient. When the "political content" of weapons transfers is low—for example, when they are not accompanied by any security commitment by the supplier—they more closely resemble other types of economic transactions taking place on the open market. Governments that allow arms producers within their jurisdictions to export their goods primarily as a means of achieving economies of scale may have little interest in the security implications for receiving states. The same is true for governments selling surplus weaponry after a military demobilization. Nonetheless, even ordinary economic transactions are strongly influenced by network mechanisms (Ward, Ahlquist, and Rozenas, 2013; Ward and Hoff, 2007), and so consequently we should expect even purely economic arms transfers to be influenced by them as well.

The types of weapons and military technology that states are willing to transfer to other states suggest something about the relative political versus economic content of those transactions. Broadly speaking, the political content of SALW transfers is lower than MCW transfers. They do not entail the transfer of high levels of military capability and need not represent a significant measure of commitment by the supplier to the recipient's security. At the other end of the spectrum, a state is unlikely to be willing to transfer (or assist in the development of) ballistic missiles, antimissile systems, or WMD—international law notwithstanding—in the absence of a close political-military relationship with the recipient. Moreover, these types of transfers take place in a context of broader political deterrence and signaling networks (Spindel, 2015). The security interests of supplier states, therefore, regulate the extent to which global weapons flows are governed by market mechanisms, political forces, or various mixtures of the two. Many of the relevant political relationships are themselves networks, formal military alliances being the most obvious.

On the demand side, both state and nonstate entities seek weapons for an admixture of functional and symbolic reasons. Security demands are frequently the most obviously apparent motive for seeking weapons, but even these can vary depending on the weapons seeker's particular strategies and repertoires for using violence—which in turn can depend on broader political network positions. The explicit or implicit security ties to the weapons source may be as or more important than the weapons themselves. Other prominent political motivations include seeking prestige through the purchase (or manufacture) of symbolically important weapons or satisfying important internal or external constituencies (Eyre and Suchman, 1996; Kinsella and Chima, 2001; Suchman and Eyre, 1992). Prestige seeking often occurs when there is a gap between actual network position and aspirational status, and diplomatic (and other) networks are central to determining the prestige of states (Kinne, 2014). Finally, weapons transfers can also be shaped by internal organizational competition for resources, such as interservice rivalries in militaries with independent branches (Buzan and Herring, 1998).

Illegal Weaponry and Networks

Illicit weapons networks materialize for fairly obvious reasons. Because global markets for weaponry do not operate freely, but are constrained by states' foreign policies and laws, some of the demand for weaponry is met through illicit channels. Black and grey markets, for weapons or anything else, form when supply and demand are sufficient to sustain profitable exchange among a collection of actors despite the risks. As in legal markets, exchange will occur when the costs of participating in the illegal market are offset by the net gains from the exchange. But the transaction costs associated with illegal market exchange are invariably higher than in legal markets—although anyone familiar with legal weapons procurement will know that it only vaguely resembles an actual market. There is a premium on information about availability, price, quality, and other matters when goods must be traded out of sight because their exchange runs counter to policy or is prohibited by law. Likewise, the costs of bargaining and sustaining agreements are higher because transactions are extralegal and therefore risky; the parties to the exchange cannot turn to state authorities for purposes of enforcing property rights and contract terms. Add to this the risk of penalty for participating in prohibited exchange and (for some) the accompanying moral costs. Yet for many goods and services, in many places, illegal markets thrive.

Although it is certainly the case that governments and weapons firms are sometimes counted among the actors participating in illicit transactions, this is often attributable to rogue individuals or entities within those organizations. Formal governmental and business organizations structured as hierarchies are not very well suited to achieve the efficiencies necessary to offset the additional transaction costs associated with exchange in illicit markets. This is because they come under the scrutiny of public policy and law, which is anathema to the functioning of illegal markets. Less formal organizations with core-periphery or cell network structures are better able to avoid this sort of scrutiny and to adapt when their illicit transactions are, or may be, exposed. Consequently, we should see illicit arms and proliferation networks adopt these types of structures.

The implications of network theory go beyond the structures adopted by these organizations. Social networks are important to those engaged in activities that must remain underground and unregulated by legal contracts and other mechanisms that attach to open market exchange. Family ties, personal friendships, and networks that are formed based on sets of common practices, such as shared ethnicity and religion, can give rise to interpersonal loyalties and the trust that reduce transaction costs when the formal rule of law is unavailable. This sort of social capital is obviously not absent from commerce in open markets, but it becomes rather more essential to the movement of illicit or clandestine goods and services by means of a multiplex of crosscutting connections (Kleemans and Van De Bunt, 1999; Lampe and Johansen, 2004; Murji, 2007; Parkinson, 2013). If nothing else, suppliers, traffickers, and consumers must instill confidence among themselves that they share a commitment to keeping the joint enterprise hidden from scrutiny by the agencies of government. About the illicit arms trade, Naylor (2004, 129) notes that "discretion is a proverb, not only with respect to one's own business but with respect to everyone else's as well. By an unwritten code, gunrunners, however anxious to cut each other's commercial throats, rarely rat out each other the way drug dealers routinely do."

Weapons Network Structures

Although at first glance organizations that are illicit and/or clandestine would seem likely to adopt different network structures than those that are not, network theory is not deterministic about alternative structures. Indeed, it recognizes both that these two characteristics may push in different directions and that organizations face a trade-off between efficiency and security in structuring their networks to accomplish their goals.

It is important to distinguish between these two characteristics—the illegal and the concealed—since they place different structural pressures on networks and produce different behavioral characteristics. They are often lumped together under the term "dark networks." Consequently, this term runs the gamut from well-developed militant political organizations carrying out insurgencies to criminal networks trafficking in various forms of contraband. It can apply to networks within or between organizations that have goals, use means, or conduct transactions that are illicit or clandestine (although the former frequently requires some of the latter).

Transfer networks for SALW and WMD proliferation networks tend to be both illicit and clandestine, but not in equal amounts. They both facilitate the diffusion of contraband weaponry. For SALW, this is often (but not always) for the benefit of nonstate actors hostile to states; for WMD, the beneficiaries are typically "rogue states" confronting constraints imposed by the most dominant states in the international community. Law enforcement and national security policymakers, in particular, have been interested in understanding the features of illicit networks that allow them to adapt to a changing environment. This includes efforts by police and military forces to defeat their activities and dismantle their organizations. Scholarship in sociology, economics, criminology, and political science is contributing to this understanding and providing a set of analytical tools to describe these networks' resiliencies and vulnerabilities (Bakker, Raab, and Milward, 2012; Enders and Su, 2007; Hämmerli, Gattiker, and Weyermann, 2006; Klerks, 2001; Koschade, 2006; Milward and Raab, 2006; Perliger and Pedahzur, 2011; Raab and Milward, 2003; Sageman, 2004). However, at least in political contexts, some analysts caution that the unreflective use of network analysis to identify and target purported vulnerabilities may be ultimately counterproductive (see, e.g., Mac Ginty, 2010).

The Efficiency/Security Trade-off

Illicit networks typically face a trade-off between efficiency and security (see, e.g., Lindelauf, Borm, and Hamers, 2009), although those operating in permissive environments or otherwise taking advantage of ungoverned spaces are less constrained. As previously discussed, organizations that rely on a multiplex of network ties allow members to overcome barriers to collective action—the production and distribution of weapons, gas centrifuges, drugs, and so forth—thereby generating collective as well as private gains for participants. But these networks typically operate in risky environments, and participants must be attentive to their exposure to external threats. Internally, trust and mutual commitment to a financially and/or politically profitable covert enterprise may be enough to maintain the concealment necessary for network security. And when it is not, the threat of violence may suffice.

A trade-off between efficiency and security exists because active networks are more likely to become exposed and fall victim to the disruptive efforts of military and law enforcement authorities. Illicit networks might generally be thought to prioritize security over efficiency, but Morselli et al. (2007, 145) suggest that this is the case only for networks with particular types of objectives:

> When the objective involves a monetary outcome, action in the criminal enterprise context is more limited in terms of time because participants expect a pay-off for their involvement in the network, and as a result, action must be played out within a reasonably short time frame. When the objective is political, time is a more extensive resource and action may be prolonged—the political cause is prioritized over any episodic action and, as a result, a network may lay low and wait for the right moment to act.

One implication of this argument is that different network structures evolve depending on the prioritization of aims. For example, economic goals may push networks toward adopting relatively efficient core-and-periphery structures that more closely resemble hierarchical businesses while sheltering the most central elements, whereas political goals might create incentives for cell structures that maximize security so that long-term goals can be pursued.

Small Arms Trafficking

Some illicit arms trafficking networks have long-term political goals, especially those connected to diasporas supporting armed groups operating in their homelands. However, most participants on the supply side of the illicit arms trade are out to turn a profit in a competitive black market. Consequently, small arms trafficking networks are more likely to be structured in ways that compromise their security, all else being equal. Some suppliers, brokers, or transporters may operate in market niches, most likely attached to particular geographic locales, and therefore face little competition, but others must devote some of their energies to outmaneuvering others for clients. They also increase their take by squeezing those they must deal with up and down the supply and distribution chain. Such imperatives are not different in kind from the competitive forces operating in legal markets, but the temptation to defect and "rat out each other" is undoubtedly present and may ultimately threaten to undermine the mutual trust and reciprocity that seem essential for the functioning of illicit networks. How this tension is resolved is likely to depend on the structural characteristics of particular networks and the attributes of those who participate in the enterprise.

Competitive dynamics within these networks, along with a generally high volume of small arms trafficking activity, work against concealment and create vulnerabilities. Bruinsma and Bernasco (2004) have examined three criminal groups whose activities have two important features in common with illicit small arms trafficking other than the need to operate underground. Heroin smuggling, human trafficking, and the transnational trade in stolen cars serve a market and involve the movement of illegal goods and services across long distances. Bruinsma and Bernasco find that activities characterized by higher levels of criminal and financial risk require collaboration grounded on substantial mutual trust, which is typically a feature of criminal enterprises that have cohesive social network structures underpinning them. In the case of heroin smuggling, the riskiest of the three criminal enterprises examined, that cohesion derives from ethnic and other demographic homogeneities. Turkish groups figure prominently in the heroin trade (at least destined for the Netherlands, a focus of the Bruinsma and Bernasco study); those who work most closely together at the different stages of the process tend to be of similar age and social class and hail from the same regions of the country.

It is difficult to say whether, in terms of criminal and financial risk, the illicit small arms trade has more in common with heroin smuggling or purportedly less-risky trafficking in humans or stolen automobiles. But a reasonable hypothesis is that illicit arms networks that operate in higher risk environments—for example, in geographic locales with a robust police and/or military presence, or spanning long distances with multiple sites of potential vulnerability—must be grounded in dense social network structures to be effective and resilient. The social cohesion created by ethnic, religious, or ideological bonds reduces the likelihood of defection and thus the risks of exposure in an extralegal setting.

In addition to dense social ties that give rise to cohesion, temporary "shortcuts" can be created in these networks to facilitate information transfer and more effective coordination within the network (e.g., Krebs, 2002). Yet even in regard to security, as Montgomery (2005, 170) points out, decentralized but densely connected networks have their own vulnerabilities:

> Densely connected, decentralized networks where no single node holds a crucial position in the network are easier in one sense to shut down: connections to additional nodes in the network are easier to discover, although this is balanced by the number of nodes and connections that need to be eliminated to dissolve the network.

Weapons of Mass Destruction Trafficking

Ballistic missile and WMD proliferation networks form around longer-term and considerably more challenging goals than do small arms trafficking networks. When proliferation networks serve the interests of states, the goal is to significantly enhance the military capability (and prestige) of the state by providing resources and know-how necessary to develop weaponry that relatively few other states possess (Kroenig, 2010). The scarcity of supply (components, machinery, knowledge, etc.) and the stringency of regulations intended to prevent proliferation require patience and perseverance over longer periods of time.

Historically, the transfer of expertise, materials, technology, or assembled weapons has been viewed as more immoral than illegal; "sensitive" assistance has long been a staple of nuclear weapons proliferation, even if the tacit knowledge requirements have

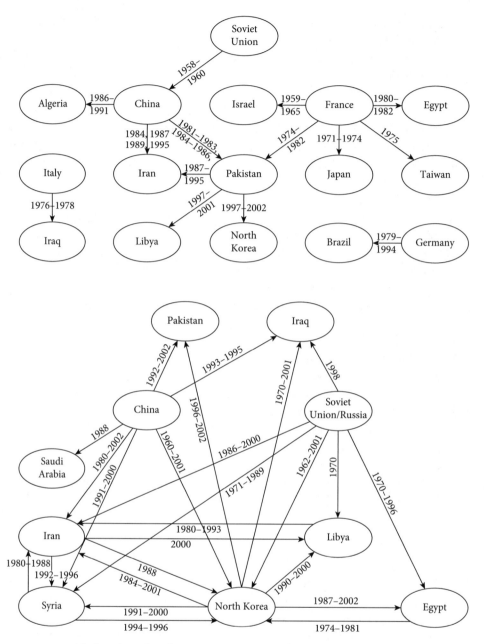

FIGURE 32.1 Nuclear (top, data from Kroenig, 2010) and ballistic missile (bottom, data from Montgomery, 2008) proliferation networks.

limited the effectiveness of these transfers, structuring the nuclear proliferation network as a set of hubs rather than the denser and more reciprocal missile proliferation network (Montgomery 2005, 2008, 2013); see figure 32.1.

The demand for WMD and effective delivery vehicles varies by type of weapon and by the particular motivations of the potential recipients. While nuclear, chemical, and biological weapons have generally been complements when states are engaged in the pursuit of such capabilities (Horowitz and Narang, 2014), countries that actually succeed in acquiring nuclear weapons have generally been willing to give up pursuit of the others. Militant organizations generally seek WMD if they are embedded in alliance structures and based in authoritarian countries with relatively strong connections to a globalized world; however, contrary to popular expectations, there is little evidence that suggests a correlation with religious ideology (Asal, Ackerman, and Rethemeyer, 2012).

When proliferation networks operate on behalf of nonstate actors—for example, attempting to acquire radioactive material for a dirty bomb[3] or chemical precursors for sarin—the goal is to enhance the group's ability to attack and terrorize its enemies rather than to provide the group with a sustainable WMD or ballistic missile capability. Nevertheless, the sort of groups seeking the ability to launch such spectacular attacks are also likely to be motivated by longer-term political goals, which suggests that, like the proliferation networks serving states, these networks are also likely to prioritize security over efficiency in meeting their objectives.

Countering Illicit Networks

Network forms of organization seem to offer distinct advantages to those engaged in illicit economic, political, and military activities. As Kenney (2007, 203) explains, compared to the hierarchically organized and bureaucratic state agencies—intelligence, law enforcement, or military—that typically oppose them, illicit networks

> contain relatively flat authority structures that facilitate rapid decision cycles and quick information flows. They compartment participants and information into separate, semiautonomous cells, often based on family, friendship, and geographic ties. They build redundancy into their operations by giving important functions to multiple groups, and they rely on brokers and other intermediaries to span "structural holes" between loosely connected nodes and networks.

These organizational structures and practices foster secrecy and secure the distribution of information and other resources necessary to accomplish tasks. State agencies enjoy a preponderance of coercive force and intelligence collection capacity. Yet their ability to employ these capacities to penetrate illicit networks and track their activities can be constrained by elaborate decision-making procedures, organizational checks, and other imperatives. And when state agencies are successful—for example, when they capture or kill a drug kingpin or terrorist mastermind and consequently are able to dismantle a portion of the illicit enterprise—this often proves temporary, as others regroup, reorganize, and recruit new members into more diffuse network structures (Johnston, 2012; Jordan, 2009, 2014). Thus, adopting network structures provides organizational advantages that can be deployed against adversaries with superior resources but operating within the constraints of bureaucratic and hierarchical organizations (Williams, 2001).

Yet these network structures can have major disadvantages in terms of command and control, information transmission, replication of roles, and even robustness against attack if critical bridging nodes are eliminated or structures are decentralized but still dense. Moreover, states can and do respond to network structures by adapting their own methods accordingly; the response to WMD proliferation networks, for example, has included a semi-institutionalized, informal set of norms and principles under the Proliferation Security Initiative (Caves, 2006). However, the overall effectiveness of PSI as a networked entity as opposed to a formal organization or simple bilateral efforts is unclear (Valencia, 2007), and formalized ties are quite useful for counterproliferation, especially in the financial arena (Schlumberger and Gruselle, 2007).

Centrality and Centralization in Weapons Networks

In addition to the overall advantages and disadvantages of adopting network forms of organization to strike different balances of efficiency and security, social scientists are interested in actors' relative power within them, the overall degree of centralization of the network as a whole, and the multiple overlapping layers that constitute most networks. Actors occupying particular central positions have access to resources that can be exploited to pursue individual and collective interests (Hafner-Burton, Kahler, and Montgomery, 2009; Kahler, 2009). The resources available to suppliers, middlemen, shippers, and others involved in the transfer of illicit weaponry are both material and social. Those who possess or can muster superior armament stocks, finance, transport, and other material resources are in a better position to exercise power within the network than those who do not. But one's access is also a key source of influence and success. Compared to legal arms markets, where openly publicizing the availability of goods and distribution services is not a risky enterprise, the contribution of social connections to one's ability to survive and thrive in the illicit market takes on relatively greater importance. Larger numbers of relationships provide more opportunities for profitable transaction, but so do the right types of relationships. The pivotal activities of arms brokers, who bring together parties that would not otherwise come into contact in an underground environment, epitomize the role that social capital plays in illicit weapons networks (Amnesty International, 2006; Cattaneo, 2004; Wood and Peleman, 2000).

Distinctive network structures arise from the frequency and intensity of interaction among network actors, whether they be individuals or collective entities. Those structures suggest certain things about the efficiency with which goods and information move from one part of the network to another, as well as the vulnerability of these flows to disruption. Second-tier nuclear proliferation networks—those that connect actors in post-1967 proliferant states and serve those states' nuclear ambitions—tend to be rather centralized, with a few highly connected nodes positioned as hubs and a larger number of nodes with links to the central nodes but few direct connections among themselves (Braun and Chyba, 2004; Gruselle, 2007; Montgomery, 2005, 2008). The A. Q. Khan network, fully exposed in 2004, displayed this sort of star structure. The network's hub was, of course, Khan himself (and Khan Research Laboratories), in Pakistan, with links to other nodes in Iran, North Korea, Libya, and elsewhere.

Ballistic missile technology has also proliferated through second-tier networks exhibiting star structures, with North Korea and Iran as hubs, although these tend to be less centralized than nuclear proliferation networks (see figure 32.1). Even "first-tier" nuclear assistance has often appeared to be centralized, with each nuclear program attempting to take advantage of prior or concurrent nuclear programs through spying (Reed and Stillman, 2009), although it is still debated how useful most of this assistance has been (Kroenig, 2010; Montgomery, 2013). The A. Q. Khan network demonstrates both the advantages and disadvantages of network structures for proliferation: while it enabled first Pakistan and then Iran, Libya, and North Korea to take advantage of Khan's diffuse supply network, it also generated a wealth of indicators and warnings for intelligence communities to map the network before rolling it up (Albright, Brannan, and Stricker, 2010; Corera, 2006; Montgomery, 2005, 2013). Similarly, Aum Shinrikyo's acquisitions could have provided early indicators of its intentions before the Tokyo subway sarin gas attacks (Picarelli, 1998).

One reason for the greater centralization of WMD proliferation networks and their tendency to manifest star structures is the importance of tacit knowledge in the development of nuclear and (to a lesser extent) ballistic missile capability (Montgomery, 2005, 2008). The components and precision machinery needed to produce nuclear bombs and rocketry are difficult to acquire, but the knowledge and experience necessary to take the intermediate steps from weapon designs to functioning finished systems may present the bigger hurdle. Yet even these two types of networks differ significantly; there are many small tacit knowledge problems with missile technologies that allow for collaboration, whereas for nuclear weapons the engineering issues provide significant barriers to knowledge transmission. There are even fewer holders and willing purveyors of tacit knowledge than there are of the other elements that must be brought together to succeed at this level of weapons development, and they are likely to be coterminous with the few hubs in proliferation networks. However, proliferants can also take the "street-legal" proliferation route by seeking to acquire capabilities through the transfer of civilian nuclear technologies, which can sometimes be an indicator of nuclear weapons intentions (Fuhrmann, 2012; Morstein and Perry, 2000).

Thus, the centralized nature of nuclear and ballistic missile proliferation networks reflects the advanced knowledge required for the development of this type of weaponry, scarcity of components and manufacturing technology, and the long-standing regulatory efforts of states. None of these apply to SALW: they are not difficult to manufacture, there is abundant surplus, and distribution is not closely regulated (the 2014 Arms Trade Treaty notwithstanding). So it is not surprising that illicit networks operating in this realm tend to exhibit more decentralized structures. The number of participants in these networks is far greater, and they are located in far more states. Although the individuals and groups involved in the illicit small arms trade do not always have many connections to other actors, some do. These networks are more diffuse than WMD proliferation networks and more closely resemble clique structures, in which nodes are connected to each other directly rather than indirectly through hubs. That is not always the case, however, and when the state is the level of analysis, some state locales are substantially more active as origination points and destinations of illicit weaponry, as well as transshipment points. States in the former Soviet bloc, for example, stand out as more central nodes in the illicit flow of arms to African conflict zones and thus form geographic hubs in an otherwise dense global network (Kinsella, 2006, 2014).

Multiplex Network Structures and Geography

Proliferation and small arms networks are not simply social or political networks; they also are—or are conjoined with—physical networks. These networks also contain multiple layers: the layer representing direct assistance between states looks very different from the layers involving, for example, middlemen who procure components, transporters who facilitate the movement of the components themselves (Hastings, 2012), and brokers who arrange financing (Group d'action financiere, 2008; Gruselle, 2007). Each country's internal and external proliferation network differs depending on political structures, international barriers, and other factors like active diasporas (Boureston and Russell, 2009). Existing smuggling networks for other goods can also be reused for the acquisition and transfer of unconventional weaponry, by both states and nonstate actors (see, e.g., Chestnut [2007] on North Korea and Frost [2014] on Latin America).

Because proliferation and small arms networks move contraband from one location to another, the physical and political geography of that space may help to explain the behavior of illicit actors and the structure of their networks. For example, several factors have conspired to make individuals and organizations in Russia and other former Soviet bloc locales active participants in illicit arms transfer networks. The most common explanations focus on the role of military and security forces, especially the incentives and opportunities associated with the political-economic transition that accompanied the end of the Cold War (Gerasev and Surikov, 1997; Holloway and McFaul, 1995; Turbiville, 1996). In addition to arms surpluses, they had access to military transport facilities or found common cause with others who had logistical expertise and experience moving cargo surreptitiously. Well-developed transportation infrastructures plus the uncertainties of postcommunism (features of multiple state locales clustered geographically in Eastern Europe and Central Asia) help to account for their emergence as pivotal nodes in illicit arms supply networks.

In regard to proliferation networks, Hastings (2012, 431) proposes a geographic approach that focuses on "how the nature of the network actors—and the spatial distribution of the technological and transportation infrastructure they use—shape the structure of the proliferation network, and, more specifically, how it is physically arrayed across the world." The structure and geographic layout of these networks depend on the extent to which the state is actively engaged in the illicit deal making, financial transactions, and physical movement of goods. In some cases, those coordinating the transfer of nuclear material, machinery, and other necessary components have access to resources of sovereign states, namely transportation infrastructure, controlled borders, and diplomatic prerogative. Weapons of mass destruction proliferation networks generally involve states, and therefore those engaged in illicit activities on their behalf have access to state resources. While working on behalf of his home government beginning in the 1970s, A. Q. Khan's network had access to Pakistan's diplomatic outposts and military transport, and once foreign-sourced materiel arrived on Pakistani territory or at its ports, there was little need to worry that state authorities would prevent it from arriving at prescribed destinations.

Non-state-based WMD proliferation networks are more like free agents and have little or no access to state resources. In conducting their illicit transactions and transfers, they are compelled to seek out the most hospitable environments available without the benefit of state sponsorship or prerogatives. These networks must therefore make use of the commercial transportation infrastructure, and in doing so they gravitate to geographic locales where their activities will be most secure from exposure and disruption. Those are the places where network hubs form. Hastings (2012) thus observes that when A. Q. Khan (as a semi-independent agent)[4] redirected his efforts to Libya's nuclear ambitions in the 1990s, he could no longer count on the resources of his home state. The network's primary hub formed in the United Arab Emirates, which attracts a large number of foreigners (and foreign companies) and whose geographic location and advanced port facilities accommodate a great deal of global commerce.

The implications for the structure of WMD proliferation networks are twofold. First, networks without access to state resources are more likely to develop global reach in order to seek out weapons components that are scarce—because of their sophistication—but nonetheless available because political and economic conditions (and sometimes personal connections) permit illicit transfer. This is not a strength; it is required to maximize network security when state resources are unavailable to the network. And it comes at the expense of efficiency. Second, although these networks may be spread thin globally, illicit transactions are concentrated at nodes that are, of necessity, established to take advantage of commercial infrastructure. In this respect, the networks are more centralized than state-sponsored, second-tier WMD proliferation networks, which are territorially diffuse because their logistics can take advantage of a multitude of diplomatic outposts and a state-controlled transportation infrastructure. Although the latter appear to have star structures when nodes are operationalized as state locales, they are likely to manifest considerably less centralized structures when nodes represent network actors operating in more precisely specified geographic locations.

The geography of ballistic missile proliferation networks, and perhaps even illicit small arms networks, ought to exhibit the same patterns that Hastings (2012) observes in the case of nuclear proliferation networks. However, compared to nuclear and ballistic missile proliferation, a much smaller proportion of total illicit small arms trafficking activity is sponsored by states. This is because states have far less need to turn to illicit networks when they want to acquire this type of weaponry, which is generally (but not always) a legitimate activity for states and easy to accomplish given the large number of suppliers. When states do engage in illicit small arms networks, this is usually in the role of covert suppliers of weapons destined for insurgencies and/or contravening multilateral arms embargoes. It follows, then, that illicit arms networks that connect to state suppliers, because they have access to state-controlled assets and infrastructure, will be territorially diffuse and less centralized. Where states are not involved, and state resources are unavailable to arms traffickers, the geography of illicit small arms networks may more closely align with the nodes and routes constituting the commercial transportation infrastructure. Thus, they should exhibit more centralized structures.

ARMS DATA AND NETWORK ANALYSIS

Implicit in our discussion of arms trafficking and proliferation networks is the notion that these are purposeful organizations engaged in collective action. That is, these networks are collective actors whose organizational forms have evolved in ways more or less conducive to the transfer of weapons, nuclear material, processing equipment, and so forth, in a covert and insecure environment. Not all participants in these networks have their eyes on the prize—the arrival of illicit weapons or components at the intended destination—and many are motivated solely by opportunism and the individual gains they derive from whatever role they play in the process. But in the aggregate, these networks resemble purposeful organizational entities; arrayed against them are other purposeful actors like law enforcement or other state agencies charged with disrupting them.

Empirical investigations into the activities and structure of A. Q. Khan's proliferation network or the arms-transport network assembled by Viktor Bout and associates, not to mention other "dark networks" like Cosa Nostra or al-Qaeda, often assume that these entities take the form of networked organizations. Social network analysis can then be applied to discover the structural features of these networks, key players within them, organizational strengths and vulnerabilities, and so forth. The outer bounds of these organizations may or may not be clearly discernible—who is part of the network, who is not—but these networks can reasonably be conceptualized as actors.

However, the application of network concepts and analytical methods need not presume that a particular collection of nodes constitutes a purposeful organization in the sense that we have been discussing illicit arms and proliferation networks in this chapter. Indeed, SNA in the field of international relations frequently examines the structure of interstate relations, such as conflict or trade, in an effort to gain empirical insights that may be missed by other methodologies, but without any presumption that states are organized (networked) for collective action (e.g., Hafner-Burton, Kahler, and Montgomery, 2009; Maoz, 2011). They may be, as would be true of states in a military alliance or a free trade association, but international interactions more generally can exhibit network-like patterns. Here "network" describes a structure of interaction without implying collective action per se.

These observations concerning networks as actors versus networks as structures are particularly relevant to arms trade research, as we describe below. Illicit small arms transfers, for example, are commonly facilitated by trafficking networks (actors), while global arms flows, both legal and illegal, exhibit patterns commonly associated with networked organizational forms (structures). To date, there have been few network analytic studies at either level of analysis.

Data Sources and Studies

Quantitative network analysis requires, at a minimum, data identifying nodes and the presence or absence of links between them. Ideally, in the case of proliferation and arms networks, we would like to have information on the individuals (dealers, brokers, financiers, etc.) and collective entities (manufacturers, transport companies, government agencies, insurgencies, etc.) involved in the transfers, as well as type and volume of what is exchanged (weapons, enrichment machinery, cash, etc.). We would also like to have data on the locations of these actors and their transactions, given the geographic factors that influence the behavior and structure of these networks. Needless to say, systematic and reliable information at this level of detail is not readily available for illicit networks like those we have been discussing. Where systematic and reasonably comprehensive data do exist, they are likely to be aggregated by state, even when states (or their agents) are not network actors per se, but merely the geographic locales within which actors operate. Finer-grained information, which is often the result of law enforcement activities or investigative journalism, is available for many networks, but these data are not very comprehensive and are difficult to assemble in a systematic way.

The most authoritative source of both quantitative and qualitative information on the arms trade is the yearbook published by SIPRI, *Armaments, Disarmament and International Security*.[5] SIPRI relies exclusively on open sources for its data and focuses its attention on the kind of information consistently available to the public, namely MCW systems. These include aircraft, armor and artillery, guidance and radar systems, missiles, and ships. In addition to those items physically transferred to recipients, SIPRI includes weaponry manufactured by the recipient under license. The MCW data come in two forms: "trade registers" of transferred military hardware broken down by model (F-16 aircraft, M-60 tanks, Patriot surface-to-air missile systems, etc.) and dollar-valued aggregates. The latter do not represent what the recipient paid for arms; they represent the "military resource value" of transferred weaponry based on performance characteristics.[6]

The few studies that take a network approach to the MCW trade all make use of the SIPRI data. Some deploy SNA for primarily descriptive purposes, especially for visualization (e.g., Kinsella, 2003), even if they go on to model dyadic relations using standard econometric methods (e.g., Akerman and Seim, 2014). That is, the importance of network-level processes in arms trading is acknowledged in these studies, but not actually incorporated into inferential models for purposes of hypothesis testing. Two recent exceptions are Willardson (2013) and Thurner et al. (2015). Both studies make use of exponential random graph models (ERGMs) to identify the covariates of arms trading while factoring in structural features of the global arms market. In terms of our discussion above, such studies treat networks primarily not as actors, but as structures. We expect that the SIPRI data will continue to be examined using these and increasingly sophisticated network analytic methods, bringing new insights to what we already know (or think we know) from the extensive quantitative literature on the global arms trade (see Kinsella, 2011).

As the attention of the academic and policy communities has turned increasingly to SALW, there has been a great deal of interest in the collection and distribution of systematic information (qualitative and quantitative) on this aspect of the arms trade. Because the SALW trade is much less regulated by state authorities than the major weapons trade, and because the weapons themselves are smaller and harder to observe by journalists and others who might want to document their movement, reliable information is very difficult to gather on a consistent basis. But researchers are now beginning to accumulate and release pertinent data.[7] Most promising for network analysis are the data collected by the Norwegian Initiative on Small Arms Transfers (NISAT), located at the International Peace Research Institute in Oslo. In addition to its document library, NISAT maintains an online database of SALW transfers, with some records dating back to 1962. These data are likely to feature in future academic and policy research and are well suited to network analysis and visualization.[8]

As an illustration, figure 32.2 maps the global trade in SALW based on NISAT data for 1998–2005. The nodes are states, which are labeled with three-letter country codes, arranged according to the geographic coordinates of their capital cities. A line connecting any two nodes means that SALW transfers between them totaled more than $1 million during the period, with thicker and darker lines indicating higher transfer volumes. The size of the nodes corresponds to the state's centrality in the network, operationalized here as outdegree: the number of other states that were recipients of that state's SALW exports. The most central nodes in this network are the United States, several states in Western Europe, Russia, and Brazil.

The value of the SALW trade amounts to roughly $4 billion per year, and probably 10 to 20 percent of this occurs in the black and gray markets. In addition to collecting quantitative data on the legal SALW trade, NISAT maintains the Black Market File Archive, a collection of news stories and investigative reports on the illicit arms trade. This material can be coded for use in network analysis (see Kinsella, 2012), although the stories and reports collected by NISAT vary widely in the amount of useful information they contain. Some articles include detailed accounts of arms shipments from manufacturer to purchaser, including any number of participating intermediate dealers, brokers, and shipping agents. Other reports include no codable event information at all. Some reports provide a wealth of background information, such as previous events in ongoing arms-supply relationships. Others pick up a particular shipment's journey midstream,

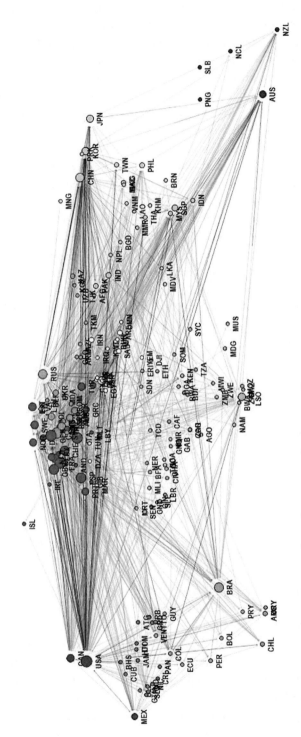

FIGURE 32.2 Legal small arms trade: node size as outdegree centrality.

such as when one militant group supplies another, without any indication of where the first group acquired the weaponry. Even when reports contain complete information, the events themselves exhibit a wide range of forms. There is substantial variation in the number and type of intermediaries engaged in illicit transfers, the nature of the illegalities involved (forged end-user certificates, arsenal theft, etc.), and whether transfers were intercepted by state authorities or someone other than the intended recipient.

Despite these limitations, this information can be used to generate binary network data, which can then be examined to elucidate the contours of illicit arms trading at regional and global levels (e.g., Kinsella, 2006, 2014). For example, following the format of figure 32.2, figure 32.3 uses these data to map illicit arms transfers between states. Here the lines connecting the nodes indicate that illicit weapons flowed from one state to the other at least once during the 1998–2005 period. Although governments are sometimes complicit in these transfers, usually they are not, so the nodes in this network are state locales: geographic spaces within which participants in the illicit arms trade operate. The lines connecting the nodes are thicker and darker if there are more illicit arms-transfer events ascertained from the reports in the NISAT archives; they do not indicate the volume of the arms flow, either in quantity or value, which is not sufficiently documented. The prominence of former Soviet-bloc countries in the illicit arms trade is noteworthy. The three locales with the highest outdegree centralities are Russia, Czech Republic, and Bulgaria, while the former Soviet bloc constitutes half of the twenty most central nodes worldwide.

Figure 32.4 further highlights the links between and among the former Soviet-bloc countries and locales in sub-Saharan Africa, which constitute over one-third of the 650 links shown in figure 32.3. Of these, over 40 percent represent outflow links from the former Soviet bloc to sub-Saharan Africa, while just under 40 percent are links within sub-Saharan Africa. Figure 32.4 also shows the substantial number of links among former Soviet-bloc locales.

As in figure 32.2, analysis of data displayed in figures 32.3 and 32.4 proceeds from a conceptualization of networks primarily as structures rather than purposeful actors. There are exceedingly few social network analyses of illicit arms trafficking networks, in contrast to other criminal organizations, despite an otherwise fairly developed scholarly and policy-oriented literature on such groups. Curwen's (2007) study of the illicit network of suppliers, brokers, financiers, and transportation agents involved in the transfer of weapons to Liberia between 1999 and 2002 is one example, although his analysis is limited to the use of network visualizations and the computation of descriptive statistics like centrality. Attempts to broaden this type of network-as-actor analysis over space and time will confront substantial data collection hurdles. However, much raw material exists in NISAT's Black Market File Archive, and text-mining algorithms designed for the extraction of network data could prove useful for systematizing it (e.g., Carley, Columbus, and Landwehr, 2013).

Finally, due to the small number of cases, WMD transfers are also primarily analyzed graphically rather than quantitatively as a network. Data sets on both sensitive (Kroenig, 2010) and civilian (Fuhrmann, 2012) nuclear transfers exist, and missile

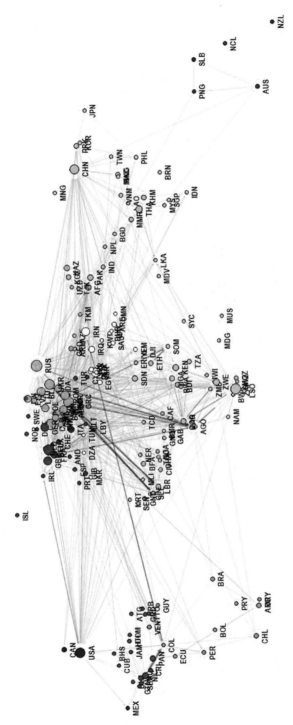

FIGURE 32.3 Illicit arms trade: node size as outdegree centrality.

FIGURE 32.4 Illicit arms trade: former Soviet bloc and sub-Saharan Africa.

transfers (Montgomery, 2008) can be gleaned from Nuclear Threat Initiative country reports. However, little or no information has been systematically collected on chemical and biological weapons transfers, although incidents of both fortunately appear to be relatively infrequent.

Conclusion

The study of the transfer of SALW, MCW, and WMD is ripe for the use of network theories and methods. Yet so far there has been little quantitative or qualitative network analysis of these networks. Rather, most work has consisted of hypotheses regarding the advantages and disadvantages of particular types of network structures for these transfers. This is partially due to a lack of reliable data sets, which is in turn due in part to the illicit and clandestine nature of most of these relationships and transactions. We have focused most of our discussion on SALW and WMD rather than on MCW because of the more extensive literature on the former two with respect to network structures. Yet the lack of analysis of the latter as a network (rather than as a set of dyads in a traditional gravity model) is somewhat puzzling given the greater availability of data and the lack of additional confounding factors.

We clearly do not lack for hypotheses regarding network structures in this area of research, just analysis. Consequently, this area is clearly ripe for the application of network theories to extant data sets using network methods and for the collection of new data for network analysis. Given the general import of these networks for both security studies and policy, we expect to see a renaissance in the study of arms supply and proliferation networks.

NOTES

1. SALW are "those weapons designed for personal use, and light weapons are those designed for use by several persons serving as a crew" (United Nations, 1997, 11); WMD are "chemical, biological, radiological, or nuclear weapons capable of a high order of destruction or causing mass casualties, excluding the means of transporting or propelling the weapon where such means is a separable and divisible part from the weapon" (United States Department of Defense, 2014, 17–18); MCW constitute everything in between (aircraft, armored vehicles, missile systems, etc.).
2. In the literature, "proliferation networks" generally refer to WMD or related delivery methods, "arms trade networks" to MCW, and "illicit arms trade" typically to SALW, although any of these terms might apply to the others. We follow this convention here, being specific wherever possible and referring to "arms transfers" when referring to the general phenomenon.
3. The most relevant extant case here is still the Chechen placement of radiological materials and dynamite in a Moscow park in 1995. Although it is still unclear where material came from, it is likely it was acquired internally by the Chechens. See Pokalova (2015, 51).
4. It is still unclear whether A. Q. Khan or his organization was acting with the knowledge of the Pakistani government, but either possibility is bad: either nonstate entities can proliferate without governmental knowledge, or the government was actively supporting proliferation (thanks to Scott Sagan for this observation).
5. Originally called *World Armaments and Disarmament*, the SIPRI yearbook has been published since 1969. Current and past data can also be retrieved from the SIPRI Arms Transfers Database online at www.sipri.org/databases/armstransfers.
6. There are two other commonly used sources of quantitative information on conventional arms transfers. The US Department of State's Bureau of Arms Control, Verification and Compliance (AVC) releases *World Military Expenditures and Arms Transfers* (*WMEAT*), which includes annual bilateral arms flows, are most useful for network analysis, but only from major suppliers (United States, France, Germany, Italy, United Kingdom, Russia, and China). The data are available online at www.state.gov/t/avc/rls/rpt/wmeat/ (United States Department of State, 2015). The Congressional Research Service (CRS), a research arm of

the US Congress, also publishes arms trade data in its periodic report *Conventional Arms Transfers to Developing Nations* (e.g., Theohary, 2016). These data are limited to transfers by major suppliers to developing countries only, but are noteworthy for distinguishing between arms agreements and arms deliveries.

7. States are invited to provide information on their conventional arms transfers for the UN Register of Conventional Arms, and although the UN register originally recorded only major weapon transfers, most reporting states now provide information on their SALW transfers as well. This reporting is completely voluntary, however, and it is not clear from the database what fraction of SALW exports and imports have been recorded. See Holtom (2009) and United Nations, Department for Disarmament Affairs Staff (2002).

8. Much of the data compiled and distributed by both the Small Arms Survey and NISAT are drawn from customs information in the UN's Commodity Trade Statistics Database (Comtrade). The NISAT Small Arms Trade Database can be accessed at nisat.prio.org/trade-database/, and visual maps of the data are available at nisatapps.prio.org/arms-globe/index.php. Other SALW data are collected by the Small Arms Survey, located at the Graduate Institute of International Studies in Geneva. The Survey's staff conducts in-depth country studies and other analyses focusing on various dimensions of legal and illicit SALW, many of which are reported in its annual review along with limited amounts of quantitative data. This information is available at www.smallarmssurvey.org/?small-arms-survey-2015.

REFERENCES

Akerman, A., and Seim, A. L. (2014). "The Global Arms Trade Network 1950–2007." *Journal of Comparative Economics* 42(3): 535–551. doi:10.1016/j.jce.2014.03.001.

Albright, D., Brannan, P., and Stricker, A. S. (2010). "Detecting and Disrupting Illicit Nuclear Trade after A.Q. Khan." *Washington Quarterly* 33(2): 85–106. doi:10.1080/01636601003673857.

Amnesty International. (2006). "Dead on Time—Arms Transportation, Brokering and the Threat to Human Rights." https://www.amnesty.org/en/documents/ACT30/007/2006/en/.

Asal, V. H., Ackerman, G. A., and Rethemeyer, R. K. (2012). "Connections Can Be Toxic: Terrorist Organizational Factors and the Pursuit of CBRN Weapons." *Studies in Conflict & Terrorism* 35(3): 229–254. doi:10.1080/1057610X.2012.648156.

Bakker, R. M., Raab, J., and Milward, H. B. (2012). "A Preliminary Theory of Dark Network Resilience." *Journal of Policy Analysis and Management* 31(1): 33–62.

Boureston, J., and Russell, J. A. (2009). "Illicit Nuclear Procurement Networks and Nuclear Proliferation: Challenges for Intelligence, Detection, and Interdiction." *St. Antony's International Review* 4(2): 24–50.

Braun, C., and Chyba, C. F. (2004). "Proliferation Rings: New Challenges to the Nuclear Nonproliferation Regime." *International Security* 29(2): 5–49.

Bruinsma, G., and Bernasco, W. (2004). "Criminal Groups and Transnational Illegal Markets." *Crime, Law and Social Change* 41(1): 79–94. doi:10.1023/B:CRIS.0000015283.13923.aa.

Buzan, B., and Herring, E. (1998). *The Arms Dynamic in World Politics*. Boulder, CO: Lynne Rienner Publishers.

Carley, K. M., Columbus, D., and Landwehr, P. (2013). "AutoMap User's Guide 2013." CASOS Technical Report CMU-ISR-13-105. Center of the Computational Analysis of Social and

Organization Systems, Carnegie Mellon University. http://www.casos.cs.cmu.edu/publications/papers/CMU-ISR-13-105.pdf.

Cattaneo, Silvia. (2004). "Targeting the Middlemen: Controlling Brokering Activities." In *Small Arms Survey 2004: Rights at Risk*, edited by P. Batchelor and K. Krause, pp. 140–171. Oxford: Oxford University Press.

Caves, J. P., Jr. (2006). "Globalization and WMD Proliferation Networks: The Policy Landscape." *Strategic Insights* 5(6): http://www.dtic.mil/dtic/tr/fulltext/u2/a521379.pdf.

Chestnut, S. (2007). "Illicit Activity and Proliferation: North Korean Smuggling Networks." *International Security* 32(1): 80–111. doi:10.1162/isec.2007.32.1.80.

Corera, G. (2006). *Shopping for Bombs: Nuclear Proliferation, Global Insecurity, and the Rise and Fall of the A.Q. Khan Network*. Oxford: Oxford University Press.

Curwen, P. A. (2007). "The Social Networks of Small Arms Proliferation: Mapping an Aviation Enabled Supply Chain." Master's thesis, Naval Postgraduate School. http://calhoun.nps.edu/handle/10945/3052.

Enders, W., and Su, X. (2007). "Rational Terrorists and Optimal Network Structure." *Journal of Conflict Resolution* 51(1): 33–57. doi:10.1177/0022002706296155.

Eyre, D. P., and Suchman, M. C. (1996). "Status, Norms, and the Proliferation of Conventional Weapons." In *The Culture of National Security: Norms and Identity in World Politics*, edited by P. J. Katzenstein, pp. 186–215. New York: Columbia University Press.

Frost, J. R. (2014). "The Nexus Between Criminal and Extremist Groups in Latin America: Implications for Unconventional Weapons Acquisition." PhD thesis, George Mason University. http://mars.gmu.edu/handle/1920/8856.

Fuhrmann, M. (2012). *Atomic Assistance: How "Atoms for Peace" Programs Cause Nuclear Insecurity*. Ithaca, NY: Cornell University Press.

Gerasev, M., and Surikov, V. M. (1997). "The Crisis in the Russian Defense Industry: Implications for Arms Exports." In *Russia in the World Arms Trade*, edited by A. J. Pierre and D. Trenin, pp. 9–25. Washington, DC: Carnegie Endowment for International Peace.

Group d'action financiere. (2008). "Proliferation Financing Report." Financial Action Task Force. http://www.fatf-gafi.org/media/fatf/documents/reports/Typologies%20Report%20on%20Proliferation%20Financing.pdf.

Gruselle, B. (2007). "Proliferation Networks and Financing." Foundation pour la Recherche Strategique. http://www.frstrategie.org/publications/recherches-documents/web/documents/2007/200704.pdf.

Hafner-Burton, E. M., Kahler, M., and Montgomery, A. H. (2009). "Network Analysis for International Relations." *International Organization* 63(3): 559–592. doi:10.1017/S0020818309090195.

Hämmerli, A., Gattiker, R., and Weyermann, R. (2006). "Conflict and Cooperation in an Actors' Network of Chechnya Based on Event Data." *Journal of Conflict Resolution* 50(2): 159–175. doi:10.1177/0022002705284826.

Hastings, J. V. (2012). "The Geography of Nuclear Proliferation Networks." *Nonproliferation Review* 19(3): 429–450. doi:10.1080/10736700.2012.734190.

Holloway, D., and McFaul, M. (1995). "Demilitarization and Defense Conversion." In *The New Russia: Troubled Transformation*, edited by G. W. Lapidus, pp. 193–222. Boulder, CO: Westview Press.

Holtom, P. (2009). "Reporting Transfers of Small Arms and Light Weapons to the United Nations Register of Conventional Arms, 2007." SIPRI Background Paper. http://books.sipri.org/files/misc/SIPRIBP0902.pdf.

Horowitz, M. C., and Narang, N. (2014). "Poor Man's Atomic Bomb? Exploring the Relationship between 'Weapons of Mass Destruction.'" *Journal of Conflict Resolution* 58(3): 509–535. doi:10.1177/0022002713509049.

Johnston, P. B. (2012). "Does Decapitation Work? Assessing the Effectiveness of Leadership Targeting in Counterinsurgency Campaigns." *International Security* 36(4): 47–79. doi:10.1162/ISEC_a_00076.

Jordan, J. (2009). "When Heads Roll: Assessing the Effectiveness of Leadership Decapitation." *Security Studies* 18(4): 719–755. doi:10.1080/09636410903369068.

Jordan, J. (2014). "Attacking the Leader, Missing the Mark." *International Security* 38(4): 7–38. doi:10.1162/ISEC_a_00157.

Kahler, M. (Ed.). (2009). *Networked Politics: Agency, Power, and Governance*. Ithaca, NY: Cornell University Press.

Kenney, M. (2007). *From Pablo to Osama: Trafficking and Terrorist Networks, Government Bureaucracies, and Competitive Adaptation*. University Park: Pennsylvania State University Press.

Kinne, B. J. (2014). "Dependent Diplomacy: Signaling, Strategy, and Prestige in the Diplomatic Network." *International Studies Quarterly* 58(2): 247–259. doi:10.1111/isqu.12047.

Kinsella, D. (2003). "Changing Structure of the Arms Trade: A Social Network Analysis." Presented at the Annual Meeting of the American Political Science Association, Philadelphia, PA. http://pdxscholar.library.pdx.edu/polisci_fac/19.

Kinsella, D. (2006). "The Black Market in Small Arms: Examining a Social Network." *Contemporary Security Policy* 27(1): 100–117. doi:10.1080/13523260600603105.

Kinsella, D. (2011). "The Arms Trade." In *The Handbook on the Political Economy of War*, edited by C. J. Coyne and R. L. Mathers, pp. 217–242. Northampton, MA: Edward Elgar Publishing.

Kinsella, D. (2012). "Illicit Arms Transfers Dataset: Coding Manual." Portland State University. http://web.pdx.edu/~kinsella/iatcode.pdf.

Kinsella, D. (2014). "Illicit Arms Transfers to Africa and the Prominence of the Former Soviet Bloc: A Social Network Analysis." *Crime, Law and Social Change* (August): 1–25. doi:10.1007/s10611-014-9531-9.

Kinsella, D., and Chima, J. S. (2001). "Symbols of Statehood: Military Industrialization and Public Discourse in India." *Review of International Studies* 27(3): 353–373. doi:10.1017/S0260210501003539.

Kleemans, E. R., and Van De Bunt, H. G. (1999). "Social Embeddedness of Organized Crime." *Transnational Organized Crime* 5(1): 19–36.

Klerks, P. (2001). "The Network Paradigm Applied to Criminal Organizations: Theoretical Nitpicking or a Relevant Doctrine for Investigators? Recent Developments in the Netherlands." *Connections* 24(3): 53–65.

Koschade, S. (2006). "A Social Network Analysis of Jemaah Islamiyah: The Applications to Counterterrorism and Intelligence." *Studies in Conflict and Terrorism* 29(6): 589–605. doi:10.1080/10576100600798418.

Krebs, V. E. (2002). "Mapping Networks of Terrorist Cells." *Connections* 24(3): 43–52.

Kroenig, M. (2010). *Exporting the Bomb: Technology Transfer and the Spread of Nuclear Weapons*. Ithaca, NY: Cornell University Press.

Lampe, K. v., and Johansen, P. O. (2004). "Organized Crime and Trust:: On the Conceptualization and Empirical Relevance of Trust in the Context of Criminal Networks." *Global Crime* 6(2): 159–184. doi:10.1080/17440570500096734.

Lindelauf, R., Borm, P., and Hamers, H. (2009). "The Influence of Secrecy on the Communication Structure of Covert Networks." *Social Networks* 31(2): 126–137. doi:10.1016/j.socnet.2008.12.003.

Mac Ginty, R. (2010). "Social Network Analysis and Counterinsurgency: A Counterproductive Strategy?" *Critical Studies on Terrorism* 3(2): 209–226. doi:10.1080/17539153.2010.491319.

Maoz, Z. (2011). *Networks of Nations: The Evolution, Structure, and Impact of International Networks, 1816–2001*. Cambridge, UK: Cambridge University Press.

Milward, H. B., and Raab, J. (2006). "Dark Networks as Organizational Problems: Elements of a Theory." *International Public Management Journal* 9(3): 333–360. doi:10.1080/10967490600899747.

Montgomery, A. H. (2005). "Ringing in Proliferation: How to Dismantle an Atomic Bomb Network." *International Security* 30(2): 153–187.

Montgomery, A. H. (2008). "Proliferation Networks in Theory and Practice." In *Globalization and WMD Proliferation: Terrorism, Transnational Networks, and International Security*, edited by J. A. Russell and J. J. Wirtz, pp. 28–39. New York: Routledge.

Montgomery, A. H. (2013). "Stop Helping Me: When Nuclear Assistance Impedes Nuclear Programs." In *The Nuclear Renaissance and International Security*, edited by A. Stulberg and M. Fuhrmann, pp. 177–202. Stanford, CA: Stanford University Press.

Morselli, C., Giguère, C., and Petit, K. (2007). "The Efficiency/Security Trade-off in Criminal Networks." *Social Networks* 29(1): 143–153. doi:10.1016/j.socnet.2006.05.001.

Morstein, J. H., and Perry, W. D. (2000). "Commercial Nuclear Trading Networks as Indicators of Nuclear Weapons Intentions." *Nonproliferation Review* 7(3): 75–91.

Murji, K. (2007). "Hierarchies, Markets and Networks: Ethnicity/Race and Drug Distribution." *Journal of Drug Issues* 37(4): 781–804. doi:10.1177/002204260703700403.

Naylor, R. T. (2004). *Wages of Crime: Black Markets, Illegal Finance, and the Underworld Economy*. Ithaca, NY: Cornell University Press.

Parkinson, S. E. (2013). "Organizing Rebellion: Rethinking High-Risk Mobilization and Social Networks in War." *American Political Science Review* 107(3): 418–432. doi:10.1017/S0003055413000208.

Perliger, A., and Pedahzur, A. (2011). "Social Network Analysis in the Study of Terrorism and Political Violence." *PS: Political Science & Politics* 44(1): 45–50. doi:10.1017/S1049096510001848.

Picarelli, J. T. (1998). "Transnational Threat Indications and Warning: The Utility of Network Analysis." AAAI Fall Symposium on Artificial Intelligence and Link Analysis. https://kdl.cs.umass.edu/events/aila1998/picarelli.pdf.

Pokalova, E. (2015). *Chechnya's Terrorist Network: The Evolution of Terrorism in Russia's North Caucasus*. Santa Barbara, CA: ABC-CLIO.

Raab, J., and Milward, H. B. (2003). "Dark Networks as Problems." *Journal of Public Administration Research and Theory* 13(4): 413–439. doi:10.1093/jpart/mug029.

Reed, T. C., and Stillman, D. B. (2009). *The Nuclear Express: A Political History of the Bomb and Its Proliferation*. Minneapolis: Zenith Press.

Sageman, M. (2004). *Understanding Terror Networks*. Philadelphia: University of Pennsylvania Press.

Schlumberger, G., and Gruselle, B. (2007). "For a Consistent Policy in the Struggle against Proliferation Networks." Foundation pour la Recherche Strategique. http://www.frstrategie.org/publications/notes/web/documents/2007/20070104_eng.pdf.

Spindel, J. (2015). "Logistics of Ballistics: Power and Politics in the Global Missile Network." Paper presented at the Annual Political Networks Conference, Portland, OR. http://papers.ssrn.com/abstract=2618827.

Suchman, M. C., and Eyre, D. P. (1992). "Military Procurement as Rational Myth: Notes on the Social Construction of Weapons Proliferation." *Sociological Forum* 7(1): 137–161. doi:10.1007/BF01124759.

Theohary, C. A. (2016). "Conventional Arms Transfers to Developing Nations, 2008–2015." CRS Report R44716.

Thurner, P. W., Schmid, C., Cranmer, S., and Kauermann, G. (2015). "The Network of Arms Transfers 1950–2013: An Application of ERGMs and TERGMs." Paper presented at the Annual Political Networks Conference, Portland, OR.

Turbiville, G. H. (1996). *Weapons Proliferation and Organized Crime: Russian Military Dimensions*. Colorado Springs, CO: Institute for National Security Studies, U.S. Air Force Academy.

United Nations. (1997). "Report of the Panel of Governmental Experts on Small Arms." UN Documents A/52/298. http://www.un.org/depts/ddar/Firstcom/SGreport52/a52298.html.

United Nations, Department for Disarmament Affairs Staff. (2002). *The United Nations Disarmament Yearbook*. Vol. 27. New York: United Nations Publications.

United States Department of Defense. (2014). "Department of Defense Strategy for Countering Weapons of Mass Destruction." http://archive.defense.gov/pubs/DoD_Strategy_for_Countering_Weapons_of_Mass_Destruction_dated_June_2014.pdf.

United States Department of State. (2015). "World Military Expenditures and Arms Transfers." http://www.state.gov/t/avc/rls/rpt/wmeat/.

Valencia, M. J. (2007). "The Proliferation Security Initiative: A Glass Half-Full." *Arms Control Today* 37(5): 17–21.

Ward, M. D., Ahlquist, J. S., and Rozenas, A. (2013). "Gravity's Rainbow: A Dynamic Latent Space Model for the World Trade Network." *Network Science* 1(1): 95–118. doi:10.1017/nws.2013.1.

Ward, M. D., and Hoff, P. D. (2007). "Persistent Patterns of International Commerce." *Journal of Peace Research* 44(2): 157–175. doi:10.1177/0022343307075119.

Willardson, S. (2013). "Under the Influence of Arms: The Foreign Policy Causes and Consequences of Arms Transfers." PhD thesis, University of Iowa. http://ir.uiowa.edu/etd/2660.

Williams, Phil. (2001). "Transnational Criminal Networks." In *Networks and Netwars*, edited by J. Arquilla and D. F. Ronfeldt, pp. 61–97. Santa Monica, CA: RAND Corporation.

Wood, B., and Peleman, J. (2000). "The Arms Fixers. Controlling the Brokers and Shipping Agents." Joint Report of BASIC, NISAT, and PRIO. https://www.prio.org/Publications/Publication/?x=658.

PART VI

NETWORKS IN COMPARATIVE POLITICS

CHAPTER 33

....

BRINGING NETWORKS INTO COMPARATIVE POLITICS

....

ARMANDO RAZO

INTRODUCTION

....

NETWORKS pervade virtually all aspects of comparative politics. For example, social ties influence the political behavior of individuals across the world (John and Cole, 2000; Zuckerman, 2005; Huckfeldt, 2009). Individuals ties underlie the social fabric of civil society, further augmented by affiliations between individuals and available political organizations (Tilly, 2005; Freidenberg and Levitsky, 2006). Private and public organizations, in turn, coordinate activities in pursuit of common goals (Prakash and Gugerty, 2010). Both individuals and organizations respectively relate to the state and public authorities in complex ways for multiple purposes (Knoke, 1993, 1996; Migdal, 2001). As a result, political processes are inherently relational by capturing the interplay of a variety of participants (Knoke, 1990). Indeed, the overall distribution of power and resources in societies, which drives many political processes, is itself often conditioned on social and economic ties (Padgett and Ansell, 1993; Collins, 2002).

However, despite ample recognition of relevant networks in comparative politics, we lack a solid understanding of which, why, and how networks matter. This is a puzzling state of affairs, because comparativists played a pioneering role in introducing networks into the discipline (Knoke, 1990; Padgett and Ansell, 1993; Tarrow, 1998). Early studies, however, did not resonate in the subfield, as one would have expected. One major impediment is that unlike in other empirical subfields of the discipline, comparativists face a more challenging task in collecting original network data. Another reason is the paucity of theoretical approaches with networks as the main object of comparative analysis. Therefore, it is not entirely clear how to reconcile extant approaches with a network perspective.

This chapter provides evidence that these long-standing barriers are slowly disappearing. In it I review recent work that pays direct attention to networks in the context of three major literatures: collective action and contentious politics, political economy of institutions, and clientelism.[1] To characterize these contributions, it is useful to review Ward et al.'s (2011) classification of political network studies under three major categories: analogical, descriptive, and inferential. Analogical studies recognize the relational aspect of networks at a very high level of generality: networks are either whole objects representing social systems or metaphorical allusions to social relations. Descriptive studies use conventional tools of social network analysis to visualize and summarize properties of some network structures. Inferential studies use statistical models that estimate either whole network structures or latent networks. For the most part, extant network studies in comparative politics are primarily descriptive, with a couple of exceptions involving inferential statistical methods.

The penultimate section of the chapter illustrates how we can apply relational thinking to sample big questions of comparative politics. My presentation highlights the fundamental problem of accurate representation (that networks can serve as realistic models of very important phenomena that interest many comparativists) as a prior step to measurement. I conclude with a brief discussion of methodological challenges for comparative analysis of networks.

Collective Action and Contentious Politics

Arguably, the study of collective action commands a central place in many comparative politics pursuits (Ostrom, 1998). Collective action affects participation and competition, and thus the quality of democracy (Olson, 1965; Van Cott, 2005; Prakash and Gugerty, 2010). Within the realm of collective action, the study of social movements warrants special attention. Social movements have enabled major political changes in the history of advanced countries (Tarrow, 1998; Tilly, 2004). Newer work also suggests that the nature and reach of social movements is rapidly changing and expanding, in response to the enlarging scope of contentious politics across the world (Tarrow, 2005, 2011). Contemporary relevance thus makes the study of social movements a fertile area for current and future research.

A comprehensive review of social movement literatures is beyond the scope of this chapter.[2] Instead, my focus is on how networks can inform key aspects of social movements, starting with their conceptual definition. A conventional definition of social movements characterizes them as "collective, organized, sustained, and noninstitutional challenges to authorities, powerholders, or cultural beliefs and practices" (Goodwin and Jasper, 2005, 3). It follows that a basic understanding of social movements requires careful consideration of how individuals and organizations come together and organize themselves for some (contentious) purpose. "Coming together" readily calls attention to a systematic study of connections or networks.

Three major paradigms underlie the study of social movements. First, in what many consider the "hegemonic" approach, scholars emphasize the importance of political opportunity structures embedded in the political process (Kriesi, 2004; Tilly, 2004). Second, the recognition that successful collective action is costly highlights the importance of securing adequate resources. Edwards and McCarthy (2004), for example, distinguish five types of resources that organizations need to be successful: *moral resources*, such as attaining legitimacy and gaining solidarity support; *cultural resources*, such as specialized knowledge and conceptual tools; *material resources*, such as property and equipment; *social-organizational resources* to build networks and form coalitions; and *human resources*, involving individual abilities to recruit new members. Finally, a third influential approach draws attention away from material-based structural constraints or organizational resources toward more subjective cultural factors (Williams, 2004). In this vein of work, the emphasis is on social movements as meaningful objects. And because social movements require sustained collective action by definition (Snow et al., 2004b), it follows that persistent meaning needs continuous legitimization, thus opening the room for dynamic discursive processes within movements and between movements and outsiders (i.e., rhetorical challengers).

Although networks have been part of the vocabulary of social movement theory, only recently have they become an object of study in their own right (Diani, 2003a). One major conceptual innovation is the integrative potential of network approaches to reconcile material and subjective aspects of social movements. Broadbent (2003), for example, in his study of Japanese environmental politics, argues that social relations provide an intermediary epistemic role between material and subjective concerns. In what he deems a *social* paradigm distinguishable from material and cultural concerns, Broadbent argues that social structure is manifested in two forms (networks and social roles) that shape both cultural and material aspects of social movements. First, dense social relations or thick networks at the community and neighborhood level make individuals more prone to social influence. An added vertical dimension, with social roles that require deference to higher social authorities, further facilitates a collective mindset to create and scale up social movements. Second, the interplay of thick networks and social roles translates into unequal distributions of power and material resource availability, which can reinforce social influence efforts. From a comparative perspective, Broadbent then argues that societies with thick networks and stringent social roles (like Japan) are more likely to articulate social movements than those societies (like the United States) with thin networks and a looser social structure that are not easily perceived as legitimate instruments to create social movements.

Social networks must be perceived as an aid rather than a threatening instrument of domination in order to reconcile subjective and material concerns. If this were not the case, then participants might have incentives to coalesce precisely to challenge such networks. In fact, there is some indication that networks can indeed be useful for participants in nonthreatening ways. In a study of Italian environmental organizations, Diani (2003b) applies network analysis to clarify the role of apparently powerful organizations within a social movement. Using in-degree centrality scores, he is able to identify movement leaders as central players whose primary role is to establish ties to other third parties. Rather than dominating, these leaders act as representatives to outside constituencies, assuming a very public role that facilitates political engagement to use existing opportunities and—from a more subjective perspective—a more cohesive communications strategy to promote movement goals. Using various measures of brokerage, Diani also documents the existence of other organizations with a less prominent role that are nonetheless critical to forging ties across various communities in order to produce valuable resources. Although network structures "empower" or otherwise make salient certain actors with prominent roles, he argues that these roles actually empower whole movements by enhancing collective action.

The ability to characterize the nature of social movements is critical to lay a foundation for systematic network studies. There is, in fact, much consensus that networks matter for the definition of social movements. Notably, Tarrow (2011) considers social movements to be a special type of contentious politics that is precisely distinguished by its underlying social networks. Along those lines, Diani (2003c, 301) claims that social movements constitute "a network of informal interactions."

What networks matter? An answer to this key question lies in the study of how social movements grow, where it is well established that recruitment is mediated by individual social ties (Diani, 2004). New members are more likely to join a movement if they have a close friend or relative in the movement. McAdam (2003) notes, however, that this conventional wisdom cannot entirely explain the rise of social movements, because it does not explain their origin. He calls for additional research that illuminates the mechanisms that explain how social ties operate at different stages of a social movement's life cycle, including but not restricted to recruitment.

Beyond individual social ties, the expansion of social movements also requires linkages across organizations. These supplementary linkages are important because organizations with limited resources rely on strategic exchanges with other organizations in order to be successful. Finally, organizations do not exclusively borrow physical resources, so it is possible to have more abstract linkages that would go unnoticed or unmeasured without an adequate analytical framework. For example, Diani (2003a) notes scholarly interest in mapping out other linkages such as events and ideas. This line of work is an at early stage of conceptual development, but these mapping exercises already establish a sound foundation for new research questions. To illustrate, we can now ask how competing social movements develop sticky ideas that resonate among individual followers, a cognitive construct qualitatively different from social or organizational ties. In many cases, analysts do not readily recognize social movements until their ideas are cemented in large groups, but with this cognitive network orientation, we can posit novel empirical questions about social cognition in the early development of social movements: Do these invariably start with a large set of potentially diffuse messages that get refined over time as individuals commit to particular messages? Are there significant differences in initial cognitive structures that distinguish successful from unsuccessful movements? Along those lines, and focusing on the distribution and coordination of information providers within a movement, is it possible to develop clusters of messages that are potentially irreconcilable—and perhaps reflect internal ideological conflict that hinders future success?

These sample questions indicate the need for a general framework to organize both extant knowledge of networks in social movements and new questions about their nature and impact. To the best of my knowledge, Diani (2003c, 2004) has provided thus far the most comprehensive outline to start developing such a framework, with a call to recognize and document the multiplicity of networks that link agents and events. He pays particular attention to the need to specify dynamic network processes that can precisely link behavior, ideas, and events; in other words, developing dynamic theories of how various networks change over time both internally and in relation to others. Homophily processes, in particular, might be important not just in seeding initial network structures, but even more in facilitating additional connections among structurally similar participants. He also argues that a dynamic network-analytic perspective facilitates multilevel analysis by recognizing the duality of network processes that include persons and groups; that is, persons are linked to others through common membership in a given group, but different groups themselves can be linked through individual personal connections.

Recent technological developments have further expanded the realm of social movements and other forms of contentious politics. First, the advent of new information and communication technologies (ICTs) has drastically altered the environment in which social movements meet their challengers. The realm of social movements is not confined to physical spaces; there are readily accessible online spaces that facilitate dissemination of messages and engagement in consequential online behaviors. For example, the Arab Spring of 2011 manifested the reality that the Internet can be a medium for significant political change. Predating this episode, however, there was already much scholarly interest in understanding how citizens could share information on a massive scale to challenge and possibly replace their governments (Kalathil and Boas, 2003; Chadwick, 2006). Especially in light of the Arab Spring, however, there is widespread scholarly and popular recognition that social media outlets have expanded opportunities for citizens to engage in online collective action on a much larger scale than was possible before (Castells, 2007; Agarwal et al., 2014).

A growing interdisciplinary literature that encompasses other fields such as political communications and informatics pays particular attention to the use of social media. Regarding the Tunisian Revolution, one successful Arab Spring case of a democratic transition, Breuer et al. (2015) analyze Twitter data to understand how in a country like Tunisia, with low penetration of ICT, protesters were nonetheless able to promote their cause through careful use of social media cyber-activism. Critically important, expert technology users played a central role in defining the architecture of communication networks to allow protesters to break past censorship mechanisms as the emerging democratic movement continually challenged the incumbent government.[3] Similar studies demonstrate that effective communication entails not just a large quantity of similar messages, but also network-mediated coordination, most notably involving the *Indignados* movement that started in Spain in 2011. A severe economic crisis that hit younger segments of the Spanish population particularly hard gave rise to sustained street protests in major cities across the country. These initial protests soon developed into acts of civil disobedience, as authorities sought to limit them in physical places, with expanded activities that moved onto online communication spaces. The use of social media, Twitter in particular, has produced massive amounts of publicly available data that have sparked multiple studies from a strictly network-analytic perspective. Among earlier efforts, González-Bailón et al. (2011) found that user centrality was not important to start the movement; but once started, centrality was critical for the spreading of information. Subsequent studies have demonstrated that these online networks exhibit "small world" features of high clustering and low average degrees, also allowing for the development of specialized roles (Borge-Holthoefer et al., 2014; González-Bailón et al., 2014).

This active line of research promises to enhance our understanding of the structure and impact of online social movements. For example, although the importance of brokers appears well established for the transmission of novel information (González-Bailón, 2013), it need not be the case that all brokering is done entirely online. Romanos (2016) argues, for example, that Spanish immigrants played a brokering role between the *Indignados* and *Occupy Wall Street* movements through personal and organizational connections. Moreover, an implicit assumption that the same information traverses different types of networks requires empirical examination and theoretical development that admits richer information configurations. For example, Bennett and Segerberg (2012) note that digital media entail two distinct logics of communication, one that lends itself to massive collective action (because presumably all participants receive and make use of the same information) and another whose participants get more personalized messages. Since it is infeasible for any individual to be aware of the complete communications work, reality might be closer to personalized rather than broadcasting channels. New research questions along these lines call for scholars to pay concurrent attention to these distinct means of communication that might coexist in the same technological domain.

Moreover, technological developments are coupled with the growing importance of nonstate actors and new ties that readily transcend borders (Tarrow, 2005). The popularity of social media might suggest that the realm of social networks is restricted to electronic settings, but this is not the case. What we mostly see in social media are communication networks that serve a variety of purposes for social movements. However, depending on the nature and purpose of mobilization, relevant networks can either be hidden from public view or otherwise activated asynchronously as needed. These possibilities are ably illustrated in a recent study of the organizational foundations of Palestinian militant networks in Lebanon, which also highlights the growing importance of nonstate actors. Parkinson (2013) seeks to understand how the Palestinian Liberation Organization (PLO) was able to rebuild its operations after it was fragmented by the 1982 Israeli Defense Forces invasion of Lebanon. Based on ethnographic research to build trust with former and current PLO members, she elicited information that revealed systematic use of "quotidian" or everyday networks to substitute for formal military hierarchies. These networks entailed a variety of otherwise ordinary family and friendship ties being used to engage in various clandestine activities, also giving a prominent role to women, who assumed both "a social and a military role" (Parkinson, 2013, 425). Although these were personal and localized networks, their widespread use allowed cross-national ties to mobilize resources and offer safe passage to persecuted militants. She concludes that the activation of these quotidian networks explains the PLO's ability to rebound. As has been hinted, the integration of ordinary networks with explicit mobilization efforts creates a dynamic that changes both sides. The nature of militant organizations changed with the more prominent role of women and routinized use of ordinary networks beyond military operations. But the social relations of women and their families also changed, as they effectively became branches of a clandestine rebellion.

These types of case studies stand in stark contrast to studies of online collective action in two respects. First, data collection is inherently more difficult. Unlike public online protests, in which salience and awareness are a valuable currency, in Parkinson's work, participants have no incentive to reveal their participation. Careful work—and the trust of participants to reveal participation—is required just to identify, let alone map out, relevant connections. Moreover, even when such data are collected, there are ethical concerns regarding the protection of human subjects that limit dissemination. Second, the scale of these studies is much smaller than studies of social media networks. Cumulating knowledge along these lines requires more intensive and extensive research.

Overall, the proliferation of new technological opportunities for interaction and new actors is both promising and challenging for the study of social movements. It is promising due to new questions about the social foundations and dynamics of modern social movements. However, there remain significant conceptual and methodological challenges to overcome. For one, the mere focus on social networks invites questions about the boundaries of social movements. Because they resist formalization while also needing more adherents, social movements are not easily contained. As scholars incorporate more heterogeneous nodes, social movements acquire a more amorphous character that blurs the boundaries between a social movement and its environment.

These observations suggest a new line of research that reverses the theoretical role of social networks and social movements. Gould (2003) has already suggested that over time, participation in social movements can alter the meaning of previous friendships. Moreover, Parkinson's (2013) study suggests that by participating in rebellious activities, the meaning and use of quotidian networks changes dramatically as well. To the extent that a single movement or multiple movements appropriate extant social spaces, the long-term impact of social movements extends beyond solving specific grievances. Over time, we see a coevolution of social networks and social movements that warrants deeper examination—not just for causal inference, but also for a better understanding of how social movements alter the social fabric of the societies in which they arise.

POLITICAL ECONOMY

The interplay of politics and economics gives rise to a variety of interactions between public and private actors. The manner in which these ties are constructed, and their specific nature, has given rise to several literatures with various normative and positive concerns regarding their impact on economic and political outcomes. In this section I briefly review three literatures that incorporate a relational perspective: corruption, political economy of institutions, and clientelism.

Corruption

Corruption is the misuse of public office for private gain (Shleifer and Vishny, 1993). The archetypal example of corruption is a private citizen paying a bribe to a public official who restricts access to a valuable public service, a global phenomenon that especially prevails in many developing societies. There are a few theoretical approaches in which key relational aspects of corruption are salient, which could serve as the basis for further empirical examination. In a seminal paper on the political economy of corruption, Shleifer and Vishny (1993) argue that the organizational context for bribe collections has major impacts on the level of corruption and economic efficiency. In particular, their analysis indicates that centralization of corrupt transactions lowers societal levels of corruption, a theoretical claim that is yet to be directly tested. From a network perspective, there is an added insight from noting that particular bribes are never devoid of social context. It is usually the case that multiple actors share bribes via social and political networks, unless bribes are collected at the highest political levels. Corruption is effectively embedded in illicit rent-sharing networks, thus warranting a more global perspective beyond dyadic interactions.

   Also informed by organizational concerns, Rose-Ackerman (1999) has advanced a theory to explain different types of corruption contingent on the relative organization of public and private actors. On the supply side, she notes that governments can collect bribes using centralized or decentralized schemes. Likewise, on the demand side, private actors can pursue corruption in an organized fashion (also limiting the number of potential beneficiaries) or not. Combinations of these supply and demand conditions translate into four different patterns. For example, when the government is better organized than private actors are, we get kleptocracy, an outcome in which political leaders drive the process and appropriate all gains from corruption. When the reverse is true, that is, private actors are stronger than the government, then we get a so-called pattern of mafia-dominated corruption. When both actors are organized, we get a situation akin to a bilateral monopoly. Finally, when neither actor is organized, we get a more "competitive" situation, with multiple buyers and suppliers, which translates into more but also smaller bribes.

These economic approaches appear to have a limited macro-level perspective that emphasizes major organizational features of a society, but their attention to bribes nonetheless facilitates the addition of an explicit network-analytic foundation. A conceptual bridge exists when we recognize that bribes, as the main unit of analysis, are effectively dyadic transactions between one private and one public actor. Clearly, aggregate corruption patterns entail multiple dyads, which can be captured with an adequate network structure. To begin, consider the relevant set of nodes to be all individuals in society. Whether these nodes have a private or public character can be an exogenous attribute. To model corruption, we can further distinguish two directed networks that account for demand (requests for bribes) and supply (an "official" cooperative response). Viewed from this perspective, the phenomenon of corruption is essentially a specialized exchange network of successful trades between private and public actors. Once we map successful corrupt exchanges, we can use relational summaries to describe general features of the overall network structure, which can then be assessed against Rose-Ackerman's typology. One major advantage of this relational approach to corruption is its flexibility, which enlarges the set of potential macro-level corruption patterns: in addition to the four prototypical configurations in Rose-Ackerman's framework, network analysis might reveal new structures that might warrant closer theoretical or empirical examination.

Although there is an extensive literature on corruption, it remains a difficult task to collect direct evidence (Treisman, 2007). It is not difficult to understand why; participants lack incentives to publicize what is often an illegal activity. In place of direct measures of corrupt transactions, there are two main approaches to data collection, only one of which is strictly relational. The most common is to calculate national-level indicators based on public opinion and expert surveys. Prominent efforts include the Corruption Perceptions Index and the Control of Corruption Governance Indicator produced by the World Bank, among others (Kaufmann et al., 2005; Svensson, 2005; Transparency International, 2014). These measurements enable cross-country comparisons, but they are nonetheless limited by their subjective nature as well as aggregations that obscure micro-level processes. A second approach occurs at the firm level. Along with other efforts to measure the cost of doing business across the world, firms are sometimes asked to report their need to pay bribes or engage in other types of corrupt practices, which captures some but not all relational aspects of corruption (Reinikka and Svensson, 2006; Clarke, 2011). In fact, measurements that are more direct are not likely to come from scholarly research efforts, but rather from political processes. A new government that comes to power might have incentives to reveal the wrongdoing of its predecessors and proceed to collect relevant evidence. For example, in a recent study that uses evidence produced by a political investigation in Pakistan, Khwaja and Mian (2005) find that public lending between 1996 and 2002 manifested favoritism toward firms with political connections that were also highly inefficient and thus not creditworthy.

A revealing example of political investigations that produced direct evidence of corruption occurred in the early 2000s in Peru (McMillan and Zoido, 2004). Peru is one of three Andean countries characterized by high percentages of indigenous populations and an incipient record of economic development. In 1990, following a decade of severe economic crisis coupled with a discredited political party system, Peru elected a political outsider, Alberto Fujimori, who stayed in power until 2000. Not only did Fujimori implement neoliberal reforms that many sectors in society found objectionable, but he also engaged in a variety of nondemocratic behaviors, most notably his dissolution of Congress in 1992. Following this self-coup, he restored nominally democratic institutions that allowed him to be re-elected a couple of times. His right-hand man, Vladimiro Montesinos, who was in charge of Peru's security apparatus, engaged in a concerted effort to pay off opponents and potential critics of the Fujimori administration. Notably, Montesinos not only recorded these illicit transactions, many in the millions of US dollars, but also kept receipts of all transactions during this period. A small cable company that was not part of the corruption network publicized video recordings of these transactions, which led to a criminal investigation against Montesinos and President Fujimori. Fujimori fled the country in 2000 to avoid prosecution for corruption.[4] Clearly, it is difficult to generalize from and replicate this type of study. Nonetheless, the existence of these detailed data enabled McMillan and Zoido to conduct two analyses that would have been impossible otherwise. Network formation followed a strict economic logic, whereby transactions were procured and financed in proportion to the political power associated with various public offices (similarly, payments to private media actors were commensurate with their market power). The evidence also served to document strategic use of documentation as a disciplining device to maintain permanent ties and to keep the secrecy of these illicit activities.

Political Economy of Institutions

The study of corruption provides a nice segue into a brief exploration of state-business relations, itself a lens to the political economy of many countries across the world. It is common to economic actors, in particular, to have close ties to government (Evans, 1995; Maxfield and Schneider, 1997; Schneider, 2004). Typically, these ties are suspicious, given a tendency to consider business interests as special interests that do not benefit the public because such ties can easily be corrupted (Hutchcroft, 1994; Campos, 2002; Kang, 2002; Bhargava and Bolongaita, 2004). There is much room to characterize and examine the nature and consequences of these arrangements. To illustrate, two related approaches are described below, which combine political economy and economic history to broaden our understanding of conditions under which private-public partnerships arise to promote economic development.[5]

One key question in studies of political economy of development is how unstable countries can promote economic development when they are plagued by major social conflicts. Haber et al. (2003) address this question with a detailed study of the impact of the Mexican Revolution of 1910. Drawing on organizational theory and theories of the firm, these authors advance a theory of vertical political integration (VPI) to characterize the incentives of political and economic actors to collaborate in the pursuit of common economic goals. Due to underlying uncertainty that inhibits cooperation, political instability actually incentivizes political and resourceful economic actors to create exclusive policymaking arrangements whereby they could better monitor one another. Although not strictly couched in network-analytic terms, this theory has two major relational implications: (1) these political networks can only be sustained by exclusive rent-sharing agreements between public and private actors; and despite the specificity of particular policy agreements, (2) access to any part of the network is carefully controlled by governments to enhance the overall credibility of a VPI system. As a result, these rent-sharing agreements are very costly to maintain. Despite their costs, these networks can be very resilient, as was the case in early twentieth-century Mexico, where a network that existed prior to the revolution was able to protect its property rights during and after this major event.

Not only are these types of political networks durable, but they can also serve as the political foundations of economic development in societies that lack adequate checks on government. Extending the work of Haber et al. (2003), Razo (2008) advances an explicit network-analytic framework to tackle a major puzzle in the literature: the ability of nondemocratic governments to promote economic growth for which conventional theory prescribes democratic institutions of limited government (North and Weingast, 1989). A network perspective is doubly useful for a realistic depiction of policymaking processes in nondemocratic regimes, which are inherently relational. Nondemocratic regimes exhibit a strong relational aspect because they tend to be selective and to be used strategically to dispense special privileges. This tendency in and of itself ties the interests of economic actors to government. However, this is not the complete story, because the question of policy credibility remains and, is in fact, exacerbated: instead of a single commitment, a government must honor multiple commitments. The author advances a network theory of private protection based on the recruitment of influential political actors with some measure of independent power to guarantee special privileges. This is primarily a decentralized process, because participants lack incentives to coordinate efforts due to their desire to capture as many rents as possible, at the expense of competitors. However, one outcome of this process is an emergent network structure that effectively ties together independent actors who recognize a common interest to protect their respective privileges. In particular, their interests overlap when private enforcers start protecting multiple economic interests, which is likely to happen in settings where power is concentrated in a few actors capable of providing third-party enforcement. This emergent structure enables two explicitly relational mechanisms that affect the incentives of governments to engage in predatory behavior. One deterrent mechanism is collective retaliation, which can occur when political actors recognize and defend common economic interests. A reinforcing mechanism is the propagation of predation risk across connected economic actors. Sufficiently high connectivity makes firms more vulnerable, but the corresponding increase in aggregate risk can also incentivize a large-scale response to discipline a potentially predatory government.

In *Social Foundations of Limited Dictatorship*, Razo (2008) offers both a general theory and a detailed study of how political-economic networks can offer viable alternatives to democratic political institutions for the narrow purpose of incentivizing economic activity. Using historical data from late nineteenth- and early twentieth-century Mexico, the author reconstructs a variety of network structures that were important for political stability and economic growth. Critical to the theory is the existence of a network of overlapping private protection that serves as a (relational) operational definition of the concept of *encompassing interests*, which Olson (1993) advanced as a necessary condition for growth under nondemocratic regimes. This is also the first work in comparative politics that uses inferential network statistics. In particular, the author estimates an exponential random graph model to test the hypothesis that political actors were critical to the existence of a network of overlapping protection that could secure the property rights of economic actors.

With its theoretical guidance and methodological template, this work stands ready for replication in other settings despite the challenging task of collecting detailed network data. Besides collecting more relational data on political-economic networks for specific countries, this line of research also invites questions that transcend the experience of particular countries. We are not there currently, but this approach makes it feasible to entertain two major comparative questions with both theoretical and empirical dimensions. Is there variation in these network structures across countries under conditions of weak democracy or nondemocratic rule? Moreover, since political-economic networks are universal, can we inject a network dimension into the difficult task of distinguishing political regimes? That is, are there significant differences in the shape and operation of these networks between democratic and nondemocratic regimes?

Clientelism

The study of distributive politics readily lends itself to a relational approach, because governments offer a variety of services and benefits to their populations (IDB and Harvard University, 2005; Robinson, 2010). Sometimes political actors condition such delivery on an exchange: an agreement or manifest political support. Indeed, there are various types of citizen-politician linkages (Kitschelt and Wilkinson, 2007). By distinguishing various exchange patterns, one can derive a general classification that distinguishes so-called programmatic policies, in which public officials offer policies in a nondiscriminating manner, from nonprogrammatic policies that are contingent on particular relationships. The latter are sometimes depicted as clientelism, a concept that has a rich relational heritage in identifying patron-client relationships, patronage networks, and other modes of delivery that make private actors dependent on political actors with valuable resources (Szwarcberg, 2012; Stokes et al., 2013).

Contemporary studies of clientelism pay particular attention to the role of brokers, which mediate exchanges between politicians and ordinary citizens. Stokes et al. (2013) have advanced a theory of "broker-mediated distribution" to explain how party elites mitigate the potential opportunism of voters who might get resources from one party and vote for another (or not vote at all). There are three main actors: party elites, brokers, and voters. Party elites recruit brokers, who in turn recruit voters. Although their model does not directly incorporate any network structures, their theory nonetheless presupposes at least two distinct network structures. First, the principal-agent relationship between party leaders and brokers is a type of partisan network that can exist on its own as current or future brokers pledge allegiance (through demonstrable activism) to a particular political organization. Second, brokers themselves have social connections to potential voters, and herein lies their potential value to political parties. Indeed, the selection of brokers is a matter of strategic choice for party elites, who decide among competing activists. In addition, this selection takes into account brokers' abilities to promise and deliver loyal followers. The term "broker" best corresponds to the notion of an intermediary agent, but if we were to take a panoramic perspective on resulting citizen-politician linkages, then it is appropriate to think of these brokers as playing a bridging role between (distant) party elites and the mass public.

Despite their linkages, party elites and brokers have conflicting goals. The former are generally motivated to win elections, also manifesting a preference to seek out swing voters. The latter seek to gain rents from their privileged intermediary position, which they can obtain by targeting the relatively more inexpensive loyal voters. Brokers recognize, however, that gaining rents depends on winning elections, so uncertainty about electoral outcomes (as well as party monitoring) can discipline their behavior to include some swing voters.

To test their theory, the authors studied distributive politics across several Latin American countries, with particular attention and more detail in the case of Argentina. For that country, these authors implemented a nationally representative survey of brokers. This survey collected information on the political history of party activists, including information on the number of social and partisan connections. Additional questions sought to understand the strategic calculus of brokers to explore how their behavior conformed to the authors' theory of broker-mediated distribution. Overall, the authors found support for their claim that brokers indeed have social connections and deep knowledge of their clients. Thus they can credibly deliver to party elites a reliable pool of committed voters.

Although political brokers receive much attention, more detailed network analysis qualifies their importance and enabling mechanisms. In a study of a working-class neighborhood in the greater Buenos Aires area, Szwarcberg (2012) emphasizes the role of problem-solving networks as precursors and mediators of clientelistic relationships. Her study entailed extensive fieldwork that included direct participation, observation, archival work, and a survey among twenty women (known as *manzaneras*) who distributed benefits associated with a large food-distribution program. With collected evidence, Szwarcberg was able to identify and map out specialized problem-solving networks that meet local needs for political advice, babysitting, money lending, and counseling. Using centrality analysis, she was further able to identify *manzaneras* who are central in both political and nonpolitical networks, a combination that allows women to become effective political brokers. One main lesson from this study is that studies of clientelism must include a detailed understanding of the social context, which extends

beyond the existence of poor voters who seek out clientelistic relationships with a particular broker. An enhanced notion of social context is necessary to incorporate and
evaluate multiple political brokers, who will not be as effective if they lack nonpolitical
centrality in problem-solving networks.

In subsequent work, Szwarcberg (2013) challenges conventional wisdom that politicians facing poor voters invariably choose clientelistic strategies. With evidence from
hundreds of interviews, she argues that politicians require access to both resources and
networks of party activists to distribute targeted goods as necessary conditions to consider clientelism as a viable electoral strategy. In addition, politicians have to be incen-
tivized to choose clientelism over more programmatic approaches.[6] These incentives are
stronger when career concerns are driven by party expectations to mobilize the largest
number of voters. Clientelism serves as a signaling device from individual candidates to
party leaders of both the desire and the ability to stay in power.

Building on this prior work, Szwarcberg (2015) advances a more general argument
about the underlying network foundations of clientelism and supporting incentive
structures that make it a persistent phenomenon in countries like Argentina. First, she
argues that clientelism is best understood not as a dyadic (and independent) relationship between one ordinary citizen and a politician, as the concept is usually defined, but
rather as an integrated system of diverse networks embedded in a hierarchical organization. Social or quotidian networks that link ordinary citizens for nonpolitical purposes
operate at the lowest level. Some of these networks are appropriated for political purposes, as poor citizens become dependent on certain local actors to meet their everyday
needs. As noted previously, social brokers can become party brokers or activists and
thus link social to political networks. Party activists who assume a brokering role can
themselves embark on a political career that might result in elected or party leadership
positions. Second, in order to attain higher positions, party brokers must continually
demonstrate their worth by gaining more voters, a recurrent task that forces them to
continuously navigate and make use of partisan network connections that provide valuable resources for electoral purposes. Unfortunately, in what Szwarcberg deems "a logic
of perverse incentives," clientelism is the most effective way both for activists to improve
their political careers and for established parties to secure large numbers of voters.

Most work on clientelism is descriptive, with a notable exception that uses advanced
inferential statistics. In a fascinating article, Calvo and Murillo (2012) develop a methodology to estimate the size of voters' social networks and linkages to partisan networks.
Using an original survey instrument applied in Argentina and Chile, these authors estimate the number of acquaintances that a respondent had based on reported personal
knowledge of people with certain names (whose population frequency is known in
advance by researchers). Additional survey questions tapped into respondents' knowledge of activists and political candidates to derive estimates of the number of party
activists as well as the relative proximity of voters to party activists. The main goal of
this study is to understand how the distributional preferences of voters (for handouts,
patronage, and pork) is conditioned on proximity to party activists, among other factors. For the most part, the authors find a greater tendency for Chilean respondents to

prefer more programmatic distributive politics. In contrast, Argentine respondents prefer more clientelistic distributions, especially when they have ties to major political parties.

As depicted thus far, clientelism entails the creation of persistent relationships of political dependence, whereby poor voters cannot reliably meet their needs without resources provided by political patrons (or intermediary agents). More work needs to be done to relax the conditions under which clientelism is studied. The deep entrenchment of historical parties in Argentina, especially the Justicialist (or Peronist) Party and its urban political enclaves, imposes major constraints on the ability of poor voters to resist clientelistic strategies. However, clientelism is by no means a phenomenon restricted to urban settings, as the case of Mexico amply demonstrates (Fox, 1994; Diaz-Cayeros and Magaloni, 2003). Moreover, the underlying economic environment mediates the impact of patron-client networks. For example, Shami (2012) studies four communities in rural Pakistan in which the unexpected construction of a major road provided a natural experiment to assess the ability of communities to connect with external actors. She finds that the negative impact of clientelism, in terms of dependence on political patrons, was mitigated in communities with better (road) connectivity to the outside economy.

Toward a Relational Comparative Politics

This section argues that many of the big questions of comparative politics are inherently relational and thus ripe for systematic incorporation of network-analytic approaches. To illustrate theoretical and empirical possibilities, I focus on two major topics in comparative politics: (1) state-society relations and (2) political organizations and political identities. I follow a simple exposition scheme, wherein I first highlight essential concepts and/or questions relevant to each topic and then proceed to describe relevant network representations. The focus here is on the initial use of networks as models (i.e., representations) of important political phenomena, prior to any research design and data analysis considerations that lie outside the scope of this chapter.

State-Society Relations

To understand state-society relations, it is useful to first define the constituent elements of this compound term. A core concept in political science is the notion of a state. The classic Weberian definition identifies a state in terms of a manifest "monopoly of violence" (Weber, 1965), but the state is generally understood to have several components that reflect a more complicated organization, including external criteria such as sovereignty, and internal criteria like a bureaucracy (Bates, 2010; O'Neil, 2012, ch. 2). Moreover, it is also common to think of the state in terms of major functions such as the provision of public goods (Hardin, 1997; Morris et al., 2004). In particular, focusing on one of the more tangible aspects of a state, namely a required bureaucracy, immediately reveals a relational foundation. Bureaucracies have two meanings that are amenable to relational thinking. One broad notion reflecting specialization and division of labor can be modeled as a two-mode structure, with individuals as one set of nodes and tasks (or offices or bureaus) as another set. A relationship that assigns individuals to various tasks effectively assigns responsibilities to get things done. Another more personal notion of bureaucracy restricts the set of potential nodes to individuals, who are then related to others within a bureaucratic context. Individuals can then be formally arranged in a *reporting* relationship of the type A-*reports to*-B or chain of command of the type B-*supervises*-A). These individual relationships correspond to organizational charts, which are typically hierarchical.[7]

Defining society is a bit more complicated, because this concept entails much more than a collection of individuals. Underlying the notion of a society is some type of social order or other mechanism that brings people together. This mechanism can be a type of social contract in which people (either on an individual basis or through group representatives) are bound by a common set of rules, but the reasons that bring people together need not be completely formal or voluntary, as long as there is some type of shared understanding (Tilly, 2005). Regardless of the mechanism, it is clear that people are brought together for a given purpose; hence, the notion of society is essentially relational.

What is more, a society proper requires that all individuals relate to everyone else. In the language of network analysis, a society is a *complete* network structure in which *all* possible ties exist. One interpretation is that individuals manifestly cooperate with one another. In that case, we would expect each individual to be cooperating with all other individuals. In large societies, however, this is an impractical requirement that would apparently challenge the notion of a society. However, a network approach serves to further characterize society as potential rather than actual cooperation. That is, all ties are realizable as long as two individuals cooperate whenever they have the opportunity.

Another way to think about society is not in terms of actual behavior such as cooperation (or public ratification of a social contract) but in terms of similar beliefs. This line of thinking suggests a more cognitive definition of society. Two people are related if they share beliefs about their mutual (two-person) association or society. Using this cognitive relationship as a building block, the scale of society enlarges if we add a third party who is mutually related to the original two parties, and so forth, as we add more agents. Although this is a rather abstract way to think about societies, its relational approach immediately reveals empirical tests for the absence of societies. As analysts, once we fix a group of individuals under analysis, we can check whether, in fact, they are related; if they are not, we would not consider that group to be a society proper.[8] This relational (cognitive) approach clarifies that patterns of ties rather than a common setting are what define the existence of a society.

Having proposed a relational definition of society in its own right, we can then explore how societies relate to their states. From a behavioral perspective, we know that ordinary citizens do not live in a social and political vacuum, and common settings induce pervasive interdependence, which makes all political behavior a function of networks (Huckfeldt, 2009). Moreover, important features of political systems need to be learned, and general social interactions can greatly facilitate social learning (Zuckerman, 2009). That is, one key facet of state-society relations involves requisite private learning about the state, which might translate into common societal expectations. Assuming the state is a known entity, there are multiple ways to engage it. In what follows, I suggest three network models (i.e., representations) of state-society engagements.

First, the simplest model is one in which the state is a monolithic and unique entity. If we let N_1 denote the set with a unique state, we can further define a second set N_2 of individuals. Then a system of state-society relations can be modeled as the affiliation network that connects (some) citizens with the given state. Readers might object that modern notions of citizenship already imply a nested structure that automatically relates citizens to the state, but this objection does not undermine this modeling exercise. If anything, the network model serves to identify the specific conditions under which one citizen gets a state (i.e., if all nested individuals are its citizens, but this may be a stringent requirement in an age of increasing globalization).[9] If we move beyond automatic ties produced by citizenship and focus on actual access to the state or protection of individual rights, which are major concerns in various democratic theories, then these alternative redefinitions of a meaningful state-citizen relationship imply that we will likely observe a lot more variation within countries in state-society relations. Indeed, one might argue that the study of state-society relations is motivated by the lack of uniform ties, which implies that not everyone in a society is equal vis-à-vis the "state." One utility of a network representation is that we can use a variety of summary properties to check for structural differences across countries. What is more, different structures can help us distinguish political regimes in which access to or control of public officials might be more limited, in particular nondemocratic regimes (Razo, 2013).

Second, we can posit a more manageable model that reduces the number of private nodes if these are already nested within organizations. Because we consider the state (or set of states) as distinct nodes, we have a two-mode affiliation network in which the other relevant actors are organizations (or mini-societies). Note that this structure assumes nested membership within organizations, or a very hierarchical form of social organization.[10] Finally, if we relax the assumption of a single state, thus enlarging the set of states, then we have a more flexible two-mode structure linking states to individuals. This type of structure models situations in which two or more states relate directly to the same individuals (e.g., dual citizenship or transnational political engagements).[11]

To summarize, the purpose of this section is not to provide specific models or network structures that fit all accounts of state-society relations. Rather, its is to illustrate how one can think about state-society relations in a very precise way using the concepts of simple or affiliation networks. The examples here, which represent only a few possibilities, serve to illustrate that there is a wide range of state-society relations across the world.

Political Organizations and Political Identities

All political systems require some degree of organization, if only to enable leaders to stay in power (Linz, 2000; Haber, 2006). Indeed, in the modern exercise of democracy through representative government, it is uncommon for individuals to interact directly with public officials or agents of the state, beyond very specific interactions with low-level bureaucrats. Viewed from a network perspective, the *organization* of political activity—whether managed through formal political parties or other organizations—is a relational phenomenon. One way to think about this topic is to understand why individuals choose to affiliate with and participate in various parties (Scarrow, 2007). In effect, political participation entails the creation of participatory networks in which individuals commit time and effort to the pursuit of goals defined by an external political organization. There is, of course, the question of how political organizations come to be in the first place, a consideration that invites questions about the dynamics of party creation and persistence without the presumption that political organizations consist of invariably supportive or participatory members. Indeed, it is widely accepted that mere common affiliations do not readily translate into group cooperation or coordination (Olson, 1965; Ostrom, 1998). Analogous to the above definition of society, we can model collective action in terms of a network structure in which desirable behavior (cooperation or coordination or a combination thereof) can be the basis for effective (shared) membership within an organization.

As suggested in the discussion of social movements, the emergence of organizations entails meaningful participation. This observation opens the room to explore other types of networks that mediate mechanisms by which individual citizens aggregate their interests or otherwise come to realize a common purpose. In other words, to understand political organization, we have to understand various processes of political affiliations. Underlying this topic is the study of political identities. This is not the place to review debates about the origins of ethnic and other types of identities, but simply to recognize that there is ample interest in constructivist approaches that offer room for individuals to choose identities (Chandra, 2012). Identity formation is analogous to a process of network formation whereby individuals (as one type of node) assume certain identities (a second set of nodes). The latter can originate from spontaneous activity as well as controlled efforts of political manipulation. The dynamic nature of these processes invites a relational definition of common ethnicity with structural properties, such as clustering of identity choices. In a context in which individuals can assume multiple identities, the relational approach offers more flexibility to identify clusters or community structures that, once fixed, can guide the behavior of participants. Once identities are fixed, we can further study how common ties can translate into important productive or unproductive behaviors. On the productive side, for example, we know that identity (affiliation) networks can mitigate problems with state failure and limited provision of public goods

(Cammett and MacLean, 2014). On the unproductive side, coethnicity can be the basis for exclusive practices, discrimination, and outright conflict (Laitin, 2007; Arriola, 2013; Cammett, 2014). Modeling political identities as networks offers the advantage of examining them as objects that can exist independently or alongside established parties, thus creating more venues for informal and formal political organizations to have major positive or negative impacts on their societies.

CONCLUSION

For comparativists, network analysis offers a systematic approach to account for (i.e., measure) the sheer diversity of relevant political networks in the subfield, both those already identified and those yet to be identified. Networks can serve as an organizing principle around which we can develop cumulative knowledge of known connections that have yet to be measured more systematically within extant literatures such as clientelism. Additionally, networks can identify similar social ties—and thus connect—disparate literatures with novel research questions. For example, under what conditions can social ties be activated for spontaneous social movements or more controlled mobilizations by political elites?

Comparativists have demonstrated a long-standing interest in relational phenomena. It is fair to say, however, that typical approaches tend to be exclusive, in that when networks are relevant, the focus remains there, with less attention given to other factors. Clearly network analysis calls for different data than many comparativists—and political scientists for that matter—are familiar with, and it is true that network methods may appear rather disconnected from conventional quantitative or qualitative methods. However, collecting relational data does not readily imply that we discard conventional attribute-based data. Instead, we need an integrative approach that incorporates all relevant factors, including variables that are not inherently relational. A network analytic perspective can provide that integrative function, thus also informing the development of better theories.

There are least three major advantages for comparativists to incorporating network analysis into their studies:

- systematic integration of social structure into existing frameworks
- a natural way to model informal structures
- the ability to systematically analyze relational data

Better theories necessarily require that relational phenomena have an explicit network structure representation. This might be an obvious point, but it also warrants some caution. Network structures provide a very natural way to model relational phenomena. Moreover, the conceptual requirements for constructing a network are minimal; we just need to posit a set (or sets) of nodes and how these can be connected (in effect, a very simple mathematical structure, only slightly more complicated than a set or collection of objects). Therefore, it is straightforward to describe complex structures because we are free to choose relevant nodes and possible connections, but herein lies a cautionary note. In general, explicit network structures are conductive to more realistic modeling (i.e., representations) of comparative politics phenomena. However, the added realism can add a lot of complexity, which may be difficult to analyze afterward. The challenge for researchers is therefore to manage the trade-off between realism and unmanageable complexity, a modeling choice that all theorists face, whether developing formal or verbal theories.

However, description is just one early phase of research. Comparativists are further interested in explaining the impact of networks (where these can be deemed independent variables) or how these are formed (as dependent variables), so there is a need for both theory building and a methodology that measures explicit network structures. There is therefore a need for empirical measurements coupled with adequate inferential methods. Adding such a quantitative network perspective to comparative politics is not without its problems, however. We are at an early stage of development, insofar as we lack standards to incorporate network approaches on a very large scale beyond existing exploratory studies. One reason stems from the noted fact that networks are pervasive; hence, data collection in and of itself becomes a formidable task even within one country—let alone multiple countries—because there is not just one network to analyze. Another critical impediment is that different research questions call for different network data types. In fact, a comparative network perspective invites serious attention to the correct identification of relevant networks. If we are not careful, which is to say that if we lack theoretical guidance, we might be measuring the wrong networks for a particular research question, or otherwise conflating a general conduit such as social media with the various substantive networks that make use of it. The general point here—which also stems from the sheer diversity of networks yet to be fully documented—is that doing network analysis will require much effort to develop data collections that facilitate comparative analysis, because extant ones might or might not be compatible with one's own research question.

Finally, there remain major obstacles in the realm of training for graduate students in political science who might want to add an explicit network-analytic perspective to their work. Relevant coursework is not readily available, because the study of political networks in the discipline is relatively new. However, this enhanced training is also strictly necessary, because adding a relational perspective to comparative politics requires new sets of tools, theories, and methods.

ACKNOWLEDGMENTS

The author appreciates feedback on an early rough draft from Amy E. Smith, Jennifer Victor, Alex Montgomery, and participants in the Handbook Authors Workshop and Panel on Clientelism and Governance of the 8th Annual Political Networks Conference, Portland, Oregon, June 2015.

Notes

1. I do not include here an emerging literature on comparative political behavior that also incorporates networks. For a review of that literature, see the chapter by Ames et al. in this handbook.

2. Interested readers can consult Diani and McAdam (2003) and Snow et al. (2004a).

3. Wolfsfeld et al. (2013) caution against the causal impact that observers have attributed to social media by noting that the political environment provides enabling conditions; in fact, protests need to attain a certain scale before social media become useful.

4. Following a self-exile of five years in Japan, the land of his ancestors, Fujimori was arrested during a trip to Chile in 2005 and extradited to Peru thereafter.

5. Indeed, scholars and policymakers recognize that these partnerships might offer advantages over strictly public or private solutions (World Bank, 2003).

6. Weitz-Shapiro (2014), also studying the case of Argentina, argues that politicians opt out of clientelism when they face middle-class voters in competitive environments, where these voters frown upon distributive politics that use clientelistic practices like individual handouts. This line of work suggests that parties explicitly choose how they will connect with voters; in effect, choosing among available network structures.

7. But see Cross and Parker (2004) for a contrary view on internal organizational relationships that actually matter to get work done. See also Thompson (2003).

8. Perhaps requiring a complete network structure is too stringent a definition of a society in practical terms, but this consideration does not undermine the utility of a network perspective. We can entertain more relaxed notions of societies with a variable threshold of sufficiently high connectivity beyond which related individuals are effectively a society proper.

9. In fact, some argue that the study of comparative politics cannot be decoupled from the international realm (Solingen, 2009), so that as comparativists we would be required to study complex network structures in which states (and people within states) have ties to and are affected by external entities. Indeed, studies of political and economic development have long noted these types of connections as in dependency theory, although now largely discredited (Packenham, 1992).

10. Although not typically used in network analysis, one could readily extend this logic to construct a three-mode network structure to represent the notion of corporatism. In corporatism, there is a center of power (call it the *state*) with a set of integrated corporations. These corporations, in turn, serve to aggregate individual interests. The three modes are therefore individuals, corporations, and state.

11. It is also possible to have a less constrained representation in which the state is not necessarily an independent, separate entity from society (Migdal, 2001). This more flexible approach does require reconceptualizing the state in terms of multiple networks to identify points of connection between "state" parts and private citizens, thus giving way to a more complex, multilayered perspective on states (Migdal, 2009). See also Anderson (2009) on the notion of nested citizens in a context of multilevel politics. Despite the entailed complexity, a network-analytic approach provides a unifying framework for empirical distinctions among these competing definitions, beyond qualitative assessments.

References

Agarwal, N., Lim, M., and Wigand, R. T. (Eds.). (2014). *Online Collective Action: Dynamics of the Crowd in Social Media*. Lecture Notes in Social Networks. Vienna: Springer Vienna.

Anderson, C. J. (2009). "Nested Citizens: Macropolitics and Microbehavior in Comparative Politics." In *Comparative Politics: Rationality, Culture, and Structure*, 2d ed., edited by M. I. Lichbach and A. S. Zuckerman, pp. 314–332. New York: Cambridge University Press.

Arriola, L. R. (2013). *Multiethnic Coalitions in Africa: Business Financing of Opposition Election Campaigns*. Cambridge Studies in Comparative Politics. New York: Cambridge University Press.

Bates, R. H. (2010). *Prosperity and Violence: The Political Economy of Development*. 2d ed. New York and London: Norton.

Bennett, W. L., and Segerberg, A. (2012). "The Logic of Connective Action: Digital Media and the Personalization of Contentious Politics." *Information, Communication & Society* 15: 739–768.

Bhargava, V. K., and Bolongaita, E. P. (2004). *Challenging Corruption in Asia: Case Studies and a Framework for Action*. Washington, DC: World Bank.

Borge-Holthoefer, J., González-Bailón, S., Rivero, A., and Moreno, Y. (2014). "The Spanish 'Indignados' Movement: Time Dynamics, Geographical Distribution, and Recruitment Mechanisms." In *Online Collective Action: Dynamics of the Crowd in Social Media*, edited by N. Agarwal, M. Lim, and R. T. Wigand, pp. 155–178. Vienna: Springer Vienna.

Breuer, A., Landman, T., and Farquhar, D. (2015). "Social Media and Protest Mobilization: Evidence from the Tunisian Revolution." *Democratization*: 22(4): 764–792.

Broadbent, J. (2003). "Movement in Context: Thick Networks and Japanese Environmental Protest." In *Social Movements and Networks: Relational Approaches to Collective Action*, edited by M. Diani and D. McAdam, pp. 204–232. Oxford and New York: Oxford University Press.

Calvo, E., and Murillo, M. V. (2012). "When Parties Meet Voters Assessing Political Linkages through Partisan Networks and Distributive Expectations in Argentina and Chile." *Comparative Political Studies* 46(7): 851–882.

Cammett, M. C. (2014). *Compassionate Communalism: Welfare and Sectarianism in Lebanon*. Ithaca, NY: Cornell University Press.

Cammett, M. C., and MacLean, L. M. (Eds.). (2014). *The Politics of Non-State Social Welfare*. Cambridge, UK, and New York: Cambridge University Press.

Campos, J. E. (Ed.). (2002). *Corruption: The Boom and Bust of East Asia*. Manila: Ateneo de Manila University Press.

Castells, M. (2007). "Communication, Power and Counter-Power in the Network Society." *International Journal of Communication* 1: 29.

Chadwick, A. (2006). *Internet Politics: States, Citizens, and New Communication Technologies*. New York: Oxford University Press.

Chandra, K. (2012). *Constructivist Theories of Ethnic Politics*. New York: Oxford University Press.

Clarke, G. R. G. (2011). "How Petty Is Petty Corruption? Evidence from Firm Surveys in Africa." *World Development* 39: 1122–1132.

Collins, K. (2002). "Clans, Pacts, and Politics in Central Asia." *Journal of Democracy* 13: 137.

Cross, R. L., and Parker, A. (2004). *The Hidden Power of Social Networks: Understanding How Work Really Gets Done in Organizations*. Boston: Harvard Business School Press.

Diani, M. (2003a). "Introduction: Social Movements, Contentious Actions, and Social Networks: 'From Metaphor to Substance'?" In *Social Movements and Networks: Relational Approaches to Collective Action*, edited by M. Diani and D. McAdam, pp. 281–298. Oxford and New York: Oxford University Press.

Diani, M. (2003b). "'Leaders' or Brokers? Positions and Influence in Social Movement Networks." In *Social Movements and Networks: Relational Approaches to Collective Action*, edited by M. Diani and D. McAdam, pp. 105–122. Oxford and New York: Oxford University Press.

Diani, M. (2003c). "Networks and Social Movements: A Research Programme." In *Social Movements and Networks: Relational Approaches to Collective Action*, edited by M. Diani and D. McAdam, pp. 299–319. Oxford and New York: Oxford University Press.

Diani, M. (2004). "Networks and Participation." In *The Blackwell Companion to Social Movements*, edited by D. A. Snow, S. A. Soule, and H. Kriesi, pp. 339–359. Oxford: Blackwell Publishing.

Diani, M., and McAdam, D. (2003). *Social Movements and Networks: Relational Approaches to Collective Action*. Oxford and New York: Oxford University Press.

Diaz-Cayeros, A., and Magaloni, B. (2003). "The Politics of Public Spending–Part II. The Programa Nacional De Solidaridad (Pronasol) in Mexico." Background Paper for the World Bank World Development Report 2004.

Edwards, B., and McCarthy, J. D. (2004). "Resources and Social Movement Mobilization." In *The Blackwell Companion to Social Movements*, edited by D. A. Snow, S. A. Soule, and H. Kriesi, pp. 116–152. Oxford: Blackwell Publishing.

Evans, P. B. (1995). *Embedded Autonomy: States and Industrial Transformation*. Princeton, NJ: Princeton University Press.

Fox, J. (1994). "The Difficult Transition from Clientelism to Citizenship: Lessons from Mexico." *World Politics* 46: 151–184.

Freidenberg, F., and Levitsky, S. (2006). "Informal Institutions and Party Organization in Latin America." In *Informal Institutions and Democracy: Lessons from Latin America*, edited by G. Helmke and S. Levitsky, pp. 178–200. Baltimore, MD: Johns Hopkins University Press.

González-Bailón, S., Borge-Holthoefer, J., Rivero, A., and Moreno, Y. (2011). "The Dynamics of Protest Recruitment through an Online Network." *Scientific Reports* 1: 197.

González-Bailón, S., Wang, N., and Borge-Holthoefer, J. (2014). "The Emergence of Roles in Large-Scale Networks of Communication." *EPJ Data Science* 3: 32.

Goodwin, J., and Jasper, J. M. (Eds.). (2005). *The Social Movements Reader: Cases and Concepts*. 3d ed. Oxford: Blackwell Publishing Ltd.

Gould, R. (2003). "Why Do Networks Matter? Rationalist and Structuralist Interpretations." In *Social Movements and Networks: Relational Approaches to Collective Action*, edited by M. Diani and D. McAdam, pp. 233–257. Oxford and New York: Oxford University Press.

Haber, S. (2006). "Authoritarian Government." In *The Oxford Handbook of Political Economy*, edited by B. R. Weingast and D. A. Wittman, pp. 693–707. Oxford, New York: Oxford University Press.

Haber, S., Razo, A., and Maurer, N. (2003). *The Politics of Property Rights: Political Instability, Credible Commitments, and Economic Growth in Mexico (1876–1929)*. Cambridge, UK, and New York: Cambridge University Press.

Hardin, R. (1997). "Economic Theories of the State." In *Perspectives on Public Choice: A Handbook*, edited by D. C. Mueller, pp. 21–34. New York: Cambridge University Press.

Huckfeldt, R. (2009). "Citizenship in Democratic Politics: Density Dependence and the Micro-Macro Divide." In *Comparative Politics: Rationality, Culture, and Structure*, 2d ed., edited by M. I. Lichbach and A. S. Zuckerman, pp. 291–313. New York: Cambridge University Press.

Hutchcroft, P. (1994). "Business-Government Relations in the Philippines." In *Business and Government in Industrialising Asia*, edited by A. J. MacIntyre, pp. 216–243. Ithaca, NY: Cornell University Press.

Inter-American Development Bank and Harvard University. (2005). *The Politics of Policies Economic and Social Progress in Latin America and the Caribbean, 2006 Report*. Washington, DC, and Cambridge, MA: Inter-American Development Bank and Harvard University.

John, P., and Cole, A. (2000). "When Do Institutions, Policy Sectors, and Cities Matter? Comparing Networks of Local Policy Makers in Britain and France." *Comparative Political Studies* 33: 248–268.

Kalathil, S., and Boas, T. C. (2003). *Open Networks, Closed Regimes: The Impact of the Internet on Authoritarian Rule*. Washington, DC: Carnegie Endowment for International Peace.

Kang, D. C. (2002). *Crony Capitalism: Corruption and Development in South Korea and the Philippines*. Cambridge, UK, and New York: Cambridge University Press.

Kaufmann, D., Kraay, A., and Mastruzzi, M. (2005). *Governance Matters IV: Governance Indicators for 1996–2004*. Washington, DC: World Bank.

Khwaja, A. I., and Mian, A. (2005). "Do Lenders Favor Politically Connected Firms? Rent Provision in an Emerging Financial Market." *Quarterly Journal of Economics* 120: 1371–411.

Kitschelt, H., and Wilkinson, S. (2007). "Citizen-Politician Linkages: An Introduction." In *Patrons, Clients, and Policies: Patterns of Democratic Accountability and Political Competition*, edited by H. Kitschelt and S. Wilkinson, pp. 1–49. Cambridge, UK, and New York: Cambridge University Press.

Knoke, D. (1990). *Political Networks: The Structural Perspective*. Structural Analysis in the Social Sciences 4. New York: Cambridge University Press.

Knoke, D. (1993). "Networks of Elite Structure and Decision Making." *Sociological Methods & Research* 22: 23.

Knoke, D. (1996). *Comparing Policy Networks: Labor Politics in U.S., Germany, and Japan*. Cambridge Studies in Comparative Politics. Cambridge, UK, and New York: Cambridge University Press.

Kriesi, H. (2004). "Political Context and Opportunity." In *The Blackwell Companion to Social Movements*, edited by D. A. Snow, S. A. Soule, and H. Kriesi, pp. 67–90. Oxford: Blackwell Publishing.

Laitin, D. D. (2007). *Nations, States, and Violence*. Oxford and New York: Oxford University Press.

Linz, J. J. (2000). *Totalitarian and Authoritarian Regimes*. Boulder, CO: Lynne Rienner Publishers.

Maxfield, S., and Schneider, B. R. (1997). *Business and the State in Developing Countries*. Cornell Studies in Political Economy. Ithaca, NY: Cornell University Press.

McAdam, D. (2003). "Beyond Structural Analysis: Toward a More Dynamic Understanding of Social Movements." In *Social Movements and Networks: Relational Approaches to Collective Action*, edited by M. Diani and D. McAdam, pp. 281–298. Oxford and New York: Oxford University Press.

McMillan, J., and Zoido, P. (2004). "How to Subvert Democracy: Montesinos in Peru." Stanford Graduate Business School Research Papers, no. 1851. Stanford, CA.

Migdal, J. S. (2001). *State in Society: Studying How States and Societies Transform and Constitute One Another*. Cambridge Studies in Comparative Politics. Cambridge, UK, and New York: Cambridge University Press.

Migdal, J. S. (2009). "Researching the State." In *Comparative Politics: Rationality, Culture, and Structure*, edited by M. I. Lichbach and A. S. Zuckerman, 2d ed., pp. 162–192. New York: Cambridge University Press.

Morris, I. L., Oppenheimer, J. A., and Soltan, K. E. (2004). *Politics from Anarchy to Democracy: Rational Choice in Political Science*. Stanford, CA: Stanford University Press.

North, D. C., and Weingast, B. R. (1989). "Constitutions and Commitment: The Evolution of Institutions Governing Public Choice in Seventeenth-Century England." *Journal of Economic History* 49: 803–832.

O'Neil, P. H. (2012). *Essentials of Comparative Politics*. 4th ed. New York: W. W. Norton.

Olson, M. (1965). *The Logic of Collective Action: Public Goods and the Theory of Groups*. Harvard Economic Studies. Cambridge, MA: Harvard University Press.

Olson, M. (1993). "Dictatorship, Democracy, and Development." *American Political Science Review* 87: 567–576.

Ostrom, E. (1998). "A Behavioral Approach to the Rational Choice Theory of Collective Action: Presidential Address, American Political Science Association, 1997." *American Political Science Review* 92: 1–22.

Packenham, R. A. (1992). *The Dependency Movement: Scholarship and Politics in Development Studies*. Cambridge, MA: Harvard University Press.

Padgett, J. F., and Ansell, C. K. (1993). "Robust Action and the Rise of the Medici, 1400–1434." *American Journal of Sociology* 98 (6): 1259–1319.

Parkinson, S. E. (2013). "Organizing Rebellion: Rethinking High-Risk Mobilization and Social Networks in War." *American Political Science Review* 107: 418–432.

Prakash, A., and Gugerty, M. K. (2010). *Advocacy Organizations and Collective Action*. Cambridge, UK, and New York: Cambridge University Press.

Razo, A. (2008). *Social Foundations of Limited Dictatorship: Networks of Private Protection During Mexico's Early Industrialization*. Social Science History. Stanford, CA: Stanford University Press.

Razo, A. (2013). "Autocrats and Democrats." In *The Elgar Companion to Public Choice*, 2d ed., edited by M. Reksulak, L. Razzolini, and W. F. Shughart, pp. 83–108. Cheltenham, UK: Edward Elgar.

Reinikka, R., and Svensson, J. (2006). "Using Micro-Surveys to Measure and Explain Corruption." *World Development* 34: 359–370.

Robinson, J. A. (2010). "The Political Economy of Redistributive Policies." United Nations Development Programme Discussion Paper.

Romanos, E. (2016). "Immigrants as Brokers: Dialogical Diffusion from Spanish Indignados to Occupy Wall Street." *Social Movement Studies* 15 (3): 247–262.

Rose-Ackerman, S. (1999). *Corruption and Government: Causes, Consequences, and Reform*. Cambridge, UK, and New York: Cambridge University Press.

Scarrow, S. E. (2007). "Political Activism and Party Members." In *Oxford Handbook of Political Behavior*, edited by. R. J. Dalton and H.-D. Klingemann, pp. 636–654. Oxford and New York: Oxford University Press.

Schneider, B. R. (2004). *Business Politics and the State in Twentieth-Century Latin America*. Cambridge, UK, and New York: Cambridge University Press.

Shami, M. (2012). "Collective Action, Clientelism, and Connectivity." *American Political Science Review* 106: 588–606.

Shleifer, A., and Vishny, R. W. (1993). "Corruption." *Quarterly Journal of Economics* 108: 599–617.

Snow, D. A., Soule, S. A., and Kriesi, H. (Eds.). (2004a). *The Blackwell Companion to Social Movements*. Oxford: Blackwell Publishing.

Snow, D. A., Soule, S. A., and Kriesi, H. (2004b). "Mapping the Terrain." In *The Blackwell Companion to Social Movements*, edited by D. A. Snow, S. A. Soule, and H. Kriesi, pp. 116–152. Oxford: Blackwell Publishing.

Solingen, E. (2009). "The Global Context of Comparative Politics." In *Comparative Politics: Rationality, Culture, and Structure*, 2d ed., edited by M. I. Lichbach and A. S. Zuckerman, pp. 220–259. New York: Cambridge University Press.

Stokes, S. C., Dunning, T., Nazareno, M., and Brusco, V. (2013). *Brokers, Voters, and Clientelism: The Puzzle of Distributive Politics*. Cambridge, UK: Cambridge University Press.

Svensson, J. (2005). "Eight Questions About Corruption." *Journal of Economic Perspectives* 19: 19–42.

Szwarcberg, M. (2012). "Revisiting Clientelism: A Network Analysis of Problem-Solving Networks in Argentina." *Social Networks* 34: 230–240.

Szwarcberg, M. (2013). "The Microfoundations of Political Clientelism: Lessons from the Argentine Case." *Latin American Research Review* 48: 32–54.

Szwarcberg, M. L. (2015). *Mobilizing Poor Voters: Machine Politics, Clientelism, and Social Networks in Argentina*. Structural Analysis in the Social Sciences. Cambridge, UK: Cambridge University Press.

Tarrow, S. G. (1998). *Power in Movement: Social Movements and Contentious Politics*. 2d ed. Cambridge Studies in Comparative Politics. Cambridge, UK, and New York: Cambridge University Press.

Tarrow, S. G. (2005). *The New Transnational Activism*. Cambridge Studies in Contentious Politics. New York: Cambridge University Press.

Tarrow, S. G. (2011). *Power in Movement: Social Movements and Contentious Politics*. 3d ed. Cambridge Studies in Comparative Politics. Cambridge, UK, and New York: Cambridge University Press.

Thompson, G. (2003). *Between Hierarchies and Markets: The Logic and Limits of Network Forms of Organization*. Oxford and New York: Oxford University Press.

Tilly, C. (2004). *Social Movements, 1768–2004*. Boulder, CO: Paradigm Publishers.

Tilly, C. (2005). *Identities, Boundaries, and Social Ties*. Boulder, CO: Paradigm Publishers.

Transparency International. (2014). *Corruption Perceptions Index 2014*. Berlin: Transparency International.

Treisman, D. (2007). "What Have We Learned About the Causes of Corruption from Ten Years of Cross-National Empirical Research?" *Annual Review of Political Science* 10: 211–244.

Van Cott, D. L. (2005). *From Movements to Parties in Latin America: The Evolution of Ethnic Politics*. Cambridge, UK, and New York: Cambridge University Press.

Ward, M. D., Stovel, K., and Sacks, A. (2011). "Network Analysis and Political Science." *Annual Review of Political Science* 14: 245–264.

Weber, M. (1965). *Politics as a Vocation*. Facet Books, Social Ethics Series. Philadelphia: Fortress Press.

Weitz-Shapiro, R. (2014). *Curbing Clientelism in Argentina: Politics, Poverty, and Social Policy*. Cambridge, UK: Cambridge University Press.

Williams, R. H. (2004). "The Cultural Contexts of Collective Action: Constraints, Opportunities, and the Symbolic Life of Social Movements." In *The Blackwell Companion to Social Movements*, edited by D. A. Snow, S. A. Soule, and H. Kriesi, pp. 91–115. Oxford: Blackwell Publishing.

Wolfsfeld, G., Segev, E., and Sheafer, T. (2013). "Social Media and the Arab Spring Politics Comes First." *International Journal of Press/Politics* 18: 115–137.

World Bank. (2003). *World Development Report 2004: Making Services Work for Poor People.* Washington, DC: World Bank.

Zuckerman, A. S. (2009). "Advancing Explanation in Comparative Politics: Social Mechanisms, Endogenous Processes, and Empirical Rigor." In *Comparative Politics: Rationality, Culture, and Structure*, edited by M. I. Lichbach and A. S. Zuckerman, 2d ed., pp. 72–95. New York: Cambridge University Press.

Zuckerman, A. S. (2005). "Returning to the Social Logic of Politics." In *The Social Logic of Politics: Personal Networks as Contexts for Political Behavior*, edited by Alan S. Zuckerman, pp. 3–20. Philadelphia: Temple University Press.

CHAPTER 34

....

DEMOCRATIC INSTITUTIONS AND POLITICAL NETWORKS

....

DAVID A. SIEGEL

INTRODUCTION

....

POLITICAL behavior does not occur in a vacuum. Our incentive to vote, or for whom to vote, depends on what our friends and family will think of our decisions and on how likely our decisions are to matter given electoral institutions. The information we use to make our decisions travels a complex path before it gets to us, echoed and distorted by the social and institutional sources we employ to obtain it. Even our very opportunities to act are limited, not only by what is institutionally allowable to us, but also by whom we know. In short, democratic institutions and social and political networks act in concert to structure our political choices in fundamental ways.

Though scholars have acknowledged the individual importance of both institutions and networks for political behavior, insufficient attention has been paid to the interaction between the two. The reason this interaction is important is that both institutions and networks affect behavior in the exact same ways: by altering individuals' incentives, information, and opportunities. It's not just that ignoring either institutions or networks introduces bias into our theories and empirical analyses; ignoring the interaction between institutions and networks does as well.

This essay is intended to be an incremental step toward incorporating the rich interaction between institutions and networks into our theories and empirics. In what follows I focus on the three common mechanisms of incentives, information, and opportunities. In the context of each mechanism I highlight several examples of possible significant interactions between the effects of institutions and social networks. First, though, I elaborate on the effects that institutions and networks have on behavior, acting through these same three mechanisms, and discuss why ignoring the interaction between them produces theoretical and empirical bias.

INSTITUTIONS AND NETWORKS

There are few words more content-rich in political science than *institution*. On one level, an institution is a physical entity that serves some role in society. Legislatures are institutions tasked with formulating laws, central banks are institutions tasked with implementing monetary policy, and national militaries are institutions tasked with national defense (and sometimes offense). Democratic institutions, on this level, are merely the formal institutions present in democracies.

Social scientists have expanded this definition of institution to include any formal or informal edifice that specifies the rules that guide "future courses of action" (Knight, 1992, 67). The logic behind this expansion is simple. Individual people are the political, economic, and social actors who operate in our world, and their behavior is structured by the opportunities, incentives, and information available to them at any given time. Institutions determine the availability of opportunities, incentives, and information and thus structure the actions we all take. For example, institutions that limit or expand opportunities alter our set of choices. Those that provide or diminish incentives alter our desires to take any particular action. And those that make available or hide information alter our beliefs about outcomes, and therefore our desire to take actions that might lead to these outcomes.

The elegance in this definition lies in the fact that it provides a unified logic to the functioning of everything from a formal legislature to an informal cultural norm. In all cases, the institution conditions the manner in which people respond to the world around them, the manner in which they make decisions and take actions. Though they serve this conditioning role in a multitude of ways, the language of incentives, information, and opportunities can help clarify the roles of institutions. To reiterate: incentives alter the desires of actors to take different actions; institutions can affect actors' incentives. Information alters actors' beliefs about the costs and benefits of taking different actions; institutions can affect actors' information. Available opportunities constrain actors' possible actions; institutions can affect opportunities to act.

To be more concrete, consider a few examples, both formal and informal. The owners of a coal-fired power plant may want to do little to mitigate the release of methyl mercury into the environment, so as to save on costs. But the institution of an environmental agency can fine them if the plant were to so pollute. These fines, if high enough, are disincentives to pollute. In other words, the agency (a formal institution) alters the desire of the power plant owners to take their preferred action via the (dis)incentive of fines.

Now introduce a judicial body with the power to proscribe the behavior of the environmental agency. If it decides that the agency has overstepped its authority in setting fines, it can in some cases remove the ability of the agency to levy them. Thus, the judicial body (a different formal institution) alters the set of actions available to the agency, limiting its opportunities to act.

Add an industry lobbying group (a third formal institution) to the mix. The lobbying group can provide information to the members of the judicial body. This information can alter the beliefs of the judicial body, which in turn can alter the degree to which it supports the justification the agency provides for its preferred action. At the same time, the group can also provide information to the agency, potentially altering the perceived benefits of its proposed plan of action.

These are all formal institutions, but informal institutions can perform the same conditioning roles (Helmke and Levitsky, 2004). A norm against polluting—or against purchasing power from or owning stock in a company that pollutes—could have a similar pollution-reducing effect to fines from a formal agency. A norm against torture might be as effective at limiting actors' use of torture as a formal convention against the practice. An international norm in favor of capitalism or democracy might alter incentives for authoritarian countries with command economies to open markets or hold elections. A tradition of transparency might produce a greater breadth of information available to the public than would be present in the absence of such a norm. Because informal institutions also constitute rules in the same manner as do formal institutions, they may have all the same effects on opportunities, incentives, and information as do formal institutions.

This addresses the role of institutions, but what about that of social networks? The answer lies in understanding that social networks act to condition behavior in *just the same way* as do informal institutions, through the same causal mechanisms. Though I do not do so here, one could therefore even refer to networks as informal institutions themselves (see, e.g., Wang, 2000). We can see this by breaking down the operation of social networks into their effects on incentives, information, and opportunities.

First, social networks alter incentives to take action by determining the set of other actors who are affected by and might respond to one's actions. For example, adoption of a policy might be a more attractive option when one is connected to many other actors already favorable toward the policy, but a less attractive option when one's connections do not favor the policy. The reason is that these connections might motivate the adoption of a favorable policy by, for example, engaging in more frequent or more beneficial interactions with the adopter, or they may demotivate the adoption of a nonfavored policy by sanctioning or limiting their beneficial interactions with the adopter. They can even alter the nature of their networks in response to an adoption, cutting ties as punishment or increasing the density of beneficial ties as reward.

Second, social networks alter beliefs about the costs and benefits of taking action by delimiting the flow of information, changing which actors learn what. For example, they may dictate that a potential policy adopter only learns about research favorable to an adoption, influencing the adopter's choice; information suggesting further costs of adoption may not be accessible via the actor's network. Networks can also delineate what each actor learns about other actors' actions, which affects the collective's ability to coordinate on outcomes. For example, participation in risky collective actions often requires the visible participation of others who are well-known to potential participants

(McAdam, 1988). Networks that limit the transference of information on participation can alter the rate of participation achieved (Siegel, 2009).

Third, social networks propagate cultural norms that limit opportunities to act and deny information that would lead to knowledge of some opportunities. The mechanism of opportunities is in a sense the extreme version of that of incentives and information: either the networks provide incentives so strong they effectively prohibit actions, or they constrain information so much that certain opportunities are not available to an actor. I treat opportunities separately because a reduction in opportunities changes the decision process in ways different from changes in incentives or information. Not only are certain actions not chosen, but reducing the set of available actions simplifies the decision process, reducing the need for simplifying heuristics. It is even possible that a reduction in opportunity could produce a better outcome if the eliminated opportunity is not optimal and the heuristics its presence would have induced are sufficiently poor.

That networks play these roles has substantial—and substantially underexplored—consequences for our understanding of democratic institutions. Extensive analysis of democratic institutions has indicated the degree to which they structure behavior and has elaborated on the manner by which they do so. Recent research has explored similar effects of social networks in a comparative context, as seen in this and other chapters. Yet what has been almost completely ignored is the interaction between the two in structuring behavior. And this leads ineluctably to bias in our study of institutions.

Why? Because networks and institutions affect behavior in the same manner, using the same causal mechanisms. Not only does this imply that omitting one or the other factor leads to bias; it also implies that failing to incorporate the interaction *between* networks and institutions leads to bias. But the problem is actually worse than this. Consider incentives, for example. As networks and institutions condition the degree to which incentives affect individual behavior, we already have to consider two-way interactions between incentives and networks and incentives and institutions. The need to incorporate interactions between networks and institutions also implies that we must include the *three-way interaction* among incentives, institutions, and social networks to obtain an unbiased model of behavior. Similar arguments hold for information and opportunities.

If this seems extreme, consider this. We may know that greater incentives increase one's likelihood to take some action, say, for instance, turning out to vote. And we may also know that some institution determines the fraction of a mandated incentive that actually makes it through to the average member of a targeted population. This would be the case whenever an institution had a hand in distributing resources to a population, as would a clientelistic party. However, we still need to know the manner in which the network in place differentially distributes incentives to different members of the population to understand (1) how any member of the population will behave and (2) how well or poorly the institution functions. In other words, without knowing its distribution network, we cannot assess how effectively a clientelistic party alters incentives to vote.

Acknowledging that incorporating this sort of three-way interaction produces a more correct model opens up numerous areas of study that heretofore have barely been addressed. The remainder of this chapter discusses a few such areas, some extant research that touches on each, and where future research might productively go in each case. I organize the discussion by the causal mechanism that drives the potential three-way interaction that includes both institutions and networks: incentives, information, and opportunities.

INCENTIVES

Electoral institutions are the class of institution perhaps most centrally connected to democracy. By electoral institution, I mean any institution that facilitates voting or affects the selection of options on which to vote. The effect of institutions of this type on electoral behavior is a well-studied topic, far outstripping the ability of a few paragraphs to do justice to it. Indeed, textbooks have been written on it (e.g., Clark, Golder, and Golder, 2012).

Less voluminous, but no less relevant for our understanding of electoral dynamics, is the growing literature on the role of social networks in every aspect of elections, from turnout to vote choice to the internal workings of parties (e.g., Koger, Masket, and Noel, 2009; Rolfe, 2012; Sinclair, 2012). What has received relatively little attention, though, is the manner in which social networks condition the effect of electoral institutions on electoral behavior. Consider first the most basic democratic behavior: voting.

A constitutional definition of the extent of suffrage is a formal institution that specifies who has the right to vote. The distribution of polling locations within a state helps to determine who has easy and safe access to vote. Increases in suffrage and in the density of polling locations help expand the pool of likely voters. Suffrage does this by providing the opportunity to vote, while a denser distribution of polling locations does this by reducing disincentives to vote.

These are institutional mechanisms that affect turnout, but we also know that social networks affect turnout: people are more (less) likely to vote when those connected to them do (not) vote (Gerber, Green, and Larimer, 2008). These effects work independently, but they are also likely to work in tandem. The overall number of polling places may affect turnout, but so may their placement. If the density of polling places in regions populated primarily by minority ethnic groups is low, or if those that are present are unsafe, we might expect to see turnout depressed by the direct effect of the lack of viable polling sites.

But networks also introduce an indirect effect. With fewer viable polling places, the cost of voting increases, depressing minority group turnout. With fewer minority group members going to the polls, the social network–driven incentive to vote among group members diminishes. As this incentive diminishes, even fewer people will want to pay the cost to vote, further diminishing incentives to vote. Thus, we see that positive feedback within the network exacerbates the detrimental effect of poor institutional access to voting.

The reverse is also true. If government makes an effort to increase the number of secure polling places in minority districts, not only will this have the direct effect of increasing turnout (an institutional effect), but also the indirect effect of increasing turnout via greater social network–driven incentives. So in both cases, the presence of social networks *enhances* the effect of electoral institutions in this context by altering the incentives of individuals to vote. Put another way, social networks and institutions designed to affect turnout play complementary roles.

Though this example was about the location of polling places, the point is more general. Any time an electoral institution acts in part by providing incentives to the public to act, social networks can change the effect of the institution by altering the nature of the incentives. When social network–driven incentives to take an action increase with the number in the network taking part in the action, then networks will prove complementary to institutions designed to support the action, as in the turnout example. So, for example, an institution like a party machine designed to increase voter support for a party will produce a complementary effect to social networks, which can encourage the same support within them (Huckfeldt and Sprague, 1995). And just as networks can condition the effects of institutions in the context of voter behavior, they can also do so in the context of electoral contestation. Prospective candidates may be differentially likely to seek office based on an interaction between the inclusiveness of the party nomination system and their networks of connections within this system, for example.

It is important to note here that the structure of the network matters. Just because the existence of a network might prove complementary to a particular institution, that does not mean that naively increasing the density of ties in that network will enhance the effect of the institution. When actors in a network are not positively predisposed toward an action or belief, increasing the density of ties can lead to less overall participation (Centola and Macy, 2007; Siegel, 2009). In other words, one can't simply assess the strength of a network in promoting an institution's effect by the density of its ties; one also needs to take into account the larger structure of the network.

To elaborate a bit, return to the example of the party machine designed to increase turnout. While it is true that existing network ties act as complements to the institution in increasing the incentives to turn out, it is not true that increasing the density of ties will necessarily enhance this effect. For example, a fractured network in which some marginalized subgroups were not directly targeted by party elites might experience a decline in effectiveness of the institution with a greater density of ties. As network connections become denser within these subgroups, exposure to others who lack incentives to vote increases, decreasing overall turnout and the overall effectiveness of the party machine.

These general insights underlie theories of civic culture as well. One argument, employed widely and particularly in regions in which a government is constructed after conflict, is that democratic institutions are insufficient to ensure a functioning democracy; one must also have appropriate democratic or civic culture. This is one example of a more general point, exemplified in Putnam's (1993) work: institutions can function differently based on the social context.

But what is social context? As Gibson (2001) suggests, social context might be best represented by concrete interpersonal social networks rather than a more abstract feeling of trust or civility. This argument leads to a falsifiable claim: one might expect better democratic performance out of strong and positive institutions the more social capital is present, as measured by the richness of social networks. If this is true even in some contexts, it implies an interaction between institutions and social networks in the context of democratic performance. While strong, positive institutions might improve democratic performance on their own, they will have more of a positive effect in the presence of rich social networks. By the same token, though, as Berman (1997) argues, in the presence of weak institutions, rich social networks might have the opposite effect, leading to civil fragmentation and the potential for extremism from one or more of the mobilized groups. Thus, as with electoral institutions, the effect of social networks depends on both the intent and strength of the institution and the structure of the network.

We can go further in assessing this claim by working out the causal mechanisms by which it might hold. One mechanism is the shifting of incentives. Civic culture is often conceptualized as a sort of norm, an informal institution that renders participation within the political system, itself established by institutions, the only viable means of contestation. Social networks can provide incentives that help to enforce such a norm. We discussed such incentives above: more frequent or more beneficial interactions within networks provide positive incentives to norm-followers, and sanctions or less frequent or beneficial interactions provide negative incentives to norm-violators. (Networks also provide the ability to observe violations of the norm, though this is more an informational role.)

In addition, as the norm becomes central to the identity of the group, the incentives to secure the norm and thus differentiate one's group from others' increases. Thus, much as with turnout-promoting institutions, strong institutions that are intended to enhance civic culture can be complementary to the social network ties that underlie and support civic culture.

These arguments rely on the positive feedback inherent in many network processes. Specifically, they require incentives to build monotonically with network participation in a group action or belief. In other words, as more people take a given action or hold a given belief, the incentives for others to take that action or hold that belief must grow. When this is true, one can generalize these points on civic culture to any situation involving the establishment of a norm of behavior. So, for example, ties between states might allow for norms of communication that improve the possibility of cooperation, which in turn would make international institutions designed to improve interstate cooperation more effective.

This complementarity need not lead to salutary outcomes, though, particularly in the presence of weak institutions that do not inculcate a single norm. In the presence of multiple, competing norms, networks with well-connected but separated subgroups can encourage the development of competing norms of behavior, some of which may be less beneficial to society. In sum, networks can lead to less-than-desired effects both because the structure of the network does not encourage participation, as in the case of institutions designed to enhance turnout, and because the network encourages too much support for splinter groups espousing extreme behavior.

In the examples above, I assume that social network–driven incentives stem from the network itself, due, for example, to the goodwill or friendship of those to whom one is linked. But such incentives may also be more concrete, such as political favors or even direct monetary payment. And networks can also enhance or reduce the impact of institutions that provide such concrete incentives.

This brings us to the realm of clientelism (O'Donnell 1996) and clientelistic networks. Here the effect of networks is straightforward: selective benefits provided within clientelistic networks have breadth limited by the scope of these networks. If an actor is not reached by these networks, then that actor cannot receive the benefits of the clientelistic system. Thus, the degree to which any such system will be effective is conditioned on the structure of the underlying clientelistic network.

Such conditionality introduces interesting interactions with institutions designed to support clientelism. Broadening the reach of the network allows for wider distribution of resources, but this might also lead to a reduction in resources granted at the individual level as existing resources are spread more thinly. This would produce a trade-off between strength of individual support (arising from quantity of resources) and breadth of individual support (arising from access to resources).

Further, if the clientelistic party utilizes individuals within the network to distribute resources, these individuals would have incentives to perform this distribution in such a way as to improve their own positions. This includes forming ties to individuals who might help the distributers gain or secure power. Similarly, others have incentives to form ties to these distributers in order to access these resources. Together, this implies that the clientelistic system will engender endogenous network formation that will come to mirror the flow of party-distributed resources. This network formation will be strategic, but the connections formed will coexist with prior, nonstrategic social connections. Unraveling this rich network tapestry will help us better understand the functioning of clientelism.

As with turnout and civic culture, this point is also more general. Clientelistic institutions betray the aforementioned interaction with network structure due to their focus on resource distribution. In essence, the clientelistic party exhibits an organizational form that relies in part on a network of connections. Any organization that has this property will show the same interactions between institutions and networks, whether the institutions and networks are within or external to the organization. So, for example, we should see interactions between institutional details and local networks in United Nations aid organizations such as the World Food Program, World Health Organization, and United Nations Children's Emergency Fund (UNICEF).

INFORMATION

Thus far the focus of this chapter has been on incentives, but information can be an even more potent causal mechanism linking networks and institutions to behavior. I start exploring this idea by returning to the example of turnout.

While it is certainly true that incentives are a significant mechanism for an interactive effect between institutions and social networks in the context of turnout, information too plays a role. It might be the case that the election or referendum at issue is one in which the minority group is invested enough to justify paying the cost of traveling to distant polling locations. In other words, the direct disincentives to vote caused by sparse polling locations are insufficient to depress minority group turnout. Even then we might see turnout decrease, though this time for informational reasons. With minority group members needing to travel farther to vote, their actions are less likely to be visible to other group members. Group members are thus less likely to obtain true information about the voting behavior of others in the group, and therefore less likely to experience the same level of social network–driven incentives they would have, had they been able to observe the true level of turnout. So, even in the case where incentives do not play a direct role, an informational argument allows us to claim that the presence of social networks *enhances* the effect of electoral institutions in this context by altering the information individuals possess. Of course, in this case the enhancement is of a normatively negative variety, making the institution of sparse polling locations more effective at suppressing turnout.

As with incentives, this argument generalizes beyond polling locations. Any time an institution acts in part by providing information to the public, social networks can alter the effect of the information by dictating the paths over which that information spreads. So, for example, whether or not alternative candidates to the status quo are known to the public depends in part on the social networks that would disseminate information about their candidacy. This informational path coexists with existing institutional mechanisms for providing the same information, leading to significant interactions between networks and institutions.

This notion has direct consequences for the institution of the media. Tasked with disseminating information, the media play varied roles in different polities. In some cases the media's goal is transparency, in others maintenance of the status quo via the selective release of information. Social networks interact with the media in a complex fashion, conditioning their effects (Siegel, 2013). At times, depending on their structure and the nature of the media, networks can support the media's message, proving complementary to it. At other times, networks can inhibit the media's message, reducing its impact. And sometimes networks have no effect on the media at all. Understanding the media's effect on behavior such as opinion formation, vote choice, or turnout and political participation thus requires understanding the joint effect of social networks and the media.

The same is true for antistate actions, ranging from protests and social movements to rebellions, insurgencies, and terrorist activity. Information and influence travel across network ties, drawing new participants into the antistate activity. State institutions designed to suppress this activity must take this into account, as the efficacy of their repression depends on network structure (Siegel, 2011). As with the media, network structure and the nature of repression dictate whether additional network ties lead to easier or more difficult repression; all one can say with certainty is that the effect of each is conditional on the other, implying a significant interaction between networks and repressive institutions of the state.

We should expect this conditionality as well with institutions designed to encourage cooperation rather than repress it. Fearon and Laitin (1996) showed that cooperation can be maintained between members of different groups as long as information about defections is available and sanctions are possible. Information of this type generally does not get broadcast globally, however; it travels via networks. Larson (2012) adds explicit social networks to Fearon and Laitin's model to show that the degree of cooperation possible depends on the network structure in potentially complex ways. As Larson (2014) shows, this sort of logic has direct implications for the efficiency of informal institutions, in that network structure must be taken into account to understand how well cooperative institutions will function.

More fully incorporating social networks can also help us parse the complicated effects of ethnicity. Habyarimana et al. (2007) probe the mechanism underlying an empirical link between low levels of public goods provision and high levels of ethnic diversity. They discover, among other things, that stronger social networks between coethnics may aid in social sanctioning. Dionne (2014) finds that social networks can even be stronger than ethnic similarity in producing trust between potential cooperators. Coupled with Eubank's (2015) finding that ethnic fragmentation and social network fragmentation are not necessarily correlated at all levels, social networks would seem to be significantly relevant in understanding the mechanisms by which ethnicity might aid or hinder the operation of cooperative institutions.

Social sanctioning, as noted above, also plays a role in the maintenance of norms and culture. Here the mechanisms of incentives and information both play a role: information to let actors know who has violated the norm, and incentives to provide reasons not to violate the norm. But cooperation need not rely on sanctioning alone. In the case of cooperation on policy, for example, information dissemination about the benefits of the policy may be sufficient. Banerjee et al. (2013) explore the diffusion of microfinance loans, a frequent tool of aid institutions, and find that the network centrality of individuals first informed about the policy helps predict its eventual adoption. Similarly, Alatas et al. (2014) show that more diffusive networks benefit more from community targeting. Perceptions of fairness can also dictate ties and alter the efficacy of governance institutions (Berardo, 2013).

Finally, simply knowing a norm exists and connecting its adoption to favored network actors can help propagate that norm (Torfason and Ingram, 2010). It is one thing for an international institution to push for human rights or labor or environmental protection; it is another for actors to which one is tied, or to which one desires to be tied, to adopt these protections. Even when adopting these protections oneself is not an explicit requirement for a network tie to continue, it can be an implicit one. Further, network ties allow for the transfer of information about how well policies and norms function and thus affect the diffusion of both, interacting with institutions tasked with the same purpose.

Moving back to more formal institutions, consider legislative bodies. Any role for networks in these institutions would indicate a potentially important interaction between institutions and social networks, since the networks operating within them would then affect their functioning. Identifying network effects is made more difficult, however, by the multiplicity of networks present within such bodies (Heaney and McClurg, 2009). Because different types of networks may serve different purposes and be formed for different reasons, it is important to clarify the causal mechanism underlying the network effect. For example, do cosponsorship networks (e.g., Cho and Fowler, 2010) affect legislative productivity because they indicate common paths along which compromises can be reached? In this case we might expect cosponsorship networks that are more dense in ties linking different parties to have potentially less gridlock. Or are they merely visible outcomes of other, deeper mechanisms that lead legislators to join in particular pieces of legislation? Assessing this question requires delving into the individual-level data on cosponsorship.

Ringe and Victor (2013) address the question of causality by looking at the particular mechanism of information transfer within legislative member organizations (LMOs), which include caucuses in the US Congress and intergroups in the European Parliament. These LMOs foster social ties, which allow for the exchange of information relevant for policymaking. In a way, these LMOs are thus complementary to the informational role some (e.g., Krehbiel, 1991) have assigned to legislative committees, as the social ties Ringe and Victor identify cut across party and committee lines, providing alternative sources of information. Institutions and social networks therefore interact within legislative bodies to affect the degree to which externally provided information diffuses through the legislature and is incorporated into the beliefs of legislators and the legislation they sponsor.

Other formal institutions possessing both internal informational structure and social networks should also exhibit the same conditionality and therefore the same significant interaction between institutional and network effects. Bureaucratic agencies are one example. Individuals working within these agencies accrue information via a combination of research, lobbying, personal experience, and the like. Institutional mechanisms exist that help determine how much and what types of information are gathered. This can lead, for example, to variation in knowledge across policy sectors (Léon et al., 2013). But social networks within and between agencies also provide alternative mechanisms of information delivery. If these networks provide information that is counter to fact, we might see worse policy outcomes. Networks would then diminish the efficacy of institutional access to information. We might also see institutional mechanisms detract from networks. This would be true if the institutional mechanisms were biased, perhaps due to dictates from political appointees heading the agencies. An intelligence analyst being prohibited from researching extremist groups that share some beliefs with the ruling party would be one example of this.

On a more normatively positive note, we might observe a statistically positive interaction between networks and institutions if network-gathered information fills in gaps left by institutional mechanisms. For example, multiple agencies might be involved in setting policy to address climate change, but few institutional mechanisms to coordinate across agencies might exist. Social networks could provide for information transfer across agencies that could improve coordination between them, enabling better policy outcomes. This sort of argument is related to that given in the literature on policy networks as well (e.g., Lubell et al., 2002).

Multiple, interacting sources of information gathering can also play a role in government formation. To address the possibility of forming a coalition, parties who may be in government must assess the costs and benefits of joining with different partners in potentially many configurations comprising ministry allotments and adopted governmental policy. While institutional mechanisms within parties to manage this complex decision certainly exist, they are unlikely to be able to provide all possible useful information. Further, the problem itself is so complex that heuristics are likely to be employed. Social networks between party leaders can not only provide additional information about potentially fruitful coalitions, but can also guide heuristics about how to propose coalitions. Under this logic, we would expect the likelihood of electoral coalitions between parties to be increasing in extant ties between party leaders. We would also expect this relationship to depend on the nature of extant party institutions.

Opportunities

Incentives and information are the two most important mechanisms driving the interaction of institutions and social networks, but changes in opportunities certainly play a role as well. A reduction of opportunities occurs in a sense at the extreme of the incentive and information arguments. At some point incentives to act in some fashion become so strong that one is effectively prohibited from acting in a contrary fashion, or information constraints bind so strongly that the choice to act in a contrary fashion does not seem to be available. At this point we may speak of a reduction in the opportunity to act in that contrary fashion.

Social network membership can produce this reduction in opportunities. Consider first the literature on political dynasties. We know that dynastic candidates have an electoral advantage (Feinstein, 2011) and that politicians in office for more time are more likely to have relatives in office (Dal Bó, Dal Bó, and Snyder, 2009). This might be true due to an incentives argument: being a member of the network corresponding to a political dynasty provides increased incentives to take advantage of electoral institutions that allow one to run for office. There are lots of reasons for this, including easier fundraising and better name recognition. Or it might be true due to an information argument: learning what running for office entails firsthand allows one to more effectively run for office oneself.

At the extreme, though, the argument becomes one about opportunities. When membership in a particular family is required for office holding, one's social network determines the degree to which institutions allowing political contestation will operate. While this might seem extreme for a democracy, replacing family with a religious sect or an ethnic group or a class, all of which may be conceptualized as social networks, should make it clearer that this network-driven reduction in opportunities can occur in democracies as well. This can be true, unfortunately, even on the side of participation. Membership in a network might be necessary to obtain the right or safe access to vote. Network ties might also limit the effect of voting institutions, as in network-driven boycotts of electoral contests or network-specific informal repression, each of which might nullify any institution-based attempt to expand the franchise.

The same reduction in electoral opportunities due to social networks can be observed in government formation. Parties linked together may be constrained by each other's preferences or prior experiences *not* to incorporate certain parties into potential coalitions. Pre-electoral coalitions (Golder, 2006) may be seen in this context as instantiations of networks that constrain government possibilities.

More expansively, the types of parties that form may be constrained by the networks in place in the broader society. While it might be natural for two distinct groups to join together in electoral contestation based on shared preferences, prior disagreements between them, exemplified by a lack of social ties connecting them, may effectively remove that option. Even the nature of salient social cleavages might be affected by social networks. Identity is socially constructed (e.g., McCall and Dasgupta, 2007), and social networks can mediate the development of identity. This in turn means networks can mediate the evolution of identity groups and the cleavages they spawn. Institutions such as power-sharing agreements designed in part to alter the salience of social cleavages, perhaps to reduce the possibility of intrastate conflict, may fail if the networks in place cannot promote changes in the salience of different elements of identity. In sum, social networks can limit opportunities for contestation, presumably granted by electoral institutions, in a variety of ways.

In a similar fashion, networks can limit the range of policies and norms that are available to implement via institutions. Policies or norms that are despised by in-network actors move off the table, as the network-driven cost to adopt them becomes prohibitively high. Similarly, policies and norms associated with out-of-network actors may be prohibited if different networks are poorly connected and their members are in conflict with each other. Further, returning to the topic of legislatures and bureaucracies, a lack of weak ties bridging different groups might not only limit information flow between groups, affecting legislative outcomes in that fashion, but also signal conflict that would make policies developed by one group untenable for adoption by the other. Additional institutions, like LMOs, might encourage ties that not only enhance information flow, but also promote less conflict between groups.

CONCLUSION

Institutions have long played a central role in our understanding of every aspect of democratic society, from participation to electoral contestation to government performance to intra- and interstate conflict. More recently, scholars have recognized the powerful role of social networks in these same contexts. Identifying the similarities between the causal mechanisms underlying the roles of social networks and of institutions raises an important point, though: ignoring either individually *or* the interaction between them introduces bias into our theories and our empirical analyses of their operation.

In this chapter I elaborated on this argument by separating these causal mechanisms into three types: the effects of institutions and networks on incentives, information, and opportunities. In the context of each of these types of mechanism I offered numerous examples of possible significant interactions between the effects of institutions and social networks. This, of course, is just a very small step toward more fully incorporating context-rich interactions between institutions and networks into our theories and empirics, but I believe the importance of these interactions makes it a step worth taking.

As the focus of this chapter has been on democratic institutions, I have stuck to examples from democratic polities—notwithstanding one's characterization of clientelism—but everything said thus far should apply equally well to the burgeoning study of autocratic institutions. For example, Malesky, Schuler, and Tran (2012) study the effect of transparency in legislatures in autocratic regimes and find it has perverse effects, leading, among other things, to reduced participation. The argument in democracies for greater transparency is an informational one, implying that *who*—as specified by networks—gains access to the newly revealed information is important. It should matter similarly who gains access to revealed information from legislatures in autocracies, as these are the individuals who will punish a wayward legislator or potentially limit the amount of punishment that autocratic leaders are able to impose. Thus, as with democratic institutions, understanding the interaction between autocratic institutions and networks should prove vital to parsing the role of institutions within autocracies as well.

References

Alatas, V., Banerjee, A., Chandrasekhar, A. G., Hanna, R., and Olken, B. A. (2014). "Network Structure and the Aggregation of Information: Theory and Evidence from Indonesia." NBER Working Paper No. 18351.

Banerjee, A., Chandrasekhar, A. G., Duflo, E., and Jackson, M. O. (2013). "The Diffusion of Microfinance." *Science* 341 doi:10.1126/science.1236498.

Berardo, R. (2013). "The Coevolution of Perceptions of Procedural Fairness and Link Formation in Self-Organizing Policy Networks." *Journal of Politics* 75(3): 686–700.

Berman, S. (1997). "Civil Society and the Collapse of the Weimar Republic." *World Politics* 49(3): 401–429.

Centola, D., and Macy, M. (2007). "Complex Contagions and the Weakness of Long Ties." *American Journal of Sociology* 113(3): 702–734.

Cho, W. K. T., and Fowler, J. H. (2010). "Legislative Success in a Small World: Social Network Analysis and the Dynamics of Congressional Legislation." *Journal of Politics* 72(1): 124–135.

Clark, W. R., Golder, M., and Golder, S. N. (2012). *Principles of Comparative Politics*. 2d ed. Washington, DC: CQ Press.

Dal Bó, E., Dal Bó, P., and Snyder, J. (2009). "Political Dynasties." *Review of Economic Studies* 76: 115–142.

Dionne, K. Y. (2014). "Social networks, ethnic diversity, and cooperative behavior in rural Malawi." *Journal of Theoretical Politics* (November). doi: 10.1177/0951629814556173.

Eubank, N. (2015). "Ethnicity and Social Network Structure." Working paper.

Fearon, J. D., and Laitin, D. D. (1996). "Explaining Interethnic Cooperation." *American Political Science Review* 90(4): 715–735.

Feinstein, B. D. (2011). "The Dynasty Advantage: Family Ties in Congressional Elections." *Legislative Studies Quarterly* 35(4): 571–598.

Gerber, A. S., Green, D. P., and Larimer, C. W. (2008). "Social Pressure and Voter Turnout: Evidence from a Large-Scale Field Experiment." *American Political Science Review* 102(1): 33–48.

Gibson, J. L. (2001). "Social Networks, Civil Society, and the Prospects for Consolidating Russia's Democratic Transition." *American Journal of Political Science* 45(1): 51–68.

Golder, S. N. (2006). *The Logic of Pre-Electoral Coalition Formation*. Columbus: Ohio State University Press.

Habyarimana, J., Humphreys, M., Posner, D. N., and Weinstein, J. M. (2007). "Why Does Ethnic Diversity Undermine Public Goods Provision?" *American Political Science Review* 101(4): 709–725.

Heaney, M. T., and McClurg, S. D. (2009). "Social Networks and American Politics: Introduction to the Special Issue." *American Politics Research* 37(5): 727–741.

Helmke, G., and Levitsky, S. (2004). "Informal Institutions and Comparative Politics: A Research Agenda." *Perspectives on Politics* 2(4): 725–740.

Huckfeldt, R. R., and Sprague, J. (1995). *Citizens, Politics and Social Communication: Information and Influence in an Election Campaign*. Cambridge, UK: Cambridge University Press.

Knight, J. (1992). *Institutions and Social Conflict*. Cambridge, UK: Cambridge University Press.

Koger, G., Masket, S., and Noel, H. (2009). "Partisan Webs: Information Exchange and Party Networks." *British Journal of Political Science* 39(3): 633–653.

Krehbiel, K. (1991). *Information and Legislative Organization*. Ann Arbor: University of Michigan Press.

Larson, J. M. (2012). "A Failure to Communicate: The Role of Networks in Inter- and Intra-group Cooperation." Working paper.

Larson, J. M. (2014). "Cheating Because They Can: Social Networks and Norm Violators." Working paper.

Léon, G., Ouimet, M., Lavis, J., Grimshaw, J. M., and Gagnon, M.-P. (2013). "Assessing Availability of Scientific Journals, Databases, and Health Library Services in Canadian Health Ministries: A Cross-sectional Study." *Implementation Science* 8(34): 1–26.

Lubell, M., Schneider, M., Scholz, J. T., and Mete, M. (2002). "Watershed Partnerships and the Emergence of Collective Action Institutions." *American Journal of Political Science* 46(1): 148–163.

Malesky, E., Schuler, P., and Tran, A. (2012). "The Adverse Effects of Sunshine: A Field Experiment on Legislative Transparency in an Authoritarian Assembly." *American Political Science Review* 106(4): 762–786.

McAdam, D. (1988). *Freedom Summer*. New York: Oxford University Press.

McCall, C., and Dasgupta, N. (2007). "The Malleability of Men's Gender Self-Concept." *Self and Identity* 6: 173–188.

O'Donnell, G. (1996). "Another Institutionalization: Latin America and Elsewhere." Kellogg Institute Working Paper 222. Notre Dame, IN: Kellogg Institute for International Studies.

Putnam, R. D. (1993). *Making Democracy Work: Civic Traditions in Modern Italy*. Princeton, NJ: Princeton University Press.

Ringe, N., and Victor, J. N. (2013). *Bridging the Information Gap: Legislative Member Organizations as Social Networks in the United States and the European Union*. Ann Arbor: University of Michigan Press.

Rolfe, M. (2012). *Voter Turnout: A Social Theory of Political Participation*. Cambridge, UK: Cambridge University Press.

Siegel, D. A. (2009). "Social Networks and Collective Action." *American Journal of Political Science* 53(1): 122–138.

Siegel, D. A. (2011). "When Does Repression Work? Collective Action in Social Networks." *Journal of Politics* 73(4): 993–1010.

Siegel, D. A. (2013). "Social Networks and the Mass Media." *American Political Science Review* 107(4): 786–805.

Sinclair, B. (2012). *The Social Citizen: Peer Networks and Political Behavior*. Chicago: University of Chicago Press.

Torfason, M. T., and Ingram, P. (2010). "The Global Rise of Democracy: A Network Account." *American Sociological Review* 75(3): 355–377.

Wang, H. (2000). "Informal Institutions and Foreign Investment in China." *Pacific Review* 13(4): 525–556.

CHAPTER 35

......

INSTITUTIONS AND POLICY NETWORKS IN EUROPE

......

MANUEL FISCHER

INTRODUCTION

......

INSTITUTIONS influence the structure of policy networks (Lubell et al., 2012), as they provide actors with opportunities and constraints for negotiation and cooperation (Ostrom, 1990, 2005). Policy networks are a specific subtype of political networks. They describe the networks of (mostly collective) actors dealing with the production or implementation of public policies. Nodes of such networks are interest groups, political parties, administrative units, experts, and other actors involved in policy processes. These actors are typically linked by ties of cooperation, information exchange, or conflict. The study of policy networks allows us to understand the production of policy outcomes.

This chapter reviews the European literature on the relationships among institutional contexts, institutional power, and policy networks. Given the more than fifty independent countries in Europe, policy networks there evolve within many different institutional settings, some of which change over time. Changes of institutional contexts are mostly due to the transformation of state structures in Eastern European countries, as well as the process of European integration. This is not to say that institutional differences and developments are always taken into account explicitly in studies of European policy networks, or that all relevant studies compare policy networks in different institutional settings. Actually, quite the contrary is true: most European studies on political networks focus on one country and are not comparative by design (for exceptions, see, e.g., Bressers et al., 1996; John and Cole, 1998, 2000; Kriesi et al., 2006; Moschitz and Stolze, 2009; Braun, 2012). Also, the relationship between institutions and networks is obviously not specific to Europe. However, given the high diversity and evolution, an institutional focus is helpful when discussing European policy networks.

More specifically, this chapter is structured along two dimensions. A first part discusses the institutional context of a country or a policy sector. On the country level, majoritarian or consensual political systems, the system of interest intermediation, the type of multilevel governance, and the level of integration in the European Union (EU) are expected to influence policy networks. As institutional conditions often vary between policy sectors, I further discuss sectoral context conditions, such as liberalization processes of industry sectors or the opportunity structures provided by institutional venues such as working groups and committees for the creation of policy networks. A second part of this chapter discusses the influence of institutional power on policy networks. Taking a micro-level perspective, state actors (including government actors and the administration), as opposed to nonstate actors such as interest groups, political parties, or think tanks, have an institutionalized influence on and a formal role in policy processes. This again is especially crucial in a European context, as the very role of state actors differs between countries.

A few caveats apply. First, the chapter focuses on the influence of institutions on policy networks, but is unable to take into account further elements of the complex, diverse, and evolving literature on different types of political networks in Europe. For example, it explicitly excludes networks among individuals, related to protest movements (Baldassari and Diani, 2007), which is dealt with in the chapter in this book on social movements and networks, or legislative networks among members of parliament (Fowler, 2006; Kirkland and Gross, 2012; Ringe et al., 2013), which is scarce for European countries, and is dealt with in the chapter in this book on legislative networks. Furthermore, a vibrant part of the European literature on policy networks deals with the EU (Börzel and Heard-Lauréote, 2009; Henning, 2009). This literature is dealt with in the chapter in this book on networks and the EU. In addition, studies dealing with transnational or cross-border networks (e.g., Kern and Bulkeley, 2009; Svensson, 2015) are explicitly excluded from the discussion, given their international dimension. Second, theoretical and conceptual discussions on policy networks are important and manifold in the European literature on policy networks. These are often related to different intellectual traditions in different countries, most prominently in Germany and the United Kingdom. The respective literature includes the influential idea that networks should be seen as an alternative to, or a hybrid between, forms of social organization along markets or hierarchies, wherein negotiation and exchange predominate (Powell, 1990; Williamson, 1991; Mayntz, 1993). Furthermore, and relatedly, important conceptual discussions include the one between the formal or heuristic use of the network concept (Dowding, 1995; Marsh and Smith, 2000; Dowding, 2001; Christopoulos, 2008), or between the network governance and the policy network analysis schools (Fawcett and Daugbjerg, 2012). Third, the direction of causality between institutions and policy networks does not exclusively lead from the former to the latter. Networks have also been described as being themselves institutions that allow actors to solve coordination problems (Blom-Hansen, 1997; Ansell, 2006; Sandström and Carlsson, 2008). Even more important, informal networks might give rise to formal institutions (see, e.g., the chapter in this book on networks and the EU), actors might rely on network contacts to construct institutions, or networks can affect the (institutional) context (see the "dia-lectical approach," e.g., Marsh and Smith, 2000; Toke and Marsh, 2003). I do not take up these discussions here, but refer to the existing discussions on the distinctive ways of using the network concept (Kenis and Schneider, 1991; Rhodes and Marsh, 1992; Börzel, 1998; Marsh, 1998; Pappi and Henning, 1998; Adam and Kriesi, 2007; Börzel, 2011).

The goal of this chapter is to review the literature on how institutions influence policy networks in Europe. Whenever possible and relevant, I mention the types of nodes and ties that define the respective network, as well as the means of data gathering. The review focuses on more recent (after 2000, with some exceptions) journal publications (with some exceptions). While it is by no means exhaustive and not based on a systematic procedure for selecting pieces of literature, I believe it includes the most relevant, recent publications related to institutions and policy networks in Europe and provides an over-view of substantive issues and methodological and theoretical approaches related to the study of policy networks in Europe.

INSTITUTIONAL CONTEXT AND POLICY NETWORKS IN EUROPE

This first section discusses the influence of the country- or sector-level institutional con-text on the structure of policy networks. The respective literature is based on the argu-ment that given types of institutional structures provide actors with opportunities to form given types of networks. More specifically, this section discusses majoritarian and consensual political systems, systems of interest intermediation, multilevel governance and European integration, democratic transition processes, liberalization processes, and venues of policy processes. Some of these influence factors are rather constant, while others change over time and across policy sectors within countries.

Majoritarian versus Consensual Systems

On the most general level of different types of democracies (Lijphart, 1999), and with a broad cross-country comparative perspective, Adam and Kriesi (2007; Kriesi et al., 2006) argue that the national institutional structure influences the structure of the respective policy networks (for an early, similar argument, see also Atkinson and Coleman, 1989). The authors expect consensual democracies with power-sharing institutions, such as Switzerland or Germany, to produce policy networks with frag-mented power and cooperative interactions between actors. By contrast, majoritar-ian democracies such as France or the United Kingdom should have policy networks with a concentration of power in the hands of a few actors, as well as rather conflic-tive relations between actors. The comparison of policy networks in three policy sectors (agriculture, EU integration, and immigration) in Spain, the United Kingdom, France, Italy, Germany, Switzerland, and the Netherlands shows that the empirical observations mostly correspond to the expected patterns. The major exception is British policy networks, which are quite fragmented and resemble more the networks of consensus democracies than of other majoritarian democracies (Kriesi et al., 2006). The authors focus on network measures such as block models, interpreted as coalitions, as well as within-coalition and across-coalition densities of cooperation and conflict relations. These measures are relatively simple but straightforward to interpret, as they indicate subgroups in the network, as well as the intensity of interaction within and across these subgroups (see also Fischer, 2014, 2015). Such generalizations and comparisons on the level of entire countries are important, as they allow us to relate macro-level formal institutional structures to more informal aspects of actors' interactions in policy networks. The combination of and influences between both elements are crucial to fully understand the functioning of political systems at the macro level. Yet as acknowledged (and partly examined) by the authors, both institutional contexts and related configurations of policy networks also vary considerably from one policy sector to the other, depending on the sectoral context (e.g., John and Cole, 2000; Kriesi et al., 2006).

Systems of Interest Intermediation

One aspect of consensual and majoritarian systems that differs between policy sectors is the system of interest intermediation. The European literature has traditionally made an important link between corporatist or pluralist types of interest intermediation and policy networks to describe relations between society and the state (Atkinson and Coleman, 1989; Knoke et al., 1996). In this tradition, different forms of policy networks have been associated with types of corporatism, clientelism, or pluralism (Schneider, 1992; van Waarden, 1992).

Corporatist traditions remain important in many European countries, and the respective processes are examined based on the structure of policy networks. For example, Svensson and Öberg (2005; Öberg and Svensson, 2010) analyze the network interactions in the coordinated market economy of Sweden, where the government, unions, and employers are involved in formal negotiations over economic and labor policies. Based on a survey among individual representatives of seventy collective actors, they show that state agencies play a central role in the influence network, but that the strongest, reciprocated relations still exist between unions and employers. Also, Beyers' (2002) analysis of Belgian policy networks (actor-event participation networks, assessed through 343 face-to-face interviews with public and private actors) suggests that access to domestic policymakers is still influenced by corporatist traditions; that is, actors traditionally defending specific interests have better access than actors lobbying for diffuse interests. On the contrary, a qualitative case study on spatial planning policy networks in Belgium shows that a regionalization of competences led to a transformation from centralized, corporatist arrangements to new forms of more decentralized and multi-level governance networks (De Rynck and Voets, 2006).

As with other institutional context conditions, the influence of (the decline of) corporatist types of interest intermediation is not always easy to isolate. For example, the influence of different types of changes in the macro-level institutional structure on the policy network in Switzerland over thirty years is examined by Fischer et al. (2009; Sciarini, 2014), who observe a decreasing centrality of key interest groups over time. Overall, while the concept of corporatism might have lost importance in the scholarly discussion, the interactions of different types of societal interests and state actors remains an important issue, not least in the context of European integration (discussed later in the chapter). As demonstrated by these studies, rather simple network indicators, such as the centrality of given types of actors, the intensity of ties between actor types, or access of actors to specific venues, can help to disentangle the more and more diverse, complex and informal relations of interest intermediation.

Multilevel Governance

Multilevel governance encompasses different aspects. On the one hand, the degree to which a state is organized in a decentralized or federalist manner is a rather constant attribute of a given country. This aspect is included in the consensual type of democratic systems as dealt with by Adam and Kriesi (2007; Kriesi et al. 2006). On the other hand, the degree to which the existence of multiple levels of decision-making affects policy networks is also sector-specific. Examples of policy network studies that examine the influence of (the interplay between) different levels of decision-making in given policy sectors abound.

First, the influence of a policy sector being (co-)regulated between a country and the EU on policy networks have been examined. The EU context is expected to influence policy networks by redistributing actors' resources and opening up new access points to decision-making (Adam and Kriesi, 2007). One of the important, early studies on the influence of multilevel governance institutions on policy networks deals with EU agricultural policy (Pappi and Henning, 1999). Based on interviews with interest groups and government actors on the national as well as EU levels, the authors find that national farmer organizations adapt their lobbying strategies as they create network contacts to both national governments as well as European-level interest groups. Not only access, but also pressure from the EU environment can influence national policy networks. Cisar and Navratil (2014) conclude that access to EU financial resources consolidates the cooperation network activities among Czech nongovernmental organizations (NGOs): intensifying their network contacts is one condition to meet their policy goals and is explicitly required as a strategy by the EU funding body. The authors' analysis is based on survey data on the cooperation and communication networks among 101 NGOs advocating for the environment, women's rights, human rights, or workers' rights. Besides societal actors, national state actors also adapt their strategies. In

Europeanized policy sectors, state actors in Switzerland are especially active in creating collaboration ties to actors that are critical of European integration in order to include them in the policy process (Fischer and Sciarini, 2013). The authors analyze the development of the network over time and focus on two subsequent networks of collaboration relations among the twenty-two collective actors dealing with the bilateral treaty on the free movement of persons between Switzerland and the EU, assessed through semidirected interviews. In a similar vein, Sciarini et al. (2004; Fischer et al., 2002) show that state actors have higher betweenness centralities (Freeman, 1978) in collaboration networks dealing with so-called Europeanized policy processes than in domestic ones, whereas the contrary is true for other actors such as interest groups and political parties. Their network data on three different policy processes were gathered through semidirected interviews with sixty-five actors.

Second, a devolution of competencies to regional levels also affects the respective policy networks. For example, De Rynck and Voets (2006) discuss the transformation of Belgian spatial planning networks from corporatist to more open networks as a consequence of the regionalization of the respective competencies. Based on a qualitative case analysis, they schematically reconstruct the network between governments and corporatist actors at different levels. However, as mentioned previously, the institutional influence of types of multilevel decision-making often interacts with other contexts. A comparative analysis of the domestic coordination of EU policies in Belgium, France, and the Netherlands suggests that network structures of information exchange and collaboration substantively derive from formal (non)federalist structures. Analyzing survey data on networks among government agencies, ministerial cabinets, and political parties, the authors find that intergovernmental relations do not only depend on the question of whether a country has federalist (Belgium) or more centralized (Netherlands, France) institutions, but also on the role of parties, the functioning and organization of the executive, and the position of the parliament in the political system (Bursens et al., 2014). In a similar vein, Jordana et al. (2012) find that the same type of EU cohesion policy program leads to different types of implementation networks in Spanish regions, depending on different roles of government actors and levels of social capital.

The institutional context also has consequences for the policy network structure at the purely local level. Ingold (2014) compares seven policy networks dealing with implementation processes in the domain of land use and protection policies in Swiss mountain regions. The respective networks include a minimum of fifteen and a maximum of thirty-nine actors, and network ties are defined by collaboration relations assessed through surveys. The author argues that local actors tend to be better integrated in the collaboration network in bottom-up-designed implementation processes, led by private and civil-society actors, as compared to top-down processes, even though the latter provide formal participation rules for local actors. In addition, at the level of cities, differences between policy sectors seem to matter. John and Cole (2000) conclude that institutions have a stronger influence on networks in secondary education than in economic development policies, because different national state traditions are more prevalent in the former than in the latter. The authors compare two city-level networks in the United Kingdom to two city-level networks in France, based on qualitative case studies. Whereas education policy networks in the United Kingdom are composed of head teachers, chairs of boards of school governors, and bureaucrats, the French policy network is more state-centered and composed of elites from the central state and the region. Finally, at least on the local level, the institutional context does not always affect policy networks. De Vries (2008) finds no effect of various institutional reforms and experiments in the form of public-private partnerships and interactive policy processes on the composition of local policy networks in the Netherlands. The study covers more than fifteen years and is based on surveys at three different time points. It finds that the local policy networks still correspond to the core-periphery structure, with state actors in the center and civil-society actors on the periphery.

Overall, the influence of European integration on the respective policy networks appears to be confirmed by the respective studies: New levels of decision-making provide new opportunities or constraints to different types of actors, and their respective positions and behavior (in terms of centrality) in the policy networks are affected. The influence of multilevel structures on policy networks within countries is less clear and seems to strongly interact with other country- and sector-level institutional factors. Whether all combinations of different types of (institutional) contexts can always be included in the respective research designs is questionable, but being explicit about the context specificity of the respective policy network seems important. Further, new methods of multilevel statistical network models could provide an important tool for examining cross-level processes in more detail. Overall, the understanding of complex cross-level networks, influenced by different institutional contexts at different levels, remains a major challenge.

Democratization and European Integration in Eastern Europe

As suggested previously, the institutional context influencing policy networks can change over time, and the networks are expected to change accordingly. Some of the most important changes in terms of macro-level state institutions in Europe are those in Eastern European countries related to the transition of former communist, Soviet (-related) states to more democratic political systems and, for some, their EU accession. Observed effects of the transition from autocratic to democratic regimes on policy networks are manifold.

For example, a study of the Russian city of Novosibirsk (based on interviews with about one hundred elite representatives) finds that already in 1997, city-level elite networks included many private actors and thus looked very similar to Western European elite networks (Hughes et al., 2002). McMenamin (2004) studies informal networks between businesspeople and politicians in Poland, which in a postcommunist context are expected to be more important than formal business associations. Some 194 businesspeople representing 144 businesses were interviewed and asked how well they knew politicians. Against expectations, the study finds that the knowledge relations between businesspeople and politicians are not based on clientelism and businesspeople's loyalty to political parties, but are promiscuous. Forest policy networks in Estonia, Latvia, and Lithuania are also affected by the transition from the Soviet system to a more democratic one. Whereas Estonia and Latvia liberalized their forest sector, the one in Lithuania remains closer to the Soviet organization. The respective networks in the first two countries are described as participatory, well-integrated, and heterogeneous, whereas the network in Lithuania is still dominated by a high number of state-related forest organizations. The study is based on stakeholder and expert interviews as well as officially available documents (Lazdinis et al., 2004). Moschitz and Stolze (2009) examine organic farming policy networks in eleven European countries based on face-to-face interviews with thirteen to twenty-six organizational actors per country. Explicitly comparing Eastern to Western European countries, they find that networks are generally smaller and less dense in the former than in the latter. The authors explain this finding by noting the short history of organic farming in the Eastern European countries, influenced by their adoption of EU legislation since their accession in 2004.

One important aspect of the transition of Eastern European countries is their integration into the EU. Jurje (2013) studies the role of Romanian state actors in the accession process to the EU and finds that due to preaccession conditionality mechanisms and their privileged access to EU policymakers, state actors are highly central in the respective policy networks, whereas their centrality decreases after accession. Her analysis is based on interviews with key organizational actors in the sectors of immigration and asylum policy, social assistance policy, and education policy. But at least in an Eastern European transitions context, EU integration has not always been found to affect policy networks. Palne Kovacs et al. (2004) study the effects of EU integration on the cooperation networks and related learning processes in regional development in Hungary. The authors interviewed thirty organizational actors from the national, regional, and local levels of policymaking. Despite EU initiatives for strengthening the regional level and its participation in national-level decision-making, their analysis shows that actors from the three levels are still only very weakly connected.

In addition to the cross-cutting influence of different country- and sector-specific institutional contexts, studies dealing with the democratic transitions and EU integration of Eastern European countries raise an additional challenge: the change of the institutional context over time. Comparisons of networks at two or more different time points, or the analysis of longitudinal data and the respective evolution of policy networks, can be appropriate strategies to deal with this challenge. However, gathering data at different points in time, or even on the past, is most often costly and difficult to do in one single research project.

Liberalization of Industry Sectors

Related to European integration and the internationalization of the economy, another important change is taking place in many European countries. Former monopolies in sectors such as telecommunications, railways, and electricity have been destroyed and the respective sectors liberalized during the last three decades. Institutional change thus happened at an ideational level, affecting the conditions for market behavior and the ideational resources of actors. These processes of liberalization are expected to lead to changes in the networks among political authorities, regulators, and state-owned and private companies (e.g., Majone, 1997). For example, Jordana and Sancho (2005) study the process of market opening in Spain's telecommunications sector. The respective networks consist of collective actors such as political parties, public bodies, and different types of private actors. The authors assess the network of perceived influence ties between actors through a survey. The comparison of two networks, one before and one after the liberalization, shows that the network after liberalization was denser, but still included a similar set of main actors, with the same few actors in highly central positions. The authors conclude that a more successful liberalization would have required a network that was more open to new competitors and less centralized in terms of power. Contrary to the Spanish case, a study on the transformation of the Swiss telecommunications sector (Fischer et al., 2012) finds that despite an overall decrease in network ties, local closure happens between actors with similar roles in the new governance structure, especially operators, as well as sector-specific regulating agencies and more general regulating agencies. Furthermore, new actors such as regulatory agencies, coregulators, and new operators were quickly integrated into the governance network of Swiss telecommunications. Fischer et al.'s analysis is based on statistical longitudinal models for network data and includes three subsequent networks of collaboration relations among twenty-three actors, assessed through semidirected interviews and surveys. Furthermore, when studying liberalization processes, the analysis of networks represents a useful approach for assessing the actual independence of the newly formed "independent" regulatory agencies from other actors (Ingold et al., 2013; Maggetti et al., 2013). Based on networks of influence and reputational power, Ingold et al. (2013) find that the main regulatory agency in the Swiss telecommunications domain is independent from telecommunication operators and policymakers, but is influenced by other regulating bodies. The network of influence relations is assessed through a survey and includes twenty-five organizational actors.

The studies reviewed indicate that liberalization processes do not always affect the respective policy networks to the same extent. This again underlines the importance of analyzing networks over time in order to be able to understand the influence of the changing institutional context. Further, the network concept proves important to evaluate the functioning of new governance arrangements in liberalized economies.

Venue Participation as Institutional Opportunity Structures

While country-level generalizations might hide sectoral differences, sectoral generalizations might hide differences between single policy processes. However, institutional characteristics also vary on the process level. For example, Leifeld and Schneider (2012) conceive of policy process venues as institutional opportunity structures that allow actors to develop collaboration contacts. Joint participation in arenas such as policy process working groups or parliamentary committees facilitates communication and thereby reduces transaction costs. In a study on the technical issue of toxic chemicals policy in Germany, Leifeld and Schneider (2012) show that coparticipation in institutional venues of the policy process, such as policy committees, even absorbs the effect of actors' preference similarity on their probability to exchange political and scientific information in a policy network. The respective study is based on interview data with thirty organizational actors. Further studies show that the specific characteristics of institutional venues seem to matter for how well institutional opportunity structures work. Fischer and Sciarini (2016) compare collaboration networks in eleven different policy sectors in Switzerland based on interview data with individual representatives of twenty to twenty-five organizational actors per process. Their analysis suggests that if a venue is important in terms of its influence on the final policy output, this increases the effect of venue coparticipation on collaboration among political actors (Fischer and Sciarini, 2016). Kriesi and Jegen (2001) emphasize the importance of policy venues and arenas for the formation of cooperative ties within the pro-ecology and pro-economy coalitions in the Swiss nuclear policy sector. They analyze the respective policy sector on the national level as well as in six cantons based on ties of close collaboration, assessed through interviews with about 240 individual actors. In a reanalysis of five policy networks at both local and national levels, dealing with both decision-making and implementation, Ingold and Leifeld (2016) find that actors participating in many institutional venues are perceived as especially powerful by other actors. Their explanation for this finding is that institutional access confers possibilities of policy influence to actors (Ingold and Leifeld, 2016). While the effect of institutional opportunity structures on policy network ties appears to be confirmed, the exact mechanism behind it needs more examination. The qualitative study of what exactly happens in venues is one promising approach, as well as the differentiation among different types of policy venues depending on their incentives to create policy network contacts (Fischer and Leifeld, 2015).

Furthermore, coparticipation in institutional venues of the policy process is sometimes used as a direct indicator of a network contact. Contrary to the literature that discusses the influence of coparticipation on collaboration, this approach directly operationalizes coparticipation as the network tie of interest. For example, Hirschi et al. (2013) analyze different scenarios of Swiss agricultural policy in the context of market liberalization. They assess the participation patterns of twenty to thirty actors in different venues of the respective policy processes. Relying on this type of data has the advantage that the data are rather easily available from documents. The Actor-Process Event Scheme (APES, Serdült and Hirschi, 2004) facilitates the systematic representation of the respective data. The respective data can also be analyzed as two-mode networks, with links representing actors' venue participation (see also Beyers, 2002).

The Role of State Actors
in Policy Networks in Europe

This second section discusses the role of state actors (government actors at different levels as well as administrative actors) in European policy networks. Even if the classical boundaries between the different functions of state and private actors have become "fluent and irrelevant" over time (Laumann and Knoke, 1987, 381; Knoke et al., 1996), state actors are special. On the one hand, their decisions are considered binding in society and are backed by the possibility of the legitimate use of force (Coleman and Perl, 1999; Adam and Kriesi, 2007). On the other hand, state actors have a crucial influence on the design of policy processes wherein decisions are made. Accordingly, state actors are often perceived as especially powerful in policy networks, as suggested in two studies on ties of influence perception, both comparing several policy domains and different levels of decision-making (Ingold and Leifeld, 2016; Fischer and Sciarini, 2015). Furthermore, differentiating between state and nonstate actors seems particularly important in the European tradition of policy networks. For example, the metaphorical use of the term "policy network" in the British literature (Dowding, 1995; Börzel, 1998) is mainly aimed at describing the specific relations between the state and society. Bressers and O'Toole (1998) define a policy network as the "pattern of relationships between a governmental authority and a set of target groups."

State Actors as Networking Targets

In an early key contribution to the field, Stokman and Zeggelink (1996; Stokman and Berveling, 1998) model the structure of policy networks based on a key driver: actors' resource dependency and their desire to gain access to powerful others. State actors often are "powerful others," and actors aim at creating network ties to them, deliver relevant information to them, or lobby for their preferences. Another early study, by König and Bräuninger (1998), examines the establishment of policy network contacts in the German labor policy domain, based on a survey among 126 organizations. They show that whereas the similarity of policy preferences is the basic predictor of the establishment of policy contacts, the "neo-institutional" aspect is important, too: controlling for preference similarity, policy actors tend to establish contacts with formal policymakers, presumably because the latter have the final vote on public policies. This finding is most important for networks of information exchange, but less for networks of exchanging favors and support. Similarly, Leifeld and Schneider (2012) study the German toxic chemicals policy sector and show that actors have a strong tendency to deliver political as well as scientific information to state actors. Their statistical network analysis (exponential random graph model) is based on data about a set of thirty collective actors, and network ties are relations of information exchange between actors. The same trends show up in a longitudinal analysis of Swiss climate policy networks, in which state actors are strongly lobbied during the decision-making phase, but not during implementation of policies (Ingold and Fischer, 2014). This study is based on interview and survey data on collaboration networks among thirty-four collective actors at three points in time. The important role of government actors in the German climate policy networks is also analyzed by Foljanty-Jost and Jacob (2004). State actors are central in network ties of cooperation, information exchange, support, and conflict, as assessed through interviews with fifty-three actors. Similar results are reported by Bursens et al. (2014), who study informal political-administrative networks dealing with the domestic coordination of EU politics. They show how societal actors target policymakers in order to influence government positions in Belgium, France, and the Netherlands. Comparing the indegree, outdegree, and betweenness centralization of networks of information exchange and collaboration in the three countries (elite survey with over one hundred actors in each country), they find that informal network practices substantively deviate from formal procedures. In Belgium and in the context of the increasing importance of the EU level of decision-making, interest groups try to diversify their strategies and establish information exchange network ties at both levels, but few are successful in doing so, and specific interests still have privileged network access to state actors (Beyers, 2002). The respective study is based on interviews with 343 private and public actors at both the Belgian and European levels. Beyers and Braun (2014) examine how coalitions among groups, and the network position of interest groups within and between coalitions, shape access to policymakers. Their results (based on 135 interviews) suggest that access to state administration is favored if actors have information exchange and collaboration ties that bridge different coalitions. Further, state-administrative actors in the domain of public health were found to be the main targets to whom actors deliver healthcare-related information in the United Kingdom (Oliver et al., 2015).

State Actors as Networking Activists and Brokers

Studies observe that besides being preferential targets for network contacts, state actors are particularly active in creating network ties. Particularly in the presence of international obligations to act, such as in the case of immigration or climate policy, state actors have strong incentives to actively look for support from nonstate actors, either already during the international negotiations or during the implementation of the policy (Fischer and Sciarini, 2013; Ingold and Fischer, 2014). Both studies are based on the longitudinal analysis of collaboration networks measured at several time points (twenty-three and thirty-four collective actors, respectively), with data gathered through face-to-face interviews and surveys with representatives of collective actors. A comparative study of four municipal employment policy networks in Denmark also underlines the importance of municipal administrative actors in terms of inclusion of nonstate actors. Still, the respective networks often have a rather hierarchical form; that is, they are dominated by municipal actors themselves (Damgaard, 2006). This study is based on qualitative interviews with twenty-six municipality and private actors. Research on individual bureaucrats and local managers in the United Kingdom, based on surveys among several hundred individuals, shows their activity in interacting with other actors such as MPs, other levels of government, or local interest associations (O'Toole et al., 2007; Walker et al., 2007).

Usually, however, state actors' active roles in policy networks are related to brokerage. State actors can act as brokers between different types of economic interests, otherwise opposing coalitions, different levels of decision-making, or different policy sectors. The idea of state actors creating contacts between opposing economic interests has already been touched upon in relation to the identification of different types of interest intermediation systems and their typical network forms, where state actors would relate to both employers and labor unions (Schneider, 1992). In Swedish labor market policy, state agencies play a crucial role in the coordination among peak organizations (Svensson and Öberg, 2005). The respective study is also based on a survey among individual representatives of seventy collective actors. With respect to other types of coalitions, Ingold and Varone (2012; Ingold, 2011) identify a center political party and an environmental administrative agency as actors able to mediate between opposing coalitions in Swiss climate policymaking. Brokers are identified based on structural equivalence of conflict ties as well as on betweenness centralities in the collaboration network, and the study is based on fifty face-to-face interviews with thirty-four key actors in the respective policy domain. The importance of brokerage ("bridge building") has also been emphasized by a study of Norwegian implementation networks of the European Water Framework Directive (Hovik and Hanssen, 2014). The more complex a network is in terms of including different types of actors and opposing interests, the more network managers tend to play the role of bridge builders. This study is based on surveys among members and managers of Norwegian water boards. It does not empirically measure network ties, but focuses on different types of strategies of actors in the network. Cross-level brokerage seems to be more tricky. Ernstson et al. (2010) discuss the findings of several case studies on urban ecosystem management in Stockholm and illustrate the need for scale-crossing brokers to connect different ecosystem scales. However, no actor currently occupies this crucial position in the ecosystem management network of Stockholm. By contrast, Swiss administrative actors at several levels play a crucial role in creating vertical cross-level interactions. This result is suggested by Hirschi (2010), who compares the development of collaboration networks involved in the planning and organization of two regional parks. His study is based on surveys among thirty-six and thirty-eight collective actors, respectively. Finally, various sectors can be connected by brokers. Papadopoulou et al. (2011) emphasize the role of state-administrative actors in representing and connecting different policy sectors ("administrative inter-sectorality") in Greek rural development projects, despite their overall weak standing in the respective power hierarchies in the networks. Their study is based on interviews with actors identified as being part of different types of projects (sixteen actors per network). Similarly, in a qualitative case study, Le Galès (2001) emphasizes the crucial role of mayors in French cities' policy networks, for both sectoral and cross-sectoral coordination. Somewhat contrary to all these studies, Edelenbos et al. (2012) find that government actors are doing worse than external network managers in terms of connecting policy networks. Finally, if they are not occupying brokerage roles themselves, bureaucratic state actors have been shown to create ties with actors occupying broker roles (Beyers and Braun, 2014). The respective analysis is based on interviews with representatives of 135 NGOs, labor unions, and business organizations, as well as elected and unelected officials.

Meta-Governance of Policy Networks

Finally, an important strand of the European policy network literature is related to the idea of brokerage in networks, but takes a broader approach. It deals with the role of state actors related to their capacity for meta-governance of networks or network management (Klijn et al., 1995; Kickert et al., 1997; Klijn, 2005; Provan and Kenis, 2008; Sörensen and Torfing, 2009; Klijn et al., 2010; Verweij et al., 2013; Van Meerkerk et al., 2015; Raab et al., 2015). The network governance literature is based on the idea that some actors can attempt to manage the interdependent relations in order to promote joint problem solving in policymaking. For reasons of resource endowment and legitimacy, this role is most often conferred on state actors (although not exclusively), or state actors are expected to have a specific interest in active network management, as they depend on the networks to govern policy processes (Klijn et al., 1995). Network management or meta-governance can be broadly defined as the capacity of the state to steer networks by influencing the context within which they function to ensure that its outcomes correspond with its broader interests (Kickert et al., 1997; Adam and Kriesi, 2007; Daugbjerg and Fawcett, 2015). It seeks to steer by initiation and facilitation of interaction processes, brokering and mediating conflicts, and reallocation of resources (Kickert et al., 1997; Klijn, 2005; Adam and Kriesi, 2007). A number of intervening factors can influence the success of network management strategies, such as the number and heterogeneity of actors in the network.

A lot of work on this issue is theoretical, but there are also empirical illustrations of the effects of network management. For example, Van Meerkerk et al. (2015) study the Dutch water sector based on a survey among two hundred stakeholders and managers of complex water projects. The analysis shows that connective management of linking actors from different sectors and different levels of decision-making by network managers influences actors' perceptions of the democratic governance process, which again has a positive influence on network outputs such as innovation or problem-solving (Van Meerkerk et al., 2015). A meta-analysis of environmental projects in the Netherlands finds that the network managers' ability to connect the important actors has a beneficial effect on the perception of project outcomes by actors (Klijn et al., 2010). Daugbjerg and Fawcett (2015) compare farming and land use policy networks in Sweden and Denmark (plus Australia and the United States) and find that the role of the state in network governance, together with the level of inclusiveness of the network, influences both input and output legitimacy. Their analysis is based on the comparison of several qualitative case studies.

This strand of the literature has developed compelling theoretical arguments and has tested them in various contexts. Most of this work, however, is based on a metaphorical use of the network concept—that is, on the assessment of policy networks as groups of actors responsible for the management of a given resource or policy—but relations in these networks have usually not been explicitly measured. Combining these theoretical arguments with explicit measurements of network ties would allow us to answer important questions about the network positions and related strategies of network managers and about the influence of network management strategies on the structure of policy networks.

Conclusions and Avenues for Further Research

Institutions have an important influence on the structure of policy networks (Lubell et al., 2012), as they provide actors with opportunities for and constraints on negotiation and cooperation (Ostrom, 1990, 2005). Given the institutional diversity and ongoing transformations, the European context provides a particularly interesting setting for studying the influence of institutions on policy networks. Policy networks describe the diverse types of interactions among actors in processes of political decision-making and policy implementation. Understanding the influence of institutions on policy networks is crucial for the design of effective and democratically anchored policymaking. In addition, studying both more formal aspects of institutional context and institutional power together with more informal aspects of policy networks allows for a more complete understanding of the functioning of policymaking. Policymaking is inherently relational, as it implies processes of negotiations and compromise finding among different types of actors, as well as the exchange of resources and information. These relational processes are at the core of democratic decision-making, and they are influenced by the institutional context in which they evolve.

This review focuses on two elements related to the institutional context and its influence on policy networks. First, studies of the influence of country- and sector-level institutions on the structure of policy networks discuss the influence of consensual versus majoritarian democracies, corporatist systems of interest intermediation, multiple levels of governance, degrees of EU integration, processes of liberalization and democratization, and policy-process-specific venues on policy networks. Second, given their formal decision-making power, state actors often play a specific role in policy networks, as networking targets, brokers, or network managers. Both institutional aspects are obviously related, as the type of macro-institutional structure influences the role state actors play in policy networks. For example, in a tradition of state-led corporatism, state actors occupy brokerage roles in the respective policy networks (Svensson and Öberg, 2005), or they are especially active in reaching out to other actors due to the pressures of Europeanization (Fischer and Sciarini, 2013).

The literature reviewed is based on different types of nodes and ties, different countries and policy sectors, different methods of data gathering (surveys, document analysis, interviews, etc.), and different methods of analysis (from qualitative case studies to statistical network models). Yet within this diversity, a rather small set of simple network concepts has proved most popular. Many of the studies reviewed in this chapter rely on indicators such as the number and types of network members, the network densities within and across groups, and measures of actors' degree and betweenness centralities. While these concepts might not capture all the complex and interesting details of network-related behavior of actors, they have the advantage of being straightforward to interpret and rather easily understandable to non-network specialists.

How institutional differences and transformations affect the incentives of actors to resort to more complex network-related types of behavior such as reciprocity, the establishment of transitive ties, bonding and bridging structures (Berardo and Scholz, 2010), homophily, or preferential attachment is certainly one of the directions that future work should explore. Furthermore, the potential and need for more comparative research designs (both over time and across countries and policy sectors) to establish the influence of institutions on policy networks are evident. However, such efforts are complicated by the costs of data gathering over time or language differences between European countries.

Finally, a review of policy networks in Europe implicitly rests on the assumption that there is something specific about policy networks in Europe, as compared to elsewhere. Given the institutional diversity and transformations in Europe, a focus on the influence of institutions on policy networks seems particularly interesting in this context. This is not to say that institutions have no influence on policy networks in other parts of the world, but the fact that European scholars deal with the implicitly top-down concept of "network management" (e.g., Klijn, 2005), while US scholars examine "self-organizing networks" (e.g., Feiock and Scholz, 2010), might be exemplary of cultural differences between the two sides of the Atlantic.

Acknowledgments

Thanks go to Dimitris Christopoulos, Karin Ingold, Philip Leifeld, Kathryn Oliver, and Paul Thurner for their feedback on earlier versions of this chapter.

References

Adam, S., and Kriesi, H. (2007). "The Network Approach." In *Theories of the Policy Process*, edited by Paul A. Sabatier, pp. 129–154. Boulder, CO: Westview Press.

Ansell, C. (2006). "Network Institutionalism." In *The Oxford Handbook of Political Institutions*, edited by Sarah A. Binder, R. A. W. Rhodes, and Bert A. Rockman, pp. 75–89. Oxford: Oxford University Press.

Atkinson, M. M., and Coleman, W. D. (1989). "Strong States and Weak States: Sectoral Policy Networks in Advanced Capitalist Economies." *British Journal of Political Science* 19(1): 47–67.

Baldassari, D., and Diani, M. (2007). "The Integrative Power of Civic Networks." *American Journal of Sociology* 113(3): 735–780.

Berardo, R., and Scholz, J. T. (2010). "Self-Organizing Policy Networks: Risk, Partner Selection and Cooperation in Estuaries." *American Journal of Political Science* 54(3): 632–649.

Beyers, J. (2002). "Gaining and Seeking Access: The European Adaptation of Domestic Interest Associations." *European Journal of Political Research* 41: 585–612.

Beyers, J., and Braun, C. (2014). "Ties That Count: Explaining Interest Group Access to Policymakers." *Journal of Public Policy* 34(1): 93–121.

Blom-Hansen, J. (1997). "A 'New Institutional' Perspective on Policy Networks." *Public Administration* 75: 669–693.

Börzel, T. A. (1998). "Organizing Babylon—On the Different Conceptions of Policy Networks." *Public Administration* 76: 253–273.

Börzel, T. A. (2011). "Networks: Reified Metaphor or Governance Panacea." *Public Administration* 89(1): 49–63.

Börzel, T. A., and Heard-Lauréote, K. (2009). "Networks in EU Multi-level Governance: Concepts and Contributions." *Journal of Public Policy* 26(2): 135–152.

Braun, C. (2012). "The Captive or the Broker? Explaining Public Agency–Interest Group Interactions." *Governance* 25(2): 291–314.

Bressers, H., Jr., O'Toole, L. J., and Richardson, J. (Eds.). (1996). *Networks for Water Policy: A Comparative Perspective.* London: Frank Cass.

Bressers, H. T. A., and O'Toole, L. J. (1998). "The Selection of Policy Instruments: A Network-Based Perspective." *Journal of Public Policy* 18(3): 213–239.

Bursens, P., Beyers, J., and Donas, T. (2014). "Domestic European Union Coordination and Interest Group Mobilization in Three Member States: Looking Beyond the Formal Mechanisms." *Regional & Federal Studies* 24(3): 363–381.

Christopoulos, D. C. (2008). "The Governance of Networks: Heuristic or Formal Analysis? A Reply to Rachel Parker." *Political Studies* 56: 475–481.

Císař, O., and Navrátil, J. (2014). "Promoting Competition or Cooperation? The Impact of EU Funding on Czech Advocacy Organizations." *Democratization* 22(3): 536–559.

Coleman, W. D., and Perl, A. (1999). "Internationalized Policy Environments and Policy Network Analysis." *Political Studies* 47: 691–709.

Damgaard, B. (2006). "Do Policy Networks Lead to Network Governing?" *Public Administration* 84(3): 673–691.

Daugbjerg, C., and Fawcett, P. (2015). "Metagovernance, Network Structure, and Legitimacy: Developing a Heuristic for Comparative Governance Analysis." *Administration & Society* doi: 10.1177/0095399715581031.

De Rynck, F., and Voets, J. (2006). "Democracy in Area-Based Policy Networks: The Case of Ghent." *American Review of Public Administration* 36(1): 58–78.

De Vries, M. S. (2008). "Stability Despite Reforms: Structural Asymmetries in Dutch Local Policy Networks." *Local Government Studies* 34(2): 221–243.

Dowding, K. (1995). "Model or Metaphor? A Critical Review of the Policy Network Approach." *Political Studies* 43(1): 136–158.

Dowding, K. (2001). "There Must Be End to Confusion: Political Networks, Intellectual Fatigue, and the Need for Political Science Methods Courses in British Universities." *Political Studies* 49: 89–105.

Edelenbos, J., Van Buuren, A., and Klijn, E.-H. (2012). "Connective Capacities of Network Managers." *Public Management Review* 15(1): 131–159.

Ernstson, H., Barthel, S., Andersson, E., and Borgström, S. T. (2010). "Scale-Crossing Brokers and Network Governance of Urban Ecosystem Services: The Case of Stockholm." *Ecology and Society* 15(4): 28–54.

Fawcett, P., and Daugbjerg, C. (2012). "Explaining Governance Outcomes: Epistemology, Network Governance and Policy Network Analysis." *Political Studies Review* 10: 195–207.

Feiock, R. C., and Scholz, J. (2010). *Self-Organizing Federalism.* Cambridge, UK and New York: Cambridge University Press.

Fischer, M. (2014). "Coalition Structures and Policy Change in a Consensus Democracy." *Policy Studies Journal* 42(3): 344–366.

Fischer, M. (2015). "Institutions and Coalitions in Policy Processes: A Cross-Sectoral Comparison." *Journal of Public Policy* 35(2): 245–268.

Fischer, M., Fischer, A., and Sciarini, P. (2009). "Power and Conflict in the Swiss Political Elite: An Aggregation of Existing Network Analyses." *Swiss Political Science Review* 15(1): 31–62.

Fischer, M., Ingold, K., Sciarini, P., and Varone, F. (2012). "Impacts of Market Liberalization on Regulatory Network: A Longitudinal Analysis of the Swiss Telecommunications Sector." *Policy Studies Journal* 40(3): 435–457.

Fischer, M., and Leifeld, P. (2015). "Policy Forums: Why Do They Exist and What Are They Used For?" *Policy Sciences* 48(3): 363–382.

Fischer, A., Nicolet, S., and Sciarini, P. (2002). "Europeanisation of Non EU-Countries: The Case of Swiss Immigration Policy Towards the EU." *West European Politics* 25(3): 143–170.

Fischer, M., and Sciarini, P. (2013). "Europeanization and the Inclusive Strategies of Executive Actors." *Journal of European Public Policy* 20(10): 1482–1498.

Fischer, M., and Sciarini, P. (2015). "Unpacking Reputational Power: Intended and Unintended Determinants of the Assessment of Actors' Power." *Social Networks* 42: 60–71.

Fischer, M., and Sciarini, P. (2016). "Collaborative Tie Formation in Policy Networks: A Cross-Sector Perspective." *Journal of Politics* 78(1): 63–74.

Foljanty-Jost, G., and Jacob, K. (2004). "The Climate Change Policy Network in Germany." *European Environment* 14(1): 1–15.

Fowler, J. (2006). "Connecting the Congress: A Study of Cosponsorship Networks." *Political Analysis* 14: 456–487.

Freeman, L. C. (1978). "Centrality in Social Networks. Conceptual Clarification." *Social Networks* 1: 215–239.

Henning, C. H. (2009). "Networks of Power in the CAP System of the EU-15 and EU-27." *Journal of Public Policy* 29(02): 153–177.

Hirschi, C. (2010). "Strengthening Regional Cohesion: Collaborative Networks and Sustainable Development in Swiss Rural Areas." *Ecology and Society* 15(4): 16.

Hirschi, C., Widmer, A., Briner, S., and Huber, R. (2013). "Combining Policy Network and Model-Based Scenario Analyses: An Assessment of Future Ecosystem Goods and Services in Swiss Mountain Regions." *Ecology and Society* 18(2): art. 42.

Hovik, S., and Hanssen, G. S. (2014). "The Impact of Network Management and Complexity on Multi-Level Coordination." *Public Administration* 93(2): 506–523.

Hughes, J., John, P., and Sasse, G. (2002). "From Plan to Network: Urban Elites and the Post-communist Organisational State in Russia." *European Journal of Political Research* 41(3): 395–420.

Ingold, K. (2011). "Network Structures within Policy Processes: Coalitions, Power, and Brokerage in Swiss Climate Policy." *Policy Studies Journal* 39(3): 435–459.

Ingold, K. (2014). "How Involved Are They Really? A Comparative Network Analysis of the Institutional Drivers of Local Actor Inclusion." *Land Use Policy* 39: 376–387.

Ingold, K., and Fischer, M. (2014). "Drivers of Collaboration to Mitigate Climate Change: An Illustration of Swiss Climate Policy over 15 Years." *Global Environmental Change* 24: 88–98.

Ingold, K., and Leifeld, P. (2016). "Structural and Institutional Determinants of Reputational Power in Policy Networks." *Journal of Public Administration Research and Theory* 26(1): 1–18.

Ingold, K., and Varone, F. (2012). "Treating Policy Brokers Seriously: Evidence from the Climate Policy." *Journal of Public Administration Research and Theory* 22: 319–346.

Ingold, K., Varone, F., and Stokman, F. (2013). "A Social Network-Based Approach to Assess De Facto Independence of Regulatory Agencies." *Journal of European Public Policy* 20(10): 1464–1481.

John, P., and Cole, A. (1998). "Sociometric Mapping Techniques and the Comparison of Policy Networks: Economic Decision Making in Leeds and Lille." In *Comparing Policy Networks*, edited by D. Marsh, pp. 132–146. Buckingham, UK and Philadelphia: Open University Press.

John, P., and Cole, A. (2000). "When Do Institutions, Policy Sectors, and Cities Matter?" *Comparative Political Studies* 33(2): 248–268.

Jordana, J., Mota, F., and Noferini, A. (2012). "The Role of Social Capital within Policy Networks: Evidence from EU Cohesion Policy in Spain." *International Review of Administrative Sciences* 78(4): 642–664.

Jordana, J., and Sancho, D. (2005). "Policy Networks and Market Opening: Telecommunications Liberalization in Spain." *European Journal of Political Research* 44(4): 519–546.

Jurje, F. (2013). *Europeanization and New Member States: A Comparative Social Network Analysis.* Oxon/New York: Routledge.

Kenis, P., and Schneider, V. (1991). "Policy Networks and Policy Analysis: Scrutinizing a New Analytical Toolbox." In *Policy Networks—Empirical Evidence and Theoretical Considerations*, edited by B. Marin and R. Mayntz. Frankfurt am Main/Boulder, CO: Campus Verlag/Westview Press.

Kern, K., and Bulkeley, H. (2009). "Cities, Europeanization and Multi-level Governance: Governing Climate Change through Transnational Municipal Networks*." *JCMS: Journal of Common Market Studies* 47(2): 309–332.

Kickert, W. J. M., Klijn, E.-H., and Koppenjan, J. F. M. (1997). "Introduction: A Management Perspective on Policy Networks." In *Managing Complex Networks: Strategies for the Public Sector*, edited by W. J. M. Kickert, E.-H. Klijn, and J. F. M. Koppenjan, pp. 1–13. London: Sage.

Kirkland, J. H., and Gross, J. H. (2012). "Measurement and Theory in Legislative Networks: The Evolving Topology of Congressional Collaboration." *Social Networks* 36: 97–109.

Klijn, E.-H. (2005). "Designing and Managing Networks: Possibilities and Limitations for Network Management." *European Political Science* 4: 328–339.

Klijn, E.-H., Koppenjan, J., and Termeer, K. (1995). "Managing Networks in the Public Sector: A Theoretical Study of Management Strategies in Policy Networks." *Public Administration* 73(3): 437–454.

Klijn, E.-H., Steijn, B., and Edelenbos, J. (2010). "The Impact of Network Management on Outcomes in Governance Networks." *Public Administration* 88(4): 1063–1082.

Knoke, D., Pappi, F. U., Broadbent, J., and Tsujinaka, Y. (1996). *Comparing Policy Networks—Labor Politics in the U.S., Germany, and Japan.* Cambridge, UK: Cambridge University Press.

König, T., and Bräuninger, T. (1998). "The Formation of Policy Networks: Preferences, Institutions and Actors' Choice of Information and Exchange Relations." *Journal of Theoretical Politics* 10(4): 445–471.

Kovács, I. P., Paraskevopoulos, C. J., and Horváth, G. (2004). "Institutional 'Legacies' and the Shaping of Regional Governance in Hungary." *Regional & Federal Studies* 14(3): 430–460.

Kriesi, H., Adam, S., and Jochum, M. (2006). "Comparative Analysis of Policy Networks in Western Europe." *Journal of European Public Policy* 13(3): 341–361.

Kriesi, H., and Jegen, M. (2001). "The Swiss Energy Policy Elite: The Actor Constellation of a Policy Domain in Transition." *European Journal of Political Research* 39: 251–287.

Laumann, E. O., and Knoke, D. (1987). *The Organizational State—Social Choice in National Policy Domains*. Madison and London: University of Wisconsin Press.

Lazdinis, M., Carver, A., Carlsson, L., Tõnisson, K., and Vilkriste, L. (2004). "Forest Policy Networks in Changing Political Systems: Case Study of the Baltic States." *Journal of Baltic Studies* 35(4): 402–419.

Le Galès, P. (2001). "Urban Governance and Policy Networks: On the Urban Political Boundedness of Policy Networks; A French Case Study." *Public Administration* 79(1): 167–184.

Leifeld, P., and Schneider, V. (2012). "Information Exchange in Policy Networks." *American Journal of Political Science* 53(3): 731–744.

Lijphart, A. (1999). *Patterns of Democracy: Government Forms and Performance in Thirty-six Countries*. New Haven, CT: Yale University Press.

Lubell, M., Scholz, J., Berardo, R., and Robins, G. (2012). "Testing Policy Theory with Statistical Models of Networks." *Policy Studies Journal* 40(3): 351–374.

Maggetti, M., Ingold, K., and Varone, F. (2013). "Having Your Cake and Eating It, Too: Can Regulatory Agencies Be Both Independent and Accountable?" *Swiss Political Science Review* 19(1): 1–25.

Majone, G. (1997). "From the Positive to the Regulatory State: Causes and Consequences of Changes in the Mode of Governance." *Journal of Public Policy* 17(2): 139–167.

Marsh, D. (1998). "The Development of the Policy Network Approach." In *Comparing Policy Networks*, edited by D. Marsh, pp. 3–17. Buckingham, UK, and Philadelphia: Open University Press.

Marsh, D., and Smith, M. (2000). "Understanding Policy Networks: Towards a Dialectical Approach." *Political Studies* 48: 4–21.

Mayntz, R. (1993). "Modernization and the Logic of Interorganizational Networks." *Knowledge and Policy* 6(1): 3–16.

McMenamin, I. (2004). "Parties, Promiscuity and Politicisation: Business-Political Networks in Poland." *European Journal of Political Research* 43: 657–676.

Moschitz, H., and Stolze, M. (2009). "Organic Farming Policy Networks in Europe: Context, Actors and Variation." *Food Policy* 34(3): 258–264.

O'Toole, L. J., Walker, R. M., Meier, K. J., and Boyne, G. A. (2007). "Networking in Comparative Context." *Public Management Review* 9(3): 401–420.

Öberg, P., and Svensson, T. (2010). "Does Power Drive Out Trust? Relations between Labour Market Actors in Sweden." *Political Studies* 58(1): 143–166.

Oliver, K., De Vocht, F., Money, A., and Everett, M. (2015). "Identifying Public Health Policy Makers' Sources of Information: Comparing Survey and Network Analyses. *European Journal of Public Health: ckv083*.

Ostrom, E. (1990). *Governing the Commons: The Evolution of Institutions for Collective Actors.* Cambridge, UK: Cambridge University Press.

Ostrom, E. (2005). *Understanding Institutional Diversity.* Princeton, NJ: Princeton University Press.

Papadopoulou, E., Hasanagas, N., and Harvey, D. (2011). "Analysis of Rural Development Policy Networks in Greece: Is LEADER Really Different?" *Land Use Policy* 28(4): 663–673.

Pappi, F. U., and Henning, C. H. C. A. (1998). "Policy Networks: More Than a Metaphor?" *Journal of Theoretical Politics* 10(4): 553–575.

Pappi, F. U., and Henning, C. H. C. A. (1999). "The Organization of Influence on the EC's Common Agricultural Policy: A Network Approach." *European Journal of Political Research* 36: 257–281.

Powell, W. W. (1990). "Neither Market nor Hierarchy: Network Forms of Organization." *Research in Organizational Behavior* 12: 295–336.

Provan, K. G., and Kenis, P. (2008). "Modes of Network Governance: Structure, Management, and Effectiveness." *Journal of Public Administration Research and Theory* 18: 229–252.

Raab, J., Mannak, R. S., and Cambré, B. (2015). "Combining Structure, Governance, and Context: A Configurational Approach to Network Effectiveness." *Journal of Public Administration Research and Theory* 25(2): 479–511.

Rhodes, R. A. W., and Marsh, D. (1992). "New Directions in the Study of Policy Networks." *European Journal of Political Research* 21: 181–205.

Ringe, N., Victor, J. N., and Gross, J. H. (2013). "Keeping Your Friends Close and Your Enemies Closer? Information Networks in Legislative Politics." *British Journal of Political Science* 43(3): 601–628.

Sandström, A., and Carlsson, L. (2008). "The Performance of Policy Networks: The Relation between Network Structure and Network Performance." *Policy Studies Journal* 36(4): 497–524.

Schneider, V. (1992). "The Structure of Policy Networks." *European Journal of Political Research* 21: 109–129.

Sciarini, P. (2014). "More Power Balance, Less Consensus: Changes in Decision-Making Structures over Time." *Political Decision-Making in Switzerland. The Consensus Model under Pressure*, edited by. P. Sciarini, M. Fischer, and D. Traber. Basingstoke/New York: Palgrave Macmillan.

Sciarini, P., Fischer, A., and Nicolet, S. (2004). "How Europe Hits Home: Evidence from the Swiss Case." *Journal of European Public Policy* 11(3): 353–378.

Serdült, U., and Hirschi, C. (2004). "From Process to Structure: Developing a Reliable and Valid Tool for Policy Network Comparison." *Swiss Political Science Review* 10(2): 137–155.

Sörensen, E., and Torfing, J. (2009). "Making Governance Networks Effective and Democratic Through Metagovernance." *Public Administration* 87(2): 234–258.

Stokman, F. N., and Berveling, J. (1998). "Dynamic Modeling of Policy Networks in Amsterdam." *Journal of Theoretical Politics* 10(4): 577–601.

Stokman, F. N., and Zeggelink, E. P. H. (1996). "Is Politics Power or Policy Oriented? A Comparative Analysis of Dynamic Access Models in Policy Networks." *Journal of Mathematical Sociology* 21(1–2): 77–111.

Svensson, S. (2015). "The Bordered World of Cross-Border Cooperation: The Determinants of Local Government Contact Networks within Euroregions." *Regional & Federal Studies* 25(3): 1–19.

Svensson, T., and Öberg, P. (2005). "How Are Coordinated Market Economies Coordinated? Evidence from Sweden." *West European Politics* 28(5): 1075–1100.

Toke, D., and Marsh, D. (2003). "Policy Networks and the GM Crops Issue: Assessing the Utility of a Dialectical Model of Policy Networks." *Public Administration* 81(2): 229–251.

Van Meerkerk, I., Edelenbos, J., and Klijn, E.-H. (2015). "Connective Management and Governance Network Performance: The Mediating Role of Throughput Legitimacy; Findings from Survey Research on Complex Water Projects in the Netherlands." *Environment and Planning C: Government and Policy* 33(4): 746–764.

Van Waarden, F. (1992). "Dimensions and Types of Policy Networks." *European Journal of Political Research* 21: 29–52.

Verweij, S., Klijn, E.-H., Edelenbos, J., and Van Buuren, A. (2013). "What Makes Governance Networks Work? A Fuzzy Set Qualitative Comparative Analysis of 14 Dutch Spatial Planning Projects." *Public Administration* 91(4): 1035–1055.

Walker, R. M., O'Toole, L. J., and Meier, K. J. (2007). "It's Where You Are That Matters: The Networking Behaviour of English Local Government Officers." *Public Administration* 85(3): 739–756.

Williamson, O. E. (1991). "Comparative Economic Organization: The Analysis of Discrete Structural Alternatives." *Administrative Science Quarterly* 36(2): 269–296.

CHAPTER 36

....

SOCIAL NETWORKS IN THE BRAZILIAN ELECTORATE

....

BARRY AMES, ANDY BAKER, AND
AMY ERICA SMITH

BEGINNING with the Columbia school's classic studies of electorates in two US cities (Berelson, Lazarsfeld, and McPhee, 1954; Lazarsfeld, Berelson, and Gaudet, 1944), a rich line of scholarship has directly measured voters' social networks and assessed the impact of these networks on voting behavior in US elections (Huckfeldt and Sprague, 1995; Sokhey and McClurg, 2012). Although this body of work has contributed countless valuable insights, one cannot help but wonder if its findings, restricted as they are to the United States context, are generalizable and universal. While a number of important studies have looked at networks and voting behavior outside the United States, these also, drawing on samples from places like France, Germany, Japan, Switzerland, and the United Kingdom, have focused on long-established democracies (Fitzgerald, 2011; Wolf, Morales, and Ikeda, 2010; Zuckerman, Dasović, and Fitzgerald, 2007).[1] Only a minority of the world's population lives in affluent, stable democracies like these, so current knowledge about political discussion and voting behavior speaks to a small slice of humanity's political experience.

In less developed countries, the primary political trend of the past thirty years has been the "third wave" of democratization (Huntington, 1991). Dozens of countries in Africa, Asia, Eastern Europe, and Latin America have moved from autocratic to democratic rule. While most political scientists view this trend favorably, a cottage industry now documents the shortcomings of these young democracies. These critical observations point, for example, to their excessive clientelism and to a lack of programmatic political competition (Ames, 2001; Keefer, 2007; Kitschelt et al., 2010; Stokes et al., 2013). They also point to poorly sedimented mass partisan identification and to the resulting instability of party systems (Mainwaring, 1999; Roberts, 2014). In other words, two features of mass politics that scholars of older democracies tend to take for granted—programmatic, policy-based competition and a large pool of stable party identifiers—are alleged to be less common in younger democracies.[2] Voters in third-wave democracies are thus less likely to call on long-standing decisions or to rely on heuristics such as party affiliation that enable voters in advanced democracies to make reasonable decisions with minimal information (Lau and Redlawsk, 2001, 2006). Instead, many voters may base their decisions on short-term influences disseminated through the media and social networks. Thus, if scholars have found social networks to be important for voting behavior in older democracies, they are potentially of even greater importance in newer ones.

In this chapter we look at the third wave democracy of Brazil, which transitioned in 1985 from military dictatorship to democracy, a democracy that today seems consolidated. We review the small but burgeoning literature that finds political discussion in Brazilian social networks to be highly relevant to mass political behavior (Ames, García-Sánchez, and Smith, 2012; Baker, Ames, and Renno, 2006). Our focus is necessarily on studies of egocentric networks—that is, studies based on sample survey respondents and the list of immediate political discussants they provide in response to a name generator query. Whole-network studies or experiments gauging the political relevance of social interaction have not been conducted in Brazil. We rely on the two data sets that are the primary workhorses for studies of social networks in Brazilian mass politics: the 2002–2006 Two-City Brazilian Panel Study (Two-City Study)[3] and the 2014 Brazilian Electoral Panel Survey (BEPS 2014).[4] We also draw briefly on other studies that examine citizens' "vertical" interpersonal connections to clergy, clientelistic brokers, and politicians.[5]

Political discussion is an important aspect of Brazilian political behavior. Most Brazilians say they discuss politics at least sometimes; the frequency of political discussion and number of discussants named in surveys are similar in magnitude to reports from the long-established US democracy. Brazilians construct political discussion networks with a balance between relatives and nonrelatives, though there is evidence of a gender skew. Outside of the family environment, men are more likely to talk politics, and citizens are more likely to report male than female discussants.

People everywhere prefer to talk politics with agreeing discussants, that is, fellow citizens with whom they share preferences on candidates and issues. Overall, however, Brazilians are slightly more likely than US citizens to have disagreeing discussants. Few Brazilians have party preferences, but partisans talk politics with other partisans. Strikingly, though, there is little evidence of party-based homophily. Among party identifiers, levels of disagreement with discussants are *even higher* than in the general population. Partisanship, in sum, neither motivates nor hinders most political discussions.

Most important, discussion affects electoral outcomes. The 2002–2006 Two-City Study demonstrated that political conversation, over the course of the campaigns, contributed substantially to voters' knowledge of the candidates and their issue positions. These effects were strongest among those lowest in education and living in low-education neighborhoods. Moreover, respondents with discussants whose preferences diverged from their own (in the early waves of the 2014 survey) were much more likely to change their vote intentions by the time of the election.

We begin by describing various aspects of political discussion and egocentric networks in Brazil, drawing contrasts with information from a variety of data sets on equivalent features in the United States. We then discuss some of the literature's findings on the consequences of social networks for mass political behavior. A subsequent section discusses the two main data sources.

THE NATURE AND STRUCTURE
OF EGOCENTRIC NETWORKS

Many of the weaknesses identified in new democracies are found in Brazil. Mass partisan identifiers do exist, but they are less stable and fewer in number than those in the United States and other developed world democracies (Baker, Ames, Sokhey, and Renno, 2016; Carreirão and Kinzo, 2004; Kinzo, 2003, 2005; Samuels, 2006). Brazil has more parties than virtually any country in the world; twenty-eight held seats in the Congress in 2015. As a result, the electoral environment can be complex and confusing for voters (Ames, Baker, and Renno, 2008).[6] Moreover, although party competition and electoral behavior are oriented to some degree around a statist-liberal dimension (Baker and Greene, 2015), politics is generally characterized by contestation over clientelistic and pork-barrel resources rather than programmatic concerns (Ames, 2001). Partly for this reason, political cleavages only weakly reflect Brazil's deep and myriad socioeconomic cleavages, such as those around class, gender, race, region, religion, and rurality (Boas and Smith, 2016).

Given this political environment, should social networks and political discussion matter more or less for voting behavior in Brazil than in older democracies? Theoretical expectations are mixed. On the one hand, the party and electoral environment might lead voters to tune out politics. With so many parties oriented around seemingly distant concerns, politics may seem irrelevant or overly complex and confusing. On the other hand, the absence of long-standing decisions for many citizens potentially leaves an important role for political learning and frequent preference change through social networks. Voters may actually rely on family and friends to help them make sense of politics precisely because it is so messy (Huckfeldt, 2001). Moreover, while Brazil's politics and party system are complex, they are also highly competitive, something that breeds political conversation (Nir, 2012).

In this section we look at some basic descriptive statistics to see if the raw materials for network influence exist in Brazil. Our descriptives answer the following two questions: Do Brazilians discuss politics with a non-negligible frequency? And if so, do they discuss politics across lines of social and political difference, so that political persuasion can spread via informal networks? To provide some point of comparison, we also report statistics on political discussion from the United States, which has a much older, simpler, and programmatic party system, one rooted in meaningful social cleavages.

The Prevalence of Political Discussion: Frequency and Network Size

How frequent is political discussion in Brazil, and with how many different people do citizens discuss politics? If interpersonal influence over mass political behaviors exists, then a society must have at least some politically relevant discussion among peers. Using data from a 2014 nationally representative survey (BEPS), table 36.1 shows the marginal distributions of self-reported political discussion frequency with family, with friends, and in social media. It also shows the distribution of discussion with family and friends from a 2012 sample of US respondents. Only a minority of Brazilian respondents say they never discuss politics, and the modal response is "rarely." Levels of reported political discussion with family and friends are fairly similar to each other and are correlated at .68. Levels of discussion in social media, however, are much lower, with 76.1 percent reporting never discussing politics in such a setting.[7]

Unfortunately, a question asked in the United States with a similarly worded stem (from the American National Election Study, ANES) does not offer the same response set, but it does allow us to distinguish those who never discuss politics from those who do. Table 36.1 shows that the percentage reporting "never" discussing politics in this US sample is virtually the same as in Brazil. This parity may be new: looking back to World Values Survey data from the 1990s, we find somewhat greater frequency of political discussion in the United States than in Brazil.[8] Still, given the dramatic changes over the last two decades in Brazil's level of social development and in the overall political landscape, we speculate that the rising frequency of political discussion in Brazil may represent real change rather than an idiosyncrasy of measurement. All told, it would surely be a stretch to say that there is "a lot" of political discussion in Brazil, but there does seem to be a moderate amount, similar in magnitude to that which occurs in the long-established democracy of the United States.

Table 36.1 Frequency of Political Discussion in Brazil and the United States by Interlocutor

	Brazil (May 2014)		United States (November 2012)	
	With Family	With Friends		With Friends and Family
Never	27.9%	33.3%	Never discusses	28.4%
Rarely	33.4%	29.4%		
Sometimes	25.7%	23.4%	Does discuss	71.6%
Often	13.0%	13.9%		

Sources: BEPS 2014; ANES 2012.

Table 36.2 Degree Distribution in Brazil and the United States: Number of Named Discussants

	Brazil	United States
	August 2002	October 1996
Zero	33.0%	17.2%
One	9.7%	18.7%
Two	10.6%	30.4%
Three	46.6%	33.7%
N	4,507	715

Sources: Two-City Study, wave 2; Spencer Foundation data, University of Wisconsin Survey Center, 1996 (Mutz, 2006).

Another way of thinking about the prevalence of political discussion is to consider the size of networks. With how many different people, on average, do Brazilians discuss politics, or, in the language of network theory, what is the average "degree" of Brazilian citizens? Higher degree generally implies a propensity to seek out more information sources; it raises the probability of exposure to disagreement and thus may lead to tolerance of political difference (Huckfeldt, Johnson, and Sprague, 2004; Mutz, 2006). The Two-City Study twice administered a name generator allowing respondents to list up to three political discussants, similar to the name generator employed in the nationally representative 1996 Spencer Foundation survey of US citizens (Mutz, 2006).[9] Table 36.2 shows the relative degree distribution, using data from the August 2002 wave of the Two-City Study.

The degree distribution of Brazilian citizens is more bimodal than that of their US counterparts. A larger minority of Brazilian respondents listed 0 discussants, but a near-majority list 3. On average, Brazilian respondents listed 1.71 discussants, virtually equivalent to the number mentioned in the US sample (1.81). We cannot, of course, conclude that this is an extremely large number of discussants, but it is moderate in size and surely enough to provide the basis for interpersonal influence.

Types of Relationships within Networks

A number of research traditions show that discussion and contacts outside the family provide a public good. They create social capital, sustain a vibrant civil society, ease the flow of information and innovation, and increase the likelihood that individuals will deliberate across lines of political disagreement. The results presented in table 36.1 suggest that Brazilians report discussion frequency to be virtually equivalent, on average, between family and friends. Do the network name generators back this finding? Are non-family members just as prevalent in political discussion networks as family members?

Table 36.3 shows these results from the two Brazil surveys and the Spencer Foundation survey. The nationwide BEPS 2014 sample had a two-name generator that asked respondents to name a relative and then a nonrelative. Given the focused nature of each question, we assess whether responses of "none" were made more frequently to the relative query than to the nonrelative query. These questions were administered repeatedly in multiple waves of the panel study, starting in July 2014 (just after the start of the 2014 presidential election campaign), and ending in early October 2014 (just prior to the October 5 first-round presidential election). Respondents were in fact equally likely to mention a relative as they were a nonrelative, confirming the findings in table 36.1. The results from the Two-City Study are similar despite differences in geographic scope and question wording. While this survey allowed respondents to mention whomever they wanted, regardless of the relationship, we still find that Brazilians construct their political discussion networks with a balance between relatives and nonrelatives. Nearly half (46.1 percent) of named discussants were nonrelatives, and 43 percent of respondents named at least one nonrelative as a discussant. The distributions in Brazil bear an overall resemblance to that in the United States.

Whereas many Brazilians clearly go outside familial bonds to discuss politics, how many cross the gender divide? Research in the United States finds that the gender divide, save for discussions between spouses, often constitutes a hidden border around an individual's pool of potential discussants (Huckfeldt and Sprague, 1995, ch. 10). In the 2014 BEPS, respondents were more likely to report male than female discussants, with men outnumbering women by roughly a 3:2 ratio. This gender skewing is more pronounced among nonrelative discussants (37 percent female) than among relatives (42 percent

Table 36.3 Percent Reporting Family or Nonfamily Political Discussants in Each Wave

	Brazil		United States
	August 2002	July and August 2014	October 1996
No discussant	33.0%	36.4%	17.2%
Only named family members	21.9%	16.3%	21.1%
Only named nonfamily members	16.3%	16.4%	23.2%
Named both family and nonfamily members	26.6%	31.0%	36.2%
Total	97.8%	100.0%	97.7%

Sources: BEPS 2014, waves 2 and 3; Two-City Study, wave 2. Percentages for the Two-City Study do not sum to 100% because not all respondents provided relationship information for their named discussants. Spencer Foundation data, University of Wisconsin Survey Center, 1996 (Mutz, 2006).

female), largely because so many men named their spouses. Outside the family, men and women each prefer same-gender discussants, but the preference is much stronger among men; 20 percent of women report an opposite-gender nonfamily discussant, while only 2 percent of men do so.

Agreement and Disagreement within Networks

Decades of research in a variety of disciplines, including evolutionary biology, have shown a human propensity toward "homophily"—meaning that individuals prefer to associate with others who are similar to them. Still, if social networks influence political attitudes, disagreement between discussion partners must exist, at least some of the time (Huckfeldt, Johnson, and Sprague, 2004). If Brazilians only forge echo-chamber networks with like-minded discussants, then social influence via ongoing discussion cannot persuade participants aside from reinforcing their prior views (Bishop, 2008). More seriously, scant rates of disagreement within networks can create a "homogeneity problem" (Mutz, 2006, 43), whereby very little deliberation occurs across lines of political difference, potentially signifying or leading to a polarized and intolerant society.

Table 36.4 shows rates of respondent-discussant agreement (in column 1) on vote intention in presidential elections in Brazil and the United States. To provide an anchor for these results, column 2 also shows the probability of agreement in dyads between any two randomly chosen voters. There are more opportunities for disagreement in multiparty systems like Brazil's than in the United States, but Brazil's most recent presidential elections have boiled down to three- or four-candidate contests. In fact, the probability of finding an agreeable discussant if choosing one randomly (based strictly on aggregate election results) was virtually the same in the two Brazilian cities surveyed in 2002 and nationwide in the United States in 1996, so these two data sets provide a nice point of comparison. The results show that a majority of dyads (.69) were agreeing ones in

Table 36.4 The Prevalence of Political Agreement in Discussion Dyads in Brazil and the United States

	Brazil		United States
	2002	2014	October 1996
Share of dyads with agreeing partners	.69	.76	.80
Probability two randomly chosen people agreed (based on election results)	.41	.33	.42

Source: Baker (2009) (Brazil 2002 and US 1996 results); authors' own calculations for BEPS 2014. Results for Brazil are from first-round elections.
Note: Calculations of agreement within dyads are based only on dyads in which both the ego and the alter have known candidate preferences.

the two cities. This figure is lower than that observed in the United States (.80). In the nationwide data for Brazil, the share of agreeing dyads was closer to that in the United States in 1996. Overall, Brazilians seem slightly more likely than US citizens to have disagreeing discussants, but there are apples and oranges issues (such as the sizes of the name generators) that make this comparison imperfect.[10]

Discussants can agree or disagree not only on vote choice, but also on party preferences. As we pointed out in the introduction, levels of partisanship are quite low in the Brazilian electorate. In BEPS 2014, partisanship hovers around 30 percent in each campaign wave (and around 35 percent among those who name at least one discussant). Given the low importance of party affiliation for most citizens, do respondents know the party preferences of their discussants? In fact, as table 36.5 shows, the percentage of respondents able to identify the party preferences of family and nonfamily discussants is nearly as high as the percentage able to identify their own party preferences.

A little over half of those who know family members' party preferences share those preferences. The rates of partisan agreement between respondents and nonfamily discussants are somewhat lower. Only 9.1 percent of respondents with two discussants report that both support the same party as the main respondent. In analyses not shown, we found that the extent to which partisans are surrounded by agreeing discussants is related to the party's support in the electorate. For supporters of the Workers Party (PT), Brazil's most popular party in terms of mass affiliation, nearly two-thirds of family discussants and nearly half of nonfamily discussants share the respondent's party identification. Among supporters of other parties, the rates are much lower.

Partisanship, in sum, is neither salient nor consistent within most political discussions. Comparatively few people have party preferences. Even among those who do, relatively high levels of disagreement persist. Levels of *partisan* disagreement are higher than levels of *candidate* disagreement, even though few people have party preferences.

Table 36.5 Party Preferences of Discussants and Agreement/ Disagreement with Main Respondent, July/ August 2014

	Family Discussants	Non family Discussants
Total respondents naming discussant	602	537
% of total reporting discussant's party preference	31.7%	30.4%
% of total reporting discussant supports same party as respondent	16.9%	11.4%

Source: BEPS 2014.

Vertical Network Ties

Citizens can talk about politics in many different places and with many different types of contacts: spouses, close family members and friends, bosses, soccer buddies, local grocers, pastors, neighborhood leaders, and local politicians. These different types and contexts of conversation may well have different effects on voter behavior. In research following in the line of Huckfeldt and Sprague (1995), social networks have been conceived as small, close-knit, and intimate groups. Studies in the American context show that networks measured with a name generator tend to be comprised of people known well, such as family and close friends (Bailey and Marsden, 1999; Bearman and Parigi, 2004; Klofstad et al., 2009). Even batteries requesting the names of *political* discussants largely elicit networks of "core" discussants (Klofstad et al., 2009). The data reviewed above indicate that the same is true in Brazil.

This approach, however, ignores the broader social and political structure in which networks are embedded. While some network members hold little social or political capital, others contribute important political resources. Though voters may not typically mention their connections to pastors or vote brokers in response to network-generator batteries, such vertical connections could be as important or even more important for electoral behavior than horizontal ties to people of similar social status and political resources. This may particularly be the case in a society such as Brazil, which is characterized by high levels of inequality and stratification.

Table 36.6 reports the percentages of respondents to the BEPS of 2010 who reported such vertical political connections. At both the beginning and the end of the campaign, over half of the respondents reported knowing "personally a politician or someone who is campaigning for a politician," while only one in ten reported hearing a clergy member in his or her church discuss the election. Awareness of clergy members' preferences is much higher, however, in certain groups. Among evangelicals, 27.6 percent had heard their church pastor discuss the election. In the 2014 presidential election, half of evangelicals responding in the postelection wave of BEPS 2014 had heard their pastor do so.

Table 36.6 Vertical Political Connections in Brazil, 2010

	August 2010	October 2010
Percentage knowing a politician or campaigner	57.2%	54.5%
Percentage hearing their own clergy member discuss the election	7.7%	11.7%

Source: BEPS 2010.

THE POLITICAL CONSEQUENCES
OF DISCUSSION NETWORKS

Do these network configurations exert a causal impact on political behavior? Assessing causality using observational data is always difficult, particularly when the independent variables are self-selected, reciprocal behaviors such as political discussion. To date, there have been no experimental studies related to the influence of mass-level political discussion networks in Brazil. However, the two survey projects on which most studies have been based are both rich panel studies incorporating many innovations that can improve causal inference. For example, assessing the impact of change in discussant preferences on change in main respondent preferences is superior to a strictly cross-sectional approach, since the former rids the analysis of the homophilous propensity to choose like-minded discussants. These innovations are discussed in detail in the next section. Based on these rich data, scholars have found that Brazilian networks at the mass level produce a number of politically relevant consequences.

Perhaps most important, political discussion seems to play a major role in shaping voter choice. In one set of self-reports from Brazilian survey respondents, discussion with friends and family was the most-used source of political information during the campaign season (Straubhaar, Olsen, and Nunes, 1993). Studies based on network name generators also find that political discussion matters (Ames, García-Sánchez, and Smith, 2012; Baker, Ames, and Renno, 2006). Brazilian voters as a collective seem prone to dramatic momentum swings during campaigns; that is, the share of likely voters reporting a preference for a particular candidate changes rapidly in a short span of time. Some of these shifts are ephemeral "fads." In the 2002 campaign, for example, presidential candidate Ciro Gomes shot from 9 percent of vote intentions (fourth place) to 30 percent (second place) over the course of eight weeks, only to fall again, to 12 percent of the vote (fourth place) on election day.[11] Other momentum swings have more staying power. Consider the wave that brought Fernando Henrique Cardoso to victory in 1994. He began the year twenty points behind the front runner, only to win by twenty points. Whether these shifts are ephemeral or durable, research suggests that preference-changing swings can be triggered by media reports (Gomes's repeated gaffes in 2002) or economic change (Cardoso's role in 1994 in ending hyperinflation). Using the Two-City Study data from the 2002 election, Baker, Ames, and Renno (2006) show that these swings occur when new information diffuses through the population via discussion networks.

Table 36.7 provides preliminary evidence from the BEPS 2014 nationwide sample that discussion mattered in the same way in 2014. We compare the vote intentions of respondents and discussants from the second and third waves, assessing whether their preferences (for the top three candidates) matched or did not match. We then link those matches and nonmatches to respondents' reported votes as measured in wave 6. The results suggest that respondents with discussants whose preferences diverged from their own in wave 2 or wave 3 were much more likely to change their vote intentions by the time of the election.

Table 36.7 Do Discussants Help Change Vote Intention?

	Discussant's Vote Intention Compared to Respondent's Vote Intention, Waves 2/3 (July/August 2014)	
	Do Not Match	*Match*
Respondent's Wave 6 Preference		
Changes from Wave 2–3 to Wave 6	335 (60.9%)	54 (36.0%)
Stable from Wave 2–3 to Wave 6	215 (39.1%)	96 (64.0%)
Number of Observations	550	150

Note: This table includes only respondents declaring an intention to vote for Dilma, Aécio, or Marina in wave 2 or wave 3. Respondents' vote intentions are measured in wave 2 or wave 3 (mutually exclusive waves), except for respondents preferring Marina Silva. The latter were selected only in wave 3 due to the death of the initial presidential candidate on her ticket, Eduardo Campos. Respondents' actual votes were measured in wave 6.

Scholars have also discovered that social networks play a role in voting behavior via clientelism, an electoral strategy in which elites attempt to garner voter support by doling out a good, service or job to particular individuals and families. In a 2010 survey, 16 percent of Brazilian respondents said that in the recent past a vote-seeking politician or broker had offered them a good or favor in exchange for support.[12] Horizontal and vertical political ties are differentially associated with being targeted for clientelistic offers. Research on Brazil and other Latin American countries shows that politicians target citizens who are high out-degree nodes—that is, citizens who have the habit of trying to persuade their peers to vote a certain way (Schaffer and Baker, 2015). With this "social multiplier" strategy, politicians pay off influential people in the hopes that, via persuasive discussion, the effect of a single payoff will be magnified, transmitting their political message to nonrecipients. Likewise, vertical ties to politicians and organizers are also, not surprisingly, associated with clientelism. However, recent research indicates that personal ties to politicians and organizers are most strongly associated with clientelistic offers precisely among those with fewer horizontal ties; high out-degree nodes are targeted for clientelistic offers even in the absence of personal connections to politicians and organizers (Smith 2015a).

Political discussion also has consequences for other aspects of mass political behavior in Brazil, namely political knowledge and turnout. Political conversations convey general knowledge about candidates and campaigns. An analysis of the Two-City Study shows that over the course of both the 2002 and 2006 campaigns, political conversation contributed substantially to voters' knowledge of the candidates and their issue positions (McCann and Lawson, 2006; Smith, forthcoming). For most types of knowledge, effects were strongest among those lowest in education and living in low-education neighborhoods, thus contributing to declining knowledge gaps over the course of campaigns. Similarly, political conversation furthers citizens' ability to use ideological labels (Ames and Smith, 2010).

Political conversations also affect turnout and other forms of campaign participation. Though voting is compulsory (and moderately well-enforced) for Brazilians aged eighteen to sixty-nine, turnout is never universal. The same individual characteristics, moreover, predict turnout under either compulsory or voluntary voting (Maldonado, 2011; Power, 2009; Singh, 2011). Research in the United States and other democracies has shown that social networks strongly shape participation. While political conversation generally boosts turnout and engagement, exposure to disagreement as well as strong ties to nonvoters can be demobilizing (McClurg, 2003, 2006; Mutz, 2002; Partheymüller and Schmitt-Beck, 2012). Evidence from Brazil indicates that, as in the United States, large political discussion networks generally boost citizen engagement with electoral campaigns, while disagreement within networks demobilizes individuals (Smith, 2011).

DATA SOURCES

This section further describes the two previously mentioned Brazilian data sets featuring political discussant name generators.[13] Both are panel studies, providing added value for understanding network dynamics during and even across campaigns.

The Two-City Brazilian Panel Study

The Two-City Study is a six-wave panel carried out from 2002 to 2006 in two midsize municipalities, Caxias do Sul (state of Rio Grande do Sul) and Juiz de Fora (state of Minas Gerais). While the two cities have similarities—populations of roughly half a million each and manufacturing-based economies—they are politically quite distinct. Juiz de Fora, like many Brazilian cities, has weakly organized parties and voted strongly for Lula, the eventual winner of both elections. Caxias do Sul features greater party organization, with the PT representing the left and the Party of the Brazilian Democratic Movement (PMDB) organizing a right-of-center bloc. Voters in Caxias do Sul defied national trends, largely voting against Lula in both 2002 and 2006.

Waves 1 through 3 occurred in conjunction with the state and federal elections of October 2002 (March and August waves before and an October wave after the first round). Waves 5 and 6 occurred in conjunction with the state and federal elections of October 2006 (a July wave before and an October wave after the first round). Wave 4 occurred in 2004, a municipal election year. A city-representative sample of about 2,500 interviews was collected in the first wave in each municipality, and a total of 21,267 main respondent interviews and reinterviews occurred across all six waves. There are limits to a study of two cities; urban networks may function differently from those in rural areas, particularly in the less developed North and Northeast, and these two cities are relatively well governed. Still, 81 percent of Brazilians lived in urban areas in 2000, and that percent continued to increase in the ensuing decade.

While the study was not nationally representative, the research design was exceptionally sensitive to micro- and meso-context. Representative samples were collected in fifty neighborhoods across the two cities, facilitating the disentanglement of the relative impacts of local social context and personal characteristics on political behavior (e.g., Smith, forthcoming). Across the six waves, moreover, respondents were asked about their contacts with a wide variety of intermediaries, from neighborhood associations to informal networks to local politicians.

Discussant name generators were included on the wave 2 and wave 5 questionnaires. Main respondents were invited to list up to three people with whom they discussed politics. Respondents were then asked to state their relationship with each named discussant, each discussant's presidential vote choice, and each discussant's gubernatorial vote choice. The batteries in waves 2 and 5 were independent of one another, meaning respondents could name an entirely different list of discussants in each. This affords the rare opportunity to analyze network stability over time (Sokhey, Baker, and Djupe, 2015).

Two other novel features of the design are also important. First, main respondents were asked in waves 3 and 6 to name the presidential and gubernatorial vote choices of the discussants they had named in the preceding wave. In analyses of network influence, this enables one to account for the confounding effect of homophily by controlling for network selection in the previous wave. In addition, two waves of data on *both* discussant *and* main respondent preferences can help improve causal inference regarding mutual influences among discussion partners.

Second, a nonrandom sample of named discussants was interviewed just after wave 3 and again after wave 4. Nearly four thousand such interviews occurred. These interviews provide an opportunity for cleaner causal inference regarding network influence, since analysts do not have to rely on main respondent reports of their discussants' preferences. Data from these interviews could be used as instruments for network members' perceived preferences. In addition, rich data on discussant characteristics can help researchers assess *which* types of discussants are most likely to be influential.

The 2014 Brazilian Electoral Panel Survey

A second valuable data set for assessing discussion effects is the BEPS of 2014, which conducted seven waves of interviews between May and November 2014. The first wave, involving face-to-face interviews in twenty-two of Brazil's twenty-six states, was representative of the Brazilian population. Subsequent waves, conducted through phone interviews, were based on subsamples drawn from the first wave. During the first interview, 79.6 percent of respondents agreed to be contacted by phone for follow-up interviews; 70.3 percent of those who agreed to a recontact were actually reinterviewed at least once. Four interim waves were conducted during the campaign prior to the first-round election: July 16–20 (wave 2), August 28–September 1 (wave 3), September 16–21 (wave 4), and September 29–October 4 (wave 5). The sixth wave was implemented in October, immediately following the first-round election, and the seventh in late October to early November, immediately following the second-round runoff for president. The list of potential interviewees was randomly split in waves 2 and 3 and again in waves 4 and 5. That is, a contact was attempted with each respondent in *either* wave 2 or 3 and then again in *either* wave 4 or 5. Thus, the maximum number of interviews per respondent is five.

In the first wave, the survey asked three questions on the general frequency of political conversation with family, with friends, and in social media. Each intermediate wave included a battery of six items related to political discussion: the identity, perceived vote choice, and perceived party preference of a family member discussant and the same three questions for a nonfamily member discussant. Interviewers did not ask for discussants' names but identified them only by relationships, such as spouse, mother/father, male colleague, or female colleague. Finally, in waves 6 and 7, the survey asked respondents about the first- and second-round presidential vote choices of their most recently named discussants, identified by the relationship. Table 36.8 lists the questions asked in each wave.

This design again incorporates a number of features that help to improve causal inference and address theoretically interesting questions. The fact that many respondents received the discussant generator twice, in wave 2 or 3 and in wave 4 or 5, provides an unusual opportunity to examine stability in network composition. In analysis of discussant influence, repeated measures of the preferences of the two most recently named

Table 36.8 Interview Waves and Network/Conversation Questions in BEPS 2014

Wave	N	Network/Conversation Questions Asked			
		General Conversation	Discussant Generator	Discussant Vote Preference	Discussant Party
1 (A)	3,120	X			
2 (B)	609		X	X	X–
3 (C)	595		X	X	X
4 (D)	606		X	X	X
5 (E)	667		X	X	X
6 (F)	1,207			X	
7 (G)	1,001			X	

discussants can again help to improve causal inference with respect to mutual influence and stability in the main respondent-discussant dyad.

CONCLUSION

Our brief review of the structure and consequences of political discussion in Brazil makes it clear that politics, while it does not dominate the day-to-day conversations of Brazilians, is not an infrequently discussed topic, and a large share of Brazilians does discuss politics at least some of the time. And while we do not mean to establish the United States as a role model of democratic citizenship for developing countries (to say the least!), one cannot help but notice that the frequency of discussion and the structure of political networks in Brazil are similar to those of the United States. Moreover, we present arguments and findings indicating that these moderate amounts of political discussion have major political consequences in Brazil, perhaps even more significant consequences than in the United States. Political discussion influences a variety of mass-level political behaviors and traits, including vote choice, political knowledge, campaign engagement, and even clientelistic targeting.

Although we are confident in these conclusions, several data and measurement challenges remain. Conceptualizing and measuring the social network as a self-reported, egocentric collection of up to three relatively close family members and friends has inherent limitations. These lists are surely truncated for many respondents, and one cannot hope to map out entire networks, even when discussants themselves are interviewed. Furthermore, we still have no nationwide samples with a full (three-or-more-discussant) battery.

Challenges also remain in terms of theory development and testing. We have indicated a number of ways in which social context may shape the nature and consequences of political discussion networks, both generally and in the specific case on which we focus. Still, the striking similarities between the United States and Brazil in levels of discussion and disagreement pose something of a puzzle and suggest the need for further theoretical and empirical work. What leads to this congruence, despite the facts that the US party system is more programmatic and less complex than its Brazilian equivalent and that the democratic regime of the United States is much older? Our answers are at this point speculative. In both countries, levels of television viewership are high, and media play a major role in campaigns; the saturation of television may contribute to moderate levels of political discussion. In addition, citizens in both countries may respond to the competitiveness of presidential elections by talking politics (Nir, 2012). At the same time, certain features of Brazilian campaigns may compensate for any downward effect on political discussion resulting from the complexity of the party and electoral systems. In particular, the famous personalization of Brazilian politics leads elites at all levels, as well as vote brokers (*cabos eleitorais*), to seek to establish personal contact with voters. Personal connections to the political world may lead to high levels of political discussion among citizens.

We also have far to go in understanding how the impacts of social networks vary across contexts. Recent cross-national work has begun to explore these issues; a special edition of the *International Journal of Public Opinion Research* contains a collection of articles devoted specifically to this question. Two further avenues for research may be fruitful in this regard. First, given the dearth of research on social networks in developing democracies, it may be particularly interesting to compare survey data from Brazil with social network data from other countries included in the Comparative National Elections Project (CNEP) (Chile, Hungary, Mexico, Mozambique, South Africa, and Uruguay).[14] Second, experiments hold much promise. Researchers could develop lab-based conversation groups in which the structural parameters of decision tasks vary in ways that mimic institutional variation. Such research should be helpful in understanding more clearly how institutions affect the outcomes of political discussion. We are confident that these and other explorations of political discussion and its effects on political behavior will add to our understanding of mass political behavior in comparative contexts.

Notes

1. Several cross-national studies based on the Comparative National Elections Project (CNEP) include developing-country democracies (Eveland, Song, and Beck, 2015; Gunther, Montero, and Puhle, 2007; Gunther et al., 2015; Smith, 2015b).
2. But see Baker and Greene (2011) for evidence of positional issue voting in Latin America.
3. Baker, Ames, and Renno (2006). Funded by the National Science Foundation (SES #0137088). Available at http://spot.colorado.edu/~bakerab/data.html.
4. Ames et al. (2016). This research was funded by the Inter-American Development Bank, the Brazilian National Research Council, and the Andrew Mellon Professorship at the University of Pittsburgh. These data are be publicly available from the Inter-American Development Bank. http://www.iadb.org/en/research-and-data/publication-details,3169.html?pub_id=IDB-TN-915
5. For national-level data on citizens' connections to clergy, see BEPS 2010 and BEPS 2014 (Ames et al., 2013, 2015). For national-level data on citizens' connections to vote brokers and politicians, see BEPS 2010 and the 2012 wave of the AmericasBarometer by the Latin American Public Opinion Project.
6. Nonetheless, see Samuels and Zucco (2014) for evidence that some Brazilian voters do use party affiliation as a meaningful heuristic.
7. For respondents in the top half of the wealth distribution, the correlations between social media discussion of politics and the other two forms of political discussion are .40 and .42. For respondents under the age of thirty, the respective correlations are .44 and .48.
8. To the best of our knowledge, the only opportunity to compare an equivalently worded question is the World Values Survey, which asked a discussion question in Brazil in 1991 and in the United States in 1995. This shows a slightly higher self-reported mean of discussion frequency in the United States (higher by about one-fifth of a standard deviation),

where the share of "never discusses" (26.8 percent) is lower than in Brazil (44.4 percent). That said, the share of "frequently discusses" responses is actually lower in the United States (16.0 percent) than in Brazil (19.8 percent).

9. These are not the only US-based network name generators available, but to maximize comparability, we use this Spencer Foundation data because, like the Two-City Study, they explicitly requested *political* discussants and capped the list at three.

10. Not to mention the fact that these were measured after election day, and thus presumably after a great degree of social influence had occurred.

11. A similar fate befell Marina Silva in 2014. She began the campaign as running mate to the then third-place candidate Eduardo Campos. Upon his unexpected death in a plane crash, she shot up in the polls to second place (34 percent), only to fall to third place on election day, finishing more than ten points behind the runner-up.

12. This datum is from the 2010 BEPS.

13. Yet another data set that included some network and social influence questions is the BEPS of 2010 (Ames et al., 2013), which included items asking for the name and contact information of a discussant in both waves 1 and 2. Phone interviews with those named discussants were attempted, but the study was unable to obtain a reasonable response rate, so phone interviews were abandoned. BEPS 2010 also contains rich information on other types of networks, including contacts with politicians and political brokers and discussions of politics in church.

14. The third round of the CNEP also studied Indonesia but, sadly, did not include any network questions.

References

Ames, B. (2001). *The Deadlock of Democracy in Brazil*. Ann Arbor: University of Michigan Press.

Ames, B., Baker, A., and Renno, L. R. (2008). "The 'Quality' of Elections in Brazil: Policy, Performance, Pageantry, or Pork?" In *Democratic Brazil Revisited*, edited by T. J. Power and P. R. Kingstone, pp. 107–134. Pittsburgh: University of Pittsburgh Press.

Ames, B., García-Sánchez, M., and Smith, A. E. (2012). "Keeping up with the Souzas: Social Influence and Electoral Change in a Weak Party System, Brazil 2002–2006." *Latin American Politics and Society* 54(2): 51–78.

Ames, B., Machado, F., Renno, L., Samuels, D., Smith, A. E., and Zucco, C. (2013). *Brazilian Electoral Panel Survey [BEPS]*. Washington, DC: Inter-American Development Bank.

Ames, B., Machado, F., Renno, L., Samuels, D., Smith, A. E., and Zucco, C. (2016). Brazilian Electoral Panel Survey 2014 [BEPS]. Washington, DC: Inter-American Development Bank.

Ames, B., and Smith, A. E. (2010). "Knowing Left from Right: Ideological Identification in Brazil, 2002–2006." *Journal of Politics in Latin America* 2(3): 3–38.

Bailey, S., and Marsden, P. V. (1999). "Interpretation and Interview Context: Examining the General Social Survey Name Generator Using Cognitive Methods." *Social Networks* 21(3): 287–309.

Baker, A. (2009). "Regionalized Voting Behavior and Political Discussion in Mexico." In *Consolidating Mexico's Democracy: The 2006 Presidential Campaign in Comparative Perspective*, edited by J. I. Dominguez, C. Lawson, and A. Moreno, pp. 71–88. Baltimore, MD: Johns Hopkins University Press.

Baker, A., Ames, B., and Renno, L. R. (2006). "Social Context and Campaign Volatility in New Democracies: Networks and Neighborhoods in Brazil's 2002 Elections." *American Journal of Political Science* 50(2): 382–399.

Baker, A., Ames, B., Sokhey, A. E., and Renno, L. R. (2016). "The Dynamics of Mass Partisanship When Party Brands Change: The Case of the Workers Party in Brazil." *Journal of Politics* 78(1): 197–213.

Baker, A., and Greene, K. F. (2011). "The Latin American Left's Mandate: Free-Market Politics and Issue Voting in New Democracies." *World Politics* 63(1): 43–77.

Baker, A., and Greene, K. F. (2015). "Positional Issue Voting in Latin America." In *The Latin American Voter*, edited by R. Carlin, M. Singer, and E. Zechmeister, pp. 173–194. Ann Arbor: University of Michigan Press.

Bearman, P., and Parigi, P. (2004). "Cloning Headless Frogs and Other Important Matters: Conversation Topics and Network Structure." *Social Forces* 83(2): 535–557.

Berelson, B., Lazarsfeld, P. F., and McPhee, W. N. (1954). *Voting: A Study of Opinion Formation in a Presidential Campaign*. Chicago: University of Chicago Press.

Bishop, B. (2008). *The Big Sort: Why the Clustering of Like-Minded America is Tearing Us Apart*. New York: Houghton Mifflin.

Boas, T. C., and Smith, A. E. (2016). "Looks Like Me, Thinks Like Me? Descriptive Representation and Opinion Congruence in Brazil." Working paper. http://people.bu.edu/tboas/looks_like_me.pdf

Carreirão, Y. de S., and Kinzo, M. D. (2004). "Partido Políticos, Preferência Partidária E Decisão Eleitoral No Brasil (1989/2002)." *Dados—Revista de Ciências Sociais* 47(1): 131–168.

Eveland, W. P., Song, H., and Beck, P. A. (2015). "Cultural Variations in the Relationships Among Network Political Agreement, Political Discussion Frequency, and Voting Turnout." *International Journal of Public Opinion Research* 27(4): 461–480.

Fitzgerald, J. (2011). "Family Dynamics and Swiss Parties on the Rise: Exploring Party Support in a Changing Electoral Context." *Journal of Politics* 73(3): 783–796.

Gunther, R., Beck, P. A., Magalhães, P. C., and Moreno, A. (2015). *Voting in Old and New Democracies*. New York: Routledge.

Gunther, R., Montero, J. R., and Puhle, H.-J. (Eds.). (2007). *Democracy, Intermediation, and Voting on Four Continents*. Oxford: Oxford University Press.

Huckfeldt, R. (2001). "The Social Communication of Political Expertise." *American Journal of Political Science* 45(2): 425–438.

Huckfeldt, R., Johnson, P. E., and Sprague, J. (2004). *Political Disagreement: The Survival of Diverse Opinions within Communication Networks*. Cambridge, UK: Cambridge University Press.

Huckfeldt, R., and Sprague, J. (1995). *Citizens, Politics, and Social Communication: Information and Influence in an Election Campaign*. Cambridge, UK: Cambridge University Press

Huntington, S. P. (1991). *The Third Wave: Democratization in the Late Twentieth Century*. Norman: University of Oklahoma Press.

Keefer, P. (2007). "Clientelism, Credibility, and the Policy Choices of Young Democracies." *American Journal of Political Science* 51(4): 804–821.

Kinzo, M. D. (2003). "Parties and Elections: Brazil's Democratic Experience since 1985." In *Brazil Since 1985: Economy, Polity and Society*, edited by M. D. Kinzo and J. Dunkerley, pp. 42–61. London: Institute of Latin American Studies.

Kinzo, M. D. (2005). "Os Partidos No Eleitorado: Percepções Públicas E Laços Partidários No Brasil." *Revista Brasileira de Ciências Sociais* 20(57): 65–81.

Kitschelt, H., Hawkins, K. A., Luna, J. P., Rosas, G., and Zechmeister, E. J. (2010). *Latin American Party Systems*. New York: Cambridge University Press.

Klofstad, C. A., McClurg, S. D., and Rolfe, M. (2009). "Measurement of Political Discussion Networks: A Comparison of Two 'Name Generator' Procedures." *Public Opinion Quarterly* 73(3): 462–483.

Lau, R. R., and Redlawsk, D. P. (2001). "Advantages and Disadvantages of Cognitive Heuristics in Political Decision-Making." *American Journal of Political Science* 45(4): 951–971.

Lau, R. R., and Redlawsk, D. P. (2006). *How Voters Decide: Information Processing during Election Campaigns*. New York: Cambridge University Press.

Lazarsfeld, P. F., Berelson, B., and Gaudet, H. (1944). *The People's Choice: How a Voter Makes up His Mind in a Presidential Campaign*. New York: Duell, Sloan, and Pearce.

Mainwaring, S. P. (1999). *Rethinking Party Systems in the Third Wave of Democratization*. Stanford, CA: Stanford University Press.

Maldonado, A. (2011). Compulsory Voting and the Decision to Vote. AmericasBarometer Insights no. 63. Nashville, TN: Latin American Public Opinion Project, Vanderbilt University.

McCann, J. A., and Lawson, C. (2006). "Presidential Campaigns and the Knowledge Gap in Three Transitional Democracies." *Political Research Quarterly* 59(1): 13–22.

McClurg, S. D. (2003). "Social Networks and Political Participation: The Role of Social Interaction in Explaining Political Participation." *Political Research Quarterly* 56(4): 449–464.

McClurg, S. D. (2006). "The Electoral Relevance of Political Talk: Examining Disagreement and Expertise Effects in Social Networks on Political Participation." *American Journal of Political Science* 50(3): 737–754.

Mutz, D. C. (2002). "The Consequences of Cross-Cutting Networks for Political Participation." *American Journal of Political Science* 46(4): 838–855.

Mutz, D. C. (2006). *Hearing the Other Side: Deliberative versus Participatory Democracy*. New York: Cambridge University Press.

Nir, L. (2012). "Cross-National Differences in Political Discussion: Can Political Systems Narrow Deliberation Gaps?" *Journal of Communication* 62(3): 553–570.

Partheymüller, J., and Schmitt-Beck, R. (2012). "A 'Social Logic' of Demobilization: The Influence of Political Discussants on Electoral Participation at the 2009 German Federal Election." *Journal of Elections, Public Opinion and Parties* 22(4): 457–478.

Power, T. J. (2009). "Compulsory for Whom? Mandatory Voting and Electoral Participation in Brazil, 1986-2006." *Journal of Politics in Latin America* 1(1): 97–122.

Roberts, K. (2014). *Changing Course in Latin America: Party Systems in the Neoliberal Era*. New York: Cambridge University Press.

Samuels, D. J. (2006). "Sources of Mass Partisanship in Brazil." *Latin American Politics and Society* 48(2): 1–27.

Samuels, D., and Zucco, C. (2014). "The Power of Partisanship in Brazil: Evidence from Survey Experiments." *American Journal of Political Science* 58(1): 212–225.

Schaffer, J., and Baker, A. (2015). "Clientelism as Persuasion-Buying: Evidence from Latin America." *Comparative Political Studies* 48(9): 1093–1126.

Singh, S. (2011). "How Compelling Is Compulsory Voting? A Multilevel Analysis of Turnout." *Political Behavior* 33(1): 95–111.

Smith, A. E. (2011). "Personal Connections to the Political World: Social Influences on Democratic Competence in Brazil and in Comparative Context." PhD diss., University of Pittsburgh.

Smith, A. E. (2015a). "People Who Know People: The Mixed Consequences of Horizontal and Vertical Social Capital in Developing Democracies." Working paper. http://papers.ssrn.com/sol3/papers.cfm?abstract_id=2704924

Smith, A. E. (2015b). "The Diverse Impacts of Politically Diverse Networks: Party Systems, Political Disagreement, and the Timing of Vote Decisions." *International Journal of Public Opinion Research* 27(4): 481–496.

Smith, A. E. (Forthcoming). "Talking It Out: Political Conversation and Knowledge Gaps in Unequal Urban Contexts." *British Journal of Political Science.* http://amyericasmith.org/wp-content/uploads/2015/07/Talking-it-Out_Smith-BJPS.pdf

Sokhey, A. E., and McClurg, S. (2012). "Social Networks and Correct Voting." *Journal of Politics* 74(3): 751–764.

Sokhey, A. E., Baker, A., and Djupe, P. (2015). "The Dynamics of Socially Supplied Information: Examining Discussion Network Stability over Time." *International Journal of Public Opinion Research* 27(4): 565–587.

Stokes, S., Dunning, T., Nazareno, M., and Brusco, V. (2013). *Brokers, Voters, and Clientelism: The Puzzle of Distributive Politics.* New York: Cambridge University Press.

Straubhaar, J., Olsen, O., and Nunes, M. C. (1993). "The Brazilian Case: Influencing the Voter." In *Television, Politics, and the Transition to Democracy in Latin America*, edited by Thomas E. Skidmore, pp. 118–136. Baltimore, MD: Johns Hopkins University Press.

Wolf, M. R., Morales, L., and Ikeda, K. (Eds.). (2010). *Political Discussion in Modern Democracies: A Comparative Perspective.* New York: Routledge

Zuckerman, A. S., Dasović, J., and Fitzgerald, J. (2007). *Partisan Families: The Social Logic of Bounded Partisanship in Germany and Britain.* New York: Cambridge University Press.

CHAPTER 37

COMPARATIVE CLIMATE CHANGE POLICY NETWORKS

JEFFREY BROADBENT

INTRODUCTION

IN the study of comparative politics, the policy network (PN) method offers unique strengths for investigating complex processes. The PN method studies a *policy domain*, which consists of the interactions among the organizations engaged in trying to shape the formation of a number of national policies around a common theme, such as energy, healthcare, labor, or climate change (Laumann and Knoke, 1987). A national labor policy domain, for example, consists of the organizational actors and their interactions as they contend and cooperate to shape the outcomes of labor-related policy measures such as the minimum wage, aid to distressed sectors, and occupational safety. In the same way, a national climate change policy domain consists of the actors and their interactions over policy measures such as carbon tax, cap-and-trade, and alternative energy and conservation subsidies. The PN approach asks questions both about actors' typical relational partners in the domain and about their specific partners, tactics, and goal attainment for discrete policy formation processes within the domain. This allows us to study both the general pattern and the discrete variations on that pattern that exist within a single national policy domain. We can then compare these domain findings either to other domains within the same country or to the same domain in different countries. This facilitates our understanding of the structures of policy formation and their degrees of generality on an empirical basis.

In this approach, the key word is *network*, indicating a pattern of relationships among members (as discussed throughout this handbook). In the study of politics, the key type of relationship boils down to power, *Macht*, the ability to get one's way despite opposition (Weber, 1978). So the PN approach is mainly concerned with power networks. We measure the relative power of actors by several types of outcome measures, as detailed in this chapter. However, when we study power closely, we realize it can be created through many different kinds of exchanges. For example, in one policy domain, the transfer of information might be the key to power, while in another, the provision of public political support or the formation of political coalitions might be key. There are many other such incentives that can constitute power, from cowrie shells to charismatic oratory. The advantage of the PN method is that it can measure these different ways of creating power as discretely composed networks. That is, the PN approach measures more than a single network, tapping into several that the researcher thinks could be relevant. Having measured these, one can re-create the social fabric of power, woven of several threads. The degree to which different societies have different social fabrics of power, once we are able to distinguish and measure it, becomes a matter of profound theoretical import.

Since the PN survey asks about a number of types of interactions, each forming a discrete network, the domain can be seen as several layers of interaction. In any domain, these multiple networks can be relatively contiguous, hanging with the same members and patterns, reinforcing each other, or relatively disparate, going off with different members in different patterns, the networks existing in tension with each other. In this way, the PN method illuminates the multiple channels by which organizations join into coalitions under the same banner, to struggle against other coalitions carrying different banners (Sabatier and Weible, 2007). The detailed tracing of many interactions among many organizations enables the researcher to view abstract causal factors as they work in the very mechanisms of the actual political process. In other words, the network represents the interactive process among many organizations, which enacts contextual factors and also through human reflexive creativity shapes and changes the contextual factors. The PN approach allows the empirical observations to somewhat more closely approach the "wicked" complexity of social and political causality, so very much evident in climate change problems (Levin et al., 2012).

DEVELOPMENT OF THE POLICY NETWORK APPROACH

The social anthropology of Radcliffe-Brown pioneered the view of social structure as a set of networks among persons in social roles. This pattern he likened to the morphology of society, and he said the idea could just as readily be considered the basis of comparative sociology. He purposely ignored the role of culture (Radcliffe-Brown, 1940). This general social structural orientation went in different directions: micro, meso, and macro. On the one hand, this idea became the basis of structural social network studies. It permitted mathematical treatments due to the assumed equivalence of relationships as the components of structures. It also supported the growth of community power structure studies (Hunter, 1953; Knoke, 1981; Warner, 1963). Building on this general orientation, but also influenced by macro views such as Parsons's systems model and Karl Deutsch's view of communication flow as the "nerves of government" (Deutsch, 1966), as well as Homan's micro-exchange analysis (Homans, 1961), Laumann began to develop his PN approach

(Freeman, 2004, 131).[1] Homans's exchange theory gave it a rational choice orientation, with networks assumed to result from the calculated choices of actors.

Laumann and Pappi's (1976) pioneering work compared "networks of collective action" in US and German community politics using quantitative network methods. This work led Laumann and his students to examine "community structure as inter-organizational linkages" (Laumann, Galaskiewicz, and Marsden, 1978) and further developments in a similar vein (Laumann and Marsden, 1979; Knoke and Laumann, 1982). Laumann and his students developed the PN method with organizations as actors in his study comparing US energy and healthcare domains (Laumann and Knoke, 1987), leading to his discovery of a "hollow core" in US politics (Heinz et al., 1993). Following Parsons's influence, Laumann and his collaborators theorized this lack of center to be caused by political modernization. In Parsons's terms, modernization leads to a differentiation or "balkanization" of the US political system into clusters of governmental units and their regulated clients. The PN concept spread to a wide range of studies (Anheier, 1987; Kenis and Schneider, 1991; Knoke, 1990; Marsh, 1998; Raab and Kenis, 2007) (see chapter by Knoke and Kostiuchenko, this volume).

Following the US study, Knoke and Pappi initiated the first cross-national PN study, with the United States and Germany as their respective cases. In 1986, when I arrived at Knoke's institution, the University of Minnesota, as a junior professor, I joined the study and brought the Japanese case into the comparison. My specialization was Japanese environmental politics (Broadbent, 1989a, 1998, 1982), not Japanese national labor politics. I recruited an expert in Japanese interest group politics, Yutaka Tsujinaka of Tsukuba University, to help in the project.

Together, our four-author comparison of the US, German, and Japanese labor policy networks accomplished the first cross-national comparison of the mature PN approach. The assumptions underlying this study were that actors created networks in the pursuit of their interests, which were given "exogenously" by their positions in social structure. The starting theoretical assumption was that all three polities would show a hollow core and a balkanization of the polity into distinct interest clusters, such as Laumann and Knoke had found in their prior US studies. However, our findings did not support this hypothesis. Instead, while the United States had many competitive actors and a hollow core, Japan had a filled core with central all-purpose ministries coordinating the whole economy. And in Germany two giant corporatist hierarchies of business and labor collaborated to run the economy, with state backup (Knoke et al., 1996).

THE COMPARING CLIMATE CHANGE POLICY NETWORKS PROJECT

Upon the conclusion of data collection for the labor study in 1991, I began to pursue my longer term goal, using the PN method to study comparative environmental policy formation. As the first version of what would become the Compon survey, I initiated the comparative environmental PN survey project. I asked my partner in the labor study, Yutaka Tsujinaka of Tsukuba University, to lead it while I cowrote the labor book with Knoke and Pappi. Tsujinaka dubbed it the Global Environmental Policy Network (Gepon) survey. With funds from the Japan Society for the Promotion of Science, he fielded the Gepon study in 1997 in Japan, the United States, and Germany. The data collection occurred at the fortuitous time just prior to the Kyoto Conference (COP3) that led to the Kyoto Protocol for emissions reductions. I collected some of the Japan survey responses for Gepon through direct interviews. Building on this experience, I started the project Comparing Climate Change Policy Networks (Compon) in 2006, recruited initial team leaders from relevant countries, and hosted the project's first international conference in January 2007 at the University of Minnesota. As principle investigator, I led the National Science Foundation application (co-principle investigators were Dana Fisher and Katsumi Matsumoto) that kick-started the project with a $589,000 grant (BCS-0827006). Since then, the Compon project has grown to include more than twenty-five direct and affiliated cases and over $2 million in funding from various governmental science research agencies. We define a *case* as the response of a political society to the challenge of climate change mitigation. The context of analysis is the nation-state, except for the region of Taiwan. As of December 2015, our website lists fifty publications from the project.[2] In the process, we have simplified the PN survey down from the original one-hour, face-to-face version to one that can be done by a respondent online in fifteen minutes with guidance from the researcher by telephone. This simplification enables a continuing expansion of the project to many more cases and to panel studies of change over decades.

The Compon project extracts PN data from the climate change domains of a range of cases, including the biggest polluters and those with interesting responses. It collects four levels of data. Level 1 tracks keyword (climate change, global warming) news share in three major newspapers per case over time from 1997 to the present. Level 2 conducts a content analysis of a sample of the keyword articles for the focus years 2007 and 2008, just before the Copenhagen Conference (COP 15). Level 2 has extracted 167 ways of framing climate change from the newspapers and compared their relative prevalence across cases (seventeen cases). Level 3 is using the program Discourse Network Analyzer to study and compare climate change actor/discourse coalitions appearing in the newspapers.

The fourth level, the PN survey per se (currently sixteen cases), includes South Korea, Japan, Taiwan, Australia, New Zealand, Canada, the United States, Brazil, Sweden, Finland, Ireland, the United Kingdom, Germany, Switzerland, the Czech Republic, and India. Using the PN data, project teams develop models of how each polity works to produce its carbon emissions trajectories. Then cross-case comparisons begin the search for more general principles.[3] The important basic shift in theoretical perspective in the Compon project from the earlier PN studies is its explicit recognition of the role of culture and discourse as a collective factor in the formation of the organizational interests and preferences that drive action. This perspective is explicitly recognized in discourse network analysis (see chapter by Leifeld, this volume). In the Compon survey instrument, it is recognized by the affinity of organizations toward different interpretive frames about climate change.[4]

As of 2016, PN surveys for the Compon climate change project are still under way, with some collected and others in process. Comparative analysis is only just beginning. Accordingly, to illustrate points, this chapter draws on data from the earlier labor PN study (1986–1990 data), an initial cross-national comparative environmental PN (Gepon) study (1997 data), and the climate change PN (Compon) study (2010 to current data).

Global Climate Change as a Quasi-Experimental Research Project

Any study and its data collection methods or instruments must, of course, be designed with the larger theoretical questions and objectives in mind. The Compon project's approaches and instruments have been designed to study the global climate change problem from a cross-national, comparative perspective. The purpose of the Compon project is to show how differences among cases in the national policy-formation process are related to differences in their mitigation policies and to their actual carbon emissions. This in turn interacts with the international and global level of climate change politics and also the grim realities of disasters ensuing from climate change. The tools provided by the PN method greatly facilitate the Compon task.

The issue of global climate change represents the most consequential dilemma of collective action (DCA) ever to threaten the whole of humanity (Olson, 1965). In the DCA situation, participants opt for short-run personal benefit maximization, even though this reduces long-run collective and personal benefits. The dilemma can only be overcome by cooperative collective action to minimize the collective costs, but participants lack the mutual trust needed to join in collective action. Climate change presents the countries and peoples of the world with just this sort of dilemma. It represents a historically unprecedented possibility of collective disaster, but also an unrelenting and intensifying prompt for cooperative collective action (Beck, 1999). Only unstinting global cooperation will avert this risk (Hironaka, 2014). Yet most societies have not accepted this responsibility. Societies exhibit a wide range of responses, a few exhibiting wholehearted acceptance and effort, but most having a lukewarm or indifferent reaction. Some societies have managed to reduce their carbon emissions, while others have increased them massively.

Societies around the world are increasingly engaged in setting up measures to combat climate change, especially since the all-inclusive Paris Accord reached in December 2015 (the 21st Conference of the Parties to the United Nations Framework Convention on Climate change, UNFCCC). A crucial factor noted in this accord is enhanced "transparency of action and support" to build the mutual confidence needed for effective reductions in carbon emissions (UNFCCC, 2015). This is necessary because each society will go about responding to this call for action in its own particular way. It will follow its own particular political processes, resulting in its own outcomes, more or less effectively reducing carbon emissions, or perhaps only pretending to do so. In its applied aspect, the Compon project is designed to provide this enhanced transparency of process and outcome. In its theoretical aspect, by the more detailed mapping of policy networks, the project must discover new political formations out of the seemingly familiar national polities, like dragging up strange creatures from the deep ocean.

Since the fit between the project methods and the real-world problem is crucial, some more detailed description is appropriate. With direct support from many member nations, in 1988 the United Nations started the Intergovernmental Panel on Climate Change (IPCC). The purpose of the IPCC is to collect, vet, synthesize, and publish reports, providing the highest quality scientific *knowledge* about climate change in all aspects. The IPCC published its first report in 1990 and its fifth in 2014. These reports have made clear to all that humans have caused the current rapid climate change, and that all countries, albeit at different paces, would eventually suffer intensifying and devastating weather disasters from climate change. Based on this science, in 1992 the UNFCCC, ratified by 191 countries (parties), initiated a new global moral injunction: all countries should reduce their carbon dioxide and other greenhouse gas emissions. The 1997 Kyoto Protocol (third Conference of Parties to the UNFCCC, or COP 3) took the next step and designated individualized specific reduction targets (averaging around 6 percent from 1990 levels) for the industrialized countries, to be met by the 2008–2012 compliance period. By 2005 most of the industrialized countries (except the United States) had officially accepted and ratified these targets. Moreover, given the rapidly falling prices of renewable sources of energy, humanity does have the technological ability to rapidly reduce our collective emissions of carbon dioxide. Yet despite these many factors supporting emissions reduction—scientific, moral, and specific normative targets—national emissions took diverse trajectories, increasing, leveling off, or decreasing. The sum total of the countries' actions led to a continuing rapid rise in total global emissions (until 2015, when it leveled off for the first time).

Some of the industrialized countries began efforts to reduce their own emissions, or in place of that, to pay for equivalent reductions in the forests and industries of developing countries (the "Clean Development Mechanism"). Overall, the Organisation for Economic Co-operation and Development (OECD) countries slowed their rate of emissions increase, but only a few attained their Kyoto targets by domestic reduction. On the other hand, the developing countries were not assigned targets under Kyoto and increased their emissions rapidly. Today, China has become the largest annual emitter of carbon dioxide, although the United States still remains by far the largest in total emissions since the 1800s. In total, global emissions have continued to rise at the "worst case scenario" rate of the early IPCC reports. This continuous increase has dimmed hopes of constraining the global temperature rise to below 2°C (IEA, 2011), a level some scientists consider a tipping point in the worsening of climate change.

Accordingly, at this point the crucial study of humanity's global climate change predicament has changed from a geophysical to a social scientific one. Why are humans doing this? Can anything change their behavior? The global dilemma of climate change provides the conditions to carry out a global social scientific experiment. In response to the same stimulus, the long-term threat and risk posed by climate change, nations have been responding in very different ways. This (un)natural experiment can be used by social scientific research to search for the causes of different response patterns through comparative cross-national research. This possibility is provided by the variation in mitigation response across nations, countries, societies, and regions (our cases). As the ultimate outcome variable, since 1990 the cases have differed greatly in their emissions trajectories, stabilizing, going up, or going down.

This global situation contains some of the elements prescribed by the scientific method: cross-case variation in response to similar stimuli. This cross-case variation sets up the conditions for an (un)naturally occurring global social scientific quasi-experiment (Campbell, Stanley, and Gage, 1966). The Compon project seizes upon this situation and uses it as the basis for a global comparative research project. The global experimental question is this: *In the face of similar scientific knowledge, moral injunctions, normative targets, and technological potentials, why do the 1990–2013 carbon emission trajectories of different cases different so greatly, going up, leveling off, or decreasing?* What factors explain this range of variation? Why do not *all* cases make reducing emissions and increasing sinks (CO_2 absorptive forests) their top priority? Answers may come readily to mind and even seem obvious, but to better ascertain their validity, a scientific approach must convert such ideas into hypotheses, testable using standardized cross-case data. The comparative method in social science refers to the comparison of huge units (countries, regions, societies, polities) with many factors considered in their full interactive complexity (Ragin, 1987). The PN method greatly enhances our capacity to trace and grasp this interactive complexity.

Once having developed this kind of detailed network data and analysis for a number of cases, the possibility of cross-case comparison arises. Researchers of anthropogenic global climate change (AGCC) have concluded that it is a "super wicked" problem because of four factors: "Time is running out; those who cause the problem also seek to provide a solution; the central authority needed to address it is weak or non-existent; and, partly as a result, policy responses discount the future irrationally" (Levin et al., 2012). From the standpoint of social scientific causal analysis, AGCC is a super wicked problem because it entails multiple levels and types of input, feedback loops, and distributed impacts.

This kind of complexity requires a new way of thinking about social causality. In order to better understand the intertwining of factors, social scientists have been calling for new inter- or transdisciplinary approaches to the problem (Broadbent and Vaughter, 2014, Manfredo et al., 2014). As the following sections illustrate, the PN method helps greatly in the empirical study of this complexity, of how diverse causal factors intertwine in a field of political contention. As an ideal type, the PN approach can carry out such a program. It can operationalize different theoretical axioms as distinct network questions in the PN survey. The resulting relational data, coupled with other data from the survey, can distinguish the relative political efficacy of different relational media (Broadbent, 1989b). The network approach can accomplish this seemingly paradoxical feat because it puts the hypothesized media from different theoretical schools, as much as possible, into a common metric: *network terms testable by network data*. In reality, the difficulties of fielding a multinational study put pragmatic limits on how fully the ideal can be realized.

Given this range of causal possibilities, we designed the Compon project to collect not only networks between the actors, but also data on the influence, ideologies, beliefs, preferences, tactics, and political participation of the actors. Starting in 2007, over the course of six international meetings the growing number of case teams collaborated to design standardized data collection methods to produce comparable data. In addition to the PN approach, we incorporated newspaper discourse using in-depth content analysis and Discourse Network Analyzer, which revealed the clustering of actors and positions in the papers. We also built a database containing relevant data for each case, such as emissions, population, economy, and institutions. We envision that when sufficient data accumulate, after a number of intermediary analyses, we will employ Ragin's method of QCA to find (perhaps multiple) causal pathways to classes of outcomes in the dependent variable: emissions trajectories (increase, level off, decrease) between 1990 and 2012 (end of the first Kyoto commitment period) (Ragin, 1987). Moreover, if we can continue the project as a panel study with repeated surveys of the same cases over time, we can address a question of the experimental dynamics: *What level, if any, of carbon dioxide atmospheric concentrations and accompanying ecological disaster will prompt the global community to take effective action to radically reduce annual carbon emissions?*

Modeling the Climate Change Domain from a Policy Network Approach

In order to run the quasi-experimental design, we have to understand the basic factors that influence the outcome in cases of climate change response. Figure 37.1 models the basic processes that make up a *case* (the response of a political society to the challenge of climate change mitigation). This model, the basic Compon ecopolitical case model, brings together different factors that bear upon a case and influence its emissions trajectories over time in a dynamic and reciprocating process. The model links a case to its internal and external dynamic influencing factors. It shows how the different cases contribution to the formation of global regimes.

The initiating factor in this model is the big arrow from geophysical climate change to scientific knowledge about it. Swedish scientists initiated climate change research and also in 1988 started the IPCC. Thus began the global learning cycle described in the figure, which has by now penetrated all countries. The meteorological science of

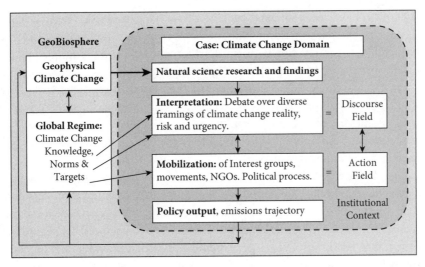

FIGURE 37.1 Climate change ecopolitical model.

atmospheric chemistry provides the only way to understand the causes of climate change, since they are not visibly obvious. Usually social contention occurs over more obvious harms like poverty, oppression, discrimination, or religious sectarianism. Even there, it may take earlier developments in moral codes and philosophy to eventually justify the "cognitive liberation" that spurs resistance (McAdam, 1982). The findings of natural science sometimes arouse mobilizing passions, as evidenced by the Copernican revolution and the reaction to Darwin's theory of evolution. Contentious passions can be intensified if the scientific information entails a change in the modes of production and consumption, as do the solutions to climate change. In this case, the climate change scientific findings set off a social process of interpreting and acting on the problem. This is the process of socially constructing the problem, framing it with degrees of reality, belief, risk, and priority for action (Hannigan, 1995). In our model, we simplify this social construction process down to the interaction of *discourse field* and *action field*.

In some cases (societies, polities of climate change process) these processes have been largely consensual, whereas in others, such as the United States, they have aroused tremendous contention. At any given point in the cycle, a case will produce some amount of carbon emissions, and perhaps some policies that will modify those emissions. The policies range from rapid growth using coal-fired energy, which greatly increases emissions, to support for solar and wind energy, which can rapidly reduce emissions. These policies and emissions in turn affect the case's stance within international negotiations. The international negotiations establish a global regime, which can be weak or strong in its effects on total global emissions and atmospheric levels of carbon dioxide. These global effects then feed back to each case in a repetitive cycle. Increasingly, especially boosted by the Conference of the Parties (COP 21) in Paris in December 2015, all cases (societies, nations) have become participants in this feedback loop.

This climate change ecopolitical model indicates (1) the interaction between case and global context, (2) the interaction within the case between active processes and shaping contexts, and (3) the interaction between the discourse field and the action field during the social construction of the problem. Figure 37.2 simplifies this process even further to show just the discourse and action fields and their interactions as networks between actors and frames (interpretive ideas, or in Latour's terms, *actants*; Latour [2005]). These actors and frames are what can be directly measured by the PN survey. *In other words, discourse meanings and actor intentions interact to form advocacy coalitions that contend to determine policy output and outcomes under institutional conditions.*

These levels must be taken into account as context when interpreting the patterns of policy networks. In the climate change domain, the active political process in a case proceeds through perception, interpretation, discourse, and sociopolitical interaction, which arise in tension with preexisting institutionalized formations. These interactions shape the actual networks that emerge to influence case policy outputs and outcomes.

Any research project and its data collection instruments must be designed to address the critical questions at stake, insofar as they can be assessed during the planning phase. The climate change policy domain is uniquely mediated by elite and public acceptance of abstract scientific knowledge. However, the translation of this scientific conclusion into a political force powerful enough to rapidly reduce emissions remains a major stumbling block. The PN method allows the researcher to trace the golden thread of scientific knowledge. It goes into and through the social meat-grinder of conflicting interpretations and contentious politics, either to disappear altogether or to come out connected to some real outcomes.

To many people in the United States, scientific findings remain wispy theory, nothing concrete and scary enough to stimulate the required changes in habits, profits, and institutions. Unlike the black smoke or toxic smell of local industrial pollution, climate change does not present any irrefutable causal evidence to the human senses. On the contrary, the resulting excess fires, floods, droughts, storms, heat waves, sea level

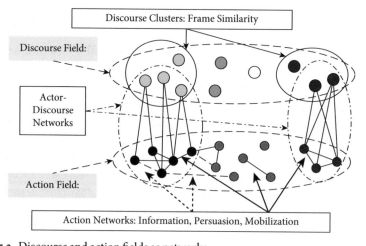

FIGURE 37.2 Discourse and action fields as networks.

rises, and many other changes can easily be written off by the nonspecialist as natural weather variation. Adding inertia to its acceptance, the idea of human-caused climate change, along with that of evolution, poses a fundamental challenge to many traditional religious beliefs. As a result, in the United States, rather than ready acceptance, the idea of AGCC often elicits rejection, denial, or numb indifference, leading to inaction (Norgaard, 2006). If people and societies do not accept the scientific findings as a palpable basis for action, they will not reduce emissions. However, the same cannot be said for many other countries, as the Compon study shows.

In empowering beliefs about climate change, including scientific knowledge as one kind of "belief," their political potency depends on their being taken up by an advocacy coalition. A previous study of national compliance with international environmental treaties concluded that advocacy coalitions are key actors (Clark et al., 2001). That study followed the theoretical lead about advocacy coalitions by Sabatier (Sabatier and Jenkins-Smith, 1993). The study also noted the importance of "multinational, multi-actor advocacy communities" in global environmental governance and the inadequacy of traditional approaches to explain these. But, it added, "*Our study was not designed as an exercise in developing or testing propositions about the growth and impacts of such actor coalitions or interest networks*" (Clark et al., 2001, 187). (It should be noted here that the advocacy coalition concept would appear to assume a pluralistic democratic political system with an active civil society. However, in this comparative study, not all societies, such as China, have such a polity. Nonetheless, even within its party-dominated power structure, different advocacy coalitions do develop and contend over proper policy directions.)

HYPOTHESES ABOUT CAUSES OF NATIONAL CLIMATE CHANGE RESPONSES

The Compon project took the baton of propositions about actor coalitions and ran with it. Starting in 2007, the project members developed a number of hypotheses about the growth and impacts of such actor coalitions (Broadbent, 2010). The hypotheses developed from the broader literature relevant to climate change politics, including empirical studies and also fields such as the sociology of science and communication studies. It was important to couch these hypotheses in terms testable by the network data that would emerge from the project. Fundamentally, given the problem, all the hypotheses concern the social conditions under which the IPCC-type scientific information could be turned into actual policy outcomes curtailing carbon emissions. Following are a few exemplary bivariate (ceteris paribus) hypotheses:

H1 *The more the culture gives legitimacy to the IPCC-type science, the more a case will mitigate its carbon emissions.*Network indicator: The proportion of organizations in the climate change domain that receive vital scientific information directly from the IPCC.

H2 *The more credible and engaged the domestic climate change science community, the more a case will mitigate its carbon emissions.*Network indicator: Degree of engagement of domestic research establishments as knowledge brokers in scientific information networks.

H3 *The more powerful the interest groups dependent upon fossil fuel use are, the less a case will mitigate its carbon emissions.*Network indicator: Relative political influence scores of fossil fuel companies and related business sectoral associations in networks of political cooperation and advocacy coalitions.

H4 *The stronger the advocacy coalitions in support of the dominant (IPCC type) climate change scientific findings are, the more a case will mitigate its carbon emissions.*Network indicator: Relative political influence scores of networked clusters of organizations advocating for climate change mitigation.

THE SURVEY INSTRUMENT AND DATA

In a cross-national comparative project, the common survey instrument has to be designed to capture the minimal information necessary for the comparison to answer the most pressing questions. That is because of the many limitations, including respondent patience, on even the best-funded survey. The PN survey has been a living, growing, transforming instrument. In the early versions, it took an hour or more to administer in a personal interview. Recently, the Compon project, aiming to make it easier for new case teams, reduced it to a fifteen-minute survey with fewer questions and networks that can be done online. The survey both enables the research and also strictly delimits it. As such, the instrument must be subjected to continual reflexive, critical, but constructive scrutiny.

A single PN survey gathers data on one policy domain (labor, climate change, etc.) at the national level in one country. A single national domain is one case of a domain that may exist in many countries. The PN survey tries to capture a set of networks among all the consequential organizations in a policy domain. The selection of organizations, or boundary-setting operation, is a crucial first step. This act establishes the list of organizations that will be included in the survey as respondents, and a longer list (mostly international) that will be included as passive partners without interviewing. This problem of boundary specification can be difficult for a large and complex polity. The list must include the most central actors, then should go down the hierarchy of organizational power until it reaches the maximal number that the average respondent can handle. In practice, this usually means a list of between 50 and 130 organizations. However, the research team starts in relative ignorance of the actual influence of different organizations within the domain. The team has to pick them out from existing studies, newspaper reports, organizational charts, a panel of experts, and other secondary sources. Once the survey goes to the field, the list is set in stone.

The PN survey instrument asks about the kinds of relational media, such as information or collaboration, that organizations transfer among themselves in the domain. Each organizational respondent checks off from the full organizational list all those specific organizations with which it transfers a specific kind of relational medium. The name of network designates the kind of relational medium, such as information, that it contains. On the survey, each type of network has its own full list of organizations in the domain. The respondent checks off all the other organizations on the list with which it has that kind of relationship. Each bit of data is a dyadic relationship of a particular content.

A wide variety of transferred media could, in principle, generate influence in a domain. The media could consist, for instance, of cowrie shells, common kin-group membership, habitual or coerced obedience, vital information, formal authority, pay-off money, trust or confidence in long-term reciprocity, belief in a common symbol, adherence to a common ideology, and many more. Given the limits of survey length and respondent fatigue, a multinational research project can actually only include questions about a few types of networks in its common survey instrument. So the project must select them judiciously based on problem, theory, or experience.

All the N organizational survey responses for a given type of network are combined into an N by N data matrix. This matrix contains all the dyadic transfers between organizations of a single medium or network type within the domain. Using this matrix data, a network analysis program like UCINet creates a graphical representation of the total pattern of social distance among all the organizations as well as statistics.

The PN survey also asks the organizational respondent about the relative perceived influence of other organizations, as well as about the respondent organization's issue-related knowledge and beliefs, solution preferences, resources, participation in specific bills, and degree of goals attained. If we want to know how a domain produces policies, a crucial piece of information is the relative power of the domain members and of the ideologies and policy preferences they carry. Political studies heretofore have often considered power in its gross, undifferentiated quantity. The main question was, who had it and who did not? But contemporary theories increasingly contend that power is relational and can be produced by different types of incentive networks, depending on the case.

The active policy-formation process is constituted by mixtures of many dyadic interactions and whole networks. The survey reveals the mixture (of measured networks) particular to a given national domain at a given time. This slice-in-time network is like a slice across a river; while the single slice cannot represent the whole river, it does represent the particular qualities of that river that would be found nowhere else. Hence it implies both the upstream and the downstream formations of the same river. The same is true for the domain network, which implies the generative past leading up to it and its future behavior as well. The latter can be captured by repeated panel surveys. Comparison of domain networks across cases reveals different mixtures in network types, patterns, interactions, and other qualities. Restricting our cases to contemporary nation-states reduces but does not eliminate this variation.

Measuring Power

The empirical study of relational power started with the community power structure research of the 1950s and 1960s. Out of such studies grew many debates about the nature and composition of power, the measurement of which is necessary to the PN approach. By asking knowledgeable respondents who was most influential, Hunter discovered a highly centralized, informal, elite power structure in Atlanta, mostly composed of business leaders who called the political shots (Hunter, 1953). He created the *reputational* measure of power, which remains a central measure in the PN survey instrument. Dahl countered those centralized findings in his study of power in New Haven (Dahl, 1961). He found that officials in the formal decision-making positions were besieged by many demands from diverse interest groups, but found a fair balance among them and made the final decisions. From these observations, Dahl created a *positional* theory of power within a pluralist polity—that the formal positions of authority such as the mayor really do exercise power. These two studies established a continuing debate about the distribution of power within a polity (political field). We can also refer to a *behavioral* measure of power, based on the self-reported political goal attainment success rates of organizations. The discussion of power and its network measurement goes much deeper and is very relevant to comparative political studies, but space limitations prevent its pursuit here (Knoke, 1990; Lukes, 2005; Scott, 2001).

The PN survey provides data on all three of these approaches to the measurement of power. One network question asks respondents to check off all the organizations especially influential within the policy domain. The sum of these checks from all respondents produces a *reputational* power score for each organization in the domain. Reputational power sounds like a weak measure built on rumor, but in the PN survey it is a very strong measure because it comes from the assessments of engaged political experts. *Positional* power is represented by the official, legitimate decision-making authorities on the organizational list (such as ruling political party or parties, president or prime minister's office or cabinet, governmental ministries and their departments). And finally, the survey asks for each organization's evaluation of its own political success by its participation in and attempt to influence the outcome of each of a number of policymaking events (such as, in the climate change mitigation domain, a decision about a carbon tax or emissions trading scheme), producing a *behavioral* measure of power.

The PN approach assumes that real power need not be confined to the formal authorities. This is, on the contrary, an empirical question. The organizations consequential to the outputs and outcomes of a national policymaking process can potentially come from any sector of state and society, domestic or even international. With independent measures of power in hand, the researcher can test the relative influence of different organizations and different networks within the policy domain network. In any domain, certain actors and types of network will show up as generating more or less power than others. These power and influence data help assess the relative validity of different causal hypotheses. Different hypothesized factors can be integrated into a hybrid explanatory model, weighted by their respective production of power in the domain.

THE NETWORK IMAGE: MEASUREMENT, INTERPRETATION, AND ANALYSIS

The basic notion of social distance is crucial to the measurement and graphical representation of social and political networks. Social distance is defined as the number of other actors A has to pass through in order to get to D. Arranging actors by social distance on a two-dimensional plane is simple enough for four actors in a string (A→B→C→D) or in a star pattern with one central hub. But when you have 50 to 130 actors with multiple connections and pathways stretching among them, the most accurate representation requires three or more dimensions, determined by computer algorithms. To inspect this visually, humans have to look at the two- or at most three-dimensional shadow cast in what the computer algorithm determines to be the least distorting projection of its optimal N-dimensional solution. Practically, this means that any flat projection of a complex network might place distant nodes near each other, creating an illusion of closeness—a caveat for visual inspection to be kept in mind.

A PN image is constructed from a whole network, or at least as close to one as the research team can approach. Within the network perspective, the network pattern is a kind of graphical statistical indicator. The network pattern is arrived at by relational statistical methods of calculating social space. Once it has been created and the types of actors have been indicated by distinguishing icons, the researcher can often visually discern qualities of the large-scale pattern: clusters in dynamic tension with others, patterns that brim with political significance. This is refreshing for the artists among social scientists, who tend to think in patterns rather than in linear correlations (Abbott, 1988). Just as the pattern itself may arise from chaotic dynamism, so too may it be irreducible to network statistical indicators such as centrality and clique analysis. Many forms of network statistics, such as betweenness measures, may be extremely helpful. But at the same time, interpretation of the pattern requires intuitive linking to larger political dynamics and to the subtleties of complex interactions through detailed case knowledge. Quantitative statistical measures cannot by themselves adequately capture this entire holistic pattern or its implications. Hence, PN research requires a creative interplay of fuzzy interpretation and precise quantification.

Quantitative Descriptive Indicators

Statistical measures provide crucial and precise information about aspects of the network that can sharply reveal differences in comparative research. For instance, one can adjust the size of the icons to reflect the amount of information they exchange with other actors or some other property. The more they exchange, the more central they are, at least within a given cluster. The distribution of sizes and patterns will differ across cases, and probably across domains within a given society. These statistical measures have been elaborated on in many books and need not be reviewed in detail here (Prell, 2012; Wasserman and Faust, 1994).[5] But a brief summary may be useful.

Network statistics produce quantitative scores for individual members, member types, subgroups, and whole networks. Individual actor scores derived from network measures include indegrees, outdegrees, centrality, and brokerage. A simple count of different types of actors in the different cases can be very revealing. Respondents may also assign scores indicating the actor's reputation for influence (as mentioned above). Subgroup indicators include cliques of different sizes and composition (k-cliques) produced by clustering (a set of actors from three to n sharing many ties within the set).[6] Whole network scores include density (percent of all possible ties actually made), connectivity (percent of all actors actually connected into the network), and path lengths (percent of actors that can be reached by one tie, by two ties, and so forth).

Once some distinct clusters in a network have been determined, one may investigate the relationships between them. Some clusters may be totally isolated from others, forming what Burt (2005) calls structural holes. Or they have one or more actors that bridge between them, crossing the structural hole, in theory giving such uniquely situated actors relatively strong social capital and power (Gould and Fernandez, 1989; Putnam, 2000).

From a different approach, block models allow the researcher to compare the joint role structures of multiple network matrices (Wasserman and Faust, 1994, 425–460). This method divides the members into groups with central actors (leaders) and groups with peripheral actors (followers). One study used this technique to compare leadership in the United States and German urban power structures (Breiger and Pattison, 1978).

In dealing with multiple networks in the same domain, the method of matrix correlation (QAP) is very useful. It shows the degree of congruence or overlap between two or more networks. It can help answer questions such as: Do the political support and information networks coincide with each other or involve different actors and/or different patterns? This can be an important theoretical question. The degree to which the same actors transfer both kinds of resources will indicate a certain type of power concentration in the system. For instance, in the climate change mitigation domain, one important subset of actors will be those who receive vital scientific information from the IPCC. If these actors are also joined by a mutual political coalition, their impact will probably be magnified.

The use of two-mode network analysis permits studying the relationships of actors to ideas or events (Breiger, 1974). This has become useful in studying the relation of actors to discourse, as pioneered in discourse network analyzer (see chapter by Leifeld, this volume). In the case of climate change politics, the organizational actors have different preferred ways of framing the issue. The earlier part of the Compon study distilled a set of 131 different ways of framing climate change from the three major newspapers

(2007–2008) of seventeen societies. For instance, some cases accepted the climate change science promulgated by the IPCC, while a few rejected it. The Compon PN survey includes questions about actor framing preferences as well. This allows us to distinguish the field of discourse from the field of action.

The discourse field shows the frames that are prominent within a domain and how they tend to cluster with each other. The meaning pattern of clusters and the holes between the clusters defines in itself a distinct "cultural" pattern of framing preferences for an issue domain (Pachucki and Breiger, 2010). The action field, in contrast, shows how actors actually establish ties with other actors by transferring or exchanging various kinds of resources and positive or negative sanctions. Each of these two fields can be analyzed separately, or they can be analyzed in tandem. In the latter approach, by analyzing how actors cluster around common framing profiles, one may distinguish potential advocacy coalitions within a domain. Then, if in their actual ties to each other, the same sets of actors also indicate that they actually do exchange vital information and join together in political advocacy coalitions, one has very strong evidence of the existence of advocacy coalitions. From this point, it is possible to measure the relative power of these advocacy coalitions in the ways mentioned above, to see which ones get their way in shaping policy. This then is the heart of how the PN approach can reveal the structure of political configurations, leading to the outcomes of emissions trajectories. These network statistics, applied to comparative PN analysis, offer powerful new tools for digging deeper into the "wicked" complexity of political systems, as exemplified by comparative climate change mitigation politics.

CHALLENGES AND NEW DIRECTIONS

Including Meaning in the Relational Social and Political Approach

As noted above, the PN method has blossomed in many qualitative and quantitative studies. One significant change has been the expansion from the study of interests and interest-based preferences to include the study of discourse and culture. This adds the dimension of meaning to the dimension of the relational. That is, it includes cultural distance and clustering based on the similarity of actors' profiles of meanings or frames about an issue. In this vein, discourse network analysis (see chapter by Leifeld, this volume) develops meaning clusters according to the number of actors sharing frames. Breiger develops "cultural holes" in parallel to Burt's "structural holes"(Burt, 1992; Pachucki and Breiger, 2010). This cultural approach provides a network method of operationalizing Bourdieu's concept of field (improving on his method of assigning positions to actors based on their quantities of economic and cultural capital) (Bourdieu, 1984, 1985). Sonnett (2015) has combined these approaches into a "netfield," and Martin

(2003) has expanded on the relational qualities of the field. As another aspect, the emergent quality of patterns in dynamic networks indicates the utility of chaos theory (Gregersen and Sailer, 1993).

Complexity and Chaos

Complexity refers to the "butterfly effect," whereby seemingly insignificant elements of a system can magnify to become determining causal factors. *Chaos* refers to activity that on one level seems random and unpredictable, but on a higher level can produce a pattern. This emergent pattern gives order and meaning to the seeming chaos below. The different types of networks and their members interact with each other in "networks of networks," providing effects of complexity and chaos (D'Agostino and Scala, 2014, Lee et al., 2014). The PN survey gathers data on multiple networks among multiple organizational actors, thereby enabling the representation of multiple networks. These representations are of course limited to the *measured* networks among the *selected* organizations asked about in the survey instrument. Each discrete network type, such as information transfer or political collaboration, contains a unique subset of actors engaged in a unique relational pattern. The researcher can view each network singly, examine the tensions between the different networks, or integrate them all into a total unified network. Multiple networks conjointly bear upon an actor (node) to affect behavior. Likewise, whole networks interact as layers within complex topologies, their tensions and synergies affecting the operation of institutions and systems (Menichetti et al., 2014).

The networks, singly and as multiple synergies, manifest patterns, often displaying densely interlinked sets of actors forming clusters, as well as sparser areas between clusters. The data allow the researcher to discern the particular ideologies and policy preferences, relative amounts of power and influence, and tactics toward discrete policy struggles of the different actors, clusters, and networks. These distinct aspects have various relationships of complementarity or tension with each other, which affect the operation of the total domain network. The special analytical capacities here described allow a more exact and differentiated tracing of the political process through to its outputs. The exercise shows why a particular national policy domain ratifies some policies and not others. Ultimately, the PN approach is about better understanding the operation of power in political systems, that is, about why political systems produce various outputs and outcomes.

New Theoretical Forms

Integrating the several dimensions provides for a fuller accounting of the deep ontological formative differences among societies and polities. Ultimately, this trend will merge social actors and cultural memes as potentially potent co-actants in multiplex, complex, and chaotic sociocultural networks (Latour, 2005). Such seemingly subtle differences profoundly affect the diversity of political system operation. While perhaps seemingly a digression, this discussion of complexity and chaos is quite indicated and required by the comparative PN study of political systems. The PN approach provides new ways to grasp these subtleties.

The key advantage of the PN approach, *as an ideal type*, then, is to let us see in one view all the relevant modes and patterns of interaction, ideology, and influence among all the relevant organizational actors and ideas in a given national policy domain. Many practical obstacles hinder the realization of this ideal, but it is the visionary goal. More exacting and precise data often, after overcoming paradigm inertia, force the creation of new models and theories. The PN method embodies this threat or promise. For example, in the network one can consider the position and operations of a single organization or a type or class of organizations. An economic ministry or a protest movement can be juxtaposed against the rest of the network. The same is true of a class or type of organization, such as business associations or labor associations. This spotlighting reveals the relative clustering, cohesion, ideologies, and political power of a class, and hence of its relevance as a collective political actor. Each of these discrete spotlight analyses invokes and enables the more refined testing of theories that have grown up around the given type of individual or collective actor, such as government bureaucracy or social movement or class. When the network is examined in total, though, the conjoint presence of the actors and their theoretical halos creates an awkward juxtaposition. This jumble, under the heat and pressure of systematic inquiry, melts and melds theoretical concepts into new hybrid explanatory models and theories. Rather than being inductive or deductive, this is best labeled an abductive process of theory building (Tavory and Timmermans, 2014).[7] To push a pun, it runs off with the best ideas.

The theoretical reformulation implied by the PN approach is profound and paradigm shaking. Political science is imbued with an orientation to "who gets what, when, how" and how rational actors attain those ends (Lasswell, 1936). To this focus on the individual actor, political sociology added attention to the "social basis of politics": large-scale social groupings, institutions, formations, and changes (Lipset, 1963).[8] The study of political networks brings a fresh third interactive perspective to this quest. The network view argues that actors are creating or embedded in sets of local, relatively stable relationships with other actors. Even if relationships are rationally and instrumentally created by individual actors, the resulting larger pattern of relationships bends back to face them with a forceful context. But the relationships may be more than rational and instrumental. They may even shape their very motivation and goals; actors may be embedded in networks and may even be their puppets (Emirbayer, 1997). In addition, multiple networks interact in complex ways. To best understand these implications, one must don a new set of relational-relativity spectacles. Despite the noted limits and cautions, the PN approach opens to our view a new social-political landscape. As we explore this strange morphology, it puts existing theories to the test and forces the generation of new, more closely hewn questions and theories.

Limits to the Network Approach

When one delves into power empirically, as this approach allows, it becomes complicated. In my extended studies of the PN data from the labor PN project, I have reached my own conclusions and speculations about the implications for theory and measurement, noted as follows and in preceding sections of this chapter.

Western political theory, located at the middle range, carries paradigmatic assumptions about the composition of political systems—of isolated, rational actors driven by interests, using instrumental, calculated tactics, and possessing powers that exert force upon each other. Each actor encounters its limits coming from the aggregate forces it faces. In addition, these actors play upon a landscape of institutionalized rules that may sanction their actions. This view is akin to Newtonian theory in physics, wherein objects exert at a distance a force known as gravity. Certainly this process can produce a type of relationship and power network. Coming from mathematical graph theory, formal terms refer to networks as consisting of edges and nodes. This projects a rather crisp image that is transitive and of equal quality throughout, like a computer network. This kind of image forms an underlying assumption for a lot of theory and statistics for social and political networks, such as centrality and betweenness. However, this assumption places more paradigmatic stumbling blocks in the way of comparative PN studies.

All social network theories, images, and statistics, unfortunately, suffer from a common debilitating, if not fatal, flaw. They tend to assume that social networks are integral and transitive (that they transfer the same relational mode throughout). This misplaced concreteness arises because many network theorists and statisticians implicitly take electrical or computer networks, with their automatic and accurate shuttling of information, as their models. Social networks, however, may work more like the game of telephone. The message degrades and changes as it passes from node to node. The PN survey (and any whole network survey) produces a network by connecting the dyadic links indicated by the survey respondents. We assume that the network is integral and transitive. But perhaps members do not transfer exactly the same information or other medium when they receive from one partner and then give to another partner. Accordingly, the researcher must maintain a skeptical awareness of the breakdown potential of social networks and look for additional evidence to justify any conclusions drawn from images and statistics.

The social and political reality is much messier and becomes more so when viewed comparatively. Harrison White laid the groundwork for contemporary mathematical and statistical studies of networks (Freeman, 2004). In the first edition of his germinal work, *Identity and Control*, he states that his work deals only with social relations, not with culture. In his second edition, he equates culture with identity which in turn reduces to control strategies (White, 2008; Emirbayer, 2004, 8). He treats actors and networks as objectively real entities as measured and hence can accept the crisp, crystalline view. And yet even he ends up saying: "*Social organization is like some impacted, mineralized goo, some amazing swirl of local nuclei and long strands of order among disor-der* (White, 1992, 127). Now, if networks were the sole reality, White might say that they resemble disconnected pick-up-sticks. But the word *goo* implies that his intuition sig-nals some inarticulate, less tangible substance surrounding the networks.

As we go into it and use it for comparative studies, the PN approach forces us to recognize more and more goo, like dark matter in physics. Actors and networks can be composed of different stuff than calculated *Macht*, than lines of power per se. In a given society, the sum total of forces at work can create valleys into which actors and relationships fall, congealing and taking shape along predetermined lines. This viewpoint of network formation parallels the Einsteinian view of gravity, which contrary to Newton, sees it as a curvature in space-time into which objects fall (Hawking, 1996). A whole national society is shaped over time by culture, social training, and a wide range of informal and formal institutions to generate certain types of actors and relationships in its political processes. Rather than rational actor theory, this reality is better approached by relational network theory (Emirbayer and Goodwin, 1994; Emirbayer, 1997), but even this fails to grasp the encompassing ontology of the social.

CONCLUSIONS

Over the past centuries (starting with the ancient Greeks), founded in cross-national comparison, the field of political studies has developed various broad (macro) theories about the drivers of policy formation, including class, culture, rational actor compe-tition, and institutions. Evidence has consisted largely of narrative case studies high-lighting certain factors or broad statistical tendencies. Both have a vagueness consistent with their lack of specific mechanisms and systematically traceable relational patterns of power. The new approach of PN research, in contrast, pushes research into unexpected, variegated, and complex dynamics, at best only partially and tangentially explained by any of these theories. Even when investigating just a single domain in a single case, the PN meso-relational perspective is eye opening. But the comparative method has always been the mother of social scientific theory building. When used to compare the same policy domain across different national political systems, the PN approach reveals dis-tinct and nuanced configurations that offer great stimulation to the exploratory mind. The variegated configurations show how subtly and deeply the actual processes may dif-fer. They can produce power and outcomes through very different mixtures of actors, motivations, discourse, and relational network modalities. Thus, peering deeply into these and comparing these complex meso-level dynamics pushes one to rethink the validity of old theories and to create new hybrid models and theories more descrip-tive and predictive of the newly observed realities. In this way, the PN approach has the potential to profoundly reshape the study of politics.

NOTES

1. In contrast, the larger school of social network analysis focuses on small-group or interindividual scale interactions (Freeman, 2004).
2. Compon project website, www.compon.org.
3. While comparing the policy networks, in the final stage the Compon project will feed them into an analytical process known as qualitative comparative analysis (QCA). This process facilitates the search for causal pathways leading cases to more or less compliance with emerging global mitigation regimes (Ragin and Becker, 1992).
4. Perhaps the deepest theoretical program on this perspective comes from Latour (2005).
5. The statistical algorithms that run these analyses on network matrices are available in network analysis software packages such as UCINet (Borgatti, Everett, and Freeman, 2002).
6. What Robert Putnam calls bonding ties (Putnam, 2000).
7. It runs directly contrary to the deductive theoretical hypothesis testing approach often taught in social scientific graduate methods courses. The latter results in the rather loose connection between reality and theory typical of macro-institutional, event-illustrative, and usually reductionist studies.
8. During his career, Lipset was president of both the American Sociological Association (1993–1994) and the American Political Science Association (1981–1982).

REFERENCES

Abbott, A. (1988). "Transcending General Linear Reality." *Sociological Theory* 6: 169–186.

Anheier, H. (1987). "Structural Analysis and Strategic Research Design: Studying Politicized Interorganizational Networks." *Sociological Forum* 2(3): 181–203.

Beck, U. (1999). *World Risk Society*. Malden, MA: Blackwell.

Borgatti, S. P., Everett, M. G., and Freeman, L. C. (2002). *Ucinet 6 for Windows: Software for Social Network Analysis*. Harvard, MA: Analytic Technologies.

Bourdieu, P. (1984). *Distinction: A Social Critique of the Judgement of Taste*. Cambridge, MA: Harvard University Press.

Bourdieu, P. (1985). "The Social Space and the Genesis of Groups." *Theory and Society* 14(6): 723–744.

Breiger, R. L. (1974). "The Duality of Persons and Groups." *Social Forces* 53(2): 181–190.

Breiger, R., and Pattison, P. (1978). "The Joint Role Structure of Two Communities' Elites." *Sociological Methods and Research* 7(2): 213–226.

Broadbent, J. P. (1982). "State and Citizen in Japan: Social Structure and Policy-Making in the Development of a 'New Industrial City,' 1960 to 1980." PhD thesis, Harvard University.

Broadbent, J. (1989a). "Strategies and Structural Contradictions—Growth Coalition Politics in Japan." *American Sociological Review* 54(5): 707–721.

Broadbent, J. (1989b). "Environmental Politics in Japan—an Integrated Structural-Analysis." *Sociological Forum* 4(2): 179–202.

Broadbent, J. (1998). *Environmental Politics in Japan: Networks of Power and Protest*. Cambridge, UK: Cambridge University Press.

Broadbent, J. (2010). "Science and Climate Change Policy Making: A Comparative Network Perspective." In *Adaptation and Mitigation Strategies for Climate Change*, edited by A. Sumi, K. Fukushi, and A. Hiramatsu, pp. 187–214. New York: Springer.

Broadbent, J., and Vaughter, P. (2014). "Inter-Disciplinary Analysis of Climate Change and Society: A Network Approach." In *Understanding Society and Natural Resources: Forging New Strands of Integration across the Social Sciences*, edited by M. Manfredo et al., pp. 203–228. New York: Springer.

Burt, R. 2005. *Brokerage & Closure: An Introduction to Social Capital*. New York: Oxford University Press.

Burt, R. S. (1992). *Structural Holes: The Social Structure of Competition*. Cambridge. MA: Harvard University Press.

Campbell, D. T., Stanley, J. C., and Gage, N. L. (1966). *Experimental and Quasi-Experimental Designs for Research*. Chicago: R. McNally.

Clark, W. C., Jaeger, J., van Eijndhoven, J., and Dickson, N. (Eds.). (2001). *Learning to Manage Global Environmental Risks. Volume 1, A Comparative History of Social Responses to Climate Change, Ozone Depletion, and Acid Rain*. Cambridge, MA: MIT Press.

D'Agostino, G., and Scala, A. (Eds.). (2014). *Networks of Networks: The Last Frontier of Complexity*. New York: Springer

Dahl, R. A. (1961). *Who Governs? Democracy and Power in an American City*. New Haven, CT: Yale University Press.

Deutsch, K. W. (1966). *The Nerves of Government: Models of Political Communication and Control*. New York: Free Press.

Emirbayer, M. (1997). "Manifesto for a Relational Sociology." *American Journal of Sociology* 103(2). doi:10.1086/231209.

Emirbayer, M. (2004). "The Alexander School of Cultural Sociology." *Thesis Eleven* 79(1): 5–15.

Emirbayer, M., and Goodwin, J. (1994). "Network Analysis, Culture and the Problem of Agency." *American Journal of Sociology* 99(6): 1411–1454.

Freeman, L. (2004). *The Development of Social Network Analysis: A Study in the Sociology of Science*. Vancouver: Empirical Press.

Gould, R., and Fernandez, R. (1989). "Structures of Mediation: A Formal Approach to Brokerage in Transaction Networks." *Sociological Methodology* 19: 89–126.

Gregersen, H., and Sailer, L. (1993). "Chaos Theory and Its Implications for Social Science Research." *Human Relations* 46(7): 777–802. doi:10.1177/001872679304600701.

Hannigan, J. A. (1995). *Environmental Sociology, a Social Constructivist Perspective*. New York: Routledge.

Hawking, S. W. (1996). *The Illustrated a Brief History of Time*. New York: Bantam.

Heinz, J., Laumann, E., Salisbury, R., and Nelson, R. (1993). *The Hollow Core: Private Interests in National Policy Making*. Cambridge, MA: Harvard University Press.

Hironaka, A. (2014). *Greening the Globe*. New York: Cambridge University Press.

Homans, G. C. (1961). *Social Behavior: Its Elementary Forms*. New York: Harcourt Brace & World.

Hunter, F. (1953). *Community Power Structure*. Chapel Hill: University of North Carolina Press.

International Energy Agency (IEA). (2011). *Prospect of Limiting the Global Increase in Temperature to 2°C Is Getting Bleaker*. Paris: International Energy Agency.

Kenis, P., and Schneider, V. (1991). " 'Policy Networks and Policy Analysis: Scrutinizing a New Analytical Toolbox." In *Policy Networks. Empirical Evidence and Theoretical Considerations*, edited by B. Marin and R. Mayntz, pp. 25–59. Frankfurt/Main: Campus.

Knoke, D. (1981). "Power Structures." In *Handbook of Political Behavior*, edited by S. Long, pp. 275–332. New York: Plenum.

Knoke, D. (1990). *Political Networks*. Cambridge, UK: Cambridge University Press.

Knoke, D., and Laumann, E. (1982). "The Social Organization of National Policy Domains: An Exploration of Some Structural Hypotheses." In *Social Structure and Network Analysis*, edited by P. Marsden and N. Lin, pp. 255–270. Beverly Hills, CA: Sage Publications.

Knoke, D., Pappi, F., Broadbent, J., and Tsujinaka, Y. (1996). *Comparing Policy Networks: Labor Politics in the U.S., Germany and Japan*. New York: Cambridge University Press.

Lasswell, H. D. (1936). *Politics: Who Gets What, When, How*. New York: Whittlesey House, McGraw-Hill.

Latour, B. (2005). *Reassembling the Social: An Introduction to Actor-Network-Theory*. New York: Oxford University Press.

Laumann, E. O., Galaskiewicz, J., and Marsden, P. (1978). "Community Structure as Interorganizational Linkages." *Annual Review of Sociology* 4: 455–484.

Laumann, E. O., and Knoke, D. (1987). *The Organizational State*. Madison: University of Wisconsin Press.

Laumann, E. O., and Marsden, P. (1979). "The Analysis of Oppositional Structures in Political Elites: Identifying Collective Actors." *American Sociological Review* 44: 713–732.

Laumann, E., and Pappi, F. U. (1976). *Networks of Collective Action: A Perspective on Community Influence Systems*. New York: Academic Press.

Lee, K. M., Kim, J. Y., Lee, S., and Goh, K.-I. (2014). "Multiplex Networks." In *Networks of Networks: The Last Frontier of Complexity*, edited by G. D'Agostino and A. Scala, pp. 53–72. New York: Springer

Levin, K., Cashore, B., Bernstein, S., and Auld, G. (2012). "Overcoming the Tragedy of Super Wicked Problems: Constraining Our Future Selves to Ameliorate Global Climate Change." *Policy Sciences* 45(2): 123–152.

Lipset, S. M. (1963). *Political Man: The Social Bases of Politics*. Garden City, NY: Doubleday.

Lukes, S. (2005). *Power: A Radical View*. 2d ed. New York: Palgrave Macmillan.

Manfredo, M. J., Vaske, J. J., Rechkemmer, A., and Duke, E. A. (Eds.). (2014). *Understanding Society and Natural Resources: Forging New Strands of Integration across the Social Sciences*. Springer Netherlands. http://www.springer.com/us/book/9789401789585.

Marsh, D. (1998). *Comparing Policy Networks*. Buckingham: Open University Press.

Martin, J. L. (2003). "What Is Field Theory? 1." *American Journal of Sociology* 109(1): 1–49.

McAdam, D. (1982). *Political Process and the Development of Black Insurgency*. Chicago: University of Chicago Press.

Menichetti, G., Remondini, D., Panzarasa, P., Mondragón, R. J., and Bianconi, G. (2014). "Weighted Multiplex Networks." *PLoS ONE* 9(6): 1–8. doi:10.1371/journal.pone.0097857.

Norgaard, K. M. (2006). " 'People Want to Protect Themselves a Little Bit': Emotions, Denial, and Social Movement Nonparticipation." *Sociological Inquiry* 76(3): 372–396.

Olson, M. (1965). *The Logic of Collective Action: Public Goods and the Theory of Groups*. Cambridge, MA: Harvard University Press.

Pachucki, M. A., and Breiger, R. L. (2010). "Cultural Holes: Beyond Relationality in Social Networks and Culture." *Annual Review of Sociology* 36: 205–224.

Prell, C. (2012). *Social Network Analysis: History, Theory & Methodology*. Los Angeles and London: Sage.

Putnam, R. D. (2000). *Bowling Alone: The Collapse and Revival of American Community*. New York: Simon & Schuster.

Raab, J., and Kenis, P. (2007). "Taking Stock of Policy Networks: Do They Matter?" In *Handbook of Public Policy Analysis: Theory, Methods and Politics*, edited by F. Fischer, G. Miller, and M. Sidney, pp. 187-200. Boca Raton, FL: CRC Press.

Radcliffe-Brown, A. R. (1940). "On Social Structure." *Journal of the Anthropological Institute of Great Britain and Ireland* 70:1, pp.1–12.

Ragin, C. (1987). *The Comparative Method*. Berkeley: University of California Press.

Ragin, C., and Becker, H. (1992). *What Is a Case?* Cambridge, UK: Cambridge University Press.

Sabatier, P. A., and Jenkins-Smith, H. C. (1993). *Policy Change and Learning: An Advocacy Coalition Approach*. Boulder, CO: Westview Press.

Sabatier, P. A., and Weible, C. (2007). "The Advocacy Coalition Framework: Innovations and Clarifications." In *Theories of the Policy Process*, edited by P. Sabatier, pp. 189–220. Boulder, CO: Westview Press.

Scott, J. 2001. *Power*. Malden, MA: Blackwell Publishers.

Sonnett, J. (2015). "Ambivalence, Indifference, Distinction: A Comparative Netfield Analysis of Implicit Musical Boundaries." *Poetics (October)*. doi:10.1016/j.poetic.2015.09.002.

Tavory, I., and Timmermans, S. (2014). *Abductive Analysis: Theorizing Qualitative Research*. Chicago: University of Chicago Press.

United Nations Framework Convention on Climate Change (UNFCCC). (2015). Paris Agreement. http://bigpicture.unfccc.int/#content-the-paris-agreemen

Warner, W. L. (1963). *Yankee City*. New Haven, CT: Yale University Press.

Wasserman, S., and Faust, K. (1994). *Social Network Analysis: Methods and Applications*. New York: Cambridge University Press.

Weber, M. (1978). *Economy and Society. Volumes 1 and 2*. Berkeley: University of California Press.

White, H. C. (1992). *Identity and Control*. Princeton, NJ: Princeton University Press.

White, H. C. (2008). *Identity and Control: How Social Formations Emerge*. 2d ed. Princeton, NJ: Princeton University Press.

PART VII

WHAT CAN POLITICAL SCIENCE LEARN FROM OTHER DISCIPLINES?

....

CHAPTER 38

WHAT CAN POLITICAL SCIENCE LEARN FROM BUSINESS AND MANAGEMENT?

An Interview with Stephen P. Borgatti

....

Which theoretical or methodological concepts do you see as the most relevant to politically oriented research?

Social network research in general has devoted itself to two generic research questions, both of which are applicable to the political setting. The first is the elucidation of network processes that account for the success (broadly speaking) of individuals or groups. This is fundamentally the story of social capital, which serves as a complement to human capital accounts of success that focus on qualities of the individual, such as experience, political skill, and so forth.

Social capital stories come in many flavors. Perhaps the most fundamental is the kind espoused by social resource theory (Lin, Ensel, and Vaughn, 1981), which focuses on the resources that an actor may benefit from by dint of having ties with the people who control them. Hence ties to savvy political operatives who know the system are useful, as are ties to wealthy donors, and as are ties to influentials who can command votes. An elaboration of this story is the notion, espoused by Granovetter (1973) and Burt (1992), that all else being equal, it is helpful to have ties to distinct sections of the network that are unconnected to each other. In Burt's account, the person who spans these different network fragments is the broker, and the lack of ties between fragments is termed a structural hole. Having structural holes maximizes diversity of information, allowing the political actor to have a broader view of the political landscape and make better-informed decisions.

However, information is not the only theorized benefit of structural holes. When first introduced, structural holes were said to provide control benefits as well, in the form of enabling brokers to play off unallied actors against each other (Burt, 1992). The general literature on structural holes has largely lost interest in this aspect of structural holes, but it is highly relevant to the political setting. Whenever two actors who are unable or unwilling to collude with each other compete for the resources controlled by a broker, the broker can exploit the situation by essentially auctioning himself off to the highest bidder. Almost any resource can be leveraged in this way, including simple attention: if you want to talk to me, you need to do me a favor, because there are others who want my time. This, of course, is the power of a larger employer who negotiates salaries individually with each employee. Once the employees start coordinating (i.e., unionizing), the employer can no longer divide and conquer, and indeed is effectively negotiating with a single collective node.

This kind of power, which hinges on having multiple alternatives, has a global aspect that may not be readily apparent. Suppose you have a network like the one shown in figure 38.1. The center node, A, has more alternatives than anyone else. However, the center is not the one with the bargaining power. The reason is that each of the three Bs that A has to play off each other has an exclusive alternative (a C) to bargain with instead of A. As a result, A finds himself in a difficult situation because the Bs would always prefer to bargain with their captive C than with the all-too-demanding A. This logic extends itself throughout the network, creating a system of interdependencies such that an actor's power can be partially dependent on nodes that are beyond the actor's horizon of observability.

The distinction between the information and control benefits of structural holes neatly maps onto two fundamental explanatory mechanisms in network theorizing about social capital. The information argument rests on an implicit model of social networks that sees social ties as providing—to use the terminology of Atkin (1974)—a backcloth along which traffic may flow. Thus, ties serve as pipes or roads that enable and constrain things to flow along certain paths. These flows include a variety of things such as information, material goods, and viruses. It is these flows that provide the proximal consequences for individual nodes, not the ties that enable them. Thus, hearing news early, before others do, can be an advantage. Receiving diverse perspectives on something, as opposed to recycled conventional wisdom, can be an advantage. Typically,

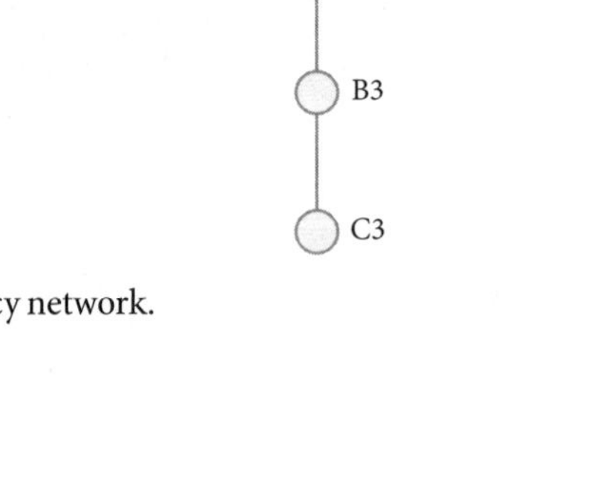

FIGURE 38.1 Dependency network.

however, researchers are not in a position to measure the timing, diversity, and quantity of specific bytes of information arriving at each node. It is in response to this problem that the machinery of social network analysis has been developed to take as input the pattern of ties in the network (which are more readily available than flows), calculate the myriad paths that something flowing through the network could take, and estimate flow outcomes such as how quickly and how broadly things are disseminated. For example, in the case of centrality measures, the interest is in calculating, for each node, such outcomes as time until first arrival (e.g., closeness centrality) and how often something passes through a node (e.g., betweenness centrality).

The control argument is different. Of course, nearly all network mechanisms involve some kind of dyadic flow, but not in the sense of the same thing moving from A to B and then from B to C. The system of dependencies by which the C nodes in figure 38.1 affect the power of the A node is not a flow, in the sense that C transfers its weakness to B, which then transfers its weakness to A, as we would see in an information flow. If anything, it is a cascade of causal reactions, so that C's situation creates a situation in B that is different from C's, and which in turn has an effect, different from B's, on A. Moreover, the effect of the structure (if unchanging) on relative power is a constant. It may take a few attempted transactions for it to affect behavior and outcomes, but the force exerted on A of having Cs on the side of Bs is as stable as the network is—it is always on.

Finally, the other canonical type of study in network analysis—the diffusion, contagion, and adoption of innovation type of study—is also highly relevant in politically oriented research. Here, the notion is that through interaction, nodes may acquire the same states as their neighbors. Over the years, a husband and wife come to like the same things, dislike the same things, and react similarly to similar stimuli. This kind of contagion is a special case of interpersonal influence, which has been well studied by social psychologists for decades. A key mechanism adopted by network theorists is Heider's (1946) balance theory, which says that if I like Corinne, and Corinne likes the Yankees, then I would experience cognitive dissonance if I didn't like the Yankees. As a result, I will either learn to like the Yankees more or learn to like Corinne less. Another mechanism is that of a relevant reference group. It may be that all of the laborers in my company have certain political views, but I find the views of my fellow middle managers especially relevant. Burt (1987) puts this more generally by arguing that it is the views of those with whom I am structurally equivalent that I take particular notice of. Structural equivalence here refers to having the same kinds of ties with the same third parties.

As political science continues to adopt network theory and methods, what do you see as the primary pitfalls or dangers the field faces?

Adoption always carries the risk of unwittingly pulling something out of context. It is obvious from the discussion above that network concepts such as betweenness centrality or measures of dependency power such as the graph-theoretic power index known as GPI (Markovsky, Willer, and Patton, 1988) are built on models and therefore carry theory. Freeman's betweenness provides an exact estimate of the number of times some-thing flows through a node, but only if what is flowing conforms to three rules: (1) it can only be in one place at one time; (2) it travels only on the shortest paths; and (3) when there are multiple, equally short paths, it chooses uniformly at random between them. If the phenomena being studied don't follow these rules very well, betweenness yields very poor estimates. If what flows does so by moving along random walks, random walk betweenness (Newman, 2005) does a much better job. Borgatti (2005) showed that for things flowing under a gossip regime (defined as copying rather than transferring from node to node and not taking the shortest paths but rather graph-theoretic trails, which can revisit nodes but do not revisit lines), Freeman's betweenness gets it wrong. In a simulation based on Padgett and Ansell's (1993) data on ties among Florentine families during the Renaissance, betweenness correctly gives the Medici family top billing but completely misses the importance of the Medici's close rivals, the Strozzi family, who were historically the dominant family prior to the rise of Cosimo di Medici. The sim-ulation puts them in second place, whereas betweenness puts them in the lower half of the pack.

The point is that political science cannot simply adopt, say, betweenness central-ity, because it is highly cited or was successfully employed in an influential study. It is linked to a model of network processes, and those should match the processes found in the research context it is to be applied to. For people new to social network analysis, it is extremely easy to see it more as a set of methods, like significant tests, than a set of theoretical concepts with associated measures. This is particularly true for fields that normally express theory in narrative form rather than in formal, mathematical, terms. I don't know political science well enough to know if it fits this category, but for fields that do, anything expressed as a formula or an equation is likely to be seen as part of statistical methodology, like a regression equation. In such fields, it is difficult to under-stand that $e = mc^2$ is a theoretical statement, not a formula used by the local power com-pany to measure output.

I think most of the math in network analysis is best regarded as formal theory. The parts of network analysis that are methodology are data collection methods, algorithmic choices, and hypothesis testing methods, such as QAP regression, exponential random graph models (ERGM), and the longitudinal stochastic actor-oriented models (SAOM) embodied in the Siena software package.

The second trap is to adopt a single idea that comes to stand for the field as a whole. The adoption process always carries with it founder's effects, such as when an island is colonized by a given pair of mating birds, resulting in sharply reduced genetic diversity compared to the parent population. I think an object lesson is pro-vided by the case of networks in the field of management research, which seems to have congealed around a single idea: the notion of structural holes. Looking at papers given at PolNet, I suggest that the incidence of ERGMs is considerably higher than in other fields. The danger, of course, is that once a concept or method becomes too dominant, it is no longer a choice; it must be used, or else you're not doing network analysis or at least not doing it right. And yet it may not be appropriate for a given research question.

What mistakes or stumbling blocks have you, or your field, faced in the study and application of network methods?

I would restate the question to include network concepts as well as methods. The mistake I notice in my field (management) is increasing myopia. Early work in management embraced the whole toolkit of network concepts. For example, early introductions to network concepts were broad and complete, as seen in classic papers by Tichy and Fombrun (1979) and Lincoln (1982). Older empirical studies adopted a variety of network concepts, including betweenness centrality (Brass, 1984) and regular equivalence (Krackhardt and Porter, 1986). Today, virtually every empirical and theoretical piece relies on just one concept: structural holes (Burt, 1992). It is almost as if the richness of network analysis was, for management, a problem to be solved. It created uncertainty about which concept to use, and in response, producers (researchers) turned to mimicking each other in search of a sense of legitimacy. It's funny, because I have often derided management's "new institutional" theory as merely an uptown version of network diffusion theory with bigger words, but I have to admit that their central tenet of mimetic isomorphism under conditions of uncertainty (DiMaggio and Powell, 1983) really nails the evolution of network research in the field of management.

As a student of Levi-Strauss, though, I have a semantic theory of what's happened to network research in management. I think what we are seeing is the power and appeal of synecdoche: a semantic device in which the part stands in for the whole, such as when we refer to workers as hands. Thus, in management today, the concept of structural holes is network analysis in its entirety. I've seen this in other fields as well, such as when Milroy and Milroy (1978), having adopted Granovetter's (1973) strength of weak ties theory, included "the network variable" in their empirical analysis—a single survey question asking respondents about their integration with their community.

What Contributions Do You Hope Political Science Will Make to the Study and Application of Networks in Your Discipline?

This is a dangerous thing to comment on. Most social science fields see themselves as fundamental and see other fields as mere branches of their own. So to list any specific contributions could easily seem to minimize and undervalue political science. But since you asked, I will suggest a few things that seem like a good fit.

The first contribution I would like to see has to do with the actions taken by political actors. Most of the research in sociology is about how certain network structures (or positions within them) have consequences for those involved. I believe that it is widely held that, in contexts like organizations, people are (variably) cognizant of their positions and seek to improve them. But research on what concrete moves people actually make to achieve and leverage these positions is scarce. How do certain senators become vastly more influential than others? How do they deploy their structural position to achieve a specific outcome? And from a whole-network perspective, what levers do stakeholders have available to them for changing the network toward a desired shape? For example, if a legislature is dysfunctionally divided into warring factions, how can this be changed? Managers of organizations have a few very effective tools, but they are also very crude: things like transferring people to different locations. I think that political arenas are particularly attractive contexts to study these questions because the actors seem—anecdotally at least—to be highly cognizant of the system of alliances and dependencies around them and consider carefully how to accumulate and on what to spend their political capital. I would especially value ethnographic research that embeds itself in a political setting and asks the actors what they are thinking as they make their moves.

The other area that I think political science is uniquely suited to contribute to is the phenomenology of social networks. A small but growing area within social network research is concerned with the perception of ties, both which ties are perceived and the consequences of perception. While it has long been known that having ties to high status people is useful, there is growing acknowledgment that being perceived to have ties to important people is equally and independently useful. A favorite quotation in the network literature is from a chapter by Cialdini (1989) on image management in which he says: "At the height of his wealth and success, the financier Baron de Rothschild was petitioned for a loan by an acquaintance. Reputedly, the great man replied, 'I won't give you a loan myself, but I will walk arm-in-arm with you across the floor of the Stock Exchange, and you soon shall have willing lenders to spare.'" However, it is not just about the benefit to self of others' perceptions. It is also about one's own perceptions. By illustration, Krackhardt (1992) sketches a case study of a failed unionization drive that might have succeeded had the union understood which of the potentially pro-union workers was central in the organization's friendship network. Instead, the union allied itself with a firebrand who was a good ideological choice and was highly motivated but had no interpersonal influence with the rest of the workers. Political situations like these seem ideally suited for exploring the perceptions of ties and the consequences of those perceptions.

References

Atkin, R. (1974). *Mathematical Structure in Human Affairs*. London: Heinemann.

Borgatti, S. P. (2005). Centrality and network flow. *Social Networks* 27: 55–71.

Brass, D. J. (1984). Being in the right place: A structural analysis of individual influence in an organization. *Administrative Science Quarterly* 29: 518–539.

Burt, Ronald S. (1987). "Social Contagion and Innovation: Cohesion versus Structural Equivalence." *American Journal of Sociology* 92: 1287–1335.

Burt, R. S. (1992). *Structural Holes: The Social Structure of Competition*. Cambridge, MA: Harvard University Press.

Cialdini, R. B. (1989). "Indirect Tactics of Image Management: Beyond Basking." *Impression Management in the Organization* 45: 45–56.

DiMaggio, P., & Powell, W. W. (1983). The iron cage revisited: Collective rationality and institutional isomorphism in organizational fields. *American Sociological Review* 48: 147–160.

Granovetter, M. S. (1973). "The Strength of Weak Ties." *American Journal of Sociology* 78: 1360–1380.

Heider, F. (1946). "Attitudes and Cognitive Organization." *Journal of Psychology* 21(1): 107–112.

Krackhardt, D. (1992). "The Strength of Strong Ties: The Importance of Philos in Organizations." In *Networks and Organizations: Structure, Form, and Action*, edited by N. Nohria and R. Eccles, pp. 216–239. Boston: Harvard Business School Press.

Krackhardt, D., and Porter, L. W. (1986). "The Snowball Effect: Turnover Embedded in Communication Networks." *Journal of Applied Psychology* 71(1): 50.

Lin, N., Ensel, W. M., and Vaughn, J. C. (1981). "Social Resources and Strength of Ties: Structural Factors in Occupational Status Attainment." *American Sociological Review* 46: 393–405.

Lincoln, J. R. (1982). "Intra-(and inter-) Organizational Networks." *Research in the Sociology of Organizations* 1(1): 1–38.

Markovsky, B., Willer, D., and Patton, T. (1988). "Power Relations in Exchange Networks." *American Sociological Review* 53: 220–236.

Milroy, J., and Milroy, L. (1978). "Belfast: Change and Variation in an Urban Vernacular." *Sociolinguistic Patterns in British English* 21: 19–36.

Newman, M. E. (2005). "A Measure of Betweenness Centrality Based on Random Walks." *Social Networks* 27(1): 39–54.

Padgett, J. F., and Ansell, C. K. (1993). "Robust Action and the Rise of the Medici, 1400–1434." *American Journal of Sociology* 98: 1259–1319.

Tichy, N., & Fombrun, C. (1979). Network analysis in organizational settings. *Human Relations* 32: 923–965.

CHAPTER 39

WHAT CAN POLITICAL SCIENCE LEARN FROM ECONOMICS?

An Interview with Matthew Jackson

WHICH *theoretical or methodological concepts do you see as the most relevant to politically-oriented research?*

Social networks are primary conduits of information and shape our opinions and beliefs. In turn, such beliefs shape political decision making. This leads to a set of basic questions that relate networks to politics: How do network structures of interaction determine opinions and beliefs? What can be said that is systematic about observed political networks and the implications for collective decision making? Which networks are most likely to form, and how does that depend on context? These are long-standing questions in the networks literatures, which have experienced dramatic advances in recent years.

The explosive growth in the collection of political network data provides new opportunities to take advantage of the rich and growing theoretical base for these questions. For example, models of the homophily that is pervasive in political networks can help in the understanding of polarization. Analyses of social learning, diffusion, and strategic communication can help in the study of collective decision making and deliberation. There are also methodological advances in detecting community structures, analyzing text, estimating network models, and measuring position and centrality in networks that are proving to be useful to network science broadly. Some of these are already proving quite useful in the analysis of political networks, as demonstrated in this volume.

As political science continues to adopt network theory and methods, what do you see as the primary pitfalls or dangers the field faces?

There are at least two substantial challenges that are faced when analyzing networks, regardless of the field.

One is that networks are formed by the actors involved, whether they be citizens, politicians, or states. This poses problems for inference, as the actors' behaviors can and will correlate with the characteristics and contexts that drive them to form relationships. Do close friends cast similar votes because they influence each other, or are they friends because of characteristics that cause them to have similar voting preferences? Of course this is not a new problem, but it is endemic to network data. Proper inference in the face of such endogeneity requires either taking advantage of some form of exogenous variation (either through controlled experimentation, natural experiments, or instruments) or a careful modeling of the full set of potential interactions and confounds. As much network data is observational, it will be increasingly important to have careful theoretical foundations that account for network formation to understand how to account for confounding characteristics and context.

The second challenge concerns a danger to all of the social sciences. The increasing availability of large amounts of data will allow us to answer many new questions, as we can observe minutiae of human behavior with huge sample sizes, in many settings, and over time. The rich data will, however, contain many spurious relationships in addition to the robust ones. The data can be extremely useful if we approach them with careful hypotheses in mind. The danger comes from starting with the data and then looking for the questions that they might answer. New data-mining and machine-learning techniques enable a researcher to search for unprecedented multitudes of correlations. We are likely to uncover a number of fascinating "facts," only some of which will be robust and truly of interest. This issue is amplified by the already documented biases in a publication system that inevitably favors uncovering provocative and significant relationships. There are appropriate techniques for correcting for such biases, so this challenge can be overcome. But the long-term solution requires social scientists to keep in mind the importance of approaching data with hypotheses, models, and theories, and placing more emphasis on replication. The deluge of data, network and otherwise, makes addressing this issue imperative.

What mistakes or stumbling blocks did you, or your field, face in the study and application of network methods?

I am not sure that I see pervasive or systematic "mistakes" in the use of network methods, but it is clear that there are still many things missing from our understanding of networks in human behavior. One is that networks of interactions are inherently dynamic, and yet most of the methods and tools developed to date are best suited for analyzing static systems. Thus, we often treat networks as if they are fixed and enduring patterns, even though they are inherently stochastic and dynamic. Although dynamic networks is an active area of current study, there is much catching up to do, and the modal network study has yet to meaningfully incorporate dynamics.

Another somewhat related challenge is that the complexity of networks necessitates that we quantify and analyze them based on relatively simple characteristics: degree distributions, clustering patterns, segregation patterns, and so forth. We still have little understanding of what is missed by the existing set of measures and which particular measures are most appropriate in which contexts. There are very few methodological studies of network tools.

What contributions do you hope political science will contribute to the study and application of networks in your discipline?

Political processes largely determine the distribution of resources in societies and the inequalities that ensue. Thus, since network structures drive the formation of the beliefs and behaviors that underlie political and economic processes, understanding political networks becomes essential for understanding the distribution of wealth and resources. Studies of the strong segregation patterns and homophily that pervade social and political networks thus hold promise in improving our understanding of the formation of political opinions and behaviors. That should in turn should help us to improve the design policies and political institutions that address regional, national, and international patterns of inequality and poverty.

A related foundational issue concerns a hole in the social learning and networks literatures: modeling the interaction among various media, forms of propaganda, and word-of-mouth communication in the formation of beliefs. As communication channels continue to evolve, so does the landscape of information to which people have access. While we are seeing many new case studies, we still have little insight into how fundamental changes in the costs of communication and the rapid access to information on a global scale are influencing the evolution of people's beliefs and behaviors, as well as how people share that information. Political models and data hold great promise in producing advances on this topic.

What types of collaborations between political science and your field do you think are the most likely to be productive? This might be particular research questions, methodological frontiers, or something else that emerges from the joint efforts of scholars across disciplines.

The divisions between fields within the social sciences are becoming blurred: network science and analyses cut across disciplines in ways that few other subjects do. More basically, it is impossible to separate political processes from their economic consequences. The study of networks should continue to bridge artificial gaps between disciplines, especially when looking at a wide variety of subjects involving politics and economics. Several obvious examples of topics that combine politics, economics, and networks are: patterns of international trade and interstate conflict, the regulation of the financial industry, the formation of political opinions and preferences, the determination of economic policies and resulting patterns of inequality, and global action concerning environmental issues.

To fully address these questions requires greater scope than has been previously employed. There is a need for more holistic and ambitious research that takes into account the social, political, and economic contexts that combine to determine many human behaviors. To date these contexts have mostly been studied piecemeal. Promising collaborations -between political scientists, sociologists, economists, and other researchers interested in social interactions will bring such broader perspectives to bear on the many questions that involve political interactions intertwined with social and economic behaviors.

....

CHAPTER 40

WHAT CAN POLITICAL SCIENCE LEARN FROM SOCIOLOGY?

An Interview with James Moody

....

WHICH *Theoretical or Methodological Concepts Do You See as the Most Relevant to Politically Oriented Research?*

I think the key problems that networks can help address in political science turn on peer recruitment and polarization. The recruitment process involves peers influencing each other to participate in politically relevant activities. These can range from voting to marching to taking up arms, but all involve the link between a personal activity and an interpersonal commitment to a fellow actor.

Modeling the recruitment process is exceedingly difficult. We can get some purchase on the theoretical process using simulations, but mapping that to particular empirical cases is tricky at best. I think the frontier for social movements research, for example, will be to link the theoretical peer influence processes involved in peer recruitment to real-world data exemplars.

Polarization is a special case of attitudinal peer influence. On the one hand, we have very well established diffusion models, mostly sundry variants on Friedkin's network autocorrelation model. But the theoretical foundation of those models generally presumes consensus. Foundational models for polarization as an influence process require an active "rejection" step; my bet is that such models can be developed building on classic balance theory, but we've yet to see much along these lines.

Note that most of this reflects a theoretical problem, not a statistical or estimation problem. We need to understand the basic actor-to-network social process first, and that work's yet to be done.

As Political Science Continues to Adopt Network Theory and Methods, What Do You See as the Primary Pitfalls or Dangers the Field Faces?

I think the biggest risk lies in rushing to adopt a technology wholesale as "standard," so that new practitioners follow that lead rather than innovating tools and ideas tailored to their problems. This is common in quantitative methods (think of the adherence to 5% alpha levels, thresholds for retaining factors in measurement models, etc.). While these sorts of essentially ad hoc conventions that become institutionalized serve to integrate and potentially help replicate across studies, they also hinder creative applications of theoretical ideas. Social network analysis should not be seen as a set of constraining tools that one must adhere to; rather, it's an approach grounded in a small number of key concepts—nodes, edges, paths, and so forth—that can be used to operationalize key social processes. The heart of the project is in the operationalization, not the application of off-the-shelf prior work. For example, the development of statistical models for networks—both exponential random graph models and latent space models—is a solution to particular problems. Rather than shoe-horning a question to fit the estimation capacity of the current models, authors need to carefully develop estimators that match the process under study. I fear that in the rush to get something out the door, we'll take the easy way out and use only preprogrammed utilities.

What Mistakes or Stumbling Blocks Have You, or Your Field, Faced in the Study and Application of Network Methods?

I think there are many idiosyncratic answers to this question that hinge on mathematical or programming acumen. Generally, I think sociologists have (1) tended to focus on direct positive social relations, (2) been slow to adapt to large online network data opportunities, and (3) been befuddled unnecessarily by issues of causal identification.

The focus on positive relations is a historical accident having to do mainly with data availability (organizations that produce data dislike collecting negative tie information), but this brought with it a focus on direct ties in single-relation networks rather than the wider questions of roles and role structures inherent in the White et al. (1976) formulations of block modeling. The real fundamental insights of networks are positional, not connectionist, but the positional side of the coin has largely been ignored. This is because to really understand positions, we need multiplex networks. Current work focused on "multi-slice" networks may help recover this (coming from math/network science), but it seems poised to be a connectionist application over differing edge colors.

Online network data are simultaneously the largest potential source for network data and the largest substantive distraction in network science. On the one hand, we are faced with a clearly network process that is fundamental in some parts of social life, but on the other we have no good way to link these cases to some level of representativeness. That is, it's fine to say we have hundreds of thousands or millions of nodes, but if we have systematically oversampled one part of the population, then any insight from that large data set is biased. This nut is hard to crack, and sociologists have largely just ignored it. I think as the adoption and use of these technologies continues to expand, this will be the next frontier for interpersonal network models. As such, I hope we see more work on what constitutes the value of such ties. (What does it mean to "follow" somebody on Twitter? Or to "like" a Facebook friend's post?)

Finally, the root of the network approach is that social life is relational—the difference between a gourmand and a glutton is company—but the methodological bias in social science is still primarily focused on the person as the key agent. This has driven what I see as a needless distraction about "selection or influence" debates that are exactly akin to the old nature/nurture debates or "genetics/environment" models. These arguments severely underestimate the interactive nature of "selection" (if one could simply select friends, we'd all have cooler friends!). In truth, the exact same logic that leads to causal nonidentification of network models due to selection (because of backdoor paths through prior contacts) leads to nonidentification of any individual level model because of unaccounted-for, prior social contacts. As such, if we take these arguments too seriously, we put ourselves in the same place as Fisher's early denial of cigarette's effects on health (see Stolley, 1991): perfectly reasonable intellectual exercises that are substantively silly and undercut our long-term scientific interests.

The entire "causal devolution" (Abbott, 1998) here speaks to a wider goal to replace careful thinking with methods, a substitution that has never succeeded. As it stands, the current requirements for causal identification result in such underpowered tests that we cannot definitively know much of anything, again gutting the larger project. This is not to say we shouldn't be attuned to issues of cause, but instead that we should not throw out the theoretical baby with the methodological bathwater; let's spend some careful time accumulating (inconclusive, "merely descriptive") evidence across multiple sources before we limit ourselves to designs that virtually ensure we won't find anything of interest.

What Contributions Do You Hope Political Science Will Make to the Study and Application of Networks in Your Discipline?

Political science has a key advantage in focusing on problems that are simultaneously clearly relational and that we all care about. For example, one empirical focus of interest will be in social influence and recruitment/social movements. The depth of contextual knowledge here in political science makes it a ripe location for identifying the key social processes embedded within political movement activity. The extent to which political activity is driven by media/money compared to interpersonal activity is a fascinating and important, open question. Similarly, network models of international relations and conflict are likely to help us understand high-stakes collaboration and conflict more broadly.

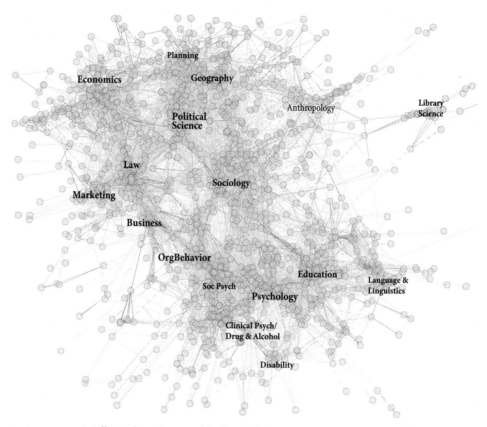

FIGURE 40.1 Intellectual Landscape of the Social Sciences

What Types of Collaborations between Political Science and Your Field Do You Think Are the Most Likely to Be Productive?

(This might be particular research questions, methodological frontiers, or something else that emerges from the joint efforts of scholars across disciplines.) Sociologists are topically omnivorous, so I expect that fruitful collaborations can be had across most of the field (and, to be fair, political science and sociology are not that distant). Consider Figure 40.1, which maps the social science disciplines based on journal co-citation patterns (tie strength is the cosine similarity score on times jointly cited by other journals).

Political science sits at a nexus of social science, anchored on issues of power and resources (law, economics, planning/policy). Sociology sits between political science and the fields concerned with meaning and mind, and my guess is that the first round of fruitful collaboration will be to embed questions of meaning and structure into network models of social action, with political action being an interesting case.

References

Abbott, A. (1998). "The Causal Devolution." *Sociological Methods & Research* 27(2): 148–181.

Stolley, P. D. (1991). "When Genius Errs: R. A. Fisher and the Lung Cancer Controversy." *American Journal of Epidemiology* 133: 416–425.

White, H., Boorman, S., and Breiger, R. (1976). "Social structure from multiple networks I: Blockmodels of roles and positions." *American Journal of Sociology* 81: 730–780.

CHAPTER 41

......

WHAT CAN POLITICAL SCIENCE LEARN FROM MATHEMATICS?

An Interview with Peter Mucha

......

WHICH *Theoretical or Methodological Concepts Do You See as the Most Relevant to Politically Oriented Research?*

All of our perspectives and answers are surely influenced by our own backgrounds. Mine as an applied mathematician—and indeed, the problems I have chosen to study in my own research—definitely influence my thinking here. So let me self-absorbedly say a few more words about this. While I surely shouldn't speak for all applied mathematicians, I see my role as inherently interested in the development of mathematical methods while also eager to cooperate with others to see those methods implemented to solve problems in various disciplines. There are many ways to achieve this second goal, but in most of my work, I prefer to partner with disciplinary experts in the areas of applications.

It is with that background that I call attention to the rapidly growing (and perhaps even accelerating) literature on methods, models, and measures for so-called multilayer networks, as a general framework that includes multilevel networks, multiplex networks, interdependent networks, and temporal networks, among many other terms that are scattered across the greater literature (see, e.g., the review by Kivelä et al., 2014). As just one sign of the weight of effort going into the study of multilayer networks currently, I note that two of the twenty parallel sessions at the NetSci conference in summer 2015 were explicitly on multilayer networks, while a third was specially focused on temporal networks.

For full disclosure (and at the risk of continued self-promotion), my very first paper about multilayer networks (Mucha et al., 2010)—though we didn't even know to call them that at the time—used similarity relationships in Congressional roll call data as a motivating example of community structure in a temporal network, and my recent collaboration with Skyler Cranmer used some of the same tools to study multiplex, international relations (Cranmer et al., 2015). So I'm admittedly very biased in favor of further development and application of multilayer frameworks within political science and beyond.

Of course, political scientists have long considered networks that include multiple kinds of actors and multiple types of connections and that have variation over time. And the political networks community is awash in such data. So I strongly believe that there are many natural points of collaboration between researchers in political networks and those in multilayer networks. Indeed, my hope is that such collaborative connections continue to work back and forth along a very inviting and busy two-way street.

As Political Science Continues to Adopt Network Theory and Methods, What Do You See as the Primary Pitfalls or Dangers the Field Faces?

As I think about my own experiences collaborating with political scientists and my conversations with my various colleagues working in political networks, I worry greatly about the unintended impacts of different publication practices, especially the typical timing of the review process at various journals. In thinking about these differences and extrapolating from my own experiences, I expect there are many manuscripts out there that could have been—and perhaps would have more appropriately been—placed in a political science journal. The fact that these papers are elsewhere, say in physics journals or other closely related fields, begs many questions. What, if anything, was lost in translation between the norms of the journals across these fields? Would it be better for political science as a discipline (and academic departments) and for the place of political networks within political science to have these papers appear in "proper" political science journals? What are the effects on political networks researchers who make their home outside political science? How might these papers have been reviewed differently if they were in the political science literature? And what other factors might be in play here? Are the disciplinary journals becoming more (or less) territorial about promoting "their own" researchers? And what does that mean for the future of interdisciplinary collaboration?

Should something be done about any or all of these issues? And if yes, what, and how? To be clear, I do not claim to have any secret solution for any of these issues. Rather, I simply note that they worry me as I look to the future, thinking about the many ways that my own research and scholarship have benefited enormously from interdisciplinary collaborations and conversations.

On a more positive note, I find it very heartening to see new interdisciplinary journals like *Network Science*, *Journal of Complex Networks*, *IEEE Transactions on Network Science and Engineering*, and *Applied Network Science* succeed. These journals and others should serve to promote interdisciplinary dialogue and advances. Of course it will be

up to each of us in our respective fields to promote the value of these new interdisciplinary journals in our home departments.

What Mistakes or Stumbling Blocks Have You, or Your Field, Faced in the Study and Application of Network Methods?

I admit that I have stumbled through different publication expectations while collaborating and mentoring across disciplines. Surely everyone reading this admission thinks
it obvious that there are many differences between the natural sciences, engineering,
and the social sciences. Of course there are. But how many of us have truly considered
the impacts or pitfalls of these differences when we embark on a new and exciting cross-
disciplinary collaboration? I have definitely been too slow to think carefully about these
differences, especially as I have transitioned from mentee to mentor (or at least from
more junior to more senior).

I have had to learn to ask myself what assumptions I or my colleagues might have
that we have all left completely unstated. When starting a new collaboration with others
within my own discipline, I've always and perhaps a little too naively taken it for granted
that we'll figure out lots of the details of publication and attribution later. It's easy in
the rush of conversations about an exciting new research direction to get completely
wrapped up in the science of it all. And if everyone is working from sufficiently similar
starting assumptions about how collaborations work, then there is very likely no problem with getting lost in that excitement. The difficulties are hidden inside the implicit
assumptions of different disciplines that we might not realize exist.

Most of these issues are relatively easy as long as we have frank conversations with our
collaborators early in the project. What is the goal of a particular project? What possible
journals should we be targeting as we do the work? If we succeed, who are the coauthors,
and in what order will they be listed? Do we expect a graduate student to write a single-
authored paper about any or all of this work? How do the publications and grants on a
project affect the tenure prospects of the junior faculty member on the team? On what
timescale does this project need to bear fruit?

You might be thinking that this all sounds like the usual stuff one deals with on any
project. But the expectations going into these conversations are very likely to be different for people from different disciplines and backgrounds. So have those conversations
earlier than you might do with a colleague from within your same discipline. If you wait
for these expectations to become issues, then it could be too late to negotiate them to
everyone's best interest.

I know that I have made the mistake of not having these conversations early enough,
and I feel lucky about how these cultural differences eventually worked out, without too
much trouble in most cases. My colleagues and I just had to be open and upfront with
each other. But it really would have been better if we had forced some of these explicit
conversations to occur earlier.

What Contributions Do You Hope Political Science Will Make to the Study and Application of Networks in Your Discipline?

There are two big general themes about which I am very excited regarding contributions from political science to the study of networks. First, as I already indicated earlier, political scientists have long considered networks that fit into the general multilayer network framework, and I think there are many natural points of collaboration there. In addition to having wonderful multilayer network data to study, political scientists have great questions that they want to explore with those data, and my hope is that many of these explorations will be done through interdisciplinary collaboration. Second, painting with a very broad brush here, I believe that as network science as a discipline becomes ever more statistical (or, arguably, returns to being more statistical), there is ample opportunity for the community to learn from political methodology as a whole.

References

Cranmer, S. J., Menninga, E. J., and Mucha, P. J. (2015). "Kantian Fractionalization Predicts the Conflict Propensity of the International System." *Proceedings of the National Academy of Sciences* 112(38): 11812–16. doi:10.1073/pnas.1509423112.

Kivelä, M., Arenas, A., Barthelemy, M., Gleeson, J. P., Moreno, Y., and Porter, M. A. (2014). "Multilayer Networks." *Journal of Complex Networks* 2(3): 203–71. doi:10.1093/comnet/cnu016.

Mucha, P. J., Richardson, T., Macon, K., Porter, M. A., and Onnela, J.-P. (2010). "Community Structure in Time-Dependent, Multiscale, and Multiplex Networks." *Science* 328(5980): 876–78. doi:10.1126/science.1184819.

CHAPTER 42

··

WHAT CAN POLITICAL
SCIENCE LEARN FROM
COMPUTER SCIENCE?

An Interview with Derek Ruths

··

WHICH theoretical or methodological concepts do you see as the most relevant to politically oriented research?

Latent attribute inference is a big one. This is the ability to infer attributes (e.g., gender and age) of users, irrespective of whether they're explicitly revealing those attributes. Online social platforms are increasingly being used as a source of observational data on which politically oriented research studies are based. This means that we're collecting data from users whom we can't see and with whom we'll almost certainly never communicate. In a typical survey, we'd collect relevant demographic variables. But if we grab tweets from 100,000 users, there's no way to ask them for this information; in fact, there isn't even a way to ask them if they're a bot.

As a result, if we want to know *who* is in the samples we collect, we need to use latent attribute inference methods. These are algorithms that typically use machine learning or artificial intelligence to infer a particular attribute of the user (Does the user live in Colorado?) from the behavior of that user (Does she mention places in Colorado? Does she have friends with geotagged tweets from Colorado?).

Of course, these inferences are never 100 percent accurate, but they can provide a powerful way of filtering users or content to build the samples we want to work with or label users with attributes that we'd like to use in our analyses.

As political science continues to adopt network theory and methods, what do you see as the primary pitfalls or dangers the field faces?

Studies increasingly are working with large, subsampled network-based data sets. Managing to collect a data set that is both incomplete and still representative is a huge challenge. Not all challenges are dangers, of course, but I do believe that this one could be. There's the nagging temptation to claim that potential sources of bias are too difficult to be controlled for—which is often implied when a study asserts that "this is all the data that could be collected."

I believe that network studies, in particular, pose this danger because they can be exceedingly difficult to collect, are often highly dependent on what people or companies make available (e.g., what data Facebook or Twitter surface through their application program interfaces (API)), and are sufficiently large as to make manual curation impossible. These and other factors create natural sympathies for researchers dealing with network data. Moreover, in many cases these factors make it impossible to control for all possible factors.

Of course, no data set is perfect—and we risk killing the whole field if we hold the work to an impossible standard. But judging when authors have done enough to control for biases must be done with tremendous care and sobriety. The alternative is a slippery slope in which research studies without adequate treatment for bias are slowly admitted into the literature, eroding data and analysis quality standards.

The middle ground between holding impossibly high standards and rejecting every study that uses large network data sets is for researchers to be mindful about how much their data allow them to claim. Studies using large network-based data sets making modest claims about particular populations under particular conditions will do much more to advance human knowledge than studies making much broader claims that cannot be reliably supported by the data.

What mistakes or stumbling blocks have you, or your field, faced in the study and application of network methods?

A lack of data and method transparency has been a persistent challenge for network-based (as well as other big data) studies within the computational social science community. A lack of transparency in either creates issues around reproducibility and enabling future research.

Reproducibility is one of the major tenants of scientific research: an experiment should yield the same results when conducted with exactly the same setup, under the same conditions. When studies do not provide sufficient details about data collection or methods used, it becomes exceedingly difficult to know even how to reproduce a study.

While ensuring that a study can be reproduced does incentivize good academic behavior, it serves an even more important purpose: fueling further research. As Isaac Newton quipped about seeing farther by "standing on the shoulders of giants," most scientific progress arises from studies building on one another. However, when the available literature is vague about what data were used and how analysis was done, the job of building on past studies becomes exceedingly difficult.

When working with network data, research pipelines can become complicated; data collection, curation, and transformation can all be highly nontrivial steps. Network methods can themselves be quite complicated beasts, involving numerous parameters and model choices. Making clear the nature of and motivation for each step in the research process will lay a firm foundation for future studies. Releasing data or methods for a particular study can also be immensely useful for future researchers.

What contributions do you hope political science will make to the study and application of networks in your discipline?

Computer scientists want to build new computational methods. Political science has the ability to motivate the search for new methods. Often new phenomenological questions that involve networks will also yield new methodological needs.

I think of there being two distinct kinds of novel methodological needs. The first, and most obvious, need arises from questions for which no computational method exists. In this case, computer scientists can collaborate in formalizing the problem and then devising a solution to it.

The second kind of need arises when a study discovers that an existing method doesn't work in the expected way—in other words, it's broken. An example here is community detection. Many methods exist for community detection, but a political scientist may find that the existing methods don't find sensible communities in her network data. This kind of finding offers the opportunity to examine why the method is failing in this case, which can yield valuable insights into the nature of the original problem and how it needs to be solved.

What types of collaborations between political science and your field do you think are the most likely to be productive?

Computer science engages with network science and network methods in a number of ways, so the opportunities for collaboration between political science and computer science seem unbounded to me. That said, here are two areas in which I think political science could provide much-needed motivation for methodological work.

Community detection This is an active area of research addressing the question: How do we find the subgroups present in a social network? The field suffers from a lack of good ground-truth instances in which the groups themselves are known, or at least could be reasoned about. Political science could provide well-motivated situations in which groups may be expected to exist within a social network. Furthermore, the results of a community detection algorithm could be assessed against what is known about the network being analyzed.

Network comparison Networks are extremely high-dimensional structures, which can make the question of how similar two networks are quite challenging to answer. Political science motivates the comparison of networks in many contexts—from international trade patterns to the structure of political movements. Each instance provides a kind of ground truth against which to compare networks (permitting the assessment of different network comparison methods). In some cases, the desired notion of similarity may dramatically differ from notions in prior work.

CHAPTER 43

WHAT CAN POLITICAL SCIENCE LEARN FROM STATISTICS AND PSYCHOLOGY?

An Interview with Stanley Wasserman

INTRODUCTION

I have been studying social networks and developing methodology for network science since 1974 ... more than forty years. I think this makes me one of the elders writing pages for this volume; it certainly gives me a longer view of what has happened in network science. I have seen methodology be born: triadic studies, blockmodels (of many different types), longitudinal models (and not just stochastic actor oriented models), and of course sophisticated statistical models (including the very detailed generalizations of the exponential family of random graph distributions, p^*). I have seen disciplines adopt the network paradigm (organizational science, epidemiology, physics, and of course political science) and have watched network science explode in size and importance. Who would have thought the small world paradigm (Milgram, 1967; Watts, 1999, 2003) and the phrase "six degrees of separation" (Guare, 1990) would become part of our culture? A movie titled *The Social Network*, nominated for Best Picture in 2011 (and winning in several other categories) by the Academy of Motion Pictures Arts and Sciences: Who would have thunk it? And social media, all based on one's networks, are so important in so many different ways, now in 2016.

Journals have been born (*Social Networks, Network Science, Journal of Complex Networks, Applied Network Science, Computational Social Networks, Network Modeling Analysis in Health Informatics and Bioinformatics, IEEE Transactions on Network Science and Engineering*, the list goes on and on . . .); some have died (*Journal of Quantitative Anthropology*, which published much network research). Conferences on network research have grown (NetSci, Complex Networks and Their Applications, and Political Networks) and overgrown (INSNA's Sunbelt Conference). There are many centers for network research at universities and even at companies. We clearly are living in an age of network research, which is exciting and overdue.

In this little commentary, I provide some perspective on the intersection of network science and political science.

Which theoretical or methodological concepts do you see as the most relevant to politically oriented research?

As mentioned, I am a methodologist, a statistician residing primarily among behavioral scientists, so I focus here on methodological issues. Political methodology, even for network data, revolves around models. It is not surprising that one of the most important developments for networks has been generalizations of p^*, as described (and researched) by Desmarais and Cranmer (see, for example, their chapter in this volume). These models are widely used in the analysis of political networks and have been developed in part by political scientists.

Network visualizations are also very important, such as those showing how partisanship in the US Congress has changed in recent decades (see the May 5, 2016, Facebook post on *Business Insider: Politics*). It's fascinating to see how the red (Republican members of the US Congress) and blue (Democratic members) nodes are almost in their very own graph components in the 2011–2012 US Congress (Andris et al. 2015) and how this is a very recent phenomenon. There was much more collaboration in earlier years, and there were fewer well-defined components based on party affiliation.

Much of the early work in network analysis focused on the network as the primary unit of analysis: which actors are most prominent, which actors are cohesively linked to others, which actors are socially/politically influenced, which are balanced structurally, which are equivalent to others, and so forth. But networks now, to a large extent, are being viewed as explanatory factors, as predictors of particular behavior, especially political. Interest in network theory and methods has boomed over the past two decades; researchers are beginning to think about relational variables, linking political actors to other such actors, as explanatory. (I prefer the words *explanatory* and *response* to the confusing words *dependent/independent*; all such variables are statistically related, so the phrase "independent variable" is incorrect.)

This research has begun to appear in a wide variety of journals (and of course in edited volumes such as this one). It has even found its way into *The Annals* (Mankad and Michailidis, 2015), in a very interesting article using network (specifically, Twitter) information to study the linkages among members of Parliament in the United Kingdom. Does "Twitter following" influence real-world votes in legislatures? It's a fascinating question, one that can now be studied.

As political science continues to adopt network theory and methods, what do you see as the primary pitfalls or dangers the field faces?

One of my main mantras is *don't reinvent the wheel!* Please do your homework and study the origins of the theories and methods used in your research. You just might find that others have been there before you.

One very good example is the work of Moreno (1934). Long before people were able to simultaneously study several structural effects (such as tendencies toward both transitivity and reciprocity), Moreno, in collaboration with his longtime colleague statistician Helen Hall Jennings, did some great, very early empirical work on networks. They were the first to look at transitivity, degree distributions, and counts of other subgroups. They compared actual counts to those expected by simple random models—the first to do so, and in a sophisticated way. Long before the physicists, Moreno and Jennings studied degree distributions with an eye toward differential popularity. The in-degree distribution was often referred to as the "Moreno distribution" and was used to demonstrate the "socio-dynamic effect" (Holland and Leinhardt, 1979): the observed distribution of in-degrees is more variable than expected by chance. People have been fitting models to degree distributions for decades! There is much in their work that has been "rediscovered" in the last twenty years.

Another example, which I will not dwell on, is the forerunner research to the so-called ERGM paradigm (Lusher, Koskinen, and Robins, 2013). These models are properly called p^*, acknowledging the earlier, pre-2005 work of Frank, Strauss, Pattison, Robins, and Wasserman (Frank and Strauss, 1986; Strauss and Ikeda, 1990; Wasserman and Pattison, 1996; Anderson, Wasserman, and Crouch, 1999; Pattison and Wasserman, 1999; Robins, Pattison, and Wasserman, 1999; Wasserman and Robins, 2005). This *exponential family* of random graph distributions is certainly *exponential*, but so are most distributions for random graphs. Clearly, later researchers have attached an unfortunate, and much too general, name to this very useful family of models. Wheel reinvention!

What mistakes or stumbling blocks have you, or your field, faced in the study and application of network methods?

I have faced few stumbling blocks, mostly because psychology, particularly social psychology, was an early adopter of the network paradigm. The intersection between network science and behavioral science is large and rich. Of primary focus are human-to-human interactions in much of the early network science research. But recently, social network perspectives have been increasingly seen as relevant in a variety of behavioral science disciplines, for example, organizational psychology, social support in clinical and community psychology, health-related behaviors, school- and classroom-based research in educational psychology, team structures in sports psychology, online Internet behavior (e.g., cyberbullying), and of course the brain and neuroscience. The network paradigm has had a large impact on behavioral science over the past two decades. Behavioral science has been very friendly to network research.

I think the same can be said for political science. It too has been very open to the network paradigm.

What contributions do you hope political science will make to the study and application of networks in your discipline?

Keep applying good and proper techniques and keep innovating! I have been impressed with the work of the political network methodologists and the new political network applications. It's all very good science.

To see how much of an impact political science has had on network science, I looked at papers published in the first three volumes of *Network Science*, 2013–2015, and the same three-year time period for *Social Networks*. Specifically, I asked the question: What fraction of articles have roots in or touch on political science ideas?

In these three volumes of *Network Science*, which are the first three volumes of this journal, there were sixty-one articles. Of these, five (8.2%) discussed political science topics. In *Social Networks*, there were 159 articles, including a special issue devoted to political networks (just as an aside, there will be a special issue of *Network Science* in 2017 devoted to globalization and networks). Of the articles in this (perhaps excessively large and of questionable quality) journal, twenty-seven (17%) discussed political science topics. If we do not count the special political networks issue, the percentage was 9.59 percent, remarkably similar to that in the other journal. Certainly, political science topics are discussed in these leading journals, but I think we can clearly state that more papers on these topics could be accommodated.

Acknowledgments

This commentary was partially supported by a grant from the US Office of Naval Research (W911NF-12-1-0176). The chapter was also prepared within the framework of a subsidy granted to the Higher School of Economics, Moscow, by the government of the Russian Federation for the implementation of the Global Competitiveness Program.

References

Anderson, C. J., Wasserman, S., and Crouch, B. (1999). "A p* Primer: Logit Models for Social Networks." *Social Networks* 21: 37–66.

Andris, C., Lee, D., Hamilton, M. J., Martino, M., Gunning, C. E., and Selden, J. A. (2015). "The Rise of Partisanship and Super-Cooperators in the U.S. House of Representatives." *PLoS ONE* 10(4): e0123507. doi:10.1371/journal.pone.0123507.

Frank, O., and Strauss, D. (1986). "Markov Graphs." *Journal of the American Statistical Association* 81: 832–842.

Guare, J. (1990). *Six Degrees of Separation*. New York: Random House.

Holland, P. W., and Leinhardt, S. (1979). "Structural Sociometry." In *Perspectives on Social Network Research*, edited by P. W. Holland, and S. Leinhardt, pp. 63–84. New York: Academic Press.

Lusher, D., Koskinen, J., and Robins, G. L. (Eds.) (2013). *Exponential Random Graph Models for Social Networks*. Cambridge, UK: Cambridge University Press.

Mankad, S., and Michailidis (2015). "Analysis of Multiview Legislative Networks with Structured Matrix Factorization: Does Twitter Influence Translate to the Real World?" *Annals of Applied Statistics* 9: 1950–1972.

Milgram, S. (1967). "The Small World Problem." *Psychology Today* 22: 61–67.

Moreno, J. L. (1934). *Who Shall Survive?* New York: Beacon House Press.

Pattison, P. E., and Wasserman, S. (1999). "Logit Models and Logistic Regressions for Social Networks, II: Multivariate Relations." *British Journal of Mathematical and Statistical Psychology* 52: 169–193.

Robins, G. L., Pattison, P. E., and Wasserman, S. (1999). "Logit Models and Logistic Regressions for Social Networks, III: Valued Relations." *Psychometrika* 64: 371–394.

Strauss, D., and Ikeda, M. (1990). "Pseudolikelihood Estimation for Social Networks." *Journal of the American Statistical Association* 85: 204–212.

Wasserman, S., and Pattison, P. E. (1996). "Logit Models and Logistic Regressions for Social Networks, I: An Introduction to Markov Random Graphs and p*." *Psychometrika* 60: 401–426.

Wasserman, S., and Robins, G. L. (2005). "An Introduction to Random Graphs, Dependence Graphs, and p*." In *Models and Methods in Social Network Analysis*, edited by P. J. Carrington, J. Scott, and S. Wasserman, pp. 148–161. New York: Cambridge University Press.

Watts, D. J. (1999). *Small Worlds: The Dynamics of Networks between Order and Randomness*. Princeton, NJ: Princeton University Press.

Watts, D. J. (2003). *Six Degrees: The Science of a Connected Age*. New York. W. W. Norton and Company.

INDEX

Page references for figures are indicated by *f,* for color plates by *cp,* and for tables by *t.*